MICA PRESS

VOICES FROM THE UNDERGROUND: —VOLUME 1 INSIDER HISTORIES OF THE VIETNAM ERA UNDERGROUND PRESS

Edited by Ken Wachsberger
with Forewords by
William M. Kunstler
and Abe Peck

ALTERNATIVE CATALOGING IN PUBLICATION DATA

Wachsberger, Ken, 1949- editor.
Voices from the underground. Tempe, AZ: Mica's Press

2 volumes.
PARTIAL CONTENTS: volume 1: Insider histories of the Vietnam era underground press; with forewords by William M. Kunstler and Abe Peck. -volume 2: A directory of sources and resources on the Vietnam era underground press; with foreword by Sanford Berman.

1. Alternative press—History and criticism. 2. Alternative press editors—Personal narratives. 3. Counterculture—Personal narratives. 4. Counterculture—Periodicals—History and criticism. 5. Alternative press—Bibliography. 6. Libraries—Special collections—Alternative press—Directories. 7. Acquisition of alternative press publications. 8. The Sixties—Personal narratives. 9. Vietnam War, 1961-1975—Protest movements—Personal narratives. 10. The Sixties—Periodicals—History and criticism. 11. Vietnam War, 1961-1975—Protest movements—Periodicals—History and criticism. I. Mica's Press. II. Title: Underground voices. III. Title: Insider histories of the Vietnam era underground press. IV. Title: The Vietnam era underground press. V. Title: A directory of sources and resources on the Vietnam era underground press. VI. Kunstler, William M., 1919- Foreword. VII. Peck, Abe, 1945- Foreword. VIII. Berman, Sanford, 1933- Foreword. IX. Title.

070.4509 or 301.2309   92-082780

ISBN: 187946101-3 (Volume 1)
      187946102-1 (Volume 2)
      187946103-X (Collection)

Both volumes are 8 1/2" x 11", softbound, Smyth sewn, with alkaline paper. The paper used in this publication meets the minimum requirements of American National Standards Institute for information sciences—permanence of paper for printed library materials, ANSI Z39.48-1984.   ∞

Cover by Merilea.

Manufactured in the United States of America.

Mica's Press
Box 25544—Library Lane

Other books by Ken Wachsberger:

Beercans on the Side of the Road: The Story of Henry the Hitchhiker. Ann Arbor, MI: Azenphony Press, 1988. Paper $8.95. ISBN 0-945531-00-1.

The Last Selection: A Child's Journey through the Holocaust, with Golda Szachter Kalib and Sylvan Kalib. Amherst, MA: The University of Massachusetts Press, 1991. Cloth $29.95. ISBN 0-87023-758-6.

Both books can be ordered from:

Azenphony Press
PO Box 15152
Ann Arbor, MI 48106

"...skillful editing and a welcome range of voices in the chorus. *Voices from the Underground* includes writers not just from big-city papers on either coast, but from small towns, military bases, even the prisons. Especially prominent are some of the feminist and gay writers who created a revolution within a revolution."

—**Abe Peck**, author of *Uncovering the Sixties: The Life and Times of the Underground Press* and professor of journalism at Northwestern University, from foreword to *Voices from the Underground: Insider Histories of the Vietnam Era Underground Press*

"[*Voices from the Underground*] furnishes the tools for students, librarians, historians, sixties' veterans, and latter-day activists and journalists to variously identify, access, use, understand, appreciate, and perhaps be energized by that still vibrant, icon-toppling, uninhibited, and hopeful corpus of newsprint called the 'underground press.'"

—**Sanford Berman**, head cataloger at the Hennepin County Library, Minnetonka, Minnesota and co-editor of *Alternative Library Literature*, from foreword to *Voices from the Underground: A Directory of Resources and Sources on the Vietnam Era Underground Press*

"*Voices from the Underground* allows 'the people who were there' to document the role of the underground and countercultural press in the development of political consciousness in the 1960s and 70s. In their own words and styles, editors and writers offer insights that scholars and students will find indispensable to the next wave of analytical writing on this important period. This is *the* volume for scholars who want to teach their students about the sixties and the underground press."

—**Barbara L. Tischler**, assistant dean of student affairs, Columbia University School of General Studies, and editor of *Perspectives on the Sixties*

"At a time when some 70 percent of Americans get all their news from network TV, with its constant diet of power elite supplied 'sound bites,' and when Third World bashing, at home and abroad, has become endemic, it is most appropriate that attention be drawn to the very vital role played by the underground and alternative press in the 60s and 70s....*Voices from the Underground* is an important guide and an inspiration for young journalism students and others who recognize the need for a media of integrity, commitment, depth, and truth; a media committed to the propagation of universal human value."

—**David G. Du Bois**, president, W.E.B. Du Bois Foundation, and visiting professor of journalism/Afro American studies, University of Massachusetts

"*Voices* is an important contribution to the history of contemporary dissent in America. Librarians should promote wide use of this insightful and unique publication."
—**Bill Katz**, editor, *Magazines for Libraries*

"The period of the late sixties and early seventies was a high water mark for American journalism. For the first time in American history, the vision of Justices Holmes and Brandeis blossomed and bore fruit. A multitude of voices, the essence of democracy, resounded through the land providing a compelling alternative against the stifling banality of the establishment press. What this nation had during the Vietnam War was exactly what the founding fathers understood the press to be all about when they wrote the First Amendment. You are to be congratulated on making a significant contribution to American journalism. I recommend that anyone who truly cares about the nation's press buy a copy and explore with your writers what journalism was really like when the alternative press flourished."
—**Art Levin**, chair, department of journalism, Butler University

"The true brief shining moment in American press history was the 1960s' voices of liberation as reflected in the grassroots press of the day. Ken Wachsberger has brought together a collection of outstanding memoirs of that age in *Voices from the Underground*: all the more important today when the shining has tarnished and the word 'liberation' is lost in the wind."
—**Barbara Grier**, author of *The Lesbian in Literature*, CEO of Naiad Press, and former editor/publisher of *The Ladder*

"This is indeed an important collection of underground press histories, and it does come with the right forewords and advance endorsements."
—**Editor**, Carol Publishing Group

"...an impressive piece of scholarship...."
—**Editor**, Little, Brown and Company Publishers

"Thank you for submitting Ken Wachsberger's impressive *Voices from the Underground*. I've hesitated to return it to you because I was busy reading it—it's a wonderful, authoritative, and much needed collection...I'm genuinely sorry that we will have to decline it. I am sure the book will do very well...Good luck!"
—**Editor**, Thunder's Mouth Press

"...couldn't put it down...extraordinary book...rave rejection...."
—**Editor**, Pantheon Books

* COLLECTIVE DEDICATION *

Contributors to this two-volume set of *Voices from the Underground* pay tribute to Tom Paine, whose *Common Sense* would not have been syndicated in England; to Upton Sinclair and other turn-of-the-century muckrakers, whose pens forced changes in labeling laws, child labor laws, and other issues that primarily affected poor people; and to all the other dissident pens throughout world history who gave us our tradition of independent reporting and analysis.

We pay further tribute to non-newspaper forms of media that complemented the underground press during the sixties, including FM-radio, poster art, and underground comix; and to underground papers that were published in Canada, France, Germany, England, China, and all over the world. Comparable books to *Voices from the Underground* that cover those topics remain to be written.

In addition, contributors have collectively dedicated *Voices from the Underground* to the following personal inspirations: David Joel and Carrie Suzanne, who hopefully will read this book someday, I.F. Stone, Abbie Hoffman, Huey P. Newton, Judy Grahn, Reed Baird, Marshall Bloom, Libby Gregory, Tom Forcade, every gay and lesbian who came out before there was a movement, Fredy Perlman, Marshall McLuhan, Russ Benedict, Emily, Zoltan Ferency, Steve Peake, Uncle Ho, John Lennon and Phil Ochs and the many other musicians and songwriters who attempted to capture the spirit of the time and whose work provided both the soundtrack and often the inspiration for our efforts in the media and the larger political movement, Mary Ellen, Myra, Annette, Max Scherr, Angela Davis, Allen Katzman, Myra Wolfgang, Clara Fraser, the Beat writers who preceded us and whose poetry and prose opened the paths to our free expression, Michael Patrick Madden, Jennifer Brooke Stanton Webb and the new generation of feminism, Scottie Remington, Richard Durham, Reinaldo Arenas, Charles P. Howard, Ti-Grace Atkinson, Elijah Muhammad, Malcolm X, Ron Ausburn, Christy and Joyce, Richie Havens and Country Joe, Sharlane, Charity, and Magda Grant, Meridel LeSueur, Agnes Tuttle, and the many prisoners whose signed articles guaranteed them gassings, beatings, endless time in solitary confinement, and sometimes death.

Finally, we dedicate the book to:

- our intergenerational peers—those students of today who are the age now that we were then, and who grew to political awareness during the Reagan years but didn't buy his explanations and interpretations;

- those heroic alternative newspapers of today that carry on the tradition of investigative journalism without being snowed under with record and movie reviews; and

- the National Writers Union (873 Broadway, Suite 203, New York, NY 10003-1209; 212-254-0279), whose leaders emerged from the underground press and whose victories are the victories of all independent writers.

MICA PRESS

TABLE OF CONTENTS FOR VOLUME 1

Voices from the Underground:
Insider Histories of the Vietnam Era Underground Press

        An alien force had taken over our country; it talked peace and made vicious war; it owned both political parties. We were all that was left of the opposition. Above all, the media had caved in and was reporting inflated, daily body counts for generals in Saigon and Washington. The press was just another chain of corporations acting like a line of skimpily dressed cheerleaders for the boys in grunt green. In such a setting, writes Peter Jensen, the Eugene *AUGUR* began publication in 1969.

        Harvey Ovshinsky wasn't happy when his mother moved to Los Angeles in 1965 and dragged along the popular senior from Detroit's Mumford High School. Wandering around town in a funk, Ovshinsky happened upon the Sunset Strip. There he saw two sights that piqued his interest: a gathering place called the Fifth Estate Coffeehouse and Art Kunkin's *Los Angeles Free Press*. Ovshinsky began hanging out at the coffeehouse and working on the *Free Press*. He was captivated by its antiwar politics, its concern for developing a radical Los Angeles community, and its coverage of the local music scene. Before the year was over, he returned to Detroit and founded *Fifth Estate*. Twenty-five years later, writes alumnus Bob Hippler, the snake oil of Reaganism is seen to have bankrupted the country, most workers do not have a union, countries still suffer under the yoke of neo-colonialism, and *Fifth Estate* is the nation's longest-lived underground paper to emerge from the Vietnam era.

        In August of 1973, Guru Maharaj Ji, the 15-year old "perfect master, arrived in Detroit to inaugurate his "Divine Light Mission"—a religious cult started in India—and to receive the key to the city. The local press hailed him as a messenger of peace and brotherhood. His disciples hailed him as the new "God." Only Detroit's *Fifth Estate* concluded that he was a hustler and a fraud. In this appendix to Bob Hippler's history of the *Fifth Estate*, Patrick Halley tells, for the first time, how he infiltrated the "Divine Light Mission" and pied the perfect master from 15 feet, and about the steel plate he wears in his head as a reminder.

to the present is told by Tim Wong, whose own 8 1/2 years of alternative journalism in Madison chronicled the transition from the sixties to the eighties.

When Paul Guzman went to Mexico for a semester of study in early 1969, he was already an experienced political activist and aspiring "black militant." After 3 1/2 months in a country where everyone was a Latino and proud of that heritage, he returned to New York as Pablo "Yorúba" Guzmán, ready to learn about Puerto Rico's ***militant*** history. In May 1969, he joined a group of college-age Latino males who would later merge with two similar groups to become the New York Young Lords Organization. His days of identifying with either black or white North Americans, even radicals, were over, he writes in this history of the group's newspaper, *Palante*; it was time to look within and without and begin organizing in the barrios, creating a ***Puerto Rican***, maybe even a pan-***Latino***, movement.

The year 1970 was a turning point for America. Resistance to the war in Vietnam had matured into a permanent institution, a persistent and articulate counterculture. A new consciousness was being developed about capitalism, racism, and sexism. And in the last eight months of the year, Minneapolis' *Hundred Flowers* blossomed, flourished, and withered. In this article, former staff member Ed Felien discusses his involvement in the paper and tells why he is neither repentant nor nostalgic for his involvement.

Women's Liberation in the nation's capital in the early 1970s was thriving. With consciousness-raising groups enabling hundreds of women to understand that the personal is political, women established rape counselling, child care, and other services, began researching The Pill and testifying in Congress, and created their own forms of media. In the winter and spring of 1972, while Richard Nixon and his minions were preparing to bug Democratic National Headquarters at the Watergate Building, 12 self-proclaimed revolutionary lesbian feminists—who were known collectively as the Furies—began putting out the first issues of what would almost instantly become *The* "legendary" *Furies*. Former collective member Ginny Berson tells her story here for the first time.

The writings of Malcolm X and Martin Luther King bump up against the poetry of Allen Ginsberg and Walt Whitman on a bookcase in Steve Abbott's house in Old North Columbus. Political extremes coexist comfortably here, from Tom Wolfe and Abbie Hoffman to Marxist and anarchist treatises, from texts on drugs and sensual massage to analyses of racism and community organizing. What may appear to be a library tour, writes Abbott, is evidence of a personal odyssey that represents the myriad influences and contending philosophies that typified the alternative/underground press during its heyday in the late 1960s and early 1970s. The *Columbus Free Press*, in its content and its internal struggles, reflected both its community and its time, a time filled with days of agony and days of wonder as the ideals of mystical transformation and principled political struggle contended for the lives of those involved.

by JoNina M. Abron

On Tuesday August 22, 1989, Huey P. Newton was murdered. The man who had been an international symbol of black resistance to white oppression was found dead on a street in Oakland, California, the same city where he had co-founded the Black Panther Party 23 years before. Six days later, over 2,000 people, including ex-Panthers from all over the country, mourned Huey's death and celebrated the enduring contributions that he and the party made to the political empowerment of black and other disenfranchised people in the United States. JoNina Abron was one of the speakers that day, along with Bobby Seale, Elaine Brown, Ericka Huggins, David Hilliard, and Emory Douglas. As she looked into the faces of her Panther comrades on the front pews, she writes, she thought about the good and hard times they had shared "serving the people body and soul," and about her experiences as the last editor of the Black Panther newspaper.

by Elihu Edelson

Jacksonville, Florida, was not the most fertile ground for an underground paper in late 1969. The city was ruled like a feudal fiefdom by a local machine that included the Florida Publishing Company, a monopoly that put out both the morning and evening papers. Three nearby military bases contributed to the ultraconservative atmosphere. New Leftists could be counted on the fingers of one hand; a handful of blacks put together the Florida Black Front, a local version of the Black Panthers; some good rock bands—like the Allman Brothers and Lynyrd Skynyrd—were to come out of Jax, but they had to make their names in Atlanta. Because none of the local hippies had any journalistic experience, they went, naively, to an editor of FPC's *Florida Times-Union* for advice. Elihu Edelson, a public school art teacher and part-time newspaper art critic, was about to get "sucked in" to the story of *Both Sides Now*.

by Michael Kindman

In September 1963, Michael Kindman entered Michigan State University, eager about the possibilities that awaited him as one of nearly two hundred honors students from around the country who had been awarded National Merit Scholarships, underwritten by MSU and usable only there. Together, they represented by far the largest group of Merit Scholars in any school's freshman class. At MSU? The nation's first agricultural land grant college? Two years later, he founded *The Paper*, East Lansing's first underground newspaper and one of the first five members of Underground Press Syndicate. In early 1968, he joined the staff of Boston's *Avatar*, unaware that the large, experimental commune that controlled the paper was a charismatic cult centered on a former-musician-turned-guru named Mel Lyman, whose psychic hold over his followers was then being strengthened and intensified by means of various confrontations and loyalty tests. Five years later, Kindman fled the commune's rural outpost in Kansas and headed west. When Kindman wrote this important journey into self-discovery, he was living in San Francisco, where he was a home-remodeling contractor, a key activist in a gay men's pagan spiritual network, a student, and a person with AIDS. He died peacefully on November 22, 1991.

by Joseph W. Grant. With sidebars by Richard T. Oakes, Warren Dearden, Bob Copeland, and Steve Levicoff

Twenty years ago, Joe Grant was a prisoner in the federal penitentiary at Leavenworth, Kansas. Back then, the feds used Leavenworth for the truly incorrigible. Leavenworth was where they sent the prisoners when they closed Alcatraz. Stepping into that prison was reminiscent of the opening paragraph of *Tale of Two Cities*. It was the best and the worst place to do time. The best place to be if you wanted to serve your prison sentence and not be bothered by anyone—prisoner or guard. The worst place to be if you were hoping to make parole. The best place for quiet in the cell blocks. The worst place for informers. The best place for food. The worst place for library books. The best place if you could learn by observing and be silent until spoken to. The worst place if you had a big mouth. It was in this atmosphere, Grant writes, that the idea began to take shape for *Penal Digest International*, a newspaper with two purposes: to provide prisoners with a voice that prison authorities could not silence and to establish lines of communication between prisoners and people in the free world.

PUBLISHER'S NOTES

Joseph W. Grant

The courage *Voices from the Underground* celebrates is ancient. That it details the times of our lives is happenstance. Walls of terrible, selfish wrong were splattered by the writers included here—writers who fought this fight with words and actions. Their assault weakened the walls of exclusion and secrecy that government had erected and exposed its military machinations.

My part is small. My contribution, as detailed in the final chapters concerning the *Penal Digest International* (*PDI*), is properly placed. Imprisonment and isolation are a last resort of the tyrant. My nobility was after the fact. I came late to the party, as a voice from the dungeon.

Twenty years later, when Ken Wachsberger asked me to write the *PDI*'s history for *Voices*, I was a different person. The *Penal Digest International* had become the *Prisoners Digest International* and had long since passed, in modern forms and under different names, to intensely ardent young women and men. I was by then suffering other lonely efforts under the ever-watchful eyes of a wife, whose intellect and field of study I greatly admire, and a college-bound daughter. At first I thought the publication of my old voice might finally enable me to explain myself to them. It was ego. I felt the pain of this reconstructed dissonance in purely personal terms. I did not see myself as one small part of a larger portrait.

Ken, on the other hand, believed that the other contributors and I were sitting on information of immense social value, especially to the younger

Grant is an artist, writer, and graphic designer living with his best friend and their daughter in the Southwest. His documentaries on El Salvador ("Prisons and Prisons: El Salvador") and author Meridel LeSueur ("Women in the Breadlines" and "The Iowa Tour") have been shown on the Time/Life and other cable networks. He believes that never before in our history has there been a greater need for the *PDI* to be publishing and providing a means for prisoners and people in the free world to communicate. He is open to suggestions.

generation of scholars and creative dissidents he calls "our intergenerational peers," who have learned about the sixties and the Vietnam era from the people we opposed then—many of whom cheered as our heads were busted and we were thrown into jail for exercising our constitutional rights to free speech and assembly.

While the writing of the *PDI*'s biography was occupying me obsessively, the original publisher withdrew from the project, citing a bad economy as the main reason and the possibility of libel as another. By the time my article was finished, Ken had found a New York agent and the manuscript was making the rounds of major publishing houses.

Ken and I talked at night long-distance. He read me the letters of rejection. The editors who wrote them were saying "No" in a wind of admiration: "an impressive piece of scholarship," said one; "much needed collection," said another; and a third—"couldn't put it down…extraordinary book…rave rejection…."

They wrote with praise and turned-away eyes as they said "No" in the "I-can't-afford-it" voice of the meek.

They were wrong, of course. For in the same way that we needed to hear history's voices from the underground that had witnessed against slavery and the Holocaust and the incidents at Wounded Knee, we must now hear these Vietnam era *Voices from the Underground*.

One night, long after these books should already have been in libraries and bookstores, after another of those midnight conversations with Ken, it finally dawned on me that I could not limit my participation to that of contributor and observer. And so again, late to the party, and worried about the insidious forms censorship—including self-censorship—continues to take in the nineties, I have become a publisher.

The voices you are privileged to read here are those of my sisters and brothers, brought together to share their dreams as well as their anger and frustration, their beatings and arrests, their triumphs and failures, and their lessons.

It's been an adventure and a challenge creating Mica's Press for the *Voices from the Underground* series. As this new publishing house continues to evolve, I hope it will do justice to the efforts of the biographers and exemplify the kind of sharing and acceptance that came of age within the underground movement of the Vietnam era. Founding and funding a publishing company is a story of its own—a story for another time.

For now, welcome to the underground of the Vietnam era and to a long overdue set of books. I hope these unimaginable experiences—these adventures—generate perilous thoughts, risky feelings, dangerous dreams, and the temptation for you to act on them.

Read them and decide. Then let your voice be heard.

MICA PRESS

FOREWORD

William M. Kunstler

It is a privilege to be asked to write a foreword to *Voices from the Underground*, a collection of alternative journalistic pieces of that portion of the 1960s and 1970s loosely referred to as the Vietnam era. This work could not have come at a more opportune time when, as starkly illustrated by the reportage of the Gulf War, the establishment media have supinely surrendered their appropriate functions in favor of accepting official briefings and handouts as legitimate sources of news. It is my hope that these fascinating and uniformly well-written pieces enjoy a wide currency, particularly among those who believe that the First Amendment means more than reprinting or broadcasting the words of Marlin Fitzwater or Norman Schwarzkopf.

It serves little purpose and probably would be a disservice to the book to attempt to discuss, in detail, every essay. It is enough to say that their subjects range from Joe Grant's long analysis of the history of the *Penal Digest International* to John Woodford's critique of the black press to Tim Wong's study of alternative journalism in Madison, Wisconsin to JoNina M. Abron's reminiscences about the life and death of the *Black Panther* newspaper. Underlying each article, however, is a common thread—the so-called underground press was indispensable in providing essential information about individuals, organizations, and subjects either totally ignored or profoundly distorted by the mass media.

In reading these essays, it is important not to contemplate the period in which their subject publications flourished in merely historical terms. The essential problem in probing any aspect of the Vietnam era is not to give the impression that corpses are being dissected. Even in the Reagan-Bush desert, there are still periodicals like *Lies of Our Times*, the *Nation*, the *Guardian*, and *In These Times*, to name but a short handful, that are attempting to give truth a chance. Perhaps, the most significant message of *Voices from the Underground* is to underscore the inestimable value of alternative journalism, especially in a period when the mass media are suffused with the antediluvian concepts of the beings they so routinely and unimaginatively classify as newsmakers, namely those sitting in high places.

Here's hoping that *Voices from the Underground* permeates upward.

Kunstler is a founder, vice president, and volunteer staff attorney, the Center for Constitutional Rights, New York, New York.

FOREWORD

Abe Peck

Another decade, another war. And another round of media coverage, warts and all.

As I write in early February 1991, reporting on the Persian Gulf war has been as whiz-bang as the technology waging it. Marshall McLuhan's prophecy about the global village has been validated in CNN real time. Hundreds of reporters have done their best to get the story, despite varying degrees of censorship invoked by every key nation involved in conflict. Skepticism of pollyanna-ish Pentagon claims has come earlier than it did in Vietnam; less than three weeks into the war, page one of the *New York Times* questioned blithe pronouncements of victory.

There's certainly more freedom to criticize one's own government in Washington than there is in Baghdad, and the Gulf War isn't a clone of Vietnam. But reading *Voices from the Underground* as somebody who was an underground newspaper editor the last time around, I've been struck by how familiar many of the limits of today's mainstream coverage seem, not only to me but to the writers who have recounted their own underground press experiences in its pages:

- The reportage that amazes also overwhelms and numbs the nervous system. minutiae from each up-close-and-personal briefing has buried discussion of whether or not war is necessary. As Chip Berlet, one-time underground news service writer turned muckraker of the Far Right, writes: "There is a distinctively American school of reporting—unconnected, ahistorical, anti-ideologi-

Peck chairs the magazine program at Northwestern University's Medill School of Journalism. He is the author of *Uncovering the Sixties: The Life and Times of the Underground Press*, which has just been re-released by Citadel Press.

cal...history and news covered as a sporting event. '[Enemies] bomb 3 ships but Navy sinks 2 gunboats...pix at eleven.' There is never time to explain why. Everything is a random events on the toteboard of history. We don't get information, we get Box Scores."

- Personalities and sidebar stories have obscured issues. As in the 1960s, there's been little mass-media questioning of whether a society in which millions are unemployed, homeless, addicted, or abused can afford to wage this war. "Only the pressing problems of the socialist countries...were (or are) described as systemic in our mass-marketing media...," recalls John Woodford, the former editor of *Muhammad Speaks* turned executive editor of the University of Michigan's News and Information Services. "If Vietnam, Laos, and Cambodia are failures of socialism, then what are Puerto Rico, Harlem, Brazil, Zaire, and the Philippines proof of the failure?"

- We've learned little about what the "other side" believes, and why. Saddam Hussein's all-too-real ruthlessness has been portrayed, but there hasn't been much insight into why he is supported by many in the Third World. Similarly, the language used to describe the conflict has had an underlying spin. Kuwaitis and Saudis have been "brave soldiers," not representatives of a tribal oligarchy or a plutocratic theocracy. The war has been one of "liberation," with little mention of a post-colonial restoration.

   No wonder underground press veterans hear echoes. As Ken Wachsberger, this book's editor, asks in his look at the East Lansing, Michigan scene: " [W]as a Black Panther described as being 'militant' or 'a black activist?' Were members of the Viet Cong 'terrorists' or 'freedom fighters?'"

- Official statements may be questioned, but they soon enter official Reality. George Bush's equation of Saddam Hussein with Adolf Hitler was debated, but in the end it made pulverizing his soldiers that much more acceptable.

- Access and predisposition have governed the spin put on stories. The missile attack on Tel Aviv rallied world opinion to Israel (and pierced my heart), in part because the Scuds landed on live television as reporters donned gas masks. But the Holocaust-laden image was based on to-date erroneous reports of chemical terror. And the missiles' explosions demolished casualty compari-

sons with the Israeli shelling of Beirut in 1982, or of news about Palestinian aspirations.

- Despite wider domestic opposition to war than existed until the Vietnam War was years old, nearly all coverage has been shot through a red, white, and blue lens. Prior to conflict, as the *Village Voice* has noted, magazine covers asked, "Will there be war?" not "Can there be peace?" With conflict on, television stations have told their audiences how to write to soldiers, but not how to contact peace activists. Peter Arnett faced backlash for his CNN reports from Baghdad, but George Bush somehow has avoided going one-on-one with an Iraqi reporter—or even with local dissident journalists such as Alexander Cockburn or Christopher Hitchens?

   Mass coverage of demonstrations has been all-too-familiar. Between the first commitment of U.S. troops in the Gulf and January 3, 1991, demonstration news ran one percent of total Gulf coverage, according to Fairness and Accuracy in Reporting. Stories lowballed crowd estimates and highlighted arrests, flag-burning, factionalism, or the supposed disillusionment of demonstrators. Meanwhile, the ideas behind the protests have been rarely discussed in mass media; of course, protest has never been advocated.

- Except for islands such as National Public Radio, mass media has assumed that its journalism is "objective"—scientific, neutral—rather than a craft based on bedrock suppositions of nationality, race, class, and culture—and on ownership, profit, and an advertising-oriented environment.

* * *

From 1964 to 1973 (and in some cases beyond), the underground press provided communities of radicals and freaks—as well as the simply curious—with alternative visions of how society might be shaped. Across the country, even around the world, these papers—usually tabloid, sometimes in color, run more on commitment than professional training—held a mirror to an America that had failed its own best hopes. War raged. Racism flouted court orders, killed those who mildly protested it, or hid behind a liberal smile. The environment was for picnicking, or exploiting. Young people were educated to be acquisitive, chaste, prematurely old. Women were trained to Stepford Wifery. Gays were told to heal their sickness.

   Though its roots extended back to Tom Paine and Frederick Douglass and *Appeal to Reason*, this underground-press incarnation began in 1964, when the *Los*

Angeles Free Press used the inexpensive new technology of offset printing to link non-sectarian leftism with the new energy coming out of the coffee houses on Sunset Boulevard. Soon after, Berkeley saw the *Barb* begin sticking it to the chronicles that demonstrators read in the dailies the morning after the big march. In East Lansing, Michigan, *The Paper* broadened the definition of what a college-town publication could cover. The *San Francisco Oracle* and New York's *East Village Other* not only noted but expressed a psychedelic consciousness.

There were five underground papers in 1965—2 of which are represented in this book; a dozen or so by 1967; 500 plus perhaps a thousand more at colleges and high schools by 1969. Whether flower power proponents or pick-up-the-gun advocates, this rainbow of protest reflected the credo expressed in *Voices from the Underground* by Nancy Strohl, who served on the staff of *Freedom of the Press*, an undergrounder published for sailors based at Yokosuka Naval Air Station in Japan, and now heads a legal services foundation in California:

"We held positions, we sought the truth, and we were part of the movement to change this country. While the *New York Times* was reporting history, the alternative press was involved in creating history. Most of us were activists as well as writers. We did not pretend to be objective, but stood for a point of view."

Those views varied, however, and this book offers testimony from a range of former underground editors and writers rather than a single narrative. But any lost continuity is made up for by skillful editing and a welcome range of voices in the chorus. *Voices from the Underground* includes writers not just from big-city papers on either coast, but from small towns, military bases, even the prisons. Especially prominent are some of the feminist and gay writers who created a revolution within the revolution. Appropriately for a time that proclaimed "the personal is political," these pieces are biographies both of young people who found themselves suddenly at odds with their Mother Country and the papers they spoke through.

* * *

"Many people recall 1967 to 1969 as a period in which events began to develop in a furiously rapid manner," socialist labor organizer, gender activist, and writer Bob Hippler recalls in his history of Detroit's *Fifth Estate*. "Demonstrations grew from 100,000 one year to 1 million two years later. Students went from peaceful petitioning to seizing university buildings, all in the same period. Black nationalists overtook the civil rights movement, and strident radical declarations were met with systematic police violence. In Vietnam, the U.S. went from rosy predictions of 'the light at the end of the tunnel' to the devastating Tet offensive that forced Lyndon Johnson from office. Time and events seemed crazily telescoped, and to many young people revolution indeed seemed possible, especially after the student-inspired general strike in France."

As the 1960s moved toward the 1970s, the Summer of Love gave way to the Spring of Assassinations, the Battle of Chicago, and beyond. The papers became more serious, more militant. They also reformed internally, as collective editorships replaced masthead hierarchy, choosing full representation over expertise if need be. Many underground writers now felt themselves members of a millions-strong world movement that was winning the war in Southeast Asia. "I was especially happy, too, because now I was part of a news staff that didn't just oppose the war against the peoples of Vietnam, Laos, and Cambodia," writes John Woodford, who'd been an editor at *Ebony* before joining *Muhammad Speaks*. "It openly supported and rooted for the victory of these nations targeted for near-destruction by the U.S...."

The underground press was the place where each new movement could declare itself without having its beliefs strained through a mainsteam filter. And so, the *Furies* was published, according to former collective member Ginny Berson, to proclaim a radical-lesbian-feminist desire "to build a movement in this country and in the world which can effectively stop the violent, sick, oppressive acts of male supremacy. We want to build a movement which makes all people free."

* * *

But as these essays also show, overthrowing both the government and all vestiges of bourgeois mentality was a high-anxiety calling. Politically, papers stretched thin to promulgate an increasing number of sometimes contradictory correct lines, or to defend groups of increasingly hazy merit. Reporting—never most papers' strongest suit—could be distorted to make the proper point. "No matter," recalls Victoria Smith, an alumna of Houston's *Space City!* turned professor of communications—"the story served our purpose, which was to trash the cops."

The cops trashed back: Underground papers felt the full range of paranoia-producing harassment, a homegrown taste of the violence the government was exporting. And if a little repression could be "tonic," as Smith says, she recalls a less dramatic problem—the limbo between "opposition and organizational collapse," between militancy and absorption, between passion and professionalism, between what tired old hands knew and the energy of less with-it newcomers.

Internal pressures grew. "Peace now" became "armed love," and some writers left after being hectored for insufficient militancy, or to avoid becoming what they'd opposed. Papers missed issues as staffers tried to incorporate still another movement into their lives. Burnout flared, desire for a personal life or personal talent rekindled. Few papers paid staffers more than a pittance, and the war's costs began to affect even a lean-and-mean counterculture. Undergrounds bit the record-company and head shop hands that fed many papers, and those ads went to more palatable print or FM-radio alternatives. Some readers also exited, turned off by too much rhetoric, too much rage.

It all added up. "By mid-1972," the *Fifth Estate*'s Bob Hippler recalls, "a whole group of staffers had left, not out of various political disagreements, like much of the 1969 exodus, but out of general exhaustion."

* * *

By 1973, Chip Berlet was in Boulder, Colorado, attending "the last meeting of the underground press in both name and form." The draft was over and the last U.S. troops were helicoptering out of Saigon, and now the workshops were less about revolutionary politics or collective acid-gobbling than community news or even how to mold a firm advertising base. Nominations were taken to change the name of the papers' association from the Underground Press

Syndicate to the Alternative Press Syndicate. "The vote in favor of the change was overwhelming," Berlet writes, "and the Boulder conference served as a line of demarcation between two eras in alternative journalism." Soon after, many of the surviving undergrounders folded their pages.

The papers eulogized in this book could descend into propaganda. They could be goofy, extreme, just plain wrong. None of their utopias came to fruition. They chewed up more than a few people. But there's also the plus side of the ledger. Commitment, conviction, and radical perspective gave the papers influence disproportionate to their small staffs and meager finances. At its best, the underground press also unveiled new vistas on What Might Be, offered an honestly subjective record of life during wartime as an antidote to Official Reality, published provocative writing and graphics. It helped to stop a war and unseat two warrior presidents. It allowed movements to discuss their politics on their own terms. It introduced feminism, gay rights, ecology, a critique of consumerism, and a sense of planetary politics to society as a whole. If this book contains recriminations, it also includes a far larger number of glad-I-was-there from people who were able to unite their work, politics, life, and art—and have some fun along the way. Warts and all, the underground press was the dissident brave enough to see through the Empire's New Clothes.

EDITOR'S INTRODUCTION

Ken Wachsberger

Voices from the Underground: Insider Histories of the Vietnam Era Underground Press is about the alternative newspapers of the Vietnam era—what we romantically called the underground press—and about its veterans, the individuals who chronicled the events and ideas and at times led the uprising in this country that toppled two presidents, ended an imperialist war, and introduced a new paradigm for the post-scarcity society.

Although several excellent histories of the underground press already have been written, for the most part their story lines are third person analyses of the "mainstream underground papers"—that is, the better known ones that published mainly on the two coasts. In this way, *Voices from the Underground* is unique among underground press histories. The strength of the underground press was the fact that there were underground newspapers on college campuses, countercultural communities, and other pockets of resistance *everywhere* in the country. Where did they come from? What did they want? What lessons can we learn from their experience? For answers to these questions, we need to talk to the people who were there.

In a sometimes structured, sometimes loose, sometimes almost mystical way, those papers united in opposition to our government's war against the people of Vietnam while calling attention to other, social issues as well—issues that the establishment press may well have ignored without prodding. This book is an attempt—and a humble one at that—to answer these questions while capturing some sense of the immense landscape of lifestyles and issues covered by that independent alternative press.

When I began laying the groundwork for this book, I intended to include representative histories of what I believed to be every component part of what made up the underground press. To that end, I've failed

Wachsberger is editor of *Voices from the Underground: Insider Histories of the Vietnam Era Underground Press* and *Voices from the Underground: A Directory of Resources and Sources on the Vietnam Era Underground Press*. His article on the underground newspapers from East Lansing, Michigan appears in this collection.

Acknowledgment: I would like to thank the following Pierian Press individuals for their assistance over the past four years: typesetter Gloria Thompson, who performs magic on WordPerfect and can read my handwriting; proofreader Sandy Stefl, whose eye for stylistic inconsistency is legendary (and frustrating during last-minute reads), and publisher Ed Wall, who encouraged me to tell this story as I lived it and supported me as it grew from an article in *Serials Review* to a special double issue to a book to a two-volume set of books, which eventually was published by Mica's Press.

and succeeded. Lack of time prevented potential contributors from completing histories that would have at least acknowledged some of the "gaps" that still remain: *Getting Together*, from San Francisco, and *Gidra*, from Los Angeles, represented segments of the Asian-American community; *Akwesasne Notes* did the same for the Native American community. *El Malcriado* is still the voice of the United Farmworkers; *Gray Panther* speaks for the senior citizens. Editors or past editors of all these papers supported this project but were unable to meet our deadline due to their own present activities. Other newspapers that were regretfully unable to be included in this volume include *Los Angeles Free Press, Rising Up Angry, Ain't I a Woman, Ann Arbor Sun, Cincinnati Independent Eye, East Village Other, The Ladder, Great Swamp Erie da da Boom, Gay Sunshine, Austin Rag, Fat Albert's Death Ship, Up from the Bottom, Semper Fi, Left Face*, and *Country Woman*. Hopefully these histories will emerge in time for *Voices from the Underground—Part 2*.

Nevertheless, what I learned in my attempt to fill those gaps is that they could never be so simplistically defined anyhow. *off our backs*, for example, was and still is a "feminist" newspaper but staff members and contributors from the beginning spoke out against racism. *Muhammad Speaks* was the newspaper of the Black Muslims but editors supported the struggles of oppressed peoples of all colors. Any artificially enforced classification on my part then would only have done injustice to the diversity of voices not only among different underground newspapers of the period but also within individual newspapers that I have tried to show through this collection.

I have gained immense insight in the course of my research, as you will also as you read these insider histories of newspapers that represented the countercultural, gay, lesbian, feminist, Puerto Rican, black, socialist, Southern consciousness, prisoners' rights, new age, student, and military alternative voices. Original copies of those newspapers still can be found in libraries and private collections around the country; the high tech revolution has put them onto microfilm. In beginning your independent research beyond this book, you will want to utilize the valuable reference guides that are found in *Voices from the Underground: A Directory of Resources and Sources on the Vietnam Era Underground Press*, which complements this volume.

I didn't ask much of contributors, merely that they look back through the haze of simplistic Reagan anecdotes that defined the eighties, on beyond the post-Vietnam Me Decade burnout that defined the seventies to what were the most intense politically defining years of their lives—and give me histories of their respective papers. "What we're looking for," I told them, "is a candid description and assessment, told in your own creative way with all the richness, resilience, texture, detail, and candor of the articles that you wrote during the Vietnam years."

What I found was a reservoir of experiences that were waiting to be tapped. For some contributors, those experiences continue to drive them today. Their articles were vehicles to self-discovery and an opportunity to untangle these confusing events. Michael Kindman, for instance, tells for the first time his story of how he went from founding East Lansing, Michigan's *The Paper*, one of the first five members of Underground Press Syndicate, to getting caught up in a personality cult in Boston and seeing his entire existence become enveloped by the negative energy of the group's charismatic leader, whose words solidified his own psychic hold on his followers through the pages of *Avatar*. Later, while living in San Francisco, he became a key activist in a gay men's pagan spiritual network. He died of AIDS on November 22, 1991, two months after completing his story.

As the stories of the other contributors show, their energies are still working for positive change. John Woodford is a member of the board of the National Alliance of Third World Journalists. Sally Gabb is a specialist in adult literacy. The day I called Harvey Wasserman—whose *Harvey Wasserman's History of the United States* begins with the line, "The Civil War made a few businessmen very rich"—I was told he had just left town to speak at a rally outside the reopening of the Seabrook nuclear power plant.

Any written history is a product of its author's bias. Thus, there are no "definitive" histories here. Jack Smith, for instance, in his history of the *Guardian*, tells about the staff dissension that led to the creation of the breakaway *Liberated Guardian*. Veterans of *Liberated Guardian* would no doubt interpret the same events differently. Harvey Wasserman writes about Liberation News Service from the perspective of its Washington contingent; veterans of its New York contingent will tell a different story. What the stories share are experiences of police harassment, internal dissension, government infiltration, legitimate reasons to be paranoid, shoestring budgets, raw energy, courage, commitment, dreams, and determination.

The period was a vision as much as a reality. It was a time of experimentation. We made mistakes and learned from them. In the beginning, men attacked sexism while women typed their articles. In the end, women founded the feminist and lesbian press and men learned that it was okay to cry. For all its faults, the sixties was a magical period. A time warp opened up and those who stepped inside glimpsed the new paradigm that brought together the best visions of the visionaries and showed us, on a small scale, how to make them work. On the pages of the underground press, writers tried to reduce the vision to the written word and apply the strategies to a larger scale. Those who were touched remain touched.

As David Doggett writes in "*The Kudzu*: Birth and Death in Underground Mississippi," "To this day, if you talk to anyone who was active in the sixties you will discover that he or she still has that vision of racial harmony, of an economic system that nurtures those at the bottom rather than adds to their numbers, of a political system with participatory democracy rather than sham republicanism, of a culture in which work and play are fun and creative rather than desperate and destructive and there is international appreciation and cooperation in maintaining the environment."

History has shown that we were correct in our overall analysis: that the personal is political, that international politics shares a bed with domestic politics. In fact, we were *too* right. We didn't just expose the dark side of America's consumerist society, we ripped it apart and tore its insides out. The Reagan years were America's plastic surgery years; the wound was covered. Under Bush, the wound oozed out from underneath the cosmetic covering.

If we made an overriding mistake, it was that we wanted change to come about faster than most people could handle change. One lesson we learned is that, even when we are operating under a sense of immediacy, other people are for the most part conservative. This doesn't mean people buy the narrow "every man for himself" philosophy of reactionary "conservatives" but rather that they want to move deliberately. In time, and with access to information, they will move along a progressive path.

The drug crisis of today is an example of information spurned. If you learned about the sixties from Ronald and Nancy Reagan you would think that recreational marijuana smoking is the cause of today's crack/cocaine crisis. Study the underground papers of the period or read the articles in this study and you'll see that, time and again, articles and special issues warned against heroin, smack, speed, amphetamines, uppers, downers, and all the other death drugs, and even were the first to point out that the CIA, which was once headed by George Bush, helped to bring some of them into the country. How many lives would have been saved and how many inner cities would not be drug-infested and crime-ridden today if in the sixties we had legalized or decriminalized marijuana and increased the budget for drug counseling and job training programs instead of prisons? Today, George

Shultz and Milton Friedman and William Buckley and other warriors from the right are finally admitting we were correct all along.

* * *

I was teaching freshman composition at Eastern Michigan University the night George Bush began the bombing of Baghdad on January 16, 1991. My students and I discussed the war and the Middle East and many related topics. Then, for an assignment, I asked them to give me 4 to 6 pages on some aspect of the war.

What I found was a passion in their writing that I seldom see in writing assignments. What they said, however, reflected tremendous confusion that blanketed their fear and anger and sadness. For instance, one woman focused her introduction on a condemnation of all antiwar protesters. In the body of her paper, she nearly came out in support of the popular antiwar position that we're only there for oil and expressed opposition to an impending draft because it might grab her boyfriend and thus disrupt her life and his. In the conclusion, she came back to her condemnation of the protesters, apparently forgetting that she had just supported them.

Some voiced opposition to the war, even considered it immoral, but said they would go if they were called, in the name of "support for the troops"—action based on guilt and military bandwagons rather than reason.

One student wrote, "If the protesters don't love this country enough to support the war, they can leave it." Déjà vu. I've heard that before.

According to popular polls, the American public registered phenomenal support for the war. I believe they supported it because they weren't aware of alternative sources of information, such as *The Progressive, The Nation, In These Times, Mother Jones, Village Voice, Guardian*, and those other independent publications and news organizations, for instance, that are challenging in court the federal government's censorship of press coverage during the Persian Gulf War. I waited in vain for polls to ask, "Have you thought critically about President Bush's decision to wage war instead of pursuing peace through negotiation?" or, "Have you looked to sources other than self-interested politicians and celebrity news people for opinions on the war?"

It's time to listen again to the poets and visionaries of the independent alternative press.

In Memoriam

Michael "Mica" Kindman

May 8, 1945 - November 22, 1991

At This End of the Oregon Trail

The Eugene *AUGUR*: 1969-1974

Peter Jensen

"Twenty years ago today," goes the Sgt. Pepper song and the memories of America's underground press. We thought we were Camus writing for *Le Combat* in Nazi-occupied France. An alien force had taken over our country: it talked peace and made vicious war; it owned both political parties. We were all that was left of the opposition, but we were everywhere in the streets in mass demonstrations and sinking new roots in old communities all over America. Above all, the media had caved in and was reporting inflated, daily body counts for generals in Saigon and Washington. For all our "freedom of the press," the press was just another chain of corporations acting like a line of skimpily dressed cheerleaders for the boys in grunt green, who were fighting against the will of eighty percent of the people in a small but tough country 9,000 miles away across the world's widest ocean.

By 1969, it was obvious that the National Liberation Front (NLF) of South Vietnam was winning its war. This fact shook the established American Empire to its core. On April Fool's Day 1968, a Democratic president resigned. On Inhoguration Day 1969, a crooked, Republican lawyer from Orange County was sworn in as president of some of the people some of the time. We knew we were in for a long airwar bombing campaign to punish the NLF for winning in the countryside and megatons upon megatons of lies (see appendix 1).

Most of the people who started underground papers in their towns were in their twenties or thirties and were veterans (since 1960) of the peace and antiwar

Jensen has been an activist for peace and freedom since 1960. In addition to teaching English at Lane Community College in Eugene, he has published three books of poems: *This Book Is Not a Mask for Tear Gas* (1970); *When Waves Sprout Birds: Twenty Years of Poetry (1965-1985)*; and *Confluence* (with David Johnson and Erik Muller, 1991). He also works as a fundraiser for the Oregon Natural Resources Council, the largest membership conservation organization in the western states.

movements. Most were also far from home trying to live in college towns after they were done with school. The people who started the *AUGUR* in Eugene represented both fronts: antiwar and alternative community. Both groups of activists were action-oriented: they set out to make the news and then write about it. This style of journalism was not new in America. American revolutionary journalist Tom Paine wrote George Washington's newsletter, *Common Sense*, after each battle explaining the strategic retreat to Valley Forge and the British warships' firebombing of Kingston, New York, a war crime to remember on the Hudson River. This kind of journalism demanded a very fierce, engaged objectivity. From the start in Eugene, antiwar demonstrations and new food co-ops, free clinics, and concerts got equal press.

What people called the "movement" of the sixties and seventies was an anti-fascist movement. Other wings of this movement were: 1) the liberation movements of Third World people and Native Americans; 2) the women's liberation movement; 3) a community-based war against narks who were dealing drugs; 4) the gay liberation movement; 5) the radical environmental movement; 6) the alternative, small business movement; and 7) what people called the hippy, alternative culture movement. Most of us tried to embrace all these wings: we wanted to forge a new majority. The *AUGUR* was started by a small crew of community activists around the Wootens' Odyssey Coffee House and the Oregon Country Fair; then it passed over to a group I belonged to—a collective of Students for a Democratic Society (SDSers) from the University of Oregon. But often, we could not serve all trends fully. At first, women on the *AUGUR* staff introduced our community to the basics of women's liberation. Later, around 1972, some lesbian and non-lesbian women broke off because they wanted to concentrate on women's issues and because they had become "separatists." They established *Women's Press*, a nationally important publication that still exists today as a regional publication. News of the women's movement, however, continued to receive major coverage in the pages of the *AUGUR*.

The streets of Eugene were filled with demonstrators—at least four major marches a year. The paper staff helped plan each march, called for it in the pages of our paper, went out and marched, spoke at rallies, took photographs, came back and wrote our stories and criticisms, sold ads, worked in the darkroom, did layout, took the paper to our printer, did distribution, and sold papers in the streets. Although some of us were experts, we held that everyone should learn to do everything. We tried to come out with a new edition every two weeks. We had a rotating editorship whose role was to coordinate the story list, and an ad sales coordinator for every issue. Most of us had other part-time jobs. Many of us counted on the income from each paper (a dime out of 25 cents) to help pay rents. We printed as many as 4,000 in each run, but we sent out almost 1,000 free subscriptions to prisoners, and we exchanged with many other collectives. Many of us got food stamps; for the first time, many of us lived below the poverty line while working hard and inventing new ways of cheaper and more natural collective living. I lived in an *AUGUR* collective house of two men and two women—a couple and two singles. I was too busy to worry.

At that time, Eugene had 54,000 inhabitants. Today, it has grown to 106,000, but it is still surrounded by a belt of farms and a further-out sea of cutover national and private forestlands. Organic agriculture and destructive forestry practices dominated our paper from the start. In 1970, women from the *AUGUR* collective attended a conference on women's health issues in British Columbia. There, they met a Cambodian woman doctor, who had walked 700 miles in the jungles of Indochina and had flown to Canada from China. She told them of the massive numbers of cancers, birth defects, and miscarriages caused by spraying herbicides (among them, agent orange) to destroy the rain forests, which provided cover for the NLF. This was a war crime we called "ecocide." That same year, Air Force doctors halted the spraying, and an Oregon State forestry professor, "Spray for an A" Mike Newton, added water and sprayed Oregon forestlands with those same, banned herbicides. Thus began a twenty-year battle to stop the use of herbicides, which caused miscarriages, birth defects, and still-to-be-detected cancers in rural communities all around Eugene. The war had come home to America in an insidious way none of us had suspected; the fetuses of our people would suffer, while the so-called "right-to-lifers" were pro-industry and full of hypocrisy.

There were plans for a system of concentric freeways around Eugene and more nuclear power plants in Oregon. The *AUGUR* staff helped lead the fight against those gross developments, and quality of life issues are still at the heart of Eugene community politics. In 1972, we campaigned for and won a citywide referendum requiring a vote on all new limited-access freeway proposals inside city limits. Some of us went into local politics: the Eugene City Council, the Lane County Commission, and the Oregon legislature. Many of us are still in activist organizations working for progressive social change, with this difference: we are now getting paid for our work.

It's interesting to note that all the underground papers had so much in common. We had fun looking over other papers; we put them on our mailing list and exchanged with most of the papers that are represented in this collection of essays, as well as others. We often took strength or articles or ideas from other papers. Some of our favorites were the *Great Speckled Bird*, the *Berkeley Tribe, Akwesasne Notes, off our backs, The Black Panther*, and the *Ann Arbor Sun*. Later, an underground press "syndicate" was born and our very own news service, Liberation News Service (LNS), was sent every week from New York. LNS provided us with the best graphics, cartoons, stories, and short news flashes from many sources. Eugene is over 600 miles from San Francisco or Seattle; we like it that way, but we needed big city information to turn out a good, small city newspaper.

There were many local roots here for radicals. Eugene was the hometown of Oregon Senator Wayne Morse, one of two senators who voted against the war from the beginning. Ken Kesey, author of *One Flew Over the Cuckoo's Nest* and *Sometimes a Great Notion*, lives up the hill in Pleasant Hill. In the early seventies, both were frequent speakers, and they represented well, for a while, two wings of Eugene's identity at that time: the serious, political activist and the jesting, cultural trickster. In addition, the Woodsmen of the World, some of them IWW Wobblies and woodproducts union activists, had built a dance hall here in 1932, and this WOW Hall was rebuilt and became a center for dances, concerts, poetry readings, theater, fundraisers, and community talent shows.

We found places in the local economy to sink our roots for money. One of the most important phases of forestry—tree planting: replacing the 200 ancient forest species with ten-inch, Douglas-fir seedling, crop trees—was an unorganized and exploited part of the economy. The Hoedads were the first forestry workers' cooperative that did quality work at a living wage. This cooperative is just one of many that formed. Food production, farming, food distribution and sales, baking, restaurants, clothing, garages, music groups—people tried out all the basic parts of the economy in cooperative form. In fact, we could not have published the *AUGUR* without these businesses. They were our advertisers; they provided our staff with jobs; their retail stores were some of our most important sales counters. And the more we developed, the more we found that we had been preceded by a wave of Eugene area cooperatives in the thirties. The local milk distributor was started by dairy farmers as a cooperative in the Great Depression. One of the plywood mills was owned by four remaining members of a larger cooperative. We found that, in many ways, the thirties had laid down a foundation for us in the sixties. We made it because they made it.

The *AUGUR* office was a confusing, exciting place to work. People with good ideas mixed with people with half-vast ideas. We were full of courage and paranoia, wisdom and foolishness. The FBI tried to shut us down. Agents approached our printer and tried to bully him, but he was an old union activist, and he smiled as he told us what he said to them: "I'm a small businessman and a capitalist. These people always pay their bills, and I need their money. Besides, I think their paper is a kick!" (Our printer had been a jazz musician in the 1930s.) He always helped us plan our color bleeds on the cover, our "tie-dyed art" covers. The IRS tried to shut us down. Agents came to our staff meeting and asked all the wrong questions, like "Who's in charge here?" A circle of rather hairy people just laughed at them. The agents had never before met a tightly knit group of anarchists, and we had a lot of fun with them.

Both narks and local hard drugs dealers tried to shut us down. Agents threatened us from both sides of the "war on drugs." We were fond of publishing pictures of undercover narks busting local pot growers and smokers, and we were fed these photos by a large, shadowy collection of people, who called themselves "People Into Sabotaging Surveillance" (PISS). When we found that the owners at one drug paraphernalia store, who advertised with us, were dealing cocaine, we picketed them and published a story on their drug dealing. When we were visited by a local hood with polished black shoes, who offered us a drug profits deal, I ran for our camera, but he escaped while threatening us harm. Of course, once the Vietnam vets were back and organized into a 400-member Lane County chapter of Vietnam Veterans Against the War (VVAW), we felt a lot safer. In fact, once they took over organizing the demonstrations, we often defeated or stalemated the sheriff's department in the streets. Soon, Vietnam vets and women were working as cops in the Eugene Police Department, and some of the police agents who attended our meetings were on our side!

One time, in 1971, we put out a paper for a demonstration that promised to be huge (4,000) by Eugene standards and, pretending this would be the start of the "revolution," we called on all demonstrators to wear wool watch caps, heavy jackets, and bandanas for tear gas. We knew no one sane would wear all that stuff on a hot, summer night in "mellow, little Eugene," so we organized a seven-person camera team that consisted of one photographer with a flash and six defenders, and we took photos of all men in watch caps and heavy jackets; they all turned out to be cops, which made a nice two-page spread of undercover cop photos. And we sang: "All we are saying is pull down your pants." When things got really heavy in Cambodia in spring 1970, a couple of us were busted as part of the Eugene Thirteen, because we were on a list of folks who had held a bullhorn more than ten times each, and we were falsely charged with felony riot—"Must bust in early May/Orders from the D.A." (Bob Dylan)—under an unconstitutional law that had been passed to bust Chinese railroad workers. They had built Oregon's early rail lines in the late 1800s and then, once they were finished, were told they were not welcome to stay. We were part of this proud heritage. Charges were dropped three years later.

By 1973, with Watergate and all, the worm had turned on our enemies. I remember one peace demonstration a month after Nixon had bombed Hanoi and Haiphong on Christmas and lost one-third of his bomber force. We were getting ready to march, but the Eugene City Council had issued us a march permit to start at 1:00 P.M., and our marchers were late in forming up. An older cop in a car told us we couldn't march, but a younger motorcycle cop with a beard drove up and asked me, "Where are we going, brother?" I nearly cried; it was such a change.

Often, we felt out of touch with modern Amerika, which we always spelled with a "k" the way Franz Kafka and my Danish grandparents had. We felt like immigrants from another time zone. The origin of the *AUGUR*'s name, meaning a bird priest from ancient Rome, was appropriate to Oregon, where there still is an environment with some birds to defend. Our paper's logo had a bearded old guy in a toga reading meanings (auguries) from the patterns of flights of birds and writing down Nature's messages. The Lower Willamette Valley used to be home to hundreds of thousands of waterfowl, hundreds of bald eagles, and the Kalapooyan tribe. Now we have a few wintering eagles we share with Alaska, 60,000 ducks in a good year in local, leftover wetlands, and nothing but stones, bones, and baskets left by the peaceful Kalapooyans.

Much has been written about the meaning of the culture of the sixties, and in Eugene, a city the *Wall Street Journal* called "a mecca for the terminally hip," that culture lives on as a mainstream for a quickly aging generation. The *AUGUR* was one of the mainstays of that culture. We always had a poetry page, and I often edited it and printed the best local poetry I could find. Many of us did music and theater reviews; most of the music was political or rebellious. Remembering is as easy as putting on a tape. The San Francisco Mime Troupe was our favorite, and some of their local income went into printing our paper. The record stores were some of our truest advertisers. I always wondered why we were called the "alternative" culture. Sinatra was mainstream for his generation; why were the Beatles and the Grateful Dead not mainstream for ours? When I think of the passions and the big ideas of my own life, the culture of my generation is my blood's mainstream. What else was there: the death kulture of the Pentagon?

Much also has been written about sex, drugs, and nonviolence, and all that was a lot of fun for some of us. In Oregon, Nature gave us a somewhat gentler ride, as we tripped and skinny-dipped and tried to keep the faith. The movement here was quite artistic, and Nature inspired many of the graphics we printed in the *AUGUR*. There is something about a full moon rising out of a snow-covered volcano that neither a coyote nor a human being can resist. Nature makes us wail, and our photography, art works, and street guerrilla theater groups were full of the sexy juice of our mother Earth. Often, I felt we were overripe fruit dribbling down the chin of some giant faces, but, when I compared that image with the body bags from 'Nam, I knew that our little messes were just humanity living it up somewhere in the surrounding galaxy. When our time is evaluated, I want to be there to make the case for our generation's culture starting the American Renaissance, no matter how long it lasts.

The underground press was full of this rebirth of science and spirit. The highs and the lows, the excitement and the bitter pain were all part of that coming out of the womb of our parents' world. They had endured the Great Depression and helped to win World War II; we inherited their survival instincts and their victories. Our paper helped to unify people and give them a shared vision of what was happening. Stories on organic gardening flowed into stories on ancient poets flowed into stories on Vietnamese villages being bombed with flaming napalm, but rebuilding into tunnels and caves flowed into feminist writings about women's orgasms and health clinics flowed into struggles of Native Americans to keep the culture of Raven and Eagle alive flowed into saving French Pete Creek with its streamside hiking trail flowed into nutritional information on organic foods flowed into medical and mental health care flowed into viewing an eclipse of the moon at 4:00 A.M. flowed into community housing and historic preservation flowed into the *AUGUR*'s cartoonists dueling the forces of darkness.

My main point is that cultural alienation ended: everything was connected to everything else, and our writing style was free to flow. Our paper layout reflected the electric rock-and-roll power of our culture. Sure it was new-lefty, trippy-hippy, but it moved us, because it was our own, and, if it failed us, we could always change. Anyway, you can't stick your foot in the same era twice. Here, by the Willamette and McKenzie rivers, its obvious reality is always on the move. Often, we had to let those changes roll over the pages of our paper. Many layout nights, we were up until dawn making changes until the car left for the printer ninety miles away just up the Yaquina River from Newport on the Oregon coast.

The *AUGUR* went under in 1974. Sure, we were burned out, but it's still hard to say why. We learned that publications also have lives of their own. *Women's Press* continued for a few more years. Some of the *AUGUR* staff helped create the next community-based paper, *The Willamette Valley Observer*, which lasted from 1975 to 1984. Some of us started *10-point 5 arts magazine*, which lasted from 1974 to 1981. In 1984, a new community paper, *What's Happening*, took over the niche first occupied by the *AUGUR*, and it is doing well today. *What's Happening* is a free paper that survives and pays decent wages on advertising income only. What a far cry from earning ten cents per copy of the *AUGUR* on the street corner to pay one's rent in the long-ago exciting times, when we thought we were making a revolution, and our excited readers thought so, too!

Now I'm forty-seven years old, teaching college and working to raise money for conservation work in Oregon. I have an interesting box of all the old *AUGUR*s in my closet with a collection of photos with waxed backs. I tried to donate the papers to the periodical section of the University of Oregon's library, but a friend there told me they didn't have the money to microfilm them. "They'll get stolen issue by issue," he said. So they're still in my closet, and almost everytime I clean, I get caught up and trapped in the past looking them over. Grassroots history is hiding in my closet. Actually, early in the history of the *AUGUR*, and I suspect this happened to most other "undergrounds" as well, Northwestern University in Evanston, Illinois, bought a library subscription and told us they had grant money (from Bell and Howell) to microfilm all the underground papers in America. So that's where our collective archives are for anyone interested in doing research on those times. We suspected that the CIA might have paid for all that microfilming, but who knows? Northwestern is one of the most heavily endowed universities. Anyway, leave it to the CIA to study the last domestic, democratic upsurge, while the next one builds behind their backs like a tsunami. It was CIA intellectuals who said that once six percent of the Vietnamese were willing to pick up a gun the war was lost, but presidents don't listen to CIA "eggheads" either. By the time the White House and the Pentagon woke up, Vietnamese teenagers were armed to the teeth.

I don't know what can re-create those times for younger folks. Despite all the strange events between 1969 (and the end of the Vietnam War in 1975) and the present, I feel a connection to those times that will not die. The revolution never happened; our generation has not come to power in America with a transforming vision for democracy. Yuppies replaced yippies in advertising. The Reagan years spread out against the sky like a war machine stalled within its own borders. The New Right enjoyed obscene amounts of media and money power—more than we even dreamed of—but what did it get them? Colonel North with chocolate cake on his face in Tehran? The idiot Contras? Reagan knighted by the English Queen? Tammy Bakker's eye make-up? Dan Quayle next to the White House? A Supreme Kourt that says you can burn the flag some of the time, but you can't control your body all the time? With these people, the right to life ends at birth! They still don't know what the hell they're doing. Remember Vietnam? Remember nuclear power? Remember Bhopal and Prince William Sound? They've been screwing up for decades and wasting the power of our country. Now, a trillion dollars deeper in debt, we still need a "rebirth of wonder."

But life, at the local level, goes on. The Vietnamese won their war for freedom and independence. The United States still needs a Solidarity movement and a radical, Gorby-type restructuring. Most of the liberation movements in the world have suffered and matured. Some have turned weird from too much pain. But the planet is in grave danger from the nonrenewable, world economy. We knew it back then, and we were frightened in the sixties by our dark vision of the poisoning of the planet. That was like a bad acid trip back then. Now, we're twenty years further into the destruction, and the living Earth is in much more serious trouble, with continental-sized holes in the ozone over both poles and atmospheric warming. The destroyers of the planet can never say they weren't warned. Just as we chanted during the antiwar movement in the streets, they still need to respond when we say, "Join us!" Sometimes, twenty years ago today seems like yesterday. In the life of our species, twenty years is just one breath in and one breath out.

As the Voyager 2 space probe rounds Neptune and dives out of the solar system, it's painfully obvious that not all blue planets support life. Thanks to Carl Sagan and many others, the technology of the early seventies is still sending us family photos from the outer planets. Thomas Jefferson wrote that each generation needs to make its own revolution. I'm still waiting and writing. Goodbye, Voyager 2! Write if you find work.

APPENDIX 1: "THE AIRWAR & THEN...MORE WAR!"[1]

by Peter Jensen

While 40 thousand NVA trash Nixon's Vietnamization, & perhaps his President[i]al hopes, along with the NLF attacks out of Cambodia & the Central Highlands, here's a review of what has led up to this massive offensive. While we were at the Santa Barbara Conference on the San Diego demonstrations, we were told that all of the scattered attacks in Indochina were carried out by local militia, & that the NLF-NVA main forces were lying low. Now we know where they were & why. But the months & years preceeding have been filled with deception & escalation by the most hated President of the United States. Using all the public relations power of his position, Nixon pretended to be winding down the war, but here are the terrible large numbers which describe an escalated war.

All the confusion about the war winding down was deliberate, guaranteed to give Nixon time to make the same devastating mistakes as LBJ. U.S. GI's killed in action did drop 90% in four years: 1968—15,000 killed, 1969—9,400 killed, & 1971—1,400 killed. & with the change to ARVN dead, the cost of the war was cut in half, from $90,000 for each American killed. Nixon, the supreme racist, had succeeded in changing the color of the corpses. Last year about 22,000 ARVN soldiers were killed, & according to Pentagon figures, total Asian military casualties per month have almost doubled: 4,300/month (LBJ) & 7,400/month (Nixon). The monthly civilian toll under Nixon is 130,000—compared to 95,000 under LBJ. The Liberal demand of 1968—that the South Vietnamese do their own fighting—has been turned into double genocide.

Nixon has also escalated the airwar & expanded heavy bombing to 4 countries. Since WW II, the U.S. Military has unsuccessfully attempted to bomb small Asian nations back into the stone age—the measure of U.S. barbarism can be summed up in this table of Pentagon figures:

KOREAN	1 million tons bombs dropped
ALL OF WW II	2 million tons
VIETNAM (1965-68, LBJ's Operation Rolling Thunder)	3,215,000 tons
VIETNAM & INDOCHINA (1969-March 72, Nixon's AIRWAR)	3,776,000 tons

On top of that, Nixon's monthly average was way ahead of LBJ's: Monthly average, LBJ years—59,704 vs. monthly average, Nixon years—95,402 tons. If we add the projected tons that Nixon will drop until Nov. 1972, there will be a total of 4.5 million tons of bombs for Nixon's "wound down" war. Nixon has ordered the Air Force & Navy pilots to double LBJ's records of their bombing of Northern Laos—he has now dropped 6,000 lbs. of explosives for every person in N. Laos. Despite the fact that Nixon never announced that he reversed LBJ's 1968 decision to halt the bombing of North Vietnam, Nixon has ordered enough "protective reaction strikes" to be near LBJ's prehalt bombing levels. Now that the NVA offensive has ar[r]ogantly been labeled an "invasion," a 500 plane raid on N. Vietnam may be in the making, if U.S. planes can save ARVN first. Of course, the N. Vietnamese are the last to be deceived by talk of a bombing halt—in Santa Barbara we saw films of a recently bombed hospital near Hanoi. Nearby, protected by anti-aircraft batteries, people were draining & rebuilding a pond in a park to make it more beautiful.

Actually, these huge tonnage levels are deceptive, since the number of real heavy bombs dropped by Nixon has gone down in favor of more fragmentation & napalm bombs. The killing power & the numbers of these horrible anti-personnel weapons have increased under Nixon. The round metal bb pellets of older fragmentation bombs have been exchanged for impossible to x-ray, fiberglass, sharp-edged fragments. Often a surgeon can only slit the stomach from top to bottom, empty the contents, search for & remove the frags, replace the entrails & sew up the stomach like a football. One frag left in can be fatal. U.S. napalm has become more adhesive, & the super napalm with white phosphorus, "willy peter," now in wide use, burns right through flesh & bones, goes on burning inside until it is burnt out.

& the Electronic Battlefield, which has only lately come to the attention of the U.S. Senate, has actually been gaining in application since the days of Robert McNamara. There are already tens of thousands of sensors scattered all over Asia. Like the plastic plants on the L.A. Freeways, they are disguised as plants & designed to pick up footsteps & trucks. The sensors are supposed to radio data to a circling plane or drone, which relays the totals back to the Air Force's computer banks in Nakhon Phanom, Thailand. This center then orders air strikes. (Incidently, these computers are linked to the ones in the underground Pentagon & probably to the computer banks in San Diego, which select targets for bombing raids for all of Indochina.) In reality, these sensors can be triggered by a child running, a water buffalo, a tiger, or the wind; & the local communist forces have learned to move quietly, so that the Pentagon had to buy millions of "button bomblets," disguised as lumps of animal shit, that pop like firecrackers if they are stepped on.

It isn't difficult to see why the NVA & NLF have launched their offensives. Hundreds of thousands of troops are no longer necessary to carry out U.S. foreign policy. S.E. Asia is one big electronic battlefield, so what the armed forces need is not large quantities of oppressed, unskilled & undedicated soldiers, but qualified technicians & pilots. While we were down in San Diego looking over the convention & demonstration sites, we saw a fascist bumper sticker, which sums up Nixon's War: FIGHTER PILOTS DO IT BETTER. It doesn't seem to matter what more than 73% of the American people want—small nazi-type clubs of pilots (the all-white Black Widowers is infamous) simply love to kill & destroy in the name of America. But since the NVA troops brought SAM missiles & anti-aircraft guns with them, it's obvious they are prepared for the sharks of the air. & the Electronic Battlefield has vulnerable connections here in America. The credit for all the torture weapons & their new-fangled surveillance-intelligence systems counterparts goes to the Military Research Network (MRN). MRN is a network of university laboratories & research institutes without which the U.S. could not have attempted to suppress Asian national liberation struggles. Across America, in sabotage attacks not always covered in the straight press, military research centers have been located & bombed by the paramilitary wing of our movement. There have also been many acts of assembly-line sabotage, & these will increase. Overground propaganda attacks have been launched against war manufacturers: a boycott has been called on Wonder-(shit) bread, a subsidiary of ITT, because Wonderbread also makes electronic sensors, which organize the destruction of healthy, innocent bodies in 12 ways. The number of U.S. companies constructing Electronic Battlefield devices is huge. Only HONEYWELL & GENERAL TIRE & RUBBER COMPANY make complete weapons systems. Other companies make only one or several components. With your help, the AUGER can do local research on industry & university projects—anyone with knowledge of local Dept. of Defense contracts should call or write us.

The result & stated goal of all this bombing has been (besides actual genocide) forced urbanization. One half of the population of South Vietnam is now homeless—there are 7 to 9 million displaced persons. In 1960 Vietnam was 90% rural—now it is 60% urban. The following figures for Saigon reflect the over-crowding in all South Vietnamese cities, however, many refugees are simply missing, with rumors of hundreds of My Lai's circulating among returning vets. Saigon, which was designed for 300,000, now contains 3 to 5 million people. It is the most densely populated city on earth, with twice the density of Tokyo. People live on rush mats in the streets as squatters, & all day & night the Saigon police are moving them out of the way of military vehicles. By the Saigon government's own figures, 60% of the people in the South Vietnamese capital have TB, & the Bubonic plague has reached epidemic proportions—10,000 cases a year reported. The streets are filled with mountains of garbage & huge rats. 50% of those who die in Saigon are under 5 years of age. There is virtually no medical treatment, since all the available doctors are in the ARVN. When there is amputation instead of death, there are no artificial limbs. Saigon is a city of orphans, amputees, & prostitutes, who, by the thousands, get their eyelids cut to have the "western look." In the cities, the destruction of Vietnamese civilization is completed by a combination of Amerikan & Japanese consumerism—Southern Comfort & Honda are making weird people out of the few urban Vietnamese who do have money. It is the progressive forces of Vietnam that are keeping the old ways alive—& this is in spite of forced urbanization & the destruction of the countryside. Since the war began, one quarter (3,000 out of 12,000) of the villages of South Vietnam have been totally destroyed. & there are 5 U.S. companies with bulldozers in the jungles, destroying 1,000 acres of forest a day. This kind of forced urbanization is a tactic that Samuel P. Huntington, chairman of the Dept. of Government at Harvard, & a long-time supporter of the war, openly advocated in Foreign Affairs, July, 1968. However, this attempt to dry up the human sea the guerrillas swim in has backfired, & the refugees may well be the quicksand that the U.S. & Saigon war efforts sink under.

Nixon still has a plan in his limp hands for neocolonialism which includes 25,000 U.S. advisors in Vietnam until 1975, $2 billion in economic aid to Saigon, & a projected strength of 1.1 million men in the Saigon army plus 147,000 men in the Saigon police force. But even before this huge offensive, things were looking very grim for Nixon. Laos is 80% liberated—the Meo tribes have largely been turned into refugees. Thai troops are the only ones really fighting the Pathet Lao. Cambodia is 67% liberated—after 10-20,000 Lon Nol troops were killed in their first big offensive, the Cambodian dictator/general brought all of his troops home to defend the capital city. & Saigon has a $760 million deficit to the U.S., & the latest figures we've found show that in 1968, South Vietnam had to import 677,000 metric tons of rice as a result of isolation from the liberated zones & U.S. spraying & bombing.

And now the NVA & NLF main forces are smashing through the illusion of Vietnamization. Actually, Nixon had asked for this offensive by showing Hanoi & the NLF how weak the ARVN is in his foolish invasion of Laos. & Nixon has proved that he doesn't want peace. Since Jan. 25th, the day when Nixon announced his new 8 point peace proposal (with which he hopes to create the illusion that he is answering the 7 point proposal of the Provisional Revolutionary Government) the U.S. has conducted the heaviest bombing raids in 4 years in South Vietnam, launched a series of new air attacks against populated areas in the North, d[i]spatched a 4th aircraft carrier, the Kitty Hawk, to the Gulf of Tonkin where normally only 2 carriers have been deployed in recent years, sent 42 new B-52's to bolster the Indochina fleet, & announced the indefinite suspension of the Paris talks. In addition, he had started a relocation program, which, according to the PRG, will move one million people from their homes in the northern provinces in order to turn the area into a free fire zone for tactical nuclear weapons. Don't forget that Nixon advocated, when he was Vice-President, that the U.S. bomb the hills around Diem Bien Phu with nuclear weapons in order to save the trapped French forces.

These are some of the bitter reasons for the NLF-NVA offensive this Spring. Those of us, who long ago saw no hope in the American government for peace, wish the liberation forces victory! We believe that the Movement in the U.S. should join the offensive with all the levels of commitment & tactics open to us. Events that were coming up anyway include: a referendum against the airwar in California; the trials of Russo & Ellsberg in L.A. in May & June: & the huge, nation-wide actions planned for San Diego. Local meetings to discuss & plan for San Diego, on the Eugene & then on the Northwest levels, should be announced & take place soon. Just in case Nixon does something crazy, we should be ready to go out in the streets at short notice now. Next Wednesday, April 12th at 2:30 at the EMU there will be a rally to support the liberation forces of Indochina & at 3:30 in 150 Science let's make the UofO faculty finally vote to off ROTC NOW! JOIN THE OFFENSIVE!

NOTE

1. From *AUGUR* 3, no. 12 (7-21 April 1972): 3, 16.

FAST TIMES IN THE MOTOR CITY—THE FIRST TEN YEARS OF THE *FIFTH ESTATE*: 1965-1975

Bob Hippler

HARVEY'S TRIP

In 1965, Norma Ovshinsky Marks decided to move to Los Angeles and take her 17-year old son, Harvey, a senior at Detroit's Mumford High School, with her. Ovshinsky wasn't too happy about going. "To begin with," he recalls, "I had to speed up my Mumford graduation by going to summer school and missing most senior class ceremonies. I was well known at school and would have been a class officer. When I got to Los Angeles, I was desperately homesick for Detroit and my high school friends."

Wandering around Los Angeles in a funk about his predicament, Ovshinsky happened upon the Sunset Strip. There he saw a couple of sights that piqued his interest: a gathering place called the Fifth Estate Coffeehouse, and nearby a functioning underground newspaper, Art Kunkin's *Los Angeles Free Press*.

Ovshinsky began hanging out with the denizens of the coffeehouse and soon began helping out any way he could on the *Los Angeles Free Press*. He was captivated by its antiwar politics, its concern for developing a radical Los Angeles community, and its coverage of the local music scene, which in coming years was to produce legendary groups like Arthur Lee's Love, Jim Morrison's Doors, and Roger McGuinn's Byrds. "Soon I became obsessed with coming back to Detroit and publishing an underground paper which would bring people together there, like the process I saw happening in Los Angeles," Ovshinsky

Hippler was a member of the *Fifth Estate* from 1970-1974. Since then, he has been a socialist labor union organizer, an activist for feminism and gay rights, and a writer for the *Guardian*.

Acknowledgments: I would like to thank Harvey Ovshinsky, Peter Werbe, and Dave Riddle, whose comments represent a major portion of this article. Ovshinsky, who founded the *Fifth Estate* at age 17, was on its staff from 1965-1969, and is now an independent filmmaker in Detroit. Werbe has been on the paper's staff for its entire 25-year existence, with the exception of two or three years in the early 1970s. He is now a radio talk show host in Detroit, expounding his revolutionary anarchist philosophy over the airwaves. Riddle was on the staff during most of the 1970-1974 period, and since then has been a Teamsters Union activist.

recalls. He wasn't even sure who his target audience would be, except that it would include freeks (with two e's, the original Detroit term for hippies) and politicos of various kinds, including civil rights activists, whose Selma confrontation during that summer got the sixties rolling in earnest. Somehow he would, as a journalist, help unify the disparate counterculture developing on the streets of Detroit.

Acting on his obsession, Ovshinsky abruptly ran away from his new home in Los Angeles and returned to his father's house in suburban Detroit. His father, Stan Ovshinsky, a noted inventor and electronics whiz, loaned him $300 for the new paper, which Harvey named the *Fifth Estate*, after the coffeehouse. The first *Fifth Estate* office was in Stan's basement.

Why the name "Fifth Estate?" A recent issue of the paper provides an explanation: "The term 'estate' harkens back to the era of the French Revolution when society was declared as being divided into the three estates of the royalty, the clergy, and the common people. By the 1920s, the power of the U.S. press was so formidable that it could make and break politicians, foster wars, create drug hysteria, etc. and so it was dubbed the 'Fourth Estate' by some wag. So, the fifth is one up in the fourth. Dumb, huh?"

Actually, the name has at times not been well understood in brass-tacks, blue collar Detroit. Jim Kennedy, who later helped distribute the paper as head of Keep on Trucking, once said that a frequent reaction he got from people was "Fifth what?"

Ovshinsky and several high school friends put out the first issue on November 19, 1965. "I decided on a tabloid form," he says. "The problem was, I didn't know a tabloid had to have at least eight pages, so I submitted only six pages to the printer. Nobody at the printer told me anything; they just ran the paper as it was submitted." So the first *Fifth Estate* had two blank pages. Good for taking notes!

"For the first issue, we stole ads from other publications and printed them, just to make it look like we had some support," he continues. "Also, we put a date on the issue, but forgot to put the year." The *Fifth Estate* announced itself as "Detroit's new progressive biweekly." Its first headline was "Bob Dylan: In Memoriam," for an article that bemoaned Dylan's switch from acoustic to electric guitar. The issue was dedicated to Norman Morrison, the American antiwar crusader who had burned himself to death right outside the office of Secretary of Defense Robert McNamara. The new paper was well received by young people in the downtown Wayne State University area, who were starved for any alternative to the dull *Detroit Free Press* and the reactionary *Detroit News*.

DETROIT—1965

Detroit in 1965 was both better and worse than it is today. It was a bustling, prosperous factory town of 1.7 million people, not the depressed, aging city of just barely a million that it is today. But politically it was more conservative than today, more dominated by the auto companies, with the Detroit Police Officers Association (DPOA) and to some extent the United Auto Workers (UAW) as junior partners.

Blacks were a large and growing minority in the city, gradually taking over the manufacturing and service jobs, and gaining political power as their numbers grew. They were about five years away from gaining a majority on the city council, and eight years away from electing Detroit's first black mayor.

As blacks gained in numbers, the white-dominated DPOA was beginning to get increasingly politicized. By 1969, off-duty police officers would spend long hours registering voters, and the DPOA would financially back a "white hope" mayoral candidate in a successful bid to prevent Richard Austin from becoming the city's first black mayor. The DPOA would also endorse eight city council candidates in that election—all white.

According to social critic Ralph W. Conant, author of *Prospects for Revolution*, as the sixties wore on, "the sharp rise in crime rates, urban rioting, student unrest, and war demonstrations...precipitated the latent political activities of the police unions." Carl Parsell, president of the DPOA, said, "We have found that our negotiating power is tied to getting greater political power."

While the police were getting more political, the blacks were getting less and less satisfied with police job performance. As early as 1957, almost half of Detroit blacks surveyed said that police service was "not good" or "definitely bad," says Conant. Two-thirds of the blacks referred to anti-black discrimination and mistreatment by police officers. A Detroit poll taken in 1965, notes Conant, revealed that 58 percent of the black community stated that law enforcement was not fair and equitable.

In 1965 this polarization was slowly developing, but to most outward appearances Detroit was still a huge one-horse factory town, the animal in question being the horseless carriage. Detroit's cultural narrowness was already then legendary, and the sense of airlessness was palpable. For baby boomers flooding downtown to escape an even more miserable existence in suburbia, the *Fifth Estate* filled a great void.

Buoyed by good street sales at 15¢ a copy, and a few head shop ads, Ovshinsky and friends produced a second issue. But they ran into the first of the *Fifth Estate*'s many hassles over the years with the commercial printers hired to run off the paper. Besides being the year of Selma, 1965 was also the year of the massive U.S. escalation in Vietnam, with hundreds of thousands of troops being deployed. "I can't print a picture of an American flag with the stripes as bayonets," declared the printer when he saw the *Fifth Estate* cover, which protested the U.S. invasion.

Finally black activist Rev. Albert Cleage, of the Shrine of the Black Madonna, agreed to print the issue. He was the first printer who stuck with the *Fifth Estate* for any period of time, and thus deserves credit for helping get it off the ground.

Creating and selling the second issue gradually broadened Ovshinsky's circle of acquaintances, and several of them commented that if he was starting a Detroit underground paper he definitely should talk to John Sinclair.

John Sinclair was a local Detroit artist, musician, and reefer-head who had started a project called the Artists' Workshop. "I remember my first visit to John Sinclair's place as wonderful," Ovshinsky says. "It was a homey yet intellectual atmosphere. John's wife Leni was cooking some exotic dish, John Coltrane was on the stereo, and we were surrounded by books. John was 24, which seemed ancient to me at the time. He was also the first adult, besides my parents, who encouraged my idea for a new paper."

Sinclair, however, had one big problem. He was targeted by the authorities because he openly promoted drug use. The *Fifth Estate* began to report on his busts and helped fight police entrapment practices in the community. This was the beginning of an adversary relationship that the paper would have with the Detroit cops for years. Crusading against police abuse was to become a big priority, especially after the Detroit rebellion of 1967.

Sinclair agreed to write a column for the *Fifth Estate*, which was originally called "Coat Puller," but was later renamed "Rock and Roll Dope." The name pretty much summarized Sinclair's political program. The role of drugs in the revolution was to be a recurring controversy on the *Fifth Estate*, with drugs definitely falling from favor by the early 1970s. Then, too, the drugs on the street in the early years—weed, mescaline, and LSD—were much more attractive than the quaaludes, angel dust, and amphetamines of later years. Who changed the supply? A good subject for another brief history.

In 1967, Sinclair founded the White Panther Party, which was to become the single most popular youth political grouping in late-1960s Detroit. The White Panther philosophy was an amalgam of Eastern religious insights, drug-oriented rites patterned after Native Americans, a love for music, including black jazz and blues, psychedelic rock and heavy metal riffs, and a long-haired hippie political militance modeled on the namesake Black Panther Party.

In 1967 the White Panther Party was probably the political group that most influenced the editorial policy and general style of the *Fifth Estate*. However, after the 1967 Detroit rebellion the Motor City political scene got too heavy for the White Panthers, and they moved to more sedate Ann Arbor, occupying a large house right across from fraternity row. The geographical distance, plus an increasing disdain for drug use on the left, reduced their influence on the paper.

John Sinclair's book, *Guitar Army*, which became popular after he began a 10-year sentence for marijuana possession in 1969, helped continue the White Panthers' popularity. As late as 1973, Jim Kennedy said that, in his travels outstate distributing the *Fifth Estate*, the strongest youth political force he saw was the White Panther Party.

Despite the encouragement from Sinclair and many new friends, after two issues, the *Fifth Estate* had a bank account of close to zero. "I didn't think we were going to make it," Ovshinsky recalls. "I went around to all the political people I knew, from civil rights groups like the Student Nonviolent Coordinating Committee to antiwar groups like the Detroit Committee to End the War in Vietnam (DCEWV). Finally I announced at a meeting at the DCEWV Building that we were closing up shop. Up stepped a guy in a t-shirt and a Beatle haircut who said he'd like to help, we should keep this thing going. It was Peter Werbe."

ENTER PETER WERBE

Werbe, 25, had been an instant convert to the *Fifth Estate* from the time he saw the first issue. "I was at a University of Detroit blues concert," he recalls. "Harvey came down the aisle selling the paper. I was flabbergasted! I'd always thought that the print media and the people in power were inaccessible, and here was a paper that said things could change. It knocked my socks off."

With new support from Werbe and other volunteers, the *Fifth Estate* moved out of Stan's basement and into an office next to the DCEWV at John C. Lodge Freeway and West Warren. The paper worked closely with the committee, and for a period devoted the middle four pages of each issue to the committee's newsletter. John and Leni Sinclair soon moved into an office upstairs, and encouraged the talented psychedelic artist Gary Grimshaw to contribute to the paper.

The *Fifth Estate* used the offset production process—in fact, the massive introduction of cheap offset technology was a major factor in making possible all the alternative presses of the Vietnam era.

The layout person worked with a row of backlit pages at light tables, applied the actual headlines, photos, and type, and had a clear view of what the final product would look like. The best layout person who ever worked at the *Fifth Estate* was Cathy West, a young woman from a working class background in the downriver suburb of Wyandotte. She also was on the staff as of the third issue, and spent more time there than any woman except Marilyn Werbe, Peter's wife. Cathy was a good friend of the paper in the years after she left the staff. Sadly, she died in Detroit in 1984.

Reminiscing on the earliest days of the paper, Ovshinsky says, "It was a thrill to be involved in it. Most of the people I was working with were older, but nobody ever treated me like a kid. Also, the essence of the sixties was a belief that things might change, as indeed they did, though not as much as we hoped for. The movements for women's rights and student rights were just taking off. It was a very optimistic time.

"Peter Werbe was radical from the start. I wanted to bring people together—he wanted them together if they agreed on a political program. He wanted to provoke people into action, which he really valued more than words. He was an angry guy at times, and I always said, 'I'm glad you're on *our* side.'"

During these years, the youth scene began to explode. According to Werbe, "People were just streaming into the downtown area, many wanting to get involved in the paper." Amid the increasingly hectic activity, the *Fifth Estate* did not even have regularly scheduled staff meetings. "We were eventually overwhelmed with material for the paper. Everyone wanted to do something. It was almost a process of automatic writing."

A POLITICAL HERITAGE

While the political establishment in Detroit was stodgy, in a longer historical perspective, and on a grassroots level, the city provided a fertile environment for a radical newspaper. Detroit was a strong union town and had a tradition of radical activity in those unions. The Communist Party had controlled the Rouge Plant local until about 1950. Sol Wellman, who went to prison as state CP chair in the 1950s, used to come by the office and discuss the issues of the day.

The Trotskyist Socialist Workers Party operated a popular meeting place on Woodward called Debs Hall, named after Eugene V. Debs, the single most dominant figure in American socialist history, who was active from the 1880s to the 1920s. Several Trotskyists were on the *Fifth Estate* staff over the years.

And there were other resources. The Catholic Worker movement had strong roots in Detroit, with activists who followed the teachings of Dorothy Day and Thomas Merton. Also, the city had one of the nation's largest liberal Jewish communities, which produced a half dozen *Fifth Estate* staffers. In 1963, the year of John F. Kennedy's assassination and Martin Luther King's March on Washington, Detroit saw a massive civil rights march of over 100,000 people, led by the late Rev. C.L. Franklin, the father of Aretha Franklin. Students for a Democratic Society started in nearby Ann Arbor, with the help of the United Auto Workers.

On a more immediate level, political opposition to the hideous day-to-day reality of the Vietnam War steadily grew, especially since the war was visible daily on television. However, young people did not need a TV to know the war was affecting them—all they had to do was read their draft notices that came in the mail. In working class Detroit, many young people knew friends who, without student deferments, were sent to Vietnam. As the war dragged on, many were killed or injured. Even all-white, middle-class Dearborn suffered heavily. Its death rate from Vietnam was twice the rate for the rest of the country.

The result of this was to breed strident revolt among many young people. "The paper was dominated by a spirit of generalized rebellion," Werbe recalls. "If you could break one rule, why not break all the rules? And if you do that, why just put a new set of rules in their place?" Even the rock music scene got increasingly political as drug busts and draft convictions produced the same repeated image: a young person led off to jail for simply trying to live freely.

With time, the *Fifth Estate* began to prosper on a modest scale. Record company media buyers began to notice the underground press and run ads there, convinced that such papers were reaching the nonconformist kids who were listening to new groups like the Grateful Dead, the Jefferson Airplane, Mitch Ryder and the Detroit Wheels, and (lest we forget) John Sinclair's high-intensity rock group, the Motor City Five, whose favorite haunt for performing was Detroit's fabled Grande Ballroom.

A typical record ad from the period read: "Country Joe and the Fish Are You—The things that you are: questioning, idealistic, involved, concerned with the love, the confusion and the excitement of the life you live today." As a result of steadier ad income, the paper even began to pay a subsistence wage of $25 a week.

PLUM STREET

Then a break came that put the enterprise on even more solid footing. In 1966, the city of Detroit decided to designate a block of Plum Street as "Detroit's Art

Community," where offbeat music, studios, bookstores, and head shops would be featured. Mayor Jerome Cavanagh even spoke at the kickoff ceremony.

After a staff debate, the *Fifth Estate* decided to move its office to Plum Street and also open a small bookstore there. "Peter was ambivalent about moving," Ovshinsky recalls, "He didn't want to lose our base near campus. But I liked the sense of community that was developing there. And also I was worried about paying our bills."

Also about this time, Werbe's wife Marilyn joined the staff and began to take an active role in writing, editing, and layout. She is still active on the *Fifth Estate* and falls about one year short of tying Peter as the staffer with the most seniority. In both cases, it's "twenty something."

Sales at the *Fifth Estate* bookstore were 90 percent periodicals, with the rest being of items like t-shirts, bumperstickers, and buttons. "The bookstore saved the paper and helped us get established," says Werbe. It also marked the high point of the *Fifth Estate*'s hippie-psychedelic era, before the politics got tougher and harder in 1967 and 1968.

After about a year, commercialism began to take its toll on Plum Street, and the flower era lost its luster as the bad chemicals drove out the good (at least they seemed good at the time). Plum Street began to seem less and less the place for a political newspaper, and the area around the West Warren office continued to take off as a center of progressive activity. The staff decided to move back to the West Warren location. "By the time we left, we were glad to get out," Werbe recalls.

Within another two years, the Plum Street scene collapsed completely, and the block became deserted as businesses moved out. Semi trucks roared by the forlorn storefronts, and it was hard to imagine how anybody thought Plum Street would last.

LOVE FOR SALE

Downtown Detroit continued to fill up with young people escaping bleak suburbs like Livonia, Warren, and Southfield. In the case of the *Fifth Estate*, many also came from college campuses and from out of state. People wanted to change their lives, and in many cases that meant forgetting hometown sweethearts and seeking out somebody new. To put it briefly, hormones raged.

Norman Mailer stated, "The middle class is preoccupied with sex; the working class is drenched in it." Nevertheless, Detroit was still an old-fashioned town, and seeking out a satisfactory love life could be a sometime thing. Amid political struggle and a subsistence living standard, sexual relationships could

be intense, but not necessarily stable. Low-rent one-night stands were not unknown. Amid a city approaching a black majority, interracial affairs were not the rule, but certainly were not rare.

Many *Fifth Estate* staffers and friends began living collectively in a big house in the Cass Corridor called Boone's Farm Commune. Shared rent and food expenses alleviated some of the financial pressures, while occasional parties and long evenings listening to rock music under the influence of mind-altering substances made it a darn sight easier to socialize. "Revolution as ecstasy" became a byword.

Despite all the factors militating against it, several relationships among the *Fifth Estate* staff and friends lasted for years and years.

In an era of sexual liberation, John Sinclair eventually concluded that the increasingly serious, Marxist-oriented *Fifth Estate* was a little staid for his tastes. In 1968, while still writing a column for the *Fifth Estate*, he started his own underground paper, the *Warren-Forest Sun*, and gave it the motto "Sex, Drugs, and Rock and Roll." The late Barry Kramer also found the *Fifth Estate* rather reserved and lacking in music coverage, and so started *Creem* rock magazine as Detroit's sensual answer to *Rolling Stone*.

Society's attitude toward sexual matters was slowly changing. Not until 1970 did the first girlie magazine dare to show pubic hair. In nearby Ann Arbor, police were busting movies and plays that would not raise an eyebrow today, and the *Fifth Estate* covered the stories. In 1967, police walked right into the projection booth and seized a soft-core film called *Flaming Creatures*. Two years later, a play called *Dionysius in '69*, which featured scantily clad actors but no nudity, was also busted. Obscenity trials followed in both cases.

Sexual variety and experimentation also became the order of the day. Detroit's gay and lesbian community, which had existed in the shadows for decades, began to come out of the closet. A gay commune was established in the Cass Corridor. A group of activists put out the first issue of the *Gay Liberator* in 1970. It published regularly until 1977.

Sometimes, in the search for sexual fulfillment, things got a little kinky. The following letter and reply were published in 1969 in the *Fifth Estate*'s "Dr. HIPpocrates" column, by Dr. Eugene Schoenfeld:

Dear Dr. Schoenfeld:

A couple of weeks ago my girlfriend and I got loaded and were making love. She told me that she wanted to show me something new that would be a real thrill to me. She said that one of her old boyfriends liked to have her do it to him often, so without knowing what it was, I agreed to let her try it.

What she did was to stretch my scrotum out tightly, then she took a pair of finger nail clippers and cut a small hole in the sac. I began to get scared then but she said not to worry, it was fun and didn't hurt much. Next she stuck a small plastic straw into the hole in my sac and started blowing air into it.

My sac got bigger than a baseball, but surprisingly it didn't hurt much and felt kind of good. I began to worry that it might burst so she stopped blowing and removed the straw. Then she quickly put a piece of adhesive tape over the hole to keep the air in. Then we continued with intercourse and I had a climax that was out of this world.

Afterwards she removed the tape from my scrotum and squeezed the air out with her hand. Then she dabbed my scrotum with rubbing alcohol (to prevent infection she said) and retaped the hole. When she put the alcohol on it, it burned like hell. The next day my penis was swollen to about double its normal size and it itched like hell, but two days later it was OK again. What I want to know is, could this practice cause me any harm? And what caused my penis to swell the next day?

Reply: I should point out firstly that more bacteria exist in the mouth than in any other body orifice. Our skin is a natural barrier to bacteria and other microorganisms which are not normally found in the bladder or scrotum. Infections of the bladder may continue up the urethra to the kidneys. Infections of the scrotum? Not a pleasant prospect. Even more dangerous is the possibility of an air embolism. Air forced into a closed tissue space may enter the bloodstream, go to the heart, lungs, or brain and cause sudden death or stroke.

Holy Toledo! How did any urban youths survive those years?

SUMMER OF LOVE?

In the spring of 1967, Detroiters decided to organize their own "Be-In," in tribute to the famous San Francisco "Be-In," which had starred Allen Ginsberg and Timothy Leary. According to Werbe, "Several thousand people showed up on Belle Isle and people were generally having a great time." Bands entertained the crowd and balloons and frisbees floated around. "It was a fusion of politics and counterculture, world revolution and the Age of Aquarius. It was all the same to us."

However, the Detroit Police Department provided a harbinger of things to come. As the crowd streamed home across the Belle Isle Bridge, mounted officers began harassing the revelers, in particular focusing on a biker element. By the time the crowd was on Jefferson Avenue, the cops were riding up and down the street, picking out individuals to sandwich against buildings, knocking people down, and even breaking windows.

The daily Detroit papers blamed the mess largely on the bikers. "They said that the Be-In crowd attacked the police, which was preposterous," says Werbe. The bias of the mainstream media, and their coverup of the police misconduct, illustrated clearly what the role of an alternative paper could be. The *Fifth Estate* provided eyewitness accounts of police beatings, and showed how the cops ruined the Be-In.

The Belle Isle Be-In was Detroit's attempt to participate in the 1967 Summer of Love. However, it was not the defining event of the summer that it was intended to be. Instead, a few weeks later in July, another event occurred that would define 1967 in Detroit history: a massive racial rebellion, worse by far than the riot of 1943. As large areas of the city burned, several square miles of the downtown were cordoned off for three days. The National Guard killed over 40 people, by official count, and finally the 101st Airborne was called in. The 1967 cataclysm was vividly described by Detroit blues artist John Lee Hooker in his song "The Motor City's Burnin'." During the rebellion, the Detroit police attacked the *Fifth Estate* office with tear gas grenades, another dose of Detroit reality during the flower power era.

The upheaval of 1967 turned the *Fifth Estate* staff into what Werbe calls "participant journalists." As Ovshinsky recalls, "We really began to go out and dig up stories about the events. There was more to the situation than met the eye."

In tone, the paper became more sober. The following editorial appeared immediately after the rebellion:

If there was any *one* thing which caused the Detroit Rebellion, it was police brutality....Most white people do not believe there is any such thing as police brutality. They have never seen it, nor have they experienced it. And as Robert Tindal of the NAACP said at a meeting recently, "Some people have got to get beat over the head themselves before they can believe anyone else was beat."

The Detroit Police Department is the epitome of systematic institutionalized racism. Twenty-four years after the race riot of 1943 when the department had 143 Negro policemen, it has today only 200 Negro officers in a force which is over 4,300, and in a city where 33 percent of the citizens are Black. It is the unbiased, the unprejudiced, and the non-sadist who is the exception in the Detroit Police Department.

The police mentality is police brutality. It goes with the badge and the gun. Especially the gun. A gun is particularly good to have and a shotgun is even better if you are sexually insecure about your virility as compared to the "natives" you are supposed to be guarding.

The "New Detroit" needs a new police department. It should be mostly Black and it should be controlled by the people it is supposed to protect. They should decide who is hired and who is fired....

It was police brutality when the police murdered three men in the Algiers Motel (during the rebellion).

It was police brutality when the police ordered William Dalton to run and then shot him in the back.

It was police brutality when Negro Recorders Court Judge Elvin Davenport was arrested two years ago and taken to the police station because he was in Lafayette Park at 2 A.M. and a rookie cop didn't know he was a judge and mistook him for a nigger in a white neighborhood late at night.

The 1967 Detroit rebellion happened in part because the nonviolent civil rights movement had failed to achieve significant change in the north, and because the society seemed to condone violence, as in Vietnam, as a means to achieve ends. Once the upheavals in Detroit and other cities happened, many nonviolent leaders "recognized the riots as a phase of the movement that...prepared the way for change in governmental action and policies," says Ralph Conant. The 1967 rebellion was a forceful assertion, however chaotic, of the black presence in the city.

THE BLACK STRUGGLE

Especially in the wake of the rebellion, the *Fifth Estate* reported on the upsurge of black activism in Detroit. The League of Revolutionary Black Workers was organized at Dodge Main, the second largest Detroit area auto plant after Ford's River Rouge complex. (It has since been closed.) The Black Panther Party was also active in the city, aiming to organize "the lumpenproletariat."

One leader of the League was John Watson, who also became editor of the Wayne State University newspaper, the *South End*, in 1968. Under Watson, the paper's masthead carried such slogans as "One class conscious worker is worth 1,000 students," and "1968—year of the urban guerrilla." Watson also increased press runs to 50,000 at times and distributed copies to Detroit-area auto plants. After leaving the *South End*, he edited an important black paper, the *Inner City Voice*.

For a time, the League had sizable support among black workers, who were an increasing percentage of the workforce. The United Auto Workers, then still headed by Walter Reuther, got worried. Peter Werbe recalls one night when some *Fifth Estate* staffers accompanied League members to a Dodge Main union meeting. The hall was guarded by a phalanx of UAW "flying squads," tough union members, some of them veterans of the battles of the 1930s.

One flying squad member came up to Werbe and said, "If you don't want to get hurt, why don't you hippies get your ass back to Wayne State University?" Werbe began to take his advice and head in the opposite direction, when he ran into an adventurist *Fifth Estate* supporter who said, "Don't worry," and showed him a weapon under his overcoat. However, cooler heads prevailed and the meeting was conducted peacefully.

The League and the *Fifth Estate* also helped to publicize the case of James Johnson, a black auto worker who, after being fired, returned to his auto plant with a rifle and killed three supervisors. Johnson's Detroit trial jury was given a tour of the plant, and, after viewing the wretched working conditions, returned a verdict of not guilty by reason of insanity. The League composed a song about the incident called "James Johnson Needed a Thompson."

Another leading League activist was the late Ken Cockrel, a brilliant young black lawyer who was undefeated in jury trials for many years in the 1960s and early 1970s. He won legal rulings that ended the practice of blacks being tried by all-white juries, something that still happens in states like Florida. From now on, a person would indeed be tried by a jury of his or her peers. In subsequent years, Cockrel was elected to the Detroit City Council.

The Black Panther Party was involved in providing free breakfasts for schoolchildren and calling for community control of the police. One time the Panthers organized 30 people to picket a local police precinct. Hard as it may be to believe, the police had sharpshooters stationed on the roof. Late one night, the Panthers called the *Fifth Estate* office and asked for armed support in an expected confrontation with police.

Werbe replied that they must be out of their minds. However, there was no organized chain of command at the paper, and indeed later that night two staffers were standing in the middle of 14th Street with rifles in their hands. Luckily for their health, the police had withdrawn from the area.

At times the League and the Black Panthers had almost a rivalry. "The Panthers were more mass based, while the League was more vanguardist," recalls Werbe. "We did more stories on the Panthers partly because they were more accessible, while the League cadre was impenetrable. I remember meeting with Watson and Cockrel. They complained about lack of coverage, but it was hard to get stories out of them."

The League did get some media exposure through a media project called "Newsreel," which was located in the same building as the *Fifth Estate*. In a film called "Finally Got the News," Watson explained the League's ideology and activities.

League activists affected a macho style. Watson went around with an attack-trained, muzzled German shepherd for a period in the late 1960s. The adventurist *Fifth Estate* supporter mentioned earlier had a muscular, aggressive Bouvier dog. Werbe recalls his own usual garb of a black leather jacket and Levis. A shotgun in a rack next to Werbe's desk was a permanent feature of the *Fifth Estate* office. The entire atmosphere was definitely pre-feminist. For both the black activists and the *Fifth Estate*, this melodramatic style led to a political approach that was confrontational and could involve a lot of posturing.

While the *Fifth Estate* and the black groups were on the same side of the barricades ideologically, they did not have a close relationship. For the *Fifth Estate*, the groups were an entree into the world of revolutionary action among oppressed people. For the black activists, the *Fifth Estate* was a way to publicize their program and give them credibility outside the black community.

There were also differences in lifestyle that caused friction. Dave Riddle recalls one argument he had with John Watson, in which Watson criticized the "poor boy act" of *Fifth Estate* staffers who lived on subsistence salaries. He tended to view some staffers as ex-suburbanites who were slumming in the inner city. "The hell with that," said Watson. "The more money I make, the happier I am."

To be fair, both sides were plowing new ground in a city that had seen two major racial upheavals within 25 years. In a catch-phrase of the day, "Nobody ever said it was going to be easy." Over the years, with the decline of the auto industry into a state of permanent crisis, auto worker militancy declined, and the League folded. However, today's workers look back to its heritage of fighting discrimination before the days

of affirmative action and standing UAW committees on the subject. As for the Panthers, soon after they started providing breakfasts, the Nixon administration decided it might be a good idea, and started the program that survives to this day. And Fred Hampton, the martyred leader of the Chicago Panthers, originated the concept of the "rainbow coalition" which has been used by Jesse Jackson.

DETROIT POLICE ABUSE

The *Fifth Estate* also worked with black activists in the years after 1967 to expose the chronic abuses of the Detroit Police Department. The paper covered the 1968 police attack on anti-George Wallace protestors, which sent people to the hospital, and the harassment of the Poor People's March the same year. With both articles, dramatic photos showed the police abusing their powers.

In 1969, a black political group called the Republic of New Africa was holding a meeting in a church when a police officer was killed nearby. The police arrested the whole church full of people—men, women, and children. The next morning, black judge George Crockett released all but three on their own recognizance, and came under attack from the white-controlled press for doing so. The *Fifth Estate* defended Crockett.

The 1969 incident galvanized the community and almost resulted in the election of Richard Austin as Detroit's first black mayor. A nonentity named Roman Gribbs squeaked by him, and as a result the Detroit police were allowed to run rampant for four more years. (Judge Crockett is now a member of Congress, while Richard Austin is Michigan Secretary of State.)

In 1972 and 1973, the *Fifth Estate* helped document the activities of Detroit's worst-ever police misconduct—the STRESS decoy unit. STRESS stood for "Stop The Robberies, Enjoy Safe Streets." One policeman would pose as a staggering drunk, and, when a mugger attacked, six or so of his colleagues would leap out of the bushes and arrest the mugger or, more often, shoot him. The decoy unit killed 14 people, almost all of them black, within one year.

Outrage over the STRESS unit and several other major police incidents finally resulted in Coleman Young's election as Detroit's first black mayor in 1973. (He is still in office.) Under his administrations the police department gradually improved, with affirmative action programs dramatically increasing the number of women and blacks on the force. Murderous stunts like the STRESS unit have been largely eliminated.

It is worth noting that, for all its support of black causes, and all the articles it printed from black contributors, the *Fifth Estate* never had a full-time black staffer in the period covered by this history, 1965-1975. Recalls Werbe, "Black journalists didn't want to work with us when the *Inner City Voice* or the *South End* existed, and that sort of separation of radicals by race on the publications of the era was overwhelmingly the rule. If there were more than a handful of black writers on any of the 500 underground papers, I'd be surprised."

SOUTH END STORY

John Watson's term as editor was only part of the picture at the *South End*. Wayne State University's student paper went through a series of dramatic changes starting in 1967. It was then that editor Art Johnston changed the paper's name—until that point it was called the *Wayne State Daily Collegian*. The new name expressed an empathy with the less prosperous south end of the campus, which bordered on the Cass Corridor. The north end of the campus abutted on the Detroit Civic Center.

Werbe remembers Johnston as a "hippie cum hillbilly biker" and "a rough-hewn writer-poet" and says that "starting with Johnston, the *South End* became an underground paper." Johnston was followed by Watson, whose term as editor shook Wayne State up completely. (Campus conservatives tried but failed to remove him from his post.) Cheryl McCall continued the new activist tradition as summer editor in 1969 (in recent years she made an acclaimed documentary on runaway kids in Seattle). John Grant was the next editor—he eventually wound up on the post-1975, anarchist-libertarian *Fifth Estate*.

A cross-pollination between the two papers went on for years. Jim Kennedy, certainly another rough-hewn working class poet, started out at the *South End*, then became a staffer at the *Fifth Estate*, and, after a brief 1970 power struggle with Werbe, left to form Keep on Trucking, which for years distributed the *Fifth Estate* and many other alternative publications to stores and head shops. Alan Franklin, a clever writer with a good touch for political criticism and satire, started at the *South End* and eventually joined the post-1975 *Fifth Estate* staff. Bob Moore left the *South End* to become a *Fifth Estate* staffer and media columnist.

Ken Fireman, a Trotskyist who was on the *Fifth Estate* staff in 1972 and 1973, left and shortly after became editor of the *South End*. During his campaign for editor, he described his politics as "left of center," which indeed they were. Fireman later worked for the *Detroit Free Press* for years, and now works for *Newsday*.

Werbe recalls participating in a virtual *Fifth Estate* "takeover" of the *South End* in the wake of murders of students at Kent State and Jackson State in May 1970. The paper had retreated politically since John Watson. It took a long afternoon of heated political argument to persuade the *South End* staff to issue extra editions about the student strikes protesting the Nixon invasion of Cambodia and the killings that followed.

Fifth Estate also had connections with another college paper, the *Michigan Daily* of The University of Michigan. The late Jeff Goodman and I were both senior editors in 1965, later becoming socialist activists and joining the *Fifth Estate*. Goodman was on the staff in 1973 and 1974. Bob Moore was a *Michigan Daily* senior editor in 1966, and also a *Fifth Estate* staffer in 1973 and 1974.

CONFRONT THE WARMAKERS

Several months after the 1967 rebellion, several *Fifth Estate* staffers went to the first really massive Washington antiwar demonstration, the "Confront the Warmakers" action described in Norman Mailer's *Armies of the Night*. Atop the building housing the *Fifth Estate* was a large billboard featuring a skull crowned by a U.S. Capitol dome. As of fall 1967, tie-dyed hippies were still putting flowers in GI gun barrels and attempting to levitate the Pentagon, but a more militant faction got into battles with the police. Most of all, the sheer size of the demonstration, over 100,000 people, showed that "things were getting heavier," in the phrase of the day.

Nobody knew how heavy things were getting, however, until the fall of 1968 at the Democratic Convention in Richard Daley's Chicago. "The Movement," as it now was called, had talked for months about how over 100,000 demonstrators would show up to demand that the war end. The unstated premise was that at least some Democrats would be willing to listen (no similar crowds went to the Republican Convention). Instead, the nation was treated to a gruesome display of Democratic police brutality against the fewer than 10,000 protestors who did show up. Added to the 1968 assassinations of Martin Luther King, Jr. and Robert Kennedy, Chicago gave the nation a definite air of political instability. The ensuing election of Richard Nixon raised justified fears that the veteran McCarthyite anti-Communist would really go after the progressive movement.

According to Werbe, "The years 1967 and 1968 were a watershed for the *Fifth Estate*, transforming us from dewy-eyed hippies to hardcore opponents to the system. Things took on more of a military aspect. The city had burned and cold-blooded murder had taken place in the streets."

"Sometimes we felt on the defense," he continues. "The forces against us were enormous, and there had been casualties. How would we keep up the pace? Somewhere in the process, we lost our sense of humor. We began to identify with the enemies of the U.S., like the Black Panther Party and the Viet Cong—and correctly, too. We were looking for allies to take part in a social revolution. When you look back, it might seem ridiculous considering the true balance of forces at the time."

It was hard to get a perspective in those days.

Many people recall 1967 to 1969 as a period in which events began to develop in a furiously rapid manner. Demonstrations grew from 100,000 one year to 1 million two years later. Students went from peaceful petitioning to seizing university buildings, all in the same period. Black nationalists overtook the civil rights movement, and strident radical declarations were met with systematic police violence. In Vietnam, the United States went from rosy predictions of "the light at the end of the tunnel" to the devastating Tet offensive that forced Lyndon Johnson from office. Time and events seemed crazily telescoped, and to many young people revolution indeed seemed possible, especially after the student-inspired general strike in France. Of course many young people had little knowledge of American history (the schools saw to that) or of radical history (the 1950s McCarthyite repression saw to that). These factors impeded their judgment, but not their enthusiasm!

During this period, the *Fifth Estate* explored topics not covered by the establishment press until many years later. One half-page article discussed anti-Semitism among blacks. Professor Leonard Fein of Harvard was quoted as saying that if every black person in the U.S. was an anti-Semite there still would be more white anti-Semites in the country. Another article described Catholic priests in Latin America who had turned to guerrilla warfare to fight social injustice. Another reported how male and female college students had protested the arrival of a *Playboy* photographer on their campus by disrobing in front of him (pictures were included).

The *Fifth Estate* was also an early supporter of Palestinian self-determination. Nick Medvecky, a supporter of the paper, made several trips to the Middle East, and was there to see the PLO's ascendance to control of the refugee camps. He provided eyewitness coverage to the paper. In September 1970, staffer Dave Riddle did an article examining the oil companies and the Israeli-U.S. alliance. The headline said: "The Middle East Will Be the Next Viet Nam."

During these years, the *Fifth Estate* changed as quickly as the times did. Tommye Wiese, who had played an important role on the paper for two years, left the staff. As well as participating in writing and editing, Wiese had typeset the entire paper every two weeks. Werbe recalls that, as a woman playing such an important role, Wiese had "democratized and collectivized" the paper, making it no longer the domain of several male political heavies. Her departure was related to the fact that, as a Trotskyist, she was becoming more and more active in the Socialist Workers Party.

Some background might be helpful here. The New Left, as the Movement had come to be called, was instinctually anarchist, anti-hierarchical, and believed in a concept called "participatory democracy," which had been popularized by the early SDS. It was radically democratic, in the sense that everybody counted and everybody was expected to take an active role in raising his or her own consciousness and participating in his or her own political destiny.

The Socialist Workers Party, on the other hand, was out of the Old Left socialist tradition, and was by definition hierarchical, since it was a type of Leninist group. Trotskyist groups such as the SWP called for defense of the Russian revolution against its enemies, but also called for a political upheaval within the Soviet Union to overthrow the government created by Stalin after the death of Lenin and the expulsion of Trotsky. The SWP very carefully planned and built coalitions around single-issue demands like "Bring the Troops Home Now." In times of mass upheaval like the 1960s, it was the most effective group around at bringing people together.

However, the SWP was notorious for not doing any education within the coalitions, which were often composed of people who mistrusted each other and had no clear reason as to why they were together in the first place, despite the fact that the SWP had ample knowledge and resources for education. Sometimes they wouldn't even admit they were socialists (of course, many socialists besides the SWP have shared this trait). The result was that their coalitions tended to fall apart after the single issue had been achieved, or even after a strong demand had been made. Also, the potential for manipulation was strong in such a situation.

Also on the political scene were the "Stalinists" (Communist Party-oriented) and the "Maoists." They had their own reasons for disliking the Trotskyists, since the "Trots" were very critical of the governments in Moscow and Beijing. Also, there was a movement hangover from decades of Moscow-Beijing propaganda that had accused Trotskyists of everything from being agents of Hitler to having contempt for peasants. The Stalinists and Maoists had a convergence with the New Left, in that at least they said who they were and did believe in education for socialism. (Their commitment to democracy was a lot less clear.)

There were further complications. The fact that Mao Zedong's ideology was actually a variety of Stalinism tended to be lost because many young activists took a positive view of the Chinese Cultural Revolution. And Ho Chi Minh's Vietnamese Communists, themselves a local variety of Stalinism, had tremendous prestige because of their heroic fight against U.S. troops. Many New Leftists and even many Trotskyists, as well as the traditional Stalinists and Maoists, thought well of the Chinese and Vietnamese. In addition, there was widespread support for Fidel Castro's Cuban revolution, which was Moscow-oriented. All this militated against the Trotskyists, who actually had better developed political ideas and better organizational skills, though the SWP made poor use of both.

On top of all this, the *Fifth Estate* had an informal policy during its 1965-1975 period that staffers could not be "card-carrying" members of outside political groups. The only possible exception to this had been John Sinclair and his White Panther Party, but most of the time Sinclair was only a columnist.

The net result was that Tommye Wiese had to choose between the *Fifth Estate* and the SWP. She left the staff and went on to be a dedicated SWP activist for many years. All the above did not prevent another Trotskyist, Ken Fireman (not an official SWP member), from moving into an important role on the paper, really steering political policy, under different conditions in 1972.

There were further *Fifth Estate* changes around 1969. John Sinclair and his White Panther Party had moved to Ann Arbor after the 1967 rebellion, and he stopped writing his column after people became more critical of the drug-oriented lifestyle. The late Sol Plafkin was a people's lawyer who had helped staffers out of many scrapes. But he was basically a reform Democrat, and stopped writing his column as the paper moved further left. Alan Gotkin, an editor, writer, and crack photographer, left to begin a career as a union printer. Political heavy Frank Joyce left the staff to help start the group "People Against Racism."

Eventually the *Fifth Estate* became too radical for its founder. "I began to withdraw around 1967 or 1968, to get a bit bored," says Ovshinsky. "I think some people on the staff also began to view me as an impediment." Finally, an issue in early 1969 featured pictures of several handguns along the bottom of the cover, with the remaining space containing the word "NOW" in six-inch high letters. "I was outraged. That

was it for me. I don't think I was missed after I left." About the same time, Harvey got his draft notice, applied for and got C.O. status, and did his alternative service at Lafayette Clinic. Then, with the help of some clinic staff, he founded the youth service group Open City. He remained there only a short time before leaving to begin his new career as an independent filmmaker.

Other staff changes included two socialist activists joining the paper in 1970. Dave Riddle arrived after a stint with Ann Arbor's Radical Education Project, and I arrived after trying to make a go of an Ann Arbor music magazine called *Big Fat*.

The political tenor of the time was getting more serious, and the paper got more serious too. Staff meetings became regularly scheduled, and decisions were now often made by votes, not just consensus. Political discussions got more urgent and sophisticated, reflecting the experience of the staff. The *Fifth Estate* was coming of age, as can be seen from a staff editorial that appeared in early 1969 (see sidebar 1).

THE YOUTH REVOLT

In the fall of 1969, *Fifth Estate* staffers travelled to Washington, DC, to attend and report on the massive Moratorium demonstration against the war, an action involving over one million people. Daniel Ellsberg later claimed that the Moratorium caused Nixon to cancel a scheduled massive military attack on North Vietnam. The 1969-1970 school year also saw an unprecedented number of college demonstrations against the war, culminating in May 1970, when four students were shot to death at Kent State and two at Jackson State for protesting the invasion of Cambodia.

During this period *Fifth Estate* staffers took a long second look at student activism and concluded that students might be a more vital "agent of change" (in the phrase of the day) than previously thought. They were influenced by writers such as Jerry Farber, whose *Student as Nigger* described the real lack of student rights, and the actual treatment students got from the authorities.

The student ferment was so intense that it began to reach into the Detroit high schools also. The *Fifth Estate* responded by running articles that criticized high school dress codes, drug busts, and the general notion that the Bill of Rights stopped at the high school door. Other articles showed how the social studies and history textbooks often ignored the lives of working people, and the cultures of blacks, Mexicans, and Native Americans.

"This demographic bubble had arrived which faced the draft and many other problems," says Dave Riddle.

Facing censorship, many of the high schoolers wanted to start their own unauthorized student papers, and the *Fifth Estate* helped by letting hundreds of students use the office mimeograph machine to run off their proud creations. The *Fifth Estate* also set up a speakers bureau, through which staffers went out to address youth audiences.

Millard Berry, who joined the staff in 1970, was important in this period of youth organizing. He also helped edit a column in the paper called "Dope-O-Scope," which ran down what kinds of marijuana, LSD, and other drugs were available on the street, and at what prices. By 1971, the title of the column was changed to "Detroit Roulette," and it soon disappeared from the paper.

"We weren't just reporting, we were going out and stirring up trouble and agitating," says Riddle. The summer of 1970 saw virtual high school youth uprisings at Detroit's Balduck Park and Memorial Park. The Detroit police, as usual, were willing to go more than halfway to quell any disturbances. Riddle himself was arrested at one of them. Though the high school activism, along with other student protests, trailed off after 1970, many young Detroiters got their first introduction to political activism through the *Fifth Estate* that year. And after the decline of student activity on both the high school and college levels (including the fall of Students for a Democratic Society) the *Fifth Estate* grew even more as a key focus for Detroit radical organizing in the 1970-1975 era.

ENTER FEMINISM

The 1969-1970 period also saw both the women's movement and the gay movement reach a critical mass in terms of their impact on the Movement. The SDS convention of June 1969, which resulted in the group splitting into "Weatherman" and Marxist factions, devoted one full day of its three days to women's issues, with women chairing the sessions. June 1969 also saw the famous Stonewall rebellion in New York City, a three-day uprising in which gays and lesbians fought back against the cops and inaugurated the modern gay liberation movement.

By 1969, the *Fifth Estate* was publishing articles with a militant feminist tone. The following is from a review by Nancy Holm of the *S.C.U.M. Manifesto*, by Valerie Solanis (Solanis, who seriously wounded artist Andy Warhol by gunfire in 1968, founded the Society for Cutting Up Men the same year): "She describes some elemental truths of our society: 'The male is...obsessed with screwing; he'll swim a river of snot, wade nostril-deep through a mile of vomit, if he thinks there'll be a friendly pussy awaiting him. He'll screw a woman he despises, any snaggle-toothed hag, and further pay for the opportunity.'"

Concludes Holm: "Paul Krassner, who comments on the manifesto, has some things to say about violence—but doesn't know much about Solanis. Both (Krassner and publisher Maurice Girodias) try to make her a fool, both laugh, but I'm really astounded that a woman hasn't killed 23 people from a tower in Houston, Texas, like [Charles] Whitman did a few years ago."

It was from such primal bursts of energy that the early feminist movement arose.

By 1970, two women who advocated strong feminist positions had joined the full-time staff—Cindy Felong and Barbara Carson. Traditionally, women on the paper's staff had done much of the necessary day-to-day work and received little credit. But now Felong, Carson, and the other women began to question this division of labor.

The nature of staff meetings began to change. "Until 1970 most meetings were basically dialogues between the men," says Riddle. Now the women began to speak up, proposing articles on feminism, and taking more of a role in writing, editing, and news decisions.

Especially in the area of feminist politics, progress often comes step by step, and seemingly small incidents have meaning. In 1970, I was doing a brief obituary for Jimi Hendrix when Felong remarked that I should comment on the occasionally sexist content of Hendrix' lyrics. Upon reflection, I recognized that she had a point, and inserted such a sentence. At that time, neither I nor any other male staffer would have come up with the idea independently.

Carson was the first staffer to argue forcefully for the inclusion of gay and lesbian news in the paper as a priority. (There had been some coverage in the past.) At first, she got some support, some opposition, and a good amount of indifference. Some of the opposition was from gays who were themselves only halfway out of the closet. These people were not really antagonistic; their consciousness had simply not reached the necessary point. Raising it could at times seem like a thankless task.

People began to grow politically as they realized what a complex struggle feminism entails, especially in a racist society. Felong at one point described the shock she and others experienced at a feminist meeting, held in one of the women's houses, when a black maid walked into the room. On another occasion, the *Fifth Estate* ran a graphic description of a local woman's experience of being raped in broad daylight. The article identified the rapist as black, and several auto workers

the staff knew complained that it only added to anti-black stereotypes.

Change brought some conflict, as it often does. At one point Carson interrupted Peter Werbe when he was criticizing a fellow male staffer. She basically told him to give it a rest, as the current saying goes. The implication was, he was overdoing his role as the dominant staff male. Another time, Werbe suggested that a certain male staffer take on the task of answering the phone whenever it happened to ring during a staff meeting, and Felong pointedly stated that it might be better to rotate the duty or leave the phone off the hook. Werbe recalls that "I tried to be true to the idea of equality of everyone no matter what their 'status' and to encourage and accept collective decision making."

Actually, Werbe tended to be a bit of a lightning rod—he was a dominant influence due to his political experience, argumentative ability, and organizational skill. The fact that his actions were more open to sharp criticism made the staff more democratic, and made everybody more willing to question and be questioned when necessary.

Riddle remembers Werbe as the staffer most vocal in support of the largest feminist project ever undertaken at the *Fifth Estate*—the Women's Issue of March 8, 1971, the 61st anniversary of International Women's Day. Written entirely by *Fifth Estate* women and their feminist associates, the issue had a cover featuring female cartoon characters such as Lucy, Blondie, Little Lulu, and Olive Oyl, all with their fists in the air.

The lead article, called "The Rising of the Women," said in part:

> We are fighting for an end to unequal wages, unequal job opportunities and dehumanizing welfare. We want an end to the "tracking" system in schools based on race, sex, or class. We want an end to the oppression of women within the family by establishing laundry and food co-ops and day care centers. We don't want our bodies used for testing untried drugs, nor do we want them used to sell the products of Madison Avenue.
>
> We want the freedom to control our bodies: to decide whether we want a child or an abortion. We want the freedom to develop our creativity and to have relationships with whomever we choose—male or female.
>
> We want to know our history....
>
> We live in a society that is historically rooted in racism and sexism. This country maintains itself by controlling and destroying the lives and resources of people in other countries....

We feel that liberation for all people can only be found in a classless society where the social system is designed to meet human needs, not profit, and where people have control over all the forces that affect their lives.

We want to come together with sisters and brothers to build a revolutionary movement for a new society. And we must create a strong women's movement to insure that our liberation will be a conscious part of the change that's coming.

The Women's Issue called for free, legal abortion on demand, with no forced sterilization—a set of slogans that would fill the banners of the abortion rights movement for the next two decades. The Women's Issue was published almost two years before the historic *Roe* vs. *Wade* decision that legalized abortion across the country. At the time, abortion was legal only in California and New York.

The Women's Issue publicized a demonstration that was to occur five days later in Lansing, the capital of Michigan. "If abortion becomes legal, fewer women will have to submit to the humiliation and danger of illegal operations," said the article on the Lansing action. "Organized crime in Michigan will take a substantial cut in its third most lucrative enterprise."

The issue also featured articles on Angela Davis, who was in jail at the time on a murder charge, and Elizabeth Gurley Flynn, the longtime Communist Party labor activist. Another essay examined day-to-day sexism at the youth service organization Open City. (Ovshinsky had by this time left Open City, and the organization was dominated by an activist named John Martin, whose leadership was criticized by many.) A "Letter from Prison" came from Jane Kennedy, a Catholic peace activist.

The Women's Issue was the only issue of the *Fifth Estate* that ever sold out down to the last copy. The standard press run was 15,000; the sellout necessitated an additional press run of 5,000.

However, the Women's Issue almost didn't get distributed at all. One article, called "Love All Ways," was written by a lesbian who lived at Boone's Farm Commune, where many members of Keep on Trucking also lived. It said in part:

We have gotten a lot of pressure about being dykes, primarily from men in our commune. Men who are insensitive to their own feelings and are not used to the idea of love not based on sex roles. At times they have succeeded in bringing me down. I've almost believed their insecure lies and ceased to trust my own feelings. But fuck that shit! I know lesbianism is not a sickness.

Lesbianism is a healthy growth of sister love. DYKE POWER!

In terms of male domination, Keep on Trucking made the macho *Fifth Estate* staff look like a feminist bastion. They were infuriated by the article, and sat on their hands for a couple of days, refusing to touch the issue. They only relented after they saw street sellers drawing crowds of young women anxious to read about feminism in Detroit.

Cindy Felong and Barbara Carson remained on the *Fifth Estate* staff until the end of 1971, when both left to embark on other projects. Following Felong and Carson, other women were full-time staffers, but none were in the same league, as far as pushing feminism.

However, the general awareness of the staff had risen to the point where the paper covered feminist issues pretty steadily over the next few years. A sample of articles includes a report of a "wet in" by Wayne State University women demanding child care and an article supporting women who protested the cancellation of a feminist radio show. Books reviewed include *Small Changes*, by Detroit's Marge Piercy, and *Complaints and Disorders: The Sexual Politics of Sickness*, by Deirdre English and Barbara Ehrenreich. A feature called "The Speculum Underground" explains the women's self-help movement, and Beth Cady of the International Socialists examines "Women's Liberation—1974." Gay and lesbian coverage also continues, but tends to be reprints from the *Gay Liberator*. The *Fifth Estate* had no openly gay staffer until I rejoined it in January of 1973, having "come out" as a gay person in 1972.

Despite the continuing articles, the paper in fact reached a plateau in terms of feminism and gay liberation, and then began to backslide, especially in the quality of internal staff relations. Riddle recalls that many forces were competing for attention—antiwar activity, labor news, police abuse, you name it. It is interesting to compare the *Fifth Estate* to the *Great Speckled Bird* in Atlanta. For years the *Bird* had a Women's Caucus that pushed feminism within the staff and in the paper. In its last two years it also had a Gay Caucus. For whatever reason, the *Fifth Estate* never advanced that far.

BLUE COLLAR BLUES

As the various waves of activism swept the Movement, the *Fifth Estate* both participated in and reported on them. But what probably made the paper unique among its contemporary alternative publications was its labor coverage.

— BOB HIPPLER —

Detroit was first of all a blue collar union town, and many staffers came from union families. In addition, the Marxist ideology that influenced the paper over the years put a strong emphasis on the working class. The result was a wide variety of worker-related coverage, some of which of course overlapped the continuing struggle of blacks, women, and students. In fact, *Fifth Estate* staffers saw the labor movement as the background, and potentially the support, for all other attempts to change society.

To begin with, the paper did historical articles on labor. In 1970, Bryce Crawford did one on the 1932 Ford hunger march, which led to four workers' deaths at the hands of Detroit police. By 1932, the Great Depression had become so severe that one Detroiter died of starvation every seven hours, according to a local doctor at the time. Workers marched on the Ford Motor Company plant in Dearborn demanding the right to unionize, jobs for laid off workers, and the abolition of spies and goons. They were met with great violence, redbaited in the *Detroit Free Press*, and blamed by authorities for the debacle. (Ford was unionized in 1941.)

In 1970, I did a piece on a big 1945 UAW strike. The demand of the strike—"Open the Books"—was actually revolutionary in nature, and has not been raised in the years since.

The extent of labor coverage in the *Fifth Estate* can be further documented by perusal of three issues from the early 1970s.

In the May 13, 1971 issue, a female Teamster member interviewed by Cindy Felong described female workers as being relegated to the lowest rung jobs, and then facing further discrimination when the union did not support their grievances. The women strongly supported male truckers then on strike, were not yet interested in feminism, and had no separate caucus. "A lot of them, when you really do get to talk to them, do resent their husbands controlling their paychecks and men controlling what they do. When you get into a one-on-one situation, then a lot of these feelings come out."

In the same issue, an article entitled "Union Democracy" examined United Auto Workers elections: "Democracy in the UAW breaks down in at least three areas. 1) Auto workers do not participate in local meetings. 2) Election procedures are biased in favor of the present entrenched UAW machine, the 'Green Slate.' 3) The union local operates as a pork barrel in many cases, with special privileges going to members who toe the Green Slate line."

The piece concluded with one worker's comments criticizing the UAW leadership: "The UAW is getting too big, self-centered and corrupt...the UAW tries to appease workers rather than represent them in dealing with the auto companies."

In the April 22, 1972 issue, an article on the UAW Convention in Atlantic City began on a historical note:

There was one Atlantic City convention of particular significance. Young rebellious members of the stodgy American Federation of Labor turned their 1935 convention into a forum of political conflict, resulting in a fistfight between the tough leader of the United Mine Workers, John L. Lewis, and Big Bill Hutchinson, who represented the pinnacle of AFL provincialism....

Out of the convention was born the Congress of Industrial Organizations (CIO) which went on to change the face of the American labor movement, leading to the growth of the UAW, and its historic Flint sit-down strikes of 1937. The CIO was led by John L. Lewis, built on the commitment of many socialists and communists, and driven by the fury and militancy of hundreds of thousands of rank and file workers.

The piece detailed the struggle of UAW opposition caucuses to democratize their union, while the leadership used the convention to indulge in nostalgia, memorializing Walter Reuther.

Another article in that issue described a boycott of food service operations by workers at the Warren Dodge Truck Plant. "While management personnel have a full-service hot food cafeteria, the production workers must put up with machine food and a sandwich line." The boycott had spread to the Chrysler Jefferson Assembly Plant (now closed) where the vending company "raised prices from 25 percent to 50 percent." The piece concluded: "The food issue may seem small, but it's a very clear-cut example of who causes inflation."

A third article described the firing of Audrey White, a black female worker at a small auto supply plant in Hamtramck. She had told the foreman where to get off when he had made a racist remark. The article goes on to criticize the shop steward, who the article charges with being an example of the poor protection Local 155 UAW gives to its members. The piece described how, earlier in 1972, 200 Local 155 members had actually been mad enough to picket Solidarity House, the UAW headquarters, and indicated that further action was planned as a result of this latest incident.

In the August 12, 1972 issue, the paper reported on the aftermath of the July heat strikes, in which 51 paint shop workers walked off the job, causing the entire Chrysler Jefferson Assembly Plant to shut down. "At a press conference called after the walkouts, United

Justice Caucus spokesman Bob Carter asserted the right of workers to leave the plant when the heat became unbearable....Jordan Sims, co-chairman of the United National Caucus, also spoke in support of these demands: 'Working people are the greatest natural resource this country has. Their lives and health must be protected above all.'"

A second piece in that issue was called "Kaymac Strike Ends...So Does Kaymac." A supposedly hip head shop supply operation in the Detroit suburb of Royal Oak, Kaymac hired very young women at very low wages. When they organized a union and went on strike, the company hired scabs from a temporary agency. That tactic was defeated when the foremen walked off the job. The strikers began to get support from other unions. Finally the company went bankrupt rather than recognize a union.

A third article reported on the Norwood, Ohio, anti-speedup strikes against the new General Motors Assembly Division, a bitter struggle that got nationwide publicity in 1972.

The *Fifth Estate* reported on and supported many other union developments, such as the spectacular rise of the public employees' unions (including teachers) in the 1960s and 1970s, the rise of Cesar Chavez and the United Farmworkers, and even attempts to unionize the prisoners at Jackson State Prison.

To sum up, the *Fifth Estate* was an alternative paper of the 1960s and 1970s, but its staff did not forget the 1930s, when industrial unionism was won, with Michigan as a main battleground. The great gains of that early period in turn made possible the progress of the later decades. The paper supported unions but, as the above articles make clear, always criticized sellout union bureaucrats, those folks known to workers as "pork choppers" or "pie cards."

In Detroit, with its boom and bust economy, unemployment was always just around the corner. It was vital to defend your basic rights as a worker—the right to have a job with decent pay, benefits, and working conditions, to join a union and strike if necessary, to participate in the union democratically, to speak up at the workplace. If you didn't have these basics, all your other rights were moot, because you were caught up in a day-to-day struggle for survival.

When Reaganism arrived in the 1980s, its first attack was on unionized workers—the PATCO strikers. The hallmark of the era was forced union givebacks and union busting. Only after that pattern was set did the right wing proceed to further attacks on civil rights, abortion rights, AIDS funding, student loans, and more. The end of the Reagan era is likely to be marked above all by a resurgence of the workers' movements. There are signs this has started to happen, with the Watsonville struggle, the successful United Mine Workers and Boeing strikes, and the sudden rise of the Service Employees International Union to over one million members.

THE TANK PLANT MARCH

While the labor movement is the background for other social changes, it is undeniable that the main background for the *Fifth Estate*'s entire existence was the Vietnam War. The first issue of the paper came out within months of the massive 1965 U.S. invasion, and the last issue (before the paper became a monthly) came out within months of the final fall of Saigon to North Vietnamese troops. Youth resistance to the continuing war was the single biggest factor that kept the paper going.

In retrospect, it is still amazing that U.S. imperialism staged such a protracted effort, and met with such complete defeat. People who were ten-years old when the U.S. invaded were in some cases parents with children when Saigon fell.

At the outset of 1971, the *Fifth Estate* staff began to plan the biggest mass action ever instigated by the paper—the march on Chrysler's Warren Tank Plant. Conveniently, the paper had moved to larger offices, at Second and Canfield, which were more suitable for large meetings. (Longtime *Fifth Estate* bookkeeper Bill Rowe quipped that the rundown West Warren building should be officially preserved as a Detroit historical site. It was torn down a few years later.)

One idea of the march was to achieve some organizational independence from the DCEWV, which had led several marches down Woodward Avenue, with speeches at Kennedy Square—a pattern that had become limiting and boring to many activists. The paper wanted instead to have a demonstration in a (then) white working class suburb that was, in effect, a main supply area for the war, sending both tanks and troops.

A series of organizational meetings with regional antiwar activists took place. Dave Riddle and I wrote a 40-page illustrated pamphlet, which showed how the war had disrupted the economy, with especially negative effects on blacks, women, youth, and older people. And, in the end, all our efforts paid off as between 2,500 and 4,000 people participated in the march, which was held on April 30 (see sidebar 2).

On a national level, spring 1971 also saw the May Day demonstration, which attempted to shut down Washington through nonviolent resistance, and used a poster of Gandhi with his fist in the air. There was also a bigger demonstration in the nation's capital, almost as big as the original Moratorium. These marked the high tide of national opposition to the war, which was being dragged out to the Nth degree by Nixon, with over a million useless casualties, as he gradually withdrew U.S. troops. Also in 1971, Daniel Ellsberg leaked "The Pentagon Papers," which documented decades of U.S. government perfidy regarding Vietnam. The uproar caused by the papers led to a Nixonian obsession with secrecy and leaks, which ultimately led to the administration's downfall.

DEE-TROIT CITY

Many exciting political events happened in Detroit during the period of this history, but what was life like on the street for the activists involved (and for everybody else, for that matter)? An essay by Jim Kennedy from the December 8, 1973 issue captures some of the ambience:

> The southwest side of Detroit is a half unnoticed slice of the Motor City that lies between downtown and the downriver suburbs....Unlike much of Detroit, people still are out on the streets shopping and looking around at 8:00 on an autumn night....
>
> Down around Clark Park is Detroit's Chicano [barrio]...Large, sprawling and mostly poor, the area has, between the cultural centers, the small businesses and the Catholic Church, held a tight sense of community. To the west, past Patton Park, is Salina, the largest Arab ghetto in the country.
>
> Scattered throughout...are small pockets or neighborhoods left over from years before. Retirees, skilled workers, Detroit cops and city workers who live isolated from the ethnic communities, grumbling and paranoid about the whole area going to hell.
>
> For sure, southwest Detroit is unique and a little strange, but if you want to spend some time and know what you're looking for, anyone can find a groove to float in....
>
> For myself I'll spend a lot of snowy nights this winter at the Bittersweet Bar on Vernor.
>
> It's mostly a young crowd—kids who work for Ford, Great Lakes Steel, move slag for Levy, or work at the railroad. That is, when they're not pissed off, laid off, or unemployed.
>
> I mean we sit around and get drunk on a drizzling Friday night, rapping and listening to a killer juke box until Marge throws us all out. Or in the summer stand around outside the Chat n' Shoot Pool Hall next door and smoke weed till the cops cruise by and we've got to move.
>
> The Bittersweet—really gets off on the name—is the place to be in this community if

you're young and crazy. Chicanos, bikers, greasers and street freeks generally get along despite the air of impending violence....

> It's strictly a West Side Doper scene—Super Fly trying to get older. Doing the West Side shuffle—all night long. Drunken haze. Marge unplugs the pinball. Snow on Vernor. Fourth Precinct rollers. 3 A.M.

> "Ooh la la
> I wish that I knew then
> what I know now
> when I was younger"

Frank Joyce once joked that Detroit activists should form a group called "radical alcoholics." Other favorite hangouts were the Jay-Cee Bar (near Wayne State University) and the Bronx Bar (across from the *Fifth Estate* office).

1972'S KEY PHRASE

The Warren Tank Plant march and the Women's Issue had been the highlights of 1971. In the months following them, many *Fifth Estate* staffers realized that the high-stress job was burning them out, the low pay (now up to $50 a week) was slowly bankrupting them, and they might want to embark on other projects (perhaps even find a real job) at least for a while. (It was the rare *Fifth Estate* staffer who lasted more than two years at a stretch.)

By mid-1972, a whole group of staffers had left, not out of various political disagreements, like much of the 1969 exodus, but out of general exhaustion. Those leaving, besides me, included Cindy Felong, Barbara Carson, Dave Riddle, Millard Berry, and—after seven and six years respectively—Peter and Marilyn Werbe.

Len Schafer, who had been on the staff since 1970, began to take on a more important role. He was skilled at investigative reporting (including an exposé of mishandled funds at Open City), editing, selling, advertising, layout, rewiring the office, and just about every other skill necessary to keep the paper coming out. Mike Neiswonger joined the staff in 1972, his main strength being graphics and layout. Ken Fireman took Peter Werbe's place as resident political heavy.

The year 1972 was slow politically, at least relative to the early 1970s. One cartoonist said that two words on everybody's lips then were "Fuck it." John Sinclair finally got out of prison after spending two years at Marquette on the "10 years for two joints" conviction. The biggest local issue in Detroit was the continuing abusive activity by the STRESS decoy unit.

One cover of the *Fifth Estate* read, "$500 Reward for Information Leading to the Conviction of Any STRESS Cop for Murder." The paper also listed the "top ten" STRESS officers in number of people killed.

At one point in 1972, a crowd of 2,000 blacks shouted down police chief John Nichols at the City Hall Auditorium after the police ransacked the black community hunting for three young men involved in a shootout following a police raid on a dope house. All three died, either in 1972 or following years, either at the hands of police or in unsolved murders.

On the national level, the Chinese Communist Party virtually assured Nixon's re-election by inviting him to Beijing. A couple of months later, the North Vietnamese destroyed his military war strategy with a big spring offensive that sent tanks right across the demilitarized zone between North and South Vietnam. Nixon responded with saturation B-52 bombing of the North and the mining of Haiphong's harbor, exhausting all ideas the Pentagon had ever suggested, as if to show he'd tried everything. Even after this, the Soviets allowed him to come to the Moscow summit. Nixon's domestic political war strategy was more successful than his military efforts: he thought that as the draft faded away so would student protests, and he was right.

The McGovern campaign drained off a lot of national political energy during the year, only to end in Nixon's landslide re-election. In June, in the middle of the campaign, several mysterious burglars were caught breaking into the Democratic National Head-quarters in the Watergate Hotel.

In Detroit, some of the baby boomers started to desert the economically declining downtown area in search of brighter economic horizons. Today's pattern of an abandoned, mostly black inner city and prosper-ous, mostly white suburbs, was beginning to take shape. This factor, along with the decline in political activity and the departure of key staff, began to give the *Fifth Estate* a case of the financial woozies. As recently as 1971, the paper had been printing 32-page issues. Now it was down to 20 or 24 pages. It pub-lished an emergency financial appeal and initiated a monthly "sustainer" program. Mike Neiswonger later recalled that some issues did not have enough ads to pay for the front cover, let alone all 20 to 24 pages.

LYNDON LAROUCHE DEBUNKED

The beginning of 1973 saw an upswing of political activity from the nadir of 1972. The Detroit black community, fed up with police abuse, mobilized to elect veteran progressive politician Coleman Young as the city's first black mayor. (Among his other accomplishments, Young had appeared as a "hostile witness" before the House UnAmerican Activities Committee (HUAC) in the 1950s, telling off the McCarthyites. HUAC was not abolished until the early 1970s.)

The *Fifth Estate* endorsed no one in the mayoral race and supported no candidates for office during its 1965-1975 history. The staff took the position that elections changed little, if anything, and only diverted attention from the source of the problems, the capitalist system. The paper preferred direct-action methods instead. Whether this was the correct policy is open to question. In the 1960s, blacks and their allies fought and sometimes died in the South for the right to vote. And the fact that blacks can now vote in most of the South has certainly brought on significant changes.

Nationally, in January, 100,000 antiwar activists went to Washington for the last major Vietnam demonstration. Peace accords were about to be signed, but activists did not trust the U.S. to abide by them. Also nationally, the Watergate scandal began to unfold in earnest, promising to render Richard Nixon more and more ineffective as president. Spiro Agnew, his vice president, resigned in a separate scandal, when it was revealed he had accepted stuffed envelopes of cash in the White House. Another major national development was the dramatic 71-day occupation of Wounded Knee by the American Indian Movement.

Dave Riddle and I decided to rejoin the *Fifth Estate*. Riddle was sick of assembling pickup trucks for a living, and I was sick of delivering pizzas. Within several months, several talented new staffers also joined, including Jeff Goodman and Bob Moore. Ken Fireman left the staff and, shortly after, badly broke his leg in the first inning of a *Fifth Estate* softball game (it was cancelled). After recovering, he went on to become editor of the *South End*.

The reconstituted staff held an emergency strategy meeting, fully cognizant that the paper had damn near folded in 1972. The staff decided that distribution was the biggest problem financially, and that if circulation went up advertising revenue might follow. This decision led to the conclusion that depending almost solely on Keep on Trucking for distribution was a mistake, and that instead the paper should start installing coin-operated (25¢) newsracks across the city. The paper ordered them in lots of ten from a small business in Georgia. By the end of the year, the 80 newsracks had more than doubled distribution income.

In this context, it is appropriate to mention the role played by unpaid volunteers in ensuring the *Fifth Estate*'s survival over the years. One such volunteer, the late Pete Kwant, donated his labor and his pickup truck to installing the first 20 newsracks across the city. The day he took out the first ten newsracks, as he rounded the first corner, two newsracks fairly leaped off the truck and crashed to the unforgiving pavement. Kwant and the staffers with him picked them up, banged them back into shape, and all ten newsracks went into operation that day.

(As an additional note, four full-time staffers who played significant roles on the paper have yet to be mentioned: Mark Mayer and Doug Larkin from 1970-1972, and Teresa Garland and Dennis Witkowski from 1973-1974.)

Several of the new 1973 staffers, along with Len Schafer, also plunged into a renewed campaign to secure paid advertising. The ad workers created an advertising brochure, which featured on its cover a picture of Canadian youths in an antiwar march at the Blue Water Bridge. The ads began to roll in.

Politically, the staff decided to concentrate on local investigative news reporting and political analysis, something readers hardly ever found in the daily papers. Issues of the paper began to appear with as many as 20 local news stories.

Soon the paper became personally involved in two controversial Detroit news stories. The first was the political exposure and debunking of Lyndon LaRouche.

The U.S. public is now familiar with Lyndon LaRouche as a right-wing extremist with neo-Nazi politics who has run for president several times. In 1973, he and his group, called the National Caucus of Labor Committees (NCLC), which had originated during the 1968 Columbia University crisis, were still posing as Trotskyists. (LaRouche got his start in the 1950s in the SWP.) Several local activists known to the *Fifth Estate* had joined the Detroit chapter, which eventually quit the national organization en masse in 1981.

The LaRouchians' strategy up to 1973 had been to subtly draw off energy and members from other progressive causes in various ways. When the National Welfare Rights Organization (NWRO) became prominent, the NCLC founded the National Unemployed and Welfare Rights Organization (NUWRO) as an ersatz clone. When Detroit garbagemen went on strike, the LaRouchians formed a Strike Support Coalition, which was used for NCLC speechifying and recruiting, rather than to aid the strikers in any material way. The NCLC joined student groups to gain use of university buildings, which were used for "classes"—mostly propaganda, finding new members, and loudly denouncing any political enemies who happened to show up. (All these tactics are similar to today's New Alliance Party, which is headed by former LaRouchian Fred Newman. For example, they formed the Rainbow Lobby, which has no relation to the Rainbow Coalition.)

In mid-1973, the LaRouchians underwent a change that strained the credulity of many observers. Their behavior became erratic and confrontational. Instead of quietly leeching off other leftist groups, they suddenly launched "Operation Mop Up," a self-described attempt to destroy the Communist Party, which by its alleged dominance was hindering the left. NCLC goons nationwide began to break up any meeting involving CP sponsorship or participation.

While seemingly "Trotskyist" in its opposition to the CP, Operation Mop Up actually more closely resembled 1930s campaigns by the CP itself to break up fledgling Trotskyist gatherings. Operation Mop Up was anti-democratic and a threat to the entire progressive movement. Activists across the country united to defend their meetings from LaRouchian goon attacks. In Detroit, people arrived at one major socialist meeting with boxes of literature, under which lay billy clubs for everybody. When the NCLC attacked the meeting, the crowd grabbed the weapons and chased the goons downstairs and out of the building.

The *Fifth Estate* saw the seriousness of the crisis, and responded by issuing a special four-page supplement, with a long staff editorial denouncing the LaRouchians, including much of the analysis just laid out. The article pointed out that, with their violent tactics, the LaRouchians were acting more like fascists than socialists. The supplement also contained an article by Keep on Trucking. While the text indicated they were partially taken in by the NCLC propaganda, the piece ended by saying that Keep on Trucking would physically retaliate for any attack on the *Fifth Estate* office. (Threats had been received.)

The four-page supplement and staff editorial put the *Fifth Estate* at the center of the controversy and made it, as Dave Riddle says, "one of the first to blow the whistle on LaRouche." The cover of the supplement had two big words in block letters—THE LEFT—with the blocks breaking up. This picture illustrated what was happening in Detroit and nationwide. The *Fifth Estate* met the crisis head on, but the nature of it did not bode well for any progressive projects.

THE GURU GETS PIED

The second controversial story involved the rise of religious cults. With the dropoff of political activity, a lot of young people were apparently still searching for something—anything—to believe in. Religious cults moved in to fill the psychological need and soak up the energy, often giving back little in return.

People in many cases gave all their worldly possessions to these groups, took part in long sessions called "love bombing," where attention was showered on them (actually a form of indoctrination), and submitted to control over the most minute aspects of their daily lives. They also worked at fundraising for next to nothing.

Some examples of these cults included "Moses David" and the early Jesus Freak movement, and Sun Myung Moon, whose church was already well enough developed in 1974 to lead demonstrations against impeachment. The black community was also affected. Jim Jones' congregation was growing in San Francisco, and Jonestown—the nation's wake-up call about the danger of cults—lay four years in the future.

In 1973, still another cult was growing in power and influence: the Divine Light Mission of the 15-year old Guru Maharaj Ji, who claimed to be God himself. The Divine Light Mission had attracted followers in chapters across the country, including Detroit, and the guru himself embarked on a national tour.

Total amazement gripped the *Fifth Estate* office when staffers first heard that Rennie Davis, an antiwar organizer *par excellence* since 1965 and an architect of the 1971 May Day demonstration, had announced in California that he was now a supporter of the young guru. Quite simply, credulity again was strained, and staffers even made several long distance calls to the West Coast to confirm the news.

Soon the guru visited Detroit on his national tour, and the Detroit City Council, not having enough to do with a major national recession and automotive slump approaching, decided to give the guru an award (for what is lost in the mists of history).

Pat Halley was another new *Fifth Estate* staffer, and the only one ever to advocate pandemonium as a political solution. He went to the City Council Chamber posing as an admirer of the guru, carrying a bouquet of flowers. However, under the flowers was concealed a shaving cream pie, which Halley placed in the face of the Guru Maharaj Ji at a strategic moment (see figure 1). [Ed.: Halley tells his own story for the first time in "Looking for Utopia" at the end of this article.]

With City Council President Mel Ravitz suddenly sounding very unliberal, in fact yelling for Halley's head, the master of pandemonium dashed down multiple flights of stairs and out of the city county building without being caught.

A Ken Kelley article describes what followed:

> "I don't want the man hurt or arrested," explained the embarrassed child-god to his followers and the press as he wiped the soap from his face.
>
> However, one week later the pie-thrower was brutally beaten from behind by two of the

Figure 1: Cover photo of *Fifth Estate* vol. 8, no. 10, August 18-August 31, 1973

guru's top devotees. The two men, one an older Indian and the other a young American, had tried to reach Halley for several days after he threw the pie. They told him they wanted to "expose" the Guru Maharaj Ji as a fraud.

The older man claimed he had traveled all the way from India for that purpose. To track down the story, and aware of warnings from other *Fifth Estate* staff members not to accompany the men alone, Halley led them to his apartment.

"For forty-five minutes or so they told me what a great thing I had done, that the guru was evil, and that they would show me hypnotic techniques he employs so that I could tell the world," he recalls. "The older man told me to close my eyes, which I did, while he walked behind me. I heard the sound of metal scraping metal, and I thought it must be some kind of flashlight they used to produce their divine light or something. Then I saw the light all right—and lots of stars. I didn't realize what was going on till I heard my blood splatter on the wall."

He screamed, the men fled. Luckily friends were next door and managed to get him to a hospital. He had received six skull lacerations and contusions; for the rest of his life Halley will have a plastic plate over his cerebrum where the skull bone was shattered....

The men were identified as 25-year old Richard Fletcher and 55-year old Jupteswar Misra....When I talked to Rennie Davis, he admitted to me that the two are still very much a part of the DLM. In fact, the Indian turns out to be Mahatma Fakiranand, one of the first two mahatmas to give knowledge in America...."Was he stripped of his mahatmadom," I asked. "No he wasn't—he was just shipped off to Europe and he's there now giving knowledge."

Rennie Davis added, "I really feel Maharaj Ji is doing everything—he had the pie thrown in his face, and he had Fakiranand do that. The whole thing is one gigantic *lila* (i.e., game) that operates on many levels." Including, apparently, felonious assault and its cover-up.

Though felony warrants were issued for their arrest, Halley's assailants were never caught or prosecuted. Following the Halley incident, the *Fifth Estate* ran a series of articles investigating the nature of religious cults. If all was peace and love, why did the bloody fangs come out so quickly when a hippie pantheist pulled a harmless prank? What else lay hidden behind the clouds of incense, the hypnotic chanting, and the beautiful altars (which in the Detroit guru house had stacks of money on them)?

The *Fifth Estate* again deserves credit for some early whistle-blowing. But again, the crisis was essentially a negative phenomenon. Young Americans were blindly following a half-baked punk from India rather than thinking for themselves how to live.

As in the case of LaRouche, people were turning to the irrational rather than to the rational, to mysticism and mindless violence rather than to struggle and analysis. The fact that Rennie Davis was now leading them down the primrose path was doubly shocking.

"ROOTS OF THE UNDERGROUND"

The third major *Fifth Estate* event of 1973 was a 15-part series called "Roots of the Underground," an in-depth look at the rise of an "adversary culture" in the United States, starting with the immediate post-World War II period, continuing through the "beat" period of the 1950s, and on into the 1960s and 1970s.

The series was retrospective in nature, raising questions such as: Where did we come from? How did we get this way? Who were the forebears of the present era of antiwar activism, sexual liberation, experimentation with drugs, and talk of revolution? The various articles examined both the political and cultural aspects. After the furor of the late 1960s and the early 1970s, it seemed a good time to reflect.

Featured were samples and analyses of works by some of the writers and thinkers whose writing has changed American life, these included the following:

- Lawrence Ferlinghetti, the owner of City Lights bookstore in San Francisco and author of *A Coney Island of the Mind* and *Unfair Arguments with Existence.*

- James Baldwin, black activist and author of *Another Country* and *Go Tell It on the Mountain.*

- Beat poet and later culture hero Allen Ginsberg, author of the famous poems "Howl" and "Kaddish."

- Jack Kerouac, author of the classic beat novels *On the Road* and *Dharma Bums.*

- Paul Goodman, the anarchist educational theorist and godfather of the New Left, author of *Growing Up Absurd, People or Personnel*, and the classic novel *The Empire City.*

- LeRoi Jones (later known as Amari Baraka), early black nationalist figure, poet, and author of *Preface to a 20-Volume Suicide Note.*

- William Burroughs, author of *Naked Lunch.*

- Paul Krassner, comedian and editor of *The Realist.*

- Diane DiPrima, author of *Revolutionary Letters.*

"Roots of the Underground" was an interesting series, but it's worth noting that, in total, it featured 14 males and only one female, a lopsided score in anybody's playbook. Early feminists such as Gloria

Steinem and Ti-Grace Atkinson could have been included, as well as black female writers such as Angela Davis and Lorraine Hansberry.

TROUBLE IN LOTUSLAND

Toward the end of 1973, something began to go wrong on the *Fifth Estate* staff, though it was hard to tell just what. Traditionally the staff operated in a somewhat relaxed manner, alternating their paid vacations as convenient.

Len Schafer took his vacation, and in his absence the staff voted 7-4 to begin running personal ads again, including sex ads. The *Fifth Estate* had banned these ads in 1969, not wanting to become a "meat market." Local gay activists had asked the paper to reinstate the personals, on the grounds that gays had fewer ways to meet than other people, but the ban had stood.

When Schafer returned, he thought something had been done behind his back. As the only openly gay staffer, I had pushed for repeal of the ban, but not because Schafer was on vacation. The issue just came up while he was gone. Both Schafer and Mike Neiswonger were incensed and threatened to quit. The personal ad ban was reinstated without a formal vote to do so.

Then I took my vacation. When I got back, Pat Halley had already thrown his pie, gotten beat up, and landed in the hospital. I probably would have voted against the pie-throwing had I been present, because that "yippie" type of activism was not my style. When I saw that Halley had almost been killed, I quickly concluded that he had underestimated the guru and his group.

During the same week as the pie-throwing incident, the staff also voted to make Cathy Kauflin a full-time member. Even though Kauflin was an excellent graphic artist, the move was a departure from common practice in that, up to that time, all full-time staffers had participated in the writing and editing processes.

As the months went on, Kauflin came under increasing criticism from several staffers (including me) for not taking part in the preparation and editing of articles. Instead, she continued to do what she had always done, mainly artwork, typesetting, and putting together the *Fifth Estate* calendar, which had become one of the big attractions of the paper. Eventually she left the staff under a dark cloud, never having been accepted as a full-time staffer. Kauflin went on to do important editorial and graphic work on pamphlets for Fredy Perlman's Black and Red Press (see final section for more on Black and Red).

The fact that staffers criticized Kauflin, or just sat and watched, rather than supporting her once she was on the staff, showed that sexism was still a problem on the *Fifth Estate*. The fact that the staff was making policy in such an erratic manner, and with so little real agreement on what should be done and so much mistrust of each other's judgment, indicated that more trouble was on the way.

As 1974 dawned, another political event took place which, like the LaRouche and guru affairs, caused staffers to question what was going on, and to examine their political beliefs. Several of the socialists on the staff decided to initiate a protest march against high energy prices and mounting unemployment. Progressive and leftist groups around the city were called and an initial meeting or two were held. To put it mildly, things went sour. The *Fifth Estate* "Detroit Seen" column of March 2, 1974 described the situation well:

> The proposed "Energy Crisis" march that we announced last issue has run into deep trouble....From an initial brainstorming group of enthusiastic independents, the planning meetings have been transformed into dialectical shootouts between small left sects, each one trying to put its pet line over....The tone of the last meeting was set by a debate over whether or not to exclude the Trotskyists from the planning sessions....The motion was defeated, but most of the original people involved in the action, including most of the *Fifth Estate* staff, have already walked out of the meetings, disgusted by this dinosaur mentality....For those who wish to try and salvage a march from this zoo of narcissistic heavies, the meetings are Tuesday nights....Earth Center spokesman Marvin Surowitz reports that the karma was so bad, the center had to be exorcised for a couple of days after each meeting....

The flop of the 1974 march, coming after the two weird episodes of 1973, had an effect on everybody on the staff. The socialists stayed firm in their beliefs, at least judged by their activities in following years. But they began to lose faith in the paper as an instrument of change.

To begin with, everybody knew that the publication's current prosperity was due to the coin newsracks, hard work hustling ads, and continuing public outrage over Watergate. It was not due to any grassroots political groundswell in Detroit—the leftist groups who were flipping out trying to organize the march were evidence of that. The largest selling *Fifth Estate* issue of 1974 had none other than a bug-eyed Nixon on the cover, with the words "Jesus F-ucking Christ" underneath. And Watergate was slowly coming to a close, with Nixon's resignation approaching. Also, all

American troops had been out of Vietnam for a year now, drastically reducing public concern over the war. And discontent over Vietnam had been the single biggest factor in the paper's survival.

Everybody also knew that a major recession was coming, and that downturns affected Detroit especially heavily, cutting into the incomes of all businesses, including marginal small ones like the paper. It seemed doubtful the publication would survive it.

Dave Riddle, a socialist, and Bob Moore, whose politics were radical-liberal, had worked together on the paper for a year and a half. They both quit within two weeks of each other, without informing each other they were going to do so. Jeff Goodman, another socialist, took on a more passive staff role, working on the office books and not always even attending staff meetings. A third socialist, myself, retreated to a part-time staff role, working mainly with the newsracks, which had been one of my pet projects from the start.

Looking back, the attitude of the socialists at the time is deserving of criticism. Socialism is a collectivist concept, with people working together in a cooperative way. Yet when confronted with adversity, the socialists acted very individualistically. Socialism also advocates progressives seizing power to effect change, outflanking the right wing. Yet the socialists passively gave away the power on the *Fifth Estate*.

Len Schafer and Mike Neiswonger reacted differently to events. They began to shed their progressive beliefs, and became more interested in the paper solely as a business proposition. Schafer was coordinating advertising, and Neiswonger directed layout, so they already had a firm grip on the financial/production process of the paper.

Both Schafer and Neiswonger began specifically to reject socialist ideas. It first came out in staff discussions, and only later in the paper itself. Two incidents were typical. A staffer did an article on the meaning of the May Day tradition, and wanted to use a drawing of a Maypole with it. Neiswonger suggested using tanks rolling through Red Square. On another occasion, a Marxist study group called, wanting to run a small ad for a meeting. Such ads were often done for a minimal rate or for free; Schafer insisted on charging full commercial rates.

When local feminists held a women-only conference, both Schafer and Neiswonger were offended and said it was sexist of the women not to admit men.

Staff meetings began to take on a backbiting tone. One disgruntled staffer described them as "litanies of bureaucratic procedure, accompanied by the hounding of singled out individuals." The quality of writing in the paper began to drop as socialist staffers and contributors stopped producing. For example, Marxist

analyst Jim Jacobs would soon quit writing for the paper.

Schafer and Neiswonger were reacting not only to the immediate political situation, but also to very real events in their lives stretching over several years. Schafer openly admitted that he had become a bit cynical after working hard on the *Fifth Estate* staff for four years, and watching the Movement decline for most of that time. Neiswonger was the victim of a bad experience before he ever joined the paper. He had arrived as a virtual refugee from the Detroit Organizing Committee, a group whose members studied stacks of Stalinist texts and held 10- to 12-hour meetings three times a week.

Both expressed some interest in anarchist ideas, as opposed to socialist ones, but neither ever wrote a major article for the paper in that vein. In reality, both were on the fast track out of politics altogether. Schafer is now a prosperous advertising executive in San Francisco, cutting a dashing figure in a three-piece suit; Neiswonger was spotted in the mid-1980s as a public spokesman for the Michigan Consolidated Gas Company, justifying rate increases.

In describing the process that went on at the *Fifth Estate*, Dave Riddle recalls Isaac Deutscher's analysis of what went on in the Soviet Union from 1920 to 1940, albeit on an immeasurably larger scale. "The class struggle receded, and bureaucracy moved in and took over. Stalin himself was a symbol of the steep decline of the class struggle." (Isaac Deutscher was the biographer of Leon Trotsky.) Schafer and Neiswonger probably would not want to be compared to Stalin, but the analogy tells as much about his politics as about theirs.

My parting of ways with the *Fifth Estate* came over the subject of whether to put the word "gay" on the cover. Since I had rejoined the staff in January 1973 as an openly gay person, the *Fifth Estate* had increased its gay coverage markedly. The gay and lesbian movement was growing stronger locally; the new Gay Community Center was only a few blocks from the *Fifth Estate* office. I urged greater coverage and wrote some of the articles myself. Gay Pride Week in 1973 was the subject of an entire centerfold.

Finally, there seemed to be enough going on in the city to merit a cover story. Tentatively called "Gay Life in Detroit," it featured a cover illustration of a cop punching a gay on the chin, and saying "Fag!" in a word balloon.

On layout night, Schafer, Neiswonger, and others began raising objections to putting the word "gay" on the cover (the word "fag" was, as noted, already there). As the staff debate went on, my position suffered from the fact that *Fifth Estate* had no women's caucus—or, for that matter, any feminist women on the staff at the time—and no gay caucus. In addition, Schafer and Neiswonger got some support from the part-timers and volunteers, who each had a vote, for the unstated reason that at least the two financial/production people were sticking with the paper, while the socialists like me seemed to be fading away.

Schafer said that "special interests" were getting too much space in the paper (a distant early warning of Reaganism). Neiswonger said that "gays have their own paper in this city" and "people might think we're a gay paper." By a narrow vote, the staff decided to strike the word "gay" from the cover. (The alternative was not designated. Cheery Life in Detroit? Deviant Life in Detroit?)

Now it was my turn to threaten to quit—leaving off the word "gay" negated the whole point of the cover story, which was that gays and lesbians were at last coming out of the closet in old-fashioned Detroit. Two hours later, the vote was reversed and the G-word went back on the cover. But the fight took so much out of me that I quit two weeks later anyway.

In retrospect, it might seem hard to believe that an allegedly radical paper was afraid to put the word "gay" on the cover. To me it was a lesson that, while change comes, it can be at an agonizingly slow pace, and at times at a very high price. To be fair, gay and lesbian coverage continued on the paper after the controversy, including another centerfold for 1974 Gay Pride Week and various other articles.

About a month after I left the staff, the *Fifth Estate* suffered its third incident of 1974 involving sexism. The following exchange of letters to the editor in June 1974 outlines the problem. The first letter was from a feminist collective that included Miriam Frank, a prominent activist in the women's health movement.

To The Editor:

Notes from the Speculum Underground was a regular column contributed to the *Fifth Estate* by the Detroit Women's Health Project from August of 1973 to very recently. This column was about the sexual politics of the American Health System and...reported research and technology on women's health as developed by local activists in the women's health movement.

One of the main provisions of our agreement to contribute to the *Fifth Estate* was that there be No Political Editing (censorship) of our copy...our experience has been that male-dominated left groups traditionally censor, ignore, misinterpret or crudely co-opt the unique voices of women...and we had no reason to believe the *Fifth Estate* would be an exception to that situation.

We have learned that the *Fifth Estate* no longer wants to keep to that original agreement of No Political Editing and would prefer not to carry Notes from the Speculum Underground without their ultimate control of our copy's political content. This is of course not acceptable to us.

The *Fifth Estate* staff made the following reply:

The last article of the column mentioned above...was not left out of the *Fifth Estate* *primarily* for political reasons [italics mine—BH]....It was much longer than the average length which was previously agreed on...it also repeated material already covered in the first installment and it had many grammatical errors....We do not share the mystifying notion that certain social, sexual or political groups have a monopoly on insights into the inner workings of human oppression—including the particular oppression of women perpetuated by the male-dominated profit-corrupted health care system. It is the editorial intent of the *Fifth Estate* to expose this system...and not to promote one group or clique's "unique voice" on the matter....

In the following issue, Jeff Goodman, the last socialist on the staff, wrote the following individual letter in answer to the staff reply:

There definitely was political editing of the last column...the changes made were not merely mechanical, shortening or grammatical in nature. They included deletion of the whole first page of the column, which basically constituted the introductory political rap and projected anger at the "male-dominated, profit-corrupted health care system" which the *Fifth Estate* deplores....The basic problem seems to have been that the *Fifth Estate*, in fact, demanded changes in the political content of the column, and the people of the Women's Health Project were unwilling to enter a lengthy struggle over these changes.

The *Fifth Estate* maintains that a newspaper must have the right to edit copy for political content; this is true but it is at best a completely ambiguous principle, which, having no political content of its own, can be used to justify anything. The real question is why did the *Fifth Estate* demand these changes in the first place? Why does the *Fifth Estate* now have only one woman on its full-time staff and not even a regular column by any of the women's groups in Detroit? Surely you can participate in the general oppression without being capable of knowing as much about the unique aspects of women's oppression as women themselves. Perhaps it is the lack of ability of some *Fifth Estate* staffers to comprehend even the general oppression of other people...which makes them so uptight that THEY take on the role of God, declaring that no other particular group of people could possibly know enough to speak for themselves.

Notes from the Speculum Underground did not run again, and Goodman quit the staff soon afterwards.

Some of the events described so far in this section were not pretty, but they did happen, and can be learned from. The saving grace is that the paper somehow came back from all these hair-raising difficulties. Even while the old *Fifth Estate* was sinking into bureaucracy and feminist-baiting, a new one—the post-1975 *Fifth Estate*—was being born within its husk.

WILDCAT AT DODGE TRUCK

The first sign of the new *Fifth Estate*, one with serious anarchist-libertarian politics, was a series of articles by Millard Berry and Alan Franklin starting on August 8, 1974. The articles analyzed the June 1974 four-day wildcat strike by auto workers at Warren's Dodge Truck plant. (A "wildcat" is a strike not authorized by the main union, in this case the UAW.)

Dodge Truck had many young white workers influenced by "countercultural" values, and many young black workers as well. They went out on strike spontaneously when five metal shop workers, including a union steward, were fired after they complained jointly about bad working conditions. The UAW did not support the walkout by its rank and file, said the wildcat was caused by "communists" and "outsiders," and actually called the local police to evict 150 striking workers from their own union hall (a total of about 6,000 were on strike).

On the fourth day of the walkout, the UAW assembled huge flying squads numbering hundreds of workers to cross the picket lines, break the wildcat, and keep the plant open. The local police arrested about 30 workers, and the company pitched in by firing another 50 to 100 who refused to return to work.

The *Fifth Estate* articles outlined the skullduggery by the UAW, and also criticized the activities of Marxist organizers who had been agitating in the plant for years, among them the original steward who was fired. The articles said that the Marxists' local plant newsletter was not critical of the union leadership, did not fight for democracy in the union, and did not win the support of the workers. They added that the Marxists themselves were taken by surprise by the wildcat, but once it started tried to co-opt its energies by appointing a steering committee and excluding all other literature besides their own from meetings.

The articles then described the fourth day of the strike—it was losing steam (partly due to the leftists' tactics) and the UAW-Chrysler-local police forces were getting ready to shut it down. The authors said that the Marxists, along with leftist allies who did not work in the plant, pushed for an ultra-Left attempt to prolong the walkout, resulting in the mass arrests and firings, and turning a wildcat that might have made a serious point to both management and union, into a rout.

Here is how Alan Franklin described the UAW:

> Any UAW member in the plant has painfully concluded that the union long ago gave up representing his interests and became instead a simple adjunct of the company, enforcing work discipline that foremen and supervisors by themselves could never hope to impose.
>
> This is the logical and inevitable result of the contradictions inherent in any organization which claims to "represent" the interests of others. Unions are not now essentially "healthy" organizations which require only a cleaning up of leadership to "begin once again serving the workers' interests." They have not been "betrayed" by the corrupt fat cats, they are the betrayal themselves.

Millard Berry criticized the Marxists as follows:

> These organizers share the basic view that the working class...is the only segment of capitalist society capable of overthrowing capitalism itself and constructing a socialist society in its place. They also believe, however, that the workers cannot properly evolve their own critical analysis of capitalism, nor any tactics or strategy to radically transform it, but must have them *injected* from outside the class.
>
> The Marxist organizers use an authoritarian, hierarchical party. This party would take on the task of administering the new society, after the overthrow of capitalism, *in the name of the workers*.

Ex-staffer Dave Riddle replied to the Dodge Truck articles in a letter to the editor. (Both Riddle and Berry had worked at Dodge Truck in the early 1970s.)

> Anarchism is the position espoused by both the authors...and by the *Fifth Estate* newspaper.

This position, which idealizes the day-to-day resistance of workers to capitalism, unfortunately provides no alternative to capitalism and no means to assure that any alternative can be reached. Not one constructive word on what to do to move beyond capitalism appears either in the pages of the *Fifth Estate* or in the writing of the people who produced the articles. Instead, anarchism condemns every initiative for change short of an unspecified scenario for spontaneous revolutionary upsurge.

So the articles condemn unions as a whole, holding that the CIO originated in a ruling class ploy to buy off an angry work force in the '30s. The authors...presumably feel that today's migrant farm laborers are fools to try to organize their own union and that mine workers would give up their union and place themselves once again in the tender care of the coal operators.

The terms of the anarchist-Marxist debate in Detroit were now defined, and the future course of the *Fifth Estate* was clearly indicated.

LONG LIVE THE *F.E.*

After the old model *Fifth Estate* heaved a great sigh and died in July 1975, the anarchist-libertarian activists regrouped. Leading the new effort were Peter and Marilyn Werbe. Franklin and Berry made great contributions, and also joining were John Grant, formerly of the *South End*, and Dave Watson, a longtime friend of the paper.

A particular inspiration for the renewed project were the late Fredy Perlman and his wife Lorraine, whose Black and Red Press published a steady stream of literature, pamphlets, and books in the 1970s, and which in fact was the fountainhead of anarchist-libertarian thought in Detroit during that decade. Black and Red Press and the Werbes helped to inform and critique the 1974 Dodge Truck articles.

The new staff tackled the problem of bureaucracy frontally by abolishing all paid positions ("We no longer will relate to people in this way") and abolishing all paid advertising. They established a bookstore with a much more complete selection than its distant Plum Street ancestor. Its purpose was to help support the publication, and to serve as a focal point for its ideas and political organizing.

The new crew brought a burst of creativity into the office at Second and Canfield, the scene of so many *Fifth Estate* achievements, and the occasional mind-boggling inter-staff argument, in the previous five years. The *Fifth Estate* continued to publish, for the first five years as a monthly and after that as a quarterly with a worldwide circulation of 5,000. Its politics could best be described as anarchist, although it has extended classic anti-capitalist, anti-statist libertarian politics to include opposition to the industrial system itself and the civilization it has spawned.

In recent times, the *Fifth Estate* has been particularly strong in supporting, and constructively criticizing, the radical environmental movement. In an issue called "How Deep Is Deep Ecology?" several years ago, the *Fifth Estate* endorsed Earth First!'s militant, direction-action tactics, but added that environmentalism should go beyond "saving wilderness" as a final objective, and should also become a revolutionary movement for social change, or there will be no wilderness left to save.

The paper criticized Edward Abbey, in many ways the inspirational godfather of Earth First! but whose views were considered by many to be racist and anti-immigrant. Similarly, it criticized an Earth First! founder: "Unfortunately, Dave Foreman and others writing in his private business, the *Earth First Journal*, continue to issue forth racist refugee baiting...and other patriotic ravings that make us barely want to be in the same room with them...."

Despite these criticisms, the *Fifth Estate* recognizes Earth First! as an important grassroots organization capable of growing out of the backward views of some of its founders. "No compromise in defense of Mother Earth" is a fine starting point, and Earth Firsters have repeatedly demonstrated a willingness to do more than talk, to put their bodies or even lives on the line. The summer 1990 issue of the *Fifth Estate* has a photograph of redwoods on the cover, with the headline "Bombing Won't Stop Redwood Summer." It stresses the importance of defending Earth First! from police attack, whatever the ideological differences.

In the winter 1990 issue, the *Fifth Estate* editorialized:

> We endorse the idea of radicalizing the 20th anniversary of Earth Week....The attempt to fashion it as a domesticated spectacle has already begun with every hack politician, mainstream institution, and even notorious polluters declaring allegiance to the 1990s as the "Environmental Decade," all the while planning business as usual. These fakes are preparing to make it a week of festivities celebrating "concern" for the earth and the system's ability to fix its problems.
>
> We at the *Fifth Estate* intend to be active in Detroit asserting the opposite contention: that the wreckage of the biosphere comes directly from the operation of the capitalist system and not from "ill advised policies," "lack of informa-

tion about sound alternatives to pollution," and the like. Industrial petro-chemical production—the cornerstone of world capitalism (even when labeled "socialism")—is incompatible with an ecologically viable world....

The 1965-1975 *Fifth Estate* did not emphasize environmentalism as the current *Fifth Estate* does. In those days, the environment was not widely recognized as the overriding issue it is today, and did not have as important a nook in the radical kitchen. On the other hand, echoing the editorial just quoted, it is arguable that moderate-to-liberal environmentalism—as opposed to the brand advocated by the *Fifth Estate*, Earth First! or even Greenpeace—is the Mom's apple pie of American "armchair radicals" today. It is a lot safer to join the Sierra Club than to picket with union strikers, defend an abortion clinic, or stop the Ku Klux Klan from marching in the nation's capital.

The current incarnation of the *Fifth Estate* is also a strong supporter of women's prerogative to control their bodies and their reproductive lives without government intervention or legal restraint. In November 1989, *Fifth Estate* staffers went to the massive pro-choice rally in Washington, DC (300,000 strong) as part of a 70-person "anti-authoritarian contingent."

While supporting women's struggles, the paper is critical of the National Organization for Women's leadership: "NOW and its liberal allies decided to forego a march, such as the one last April which brought 600,000 people to the capital in support of abortion rights, and instead have the only event of the day be a rally where those attending would be held captive to speeches by an endless parade of mainstream feminists and Democratic Party politicians. It is usually the case that after experiencing the exuberance of a mass march, participants tend to drift away as rally speakers begin to drone on. This time, NOW assured that to attend was to sit and passively listen."

The anti-authoritarian contingent's leaflet explained the group's position: "In order to create a lasting community of resistance, we must establish systems for health support (midwives, health collectives, etc.) so that we are no longer vulnerable to the patriarchal medical establishment or an oppressive government.

Why grovel before the courts and legislatures again to ask for that which is *already ours*? Let's take control of our bodies and our lives!"

The winter 1990 issue is dedicated

> ...to the memory of the 14 women slaughtered in Montreal December 6 at the hand of a patriarchal maniac. As he lined up his victims and methodically shot them, he expressed a hatred for all women and said he wanted "to kill feminists."
>
> In the memory of these dead sisters, we pledge, "We're all feminists here!"

This last, brief section has been a glimpse into the post-1975 *Fifth Estate*; its more detailed history must be written by somebody who knows better the events and issues of these years in Detroit.

As a veteran of the early *Fifth Estate* days, I look forward to another season of social change in the United States. Karl Marx's "old mole of revolution" has been burrowing for quite a while now, and she may pop her head up at any moment. Now that the snake oil of Reaganism is seen to have bankrupted the country and led it into economic decline, there are great opportunities for progressive organizing. The true agendas of the 1930s and 1960s have yet to be fulfilled: Most workers do not have a union, countries still suffer under the yoke of neo-colonialism, and politicians still win elections by appealing to racism.

Many activists are working to accomplish the needed changes—feminists defending abortion clinics and causing "pro-life" political hacks to run for cover, young gays of ACT-UP demanding AIDS funding, blacks pushing George Bush into a corner on civil rights and defending the great South African revolution, immigrant labor organizers winning the basic rights of workers (again) in the fields, factories, and offices of this vast country. Most important, students and many other protesters are working to turn Bush's war against Iraq into a political defeat for the militarists.

It is for my *Fifth Estate* comrades, and all today's progressive activists ("those infinitely different from us, and infinitely like us," in the words of novelist Victor Serge) that I have written this history.

by Patrick Halley

In 1973 I decided that I *had* to start writing for the *Fifth Estate*, Detroit's revolutionary, "underground" paper; or become a werewolf and fade into some wilderness unknown. The times were ablaze with change, and the world was but a tinderbox only waiting for the right match.

I had been on the road, a la Jack Kerouac, for six months, hitchhiking up and down the West coast; singing for quarters on street corners from Vancouver, British Columbia, down to L.A. and in major cities between Detroit and the coast. My little theater troupe, "The Shadow People," also took me around the Midwest where we performed wild skits and bizarre "assaults on Western Culture" on the streets, in coffee houses, bars, and outdoor concerts—wherever and whenever we had the slight-est opportunity to vent creative spleen. In a word, I was afire.

But working for a biweekly underground paper was a more disciplined pursuit, with deadlines, heavy scheduling, and editorial responsibilities that forced me to hone my writing skills and adapt to compromising with a collective of equally imaginative and fermentative individuals. I couldn't be as crazy, yet I could be more effective because we had a wider audience with the *Fifth Estate*, and other members of the collective were very talented people with experiences in teaching and writing. One fellow, Michael Neiswonger, was a former head of the English department at Cass Technical High School in Detroit; another, Bob Hippler, was the former editor of the University of Michigan's college paper; another guy had a Ph.D. in economics, and so on, and all of us had a slightly different view of Utopia—though we were certain that it was "just around the corner."

I was certain that "Utopia is already here, but people just don't know it yet."

Via the *Fifth Estate* we not only worked frantically to end the war in Vietnam; we also wanted civil rights, economic justice, women's equality, gay liberation, ecological awareness, free thought, legal drugs, and all manner of New Left issues. We were on a tidal wave of change and were more than willing to sacrifice not only our careers but our lives to make the world a place where we could live for love and creativity and not merely for economic prosperity—with all of the social evils that unrestrained capitalism necessitates.

Working on the *Fifth Estate* was rewarding and stimulating but it wasn't so very easy, largely because the paper was (and is) collectively run. Every rule, every single article that we printed, was debated and voted upon, because the operation of our paper was itself a socialist experiment. Begun in 1965, the *F.E.* by 1973 was staffed by anarchists, socialists, liberals, and even apolitical activists oriented by single issues. Arguments often raged into the night. Sometimes fisticuffs would come into play, only to be broken up quickly and settled eventually with marijuana or a trip to the bar. Despite our different backgrounds and political orientations, however, our first principle insisted that we operate with no boss or editor-in-chief to make anyone tow the line. It worked. We fought, but we wanted history to show that a socialist experiment could work and that's why we made it work!

THE GURU COMETH

I made myself and the *Fifth Estate* world-famous in 1973, in one of the many bizarre instances of Detroit politics, when I threw a pie in the face of a renowned guru. The year before, the Supreme Court had broadened the scope of U.S. tax exempt laws to enable obscure religious groups to receive tax-deductible donations that previously only traditional major Judeo-Christian religions had been entitled to. One immediate result was the rise of the "Moonies," the "Krishnas," and various fundamentalist Christian groups that seemingly surged from nowhere.

In August of 1973, guru Maharaj Ji, the 15-year-old "perfect master," arrived in Detroit to inaugurate his "Divine Light Mission"—a religious cult started in India—and he was to receive the key to the city. The *Fifth Estate* was alerted of his coming by the Yippies in New York, who indicated that this guru was a hustler and a fraud, and I volunteered to investigate him and his sect. Having been involved with Buddhist and other Eastern religions, I felt that I could at least feel out this sect and determine if it was a genuine movement for peace or another capitalist scam.

I went to a meeting of the Divine Light Mission, previous to the guru's coming, and found that the Yippies were correct. The guru's technique was to attract affluent suburbanites into the cult, indoctrinate them, and then get them to donate all of their money to him, even to work in businesses that he started. It worked. Even George Harrison, the erstwhile Beatle, gave a Rolls-Royce to the corpulent mogul of spirituality. But I could see at their meeting that the deceptive methods of recruiting were more like a pyramid scheme than a truly religious function. My friend and I were ejected from the meeting for heckling the guru's head Detroit disciple.

When the guru came to town a few days later, on August 7, 1973, the local press hailed him as a messenger of peace and brotherhood. His disciples (advance men) hailed him as a combination Jesus, Buddha, and Krishna, the new "God." The Detroit City Council had plans to give him a testimonial resolution and the key to the city, but my radical friends and I were ready to give him hell. At the foot of the City-County Building in Detroit, we passed out leaflets to satirize the occasion. Since this guru was "God," our leaflet had a list of demands that "God must meet, or leave the Universe in shame." It was signed, "No-Name, Ambassador of the Animal Kingdom."

In compiling this list, knowing that the major press would most likely pick it up, I decided not only to satirize the guru and religion in general, but also to throw in some anarchist concepts to prick society as a whole. The demands were: "End to all suffering, pain, and hostility immediately ...Money should grow on trees...God must clean house—no more pollution...No more work—let the angels do it...Extend the life span of people, with perpetual youth...Large mountains in Michigan...No more gravity—let people fly...No more winter...Free the Devil and all political prisoners...Abolition of all private property, bosses, and government...More money for teeth from the Good Fairy...No more premature orgasms...Communications with all civilizations in the Universe...PEACE, PEACE, PEACE, PEACE, PEACE, PEACE, PEACE, PEACE."

This was participatory journalism, radical in itself at the time. Not only did the New Left writers write news; we also tried to make news. After our brief demonstration, we alerted the media that an event was to occur with the guru that shouldn't be missed. In the council chambers, surrounded by gushing worshippers of the guru, I sat with a corsage of flowers that concealed a cream pie. When the guru entered the dais, surrounded by aides, I came forward with the corsage. He glared disdainfully down at me, in his expensive suit, as I approached him, so without hesitation I launched a perfect throw from 15 feet that hit him square in the face.

Pandemonium ensued as I flew out of the council chambers. My friends in the balcony laughed uproariously; furious disciples clutched at my arms as I raced down the aisle with a mob of screaming "gurunoids" and policemen following in hot pursuit. I raced down thirteen flights of stairs and out the door, and lost myself in the swirling crowds of downtown Detroit citizenry. I did it; I didn't even wind up in jail!

SERIOUS REPERCUSSIONS

My friends and I had a great time watching the videotaped event on the evening news. I was particularly satisfied when Bill Bonds reported the list of demands on the channel 7 news at 11:00 o'clock. My momentary utopia was sobered out of me the next day when I read the newspapers. I had carefully prepared a statement to the commercial press: "This pie should be seen not only as a protest against the guru, who I consider a fraud, but also against what I consider to be thousands of years of illegitimate religious authority." The *Detroit Free Press* quoted me as saying, "I hate authority. God is an authority. Therefore, I hate God."

What I thought was a perfectly quotable anarchist statement for all time was instead twisted into a grotesque statement of someone who is insane, or worse. The *Free Press* used this misquote to attack me in the editorial page next day as a racist and religious bigot. They said that the "guru only came to town preaching brotherhood and peace, which Detroit needs so badly, only to be insulted by a misguided and confused zealot."

Of course the *Free Press* had no way of knowing that people would pay good money a few years later to kidnap their own children from the guru and other cults, and have them "deprogrammed," because they didn't investigate him. But they did investigate me, and I still don't know if it was merely sloppy reporting on their part, or an attempt to get back at the alternative press for our constant harping about them and the commercial press at large. A revolution is never without enemies.

A week later, however, I was vindicated, because the press had to report that I was beaten and almost killed by two of the guru's disciples, who attacked me with crowbars and crushed my skull. This was the first battle in the war against cults and represents a real "scoop" by the alternative press. Because the New Left and the alternative press were really at the forefront of peace and equality in the early seventies, we had to constantly be on guard against opportunists attempting to co-opt these trends for personal, political, and corporate gain.

BACK TO THE PRESSES

The notoriety of this pie-throwing incident helped expand interest in the alternative press, and that is one of the reasons we did it. *We* did it, as I've always insisted, because, like everything associated with the *Fifth Estate*, the pie-throwing was a collective effort. I depended on others to help defend me physically, and also the paper retained a lawyer and guaranteed me money for bail, fines, and other related expenses. In fact, while I was being besieged by howling gurunoids in the council chambers, one of my comrades knocked down two assailants who would have hemmed me in. I would have been torn-up badly if that mob had caught me in the aisle.

But everything the *Fifth Estate* did was a result of collective effort. As I said, we wanted to prove that we could manage a business without a boss, demonstrating in practice one of the concepts we professed, workers' control, or self-management. We *had* to prove that anarchy was not chaos, not pie-in-the-sky (or in the face) idealism, but a form of organization that is viable, practical, and desirable.

Working on the *Fifth Estate* showed that I could be imaginative and daring as an individual while still functioning within a socialist group. We were then at the crossroads of many political movements and groups and for the sake of internal harmony maintained an "independent socialist" philosophy. All of us were convinced that some sort of socialist form of organization must replace the capitalist structure on a national and local level. Some staff persons were hardcore anarchists, but some were active in Communist or Socialist parties. A few of us were even liberals, working for a more benign capitalist government. The *F.E* was so fluid, it was constantly reflecting the personal evolution and transformations of about thirty or more part-time and full-time writers.

But we did function as a classic anarchist group, in the sense that we didn't, in principle, affiliate with any outside group or party, and we did not have any chairman or editor-in-chief. Instead, we voted on every decision, and even edited each article collectively. This did indeed make for lively arguments, and, I think, contributed to a creative atmosphere, providing one had a thick skin and could defend one's own perspective.

The topics we wrote about reflected this diversity and combativeness. We would publicize such events as gay rallies, drug busts, feminist activities, antiwar efforts, union strikes, government corruption, new publications, films, and art gallery openings. At the same time, we never hesitated to cross horns with other groups in the New Left movement and, in fact, considered it necessary, in our role as newspaper people, to help foster internal criticism and debate, as well as to confront frauds and opportunists on the left.

For instance, during the Patty Hearst debacle, when she declared her mission to join the S.L.A. (Symbionese Liberation Army) and then joined them in bank robberies and socialist communiques, I contrived, and we printed, a "Patty Hearst Look-Alike Contest" that savagely ridiculed her and the S.L.A. and

which was reprinted in other alternative papers. Another staffer, Bob Moore, maintained a media column that constantly rated and berated commercial and socialist radio, television, and print media.

The *Fifth Estate* was only one of many alternative papers, and I was only one pie-thrower. Aron Kay, a Yippie from New York, pied George Bush in 1974 while Bush was CIA director. Numerous mayors and small town politicians around the country have been pied since, and I hope the tradition continues. I won't pick up the pie again because its singular use was appropriate for the time and I find its echo in numerous performance art pieces that have merged theater with life, but that's another topic. Besides, becoming a cult hero goes against the grain of an anarchist-communal viewpoint and would have vulgarized and trivialized the purity of that particular moment.

Thus, when that very *Free Press* reporter who had misquoted me called to tell me he had been commissioned by *Rolling Stone* magazine to do a cover story on me, I refused to cooperate. It reflects the mercenary nature of the commercial press, and a lack of integrity, that a reporter can switch sides on an issue abruptly and without consequence to himself while his subject's very life may be radically influenced by his coverage of events.

The major function of the underground press was to scoop up the life that falls between the cracks of our dehumanizing, corporate mass media and to publish information in defiance of that press and the large corporate advertisers who influence its tone and content. The shareholder-owned Detroit commercial press has Chrysler Corporation and Ford, for instance, who profited handsomely in the manufacture of tanks and army trucks during the Vietnam days. So the *Fifth Estate* people were not surprised when certain antiwar demonstrations were never reported by the *News* and *Free Press*. We could also write virulently against the oil companies and the food processors, or against union busting firms that the *News* and *Free Press* conveniently overlooked. We would even reject lucrative advertising money from companies we thought to be sexist or racist or big war supporters. Needless to say we never made any money, and that no doubt contributed to our attrition.

Some of the issues we confronted and prompted seemed too fringe or extreme for the commercial papers at the time, but we can see now that we were merely ahead of our time. We remember when nuclear power seemed inevitable and how we were labeled kooks for opposing it. We were advocacy journalists, a new concept at the time, and promoted feminism, gay liberation, nuclear disarmament, and other facets of the waves of change. We didn't start these movements but we actively publicized groups and events that worked toward progressive change when the commercial media ignored or ridiculed them. Much of what we helped accomplish is taken for granted now and our ideas have influenced the mass editorialists who are still trying to catch-up with the waves of change that occurred in the sixties and seventies.

One of the best examples of the damage caused by the negligence of the commercial press is the present ecological crisis. It was the alternative press that warned, even screamed, of the dangers of a mass consumption society; of off-shore drilling, factory pollution, and uncontrolled growth. As the greenhouse effect starts exacting its toll on the world, I get no personal satisfaction knowing that my own small efforts for ecology were ignored or scorned, but I sometimes wish I had been wrong.

If the efforts of the men and women of the underground press haven't succeeded in overthrowing capitalism or disarming the militaries of the world, they may have at least spared Nicaragua and other small countries from invasion by Old Glory. We helped stall the nuclear industry. We helped the women's movement get respect and helped swell its ranks by covering feminist events in the early days when no one else would. The list of victories goes on, but the struggle for ideas is a continuous process and *our* best hope is that our contributions may have influenced other people to continue the struggle in whatever societal roles they play today.

America is still dominated by the interests of enormous corporations and by a vast bureaucratic government that is actually remote from the average working person. The newspapers in this country, already huge corporations, are themselves merely links on a chain pulled by overlapping mega-corporations that may own several factories, oil companies, and international investment firms as well.

Today the media is still the "watchdog" in America—but for big business, not the common people. The *Fifth Estate* and a few other small presses still exist, but in emaciated form, a victim of the times. I do hope, and dare predict, that the underground press will rise again, to greater heights and influence in the future. The ecological and political awareness fostered by the alternative media has affected society and we can see its influence. But a few generations down the road? New wars and new issues, plus the inevitable destruction of a capitalist system that *requires* continual growth, will necessitate another popular uprising.

I know that someone will be there to challenge unbridled power and to fight against the enemies of freedom and natural integrity. I know because it has always been such fun all along.

Halley is a playwright, dramatist, and truck driver from Detroit who wrote and produced "Werewolf of Grosse Pointe," "The Canary House," and numerous articles, skits, and irate "letters to the editor."

A Fowl in the Vortices of Consciousness:

The Birth of the *Great Speckled Bird*

Sally Gabb

Gabb is a former staff member of the *Great Speckled Bird* and a co-founder of the Atlanta Lesbian Feminist Alliance (ALFA). She is currently a specialist in adult literacy in Providence, RI. She views herself as a refugee from revolution who has found momentary meaning and fun through learning from her students in basic literacy programs. She has spent half the last decade completing an academic thesis on what adult new readers have to teach us about learning ("words get in the way") and is now in recovery. She leads a life based on a variation of the Laurie Anderson credo: "I like subversion. The world needs it, and I like doing it." Like Anderson, she believes the best efforts for revolution are those that work "...in little ways that creep in."

I took a trip to Connecticut and read dog-eared issues of my old friend, that notorious radical rag from Atlanta, Georgia, the *Great Speckled Bird*, issues dated from 1969 to 1971. I sat in the special collections room of the giant university library. The young woman librarian with a shirt that said "Contra, no!" glared at me when I laughed out loud. She looked away when I cried.

During that warm lazy afternoon last summer, I visited a world that was full of useless war, of labor struggles, racist violence, sexism, and economic oppression. I examined a response to that world that was filled with passion, with humor, with anger, with love. I leafed through pages filled with creative energy, with raw and bold expression. I saw the grace of highly trained talent placed next to the raw ugly beauty of untrained creation.

I heard my own voice of twenty years ago and met myself face to face with a combination of the contempt that accompanies spine chilling familiarity and the affection of vital, connected recognition. In the spirit of this time warp, I came home and watched *Soylent Green* on my VCR. Charlton Heston, looking young, talked about women as furniture and the greenhouse effect. The film was released in 1970 or so. The past became the future. Is this 1989, or did I ingest orange sunshine today as the government was bombing Cambodia? Really? Anything is possible.

In 1968, a collective of young type humans in Atlanta, Georgia, spit out a response to the then-present insanity because they believed in possibility. As Tom Coffin, founding member, wrote for the final issue in 1977:

> The creation of the *Bird* in early 1968 was a political act engaging numerous people from diverse backgrounds suddenly thrown together in the vortices of consciousness and commitment emanating from the Civil Rights movement, and the Anti-war Movement, coinciding with (and participating in) the less coherent and rootless mass defection of American youth in the late 60's and early 70's.
>
> The *Bird* survived and even thrived for a time in that somewhat inchoate movement, constantly struggling to instruct and inform and somehow meld the all too confused and confusing cultural expressions of disgust and revolt into political expressions of anger and revolt. For the system, in that period, lay fully exposed, for all who cared to see. We learned a great deal...we fought, we struggled, seeking clarity and directions in a climate of historic events beyond our control, rushing blindly hysterically by us, before our eyes.
>
> We created a new journalism to deal with it—personal, participatory journalism. We milled personal experience, fragments of the whole, for all they were worth evoking grand themes and large concepts from bits and pieces we experienced. And thereby experienced deeply, learned great truths, clarified our vision, and so on.

So wrote Tom Coffin.

It was, naturally, a collection of graduate students. Who else has been so groomed to take themselves so seriously? Budding historians and philosophers they were, mostly men, with women in the shadows, women on the brink of bursting forth to be heard. They were men and women joined by a certain lesson: the South.

The civil rights movement was the birth of my consciousness, as it was for most early *Bird* staffers. Most early staffers were white Southerners, or reared in the South, bred to contradictions that exploded on our consciousness when we, the golden sons and daughters, entered college—that promised land of our parents' dreams. In colleges throughout the South, we were schooled in activist politics.

Some of us had participated in the rather late development of southern chapters of Students for a Democratic Society (the chapter at my university, Duke in North Carolina, was established during my junior year). Many had been part of the development of an alternative southern student movement, the Southern Student Organizing Committee (SSOC). A few had worked with the Southern Conference Education Fund (SCEF), a strong organizing group affiliated with the southern branch of the American Communist Party.

We had marched, we had sat in, and we had upheld the breaking of bondage for southern blacks. We had also been invited out of the radical student wing of the black movement when the Student Nonviolent Coordinating Committee (SNCC) announced to young whites in 1966 that they were no longer welcome, that they should instead attend to issues in the white community. Beyond race lay poverty and war and, finally, the sexism that was used against us all.

Although I had participated in civil rights sit-ins, marches, and tutoring programs during my undergraduate days, I was not active in the college New Left movement. My radicalization occurred while at graduate school in New York—and even there, it was radicalization of my thoughts, but not yet my actions. Original *Bird* staffers had been much more active in the student left. Nan (now Orrock) Guerrero and Gene Guerrero, Anne and Ted Brodak, Howard and Anne Romaine, Pam and Jim Gwynn had evolved politically in the growing New Left movement at Emory University.

It was from this student left orientation, combined with a broader cross section of alienated radicalized intellectuals and professionals, that the *Bird*, as Tom Coffin noted, had emerged.

Like the New Left nationally, we were socialist explorers, but our southern experience gave us a fortunate depth not availed many in the North and West. We had teachers. The civil rights movement did not spring up whole cloth in 1960. Rosa Parks was not an isolated individual too tired to stand on the bus. She belonged to a network of left political organizers who had worked for several decades to prepare us for the sixties. These older, experienced footsoldiers for social and economic justice gave us the advantage of history. The *Bird* staffers were welcomed into a community of struggle in the South.

The early *Bird* staffers had as teachers such leaders in the southern movement as Anne and Carl Braden from the Southern Conference Education Fund, out of Louisville, Kentucky; Virginia and Clifford Durr, veterans of the New Deal, and close associates of the Highlander Center; Miles Horton, founder of the Highlander Center; and many more. We knew we were part of a tradition. Some of them, from the conservative old Left, looked askance at the beaded, bearded, tiedyed motley crew of hippie radicals. For the most part, we won them over. Those who couldn't take a joke, well.....

Our lives were our statement of our commitment to change. We immersed ourselves in our counter culture—we wanted to live our revolution, singing and dancing, not wearing lipstick and heels, girdles and garterbelts, ties and three-piece suits. We were stridently "freaks."

> Freaks are not dropouts. We're members of the working class. It's just that we're on permanent strike.—Abbie Hoffman

> Sometimes we get so wrapped up in our own struggle to survive...that we forget about other people who are fighting their own struggles. *Freaks are not the only people who get put down when they try to live the way they want to.* (author's emphasis)—Bob Goodman, *Bird*, July 6, 1970

Bird staffers like Bob Goodman were unlikely freaks. Bob was a Harvard history grad student who had come to Atlanta to teach at one of the black colleges. A scholarly, personally conversative fellow with a radical mind, he never seemed quite comfortable in bell bottoms and beads, but spoke eloquently for the lifestyle. The article quoted from above was one of many designed to bring "freaks" closer to the struggles of others, in this case, the labor movement.

We were a fortunate collective of words and images and actions. The major wordsmiths were graduate students Coffin, Gene Guerrero, Howard Romaine, Jim Gwynn, Don Speicher, Dottie Buono, Anne Mauney, Ted Brodek, and Steve Wise. Also writing down the bones were local college faculty Goodman, Barbara Joye, Bud Foote. Then there were the images, photographic and graphic, of Bill Fibben, Ron Ausburn, Vicki Shanholtzer, and Nancy Jones; the graphic expertise of Stephanie Coffin and Linda Fibben in layout design; the poetry of Harvey Mertz; the humor of OG King of Bhashan (Bud Foote, prof at Georgia Tech). To hold it together was the business acuity of Anne Jenkins and Nan Guerrero, and the patient, arduous typesetting and office management of Becky Hamilton and Pam Gwynn.

By summer 1969 (when I officially joined the staff) we were living in communes (the Heathan Rage and others), making decisions by consensus—ahhhhhhh-hhh, endless consensus—and throwing ourselves into merciless critical exchange (barring vicious personal attacks). And, we survived. Thanks to public outrage.

Initial issues (before my time, in 1968) were supported by staff "investment" and surprising reader response. Apparently the irreverent alternative reporting filled a news void in Atlanta. What brought us a landslide sell out audience was our lack of respect: for mother, for the King's English, and for the Atlanta Holy family—Coca Cola. The cover for the May 26, 1969 issue, masterfully executed by our staff artist Ron Ausburn, depicted a Cuban revolutionary type foot-soldier, complete with Tommy gun, bursting through a Coca Cola sign (classic), and inviting the person who violated a female parent to come forward (as in "Come and Get It, M------- F-------!").

The good mayor of Atlanta saw fit to step forward with a warrant for the arrest of staff for "distribution of obscene literature to minors, and public profanity." (Never mind that the same Coca Cola was supporting the obscenity of the Asian conflict, where numerous American young men with Tommy guns were coming and getting it, and many were violating the mothers of unknown residents in said foreign land.)

To shorten the account, the *Bird* lost the case in court, but appealed, and finally won a year down the line. The Atlanta printer who had reproduced this work of art, New Era Press, claimed we were a "detriment" to their image and refused our subsequent patronage. We found a friendly first amendment printer, Southeastern Publishers, in (of all places) Montgomery, Alabama, and proceeded to raise our circulation to a high of 20,000. We maintained a steady 13,000 press run during several years of our peak popularity.

ANTI-ORGANIZATION ORGANIZATION

We were anti-institutional but developed the institution using effectively those lessons we had dutifully learned. Nevertheless we fought centralized power, and were still able to produce a *weekly* publication for years.

We were a collective. All positions rotated—at first every six months; later, for some positions, every year. We negotiated between our fear of centralized power bases and the need for talent and expertise. We were fierce in our attempts to keep ourselves and each other honest.

Collective meetings were theatre. An ad hoc chair kept the dialogue moving; each speaker called on the next. Criticism was the demand of the hour, as cutting and harsh as could be evoked, but the cardinal rule was, "No vicious personal attacks." The personal was political, but no one was allowed to use the personal as a political weapon.

The staffers demonstrated potential administrative abilities, notably Gene Guerrero, Nan Orrock, and Stephanie Coffin (the hardline business guru). A collective meeting might have had a lengthy debate on the position of Students for a Democratic Society (SDS) on imperialism, versus the position of Southern Student Organizing Committee (SSOC). Nevertheless, reports were made about costs, pleas were extended for workers to bind and label mailing bundles, and discussions were held about design and graphics. We were a business whether we wanted to be or not.

ENTERPRISE AGAINST CAPITALISM

The free speech controversy, the publicity, and our flight to the Alabama publisher also ironically increased our circulation and therefore our revenue. But publishing a 16- to 24-page weekly issue required dedication beyond a solely volunteer staff. The *Bird* employed between three and ten staffers at wages of from $25 to $75 a week during the seven years between 1969 and 1975. Despite an arson fire and eviction for real estate development, the paper as a business entity rented office space, rented IBM typesetters, purchased layout materials, paid the printing bills (not to mention gas mileage to Montgomery) and paid bulk mailing fees for up to 10,000. Despite our earnest politics, we had no choice but to participate in the capitalist economic system which we despised, criticized, and exposed at every chance.

Our true identity as a business thus involved us in issues that created passionate exchange and policy debate. A key issue, beginning early in 1969, and continuing throughout the life of the paper in some ways, was the issue of advertising as the paper's primary income. On one side of the issue were purists who favored reducing the paper to mimeographed sheets cranked out by loyal volunteer cadre rather than stooping to advertising. On the other were pragmatists who favored building a thriving "personals" ad base to bankroll our operation. In between these two extremes were the rest of us who enjoyed the economic "freedom" allowed by our advertising base—freedom to print photographs, freedom to use color in an issue, freedom to have (poorly) paid staff. At the same time, of course, we chastised ourselves for this collusion with the profit-seeking oppressors.

We did establish policies that would draw the line at advertising that blatantly contradicted our politics. An initial focal point for the Bird Women's Caucus, a group that emerged in early 1969 to deal with inherent sexism on the staff, was the problem of sexist content in advertising copy. Despite the refusal of some *Bird* men to concede, the *Bird* women gained the right to pass on acceptable gender-related content in advertising.

The choices weren't easy, however. The *Bird* was heavily supported by advertisements from so-called "Hippie capitalism"—the clothing stores, head shops, and music-related businesses that knew they could reach their consumers through our pages. Such advertisements often appealed to traditional male domination and to the view that women exist as sex objects for men. "Sexy" pictures of women were submitted to attract male buyers, no matter what the product. Ads to attract women often focused on the ability of the women to please men.

In addition, the "art" faction of the staff, who often submitted work depicting nudes, were sometimes in conflict with the more radically feminist of the women, who felt such illustrations, no matter how beautiful, would feed into the learned sexism of the readership as a whole, and thus reinforce the attitudes that it's okay to objectify women. The battle continued to rage throughout the life of the *Bird*, and was never more fully resolved than the sexual tumult in the world around us.

POLITICS: HARD LINES, DIALOGUES, DEFECTION, AND REVISION

The early issues of the *Bird* reflected the student politics of its founders: the civil rights fervor of white supporters; the growing outrage at the war in Vietnam; the connection between discrimination, economic oppression, and war through history and in the present. As *Bird* staffers, we always prided ourselves on expressing both "alternative lifestyles" (we were indeed…and proudly so…"hippies") and our independent New Left politics. Through the course of the paper's life, numerous political debates were carried out, some of them sectarian, but most related to issues. The *Bird* identified itself as representing an "independent left" position, free of party affiliation or "line."

Early issues reflected awareness of left "party" groups that were emerging into the New Left arena. The Socialist Workers Party (SWP) was ever present at actions and demonstrations, yet generally misunderstood and mistrusted. The feeling was often expressed within the *Bird* staff that SWP members "used" actions and issues to recruit members, rather than vice versa. While the American Communist Party was seldom if ever mentioned, the presence of "fellow travelers," or at least sympathizers, was clear. (Even mentioning the "party" here seems scary—like a betrayal.)

I was one of the *Bird* staffers educated by collective members and friends who had worked with the American Communist Party in the South, in both civil rights and labor struggles. These members brought with them a sense of history of the struggles that informed us all. Among the strongest of these members was Lynn Wells, child of old Left labor organizers, who had worked for the left labor movement as an organizer at age 16. She shared her knowledge of early struggles through pages of the *Bird*. In an early issue devoted to women's issues, she wrote an article about the New Left women's movement. In this article, she quoted

Sarah Grimke, an early abolitionist who, I learned, had become a feminist when she was barred from speaking out about her views on slavery because she was a woman.

Through Lynn and others, the old Left armed us with these and other pieces of history, and gave us the knowledge of a tradition of struggle for change. I believe that this knowledge, this sense of history, kept the *Bird* politics grounded and tied to real issues—not mired in specious New Left sectarian diatribes or flying about in utopian "hippie" lifestyles nonsense.

The fears of McCarthyism were apparent: accusations of "Redbaiting" surfaced in debate, and old antagonisms from the Left splits of the forties and fifties occasionally seemed to arise in dialogue. After all, the original Students for a Democratic Society groups were organized by a group strongly opposed to the American Communist Party. The history of "Red Baiting" also was reviewed: a piece in February 1970 quoted Robert Baden Powell about organizing Boy Scouts in the slums of London in 1928 in order to combat the "red peril."

With more current contacts, and the power of information about the present, an article in December 1970 reported the trial of Alan and Margaret McSurley, labor organizers for the coal miners in Kentucky. The McSurleys were imprisoned for contempt because they refused to testify about leftist political materials seized in a raid on their home. They had been charged under a Kentucky law prohibiting "sedition." Although this law was struck down, their papers, including books and pamphlets written from a Marxist analysis, were retained, and the "contempt" charges sustained. Such reporting continued to energize the young Left throughout the South, with the *Bird* functioning as a source for progressive history, for current events about progressive action and struggle in the present, and for information to aid in organizing the antiwar efforts, the continuing black and civil rights efforts, the newly developing women's movement, and the beginnings of gay rights.

CIVIL RIGHTS, BLACK POWER, AND THE (WHITE) UNDERGROUND PRESS

Although many early *Bird* staffers, myself included, had worked closely with the early sit-ins and black civil rights efforts, including Mississippi Summer—that special organizing effort by civil rights groups through which dozens of activist students were brought in to Mississippi to organize and do voter registration—the *Bird* seldom had black staff members. Nevertheless, we reported regularly on both black community actions and the Black Panthers. There was a recognition of different fronts but one struggle.

A review of issues from 1970 and 1971 revealed a wide variety of articles recounting the various struggles in Atlanta's and Georgia's black communities. I found pieces I had done on Atlanta school desegregation and its limits, on the lack of summer jobs programs for black youth in Rugglestown, an inner city black community, on the strong chapter of National Welfare Rights Organization, on the inner city black housing crisis created by "urban renewal" (known as Negro removal in the Movement), and black busting.

Others followed the spread of civil rights organizing and "first time" marches by black community groups for basic rights in small Georgia towns. We carried news of the black colleges movements—the growing voice of black youth in the South. "Correspondents" chronicled actions by black students to bring about equity in elementary and high schools in the small towns. We carried news of and articles from the outspoken Julian Bond, most radical of those young black leaders who moved into traditional politics when he was elected as Georgia's first black state representative in 1964.

The *Bird* also provided a running account of the continuing harassment and atrocities against blacks within the city, throughout the state of Georgia, and in the entire South, including the killings of black teens who spit or threw rocks, and the jailing of dozens for small accusations.

Through the years, the paper became a center for dialogue, and a vehicle for airing views not available in the daily press. Politicians, community leaders, and angry citizens sought out the *Bird* to express views not publishable elsewhere. The black community in Atlanta never embraced the *Bird*—it was not theirs. However, it was seen by most black citizens as a voice of friends from one community to another—a paper with news of the black community that was read at least by some whites.

The *Bird*, like other "underground" media around the country, carried regular news from the Black Panther Party, both in Atlanta and across the country. With many of us graduates of early civil rights organizing, the paper reflected with respect the continuing activities of King's organizers and the Southern Christian Leadership Conference (SCLC). Many of us believed that the struggle had reached new levels, however, and that "revolutionary" action was in order, in all struggles. The Panthers represented the front lines of the revolution against racism. In an article about Panther leader Huey Newton, in 1971, Lucille wrote:

> Our revolution requires participation and
> dedication by all of the people and we must find

a way to work and fight together. Huey wrote, '"the ideas which can and will sustain our movement for total freedom and dignity of the people cannot be imprisoned, for they are to be found in the people, all the people wherever they are.'" It is now time to turn those ideas into practice. Collective action is revolutionary action.

From 1970 on, however, the *Bird* and the underground press served to record the systematic campaign by the federal government against the Black Panther Party. The *Bird* staff were in contact with the local Panther group, and wrote about the busting of their headquarters, the arrests for weapons, and the constant harassment. As a staff we thought we were putting ourselves on the line. According to Lucille, "The question for white people, of course, is how can we prevent the annihilation of black people? What part do we play in support of these programs that serve the people?"

I recall a meeting in 1971 with Atlanta Panther party leaders. We were pressed about our support for their movement, our defense against persecution. We were pressed about our commitment to revolution. The posturing was grandiose. The questions were startling and dramatic. The hypothetical seemed real. The United States had become an armed camp against black people. Were *we* ready to take up arms? If there were armed conflict were we ready to declare our loyalties? I will never forget a direct question from one Lieutenant: "If the movement needed supplies, and your family was armed, working against us, would you challenge them in our name? Are you ready to shoot your grandmother?"

This meeting was not reported in the *Bird*, but it was part of the fabric of the politics. Most of us had already been arrested at least once for civil rights actions. Several members had heard bullets whistle by their ears when attending marches in south Georgia and other southern states.

The early civil rights activism of *Bird* staffers also provided contact with black leadership in the Atlanta area. In January 1981, *Bird* collective members Sue Thrasher and Reber Boult (an attorney) interviewed Howard Moore, a black attorney who was leading the defense of Angela Davis in her trial for murder, kidnapping, and conspiracy. The *Bird* provided a forum to air the defense perspective, that Angela was set up, charged through invalid statutes, and railroaded because she was working with black radicals in prison, because she was a member of the Communist Party, and because she was black. This important interview was not unique in the pages of the paper. The *Bird* held legitimacy as a progressive publication for many groups in struggles for social justice, including black groups,

despite the "alternative lifestyle" hippie character of its staff and style which was clearly a mostly "white" phenomenon.

Many a collective meeting was spent in debate about our relationship to the black community and the black struggles. Were we too "liberal"?—the word had a negative connotation because it suggested that we weren't revolutionary. Were we racist in our white hippie identity? The dialogue continued, but so did the reporting, energetically and consistently through the nine years of publication. A unique combination of political persistance and play existed throughout its history. Perhaps this strange polygamous marriage of many spirits accounts for its strength, appeal, and longevity.

In later years of the *Bird*, black writers actually joined the staff. While this change gave some credibility to the political positions we took, the paper was never fully embraced by the black community, yet it was seen as an effective communicator across the lines.

LABOR STRUGGLES: BEYOND STUDENT POLITICS, WHAT IS TO BE DONE?

Reporting on labor issues became a major function of the *Bird* in its latter years; in the early months, student politics, civil rights struggles, and the war in Vietnam took precedence. Liberation News Service consistently carried labor news, however, and early *Bird* collective members saw the significance.

From the civil rights movement, to the war in Vietnam, to labor struggles, women's rights, and finally gay rights, the *Bird* collective grew politically in awareness of how seemingly disconnected issues are actually intimately related. In February 1969, the *Bird* reprinted a piece from LNS on the General Electric strike in New York. From that article, both our readership and the staff learned that "this GE strike is the largest and the longest strike ever against a major American defense contractor during wartime."

As *Bird* staffers, we learned that we ourselves were hardly ahead of the workers who "don't particularly see it as unfair that the boss owns the plant and that they work....They don't recognize the historic gigantic unfairness of that to themselves and to the whole working class and to the whole population."

A turning point for the Atlanta youth/antiwar troops was the city garbage collectors' strike. The *Bird*, in covering the progress from the start, reflected the issues, the attitudes, and the violence. After several weeks, a joint strikers/antiwar rally came together. *Bird* writer Barbara Joye saw tremendous hope for unity in the mutual support: "hopefully Saturday's march was more than just a catharsis for the participants. It may have strengthened the city workers, and laid groundwork for future coalitions and new strategies for the Left in America."

Labor coverage continued throughout the life of the *Bird*, and grew, as the consciousness of *Bird* staffers grew and changed. Several staff members became seriously involved in the growing radical labor left, in groups such as the October League, which later transformed as the Revolutionary Communist Party. These staffers eventually left the paper, turning to in-plant organizing, and publishing more sectarian "Marxist Leninist" organs such as *The Call*. Former *Bird* staffers who wrote for *The Call*, such as Steve Wise, were strong in their belief that "Marxist Leninism [is] the only ideology proven (sic) capable throughout the world of leading the working class to victory."

Labor politics was not the only movement leading staff members away from the *Bird*. The collective was the center for intense dialogue on two other primary issues that highlighted the era: the issues of women's rights and the right to freedom in sexual orientation.

WOMEN, FEMINISM AND THE *BIRD*: REFLECTING THE REVOLUTION WITHIN

In the final issue of the *Great Speckled Bird*, October 1976, I wrote these words:

> It wasn't exactly a bloodless revolution. There were casualties. But the results were real for us. No more were women to be the shit-workers, the silent support for male voices. We were the Women's Caucus, our cause was to fight the sexism, our duty, to take leadership.

The Bird women's caucus was a major piece of the progressive development of the collective. Strong women—Nan Orrock, Stephanie Coffin, Sue Thrasher, Anne Jenkins, Anne Mauney, Lynn Wells, Nancy Jones—seized the time. Other women of the *Bird* staff gained strength from the leadership. The movement of the women made a difference in the internal workings of the staff, and in the copy we printed.

The New Left women's movement had been spearheaded by female members of Students for a Democratic Society, who recognized the silent subtle oppression doled out by the male Left and pushed forward a new agenda for feminism. With Rousseauean feigned innocence, the male Left responded with surprise and not a little indigence. The underground press reflected this growing consciousness and struggle; the *Bird* caucus was an early institution for defining theory and practice, and for providing strength for growth.

"not exactly bloodless."

Advertising was only one of many areas of the paper that presented sexist contradictions.

The raising of feminist issues interrupted a fairly stable pattern of heterosexual coupling on the early *Bird* staff—male active initiative, assertively "revolutionary"; female passive support, submissively servile. These "couples" indeed built the paper in its first year: men led meetings, wrote articles, defined politics; women typed, did lay out (!), mailed papers, cooked, cleaned, and had babies.

I was among the first non-coupled women to join the staff. In addition, I was among few with a journalism background. In some ways, I became their token female member of the staff leadership. Later I had to mend fences, having alienated sisters through my easy entrance into the male journalistic provinces. In reality, I had training for journalistic writing, but was far weaker in organizing and administrative skills than other women on the staff. It took several years for the learned "life in the shadows" to be erased for some.

In an early issue of 1969, we had declared our existence as a women's support group within the staff in an article to our readership. We presented demands to the collective: no male dominance of meetings through stronger vocal cords. Shared shit work. Shared child care by males in families. Editorial presence of women's perspective at all times.

In those early years, we sought to follow suffragist Lucy Stone's words, "In education, in marriage, in everything, disappointment is the lot of women. It shall be the business of my life to deepen this disappointment in every woman's heart until she bows down to it no longer."

Beginning in 1969, the *Bird* became the journal of struggle in women's issues. The earliest reproductive rights efforts were recorded and promoted. Women in the labor movement, women in education, women in Cuba, women in Vietnam, all were celebrated in our pages.

> Bread and roses, bread and roses, we want bread but we want roses too...

The *Bird* became a history text and a modern record of the strength and gallantry of women. In addition to stories of sisters Sarah and Angela Grimke, we were able to glorify the strengths of women leaders such as Jeannette Rankin, Anne Braden, Ella Mae Wiggins, Nannie Washburn, and many more.

We chronicled events in the growing New Left women's movement. Anne Braden herself, leader in Civil Rights and progressive politics, wrote a report of the women's conference held by SSOC. Reading it in 1989, I was fascinated to hear her voice of twenty years earlier, a voice reminiscing about involvement in the New South progressive movement, projecting about the future:

> We too thought we were part of the 'New South' and did not intend to be forced into traditional roles of Southern white women.
>
> Most of the "liberated women" of my generation [she was 44]—these girls' mothers perhaps—after a period of youthful rebellion, faded back into the scenery of Southern life.
>
> Will the young women of 1969 fade back into the scenery too? Some will—but some way I think they have a much better chance.

Braden noted that the organized women's liberation groups gave young women strength. However, she criticized the groups in their white middle class isolation. She noted that the conference organizers had discussed inviting black women's groups to the session, but decided against it after talking with some black radical women. The black women had insisted that the experiences were too different.

> That may be true for now, but I have always found that the experiences black and white women share as women are more powerful than the ones that divide them.

Anne Braden brought her own history as a fighter for social justice to us as young women. Her participation and that of other strong older women gave depth and substance to our movement, our search for definition.

Jeannette Rankin in particular represented living history. I had the honor to interview her in her ivy covered home near Athens, Georgia. A former congresswoman, she holds the record for legislative votes to promote peace in the world. This tiny ancient indomitable woman described for me how she stumped for congress in her home state of Montana, which gave women the vote before national suffrage. She immortalized herself by persisting as a peace candidate throughout her life and legislative career. She *refused to vote to support the entrance of the U.S.A. into World War I*. She was a leader in the International Women's League for Peace and Freedom, a worldwide women's group for peace.

Other women staffers and I also had the honor of interviewing Nannie Washburn, a fighter for peace, freedom, and social justice from her early days as a mill worker's daughter. In the article that resulted from that interview, she describes how as a teenager she learned to read from a black Communist labor organiz-er, Angelo Herndon. She spent her life participating in movements, demonstrations, and actions for social justice and radical change. On her 72nd birthday she was imprisoned during the May Day demonstrations. At 75 she visited China with a group of American "friends of China" from Atlanta. We were able to share and preserve her words of strength and leadership, to expose to the light of day the history of strong women, the models we have been denied through the tradition of patriarchy and the shaping of reported history by men.

The May 1970 issue reported our attendance at the Liberation News Service Women in Media Conference in New York City.

"We are everything they say we are—tough, strong, grim, willing to struggle with men," wrote *Bird* staff woman Becky Hamilton.

Those were the words of the battle-scarred. Seven of us had traveled from Atlanta to NYC in a Volkswagen bus with flowered curtains blowing in the windows. Seven hippie women complete with the gentle outfits of our "culture," the india print shirts and skirts, the beads and headbands, the embroidered bell bottoms. We had picked up a longhaired teenage boy somewhere in Maryland. We had music and heavy conversation. Then we were stopped on the New Jersey turnpike. The highway cops invaded our van, threw open all our duffles and packs—and found one lousy joint.

We were prepared. None revealed the identity of the traveler owning the joint-bearing pack. For five hours, we were grilled in the turnpike jailhouse (exit eleven, to be exact). Finally allowed to make a phone call, we contacted the New Jersey ACLU. "Contact the Atlanta branch," we gambled. (We had friends there.)

Luckily, the friendly New Jersey ACLU followed through. A male freak friend *Bird* staffer (hair to his shoulders) was working as a *secretary* for the Atlanta ACLU. When the New Jersey counsellors contacted the office, a male voice answered the phone. "Go ahead, take the case, we'll back you," offered our friend. Thank Saint Susan B. for those remaining stereotypes. The New Jersey *male* lawyer-type assumed that any male voice in a law office was a lawyer!

Actually, the New Jersey ACLU lawyer was a friend of the times. After our call for help, this affluent liberal man of the Bar came and picked up our motley crew of eight, sprung us, and brought us to his *home* in posh New Brunswick. There we spread our sleeping bags on his orientals while his dutiful wife fixed us bacon and eggs. We were out on personal recognizance; we travelled to the city with renewed fervor for the revolution.

Having braved this ordeal, we immersed ourselves in the intense feminist dialogue of the moment. As staffer Becky Hamilton wrote:

> Rat and Off Our Backs women offered the all woman paper as a solution to the energy consuming hassles of working with men. Rat women spoke about the final necessity of women assuming control of Rat and the liberation and freedom involved. The Rat men seemed committed in individualistic ego ways to a sick structure (i.e., one that gave men privileges and kept women down). While the women, together as a unit, were involved in putting out a revolutionary newspaper collectively. When the differences became clearly unresolvable, the women took control, began to erase the dichotomy between "creative" work and shit work, and for the first time, really dug putting out a paper.
>
> But we at the Bird want to make our man/woman paper work. Men are beginning to type, women are writing more. Men help with children, women do daily business and circulation. But before the men typed or participated in child care, or talked about exploitative advertising, the women had to get together, make demands, explain, threaten, etc. First we had to be united as women.

In later years of the Bird publication, long after I had left the staff, women achieved full partnership in decisions, and claimed rightful ownership of the politics and positions. In fact, in the attempted rebirth of 1984, almost a decade after the initial demise (or long sleep), half the resurrection crew were women once again. In retrospect, I venture to speak for women of the Bird.

The collective served as a site of mutual consciousness raising, providing us with a support group within which many of us could grow and develop our self definition. The Bird spirit of critical exchange persisted within the women's caucus, and we challenged each other and ourselves through the dialogue. Many of us left to pursue further our identities as women. I like to think, however, that our process of growth was shared by the men as well.

I wrote in the "closing" issue of 1976, "women on the Bird have refused to allow the male *left* to relegate women's issues to a back seat position." In returning now to that issue, however, I note that none of the men mention any effect of the women's movement on their lives. Perhaps it was too soon to tell? (We were indeed an optimistic generation...)

GAYLY WE MARCHED ALONG: COMING OUT AHEAD???

The "gay rights" movement's official beginning, with the Christopher Street response to police violence in 1969, corresponded with the birth of our fine feathered publication. The coverage of gay rights issues did not fully develop, however, until well into 1970, when gay rights groups challenged the staff. An article in October 1970 notes that the staff was criticized by a gay rights activist for the lack of lesbian and gay coverage in the 1970 Women's Festival issue.

In November, the Bird reprinted an article by Martha Shelley/Rat (NYC) that began:

> Look out straights. Here comes the Gay Liberation Front! springing up like warts all over the bland face of Amerika causing shudders of indigestion in the delicately balanced bowels of the Movement. Here come the Gays, marching with six foot banners, in Moratoriums, and embarrassing the liberals.

The Bird's own Miller Francis, arts and music commentator, came out in print, and provided eloquent support for the gay rights movement in Atlanta. In the same November 1970 issue, Francis noted that city hall had closed a gay club, but provided a radical analysis—that bars and clubs cannot be the center of change, as they are never controlled by patrons.

"Out of the bars and into the collective consciousness," wrote Francis.

Among the strongest spokeswomen for the growing radical lesbian community in Atlanta was Vicki, a long time Bird staff member. Vicki made sure that gay and lesbian news was well represented in the Bird. In March 1971, she reported the New York press conference at which a number of women's liberation groups publicly stated support for gay and lesbian liberation movements. She quoted the press release as consistent with the Bird policy, that:

> Women's liberation and homosexual liberation are both struggling towards a common goal: a society free from defining and categorizing people by virtue of gender and/or sexual preference.

In latter years, this independent left position on gay rights was maintained and extended. Many of us who were exploring our personal, political, and sexual identities left the Bird to pursue other needs. Francis, the early eloquent gay rights advocate, joined a revolutionary socialist labor group that renounced homosexuality. I myself first worked for a lesbian print collective before settling into adult literacy as my life work.

There is much that the *Bird* provided that is not discussed here. The art and photography elements were unique and superb. Ron Ausburn's comix rivaled Furry Freak Brothers and R. Cobb. His early demise shocked and saddened us all. The exquisite photography of Bill and Linda Fibben, Vicki Shanholtzer, and others made our publications works of art.

In addition, the pages sang with reports of music—rock, country, blues, jazz, and soul. For *Bird* staff, the movement definitely had a sound track. And the voices of the people came through the melodies and lyrics of Southern music.

Anne Romaine still plays country. Bernice Reagan, friend of *Bird* staffer Sue Thrasher, founded "Sweet Honey and the Rock." And all of us have indelible memories of the *Bird* encampment at the Atlanta Pop Festival in Byron, Georgia, 1970.

Gene Guerrero sings a different tune now, as lobbyist for the ACLU in Washington. Nan Orrock is a Georgia state representative. Howard Romaine plies the legal trade. Steve Wise hopes to teach real history. Ted Brodek and Neal Herron organize labor. Anne Mauney and Stephanie Coffin (and I) teach, teach, teach.

In the last issue, Jon Jacobs wrote, "And now, the *Bird* is dead. Just writing the sentence brings a twinge. It partially filled a great need for some time, and it schooled some of us in skills which we now consider most important. It helped win the war in Vietnam, it helped diminish the brutality of the Atlanta Police Department, and it opened up the Atlanta of the late sixties in a dramatic way which those who were not around for it cannot comprehend."

And finally, Tom concluded:

> We are, by the way, a part of a generation of Americans who have by no means had their last say.

THE JOY OF LIBERATION NEWS SERVICE

Harvey Wasserman

Copyright © 1990 by Harvey Wasserman

Wasserman continues to be active in peace and ecology issues. His *Harvey Wasserman's History of the United States* was written in the LNS garage at Montague Farm, and has been reissued by Four Walls Eight Windows Publishers (New York: 1989). He co-authored *Killing Our Own: The Disaster of America's Experience with Atomic Radiation* (New York: Delta, 1982), the first full-spectrum account of what radiation has done to the American people. That project grew out of the successful campaign to defeat a nuclear power plant slated for a site four miles from Montague Farm. He currently speaks on college campuses about American history and the global ecology. His twin daughters, Annie and Abbie, were born on Rosa Parks' birthday (February 4) 1987.

Liberation News Service! Founded in youthful genius, LNS moved this country as few other rag-tag operations ever did. It was the AP and UPI of the underground, supplying the counterculture with a wide variety of articles and essays, proofs and spoofs that were read and loved by emerging millions. When it fissioned, after less than a year of pure blinding light, its fallout comprised yet another news service (that lasted another decade) and a magnificent communal farm with a compelling activist destiny of its own.

What we didn't know about that explosion at the time, however, was the malevolent role played by a cynical, vicious, and extremely dangerous network of covert U.S. government operatives. These FBI thugs, financed by our own tax dollars, lied, cheated, stole, committed acts of violence, and made a mockery of the spirit and letter of every law on the books, not to mention all the precepts of common decency. And they're still doing it.

But first to the happy stuff. So much has been written about LNS I won't try to duplicate the telling. Please read Raymond Mungo's wonderful *Famous Long Ago*, first published by Beacon Press, and Stephen Diamond's *What the Trees Said*, a superb sequel produced by Seymour Lawrence/Dell shortly thereafter. They tell the early story of LNS and Montague Farm far better than I ever could.

But in 1969, shortly after the suicide of Marshall Bloom, LNS co-founder and one of my dearest brethren, I sat down to write an autobiography. It was essentially designed to clear my psyche, to make sense of some of the astonishing events that had happened since 1966, when I turned 21.

What emerged was a book variously called *Young Thunderbunny* or *The Adventures of Sluggo*.

Gratefully, it was never published in toto. But I present some of the passages because they may capture some of the spirit of what we did back then as told on the scene, in the terms and mindset of the day.

LNS was a joyous, thrilling, uncommonly powerful rocket ship we got to ride, as a blessing of youth and of the rare brilliance of the time. May we never lose the essential magic and humanity of either.

* * *

It is October 19, 1967, the eve of our first mass attempt to end the war in Vietnam. In this particular Washington, DC house, the assault on the Pentagon by more than 100,000 peace marchers from all over America is being orchestrated to accommodate the founding of Liberation News Service as well, that being a movie directed by Marshall Bloom and Ray Mungo and involving a cast of millions, including yourself.

Bloom is crazy but smart like a good Jewish boy from Denver, Amherst College, and the London School of Economics should be. You've read about him in the *New York Times*, saw his picture in *Time* magazine, gasped at his suicide in Leverett. We thrilled to his insanity, chortled at his insufferability, were dazzled and infinitely warmed by his loving genius, and were confused by where he dragged us.

On the morning of the twentieth, we all went to the big meeting. It was in a loft somewhere on the Northwest side, and everybody was there. Marshall had been ejected from his promised post as head of College Press Service, which serviced college papers, and had followed with the typically brilliant idea of establishing a service for the young but burgeoning underground press. So he gathered together all the editors who would come and/or would be in Washington anyway and would today declare, with their support, that the news service had been wrought.

Marshall liked some of my articles from when I was an editor of the *Michigan Daily*. When I passed through London early in that 1967 summer of love he asked me to work with him at College Press Service. Now he wanted me in the new LNS office. I told him I'd send him my articles and my fellowship money from The University of Chicago where I would study history, and we agreed this would be all right.

You can read all about the founding of Liberation News Service in *Famous Long Ago* by Ray Mungo. Marshall burned his draft card in his Sgt. Pepper jacket, Kenneth Anger sputtered something from the top of a ladder down at Shirley Clarke, who was taking

pictures. Oh, it was a fine time. On the wall was a funky picture of a woodlands scene (a Karmic glimpse of our future at Montague Farm, of course), which provided the backdrop for Marshall's flaming Selective Service card. Walter Bowart of *East Village Other* had on a really neat jacket made out of an American flag and there were a lot of new words flying around.

Basically what happened was the editors of the underground papers told Marshall that if he wanted to do Liberation News Service that would be fine with them and he should wire for money.

Most writers on the left felt that the Pentagon demonstration would call an end to non-violent protest, but this wasn't the case at all. The most popular variety of antiwar demonstration through the years 1967-1968 was the anti-draft celebration. This usually consisted of people turning in or burning their draft cards or refusing induction with a flourish. Ray refused in Boston with friends and followers joining him afterwards for a happy ceremonial breakfast.

Most of us who had been Kennedy liberals or worse were finding out in various ways that Vietnam was neither an accident nor LBJ's war. The war and racism made sense in the framework of the government's historic domination of smaller nations and minority groups—a framework assiduously couched in tons of textual and electronic bullshit, stuff we could no longer stomach once stoned.

My own radicalization was typically intellectual —it occurred to me that what the United States was doing in Latin America was remarkably similar to what it was doing in Vietnam. From then on the ball began to unravel. For others in school I think the draft or the black revolt were the events that struck closest to home and that started the change in analysis. When you exploit that many people it's bound to dawn on some of them that there's a pattern to it.

As for the sell-out of the 1964 election, it was just beginning to dawn on us that other elections had been sold out too. Professor Hans Morgenthau dropped on us one day that, had Nixon rather than John Kennedy been elected president in 1960, his choice for secretary of state would most likely have been the same man JFK had appointed—Dean Rusk.

The social sciences all began to get a radical working-over and departments in most of the universities began to divide and choose sides. Fanon and Che became culture heroes and SDS chapters started springing up everywhere. For a generation, graduation from college coincided with events that demanded we break almost totally from what we'd been taught there.

For there was something in the air. It was joy and hope. We were finally shaking the mindlessness of the fifties and the premature confusion of the early sixties. We were coming fully alive, for the first time. We were claiming our independence and we were young and strong.

There was new music and new art; we learned to slow our senses and see into the back and bottom of our perceptual and spiritual lives. There were colors and sounds and sensations and emotions all in and around us that had only registered before; now we were learning how to grasp and enjoy them.

We started making love without guilt or even looking back. They were our bodies, we could use them. We could sleep together and feel neither obligation nor embarrassment.

Behind it all was a group of people developing a feel for themselves as human entities with individual needs and quirks, but most importantly, a common bond of humanity. Not that the idea was new—just to us, as a generation of young people. The rhetoric has always been around but we were making it the reality of our lives. Our hair could grow and we could dress comfortably, smile and just not give a shit about booger cars and tv stars. It was freedom from the sleazy side of America.

We could taste it.

We wanted it.

The media that had dominated our lives became our stage. Jerry Rubin showed up at a House Un-American Activities Committee hearing in full Revolutionary War dress. Later he and Abbie Hoffman varied their costumes—Che Guevara guerrilla suits, bare chests, toy machine guns. Remember the pictures? In a stroke they destroyed an inquisition that had repressed liberal intellectuals for a decade.

Then they dropped money on the floor of the New York Stock Exchange, precipitating a riot among the moneychangers. People started turning up nude at highbrow parlays, dumbfounding even the most verbose.

We caught them completely by surprise. They were vulnerable and it was easy. One weekend in Ann Arbor I figured things were too dull at the *Daily* and decided a marijuana editorial might be nice. I wrote a demand for legalization and called it in to United Press International before it was even set in linotype. Six hours before the paper was printed the article was national news.

Bullseye in the game was Lyndon Johnson. He lied badly, took criticism like a child, and was a mass murderer to boot. I think he went really crazy. The more it got laid on him the clumsier and crazier he got. If you compare pictures of him in 1964 with ones from 1967 and 1968, I think you'll see he was really flipping out.

By the time he'd given a gold bust of himself to the Pope we figured we had him beat. And we did.

Fighting LBJ had an air of unreality about it that kept a lot of the struggle in a stage of suspended innocence. I visited Ann Arbor a lot and found it never better. There had been a film bust, big anti-draft actions, and some anti-university stuff, somehow all without serious violence.

Everybody was really high, like when you play on a team and find yourself winning without casualties.

There were rock festivals every week in the park, stoned football games, and Mark's coffeehouse. It was a looking-glass war.

I spent part of the winter in Berkeley. Writing and organizing flowed naturally with meeting and enjoying the people. Haight-Ashbury was showing definite symptoms of dying but the daily love picnic in Golden Gate Park was unaffected. You could walk into the big grass bowl next to strangers, and listen all day to the conga drums. Usually in the late afternoon freaks with saxophones, guitars, or clarinets would join in and jam for hours. The Airplane and the Dead were in town as a part of the community. When you got hungry you sat down next to the Hare Krishna freaks and waited for the announcement of the love feast only four blocks away.

The scene in Washington, at Liberation News Service, was more of the same. Ray and Marshall were now joined by Verandah Porche, Queen of the Bay State Poets for Peace. LNS and the underground press were growing like a magic mushroom. The news service was colorful, lively, obscene, and funny. Feature stories included demonstration scorecards, exposés of the insidious tentacles of foreign and domestic imperialism, caricatures of official buffoonery both local and national, denunciations of drug laws, true tales of military insubordination, and long tomes of righteous doctrine.

Also stuff like: "Kevin Simpton, editor of the *Fuckoff*, the underground paper in St. Rouet, Arkansas, was run out of town last week after being tarred and feathered by angry residents of this backwoods southern town." The story was the product of Ray and Marc Sommer's imagination; I hope the guy that wrote us for directions to St. Rouet (that does not exist) didn't try to go there.

We also had Allen Ginsberg writing about his encounter with the Maharishi, who was touring the country with the Beach Boys. And some true science facts, like the desert rainstorm of dried beef and the German carpenter who was killed by a six-foot icicle that fell from the sky.

While I typed rock-and-roll lyrics in the margins of the mailings, Marshall was holding the operation together with mirrors in a way that would put Jay Gould to shame. He got money from nowhere, sent it somewhere else, and two days later equipment would arrive. Magic!!

Meanwhile he took acid while Washington burned and tried to walk the streets in his Moroccan challaba carrying a little toy bird that dangled from a string. No cop in the world would arrest him.

Ray and Marty Jezer were busted for grass while driving cheerfully through the riot zone, checking out the scene. When they came up for trial the dope had been smoked and they were released for lack of evidence.

Pie-throwing became a popular political activity. Army recruiters and even colonels became unwilling recipients of whole custards.

Paul Krassner said Lyndon Johnson hunched John Kennedy in the neckwound and millions believed the story. Some were even offended.

Hair got longer and the sweet smell of marijuana began filling high school johns.

Demonstrations got bigger and more aggressive, especially in places like Oakland and Madison. The list of draft resisters swelled immensely.

Then the first stories of GI resistance within the army began to filter back. So did large quantities of Vietnamese grass.

Everywhere underground papers were springing up, some of them printing as many as four and five issues.

In the spring McCarthy began winning support to be the next Democratic presidential nominee. When Bobby Kennedy announced, it was clear either he or Cleangene would be the next president. What it meant was that our suspicions were right—either LBJ or the war or both were making the rest of the country completely nauseous.

Then Columbia. University buildings had been occupied before, but never for more than a few days and never so many. Not one, not two, not three, but five buildings overrun and held for a week. New Yorkers flocked back for a new Rosh Hashana.

Columbia sent a feeling of power into us that was only duplicated in moments that summer when it seemed the French students had succeeded in toppling the Fifth Republic. It was the spring and summer of the revolution's first wave. By the middle of 1968 we were fully aware of ourselves as a nascent class with boundless potential. We had confronted the world's largest military machine at its doorstep, black uprisings had ripped apart the empire's greatest cities, we had occupied the imperial academies, and we were ending at home a war that would mean the end of the empire.

On April Fool's Day LBJ quit. We had ripped into the nation's ruling party and split it. In the summer we threatened to bring revolution to Western Europe and to force reform in Czechoslovakia, inside the monolith where the dream of our parents had died.

It was power! Our hair, our very walking down the street constituted a threat to the national security. We'd been slated to be the new working class of the technological empire and we were telling it to Fuck Off. We were a worldwide fraternity of the young and the bright, our weapons our spontaneity and humor, our rewards the joys of new liberation, our stage the planet.

The next battle would take shape after another summer of black insurrection, in Chicago, where they slaughtered the pigs. There the past would demand payment.

...In Ann Arbor, I had worked for *Time* magazine as their campus stringer. In the fall of 1966 they sent out memos to all their campus stringers to do a general evaluation of what was going on with the student bodies in their towns.

I knew a long memo would be no problem but I wondered what they would actually print. It hit me walking out of the Undergraduate Library (UGLi), a druggy Madison Avenue bit: "Said a University of Michigan acid head, 'LSD is like Ban deodorant. Ban takes the worry out of being close. LSD takes the worry out of being.'"

Of course they printed it. You can find the sentence somewhere in the 1966 "Man of the Year" article.

When you work for *Time* you write them long memos in article form and style that they collect from their network of reporters. All the memos are then gathered in New York and someone (personally I think it's a machine) blends them and spews forth a *Timese* piece maybe one-one hundredth the length of all the verbiage they originally received. It was a big event at your bureau when something got quoted directly—it proved you existed.

By the spring of 1968, I was on the other side of the fence. When Liberation News Service covered the Rusk-Fulbright hearings I led off the article thusly: "Dean Rusk sang and danced for some ten hours these past two days. Among his favorite numbers were 'Halt Hanoi, Harry,' 'The Yellow Peril Polka,' and that old standby of the Johnson administration, 'Lies, Lies, Lies.'" You can find that one in an early 1968 issue of *Time* under a picture of Marshall Bloom and Ray Mungo with their names reversed in the caption. *Time* quoted it to show how shitty we were. Little did they know where the creep who wrote that had learned his stuff.

The *Time*-game isn't hard to learn. What you do is take the heart of an event/place/person and compose a catchy little phrase that captures part of the object's essence while at the same time making it slyly humorous and absurd. This allows you to destroy that object while leaving yourself both superior and witty.

The object of the game is to amuse the reader, giving him the illusion that he is being informed while meticulously protecting him from the reality of the situation.

Through 1967-1968 we engaged in media warfare, creating our own images and symbols and destroying others. The organs like *Time* and the networks did the same with opposing values.

It was a game we could play with little cost. But as the realities of the Chicago Convention and what lay beneath it began to make themselves felt, it became clear we would have to tie our lives to something stronger. If most of this nation yields its freedom to the media in exchange for an escape from the pains of daily life, the one thing we learned just before, during, and since that convention was that this is not life. Painful days were upon us and more were yet to come, but the last thing we could do was deny their existence.

As a result, these were the days that solidified our identity, not in telling us what we were, but in closing doors on what we could never be again.

It was spring now in Chicago, 1968. The city was tensing for the convention. I wrote an article for Liberation News Service: "There are many things Chicago may be, but one of them it is not now and never will be is a picnic...."

We were getting ready, growing more militant. We continued the SDS debating society with growing grimness in the face of a city girding for war. It was pretty frightening. You could feel the urge to kill in the air. Race war was already a daily part of life in Chicago; now something else was coming and nobody knew quite what but everybody knew it was going to be bad....

Marshall was thin and wiry, with electric hair and warm eyes. The last time I came to Washington I walked into the office about ten at night. He dropped the phone, leapt out—stark naked—from behind his desk, shook my hand, and then raced back to finish burning whoever it was on the other end. Hi, Marshall.

Ray was the writer. Short, dark-haired, and of Catholic descent from Lawrence, Massachusetts, he'd freaked out Boston University and most of the city of Boston besides as editor of the *B.U. News*, then went on to Harvard in Keats-Thoreau to partake of their fellowship trough until it got to be too much of a drag.

Ray and I met, of all places, at a student editor's conference, at one of those fat-cat Washington hotels. It was 1966 and Ray was put up on a panel with key Johnson and Kennedy advisors Walt Rostow, John Roche, and Richard Goodwin to discuss the war in Vietnam, which was just starting to get bad reviews.

Ray gave a brilliant inflammatory speech against LBJ and his bloody hoax, concluding with a demand for impeachment.

The student editors gasped with disbelief.

Roche and Rostow were known reactionaries even then, so it was up to the liberal to put Ray down. Goodwin, the Kennedy man, waltzed in: "Now you all know I have strong disagreements with the way the Johnson administration is pursuing the war in Vietnam. But I hardly think any sensible, serious American could endorse the substance or the tone of Mr. Mungo's speech. Let's see now. How many of you out there think the president should be impeached?"

Four of us raised our hands. Ray and I looked at each other and became friends.

Later that day I sputtered into a microphone at Rostow, whom I particularly despised for some various academic reason, about a peace feeler (remember these?) the United States had spurned. The *Washington Post* had exposed the affair the day before.

"You prick! You jerk! You motherfucking bastard! What about this stuff, huh, huh, well, what about it, huh, huh?" (Those were not my exact words.)

Rostow smiled in a fatherly way and explained that I didn't know all the facts, and that, indeed, I was lucky not to have to suffer, as he did, with the burdens of such decisions.

By the following summer (of 1968), events had long since sped by the college editors, as well as John Roche, Walt Rostow, and Richard Goodwin, and left them all deep deep in the dust. The Democratic convention loomed in the future and, with scores of campus confrontations to its credit, the movement was beginning to take definite shape. Many of its members were now no longer students and were dedicating their lives full-time to political organizations of one sort or another.

By June, Martin Luther King was dead. The Poor People's Campaign, which had begun in hope and good faith, died stillborn in fragile tents and huts by the reflecting pool where the Pentagon March had started. It rained and there was mud all over the place.

Marshall decided we should camp with the California people. There was free food and clothing, some camaraderie.

But the mud was everywhere and there was no leadership. Dr. King was dead. We all just wallowed. It was the end of coming to Washington to ask for help.

Shortly after that, at the beginning of the summer, we moved the news service to New York.

The heavies were waiting for us.

Allen Young was in charge of the takeover. Allen is of Communist Party parentage with an impressive journalistic background. Before LNS he'd written for the *New York Times*, the *Christian Science Monitor*, and the *Washington Post*.

Allen came to the Washington office from the *Post*, and his hard work, competence, solid backbone, and impeccable character led Marshall to invite him into the circle of directors.

But Marshall and Allen, though each devoted beyond question to the news service and the movement, embodied almost perfectly its opposite poles.

Marshall had that wild, curly hair out to here. From one minute to the next you could never guess where he was going or what he was thinking. He was completely capable of interspersing long, heartfelt compliments of your work with totally outrageous demands on your life without changing facial expression. He and Ray put music on the automatic telephone-answering tape, would fly anywhere on LNS' last cent ("dancing instructions from God"), printed copy on paper of only the wildest colors, and were generally, well, quite spaced.

Allen was down-to-earth, believed in carefully thought-out positions and political consistency. Marshall was an affront to Allen's sensibilities; Allen was an affront to Marshall's taste in art.

By spring the news service was in need of added manpower and money so Marshall decided to move to New York. There was already an office there. By the time the move was made the New York people outnumbered those from Washington. Ray was splitting to a farm in Vermont and Steve Marsden, Lazarus Quan, and I were the only people coming to the Apple who had been with Marshall from the start.

A few days after we arrived, Allen announced at a staff meeting that he thought Marshall should split. There was already a subtle struggle going on; George C. had controlled the money in New York and now the control of funds overall became a grey area, with little day-to-day conflicts popping up. By the time Allen brought it up, things had pretty much surfaced anyway.

We all sat around feeling each other out for the first time. By the time that meeting was over it was pretty clear the divisions in the office were serious. The idea of ousting Marshall was quickly dispelled—his personality so permeated the news service that the idea of his being expelled from it was almost a contradiction in terms.

But control? Sheila R., George, and Allen moved in the next meeting to turn control of the office over to a committee to be elected by the whole staff, and to turn editorial decisions over to a special editorial committee. Marshall was now on the spot, because the struggle appeared to be democracy versus elitism.

A long, hairy series of debates ensued. Almost immediately the two groups formed, each eating and living together, spending time working out the fine points of debate. They were the politicos (our name for them), we the insufficiently militants (theirs for us).

Debate, which carried on for about two weeks and often went on for as long as eight hours straight, ran through Cadres, Lenin, Marcuse, Cuba, North Vietnam, Algeria, democratic centrism, Russia, participatory democracy, Haiti, the Panthers, our parents, bourgeois democracy, Mr. LSD, LBJ, the sanitation department, John Stuart Mill, Bugs Bunny, and the people's struggle to off Porky Pig. The walls shook with college rhetoric.

The killer came one really muggy night, at a point when the crowded basement office was completely unbearable anyway. Ray came in and made a speech. "Now I've worked with Marshall a year, and there are times when it's been really rough. But that Bloom, you know, he's got magic. It comes from somewhere, and it's what LNS is, magic."

Booooom. They hit the ceiling. Sheila screamed that they had magic too, godammit.

By this time we'd lost anyway. I wish I could convey to you more than just the gist of the discussions, but of anything in my recent past I would say that the actual words that passed in the LNS meetings and in others like it are most easily and gratefully forgotten.

At the end of two weeks of discussion, they outvoted us. The same people voted in exactly the same manner as they would have when debate began.

The committee to run the office included only Marshall from our faction. The editorial committee had only Marshall and me out of seven people.

In the first editorial meeting Sheila proposed that all copy be subject to approval of the editorial committee. I objected. We had unlimited copy space and for me at least the one thing that had made the news service valuable was our freedom to print anything that happened to fall into our hands. We had a lot of misses, but then, who were we to judge?

When Sheila won that point I finally decided it was all over.

Marshall and Ray had decided earlier. The night of Ray's "magic" speech we—Marshall, Ray, and I—had a little meeting in the conference room and voted Allen off the board of directors. This didn't go a long way to winning us friends in the office, but it did throw the whole thing in doubt. The corporation was now clearly ours, the office theirs, and everything else was in suspension.

There were a number of good people caught in the middle who, while wanting a share of the power, would have been more than willing to allow us to continue in our modified roles. But as the days after the final meeting went on we all began to feel more and more uncomfortable and insecure. Clearly, the news service was no longer our home.

Meanwhile, Marshall had an outrageous idea that he would confide to you quietly, in a moment when he was sure his credibility was strongest. He wanted to take the news service out of the city, where all the news was, and into the countryside, where everybody knew nothing was happening. Usually he got told he was crazy.

But now there was a plan. The Beatles gave the news service their home movie, *Magical Mystery Tour*, to show at the Fillmore East, Bill Graham's psychedelic dungeon on the lower east side. Income from the benefit would go to about $15,000.

Stephen Diamond was in charge of it because he was thought to be a neutral in the faction fight.

But in fact he was of the virtuous caucus (us).

When $5,000 had been collected in advance ticket sales Steve and Marshall went up to New England and put a down payment on a farm in western Massachusetts. The place was near the Amherst-Northampton university center and about 30 miles south of Ray's farm in Vermont. It was also, according to Marshall, quite beautiful.

The morning of the Beatles movie our number swelled to twenty and we cleaned out the office —paper, machines, everything. It was Sunday morning August 11, 1968, and broad daylight, not even very early because we had to wait for the building manager to go to the beach. We piled everything into a Hertz rent-a-truck, I poured duco-cement into the lock on the front door, the truck drove off to the north.

That night some of us had the gall to stay in New York and go to the movie. If anybody from the other side had happened by the office that day we were bound to get the hell beat out of us.

But nobody knew. Everybody was all smiles. The movie was good. Freaky. But good.

Next morning the New York people found their empty office. An expedition went up to the farm and held everybody hostage and hit Marshall a few times. But the farm and the printing equipment remained ours and within a few weeks they had new stuff and had got their own service going.

It was big news. The straight media loved it. The left was stunned.

I met with a few of the people from the New York faction. They were completely pissed. Allen was appalled. In the West End Bar he told me that he had grown up on a farm.

Later, in the fall of 1970, Allen left the news service, moved to a farm near us in western Massachusetts, and became an outspoken and very effective leader in the gay liberation movement. When the farm became a center of the anti-nuclear movement, Allen worked with us.

Life is full of surprises!

...At the end of August 1968, we all went to the Chicago convention like moths to a flame.

Immediately we got caught up in the LNS thing. Everybody on the left was upset about the split. LNS had been a valuable organ to the movement and the vibrations that came out of the heist and its aftermath were bad, especially at a time like this.

Abe Peck of the *Chicago Seed* set up a meeting for us in some psychedelic theater north of the loop. Everybody looked at everybody else and the glances varied from hatred to dismay to embarrassment to puzzlement, depending on who was looking at whom. The walls were shiny aluminum for a light show; the meeting was held on a stage.

It took about two exchanges to ascertain for good that it was all over. Marshall said the New York people could send their copy to the farm and the New York people said Marshall could send the farm copy to New York. Oh man, why bother?

The symbols began flying again. Country/city, freak/militant, you did this/you did that, honorable/thief, bourgeois/revolutionary. What a drag.

Some of it really hurt. We had all shared some really good and some really hard times. We had been brothers and sisters in as true a sense as you can find.

Now we were at each other's throats, demanding to know whose fault it was.

I suppose the burden lay definitely on us for taking first action and ripping off the stuff, but I don't think a quiet squeeze job is any more legitimate. As for the outcome, that, it seemed to me, made sense. It was clear that continuing as we had in New York was a lie, that our styles of life had spread as far apart as our styles of journalism, and that attempting to stay together might well have meant death for both.

As it was, they kept the New York office and the news service and we got a farm. Events and the growing demands of a maturing movement were the political realities; we just happened to be the people involved. We had acted; now the wave was beyond us.

At least it was finally over. It didn't take long to stop worrying about it, either, or even to find greater ugliness. When we walked out of the theater and into the Chicago streets, we found ourselves all right back together in the same bag. There were troops and cops everywhere. They were after *US* and they didn't care who ripped off what from whom or why.

* * *

In the winter following the Chicago Convention, the Montague LNS ceased publication. The cold New

England winds pouring through our beautiful but uninsulated farmhouse and garage were a reality on which we urban and suburban refugees could not have counted.

I stayed in New York that year to teach elementary school, and, ostensibly, to set up our own New York bureau. Up north, my brothers and sisters in arms were burning furniture to stay warm. A great future lay in store there for us in organic farming, fighting nuclear power, and more.

LNS New York also carried on. Over the years its dogmatism softened and it resumed a highly productive role as a source of information and inspiration on the humanist left.

In the late seventies, as short of money and energy as we had been when we first moved to New York, LNS made a graceful exit, having served a remarkable set of purposes through a remarkable era.

But something had happened back during the split that all of us suspected but none of us could really confirm. To this day we don't know the full story.

But thanks to the efforts of a handful of dedicated researchers such as Chip Berlet and Angus MacKenzie, we discovered that the FBI had deeply penetrated our news service, and may well have been at the root of the split.

Berlet published a number of pieces in the late seventies documenting the role played by the FBI's COINTELPRO operation in subverting a wide range of movement organizations and publications.

In 1981 MacKenzie wrote in the *Columbia Journalism Review* that documents obtained under the Freedom of Information Act showed that "by 1968, the FBI had assigned three informants to penetrate the news service, while nine other informants regularly reported on it from the outside."

Their reports were allegedly forwarded to the Secret Service, IRS, CIA, Air Force, Navy, and the Army's Counterintelligence branch.

But that wasn't all. Monitoring for information is one thing. But the FBI also "attempted to discredit and break up the news service through various counterintelligence activities, such as trying to make LNS appear to be an FBI front, to create friction among staff members, and to burn down the LNS office in Washington while the staff slept upstairs."

MacKenzie and Berlet both published articles based on FBI documents indicating that agents within the news service had done their best to bust it up. During the fight some of Marshall's "critics" charged him with being a homosexual. The term "gay" was not yet in use. Some on the left of 1968 apparently considered it some kind of a crime.

Certainly the FBI did. Undoubtedly their agents inside the office led the assault. Later, Allen was forced out partly on the basis of the same "charges."

When LNS split, J. Edgar jumped in to take full advantage. A memorandum to him from his New York office dated 10-7-68 included a vicious article "written in the jargon of the New Left, necessitating the use of a certain amount of profanity."

The outwardly prudish Hoover didn't like dirty words. But copies of this article—titled "And Who Got the Cookie Jar?"—were "sent to various 'peace groups,' New Left organizations and individuals in the New York area anonymously." The piece was "designed to take advantage of the recent split in the Liberation News Service."

That it did. I remember it clearly. It was published all over the country, and it dug into Marshall like a dagger. [An exact reproduction of the article, obtained through the Freedom of Information Act, appears in figure 1.]

The article was such a perfect mirror of the type of writing being done at the time it never occurred to me that it might be the product of the FBI.

But it almost certainly helped kill Marshall Bloom. On November 1, 1969, after nearly fifteen months at the farm, Marshall drove to nearby Leverett early that cloudy morning, hooked a pipe to the exhaust, and left us his body. It rained for the next ten days.

Many theories have emerged about why Marshall died (see sidebar 1). Some have blamed "other hands." Until reading this FBI material, I doubted them.

But it is now very clear that the federal government actively attempted to destroy our organization. If the FBI actually pushed us over the brink, then the agents involved should kick themselves, because the split itself actually proved to be a wonderfully progressive event. It gave birth to what became a stronger, more consistent New York-based LNS and to a communal farm that proved a vital center in the movement to stop nuclear power.

But I also remember quite clearly that Marshall was deeply wounded by that "Cookie Jar" article. What else was done to him over the months at the farm by FBI and other government agents remains to be discovered. Any regime crazed enough to try setting fire to our office while people were sleeping in it, and slick enough to penetrate our organization's endless debates without being found out, was clearly capable of subverting the psyche of a man as sensitive and vulnerable as Marshall Bloom.

I still haven't seen Marshall's FBI file, or been granted access to my own. But can there be any doubt these people were capable of killing him?

Indeed, did not these same people destroy the democratically elected government of Chile in 1973?

Sidebar 1: "Marshall Bloom: Gay Brother"[1]

by Allen Young

It's more or less an unwritten rule among gay people, "liberationist" or not, that you don't talk about someone's being gay in a public way unless we know for sure that the person wouldn't mind.

Marshall Bloom was still in his closet when he committed suicide on November 1, 1969, yet I am confident that his spirit is with me as I write this.

Marshall Bloom was a faggot, and his faggotry was part of his life, as it was part of his death. This wouldn't be an article in *Fag Rag*—many faggots live and die as Marshall did—except for one fact: Marshall has become a minor folk hero and symbol of "the movement," and yet everyone who writes about him ignores the fact that he was a faggot. It is a farce that pains me each time I become aware of it.

Very recently, Marshall was the subject of a series of articles on the Op-Ed page of the *New York Times*. David Eisenhower, who met Marshall briefly at Amherst College, wrote an essay, published in the *Times* April 30, pointing to Marshall's death as a symbol of the emptiness and evil of the movement. Two of Marshall's friends wrote responses to the Eisenhower piece disagreeing eloquently and putting down Nixon's son-in-law.

At Amherst College—Bloom's alma mater, Class of '66—he is something of a legend. At the college library there is a fine collection of underground newspapers officially known as the Marshall Bloom Memorial Collection.

Who, in God's name, you may be asking, was Marshall Bloom?

I suppose Marshall is best known as the founder and, for a time, prime mover of Liberation News Service (LNS). Some may remember him as one of the leaders of a student uprising at the London School of Economics. At Amherst College, he had been editor of the *Student*, bringing a radical viewpoint to its page well before student rebellion was a national phenomenon. Marshall was a featured character in Ray Mungo's popular autobiographical book, *Famous Long Ago: My Life and Hard Times with Liberation News Service*. He is mentioned prominently in other books by Mungo, as well as in *What the Trees Said*, by Steve Diamond.

In mid-1968, LNS, then still in its first year of publishing, broke into two feuding camps. The Bloom-Mungo-Diamond camp bought a farm in Montague, Mass., with money secretly funneled off from a benefit film showing. They shocked the opposing faction by literally heisting everything from the New York office to their farm. For awhile, there were two competing LNSes: one on the farm, the other in New York City. The New York LNS carries on to this day, but by February of 1969, the farm LNS folded and became just a farm (which it still is).

The following fall, sometime after All Hallow's Eve (the traditional gay holiday), on All Soul's Day, Marshall Bloom ran a vacuum cleaner hose from the exhaust pipe through a window of his little green Triumph. When his friends found him, he was dead.

I heard about his death in Chicago. I was covering the Conspiracy Trial for LNS, and it was in Judge Hoffman's neon oven courtroom that Abbie Hoffman and Jerry Rubin, wearing black armbands in Marshall's honor, told me about it.

Although Marshall was indeed a Yippie, I find it rather incredible, if not stupid, that some of Marshall's friends, particularly Ray Mungo, treat his suicide as though it were some kind of ultimate yippie stunt. They make Marshall a mysterious magical figure, a shaman, which is not all that surprising as this is a traditional role for homosexuals in many cultures.

I knew Marshall Bloom not as a shaman but as a human being. I worked with him at LNS for nearly a year. But we were not friends. For a good part of that time, in fact, we disliked each other, though I'm not quite sure why. Partly it was because at the time he was more into being an anarchist, and I was more into being a communist. We had very different ideas about society, collectivism, and the individual, though I'm sure we would agree about much more today. We were on opposing sides of that awful split in 1968, and we never spoke to each other after that.

Did I recognize that Marshall was gay? Not on any conscious level. I was a desperately frightened and lonely closet case myself in those days. I couldn't deal with missing my gay life and my straight life; they were never allowed to mix (a situation enforced by the straight environment of "the movement"). Consequently, I just assumed that Marshall was straight.

The truth is that Marshall had GAY written all over him, especially when he talked and moved. Once I heard someone make a nasty comment about Marshall being a faggot, and I voiced my objection by replying something like, "Just because someone is effeminate doesn't mean he's homosexual." I helped to kill Marshall Bloom by hiding in my closet, and by saying things like that. I'm not going to hate myself for it—I was a victim of my own justifiable fears—but I think it's high time for Marshall's straight friends and bisexual friends (like Ray Mungo) to admit that they, too, in their straightness and in their closetry, helped take Marshall to his death.

It is not enough to say that Marshall was a lonely, unfulfilled person. Marshall was a lonely, unfulfilled *faggot*. In fact, he killed himself shortly after a last-ditch unsuccessful attempt to make a go of it romantically and sexually with a woman friend. For years, he had carefully surrounded himself with attractive young men, yet he could not (as far as I know) bring himself to tell them how much he loved them and how much he wanted to kiss them and lie with them.

When Steve, one of these young men, was killed in an automobile crash, Marshall expressed his sadness and love in an LNS article. Maybe you can perceive the gay love as I do hidden inside this paragraph from that "obituary": "For his seventeenth birthday, we got him a light meter; and a week later his camera was stolen from where he had (too casually?) left it in the office. By now he needed, beyond a family, a lover, or two, and he changed our house into his lair with other rooms appendaged. He touched secret truths with a bewitching poetess, and she opened her most delicate self to their shared trust. And then he violated everything temporarily for another. Never would she forgive him—how could she?—but her parting goodbye to Washington was to tear the only photo of him from my wall and put it in her purse."

Suicide is a complex thing, and I am not saying that Marshall took his life "just" because he was gay. But I am convinced it is an important part of the story. I believe this because I shared Marshall's life for nearly a year and because I have talked about this very topic with several of his closest friends.

Is it in "poor taste" to bring this all up? I suppose some people will think so. It interferes with some people's notions of myth and magic. But remember, it's in "poor taste" to commit suicide; like homosexuality it's an act condemned by church and State. The poor taste in this matter, as far as I am concerned, is that of the "movement people" and the "friends" of Marshall Bloom who wish to romanticize his life and death while they hide the very unromantic but crucial fact of his faggotry.

This same faggotry was crucial, I want to add for the record, to the very beginnings of Liberation News Service. Marshall founded LNS in the summer of 1967 after he was kicked out of his position as Director of the College Press Service. In writing about Marshall's ouster from that position with the establishment colle-

giate press agency, Mungo and others point to Marshall's radical politics and his pot-head acid-freak lifestyle. Yet I know from talking with people intimately connected with the incident that Marshall's faggoty manner was a major factor in some people's negative attitudes towards him and in the eventual decision to fire him.

To tell the history of LNS while deleting this fact is akin to telling the history of America while deleting the struggles of women, blacks, and workers.

Marshall Bloom died only four months after the Stonewall uprising, and two months before I got up the nerve to attend my first Gay Liberation Front meeting. Perhaps Marshall and I would never have become friends, but I like to think that the reality of gay brotherhood (with all its shortcomings), which I feel has saved my life, would have saved Marshall's life too.

NOTE

1. From *Fag Rag* no. 5 (Summer 1973): 6-7. Reprinted with permission from Allen Young.

Young lives in Royalston, Massachusetts, where he is active in community life and environmental politics. He is chairman of his town's zoning board of appeals and is a member of the board of directors of the Mt. Grace Land Conservation Trust. After 10 years as a reporter and assistant editor for the *Athol* (MA) *Daily News*, he took a new job in 1989 as director of public relations for the Athol Memorial Hospital. The pioneering anthology he co-edited with Karla Jay, *Out of the Closets: Voices of Gay Liberation*, will be issued in a special 20th anniversary edition, with a new introduction by the editors, in 1992 by New York University Press. He is the author of *Gay Sunshine Interview with Allen Ginsberg* and *Gays under the Cuban Revolution*, coauthor (with Jay) of *The Gay Report*, and has also written, edited, and/or published more than a dozen books of regional interest in New England.

Did they not put Pol Pot on the throne in Cambodia, undermine countless elections overseas in the name of democracy, while destroying scores of peace and equal rights organizations here at home?

And didn't we learn that these so-called protectors of the domestic peace covertly committed innumerable acts of violence to push otherwise peaceful organizations and demonstrations into bloody conflict right here at home?

One can calmly say that this all "comes with the territory." But in whose territory is it that taxpayers' money goes to subvert non-violent organizations committed to social justice and peace, or merely to

publishing information and opinions that may not conform to the current official line?

Two decades later we are asked to believe that the Contras, who were funded to overthrow a democratically elected government in Nicaragua, were not also dealing large quantities of cocaine, an assertion for which there is more than ample evidence.

There is also substantial proof that in 1980 the Reagan-Bush campaign persuaded the Ayatollah Khomeini to KEEP 55 hostages in Tehran until after our November elections, thus assuring a Republican victory over the hapless Jimmy Carter. We are asked to discount Barbara Honneggar's book, *October*

"........And Who Got The Cookie Jar?"

We see by the papers - New Left Notes, Guardian - that the Liberation News Service has been screwed into the ground while the peace movement has just been screwed. A real kindergarten performance by all concerned. See the cats run from the LNS office with the typewriters. See the girls dash away with the office supplies. See ███████████ carrying the check for £6,000 skins. See SDS people weeping and grinding their teeth. (Scene change)

See the farm at Montague, Massachusetts. See the hip confrontation. What language! Now, all the men are fighting. Now the pigs are near. Will the State of Massachusetts charge ████ with kidnaping? Will he be executed in public? Will LNS survive? Baby, at this point we wonder.....

New Left Notes described ███████ - one of the founders of LNS and onetime member of SDS - as suffering from megalomania. Could be. ██████████ has always been a bit of a nut. Nice guy, understand, but just a little uptight where LNS was concerned. He has screamed charges of SDS take-over and conspiracy. He's named ██████████ a traitor. With it all, he's managed to turn LNS from an efficient movement news service into a complete mess. The establishment of a bastard LNS at "Fortress Montague" is the most unrealistic bag of all. ██████████ you've left the scene of the action in exchange for assorted ducks and sheep.

██████████ has used the old bat "doctrinaire propaganda" to describe the monthly contribution of SDS to the LNS subscriber packets. It just ain't true, ██████████ and you know it. SDS contributed meaningful ideas, yes. Maybe just a squib of intelligence. A little color. Some meat. How many of the 400-odd subscribers complained? One? Two? The office staff saw the response to the monthly mailing. Most was favorable, some not so hot. But not one letter was received by the New York office accusing LNS of engaging in SDS propaganda. Actually, after Chicago, what's wrong with a little SDS spiel?

"We saved LNS from withering away", says ██████. Not so. To say he killed it dead. Sort of a literary euthanasia. The New York staff is trying to keep one limb alive at ██████████████ under the medical care of ████████████. Will it live? Frankly, we don't know.

It's a bad scene when a good movement organization engages in civil war. Some of the details might be termed funny (We like the kidnaping bit), but dirty wash in public can only hurt. The situation was stupid, stupid, stupid.

What now? ██████ got the bread. Others got the office junk. ██████ got the finger. A fink ran off with the water cooler. And we got the cookie jar. LNS seems dead. Long live, LNS.

                            - A former Staffer

Figure 1: Reprint of "And Who Got the Cookie Jar?"—obtained from
Liberation News Service's FBI file through Freedom of Information Act

Surprise, the first book to raise this claim, and believe instead that our government could never do such a thing.

But how does that differ morally or spiritually from what was done at LNS, or from the cynical document shredding by Oliver North, who was virtually canonized for his contempt for democracy?

We also have to remember that serious questions remain about the murder of John F. Kennedy, the single most important political event of our generation.

Unanswered questions also linger about the Gulf of Tonkin incident, the full context of the Watergate break-in, and a litany of dubious occurrences during the Reagan years that will take decades to unravel.

Now that a former CIA chief is president of the United States, we might also ask about the Dukakis campaign he defeated. Were the Democrats really that inept? Or did some youthful LNS infiltrators merely graduate to the McGovern, Carter, Mondale, and Dukakis organizations, there, again under the guise of sincere reformers, to wreak the same kind of CO-INTELPRO havoc?

Think not?

Just remember LNS.

Remember also: flashes as brilliant as those that shaped us in the age of the underground press never really disappear. They burn in all of us, ebbing and flowing on the outside as the times warrant, but remaining an unquenchable core of joy and hope.

In his zeal to destroy us, J. Edgar actually helped fan and spread those flames. I suspect George Bush will ultimately do the same.

Spirits as potent and fertile as LNS's inevitably bloom with the return of spring.

REFERENCES

The most complete collections of LNS papers and related materials reside at the Marshall Bloom Memorial Collection at Amherst College, Amherst, Massachusetts, and at the Contemporary Culture Collection in Paley Library at Temple University, Philadelphia, Pennsylvania.

Berlet, Chip. "Boston Media and the FBI." *The Real Paper* (4 November 1978).

Berlet, Chip. "COINTELPRO: The FBI's Zany and Disruptive War on the Alternative Press." *Alternative Media* (Fall 1978): 10-13, 26.

Berlet, Chip. "Journalists and G-Men." *Chicago Reader* (2 June 1978).

Glick, Brian. *The War at Home*. Boston: South End Press, 1989.

Lerner, Steve. "The Liberation of the Liberation News Service." *The Village Voice* (22 August 1968).

MacKenzie, Angus. *Sabotaging the Dissident Press*. San Francisco: Center for Investigative Reporting, 1983.

Muckraking Gadflies Buzz Reality

Chip Berlet

One by one we left home.
We went so far out there.
Everybody got scared....

Something about the danger zone
Wouldn't leave the bunch of us alone.

> Terre Roche, from "Runs in the Family"
> © 1979 DeShufflin Inc.—ASCAP,
> on Warner Bros. album, "The Roches,"
> all rights reserved, used by permission.

Berlet is an analyst for Political Research Associates, a Cambridge, Massachusetts institute that monitors authoritarian and right-wing political movements. He freelances articles to a wide range of publications, from mainstream dailies to alternative monthlies.

Portions of this article are adapted from material that previously appeared in *Alternative Media*, *National Reporter*, and *Library Quarterly*. Appendix 2 is adapted from two pieces that, when they first appeared in *Alternative Media* and *Public Eye*, were the first major documented studies of FBI harassment of the alternative press.

How does an Eagle Scout and church youth group leader end up hawking underground newspapers with nudes and natural food recipes? In the 1960s the transition seemed, well, organic. In fall 1967 I was a senior in high school. I still recall clearly the night I decided that the underground press was the most exciting occupation in the world—and for many of us then it really was. There was an exhilarating sense of immediacy and danger that seems almost naive today, and hard to comprehend for people who did not share the experience.

In 1967 the debate over political versus cultural coverage was already causing staff splits on U.S. underground newspapers, and in Washington, DC, Ray Mungo and Marshall Bloom were moving down Church Street to set up Liberation News Service (LNS) after being fired from College Press Service for being too radical. I learned about LNS and the mysterious world of the underground press as one of several token youth delegates to the 1967 National Council of Churches

(NCC) Conference on Church and Society in riot-torn Detroit.

A group of seedy-looking underground writers and activists had stopped at the meeting on their return to San Francisco from the exorcism of the Pentagon outside Washington, DC. They talked about a tumultuous meeting where LNS and the Underground Press Syndicate had vied for the loyalty and support of the assembled underground newspapers (see appendix 1). They handed out colorful street sheets with arcane messages such as: "We are trapped in disappearance—sighing, screaming with it. Buying and selling pieces of phantom—worshipping each other," and "The government of America will rise and fall in episodes of political struggles. And Hollywood whose movies stick in the throat of God will rot on windmills of eternity." This message was handed out by the Diggers, who patiently explained to everyone their anarchistic ideas about a moneyless society based on love and selflessness, a message not totally alien to the religious set.

The counterculture crowd hung out with the more unusual ministers and nuns at the conference, and had a peculiar habit of passing their cigarettes back and forth during meetings. Everyone thought it was exemplary how they shared possessions. Reverend Harvey Cox of the Harvard Divinity School produced a lush and powerful multi-media extravaganza documenting social problems, Sister Corita built a collage wall of decorated boxes, Margaret Mead strolled purposefully through crowds with her walking stick; it was, pardon the expression, a mind-expanding experience.

The clique that formed around the underground writers included those conference delegates who challenged policies and forced heated debate on issues at every meeting. They were articulate and outrageous at the same time. No topic was too sacred to be profaned. I was fascinated. One night a huge black man stepped on the elevator as my friends and I headed for bed. He smoked a large gnarled pipe and wore a Cheshire Cat grin. As a fledgling pipe smoker myself, I asked innocently what blend of tobacco he smoked. "It's a special blend," he said slowly after inspecting me for several seconds. Then, between puffs, he added, "If you would like to try some, follow me. Some of us are having a little party." Thus began my descent into demon drugs, sinful sex, raucous rock and roll, cataclysmic communism, and the general subversion of authority that was to lead me to the underground press.

At the party I got stoned for the first time and was whisked away on a tour of Detroit's underground newspaper, the *Fifth Estate*. We were met at the door to the paper by a gun-toting editor who suspected another police raid, but instead found several old friends from the San Francisco underground scene accompanied by some very straight-looking and awe-struck teenagers.

Upon returning to high school, it was clear that we had tasted the forbidden fruit. The counterculture was already spreading its poison. The progeny of suburban New Jersey, we betrayed our parents' dreams and began to drive into Greenwich Village and march in civil rights demonstrations. Three of us who had attended the NCC conference even started a church basement coffee house—The Purple Kumquat. Curt Koehler was master of ceremonies, Sue Kaiser kept the coffee flowing, and we roped in half-a-dozen friends to help. We shared entertainers with another local church coffee house. I went and recited poetry and in return the sister act of Maggie and Terre Roche visited to sing folk music.

INK IN THE VEINS

Even though I was clearly on the road to ruin, I somehow rationalized the idea that an underground journalist first needed to get a good college education. Arriving on campus at the University of Denver in the fall of 1968, I soon gravitated to the school newspaper, *The Denver Clarion*, where I began by submitting photographs. My first editors, Carol Carpenter and Bill Zalud, soon coaxed me into writing articles, and spent long hours patiently (and sometimes exasperatedly) teaching the craft and ethics of print journalism.

Some of the copy we published at the *Clarion* came from College Press Service, a Washington, DC-based news outlet that mailed out twice-weekly packets. College Press Service had a now-defunct parent group, the United States Student Press Association (USSPA), which held summer and winter conferences. The conferences were a breeding ground for advocacy journalism where college reporters met mentors ranging from liberal mainstream journalists to radical underground writers. The August 1970 USSPA conference in Manchester, New Hampshire, not only spawned a flock of underground journalists, but an alternative newspaper, *Manchester*, published as part of a five-week summer seminar on college journalism. After rabid attacks on the paper, USSPA, and liberalism in general by the infamous right-wing daily *Manchester Union Leader*, several project members stayed on and continued publication for over a year.

Returning from the USSPA conference, a group of us under the leadership of college journalist Diane Wolfe formed the Colorado Media Alliance (CMA), a coalition of college and underground newspapers. CMA immediately became embroiled in a controversy with Southern Colorado State College in Pueblo where the SCSC *Arrow* had been censored when an article by Managing Editor Dorothy Trujillo was cut and Trujillo was suspended for protesting. Diane and I, representing CMA, drove to Pueblo and lent moral support to Trujillo at a student senate meeting. We then helped arrange for her to be represented by the ACLU of Colorado. Eventually the case reached federal court where in a precedent-setting case Judge Alfred Arraj ruled Trujillo's rights had been violated.

In the spring of 1970, I was named editor of the *Clarion* just in time for the murders at Kent State and Jackson State to spawn a vociferous student strike where the center of the campus was seized and turned into an encampment dubbed "Woodstock West." We transformed the *Clarion* into a forum for the debate that tore the campus into opposing factions, and even barricaded the press room to ensure we could complete production the night the National Guard arrived to take over the campus. The *Clarion* gained a reputation as an ardent advocate for peace and social justice, with devastating cartoons by Ed Stein.

In February of 1971 USSPA/CPS held its winter conference in Hollywood, California. One of the workshops was led by Michael Aldrich, professor of psychedelics at the California Institute of the Arts. Aldrich told the assembled editors about research he and Poet Allen Ginsberg had conducted showing links between the CIA, the Saigon regime, and the opium smuggling of Meo tribespeople in Laos. Ginsberg had stumbled across the patterned outline of the story while sorting his massive newspaper clipping file. He noticed that, when arranged chronologically, clippings reporting that American and South Vietnamese forces controlled the Golden Triangle opium-growing area in Southeast Asia were followed a few months later by a significant increase in clippings detailing a rise in heroin overdose deaths in American cities.

After attending Aldrich's session, I joined several other college and underground editors and put together enough money to purchase one-time reprint rights for Aldrich's manuscript, a much-corrected single-spaced document bearing the letterhead, "Marijuana Review." We agreed to print an edited version in early March and my college newspaper, *The Denver Clarion*, became the first U.S. publication to run a documented story about the CIA-heroin connection. We thought that was pretty nifty.

At the Hollywood conference, I was recruited to write for College Press Service. One night I sat down with Aldrich, Carl Nelson, and Barry Holtzclaw of CPS and former CPS writer Frank Browning who at the time was an editor at *Ramparts* magazine. (Browning now reports for "All Things Considered" on National Public Radio.) Talk turned to the Aldrich story and the CPS editors were hot to run it if some information holes could be filled. Browning suggested that *Ramparts* research the story and that CPS wait and release the text of the *Ramparts* article timed to coincide with the magazine hitting the newsstands. An agreement was struck and Browning enlisted Banning Garret of the Pacific Studies Center to co-author the piece.

The May 1971 issue of *Ramparts* featured the story on its cover with the headline "Marshal Ky: The Biggest Pusher in the World." CPS mailed out the text one week before the magazine was released and told its subscribers, "News of the story has already stirred considerable interest among Capitol Hill doves, and both Sen. George McGovern and Rep. Ronald Dellums say they will announce it in press conferences at the end of this week and press for hearings on the issues raised in their respective houses of Congress. In light of President Nixon's claims for a new world-wide effort to fight the international drug trade, the revelations in this story easily point out U.S. hypocrisy."

Just before publication, CPS editor Carl Nelson took a copy of the story to his father, a ranking CIA official, to get his reaction. Carl told us his father seemed genuinely astounded by the story, and at first simply didn't believe a word of it. Other sources told us that only a handful of people at CIA headquarters knew the extent of the drug deal, although in Southeast Asia it was a poorly kept secret.

The CIA/heroin story was a well-documented blockbuster, but the mainstream press virtually ignored it at first. There were a few column inches about congressional hearings being called for, and then the story vanished. A few months later, Senator Albert Gruening of Alaska opened hearings. Suddenly the story was "discovered" by the *Washington Post* and "NBC News." After a burst of coverage, however, the story received continued coverage only through alternative sources.

For instance, Professor Peter Dale Scott, who was credited with providing material on Laos and the China Lobby for the *Ramparts* article, authored his own piece in *Earth* magazine in early 1972. The alternative Dispatch News Service International, which broke the story of the My Lai massacre, ran follow-up articles on the CIA/heroin connection by T.D. Allman and D. Gareth Porter, who also wrote for CPS from Vietnam. Another Dispatch freelancer, John Everingham, served as a photographer and guide to author Alfred W. McCoy while he researched his book, *The Politics of Heroin in Southeast Asia*, published in 1973.

The McCoy book showed the connection between anti-Communist foreign policy objectives, U.S. intelligence intrigues, and the flow of heroin into the ruptured veins of addicted Americans. Despite its 70 pages of footnotes, other documentation, photographs, and first-hand accounts, the McCoy book was soon out of

Sidebar: Sex, Drugs, Rock & Roll, Revolution, and Readership

by Chip Berlet

Reminiscences by underground and alternative journalists are sometimes shaped by self-censorship resulting from increased age, higher socio-economic status, peer pressure, the arrival of children and parenting responsibilities, and continued societal disapproval of drugs, sex, rock & roll, and revolutionary ideas.

"How can we write or even talk about our use of drugs or knowledge of the drug trade when we're trying to keep our teenage kids from hurting themselves by using the kinds of really dangerous drugs that are popular today?" asked one underground press compatriot now working in the computer industry. "I don't even smoke pot anymore because of the kind of negative example it would be for the kids," he said, admitting he was somewhat incredulous at his own changed values.

One of the few books to honestly and accurately capture the capricious lifestyle of the underground press was written by Abe Peck whose journalistic career included stints on the early underground *Chicago Seed* and who now is a professor at Northwestern University in Illinois. His *Uncovering the Sixties: The Life and Times of the Underground Press* has recently been reprinted by Citadel Underground Press.

Peck's technique of interviewing dozens of underground and alternative writers and editors and incorporating their coaxed comments in his narrative provides many valuable insights into the culture and politics of underground reporting.

Until Peck's interview, I had never discussed my role in an obviously illegal antiwar project with a group of other Denver alternative press regulars. In the early 1970s, we pooled our graphic arts and printing skills to design, print, and assemble complete sets of phony ID-birth certificate, drivers' license, bills, mail, clippings, letters, business cards—used exclusively (and successfully) to assist military deserters in crossing the border into Canada.

My favorite personal story, however, is more mundane. In the mid-1970s, the staid Conservation Foundation (CF) hired a Washington, DC printing consultant with his roots in the alternative college press to crash produce a book to salvage an impending default on a grant-imposed deadline. He hired me as production coordinator and I hired my friends in the DC area alternative press—College Press Service, *off our backs*, Source Publishing Collective—along with staffers from other alternative and political publications, thus creating a wild and wacky crew. The deal was that the consultant would be the exclusive interface with the CF staff, who were forbidden from even setting foot in the studio, a converted garage in the alley behind CF.

One day the Conservation Foundation representative broke the agreement and visited. The stereo system was blaring rock music, the flaming kerosene furnace was leaking fumes and smoke, a lesbian couple was just kissing goodbye as one left to shop for dinner, one typesetter was smoking a joint, on the light table we were working on a flyer announcing a demonstration in support of the striking *Washington Post* pressmen's union, the illegal Chilean refugee raced out the back door yelling in Spanish that it was an Immigration raid, and a six-foot-high poster of Lenin looked sternly down from the wall. The CF representative fled in horror and once back in the office threatened to cancel the deal. But we knew the deadline was near and our production team was the only hope of meeting the contract. We threatened to strike if another CF staffer set foot in the office. A truce was arranged. The result was the classy-looking "Sanibel Island Report." The nervous Conservation Foundation proofreaders did find and excise the lobster waving an NLF flag, but look for the dancing starfish!

In an effort to assemble other colorful stories, and with the promise of utter anonymity to those who regaled me with these tales, here are some other incidents from the cultural side of the underground press. I, of course, refuse to identify those stories in which I may have had any personal knowledge or involvement....

What underground journalist didn't engage in manic sweeping and vacuuming in an attempt to remove every last marijuana seed from tiny cracks and crevices in his or her car, home, or underground newspaper office the night before publishing an article calculated to drive government officials to the brink of madness? While not every underground journalist smoked dope, and many papers instituted "no drugs in the office" rules, the cultural milieu of the late sixties and early seventies was such that soft drugs were otherwise ubiquitous.

print, and the CIA was off trading guns for heroin in another part of the globe. The CIA/heroin story did, however, add one more straw to the heap of revelations that eventually broke the back of public support for the U.S. role in southeast Asia.

BIG BROTHER IN A COP'S UNIFORM

Another underground press scoop also came in 1971 when *WIN Magazine*, College Press Service, Liberation News Service, and several other alternative

One underground editor used to treat his paste-up production staff to lines of cocaine to boost morale and productivity.

Another underground editor borrowed from classical legend and decided that all important decisions should be made twice, first while straight, and then reconfirmed with chemical assistance. If the decision was the same both ways, he figured, it had to be right.

A common example of early underground press humor was running ads announcing that subscriptions would be "personally delivered to your door by a uniformed agent of the federal government." This prospect horrified the average underground newspaper readers until they realized the agent was a postal carrier.

Several early underground newspapers ran little boxed notices with a small circle advising "Lick this spot, you may be one of the lucky 25." Some say it was always a gag, others insisted that liquid LSD had carefully been eyedroppered onto 25 copies of the paper in that exact spot.

One writer remembers wistfully that a local dope dealer would regularly drop by to congratulate the staff for a particularly fine piece of writing—and leave behind a donation of cash and product.

There was indeed a lot of sexual activity in the underground press, but it was freewheeling in the spirit of the times, not casual in the sense of indifferent or uncaring, but often serendipitous. There was an openness to experiment, a freedom with body, a sense that sex could be the logical extension of a friendship and not necessarily interfere with other relationships. Sexuality was expressed in many forms—heterosexual, homosexual, bisexual, sequential, multiple, group, polymorphous, the mind reels. To be honest, male chauvinism and sexism abounded, and what was common behavior then would be considered dangerous or date-rape today. Still, the stories remain to mark the milieu:

One pert young woman dressed in fringed leather and bedecked in beads arrived at an underground press confab with an alternative radio journalist (now a well-known rock music critic) and, being upwardly mobile, left with Tom Forcade, head of the Underground Press Syndicate. (Sorry, Tom, but dead friends forfeit privacy rights.) Most conference attendees slept in sleeping bags in one large room, so nocturnal activities were easily documented by moans, loud panting, and thrashing of limbs. A particularly dramatic performance garnered a round of applause.

One young underground newspaper staffer (now a respected radio journalist) decided she was tired of being a virgin and presented herself to the local underground editor as a gift, figuring it was a romantic-sounding and incredibly hip way to be deflowered.

A well-known Rocky Mountain graphic artist, who first published her work in an underground newspaper, felt a local Baptist Temple under construction needed a proper consecration. One fully mooned night, she and her lover snuck into the as-yet-unfilled full-immersion baptismal pool near the altar and then proceeded to see how many times in different positions they could reach orgasm before dawn.

After meeting and making love to a sophisticated-looking blond activist at a peace encampment, one underground writer recounts how he invited the young woman to drive over and visit the office sometime. He was dismayed when she replied that would be impossible since 13-year-olds still could not obtain drivers' licenses.

One perk of the underground press was that promoters advertising their rock concerts often gave several passes or free tickets to the paper beyond those required for the reviewer. One group of underground journalists went to see Cream and sat in front of sets of six-foot-high speakers. The next day they had trouble answering the office phones because they were all temporarily deaf.

Staff training at one underground newspaper included use of small arms, and several newspapers had plans to relocate their offices if raided, plus pre-arranged telephone codes and gathering points.

Handling of underground communiques became such an issue that the UPS newsletter carried an article on the subject. When the FBI sent two agents to retrieve a communique published in one alternative newspaper, they were outraged when a staff person blandly informed them of the paper's standard policy of copying then destroying the original communique to destroy any fingerprints or other forensic evidence.

C'mon folks, send in your other anecdotes, maybe we can sell the movie rights and host a reunion.

---

newspapers revealed the existence of a mysterious FBI Counterintelligence Program (COINTELPRO) to disrupt dissident activists in the United States (see appendix 2). Documentation for the story arrived at alternative publications in plain brown envelopes stuffed with pilfered files from the Media, Pennsylvania, FBI offices. One packet arrived at CPS with a cover letter from the Citizen's Commission to Investigate the FBI that stated: "We believe that surveillance…violates individuals' basic rights to participate in organizations of their choice. It must be stopped if we have the just, peaceful society we all hope to live in."

By 1971, I had become completely committed to the antiwar movement, and as editor of the *Clarion* I pushed that view editorially and in long essays and articles on the war in Vietnam. One professor at the college was so moved after one antiwar demonstration that in frustration and anger he turned over his Korean war medals to me with a letter saying he didn't have the guts to get arrested but was turning in his medals to me as his symbolic protest. The next morning the *Clarion* ran his letter on the front page and I sat down in the entrance of a federal facility outside Denver and was arrested with a handful of others in an act of non-violent civil disobedience. A few months later I was sentenced to three days in jail by the same Judge Arraj who rendered the decision in the Trujillo case.

For some time, Carl Nelson, Diane Wolfe, and I had talked about ways to save the nearly bankrupt College Press Service. Our hope was to preserve the role CPS played in spreading information about the war and antiwar protests. With considerable fear, I dropped out of school to work with Diane and a group of our friends to form a collective to move CPS to Denver and continue publishing with lower operating costs. My high school buddy Curt Koehler came out from Columbia University and Diane coaxed her friend Steve Hatch to join us. Suddenly I was in a collective. Carl became our Washington correspondent. During the summer of 1971 we learned how to run a printing press and invited other alternative news service staff to a Rocky Mountain meeting to discuss increased cooperation, technical skills, and antiwar organizing. The night the meeting ended, while waiting for a bus with Elaine Elenson of Pacific News Service, I confessed to cold feet about dropping out of school to become a full-time movement journalist. As would many others over the next few years, she took the time to offer words of understanding and support that helped give me the confidence to stay the course.

CPS quickly re-established itself and began churning out news packets that included graphics and cartoons by Ed Stein, Doug Marlette, and others who are well known today but once were struggling campus cartoonists. Marlette served his two years of community service as a conscientious objector by providing educational materials to CPS.

One of the first major stories the new CPS collective in Denver encountered in fall 1971 was another piece of the puzzle detailing domestic Counterintelligence operations. Louis Tackwood, an undercover agent and informer for the Los Angeles Police Department, had flipped out and revealed to a group of alternative writers details about a plot by "Red Squad" agents to disrupt the San Diego Republican Convention in 1972 and blame it on radical groups. The bosses of the conspirators allegedly planned to use the event to legitimize repression against leftists and gain sympathy for Nixon and other conservative politicians. Tackwood claimed the plan had its roots in the White House. Unknown to the alternative press, it had stumbled onto the first evidence of a "dirty tricks" campaign coming from the Nixon White House.

Alternative Features Service (AFS) covered the breaking story on the West Coast in October 1971 and rushed a release into the mail. Recognizing the importance of the story, AFS phoned their subscribers, including the Denver underground *Chinook*, which alerted College Press Service upstairs in the same building. *Chinook* and CPS decided to cooperate in further researching the story. After a quick briefing from AFS, CPS patched into a live press conference with Tackwood on the West Coast through a hook-up with a Pacifica radio network station in Houston.

Meanwhile, Carl Nelson was collecting vehement denials from various government officials. He also slipped into the office of the *Washington Post* with the help of a friend in the newsroom and read the *Post* article on Tackwood over the phone to CPS in Denver. Working all night, CPS and *Chinook* writers managed to piece a lengthy story. I condensed the article for CPS and our release was in the mail the next morning. Then we moved over to a local college typesetting collective and, with some help from a sympathetic *Denver Post* editor, *Chinook* staffers re-wrote the story for a special edition. We missed our printing press deadline and the printers called to say they were going home. After a few minutes of negotiations on the price of the bribe ($50 and a bottle of top-shelf scotch), they agreed to stay near the presses. As dawn lit the Rocky Mountain backdrop of Denver, *Chinook* breezed into town with a four-page special edition. Ours was the first version of the story to appear in print. We even beat the *Washington Post*. Scores of underground and college papers from as far away as Alaska ran the CPS version of the article. Most mainstream media reported the story by stressing the denials. Yet the *Chicago Journalism Review* praised both the CPS and AFS for their handling of the story, saying the two alternative services "acted truer to the tenets of good journalism than most established services."

SHEETS FOR THE STREETS

In 1972, I covered the Democratic convention for CPS and Denver's *Straight Creek Journal*, which had been formed by new blood and the traitorous remnants of the writing staffs of *Boulder Magazine* and *Chinook*, which published a final issue on Valentines Day 1972. While in Miami I decided the demonstrators needed their own newspaper; so, when I drove back to Miami Beach for the relocated Republican convention, I loaded up a borrowed VW bus with the CPS mimeograph machine and 20,000 sheets of paper expropriated from the Colorado McGovern campaign after Gary Hart and his friends booted us out of our campaign posts following the surprise McGovern nomination.

Publishing the *Flamingo Park Gazette* was a group effort by assorted alternative journalists including Henry Doering, a friend and copy editor from the *Clarion*. The *Gazette* became quite popular, especially on the last night of the convention when we went mobile and issued hourly updates for the demonstrators who were being chased all over the island by enraged police firing tear gas. For some reason our van, with *Flamingo Park Gazette* signs posted all over the sides and roof, was allowed through the police lines.

We would dash through a line of police, then fling leaflets through the windows telling demonstrators to regroup with Dave Dellinger at the Doral Hotel for a sit-in or that the Zippies were heading back to the park. One clever but useless leaflet was our map of fountains and water hoses to aid demonstrators in washing the mace and tear gas out of their eyes. When they needed the information...they couldn't read the map. One idea that worked better was our "Special Incarceration Supplement" of poetry for people busted during the demonstrations. Included was a page of Ho Chi Minh's prison poetry. We later heard that whole cells filled with arrested demonstrators would chant the poems in unison to the dismay of the jailers.

In Miami I re-established ties with the Underground Press Syndicate through Tom Forcade and Ron Lichty, and, when I moved to Washington, DC, in late 1972 to run the CPS office there, I started writing for UPS. Both Lichty and Forcade came to Washington in May 1973 to attend the second A.J. Leibling Counter-Convention sponsored by *More* magazine, a trendy journalism review.

The year before the underground press had terrorized and guilt-tripped the gathering into scheduling a workshop on the alternative media. Writing in the *Underground Press Review*, Lichty and Forcade described the meeting:

> The alternative media workshop offered a sharp visual contrast to the others, if nothing else. Instead of having the "panelists" on a stage addressing the "audience" thru microphones, the chairs were rearranged in a circle, and the panelists sat in the audience, indistinguishable from anyone else. While the smell of Bolivian reefer permeated the large ballroom, the gathering resembled a revival meeting in spirit as the underground writers laid out their trip. Rex Weiner of UPS non-moderated. Beryl Epstein of LNS patiently and precisely explained how LNS functions collectively, what it means to be a radical news service, and so on. Frances Chapman from *Off Our Backs* explained the goals of a women's paper. Steve Foeher [sic] of *Straight Creek Journal* delved into some of the changes

the underground press has been through. Roger Cranz from *All You Can Eat* contrasted the straight press with the underground press, and rather harshly. Jack Schwartz, formerly of Albany's *Sweetfire*, spoke of the problems of underground papers in small towns. Art Kunkin of the *L.A. Free Press* held the audience spellbound as he reeled off long lists of stories of national importance that had first broken in the underground press, proving it with copies of the papers.

Individual alternative journalists raised criticisms at other panels but the overall impression was that, although some of the attendees had a greater respect for the alternative media, they were not about to challenge official reality themselves. As Paul Krassner put it, "The underground press has its force and impact because it began with the supposition that the government is corrupt and writes from there."

Summer 1973 saw the last meeting of the underground press in both name and form. The Boulder conference was sponsored by *Straight Creek Journal*, itself showing the signs of transition. Editor Stephen Foehr had originally targeted the paper at educating the regional "antiwar community and politically-motivated long hairs." With the recall of U.S. troops from Vietnam "we all had to find a new *cause celebré*," he recalls. "At *Straight Creek* we decided to become a community weekly." At the Boulder conference, *Straight Creek* and Tucson, Arizona's *New Times*, with its focus on investigative journalism, were heralded as new role models for the underground press. A move towards community focus and firm advertising bases confused some of the older "movement" and "counterculture" journalists. Despite the changes, Rex Weiner pointed out that "over fifty papers and 150 people gathered in Boulder was in itself affirmation of purpose...the Alternative Press remains as the one viable institution created from the counterculture of the '60s."

Also at that conference a group of us argued that the term "underground" was a dinosaur and suggested changing the name of UPS to Alternative Press Syndicate. The vote to change was overwhelming, and the Boulder conference became a line of demarcation between two eras in alternative journalism.

FROM UNDERGROUND TO ALTERNATIVE

In December of 1973, I wrote a two-part article on the Teamster/Nixon connection for Washington, DC's *Daily Rag*, an alternative weekly. The story detailed how the Teamsters Union had paid a Nixon slush fund to obtain both the pardon of Hoffa and the restriction against Hoffa running for union office. I had audio tapes, sworn depositions, court records, and a zillion interviews, and even had cross-checked the allegations with my very own secondary source on the Watergate Committee (every journalist in DC had one…the committee was a sieve…my source had gone to school with another alternative journalist). The only attention the Teamster article got me was someone breaking into my apartment building and yanking my fuses, and my primary source fleeing in hysteria when someone re-wired his car's ignition. A few months later I was watching the "exclusive" story on "ABC News."

The Teamster/Nixon research was prompted by an unlikely meeting of interested persons in my apartment with folksinger Phil Ochs arguing with *Yipster Times* writer A.J. Weberman over Nixon, the Mob, the Kennedy assassination, and general conspiracies. I remained friends with both Ochs and Weberman, but they never occupied the same space again without sparks flying. Later, Weberman would spend a summer at my Washington, DC apartment collecting research at the National Archive for his book on the Kennedy assassination, *Coup d'État in America*. Ochs would drift through for benefit performances at events urging the end to the war or the impeachment of Nixon.

SPOOKS FOR SCOOPS

The Watergate/Church Committee revelations were grist for the muckrakers mill, and led to the discovery that College Press Service had made a big mistake when it hired a nepharious character named Sal Ferrera to run a European stringer operation out of Paris. LNS and several other alternative newspapers also used Ferrera as a stringer until Ferrera vanished shortly before former CIA agent Phillip Agee identified the intrepid journalist as a CIA operative who had helped plant a bugged typewriter while Agee was writing *CIA Diary*. One of my most painful memories is explaining to Agee how I had gone about my background check of Ferrera prior to his hiring by CPS. Indeed, Ferrera had worked for several underground newspapers prior to his CPS stint, and had even written a college essay on revolutionary political views.

Ferrera also worked with a debugging outfit that supposedly checked local DC movement groups for possible wiretaps. This operation has also been identified as having CIA connections. The most offensive part of this turgid story is that Ferrera, while working for CPS in Paris, managed to gain the trust of the Paris headquarters of the Provisional Revolutionary Government of South Vietnam and on several occasions was given exclusive stories to forward to his U.S. contacts,

which now appear to have included far more than some alternative news agencies.

Out of curiosity, I began researching government intelligence abuse, while editing a magazine for the National Student Association, itself a victim of CIA manipulation, as was exposed in 1967. *NSA Magazine* reflected the antiwar politics of NSA and included articles by Don Luce and other antiwar activists along with cartoons by Doug Marlette, who had moved on to the *Charlotte Observer*. NSA ran summer conferences where dozens of movement activists and ideologues would mingle with academics and student leaders. Assigned to handle film showings and entertainment at the 1974 convention in addition to editing a series of booklets, I roped in Curt Koehler to assist, and together we connived a booking for Maggie and Terre Roche, who had decided to dive into the folk scene with all four feet. They picked my candid photo of them sitting on a couch at the St. Louis NSA convention for their first Columbia recording, my first (and last) album cover (now replaced in re-issue).

While negotiating an NSA convention film showing with Emile de Antonio we drifted into an exchange of letters over government spying of antiwar activists. He gave my name to Jane Fonda, then working with the Indochina Peace Campaign. In addition to showing an antiwar film she had worked on, *Introduction to the Enemy*, at NSA meetings, we cooked up a publicity campaign around the issues of political prisoners in South Vietnam with a special focus on student leaders jailed for their activities. One of my favorite momentos is a letter from the student newspaper at New Hampshire's Plymouth State College asking to reprint an article from *NSA Magazine* saying, "Your damn article was the last straw in a long line of eye-opening stories."

What opened my eyes was my research into the intelligence community. I began hanging out with the staff of the original *Counterspy Magazine* and volunteering as a proofreader. Tom Forcade hired me to write articles on government misconduct for his *High Times* magazine and then gave me an office and phone as "Washington Editor" to gain visibility and tweak the nose of official Washington. He also wanted to support my research into surveillance and repression, and provided quiet support for my movement activity as publicity coordinator for striking *Washington Post* pressmen.

At some point in the 1970s, the underground press as a national institution slipped away. I know I felt it was finally over when I wrote obituaries for Ochs and Forcade. But while the sorrow of losing such friends still pains, I am encouraged to still see the bylines of many of my comrades from the front lines of the era of barricades journalism, especially the cartoons of

Stein and Marlette, which continue to reflect their strong commitment to peace and social justice.

Looking back I am struck by how much those of us in the movement for social change counted on each other and helped each other along, especially so in the underground and alternative press. I may have evolved into leadership positions, but never alone, never without mutual support and sharing, always with trust and love. We tried to define new ways of relating to each other and the world around us that were progressive not aggressive, and we used words as our implements of construction. We were not wrong, and I believe history is on our side, albeit a little late on the upswing.

Still, I am an optimist. And in twenty years I am confident I will see some of us aging rebels with a cause still writing, still cartooning, still muckraking, still pursuing in print a slogan of the early civil rights struggle: "Speak Truth to Power."

POSTSCRIPT

While the muckraking influence of the underground and alternative press has spread to some degree to mainstream media, there is still a chronic lack of contextual reporting.

In 1980, after five years of researching and writing articles about perennial presidential contender Lyndon H. LaRouche, Jr., I joined two other alternative journalists, Dennis King and Russ Bellant, at a press conference in Washington, DC.

Having concluded that our stories calling LaRouche a neo-fascist cult leader hadn't sparked any sustained interest by the mass media, we produced evidence indicating the LaRouche network was a $10 million-per-year operation potentially violating laws governing fundraising, financial operations, and taxes. Despite the sensational nature of our charges, not one major media outlet reported the story.

In October 1986, the mass media finally discovered the LaRouche financial story following the indictment of ten top LaRouche lieutenants stemming from a federal investigation into the same type of financial irregularities we cited in our press conference. Many newspapers noted with irony that on the same day the indictments were revealed the U.S. Supreme Court refused to hear arguments stemming from a LaRouche slander lawsuit filed against several NBC television reporters, the Anti-Defamation League of B'nai B'rith, Dennis King, and myself.

A few newspapers made the connection, but most still failed to mention what the NBC lawsuit case involved: a federal jury decision that NBC had not slandered LaRouche by airing charges that he ran a financial empire that appeared to be operating illegally.

The broadcast had also alleged that LaRouche was a "small time Hitler," who headed a thuggish anti-Semitic cult. That these small details would have significantly expanded the depth of the main story did not seem to occur to most reporters. As for LaRouche's ideology, most reporters were stumped. Some even applied the monumentally inaccurate term "extremist conservative" to this authoritarian who in many ways represents the antithesis of small-government political conservatism.

I began to collect examples of this type of "news-from-nowhere." Here are two recent favorites.

The news that Panama "strongman" Noriega was a mega-dealer in death-drugs with the complicity of the CIA was treated as shocking news and an abberation by the mainstream media. Don't these journalists own a library card?

The Politics of Heroin in Southeast Asia, by Alfred W. McCoy, prompted by the *Ramparts* article, came out in paperback in 1973 with meticulous documentation of the connection between anti-Communist foreign policy objectives, U.S. intelligence intrigues, and the flow of heroin into the ruptured veins of addicted Americans.

FBI spying on the anti-intervention group CISPES (Committee in Solidarity with the People of El Salvador) has been revealed over the past few years by both the Center for Investigative Reporting and the Center for Constitutional Rights. The spying grew to encompass hundreds of groups and thousands of individuals. Yet the mainstream media treated the incident like a novelty. Frank Donner's *The Age of Surveillance* (1981) is a virtual encyclopedia of the FBI's 40-year history of unconstitutional attacks on dissidents. It is one of perhaps another dozen books on the same subject. Why the short memory?

There is a distinctively American school of reporting—unconnected, ahistorical, anti-ideological...history and news covered as a sporting event. "Iranians bomb 3 ships but Navy sinks 2 gunboats...pix at eleven." There is never time to explain why. Everything is random events on the toteboard of history. We don't get information, we get Box Scores. Why?

In his book, *Inventing Reality*, Michael Parenti regales us with scores of examples of this phenomenon, and offers an explanation. Parenti sees in the American media a "tendency to favor personality over issue, event over content, official positions over popular grievances, the atypical and sensational over the modal and systemic." He argues that these persistent media failures, when taken in the aggregate, serve as a conscious reification of the political and social status quo in America—a conservative force rather than a liberal one. Parenti's examples persuasively buttress his contention that the mass media "exert a subtle, persistent influence in defining the scope of respectable political discourse, channeling public attention in directions that are essentially supportive of the existing politico-economic system."

In his acknowledgments, Parenti notes the influence on his work by journalist George Seldes, an early mass media critic whose books occupy several feet of shelf over my desk. Seldes gained fame in the 1930s and 1940s by scolding reporters for suppressing information about authoritarian or fascist leanings among corporate and political leaders in America—even during World War II. Seeking to better understand these issues, I visited Seldes in 1986 with a briefcase full of LaRouche's writings. Clearly a "Mussolini-style fascist," agreed Seldes, but why the mass media still seemed unwilling or unable to accurately report on right-wing ideologues left us stumped.

Seldes contended that, since his newsletter *In Fact* ceased publication in the early 1950s, the mass media had grown more professional and less willing to be overtly manipulated into suppressing news. He felt his theories of heavy-handed corporate and government interference and influence no longer adequately explained what he saw as a continued media bias favoring the political status quo. The influences and biases today seem much more subtle to Seldes.

The Parenti book addresses that issue by showing how even subtle pressures, if pervasive enough, can have the same effect. "What is it about the dynamics of news gathering and the foibles of reporters that obliges the press to treat capitalism as a benign system and socialism as a pernicious one?" asks Parenti. "Not much. But there is plenty to explain that bias in the pattern of ownership and control, the vested class interest, the financial muscle of big advertisers, and the entire capitalist social and cultural order."

Parenti does have a one-track mind on this question, and there are undoubtedly other reasons, especially on network television. For instance, a structural bar to intelligent reporting on TV is the segmented commercial market system that financially supports news broadcasts. You can't sell deodorant if viewers are bummed out by reality. But the bottom line is the same. Happy talk. There are rare and noble exceptions such as "Frontline" on PBS, the Civil War series, and anything by Bill Moyers, but they are not where most Americans get their news. This carping does have a point, which was best articulated by James Madison, number four on the charts as President of the United States:

> A popular government, without popular information or the means of acquiring it, is but a prologue to a farce or a tragedy or perhaps both. Knowledge will forever govern ignorance, and a people who mean to be their own governors must arm themselves with the power which knowledge gives.

A tragic farce? Sounds right to me. Now let's figure out what to do about it.

APPENDIX 1: NEWS DELIVERED BY A UNIFORMED AGENT OF THE FEDERAL GOVERNMENT: THE ALTERNATIVE NEWS SERVICES

by Chip Berlet

The underground press has a distinct and short historical period from roughly 1964 to 1973, when it was in part absorbed and in part supplanted by what is now called the alternative press. The first handful of undergrounds in the early sixties often shared stories and graphics. News of a demonstration scheduled for Boston would magically appear in an Ann Arbor underground; notices of marches on Washington would sprout across the country and result in a bountiful harvest of demonstrators.

In 1966 the underground news-sharing arrangement became more formalized when Walter Bowart, Allen and Don Katzman, and John Wilcock of the *East Village Other* in New York concocted the Underground Press Syndicate. Originally it was a hype to create the spectre of a national network of freaky newspapers. A straight reporter had asked if such a network existed and the *EVO* staffers felt it was an idea whose time had come, so they invented it on the spot. The fantasy quickly turned into reality when *EVO*, *The Paper* in East Lansing, Michigan, the *L.A. Free Press*, *Berkeley Barb*, and the *San Francisco Oracle* all agreed to an exchange of papers and free reprint rights among members. This agreement produced an immediate quantum leap in information dissemination, with some stories reaching the full 50,000 circulation of the five founding undergrounds.

The undergrounds flourished along with the counterculture of the sixties, and when that decade ended there were over one hundred regularly published undergrounds, plus hundreds more that appeared sporadically. This burgeoning underground press movement created a national information vacuum that pulled groups of diehard underground journalists together in decayed offices to create alternatives to the lockstep offerings of AP and UPI. These alternative news services linked the undergrounds into a national network that educated, entertained, and enhanced the political and social movements they reflected.

Some of these news services grew into established organizations with full-time staffs and realistic budgets, others operated as collectives with subsistence salaries, a few were held together only by staff dedication and a handful of brown rice; but all of them shared a rich history filled with feuds, friendships, outrageous personalities, and the efforts of progressive journalists to create a national distribution system for news, features, and graphics to the alternative press.

Actually, a forerunner of the alternative news services was formed in 1962 when a group of college editors met at a National Student Association conference and formed the United States Student Press Association (USSPA). USSPA's first priority was the establishment of a campus news link dubbed Collegiate Press Service. At the time, the National Student Association was receiving generous financial support from the Central Intelligence Agency, and one of the strongest backers of the fledgling CPS was the right-wing *Reader's Digest*. USSPA also received CIA funds laundered through dummy foundations, but this cozy relationship was not long to last. CPS began drifting leftward, and by 1966 had a Vietnam correspondent with a jaundiced view of U.S. foreign policy in Indochina. When *Ramparts* magazine revealed the covert CIA funding of various NSA international programs in 1967, USSPA and Collegiate Press Service severed their ties with NSA and moved into a headquarters on Church Street in Washington, DC.

Senators Scoop Jackson and Barry Goldwater provided the comic relief for the affair on "Meet the Press." Jackson defended the spy agency for funneling funds, while Goldwater condemned the CIA for not funding conservative groups "like the Young Republicans." Goldwater charged the CIA was paying "to finance socialism in America."

Into this scene stepped Marshall Bloom and his sidekick Ray Mungo. Bloom had been chosen to be director of the United States Student Press Association and Mungo, fresh from a tumultuous editorship of the *Boston University News*, was to run College Press Service, but the pair proved too radical and spacy for the college crowd. Upon returning from a conclave with the North Vietnamese in Czechoslovakia, Mungo joined Bloom for the annual meeting of the student press and they were promptly purged for political and personality problems.

Undaunted, they moved across Church Street from CPS and began laying the groundwork for the first alternative news service. They formed the New Media Project and sent out a release under the name Liberation News Service. The first packet was printed in gold and black ink on magenta paper and carried a story on hospital LSD experiments on cancer patients. Accompanying the release was an invitation to an underground editor's conference on October 20, 1967, at the Institute for Policy Studies.

Many underground journalists had already planned to be in DC that weekend for the exorcism of the Pentagon. The crowd arriving for the conference was so large that the site had to be changed to an old school gymnasium on Church Street. Seated among the rafters were many of the original underground staffers, along with a number of more politically oriented journalists. A riot scene of conflicting politics and competing egos ensued. The original UPS crowd wanted a news service published from within that group; Mungo and Bloom wanted more politics and less incense. The result was two news services: UPS stepped up their sporadic publication of news and features in New York, and LNS began regular publication from Washington, DC. Soon papers all over the country were reprinting LNS stories and even I.F. Stone began dropping in on the LNS offices, which had moved to Thomas Circle. When the Columbia University strike and sit-in began attracting national attention, LNS set up a New York office with some funding from liberal church groups.

Meanwhile, the Underground Press Syndicate had changed staffs several times, and briefly relocated in Phoenix, Arizona, at the offices of *Orpheus* magazine, a digest of underground writing edited by Tom Forcade. Forcade was a key person at UPS during this period, instituting many valuable services, including the microfilming of underground papers by Bell and Howell. He also gained a reputation as one of the underground press' most flamboyant figures. The radical antagonist in the film *Medicine Ball Caravan* and Zippie field marshall in Miami Beach during the 1972 conventions, Forcade gained notoriety by tossing a pie in the face of a commissioner on the president's Obscenity Commission following his testimony on behalf of the underground press. Forcade even successfully sued the White House to gain press credentials for APS. After he won a similar credentials battle with the Congressional Press Corps, horrified legislators began enforcing the "Forcade Rule" requiring a tie on all newspersons in the gallery. Forcade complied by appearing in black tie—and black shoes, black pants, black shirt, black frock coat, black cowboy hat, and black glasses.

In the late sixties a new generation of underground editors appeared. Motivated more by political than cultural causes, they began an era of muckraking and political analysis. This shift prompted many bitter disputes over control of underground newspapers and led to a split in Liberation News Service.

In the spring of 1968, the Washington office of Liberation News Service shut down and the staff moved to New York and combined with that office. Staff size multiplied and the New York workers began demanding greater decision-making rights and increased political coverage. Personalities clashed. Ray Mungo, in his book *Famous Long Ago*, described the split as between the Vulgar Marxists and the Virtuous Caucus—a self-serving but not entirely inaccurate description. Bloom operated on an almost mystical level of frenetic organizing and had an intensely personal view of LNS. Many of the new staff wanted to integrate their radical politics with their working arrangement by operating collectively. Bloom tried to integrate his philosophy with his actions, but his was a passing order based on anarchistic cultural zaps rather than methodic Marxist analysis. Bloom became outmoded in the environment he had created.

After several bitter meetings the staff voted to collectivize. Bloom and Mungo with Virtuous Caucus loyalists responded by loading the printing press and other equipment onto a truck and, with the box office receipts from an LNS benefit showing of a Beatles movie, stole away to the pastoral Berkshires in Massachusetts. A series of midnight raids between the two groups landed the entire matter in court and for a few months LNS-Massachusetts and LNS-New York published competing packets. But with winter's icy arrival the Massachusetts press froze solid. Mungo and Bloom became farmers.

One of the people who helped keep LNS-New York together after the split was Allen Young, a refugee from the *Washington Post*, who reflected the growing trend in the underground press toward a more serious coverage of local, national, and international news from a progressive prospective. This new level of political sophistication created a demand for a variety of specialized news services, which began to appear at the turn of the decade.

In 1969, John Schaller, a student in Naperville, Illinois, founded the Chicago-area High School Independent Press Service (CHIPS) to serve the region's mushrooming high school undergrounds. Word spread about CHIPS and by late 1969 its pamphlet, "How to Start a High School Underground Newspaper," had been distributed nationwide to the dismay of many school principals.

CHIPS dropped "Chicago-area" from its name and added "Cooperative" to accurately reflect its role as a nationwide high school news exchange which served as a distribution center for papers and articles published by student journalists. CHIPS migrated to Houston in July 1970 where it began publishing FPS, a news service covering national and local events from a youth perspective. In January of 1971, CHIPS/FPS moved to Washington DC, and then, after completing thirteen issues, CHIPS and FPS moved to Ann Arbor where they eventually merged with a project called Youth Liberation. FPS later became the "Magazine of Young People's Liberation" with CHIPS filling six or seven pages of the monthly publication with reprints from the then active high school underground press.

FPS is an acronym that translates differently depending on who is asking or explaining. It has variously stood for Free Public Schools, Fuck Public Schools, or Freedom, Peace, and Solidarity. Take your pick.

In 1969, two groups were formed as outlets for frustrated progressive writers in Southeast Asia who found their copy butchered and distorted by daily press editors who couldn't stand the reality that we were losing the war in Vietnam. Both Dispatch News Service International (DNSI) and Pacific News Service (PNS) started with help from progressive foundations concerned with U.S. foreign policy in Asia.

Dispatch, originally tied to International Voluntary Service, scored its biggest scoop with the My Lai story. Originating in Saigon, the group of freelance writers eventually set up a Washington, DC office to coordinate production of a mailed news service to subscribers who were predominantly daily newspapers in the United States and abroad. Unlike many mainstream correspondents, Dispatch reporters were required to know the language and customs of the people they covered, and thus were able to turn out some of the most perceptive and prophetic articles about the war, including overlooked masterpieces on the secret wars in Laos, Thailand, and Cambodia.

After the move to DC, Sy Hersh and David Obst left the basement offices of Dispatch to set up Reporters News Service, a short-lived project that tried to duplicate Dispatch's formula while covering domestic rather than Vietnam War and Asian news. Reporters News Service faded away after Hersh joined the *New York Times* and Obst went into publishing.

Pacific News Service, like Dispatch, aimed their articles at established newspapers with their politics reflected in story selection rather than rhetoric. Starting with help from the Bay Area Institute in San Francisco, Pacific News Service began by supplying coverage of Asia that "provided a counterweight to the news monopoly of the media giants." Pacific has since moved into coverage of U.S. foreign and military policy around the world and also domestic issues such as nuclear power, agribusiness, the food crisis, and minority and social conflicts. It is one of the few services to survive into the 1990s.

Earth News Service in San Francisco started as a public relations gimmick in 1970 for the now-defunct *Earth* magazine. The idea was to send free pre-publication articles to progressive FM radio stations in return for plugging the magazine. The magazine later went bankrupt, but Earth News Service managed to survive and became the longest surviving alternative service aimed primarily at a radio audience.

Alternative Features Service was going to be the "King Features Syndicate of the underground press." Begun in Berkeley during June of 1971, it served as an outlet for West Coast writers, dishing up a potpourri of cultural tidbits through philosophical columns and news analysis. Originally aimed at underground papers as a supplement to LNS, the feature service soon shifted its emphasis to include college newspapers as well. It died in 1973.

College Press Service survives to this day having metamorphisized several times. CPS was still part of the United States Student Press Association when USSPA went bankrupt in 1971 to the tune of $15,000. Dedicated staff members collected unemployment while trying to continue publishing CPS through the end of the academic year by selling the office furniture piece by piece. In June, what was left of CPS was shipped to Denver just hours before enraged creditors descended on the Washington office with padlocks. A collective was established in Denver and the next September CPS began publishing as if nothing had happened except an address change. During that first lean summer, while the CPS collective waited for college papers to pre-pay their bills and fill the empty bank account, a letter arrived from the Carnegie Foundation; the foundation wanted to know what had happened with the $23,000 grant they had issued to USSPA in Washington—so did the Denver CPS collective, which was living on $23 a week. The letter was tacked up on the CPS bulletin board for years.

From 1968 to 1971, as a result of multi-level feuds over politics and personalities, the three major services—CPS, LNS, and UPS—had little contact with each other. By the summer of 1971, however, time and staff turnovers had mellowed the original feud so the new CPS collective decided to invite representatives from all the alternative news services to a Colorado meeting to discuss common problems and goals. CPS, LNS, UPS, Dispatch, Pacific, AFS, and FPS all sent people and a half-dozen other alternative media groups also showed up.

The three-day meeting was held in a log cabin 10,000 feet up into the Rocky Mountains. Participants lived communally, sharing food and dope and helping to chop wood for the blazing fireplace—the only source of heat. Memories of past squabbles became dim and the alternative services buried the hatchet. The last night was spent clustered around the fireplace melting marshmallows and chocolate onto graham crackers and singing songs. Three generations of alternative journal-

ists sang while pounding pots and pans accompanied by two flutes and a guitar in a serenade for the forest two hundred feet from the continental divide.

At the meeting, the services agreed to exchange news packets regularly and most agreed to a mutual reprint rights arrangement. Pacific, Dispatch, and CPS worked out a syndication deal for college newspapers and CPS set up a Washington Bureau at Dispatch headquarters in DC. Some of the services began sharing their news gathering resources and cooperated on hiring reporters to cover political trials and demonstrations.

Following the Rocky Mountain meeting, seven more alternative news services emerged:

- In late 1971, Community Press Features began to publish working class-oriented material out of the federally funded Urban Planning Aid in Cambridge, Massachusetts. Although tied to the activist community and tenant organization, CPF established itself as a separately financed news service supplying well-researched news and features to the growing number of community and workplace publications until its demise in the mid-1970s.

- In April 1972, during the death throes of *Earth* magazine, two of the original staffers on Earth News Service established separate news agencies aimed at the FM market; John Newhall began Zodiac News Service with two friends, and Tom Newton invented Zoo World Newservice. The spacy Zoo World barely lasted a year, but surprisingly a freelance magazine writer named Jon Stewart salvaged the tottering Earth News Service and turned it into a successful organization offering diversified services including an entertainment blurb sheet edited by a former CPS staff member. Earth News Service and Zodiac News Service battled for several years for control of the nation's hip airwaves.

- People's Translation Service (PTS) was formed in 1972 by Americans who had lived abroad, and foreigners living in the United States. Their goal was to translate and distribute feature articles from foreign-language publications. PTS started several different services but by 1974 financial stringencies had forced the Berkeley-based group to consolidate into a weekly packet of news and features. For a time they continued to publish a hefty collection of foreign items with most articles originating in Europe, but eventually they disbanded.

- An effort similar to PTS but with an emphasis on Latin America, Asia, and Africa was started in 1973 as Tricontinental News Service. Utilizing a magazine format to attract individual subscribers, the 24-page publication lasted slightly over one year and then vanished.

- The first packet of Appalachian News Service rolled off the presses in Charleston, West Virginia, in January 1974. Aimed at a mountain audience of dailies, weeklies, and libraries, the foundation-funded project garnered the attention and respect of many underground editors before quietly slipping into non-existence about one year later.

- New York News Service also published for only a year. It started in 1973 as sort of a relief agency for starving Big Apple alternative writers left homeless by the demise of the *East Village Other* and New York *Ace*. The service was the brainchild of Rex Weiner and Deanne Stillman who also founded "Pie Kill Unlimited"—the first and foremost group of pie-throwers for hire. Outrageous articles and general craziness were the hallmark of the all-too-brief service.

The year 1973 marked the end of two other alternative news services. Both Alternative Features Service and Dispatch News Service International failed to find adequate financial support for their operations. When Dispatch closed down its dank office and unplugged its teletype, the Washington office of College Press Service was forced to relocate. The added expense made the venture too costly and eventually the CPS Washington "bureau" was demoted to "correspondent" and then rolled up entirely when *Higher Education Daily* newsletter began publishing.

The Underground Press Syndicate was renamed the Alternative Press Syndicate (APS) after the 1973 Boulder meeting, and turned its energies for several years into producing a sporadic magazine, with office space at the offices of Forcade's successful *High Times* magazine. After Forcade's suicide, there was not sufficient energy and commitment to keep APS functioning as the collector of newspapers for microfilming or a network for the alternative press, and APS became a paper organization lost in a busy magazine's office desk drawer.

Although short-lived, the alternative news services produced several journalistic scoops as well as serious coverage of many overlooked and misrepresented issues.

Liberation News Service's coverage of the war in Southeast Asia was controversial, but in retrospect it is seen to be an accurate account of what was happening. LNS frequently carried the first reports of renewed bombings or offensives by the U.S. forces. Asian coverage by Dispatch and Pacific was also generally ignored or disbelieved by most of the established media until quite late in the war. AP and UPI reports during the sixties often parroted administration press releases about "pacification," "Vietnamization," and "body counts" that would have accounted for the entire armed forces of North Vietnam had the wire services bothered to keep a running total. During that same period, both LNS and CPS had Vietnam correspondents who were writing a totally different story. Several researchers have suggested that one reason the youth of America were the first to massively protest the war was that their college and underground newspapers were telling the truth about Vietnam while established media continued to be fooled by (or actively assist in) the government's deception.

The more established services during this period often ignored stories exposing corruption in government or corporate circles. The CIA-Heroin story was not picked up by the straight press until Senate hearings were convened as a result of the *Ramparts* story syndicated by CPS months earlier. Sometimes the straight media would ignore a story in the alternative press and then later "discover" it and release it, with much breast-beating, as a major scoop. This was the case with the FBI's COINTELPRO operation, which was aimed at disrupting the New Left. Both College Press Service and Liberation News Service had circulated stories about COINTELPRO based on files stolen from the Media, Pennsylvania FBI office. Several years later, during the Watergate exposés, this same story was released by the wire services as an earth-shaking revelation. One wire service reporter explained that AP and UPI were often hesitant to carry controversial stories unless some other source, such as a Senate hearing, surfaced the material first.

The alternative services were not afraid to cover controversial stories, along with analysis to put them in perspective. As LNS explained: "When Nixon cuts the budget to eliminate poverty programs, it is a class and race issue. And when day-care facilities are shut down, sexism is there. U.S. involvement in Vietnam is not an unfortunate mistake, it is the policy of imperialism. Of course, the burden of proof is with us. We have to show imperialism at work, not just announce that it exists. We can't depend on political rhetoric and jargon to do our work for us."

At a 1973 summer meeting in Boulder, Colorado, over one hundred progressive journalists from newspapers across the country had both praise and criticism for the alternative services. Accountability was one problem mentioned—editors thought the services were too remote. They also detected a tendency to rewrite the *New York Times* from a radical political perspective. This was glaringly true during the revolution in Thailand when several services lifted entire sentences from the *New York Times* without attribution. One assumes the *Times* stringer was not freelancing. Editors suggested the news services either attribute their sources or be more clever with plagiarism. The worst offenders in this area were Earth News, Zodiac News, and LNS.

Several services had rather cavalier attitudes about copyright laws—especially with reprints of syndicated cartoons. Chronic offenders were Community Press Features and LNS, but there seemed to be little hassle from large publishers. Some services carried original cartoonists, notably CPS and LNS. Several CPS cartoonists now have successful careers, including Ed Stein at the *Rocky Mountain News* and Doug Marlette at *Newsday*.

Stories sometimes would materialize out of thin air. One famous incident was when CPS ran an article by Tom Miller about a man electrocuted when his leaking waterbed shorted out his stereo. CPS forgot to mention it was a satire that Miller had originally prepared for Paul Krassner's *Realist*. That story was republished internationally and was even picked up by top-40 radio news programs. According to Miller, one California legislator heard the story and promptly proposed waterbed safety standards.

Other gems include an LNS story about federal agents bursting in on a couple making love in their bedroom, and seizing their young daughter because her parents were contributing to her moral decay. That story was written to scare people into considering legal implications of their lifestyle by a Madison, Wisconsin radical lawyer who thought it was dandy that people believed it.

CPS made the AP wire twice after running a totally fraudulent interview with Selective Service director Lewis Hershey announcing massive draft call-ups. AP picked up the story and then ran a special kill alert and follow-up article after the Selective Service was deluged with outraged callers. The CPS story had inadvertently been plucked from the April Fools edition of the Rutgers *Daily Targum*.

These lapses point up the human frailty of the services, which were run by flesh-and-bones people. And there was a lot of shit-work and alienation for service staffers:

- working until 2 A.M. stamping out names onto envelopes on an addressograph and watching, frustrated, as the machine turns an address plate into a twisted shard of tin,

- the dull, pounding monotony of running a press held together by coat-hangers and thick grease,

- eagerly scanning the mail to see if there is a check so salaries can be met; an escape from lentils and soy beans, and

- spending days piecing together a story only to have it vanish into the mail with no feedback for several weeks until a subscribing paper arrives in the office with the story cut in half and buried on page six without a credit line.

The isolation of working at the alternative news service was very alienating—there were no local repercussions from running a story, so service staffers seldom had any contact with real, live readers.

Still, the LNS staff would take time to have picnics in Riverside Park before returning to their red-doored basement offices; CPS used to troop down to a flea-bitten hotel to have their weekly collective meetings over the $1.25 luncheon special; New York News Service always had a case of genuine Seltzer spritzers on hand; and UPS had a big green tank of nitrous oxide in the office. We all had the time of our lives.

APPENDIX 2: THE FBI, COINTELPRO, AND THE ALTERNATIVE PRESS

by Chip Berlet

The FBI in the 1960s and 1970s carried out a large-scale campaign of intelligence-gathering and disruption specifically aimed at crippling the alternative and underground press. The FBI targeted what they called "New Left" publications along with old-line Communist periodicals and underground newspapers as part of its COINTELPRO program. These publications were seen by Hoover as a threat to democracy, so he ordered his agents to violate the First Amendment rights of alternative journalists to suppress their newspapers.

Surveillance of the Underground Press Syndicate was documented through a lawsuit filed by former UPS kingpin the late Tom Forcade, whose files show that the UPS was subjected to mail openings, physical office stake-outs, staff surveillance, and the obtaining and copying of bank records, credit card records, postage meter records, car rental records, telephone call records, traffic ticket records, income tax records, and more. Some of the UPS files which re-surfaced in the FBI files include documents that appear to have been obtained through illegal black-bag jobs.

The *Yipster Times* file shows the FBI obtained its mailing list and harassed subscribers through interviews and heavy-handed investigations. At one point certain *Times* staffers were considered such a threat to national security that their names were added to the FBI's ADEX (Administrative Index) list of activists slated to be rounded up in case of insurrection. The publisher and a staff member of the *L.A. Free Press* were also ADEX'd.

Disruption

Using anonymous letters to increase factionalism among leftist groups was a popular COINTELPRO tactic and the alternative press was no exception. In 1968, Liberation News Service experienced a staff split and Hoover used the occasion to suggest an operation against the news service. "Recent issues of the underground press have carried articles relating to the split which has developed within the Liberation News Service (LNS)," wrote Hoover in a memo to the New York office. "It would seem this is an excellent opportunity to take advantage of the split to further disrupt the underground press and to attack the New Left."

The New York FBI office promptly invented a letter titled "And Who Got the Cookie Jar?" which ridiculed the situation and criticized the LNS staffers who left the New York office for a farm in Massachusetts. [See "The Joy of Liberation News Service," by Harvey Wasserman in this collection.] "The letter is written in the jargon of the New Left, necessitating the use of a certain amount of profanity," admitted the New York FBI office apologetically.

The letter, signed "a former staffer," was circulated among various progressive groups and alternative newspapers in an attempt to win support for the New York faction. At the time both factions were publishing under the name LNS. "A real kindergarten performance by all concerned," said the letter, which called one of LNS's founders, who had moved to Massachusetts, "a

bit of a nut." The letter went on to charge the farm-bound crowd with leaving the "scene of the action in exchange for assorted ducks and sheep," and turning LNS "from an efficient movement news service into a complete mess."

When LNS-New York survived the split and continued publishing, the FBI contacted the Internal Revenue Service, which obligingly began auditing LNS for possible tax law violations. The FBI used at least two other federal agencies in its vendetta against the alternative press.

Progressive radio station WBAI in New York came under FBI scrutiny after broadcasting portions of a Communist convention. The FBI began monitoring its bank account and contacted the Federal Communications Commission. The San Diego FBI office requested that postal inspectors be used to harass the *San Diego Door* and the *Teaspoon*, along with a newsletter published by SDS at San Diego State College.

Reports submitted to a Senate committee investigating intelligence abuse have indicated that FBI funds were used to finance paramilitary operations by two right-wing groups in San Diego. These groups physically attacked the *Street Journal*, destroying on one assault over $5,000 worth of typesetting and production equipment. After they forced the *Journal* out of business, the *San Diego Door* became a target, with equipment vandalized and cars fire-bombed.

The San Antonio FBI office took credit for coercing a printer into refusing to continue publishing the *Rag*, in Austin, Texas. Printer cancellations were a constant headache for underground papers, and now it appears they were induced in part by visits from friendly feds.

The New York office tried a more subtle approach to disruption by contacting the shipper who transported bulk copies of the Black Panther Party newspaper into the city. After the contact, the firm raised its rates to the highest legal fee. "This will amount to an increase of around $300 weekly in shipments to New York City alone," gloated an FBI memo. "This counterintelligence endeavor…will definitely have an adverse effect on the amount of incendiary propaganda being published by the BPP," said the memo, which accurately notes: "The group suffers from a constant shortage of funds."

Most alternative publications were operated on a shoestring budget in the 1960s and early 1970s, and there is little doubt that the added expense caused by FBI-inspired tax audits, postal hassles, price hikes, evictions, and arrests forced many publications into insolvency. Distribution hassles were frequent among underground newspapers and the FBI played its part by encouraging local authorities to enforce vague and usually unconstitutional ordinances concerning pornography, obscenity, and hawking without a license.

Details of this type of FBI role are incomplete but one incident in Milwaukee shows how the FBI succeeded in tipping the scales against two undergrounds.

"On 12/6/68, a copy of *Kaleidoscope* and a copy of *The Open Door* were anonymously mailed to Miss Lauren Dixon, Principal of Homestead High School, with certain objectional statements and pictures indicated in red pencil," reports an FBI memo. A few weeks later Homestead High instituted a new dress code which forbade pupils from distributing "newspapers, magazines and pamphlets without permission from the administration," according to a news story that quoted the principal saying both underground publications could possibly have a bad effect on students.

One suggestion for disruption that was apparently turned down by Hoover was to spray alternative newspapers with a chemical stench. "A very small amount of this chemical disburses a most offensive odor," wrote the Newark FBI office, "and its potency is such that a large amount of papers could be treated in a matter of seconds. It could be prepared by the FBI laboratory for use in an aerosol-type dispenser."

If You Can't Beat Them...

On several occasions the FBI used alternative publications for counterintelligence operations by placing advertisements or submitting ersatz letters to the editor. In Los Angeles, for instance, the local FBI office concocted a byzantine plan to use the *Los Angeles Free Press* in an attempt to cause friction within the Communist Party USA. This escapade characterizes the zany and sophomoric side of COINTELPRO.

In 1966, the chairperson of the southern California branch of the Communist Party, Dorothy Healey, prepared a report that was "critical of CPUSA leadership," according to FBI documents. The "Healey Report" was allegedly suppressed by CPUSA officials and the FBI decided to print up copies of the supposedly secret report and distribute them. By circulating the report, the FBI hoped to embarrass the CPUSA leadership and cause dissension in the ranks.

The Los Angeles bureau was authorized to place the following advertisement in the personal classified section of the *L.A. Free Press*:

> Banned by the Communist Party National Secretariat. Get your copy of Dorothy Healey's controversial report. Send $.15 in stamps to cover mailing costs to Ivanova care of *Free Press*.

The FBI chose the *Free Press* to reach its target audience of leftists because it was ultra-liberal and its classifieds already contained unusual notices. As the FBI observed in a memo: "A good portion of the paper is devoted to a 'personal' section of classified advertisements. The wording of these 'personals' is quite uninhibited and ranges from invitations to sex orgies and LSD parties to guitar lessons."

The dubious contention was that such ads were read by Communists and others who would be interested in the Healey report. There was more, however, to the operation than just distribution.

The ad was signed "Ivanova" because the FBI wanted Communist officials to believe that the report was being circulated by "disgruntled comrades." To enhance this aspect of the operation the ad was placed by a "Russian speaking agent and an experienced, older female clerk with a heavy Russian accent" who were instructed to converse in Russian while placing the ad. *Free Press* ad-takers were supposed to immediately assume the ad-placers were dissident members of the CPUSA.

The FBI figured that Communist Party officials would contact the *Free Press* and ask who placed the ad. The *Free Press* would then tell them about the Russian-speaking duo. The Communist officials would suspect unhappy party members, and this would "cause consternation among local comrades...cause further internal dissension within the Party and possibly have internal ramifications," predicted an FBI memo.

Now you have to be pretty dumb to think American Communists speak with a "heavy Russian accent," or that the *Freep* staff would care who placed a particular advertisement, especially when the weirdest casualties of the hip scene frequently flowed into the *Freep* offices to place improbable sex ads. Nonetheless, J. Edgar Hoover was delighted with the plan, saying: "This suggestion by Los Angeles appears most imaginative and should have disruptive results."

The ads appeared in the 2/17/67 and 2/24/67 issues of the *Free Press*. There is no indication whether or not "Ivanova" got any requests for the suppressed report from disgruntled Communists, fellow travelers, or sex-cult fetishists who misunderstood the ad.

Signed: A Friend

The FBI sent phony letters to the editor to commercial and college newspapers, as well as underground publications. The letters generally revealed embarrassing information or made false charges against progressives. The letters were usually signed with aliases or phrases such as "A True Progressive."

When Angela Davis was arrested with Panther David Poindexter in New York in 1970, the FBI sent letters to the *Village Voice* and *Ebony* magazine. The FBI revealed a certain lack of cool by identifying *both* as "published by and primarily for Negroes, but in any case the letters painted Black Panther Party leader Huey

P. Newton as an informer who was paid to rat on Angela by the feds. The letter to the *Voice* reads

> Sister Angela is in jail. Poindexter is free. Huey Newton is free. David P. [Hilliard, a Panther leader] is a dumb-head and a hop-head. Forget him. But Huey is smart. Gets along well with the MAN. The question is: Did this cat bank five big bills lately....a gift from the federal pigs?

The letter is signed "Concerned Brother." Hoover instructed the agents sending the letters to "Take the usual precautions to insure that action taken cannot be traced to the Bureau."

Wanna Buy a Paper?

In Charlotte, North Carolina, the FBI published a newsletter distributed in Winston-Salem called the *Black Community News Service*. The "newssheet" was aimed at disrupting the Black Panther Party and winning readers away from the Panther newspaper. The ostensible publisher of the newsletter was a fictitious FBI front called the "Southern Vanguard Revolutionary Party," which the FBI hoped would be seen as "a black group at Winston-Salem of a slightly higher calling than" the Black Panther Party.

New York Press Service, a photo agency that sent photographers to demonstrations and then offered the photos to alternative publications, also sent pictures to the FBI. The photo agency was subsidized by the FBI with $10,000 between 1967 and 1969 before the owner surfaced at the Chicago conspiracy trial as a government witness. Even the staff photographers had not been aware of the FBI connection.

Ever alert for an opportunity, the FBI seized the revelations about New York Press Service that appeared in the *New York Post*, and used them in a plan to discredit Liberation News Service. An FBI-authored letter signed "Howie" was sent to the Student Mobilization Committee. The letter asked, "How has the Liberation News Service survived these many years?" and supplied the answer: "federal bread constitutes its main support." The letter pointed out that "LNS is in an ideal position to infiltrate the movement at every level" and ended with a P.S.: "LNS representatives all carry police press cards too."

The FBI apparently produced bogus editions of Liberation News Service in the FBI laboratory by matching the paper, ink, and format and thus creating releases that contained counterintelligence misinformation in rewritten stories. One such release was used to

discredit a leader of the Revolutionary Union in San Francisco. In another incident, the Cincinnati office proposed sending LNS a phony message from the Weather Underground containing retouched photographs showing an activist supposedly passing information to a police agent. The note charged the activist with being a police spy. It is not clear from the FBI files if the plan was carried out.

The San Francisco office proposed printing "bogus copies of the Revolutionary Union (RU) pamphlet, 'The Red Papers'" to discredit the organization by changing the content and distributing the new version "to Marxists, Black militants, SDS, left publications, etc. throughout the country." The Chicago office called the idea "outstanding" and suggested the alterations "distort the political line of the RU and, in fact, turn it into a revisionist line in a subtle manner."

Avid Readers with Avaricious Appetites

The bureau found the alternative press to be a valuable source of information about progressive activities and subscribed through aliases to many newspapers and news services. It learned about a growing feud between SDS and the Black Panther Party through the *Guardian*, which it read avidly, and alerted its agents to encourage the split. The San Francisco bureau began its campaign against the Revolutionary Union after reading advertisements placed by RU in *The Black Panther* and the *Movement*.

A letter to the St. Louis bureau suggests the agent in charge instruct an informant to "review a number of locally available publications of New leftists, Negro militants, underground-type organizations, and other extremists in an effort to develop targets of intelligence interest with whom he may initiate correspondence."

The FBI maintained a clip file of underground publications and sent clips to commercial newspaper reporters for background, and to parents and school officials to encourage them to take action against activists. Clippings and entire publications were also distributed to various political groups to cause factionalism. When the RU published "The Red Papers" the FBI had its San Francisco office send copies to the political groups whose ideology was criticized in the pamphlet. "San Francisco, for additional disruption, should anonymously forward copies of 'The Red Papers' pamphlet to one or several of the addresses listed in PLP (Progressive Labor Party) publication, *Progressive Labor*. Appropriate sarcastic or warning notes should be included seeking to aggravate as well as alert PLP to the RU attack," said the memo.

MESSAGING THE BLACKMAN

John Woodford

H. Rap Brown was in jail in Louisiana on trumped-up charges. The Black Panther Party was striding around northern California declaring it the right and duty of our ethnic group—the African-American people—to defend itself with arms against brutal police. And there sat I, in what I thought would be a good position to cover the freedom movement, as an editor/writer for *Ebony* magazine in Chicago.

The problem was, in 1968 both Rap Brown and the Panthers were strictly *verboten* as topics for our country's biggest magazine aimed at African-American readers. *Ebony*'s publisher, John H. Johnson, not only regarded the Panthers as bad apples, but also considered covering them as not worth the financial risk. The advertising leash constrains most mainstream media in the land of the avowed freedom of the press, and a black publisher runs on the shortest leash. (Which is not to say that there have not been many dauntless and high-principled black publishers who have sacrificed riches to carry the real news, from Joseph Russworm's *Freedom's Journal* in 1827 and Frederick Douglass's *North Star* in 1857, to Robert S. Abbott's *Chicago Daily Defender* in the early decades of this century, to Carlton Goodlett's *Sun Reporter* in Oakland, California, and Andrew W. Cooper's New York *City Sun* today.)

Regardless of the rationales behind *Ebony*'s censorship, all I knew was that it was barring me and other young writers from covering two of the biggest stories for black Americans in 1968. I was 26 years old, the same age as Huey, and there he was showing the guts to defy a bunch of "racist pigs," and here I

Woodford is executive editor of The University of Michigan's News and Information Services, where he produces *Michigan Today*. He is also a member of the board of the National Alliance of Third World Journalists.

was, muzzled while working for a black publication when I could have worked anywhere else in the country. I'd quit grad school and law school to enjoy the satisfaction of being in on "the action" via journalism. I knew something had to give. (The *Ebony* staff did get some meaty assignments, but none of them was near the battle zones; any story with teeth was usually historical.)

I'd already been bugged by an earlier demonstration of *Ebony*esque servility that has never been reported until now. *Ebony* had surveyed its readers in 1967 on their preferences in the 1968 Democratic presidential primaries, promising to report the results. President Lyndon B. Johnson and his aides didn't like the results of the poll, however, because it indicated African-Americans strongly favored Robert F. Kennedy over LBJ. The story was written, and the ear of the front cover (the ear is a headline summarizing a key non-cover story) announced that the issue contained the results of the poll. Suddenly the presses were stopped. The poll was cut out of the issue, and the cover was reprinted with a new ear. This maneuver had to cost Johnson Publishing Company plenty in production charges. I don't cite this incident to knock Mr. J. personally, however, for he was following the same pocketbook-first principles of U.S. journalism as the heads of publications like *New York Times* and *Time* magazine, both of which received evidence of the killing of the *Ebony* readers poll, but chose not to follow up with an investigation and news story.

In any event, these and similar practices of American mainstream "free" journalism—whether the owners of the presses were black or white—were goading me to seek an employer with more guts to cover stories that needed to be told. One late spring day I picked up another Chicago-based publication that I'd previously enjoyed reading only for its kookiness—*Muhammad Speaks*, a weekly tabloid published by the Nation of Islam (a.k.a. the Black Muslims) under the leadership of the Honorable Elijah Muhammad.

I'd read with a sort of scoffing amazement the newspaper's religious columns that explained the Messenger of Allah's distinctive mythology—how people who considered themselves to be whites were somewhat artificial beings created by the superb surgical grafting and bioengineering of the arch-scientist and chief devil, Yakub. Yakub had accomplished this feat 6,000 years ago by engineering pig genes, or portions of pig anatomy—something like that. This passage from "Muhammad's Message to the Blackman" offers a sample of the apocalyptic rhetoric of the Messenger of Allah:

> Their history shows trouble-making, murder and death to all darker people from the far-off islands and mainlands of Asia as well as the South Seas and the Pacific and Atlantic Oceans.

All have been touched by their destructive hand and evil way of civilization and finally the bringing of my people to make their destruction sure.

Actually it was suicide for them to have brought our fathers in slavery. This act was charged to them by the Divine Supreme Being as being the most wicked people on the earth. Now we see the results in the fight of the ignorant among our people to gain sincere love from a people who have no sincere love among themselves.

And then there was the Mother Plane, an invisible aircraft that would take all true-believing Original People to paradise on Judgment Day. One cartoon that appeared every week showed Uncle Sam as the head of the World Serpent—the European and Euro-American coil around the peoples of the Third World.

Another regular-running cartoon showed mini-skirted black and white women, and denounced this revealing fashion as "the filth that filth produces." Another doctrine held that all natural disasters were unleashed by Allah to weaken, and ultimately to destroy, the rule of the Devil. The doomsday disaster would mark the arrival of the Mother Plane, which got you your ticket to ride via Islam.

The word among the more privileged ranks of the "so-called Negroes," as the Muslims dubbed them, was that the Black Muslims were ignorant, fanatic, violent, a haven for ex-cons and confidence men who could get by in any setting that let them perform their special form of salesmanship. The women were said to be better educated than the men, but appreciative of a rigid system that would prescribe a husband's behavior and, presumably, punish a husband who strayed from the *Quran*'s moral code.

THE BLACK PANTHER TABOO

I'd been as indoctrinated as the next person to accept the mass media's simplistic image of the Black Muslims. But I felt the poetic force, and poetic accuracy, in much of Elijah Muhammad's prose. Furthermore, any condescending smile that broke my face as I read this particular issue slid away when I saw an interview a *Muhammad Speaks* correspondent had conducted with Rap Brown in prison, detailing the racist practices in Louisiana that had drawn Rap and other civil rights fighters to challenge the brutal bigotry and other apartheid customs. Other articles in the same issue told about the Black Panthers' fightback against police violence in Oakland, California; about liberation struggles in Africa; about evidence that showed African voyagers had landed in Mexico and other parts of the Americas long before Columbus. Fascinating stuff, and in a publication circulating at 300,000 copies a week, which rivaled, if it didn't surpass, *Ebony*'s figure. (*Muhammad Speaks* had the largest circulation of any weekly newspaper in the country except *Grit*, a rural weekly that has never made any journalistic waves strong enough to bring it to general attention.)

In one of those fateful coincidences, not many weeks after I'd begun to read *Muhammad Speaks* with real interest and respect, I learned that the Nation of Islam was looking to hire more aggressive, skillful young journalists to further boost its circulation and reputation. I learned about this plan from what may seem to non-Chicagoans to have been an unlikely source. He was a Chicago black Republican associated with certain Black Muslims in a number of businesses, one of which was rumored to be fencing stolen goods. In many ways, the Nation of Islam was a microcosm of the nation at large; in other ways, influenced by the separatist ideology of Elijah Muhammad and Malcolm X, it was an anti-nation.

Like most young African-Americans, I had been captivated by Malcolm X's sharp refutations of mainstream racist lore in his speeches, TV appearances, and interviews in the print media. The fearless eye-for-an-eye militancy of Malcolm X, who was the Nation of Islam's chief minister, and Robert Williams, the North Carolina freedom fighter and author of *Negroes with Guns*, was inspiring to a generation that was not going to do any stepping, fetching, or "yassuhing." This new militancy also had an international component. Blacks were no longer going to kill so willingly or proudly for Uncle Sam overseas for "freedom" we didn't have at home. As Muhammad Ali had put it when he rejected his draft notice inducting him into the U.S. Army: "No Viet Congs ever called me nigger." Ali's pithy expression of political wisdom soon became a political aphorism in the black community, and it remains so to this day despite efforts to subvert it via slick armed forces recruitment ads, movies like *Glory* and *A Soldier's Story*, and the elevation of General Colin Powell to head the joint chiefs of staff.

I was well aware, however, of the contradictions within the Nation of Islam. I'd heard Malcolm X lecture at Harvard four years earlier, in 1964. This was before he'd gone to Mecca and decided that counter-racism was a poor excuse for a revolutionary or uplifting ideology. He'd laced his lecture with a lot of spiteful reverse-racist and cultural separatist talk that continues to be recirculated today, though in ever-cheaper coin.

Before his self-proclaimed enlightenment in Mecca, Malcolm had been most effective when he spoke on talk shows with plenty of arrogant whites whom he turned into straight men, hoisting them on the petard of their own blind bigotry. But Malcolm had no straight men at Harvard that evening. Much of his speech was disappointing.

Even if my own beloved classmate, Elizabeth Duffy (we celebrated our 25th wedding anniversary in 1990), had not been of Irish-Bulgarian ancestry, I would have been repulsed by Malcolm's or anyone else's efforts to unite blacks by fomenting enmity against whites, Jews, Asians, Latinos, or any other ethnic groups. When the person closest to you in the world is described as being of "another race," it makes the concept of "race" pretty silly, if not—considering the damage under the myth of race—downright disgusting. Progressive organizations can't be built on mirror-image-of-the-oppressor dogma.

That's not to say I was a Martin Luther King devotee. To me, nonviolence as a strategic principle is wimpy, attractive only to those who don't mind being psychological and physical whipping-boys. I'm not one for turning the other cheek, which is why in the summer after Malcolm's speech, following graduation, I went to Mississippi with a group other than the Student Nonviolent Coordinating Committee. I wanted to make sure I'd be around black Mississippians who would bear arms and return fire in a situation calling for self-defense.

But back to the Muslims and me. I had reviewed *The Autobiography of Malcolm X* for Johnson Publishing Company's literary journal *Negro Digest* (later *Black World*) in 1965, during my first stint at *Ebony*. I argued that Malcolm's significance to blacks and the nation at large was being trashed by establishment journalists like the columnist Carl Rowan, a favorite of the white media barons because he espouses their foreign policy line. A black American doesn't get far up the media ladder unless he or she is something of a my-country-right-or-wrong America-Firster in international affairs, or shuts up about any differences with the establishment save those that are conceded to be "black issues," such as South Africa. The network of enforcement of this hush-your-black-mouth policy is tangled. I consider it no coincidence that, just as Malcolm X was trashed by the Rowans, he was also ejected from the Nation of Islam, or driven to leave it, after he described the assassination of President Kennedy by a screwball FBI-informer and CIA-maverick as an example of "the chickens coming home to roost." Malcolm meant that the United States under JFK had attempted to assassinate Fidel Castro, had attacked Cuba, and was keeping in place a violently repressive and impoverishing stranglehold throughout the Third World—and on the African-American citizens of the "land of the free."

MALCOLM X MUZZLED

Malcolm's barnyard aphorism—like Muhammad Ali's summing up of black America's relationship to the Vietnamese—was met with overwhelming assent by most blacks I've known, even those who disapproved of his audacity in saying so publicly. But, his comment upset the Black Muslim leaders, who followed the unwritten policy that they should not "interfere" in mainstream American politics. Elijah Muhammad ordered Malcolm to make no more public comments. I've always interpreted this harsh punishment by the Nation of Islam as evidence that some influential Black Muslims, perhaps the same ones who accepted donations from the American Nazis and other white racist-separatist groups, didn't want the group to become a *politically* militant force. Separatist propagandizing was OK, but independent political organizing was a no-no. For example, Black Muslims were under orders not to vote in any U.S elections. And the Muslims never did use their economic base to support independent African-American political mobilization. (I'm convinced that African-Americans will gain the leverage to attack and change the systemic causes of racism only after we form a grassroots-based, militant, programmatic, democratic but non-preacher-led organization like the African National Congress of South Africa.)

Malcolm soon defied the Messenger's gag order, however, and was ousted from the Nation as a "hypo-crite," a category, under Muslim terminology, that puts one in the position of other renegades from secret organizations, from the Mormons to the Scientologists to the Mafia: that is, the position of being marked for death. For several months, Malcolm escaped a few assassination attempts and founded a quasi-Pan African-ist/socialist organization; men linked to the Muslims killed him as he was delivering a speech in Harlem in February 1965. Whether any of the triggermen were also in the FBI, or were pawns of an agent inside the Nation, has not been proved; but neither of these scenarios strains credulity. J. Edgar Hoover's writings and sundry freedom-of-information documents show that the FBI had several operatives in the Nation—and who could expect it to have been otherwise, for this was a powerful organization capable of affecting the sailing of the ship of state.

These individuals, events, and intrigues formed the background against which I had to decide whether to go for a job on *Muhammad Speaks*. And if I hadn't already known what a mixed bag the Nation of Islam was, all I had to do was take a look at the news of the day. As I contemplated joining *Muhammad Speaks*, the Black Muslims were punishing Muhammad Ali for his "No Viet Congs ever called me nigger" statement. Like Malcolm X before him (and it was Malcolm who had converted the Champ to Islam), Ali was being shunned and silenced by his co-religionists under Mr. Muhammad's orders. One friend of the Champ's told me Ali was too vulnerable psychologically to break away from the Nation as Malcolm X had. That may have been true. But Ali may also have felt much more vulnerable physically than Malcolm had been. A healthy percentage of his many multimillion dollar prizefighting purses went to his managerial team of Muhammad family

members and their top aides, so Ali was the chief money-earner for the entire elite of the Nation of Islam, far surpassing rank-and-file tithers and contributors from white separatist groups.

So what was I to do? I've never been one to idolize or idealize the sources of my paychecks. I had no reason to hold Mr. Muhammad to a higher standard than I'd held John H. Johnson of *Ebony*. In subsequent years my labor power has been owned by a Marshall Field of some numeral (a Harvard classmate unknown to me, but who happened to inherit the *Sun Times*); the *New York Times*' "Punch" Sulzberger; and Henry Ford II, among others. Does being a worker of the brain oblige you to identify with and share the ideological thinking of your employer, any more than working in a mine or factory does? I say an emphatic "no," so I didn't feel that working for the Black Muslims would pressure me to espouse separatism any more than working on the *Christian Science Monitor* would force me to back the tenets of that sect. I have found, nevertheless, that almost everyone, black or white, who learns of my association with *Muhammad Speaks* assumes I've gone through a series of integration-ist-separatist-integrationist transformations—identity crises or something of that sort. I never bought into the widespread, simple-minded integrationist-separatist pseudo-paradox. I've always been for desegregation as a means of improving democracy, which is a horse of another color—plaid.

What cinched my decision to seek a job on *Muhammad Speaks*, despite most of my family's and friends' advice that a job there would be a foolhardy step "career-wise," was the hard fact that it was presenting more stories about issues and events that concerned African-Americans and Africans than any other publication, and that it was doing so in a more forthright, more "together" way (to use a term that was popular back then and that still expresses the material and spiritual quality of integrity) than any other highly circulated publication in the country—black or white.

A trivial flare-up at *Ebony* was the spark that shot me toward my new objective. I can't remember the episode, but an editorial decision in the censorial mode led me to post a Martin Luther-like manifesto, defiant and full of invective, on several walls in *Ebony*'s offices. I left the building and didn't return (at least not till a visit 12 years later, when I patched things up with Mr. J., who tolerates expressions of youthful rage surprisingly well, perhaps because he, himself, had to bottle up his own emotions and remain coolly disciplined to build and sustain a successful publication).

I went to *Muhammad Speaks*' storefront-size office on 79th Street near Cottage Grove in the heart of the South Side for an interview with its editor-in-chief, Richard Durham, a former union organizer in the C.I.O. Durham was a playwright and author (he wrote Ali's autobiography, *The Greatest*), as well as an outstanding journalist. He hired me and said I would begin to draw a paycheck, but that I couldn't work in the office until Elijah Muhammad had interviewed me personally. In the meantime, he arranged for me to spend several days in New York with our United Nations correspondent, Charles P. Howard, while he arranged for the interview.

Howard was one of the nation's greatest unsung newspapermen. He covered the African liberation movements for *Muhammad Speaks* and for those few other black newspapers who continued to print his column and articles despite pressure from the anti-communist Thought Police who objected to his viewpoint. Howard consistently analyzed events as they affected the interests of the oppressed, not how they affected the line of the State Department, Pentagon, White House, and the fat cats' twin holy cows, the "two-party system." Several of the toughest-minded black journalists and literary figures, including the cartoonist Ollie Harrington, had been forced into exile by the anti-Communist Redbaiting witchhunt spearheaded by Senator Joseph McCarthy, which prodded many an employer to bar "subversives" from jobs. Thanks to Durham's guts and savvy, Howard enjoyed an income that permitted him to stay in the States without compromising his politics.

"WHAT ABOUT YOUR WIFE?"

When I returned to Chicago and began going to the editorial office, my first story was an interview with the African-American poet Ted Joans, who'd been living in Timbuktu, the village in Mali that before its decline was the most renowned city of medieval Africa. Meanwhile, I awaited my official hiring interview with the Messenger of Allah, the Honorable Elijah Muhammad, which I thought would be a mere formality. On the appointed day, Durham accompanied me to the Messenger's splendid brick home in Chicago's Hyde Park neighborhood near the University of Chicago. Security was efficient and tight at the Messenger's house. As we made our way toward the den where the meeting would take place, I saw out of the corner of my eye several tall, attractive women in full-length dresses and unveiled Muslim headcloths, who seemed to be sizing me up from half-concealed vantage points like schoolgirls peeking at the new boy in town.

Durham, Mr. Muhammad, and I chatted for awhile. The Messenger said he was happy to see that a young black person who had had considerable economic and educational advantages wanted to work with him "to free our people." Then he asked me where I was working now. I said for *Muhammad Speaks*. "Oh, no you don't, brother," he said with a reproachful look. "You can't be working for *my* newspaper because I haven't hired you."

I almost blurted out that I'd already received a paycheck, but I looked at Durham, and luckily I read in his face an expression of regret that he'd failed to tell me something. "Well, I really don't have a job now," I said. "I recently quit *Ebony* and I'm looking for work."

"And are you married?" he asked me.

"Yes."

"Well, what about your wife? What is she?"

"Her father is of Irish ancestry and her mother Bulgarian, although her mother's father probably migrated to Bulgaria from Albania." (I *had* been coached in this area, so I knew that the Messenger's view of "race" was by no means as simple as the mass media made it out to be and that the wandering orphan Nikolai Subev's likely Albanian origin would put him in Mr. Muhammad's racial pantheon rather than its bestiary.)

"Those are Asiatic peoples," the Messenger said, "and many of the people in Bulgaria and Albania are Muslims and followers of Allah, as we are. They are part of the Black Asiatic people, the Original People, as we call them, but some don't know it or admit it. Anyone can be a black man or woman to us who recognizes that man and woman arose in Africa, which was one with Asia then. Anyone who accepts their ancestry as from the Black Asiatic people—and not from the Devil's grafting—is one of us."

"I think pretty much the same thing," I said quite truthfully, for I took this part of his doctrine as essentially anti-racist; it was a rejection of the pseudo-scientific concept of races and an assertion of the historic role of the Afro-Asiatic peoples in human history.

"My wife agrees with this, too," I continued. "We don't see each other as belonging to different races. Our ancestors had to arise in the same place, Africa, long ago."

"Well, brother," the Messenger smiled. "Your wife is fine with me. I hope you will accept a job on our newspaper. All we want you to do is tell the truth and bring freedom, justice, and equality to the black men and women of America. The Devil has built his empire on lies, and we can destroy it with the truth."

And so began my very exciting and rewarding four years. *Muhammad Speaks*—which was at that time a 48-page weekly—sent reporters to Cuba, the Soviet Union, Puerto Rico; to Africa to tell of the freedom struggles of South Africans, Mozambiquans, Zimbabweans, and Angolans; to England, Mexico, and both Germanys—any damn place we wanted to go, even North Vietnam and North Korea and other places our government said Americans were not permitted to go.

I was especially happy, too, because now I was part of a news staff that didn't just oppose the war against the peoples of Vietnam, Laos, and Cambodia, it openly supported and rooted for the victory of these nations targeted for near-destruction by the U.S. money-bags who today are calling the ravaged economy of these countries proof of the failure of socialism. (Oh yeah? Then what are Puerto Rico, Harlem, Brazil, Zaire, and the Philippines proof of the failure of?)

"The enemy of my enemy is my friend," was one of the Messenger's favorite expressions, meaning he and his newspaper were enemies of all enemies of the Third World struggling against racist-imperialism. The Third World was our friend and—by syllogism if nothing else—the socialist-communist camp, to the extent that they supported the interests of the Third World, was also our friend.

Our staff never fantasized the Third World into realms of utopia, the way Joan Baez, Jane Fonda, and the others who've recently flagellated themselves for "sins of their youth" seem to have done, judging from their "recantations" in this period of Inquisition by the powers that be. We never supposed that the nations we supported were chock full of selfless, flawless peasant heroes and heroines. We supported their right to get Uncle Sam & Co. off their backs.

In my early months on the job, the issue that I took aim at as my very own was the Nigerian civil war. The U.S. media were proclaiming that Nigerians were trying to commit genocide against the "Biafrans" (I always put the term in quotation marks for reasons that will soon become clear). I'd first tuned into the situation during my pre-hiring visit with our UN correspondent, Charles Howard. I told Howard that the "Biafrans" must be in the right because the Chinese were backing them, while the Soviet Union supported Nigeria. I can see now in hindsight that, confronted with events I knew nothing about, I resorted as readily to simple-minded racist, or racialist, formulae as the next yahoo: The Chinese were "colored people"; the "Russians" were near-white, at the least; therefore, the "Biafrans'" cause was probably just.

Howard looked at me impassively. "You know," he said, "these conflicts can be really interesting when you study up on them a bit. Have you ever read any literature that either side put out, or talked to a representative of either side?" I said no, I hadn't, that I'd only read about the war every now and then in the *New York Times* and seen some of the starving children on TV programs and in the appeals for money by several charities.

"Well, since you're in New York for a few days," he said, "why don't you spend some time at the UN talking to the representatives of both sides?"

Without my knowing it, Howard had just given me the most fruitful lesson in my profession I've ever had. Despite my Ivy League "edgy-cation," this was the first time I was made to think for myself from scratch. I went to the UN and spoke to key public information specialists from the "Biafran" secessionists and from the Nigerian federal government. I also spoke to nonofficial supporters of both sides. I became convinced that the mass media's "Biafra" story was a hoax, as was the "Biafran" cause. In my first series of articles on the war, I explained why none of the readers had ever heard of the so-called "Biafran" people before the secession. The "Biafrans" were in reality the Ibo nationality. A section of the Ibo elite wished to secede with the richest Nigerian oil fields and form a small wealthy state. They had support from such champions of African progress as the CIA, Israel, South Africa, and Portugal—plus China.

What the U.S. media weren't reporting was that the Ibos had invented the name "Biafrans" for their nationality because Biafra was the name of the bay holding oil deposits, wells, and refineries. These oilfields and other key "Biafran" resources did not lie in the Ibos' home state, however, but on territory of the minority nationalities in the Eastern State—the Effiks, Ijaws, Ibibios, and others. The Ibo rebel government suppressed, jailed, terrorized, and starved these minorities; meanwhile, they drew the "Biafran" boundaries around their victims' territories. Most of the starving children used in hype photos by "relief agencies" (some of which were later exposed as swindlers) were non-Ibo. But the phony name "Biafran" concealed to the uninformed non-African public the fact that the Ibo plotters used the starving "Biafran" photos to raise money for weapons and for their own food. The more starvation, the less resistance by the nationalities opposing the Ibos, and the more relief money via the charity-conspiracy. (Gladys Riddle, a woman from my hometown of Benton Harbor, Michigan, died in a "relief" plane that the Nigerians shot down. The pilot, her male friend, was a CIA/mercenary-type hoping to strike it rich ferrying weapons in "relief" shipments to "Biafra," her friends told me.)

The U.S. media refused to report the ethnic, historical, and political facts that would have shed light on that complex civil war; nonetheless, the African-American community never swallowed the "Biafra" story. *Muhammad Speaks* played a key role in building up an immunity to this specific germ carried in the constant, infectious spewing of disinformation and brainwashing that our press and TV networks disguise as "news." Sometimes I traveled to community organizations or college campuses with Nigerian graduate students. As part of this volunteer truth squad, I found that most African-Americans were naturally skeptical of and suspicious about the "Biafran" genocide story. They knew by mother-wit alone that the racist American establishment had never showed concern for starving blacks at home or abroad before "Biafra," just as they know today that there's bound to be a lot of bigoted bunkum and pure baloney spread in the Ethiopian starvation story and every other feature story about Africa.

Blacks knew that the Africans struggling against apartheid and against Portuguese colonialism in Mozambique and Angola, and against the British in Zimbabwe, were as hungry as the "Biafrans," whoever the people so-named might be, but none of these starving people were receiving publicity or aid that approached "Biafran" levels.

We didn't cover only international events at *Muhammad Speaks*, however. We covered hot domestic stories, too, and not just the Black Power movements but also big strikes and union-organizing drives, the campus and antiwar movements, the fightbacks against police brutality, and the activities of U.S. organizations formed in solidarity with the Third World.

THE ANGELA DAVIS STORY

Our biggest national impact was probably the Angela Davis story. Sometime after the capture of this leader of the Communist Party, Joe Walker, our New York editor (as well as one of the nation's greatest unsung journalists) got permission to interview her in prison. It was the first big story with Davis, who had been accused of taking part in the assassination of a California judge by Jonathan Jackson, the deranged brother of George Jackson, a prison activist Davis was involved with. Many news organs picked up this interview, and a special reprint was snapped up across the land and overseas.

The Muslims didn't agree with Angela Davis' political philosophy, and not a few of them were displeased to see *Muhammad Speaks* spearhead a media campaign to defend her; they felt it might draw extra scrutiny and perhaps intrigue from the FBI, CIA, or some other arm of the secret right-wing political forces in the Land of the Free. What's more, the Nation saw Davis' Communist class analysis viewpoint as an incompatible ideology competing against nationalist separatism for the allegiance of African-Americans. But to the Muslims' great credit, they never said, "Don't defend her" or "Cool down your free-Angela stories." I doubt any publishing group in this country has honored freedom of speech, information, and publishing with more integrity than did the Nation of Islam in the Angela Davis case.

The story built tremendous sympathy for Davis and led to wide-based popular involvement in her defense committees. The photograph our New York freelance photographer Joe Crawford took of her, which Crawford and *Muhammad Speaks* released at no charge, became the main image for the buttons sold by her defense committees. (When I visited Mongolia in 1971, I occasionally wore one of the several dozen "Free Angela" buttons I'd brought as gifts, and even shepherd families living in isolated yurts in the vast and near-empty plains recognized Angela Davis and were overjoyed to get a memento. Billions of people probably recognized Angela Davis in those days.) It was a great day when Davis was released from prison. My wife and I dined with her and the Rev. Ben Chavis—who'd overcome similar trumped up charges in North Carolina—in Chicago not long after she was

set free. To have played a part in the Free Angela movement remains one of my most satisfying journalistic experiences.

Perhaps *Muhammad Speaks*' most distinctive feature, the one that aroused most animosity in the political and journalistic establishment and in various black cultural nationalist groups, was our appreciation of the positive traditions and socioeconomic accomplishments of the socialist countries. Here was an exercise in real press freedom, for we were rebutting the Red boogey-men demonology spread by the U.S. brainwashing mass media and educational system.

Maybe, in retrospect, we sometimes leaned too far the other way to counterbalance the weight of the domineering Daddy Warbucks culture. Maybe there were aspects of life in the socialist countries that we should have probed more deeply. In my five or so trips to the Red lands of the USSR, Czechoslovakia, Cuba, Mongolia, and the German Democratic Republic, I got glimpses through the cracks of officially sanctioned and arranged tours to sense the rising resentment against thought control, the lack of freedom to travel, the punishing of free thinkers in art and politics, the economic backwardness, animosity among nationalities, manipulation of Third World progressive groups, the rise of yuppie-type careerists in the supposedly vanguard revolutionary parties, and a sort of craven fawning for approval from the anti-communist elites of the West. Yet I never interwove these observations in my stories. I suppose I assumed that such problems were atypical and/or curable, and also that to open up such subjects would provide ammunition for the enemy and make me indistinguishable from the mammoth stable of kneejerk anti-communist journalists.

But that's proverbial 20-20 hindsight. The key point to me is that we strengthened the democratic principle of freedom of the press by exercising it against the Big Brotherism still ruling the roost in the mass commercial media. Therefore, from the standpoint of the interests of our country, I'd say we practiced patriotic and anti-totalitarian journalism of the highest order because we kept out of the rut dug by the Sacred American Two-Party Big Biz establishment, which is that, in the formation of the United States, humankind has exhausted the possibilities of democracy. This attitude does to the body politic what cholesterol does to the human bloodstream.

One of the *Muhammad Speaks* staff's main objectives was to inform blacks and other citizens about the harm their government was doing in their name to many millions of people in other countries. In a healthy democracy, citizens know what The State is doing in their name. Such information is always hard-won because in virtually all countries the political and military groups pulling the levers of state power condone secret diplomacy and try to conceal their intrigues from the people.

by John Woodford

Charles Greenlee, a giant Black physician, sat behind the desk in his austere office on Franktown avenue in Pittsburgh's Homewood-Brushton area. He pounded the book on his desk and launched into his attack:

"**DO YOU KNOW** how these white colleges and universities are supported? By government grants of all our money. The Harvard Medical School alone received a $31,000,000 research and development grant. That's just the medical school.

"But the Black schools in the United Negro College Fund don't receive that much money combined! The U.S. gave someone else a $2 million R&D (research and development) grant to check a rectal temperature of a hibernating bear. But Black colleges don't have one R&D grant. They spend more to check a bear's a— than they do on the Black man.

"The thing that's important is that this shows how the Black man is planned out. So when the U.S. began to plan the Black man in several years ago in their big birth control programs, Black people should have known to GET OUT OF THE WAY."

Dr. Greenlee paused and opened the book he had pounded on. "There is lots of evidence you can dig up to support the claim that there is a conspiracy to get rid of the black and other dark races of the world," he said as he leafed through **Population Crisis, Part 4—1966: Hearing before the...Committee on Government Operations, U.S. Senate.**

"And one of the handy things," he went on, "is that they give you all the evidence you need themselves." Then he read a section of the report describing how the absurdly named "maternity and infant care program" was jammed into every Afro-American community. The program's name is absurd, he said, because the goal of the program is to prevent motherhood and infants from existing and not to care for them at all.

"**WHEN A BLACK** woman has a baby, under this program she is then tricked or brainwashed into getting her tubes tied or a birth control device inserted in her." (Tying and cutting the fallopian tubes ends a woman's fertility.)

The result of this program, said Dr. Greenlee, is that the 1966 U.S. population growth reduced the 1965 level by 0.4 per cent, and the 1967 growth rate was 1 per cent lower than the 1.7 per cent 1966 rate.

Yet, as the United Nations Food Production Committee proved, there is no "population crisis" or "food crisis" at all. Dr. Greenlee said the food committee found that if the population and food supply continue to grow at the same rate in 1979, the problem will be, "What will we do with all this food?"

This view is supported by the exhaustive study, "The Dimensions of World Poverty" in the November 1968 **Scientific American.** That magazine article reports a study which shows that there is actually a surplus of basic calorie-requirement food in the world. But 1.8 billion peo-

ple live in calorie-deficient countries. The "food problem," the article concludes, "is really a distribution problem rather than a production problem."

But the "maternity and infant care officials do not work to distribute food or medical care to Black families. Instead, the costly program has tied the tubes of Black women only 23 years old. And when two Black women drug addicts came under this federal program, they received no treatment designed to end their addiction. They got their tubes tied.

Dr. Greenlee said that women all over the nation are subjected to films designed to convince them that they should stop having children. These films are frequently shown to women right after they are wheeled out of the delivery room where they have been doped up after enduring lengthy contractions. The federal program also pays for babysitters while Black women go to one of the "pill mills." And if they can't get out of the house, the government pays female aides to go with Black bags full of every kind of birth control device right to the Black women's homes.

Although Dr. Greenlee (who is not an opponent of birth control but of the genocidal use of birth control) has offered to pass along his information to students at Black colleges, no Black college administration has, as yet, allowed him to lecture before its students. Dr. Greenlee said that this certainly indicates that top government officials do not want Black Americans to begin analyzing the programs.

The U.S. government has not always openly pushed birth control. In fact, President Eisenhower said in 1959 that he thought that no political concern of this sort was justified. So, Dr. Greenlee said, the Ford Foundation kept the ball rolling until President Kennedy, a Catholic, came along and picked up the program on the government level.

"**IT WAS KENNEDY** who opened the war against us," Dr. Greenlee revealed, "and his allies were the Rockefeller and Ford Foundations. They even got old Ike to mutter something in favor of it.

"To show what kind of progress they've made; in 1966 the U.S. specialized in intra-uterine devices on Indians; now they've moved up to sterilization."

The Agency for International Development (AID) runs the U.S. birth control program in foreign lands. To the U.S., Dr. Greenlee noted, developing another land "means nothing but birth control." He cited statistics showing that the U.S. gave 900 jeeps to Turkey, and pays the upkeep and the drivers for the jeeps. The jeeps are used to take women to birth control clinics.

"The U.S. gave $4 million in birth control pills to Egypt. At the same time, Israel received Phantom Jets.

"In white nations AID is studying to explain the differences in the levels of European versus United States infant mortality rates. But in all the Black and Brown nations, the AID programs are run to prevent infants from being conceived."

It takes a different kind of economy to feed a large and healthily expanding populace than it does to feed a class of elitist exploiters. The U.S.

government and ruling class do not want the nations they control to have to devise economics based on cooperation and an end to exploiting classes. Therefore, as Dr. Greenlee's facts show, the U.S. will go to any length to limit or reduce its puppet-nation's population growth.

Then he began to show how, as a colony within a nation, the Black communities in the USA are victims of the same kind of extermination policy—and for the same economic reasons.

On the domestic front, U.S. politicians and their agents in college and university sociology departments conduct studies of "trends of illegitimacy" or of Black infant mortality rates or of child disease in the Black community.

AFTER PILING up enough "negative" data they ignore the racism and exploitation which attack the Afro-American colony. They tell the brainwashed public—Black and white—that children born out of wedlock are by that very fact alone exposed to ill-health. To combat high infant mortality rates and diseases afflicting children, they tell the U.S. public, the main weapon is to keep babies from being born or conceived in the first place.

Therefore, said Dr. Greenlee, when President Johnson said that "our response (to the problems of poverty, disease and joblessness in the Afro-American community) must go to the root causes," he was backing a program aiming to sterilize mothers with no husbands and to spread birth control and sterilization programs throughout Black communities whether the men and women, husbands and wives, wanted them or not.

A large and growing Black population is a force potentially strong enough to rearrange the U.S. exploitative economic system so that the real causes of high infant mortality, disease, and joblessness can be attacked. With things going on as they are now, Dr. Greenlee said, the combination of birth control and sterilization programs joins with the conditions causing disease and infant mortality "to exterminate our people."

"I might be wrong," Dr. Greenlee said, with his voice carrying his discouragement with most Black people's willingness to accept the white man's "solution," "but I get the idea that someone is smart enough to understand this sort of thing."

The U.S.'s massive investment in improving the delivery and power of birth control and sterilization devices is only matched in intensity by its efforts to improve the delivery and power of atomic missiles.

Dr. Greenlee said that "they have already a serum which will cause prolonged sterility after one injection. In five to six years, they'll be able to sterilize a person for 15 years with one injection, almost a generation.

"Now consider the fact that there are only 5,000 Black doctors in the USA because there is a definite limitation on the number of Blacks allowed in the medical field. This means that 95 per cent of us go to white doctors and institutions where only one injection can take you out. And, of course, I've talked to some Black men who support the extermination of poor—that is most—Black people, too."

Dr. Greenlee relaxed for a moment: "You know, the more I learn about this the more I think that there is no difference in these white people in power; they argue about methods of killing niggers, not whether they should do it.

I believe they have every intention to get rid of us and our brothers and to take over the world."

NOTE

1. From *Mohammad Speaks* (24 January 1969): 7-8, 37.

The mass media usually abet this secrecy by publishing stories whose "spin" meshes with the Official Story. In this situation only a truly oppositional press can defend democracy, and we *were* that opposition, using the weapons of hard-hitting prose, strongly editorialized but accurate stories, potent cartoons, reprints from people's organizations from around the world, and lots of action photos. We also provided prolonged coverage of key issues so that the systemic context, the many strands of an issue, could be untangled and analyzed. This practice enables readers to learn about the causes and possible cures of societal problems, rather than to present readers with a media world in which events are disjointed, arbitrary, and, therefore, seemingly beyond understanding and correction.

Jimmy Breslin, the New York columnist and author, was scanning a *Muhammad Speaks* issue beside our triple-threat New York editor-reporter-photographer Joe Walker at a press conference one day. After reaching the last page, he turned to Joe and said, "Hey, you guys don't ever let up, do you?" One of the most controversial subjects we never let up on was population control. We didn't oppose birth control in principle, but we did attack the unusual Population Control alliance among our country's liberal-moderate-conservative-reactionary elite. Around no other issue—not even in their opposition to Nazi Germany—have these strata reached such unanimity as they have concerning the genocidal "eugenic" and Malthusian policy of population control. I'd held the standard liberal view on this subject, that any birth control program is by definition progressive, until I studied the politics and arguments of the originators and continuers of the U.S./West European population control programs.

Anyone who examines the record of the founding of the international Population Control programs (they are so-named) will be struck by a big fishy fact: The pushers of population control have funded the pill, intrauterine devices, surgical abortions, and sterilization—be they ever so expensive—to the nations containing most of the world's large, poor, dark-skinned families. But when these same population controllers put on their World Bank and heir/heiress hats, when they vote for party platforms in their own countries, they deny funds that would help the Third World stand on its own feet technologically and economically (see sidebar 1).

The same forces that have looted the poor countries, driving people off self-supporting farms and into shanty towns, sold them rotten food and inferior medicines, while propping up their repressive military and police—these are the people who ask us humans they regard as "lesser breeds" to believe that they want to improve our living standards by limiting our numbers. Nonsense! First let them pay back the wealth stolen over 500 years of imperialism, colonialism, and neo-colonialism. Then let's talk about population control and conservation and curbing growth and all the rest of the sanctimonious ecological doomsday blather. When they talk about making sure Starship Earth can fly in ship-shape, they are thinking about jettisoning the excess baggage, the dead weight of "marginal populations" (how gentler a term than "lesser breeds"). Why else are the American plutocrats more eager to build additional prisons than to recognize the human rights of black Americans to education, housing, and jobs?

Any black person in America can testify to the world that the African-American people are limited to housing in *de facto* prescribed areas/compounds of this country. This territory makes up less than five percent of the habitable real estate in this land that is your land, my land, the land of the free. Except in certain middle-size, middle-class liberal cities, any black Americans who venture to live outside these black compounds—in "white" territory (assuming a housing purchase or lease can be obtained)—subject themselves and their families to constant anxiety, for Uncle Sam condones this separatism, this apartheid, and the intimidation and violence needed to maintain it.

This is the American Reality that has given and will give rise to nationalist, separatist, and radical black organizations; this is what sparked in the Black Muslims that emotion that the sociologists and headline writers called in their first articles about the Nation of Islam: "The Hate That Hate Produced."

But before Elijah Muhammad formed the Black Muslim movement as a negation of Christianity, of the two-party straightjacket, and of the food, the music, and other mores of the self-styled Judeo-Christian America, no white sociologist looked at white racist America and wrote about: "The Hate That Produces Hate." And none has to this day. Yet it is the white skin/feature fetishism and psychosis that is the cancer rotting this nation at the bone; that is the root hatred. But the racially obsessed, from the Wall Streeters to John Doe, still point the accusing finger first at African-Americans, who are reacting to racist ignorance, insanity, and hatred as "the problem." Too many

European-Americans avoid looking in the mirror. A culture that entertains such terms as "mixed-race" children, of "mixed marriages," of "biracial" people, of "someone of a different race" (in scholarly circles, they now call it the "problem of the other") is sick in its heart and mind.

"DO THE OPPOSITE!"

I'm trying to convey the mystique of *Muhammad Speaks* here, so you, friend reader, can understand its popularity among blacks as well as the reasons why blacks keep their affinity with these sorts of doctrines private, or may even disavow them in public. And I want you to understand why, if you are young and white and perhaps studied the sixties and seventies in high school or college, or if you've read the many media rehashings of those days, you have never heard of *Muhammad Speaks*. I would paraphrase the appeal of *Muhammad Speaks* and other African-American nationalists to African peoples everywhere—including those who migrated long ago to India, Southeast Asia, and the Pacific, as well as those in South, Central, and North America—in this way:

> Look at the White power structure and White masses. The majority of them hate us. They don't want us to breed. They don't want us to read. They don't want us to act reserved and proud. They don't want us to unite and plan among ourselves. And they want us to love them in the name of Jesus Christ. That's a hell of a system to buck, and there are no guarantees of success in changing it. But there is one thing we can do that is likely to give us some leverage, and that is, DO THE OPPOSITE!

This is both an emotional and intellectual appeal, one that has had an impact on how black people analyze population control and other programs launched here and abroad by social engineers—including those Mr. Muhammad called the "mentally dead Negro"—that is, the non-Muslim black. The objective of this do-the-opposite tactic (and like components of any mythological mode of thought, it has severe limitations) is not so much to make all black people shun birth control, or even pork flesh, for that matter, as it is to endow them with a central nervous warning system that can alert them to the genocidal aspects of so many of the experiences they will encounter, given the socioeconomic and political realities of American life and other coils of the World Serpent.

Nationalistic consciousness is not a be-all, end-all, but a prerequisite in "the world as it is." It arms the black individual against the media and academic and political establishment. It helps them "Do for self," another one of Mr. Muhammad's pithy slogans, one that is much more healthy and positive than Jesse Jackson's pitiable moan out of an inferiority complex: "I may be black, *but* I am somebody."

(Speaking of phrase-making, Mr. Muhammad coined many terms that a scholar interested in the politics of psycholinguistics would find an illuminating subject of study. He advocated book-learning and study, but he warned of the Devil's "Tricknology"—the abuse of knowledge through trickery, especially trickery of a racist sort, such as the pseudo-theories on genetic racial intelligence. His essays in the centerspread of *Muhammad Speaks* were full of rhetorical wonders, such as this title of one of my favorites, about the psychology of the White Western Free World: "Disagreeable to Live with in Peace.")

When I joined *Muhammad Speaks*, there were no Muslims among the central writing crew in Chicago; we heard that Mr. Muhammad didn't want a second coming of Malcolm X, who had used the newspaper to increase his popularity within and outside the Nation at the expense of the movement's founder, the man who Malcolm had said "taught me everything." Malcolm had launched a magazine called *The Messenger* in 1960, and it was vastly better than two short-lived publications started a year earlier by other members of the Nation—the *Islamic News* and *Salaam*. Malcolm had written a column for the *Amsterdam News*, following a precedent set by Mr. Muhammad, who had published a column from time to time in many African-American newspapers for the previous dozen or so years. (Publishers of these papers found their circulations rose dramatically when the Messenger's column ran because Muslims bought all available copies and resold them, at no mark-up, to disseminate their faith. Mr. Muhammad probably saved or prolonged the life of many a black newspaper, although white advertisers and politicos occasionally succeeded in intimidating the black publishers into dropping the column because of its vilification of "the Devil.")

In 1960, Malcolm got the green light from the Messenger to edit *Mr. Muhammad Speaks to the Blackman* in Harlem, where he headed the mosque. Soon the publication became simply *Muhammad Speaks*. Malcolm was succeeded after a couple of years by Dan Burley, a veteran Chicago journalist, and the news offices moved to Chicago. Dick Durham took over around 1964.

By 1969, one might say that *Muhammad Speaks* was no longer a paper that fit the description of an unidentified critic quoted in R.E. Wolseley's *The Black Press, USA*: ["It is] a shallow publication playing upon racial feeling in such a way as to be nauseous even to some Muslims." Interesting, isn't it, how such critics, black or white, are so disturbed when African-Americans dare to "play upon" feelings of solidarity, of nationalistic identification and pride—feelings that are assumed to be natural and beneficial to other ethnic groups. I would say that if the paper indeed had been

narrow, not "shallow," for awhile, it had improved considerably before I got there. Nauseating we might still be, but not to anyone whose stomachs we had any regard for.

No Ciggies, No Pork

By 1969, the Nation was solvent enough to buy its own 4-color press and a plant to hold it and the editorial offices on 23rd Street, and we moved from our storefront office on 79th Street between State Street and Cottage Grove into the new building just south of the Loop.

Before the move, no meal was sweeter for us half-dozen or so "mentally dead" (Mr. Muhammad's term for black non-Muslims) staffers than to spend an afternoon chewing through a heap of barbecued pork spareribs hidden in our desk drawers to escape visual detection by Muslim visitors. We complied with the ban on alcoholic beverages, however, and with other prohibitions, such as curbing profanity around the Muslims and especially avoiding "loose talk" around Muslim women. Anyone who has labored under any authoritarian-cum-puritanical party, church, or boss will easily understand how good forbidden hog tasted under these circumstances. The smokers, however, didn't compromise. The little office was as hazy as any other newspaper room back in those days when the Marlboro Man still meant something.

But with the move to the new plant came direct surveillance by the Fruit of Islam—the Nation's semi-military fraternity to which all men belonged (the women were in the Muslim Girls Training Corps, or MGTC, as it was usually known) and by all of the other Muslims, who were trained to keep a vigilant eye on everyone and everything happening around them at all times. For the mentally dead, this meant no more pig flesh on the property, a prohibition all of us could adjust to since we could still work the afternoon with plenty of ribs inside us from lunches in local soulfood restaurants. But no more smoking? This was the ban that unexpectedly propelled me after only a few months on the job into the editor-in-chief's spot. Marlboro Men were not to be fenced in back then!

Cigarette puffs must be included among the ill winds that can blow some minimal good. At least it worked that way for me. The smoking ban riled our chief, Dick Durham, and the three top editor-writers who had seniority over me. Another irritant was the psychological atmosphere: Being spied on, and being glared at as if one were hopelessly fallen, are among unsung sources of the blues. I didn't like having to be so cautious any more than my colleagues. I spent considerable time in sophomoric debates with Muslim co-workers about devils, and grafted races, pork, and so on. They had received readings from many sources that supported their views and did a lot of side reading on their own. They had excellent memories and were good arguers, and in puritanical movements, bull sessions become a chief form of the devotees' entertainment.

I think the Lost-Found, as the Muslims called themselves, enjoyed getting a chance to hear someone voice so many views counter to their orthodoxy—not that they all had only one line of talk or analysis, for they were individualistic within the orthodoxy and entertained a full range of views from left to right. They knew I didn't claim that my views were better, that I wasn't biased against them individually or collectively, that I shared some of their critiques of American society, and that I admired the achievements of their organization in rehabilitating prisoners, building a successful economic complex, stressing literacy and high education, and introducing new ground to the debate on "race" with those whites who proclaimed or exhibited white supremacism.

So I was working and gabbing, digging the scene, while my colleagues were laying escape plans. After a month or so in the new plant Durham surprised me one day by saying he'd been granted an indefinite leave from the chief editorship for reasons of health (and he did have a bad heart, which brought his premature death). Bossette, Landry, and Casimere—the veterans—insisted to management that they be free to smoke at their desks, or else they'd go work someplace where tobacco was honored. The Muslims said walk. They walked. That left me. The last one in the pool. I just wasn't a heavy enough smoker to be motivated to hunt for a new job, always an unpleasant experience.

INTO THE LION'S DEN

I functioned as editor for a week or so, and then in the spring of '69 some top aides of the Messenger said he wanted to see me. Durham and one or two of the Muhammad's sons and sons-in-law, the National Secretary, and the Captain of the Fruit of Islam accompanied me to the Messenger's home. After several minutes of pleasant chatting about how we were kicking one side of the Devil's rear end with the newspaper while Allah was kicking the other side with tornadoes, droughts, avalanches, and other natural disasters, Mr. Muhammad said, "Well, I understand we are getting a new chief editor. Now who might that be?"

I remembered my earlier premature statement of employment and remained silent. He looked at me and said, "Why aren't you speaking up, Brother Editor? This is the den where lions roar." I said I would be proud to serve as editor-in-chief and thought I could handle the job quite well. The main qualification for the post, Mr. Muhammad said, repeating his admonition from my hiring-in day, was "to tell the truth and

to fight for freedom, justice, and equality for the black man and woman."

He said he'd decided to start publishing a 16-page insert "advertising" the Nation of Islam. The Nation would also continue to take up four or so news pages with religious essays and the Messenger's centerspread column. I was to see that these were typeset accurately, with no spelling or grammatical errors. An error of any kind in the Messenger's column would bring immediate dismissal to the editor and anyone else found responsible. The rest of the 28 or so pages were to be filled with coverage of the Black World (which was, by doctrine, the Whole World) as I saw fit. What I saw fit was fit to print.

I made few changes in the regimen set by my predecessors. I used more freelance correspondents, including those from the Nation of Islam, to increase on-the-spot reporting of the struggles in the American cities. I also began to hire members of the Nation as staff writers, a move that Mr. Muhammad never objected to and which the rank-and-file greatly approved. It didn't make sense to me to have a non-Muslim caste of writers and a Muslim crew of typesetters, keyliners, layout people, and pressmen. Diane Nash Bevel, the civil rights heroine of SNCC days, and a non-smoker, continued as librarian, as well as a source of wisdom and courage and information. Lonnie Kashif was our Washington correspondent; Joe Walker remained in New York.

Many of the former freelancers are still writing today; some are still presenting themselves as former full-time staff members or editors of *Muhammad Speaks*, and getting jobs via this exaggeration. I point this out only to indicate the newspaper's strong reputation at home and abroad in the African states, among African peoples in other lands, and among other resurgent peoples of the Earth.

Muhammad Speaks' circulation rose to 650,000 copies a week during my three years as editor-in-chief. We were widely known on college campuses, military bases, prisons, and in the neighborhoods, marketplaces, and transportation centers where the street salesmen hawked it. The Muslim men had to buy the papers at a discounted price, and therefore were strongly motivated to sell it for 25 cents. Some felt coerced, far more seemed motivated by zeal and a drive to augment their incomes, which were hardly conflicting motives to the highly Calvinistic Muslims. These salesmen were a significant force behind our mighty circulation. In addition, almost every leader of every liberation group or progressive Third World country subscribed to *Muhammad Speaks* in those years.

The Muslims didn't like European-American leftist hippies or African-American radicals very much (in fact, Mr. Muhammad tried to dissuade the Black Panthers from taking the revolutionary-leftist course they chose), but I covered some of these groups more often and more sympathetically than had been the case previously. We subscribed to the Liberation News Service (LNS), used many of its international stories and graphics, and published its credit. I chatted with some of the LNS folks by phone from time to time, especially Alan Howard, and felt that on some fronts we were comrades in arms, using the weapon of the pen. We also had good ties with the Venceremos Brigade movement, with various offshoots of the socialist movement—for it was the biggest and strongest foe of the racist establishment—and with black, Africanist, and Third World groups of all kinds except two: Bible-thumping preacher-hustlers and mean-spirited ultra-nationalists, virtually all of whom fall into two of three categories: screwball reverse-racists, police informers, or agents-provocateurs (see sidebar 2).

There were countless satisfactions on the job, from relatively personal ones like helping Ladell McBride, a soldier from my hometown of Benton Harbor, Michigan, avoid being swept into combat in Vietnam despite his debilitating back injury; to publicizing the research of Dr. Tom Brewer of San Francisco about the increase in low-birth-weight babies in the African-American community. Dr. Brewer showed that inadequate prenatal and infant care was so widespread and systemic that the fatal results smacked of genocide, and in fact should be pursued as such under the UN Treaty Against Genocide.

Many world leaders visited our offices, including Oliver Tambo of the African National Congress of South Africa; Shirley Graham, the widow of W.E.B. DuBois and a powerful thinker and freedom fighter in her own right; and Sam Nujoma, the South West African People's Organization leader who returned from exile in September 1989 to head Namibia's government. We also got suspicious visitors. Once a guy called me up and said he and some fellow Nebraska wheat farmers were in town on business and wanted to talk about the diet articles in *Muhammad Speaks*. When they arrived—five well-fed men with flat-top haircuts and clad in conservative suits—they opened up on a different topic: Did I really think that giving Ritalin to unruly black schoolchildren was making them hyperactive?

Soon the conversation shifted to questions about my views on the economy and whether they squared with Elijah Muhammad's. And what about Mr. Muhammad, what was he like, they wondered. Did I find him intelligent? Was he healthy? Was he senile? I still don't know who these visitors were, but I treated them as if they were really good, honest, curious Nebraska farmers. (I still like to believe they were, for their sake. It's possible.)

Another odd visitor was a young white man who'd been in Europe with a self-styled revolutionary group. He called to say he'd liked my editorial condemning Nixon's bombing of Cambodia (it was titled, "Those Who Wink at Murder Swim in Blood!") and wanted to drop by to talk. Soon after sitting down in my office, he said he wanted to tell me about the Soviet-Chinese border dispute, so I'd know why I should condemn the Soviets. The TV clips showed Soviet troops turning water hoses on the Chinese to drive them back across the Amur River, he noted, neglecting to mention earlier Chinese assaults on Soviet-Asian farmers.

"You know what I couldn't help thinking?" he said in a patronizing tone, as if he were drawing a picture for a schoolchild. "I couldn't help thinking that the Russians were white, and they were turning hoses on a colored people—*just like Bull Conner did in Alabama.*"

He figured this was the right bait for someone in my position, but my experience with the Chinese-Soviet split over the Nigerian civil war had immunized me to color-coded political analysis. I told him, on the way to showing him the door, that, except for the usual lunatic fringe within any nationality, African-Americans had a more complicated outlook on international affairs than he gave us credit for. I was never surprised in the following years to find the Chinese government praising Pinochet in Chile, funding the CIA-supported black traitor-guerrillas in Angola and Mozambique, slipping support to the Nicaraguan Contras, and aiding and abetting the phony Pakistani-U.S. "holy war" against Afghanistan's Sandinista-type government.

(Today, a stratum of Chinese students—many of them trained by the U.S./NATO academic establishment—parade around as champions of liberty, but they have never criticized their government's repression of Tibet, its attacks on Vietnam, or its funding of Pol Pot's Khmer Rouge and other renegades and mercenaries. The American scholars who assisted the Chinese "democratization" almost to a person do not support real Third World liberation movements, especially those of the Palestinians and Africans. I think the actions you take toward your own country's treatment of other peoples is the litmus test for the sincerity of your support of liberty and democracy.)

Muhammad Speaks staffers began to play an active role in all of the major black press conventions. I even went to the Alternative Press Convention in Ann Arbor, Michigan, that was attended mainly by the white radical and/or hippie press. The highlight of the meeting was looking out the window of the farmhouse in which we met and seeing Abbie Hoffman prancing nude in a glen with two naked young women.

Lots of toilers in the alternative media hoped that there might be a way to coordinate the journalism of the antiwar movement and campus with that of the Third World, anti-racist, and black liberation struggles in this country. Some link-ups took place, but in general the many divisions within the progressive movement—the American penchant for hyper-pluralism—made long-term coordination impossible.

Nevertheless, all of us in the alternative press seemed independently to have reached certain common

Sidebar 2: "Those Who Wink at Murder Swim in Blood"[1]

by John Woodford

The wanton slaying of four Kent State college students in Ohio is simply the latest and therefore most dramatic sign that the world serpent of U.S. racist exploitation cannot replace its tentacles as fast as they are being hacked off.

The youths of this country are refusing to carry on the devilish work of desperate and dying U.S. leaders. Young people are rising up in the factories, on the campuses, within the cities, and out of the military force itself.

They are uniting across many ranks and they are shouting, "No, we will not accept the inheritance you leave us; we will not accept your blood money."

And as in all struggles both in the United States and around the world, it has been progressive Black people who have set the pace in the battle against the forces of genocide, hatred, and plunder.

The Kent State incident is the latest wave in a tide that also included the Fort Hood (Texas) mutiny and the armed assaults at Texas Southern University, South Carolina's Voorhees College and Pendleton (Ind.) Reformatory to name only a few of countless incidents where Black youths and men took principled stands against inhuman officials of the ruling racist elite.

Remember that at Fort Hood Black soldiers refused to accept guard duty that they saw could possibly find them ordered to shoot down their brothers and sisters in Chicago during the infamous Democratic Convention of August 1968.

It was unfortunate for the dead and wounded Kent State students that the virtually lily-white Ohio National Guard did not have among it young men of equal human compassion.

But the National Guard, as all know, is made up of privileged, well-to-do, glorified draft dodgers who are permitted to serve their military duty without exposure to the Vietnamese, Cambodian, Laotian, and Thai liberation fighters.

Cannon fodder from the wage-earning and underemployed classes are ordered to fight in a war in which the National Guard types have all the economic interest but none of the military risks.

For those who have been tricked into calling for an end to the draft and the beginning of a volunteer army, consider this: the frenzied and mercenary reaction of the National Guard of Ohio is what you will see more of if the government builds a volunteer army.

The drafted army expresses more clearly the will of the people. And the will of the people is to lay down the arms that Wall Street financiers and military-industrial monopolists forced them, through hireling politicians, to pick up.

Black people have usually been killed by vigilante forces—Klansmen and other scum who murder while the "lawmen" look the other way.

But at Texas Southern, Voorhees College, and Pendleton Reformatory, Blacks, too, were confronted by deputized forces of repression. And the National Guard has frequently gunned down Black people in many cities where mass protests against poverty, war, and racism gave way to uncontrollable frustration and rage.

The remarks by the president and the vice president following the Kent State killings indicate that those who now rule welcome uncontrollable protests and the police state atmosphere that follows them.

Both men assumed, as their statements show, that the Kent State protest against the illegal, inhuman use of violence in Cambodia was itself an example of "violent dissent" that necessitates "justifiable homicide."

But eyewitnesses say that the protests were not violent, that National Guardsmen were themselves the so-called "sniper." Like countless Black people before them, the four college students, two boys and two girls, were exercising their right to free assembly to protest unconstitutional genocidal actions of their government against Asians.

It remains to be seen whether those who wink at murder and swim in blood will be able to "justify" the slaughter of unarmed white youths as they have so many times in the past when the victims were civil rights workers, little girls in Sunday school, Vietnamese mothers and their babies, Arab schoolchildren, unarmed South African demonstrators, or a Black girl running playfully down a street in Omaha, Nebraska.

NOTE

1. From *Muhammad Speaks* 9, no. 35 (15 May 1970): 17.

---

opinions and to have formed common values. We all saw class oppression and racism as interlinked; we saw dog-eat-dog individualism and racism as interlinked. We saw the joblessness, hunger, military aggressiveness, criminal activity, high infant mortality, and poor education that plagued so many Americans as systemic problems. And we saw how the U.S. mass media goes to any lengths to avoid describing America's problems as systemic. Only the pressing problems of the socialist countries—stifling cultural systems, low productivity, bureaucratic parasites, inability to put scientific and technological innovations into practice—were (or are) described as systemic in our mass-marketing media.

TOO MANY WHITES?

A few high-ranking Muslims began to hint to me that some Muslims felt I had too many pictures of whites in the paper. In fact, only two or three such photos were likely to appear, I said, and besides, I wasn't the one who'd put Nixon on the cover as they had required after his first inauguration! They also complained that I published too many stories that seemed to support socialism and communism. Some objected when I editorialized that, rather than wait for a separate state before they developed political savvy, Muslims ought to register and vote so they'd gain experience in how to fight for freedom, justice, and equality through political action.

College organizations invited me to speak periodically and, when I did, the question of Muslim and black nationalist views on marriage often arose. The separatists didn't like my position on this question, which was: Anyone who wants to tell you whom you should or shouldn't marry can't be sincerely interested in your freedom. I argued that black and white separatists shared the same mental impairment, the belief that white women have the sexual power to "undo" the black man. Staking out some women as "our" women is the refuge of men who fear both their own impotence and the rejection of women.

Another issue over which I bumped against the Nation of Islam's dogma was Bangladesh. My support of the independence of Bangladesh from Pakistan irritated them. They told me W.D. Farad (a.k.a. Fard Muhammad), the traveling salesman who, as an incarnation of Allah, designated Elijah Poole as his Messenger, renamed him, and inspired him to found the Nation of Islam in the early 1930s, had been a Pakistani. They implied that a Pakistani group regularly donated money to the Nation. As for Bangladesh, it was backed by Indian Hindus, and so on in the usual litany of religious bigotry. I told them that being an Islamic theocratic state did not give a government the right to oppress a minority or to commit genocide. Let the champions of Pakistan send letters to the editor pointing out anything untruthful in our coverage, I added. I always came out of such encounters O.K. because none of the Muslim leaders was in a position to risk the Messenger's wrath and suspicion by attacking me to him. His vigor was my shield.

And then there was Israel. I consider zionism to be an ideology highly infected with racism, as have many anti-zionist Jews. I oppose the existence of a racist-exclusivist state like Israel, just as I oppose a racist-exclusivist South Africa, or an exclusivist Islamic state, as so many Muslim-majority states are. I knew, however, that many Muslims were vulnerable to a lot of Jew-baiting propaganda, from the *Protocols of the Elders of Zion* to neo-Nazi propaganda. I made sure that any hatemongering anti-Jewish statements, bigoted stereotypes, and references to Jewish "conspiracies" or presumably inherited Jewish traits were stricken from any copy I received.

I did and do not include as impermissible or biased those inquiries that objectively examine certain actions of the Jewish-American elite or of Israeli zionists. My journalistic code has always boiled down to "What's good for the goose is good for the gander," so my policy was, "We will treat the Jews for what they are—people like all other people, innately no better and no worse." The main issue, however, is that such analysis and discourse should never be carried out as a means to foster hate, divisiveness, vengefulness, or arrogance. No one should whip up animosity in one

nationality against another, for such passions represent the foulest depths of the human personality. The current vogue in some quarters of inviting obscure, headline-seeking black hustlers to college campuses to incite hatred among African-Americans against Jews is a symptom of a sick and repulsive mindset. This mindset, however, is an effect—not the cause—of the racism in society at large, and, although I don't share it, I advise Jews and whites to make a more open, vigorous, sincere, and SUCCESSFUL fight against American racism before they publicly demand that African-American leaders "prove themselves" by taking on bigots in the black community.

For my part, I tried to ensure that *Muhammad Speaks* did not imply that Jews had a worse record in relationships with the African peoples than did Latinos, Asians, West/Central/East/Southern Europeans, or Arabs. I pointed out to the Black Muslims that it would be especially hypocritical for them to smear Jews, for I had seen Jewish-American businessmen in Mr. Muhammad's home. They were in an investment firm, the Wolverine Acceptance Corporation, that lent money to the Nation for many of its purchases of properties.

I also reminded Muslim Jew-baiters that it was the printing house of Lerner Newspapers in Chicago—Jewish-owned—that first printed *Muhammad Speaks* when it was launched in the early sixties under Malcolm X. Other printers had refused to print the "un-American" Muslim newspaper, but the Lerners were a progressive family and felt that freedom of the press should mean the freedom to get in print what you had the money to put into print. They defied racist comments and threats of sabotage and took on the job. It probably cost the Lerners many jobs over the years, and the Muslims didn't think the higher price the Lerners charged was unfair, in view of the risk.

Still, a few Black Muslims and nonMuslims would occasionally toss out a "joke" about how I was soft on the Jews. They'd say it must be some whammy from Karl Marx or other Jewish communists. What a brotherhood there is beneath the skins of racists of diverse shades! who share the belief that hatred, discord, and rivalry are the "natural" conditions under which different peoples interact.

I held to what I considered as my principled stand on our treatment of Jews and other nationalities until mid-1971, when I went to Mongolia for 17 days with my wife to see how the economic results of Mongolia's "non-capitalist path of development" compared with the living standards of Third World countries that remained tied with the capitalist bloc.

Authoritarian single-party rule has caused many problems for the Mongolians, as it has for people in other left-wing or right-wing totalitarian states, but I found then and still believe that the Mongolians, and the Cubans, and the Vietnamese stand a better chance of overcoming those problems and expanding democracy with full stomachs, good educational systems, and relatively full employment than they do in the debt- and crisis-ridden Third World countries dominated by the transnational monopolies and native profiteers.

My trip to Mongolia was as close to a vacation as I had during my four years at *Muhammad Speaks*—and it was definitely a working one, for I compiled three feature stories cum photos while there. Until this trip I had edited and rewritten every piece of copy, overseen the layout of every page, and stayed through the paste-up of every issue. In my absence two or three bigoted anti-Jewish statements had appeared in the newspaper, and at least one was immediately played up by the *New York Times*, via an Anti-Defamation League report, in an article about "Black Anti-Semitism." I regretted that the *Times* had been given this ammo, and didn't blame them or other Jewish-Americans for investigating these and similar statements by other African-Americans. But their approach to the subject was, and is, fundamentally unethical because they do not give similar attention to "Jewish Anti-Black Racism," which, given the relative wealth of the two communities, has a far greater impact on society.

I did not see much of the Messenger over my last three years at the paper, though we did have some brief talks by telephone. Certain Muslim factions that vied to influence him and enrich themselves off him as he grew feebler didn't want any outsiders around him. Still, I was able to follow his physical decline.

MALE PROBLEMS

The divisions were sharpening so much that one day the head of the Fruit of Islam was wounded slightly outside our plant in gunfire from an angry breakaway unit. During this period someone fired a rifle bullet through the office of his window; the shot came from a highway overpass about a half-mile away. The window was directly above mine, so it should have been obvious to the various rivals why I had no intention of getting into this internecine struggle by becoming a confidant of Allah's Last Messenger.

A few mosques harbored a criminal network that I don't think the Messenger ever knew about. Some older members of the Nation in various Southern cities used to write me about physical abuse of women in their temples or mosques, of beatings of men who objected to certain actions of these thugs and petty criminals, who seemed to operate with the approval of certain elements in a few mosques. Four representatives from a mosque in Florida came to my office to tell me they couldn't make their way through Mr. Muhammad's rings of aides to tell him their complaints. If the Messenger knew of their difficulties, they said, they were sure he'd straighten matters out as he had in the past, so would I please inform him of them? I

said I'd try if the opportunity arose, but that I doubted it would.

I received similar complaints from a few Muslim women who worked in the plant. The Nation, like most religious organizations, espoused and imposed a strongly patriarchal social order. As elsewhere, this ideology boiled down to condoning violence by husbands against wives.

The Muslim women had hoped that the Nation's emphasis on family harmony and achievement would mean that they were less likely to be beaten by a Muslim husband than by a "mentally dead Negro" spouse. Maybe they were right, I don't know. But there was wife-beating, nonetheless, and what galled the women who complained about it to me was that when they reported it to certain high-ranking men they had been laughed at.

"They told me that, because of the way the black man has been abused in the Devil's society, I should understand how my husband might lose his temper easily," a clerical worker told me. "They said I should take it 'for the good of your man.' And then in the next breath, they said that black women are like children, and the man has to discipline a child with a whipping. The truth is, most of the Muslim women are better educated than the men, and a lot of the men have been in prison, where they get conditioned to dishing out or taking physical abuse."

One of my relatives joined the Nation of Islam during my years there (some of their recruits I label as "flip-outs," and I'd say that, for a time, she fit that category), so I've learned more about male-female relationships and other aspects of Muslim customs than most outsiders. I remember how her 9-year old son was routinely punished in the Muslim cadre of boys—considering his age, tortured would not be an extreme word—because he had an assertive and independent spirit. Failure to follow some petty instruction or ritual could result in any one of several punishments-that-leave-no-telltale-marks common in the prisons that produced many Muslims, such as twisting limbs, squeezing fingers, and rapping the ribs. (These same prisons are filled to bursting now, and what spills out of them in the coming days will make the unpleasant idiosyncracies of the Nation of Islam seem tame because the conditions are more crowded, jobs are scarcer, and the mood of the incarcerated is more coldly violent and vengeful than ever.)

I don't wish to imply that petty crime, family violence, and hypocrisy were more serious problems within the Nation than outside it. But these violations of the utopian image of Islamic life did occur, and there was no mechanism for dealing with them under an autocratic system in which the autocrat was weakened by old age. One-man-rule and its corollary cult of the personality were two of several aspects of the Nation that seemed to assure its self-destruction once Allah's Last Messenger had left the scene.

Very few Muslims would complain to an outsider, however, and I was of little help to those who confided in me. All I could do was to suggest that they quit the organization if they didn't like what was happening or unite with other critics to improve it from within. The problem with that advice, some said, was that they could be accused by their tormenters of being "hypocrites," and a hypocrite could be severely punished, even fatally.

With Mr. Muhammad's asthma and other ailments taking their toll on him, I remembered Dick Durham's advice: "When it's time to quit, it's better not to quit. It's better to be let go. If you quit, you may be accused of being an enemy. But if they push you out, then they are in control."

I didn't know where I wanted to work next, but I definitely knew I didn't want to be around when Mr. Muhammad died. I thought his followers might plunge into dangerous hysteria if he died unexpectedly (a fear widespread at the time, though it proved to be groundless). One day in 1972, the assistant editor, Leon Forrest, came into my office and said he had something confidential to report. A few top Muslims had come to him to say that our news content was contradicting the Muslim point of view. They were going to denounce me to the Messenger on the grounds that I had made sexual advances toward Muslim women and had stated that the Messenger was senile and a drug addict. Forrest said that Charles Wartts, one of our poorest reporters at the time, would "verify" that I had made these statements about Mr. Muhammad at a luncheon. (Whether Wartts was an FBI informer or just dim-witted I never learned; I do know that, only a few months earlier, I'd managed to get his brother some good, free legal assistance in Minneapolis, which prevented his expulsion from college.)

I remembered the fateful luncheon. It was months earlier, after Savior's Day, the annual February celebration of the birth of W.D. Farad, the twentieth-century incarnation of Allah, according to the Nation's tenets. All of the faithful from Muslim mosques throughout the land gathered in Chicago every Savior's Day. The best orators among the ministers would deliver powerful speeches. Then, as they awaited the appearance of the Messenger of Allah, the throng of twenty thousand or so would shout repeatedly in strict martial cadence, clapping and stomping their feet on the stressed syllables:

All praise
Is due to Allah
For the Honorable Elijah Muhammad!

The chant becomes hypnotic after the first five minutes—then goes on for another five or ten. The fervor of true belief manifested in the unity of sound and in the sight of uniformly gowned women and the lean, stern-looking, neatly dressed men could shake the most irreligious soul. I wondered to myself if I would have been better off in some way if I had a mind that succumbed to the intoxications of religion. It was, as Mr. Muhammad intended it to be, a spiritual manifestation of Black Power.

A day or so after Savior's Day, we non-Muslim staffers were lunching in a local restaurant. I don't remember if it was Wartts or someone else who said: "The Messenger had asthma so bad a few days before Savior's Day that he was wheezing with every sentence. Then he got up there, delivered that fiery speech, and stood up the whole time. How could he do that? Is he on drugs?"

I reminded them that as he began his speech Mr. Muhammad had said, "They told me I should deliver my talk to you from my seat, but my doctors have given me something that could make any man stand." I told them that I had had asthma as a boy, and that the Messenger might have received an injection of adrenalin, a common treatment for severe asthma, so if he was "on drugs," it was probably adrenalin.

Someone else commented, "The Messenger is looking so weak, I think he must be getting senile." I said I doubted that because no senile person could have given a speech that was so clearly improvised and yet well-fashioned, dotted with reminiscences from readings and from earlier incidents in his life, as Mr. Muhammad had on Savior's Day.

True, I had uttered the words "drug" and "senile" in statements about Mr. Muhammad, but I certainly had not used the terms in the way my accusers charged. As for the claim that I'd flirted with Muslim women, I never learned what that was about. I could guess only that one of the Muslim reporters knew that Sister Cleo, my secretary, had told me about beatings administered by her new husband. Nothing could make me believe that Sister Cleo would lie about our chats, most of which were about pleasant topics. We did laugh a lot, however, and that was probably enough to rile a certain variety of Muslim male, the ones with sexual hang-ups that made their jaws tight any time they saw a Muslim woman look happy in public, period, let alone in conversation with an infidel.

"I don't want to stab you in the back," Forrest told me after describing the planned steps in the coup. "So what do you want me to say? They want me to say I heard you make these statements, and I can become editor after you're gone. But if you want to fight it, you know I'll back you all the way."

I told Leon that, as far as the intrigue went, they could throw this Brer Rabbit right into the briar patch, but at the same time I resented being pushed out under false charges. I said I would deny the charges, and he needn't say anything one way or the other, because if the charges stuck my exit would flow as Durham had advised. I would be the rejectee and not the rejector.

Word came to me the next day from one of the top officials that I was hereby suspended on the charges

Leon had cited until my "trial" at the Messenger's house, where I could defend myself. Meanwhile, he advised, I would be wise to look for other work.

"IF YOU WERE A GOOD EDITOR..."

Two weeks later—during which time I'd begun talking with the *Chicago Sun-Times*—I went to the Messenger's home for the last time. He looked unwell (though he was to hang on for three more years). "Well, Brother Editor," Mr. Muhammad began, "they've made some serious charges against you." Then he instructed an aide to describe the allegations briefly.

"All I can say, sir," I replied, "is that all three charges are false. I can explain my statements. And as to the accusation that I flirted with the sisters, I don't know which sisters I'm accused of doing what with or when I was supposed to have done it."

He said, "You have worked very well and faithfully for me." He paused, gave me one of his stony, piercing stares, then delivered a typically succinct, commonsense lesson on How To Manage People: "Brother Editor, if you were being a good editor the way you should, no one would be able to bring charges like this against you. You shouldn't be eating with these people who work for you. You shouldn't be laughing with our women. I'm going to have to suspend you until such time as I look into this further."

"Yes, sir," I said, silently recognizing my constitutional inability to profit from such advice.

So here was I, facing trumped-up charges just as H. Rap Brown had done in Louisiana when his predicament had altered my career and sent it careening toward the Nation of Islam. I could have quibbled with the Messenger. After all, hadn't he himself been accused by Malcolm X in 1964 of hanky-panky with several Muslim women? Hadn't others more recently claimed that he sired several children with several of the young women working in his house? Did an accusation prove guilt? But this was hardly a time even to think about quibbling. It was, in fact, one of the few times I've kept my mouth shut when that was the wiser course. Besides, I had no hard feelings. Mr. Muhammad had certainly been an honorable employer to me. It was his press, after all, and yet for four years he had let me feel as free as the man who owns one.

POSTSCRIPT

Muhammad Speaks withered away in the months following Elijah Muhammad's death in 1975. Wallace Muhammad, the son who inherited Elijah's religious leadership, changed the paper to *The Bilalian News* (named for Bilal, an African who was one of the first prophet Muhammad's top disciples), a newspaper which faded away over the next three or four years.

A schism took place that saw one branch of the Black Muslims leave Wallace (Warith-Deen) to follow Minister Louis Farrakhan. Farrakhan founded in the mid-eighties *The Final Call*, a weekly newspaper that is published in Chicago and distributed to most major cities. Farrakhan's newspaper is not a clone of *Muhammad Speaks*, but of all the would-be successors it most closely resembles the original. Farrakhan attracts a lot of publicity with his remarks that appear to be designed to whip up hostility against Jews. I met Farrakhan several times in my *Muhammad Speaks* days and, although I don't know him well enough to identify the motives behind his controversial statements, I do feel that his portrayal as some sort of monster is simplistic. I think he is practicing, quite sincerely, an eye-for-an-eye/tooth-for-a-tooth brand of ethnic relations that he was not the first to invent.

Like Meir Kahane of the Jewish Defense League and many extreme nationalists the world over, Farrakhan has a lot of raw courage. When he headed the New York temple of the Nation in the late sixties, Farrakhan and three or four of his aides held off the New York police when they attempted an illegal, provocative raid of the religious buildings. And he and the Black Muslims did so without weapons. Eyewitnesses reported to me that the Muslims' obvious willingness to die in unarmed singlehanded combat with the police seemed to stun the police into halting their action. A similar incident occurred in New Orleans in 1971, although Farrakhan wasn't present at that time. Unarmed Muslims confronted armed mad-dog police and even disarmed them despite taking several gunshot wounds.

Farrakhan's approach to me seems to be: "We didn't invent racism or the notion that this is a dog-eat-dog world with a hierarchy of nations that operate under the rule the devil take the hindmost. But if that is the world as our foes see it, then Africans, African-Americans, and other people holding the short end of the stick had better unite and come up with the intellectual, political, military, and any other kind of wherewithal required to protect their people and enhance their chances of holding the big end of the stick."

If my family or I were under any threat of violence, and I was in a position to turn to Farrakhan or Jesse Jackson or any other black leader for help, I would choose Farrakhan. I think a lot of black people who are under many kinds of threats to their existence more concrete than any I face feel the same way.

After working for the *Chicago Sun-Times*, I moved to the *New York Times* as a copy editor on the national desk. I have since pursued public relations journalism at Ford Motor Company, worked as an editor and writer for the *Ann Arbor* (Michigan) *Observer*, taught writing and African fiction, and served as executive editor of *Michigan Today*, a 300,000-circulation tabloid published by the University of Michigan.

THE *GUARDIAN* GOES TO WAR

Jack A. Smith

America's "underground" press of the 1960s and 1970s played a key role in building domestic popular opposition to the Vietnam War—an important factor leading to the defeat of Washington's imperial adventure in Indochina. Within this assortment of several hundred alternative publications, none matched the antiwar influence exercised by the independent left-wing weekly, the *Guardian*, published in New York for a national audience (at the time) of 24,000 paid subscribers and an estimated 75,000 readers.

Week after week between the main antiwar years of 1965 and 1975, the *Guardian* unfailingly focused on supporting the Indochinese liberation forces and on convincing the American people to oppose the war. The paper's influence was based on the fact that it was able to publish exclusive articles from the battlefields and capitals of Indochina throughout the war; on its independent, anti-imperialist analysis of Washington's policies, backed by solidly researched news reporting; on its in-depth, nonsectarian coverage of antiwar activities in the United States; and on the fact that its reporting of the war was considered essential reading by leading activists and decision makers within the various antiwar, civil rights, student, feminist, and progressive movements throughout the country.

Underground newspapers of the period were unanimously against the war—but their respective influences largely were upon local or regional audiences and the individual papers varied greatly in their political character and journalistic calibre. The left party papers—*The Daily World* (Communist Party), *The*

Smith was an editor for United Press International before serving a year in federal prison as a conscientious objector. Leaving prison in 1963 (and "blackballed" in the commercial press), he joined the staff of the the *Guardian* weekly, where he remained until 1983. He was managing editor and chief editor from 1967-82. In recent years he has been the editor of several trade magazines and presently serves as editorial director for a nonprofit organization.

Militant (Socialist Workers Party), *Workers World* (Workers World Party), and several others—all had strong antiwar positions and represented organizations that played important roles in building opposition to the war. Still, none was able to match the *Guardian* in terms of reaching the forces of the developing "new left" for several reasons. One was the fact that the *Guardian* published supurb antiwar material, spoke directly to the political concerns being raised by the "new left" and other militant forces, and remained independent of organizational control. Another was that many members of the "new left" distrusted established leftist parties and rejected many of the lessons they sought to convey to the young activists. The positive side of this phenomenon was that the "new left" for a few years tried to open some original territory for practical and theoretical exploration and created innovative techniques for confronting the power of the state at various levels. The negative was that a great deal of important knowledge and history was ignored to the ultimate detriment of the "new left" itself, a contributing factor to its demise in the early seventies.

Even though the *Guardian* metamorphosed from "progressive" to "radical" to "Marxist-Leninist" during the decade from 1965-1975 (see sidebar 1), it retained its political and organizational independence, did not deviate from its stress upon "uniting all who could be united" in the fight against the war, waged combat against "right opportunism" and "left dogmatism" within the movement, and—perhaps above all—continued to publish timely and superior articles, commentary, and polemics about the war for over 10 years.

The *Guardian* remains publishing to this day, of course, one of the few non-party radical newspapers to have continued into the 1990s. It was formed as the *National Guardian* by James Aronson, Jack McManus, and Cedric Belfrage in 1948 to generally reflect the views of supporters of the short-lived Progressive Party of Henry Wallace. The PP constituted a progressive political alternative to the Democratic Party at the dawn of the Cold War when it was clear both major parties were pushing nuclear-armed America toward confrontation with the war-weakened Soviet Union. The party advocated economic justice, racial equality, and a continuation of the wartime cooperation and friendship between the U.S. and the USSR. Communists were involved with the party but did not control it. The *Guardian* at the time described its politics as "independent progressive" and viewed itself as a transmission belt from liberalism to a more enlightened progressive politics. The paper enjoyed the support of a broad spectrum of the left from disenchanted liberals to communists. Marxists were represented on the *Guardian*'s staff and in the leadership from the beginning, but the paper did not openly advocate revolutionary

politics for another 20 years. The paper survived the 1950s despite the dissolution of the PP, the period of political witch-hunts in America (which resulted in the deportation of one of its three editor-owners), the Korean War (which the paper strongly opposed, virtually alone), the Rosenberg execution (the *Guardian* was the first to take up their cause and remains its champion to this day), and a Cold War atmosphere that resulted in a sharp drop in circulation, money, and political influence.

The *Guardian* published articles during the 1950s supporting the Indochinese liberation struggle against the French before most Americans ever heard of Vietnam. Correspondent Wilfred Burchett, who began writing for the paper from North Korea during the U.S. "police action," began to supply the *Guardian* readers with accounts from Indochina in the later fifties and was among the first to point out growing American involvement in Indochina after the French defeat in 1954. He had excellent connections with all the top leaders of the Indochina struggle, starting with Vietnamese President Ho Chi Minh.

By 1962, when the anti-Vietnam War movement was just beginning to stir ever so cautiously, the *Guardian* was publishing long articles from Burchett datelined, "From the Liberated Zones" of Vietnam. Burchett's extraordinary *Guardian* dispatches from Vietnam, which continued until the end of the war in 1975, were instrumental in developing what the Vietnamese termed their "second front" in the war: the antiwar movement in the United States. Years later, activists of the period point to Burchett as the author and the *Guardian* as the newspaper that first opened their eyes to the truth about the conflict.

Likewise, a great many of the new underground papers took their lead from the *Guardian* when it came to facts, figures, and analysis about the war. The paper's articles were reprinted frequently in scores of local alternative publications, even some "countercultural" journals that had little affection for much else about the openly Marxist *Guardian*.

The *Guardian*'s long-time point of view about the outcome of the war, first put forward in the mid-1960s, was that Vietnam would win eventually, no matter how many troops and weapons the United States dispatched to Indochina. Indeed, *Vietnam Will Win* is the title of a successful book by Burchett published in 1968 by the the *Guardian* and distributed by Monthly Review Press.

In addition to Burchett's reports from the war zones and from Hanoi, Phnom Penh, Vientiane, Beijing, Paris, and elsewhere, the *Guardian* published frequent editorials about the war, detailed analyses of Washington's political, diplomatic, and military maneuvers, and not only coverage of demonstrations throughout the country (one issue alone has individual

Sidebar 1: Brief Directory of the *Guardian* Goes to War Definitions

A few informal 1960s-70s definitions may be in order to better understand some of the terms used in this article:

"Progressive" meant a position that was considerably to the left of Democratic Party liberalism on domestic issues and was opposed to the U.S. role in fostering the Cold War internationally. In certain cases it described non-communists who tended to support the USSR as well. The *Guardian* defined itself as a "progressive newsweekly" from 1948 to 1967 when it changed to "radical newsweekly."

"Radical" politics at the time was considered to be to the left of progressive politics. Domestically, the term embraced those who advocated not just major reforms in the capitalist system but fundamental (to the root) changes in U.S. society by various means, including, in some cases, mass strikes, civil disobedience, social rebellion, and armed struggle. In international issues, radicals generally supported Third World revolutions, defended the socialist countries, and sought the defeat of U.S. imperialism. The *Guardian* changed its self-definition from radical to Marxist-Leninist around 1974 but continued to refer to itself as independent radical on its page one nameplate—an indication of the elasticity of the word radical. (The paper always retained the word "independent" in front of either progressive or radical in order to indicate that it made up its own mind and did not follow the dictates of this or that party or organization.)

"Anti-imperialism" signified opposition to Washington's military, economic, and political activities abroad. One of the struggles within the antiwar movement at the time was between those who opposed the war because they wanted the killing to stop or thought the United States made a bad error getting involved in Indochina and those (such as the *Guardian* and much of the left) who viewed the United States as an imperial aggressor which should be defeated politically and militarily.

"Marxism" generally defined the economic, philosophic, and historical doctrines of Karl Marx, and Frederick Engels, which were undergoing a revival in the United States during the late 1960s—largely from within the radical student, civil rights, and antiwar movements—after a marked decline in the repressive 1950s.

"Marxism-Leninism" indicated the merger of Marxism and V.I. Lenin's (and the Bolshevik Party's) theory and practice about revolution, imperialism, party organization, the dictatorship of the proletariat, and the building of socialist society. By the late sixties, Stalin's negative contributions to Marxism-Leninism were rather universally criticized in form but continued to be tolerated to a greater or lesser extent in practice. The term "Marxism-Leninism" was upheld by a number of sharply opposed political formations from the Communist Parties of the USSR and other members of the "socialist camp" to that of China (the leftist archenemy of the "camp" at the time) or of Trotskyism, which criticized the parties of both the USSR and China (and most other communist countries and movements) from the perspective of Leon Trotsky, whom Stalin hounded out of the USSR and arranged to have murdered.

"Mao Tsetung Thought," the Marxist-Leninist varient in China, became popular with a fairly large section of the new left (and the *Guardian*, among others) in the late sixties and early seventies because of its direct call for revolution, its dedication to building what was viewed as a "purer" form of communism than existed elsewhere, and its criticism of the USSR for distorting socialism ("revisionism"), for dominating other socialist and noncapitalist countries ("social-imperialism"), and for "colluding and contenting" with the United States. The term "Maoism" was not used by its most serious devotees in the United States because the "ism" denoted a finished, closed system and the "Thought" was evolving. The Sino-Soviet split doesn't exist now but it was a major element in world affairs from the late 1950s to the early 1980s.

The "new left" was a broad term for younger radicals in the United States and abroad who sought fundamental and revolutionary changes in capitalist societies and in the oppressed Third World but who frequently rejected the established communist organizations as too dogmatic or sectarian or reformist or counter-revolutionary. The new left in the United States, largely associated with the Students for a Democratic Society, existed for only a few years until SDS self-destructed in a binge of ultra-leftism fostered by many of its leading elements in the early 1970s. A number of those who remained politically active after this debacle were drawn to the Maoist varient of Marxism-Leninism, organizing several national parties and regional groupings in the United States which lasted several more years. The *Guardian* played an important role in this process. The new movement declined in the mid-seventies when China began cozying up to the United States and started misidentifying the USSR as not only "capitalists" but the "main danger" in the world. The *Guardian* never bought the "capitalist" and "main danger" lines but—in keeping with its Third World orientation—didn't make an overt break with China until the Beijing government started undermining certain revolutionary movements and governments in Asia, Africa, and Latin America.

reports of antiwar actions from over 25 different U.S. cities), but also inside reportage about the prospects and problems of the antiwar movement itself. Even activists who had little political use for the *Guardian* (pacifists who disagreed with the paper's support for violent revolution; liberals who thought it was too radical; single-issue supporters who opposed the paper's dedication to building a multi-issue antiwar movement; supporters of the Communist Party who thought the paper was ultra-left and too critical of the USSR; pro-Maoists who claimed the *Guardian* wasn't "Maoist" enough, etc.) felt the need to read the paper because its Indochina coverage was peerless.

The war in Indochina was only one of the *Guardian*'s editorial concerns, of course. By the mid-sixties the paper was reporting intensively on the civil rights struggle and the student rebellion, among other activist causes of this incredible era. At the same time, a battle of sorts was taking place within the *Guardian* itself between a majority of its 25-person staff and the remaining founder-owner, editor James Aronson (of the other founders, Jack McManus had died and Cedric Belfrage was in exile in Mexico). The principal issue, as defined by the staff, was that the *Guardian* "was not growing with the movements"—a reference not only to the fact that the paper was still only 12 tabloid pages a week (too small to adequately cover all the struggles) but much more importantly it was not taking a "radical enough stance on the domestic movements for social change" and on "certain international developments."

Differences between the staff and the editor actually had begun during the summer of 1964 when Aronson fearing that right-wing Republican candidate Barry Goldwater might win the November election advocated that the *Guardian* call for the reelection of Democrat Lyndon Johnson. Until then, the *Guardian* prided itself on the fact that it never supported a candidate of either big party for the presidency—a position consistent with its expressed mission of breaking the two-party monopoly in U.S. politics. Virtually the entire staff disagreed with Aronson, including Russ Nixon (an academic and union educator who was active with the old Progressive Party), whom Aronson had recently brought to the paper as general manager and intended coowner. Editor Aronson was so soundly defeated in the debates that the *Guardian* did not champion Johnson (who soon escalated the Vietnam War to an extent Goldwater never could have matched).

The owner removed Nixon from the *Guardian* not too long after the showdown over the election. The grounds put forward had nothing to do with the election struggle, but some staffers were convinced there was a direct connection. In order to obtain approval for the firing, Aronson offered the staff committee (a kind of in-house union) the one-half stock ownership that had been promised to Nixon. The committee accepted the offer and Nixon was purged—an action that ultimately brought together several staff members who found they shared a critique of the way the paper was developing politically and journalistically.

In essence a "new left" vs. "old left" disagreement, some staff members began expressing the view that the *Guardian* was too concerned with the defensive politics of the 1950s to the detriment of its coverage of the more assertive movements of the 1960s. By the mid-sixties, Aronson was being directly urged by many on the staff to adopt an explicit stand in favor of the more radical movements for social change in the United States and open support for socialist revolution to the world.

As time went on, a majority of the staff aligned itself behind a program demanding three specific changes: 1) a political move to the left editorially; 2) improvements in the paper itself, including a new design, the addition of columnists, more controversy, the hiring of a foreign editor to improve coverage from abroad, and broader, deeper coverage of domestic left movements; 3) more internal democracy and worker participation in political, editorial, and business decisions. (Indeed, some within the staff also had the objective of transforming the ownership and organizational structure into a cooperative based on workers' control, which ultimately is what took place. The *Guardian* remains a cooperative with an elected leadership to this day.)

Aronson, an experienced and respected journalist, a dedicated progressive, and a favorite of the "old" left, was unable to respond creatively to the changes sought by the staff. He saw the challenge to improve the *National Guardian* (as it was still called) both as a personal attack and a reflection of the "immaturity" of the developing new political forces that in the next several years would shake America to its foundations. He rejected all the requested changes.

The staff majority continued to press its demands, however—respectfully but with additional urgency by the beginning of 1967. Then, totally unexpectedly, Aronson announced his resignation, turning over all stock in the company to the staff committee. There were those who suspected the resignation was a ploy to bring the staff to its senses, to force it to withdraw its demands, and to insist that the editor remain in place. But no such sentiment arose, though the paper the staff was about to inherit was deeply in debt and may not have been able to survive the year, especially with the prospect that "old left" money sources inevitably would be encouraged to stop making contributions now that the *Guardian* was about to repose in alleged "new left" hands. Within two months, most of the paper's big contributors withdrew their support, leaving the *Guardian* near destitution. In another two months virtually the rest of the support network disintegrated when the *Guardian* decided for the first time (in

— Jack A. Smith —

response to the June 1967 Mideast war) to support the national rights of the Palestinian people—a position the previous ownership had not thought wise to articulate.

The *Guardian* staff took immediate measures to save the paper—tough, innovative measures that worked. The business was reconstituted as a staff-run cooperative with equal (valueless) "shares" to full-time workers and an elected leadership responsible to the members. One of the first acts by that leadership was to change the pay structure to one of complete equality—the top editors and the mail room clerk now earned the same amount of money each week—$60 (with a small child-support allowance for parents). The new pay scale was a big step down for most of the staff. Editors and senior employees had been earning between $120 and $135 a week (pay was pegged at two-thirds of Newspaper Guild standards before the change). Work hours were extended as well—from a 35- to 40-hour weekly average to between 50 and 70 hours, depending on position. Several major cost-cutting measures were introduced at the same time. The reforms even included knocking down the walls separating the editor's office from the newsroom. Those were heady days of endless work and collective discussion and struggle for the *Guardian* staff. In retrospect, while some of the reforms were clearly utopian, most of them served the very practical purpose of keeping the paper alive in addition to fulfilling aspirations for a socialist-type collective enterprise.

The importance of this revolution within the *Guardian* (the "National" was dropped as part of developing a new political image) was several-fold:

- The new pay and hours structure enabled the paper to withstand the financial blow caused by Aronson's resignation and the reaction among some previous supporters to the *Guardian*'s criticism of Israel (thousands of subscriptions were cancelled because of the criticism as well).

- The *Guardian* quickly became identified as much more of a "movement" newspaper and no longer the organ of the "old left" by taking certain stances to the left of its previous positions and by developing "comradely" ties with many of the more radical movement organizations. For example, the paper began providing increased coverage of the activities of Student Nonviolent Coordinating Committee (SNCC) and Students for a Democratic Society (SDS). SDS was reported upon in minute detail. Elected leaders of the paper were assigned to develop "organization-to-

organization" ties with several political groups and antiwar coalitions.

- As such, the influence of the paper greatly expanded and circulation grew in the politically explosive years of 1967-1969.

One result of these developments was that a large portion of the lost financial support was replaced by many new "movement people"—thousands of "sustainer" readers who now donated a few dollars each month in place of several large contributors to the "old" *Guardian*. (A number of these small givers, by the way, remained with the paper from the old days.) A year after the cooperative took over, the paper had increased in size and circulation was healthy—largely through great staff sacrifices and (non-financial) support from the broader movement. (For instance, SDS student activists began selling the paper on scores of campuses for the first time, contributing to the gain of thousands of new subs that made up for the losses due to the paper's support for Palestinian rights. Radical students also began sending in news about demonstrations and the like. Further, a dozen *Guardian* news/circulation bureaus—staffed by volunteer activist-journalists—were opened in cities around the United States, greatly expanding the paper's coverage of the domestic antiwar struggle.) Previously two or three individuals outside the New York office helped with circulation and occasional reporting.

Throughout this time of change at the *Guardian*—a period that saw enormous staff turnover as people burned out quickly from overwork and underpay or from mounting political tensions and diversions—the paper continued to deepen its antiwar perspective and broaden its coverage. Burchett not only remained with the paper after the change to a cooperative but increased his articles to more than one a week at the request of the new editors. Such coverage was expensive since Burchett was constantly traveling to exotic locations and communicated via commercial cables, but the paper gladly paid the bills in order to fulfill its political responsibilities to the antiwar movement.

By the end of 1969, after much turmoil, the *Guardian* had not only doubled in size but attained a paid readership of 24,000—the highest since the early 1950s.

Along with its more radical politics and new free-swinging manner, the *Guardian* was becoming a serious political force within the people's movements in the United States. The paper's elected leadership was taking part in important movement discussions and decisions, especially in the antiwar and student movements. In this connection, the *Guardian* became an even greater asset for the Indochinese revolutionaries because the

January 25: "The National Mobilization Committee to End the War in Vietnam, the coalition which has presided over the growth-to-relevance of the U.S. antiwar movement, is in serious trouble....Where has the mass support gone? Why are so many active peace workers no longer showing up at protests? Why are radicals turning away from mobilizations?....The organized antiwar movement began to decline when its liberal base, never politicized, withered away when the U.S. government undercut its moderate demands with moderate action. This cannot be permitted to happen again, assuming the antiwar forces grow large enough to worry about a new decline. The antiwar movement must become a consciously anti-imperialist movement. New strategies, new tactics, must be devised in coming months to achieve this objective."

March 3: "The change in administrations [which some peace forces thought would help end the war] has changed nothing in Vietnam except that the imperialist adventure known as Johnson's War has now become Nixon's War."

May 17: "On May 8, the National Liberation Front [of South Vietnam] submitted a 10-point proposal for ending the Vietnam war. The *Guardian* endorses the proposal absolutely and calls on the antiwar and radical movements to support the Front document as the basis for peace in Vietnam."

May 24: "The NLF call for a provisional coalition government must be supported by the U.S. movement. Only such a government, based on the broadest popular mandate, can oversee elections for a permanent government and finally determine the reunification of Vietnam."

June 14 (Written to counteract a trend in the student movement and the broader mass movement to disengage from mass antiwar demonstrations to turn attention to "local organizing"): "With a few laudable exceptions, the new left is failing its responsibility to Vietnamese national liberation. National SDS's indifference to serious involvement in the antiwar struggle is...reckless....The war for independence and freedom of South Vietnam is being waged on three fronts [a continual *Guardian* refrain]—on the battlefields of Vietnam, across the conference table in Paris and by the movement in the U.S. These fronts must be synchronized to produce the swiftest victory possible for the people of Vietnam behind the leadership of the NLF."

June 21: "Nixon has no intention of ending the war any earlier than he is forced to on the battlefield, in Paris and by opposition to the war at home. The struggle against the war at home is now central to a swift people's victory in Vietnam. Nixon thinks he can bluff it out, neutralizing antiwar opposition by engaging in meaningless troop withdrawals."

July 12 (Written in response to movement forces that wanted to remove the struggle against imperialism from the overall "peace" struggle): "The struggle against imperialism and its concomitant racism is the primary revolutionary struggle of today in the oppressor as well as the oppressed nations....The struggle against imperialism and racism transcends the quest for peace. While imperialism and racism stand, there can be no such thing as peace."

September 13 (On the death of Ho Chi Minh): "The liberation of the Vietnamese people and the people of the world will proceed. Ho Chi Minh is no more dead than man's eternal quest for freedom."

---

paper's line on the war was extremely close to that of the patriots who were waging the military and diplomatic offensive. The paper was also in communication with the Indochinese leadership, with whom it occasionally exchanged opinions.

As the sixties closed, the *Guardian* was in the thick of the antiwar struggle, putting forward a very specific political line and fighting for it within the movement. Sidebar 2, for instance, shows a sampling of excerpts from antiwar editorials published during 1969.

No other U.S. publication at the time could rival the *Guardian* in its weekly quest to represent the interests of the oppressed Third World "within the imperialist heartland," especially those of the Indochinese peoples and their revolutionary leadership in the fight for national independence against the American war machine. The *Guardian* saw this as its special task and went about it with single-minded discipline, helping to change positively the nature of the antiwar struggle and to make a contribution toward the Indochinese

victory at the same time—no insignificant accomplishment for a small, overworked cooperative of independent left-wing newspaper workers without a party, organization, or funds.

At the same time that it focused principal attention on the antiwar struggle, the paper was taking a number of controversial positions within the left that were earning it enemies as well as friends. It was fighting hard against ultra-leftism within the movement on the one hand while developing openly Marxist-Leninist politics on the other. In the process it began launching attacks against the ultra-left Weatherman faction of Students for a Democratic Society in 1969, for instance. The *Guardian* saw Weatherman for the totally destructive force it was—destructive of the antiwar and student movements and the developing "new" left Marxist-Leninist movement as well.

In October 1969 Weatherman held a provocative demonstration in Chicago which inspired this comment from the *Guardian* October 18: "The most significant aspect of the surrealist contretemps created by the

October 25: (Written to counteract a radical trend toward viewing liberals as enemies): "Radicals have a dual task....First we must help continue the expansion of the antiwar movement until political pressure and fear of domestic turmoil is such that the ruling class brings the troops home. Second, we must increase attempts to propel the movement to the left. Thus, the radical left will find it necessary to work with liberals to broaden the base of the antiwar movement. At the same time, the radical left will have to engage in political struggle with these liberals to stem the rightward drift and to resume the movement's developing anti-imperialist identity."

November 22 (Written to attack "right opportunism" in the movement): "The major political question raised by the Nov. 15 action is the rightward direction of the leadership of the antiwar coalition. The liberal Vietnam Moratorium Committee, despite having hardly organized for the Nov. 15 demonstrations, gained significant influence with the Mobilization Committee coalition in the days leading up to mid-November. This was more covert than overt. The existence of the Vietnam Moratorium Committee and the millions who attended the Moratorium demonstrations in October gave considerable leverage to liberal elements within the Mobilization coalition and the more conservative left wing elements which traditionally seek the opportunity to minimize radical politics to attract greater numbers....We believe the antiwar movement will continue to grow. But an intelligent left—one capable of dealing both with the mindless tactical militancy of the ultra-left and the liberal accommodations of the conservative left—is essential to this process."

November 29: "The calculated slaughter of the innocents of Songmy, the tiny South Vietnamese hamlet of the lyric name, is neither a mistake nor an aberration, neither a temporary moral lapse on the part of weary GIs nor the debased sadism of a few perverts. The murder of more than 500 civilian residents of Songmy—children in arms, women and men—is the quintessential expression of American imperialism and racism directed toward one hamlet in ravaged South Vietnam."

December 13: "America is defeated in Vietnam, defeated by the most important invention of the 20th Century—people's war [the war went on for several more years, of course, but to the Guardian defeat was a given]. The U.S. is resorting to genocide because the 'enemy' is the entire people of Vietnam, not simply a hundred thousand guerrilla soldiers. It is a war to exterminate a people. And, through incredible hardship, sacrifice and heroism, the people are winning."

December 27: "The movement must not underestimate the importance of nationally coordinated mass marches and rallies around the political slogan of immediate withdrawal from Vietnam. Granted no mass demonstration is going to end the war and granted that some movement veterans may be bored by 'the same old peace rally.' The point remains that the vehicle of the mass demonstration is effective and the best method found so far to increase the numbers of the movement and to make the movement visible—not only to the White House and to world public opinion but also to our Vietnamese comrades." (Regarding this last point, the Guardian fully understood just how important it was for the morale of the Indochinese people—and thus their fighting spirit—to know about continual mass opposition to the war in the U.S.)

Weatherman microfaction of SDS last week was that the rest of the movement had the revolutionary wisdom to stay away. It amounted to a movementwide boycott of left adventurism....Regardless of Weatherman's deserved isolation and small group mentality, the fact remains that through the inexcusable folly of SDS as a whole, the Weatherman microfaction is in control of the largest white radical organization in the country [SDS had 100,000 members in the late sixties]....It is to be hoped the whole radical movement has learned some lessons during the organizational rule of Bonnie, Clyde and Our Gang [insiders understood who was meant]. First, 'left' adventurism is the quickest road to irrelevance. Second, sectarianism, dogmatism and opportunism are not substitutes for developing a revolutionary Marxist-Leninist ideology suitable for America."

Over the next few months, some ultra-leftists and anarchists within the "new" left (cheered on to a certain degree by some social-democrats who did not fully appreciate the actual stakes involved) were beginning to develop reasons for desiring to curtail the paper's influence—the ultra-left because of the Guardian's attacks on "infantile leftism" and small group violence; anarchists because while the paper was organized along cooperative, egalitarian lines it politically opposed syndicalism, the notion of "skipping stages" in the development of the stateless society, and the concept of "absolute equality"; the social-democrats because the Guardian was beginning to declare itself openly Marxist-Leninist. All of these essentially contradictory forces seemed to join in a critique of the Guardian that nearly resulted in the ruin of the newspaper in April 1970.

The precipitating event appeared to be a front-page editorial in March attacking the tactic of "individual [small group] terrorism" from a Leninist point of view. The editorial was occasioned by the deaths of three Weathermen in a bomb explosion. A couple of weeks later, the Guardian office, located on three floors of a tenement in New York's Lower East Side, was broken into and (as was reported at the time) stormed by "about 50 assorted ultra-leftists, anarchists and other self-styled 'revolutionaries'...in an effort to prevent the paper from going to press."

This group occupied the offices, destroyed equipment, scattered (or stole) files, and threatened dire consequences if any of the staff returned. They had intended to seize control of the paper before it went to press, change its political contents, and continue to function as the publisher of the newly titled *Liberated Guardian*. The new publication was to have reduced the amount of space given over to the antiwar struggle in order to concentrate more on "revolutionary" domestic political and lifestyle affairs.

Fortunately, the *Guardian* staff anticipated the office would be attacked shortly. Thus, while it conveyed the public impression of business as usual inside the building, much of the staff was in hiding in a secret Brooklyn apartment producing the next issue. The workers brought some key equipment and the precious mailing list with them. As soon as the attack came, the front page and three inside pages were quickly made over for an account of the invasion and the paper went to press (thanks to a different printer who had been alerted that a job might come barreling in at the last moment).

Without being able to dictate their version of the story to the *Guardian* readers as they had planned, the "liberators" decided to publish another newspaper titled, the *Liberated Guardian*. This publication came out for several issues before suspending publication.

The *Guardian* survived—but the next year was difficult indeed. With no money to replace much of the lost equipment, many jobs now had to be done by hand. The mailing list was saved but contributor files had been destroyed (a very serious blow). The threat of violence hung in the air for months. The new office was about as dark and dingy as they come. Staff pay had to be cut—this time below the sub-minimum wage for people who were working astronomical hours.

The early 1970s seemed to be more difficult for many of the progressive movements than for the *Guardian*, however. The period saw the near collapse of the broad antiwar movement (but it revived in lesser form and continued the struggle until the end of the war), the virtual liquidation of the civil rights movement combined with the intensified repression against what was left of the black liberation struggle, the self-destruction of the student movement, and the total fragmentation of the "new" left.

Despite these problems, the *Guardian* never skipped an issue and its antiwar coverage throughout the period was spectacular. In about a year the *Guardian*'s internal wounds healed and the staff decided to celebrate by redesigning the paper, again making it more lively, and expanding the size once more. The new "look" was a big success with the readers, many of whom now found the *Guardian* their only lifeline to what remained of the movement.

By 1973 the *Guardian* began to develop influence in the emerging "anti-revisionist" Marxist-Leninist movement, an outgrowth of a section of the "new left," which lasted for several years—but that's another story, as is the frequent saga of political splits and difficulties within the cooperative itself. Suffice to say that the paper continued to put antiwar coverage first and to place the main emphasis on uniting the left and progressive forces to defeat U.S. imperialism. It continued with this orientation until that extraordinary day in the spring of 1975 when it was no longer necessary to predict "Vietnam will win," because Vietnam actually did win at long last.

People in the *Guardian* office were weeping the day it became official. Everyone who stuck with the paper through those tough, exciting years was proud. They knew they had played an important role in helping to mobilize the "second front" that their Indochinese friends said was vital so long ago. The *Guardian* went on to report many different struggles and is still doing so, but to those who were fortunate enough to have played some role in guiding the paper during those incredible antiwar years, the struggle against imperialism in Southeast Asia was this great "underground" newspaper's finest moment.

OFF OUR BACKS: THE FIRST DECADE (1970-1980)

Carol Anne Douglas and Fran Moira

off our backs was founded in late 1969 with $400 that had been collected to start an antiwar coffeehouse for GIs. The women who started it felt that, since the Left press was not covering the new women's liberation movement adequately, a women's newspaper was essential. Marlene Wicks was one of the co-founders.

Ten years later, in an interview that appeared in *oob*'s tenth anniversary issue, she remembered the circumstances surrounding that decision

> The paper really started because Marilyn Salzman-Webb [see appendix 1, "*off our backs* and the Feminist Dream," for Webb's own story of the founding of *off our backs*] was writing for the *Guardian* in New York and every time she would send articles having to do with women they would be totally screwed up and edited to the point that they wouldn't make any sense at all. So after a meeting at the Womens Liberation Center on Mintwood Place we were rapping about what we could do about that and I don't know who said first, "Why don't we start our own?" but the response was "Yes, let's do that."

The first issue, a 12-page tabloid, burst onto the scene on February 27, 1970, with articles that covered abortions at a DC hospital, medical problems with the pill, and how to use the diaphragm, plus an editorial calling on all women to join in a celebration of International Women's Day March 8.

Douglas has worked on *off our backs* since 1973. She supports herself with a reporting job for a non-profit magazine. *Moira* worked on *off our backs* from 1971 to 1986. She is a professional health journalist.

Portions of this article appeared in *off our backs*.

Also in that first editorial, the editors explained why they had chosen the paper's name:

> The name *off our backs* was chosen because it reflects our understanding of the dual nature of the women's movement. Women need to be free of men's domination to find their real identities, redefine their lives, and fight for the creation of a society in which they can lead decent lives as human beings. At the same time, women must become aware that there would be no oppressor without the oppressed, that we carry the responsibility for withdrawing the consent to be oppressed. We must strive to get off our backs, and with the help of our sisters to oppose and destroy that system which fortifies the supremacy of men while exploiting the mass for the profit of the few.

As Marlene recalled, the name "reflected three things: We wanted to be off our backs in terms of being fucked. We wanted to be off our backs in terms of being the backbone of American or every society or culture with no power. And we wanted the flack we would get from everyone about being strong to roll off our backs."

The subtitle, "a women's news journal," was an attempt to convey that it would carry as much news as possible about *all* women and that women and groups from all over the country were invited to contribute articles. Over the course of the first volume, it was called "a women's liberation bi-weekly," a "women's liberation newspaper," and then again a "women's news journal," which it has remained to this day. According to Marilyn, the initial community response was "overwhelming." "I don't remember exactly how many mailings we sent out—we sent to women's groups all over the country plus the names from our Vietnam Summer mailing list—but the response was almost 100 percent."

Women became *oob* collective members in those days simply by being there. In fact, said Marlene, "We gave credit to anyone who walked in and typed a few dots." Fran Moira's entry onto the staff agrees with Marlene's memory. "When I walked into the *oob* basement in May of 1971 in time to help put out issue number 22 and asked how to join the newspaper, a collective member brought me the roller-dex and said if I was willing to put my name and phone number in it I was on the paper. My name appeared on the masthead from that issue on."

Most of the early staff members came out of the antiwar movement, though not as participants in the New Left. According to Marlene

Marilyn was an intellectual and she was about three years ahead of us politically. I wasn't part of the New Left because I was out of that age bracket. Reading Betty Friedan really turned me on and then Doris Lessing. I was hanging around being a pissed off housewife and when the women's movement came it really grabbed me. I had gone to demonstrations against the war but didn't really work at it.

I was working-class and "climbed" to the middle-class through marriage. Marilyn was middle-class. Onka [Dekkers] was working-class. I don't know what you'd call people who were very well educated and doing well financially yet are socialists. They wouldn't want you to call them middle-class. Heidi and Nan were from that background. Coletta was working-class. Norma went to college but I think her background was working-class.

There was a spirit of iconoclasm, looseness, and humor among the women and throughout the pages of the newspaper then, no matter the serious internal struggles or the weightier contents of each issue. We spent as much time creating colorful, imaginative covers and centerspreads as we did agonizing over the substance of collective articles. "Culture Vulture," our special culture section, was flying in the sixth issue, and "Chicken Lady," our listing of events and new publications, was hatched in the twelfth issue. For members like Marlene, the work day was pretty much "from nine in the morning until eleven at night and it was *not* a drag!"

I was totally high on the paper. I wanted lots of people to come in and put out! Frances Chapman was wonderful in this way. She would come in, edit, be very consoling too. Johanna Vogelsang was a wonderful discovery for us. She's the artist you saw so much in the early issues.

I believed that keeping the paper going was a matter of survival for us all. I felt as if we were in Hanoi and we were going to be bombed at any minute. That wasn't paranoia. It was really intense. I wanted people to be serious.

Organizationally, Marlene credits Marilyn with being "the unacknowledged editor and leader of the collective."

We didn't want to use terms like that—we thought that we wanted to use non-male, non-elitist ideas and terms and not have hierarchical positions—but what actually happened in terms of the work was that a few of us worked a lot and others may have come in only once and everyone's name appeared with equality as staff members. Marilyn and a few others wrote most of the substantive articles, and we got a lot of other material from the news services like Liberation News Service.

> I was the backbone who made it happen. I designed it. I did most of the typing. I edited. I really didn't do much writing except for an article on diaphragms, and another asking our readers for support and contributions, written contributions. Mostly, I wanted to do layout, keep the books, make sure there were plenty of graphics. I was constantly poring through books, cutting things out, or sending Bobbie [Spalter-Roth] out to take her wonderful pictures. I was concerned with production, systems, deadlines, keeping things efficient enough so that *oob* would last forever.

Many of the early articles were devoted to women gaining control of our bodies, with an emphasis on reproductive health and contraception. Survival articles, in addition to laying down how to change a tire and similar skills unfamiliar to many women, focused most often on the different methods of birth control, emphasizing the dangers systematically withheld from women by the drug companies and the government. Protests, demonstrations, and disruptions around the issue of abortion were major items. Abortion and birth control were consistently linked with issues of population control and genocide throughout the pages (contrary to later leftist criticism that feminists ignore such atrocities as forced sterilization).

Along with these special articles, we ran a number of special issues during that first volume that mirrored the self-definition women were undergoing, as individuals and as a movement. Themes of these special issues focused on in-depth examinations of women and ecology, women and the media, women and social class, women and the church, and women working. Other groups were given the space to put out children's liberation and women's health supplements, and an entire issue was given over to another women's collective to analyze women and imperialism.

The relationship of the women's movement to the Left was the stuff of many long, opposing pieces. The Black Panther Party's Revolutionary People's Constitutional Convention epitomized, to a group of New York lesbians, the complete contempt with which so-called revolutionary brothers held women; other wo-men, however, emphasized the need for revolutionary women to join in the struggles of all oppressed people.

The Vietnam War was very much with us during our first year, as is reflected in the many accounts of both government actions and antiwar marches and demonstrations, along with the fractured accounts of meetings between North American and Indochinese women in Toronto and Vancouver that took place in April 1971. After the Toronto meeting, *oob* published two short pieces and the following editorial comments:

> After nine months of intensive work involving thousands of women in the U.S. and Canada the conferences in Vancouver and Toronto with Vietnamese and Laotian women actually happened—are over—and can finally be talked about. Women's liberation people returning to this city from Toronto talked about tensions, alienation, anxiety and confusion coming out of factionalism, racism, liberalism and other movement maladies. There were devastating problems (as yet undefined or at least unanalyzed) between women's liberation and third world (black, Puerto Rican and Chicana) women. *off our backs* is handicapped in its reporting since media was effectively excluded. It is the day after the conference and the night before we go to the printers and we can't sort it all out. In this issue we're printing some of the Washington, D.C., delegates' impressions of several of the Indochinese women—which seemed the only clear positive aspect of an embarrassing fiasco.

Because the straight media liked to spotlight photogenic feminists like Gloria Steinem and Jane Fonda and designate them as "feminist leaders," we warned against media stars and the media. Perhaps the only famous living women to be pictured on the paper's cover were Jane Fonda and Mme. Binh of Vietnam, in a split cover in March 1974—and some of us weren't too happy about the Fonda picture at the time. In fact, the antagonism toward media stars was so strong that it ultimately led, in fall 1970, to Marilyn's decision to leave the paper she had helped found. As Marlene explained

> She was a very articulate, powerful woman and we were individuals with differing philosophies of practicing our consciousness. We were turned on to doing things collectively and not having stars. That was a big issue. I really welcomed her direction and her thought. She was a great asset to *oob*. People like Onka and Norma, however, were really turned off and there were other people in the women's movement in

DC—not particularly on the paper, who encouraged censuring Marilyn and telling her that things would be decided collectively. Their ultimatum was that the direction of the paper would be more collective or they weren't going to work on it. Marilyn was absolutely devastated.

Other warnings that we issued then focused on fears that members of the feminist right wing would co-opt the women's movement. An angry report on the August 26, 1970 coalition between DC Women's Liberation, NOW, and the Young Socialists Alliance (YSA) condemned NOW for focusing only on the Equal Rights Amendment and selling out welfare women, lesbians, and Black Panther women. The report further condemned the YSA for being interested only in increasing party membership.

oob achieved early fame for its irreverence toward men in two of its more notorious centerspreads: Issue number 4 bared Mr. April, *oob*'s bearded playboy of the month, whipping up a souffle, reading Valerie Solanas' *S.C.U.M.* (Society for Cutting Up Men) *Manifesto,* and kneeling on his bearskin rug sniffing flowers; Issue number 13 carried the centerspread ad for Butterballs, the genital deodorant for men, which featured two naked men, arms linked and smiling, daisies shielding their more private parts, and hilarious copy. Although we met all our editorial deadlines for that issue, a feat obviously not always accomplished during the 18-month life of *oob*'s first volume, Issue number 13 came out late nonetheless because *oob* had to trudge to New York to get it printed: the regular printer was too offended to print it (unless a particular collective member jumped into his bed) and other local printers refused also after they had ascertained what kind of publication *off our backs* was—because, levity aside, *oob* was a threat to male dignity and male supremacy.

In spite of our irreverence toward men, however, a handful of men did play roles in our early years. Marlene's husband built the layout tables. Jim True shared his knowledge of graphics. A man from *Quicksilver Times* agreed to distribute our paper along with that paper. Although some staff members, including Marlene, considered themselves "anti-men," an official statement on page one of the first issue declared that "We are not anti-men but pro-women." Both Marlene and Marilyn were married when the paper was founded, although Marlene's marriage lasted only until October of that first year. Norma was married, had a little baby, and didn't work outside of the home. Coletta was married. Nan and Heidi weren't married but they were young and were still dating men.

Later, though, the institution of heterosexuality would be attacked, along with racism and classism, in two political commentaries, written by two non-*oob* women, on the need for an autonomous women's movement and the radical restructuring of society. In the first, "Hanoi to Hoboken, a round trip ticket," Rita Mae Brown advised American women that working on their own oppression, while less glamorous than a trip to Hanoi, would help Vietnamese women more and would serve feminists better in their fight against capitalism and male supremacy. "Why the persistent enthusiasm for far-away places and distant struggles with imperialism?" she wrote. "Why travel to Hanoi when you can go to Hoboken and see the same show?...the plot is still the same: Oppression."

In the second, "Subversion in the Women's Movement," Martha Shelley wrote, "The women's movement is being co-opted, ripped-off, patronized, seduced and raped." Her article was critical of connections with liberal candidates, the government, and left-wing men who want to use women as "cannon fodder."

"At that time, the women's movement was still 'thinking about' addressing itself to lesbian issues," Marlene remembers. "We were all beginning to believe that 'if women are really going to support women then women need to deal with having sex with women.'"

An *oob* commentary called "Mind Bogglers" referred to the "heavy thinking" our staff had been doing and attempted to "share our confusion" with the community. Later as a result of our need to resolve some of these unsettled thoughts, some of us decided to live together in a woman's commune for a month. The resulting article, which appeared in July of 1970, was signed by Women's Commune and was one of the few harbingers of the "gay/straight split" that would happen soon on *oob*.

Ten issues later, the article "Goodbye Ruby Tuesday" announced that five of *oob*'s 12 members had quit. This article was written by one woman "with spirit" from another woman. The author said:

> Simply, I saw the split as us, those who want to put out a radical women's newspaper and who want to involve themselves in other things including living and working with men. And the heavies, those who in most cases want to relate to women exclusively, in their work and all areas of their lives. I had many problems with what I thought were the politics of the second group. I say thought because we never talked. Each side was afraid of the other. Staff meetings were a disaster, with side comments and dirty looks. I feel they place restrictions on their lives that I don't want to place on mine....On Tuesday all the heavies left the newspaper. I was hurt....

The women who left *oob* began the lesbian-feminist newspaper, *The Furies*, because, they said, on *oob* they felt pressured to suppress their lesbian politics. [See Ginny Berson's story, "The Furies: Goddesses of Vengeance," in this collection.] *oob* printed a letter in the next issue that criticized the paper's politics for being sexist, anti-lesbian.

The staff never responded publicly to the letter. However, two months later, in January 1971, Marlene quit *oob* and joined the staff of *Furies*.

> Personally, my lesbianism didn't have anything to do with my reasons for leaving. I was, however, really pressured for being the only so called "pro-lesbian." I left because we had a big "blow up" and I just said fuck it and walked out. The big "blow up" was some trivia—some disagreement among us about the printers. Underneath, all the hours, the intensity, the tension of the times, my personal struggles had taken their toll. On the surface, I felt that I was doing most of the work. Others were good at making decisions but I was the one who ended up carrying them out. It's so sad. I just walked away from something that meant so much. I walked away from a part of myself. I have never found a substitute to being turned on to the hours and hours of work on *oob*.

Later in the decade, many women on the collective became lesbians, other lesbians joined the collective, and it is currently all lesbian, although other women are welcome.

1971-1972

An exact rundown of statistics from our first year's financial record is lost to history, but we certainly didn't get rich that year. One reason was that we mailed out most copies of each issue so we had tremendous postage expenses. In addition, because printers didn't like what we were publishing, they charged us premium prices—or refused to print us altogether, in which case travel expenses increased as we drove further from the office to find a willing printer. These facts combined forced us to raise our cover price at the beginning of Volume II—which covered the period from September 1971 to Summer 1972—from 25¢ to 35¢. In order to attract more subscribers, we also lowered our subscription rate from $6 to $5. Volume II also found *oob* in an actual office on Dupont Circle.

oob continued to get letters critical of its coverage and understanding of lesbianism. Especially upsetting to readers was the final article on the Venceremos Brigade by an *oob* collective member that explained, but disagreed with, the Cuban perspective of homosexuality as a sickness and counterrevolutionary and the brigade's decision not to accept any representatives of gay organizations.

Some readers also saw an inadequacy in coverage of race, class, international news, and problems related to being older or a mother.

But the heaviest criticisms came in person from women in the DC community who were furious over *oob*'s coverage of the movement to repeal all abortion laws—or, more specifically, of the structure and politics of the Women's National Abortion Action Coalition (WONAAC). WONAAC had been organized for the sole purpose of working to repeal all laws restricting abortion. *oob* coverage of conflicts surrounding the formation of WONAAC and a split in the local abortion group had favored the women who supported the concept of a nationally based single-issue-oriented organization, such as WONAAC. Most of these women were members of the Socialist Workers Party (SWP) or the Young Socialist Alliance (YSA). In angry letters to the paper, readers questioned whether it was a good idea to have a national organization devoted to any single issue, even abortion rights, whether large demonstrations were the best tactic, and whether to have anything to do with a group that was influenced by the SWP. Further, it was implied that *oob* had been infiltrated by a member of the SWP.

These readers believed that working with SWP was inimical to an independent women's movement. In a confrontation with a group of these women, we explained that the politics of *oob* was defined by the spectrum of women who were on the collective. Although most of the women on the collective did not favor mass actions or single-issue campaigns, a staff member who thought there was a place for that sort of activity would not be denied space to say it (and, of course, other approaches were always aired). One article did in fact support the sort of work the SWP was doing on abortion, though not the SWP as an organization. Whether that sort of sisterhood would have been sustained had the *oob* reporter in question actually been an SWP member is speculation.

In fact, however, during that period the pages of the paper reflected the growing awareness of women around the country that SWP tactics of bloc voting and of working with women to increase its own numbers and further its interests made working in groups with SWP women self-defeating. Independent women were developing ways of functioning that did not include majority rule or a follow-the-leader philosophy.

oob articles reflected this change in women's consciousness. Rather than giving major coverage to party politics, for instance, *oob* devoted many pages to women's emerging culture, printing the summer tour scrapbook of Earth Onion, a women's improvisational theatre; and publishing a previously unpublished series of poems called "Laying Down the Tower" by Marge Piercy, as well as poetry and fiction of dozens of women.

Volume II also saw not only *oob*'s first major political analysis of rape and the victimizing of women on the streets, but also calls to establish rape crisis centers and all-women anti-rape squads of a vigilante nature. *oob* investigated and exposed the nature, history, and current usage of psychosurgery; and discussed the positive uses to which videotape technology could be put.

Coverage of women in prison expanded: the first issue of Volume II was a poster issue urging women to demonstrate at the federal women's penitentiary in Alderson, West Virginia; the eighth was a special issue on women in prison produced by non-staff members with staff help. *oob*'s policy of making the feminist press available to as many women as possible was also acted on in a special issue on Jewish women, produced mostly by women not on the newspaper.

A special issue on women learning launched our coverage of women's studies. Two others, on women loving, explored lesbianism, lesbian separatism, mother-love, sister-love, "love" in marriage, the need to love, and the exercise of power in love relationships. The collective was generally dissatisfied with the contents of the loving issues, feeling most were too superficial because our understanding of love fell far short of our presumed experience with it.

oob scurried around DC to get firsthand knowledge, which usually turned into rather wry coverage, of how the Supreme Court operated when it heard arguments in the case resulting in the 1973 abortion ruling. We were there when the National Women's Political Caucus launched itself with a posh fundraiser and speakers that belied any pretension to radical feminist concerns and focused instead on merely electing women to political office. And we exposed the sexism in the policies and structures of the radical/leftist Institute for Policy Studies, where, despite its rhetoric, women were given positions of considerably less authority than men.

oob was one of nine media organizations in DC that were sent the key to a bank vault in which a bomb had been placed by an individual who wanted political prisoners freed. In typical *oob* fashion, not having regular office workers, we did not open our mail until after the story broke in the establishment press (the *Washington Post* also got a key). We called a lawyer for advice on what to do with the letter and the key; we xeroxed the original for publication in the paper,

key and all; and we came up with two commentaries that covered the two general feelings various collective members had about bombing as a means to an end: that it was simply unconscionable, regardless of how sure the bomber was that people could not be hurt; and that bombing property not only could damage some particularly insidious property but was also a logical recourse when other measures to stop truly atrocious government actions failed.

That first volume of *oob* consisted of 24 issues, most 12 to 16 pages long, and spanned the period from February 27, 1970, through the summer of 1971—the staff apologized for being five months behind their intention of coming out every two weeks and assured their first-year subscribers that they would receive 24 issues regardless of how long it took *oob* to produce them. The entire first volume was put out from the basement of a collective member's house.

1972-1973

During the summer of 1972, the DC women's community was looking for a place to establish a new women's center and hoped *off our backs* would move there once a building was found (*oob* was one of the few marginally solvent feminist groups around). After much discussion, the collective decided to remain physically removed from groups we would undoubtedly be covering in the newspaper. The next summer, we moved into a new office on 20th Street NW.

However, because our decision antagonized many DC feminists, Volume III, which covered the period from September 1972 through 1973, began with an editorial explaining *oob*'s position and politics. In part the editorial said that

> producing a women's paper that (does) not shrink from evaluating women's theories and actions necessarily entail(s) that a certain distance be maintained from all institutions, albeit feminist....We have, on occasion, been admonished for "failing to develop a consistent politics." This fact is not a failure, but rather a conscious decision that any line would destroy our ability to view critically what we are covering, would, in fact, predetermine what received space in this newspaper, what was trashed, and what was proselytized. We are not an organizing tool for any one tendency in the women's movement—or for any one women's organization.

Instead, we attempted to provide as broad coverage of the women's movement as our resources would allow. International news got a space of its own, though it was still a relatively small space.

But *oob* did go to lots of conferences—and wasn't very pleased about them: the Democratic National Convention in Miami Beach in the summer of 1972, aided by the National Women's Political Caucus (NWPC), was graced only by vastly amusing reporting that included NWPC's Liz Carpenter, Lady Bird Johnson's former press secretary, saying, "It is the white women isolated in the suburbs that we have to reach" and NWPC women assuring everyone that feminists weren't against men and, in some cases, even being flirtatious with the male delegates; the MORE counter-convention for nonestablishment press was revoltingly sexist in that organizers took the attitude that the Vietnam War was the only important issue, and that women's issues were trivial; the Women as Economic Equals Conference, sponsored by BankAmericard, was an incredibly obnoxious rip-off because it was only concerned with upper-class and upper middle-class women's issues (but we did get to hiss HEW Secretary Weinberger for lunch and offend everyone); the national NOW convention was top-heavy, nonresponsive to minorities, and insulting to lesbians; the National Welfare Rights Convention told it like it was, but, of course, "it" remained that way; and the International Childbirth Conference enlightened attendees with information on alternate methods of prenatal care, childbirth, and feeding, but it failed to discuss midwives or self-exams, gave women no information to empower themselves in questioning doctors, and as a whole didn't go far enough in getting men out of women's bodies.

oob did not cover the West Coast women's studies and lesbian conferences but printed several conflicting accounts of each: culture versus race and class issues abounded.

Volume III also carried in-depth investigative articles of health issues involving feminist groups, sometimes in opposition to one another: menstrual extraction was thoroughly researched; and the supercoil abortion disaster—which concerned whether an abortion-inducing product called the supercoil was safe and whether black women had been used involuntarily as guinea pigs to test it—included perceptions and statements by the opposing factions in the women's health movement, which drew criticism from one of them for not having had its views take precedence.

Our coverage of struggles to change the laws related to rape trials strongly advocated self-defense and increased visibility of maimed and mutilated would-be rapists as a stronger deterrent than the law regarding rape attempts.

oob came out with a special holiday issue in December of 1973—a novel called *Mary anti-Mary*

written by Carol Anne Douglas and illustrated by Mecca Reliance.

In interviews, members of a feminist counseling collective discussed their views of feminist therapy; and a co-founder of the newly formed National Black Feminist Organization (NBFO) explained that the organization had been started by committed feminists who were nonetheless tired of the covert and overt racism they encountered in the predominantly white women's groups, where they believed that issues of major importance to black women achieved only low priority. In-depth interviews with Bev Fisher, in DC, and Brooke, and with other committed feminists whose names never made the headlines, complemented our usual criticism of media-created superstars such as Gloria Steinem and Germaine Greer.

In November, *oob* suffered a form of "culture shock" when one layout night, in the wee hours of the morning, the woman who had been coordinating the paper's "Counter Vulture" section (another name for the previously mentioned "Culture Vulture" section) took her name off the masthead, placed it on the "Counter Vulture" section with the word "editor," and accounted in that section that

> Counter vulture gets a room of her own...Peer group controls fell apart leaving counter vulture free to grow into a self-contained monthly pullout section. The goal of this section is to both present and analyze the arts, aesthetics, rituals, values, and belief systems of an emerging feminist culture.

Since having "editors" was contrary to our belief system, she was absolutely correct in her statement that peer group controls fell apart. But she had a vision of what she wanted to explore in that section—a sort of anthropological view of feminist culture—which no one else wanted to really commit themselves to—and she agreed to take on that task only if she could claim the attribution. We agreed, reluctantly, but resentment kept building, especially when reviews of feminist books and movies, which we had always done, were placed in this separate section. We seemed no longer to be writing these pieces for *off our backs*, but rather for an individual's enterprise. This section's name was soon changed to "Culture(s)," and the editor's position remained until February 1974, when members mutually agreed that the situation was no longer tenable.

During the time of the editorship, some of the more controversial items ran. One, "experiments in hostility," was a series by a New York writer that featured a logo that some of our readers found overdone—it pictured a woman holding up a just-ripped-off-and-dripping-blood penis. (Remember, this was on a collective with several married woman—how many heterosexual feminists would think this graphic was funny today?) Another was a several-page spread on women's erotic art, called "another cuntree," that was replete with explicit genital/sexual women's art, which some readers found overdone also, and which our printer refused to print ("women impaled on new york" and similar painful pictures were not found objectionable by him, but he was thoroughly offended by a piece called "red flag," which showed a woman removing a tampax).

But perhaps the most sensational articles to appear in *oob*, in May 1973, were Jane Alpert's letter to her "sisters in the weather underground" and her manuscript on "Mother Right: A New Feminist Theory." In her cover letter, she said that she had gone underground three years previously as a committed leftist and had since become a radical feminist. She concluded with the statement, "I will mourn the death of 42 male supremacists no longer," a reference to the prisoners killed at Attica State Prison, one of whom was her former lover Sam Melville. In her manuscript, she stated that bearing children was women's right and that patriarchal society had injured women by constraining that right and shaping it to men's needs and institutions.

The closing statement to her letter horrified many readers. Responses filled *oob*'s letters pages for several issues afterwards. Her theories of matriarchy and mother right inspired some and worried others. Later, when she surfaced in late 1974, her position in the movement became a source of polarization among feminists.

1974

Volume IV began with tortured coverage of the first conference of the National Black Feminist Organization. Because some of NBFO's founders were well-known lesbian feminists, we had assumed that most of the women who would attend the first national conference would also have feminist politics and some previous contact with lesbian feminist women. We were therefore totally unprepared for the intense hostility directed against white feminists, who were accused of being interested in getting to know black women for the sole purpose of slipping into bed with "their men." Blanket statements were made to the effect that any criticism of a black man by a white feminist was racist, and that women who sought money from the same source or who ran for the same office as black men were racist. Because these statements had been made during large plenary sessions, and the workshops were closed to us, we—the few white feminists in attendance, all of us reporters—had no way to respond. In retro-

spect, we saw that we should not have been at the conference at all, but we had not been led to believe beforehand that our presence at those sessions that were specifically open to us would be so antagonizing.

After the conference, still feeling frustrated and angry, and despairing of the possibility of creating strong coalitions between white and black women in the very near future, *oob* wrote our first editorial in two years. In the editorial, called "uniting and conquering," we made a plea for an end to the divide-and-conquer strategy, recounted the misconceptions of our motives in attending the conference, and expressed the genuine desire that the NBFO make known its program for actions so that white and black women could work together for them. We made several attempts afterwards to follow up on developments generated in the workshops, but were told that no information was yet available. We received little response to the editorial or to the conference coverage.

That issue, however, seemed to be the exception in 1974. We covered other controversial issues—and were pleased to receive heated responses: we usually see the fact that both sides of an issue are annoyed at us as a sign that we are doing a good job.

In June, we made women's movement enemies with our printing of "testimonies" from women who had been fired from or quit the Feminist Women's Health Centers (FWHC) in California over issues involving the FWHC's hierarchical structure and personal manipulations of low-status workers. In an editorial, we criticized: 1) the FWHC structure, as described by these women and corroborated by FWHC founder Carol Downer in her writings on FWHC structure, 2) the idea that the concept of self-help was under patent to the FWHC, and 3) the practice of Downer's awarding medals to women she decided had "dared to be great." In the next issue, we were criticized at great length by the California FWHC hierarchy, who had refused to talk to us on the phone when we were doing the story.

In October, we covered the suit brought by Lucinda Cisler against Robin Morgan and the Sisterhood Is Powerful, Inc., fund for alleged plagiarism without credit or compensation of Cisler's bibliography. Neither "side" was pleased by the coverage, and the best outcome of that story for us was Ti-Grace Atkinson's proposal for feminist arbitration in future similar cases.

In an editorial on the decimation of the Symbionese Liberation Army (SLA), we lamented that women with a feminist consciousness who were ready to take direct action against the state had no place within the women's movement, which had grown too respectable to even be disruptive.

In July, we published the C.L.I.T. (Collective Lesbian International Terrors) papers, which may or may not have had a profound effect on the women's movement, but which certainly had a profound effect on us. We were nearly torn apart during our discussions with the C.L.I.T. women and with one another on the content of the papers and on whether or not to publish them at all. The C.L.I.T. papers were a series of articles that presented the political philosophy of "drastic dykes" who would speak to and listen to only other "drastic dykes," lesbians who separated themselves completely from men, straight women, the straight media, and the straight culture. One article in the series, called "straight women," began with "the danger of straight women is their disguise. They look like women," and got more vituperative from there. At that time, the collective consisted of about equal numbers of women who considered themselves lesbians, women who considered themselves straight, and women in some sort of transition period. We felt intimidated by the C.L.I.T. women and by one another to make some sort of declaration of our position—which ended up being that to say one was straight implied one rejected lesbians, and vice versa.

We published the papers, unedited as demanded and in their entirety because, as we stated in an *oob* editorial: "the issues they speak to are important enough to all women relating to other women and concerned about the state and future of the women's movement to warrant *oob*'s printing it. We recognize the importance of dykes communicating with dykes and the fact that such communication is possible neither through the straight media nor most alternative papers." The editorial also describes how the collective nearly drowned in debate and then managed to pull one another to shore.

Other reader comments, in response not so much to *oob* articles as much as to issues within the feminist movement, showed the community force that *oob* had become in its first four years. For instance, in one issue we published an angry, long open letter that attacked women in the movement for failing to put into action lip-service theories about the destructiveness of the nuclear family and the need to raise children communally. Responses from readers objected to guilt-tripping and affirmed their rights to remain childfree, even if the writer of the open letter had not.

Two collective members, tired of missing theory articles, wrote some themselves on feminist views of the future: one analyzed current hang-ups, posed hard questions, and projected ways of thinking and acting in the future; the other elaborated in concrete terms upon the feasibility of actually establishing a feminist territory. A reader responded with a commentary elaborating on the military implications of a feminist nation.

We got more letters objecting to our lesbian tendencies than we got calling us tools of the Left. As a result of the controversy our articles were causing or our readers' letters were generating, *oob* meetings in 1974 were fairly heavy in content and tone, both at regular meeting times and at special meetings, on collective process, anarchy, true consensus, commitment—politics in general. As a result of one member's suggestion that we read the pamphlet *anti-mass* and follow its recommendations, we instituted the process of criticism/self-criticism into meetings, generally at the end. Each member was supposed to analyze her contribution to the meeting or to the newspaper in general and to bring up any problems she had with anyone else or with the collective's process. At best, these sessions sometimes brought up and resolved tensions between members, with neutral members serving as mediators. At worst, they were painful criticism sessions, with almost everyone feeling compelled to repeat a criticism one member made of another.

In other issues throughout Volume IV, which coincided with the year 1974, *oob* increased its coverage of labor union and working women, with in-depth stories of the newly formed Coalition of Labor Union Women (CLUW), the struggle of hospital workers union 1199, and the Farah strike. We also covered the sexist browbeating of women trying to gain entrance to traditionally all-male unions, and the activities of an all-women's trucking collective.

We reported on and took pictures of the first horribly visible signs of a major abortion backlash in a mass right-to-life demonstration in the beginning of the year. We ran an article by a support group of the Native American women at Wounded Knee, which was subtitled "notes to confused white feminists."

Aside from covering a good many issues from a lesbian feminist perspective, we also interviewed lesbian feminist musicians on their politics, their music, and their plans for the future: Lavender Jane (at that time Alix Dobkin, Kay Gardner, and Patches Attom); the women who were in the process of forming Olivia Records; and Casse Culver and Mary Spottswood Pou (Spotts). We also interviewed Willie Tyson and sat in as she cut her first album on her own Lima Bean label. Unlike the politics expressed then by the other musicians, Willie's work did not preclude working with men.

Other interviews were with Nguyen Thi Ngoc Thoa, a Vietnamese woman working with the Committee of Responsibility; Jane Fonda, on the Indochina Peace Campaign; and Shirley Chisholm.

Clearly, *oob* was making an impact on the feminist community. And so in 1974 we made one move to expand and one move to close ranks. When a former, newly returned, collective member who was moving to Chicago presented the idea of starting an *off our backs* branch in Chicago, we talked about the idea at great length and came up with the concept of an autonomous sister collective. It was launched at the end of the year with great hopes from some of us and a hesitancy bordering on foreboding from others of us.

On the other hand, when in November a rash of new women wanted to join the paper, we decided the door would have to close behind them. We were at a very serious phase in the development of *off our backs*, we thought. We needed to really know one another and our sense of things so we could get down to the serious business of making a women's revolution.

1975

It was in 1975 that the feminist movement and *oob* were most concerned about infiltration. Jane Alpert had just come up from underground and many people believed that the subsequent arrests of two Weather Underground women, Pat Swinton and Susan Saxe, were connected to her. *oob* went through many painful meetings debating whether there should be an editorial condemnation of Alpert, as some wanted, or an editorial condemning the practice of informing to the FBI without naming and judging any particular individual, as others wanted. People were perceived as taking "strong" or "weak" positions on collaboration with the government. There was also discussion about whether *oob* had been irresponsible in printing Alpert's 1973 letter rejecting the men of the Weather Underground because the letter might have had information that the FBI could have found useful, such as descriptions of individual behaviors.

In the editorial that finally emerged from those meetings, *oob* condemned cooperation with the state in general, but also said that Alpert did not "represent our concerns or our goals when she chose to provide the state with information" by writing a public letter, and that our printing of her letter to the underground was "dangerously sloppy" because

> our basic feeling is that the state is a great enemy to feminists, by virtue of its measurably greater power, than any sexist man or male-defined left power, both of which would wield power over us if they only had a chance.

Some angry responses supported Alpert. One letter said, "to fear Alpert is to fear ourselves." The *New*

Women's Survival Sourcebook changed its rating of *oob* from its first edition comment—"the New York *Times* of the women's movement"—to its second edition comment—that some publications continued to grow but *oob* had "switched from national news reporting with a radical feminist slant to focusing on intermovement factionalism from what appears to be a predominantly male left perspective."

Charged with being one-sided, *oob* published an interview with Alpert that had been submitted to us, and in which she claimed she had not betrayed anyone, but we set it in itsy bitsy type.

Still, fear of possible FBI and also CIA harassment was always with us and was reflected in a variety of articles that discussed FBI and CIA tactics in infiltrating the feminist movement, and that gave coverage to grand jury defense committees.

An essay by Redstockings, one of the earliest radical feminist groups founded in New York—or anywhere, charged that Gloria Steinem had once worked for a CIA front organization and still had connections with the CIA, and that *Ms.* spread a reactionary ideology. *oob* ran most of the text of the essay. First, however, we did a small investigation of our own. In an analysis that accompanied the Redstockings essay, we said that Redstockings had not proved Steinem was an agent but that they had nevertheless raised questions that Steinem should answer, such as why she had as a student gone on a CIA-sponsored trip to Europe and whether she still had connections with the CIA. Some of Redstockings' research was well done, the analysis noted, but other parts were based on guilt by association. In Steinem's response, which we also ran, she said that many students did the same at the time—the late fifties—but that she had had no further ties to the CIA.

oob also wrote about WASP, Women Armed for Self Defense, a Texas group of women who had guns, and reviewed "A Call to Arms," a women's pamphlet about guns: *oob*'s review said that getting killed was an occupational hazard for rapists. *oob* interviewed karate teacher Dana Densmore on self-defense.

oob covered the story of the feminist institute Sagaris, which taught classes that summer but was closed because some of its students and teachers protested hierarchical classroom arrangements and the fact that the school had taken $5,000 from *Ms.* and would have to take more in order to stay open. Some felt that they had gained much at Sagaris.

oob attended the Socialist Feminist Conference and reported that only the lesbian caucus at the conference seemed to see male supremacy and capitalism as feeding each other.

Other issues and topics covered or discussed by *oob* in Volume V include the following:

- Joanne Little's trial and acquittal in North Carolina;
- Racial discrimination in DC's gay bars;
- The stealing of Indian women's children to be raised by whites or in institutions;
- A Dayton speech in which Ti-Grace Atkinson said that female nationalism was eroding militancy in the movement;
- A debate between Kate Millett and Herbert Marcuse;
- The belief that Ethel Rosenberg had been framed;
- "Operation Babylift," which brought many Vietnamese children, including some who still had parents, to the United States;
- Women in China, Guinea Bissau, Portugal, and Puerto Rico;
- International Women's Year as a government-controlled event;
- Women ex-convicts;
- A sit-in in a women's prison in Raleigh;
- Feminist alternatives to mental institutions;
- Andrea Dworkin's problems in publishing *Woman-Hating*;
- An interview with Shoshana (Pat Swinton);
- The founding of the Washington Area Feminist Federal Credit Union; and
- Iris, the feminist film distributing company.

oob Chicago collective became active in 1975 and problems between the two collectives developed right away. *oob* Washington collective controlled the paper's means of production and had most of the experience, so the relationship quickly became hierarchical. Washington *oob* members found they wanted to do both technical and sometimes content editing of articles coming from Chicago and Chicago women sometimes resented the editing suggestions. Further, because most communication was done by telephone, and because other expenses were incurred as well—especially when *oob* wound up paying for three Chicago members to take a plane trip to DC for a weekend discussion of process—expenses were run up so quickly that one of our two office workers had to give up her salary. *oob*, a marginally self-supporting organization, had taken on a major expense.

Communication between the two groups was difficult, especially since it had for a long time gone through the woman who founded the Chicago collective. When Chicago and Washington women met face-to-face, the atmosphere became more pleasant, but the problems proved insurmountable and the Chicago collective eventually dissolved itself. It had provided some good coverage of Chicago news.

In 1976, *oob* commentaries debated the pros and cons of feminist businesses, such as whether they are part of the feminist political movement, and whether creating an alternative network of feminist businesses is a revolutionary strategy, or whether feminist businesses provide jobs and benefits for more than a few women. Both viewpoints were expressed intensely, and one bookstore stopped selling *oob* because its owners felt that it, as a feminist business, was being insulted.

Several articles described and analyzed a specific feminist business, Detroit's Feminist Economic Network (FEN), and emerging feminist credit unions that both were and were not related to it. Some considered FEN and/or other credit unions to be creative endeavors that would fund and support many women and women's enterprises. Others maintained that FEN was authoritarian or that credit unions could not both effectively redistribute income and succeed financially. In September 1976, after ten months, FEN folded. A FEN supporter wrote that irresponsible criticism in the feminist media killed FEN.

Commentaries by a former therapist and women who had gone to therapists laid strong criticism on feminist therapy as frequently being insufficiently feminist, contributing to dependency, and supporting women more in traditional relationships than in their movement work. Responses maintained that feminist therapy was useful and healing.

As a result of collective discussions on the need to report on practical problems in women's daily lives, *oob* published articles on the problems of older women, crackdowns on welfare mothers and food stamps, workplace health and safety hazards, battered women and emerging feminist shelters, housing pressures on women, and nursing homes. A commentary called for more outreach to other women and for being like Mao's proverbial "fish in the sea" of the people.

oob also debated implications of various sexual practices and ran our first article criticizing sadomasochism. Counter-commentaries portrayed sadomasochism as a depressing inheritance from a male-shaped sexuality involving dominance and as a harmless practice no different than other sexual acts. Coverage of a prostitutes' convention took the perspective that prostitution had to be accepted and decriminalized in order to end the stigmatization of prostitutes, but added that decriminalization was not part of a revolutionary strategy to end male supremacy. A 1977 article discussed bisexuality sympathetically but with criticism; though there was no counter-commentary, there was disagreement in the collective.

oob attended and reported enthusiastically on the Women in Print Conference, which created a network of the many feminists involved in publishing. We also reported on the trials and confinements of Susan Saxe, Assata Shakur, Dessie Woods, and Cheryl Todd. We wrote about black women in South Africa's Soweto district, French women's strike at the Lip watch factory, Swiss women occupying a building in Geneva, Australian women accused of false arrest for charging men with rape, and the Chilean government's killing of Ronni Moffitt just a few blocks away from us. A commentary protested taking blanket lines for or against sterilization for Third World women, rather than letting the individual women decide. The collective debated whether sterilization should be assumed to always be genocidal or whether some Third World women might prefer it to contraception if given the choice.

oob interviewed a militant coal miner's wife from Harlan County, Kentucky, covered local demonstrations against the Veterans' Administration Hospital's firing of a nurse who refused sexual advances from her supervisor, and wrote about Women in Construction, a local group of women involved in the building trades. *oob* covered the founding convention of CLUW, the Coalition of Labor Union Women. Another article pointed out that self-defense can get you jailed, and that it is illegal to carry a concealed weapon or resist physically someone who has assaulted you verbally.

The C.L.I.T. statement # 3 said that bourgeois feminists had sold out to the state, and that dykes had saved the women's liberation movement from both the Left and the Right. It called on proletarian feminists to confront patriarchy in prisons, mental institutions, the welfare system, and other government institutions. *oob* staffers wrote counter-commentaries, one saying that separatism was not the way to change but that the Left should unite, and the other saying that a politics of confrontation with men was welcome but that lesbians had pursued many different kinds of politics.

oob covered the "People's Bicentennial" celebration in Philadelphia. There was a great debate about whether to print a picture of a man carrying a sign saying, "Fight sexism." Some felt that printing the picture endorsed the idea that men are feminists, and objected; others felt that not printing the picture amounted to censorship. The picture was printed.

1977

Some issues of *oob* in these years seem almost schizophrenically split between "heavy leftist" articles and goddess, back-to-the-country articles—the splits reflect real differences on the *oob* collectives, though not everyone took one of these positions. In fact, perhaps a "majority"—though we don't often talk in terms of majorities—never took either.

Collective members agreed we had waited too long before covering the women's spirituality movement because none of us was much interested in it. In December 1976, *oob* covered a spirituality conference in New York. The reporters liked the affirmation that we are more than intellectual beings but called goddess worship a sham. Books about goddesses and the moon were reviewed, though not always favorably. One article described the process of parchenogenesis, by which ova can become babies without the intervention of sperm. Another told how women went about setting up land trusts in the country and described different land trusts. A commentary protested that radicals should get off the mountains and into the streets. Reader responses said the spot between politics and spirituality was too dualistic.

Around the world, the paper reported on women in Argentine prisons, the Spanish feminist movement, a rape trial in Italy, an Italian women's health conference, and a West German feminist conference.

At home, *oob* wrote about the new movement of the disabled, revelations about D.E.S. daughters, estrogen marketing, and spraying of the herbicide dioxin. We covered the trial of Wendy Yoshimura, who was charged with helping the Symbionese Liberation Army (SLA). Inez Garcia was acquitted. The Bakke case began. The anti-gay movement won its first referendum in Miami.

There was an open call to power and to think more, an invocation not to panic in a time of reaction, as commentaries suggested forming study groups, said we are all political thinkers, and advocated becoming long distance runners since the revolution won't be tomorrow. On the other hand, more group actions seemed to be developing. *oob* covered a large ERA march on Washington, the beginning of the "take back the night" marches, and the Kitty Genovese project, a group of women who had published the names of all Dallas' indicted rapists.

oob ended the year with an insert entitled "The Washington Pits" that featured headlines saying "Women Declare '78 Year of Armed Struggle," photographs of *oob* staffers "storming" the U.S. Capitol, and stories about massive prison escapes, small bands of armed women prowling through the country, and a condom stuck on the Washington Monument.

Gradually but steadily, women who felt that *oob* was insufficiently socialist left the newspaper. Personal reasons were also a factor.

1978

oob began 1978 by covering the November 1977 National Women's Conference at Houston. Reports commented that the process was unnecessarily rigid. A later commentary questioned the emphasis on bargaining and asked when radicals who push for reforms become assimilated.

In December 1977, *oob* had written critically about an Olivia Records workshop on feminist business. The reporters said that Olivia's music focused too much on love and did not deal with other political issues such as race and economics. In 1978, Olivia replied that the criticisms were rhetorical, perfectionist, and unfair, and said that Olivia was bringing Third World women onto its collective. *oob* staff members worried that the initial report might have been too harsh and did not want to have a split with Olivia. We pointed out that we had written many favorable reviews of Olivia's music and sent letters to Olivia trying to clarify our position and avoid a split.

Other *oob* commentaries discussed the ethical questions involved in killing, even in self-defense, the difficulties inherent in combining lesbianism and feminism, and the ways that love and break-ups can make us angry at each other (which had been a problem on the newspaper). Several articles debated the pains, problems, and joys of motherhood, child-rearing, and being a daughter; the articles reflected great disagreements over whether the process of motherhood was primarily pleasant or oppressive.

In October 1978, we published an issue focusing on work. *oob* described its process of putting out an issue. Articles discussed jobsharing, increasing automation in offices, women in blue-collar trades, and the idea that feminist activist work is non-alienating, that work does not have to be unpleasant. A film about women participating in the General Motors strike of 1938 was reviewed. There were interviews with a woman who repaired railroad freight cars and with a West Virginia coal miner's wife. Also that year, *oob* interviewed a woman truck driver and a woman welder, and wrote numerous articles analyzing the Bakke decision.

oob articles took different perspectives on the question of whether there are inherent differences between women and men. For example, coverage of the American Association for the Advancement of Science (AAAS) conference in 1978 criticized the views of a male sociobiologist who maintained that inherent differences justify the current division of power, whereas 1979 coverage of the AAAS meeting focused on women who were trying to create a women's substitute for the scientific method.

oob staffers did not maintain a distance from the news but, as usual, became involved in it. An *oob* staffer who was attacked when leaving a lesbian bar began WomanAlert, a group whose purpose was to demand action from bar owners and police on violence against lesbians and gays.

In fall 1978, *oob* was confronted by a woman after we had suggested changes in an article she had written in which she charged that the lesbian community had been racist. When we asked her to mention specific instances, a misunderstanding arose because the woman, who was a Filipina-Indian, felt we were trying to do cultural editing while we thought we were asking for information. A group of women of color and white women supported her. After an agonizing series of meetings among ourselves and with the group, which took the name Ain't I a Woman?, *oob* decided that we should print her article and allow Ain't I a Woman? to put out a special issue of *oob*, which became the June 1979 issue. We also set the goal of having women of color on the collective. Although our subsequent outreach in the community did not move us any closer to realizing that goal, we did begin looking more vigorously for articles by and about Third World women. In November, *oob* published an issue on racism and sexism. The whole process involved in the confrontation was painful for us, but for most of us it was part of our continuing process of learning to trust each other.

1979

Over the course of these last few years, our international news coverage was growing considerably. In 1978, we had published long articles about repression and women prisoners in Chile and Argentina; covered an American feminist anti-shah demonstration in New York and a conference on women and multinational corporations; discussed obstacles to abortion rights in Britain, Italy, and New Zealand; and written about the struggles of Palestinian and Algerian women against their oppression as women. In 1979, still more coverage was given to international news and analysis, often three or four pages per issue. We ran numerous articles on women in Iran and wrote about clitoridectomies in many nations. We wrote about women in Botswana's economy, women in the liberation movement in Guinea Bissau, repression in Chile, interviews with Egyptian and French feminists, articles on anti-rape demonstrations and murders of daughters-in-law in India, a national feminist conference and the founding of a lesbian organization in Mexico, a feminist's trip to China and analysis of the "rebourgeousification" of China, the effects of the pill in Bangladesh, a conference of black women in Britain, and the lives of Muslim women.

Pornography became a subject of much debate in the movement, and *oob* reported on the debate. *oob* covered the Feminist Perspectives on Pornography Conference in San Francisco and the New York University School of Law's colloquium on pornography. Questions were raised about how pornography can be eliminated, what constitutes censorship, and whether pornography causes or abets violence. Some *oob* staff members wrote a commentary saying that they hated pornography but would not ban it and worried about the commitment to civil liberties of those who would ban it. Other *oob* staffers disagreed strongly with the commentary and said instead that it might be possible to differentiate between different kinds of pornography, such as violent as opposed to non-violent. A later commentary said that the First Amendment had never been absolute and had never been intended to cover pornography. In November, *oob* covered the New York conference on pornography and marched against pornography.

Health issues that *oob* covered included the progress of the anti-abortion movement, aspects of the reproduction industry such as fetal monitoring and sex selection, and the reconstruction and construction of women by moving the clitoris to the vagina and by creating transsexuals. *oob* readers contributed much mail on the transsexual issue. In April 1979, *oob* ran articles about fat as a feminist issue, fat liberation, and anorexia nervosa, compulsive rejection of food. This issue drew more mail than almost any issue up to that time.

oob, like the rest of the country, was shaken by the nuclear accident at Three Mile Island and *oob* carried articles discussing the mechanics of and problems with nuclear power, the May 6 protest march, demonstrations at Virginia's North Anna nuclear plant, and the subsequent jailing and trial of women who were arrested for civil disobedience. Letters both supported and criticized the women for becoming involved in the struggle against nuclear power and for forming an all-women's affinity group. Collective members discussed whether nuclear power was even a feminist issue.

The October issue published another set of controversial articles, about heterosexuality, one by a heterosexual feminist and one by an ex-heterosexual lesbian feminist. In several discussions on sexuality, collective members expressed great differences in perspective and some anger, but the atmosphere was good because it showed how much we cared about each other.

Nevertheless, by the late seventies, *oob* had stopped writing editorials and had begun instead writing signed commentaries, since we often tended to disagree on issues anyway. People worried less about hammering out a common line and simply wrote counter-commentaries if they disagreed with each other.

1980

The year 1980 began with Dustin Hoffman playing Mother of the Year and ended with Ronald Reagan playing Father of the Country.

Soon after *off our backs*' tenth anniversary issue, the *oob* collective, always hardpressed for money anyhow, suffered our most horrifying money crunch when we discovered that one of our members had embezzled about $5,000 from *oob*. After she admitted it, the other members of the collective decided to suspend her membership. She had done much good work, been a friend, and been a collective member for a number of years, so we decided that she could be a member again if she repaid the money over time. She did not.

The loss was a real financial blow. Traditionally, we have managed to earn just about as much for each issue as we needed to put it out. Since our founding, we had never had the money to pay anyone a decent living wage, but office workers accepted the low "movement" wages out of the satisfaction they derived from their work and because of the skills they learned on the job. Over time, some of us had evolved a fairly casual style, not worrying about such issues as less than perfect records, while others found such attitudes undermining to the point of preventing good work. Perhaps the "casuals" had been in the movement or on the paper longer and accepted a certain amount of chaos as movement style and as acceptable amidst the frenzy of putting out 11 newspapers a year. In any case, by 1980 the collective consisted largely of "casuals." Through this experience, we learned one more time that we could get through even the most serious of troubles. We survived this experience after four collective members lent the newspaper money to keep it publishing and our office worker, Tacie, took no salary for several months.

oob moved into its second decade with articles cautioning young women not to join the military just because then-President Jimmy Carter was demonstrating his commitment to equal rights by suggesting that women be drafted. Instead, *oob* members did not think that anyone, woman or man, should enlist in the U.S. military because it so often engages in imperialist ventures. Some Washington, DC feminists, including some *oob* collective members, organized a conference on women in the military that was held on the day of one of DC's few blizzards.

On the international scene, *oob* interviewed Madhu Kishwar, an editor of the Indian feminist magazine *Manushi*. Besides discussing the condition of women in India, Kishwar criticized *oob* for making favorable comments about Indira Gandhi in a review of a biography.

We also covered the following international topics:

- the existence of movements urging women in Egypt to return to the veil;
- more restrictions on women in Saudi Arabia;
- Iranian women civil servants' protests against being forced to wear the veil;
- the arrests and expulsion of Soviet feminists;
- the press conference held on Capitol Hill by Tatyana Mamonova, one of the expelled Soviet feminists;
- Sandinista women in Nicaragua;
- women freedom fighters in Zimbabwe (then not yet liberated);
- the situation of women in Spain and Argentina (the latter in an interview with Celia Guevara, Che's sister); and
- the French group Psychoanalyse et Politique's legally successful copyrighting of the term "women's liberation movement" despite other groups' opposition.

In October, *oob* carried a report on the United Nations conference on women held in Copenhagen. A major political split developed over the issues of denouncing Zionism and saying that all aid for Palestinian women should go through the PLO. The coverage also discussed topics such as how to improve the economic situation of women in Africa and the experiences of lesbians from different countries (discussed at an alternative conference, not the UN-sponsored one).

Other conferences covered by *oob* included the second National Women's Studies Association conference, the first national black lesbian conference, the first national battered women's conference, a national conference on Third World women and violence, an Hispanic feminist conference, Barnard's conference on racism, classism, and sexism, and a conference on workplace health. The black lesbian conference was a welcome change from the earlier NBFO conference, where the issue of lesbianism had been muted.

In 1980, the debate between anti-pornography/critique of sexuality feminists and sexual libertarian "if it feels good do it" feminists was starting to heat up. Alice critically reviewed a lesbian sexual manual that included a positive chapter on sadomasochism. In her review, she called sadomasochism "silly sex." That article drew angry responses from several readers, including author Pat Califia, who suggested that Alice must really be unconsiously attracted to sadomasochism.

oob also covered rising feminist activism on pornography, including the Preying Mantis Brigade in Santa Cruz that attacked pictures showing women as dead food. Feminists and lesbians demonstrated against the movie *Windows* for its depiction of a lesbian who hired a man to rape a woman who had refused her, and against *Dressed to Kill*, a movie about murdering models. *oob* also criticized the somewhat subtle extinction of women in *Kramer vs. Kramer*.

Health issues we reported on included estrogen replacement therapy, which Fran criticized as dangerous because it required "risking your life to avoid hot flashes"; the new cervical cap; tampons, which we suggested could cause infections; and toxic shock syndrome.

In articles about women's workplace issues, women carpenters, a truck driver, and coal miners told about sexual harassment and other job hazards. Another article described the difficult lives of migrant farm worker women on the Delmarva Eastern Shore. *oob* covered the strike at Sanderson Farms' chicken packaging factory in Laurel, Mississippi, and interviewed union leader Gloria Johnson.

oob ran a commentary by Vickie, based on her experiences in the environmental movement, on how unrewarding it is to work with men because the men did not listen to what she had to say. We ran more papers by C.L.I.T., the lesbian separatist group whose work we had published in the seventies. This time, they slashed fame discos, therapy-type groups, and the hooker look, among other topics.

Throughout most of our herstory, students had on occasion worked at *oob*. In 1980, Tacie formalized the process by beginning a program that regularly brought student interns to *oob*. Many women have helped us greatly with fine reporting and generous attention to office work, beginning that year with Brenda Marston.

Also that year, *oob* tried to make our issues available on tape for blind women. Wendy helped begin this process.

The year 1980 ended with the first election of Ronald Reagan as president. In *oob*'s article that we ran in honor of the election, we discussed how German "moderate feminists" mostly failed to oppose Hitler.

WE'RE STILL OFF OUR BACKS: A BRIEF OVERVIEW TO THE PRESENT

It has been difficult to write about our memories of producing *off our backs* during our first ten years simply because we have continued to publish through the present day. In some ways, that era seems different, but in other ways it seems as if we are just doing the same things we were always doing.

We still have an almost entirely unpaid staff, with just one (poorly) paid office worker. We have had an office worker since 1973, but in the seventies we were able to pay two of us a measly salary rather than one. There used to be intense competition for the job, so we were only allowed a six-month term at a time, after which we would have to ask whether we could continue it. Now, with inflation forcing all of us to hold full-time jobs, most of us would enjoy the office worker job but cannot afford to leave our jobs to take it. We ask that a collective member make a commitment to take the job for at least one year.

Perhaps the greatest change has been in our concern about the government. In the early years, we were very concerned about the possibility of government disruption of *off our backs*. Several times, women worried that other women who had contact with the newspaper might be government agents. That concern generally has faded, in part because of the changing times and in part because fewer women come around the newspaper. Those who join tend to work with us for quite awhile first, so we know them better than we knew each other when we joined in the seventies.

In the seventies, feminist radicals who were trying to operate underground sent their material to be published in *off our backs*. Both Jane Alpert and the Weather Underground sent us statements, which we published. After we published a Weather Underground communique, we found that our offices had been broken into and our paperwork had been gone through, but no money had been taken. We were sure that this was the work of the government, and were quite alarmed, but so far as we know it never happened again.

At one point we went so far as to discuss designating ourselves by code names when we talked on the telephone because we assumed that our telephone was tapped. However, we never actually used the code names.

We spent a good part of the seventies deciding what it meant to operate collectively. Our forays into criticism/self-criticism in 1974 were an attempt to deal with this issue. As time went on, however, at least in part because members resisted speaking honestly, criticism/self-criticism got left by the wayside, both the good and the bad of it. We may be somewhat less frank in the nineties, but we certainly are less brutal also.

Meetings in the seventies were intense in a number of ways. During one year or so—around 1974 and 1975—we passed a brandy bottle around the room, which did not make for cooler meetings. Now, a number of collective members either do not drink alcohol at all or seldom drink, and we never drink at meetings or layout.

In the 1970s, it was more common for members of the collective to become romantically involved with one another, which contributed to tensions as relationships broke up and new ones began. Now that still happens, but much less frequently.

The intensity of the 1970s, including the ongoing romances and perhaps also the greater suspicions about whether women were going to be politically acceptable, probably led to more cliquishness. It used to be that during layout weekend women on the paper went out to dinner with their particular friends. In the early eighties, we instituted the practice of going out to dinner with whoever came to help us put out the issue, so they could get to know us; anyone who is working in the office is welcome to come. Of course, we have different degrees of friendship with each other and see each other to a greater or lesser extent during the rest of the month, but Saturday night dinner on layout weekend is open to everyone.

In content, the newspaper in the early seventies reflected the belief that focusing on what the government was doing was simply reacting to it, and there was not that much mention of what the government did except for the war in Vietnam. Beginning with Ronald Reagan's election in 1981, however, we began to write about what all levels of the government—federal, state, and sometimes local—were doing that had a direct impact on women, and how citizens were demonstrating against these activities. We no longer felt that writing about pending legislation and court decisions somehow made us complicit with the system. You might say that Reagan brought *oob* into the mainstream.

For instance, by spring, *oob* was carrying articles on how Reagan's budget cuts affected women. The urgency with finding direct alternatives to Reagan's policies prompted *oob* to carry more articles on leftist theory, including coverage of a conference on capitalism and reviews of books on anarchism and non-authoritarian socialist theory.

In 1982, we looked at some of the more dismal aspects—which would become more dismal yet—of Reagan administration policies like "workfare" for AFDC mothers and anti-abortion legislative pushes; and in July we carried stories on the end of the failed effort to get the ERA ratified.

Analyses of the impact of Reaganomics in this country became regular features. In 1982 alone, Denise dissected the effect on women of Reagan's budget proposals; Tricia exposed his elaborate war on children; Lorraine followed the organized efforts of working women to achieve comparable worth compensation; and we ran countless news articles on fights for liveable wages and decent working conditions.

oob also covered activities of the right wing outside the White House, and its new strategy of promoting a constitutional amendment to give decisions on abortion back to the states. Janis reviewed right-wing author George Gilder's book *Wealth and Poverty*. Several women, including *oob*'s Tacie, disrupted a Senate Judiciary Committee subcommittee hearing on "when life begins" because the chair, right-wing Sen. John East (R-NC), only invited testimony from those who believe that life begins at conception. The women were arrested and found guilty, but only fined.

We kicked off 1983 with a long round-up by Tacie of abortion strategies—federal, state by state, legal—contemplated by radical and more mainstream pro-abortion groups. Within that round-up was a foreshadowing of the anti-abortion violence that was to explode onto the public consciousness. Abortion coverage was continuous throughout the year, as the Right escalated its attempts to undo, but never quite successfully, the 1973 Supreme Court decision, a conservative Supreme Court reaffirmed it in mid-year, and Ronald Reagan equated abortion with slavery in his seminal piece in the *Human Life Review*. Practically every 1984 issue of *oob* reported more abortion clinic bombings.

In 1989, the Supreme Court's *Webster* decision gave states more power to curb abortions. *oob* covered the Supreme Court decision and continued what by then had become its usual state-by-state coverage of legislation on abortion. We covered the 600,000-strong April march in support of reproductive rights and the November demonstrations around the country for abortion.

Also on the issue of reproductive rights, in December of that year, we carried a lengthy report on the double bind of pregnant women on drugs: they are excluded from most drug treatment programs but are increasingly held by courts to be child abusers because they are on drugs.

Although our coverage of government activities has increased since the beginning of the 1980s, our main focus still, as it always has been, is on what the feminist movement is doing.

In 1984, *oob* delved into personal politics while continuing to report on national and international issues. Our February issue on love and sexuality included Tricia's discussion of lovers who no longer make love, Fran's article about relationships with large age differences between partners; and shorts by collective members about most embarrassing sex-related moments, and how we felt about flirting, breaking up, and related topics.

As the year went on, *oob* moved on to the subject of motherhood. We reported on a summer conference on lesbian co-parenting, and ran critical discussions on the decision to have a baby for lesbians and feminists. Vickie wrote that she wished women would choose politics over having children. Fran reported on the state of research in and practice of in vitro fertilization, surrogate mothering, frozen sperm, and related topics.

Meanwhile, *oob* continued covering the anti-pornography movement, including the Minneapolis ordinance that defined porn as a violation of women's civil rights (and was vetoed by the mayor). Alice interviewed Catharine A. MacKinnon, who had co-written that ordinance along with Andrea Dworkin. A later article by Alice disputed research used by anti-pornography activists to claim a causal link between pornography and male violence. Feminist sociologist Pauline Bart wrote saying it had been proven.

Most of our June 1985 issue focused on pornography, stemming from our coverage of the Women and the Law Conference, which featured a debate between MacKinnon and Nan Hunter, the author of a brief opposing the Minneapolis ordinance. We also printed the text of the ordinance, as it was passed by the city of Indianapolis (and later overturned by the courts), and excerpts from Hunter's opposing brief for the Feminist Anti-Censorship Task Force (FACT). The issue included articles about the Washington area group Feminists Against Pornography and an article by feminist lawyer Ruth Colker, in which she attempted to find a common ground on pornography.

In that issue, *oob* also ran a collective statement that said

> Although everyone at *off our backs* agrees on the need to fight pornography, we have strong disagreements about conclusions reached by current research on pornography, the legal strategy proposed by MacKinnon and Dworkin, and the issues raised by the FACT brief. Some of us also have misgivings off and on about the emergence of pornography as a central focus of feminist activism and controversy within the feminist movement—some do not.

> This has often taken concrete form in arguments not only about the content, but about the length of our coverage. We know the divisions among women on the paper reflect many of those within the movement; and, like so many other women, we are simultaneously fighting over them and trying to hold on to the common ground we know we still share.

In July, we interviewed Nikki Craft, who used civil disobedience as a form of protest, against pornography and in favor of nudity. We also printed a commentary by Adrienne Rich, "We Don't Have to Come Apart over Pornography." In her commentary, Rich said that she opposes pornography, but she also criticized the use of laws to fight it during the Reagan years. Three months later, we printed an open letter to Rich from MacKinnon saying that Rich still did not explain why she had signed the FACT brief although she disagreed with many points in it.

In the mid-seventies our focus on movement content included a number of "exposés" of political disagreements within other feminist groups, a subject to which we devoted much less attention in the eighties. As a matter of fact, we did more investigative reporting in general in the seventies than in the eighties, simply because we had more members who were semi-employed or collecting unemployment then. Inflation and other economic pressures have made it harder for us to have time for investigative reporting—book reviews and interviews are easier to fit into an employed woman's schedule, though we have tried hard to maintain

our extensive conference coverage, as well as our reports of women's struggles worldwide and our interconnectedness, especially regarding economics and armaments.

Overall, in looking back through our first two decades, we find truth in the old saying that "the more things change, the more they stay the same." We have changed in some ways, but we still are operating on a shoestring, still being political, yet still trying to look at politics, no matter how serious, with a journalist's weird sense of humor.

As we begin our third decade, we aren't tired yet. (Well, maybe in the wee hours, but not basically.)

APPENDIX: *OFF OUR BACKS* AND THE FEMINIST DREAM

by Marilyn S. Webb

off our backs, the first national feminist newspaper to emerge on the East Coast during the Vietnam era, is a quintessential child of the sixties—born of enthusiasm, a pinch of planning, and a lot of idealistic vision.

Although no one recognized it at the time, the paper's beginnings can be traced to the summer of 1968. Elsewhere, hippies were giving up the Haight, police were rioting in Chicago, and the Weather Underground was beginning to form. But in Washington, DC, it was hot. Sticky hot. And muggy.

The women's movement had already been a year in the making. During the winter and spring a small group of women had begun meeting in my DC living room—where it was cold at the time—to form what was one of the first consciousness-raising (CR) groups in the nation. We talked about our lives, about work, about children, and about men. Some of us were loosely connected with the Institute for Policy Studies, a liberal think tank run by people who had been involved with the Kennedy administration.

I was 25 at the time, and in Washington because my then-future husband, Lee Webb, was visiting fellow at the Institute. Lee and I had met in 1965 at a meeting at the University of Chicago, where I was a graduate student in educational psychology. The year before he had been national secretary of Students for a Democratic Society (SDS), when it was still an idealistic national youth organization concerned with civil rights. We fell in love, so when he moved to Washington in 1967 to work at the Institute I went along also, with plans to finish my doctoral dissertation. I thought I'd be there just temporarily. The war, however, seemed to get in the way.

During the summer of 1967 Lee and I both went to Cambridge, Massachusetts, to work in the headquarters of a national antiwar organizing effort called Vietnam Summer. Lee was the national director. My job was to direct an organizing effort aimed at high school teachers and to create a curriculum on Vietnam that could be used in high school classrooms. Since I already had a master's degree, I knew something about curriculum planning, but I also knew about organizing since I'd already helped found and then directed two preschools in a poor, black Chicago community (that were later prototypes for national Head Start) and an early women's group at the University of Chicago.

To do this for Vietnam Summer, I developed a thick file of contacts among teachers around the country. For some reason, I quickly added the growing list of women who'd also begun meeting in CR groups in Chicago, New York, San Francisco, and elsewhere. These were women who had been involved in the civil rights and antiwar movements but were now meeting on their own.

That fall, when I returned to Washington, I built up a regular correspondence with these women, all of us sharing ideas with our various groups. I was very actively against the war, but I was growing enormously interested in the lives of other women. Maybe that interest stemmed from the civil rights movement, where black men and women began redefining their own history and experience. Maybe it grew from interest in what the mothers at the preschools were saying and experiencing. Or maybe it grew from SDS, a liberal student organization that—though it called itself progressive—seemed unable to view women as anything more than observers on the scene of real action; the action was what the men were doing. Women's viewpoint was usually left out. We were always fighting other people's causes, but we also had some real problems of our own. We wanted to define what they were and to do something about them. Other women felt that way too.

Our Washington women's group began a speakers bureau around the city and in the suburbs to talk about these concerns—about equal pay for equal work, about health care, about child care, about life as other than being just a wife. We started an informal abortion counseling center and began to organize a growing national movement to legalize abortion. We also began to write articles for various publications, including *Guardian, Ramparts,* and other liberal magazines. That fall I also managed to get married.

As the temperature hit ninety in the beginning of June 1968, my friend Margie Stamberg and I sat around in the living room and decided an air conditioner was the only possession worth having. By this time I had stopped thinking about my dissertation and had become the *Guardian's* "Washington Bureau." Margie worked for a newspaper in Washington called *Quicksilver Times* and with Liberation News Service, which was kind of the AP of the underground press. She and I were also both loosely affiliated with SDS, which was by now focused on the mounting number of national antiwar demonstrations in Washington.

Anyhow it was hot. Margie and I sat around complaining about the heat, while Lee sat in the next room trying to work and also trying to ignore both of us and the heat. We weren't exactly rich, so to get an air conditioner Margie and I conceived of a plan. I wore my shortest mini-skirts and got a job waitressing at nights at a posh restaurant in Georgetown. By July, I had made enough to buy the air conditioner, so I quit. Hardly a feminist act, but it paid the bills.

The rest of that summer, Margie and I spent our days staying cool, sitting by the air conditioner, and talking feminism. But we were also concerned about the war and wrote numerous articles for our various newspapers. Nights, when the heat let up, we set up movies borrowed free from the local library, charged admission to a room we used at the Institute for Policy Studies, used one of the Institute's projectors, and advertised that we planned to open a coffee house for GIs so we could talk to them about why we were concerned about the war.

By the end of the summer, the idea of a coffee house had been set aside. Research showed that licensing requirements in Washington were more than we could afford, and there didn't seem to be enough GIs in the area to warrant the coffee house anyway. Who would come in and talk? This model had been successful for antiwar work near army bases elsewhere, but somehow it didn't seem right in DC. Nor, we

realized, did we want to spend our time sitting in a coffee house talking with soldiers. We really wanted to be talking with women, to find out how they'd been brought up, how their dreams were shaped, what school was like for them, what their plans were for their lives. We wanted to understand how women were being socialized that made them so different from men. By the end of the summer, we had the beginnings of a feminist understanding hashed out. And $400 in cash. Then Margie left for San Francisco and the money stayed in the bank for a long time.

One of the few times I did go out that summer was to a women's conference in Sandy Springs, Maryland. Most of the other times were to go to a small office the Institute had given Charlotte Bunch (who had worked with a liberal Methodist youth organization) and myself in order to organize that conference. This conference at Sandy Springs ended up being the first of many national conferences the fledgling women's movement would have. But it was important to us then because it was held in August to commemorate the 120th anniversary of the Seneca Falls Convention, the meeting that had sparked the women's suffrage movement.

This meeting was also the first time representatives from the consciousness-raising groups in the cities we'd been corresponding with had gotten together to talk face to face. They too had been sitting around—like Margie and me, and like my group that met in the living room—talking about women's experience, and they all had developed philosophies and ideas. At that meeting of about 20 were women who would later help shape the more radical wing of the women's movement: Shulamith "Shulie" Firestone, author of the book *The Dialectic of Sex*; Kathie Sarachild, author of the term "consciousness-raising"; Roxanne Dunbar, founder of a radical feminist group in Boston called Cell 16 and proponent of Valerie Solanas' (the woman who shot Andy Warhol) *S.C.U.M. Manifesto*; Judith Brown and others from Gainesville, Florida, who created what later became known as the "pro-women line"; and Charlotte Bunch and myself, both of us still loosely affiliated with the antiwar movement. Because of these differences in thinking, which became apparent at this conference, we realized there could be in the near future a split between women who wanted to go it alone as a separate movement and women who wanted to think about feminist issues in coalition with men. For the time being, though, we let such a split lie dormant.

The next whole year was a milestone because of Seneca Falls, we thought, so we busily spent the fall organizing a larger national conference to be held in a YMCA camp outside of Chicago at Thanksgiving time. About 200 women attended this second major conference, including others who were formative thinkers in the movement, such as Ti-Grace Atkinson, author of *Amazon Odyssey*, and Kate Millett, author of *Sexual Politics*. We held consciousness-raising groups and gave workshops, speeches, and papers. The splits that had first become noticeable at Sandy Springs began to appear larger. But the main outcome was the realization that we had a real movement here, one with enormous excitement, ideas, and cohesion. Women, it seemed, had a shared body of experience and knowledge, and our lives enormously mattered, at least to us. The energy and good feelings were very high. Meanwhile, the money that Margie and I had stashed in that bank in Washington just sat, collecting a few pennies in interest each month.

In January 1969, at the time of President Richard M. Nixon's inauguration, a national organization called the Mobilization Against the War held a demonstration in Washington. Speeches were given under a huge circus tent. Among those invited to speak as representatives of the emerging women's movement were Shulie Firestone and myself. We had taken pains to be sure both the antiwar and separatist sides of the women's movement were represented here. I spoke first.

In a scene that has since been much referred to in books on the sixties, I began to talk about a woman's right to control her own body, mentioning abortion, rape, and equal work for equal pay. It was a mild speech by today's standards, but in 1969 it infuriated that crowd of some 20,000 people. Fist fights broke out, with men yelling, "Fuck her. Take her off the stage." I was 26. It was my first speech ever and I was terrified. As some men yelled, other men, and women, began shouting them down or hitting them. I finished and Shulie took the microphone. She gave an even more "feminist" speech than mine—though it too was mild by today's standards—about building respect for a feminist culture. The fights got so bad that Dave Dellinger, a long-time pacifist and the demonstration's master of ceremonies, interrupted her and tried to get her to stop speaking. Other women intervened to ask him to stop trying.

In the aftermath, we were accused of being divisive to the antiwar movement. I received one phone call in particular while we were still holding women's meetings before the weekend's events had ended. I thought it was from a woman I knew who was involved with what would later become a militant offshoot of SDS called Weatherman. As a result of these accusations, a decision was made by representatives of women's groups from around the nation that we would indeed begin organizing for our own interests on our own, that the New Left and antiwar men were not necessarily our friends, as we'd thought. That isn't to say that most of us believed them to be our enemies, but it meant the women's movement was officially born

as separate and independent. In Washington, however, we were not as militantly separatist as women from other cities, probably largely because, like me, most of the leaders were newly married.

By Thanksgiving of 1969, Washington Women's Liberation had blossomed. It included a series of projects—abortion counseling, a rented space for a women's center, a health group, and demonstrations at the Senate hearings on birth control pills. During all that time, I worked as a reporter for the New York *Guardian*, then the "organ of the new left," as it liked to be known [see Jack Smith's "The *Guardian* Goes to War" in this collection]. As radical as it supposedly was, however, the newspaper had an unconscious black-out on feminist news. While demonstrations might be newsworthy, the editors did not consider issues about women—like news on abortion counseling or issues of consciousness-raising—important enough to write about. There was some coverage on the Senate hearings against the pill, but basically the kind of thinking that was beginning to go on in the women's movement seemed beyond the interest of the *Guardian*, beyond the interests of even this most widely read paper of the New Left.

By December, the time seemed right to start a paper of our own. That's when Margie and I agreed to spend the cash. She was still in San Francisco, where it turned out she was organizing telephone workers. Because both our names were on the savings account that held the $400, I wanted to talk with her about using the money to begin a paper that would later be called *off our backs*. When I dialed information, a San Francisco operator said to me, "Oh, Margie, she's great. Her number's unlisted, but for old friends, here 'tis." So that's how I got back in touch with Margie. And she said yes.

It was Christmas and I was seven months pregnant. Shortly after I reached Margie, Heidi and Nan Steffens, Norma Lesser, Nancy Ferro, Marlene Wicks, and I were sitting around my dining room table. Heidi and I were best friends, but we all knew each other through the women's center. Coletta Reid joined our group a few days later. But on this day, we were brainstorming and writing down names on pieces of paper. In between names for a paper, we listed names for my baby as well.

Those were the days of disparities, where we tortured ourselves, denigrating what we actually believed in favor of what we fully thought we should believe. Like with the baby, for instance. I kept on saying that I wanted a girl, but secretly I never once considered a girl a decent way for a person to enter the future, which is what the women's movement was supposed to be all about anyway. For my own child, I wanted a boy so that he would have a fighting chance.

I had already decided to name him Matthew. Yet part of me hoped desperately that we really would create a solid movement so that a daughter of mine could grow up proud to be female.

And the table we sat around was another source of double-think. I had carefully painted it deep blue to hide the gouges from Hoffman's Used Furniture store, but it was an embarrassment for other reasons. In those days, any sign of artful decoration was regarded by local SDS members, at least the ones who lived around the corner and were soon-to-become Weathermen, as decadent symbols of bourgeois lifestyle and politics. Above all, I did not want to be known as decadent, but I did love my table. Except when my mother came, that is. She thought it was an astounding piece of junk.

There was always a gap between what we thought "should be" and what actually was, whether the issue was a beautiful table or a girl child, or, later, so-called armed struggle and the rising up of the masses (as Weathermen were proponents of when they finally split off from SDS), or separatist, lesbianism, leadership, elitism, collectivity, or a middle-class, professional way of life. At the time, though, we kept all these ideological contradictions to ourselves. A few months later they would erupt, causing divisiveness and personal anguish among those of us on the Left.

Men were involved at the very start of *off our backs*. One very talented graphic artist named Jim True, then my downstairs neighbor, designed the paper. He picked typefaces and created the logo and page layouts. We didn't want *oob* to look like the local hippie underground, so Jim gave us the kind of neatness we imagined we needed and a layout that was easy to follow. More than twenty years later, this design has remained basically the same. In addition, our husbands did plenty of childcare, easing up the cries of "Uppy" from 1 1/2-year-old Natasha Lesser when she wanted to be picked up, and the squawks of hunger from Kara Reid and Jennifer Webb, born to Coletta and to me during the preparation of issue number one. Although our marriages didn't survive, Kara, Jennifer, Natasha, and *oob* are all grown women now, a tribute to all our love and stamina. I don't know where Kara is, but Jennifer is in college and considers herself an active feminist. Natasha has just graduated, ready to launch a high powered career.

In putting out the paper, we got by with no cash whenever we could and hoarded the $400 only for the essentials. For office space, we used the basement of a house rented first by Heidi and Nan Steffens and then by the Lessers. We paid no rent, unknowingly broke all zoning regulations because we had no idea there were any, and got no salaries. We ended up using the money for printing and mailing the first issue. We blithely hoped we'd get back enough money in subscriptions to put out a second issue, and we did. Although no decent business would ever begin that way, it actually worked.

The early mailings came from my phone list from Vietnam Summer, that leftover address list of antiwar contacts from the summer of 1967. Added to that was a mailing list from the national conference at Thanksgiving held outside of Chicago in 1968. Since there were no other national feminist publications at the time, although shortly afterward *Ain't I a Woman* and *Rat* appeared, we benefitted largely by excitement and word of mouth. *Ms.* wouldn't appear for another two years.

Staff operations were equally as unplanned, although it fell to Marlene to take charge of the business side of the operation and me to work on editorial content. Specific tasks were done by whomever happened to be in the office at the time the tasks needed doing, but this loose organizational formula only worked well for the first several issues. After that, tensions began growing over how decisions got made (usually by whomever was around when they needed making), over who was or was not doing her share of the work, and over what work did or did not need to be done. Had there been specific job assignments, each collective member could have gained expertise in a specific area and planned out her own job schedule. But because we feared the establishment of some formal hierarchy, jobs were never assigned. An informal hierarchy developed instead, based only on who did the most work. This structure opened the way for guilt trips and unplanned methods of decision making. It later caused divisions over total commitment to feminism versus family responsibilities, outside interests, and the very real requirements for earning money.

By the spring of 1970, two events occurred to precipitate a break. First, a growing feminist rhetoric, later to develop into lesbianism, stipulated that women should spend time only with each other. Second, marriages ended for three out of the four women who were most central to the paper. These two factors threatened everyone. Those who were single generally did not want to give up the hope of having a family. Those who had been married and seen relationships go sour were feeling distant from men and were looking for other ways to live their lives. Children in all these marriages compounded everyone's guilt, as there were also discussions on whether feminists should be raising their own male children or whether women should be raising any children to begin with.

In June, Coletta, Marlene, and I set up an experimental, two-week live-in commune at Marlene's house. It was planned so we could hammer out a philosophy of feminism and so we could take a retreat from work and politics and live in an all-female environment.

Joining us were Charlotte Bunch and Judy Spellman, both key people in other women's liberation projects in DC, and Susan Gregory, Betty Garman, Tasha Peterson, and Susan Hathaway, all antiwar activists newly on the verge of feminism. Tasha, who is Dave Dellinger's daughter, and the two Susans had recently moved to Washington fresh from working on the Chicago 7 trial.

We made presentations and studied, and what emerged from this retreat was a new understanding of feminism that has since evolved, with the research of other feminists, into the more sophisticated philosophy of anthropology now taught in feminist studies courses. It harked back to pre-patriarchical days, when matriarchies were supposedly key, and it viewed sexism as the first real division between classes of people—later followed by racism and classism. Also at the retreat we began developing ideas that would later blossom into feminist spirituality, ideas about the basic female desire for the preservation of nature, of the species, and of the environment.

The retreat unfortunately created hostilities amongst other local feminists. Women who refused to participate felt antagonistic, usually because they were opposed to fledgling separatism. Those who hadn't been invited felt understandably excluded. What we actually did on the retreat was talk theory and practice, eat, clean, take care of children, cook, and dance, all of which had the effect of welding us together in an intense and inexplicable closeness. Lesbianism was not on our agenda, although in retrospect it should have been obvious that homosexuality would be a future result for some.

At the time, part of the hostilities came from an unconscious fear of lesbianism, that if women spent time with one another it had to do with sex. The fear wasn't totally unfounded, as that spring two women very central to DC Women's Liberation had become lovers. Since one was married, and since homosexuality was not mentioned in political circles prior to that, their coming out was shockingly unexpected. But time spent together, of course, did not necessarily mean women had only sexual interests. Additional hostilities and fear arose when, as a result of the retreat, some members of the group decided to form a more permanent communal living situation. Tasha, Betty, and Susan Hathaway rented a house, with the understanding that Susan Gregory, Marlene, and I would all move in. We wanted to experience an all-female culture. In addition, several of us were by then single mothers. My own marriage seemed to be in question, although not because of anything to do with lesbianism, and Lee and I were living apart. It was a tough time for marriages, but at the time I just viewed what I was doing as a temporary experience.

In the meantime, Susan Hathaway, Tasha, and Betty quietly invited a woman alternately named either Beth or Dee from Chicago to join the house commune. She too was a young, single mom. They knew her only distantly from their work on the Chicago 7 trial, but suspicions soon arose about her credibility. An investigation was done on her and it seemed she may have had some connections with the Chicago police and the FBI. Although none of these suspicions were ever confirmed, one result of our concern was that Susan Gregory and I ended up never moving in. It was the first time that any of us had ever thought about the possibility of police infiltration.

At the same time, Tasha, Betty, and the two Susans wanted to join the *oob* collective. We had not set up any internal screening procedures for how new members could be taken on, so they simply began coming to meetings, as new members had done in the past. With the introduction of so many new members at once, other *oob*ers became understandably resentful and suspicious of some planned takeover. In addition to already existing tensions, the break-ups of Coletta's, Marlene's, and, finally, my own marriages left us raw and rather ill-equipped to handle such serious conflict.

Years later, I received some FBI files in the mail that detailed conversations held that summer amongst *oob*ers. At the time, we didn't really worry about police involvement, but I do not know how that information got out, or whether the tensions were purposely exacerbated, or by whom. I later learned the CIA and the FBI both had very sophisticated domestic programs that included placing not only surveillance and provocateurs in the New Left and in the women's movement, but actual political manipulation. One of these programs was called COINTELPRO, but I don't know whether what happened here came under the aegis of that particular program or not.

Just in the past two years I also learned that the phone call made after the speech at that 1969 demonstration may not have been made by the soon-to-become Weatherwoman, as I'd thought, but by very sophisticated intervention on the part of either the FBI or the CIA. The woman I believed made that call, a person with a very distinctive voice, recently surfaced and denied ever making it. Either she is wrong or the key call that ended up dividing the entire movement was made by a paid government provocateur. It turned out there was indeed such a covert action program like that in place at the time.

By fall, however, the *oob* collective was on the verge of splitting apart entirely and I was asked to leave. The issue was ostensibly over elitism, but it also involved a scapegoating mentality, that things could get back in order if I wasn't there. Partly this feeling came from the fact that I had been a key founder of the paper, I was told, and therefore had tremendous power. Partly it existed because I was the only one with prior journalistic experience. But I suppose the notion of anti-elitism was very central to all collectives at the time. Our lack of structure paved the way for informal leaders to emerge, however. With no formal structure there was no formal definition of responsibilities and therefore no way to set limits or grant privileges to informal leaders. The only means for group control was resentment and/or purge.

The specific issue we argued over was my giving a keynote speech at a National Student Association convention and sharing a platform with Betty Friedan. The collective knew I had been asked to speak and had approved of the format. But when I returned, some members were outraged. I was a representative of young, radical feminists. Betty Friedan was a representative of the more moderate, National Organization for Women. The *oob* collective, now enlarged with Tasha, Betty, Susan Hathaway, and even Beth/Dee, made a decision against public speaking so that no one would ever become a personal media star from the feminist Left. This view was repeated in collectives across the nation. The result was that national spokeswomen's roles—and indeed, the national feminist agenda—were taken over solely by political moderates. Indeed, even family issues like guaranteed, quality childcare programs ended up being ignored in the moderate melee, as feminists like Friedan began to focus solely on equal pay and women's career advancement.

In addition to a negativity toward spokeswomen, we also had an unstated assumption that expertise should not be developed by one person but shared by many. This view was originally developed during the revolution in China. We all thought that, because I had been a journalist, for example, others should be encouraged to write and I should do different kinds of jobs.

Thinking about all this now, both ideas sound absurd, although I fully believed them at the time. Our denigration of leaders and skills could only force us into mediocrity (as they, too, later discovered in China) while those women who did not accept this "collectivity-edict" were the very ones who went on to develop a new feminist psychology or history and made advances in medicine or health. They helped us to advance our knowledge about women, while the rest of us had to constantly pick ourselves up off the floor, reeling in guilt and sorely lacking in confidence.

I don't think we needed the women's movement to make us feel low. Since then, all of us have gone through many metamorphoses. Some have been gay and still define themselves that way. Others were gay because politics forced their hands, so to speak, as ideology forced political women to turn to each other.

Still others have returned to careers or found new ways to pursue feminism, excellence, and the need to earn a living. Probable police infiltration of the movement, a tightened economy, a lust for knowledge and skill, the disintegration of marriages, and the very real demands of motherhood all forced us apart as a collective from that very close period of time.

Luckily for *oob*, other women came and took our places. I left in the fall of 1970 and moved with Lee (we'd reconciled for awhile) and Jennifer to found a women's studies program—one of the first in the nation—at Goddard College in Plainfield, Vermont, where I taught for the next five years.

Since then I have moved in and out of another marriage as well as other feminist organizations and programs. Professionally, I've been a newspaper reporter and a magazine writer and editor, serving most recently as editor-in-chief of *Psychology Today*. It has been my experience that as feminism has become part of the mainstream agenda for millions of American's my best work is to help people successfully adapt and incorporate it into their lives letting them use the mass media—especially the women's service magazines—as places to glean important information and as interesting sounding boards. But I also find that, as a reporter, the news of feminism is still not "fit to print," although far more women than ever are journalists. There is still news censorship and/or sensationalism in the reporting of rapes. Women still earn 64 cents to every dollar men earn, there is still a shortage of childcare, the right to abortions—since legalized after much struggle—is now in real question, and there are still few women at the top of major corporations or in very high national political office.

In some very basic ways, there is still no essential change in the status quo: women still have the major responsibility for childcare, and when the economy slows women's jobs are often the first to go. Projections are that poverty in the year 2000 will reside mainly among single mothers and children, and aging divorcees and widows. We might in fact be backtracking.

This makes *oob* all the more crucial, and for 22 years now, indeed it has continued to survive. Our own in-house antagonisms and power struggles may have reduced the cohesiveness of the women's movement but, as time passes, I for one feel nostalgia for the way things were in those earlier times.

In other ways, however, we and other women of the time may have helped to completely overhaul the role of women in American culture. A next generation of feminists seems to be emerging. Hopefully they will pick up and go forward with whatever gains have already been made. My hope is with these women, women of the generation of Jennifer, Natasha, and

Kara, the first daughters of *oob*. They take reproductive rights as a matter of course, they expect equal pay for equal work, they expect to be equal partners in their families and to enter the careers of their choice. They have faith in societal responsibility for childcare and in a woman's independent future. This is the next generation of feminism, ready to go beyond what we fought for. They accept what we won as their starting point and their birthright. When I look at that I realize that, despite our pains, we did our job well.

But I also still wonder: Whatever happened to Margie Stamberg? I sure miss those long, air conditioned nights, those times when we first talked long and hard about a future where women didn't have to go through such struggle. I think it's still a viable dream.

Webb co-founded *off our backs* in 1970. She went on after that to found and teach in one of the first women's studies programs in the country—at Goddard College—and to write for many national magazines. She was features editor of *Woman's Day*, a magazine read by 19 million women and one million men, and recently was the editor-in-chief of *Psychology Today*. She also teaches at the Graduate School of Journalism, Columbia University. In all this, Webb is proudest of her daughter, Jennifer, born during production of the first issue of *off our backs* and today an active feminist at a college in Massachusetts.

THE SAN FRANCISCO ORACLE: A BRIEF HISTORY

Allen Cohen

It began as a dream and ended as a legend. One morning in the late spring of 1966 I dreamt that I was flying around the world. When I looked down, I saw people reading a newspaper with rainbows printed on it—in Paris at the Eiffel Tower, in Moscow at Red Square, on Broadway in New York, at the Great Wall of China, everywhere—a rainbow newspaper.

I told my friend and lover, Laurie, about the dream and she went out early for a walk up the Panhandle of Golden Gate Park to Haight Street telling everyone along the way—artists, writers, musicians, poets, dope dealers, merchants—about the rainbow newspaper. When I went out later, people were exploding with rainbow newspaper consciousness.

I strolled into Ron and Jay Thelin's new Psychedelic Shop where the icons of the new emerging culture were gathered, displayed, and sold—books on Eastern religion and metaphysics and the Western occult, Indian records, posters, madrases, incense, bead necklaces, small pipes. Ron Thelin immediately offered start-up money for publishing a Haight-Ashbury newspaper. Ron called his brother Jay, who had a weekend car parking business in Lake Tahoe to supplement the losses at the Psychedelic Shop, and Jay sent about $500. I was stunned to see how quickly a dream could begin to become reality.

THE HAIGHT-ASHBURY SEEDPOD

The Haight-Ashbury was still unknown to the world. It was an artists' bohemia, and a seedpod that was destined to catch the wind and blossom throughout the world. Since World War II, the Haight had been

Cohen is the author of *Childbirth Is Ecstacy*, the first of the new wave of books on natural childbirth; and *The Reagan Poems*. He also was founder and editor of the *San Francisco Oracle*. The following history is from *The San Francisco Oracle Facsimile Edition*, a complete reprinting of the entire run of the *Oracle* in book form that was published in 1990 by Regent Press, Oakland, California.

an interracial, working class neighborhood bounded by Golden Gate Park, the upper middle class Victorians on Ashbury Heights, and the mostly black Fillmore District.

San Francisco State College's campus had been located on lower Haight Street before it moved to the southern outskirts of the city, so its students, teachers, dropouts, and alumni were still living in the Haight. Artists and poets who had escaped the police crackdown of the North Beach Renaissance several years before had also taken refuge in the Haight. Rents there were cheap—$120 for six rooms in elegant Victorian and Edwardian houses built after the earthquake. The houses and apartments were large enough to be shared, and cooperative living was common. Later, when the world descended upon the Haight, many flats would become crashpads to house the new multitudes.

It wasn't difficult at that time to work occasionally, and sell marijuana or LSD intermittently, thereby maintaining oneself and others economically. One could devote most of one's time to art, writing, or music, experience the enhanced and ecstatic states of mind accessible through the use of marijuana and LSD, and interact with other artists, talking, talking until the sun's rays erased the night. In these years and in this way the particular styles of music, art, and the way of life that are identified with the Haight, the sixties, and the hippies developed.

THE DIALECTICAL PENDULUM

The years 1963-67 were formative to the Haight-Ashbury hippie phenomenon. Swings of the dialectical pendulum of American history underlie the extraordinary changes that were about to occur in America. World War II had been an abyss of planetary violence ending with the development and use of the atomic bomb. The United States emerged from the war as the economic and military leader of the world. The generation that fought the war became the conservative builders and maintainers of an economic empire whose worldwide interests had to be defended, while in their off hours they engendered the largest generation of children in our history.

Women returning to traditional family life relinquished the workplace to the men, and a housing boom brought jobs and homes for the new post-war families. The faceless suburbs arose on the farmland surrounding cities. TV emerged and began to dominate human communications. Grey flannel suits defined the rising middle class, and the cold and sometimes hot war gave us the military-industrial complex. Protecting American capital interests around the world from the rise of

socialism and communism became the obsession of our political, economic, and military policy.

But the sixties would bring pivotal and generational change to America. The fifties of the Cold War, the inquisitions of McCarthy, the Eisenhower uniformity, and America's rise to economic world dominance started to give way to a new social energy with the election of John Kennedy, racial crises, and the renewed idealism of the civil rights movement. The assassination of Kennedy and the buildup of colonial war in Vietnam were counterattacks intended to rein in the forces of cyclical and generational change that had begun to emerge. Though the seat of government was back in the fists of the military-industrial junta, the streets and the campuses were occupied by a new idealistic generation who thought they could taste and control the future.

DIONYSIUS RISING

In the late fifties from the fringes of bohemia came the torrential Dionysian winds that would shake the tree of history. The American yearning for liberty and rebellion burst forth in the poetry and prose of the Beat Generation and the painting of the Abstract Expressionists. These creative energies erupted within a culture gone rigid with profits, conformity, weapons of destruction, and the politics of suppression of dissent.

These buried, unconscious energies could not be confined. They called forth the primacy of the individual and the sensual experience of the body as universe center. All forms and institutions seemed ready to fall away and dissolve before the soaring experience of the Whitmanesque Self and its sensual delight in the American earth. These rising vital energies found their correlatives in the occult philosophies of the West, the meditative philosophies of the East, the romanticized sensuality of the Afro-American ghetto culture, with its improvised jazz and marijuana high, and the ancient tribalism of the oppressed American Indian.

LSD—THE ROCKET ENGINE

The Rise of the Universal Self has had its ups and downs since the late fifties, but its peak came with the discovery and use of LSD by American youth and intellectuals during the sixties. The rebellion, insight, and visionary experiences of the artists of the late fifties would come wholesale to those individuals who wanted or needed to get out on the edges of the only frontier left in America—their own minds and their own senses.

Harvard University, in its suppression of the psilocybin and LSD experiments of Drs. Timothy

Leary, Richard Alpert, and Ralph Metzner, brought instant Universal Selfhood and Dionysian release from social constraint to the awareness of anyone with the urge to step out of his or her grey flannel world and journey to the frontiers of the mind.

LSD was the rocket engine of most of the social or creative tendencies that were emerging in the sixties. It sped up change by giving the experiencing self a direct contact with the creative and mystical insights that visionaries, artists, and saints have sought, experienced, and communicated through the ages. But there were casualties of the LSD voyages—those who were too psychologically wounded, or badly guided, or severe overusers, or victims of the CIA's irresponsible experiments with the psychedelic.

Millions of people took LSD, and for most of them it was a decisive instrument that accelerated change. It released energies that are still reverberating both positively and negatively through our world. This brush with cosmic consciousness stimulated the pagan and Dionysian energies, but it also resulted in the rise of authoritarian religious cults and the social and political reaction of religious fundamentalism. A vision of eternity and freedom was revealed to some while others in fear of such a vision sought the protection of authority and the old dogmas.

P.O. FRISCO—THE PRE-ORACLE

At this historic crossroads during the summer of 1966 in a small neighborhood called the Haight-Ashbury, people began to attend a series of meetings to discuss starting a newspaper. Some of those who attended wanted to do a politically radical but formally traditional newspaper; others wanted the same revolutionary rage but with a more innovative McLuhanesque punch. But there was a third group of poets and artists who felt the world changing in more ways than the confrontational political dualisms of left and right, us and them, and capitalist and socialist.

A deeper revolution was being nurtured in the Haight based on the visionary and mind expanding experiences with LSD, the cooperative living environment, and the exuberance of youth. These poets and artists envisioned a revolution of love and peace starting in the Haight and engulfing the whole planet. The newspaper format was one of the vehicles of the oppressions and materialism of the past. They were searching for a form that would annihilate the phony plutocratic "objectivity" of most reportage, and the lockstep military-industrial rigidity of the column form. This visionary group didn't know what would lie ahead but they knew it wouldn't look like a traditional newspaper.

The meetings were stalemated as a result of these clashing ideas. They wore on and on. Finally, the political group joined forces with the McLuhan group. They secured Ron Thelin's capital without revealing their goals, opened an office in a Frederick Street storefront, and began to work on what was to become the renegade *P.O. Frisco*. The title was an ironic slap at the unwieldy name *Psychedelphic Oracle* (suggested by Bruce Conner, the moviemaker and artist) that the sense of the meetings had been leaning toward.

When *P.O. Frisco* came out in September, it created a shock. There was the same old parade of black and white columns, a cartoon of a naked woman with a Nazi armband on the front page, an article on the concentration camps that some militant groups with a strange mixture of self-esteem and guilt saw awaiting them and all dissidents, and an article on masturbation and its pleasures. It also had a decent remembrance of Ron Boise, the metal sculptor who, after fighting the blue noses and rednecks for many years, had just died of an inflamed heart. His erotic sculptures based on the Kama Sutra had been busted by the San Francisco police at the Vorpal Gallery.

Ron and Jay Thelin and many others felt betrayed by the lack of vision in this renegade paper and withdrew support from the editors, Dan Elliot and Dick Sasoon. The Thelins insisted on a more open decision-making process and *San Francisco Oracle* was chosen as the symbolic designation for the prophetic ideals we wanted to express.

ORACLE #1—LOVE PAGEANT RALLY

The first two issues of the *Oracle* were edited by John Bronson and George Tsongas, but they were still working in a hierarchical and familiar tabloid style. Bronson knew the Chinese language well enough to have worked on a Chinatown newspaper. His priorities were political, but he also had leanings toward the non-linear McLuhanesque aesthetic, as did George Tsongas, who was a poet and novelist of Greek heritage. A more graphic tone came into the paper, and some of the artists who had been alienated by *P.O. Frisco* began to contribute their work. Bruce Conner and Michael Bowen both had full page works in *Oracle* #1 and *Oracle* #2.

The paper picked up some local advertising from the new Haight Street hippie boutiques and the Avalon Ballroom. But the tone of the paper was still hooked into the anxiety of confrontation—that only bad news is worth communicating; that there is only them and us, and them is the POLICE and US is always persecuted. During this period, however, the visionaries developing the *Oracle* and active in the Haight were seeking a form of social development and a vehicle of expression that would make the seemingly endless class and culture clashes obsolete. They imagined the creation of a new transcendental humanity in a society and world freed from the scourges of war and racism.

There was certainly enough persecution around to keep us in perpetual duality. *Oracle #1* featured a defense of Michael McClure's play "The Beard," which had been busted by the San Francisco police. The play was a blunt and raucous dialogue between Billy The Kid and Jean Harlow as they meet and fall in love or lust in heaven, and at the fadeout appear to perform oral sex. Even though it had won two Obies in New York, the San Francisco police threatened to remove Bill Graham's dance permit when he produced it at the Fillmore. Graham moved it to the Committee Theatre on Broadway where it was summarily busted. Letters of support and acclaim for "The Beard" and the First Amendment from Allen Ginsberg, Norman Mailer, and Robert Creely are printed here.

The front page lead story was an account I wrote about a police community relations officer giving a talk at the I-Thou Coffee House during which he commented that the cigarette he was holding was probably more harmful than smoking marijuana. This comment caused an uproar downtown and the officer was removed from public relations.

The backpage of *Oracle #1* had the announcement for the first public outdoor rock concert. The concert, which was called the Love Pageant Rally, was performed on October 6, 1966, a date chosen to suggest 666, the number of the Beast in the Book of Revelations. It also turned out to be the day LSD became illegal in California.

The idea for the event originated with a conversation I had with Michael Bowen, the visionary artist and Mage. We were sipping coffee and watching a group of angry, sign-carrying hippies marching and storming the Park Police Station in protest of the busting of their commune. We saw the futility of this endless confrontation with authority and decided that we needed to invent a new mode of celebration that would energize change more than anger and hate engendering confrontations.

With a group of writers and musicians, and with support from the *Oracle*, we organized the Love Pageant Rally in the Panhandle of Golden Gate Park. We brought flowers and mushrooms (symbolizing the now illegal LSD) to the mayor's office, the police chief, and the U.S. attorney general. People were asked to "bring flowers—flutes—drums—the color gold—pictures of personal saints and gurus and heroes of the underground...." Some of the new emerging bands played, including Big Brother and The Holding Co. with Janis Joplin, and the Grateful Dead.

Two or three thousand people came, danced, turned on, and gawked at each other. Ken Kesey's psychedelic bus, "Further," was there, as were the Hell's Angels, whom Kesey had befriended and turned on to LSD after they had stormed a peace march in Berkeley. The police looked in vain for Kesey, who was rumored to have returned from Mexico even though he was a very wanted man for having jumped bond following a marijuana bust earlier in the year.

The media loved the circus but were confused by it. The *Oracle*, considering it to be a second Boston Tea Party, published a new Declaration of Independence that read in part:

> We hold these experiences to be self-evident...that the creation endows us with certain inalienable rights that among them are: the freedom of body, the pursuit of joy and the expansion of consciousness...

The event had the feel of a new community ritual, and the idea for the "Human-Be-In," a larger more inclusive event that would rock the world, was born.

ORACLE #2—YOUTH QUAKE

Oracle #2's headline story, "Youth Quake," covered the National Guard's invasion of Hunter's Point, the Fillmore, and the Haight-Ashbury on the occasion of September's insurrectional ghetto burning that was caused by the police shooting of a Hunter's Point youth. Red-cheeked boys of 18 with rifles occupied Haight Street, and were met by long-haired girls and boys with LSD, while Hunter's Point burned. Authorities were baffled by both a smoke and brimstone insurrection, and a Dionysian uprising.

The first public act of the Diggers occurred the first night of the martial law when Emmett Grogan taped signs to lampposts urging hippies to "Disobey the Fascist Curfew." While putting these signs up, he was also tearing down signs put up by Michael Bowen. Bowen's signs urged hippies, who he thought might be oblivious to apparitions such as soldiers with rifles, to stay home and out of harm's way. Bowen, while putting up his signs, was tearing down Grogan's signs. They met at a telephone pole and began an angry dispute about style and purpose that would persist till they left the Haight.

A large detailed pen-and-ink drawing by Bruce Conner occupied the entire centerfold of *Oracle #2*. This is the first use of the whole centerfold for a work of art.

ORACLE #3—KEN KESEY'S
GRADUATION PARTY

In the interval between the second and third issue, I had met Gabe Katz, a dropped out advertising artist from New York. Gabe was an expert layout artist who agreed with me on the necessity for aesthetic redirection of the *Oracle*. Gabe had taken LSD and had seen the Light through New York's polluted skies. During his trips he had envisioned Timothy Leary as a being whose existence was on a plane somewhere between an idol and a guru. Gabe gave up his career and the desire for material success and headed for San Francisco.

When the printing deadline for *Oracle* #3 approached, there was a confrontation between Bronson and Tsongas, and Gabe and me over style in general and the inclusion of my long descriptive piece on the Kesey graduation in particular. In a daring gesture, or perhaps in a state of frustration, Bronson and Tsongas walked out. With Gabe's expert layout designs and a shared sense of the necessity to jujitsu the dreary newspaper format, we began our evolution toward the rainbow *Oracle*.

I wanted the content of the *Oracle* to cover two aspects of our new culture: to provide guidance and archetypes for the journey through the states of mind that the LSD experience had opened up; and to invent and examine the new social and cultural forms and institutions that we needed to make the world align with our vision. No small order!

The new design of *Oracle* #3 had a full-page picture of Ken Kesey on the cover. Inside, the paper reported and interpreted his return from Mexican exile. After his San Francisco rooftop bust for smoking marijuana in January 1966, Kesey had jumped bail, feigned suicide, and escaped to Mexico with Neal Cassady.

But America beckoned and Kesey devised a plan for his return: he would have a gigantic dance hall party like the Acid Tests, but, instead of the participants imbibing LSD punch, he would tell everyone to graduate from using LSD. The idea was good enough to keep him out of jail while the wheels of injustice turned. He held a news conference announcing to the world that it was time to graduate from using LSD, though he never did say what to graduate to. After much debate and chagrin, Bill Graham decided against letting him use either Winterland or the Fillmore ballrooms. He thought that Kesey would dose the world again and in particular dose the state Democratic Party, which was due to use Winterland the next week for a convention.

Kesey held the graduation on Halloween in a spontaneously decorated warehouse south of Market Street. Lots of acid was there, along with zany costumes, the first Moog synthesizer used in a rock and roll band, Neal Cassady rapping his ambiguous rhapsodies, and the ominous-looking Hell's Angels. Many people got graduation certificates, and I walked home about four miles to the Haight with a police car slowly following me. I wore bright red chinese pajamas with a dragon embroidered on them and chanted the new Hare Krishna chant, while the whole world turned into a crystalline paradise.

The centerfold of *Oracle* #3 was a collage by Michael Bowen surrounding an article by Gary Snyder. In his article, "Buddhism and the Coming Revolution," Snyder criticizes traditional Buddhism because it has no analysis of how suffering and ignorance are caused by social factors, and has ignored and accepted whatever political tyrannies it found itself under. Once a person has insight from meditation and/or faith, Snyder writes, that person must be led to a deep concern with the need for radical social change, through a variety of hopefully non-violent means. "The mercy of the West has been social revolution. The mercy of the East has been individual insight into the basic self-void. We need both."

During the martial law and curfew many hippies decided to hit the streets and denounce the curfew. Others were oblivious that anything unusual was happening and were caught up in the real world martial law. One of our staff artists, Alan Williams, was one of the oblivious ones. He was busted by the police and beaten in the police station. In "Yogi and the Commissar," he describes his arrest; an accompanying photograph shows him demonstrating the yogic posture he used to withstand the police beating.

When the issue came out, I ran into the captain of the Park Police Station on the street and asked him how he liked the new *Oracle*. He said that it was fine except for the article alleging police brutality. A week later I would be busted for selling *The Love Book*, a book of erotic poems with transcendental invocations, by Lenore Kandel.

ORACLE #4—TIM LEARY COMES
TO THE HAIGHT

In December, Tim Leary came to San Francisco for the first time since the emergence of the Haight as psychedelic central. He had come to perform and promote his travelling, multi-media, psychedelic road show and ritual, "The Death of the Mind." Gabe Katz wanted desperately to draw Tim on the cover because of his almost worshipful admiration for him. Though the rest of the staff didn't want to add to Tim's guru and leadership status, Gabe was very insistent and he was the art editor. His original drawing had multiple halos and rays but we prevailed upon Gabe to cut it down to just a pronounced aura and a few rays.

Dr. Leary discussed his new religion, the League of Spiritual Discovery, which used LSD, marijuana, peyote, and other psychedelic substances as sacraments:

> We urge our fellow Americans to consider forming their own religions...i think the social reality is that more young people are going to be using these drugs and the way to handle them is not to imprison them, but for the universities to run courses on the visionary experience, on the mystical experience, on the methods of using these microscopes of experience.

Applying the teachings of the Eastern religions in meditation, yoga, chanting, and so on to the extraordinary transcendental experiences with LSD was an essential concern of the *Oracle*. Bob Simmons, a yoga teacher, painter, poet, and world traveller, wrote, under his penname Azul, our first article on yoga. In his article, he explores his initial discovery of yoga and meditation for the expansion of consciousness.

He writes, "Yoga is based on the Hindu idea of the perfect state of being, living in accord with the infinite wisdom of the universe. This wisdom is inherent in every molecule, rock, tree, leaf, flower, insect, animal and person."

The "Gossiping Guru" was Carl Helbing, an artist and astrologer who lived in the Haight. He would provide gossip of the inner planes, announce flying saucer landings, suggest astrologically significant dates, and pinpoint the coming of the next avatar. When he reprinted a letter that asked, "Who then can tell us further of Him who was born February 5, 1962, when 7 planets were in Aquarius?", he received a long answer from Kitty McNeil, who described a joint meditation on the inner planes with all the world's adepts providing the spiritual energy and will needed to bring about the birth of the next avatar. Of course, we made her a columnist and called her column "The Babbling Bodhisattva." Kitty was a suburban housewife, theosophist of the Alice Bailey variety, psychic, and lover of LSD and hippies.

The centerfold of *Oracle* #4 was Lawrence Ferlinghetti's poem "After the Cries of the Birds Has Stopped" placed inside a stunning border collage by Michael Bowen. "I see the future of the world in a new visionary society," Ferlinghetti writes. The poem ends with the Chinese invading Big Sur in junks: "Agape we are and Agape we'll be."

The Love Book

The police and City Hall were not pleased with the brashness of this very public bohemia arising in the Haight. They had attacked the Beat scene in North Beach in the late fifties when it rose to national notoriety, and now they were trying to prevent another flourishing of an unconventional culture. The Haight was the geographical center for a new physical bohemia with its own lifestyle, drugs, dance halls, newspaper, customs, flare for public relations, belief in free love, and tremendous appeal to the disillusioned and alienated youth of America.

Ron and Jay Thelin's Psychedelic Shop was the psychic center and meeting place of the Haight, and the first of a multitude of shops and boutiques for the new culture. I was working there part-time for rent money while editing the *Oracle*. The police, who didn't like the *Oracle*, particularly the police brutality story in *Oracle* #3, or the activity around the Psychedelic Shop, or free love, or poetry, contrived a plan to bust us all at once.

On November 15, about a week after *Oracle* #3 came out and a week after the election of Ronald Reagan as governor of California, San Francisco Vice came into the Psychedelic Shop on my shift, leisurely looked around, and with pre-determined intent picked out Lenore Kandel's *The Love Book* from amidst the esoteric and occult books on the display table. They strolled to the counter, paid me for it, handcuffed me, and uttered Kafka's refrain so symbolic of our age, "You are under arrest!"

The Love Book was a long poem about the beauty and spirituality of the sexual act. It used the common names for our physical parts and an encyclopedia full of Tantric and Hindu symbolism. The poem had been read at the Berkeley Poetry Conference in 1965 before an audience of 1,500 people. Of course, the police and whoever had ordered this brilliant maneuver had handed us a sword of righteousness. We had a national first amendment issue, a giant press conference in an old firehouse transformed into an elegant hippie pad, a defiant public reading of *The Love Book* by university professors, and a seminar with professors and poets at San Francisco State College. We published the seminar in full, and relished it down to the last syllable and the smallest print. *The Love Book*, of course, sold thousands of copies.

I wrote a lyrical article, "Notes of a Dirty Bookseller," about my arrest and arraignment. It was full of the ironies of being young, innocent, and unjustly busted: On the day I was arraigned my first teenage love, now a pop singer on her way to minor stardom, had come coincidentally to San Francisco. I remembered the thrill of our hands touching, when I was 15 and she was 13, as we left synagogue after Yom Kippur services. Though I hadn't seen her in ten years, she had changed her name to Tarot Delphi and I was editing the *Oracle*.

The *Love Book* trial held a few months later lasted five weeks, as a parade of scholars, priests, nuns, sociologists, public health officials, doctors, poets, and psychologists testified on the nature of love and poetry. I brought roses to the courtroom from Jay Thelin's garden and gave them to judge, prosecutor, and jury. It was cosmic!

Ironically, despite San Francisco's reputation for liberalism, we were found guilty. Such was the tenor of the time. A higher court later reversed the decision on first amendment grounds.

Lenore Kandel wrote an article in which she describes *The Love Book* as being about: "...the invocation, recognition and acceptance of the divinity in man thru the medium of physical love ...Any form of censorship whether mental, moral, emotional or physical, whether from the inside out or from the outside in, is a barrier against self-awareness."

In another article, Lee Meyerzove discussed the atmosphere of censorship in San Francisco that was apparent in the busts of *The Love Book* and, the previous July, Michael McClure's play, "The Beard," during its performance at the Committee Theatre.

At the Handle of the Kettle: The Diggers

There were two visible handles on the symbolic kettle of the Haight as it boiled its way into history. They were held by the Diggers and by the *Oracle*. But the Diggers and the *Oracle* each represented a different philosophy and lifestyle. The Diggers were a loose association of non-members who were inspired by some former Mime Troupe actors, including Peter Berg, Emmett Grogan, Peter Cohan, Kent Minnault, Billy Murcott, and a dynamic Hell's Angel poet, Bill Fritsch. They brought improvisation, dramatic confrontation, and ritual from their theatrical background into the everyday life of the Haight. They were anarchistic, original, and intellectually insightful in their criticism of society. They intended to act out and bring into existence a total transformation of economic and human relations in our society.

They were "psychedelic" but did not exclude harder drugs and alcohol from their pharmacology. They were passionately critical of the commercialization of the Haight and of the otherworldliness of the more transcendental school of psychedelic rangers. They wanted to abolish social authority and class structure by eliminating the use of money. "Freedom means everything free," said Emmett Grogan to emphasize their radical common sense. Emmett was not adverse

to refusing donations of money, or even burning it to make the point.

The Diggers began giving away free food daily at the Panhandle the week after the Love Pageant Rally. They opened a free store and continued putting on free events, rituals, and actions, including the Death of Money parade at which two Hell's Angels were busted and bailed out with a hippie bail money collection.

The Diggers had a tendency toward anarchy that bordered on violence. They once planned a street happening during which mirrors were to be shined from Haight Street rooftops into the eyes of drivers going up the street. The Hip Merchants, in defense against the Diggers' demand to share their profits with the community, accused the Diggers of threatening extortion and violence.

Though the Diggers' sense of altered reality conflicted with the Love and Nirvana Now view of many other hippies, the *Oracle* was receptive to their input, and they often sat in at our editorial meetings. At one junction when a Be-In was being planned on Hopi Indian land, Emmett Grogan convinced me of its colonialist connotations and its physical impracticality. I presented that view to the *Oracle* staff, and it prevailed. Our refusal to support the proposed Hopi Be-In canceled the project. Generally, the atmosphere around the Diggers was desperate, dark and tense, while at the ordinary hippie pad it was light, meditative, and creative with a mixture of rock, oriental aesthetics, and vegetarian food.

Steve Lieper, in "At the Handle of the Kettle," described the Diggers providing free food at the Panhandle and for Thanksgiving at their Free Frame of Reference garage. Just before we got to press the Health Department closed down the Digger garage. Lieper reported the dark confusion and revolutionary anarchy that hovered around the Diggers.

THE *ORACLE* STAFF

By the time our fourth issue appeared, most of the artists and writers, secretaries, and business people who were to steer the *Oracle* on and off course in the year and a half to follow had gathered together: Stephen Levine, a New York poet who had moved to Santa Cruz and then to San Francisco; Travis Rivers, a Texan who brought Janis Joplin to San Francisco and managed Tracy Nelson, another blues singer; George Tsongas, a poet and novelist from Greece and San Francisco (though Tsongas had left after *Oracle #2*, he would return later and play a major role both artistically and editorially); Hetti McGee, one of our staff artists originally from Liverpool, England; Ami McGill, another staff artist and designer from San Francisco;

Harry Monroe, poet, world traveler, and inspiration to all who would sit through the night and listen to him talk; Dangerfield Ashton, the best pen-and-ink artist South Carolina ever gave to America; Gene Grimm, a 6-foot, 6-inch ex-marine who had become as gentle as a butterfly; and Steve Lieper, a lanky Tennessee hillbilly who did a lot of everything.

Artists who designed and illustrated many *Oracle* pages, often anonymously, included Mark DeVries, Steve Schafer, Michael Ferar, Armando Busick, and Gary Goldhill. Those who typed and organized our words, business, and circulation, many of whom were also artists and writers, included Tiffany, Lynn Ferar, Joan Alexander, Alan Russo, Arthur Goff, and Penny DeVries. There are many others too numerous to mention, some who were anonymous and others whom you will meet in the following pages. All their collective, selfless, and creative work built the *Oracle* into a unique monument of American arts and letters.

Our first offices were the small upstairs spaces behind the Print Mint, a large poster shop on Haight Street that Travis Rivers managed. We converted even the tiny bathroom into an artists' workroom. Dangerfield would stay in there all night working on his elaborate mandalic designs.

ORACLE ECONOMICS

Around this time we got some cash donations from marijuana dealers to help us expand from twelve pages to sixteen. Alex Geluardi, who was a benefactor and comforter to many San Francisco writers and artists, also donated money toward the *Oracle*'s growth. Cashflow never did catch up to costs, so we occasionally had to borrow money to print. At one point Jay Thelin would get an unsecured $6,000 loan from the local Haight Street bank. One of the bank executives was pleased to lend the *Oracle* money, because he had just won a free trip to Hawaii for opening more accounts than any other bank in the state. Even Bill Graham, the rock impresario, with his reputation for realism and grouchiness, lent the *Oracle* $1,000. But after the first few issues the only outright donation we got was $5,000 from Peter Tork, of the TV rock group, The Monkees. Unfortunately, that contribution had a karmic retribution: my friend and lover, Laurie, fell in love with Tork's business associate during an LSD trip, and on Christmas day drove away with him to Los Angeles in his Mercedes.

But by *Oracle* #8 we would be mostly self-sustaining. The paper was able to pay the rent and food costs for most of the staff, who were living together in several small communes. We had started the paper printing 3,000 copies and grew gradually to about 15,000 by *Oracle* #4. We jumped to 50,000 for #5, the Be-In issue, and grew to almost 125,000 by about *Oracle* #7. We estimated that five or more people read each issue, lifting circulation to over 500,000. We sent *Oracles* as far west as New Zealand, India, and Vietnam—we would receive Vietnamese marijuana from soldiers in return—and as far east as Prague and Moscow, hidden in the bottom of boxes of secondhand clothing.

Oracles were sold in the streets of San Francisco and Berkeley by hippies for whom it was often the sole means of support. We let anyone take a free ten copies to sell in order to get a stake, and then buy more. The *Oracle* was the largest employer on the scene. We had a large worldwide subscription list, and backpackers and gypsies would buy as many as a hundred to take back to their hometowns.

THE *ORACLE* AESTHETICS

The *Oracle* would go from hand to hand and mind to mind in the evocative states unveiled by marijuana and LSD. It was a centering instrument for that intense, aesthetic, and expanded perceptual universe. To this day I meet people who tell me how they had seen an *Oracle* in some small town in West Virginia, or thereabouts. They attribute to that sighting of the *Oracle* their recognition that they were not alone on a dark planet in an empty universe. From that moment on they date the beginning of their journey toward self-realization.

To achieve the oracular effects we wanted we would give the text, whether prose or poetry, to artists and ask them to design a page for it, not merely to illustrate it, but to make an organic unity of the word and the image. Most of the artists would conceive and manifest their designs in a state of expanded awareness. Thus, the *Oracle* pages correspond to the methodology of the Thanka art of Tibet and Byzantine art in which the artist established a visionary state of mind, through meditation, chanting, and/or prayer, and tried to convey that vision in his painting.

The perceivers of the art then could mount to that same elevation, and experience within their minds the same visionary state. So, looking at an *Oracle* could be a sort of occult trance experience communicated across the dimensions of space and time, through the tabloid medium, from one explorer of inner worlds to another. That was the magic, the fire, that spread from mind to mind with the *Oracle*. Motifs and techniques were universal—from ancient Chinese spirals to Sci Fi—all brought together in multi-dimensional depth, pattern, and flow; wings, rays, auras, arabesques, swirls, unicorns and centaurs, mandalas, collages, flying saucers and their inhabitants, op-art, flowers and paisley, nudes, feathers, and ghosted images all interwoven into a dazzling cross-cultural spectacle.

ORACLE #5—HUMAN-BE-IN ISSUE

Issue #5 established the basic format that the *Oracle* was to develop for the next seven issues. The front page announced the Human-Be-In with a purple, ash-covered saddhu with three eyes and matted hair staring at the reader. This was our first color experiment with eight pages in two shades of purple. The color pages—the first four, the last four, and the centerspread—were our rainbow brush. These pages—the head, feet, and spine of the *Oracle*—were used for major art work, articles, and poetry. They were never used to enhance advertising. The centerspread was used especially for a central theme or important poem, and always received a lavish design. Most of these principles of format had appeared in the previous issues, but were now consciously solidified and enhanced. Our use of shaped text instead of straight columns appears here for the first time.

Another practice we had begun in *Oracle* #4, with the Leary press conference and the symposium of the "Six Professors in Search of the Obscene," was to print all interviews in full except for stuttering and repetition. This practice would prevent such common newspaper terrors as quoting out of context, downright misquoting, and a reporter's subjectivity or political leaning from distorting the actual spoken word. All *Oracle* interviews are printed as they were spoken even if we had to continue them in small print to fit. Interested readers might have to squint, but what they read was everything that was said, warts and all.

By *Oracle* #5 we realized that, in order to publish with the artistic and visionary quality we intended, we could not be bound to the everydayness of the tabloid format. We would be lucky to publish every six weeks. Even to meet that schedule, we would have to lift our binoculars to the prophetic horizon. From here on all resemblances to an ordinary newspaper were purely coincidental. We would not be co-opted by commercial interests and we would not add to the fear and anxiety in America—TV, newspapers and movies did a fine job on that end of the stick. The *Oracle* was now a journal of arts and letters for the expanded consciousness—a tribal messenger from the inner to the outer world.

Though the *Oracle* staff didn't have a political program, we did feel that we were part of a worldwide process of transformation—part revolution and part renaissance—originated by this new generation of youth. A mystique of youth began with the conception

that the world and the powers that ruled it were decadent, corrupt, and calcified. Therefore, the future was perceived as youth's responsibility to create and remold.

Staff members felt a moral revulsion against modern technological civilization for its failure to regenerate the world according to the principles of economic justice and peace. Most of us wanted the conversion of the dying past to come about through a spiritual transformation that fostered the values of love, peace, and compassion. The *Oracle* would be a vehicle for new and ancient models that were needed to guide these changes in consciousness and to reconstruct our world.

Some writers have seen an escapist gap between the *Oracle*'s point of view and the antiwar movement, but the *Oracle* was as committed to the movement as anyone else. We emphasized the unity of political and transcendental ideals, and we had a preference for non-violence. The mass movement against the war had equal parts of LSD vision, marijuana sensory delight, political ideology, and moral rage.

The purple saddhu cover of *Oracle* #5 was also used as one of the posters for the Human-Be-In. The *Oracle* sponsored, announced, and was given away free at the Be-In. We printed about 50,000 copies of this issue and the circulation would continue to build until it reached almost 125,000. The cover was designed by Michael Bowen, and included a photograph by Casey Sonnabend and artwork by Stanley Mouse.

The Human-Be-In developed out of the success of the Love Pageant Rally, and the realization that the change in consciousness and culture we were experiencing had to be communicated throughout the world. We felt that the ideals of Peace, Love, and Community based on the transcendental vision could transform the world and end the war in Vietnam. In short, we wanted to turn the world on and to do it we would need to attract the spotlight from centerstage Washington and Vietnam to centerstage Haight-Ashbury.

Michael Bowen centered much of the organizing energy for the Be-In from his pad at Haight and Masonic. In addition to his expressionist painting and drawing, he was friends with the Beat poets from the North Beach era, and had spent time with Tim Leary at Millbrook. He was a mystic hustler whom Allen Ginsberg had called the most convincing man he had ever known. He could charm the press and turn on a square. And he did. He invited Leary and the Beat poets to the Human-Be-In, and arranged for it to be a worldwide media event.

Bowen and I had become concerned about the philosophical split that was developing in the youth movement. The antiwar and free speech movement in Berkeley thought the hippies were too disengaged and spaced out, and that their influence might draw the young away from resistance to the war. The hippies thought the movement was doomed to endless confrontations with the establishment that would recoil with violence and fascism. We decided that to strengthen the youth culture we had to bring the two poles together. In order to have a Human-Be-In we would have to have a powwow.

We met with Jerry Rubin, Max Scherr, and other Berkeley activists, and shared our ideas about directing magical and conscious energy towards the Pentagon as a way to overcome its impregnability as both the symbol and seat of evil. We had developed this magical concept to exorcise the Pentagon from the writings of Lewis Mumford and the visions of Charlie Brown, the peyote shaman. We turned Rubin on to marijuana and then Bowen turned him on to LSD. The idea to exorcise the Pentagon would be realized in the March on Washington in October. Rubin and Jack Weinberg were invited to speak at the Be-In, and Max Scherr agreed to announce and support the Be-In in the *Berkeley Barb*.

The Gathering of the Tribes in a "union of love and activism" was an overwhelming success. Over twenty thousand people came to the Polo Fields in Golden Gate Park. The psychedelic bands played: Jefferson Airplane, the Grateful Dead, and Quicksilver Messenger Service. Poets Allen Ginsberg, Gary Snyder, Michael McClure, Lawrence Ferlinghetti, and Lenore Kandel read, chanted, and sang. Tim Leary told everyone to Turn on, Tune in, and Dropout. The Diggers gave out free food; the Hell's Angels guarded the generator cables that someone had cut; Owsley Stanley gave out free acid; a parachutist dropped like an angel from the sky; and the whole world watched on the evening news. Soon there would be Be-Ins and Love-Ins from Texas to Paris, and the psychedelic and political aspects of the youth culture would continue to grow hand in hand everywhere.

Renaissance or Die

Other contributions to *Oracle #5* included an interview with Richard Alpert, a centerfold speech by Allen Ginsberg, a poem by Michael McClure, and mandalas by Dangerfield Ashton.

Alpert was a psychologist at Harvard who had participated with Tim Leary in the early research and experimentation with LSD at Harvard and Milbrook. The title of the article is "See Opposites" spelled backwards. The mandalic art was drawn by Dangerfield Ashton.

"The Haight-Ashbury is...the purest reflection of what is happening in consciousness at the leading edge of our society," Alpert says. "This is an interesting question: Whether we westerners can ever take on a master...master roles really don't fit into Western culture...Meher Baba says 'love me, turn your whole consciousness over to me and you'll get enlightened.' But that's not going to work here and Tim doesn't take on masters. I mean I can't do it, just constitutionally at this point in my development, I can't do it....A guide is a guy who's been there before and will help you but he's not somebody you turn over your spiritual development to."

Of course, Dr. Alpert would go to India, find a guru, change his name to Ram Dass, return, and educate thousands on the virtues of guru worship and the spiritual life.

The Ginsberg centerfold, "Renaissance or Die," was a reprint of a speech he gave in Boston in November 1966 to a convocation of Unitarian ministers. The incredible drawing is by Rick Griffin. Ginsberg speaks of the poet's role as prophet:

to trust my own fantasy and express my own private thought...How can we Americans change theme? I will make a first proposal: that everybody who hears my voice...try the chemical LSD at least once, every man, woman and child over 14 in good health....then I prophecy we will all have seen some ray of glory or vastness beyond our conditioned social selves, beyond our government, beyond America even, that will unite us into a peaceful community....there should be within centers of learning facilities for wisdom search which the ancients proposed as the true function of education....There is a change of consciousness among the younger generation toward the most complete public frankness possible....Likely, an enlarged family will emerge for many citizens...with matrilineal descent...children held in common with the orgy an acceptable community sacrament. America's political need is orgies in the parks, on Boston Commons, with naked Bacchantes in the national forests....I am acknowledging what is already happening among the young in fact and fantasy....

He speaks of ancient forms of Indian, African, and Eastern culture being practiced by American youth, and continues:

....I am in effect setting up moral codes and standards which include drugs, orgy, music, and primitive magic as worship rituals—educational tools which are supposedly contrary to our cultural mores and I am proposing these standards to you respectable ministers, once and for all, that you endorse publicly the private desire and knowledge of mankind in America, so to inspire the young.

Michael McClure's poem, "The God I Worship Is a Lion," is an expression of two major themes in the developing philosophy of the period: a pantheistic identification with nature perceived as an alive and conscious organism, and a totemistic empathy with the other creatures of our world revered as aware and admirable beings; and the second theme was the felt identity of the human body and the human spirit replacing the dualistic notion of the separateness of the spirit and its supposed superiority. McClure's poem captures these ideas. It is embraced by a collage by Michael Bowen:

The God I worship is a lion
and I pray to him for
Speed
Power
& Courage...
In the meekness of May
I'll sing all the day
in the throne of my flesh
freed of the mesh
and the gins and the traps
that bind me!...
There shall be a new image of God!...

The back cover was another mandala by Dangerfield Ashton. Dangerfield was a young southern boy about 19 who was AWOL from the army. Even at that young age, he was a great pen-and-ink artist. Unfortunately, he was taking a lot of amphetamines, which made him overwork some of his drawings. He lived in the *Oracle* office for awhile, and worked in a small bathroom that we converted into a studio for him. We had to keep an eye on his work, though, and grab it away from him before he turned it into a blot. One day the FBI came looking for him, but he had grown a beard since he had taken his enlistment pictures. They showed Dangerfield his own picture, but failed to recognize him.

THE TRANSCENDENTAL RED CROSS

Before the production of the sixth *Oracle*, we moved our offices to larger quarters in Michael Bowen's former flat on Haight Street just off Masonic. Bowen moved to Stinson Beach in West Marin. The Be-In media blitz had brought the Haight-Ashbury to the center of America's consciousness. The disaffected, the disenchanted, the mafia, the mad, the CIA, the FBI, the sociologists, poets, artists, American Indian shamans, East Indian gurus, TV and movie crews, magazine and newspaper reporters from all over the world, and tourists riding through and staring at it all descended on the tiny street called Haight. The result was a monumental traffic jam on all levels.

The *Oracle* kept its new offices open 24 hours a day. We had a day crew who were mostly engaged in producing the *Oracle*, and a night crew who were a multi-purpose transcendental Red Cross. They fed the hungry out of a giant pot of rice and beans, eased down and straightened out the bad trippers, and gave impromptu seminars in cosmic consciousness for the heads, the FBI, and the undercover cops who wandered through.

The night crew were chosen to be guides and nurses to the mind hurricane that blew through our open door. Twenty or thirty people a night were fed by Jim Cook, a Big Sur mountain man and peyote eater. Alan Williams, a painter, sculptor, and yogi, painted an eight-foot high mural of the new Adam and the new Eve, muscular and naked, on the kitchen wall. Alan and Jim and others would spread a non-stop rap of cosmic love and cosmic dust from dusk to dawn. They were healers and tricksters who could help people kick methedrine and heroin, turn bad trips into ecstasy, and give comfort to the confused and lonely.

The presence, use, and abuse of methedrine and heroin soon became a problem in the Haight. Methedrine caused anxiety and paranoia and severe depression during the comedown. It was known to be a brain cell destroyer in whose wake violence often erupted. We looked upon heroin as an anti-consciousness drug, because its addictive properties and expense would turn people away from their goodness for the sake of their habits. In the Haight a heroin addict might steal your hi-fi, forge your check, and most frequently take the drugs or the money in a marijuana or LSD deal.

Most of us felt that some drugs were positive, therapeutic, and physically harmless, while others were harmful to the human body and/or mind. Generally, we thought, as shared victims of the legal prohibition against drugs, that all drugs should be decriminalized, and addiction treated as a medical problem.

At the *Oracle*, we decided that we had to get the worst cases of psychotic breaks and drug abuse out of the increasing pressure of urban life. In late spring of 1967, Amelia Newell donated the use of thirty or forty acres, and what was known as the Stone House near Gorda, a tiny town just south of Big Sur, for an *Oracle* retreat.

Jim Cook went there to keep the action flowing and we sent people there every weekend in a truck along with a hundred pounds of brown rice, beans, and vegetables. At times there were a hundred people at

Gorda recovering and recuperating, taking LSD and peyote, drumming and dancing around nightfires, meditating and hiking in the Big Sur wilderness. It was a free pre-Esalen experience for those who really needed it.

The retreat functioned well for about nine months until early 1968, when a young man came through with a rifle, took LSD, and shot a neighbor's cow that in his hallucination was turning into some unruly beast. Then, the highway patrol with cars, motorcycles, and helicopters descended on this Haight-Ashbury extension, hostel, and dry dock, sending a hundred hippies scurrying into the hills in the nick of time. Amelia Newell, who was innocent of everything but a charitable heart, went to court, and had to make restitution for the cow.

THE RAINBOW UNVEILED

In the meantime, during the daytime and one hundred miles north in San Francisco, we were creating *Oracle #6*. We switched our printer from Waller Press to a 7-web press at Howard Quinn Printers. Because of the size of the press we could expand our use of color. We would print the paper on Sundays and the printers would allow our staff artists to use the presses like a paint brush. Our first experiment was to divide the ink fountain of a web into three compartments with metal dividers and wooden blocks, put a different color ink into each compartment, and run a rainbow over eight pages of *Oracle #6*. Thus the dream I had in the spring of 1966, of a rainbow newspaper being read all over the world, became a reality.

We soon discovered that, where two colors came together in the fountain, the inks would blend to make a third color. When we had blue and yellow in adjacent compartments, they would seep beneath the dividers during the run and produce a strip of green on the image. We devised ways of controlling this fortuitous accident that enabled us to bring forth five colors on a page, but with the drawback of having only stripes of color.

Although the records have disappeared, I think we wanted to produce 60-75,000 copies of *Oracle #6*, but we didn't have enough money for such a big printing. We printed as many as we could pay for, sold them, collected our advertising money, and then came back on subsequent Sundays to print more. In the interim we could make changes in colors, and even in content. So *Oracle #6* has at least three different printings that I have found, and the next six issues have two or more different printings.

Because the press had so many webs, we could also separate parts of the image and run them in different colors. Therefore one image could have both a split fountain and separated colors that were printed in a specific part of the image. This ability gave us the potential for six or more colors on a page, and more control of where some of the colors would be placed. The manipulation of this palette on a press that was usually used for supermarket advertisements was the unique signature of the *Oracle*. To top it off, as a special talisman, we would sometimes spray the papers with Jasmine perfume when they came off the press.

ORACLE #6—THE AQUARIAN AGE

Oracle #6 was our first theme issue. In our theme issues we would try to present various aspects of a theme but never all sides of a theme. We weren't interested in a pro or con presentation. We presented a theme because a consensus of interest existed in the community and on the editorial staff. Actually the editorial meetings included everyone—editorial and art staff, secretaries, circulation and business people, invited guests, and anyone who happened in the door. We felt that, if the flow brought a person there, that person was supposed to be there. Therefore, he or she was also allowed to vote on whatever issue was being decided. We thought of these guests and drop-ins as representatives of the rest of the world.

The theme of *Oracle #6* was an astrological speculation on the Aquarian Age. Three astrologers presented their views on what the Aquarian Age meant, and whether we were in it, or approaching it. A member of our staff quipped that the Aquarian Age had arrived, lasted six months, and we were now in the Age of Capricorn. The front cover was the symbol of the Aquarian Age drawn by Rick Griffin (see figure 1) and the back cover was the feminine representation of the Aquarian Age drawn by Ida Griffin.

The three astrologers were Ambrose Hollingsworth, Gayla, and Gavin Arthur. Ambrose Hollingsworth was a young man in his thirties, who used a wheelchair due to paralysis caused by an auto accident. He had been a writer in Greenwich Village and North Beach and had participated in many artistic circles during the fifties and sixties. He claimed to be an initiate in an occult group called The Brotherhood of Light and had begun an occult school in Marin called the Six Day School. Ambrose had astrologically chosen the date of January 14, 1967, as the most propitious date for the Human-Be-In.

Gayla was the pen name of Rosalind Sharpe Wells, a medium and astrologer who had received the New Aquarian Tarot Deck through the Ouija board and automatic writing. Rosalind claimed to possess the psychic capability of distant viewing. During her adol-

Figure 1: Cover for *Oracle* #6: Symbol of the Aquarian Age. Copyright © 1967 by Rick Griffin.

escence in the Forties, she could envision the bombings of World War II as they occurred, and felt great consternation and pain seeing the destruction of life flash across her mind. She began to suppress her psychic abilities with alcohol and drugs until she met the occult teacher, John Cooke, who encouraged her abilities. Together they commenced their work on the "New Aquarian Tarot," which we introduced in *Oracle #9*.

Gavin Arthur was a well-known astrologer, philosopher, and raconteur. His flat above a Japanese restaurant on Buchanan Street was a gathering place for artists, occultists, hippies, international vagabonds, politicians, and the upper crust of San Francisco. He was the great-grandson of Chester Arthur, the twenty-first president of the United States. He had been in W.B. Yeats' circle in Ireland, and claimed to be a disciple of Walt Whitman through the English mystic, Edward Carpenter, a friend, student, and, perhaps, lover of Whitman's. In our interview Gavin says the Aquarian Age wouldn't come until 2660: "until science, religion and philosophy are one, mankind will not have reached his coming of age, his maturity."

New Geology, Paul Krassner, Dr. Mota—and Methamphetamine

"New Geology," by Chester Anderson, is the classic ode to acid rock. Anderson, as founder and editor of the Communications Company, wrote and printed mimeographed diatribes and newsflashes, and distributed them instantaneously on Haight Street. The Communications Company was also the Diggers' instant telegraph and some of its output is known as the Digger Papers. Chester writes in *Oracle #6*:

Rock is head music, psychedelic music.
Rock is legitimate avant garde art form.
Rock shares most of its formal structural principles with baroque music.
Rock is evolving homo gestalt configurations—the groups themselves living together—super-families—pre-initiate tribal groups.
Rock is participational and non-typographic art form.
Rock is regenerative and revolutionary art, not degenerative or decadent.
Rock principles are not limited to music.
Rock is an intensely synthesizing music able to absorb all of society into itself.
Rock has reinstated the ancient truth that art is fun.
Rock is a way of life—international and universal.
Not even the deaf are completely immune. (IN THE LAND OF THE DARK/THE SHIP OF

THE SUN/IS DRIVEN BY THE GRATEFUL DEAD)

Paul Krassner also appeared on the pages of *Oracle #6*, and spoke not about acid rock but about acid, the street name for LSD. Krassner, the satirist and editor of *The Realist* magazine, was visiting San Francisco for the first time. He would later be one of the founders of the Yippies, raid Chicago, and move to San Francisco.

"I was never high before I took LSD," he confessed in an interview entitled "LSD, Revolution & God." "I had all kinds of reverse paranoia on my first trip. I thought people were doing nice things for me....I called my wife and thanked her for it but she didn't know what I was talking about....I don't look upon youth as a panacea, because at every demonstration I've been in there's been a lot of youthful counterdemonstrators filled with hostility, filled with a kind of fierce patriotism....Well, Alpert talks about a serenity on the West Coast; I get that feeling....But I hear from people on the West Coast that they're imitating people on the East Coast, and I hear from people on the East Coast that they're imitating the West Coast...and I begin to think that it's really happening in Denver..."

At this moment two nuns walk into the *Oracle* office and Paul remarks, "It's hard for me to imagine two nuns walking into the office of the *East Village Other*."

One of the nuns was Sister Mary Norbert Korte, a nun in the Dominican order. Sister Mary Norbert was a fine poet as well as a rather unorthodox nun. She would climb out of her nunnery window at night, and come to poets' houses to talk, read, and turn on. We would bake marijuana brownies and bring them to her in the nunnery. Though she came from a long line of priests and nuns, she did drop out to live a sectarian life as a poet.

The *Oracle* asked Krassner, "Did your atheism change after LSD in any quantitative way?"

Paul answered, "No, no! How could it change? There was a different God I didn't believe in."

Another call to higher consciousness in *Oracle #6* was John Phillips' drawing of the broken down bus that resembles an old medicine show wagon with signs all over it saying, "Cannabis Cure All, Cactus Therapy, Peyote Practice, Nature's Chemicals, etc." "Dr. Mota's Medicine Show Bus" was a representation of the general attitude toward drugs, particularly natural drugs, but including LSD. These drugs were seen as medicines for the sick spirit of western civilization that was suffering from the disease of alienation and the domination and destruction of nature. Our psyches also were sick with alienation, bound in the nutshell of the

Ego, and cut off from the repressed, personal, and collective unconscious.

These medicines allowed us to experience the depths of the unconscious, intensified our sensory delight in nature, and aided the integration of the severed psyche. Visions of gods in all their forms and ecstasies were being experienced widely. An awareness that humanity was able to reach a potential fulfillment—a world at peace, human relations based on love and brotherhood, and communities based on compassion—drove this whole generation to its mostly non-violent battle against the war in Vietnam.

One drug, however, was not glorified by Phillips' drawing, but was discussed in an article by Kent Chapman entitled "Ecstatic Isolation & Incarnation." Methamphetamine was the crack of the sixties. When injected it produces a flash high and a long stimulation effect that gives the sense of a godlike mental acuity. It was invented by the Nazis in the thirties, and used by Hitler, his associates, and the SS. It causes brain cell damage, depression, and an addictive need to use more. Often, the user will go for days without sleep. In *Oracle #4* we had published an article by Dr. Joel Fort, "Methedrine Use and Abuse in San Francisco," that discussed the possibility of a therapeutic cure for this addiction. Chapman's article, written originally as a letter to Michael Murphy of Esalen Institute, was a lyrical confession after three years of methamphetamine abuse.

Chapman writes: "I have been at a standstill in my flesh as a person incarnated...For me hell was the ecstasy that rots teeth and person. I didn't live in the seasons of the sun but in the changes of my metabolism."

Alan Watts' Basic Myth and Tom Weir's Photo Lovers

Alan Watts, a former Anglican priest, was America's foremost authority on Zen Buddhism and Oriental mysticism. He lived in a houseboat in Sausalito, and was the resident philosopher for the hippies and the Beat poets. "The Basic Myth—According to the Tradition of Ancient India" was the first of Watts' several contributions to the *Oracle*.

He writes: "In the beginning...is the self...Because of delight the Self is always at play, and its play, called LILA, is like singing or dancing which are made of sound and silence, motion and rest. Thus, the play of the Self is to lose itself and to find itself in a game of hide and seek without beginning or end."

Many other spiritual paths were also being explored and invented in the Haight during this period, but the preponderant view favored an intense sensuality. Experiences with both LSD and marijuana seemed to unveil a world of sensory splendor and spiritual depth that had been absent from most people's Judeo-Christian expectations. Our religions, philosophies, and social conditioning had not prepared us for such experiences as the whole planet being one living and breathing organism, with our own beings melting into it, or every atom of our bodies merging with our sexual partners' bodies so that their thoughts became ours, as if there weren't two different beings, or seeing God or gods and talking to them, or realizing that you and everyone else were God. These kinds of visions inspired a search through the literature and religions of the world for guideposts and maps for these ancient journeys.

One of the most generally preferred and admired spiritual paths was Mahayana Buddhism (from which Zen developed). Mahayana Buddhism teaches that the experience of the Void, or God, or the greatest Bliss, is a unified field identical with our everyday experience of the material world. When the veil of separateness lifts, and we experience reality without the interference of egotism, desire, and its consequent suffering, and without the shadow of concepts, the blending of the material and spiritual will fill every instant with wonder. The Mahayana ideal of the Bodhisattva, who achieves enlightenment, but returns to the world to compassionately serve humanity, appealed to the spiritual seekers of the Haight.

Hinduism also has a sensual and sexual school of thought and practice called Tantra that influenced those who wanted to bring together the body and the soul, and the material and spiritual worlds. The word "LOVE" was a symbol or code for these ideas, mystical experiences, and practices. "Love" was the universal principle merging all and everything in an ecstatic unity. Thus the phrase often used by hippies, "It's all love," had a more precise meaning than was generally understood.

Tom Weir's full-page photomontage of a couple making love with multiple sets of arms and legs in motion and, in issue #7, Paul Kagan's "Yab-Yum" (see figure 2) epitomized the *Oracle*'s dedication to this ideal of the unity of body and soul.

ORACLE #7—HOUSEBOAT SUMMIT MEETING

Our longest issue, 52 pages, was the Houseboat Summit Meeting with Allen Ginsberg, Alan Watts, Gary Snyder, and Tim Leary that was held, I must admit, in Top Secrecy aboard Alan Watts' houseboat in Sausalito (see figure 3). The four mentors, poets, and philosophers were the most respected voices in the Beat-Hippie-Psychedelic movement. We intended this issue to be the ultimate roundup of the hippie philoso-

AMERICAN TANTRIC #2   (YAB-YUM)
PHOTO: PAUL KAGAN
      51   Available in poster form from Berkeley Bonaparte
                                 P.O. Box 1250 Berkeley, Calif

Figure 2: From *Oracle* #7: "Yab-Yum." Copyright © 1967 by Paul Kagan.

phy. It came out just before Easter week when a huge influx of the young, the curious, the pilgrims, and tourists were expected to descend upon the Haight.

The idea of bringing Leary, Watts, Snyder, and Ginsberg together originated with art editor Gabe Katz. Gabe had become dissatisfied, even a little paranoid, that others were seeking his position, particularly Neil Rose, an abstract painter from Big Sur with a passion for the Tarot and the *I Ching*. This would be the last issue whose design was administered by Gabe and he would resign with bitterness after its completion.

Most of the Houseboat discussion circled around the problem of whether we were going to drop out or take over.

Leary and Watts criticized the moral violence and anger of the antiwar movement while Ginsberg and Snyder defended the movement. Snyder said that political utopianism and mysticism have common historical roots.

Leary was questioned by Snyder and Ginsberg about what "drop out" really means. He prophesied small groups dropping out, like ten MIT scientists, and forming small tribal groups.

Watts criticized our educational system for not giving us any material competence: how to cook, make clothes, build houses, make love, or be a father or mother. Meanwhile, he added, we are a rather small movement involved in the midst of a multitude of people who can only survive if automated industry feeds, clothes, houses, and transports them by means of the creation of ersatz materials. Snyder brought up the necessity of stopping population growth because it destroys other species; and Leary suggested putting all technology underground.

Watts continues, "If we don't have the political catastrophe of atomic war, we will develop a huge leisure society that pays people for the work that machines do for them."

Leary suggested that two or more species may be evolving—one an ant hill species with a technological king and queen, and the other tribal and basic.

Snyder answered that this is a negative view of human nature, and that all people want to be in touch with what is real in themselves and nature. "People will consume less, if what is exciting to them is not things but states of mind," he said.

Watts and Snyder spoke of organic original intelligence in so-called "primitive society"—an intelligence based in experience and vision, not abstract thinking. Snyder rhapsodizes, "The Comanche or Sioux demand that everybody go out and have his vision and incorporate and ritualize it within the culture. Then a society like India, a step more civilized, permits some individuals to have these visions, but doesn't demand it of everyone. And then later it becomes purely

eccentric."

Snyder related what he was telling people who asked him how to drop out:

> Get in touch with the Indian culture here....Find out what the mythologies were. Find out what the local deities were. You can get this out of a book. Then go and look at your local archaeological sites. Pay a reverent visit to the local American Indian tombs, and also the tombs of the early American settlers. Find out what your original ecology was. Is it short grass prairie or long grass prairie? Go and live on the land for a while; set up a tent and camp out, and watch the clouds, and watch the water, and watch the land, and get a sense of what the climate here is....Then decide how you want to make your living here.

They all talked about practical steps, like meditation centers in the city; Human-Be-Ins in all cities; groups, tribes, and clans forming out of these meditation centers; people living together, working together, sharing money, and becoming extended families.

Snyder summed it up with: "the extended family leads to matrilineal descent, and when we get matrilineal descent we'll have group marriage...with group marriage capitalism is doomed and civilization goes out."

The discussion continued with elaboration of these themes, Ginsberg's conversations with Mario Savio, and who their grandfathers were.

It ended with Tim Leary saying, "The seed carrying soft body should not be embedded in steel...I have no intention of going to jail and I won't go to jail. No one should go to jail." Of course, Tim went to jail but not until he announced that he was running for governor.

Bom Bom Mahadev, Prajna Paramita Sutra, and Lucifer Rising

In addition to the Houseboat Summit Meeting, *Oracle* #7 contained a review, a preview, and a prayer. "Bom Bom Mahadev—A Mantra for Marijuana" is the title of the review article. "Bom Bom Mahadev" was a mantra for marijuana intoned by Indian holy men who smoked ganja (strong Indian hemp). It meant "Hail, Hail great god." This article is an extended review of David Solomon's book *The Marijuana Papers*, a collection of most of the pertinent literary, historical, political, and scientific documents available at that time about marijuana use.

The review was written by Harry Monroe, a lyric poet who had been involved with Bohemian culture for

Figure 3: Cover for *Oracle* #7: Houseboat Summit Meeting. Left to right: Timothy Leary, Allen Ginsberg, Alan Watts, and Gary Snyder. Photo copyright © 1967 by Paul Kagan.

20 years and had inspired many young poets in the Haight. According to his review, "Mr. Solomon has collated a massive volume of absolutely convincing evidence that marijuana is good for you, good for your health, good for your mind and good for your world."

A full-page collage, "Lucifer Rising," was an announcement for Kenneth Anger's new film, *Lucifer Rising—A Love Vision*, that was to be previewed at the Straight Theater on Haight Street. The artwork is by Rick Griffin using an old print by Gustave Doré. Anger was involved with satanist cults, as well as being a leading underground film maker. Along with the film, he performed satanic rituals. After the showing, the film was stolen and didn't reappear for many years.

The centerfold of the Houseboat Summit was the "Prajna Paramita Sutra," the Buddhist prayer considered to embody the most profound insight of Buddhist thought: "...form not different from emptiness. Emptiness not different from form. Form is the emptiness. Emptiness is the form. Sensation, thought, active substance, consciousness also like this.... Gone, gone to the other shore. Reach, go enlightenment, accomplish...."

The artwork is by Ami McGill, one of our staff artists. Some of the conservative elements of the Buddhist community weren't too pleased with the naked butterfly lady standing in the middle of the highest perfect wisdom.

The back cover was Rick Griffin's magical peyote Indian.

THE UNDERGROUND PRESS SYNDICATE

Many major American cities now had underground papers. Most of them were political, or had originated as a political response to the war in Vietnam, but some, like the *Seed* in Chicago and *East Village Other* (*EVO*) in New York, had begun to introduce cultural and aesthetic innovations similar to the *Oracle*. The papers tended to bring communities in rebellion together using passionate advocacy and direct coverage of movement plans, debates, and demonstrations. Through these papers, the war against the war progressed and the new world that we felt would replace the old world of imperialism, materialism, and privilege was being envisioned and defined.

The growth of underground newspapers was mushrooming—every major city, most universities or university towns, at least 500 in all, and about 500 high schools would have underground or alternative papers over the next five years. These papers were a training ground for the creative people in each community—writers, artists, cartoonists, and poets could publish their work in these open fields of opportunity, and communicate with their peers. By the spring of 1967, with about twenty underground papers, a shared vision of political and cultural rebellion began to focus.

A political movement that was radical with an extreme democratic openness, mistrustful and independent of political parties or dogmas, anti-authority and non-hierarchical, generally non-violent, and dedicated to the values of equality, justice, and peace had been forged in the civil rights struggle, the SDS Port Huron Statement, the Free Speech Movement in Berkeley, and the beginning of the antiwar movement.

A cultural identity that was anti-materialist, idealistic, anarchistic, surreal, Dionysian, and transcendental had been birthed through the Beat literary explosion, the Leary LSD experiments at Harvard, rock n' roll music, the Haight-Ashbury Renaissance, and the Human-Be-In. This two-headed rebellion was now the greatest threat to the American status quo since the Depression.

The *Oracle* staff, motivated by Ron Thelin's vision of a nationwide "tribal messenger service," decided to host an underground press conference. We invited all the papers that were already loosely allied as the Underground Press Syndicate. We also wanted to show the editors how to adapt the innovations we were making in the *Oracle*, and expose them to the burgeoning Haight-Ashbury community that was then at its peak of creativity and spontaneous interactive compassion.

The first UPS conference was held at Michael Bowen's house on Stinson Beach and the *Oracle*'s offices, Easter 1967. Some of the participants included Art Kunkin of the *Los Angeles Free Press*, Allan Katzman and Walter Bowart of *EVO*, Max Scherr of *Berkeley Barb*, and representatives of Detroit's *Fifth Estate*, Chicago's *Seed*, Mendocino's *Illustrated Paper*, Austin's *Rag*, and a few other papers.

We had invited Rolling Thunder, a Cherokee medicine man, to talk about the plight of the American Indian in the face of yet another legislative attack on Indian treaty rights. He also affirmed what had become the hippie creation myth—that hippies were reincarnated Indians returned to bring the American land and peoples back to traditional tribal ways.

Some of the Diggers, including Peter and Judy Berg and Chester Anderson, barged uninvited into the conference with the intention of exposing our elitism and to make their case for the underground press to write about feeding and housing the hundreds of thousands of kids who were about to break loose from home and social expectation in order to adopt the life of rebellion, free love, and LSD visions.

Several important and practical decisions were made amidst the beach walks, tripping, hippie sightseeing, and vegetarian meals. The basic principle of article-sharing without copyright infringement was adopted along with the sharing of subscription lists. It was also agreed that *EVO* in New York should explore the selling of national advertising, which then would be printed in all participating underground press papers. This was seen as a way of securing much needed advertising revenue for member papers. There was, of course, some argument about the potential of selling out by taking corporate ads, but it was reasoned that ads for products like rock records or books would further undermine the corporate state. Furthermore, each paper would have a choice whether to run an ad or not. It eventually turned out that the advertisers were unreliable or late payers and little was gained from this financial gambit.

The major accomplishment of the conference was the reinforcement of the mission we all shared, whether our emphasis was psychedelic cultural, or political. We were creating, maintaining, and informing a new international community that would ultimately replace the crumbling status quo. A UPS statement of purpose was agreed upon:

> To warn the "civilized world" of its impending collapse, through "communications among aware communities outside the establishment" and by attracting the attention of the mass media.
> To note and chronicle events leading to the collapse.
> To advise intelligently to prevent rapid collapse and make transition possible.
> To prepare the American public for the wilderness.
> To fight a holding action in the dying cities.

This statement indicates clearly the apocalyptic feeling of the time. Even the war seemed to us to be a symptom or symbol of the general fall of the American civilization.

ORACLE #8—INDIAN ISSUE

Not only did the hippies have a Creation Myth concerning the American Indian, but they also shared with the Indians a sense of cultural alienation from American society. There was a general perception that urban society was a cancer and a scourge upon the American earth, and that the destiny of the hippies was to begin a gentle reinhabitation of the land. A shared vision of the unity of earth and humanity as a living harmonic organism began to develop. The American Indian tribal life before the Europeans came to this continent appeared to be the ideal expression of that harmony. Many people were studying with, and learning about, the American Indian. To prepare for our Indian issue the *Oracle* sent a small group of artists and writers to the Hopi community for inspiration and study.

Oracle #8 was dedicated to the American Indian Tradition. In the article, "Sun Bear Speaks," we profiled Sun Bear, an Indian medicine man who had begun teaching white youth the way of the American Indian. At one point, Sun Bear discussed the traditional understanding of what a leader should be:

> When a man went to become chief, he would fast and say "What can I do that will best serve my people?" The Indians fasted because, when you take no food or water, you are closest to the Great Spirit and your mind is not dwelling on things of the belly. A man was chief only so long as he did the will of the people. There were cases where a chief got too chiefy and arrogant. He would go to sleep at night, but while he slept, the band moved away, leaving him to be chief all to himself.

An anonymous artist designed the page so that the type would lay in arrowhead shapes.

Another non-fictional piece, "Tuwaqachi—The Fourth World," by Richard Grossinger, contrasts the life of native peoples with the rapacity of the white ruling class:

> Do you not see that in mythic time a broken bargain with Hopi priests can be repaid by Vietcong warriors?…Myth kicks you in the ass, man; knocks you down from those high towers and missile sights. You think you can bury a tribe, reduce it to a rare language, quaint religion, a few dancing dolls, remove it thus from the earth?

The front and back covers of *Oracle* #8 are a continuous image that represents a vision of the ghost of Chief Joseph at Mount Shasta with flying saucers. Image designer Hetti McGee also contributed "The Hopi Life Plan," a rubbing from a petroglyph on a rock at the Hopi village, Old Oraibe. The Hopi elders sent a verbal interpretation of the petroglyph to us via the Hopi messenger, Craig Carpenter. The petroglyph symbolized the history of the intersection of the Hopi people with the white man. It prophesied a terrible world destruction wherein a gourd of ashes would fall from the sky, if the white man didn't respect the ways of nature, the earth, and the Indian peoples.

Hetti was originally from Liverpool and was a prolific and fine artist working on staff for the *Oracle*.

Dedicated to the muse as Hetti was, and as many of us were, she rarely signed her work. When the *Oracle* meteor flamed out, she and her husband Angus Mac-Lise, who was a poet and musician, went to Katmandhu, Nepal. They lived inexpensively in the midst of the Buddhist culture they loved, and published limited edition books of poetry there. Angus died, though, leaving behind their newborn son. When he was a toddler, the boy was chosen by Buddhist priests to be the first western incarnation of a deceased high lama. To the Buddhist understanding this is the equivalent of a living god.

A Curse on the Men in Washington, Pentagon and Other Poems

Three poems rounded out the thematic element of *Oracle* #8. The most controversial of these was "A Curse on the Men in Washington, Pentagon," which Gary Snyder sent us from Japan. I knew that this was a well thought out, shamanistic poem in a long tradition of curse poems, chants, and incantations. But many people on the *Oracle* staff didn't want to violate their commitment to the ethic of love and non-violence. One of our staff members was the son of an Army captain who worked in the Pentagon, so the curse would have reverberated upon him. We had a formal staff debate and a vote. The poem won by one vote. The photographer whose father was in the Pentagon left the *Oracle* along with several other people:

> As I kill the white man, the American in me
> And I dance out the Ghost dance
> To bring back America, the grass and streams,
> To trample your throat in your dreams.
> This magic I work, this loving I give
> That my children may flourish
> And yours won't live.

We went to press for the first printing with the poem included. Thirty or forty thousand copies were printed and sold in order to get the money necessary to print more. In the interim we received a telegram from Gary asking us not to print the poem because of a copyright dispute with a poster company. We took it out of the second edition and replaced it with a photograph of a naked Madonna with Child. When the rest of the editions came out without the poem, it was falsely rumored that we had bent under some kind of political or spiritual pressure. The Communications Company mimeographed the poem and distributed it on the street.

The centerfold of the Indian Issue was a poem, "Who Is an Indian?" by John Collier, Jr. The page was lavishly designed by Ami McGill. John Collier, Jr.,

was a teacher of anthropology at San Francisco State College. He was half Zuni Indian, the son of John Collier and his Zuni wife. John, Sr., was a scholar of Indian life, the first white man to be initiated into the Zuni Tribe, and Franklin Delano Roosevelt's head of the Bureau of Indian Affairs. He was the first bureau chief who tried to bring the bureau out of the nineteenth century Indian wars, and into the twentieth century. John Collier, Jr., sings:

> We were suspicious of your God,
> who never failed you
> always loving, a Christ with no human faults.
> We knew there was a terrible truth
> you did not want us to hear.
> For there are no gods
> or people without fault.
> The terrible truth was that your Christ
> carried Hell with him, and that each of you
> had a hell, a darkness.

"Sioux Songs" is the highly charged sung poetry of the Sioux Indians translated from the Sioux language by James Koller, a poet and editor of *Coyote Magazine*. The drawings, reminiscent of cave paintings, were done by an anonymous artist:

> Here I am
> look at me
> I am the sun
> Here I am
> look at me
> I am the moon
> look at me.
>
> I thought
> I saw buffalo
> and called out
> I thought
> I saw buffalo
> and called out
> "Let them be buffalo!"

Dialogue with a Western Astronomer and an Eastern Philosopher

Three other poems, not directly related to the Indian theme, also appeared in *Oracle* #9. "Astromancy" is a poem written by Phillip Lamantia, one of America's leading surrealist poets. He was in Europe during the sixties but is now living in San Francisco:

> Another civilization
> secret for six thousand years
> is creeping on the crest of future,

I can almost see
the tip of its triangular star....
No matter, I'm recovering
from a decade of poisons.
I renounce all narcotic
and pharmacopoeic disciplines
as too heavy 9 to 5 type sorrows....

Kirby Doyle is a poet who had been living in Big Sur tending his own garden but decided to come to the Haight to tend the bigger garden. His essay, "The First Sound," is his personal invocation to the natural order of things:

Well you had better wise up, honey and for a start listen within—it ain't no group thing and as you listen you will find two tools of yourself immediately available for your use on you—your Focus and your Balance...To use them you must sit still, sit down, don't fake no lotus like you been doing, you bunch of basketcase buddhas. Just stop and listen—pay attention to yourself and protect your heart from your head until you can fill that damned and noisy dome with the warmth and silence of the heart.

"Plea" is a poem by Bob Kaufman, the innovative, maverick surrealist, street poet of the San Francisco poetry renaissance who was often arrested and beaten by the San Francisco police. At one point he was hospitalized and given shock therapy. His later years were haunted by illness and alcoholism. He died in 1986. A funeral procession with over 100 poets accompanied by a jazz band marched around North Beach reciting poems at Kaufman's favorite hangouts. His ashes were thrown in San Francisco Bay while KJAZ radio station played the Charlie Parker music he loved.

The art illustrating Bob's poem was drawn by Michael X, a young man who had walked into the *Oracle* office carrying a large black notebook under his arm and proclaiming himself to be a messenger from Mars. His black book contained elaborately intricate drawings that, he said, were designs of Martian technology. He had brought them from Mars to help advance earth's civilization. Some of our people took LSD with him, and came back from wherever they had travelled thinking that Michael X was nuts, not Martian. Bob Kaufman's poem begins:

Voyager, wanderer of the heart
off to a million midnights, black, black
Voyager, wanderer of starworlds,
off to a million tomorrows, black, black

Seek and find Hiroshima's children
Send them back, Send them back.

"Dialogue with a Western Astronomer and an Eastern Philosopher" was written by Dr. Ralph Metzner, the Harvard psychologist. This article is one of the first attempts at comparing the findings of contemporary astrophysics with the metaphysics of Hinduism and Buddhism. In response to the astronomer describing the mysteries of the recently discovered quasars, in particular, that they seem to possess a "definite, as yet undetermined plan of arrangement," the eastern philosopher compares it to an ancient Hindu idea:

After 100 Brahma nights and days, we reach the end of the kalpa (5 billion years) and all matter, all forms, are withdrawn into a sort of super-condensed state, which the Buddhists call "the seed-realm of the densely-packed." All creation and destruction, evolution and involution come to an end; only pure energy consciousness is maintained. Vishnu, the preserving principle, sleeps at the bottom of the "Milk Ocean," until such time as at the beginning of a new Kalpa, the observable forms of the universe manifest again, like dreams out of his quiescent consciousness.

"1984" was Armando Busick's vision of a sensual, rural, natural, neo-primitive future that we grasped for in the seventies, but that seems to have disappeared in the eighties.

Summer of Love Poster

The "Summer of Love Poster," by Bob Schnepp, showing St. Francis in the Sky, was part of our attempt to deal with the expected influx of young people into San Francisco in the summer of '67. Despite our pleas for America's young and adventurous to stay in their hometowns and begin the new world where they were, we were expecting an avalanche to fall upon the Haight. We asked the city to help by allowing the establishment of tent cities in Golden Gate Park, but their reaction was far from sympathetic. One supervisor said, and I closely paraphrase, "Would you let thousands of whores waiting on the other side of the Bay Bridge into San Francisco?"

The community had to band together—a "Council for the Summer of Love" was formed to coordinate activities and raise funds. An educational group called "Kiva" intended to build a geodesic dome in a vacant lot on Hayes Street that would be used primarily as a school for rural skills and communal living. Its dream was never realized. "Happening House" was a college in the street (later in a house) started in collaboration with San Francisco State College through the efforts and inspiration of Leonard Wolf, an English professor, novelist, and Chaucer scholar.

Local churches and ministers started to feed and house people. An Episcopal priest, Father Leon Harris of All Saint's Church (acting like a saint), turned his whole church over to the effort. There were crashpads, free food, concerts in the park and every night at the dance halls—youth gone wild with the exuberance and risk of love and adventure.

Of course, the city tried to ban amplified music from the park, but they relented under pressure and demonstrations. The *Oracle* fed and crashed people, and sent those who had burnt out from drugs or the urban chaos to a piece of land in Big Sur donated to us for that purpose. The Diggers had occupied Morningstar Ranch in Sonoma to pick apples and grow vegetables. The ranch originally belonged to Lou Gottlieb, of the popular folk group, the Limelighters. Gottlieb was constantly defending his acceptance of hundreds of refugees and back-to-the-landers from the attacks of the Sonoma authorities. He eventually would deed his land to God, causing Sonoma to challenge in court the right of God to own land. The Haight-Ashbury was a gigantic media magnet, and now we would drown in the media flood. It would never be the same.

ORACLE #9–PROGRAMMING THE PSYCHEDELIC EXPERIENCE

Oracle #9 was perhaps the most wide ranging *Oracle* in its content but, at the same time, the most carefully designed in its aesthetics. The cover, by Bruce Conner, was our only abstract cover, though I call it "infinity billiard balls." The content ranges from psychedelic to occult, and from analysis of happenings on Haight Street to a passionate poem against the war in Southeast Asia.

"On Programming the Psychedelic Experience," by Tim Leary and Ralph Metzner, sums up the results of their earlier scientific research with LSD. Given the tremendous therapeutic and spiritual breakthroughs that LSD effected in the human psyche, and its easy availability and the occasional negative effects of its misuse, Dr. Leary did his utmost to consistently provide the best guidance from both a scientific and aesthetic point of view to those who would take LSD and other psychedelics.

In formal, double blind experiments at Harvard with students, faculty, theological students, and even prisoners, they discovered that the most positive experiences—ecstatic, joyful, religious, poetic—could be induced and predicted if the psychedelic was taken with the guidance of an experienced and trusted guide, and with the careful preparation of the "set and setting."

"Set" refers to a person's mood, expectations, and emotions. The voyager and/or guide would want to begin the inner journey with a calm state of mind, not an anxiety state caused by a negative circumstance like a death or illness in the family, or separation from a lover.

"Setting" refers to the physical environment of the trip—that it should be prepared for a relatively undisturbed eight hours of spiritual experience and be aesthetically designed to enhance that experience. A natural setting for part or all of the trip often seemed to enhance the experience.

Drs. Leary, Metzner, and Alpert wrote and spoke widely and often about "set and setting" and the need for an experienced guide. They published a professional journal, *The Psychedelic Review*, and psychedelic interpretations of the *Tibetan Book of the Dead* and the *Tao Teh Ching*, ancient texts that were symbolic versions of the psychedelic journey. The concepts of "set and setting," and their books guided hundreds of thousands of people on these voyages through the mind and the deep self. Despite the current view of many that Leary was the Pied Piper of the sixties, the fool or chameleon of the seventies, and irrelevant in the eighties, literally multitudes know that they owe him the deepest gratitude for his fortitude in staying the course in those halcyon days, when paranoia sought to replace reason, and the gods of war did battle against the higher virtues.

There was also another view of "tripping" that was advanced especially by Ken Kesey and the Merry Pranksters in the "Acid Test" period in 1965 and 1966. Kesey's view was that the visionary state and the randomness of everyday life should not be separated; that we should come to every moment, every surprise encounter, and every emotion with that state of ecstatic presentness fully turned on. Also, if someone was blocked from that transcendental experience by his or her own psychological preoccupation, fear of letting go, neurosis, or even psychosis, reality might cast up a surprise event or unexpected stimulus that would cause the person to break through into the expanded awareness of "cosmic consciousness."

Most people used both the controlled and uncontrolled methods of turning on. They would save the higher dosage trips (300 or more micrograms) for a controlled "set and setting," and a lesser dosage (100 or 150 mics) for tripping lightly around town. Many did use LSD indiscriminately and indiscreetly, even as a challenge or test of their mental powers or self-control. Generally, I would say that there were more bad trips and even psychotic snaps, when medical attention was felt to be needed, with the uncontrolled method of tripping.

Many of the writers in the *Oracle*, including Allen Ginsberg, Alan Watts, and William Burroughs, suggested that these psychedelic journeys are basic to psychological integration and to human evolution. They felt that courses should be given in which psychedelics would be used within the university system and/or private academies along with the teaching of various mental disciplines such as yoga and meditation.

Estimates of how many people took LSD in the sixties and early seventies vary from seven to twenty million people. A resurgence in the eighties has added to that number. A poll in the early eighties revealed that 8 percent of college seniors were taking LSD and 25 percent of those between the ages of 18 and 26 had taken some hallucinogenic drug. For such massive use with dramatic mind altering effects under the glaring spotlight of paranoid propaganda, LSD turns out to have been a relatively benign national trauma.

Psychologists had been working therapeutically with LSD with great success in treating everything from alcoholism to schizophrenia, but unfortunately almost all research ended when LSD became illegal. Therapeutic aid and possibly even cures of addictions and severe mental illnesses might have been found if this research had been allowed to continue.

The battle over LSD is another chapter in the age-old war of who controls what people think and experience. The Catholic church during the Middle Ages resisted and oppressed the rise of heretic sects, because the protesting sects wanted to experience the deity themselves without the intercedence of the church and its priests, rituals, and dogmas. Similarly every establishment group was threatened by the tremendous release of spiritual, psychological, political, medical, creative, and intellectual autonomy available to the individual through the use of LSD and other psychedelic substances. Fortunately, though to a lesser extent, the search for authentic experience continues for those who want to find their own way.

Poisoned Wheat, Superspade, and the Buddha Mind

Many of us on the *Oracle* staff were dedicated poets and artists, so we featured certain poetry, often complemented by artwork, and sprinkled other, smaller poems around the *Oracle* pages. In *Oracle* #9, two utterly different poems—"Park Songs for Two Kinds of Voices" by Pamela Milward and "Aaron M., April 1967" by Bill Dodd—meet a design by John Thompson that incorporates the meaning of both poems. Aaron Mitchell was the first man executed in many years in California, and it was at the command of Governor Ronald Reagan. Bill Dodd writes prophetically:

Reagan himself killing
Communists by the millions in his head,
but who knows what awaits to slay him,
of the living or Aaron,
or any of 59 others,
the dead in their graves.

A third poem was Michael McClure's antiwar poem, "Poisoned Wheat," which we spotlighted in the centerfold along with the art and design skills of Billy Jahrmacht, an innovative artist with an addiction to heroin. Billy, whose nickname was Batman, had opened an art gallery on Fillmore Street called "Batman Gallery." Around this time we asked him to be art editor, but his addiction made him too unreliable. Billy would die a few years later in Hawaii. McClure, in his passionate poem about America losing its soul in Vietnam, writes:

There is death in Vietnam!
There is death in Vietnam!
There is death in Vietnam!
And our bodies are mad with the forgotten memory that we are creatures!

Blue black skull rose lust boot!....
...Withdrawal from information is Escapism
Escape from the ears that hear the bombers pass?
Evangelism—whether it be of art or religion—is Escapism

"Notes from the Genetic Journal" was one of a series of columns by co-editor and poet Stephen Levine. Stephen has since become well known for his work with people with terminal illnesses and his writing on the psychological and spiritual dimension of the transition between life and death. He writes:

Suspended between supernova and atomic dervish,
I am Man, center of the universe,
disproving Copernicus after all,
cosmic acrobat trapezing on the tendency toward rebirth.
Poised between whirring mass at either end of infinity.

"Flowers from the Street" is a lyric analysis of life on Haight Street by Richard Honigman:

The street can be a classroom, a zoo, a stage,
an asphalt padded cell, a whorehouse, a folksong,

or the traverse of Scorpio. They leave jobs, armies, schools to turn their lives and psyches inside out.

Two interpretations of the Tarot cards were "The Aquarian Tarot Cards" and "The Hanging Man." "The Aquarian Tarot Cards" was developed by Gayla, who channeled her imaging of the Tarot through the Ouija board while occultist John Cooke painted the cards and wrote the text from Gayla's descriptions. "The Hanging Man" was drawn by Bryden, a San Francisco artist. The philosophy of the deck emphasized the harmonizing of soul and body in a new non-hierarchical age.

"In Memoriam for Superspade and John Carter" is an article I wrote on the occasion of the murders of these two dope dealers in early August 1967. The murders were a turning point, a signal that flower power might be wilting, allowing old-fashioned power and greed to supplant it:

> All energy and thought forms devoted to commercial dope game and increasing fear and paranoid actions produce hell lives and bad trips....Let's disengage ourselves from the commercialization and the bottomless desire for more dope. That will devalue dope. Organized business and crime and government would murder for bat shit...if someone would convince them of its value, just as we have created the illusion of the value of Dope.
>   GIVE YOUR DOPE AWAY—DO NOT BUY OR SELL.

"The Buddha Mind," by Dane Rudhyar, the well-known philosopher and composer, is a detailed analysis of the essential meaning of Buddhism. Mr. Rudhyar writes:

> If Nirvana, which Buddhists say is the goal of everything, and which the Buddha had reached, is the supreme value, then why did the Buddha return? And if the Buddha returned out of compassion or something, then that something is greater than Nirvana, or else he wouldn't have returned from it. If compassion...makes one sacrifice Nirvana, then that compassion is greater than Nirvana; it is the most supreme value.

The drawing used to illustrate "The Buddha Mind" was from the strange notebooks of Michael X, the self-proclaimed Martian. This drawing was one of his Martian Machines that would save humanity.

"Alice in Wonderland" is a delicate drawing illustrating *Alice in Wonderland* as seen under the influence. A young man named Owen dropped into the office, told us he was working as a janitor, and gave us this drawing.

The back cover was a drawing called "Kali, the Hindu Goddess," by Bob Brannaman, one of the School of Backwoods Hermit Big Sur Artists.

ORACLE #10—THE PENTAGON

Oracle #10 was another issue without a specific theme or focus but it contains some of our boldest artistic experiments, including our peak experiences in design, particularly in the relationship of print to image. The two editions, which bridged the Pentagon Demonstration and Exorcism on October 21, contained drastically different images and colors. The cover of *Oracle* #10 is an exploding expressionistic mandala by Bob Brannaman.

As you can see by now, the *Oracle* and many of the thousands of underground papers in cities, colleges, and even high schools across the country were centers for a renaissance of art, ideas, and poetry. Writers and artists contributed their work mostly for free, though the *Oracle* toward the end was able to pay the rent and food costs for several communes of staff and artists. Many artists and some writers didn't sign their names to their works because they felt that the works came through them from a higher consciousness, or Muse, and thus belonged not to them but to the world. Many of the writers and artists wanted to act out the human potential for selflessness. The styles were eclectic, drawing upon the whole history of human artistic expression—realism, art nouveau, surrealism, illuminated manuscripts, expressionism, collage, photography, Indian and Tibetan art. All the archetypes hidden in the human mind were gathering in the *Oracle* and reentering the world.

"Temporary Flight" and "Fuclock" are two poems by Lawrence Ferlinghetti that are accompanied by a startling drawing that is unsigned but is probably by Mark DeVries. In "Temporary Flight," Ferlinghetti recreates a flight to Chicago while under the influence of LSD. In "Fuclock," he imagines a production at the Fillmore Ballroom where a man and a woman would be tied to the hands of a giant clock. At the hour of midnight, amidst crescendos of raga rock and flashing strobe and color lights, they would meet in an embrace. But it only happened, I believe, in Lawrence's imagination.

"Janus" is a lyrical poem by Pat Sweeny, whose sci-fi theme was prophetic of current strains of flying saucer tales. He tells of visitors to our planet taking our:

sperm and ova
that unite on some congenial
planet where our telescopes
end....you steerers of our
planet off into another
part of the galaxy to
replace the ailing sun. I
can guess your joy in
risking it....

The centerfold of *Oracle* #10 was another lyric poem, simply called "Poem/Exhortation," by Janine Pommy Vega:

inherent blossoms emblazon the moment flown
this silent portion of eternity Rising. How much
I love your creation! How much I love it.

The design for "Poem/Exhortation" was done by Bryden, who also contributed "Ganesha as the Fool," another of the several full-page images in his Tarot series. "Ganesha as the Fool" symbolizes Ganesha, the Hindu elephant God, son of Shiva, remover of obstacles, god of letters, and supposed author of the epic *Mahabarata*, envisioned by Bryden as the Fool in the Tarot.

"Abstract Mandala" is an intriguing work that was unsigned but was probably by Frank Berry. It is part of a two-page layout that is the height of the *Oracle*'s design experiments in restructuring viewing space. The facing page has continuations of articles by Lew Welch and William Burroughs, but they are placed in circles around a bullseye with a lot of white space around them instead of the usual long columns surrounded by ads.

Greed, Deconditioning, Leary, and Chinmayananda

Lew Welch's article, "Greed," discusses the origins and pervasiveness of American greed. Lew was one of the most lyric of the Beat poets. He was a warm sensitive being who would cry if he saw or heard something sad or terrible and cry also when he saw or heard something beautiful. In 1971, after writing poems prophecying his death, Lew walked off into the Sierra Mountains and disappeared.

"When did America go wrong?" he asks. "Is a question easily answered. It was never right. Greed then and usury (the most pernicious form of greed, the selling of money) have always been the carbuncles on the neck of America. We have never been free....It is now time for America to give away its corporations."

William Burroughs' article, "Academy 23: A Deconditioning," was widely reprinted in the underground press. Burroughs analyzes the criminalization of drug use and concludes that "Any serious attempt to actually enforce this welter of state and federal laws would entail a computerized invasion of privacy, a total police terror...."

He criticizes the press for sensationalizing drug use and calls for a halt to the manufacturing of benzedrine and all variations of the formula. Cannabis, on the other hand, should be legalized, he says, and academies should be set up for use of psychedelics:

This is the space age. Time to look beyond this rundown, radioactive, cop rotten planet. Time to look beyond this animal body. Remember anything that can be done chemically can be done in other ways....Students (in the academy) would receive a basic course of training in the non-chemical disciplines of yoga, karate, prolonged sense withdrawal, stroboscopic lights, the constant use of tape recorders to break down verbal association lines.

He talks about propaganda and opinion control and breaking its power through General Semantics study, then adds: "The program proposed is essentially a disintoxication from inner fear and inner control, a liberation of thought and energy to prepare a new generation for the adventure of space....Remember junk keeps you right here in junky flesh on this earth where Boot's is open all night."

In "Another Session with Tim Leary," which took place in the *Oracle* office, Leary charges that the stories in the press about LSD and chromosome breaks are all lies, hoaxes, and manipulations by government agencies intent on frightening those who are using LSD. Nevertheless,

The old temptation to build a religion, a dogma around your way of getting high is the oldest cop-out in history....The highest form of psychedelic wisdom that man has developed in my opinion is the Sufi. The Sufis tell you it's all energy, it's all work. You don't have to drop out at all, visibly. You can be a rug weaver; you can do the *Oracle*; or you can drive a cab in SF... The great masters are to be found in every walk of life—just doing their gig as an act of grace and gratitude and beauty.

A second interview in *Oracle* #10 was with Chinmayananda, one of the first of the Indian teachers to come to America in this generation. Chinmayananda was a philosopher of the Vedanta non-dual school of Indian thought and a practitioner of Jnana Yoga, the yoga of knowledge. He had a good command of the English language and was well known in India for giving long philosophical talks to audiences of thousands. During his interview, Chinmayananda said that he was very much against the use of LSD for initiating spiritual experience, and thought it to be a shock to the nervous system and dangerously addictive. He admired the renewed interest in spiritual ideas but advised spiritual study instead of drugs.

Death of a Hippie, Birth of a Freeman, and the Politics of Ecstasy

By the time *Oracle* #10 appeared on the streets of San Francisco, the Summer of Love had come and gone. Perhaps 100,000 people had come to the Haight on a pilgrimage to see where and what was happening. Just about every group or organization the Haight had developed to deal with the influx had dissolved, burnt out, or divided under the strain. Hard drugs had infiltrated the area, and the veins of some of the best players. The FBI, the CIA, and the Intelligence divisions of the San Francisco police were rumored to be involved in the sudden availability of heroin and methamphetamine, and the rash of arrests and civil disturbances that had begun to plague the Haight.

One of the provocateurs' favorite sports occurred regularly on weekends, when a handbill would mysteriously appear on lampposts urging "the people" to take over the street at 12 noon. At the appointed hour the police and the crowd would dutifully appear. The Tac Squad, the police riot control unit, would surround the crowd with one contingent of troops with motorcycles at the end of Haight Street near the entrance to Golden Gate Park, and another contingent at Haight and Masonic.

At 12 noon, hundreds of people would walk into the street and block the voluminous traffic. The police would then sing a few operatic warnings and charge up the street swinging their nightsticks while the motorcycle cops rode into and over people on the sidewalks. Then tear gas would be thrown into the crowds and stores. Once it was even thrown into the Straight Theater, where people had gathered to escape the onslaught.

Because no organized group took responsibility for these street takeovers, it was widely presumed that government provocateurs were causing this chaotic atmosphere of fear and intimidation in order to dissolve the delicate bloom of hope that had catapulted the Haight to international prominence. Unfortunately, their tactics were succeeding—by the fall many people were looking to move on, usually in small groups, to communes in rural areas. They wanted to advance their new tribalism outside the glare of the spotlight. Others were having apocalyptic visions and waiting for the world to end, or at least for an earthquake to strike San Francisco down to the primeval sand and ashes.

The Diggers developed another approach. Appalled by the spotlight of the media on the Haight, and eager to attract it at the same time, they staged a "Death of the Hippie" ceremonial march down Haight Street with a coffin filled with hippie paraphernalia and flowers signifying the death of the media-generated hippie, and his rebirth as a Freeman in a Free city with Free necessities provided to all.

At the march, I ran into one of the Diggers' anti-leaders, Peter Berg, and we exchanged symbols to commemorate the event. He gave me a yellow, wooden, six-inch square Free Frame of Reference that he was wearing on his belt, and I gave him a rough cut, Nepalese-made, soapstone Buddha Ring that I was wearing. Later at a Berkeley Metaphysical bookstore, where I was buying a rare book on Tibetan ritual called *The Hevajra Tantra*, I exchanged the Free Frame of Reference for the beads the salesgirl was wearing. She said the beads were blessed by Meher Baba. I then learned an ancient Tibetan purification mantra from the book. A few weeks later I went with a few of the *Oracle* staff to the Exorcism of the Pentagon, and, with Stephen Levine, chanted the mantra on the steps of the Pentagon just before any other demonstrators arrived.

The collage "Death of a Hippie—Birth of a Freeman" was done by Martin Lindhart from photographs taken by Stephen Walzer. It portrays the transition and is accompanied by my lyric essay, "Politics of Ecstasy":

> Secretly, behind all illusions of order, civilization, law, and tongue wipings of rhetoric, the anarchic, natural, wild condition of body exists....The body and being of man is all fountains of youth and heavenly apparitions.

Pentagon Rising

"Pentagon Rising," an article by Richard Honigman, is an announcement of the Exorcism of the Pentagon that appeared in the first edition of *Oracle* #10. The artwork, by Mark DeVries, envisions the post-Exorcism Pentagon floating in the air. Jerry Rubin had taken the magical idea to exorcise the Pentagon that Michael Bowen and I had suggested during our meetings before the Human-Be-In and incorporated it into the official program for the March on the Pentagon on October 21, 1967.

The *Oracle*, along with all other underground papers, supported and announced the March and the Exorcism. We had envisioned thousands of dancing and chanting hippies joining hands in a gigantic circle around the Pentagon invoking gods and spirits to exorcise the demons within the Pentagon, and make it rise. When the General Services Administration finally granted the permit for the march, the one action they refused to allow was the hippies' encirclement of the Pentagon.

Another Underground Press Conference convened the day before the March on the Pentagon. It was attended by what was now well over a hundred underground papers, whose combined readerships were estimated at anywhere between 330,000 (*Wall Street Journal*) and 15 million (Walter Bowart, editor of *East Village Other*).

The conference was as raucous as the rage encircling it, but out of it came two important decisions: the extension of free reprint rights to college newspapers and the formation of Liberation News Service. Based in Washington, DC, LNS would reprint and distribute the best of the underground press, and originate material that could be reprinted by member papers.

At the demonstration every faction had a chance to act out its outrage at the ever growing horror of the war: the more moderate marched and listened to speeches; the more radical broke through the lines and into the hallowed halls of the Pentagon wherein they were beaten by soldiers; occultists and poets like Ed Sanders and Kenneth Anger chanted and did exorcism rites; the hippies threw flowers at the soldiers and marshalls, and placed the flowers delicately in the barrels of their rifles.

The flowers came to the Pentagon as a result of the FBI thwarting the attempt of Michael Bowen and Bill Fortner, a large, loud, Texan adventurer, to circumnavigate the Pentagon by plane, and bomb it with bushels of flowers that were to be dropped into the hole in the Pentagon's center. When the hired pilot didn't come to the airport (probably because he was an FBI agent or was stopped by the FBI), they had no alternative but to truck the flowers to the steps of the Pentagon, causing rifles and helmets to blossom. In the evening Mayan Indians in native dress gathering around dusk campfires on the Pentagon lawn watched intently and said "La gente es uno" (The people are one).

In the post-Exorcism edition, which we published after returning to San Francisco from Washington, DC, Ralph Ackerman's photo of the Buddha in the Tea Garden of Golden Gate Park replaced the Pentagon Rising page.

Back Page Poster and Collage

The back page of *Oracle* #10's pre-Exorcism edition was the poster announcing the March on the Pentagon, by Peter Legeria. The text with it is the same text I read to Jerry Rubin at that first fateful meeting

in Berkeley. It was from Lewis Mumford's *City in History*:

> The Pentagon...an effete and worthless baroque conceit resurrected in 1930s by US military engineers and magnified into an architectural catastrophe. Nuclear power has aggravated this error and turned its huge comic ineptitude into a tragic threat...The Bronze Age fantasies of absolute power, the Bronze Age practice of unlimited human extermination, the uncontrolled obsessions, hatreds and suspicions of Bronze Age gods and kings have here taken root again in a fashion that imitates and seeks to surpass the Kremlin of Ivan the Terrible and his latter day successors. With this relapse... has come one-way communication, the priestly monopoly of secret knowledge, the multiplication of secret agencies, the suppression of open discussion and even the insulation of error against public disclosure and criticism through a bi-partisan foreign policy...the dismantling of this regressive citadel will prove a far harder task than the demolition of the earlier Baroque fortifications. But on its performance, all more extensive plans for urban and human development must wait.

In the post-Exorcism edition, the back cover was a photo collage of Haight-Ashbury resident, Gandalf, meditating in front of marshalls at the Pentagon.

ORACLE #11—THE CITY OF GOD

In the City of God Issue, beginning with a cover by Steve Schafer that was symbolic of renewal and rebirth (see figure 4), we attempted to explore how individuals and society in this coming age of computerized technology could transform the mores, values, and institutions that are based on the paradigms of scarcity and the survival of the fittest. How could we destructure ourselves and our societies to live more harmoniously with each other and with the earth?

Articles by Bill Dodd and George Tsongas and poetry by Michael Hannon explore the spiritual and political dimensions of these new potential relationships. Gary Snyder tells of a Japanese commune on Suwa-no-se Island. Robert Theobald reflects on a surplus economy bringing on the necessity of a guaranteed annual wage to free people for spiritual and intellectual development, and Neill Smith, an architect, invents "Environments for Expanded Awareness."

"How Long, O Lord, How Long?" is a full-page original design by Hetti McGee, while "City of God," our centerfold, was the visionary city of Jerusalem from the Book of Revelation as envisioned by Bryden. "Abstract Kundaline," by Ami McGill, could be a view of the Kundalini energy bathing the spinal column.

A fourth piece of artwork, an unsigned mandala, was given to us by a lovely young woman who came into our office one day while we were working on the issue. She was glowing and vibrating and asked if she could do a drawing for us. She worked for a couple of hours, gave us the drawing, which was of herself in the midst of a mandallic universe, and left. She wrote beneath it:

Float Beyond Time: We are ageless, timeless
We have been here always and will be
here always in one form or another.
We created ourselves to be ourselves.

The back cover is a cautionary vision of the earth engulfed in the fires of war. The artist is unknown.

Bucky Comes to the Haight

In November, Buckminster Fuller came to the Haight, spoke at Hippie Hill, and did an interview with the *Oracle* staff. "Bucky" was the philosopher and visionary who best represented the western aspect of the ideals of the sixties. As an inventor of the geodesic dome and a philosopher of technological change, he optimistically envisioned a world where more could be done with less resources to feed and house everyone.

He was legendary for his eight hour long talks and his charismatic joy and energy. When he came to our house for the interview, he was already talking as he came in the door. When he noticed that the tape recorder wasn't turned on, he playfully scolded us because we hadn't recorded what he had already said. The air brush designs for these pages were done by Mike Ferrar:

I would suggest that all humanity is about to be born in an entirely new relationship with the universe....We have gone in this century from taking care of less than 1% of humanity to taking care of 40% of humanity. We have done more with less....What I want the young world to realize is that actually we're right in screaming that we ought not to have war. The way you're going to get it is by a design revolution where you do more with less...I've discovered that it takes 22 years to go through the cycle—through weaponry and to fall out into what we finally call "livingry." We can save 22 years by simply deliberately setting out to redesign the use of the

world's resources to take care of 100% of the world's population.

The final two articles in *Oracle* #11 were by Harry Monroe and Alan Watts. Monroe's "Instrument of the Womb" is an anthropological study of the Earth Goddess and Matriarchal Society":

She had many names as many as there are peoples over whom she reigned and who worshipped her—Great Goddess, Divine Goddess, White Goddess, Earth Goddess, Moon Goddess, a triple goddess always...whose three aspects of maiden, matron and crone are the anthropomorphisms comprehensible as beauty, birth and death. Her influence was absolute over peoples whose concerns remained the simple ones of agriculture, grazing and hunting...All the totem societies of ancient Europe were under the aegis of the Great Goddess.

Despite Harry Monroe's efforts here to realign the chairs in heaven and place women in their rightful place among the gods, there was still much to be desired in the position of women in hippie culture. Generally speaking, women were respected more as a result of men and women experiencing each other in their symbolical divine aspects during psychedelic visions.

In fact, creative work overall was respected more as a result of those experiences regardless of which gender originated the work. Still, women all too often found themselves playing the role of hausfrau, while men just played. At the same time, many women, in the pervasive atmosphere of sexual and psychological freedom, also played in the open, deep, psychic spaces, and began to find their personal and social power. These factors, along with the politicization of women in the movement against the war, would lead to the women's liberation movement that began to shake the status quo in the early seventies.

Unlike the more ascetic and even nihilistic varieties of Buddhism, Alan Watts' Zen Buddhism was a practical, life-loving, and sensuous philosophy. "Food Is God" catches Watts in his most informal and playful mood. "When people announce that they are intent on the spiritual life and are going to practice universal love," he writes, "I lock my doors, bar my windows and get hold of a gun....When people do the most appalling things people can do, it is always in the names of the highest ideals, like the purely unselfish ideological war in Vietnam....This is why the US is such a danger to the rest of the world...Scratch an American and find a Christian Scientist because we

Figure 4: Front cover for *Oracle* #11: Symbol of renewal and rebirth. Copyright © 1967 by Steve Schafer.

have a national belief in the virtue of being above mere materiality."

Then Watts goes into an exposition of Chinese cooking for its taste and simplicity; puts down macrobiotics as ending in malnutrition; and continues:

> Make your chopping board and stove your altar at which you celebrate divine mysteries with the utmost devotion. But because you must kill to eat, always remember that to some extent you are an irremediable rascal. This will season your holiness with a certain twinkle in the eye, a sauciness which will preserve you from the abominable cruelty and thoughtlessness of those who aspire to be 100% sweetness and light. Do not try to be saints; be content with being completely human. For true sanctity is a divine gift which when imitated is only a plastic flower.

ORACLE #12—RETURN FROM MEXICO TO DARK VISIONS

Oracle #12's front cover photo by Tom Weir, of a sleeping woman on Marin Headlands, symbolized, perhaps, the fragility and exhaustion of the vision. The Haight and the counterculture had been under severe attack from both local and national authorities. Issue #12, published in February 1968, was to be the last *Oracle*. San Francisco Mayor Joseph Alioto hated the hippies. It was rumored that he had been prevented from being vice president by the Democratic Party bosses, who had told him that if he couldn't control his own city he couldn't be entrusted with the nation. So he put the Tac squad on alert.

COINTELPRO, the FBI and CIA program (in association with local police agencies) to infiltrate, disrupt, and destroy the civil rights, black liberation, and antiwar movements, was also committed, I believe, to breaking up the Haight-Ashbury. Ronald Reagan was creating Communist conspiracies in Sacramento. The Black Panthers had made self-defense the priority for revolution instead of non-violence. Hard drugs were rampant on Haight Street and were creating casualties.

The Haight had been a success nevertheless—hundreds of thousands of young people had come through the Haight and had spread its message of peace, love, and community across the country and across oceans. But the visionaries and pioneers in the Haight were tired and needed renewal. Declining energies were being replaced by dark visions.

Many of the originators left San Francisco for new rebirths. Steve Levine and I went to Mexico for a couple of weeks. We spoke at universities and were interviewed by newspapers and TV. We read poetry, generally stirred up activity, and spread the word.

When we returned, we discovered that a street guru with a following and a combative manner had moved himself into the *Oracle* offices, and was making it difficult for staff members to work or even think. The *Oracle* staff had exhausted its vision of the future. Most of us felt it was time to act out what we had already dreamed. *Oracle* #12 reflects this mood.

In "Final City, Tap City," Lew Welch speaks of the vulnerability of cities as polluted and dependent living environments: "And there will be signs... We will know when to slip away and let these murderous fools rip themselves to pieces. For there must be good men and women in the mountains, on the beaches, in all the neglected, beautiful places, who one day will come back to ghostly cities and set them right at last...And there must not be a plan. It has always been the plan that has done us in. Meanwhile—(1) Freak out (2) Come back (3) Bandage the wounded and feed however many you can (4) Never cheat."

In "Drop City," Bill Dodd describes his visit to Drop City, New Mexico, one of the first of the new rural communes. All the houses there were geodesic domes, a type of round house invented by Buckminster Fuller that combined advanced engineering and the spiritual simplicity of a primitive dwelling. They were also simple and inexpensive to build. The communards at Drop City had used abandoned car tops overlapped like wood shakes for the domes roof.

In Mexico, I had been impressed with the way all of human history is layered, visible, and touchable—a revelation in the transitory nature of human culture, but also in that feeling that everything exists at once in an eternal instant, all of history montaging, while no one watches and the universe breathes in and out.

I wrote "Return from Mexico" on the flight back from Mexico. The Flying Saucer drawing was by Steve Durkee, a New Mexican artist and occultist, who would later design Ram Dass' book, *Be Here Now*. When we crossed the border, champagne was served and I wrote:

> I toast the sea, the desert below
> the air for our safe flight.
> I toast the happiness and bliss
> of all sentient beings.
> I toast the victory of the Viet Cong
> and the Johnson gang's graceful surrender.
> I toast the opening of the compassionate chakra
> of the heart before America
> falls into time's abyss for empires.

Esalen had just been started and some of the *Oracle* staff had been doing encounter group work with them. In an article entitled "Esalen," Esalen co-founders George Leonard and Michael Murphy write: "How can we speak of joy on this dark and suffering planet How can we speak of anything else?"

When Mark DeVries, who had done many designs for the *Oracle*, originally brought his drawing "Evolution?" to the office, the word on it was "Revolution" without a question mark. After witnessing all the police raids and tear gassing on Haight Street, Mark felt that the time and opportunity for peace and love had passed. The question of whether to print this piece initiated another big staff argument and a vote. Had we dreamed these ideals, tried to manifest a new hope for humanity, only to revert back to war, gas, and brutishness? With Mark's approval we changed the lettering to a cautionary "Evolution?"

Other artwork also reflected the desperation we were all feeling. The centerfold of the last *Oracle* was "A Mandala for Those in Psychic Agony," by Red Dog Pieface. The center of the mandala says, "The meaning of life is the celebration of it." "Johnson's Universe," a collage by Martin Lindhart, is the perfect example of a picture being worth a thousand words. It shows a picture of Lyndon Johnson and Dean Rusk on either side of a map of the United States. Reaching upward from the map to the stars is a pile of naked human bodies. "The Tree of Death," by R.J. Grabb, Jr., is another symbolic representation of the disintegrating vision.

"In Memoriam for David Sandberg" contains excerpts from letters David had sent me before he committed suicide. He was a dear friend, a poet, and an editor of several poetry magazines. His death, I believe, was caused by the speed plague that had descended upon the Haight, a broken love affair, and the general desperation. The portrait was by John Paul Stone:

> I don't know what I'm saying half the time; don't know what it's all about and run screaming thru labyrinthine corridors of my cell body, holy ordering of things, grasping at flashes of light which are bloody fish, which disappear as I reach out for their lantern cave-like eyes.

In "Black Rose of Thunder," a short poem by Michael McClure, the desperate decline of the human spirit and the bottomless war in Southeast Asia are expressed with a purging directness. The art, by Azul, provides an almost perfect integration of art and word vision:

> Jesus, I am sick of the spiritual warfare.
> Yes, here we are in the death of hell.
> O.K., Black rose of thunder!
> O.K., Black rose of thunder!

> O.K., Black rose of thunder!
> Your Bodies and kisses are my eternity
> Fleck! Boot! Mercury! Vapor!

Each issue had a letter page that we called the "Love Haight Ashbury Bush." The word-image in the center is a letter that says, "Virgo, 22 years. Dear Oracle. Are you still there or were you swallowed in last summer's plastic deluge? There is no life nowhere in Boise, Idaho. If Haight-Ashbury still lives, I'm coming. Does anyone need a bass player, who's a chick, also sings, does artwork etc."

Another letter is from R.N. Rogue of West Covina, who announces that his friend, Dr. Matthew Reinhart, has invented a time machine:

> It's a 9 foot capsule with $50,000 worth of equipment and it's stored in a barn. I was with him on September 19, 1967, when he was transported into the year 2000....He said that in the next few years, nations will fall but not by atomic war. The people who survive will evolve into superbeings. They will live a similar life to that of the Hippies in the Haight Ashbury but better. No one will have to work to survive, no fighting, no wars, and a complete anarchy...no boredom, no jealousy, but a large abundance of love and brotherhood. They won't need any drugs because they will be superconscious and won't need them.... As soon as the machine has been patented and approved by the government, he will be able to have visitors to his secret barn. (the time machine) is called Nero.

AD 2000—A Symposium: Watts, Rogers, and Kahn

Alan Watts, Carl Rogers, and Herman Kahn had spoken at a symposium called "AD 2000" in Masonic Auditorium. Their purpose was to try to envision that millennial future. It was symptomatic of our failing energy and vision that we used such a canned feature. But we did present the transcript of the entire symposium without cuts. The art and design for this section were done by Alton Kelley and Stanley Mouse.

Carl Rogers was among the great innovators of modern psychology and was one of the originators of the encounter group method. He emphasized here that the most important problem of our time was whether people would be able to accept and absorb change at the rate it's occurring. He saw intensive group experience as the most significant social invention of the century:

> Religion as we know it today will disappear and be replaced by a community based not on

a common creed nor an unchanging ritual but on the personalities of individuals who become deeply related to one another as they attempt to comprehend and to face as living men and woman the mysteries of existence.

Alan Watts said with some skepticism that we would survive the year 2000 only if:

> ....we begin to think of the US not as an abstract political nation but think of it instead as real physical people and a real physical environment and the love of it...Man is so embroiled in his abstractions that he represents the physical world in the same way as the menu represents dinner...He very easily confuses the symbols for what they represent and so has a tendency to eat the menu instead of dinner.

He speaks of money as a symbol that is mistaken for wealth: "We have the capacity to wipe poverty from the face of the earth. We are long past the age of scarcity....The money we have spent on war since 1914 could have given everyone on earth a comfortable independent income."

To the question "Where is the money going to come from?" he answers, "Money doesn't come from anywhere. We invent it....It is a measure of wealth. Real wealth is energy, technical intelligence and natural resources."

Herman Kahn was the author of the notorious book *On Thermonuclear War*, wherein he sought to justify the use of nuclear weapons and the winnability of nuclear war. He also founded the right-wing think tank, Hudson Institute.

He idealized the Los Angelization of the world as a desirable future for all of us, and perceived human history as having two incidents of interest—the agricultural revolution and the industrial revolution: "In America we all have faith in the future—from the middle class person who borrows right through next year's salary to the hippie—We all know the system's going to work."

He speaks about the computer revolution and predicts that computers will improve by a factor of ten every two or three years:

> Outside of divine revelation...we don't know if there are any characteristics of a human being including the most intimate...which could not be duplicated, or in some reasonable sense of the term surpassed by computers. And when computers get better, who needs humans?.... We know where the human pleasure centers are...get them wired to a computer on your chest or a

console. I'm a prudish type, not free, so I won't let you play your own buttons. That's depraved. But get yourself an opposite number, hopefully of the opposite sex,...and play each other's buttons....I would bet you even money that there will be a new human being in the 21st century. But I really doubt that he'll be a hedonist or a dropout...I rather suspect he'll be a little like me.

Back Page—Cosmic Village

The last page of the last *Oracle* was Azul's plan for a cosmically attuned village perfect for reinhabitation within a natural environment along with some of the text of the *Oracle* staff's last *I Ching* change. The *I Ching* is the ancient Chinese book of divination that was widely used because it contained a profound view of humanity woven into the cycles and processes of nature. Its use was based on a system of patterned randomness and chance:

> 43 Kuai—Breakthrough, Danger—It is necessary to notify one's own city. It does not further to resort to arms...Therefore, it is important to begin at home, to be on guard in our own persons against the faults we have branded. In this way finding no opponent the sharp edge of the weapons of evil become dulled. Finally, the best way to fight evil is to make energetic progress in the good.

CONCLUSION

The *Oracle* and the Haight-Ashbury were a manifestation of forces that are rare in human history. These forces carried vast undercurrents of unfulfilled need that caused new ideas and ideals to burst forth in the creative work of artists, poets, musicians, and philosophers. The energies and echoes are still reverberating through time and cultures.

Few people realize the tremendous influence that the Haight-Ashbury community and its voice, the *San Francisco Oracle*, had as both symbol and focal point for the social, artistic, psychological, and spiritual changes in that chaotic period. The sixties came close to bringing about a revolution, and, looking backward, perhaps the period's failure was a consummation sorely missed; but the sixties without a doubt brought forth a renaissance and a revitalization of American and world culture.

When I look around and speculate what America would be like if we had somehow gone from the grey flannel Eisenhower-McCarthyite fifties to the 3-piece-suit Reagan eighties without the intercedence of the

Beat, hippie, civil rights, and antiwar movements, I wonder if the result of such a time warp would have been a direct line without much resistance to fascism or even holocaust.

The Beat and hippie movements brought the values and experiences of an anarchistic, artistic sub-culture, and a secret and ancient tradition of transcendental and esoteric knowledge and experience into the mainstream of cultural awareness. It stimulated breakthroughs in every field from computer science to psychology, and gave us back a sense of being the originators of our lives and social forms instead of the hapless robot receptors of a dull and determined conformity.

The sense of personal and social freedom manifested in the sixties has had its antithesis in the reaction of the eighties trying to block the road to personal and social evolution. But the freedoms that have become real to us cannot be beaten back. The values of compassion, creativity, social equality, love, and peace will be victorious over war, fear, control, and injustice. In the sixties in all the different move-ments—from the sacrifices of life and limb of the civil rights movement, and the solidarity and commitment of the antiwar movement, to the cultural warriors and internal pilgrims called hippies—we showed that we must, each of us, work together to create a world that will survive and flourish.

REFERENCES

Harrison, Hank. *The Dead*. Millbrae, CA: Celestial Arts, 1980.

Lee, Martin, and Bruce Shlain. *Acid Dream, The CIA, LSD, and the Sixties Rebellion*. New York: Grove Press, 1985.

Peck, Abe. *Uncovering the Sixties: The Life and Times of the Underground Press*. New York: Pantheon Books, 1985.

Perry, Charles. *The Haight-Ashbury: A History*. New York: Rolling Stone Press, 1984.

SPACE CITY!:

FROM OPPOSITION TO ORGANIZATIONAL COLLAPSE

Victoria Smith

Space City!, one of several hundred counterculture newspapers spawned by the New Left during the late 1960s, was conceived in Nirvana—the Nirvana coffeehouse in midtown Manhattan, that is, located in the basement area of an apartment building in the West Seventies just off Broadway. A holdover from the beat era, the Nirvana served espresso, cappuccino, and other exotic coffees. For some reason, Thorne Dreyer, a Texas radical, my coworker at Liberation News Service, and the man I lived with, took a fancy to the place. I wasn't all that wild about the Nirvana, but it was a convenient place to take Thorne's visiting Texas friends, Dennis and Judy Fitzgerald, night after night, in an undisguised effort to persuade them to do something they swore they'd never do—return to Houston, Texas.

After less than a year in New York, Thorne and I were getting burned out on the city (even back in the late, less economically demanding 1960s, New York wasn't a terrific place for the impoverished). We had this great idea of going to Houston to start an underground newspaper. Houston, we reasoned, as the nation's sixth largest city, *needed* an underground newspaper. Houston was Thorne's hometown, and, while I was from Minneapolis, anything west of the Mississippi sounded good to me at that point. Thorne believed—and I soon came to agree—that the Fitzgeralds were indispensable to this project.

Thorne, Dennis, and Judy had been prime movers behind the Austin (Texas) *Rag* in the mid-1960s, back when all three were dropping in and out (mostly out) of the University of Texas. Dennis, Thorne told me,

Smith teaches mass communication at the University of North Dakota in Grand Forks. She is completing her doctoral dissertation at the University of Minnesota. The topic is American unions, empowered expression, and the First Amendment.

was a first-rate writer and Judy had stellar organizational and management skills. The problem was, they both hated Texas, especially their native Houston. They'd been in San Francisco for the last couple of years, working at what Judy referred to as "grunt" jobs to save up enough cash to go to Europe. They'd met their goal and were more or less on their way overseas, when they decided to visit New York for several weeks, to see Thorne, experience the city, and help out at LNS.

We began talking up the newspaper idea almost from the start, knowing it would be a hard sell. Judy, in particular, was determined to go ahead with the European trip, and she was dead set against returning to Houston, a location she regarded as only slightly more desirable than hell. But we kept at them, over mugs of the Nirvana's sweet, foamy coffee.

We pointed out how much fun we would have putting out a newspaper in Houston, how historically important our role would be, and how the city was a radical journalist's dream town, with all those major power centers (big oil, big construction, big banking) just waiting to be attacked. We talked about the different kinds of stories we'd do, who might advertise in our pages, graphic artists we might enlist in the cause (like Dennis' Austin-based hippie brother, Kerry). We speculated on various names. Plus, it was a lot cheaper to survive in Houston than in most American, and certainly most European, cities. And Austin, a cherished oasis in the cultural and political desert of Texas, was only a few hours away. Finally, we prevailed. One night in late January 1969, Judy announced that she and Dennis had decided to commit at least a year to the newspaper project, and, yes, they would go to Houston with us. Thorne and I were delighted (despite the edge of hesitancy in Judy's voice), and the four of us started getting down to some serious planning.

By April, we were on our way to Houston, packed sardine-style in an ancient Chrysler something-or-other driven by an acquaintance of Thorne's. Before that, though, we had taken a short trip to a regional underground press conference in Atlanta, where we met two VISTA workers from Houston, Sue Mithun Duncan and Cam Duncan. We told them of our plan, and within hours they were part of the scheme, too. We all agreed to meet in Houston in April.

We had our first "collective" meeting at Cam and Sue's big, old, rickety house in Houston's second ward, one of the two Chicano barrios in the city. We started hashing out some of the basics, like our organizational structure (no division of labor, no hierarchy, no single or permanent editor). We debated long and passionately over the name for our paper-to-be. We finally came to a consensus on *Space City News*, which was intended

as a satirical statement about Houston's pre-eminence as a space center, with NASA and the Apollo program. I alone didn't like the name and wanted to call the paper *The Houston Free Way* (a satirical statement on Houston's growing gridlock problem, I thought). But in the spirit of democratic consensus—and, more compellingly, because I was tired of arguing—I gave in. (As it happened, we were able to keep the name *Space City News* for only a few months, because of threatened legal action by a UFO newsletter with the same name. We changed the name to *Space City!*, with the exclamation point an inexplicable flourish added by artist Kerry Fitzgerald).

Thorne and I had to go back to New York to collect the rest of our possessions, and Dennis and Judy had to return to San Francisco for the same reason. Cam and Sue said they'd look for an office and start trying to line up a printer and some advertisers. We all reconvened in Houston about a month later and immediately began functioning as the close-knit collective we would remain for more than a year.

It might be useful at this point to describe briefly the collective members and the motivations each of us had for embarking on this rather uncertain project. Of course, I can speak only for myself with any accuracy (and even there, I have some doubts), but I knew the others intimately enough (especially Thorne) that I think I can make some reasonably reliable assessment of the roots of their radicalism. All of us were in our early twenties, and all were revolutionaries of some sort. Each shared the same passion for social justice and, above all, human freedom. But in many important respects, we were quite different.

I was probably the most politically doctrinaire of the group, admittedly more because of my own intellectual confusion and quest for certainty than historical understanding of revolutionary change. In recent years, I've developed a stronger appreciation of the early Marx and Marxist humanism. But back in the late sixties, I considered myself a Marxist-Leninist, although I never was quite sure what that meant in practice.

I had left the University of Minnesota in 1967, nine credits shy of a bachelor's degree in English. That didn't seem to matter much, though, because I'd already established myself professionally as a newspaper reporter at the *St. Paul Dispatch*. Journalism jobs were plentiful then, especially for those who could write decently. I quit the *Dispatch* abruptly that year (and broke off an engagement) to work in Chicago at the national headquarters of Students for a Democratic Society (SDS), where I ran the print shop for about ten months. Since high school, I had been a red (although my communism was modified—some would say contaminated—by Romanticism and a strong

Thoreau-type anarchism). I had become bored with both the middle-class and hippie lifestyles I found in Minneapolis, and I wanted to be a professional revolutionary. And in the late 1960s, that didn't seem such a far-fetched notion.

I met Thorne in the late spring of 1968 at an SDS convention in East Lansing, Michigan. Since both of us were heading to New York and LNS at the time, we decided to live together. What began as a marriage of convenience quickly developed into a close, often tumultuous relationship that was to last several years.

Thorne was a college dropout who had long been involved in New Left politics and had achieved some measure of prominence in SDS. But his real claim to fame in the movement was his pioneering work with the *Rag*, one of the first and most successful counter-culture (or "underground") newspapers of the era. Thorne was really more of an actor than a writer, but he found an important outlet for his unique brand of anarcho-communist views in journalism.

Dennis and Judy Fitzgerald, whom I regard as perhaps the finest, dearest people I've ever known, were peculiar in many respects. As close as we became, it was never entirely clear to me what they sought in revolutionary change. I guess that's not surprising, since most radicals then (and now, I think) really talked less about the nature of society they envisioned than the deficiencies of existing institutions, frameworks, and relations. In the jargon of the time, the Fitzgeralds were more cultural than political revolutionaries. How strange we made such a distinction then!

Judy Gitlin Fitzgerald, unlike Thorne, Dennis, and me, was a child of the petite bourgeoisie. Her father owned a dry cleaners, and he and his wife lived in a small ranch-style bungalow in a modest Houston suburb. Money seemed to be something of a problem in the Gitlin household, and, in fact, Judy's mother Jean was to become one of the few *Space City!* workers who actually got paid, typing endless columns of copy on an old IBM typesetter. Like Thorne, Judy was an actor, and a very good one. She never seemed to want to try her hand at writing and editing, though, so she devoted herself more to *Space City!*'s business side (such as it was).

Dennis came from a middle to upper middle-class background, and, accordingly, his family lived in a more prestigious Houston suburb than Judy's. He was (still is, I'm sure) a highly skilled, facile writer—one of the best I've ever known. Some people seem to be born with that talent, and Dennis was one of them.

Cam Duncan and Sue Mithun Duncan literally were of a different class from the rest of us. Cam (his full name was Green Cameron Duncan III) was from the real ruling class: people of wealth and power who owned, among other things, a major steamship line.

Sue's background was only slightly more modest. Her father was a Minneapolis attorney who at one time was chief counsel for the Minneapolis *Tribune*. Sue and I didn't know each other in Minneapolis, even though it turns out we lived only blocks apart. Her family had a large, expensive home on Lake Harriet, while mine lived in a less wealthy, though nearby, neighborhood. Sue attended a private school, and I went to public school, so our paths never crossed.

Cam and Sue's commitment to revolution (or radical reform) had a relentless, disciplined, pragmatic quality. They were among the most respected people on the Houston left. They were never ideologues, but they knew how to relate to ideologues. They were about as close to selfless as one can be in contemporary America. One illustrative incident in particular is burned in my memory. During her *Space City!* years, Sue spent some time working in Cuba as part of the Venceremos Brigade. She was a tiny, slender, athletic woman whose most distinctive feature, perhaps, was her long golden hair, which fell well past her waist. The first time I saw her after her return from Cuba was at an antiwar rally in a large Houston park. As she came running across the grass, I could scarcely believe my eyes—she'd cut off all her hair! She looked like a little boy. I don't know whether she actually said this, or whether I just inferred it, but she did it because it got in her way when she was cutting sugar cane. And because it was a bourgeois indulgence.

This, then, was *Space City!*'s founding collective. We began bimonthly publication June 6, 1969, with a smattering of advertising (not prepaid, of course) and about $1,000 in the bank. Our struggle to keep above water financially would never cease, but, as it turned out, the big threat to *Space City!*'s existence was not money, but something far more complex and illusive. As for so many underground papers, *Space City!*'s real nemesis was what sociologists call organizational failure. Each group that goes through organizational collapse does so in its own way, but there are some common characteristics. To explain this, I need to indulge in a brief theoretical digression here. This discussion might be a little more abstract than one would expect in a personal narrative, but I've found that analyzing our paper's rise and fall through the social movement research literature has helped me understand what we did right and, more important, where we went wrong.

SOME REASONS SOCIAL MOVEMENT ORGANIZATIONS FAIL

Any organized group is a potential victim of organizational failure, but social movement organizations seem especially vulnerable. People who come together in more or less formal groups for social change often are so determined not to fall into conventional patterns of division and hierarchy that they may not notice when these patterns start creeping into the group. Or, perhaps, their resistance to mainstream structures is so intense, they fail to take advantage of the valuable aspects of a little conventional organization. Or maybe many people who get involved in social movements are so individualistic and creative, they just have trouble functioning in *any* sort of organization. In any case, the problem of organizational failure in social movements has generated a great deal of scholarly interest. What follows is based largely on the work of several social movement theorists, mainly Frederick Miller, Roberta Ash, Mayer N. Gold, Frances Fox Piven, and Richard A. Cloward.

Organizational failure can take at least four different forms: factionalism, encapsulation, bureaucratization, and short-term success.

Factionalism, both ideological and practical, is one of the most common of social movement ills. Factionalism typically occurs when members cannot agree on means to an agreed-upon end, although it also may involve disagreement over the end itself. Most groups can tolerate a certain amount of factionalism and can even benefit from internal debate, but factional disruption can destroy an organization by diverting resources and energy from the group's main goals.

Encapsulation, or self-isolation, occurs when a movement develops an ideology or structure that discourages new members or interferes with the group's ability and desire to communicate effectively with the outside world. A movement may become encapsulated for many reasons—fear of infiltration, for instance—but whatever the cause, the effects typically are debilitating. An exceptionally strong encapsulated movement may survive for a time, but, as a rule, a movement that does not grow, dies.

Bureaucratization is a form of oligarchization, which is the concentration of power in the hands of a minority of the group's members. In bureaucratization, the group establishes a hierarchy of positions, specified roles, and rules that must be kept.

Robert Michels, in his famous book on political parties and oligarchy (see "References and Suggestions for Further Reading" at end of article), contends that all social movement organizations tend to centralize authority and become bureaucratic, a tendency he labels the "iron law of oligarchy." Whether this tendency is truly an iron law, and thus unavoidable, is open to debate. I would argue that a group committed to democratic structure can keep oligarchy at bay, but it takes much conscious effort and a willingness to endure almost endless political struggle. In any case, olig-

archization and bureaucratization seem to be major causes of social movement decline. By focusing on organization building, leaders drain energies from the struggle, blunt the edge of militancy, and open themselves to cooptation.

The tendency toward organization-building is difficult to avoid because movement leaders often are drawn toward traditional power elites and elite definitions of reality. The reasons for this are mainly practical. To build a permanent organization, movement leaders seek acceptance and legitimacy from these elites through their material and symbolic support. This strategy fails more often than it succeeds, however, because the power structure historically has been more responsive to mass disruption than to bureaucratic competence in a movement organization.

Short-term success, the fourth form of organizational failure, is closely related to the other three. For a single-issue movement—one seeking to halt the construction of a rural powerline, for example—success is an unqualified good: The demand is met, the movement disbands, and members return, satisfied, to normal life. Many movement groups, however, press several demands, some of them long-term or vague. Satisfaction of some demands may come at the expense of others, through deals struck with those in power. These compromises activate a process of absorption that draws movement organizations into the structured interests of the establishment. Before long, the movement has streamlined its operation, hired professionals, abandoned voluntary labor, and, in the process, dampened its unique creativity and openness. The group's oppositional character has vanished and with it, perhaps, its reason for existence.

Membership growth is another, very important, form of short-term success that, ironically, can lead to movement decline. To survive and expand, voluntary movements must attract new members, but growth can cause serious problems. New members may lack the commitment of older members or may differ on how to wage the struggle, and factional splits may result. A movement organization may attract additional members before new roles can be created for them, and this can force the group to focus on organizational problems and neglect the political battle.

Finally, short-term success, either through recognition from the power structure or through membership growth, can be deceptive. Believing that in winning a few battles they have won the war, movement members may relax their guard in various ways. The austerity and pressures of the constantly politicized life make this especially tempting for full-time movement cadre.

There are two other, related causes of movement decline I should mention, because both played some role in *Space City!*'s lifecycle. They are repression and what might be called accommodation strategies.

We all know generally what repression is. Repression is direct or covert coercive actions by the state (or its agents) against social movements and their members. Repression can be official (e.g., criminal indictment and imprisonment, direct physical violence, the raiding of offices, destruction of equipment and similar property, spying, infiltrating, intimidation, and petty harassment), or it can be extralegal. Here I'm thinking especially of vigilante violence, which the state sanctions or ignores, such as the bloody assault on northern abolitionist editors, black and white, that preceded the American Civil War.

The main purpose of repression is to disrupt or curtail movement activities and hinder recruitment efforts. It doesn't always work, however. Moderate or mild repression may have the unintended effect of increasing movement solidarity and rallying popular support for the beleaguered organization. Consider, for instance, the boomerang effect of recent state violence against the Miami rap group, 2 Live Crew. Largely as a result of arrests and court actions, the group has become an emblem of today's embattled civil liberties *and* civil rights, and its album sales have soared.

But when the state gets serious about crushing dissent or subversion, repression can be severe and deadly. Under certain conditions, repression can be a highly efficient way to cripple or kill a movement or organization. Moreover, strong repression, particularly if it involves physical violence or imprisonment, can aggravate a group's organizational problems through a kind of whipsaw action, by picking off leaders, destroying movement property, depleting resources through legal defense costs, and leaving the rank-and-file fearful, impoverished, and confused. Surely the collapse of the Black Panther Party in the 1970s is a case in point.

While repression is something done *to* a group, and organizational failure something the group does to itself, accommodation strategies involve a subtle collaboration between those in power and the movement group. Accommodation is a slow, interactive process that, in the words of Berkeley sociologist Todd Gitlin, "unites persuasion from above with consent from below." That consent may be active or passive, but it must be present for accommodation strategies to operate. These strategies depend heavily on persuasion techniques but also on a more amorphous cultural process that tends to defuse popular discontent and reproduce existing class, race, and gender relations.

Some people call the accommodation process cooptation (the buying out of movement leaders), but it's much bigger and more insidious than this. It can poison an entire group, or an entire movement, from top to bottom.

Accommodation strategies can scuttle movement opposition and militancy, increase movement dependence on those in power, minimize real political differences and structural contradictions, and, in general, reinforce the (false) belief that the interests of society's elites are the interests of all.

In general, then, accommodation is a dynamic and powerful process of social control that goes beyond social movements. It operates throughout the entire society, to create and reinforce a dominant consciousness (or a consciousness becoming dominant) that is continually recreated, reinforced, and, for most, internalized. This consciousness—this cultural hegemony—thus becomes synonymous with common sense, as revealed in expressions such as "they say," "it's self-evident," or "everyone knows." Further, because the process is so effective in presenting the elite interests as common interests, people under its influence frequently will collude in their own oppression.

Most people in mass society can be expected to internalize the dominant consciousness, to greater or lesser degrees, but when radicals and revolutionaries do this they've suffered a defeat more certain and devastating than guns, tear gas, and jails can bring about. The only real defense, as the Italian Communist Antonio Gramsci observed, is to build a genuinely oppositional social movement, which then would be able to exert sustained resistance to the mainstream. In Gramsci's view, this meant the building of a powerful *counter-hegemony*, capable of fulfilling all the emotional, intellectual, and physical needs of a revolutionary class.

Space City! lasted a little more than three years. I think its death was untimely by at least two or three more years. So in moving from theory to practice, I've tried to explain our too-early collapse in light of what I've learned about social movements and revolutionary change. In general terms, it happened something like this: During its three years, *Space City!* moved from its original incarnation as an organ of militant opposition to local and national power structures to a more moderate, "alternative" stance. It finally ceased publication in September 1972, after a series of financial crises and internal disruptions.

All the influences I just described, except repression, contributed to *Space City!*'s early death. Although we experienced considerable repression (which I'll describe shortly), that repression tended to strengthen, rather than damage, us, individually and as an organization. Accommodation processes indirectly contributed to the paper's demise by generating the conditions for organizational failure. Houston's traditional conservative community made no direct effort to absorb us, but an emerging liberal elite drew us inexorably into habits and values of bourgeois legitimacy. As a result, the paper lost its raw spirit of opposition, its distinctiveness, a clear sense of purpose, and, ultimately, its reason for being.

I have found it useful to divide *Space City!*'s short history into four phases: opposition, redefinition, alternative, and collapse. These are organizational and ideological categories, but they also have fairly distinct time lines. I suspect many former underground editors could identify most, if not all, these phases in their own publications.

OPPOSITIONAL PHASE: JUNE 1969-SEPTEMBER 1970

From the start, we made it clear that *Space City!*'s central purposes were to serve as a "focal point" for movement organizing and to raise revolutionary consciousness among the city's disaffected, primarily a fragmented youth population that expressed defiance through sex, drugs, and rock 'n' roll. Sex, drugs, and rock gave us something to go on, but we hoped to infuse that youthful rebelliousness with political awareness as well. As we wrote in an open letter from the collective in the third issue:

> For us, putting out a newspaper can't be an end in itself, and we sure ain't doing it to make money! We want to build a movement in Houston. We want our paper to serve as a catalytic agent, stimulating radical activity. And as a coalescing point, around which an alternative community can grow.

The paper expressed its oppositional stance both in content and in organizational structure. For example, one of the earliest issues featured two lengthy articles on media. The first was a detailed analysis of the corporate and social power structure undergirding the two local dailies and several radio and television stations. The second was a history of the underground press that described its function this way:

> The underground press was born of necessity. Something was happening and it demanded visibility....
>
> Kids began to discover their heads and their bodies and, most important, their lack of freedom. And as they came together, the man came down—making joy and paranoia the bedfellows of the new awakening.
>
> It was these two states of mind that demanded expression. To spread the glorious word and

to publicize the harrowing realities of the system, a medium was needed.

Together, the articles expressed the kind of journalism we opposed and the kind we intended to practice.

Organizationally, the *Space City!* collective rejected hierarchy (as was the case with many underground papers of the era). Division of labor was minimal, an arrangement that was remarkably successful, at least in our oppositional phase. Each collective member performed every task involved in putting out the paper, from planning to editing to layout to distribution to selling the paper on the streets.

Sexist content and practices were forbidden. The rule that none of the three male collective members could act as *Space City!* spokespersons bemused and occasionally angered local commercial journalists writing feature stories on the paper, because they were accustomed to male leadership and reasonably cooperative sources. Participation in collective meetings was mandatory. And the meetings were almost continuous because, within a few months, all six of us were living together, in a big old house near the newspaper office. To a large extent, we shared resources, since there were no staff salaries. In fact, as I mentioned earlier, Judy's mother Jean, our typesetter, was the only regularly paid staff member. Given the Gitlins' economic situation, we never would have considered asking her to work for free. Advertising salespeople and newspaper vendors received a percentage of their sales, but, aside from these people, no one made any money off the early *Space City!*

We sought only as much advertising as was necessary to cover printing and miscellaneous costs and relied heavily on street sales and subscriptions. This, in itself, set us apart from just about any other publication in the city.

While collective membership, with its ideological and lifestyle rigors, was all but closed, anyone could be a street vendor. Vendors were allowed to keep ten cents for every twenty-cent paper sold, and many young people were able to support themselves selling *Space City!*. The vendors, most of them long-haired, teenage males, would pick up their bundles as soon as the paper left the printer. We asked new vendors unknown to us to pay in advance, but, in fact, most of the papers went out on consignment. Then, the vendors would spend the next several days hawking the paper like nineteenth-century newsboys on downtown street corners, at busy intersections, concerts, movies, and wherever else prospective customers might happen by.

As one might expect, Houston in the late sixties and early seventies provided an inhospitable climate for radicalism. Already the nation's sixth largest city, it was growing rapidly and almost uncontrollably, which meant the general population was unstable, and communication and transportation difficult. Politically, Houston was dominated by extreme conservatism. The white left-liberal movement consisted of a few older antiwar activists, staff members of KPFT-FM (the local listener-sponsored Pacifica radio station), a small Socialist Workers Party group, and some five or six ex-SDSers who recently had broken with the militant Weatherman faction.

While the city could no longer maintain segregation in public places, the neighborhoods were not integrated. Entering a ghetto or barrio in which Houston's blacks and Chicanos dwelt, you had the sense of stepping, quite literally, into another country. The police force was widely known to be vicious when it came to controlling minorities and dissidents. Black activism, in particular, was discouraged. In 1968, for example, Lee Otis Johnson, a local organizer for the Student Nonviolent Coordinating Committee, was sentenced to thirty years in federal prison for passing a marijuana cigarette to an undercover narcotics agent at a party. The specific charge was sale of narcotics, and the conviction was based on the testimony of a single material witness.

Despite the drawbacks, we saw Houston as a challenge as well as a tremendous opportunity. The booming economic climate initially helped nourish *Space City!* and the city's growing movement. Houston had shocking poverty but also enormous and frequently conspicuous wealth, most of it from oil, gas, and land development. Partly because of this, the cost of living was relatively low, making it easier for counter-institutions to develop.

Early issues of *Space City!* focused on the struggles of Third World peoples, workers, and women, and included features catering to the counterculture, such as Gilbert Shelton's "Fabulous Furry Freak Brothers" comics, a poetically composed column on whole foods (including recipes), and an "Advice to Dopers" column (the idea here was, if people were going to do drugs, they should do them responsibly).

The *Space City!* collective, directly or through the paper, helped start a drug crisis center, a food coop, and a people's rock hall called Of Our Own. We also organized Houston's first guerrilla theater skits, a women's liberation group, and some of the city's first big antiwar marches. *Space City!* also provided moral and material support to movements and actions it did not initiate, such as a high school underground newspaper and spontaneous riots in parks and at rock concerts.

It is hardly surprising then that *Space City!* experienced repression during its oppositional phase. While the notion of armed revolution, or even insurrection, in the United States may seem preposterous today, back then it seemed just around the next bend, not only to

revolutionaries, but also to those in power. At home, the nation was undergoing a legitimation crisis, with growing opposition to American troops in Vietnam, public revulsion at the assassinations of Martin Luther King and Robert Kennedy, and the televised spectacle of troops and demonstrators clashing at the 1968 Democratic National Convention in Chicago. Internationally, Vietnamese liberation forces were holding at bay American military power, revolutionary groups were appearing throughout the Third World from Mozambique to Uruguay, and a worker-student alliance had come close to seizing state power in France. Richard Nixon's election in 1968 seemed to herald an intensification of the conflict, with a growing schism between the forces of reaction (much of the United States with its law-and-order president) and of international revolution. With the Nixon administration came a more serious and more deadly wave of repression, and, in May 1970, during demonstrations protesting Nixon's decision to invade Cambodia, four students were killed at Kent State and two were killed at Jackson State.

Violence against *Space City!* came from civilians rather than police. One steamy night in July 1969, individuals later identified as members of the local United Klans of America chapter pipebombed our office. At the time, the collective was meeting in a nearby home, but Sherwood Bishop, a volunteer and later a collective member, was on the premises. Sherwood was unhurt but, understandably, pretty upset. Nevertheless, he remained one of *Space City!*'s most courageous Klan-fighters.

Over the next several months, we endured break-ins, thefts, tire-slashings, potshots (including a steel arrow fired from a crossbow through the front door), and threats, both to staff members and advertisers. We acquired the habit of never walking in front of an open window after dark. (I visited my family in Minneapolis in early 1970 and kept finding myself ducking when I passed the picture window in the living room. Fortunately, my parents didn't ask why I was spending so much time on the floor.) The Houston police generally were unresponsive to *Space City!*'s complaints, and soon we were forced to install floodlights and keep an around-the-clock armed watch on the office. More than once, we actually returned a shot or two. But, in fact, this whole episode was pretty exciting, exhilarating, and, oddly enough, almost fun at times.

Our relations with the Klan members gradually changed, as they came to realize we were formidable opponents and not to be trifled with. Also, some of the Klansmen were not too bright, and they'd actually hang around the office during the day, masquerading as working-class folk. One of them, a wispy, spaced-out-

**Figure 1: Mike Lowe in full regalia poses with Rev. Kitt
at Klan rally near Crosby. Reprinted from *Space City!* June 1, 1971.**

looking blond named Mike Lowe, was especially persistent. We assumed he was Klan, because we had obtained a photo of him in Klan regalia, with the hood up to reveal his face (see figure 1). One day, while Mike was in the office, Cam suddenly started snapping pictures of everyone, and insisted on getting Mike's as well. He resisted. Cam persisted. Finally, Mike dashed out the door and down the street, with Cam and Dennis right on his heels. They caught him easily, and, laughing gleefully, held him down while Sue took his picture. We ran both Sue's photo and the Klan photo in the paper, with a long story about how we caught the Klansman (and let him go, of course—I mean, what would we do with a dopey, 20-year-old Klansman?). (See related article in appendix 1.)

So, the kind of repression we experienced had a tonic effect on us; it didn't crush the paper or our spirits by any means. In fact, the attacks brought us sympathy and support from Houston progressives and civil libertarians. And eventually, the Klan left us alone, preferring more passive targets and unguarded facilities (like KPFT's transmitter).

Other radical groups in Houston had a much different experience with repression, however, and their ordeals touched us profoundly. The most deadly action was aimed at People's Party II, a fledgling black revolutionary group with which *Space City!* was allied. In August 1970, police snipers shot and killed Carl Hampton, the party's charismatic young leader. Several others also were injured, including a white radical. The shootings severely crippled the black revolutionary group, but the incident seemed to strengthen the *Space City!* collective, both internally and in its ties with other radicals. In the August 1-21, 1970, issue, we accused the Houston police of premeditated murder and declared:

> The war of the poor people of the world against the Amerikan Leviathan is now, and will continue to be, the most important, the most difficult, and the bloodiest in history. Amerika will not relinquish control without a deadly fight....
>
> If there was ever a time to get serious, it's now. If there was ever a time to get together, to

suspend our ideological differences for a while, it's now....We need to re-recognize our common struggle, if any of us are to long continue in that struggle at all....

[I]f we don't live our lives fighting this American monster that killed Carl, that is killing people all over the world, that is destroying the planet, that is twisting people's minds—well, then our lives aren't worth shit.

REDEFINITION PHASE: OCTOBER 1970 - APRIL 1971

By fall 1970, *Space City!* had developed a respectable following of newly politicized young people who, like their paper, regarded themselves as revolutionary. Inspired by the flamboyant political style of the Youth International Party, or Yippies, who were trying to combine radical and hip cultures into an ongoing stream of public relations stunts, the *Space City!* collective organized the Red Coyotes, a Yippie-inflected antiwar group, and attempted to publicize it into existence through guerrilla theater forays and prominent coverage in our own pages. The Red Coyotes was somewhat successful and, in January 1971, mobilized several hundred people who blocked streets and fought with police during a demonstration against a visit by Vice President Spiro Agnew.

Yet we rapidly lost interest in the Red Coyotes, perhaps because such youth-oriented "media-event" groups like the Red Coyotes seemed too insubstantial and impermanent, even too childish, for what we perceived as our political coming-of-age. Perhaps, too, we felt uncomfortable, to varying degrees, with the boisterous Yippie style, which demanded a constant and exhausting level of outrageousness. At the same time, some of us—mainly Thorne and I—were developing an interest in Houston's emerging avant-garde arts community. We were attracted to the polished professionalism of Pacifica radio and two progressive rock stations, which seemed to be reaching a far broader audience than *Space City!*

We sought a new identity for *Space City!*, one that would project a more sober and responsible image. Moreover, the internal collective unity that had worked so well in the beginning was becoming burdensome. Cam and Sue had moved to Austin, and three new collective members had been added, but we still felt isolated and unable to expand. In short, we were weary of being cast as youthful deviants and began looking for legitimacy and acceptance from more moderate groups and individuals. It was a moment of fatal hubris. We were starting to reject our natural youth constituency and to look outside ourselves and our loyal followers for support. At the time, we believed we wanted simply to reach more people with our revolutionary message. But in ways we couldn't see or admit, the revolutionary message was losing its clarity and toughness.

In February 1971, *Space City!* suspended publication to reorganize and raise money. An open letter from the collective in the February 14, 1971, issue reflected the group's ambiguity and vague malaise:

[W]e've come to the end of something. This issue of Space City will be the last issue for...well, we're really not sure. Whether this ending will be a death, or whether it will be the quiet before a new, better rebirth depends mainly on you....

If it were just a matter of raising a little more money, adding a few more pages to every issue, and getting the whole thing a little more together, we could probably do that, just like we've done it before. But it's not that easy.

If you want it we're stuck in a rut and freakin' out. Also we're broke like we've never been before.

During the two-month redefinition period, we held several fundraising events, from rock concerts to cocktail parties, and raised just under our goal of $3,000. We also began to forge new links with influential liberals who, if not wealthy themselves, knew people who were.

Soon after suspending publication, we held a series of closed collective meetings to plan the new *Space City!*. We decided the paper should expand its appeal to include essentially the same audience Pacifica reached, the socially conscious liberal and artistic intelligentsia. Editorial changes involved increasing the amount of local news coverage and investigative reporting, plus adopting a more objective tone and consistent writing and editing styles. To carry out the new editorial policies, we established a hierarchy of positions, including a city editor, managing editor, production chief, and photo editor. The business side also was to expand to include advertising and circulation managers (previously there had been only a bookkeeper, a few advertising salespeople, and an army of street vendors). Finally, *Space City!* would appear weekly, to increase the immediacy of its new impact. As the collective put it in an open letter in its first new issue on April 6, 1971, the changes were made so "we could be more of a *newspaper*, more immediate."

During *Space City!*'s redefinition phase, symptoms of what would later develop into complete organizational failure had begun to appear. As I mentioned earlier, we had succeeded in helping organize some semblance of a radical youth movement. Whether this success was too much or not enough, it apparently contributed to the paper's bureaucratization and legitimation seeking. These developments may have been related to our growing internalization (or re-internalization) of bourgeois standards and values, particularly the drive for public approval and acceptance from increasingly broader, non-deviant segments of society. Meanwhile, the underlying conflicts and uncertainties that had forced redefinition went unresolved and, in large part, unexamined. These conflicts chiefly stemmed from a central emotional and ideological tension with which all social movements must contend: the difficulty of maintaining a consistently oppositional movement (with a mostly intangible reward system) in the face of a subtle, all-encompassing cultural hegemony (with a very tangible reward system).

The forces of accommodation had not actually set in yet, but the nature of the reorganization scheme suggests that some of us anticipated or even unconsciously invited those forces. I know that, at that point, I found legitimacy and acceptance by the larger society enormously attractive. We never discussed these forbidden yearnings openly, or at all, so I really can't say whether the others shared them. I think Thorne did, to some degree. But, for me, the strain of being constantly so far outside the mainstream was wearing me down, and, at the time, I believed the strain was undermining *Space City!*'s effectiveness.

The reorganization did allow us to break out of our encapsulization, but, as it turned out, the expansion was only temporary. And, ironically, it set the stage for further short-term success and factionalism.

ALTERNATIVE PHASE: APRIL 1971 - DECEMBER 1971

The spring and summer of 1971 was a wonderful, stimulating time for many of us. Although the visible changes were subtle, the new *Space City!* enjoyed great success. Actual subscriptions and sales did not increase substantially, but the paper's more subdued and balanced tone and content selection won praise from mainstream journalists, some local progressive politicians, and experimental artists. Where the old *Space City!* had attracted mostly street people and "heads," new kinds of volunteers began to offer their services. The new volunteers were typically young, hip, professional, and educated—in short, proto-yuppies. They included a talented commercial artist, a civil liberties attorney, and an entrepreneur who tried, with limited success, to restructure *Space City!*'s business end.

Most of us were satisfied with the new editorial structure, style, and emphasis. For once, the newspaper seemed to run smoothly, now that we had a more structured organization. Meanwhile, the extralegal violence had ended, after the arrests of two Klan

members for dynamiting Pacifica's transmitter, literally blowing the radio station off the air on two separate occasions. One of the two men was convicted in federal district court of attempting to blow up transmitters in another state in September 1971.

In many ways, 1971 was a year of adjustment, even complacency, for *Space City!*. Houston's radical movement, which never had been strong, was dwindling further. More important, perhaps, were developments in the national movement. SDS had died in 1969, a victim of internecine factional warfare, and by 1971 the more important Weatherman faction was operating largely underground. Further, the mass media had ceased its intensive coverage of the national movement, which prompted many people, including *Space City!* staff members, to start losing interest as well.

A comparison of two articles on the police illustrates the contrast between the old and new *Space City!*. The first story, in the January 30-February 13, 1971, issue (the old *Space City!*), is a report on the Red Coyote demonstration against Spiro Agnew, who was addressing a group at Houston's Astroworld Hotel. At the demonstration, several participants were beaten and arrested. The lead reads, in part:

> Houston hippies got unruly and Houston pigs ran amuck Thursday night, January 21, at the Asshole World Hotel right here in Space City. Seems Spiro came to town, to give the Vince Lombardi award to the college football lineman of the year....

An accompanying story describes an alleged beating incident at the police station. The headline screams, "'I Thought They Were Going to Kill Her.'" Thorne and I cowrote both stories, and, to be honest, we even then doubted the credibility of the witness to the beating. But no matter—the story served our purpose, which was to trash the cops.

The second story, which I wrote for the April 20, 1971, issue, deals with what I perceived to be a *real* police beating of a local black youth. It's a report on an upcoming trial of two Houston police officers charged the year before with first-degree murder "after they allegedly beat and stomped to death 22-year-old Bobby Joe Conner in the Galena Park police station."

In the same issue, an unsigned editorial—the newly established "*Space City!* Viewpoint"—denounces police brutality and calls for fair and impartial administration of justice in the Conner case. Both sound like something you'd read in the *Houston Chronicle*. I wrote the editorial, too, and I knew damned well those cops would get off (which they did), just as I had little doubt they were guilty. But, of course, I had no proof of either assertion, and bald opinion not grounded in fact was to play little or no role in the new *Space City!*.

The new *Space City!* still stressed interpretive and analytical stories, such as a lengthy feature on the involvement of the construction giant Brown & Root, Inc., in the Vietnam conflict during the Johnson presidency, and a splendidly researched series on irregularities in the city's tax assessment office. But although we claimed our new plan was to provide more local "muckraking," the paper actually ran a greater number of substantial investigative pieces *before* the redefinition period, including three major pieces on ownership and control of Houston's media plus in-depth articles on Rice University, the Houston Endowment (owner of the *Houston Chronicle*, among other properties), and the mayor.

Instead, the new *Space City!* was dominated by more traditional, objective, "hard" news. We established a system of beats, and *Space City!* reporters began covering and quoting conventional sources of institutional power, as we took our places at local government meetings along with the rest of the press corps. Monday after Monday, I showed up promptly at 9 A.M. for the weekly meeting of the Harris County Commissioners, took extensive notes, asked questions, and hobnobbed with the other reporters. I loved it. It reminded me of my days as a "real" reporter at the *St. Paul Dispatch*. It gave order and meaning to my chaotic life.

(Part of the reason my life was so chaotic at this time was that Dennis and Judy had left the paper. Judy had a baby in early 1971. If memory serves, it was during Judy's pregnancy that Dennis became romantically involved with a beautiful young *Space City!* volunteer in her late teens. The emotional fallout was devastating, and Dennis and Judy left the paper to resume "grunt" jobs in San Francisco. I missed them both desperately, and I still believe losing our two most rock-solid, talented people was one of the paper's greatest disasters).

Visually, *Space City!* acquired a more polished look, with preference given to photos over drawings. Production increasingly became the responsibility of specialists, where before the entire collective participated in the layout process. For me, this was an enormous relief. I loathe layout and keylining and all that. With the new structure, the major layout challenge was a diplomatic one—ensuring that our two hotheaded designers, Gavan Duffy and Jim Shannon, didn't spend production night screaming at each other over god knows what, instead of getting the paper ready for the printer. Their fights were so loud, so intense, and so seemingly pointless, they nearly drove away new volunteers, including Bill Narum, an extraordinarily gifted and peace-loving graphic artist. Nevertheless,

Shannon and Duffy did fine work, and the paper never missed a deadline, despite all the ruckus.

In late summer of 1971, the collective made the most dramatic change in *Space City!*'s content and political direction up to that point: We began covering the city elections as though we believed they mattered. This was an abrupt and controversial departure from our previous stand on the electoral process—that elections were a sham and merely reinforced the illusion of power and participation. Although several black and Chicano activists were running for offices, *Space City!* took special interest in the mayor's race and began covering it in earnest, all but endorsing the Democratic candidate—a slick, young, white liberal who also was a scion of the local Astrodome/Astroworld dynasty. At my behest, we devoted almost the entire November 11, 1971 issue to the elections, with a half-page photo and lengthy interview with the liberal mayoral candidate. After the city elections, we began covering the state election campaigns, devoting substantial portions of the paper to progressive liberal candidates.

Significantly, it was the election coverage that, for the first time, provoked protest from many non-collective members. Indeed, even some of the new collective members were skeptical. For whether we called ourselves communists or anarchists (or some creative hybrid thereof), we were supposed to be unequivocally opposed to the hypocrisy of elections. The problem was that some of us had unwittingly ceased to believe in communism or anarchism (although I must add that, in my case, the lapse has proved temporary).

Space City! had changed in content, style, and appearance, and had won admiring comments from local liberals, but by the end of 1971 the paper suddenly found itself in deep financial trouble. Since revenues appeared to be slightly ahead of expenditures and press runs higher than ever, we were perplexed, until we discovered that two new collective members—one of them the new bookkeeper—had embezzled close to $2,000 from *Space City!* funds. Now, I must admit there was a certain poetic justice in the rip-off. How symbolic of the new, more bourgeois *Space City!* to uncover embezzlement, which, after all, is a deed motivated by desire for personal gain, rather than the ethic of revolutionary virtue and cooperation. The incident also highlighted the unavoidable fact that we, like so many of our journalist comrades throughout the country, had failed ourselves and our recruits, by not finding ways to pay people a living wage. I never have been able to work up much anger or resentment towards the two kids—and they were only kids—who took the money. They felt they needed it, it was there, and apparently the temptation was just too great.

In December 1971, because of the financial crisis, we again suspended publication to reorganize. This time, however, only two of the original collective members remained, and morale and energy were perilously low.

Before I continue the story, let me sum up *Space City!*'s alternative phase. We had moved away from our radical youth constituency in an attempt to escape encapsulation and broaden our economic and political base of support. To do this, we altered the paper's entire journalistic strategy, from a combative, oppositional style to a more reasoned, "alternative" approach, structurally supported by division of labor and hierarchy. But the more the paper assumed the outward form of a serious, news-oriented, and increasingly moderate publication, the more we, the collective members, seemed to internalize the outward forms.

Initially, we absorbed conventional standards of newsworthiness and organization, and then conventional definitions of politics and social reality in general. Further, the initial contacts some of us had with members of the paper's new constituency led to intimate social and political relations with the liberal bourgeoisie. These ties, in turn, were reinforced by the new, increased legitimacy we received (or thought we received). The embezzlement crisis painfully illustrated the degree to which the paper's original identity had been submerged in bourgeois ideology and practices. This incident also was related to our short-term success of membership growth. When you open yourself to new members, you can't always be certain the newcomers have the same depth of commitment, same values, and same understanding of goals and means as the original members.

THE END: JANUARY 1972 - SEPTEMBER 1972

Space City!'s December hiatus lasted only a week, and the paper resumed publication on December 16, 1971, with a new business manager named Bill McElrath. McElrath was given absolute control over advertising, circulation, and long-range planning to carry out his promise that *Space City!* soon would be making a profit. (The eagerness to make money also reflected a profound internal change in the collective's values, because we previously had rejected the profit motive and profits themselves, as the summer 1969 collective letter, which I quoted earlier, makes clear.)

Through the early part of 1972, we considered folding the paper and starting over again. We consulted with liberal attorneys and businessmen interested in backing a new paper modeled after the *Village Voice*, but nothing came of the discussions. Content continued much the same as in 1971, with increasing coverage of local politics, and a new, controversial emphasis on the fine arts and high culture.

As *Space City!* tumbled from one financial crisis to another, however, some of us began to lose interest in continuing this or any publication. I know I was losing interest, as well as weight, sleep, and energy.

We also began to lose control over the entire operation. Our new business manager didn't make any money for the paper, but he certainly was busy behind the scenes, organizing opposition to the collective. Consequently, a factional split developed between staff members backing the collective and those supporting McElrath. Interestingly, his team was arguing for a return to the paper's old, more radical image, while the collective wanted to continue the more moderate direction, with expanded contemporary arts coverage.

The dispute smoldered through the spring and erupted into near violence in early summer. I'll never forget the vision of the balding, chain-smoking McElrath, screaming at me and throwing ashtrays across my living room, in a fit of rage over my evident intransigence. After mutual legal and physical threats, frozen bank accounts, and many angry meetings, McElrath was fired. Unfortunately, the only way the collective could oust him (short of something illegal, like kidnapping) was by a civil maneuver: a vote by the *Space City!* board of directors, including proxies from Dennis and Judy. To say this action damaged the collective's fragile credibility with staffers is a vast understatement. Even those sympathetic to our plight were shocked by such a blatantly bourgeois move. But we believed we had to get rid of this Machiavellian business manager, and this tactic seemed the only peaceful, legal, and permanent way.

After McElrath left, he and his people started a new paper (I forget the name), but it lasted only a few issues. We still had *Space City!*, but the conflict had taken its toll. The paper folded in September 1972, awash in unpaid bills and back taxes.

POST MORTEM

So what happened? Why did *Space City!* die, just when it seemed to be gaining a measure of credibility? There is no single reason, of course. Recall the three general sources of movement decline I outlined earlier: organizational failure, repression, and accommodation. Organizational failure appears to have been the primary source of *Space City!*'s collapse, but some accommodation processes seemed to create a climate in which organizational failure could flourish. Repression, however, seems not to have had a negative effect on the paper. Instead, repression increased our internal solidarity and popular support. Of course, repression against *Space City!* was far less severe than that experienced by some of Houston's other radical groups, and by much of the underground press and New Left in general. Also, no one was killed or injured in the extralegal violence against *Space City!*. Had there been deaths, or had we experienced official state repression, the outcome might have been different.

As for accommodation, there were few explicit attempts to coopt *Space City!* collective members during the paper's three years of publication. We were frequent radio talk show participants and guest speakers, and often were interviewed by local mainstream journalists. These relationships did not constitute cooptation as such, but were more a function of what Todd Gitlin calls the commercial media's need to "certify leaders."

But despite the apparent lack of intention on anyone's part, I believe the collective and some staff members were, in fact, absorbed and accommodated, and for one overriding reason: We simply could not resist the pull of one important segment of the dominant belief system—progressive liberalism, both political and artistic. Our inability to resist no doubt had many causes, and ours is not the only underground newspaper group that gave in to this hegemonic sway. One problem was that we were young and, more important, terribly immature, politically and emotionally, but we didn't realize that. We were unsure of our individual *and* collective identities, and that uncertainty left a kind of vacuum to be filled by other, less progressive ideas. Still, we might better have been able to retain our integrity had we been able to rise above our insecurities and build an effective alternative culture and, thus, find the acceptance, reinforcement, and legitimacy we longed for *outside* the dominant system.

For *Space City!* the accommodation sources of decline and organizational failure fed on each other. We were unable to use the paper to build a counterculture with which we could feel comfortable because we were encapsulated. But to break out of our isolation and build a broad base of support, we had to open ourselves to bourgeois values, beliefs, and individuals. Without some sort of alternative support structure, however, we were likely prospects for absorption into the dominant system. Other elements of organizational failure, notably bureaucratization and short-term success, exacerbated the problem until factionalism dealt the final blow.

From the vantage point of some two decades after *Space City!* folded, I find it relatively easy to identify, in the collective's efforts to propagate its message and broaden its base, the germ of destruction. And while it is a little sad to reflect on those innocent, disastrous mistakes, I think I've learned some valuable lessons in the process—about myself, the other collective members, and social movements in general. It is not so easy to point to things we should or could have done differently, however, particularly when I know that other underground papers had gone through similar experiences of disorganization and disintegration, and many were also unable to recover.

Perhaps the mature, rational, and right position would have been for us to realize and accept that we were bound to feel isolated in the early years of movement building and, summoning all the self-discipline we could, cultivate the radical youth movement that had begun to coalesce around the paper, instead of trying to generate a popular front. Only after that community was firmly established as a countercultural and political force should we have attempted to expand the paper's appeal to the liberal intelligentsia. I don't know if we could have acted with such discipline at the time, though, considering how isolated and jaded we felt in early 1971.

A few years ago, when I was a graduate student at the University of Minnesota, I had the good fortune to be able to escort Stuart Hall, the great British neoMarxist sociologist, around campus, where he was visiting as part of a speaking tour. We talked extensively about this problem of movement isolation versus expansion. Hall, who like many of us is continually exploring new avenues for change, takes the position that, at some point, any social movement or organization *must* attempt to move out into the mainstream. That, after all, is the whole point of a revolutionary movement—to establish a new way, a new society, and, yes, a new hegemony. When I protested that, in my experience, moving into the mainstream is a recipe for disaster, Hall suggested that we acted too soon. He pointed out that, in such matters, timing is critical. And I have to agree. You don't expand outward until you are ready and have a solid base of your own support—until, in Sun Tzu's now trendy words, you "know the enemy and know yourself." And you never, *never* seek your really fundamental support from those you're opposing and striving to supplant.

REFERENCES AND SUGGESTIONS FOR FURTHER READING

Ash, Roberta. *Social Movements in America.* Chicago: Markham Publishing Co., 1970.

Dennis, Everette, and William Rivers. *Other Voices.* New York: Harper and Row, 1974.

Gitlin, Todd. *The Whole World Is Watching: Mass Media in the Making and Unmaking of the New Left.*

Berkeley: University of Southern California Press, 1980.

Gramsci, Antonio. *Selections from the Prison Notebooks*, ed. by Quintin Hoare and Geoffrey Nowell Smith. New York: International Publishers, 1971.

Leamer, Lawrence. *The Paper Revolutionaries: The Rise of the Underground Press*. New York: Simon and Schuster, 1982.

Michels, Robert. *Political Parties*. New York: Free Press, 1962.

Miller, Frederick D. "The End of SDS and the Emergence of the Weatherman: Demise Through Success."

Social Movements of the Sixties and Seventies, ed. by Jo Freeman. New York: Longman, 1983.

Piven, Frances Fox, and Richard A. Cloward. *Poor People's Movements*. New York: Random House, 1977.

Sale, Kirkpatrick. *SDS*. New York: Random House, 1973.

Sun Tzu. *The Art of War*, trans. by Samuel B. Griffith. Oxford: Oxford University Press, 1963.

Zald, Mayer, and Roberta Ash. "Social Movement Organizations: Growth, Decay and Change." *Social Forces* 44, no. 3 (March 1966), 327-41.

APPENDIX 1: LOWE-DOWN[1]

by Victoria Smith

We last saw Mike Lowe, young Waco carpenter and known Klansman, just a few weeks before he was arrested with materials to make a bomb.

He and some friends dropped by to purchase some papers Saturday, May 8. Lowe was smiling and cocky, as usual. We were downright hostile, angrily snapping photographs of him and his colleagues. After it became clear to them that we were in no mood for playing games, they left in a hurry without even paying for the papers.

This encounter was certainly not the first. We've known Mike Lowe for nearly two years. He has been around *Space City!* from time to time just about as long as *Space City!* has been in Houston.

The story of our acquaintance with Lowe is at times comical, more often hair-raising but generally revealing. He has visited us more often than have Jimmy Hutto, Louis Beam or any of the others, sometimes under the cover of night, sometimes in broad daylight when he would drop in for a little chat. And while he never openly admitted what he was up to, he was apparently so taken with himself that he could scarcely conceal it; we got the message through innuendo and thinly veiled threats.

We were barely into our second month of publication when Mike first came by the *Space City!* office. He told us he was a carpenter and wanted to help. But he seemed more interested in just "hanging around" and eyeing people as they worked than in performing the little tasks we set out for him.

He especially liked to hang around Judy Fitzgerald's office, where most of the business and subscription records were kept. Lowe gave Judy the creeps from the very beginning.

One day, late in July of 1969, after Mike had spent the day watching Judy work, the subscription files mysteriously disappeared. The next morning, the tires on one of the staff cars were slashed. But no one was particularly suspicious of Mike, and he just kept hanging around.

The following evening staff members Sherwood Bishop and Gavan Duffy were working downstairs in the office when there was a strange noise at the front door. Sherwood went to investigate. He found a funny-looking cylindrical package just inside the door. Fortunately, he didn't pick it up, but stepped outside to catch sight of a figure beating a hasty retreat to a car parked in front of the office. The license plates were covered with white cloth.

Then the little package exploded. Glass in the front door and in most of the downstairs windows shattered. Smoke filled the office.

Gavan called the police and summoned the rest of the staff which was meeting at a nearby home. When we arrived the place was crawling with police, who were busily probing through the debris with flashlights. Just then the phone rang. Gavan answered it and nervously conveyed the caller's message: "You're going to be dead motherfuckers if you don't quit messing around."

"I know who it was, too," Gavan whispered. "That was Mike's voice." (Lowe has a distinctive voice: deep, deep Southern accent complicated by what sounds like a speech impediment, making it difficult to understand what he's saying. He also maintains a saccharine-sweet intonation that bugs the hell out of you.)

But we didn't tell the police; we didn't want to get any possibly innocent people in trouble. (Little did we know that it would prove next to impossible to get any possibly guilty people in trouble with the Houston police.)

We should have listened to Gavan. He was a SDS member that summer and was living in an apartment with Bartee Haile and Jimmy Dale Hutto, a rather odd couple as it turns out, Hutto was also "an SDS member" that summer. That was the summer that SDS was trying to organize a work-in and Hutto was a worker at Shell and how was anyone to know that he was a Klan infiltrator? Gavan says he was suspicious of Jimmy Dale from the beginning.

Some of us stubbornly refused to jump to nefarious conclusions about Lowe until a few months later when Cam Duncan, then a member of the *Space City!* collective, met up with him at a high school rally at Jubilee Hall. Cam and Mike took a little walk into the night, during which Mike, in his own inimitable manner, made some pretty provocative statements. Cam, while a little nervous about his physical safety during the jaunt, courageously persisted in his "investigation," and returned convinced that Lowe was involved in right-wing terrorist activities.

On October 4, 1969, SDS and *Space City!* held an "anti-imperialist" rally in Hermann Park. Several carloads of anti-war GIs from Ft. Hood, travelling in caravan to Houston for the rally, were attacked and fired upon in broad daylight on the highway near Temple. (The attack was extremely nervy.) One car was seriously damaged, but no one was hurt.

Interestingly enough, the GIs' description of one of the occupants of the car resembled that of our friend Mike. The victims said this man had been hanging around the Oleo Strut GI coffeehouse near Ft. Hood, asking about the rally. (Lowe's physical description, like his voice, is rather unique: moderate height, wavy reddish-blond hair and startlingly piercing blue eyes. When he smiles, you just *know* he's not your friend.) Later, when we showed the Strut folks our photographs of Mike, they said they couldn't be absolutely positive, but they thought it was the same man. They also described the attacker's car as deep red with a black vinyl top, a vehicle that was to become all too familiar to us in the next several months.

Mike put in another appearance at the *Space City!* office November 8, 1969, at a meeting to discuss a large anti-war march and rally scheduled for the next day. There was quite a little flurry as Mike sauntered in. It was a large meeting and those of us who knew Mike went around whispering to those who had not yet had the pleasure. Lowe seemed amused. He kept asking me which one was Dennis (presumably Dennis Fitzgerald, another *Space City!* collective member). I told him coldly that I didn't know any Dennis.

The meeting broke up and we all moved outside. I overheard Lowe asking someone why the *Space City!* people were so uptight. He also told this same person that he knew the guys that shot up those GIs on the highway. It was a clear case of he knew what we were thinking, and we knew he knew, and he knew we knew he knew....

So there we were, sitting around on the front porch, exchanging abstruse but leading comments about guns and paranoia, when all of a sudden Mike stood up, bid us an abrupt farewell and split. We watched him walk down Wichita St. and turn the corner at San Jacinto. The instant he passed out of sight, Kerry Fitzgerald took off like a shot after him. But he had disappeared, seemingly into thin air. There was no chance of trailing him.

Early the next morning, a car was burned and gutted outside the front of the *Space City!* office. Lest this sound too incriminating, we still don't know who did it. But we have our suspicions.

We didn't see much of Mike until the beginning of 1970. It was Christmas vacation time and Thorne Dreyer and I were just about the only *Space City!* people in town. We were sitting around the office one afternoon when Mike came by, ostensibly to purchase some papers. He and Thorne (or "Thornton," as the Klan is wont to call him) fell into a heavy discussion.

The message was increased terrorism and the medium was snide innuendo. Mike spoke extensively of right-wing groups, particularly the Minutemen, but he never used the first person plural. It was always "them," with the "we" heavily implied. In addition to the usual right-wing analyses (like it's the Communists who are stirring up all the trouble among the blacks), Lowe submitted that the right-wing was using Houston as a sort of testing ground, to demonstrate how a city could be purged, one way or another, of leftist elements. He also told Thorne that he thought the terrorism would quickly rise to more serious levels; they're going to start killing people, he said. He painted a vivid picture of one of these "nice young girls" around *Space City!* being whisked away one night and later turning up with a slit throat.

Well, we just didn't know what to think. We felt that Mike was bluffing, but then, one couldn't be too cautious. After all, the man was clearly mad as a hatter. No telling what he might do. After that, we forsook those lonely evening walks, travelled everywhere in pairs, religiously locked doors and windows. And you can be sure that we always knew where to find a shotgun quickly.

The next time Lowe made the scene, however, we were ready for him. He appeared one afternoon in February 1970. Dennis Fitzgerald kept him occupied with idle chatter downstairs while Judy Fitzgerald contacted Cam and Sue Duncan on the phone. "Mike Lowe's here," she said. "Get over here with your camera." Cam and Sue took the long route, via the Sears parking lot where their suspicions were confirmed. There was that notorious red late model car with a black vinyl top: the license plate spelled out, most appropriately, NEVER.

Sue snapped a few pictures of the car as well as some of a couple in the car parked next to it. Sue said she had seen the people, a man and a woman, observing anti-war demonstrators at a peace march some months before. When the couple realized what was going on, they became angry and chased Cam and Sue's Volkswagon up Fannin to Wichita where the VW turned off and the other car drove on.

Cam and Sue burst into the *Space City!* office with the camera. Mike started getting a little jittery. Cam suggested that Mike let him take his picture, but Lowe didn't go for that idea at all. He dropped his papers and darted out the front door, with Cam, Dennis, Sue and the camera right behind him. The *Space City!* folks caught up with the suspect a few blocks from the office. Cam and Dennis wrestled him gently to the ground while Sue snapped his picture. They said that Lowe kept telling them that he "couldn't be our friend" after this. Was he mad! (We later traced the NEVER license plate to a Waco registration under the name of Michael Lowe and the plate on the other car to a Houston firm, the Brown Fintube company.)

Later that night, Mike and his friends drove by a few times in the never, never car. At one point, the intrepid Lowe marched up the front walk to reclaim the papers he had lost earlier. Every time the car drove by, we stuck a warning shotgun out the upstairs window. We didn't notice the Klan hanging around for several months after that. Forewarned is forearmed, and all that.

True to his word, Lowe was apparently no longer our "friend." We would only see him at large public gatherings, like anti-war rallies. The notorious red and black car was replaced by a goldish-brown car, which always seemed to be cruising around whenever bullets or arrows were fired at our office.

One of our cagey short-haired photographers did manage to snap a shot of Lowe in United Klans of America regalia posing with a right-wing minister at the Klan rally near Crosby last year. "Here, Reverend, let me take your picture with the nice young Klansman here." They both beamed (no pun intended).

At any rate, we were happy when we found that Lowe had been picked up by the police and put behind bars.

We don't have much of an analysis of this man, except that he's dangerous, disturbing and probably very sick. We never could quite figure out what drove him to play those games with us, to blow his cover almost from the first time he came around. Surely he must have known that we weren't your traditional peace love stoned freaks, that we strongly believed in armed self-defense, particularly where right-wing terrorism is concerned.

I have since learned that they call him "The Kid" in the Klan and that he is generally considered to be pretty wacko. In fact, when Klan Grand Dragon Frank Converse was interviewed recently by Pacifica radio's Gary Thiher, he said, "I hope that little sonofabitch gets what's coming to him." Converse claimed that Lowe was an upstate Klansman and had never been a member of a local Klan "unit," and that even the Klan considers him pretty crazy.

Whether that's on the level or just Converse covering his tracks, we don't know. It's kind of hard to read those folks. But we have to agree with Converse on one point: Mike Lowe certainly *is* a crazy sonofabitch!

NOTE

1. Reprinted from *Space City!* June 1, 1971.

SOLDIERS AGAINST THE WAR IN VIETNAM: THE STORY OF *ABOVEGROUND*[1]

Harry W. Haines

"Tell us about the plan to burn down barracks buildings at Fort Carson." The army intelligence officer wasn't keeping notes during the interrogation, so I figured the gray room had a microphone hidden somewhere, recording my answers. My cover was blown, and here I sat in my dress uniform, summoned to explain my role in the publication of *Aboveground*, an antiwar paper directed at soldiers stationed at Fort Carson, Colorado.

Aboveground was the brainchild of my buddies, Tom Roberts and Curt Stocker. Intelligence officers had already questioned Roberts and Stocker, and now it was my turn. A couple of my articles, written under the name "A Fort Carson GI," rested on the table. The intelligence officer sat directly across from me, and the articles were spotlighted by a single bulb that hung from the ceiling. "I need to know about the plan to set fire to the barracks," he repeated.

"I don't know anything about setting fire to barracks," I said.

"I understand how you feel about the war, but these barracks buildings are tinder boxes—do you realize that men could die?"

"I know the buildings are very unsafe, sir."

"But you won't cooperate."

"As far as I know, there is no plan to set fire to anything at Fort Carson, sir." I wondered how much he knew. A few weeks earlier, somebody actually suggested that we do just that—torch a few barracks. The suggestion came from a GI during a meeting at

Haines is a communication researcher who writes about film and television portrayals of the Vietnam War and veterans. He was drafted in 1969 and took part in the GI Resistance to the war in Vietnam. He lives in Sacramento, California.

the Home Front, the GI coffeehouse in nearby Colorado Springs. The Home Front, one of many coffeehouses operated by the United States Servicemen's Fund (USSF) and located near army posts across the country, served as a base for all kinds of antiwar activities, including the publication of *Aboveground*. We'd gather each month at the Home Front to talk about articles for the coming issue of the paper. Sometimes the meetings would develop into lengthy discussions about the war and what we should do to end it. The suggestion to torch a barracks came at one of these meetings.

The GI who proposed the idea seemed especially weird to me. No one at the coffeehouse knew him, and he didn't seem to know much about Fort Carson or Colorado Springs. More important, his suggestion was truly reckless. The Fort Carson barracks were World War Two structures, and their estimated burn time was about ten minutes, max. Burning a barracks meant more than arson. It meant murder. It meant killing GIs, guys like us. We ignored the suggestion and went on with the meeting. And here, a couple of months later, an army intelligence officer alluded to the same bad idea.

What I didn't know was this: at the precise moment I was being questioned, an anonymous clerk in Fort Carson's headquarters company was passing an envelope to Roberts and Stocker. The envelope contained the identifications of military intelligence agents who worked undercover. The guy at the meeting—the guy who tried to get us to set fire to barracks buildings—was an agent. Our little band of dissidents was so potentially threatening that military intelligence actually risked the incineration of U.S. soldiers in order to discredit us! This incident provided some insight into the nature of political power in the United States.

"Well, if you don't know anything about the plan to burn down barracks, tell me about the money. Where does *Aboveground*'s money come from?"

"You mean the money to finance the paper?" I asked.

"Yes. How much support comes from the Communists?"

My fear was turning to anger. I was just out of college. I majored in communication and I was on my way to a radio news job when the draft got me. Back in school, I decided on a career in broadcast news the day I saw the tape of Edward R. Murrow's famous "See It Now" program about the dangers of Joe McCarthy. The interrogator's question revealed the same kind of contempt that McCarthy and his supporters shared for their opponents, or so it seemed to me.

"I don't know what you mean about Communists, sir." I said.

"We know there are Communists in *Aboveground*'s organization," he said. "Why don't you help

the country by identifying them? You'd also be helping your buddies Roberts and Stocker. We don't think they know what they're getting themselves into."

I smiled at the thought of "*Aboveground*'s organization" and was tempted to say, "*What* organization?" Roberts and Stocker operated *Aboveground* on the principle of democratic participation. If you contributed to the content or distribution of the paper, you had a say about how things were done. Staff volunteers discussed and voted on the content of most of the nine issues of *Aboveground*. Although Roberts and Stocker maintained editorial leadership, they often published opinions with which they strongly disagreed, and these opinions often came from the civilian antiwar activists at the Home Front. The newspaper's volunteer staff had a core group of five or six, plus several others who came and went according to military reassignments and the transient nature of the Colorado counterculture in 1969 and 1970. To talk about "organization" was to miss altogether the amorphous nature of the "movement" and the broad spectrum of political viewpoints that swirled around *Aboveground* and became represented in its pages.

Four political factions were involved in the paper's operation, and all of them were based at the Home Front. First, there were the civil libertarians. Like me, these were dissident GIs who agreed that the Vietnam War was essentially illegal and immoral. We doubted that the war was even constitutional, and we were certain that it violated our country's values. Our experience in the army led us to distrust the military hierarchy. This political viewpoint was strongly influenced by men like Roberts and Stocker, soldiers who had already pulled tours of duty in Vietnam and who were now reassigned to stateside posts.

Ironically, the army had trained Roberts and Stocker to do journalistic work! They had both been assigned to the Tenth Psychological Operations Battalion in South Vietnam. Based on their war experience, they concluded that the corruption and brutality of the South Vietnamese government precluded victory, because the vast majority of the South Vietnamese didn't support the Saigon regime. Simply, GIs were fighting and dying for a government that wasn't worth the sacrifice of *one* American life. Roberts and Stocker—and other soldiers who had already been to 'Nam—were potentially dangerous, and the army made a mistake by reassigning them to stateside posts where they could talk about the war to recently drafted troops. Stories of corruption and atrocities spread throughout the army as the returning GIs tried to warn the rest of us about the war's realities. *Aboveground* and the other 200 or so GI underground papers helped spread the word to soldiers who were headed to Vietnam. So the civil libertarians wrote articles for the paper that stressed the history and nature of American involvement and how the war violated the Constitution and traditional American values.

The second political faction was called the "radicals," a very imprecise term that covered a variety of viewpoints and that seemed to change daily. The antiwar movement was composed of numerous political groups that sometimes cooperated and often competed for political leadership. The term "radical" was used at the Home Front to identify a wide assortment of these groups, all of which shared a generally Marxist orientation. The "radical" faction included members of the Weatherman group of Students for a Democratic Society, the Young Socialists, and the New York-based American Servicemen's Union (ASU).

The term was by no means negative. On the contrary, much of the Home Front's continuing debate focused on the meaning of "radical," and on the best "radical" strategy—including violence—to help end the war. One radical plan involved the organization of U.S. troops as the vanguard army of an armed revolution in the United States. The idea was to turn the guns around. This plan made more sense to some of the civilian volunteers than to those of us in the army. In 1969, most GIs simply wanted to be liberated from the army, not involved in armed revolution. It was also very difficult to organize GIs in an effective way. Once the military command identified a GI organizer, that person would be imprisoned, roughed-up, or reassigned to some other post. What many of us hoped for was simply an increasing unwillingness by soldiers to comply with the war effort. And gradually, that's what happened throughout the ranks.

The biggest difference between the radicals and the civil libertarians was the radicals' emphasis on what they viewed as class distinctions in the military social structure. For example, the ASU viewed the military caste system as analogous to the system of exploitation in civilian life. The officers were the bosses while the enlisted men were the workers. This particular position didn't make much sense to me, because many of the officers were themselves from lower-middle and working class families. More important, many of the officers had already turned against the war and were actually participating in the antiwar movement. Officers were potential allies in the movement to end the war. As a draftee, I was less interested in union-like organizing than I was in simply ending the war and getting out of the army.

The ASU attempted to establish a local chapter at the Home Front, but this attempt failed to generate interest among more than a few soldiers. Nevertheless, the radicals' emphasis on class analysis profoundly influenced *Aboveground*, because the analysis introduced considerations of social structure and the distribu-

tion of power. The faction compelled the rest of us to start linking the destruction of Vietnam to patterns of repression at home and in other parts of the world.

The third political faction that influenced *Aboveground* was a group of United States Servicemen's Fund (USSF) organizers who were also activists in the emerging women's liberation movement. This group, which included persons sent to Colorado Springs by the USSF to establish and operate the Home Front, began to influence the newspaper when Roberts and Stocker agreed to base *Aboveground* at the coffeehouse. These women were the first feminists I had met, although the term "feminist" was hardly in widespread use at this time. This faction attempted to link U.S. policy in Vietnam to women's oppression. They took the difficult task of attempting to educate men (young GIs) about feminist issues.

Because the editorial decision making of *Aboveground* was based upon group consensus, these three factions exercised varying degrees of influence upon the newspaper's political orientation and content. The fourth group, less well defined than the others, shared a countercultural orientation with interests in Eastern spiritualism, the development of a communal society, and the use of hallucinogens as religious sacraments. This countercultural influence was a product of the social environment existing in the mountains of Colorado and was sometimes viewed by the other factions as anarchistic and politically unproductive.

What we had at the Home Front was a microcosm of the antiwar movement. So when my interrogator asked me to identify the "Communists," I was understandably amused.

"We have at least one of everything at the Home Front, sir," I said, "so there's probably a Communist there somewhere. I think Stocker is a Republican."

"So you don't care about the possibility of Communists taking over the newspaper and using Roberts and Stocker to spread anti-American sentiment at Fort Carson?"

"It's not anti-American sentiment that's getting spread," I said. "It's antiwar sentiment. And the troops don't need Communists to tell them that the war is wrong. The troops already know that it's wrong, and very soon you—the command, that is—will have to come to grips with the fact that a lot of us know that you've already lost the war. We *know* that guys are dying for no reason, sir."

"Uh huh," he said. "If you won't identify the Communists, at least tell me where the money comes from. We know that USSF is supplying cash for the newspaper. What are the other sources?"

From August 1969 to May 1970, Roberts and Stocker produced nine issues of *Aboveground*. Most of the issues were between 4 and 8 pages, and the press runs ranged between 3,500 and 10,000 copies, distributed at Fort Carson and in Colorado Springs. The USSF support began in November 1969 (starting with issue number 4) and other sources of support included limited donations and subscriptions. Roberts and Stocker paid for the first two or three issues out of their own pockets. What made the October 1969 issue (number 3) unique was its partial funding by a Vietnam War widow who donated a portion of her husband's $10,000 military life insurance payment (GI "blood money") to the paper's operation. I decided to elaborate on this unusual, one-time source of revenue.

"War widows, sir."

"What?"

"The paper is supported by donations from war widows throughout Colorado and a few other places. Their husbands get wasted in Vietnam, and they turn over the blood money to *Aboveground*."

"You mean these women give up a portion of the money that's supposed to be used to bury their husbands?"

"They go easy on the funeral expenses and donate what's left to *Aboveground* and to the Home Front," I lied.

"That's the most disgusting thing..."

"They feel very strongly about the war."

"They're disgusting. All of you are disgusting. And you're...confused. You're confused about what the war is all about."

"What *is* the war all about, sir?"

"It's about democracy. The Vietnamese don't know the difference between communism and democracy. We're in Vietnam to help give them the opportunity to decide for themselves, without being forced. If they decide to go Communist, well, that's OK. That's up to them. We just want to give them the chance to make up their mind. We're not trying to force anything on them. That's what the other side is trying to do, to force something on them. And you people are using the insurance money of the war dead to..."

"All of the war widows tell us that their husbands would approve of it."

"How much money has been...how much has been donated in this way?"

"Thousands," I lied. My interrogator left the room for about twenty minutes, and I had the feeling I was being observed by lenses embedded in the walls. Paranoia washed over me, and I imagined electrical currents running through the bars on the window. It was total vulnerability, the kind of vulnerability that the Home Front civilians never quite understood. To be in the army was to be totally vulnerable, observable at all times. And they could do things to you that they couldn't do to regular human beings outside the Green Machine. Once you stepped forward and took the oath,

your "ass was grass" (just like the boot camp saying pointed out) and the army was "the lawnmower." The United States Constitution didn't mean much here. The interrogator returned and sat again, facing me at the small table with the light bulb hanging overhead.

"I suppose people at the Home Front have sex. I mean, who do they have sex with? Do they have sex with each other?"

"I don't know, sir. I don't have sex with Home Front people."

"Who do Roberts and Stocker have sex with? Do they have girlfriends at the Home Front?"

"They have girlfriends, of course. They date. I don't know about their sex lives. It's none of my business."

"Do they have sex with any of the war widows?"

"I have no idea."

"Do any of the GIs at the coffeehouse have sex with each other?"

"Not to my knowledge."

"How about the women's libbers? Are any of them lesbians?"

"I don't know, sir."

"I'm only asking these questions so I can help Roberts and Stocker. They're in over their heads. You can help them by cooperating. If you're their friend, you'll cooperate."

"I don't know anything about sex."

"Who uses drugs at the Home Front?"

"Nobody. There're no drugs at the Home Front."

"There are drugs all over Colorado Springs. You mean the Home Front is the one place in town where there are no drugs?"

"We police the area. The Home Front staff keeps out drug users. We know that the police could use drugs as a way of closing down the coffeehouse. The military could put the place off limits. Nobody uses drugs at the Home Front."

"Nobody?"

"The only way that drugs will get into the Home Front will be if the police plant some there, sir."

"I understand that *Aboveground* has a new printer. Who's the new printer?"

The paper's initial printer, a company in Colorado Springs, was discouraged by agents and police officers and halted production of issue five (December 1969-January 1970) following a visit by agents from the Federal Bureau of Investigation, Military Intelligence, and local Colorado Springs police officers. The company broke its agreement to print *Aboveground* as a result of the visit, and no other printer in Colorado Springs would agree to print the paper.

Roberts and Stocker eventually found a printer outside Colorado Springs who, although he favored U.S. policy in Vietnam, was willing to print *Above-*

ground at about half of the original cost. The name of this printer was kept secret. Twenty years later, Roberts and Stocker will say only that the printer was located in the Boulder, Colorado area.

Roberts believed that action was taken to suppress issue five because it contained a story potentially damaging to a former commanding general of Fort Carson. The story resulted from materials passed to Roberts and Stocker by another serviceman with access to the general's flight records. These materials indicated that the general may have violated army regulations by piloting helicopters at Fort Carson. Roberts assumed that Military Intelligence learned of the decision to print the story from undercover agents assigned to the Home Front coffeehouse.

"Not many people know who the printer is."

"You must have some idea, though."

"Well, I know that they ship the photo-ready stuff to Omaha, so maybe the printer is there," I lied. "Why do you want to know who the printer is, sir?"

"In case we have to protect him. These antiwar groups have falling-outs, you know. Which is one thing you might keep in mind. Communists will do anything to reach their goals, anything. You probably think you're doing the right thing, and I certainly respect that. But even if your heart is in the right place, I have to say that you may be hurting the interests of the United States, and you may be jeopardizing the lives of your fellow soldiers."

"I don't think so, sir."

"Maybe you'll change your mind...later."

The interrogation was over, and I returned to my unit. By anybody's estimation, I had lucked out in the army. My duty assignment was a closed-circuit radio station established during World War Two at the Fort Carson army hospital. Back in the '40s, there were few radio stations in the Colorado Springs area, so the army operated the closed-circuit station as a morale booster for patients. The station had its original control board, a beautiful mahogany and brass Stromberg-Carlson board and turntables big enough to play the huge hour-long transcriptions that used to be the mainstay of network radio drama. The station also had a great collection of 1950s Cold War propaganda dramas aimed at soldiers. One dramatic series was about life in the U.S. after a Communist coup! Commissars were fixing little league baseball games, and the party decided who married whom and when. I and the other GIs assigned to the station would sit for hours, howling with laughter at Cold War plays.

By 1969, many commercial stations were on the air, so no one—*no one*—listened to the closed-circuit station, not even the aged civilian manager who nominally ran it. Nevertheless, the army was concerned that I might pump the *wrong* propaganda into the

closed-circuits, so I was removed from the radio station and sent into army limbo. For a time, I was reassigned to the hospital admissions office where I worked as a clerk. And a few weeks after my interrogation, orders for Vietnam came down.

The conflict between Roberts and Stocker and the so-called "radical" faction at the Home Front eventually split *Aboveground*'s volunteer staff. Roberts and Stocker decided to move the paper out of the coffee-house, and the final issue (number nine) was published in May 1970. By that time, I was in Vietnam, assigned to a medical unit at Cam Ranh Bay. Stocker told me that, from his point of view, the "radicals" alienated many GIs who might have gotten involved in the movement, which, by that time, was called the GI Resistance. The feminists increasingly challenged young enlisted men unaware of the political basis of feminism and unconvinced of its relationship to their own situation in the army. And there was a serious ideological split among those who argued in favor of armed revolution and those (including Roberts and Stocker) who saw no indication that soldiers would take part in a widespread armed insurrection. Roberts said, "Some of the Home Front people couldn't understand why GIs wouldn't turn the guns around, because they were never in the army themselves. We knew what was going down in Vietnam, and we didn't wish the same hell on the United States. We just wanted to end the war, get out of the army, and get on with our lives."

Despite the factional split, *Aboveground*'s short-lived operation (August 1969 to May 1970) was successful. Like the other 200+ antiwar papers published by service personnel throughout the United States and overseas, *Aboveground* signaled a willingness of soldiers to take responsibility for the ill-conceived and disastrous policy that brought so much misery to the people of Vietnam and the United States. At the Home Front, and at the other GI coffeehouses sponsored by the USSF, coalitions developed between civilian and military groups, and strategies were developed to stop the war. The coffeehouses and the GI undergrounds introduced many of us to the methods of political organizing that sustained us through the mean-spirited years of the Reagan-Bush regime.

The GI underground papers, along with acts of civil disobedience committed by individual soldiers, encouraged other service personnel to act in varying degrees against the war effort until military discipline was severely eroded. Simply, the generals and politicians could no longer depend upon the troops to carry out orders, the real significance of Nixon's euphemistic "Vietnamization" plan.

Ironically, the brass viewed this process as a deterioration of morale, when actually our morale was increasingly strengthened by what we read in the papers. The GI papers were the tip of an iceberg that went very deep into the structure of the American soldier's experience of the Vietnam War. Antiwar soldiers had allies throughout the ranks and among the officer corps, but these allies had to be quiet and anonymous, something that our civilian comrades could not fully appreciate.

Our power was in our anonymity and in our willingness to act when specific opportunities developed. Acts of sabotage and fragging have received attention in the histories of the war, but the written record has necessarily avoided the more difficult subject of a generalized noncompliance among the troops to follow orders, a more challenging topic to pin down because its significance is not readily quantifiable.

Additionally, many antiwar soldiers remain, twenty years later, quiet about their activities. Like people in any organizational structure, antiwar GIs learned how to stand-in-place, as it were—to give the minimal effort to the war, except when the effort was a matter of life or death for a fellow soldier. In this way, the Green Machine slowly ground down. The papers fed the process. Papers like *Aboveground* contributed to this generalized noncompliance by letting antiwar GIs know that they were not alone, that there were many of us throughout the ranks, and that we were not crazy or un-American. The papers gave us a sense of solidarity and purpose, a way to focus the anger and profound sadness we shared as victims of the same policy that turned much of Vietnam into moonscape.

To my knowledge, only one group fully conceptualized the role of the GI underground papers in this particular way, a result of their early incorporation of Vietnam veterans into their operation. The group was based in Berkeley, California, and published *The Ally* from 1968 to 1974 (perhaps the longest run of any of the GI papers). *The Ally* was distributed among GIs throughout Vietnam. The group's initial objective was to encourage widespread desertion. To this end, they published addresses throughout the world where deserters might be expected to find help. As the group expanded its membership to include Vietnam veterans, they gradually understood that no widespread desertion would occur, so they redefined their role as one of competing with another information source—the military—for the mind of the individual soldier.

The Ally was probably unique among the GI papers in that it consciously focused on the soldier's position in a war that questioned traditional American values. *The Ally* gave legitimacy to the antiwar soldier's sense of ideological contradiction and isolation. *The Ally*'s editor, Clark Smith, explained to me that staff members gradually discovered that the paper represented a kind of comfort to some readers who "received *The Ally* as a kind of blessing...which made them feel better about themselves and about where they were." By attempting to undermine military morale, Smith said, the staff came to feel they were inadvertently helping some soldiers cope with the peculiar emotional stress of the war's ideological crisis. After shifting away from the desertion objective, the paper focused on ways that GIs could legally slow-up the war effort from within the military. By late 1969, *The Ally*'s circulation varied between twenty and twenty-five thousand copies a month, most of them distributed in Vietnam. The distribution method itself fed the soldiers' growing sense of power.

Initially, *The Ally* staff planned to ship portable printing presses to dissident soldiers in Vietnam so they could publish their own antiwar papers in the war zone! The staff soon figured out that this plan was not workable because conditions in Vietnam precluded underground printing operations among the troops. (Roberts and Stocker, who met in Vietnam, considered the publication of antiwar material in the combat zone but concluded the operation would be too difficult.) Combat troops, because of their fairly constant movement, would not have time to use the presses, and troops in the rear areas were subject to observation by commanders and South Vietnamese police. In addition, for troops in the rear, the operation of a printing press would be a one-way ticket to the war zone. *The Ally* staff soon shifted to a method of clandestine distribution, which challenged the ability of commanders to control their men.

At first, building *The Ally*'s Vietnam circulation was a slow and difficult task, because the staff had to depend upon making contact with potential readers and distributors through the newspaper itself. Subscription coupons were published in each issue. By returning a coupon, an individual subscriber decided for himself whether or not he would receive the paper through the mail. Subscribers were, of course, subject to harassment if their commanders found copies in their possession, despite army regulations that allegedly protected GIs from such abuses. By checking the appropriate box on the subscription coupon, a reader could also indicate his willingness to distribute *The Ally* to other servicemen. Bundles containing up to one hundred copies of *The Ally* would then be mailed each month to these distributors. The bundles were disguised as care packages from home. Gradually, a distribution system developed among troops in Vietnam, and the paper encouraged soldiers to pass along individual copies to other readers. Dated subscription coupons indicated that some copies of *The Ally* were still being circulated hand to hand as much as six months after publication.

The covert distribution was an important part of the newspaper's function as a political tool. Attempts by military commanders to limit the distribution of *The Ally* and other GI papers resulted in conflict, tension, and the gradual erosion of military morale and authority. Attempts by commanders to seize copies of *The Ally* added to dissatisfaction among the paper's readership and aroused curiosity about the paper's contents.

Clandestine distribution also afforded GIs the chance to fight the system of which they were an unwilling part. The contents of the paper sometimes prompted discussion between dissident lower ranking soldiers and their potentially sympathetic commanding officers. The distribution method "was a form of counter-harassment," Smith told me. "In a sense, *The Ally* was an organizational weapon."

Distribution of *Aboveground* probably functioned in a similar way. Volunteers, acting in violation of military regulations, distributed copies throughout Fort Carson. Roberts and Stocker handed out copies to motorists entering and leaving the main gate of the post. They could usually distribute the paper for about twenty minutes, before military police would arrive and pack them off for interrogation sessions. The reaction of the military, of course, would spark interest in the paper by the straight media concerned about First Amendment protection. In turn, this interest gave the paper a higher profile even among soldiers who had never read a copy. Mere distribution of antiwar papers challenged the military's authority and helped strengthen the morale and solidarity of antiwar GIs.

And it was very satisfying to tweek the brass! As Stocker said, "I didn't start having fun in the army until we began publishing *Aboveground*. I came back from Vietnam with the intention of declaring myself a conscientious objector, so I could get the chance to tell people about what was actually happening to the Vietnamese. Roberts convinced me that it would be more effective to put out a paper, to spread the word among troops who hadn't gone to Vietnam yet....and to fuck with the commanders' minds a bit." On one occasion, Roberts folded copies of *Aboveground* into paper airplanes and sailed them over the stockade fence to inmates.

Twenty years later, I look back on my brief experience as an antiwar GI, and I recognize how lucky I was to get caught up in the effort to publish and distribute *Aboveground*. Despite current attempts by craven politicians, revisionist intellectuals, and mindless media operatives to reposition the Vietnam veteran as a World War Two hero, those of us who worked in the GI Resistance know that many GIs risked everything they had to limit our country's ability to wage war in Vietnam. Our experience is largely hidden, a secret part of the war's history that embarrasses and threatens the regime that rules America today. We now face the challenge of using what we learned in those years to help guarantee that state power is used legally, morally, and with a sense of compassion.

NOTE

1. A complete collection of *Aboveground* is deposited with the William Joiner Center for the Study of War & Social Consequences at the University of Massachusetts Harbor Campus, Boston.

APPENDIX: THE GI RESISTANCE: MILITARY UNDERGROUNDS DURING THE VIETNAM WAR

by Harry W. Haines

The following list identifies 227 GI underground, antiwar newspapers aimed at members of the U.S. armed forces during the Vietnam War. The list is divided into two groups: (A) 212 newspapers with distribution limited to specific military posts, bases, or ships; and (B) 15 newspapers with national or international distribution, including U.S. military units in South Vietnam. The list is a compilation of GI undergrounds identified by James R. Hayes in his 1975 doctoral dissertation, *The War within a War: Dissent in the Military with an Emphasis on Vietnam* (Department of Sociology, University of Connecticut) and in my master's thesis, *The GI Underground Press: Two Case Studies of Alternative Military Newspapers* (Department of Communication, University of Utah).

Additionally, several newspapers and their organizational affiliations were identified in two government documents: the *Annual Report for the Year 1972* of the House Internal Security Committee and *Organized Subversion in the U.S. Armed Forces* (25 September 1975), based on hearings conducted by the Senate Subcommittee to Investigate the Administration of the Internal Security Act and Other Internal Security Laws.

These newspapers were ephemeral publications. Only a few of them maintained continuity over extended periods of time. The normal turnover in military personnel and the systematic re-assignment of malcontents by commanders made it difficult to sustain the papers. Some papers were published anonymously with only the name of a disbanded activist coalition and an expired post office box as clues to the mystery of their origin. The political and organizational complexities of the antiwar movement also made it difficult to identify the papers' affiliations.

Hayes' sources included the Chicago Area Military Project, volumes one, two, and three of the U.S. House Committee on Internal Security reports (1972), and the archives of the Wisconsin State Historical Society at Madison.

My work relied heavily on Clark Smith's private collection at Berkeley and the Contemporary Issues Collection (organized by Russell G. Benedict) at the University of Nevada Library at Reno. In most cases, information included in the list was gathered by Hayes or myself directly from copies of the newspapers. The list identifies each paper's place of publication and distribution and, in the case of locally distributed papers, service branch and organizational and coffee-house affiliations.

During the Vietnam War, several antiwar organizations used off-post coffeehouses as centers of operation. Most sources agree that the first GI coffeehouse was founded in January 1968 by United States Servicemen's Fund (USSF) activist Fred Gardner. Called the UFO, it was located in Columbia, South Carolina, and was operated by a coalition of dissident GIs from nearby Fort Jackson, USSF organizers, and University of South Carolina students. Gardner later moved on to help establish USSF-sponsored coffeehouses in other towns near military installations. GI newspapers sometimes evolved out of the organizations responsible for operating the local coffeehouses.

The newspapers were seen as part of the educational or propaganda function of the coffeehouses. Often, the newspaper was the prime factor around which several organizational functions rallied for a time. The role of the coffeehouse is described in the literature of the Nonprofit Service Corporation (NPSC), an incorporated arm of GIs United, a group that operated both Quaker House and Haymarket Square in Fayetteville, near Fort Bragg, North Carolina. The NPSC saw the coffeehouse as "an educational center where GIs and students can rap about common problems" and as "an alternative to downtown Fayetteville and Fort Bragg which exploit the isolation and depression of GIs."

The NPSC also purported to create in their coffeehouse "an atmosphere in which we can all begin to understand what this country is all about, and out of which a sense of solidarity, struggle and understanding will develop." Weekend rock concerts were provided, along with "cheap thrills, relevant entertainment, and raps about the problems we face in society, and how we together can deal with those problems: the war, the army, racism, sexism."

Like most other GI coffeehouses, the Quaker House and Haymarket Square provided reading material including *Bragg Briefs*, the underground paper produced by the local members of GIs United. The "FTA Show," a celebrated variety program critical of the Vietnam War and starring Jane Fonda and Donald Sutherland, was first performed at the Haymarket Square on March 14, 1971.

The emergence of coffeehouses near military posts and bases was a significant development in the history of the general antiwar movement. Until the USSF began channeling funds to sponsor coffeehouses and thus provide a nationwide base for organizing antiwar soldiers, members of the armed services were essentially ignored or denounced by many campus-based antiwar organizations. Fred Gardner, a former army draftee, played a major role in the antiwar movement by recognizing and tapping potential dissent within the younger enlisted ranks of the military itself. As centers of dissident political activity and strong objection to the Vietnam War, the GI coffeehouses were likely places for underground papers to flourish.

The titles listed here require an explanatory note. The GI press embodied an imaginative use of ambiguity in its selection of titles, whose meanings may be quite obscure to readers unfamiliar with military life during the Vietnam War. Reflecting the radical political consciousness of the 1960s, these titles often combined contemporary hip slang with military jargon in the creation of hybrids unique to the American military experience of Vietnam.

GI papers were often named by placing in a new context slang phrases and military jargon familiar to the intended readership: younger, lower ranking enlisted personnel. For example, military commands such as "about face," "as you were," "eyes left," "left face," "open ranks," "open sights," "head-on," "forward," and "all hands abandon ship" were used as underground titles. The use of these typical military commands as titles of anti-military newspapers was an element of irony and ambiguity in the GI press, identifying the general nature of the papers to prospective readers and capitalizing upon possible anti-military dissidence already experienced by alienated or otherwise dissatisfied members of the armed services.

Hence, new connotations were given to military jargon. In the process, the phrase "about face" refers both to the command shouted at basic trainees as well as to a change in direction of United States policy in Southeast Asia, an "about face" promoted by most GI undergrounds. "As you were," a command given to lower ranking military personnel to resume activity following their coming to attention at the arrival in their work area of a high ranking officer, became a reference to the reader's prior status as a civilian. "Eyes left" and "left face," when used as underground titles, referred to the generally leftist political orientation of the papers.

All Ready on the Left, the title of a GI paper produced by Marine corpsmen at Camp Pendleton, took its name from an important response in a structured series of commands and responses shouted during weapons practice on a rifle range. The response denotes the readiness of soldiers located to the left of the range's commanding officer in anticipation of firing at targets.

"Your military left," a phrase used as the title of a paper published at Fort Sam Houston, Texas, originated from military slang that recognizes qualitative differences between civilian and military society. In its original context, the phrase is used to elicit a desired behavior: physical movement to the left by a basic trainee who has difficulty identifying left from right. Used by a drill sergeant, the phrase denotes desired movement in a particular direction and connotes a difference in reality between military and civilian life, as if one's *military* left or right were somehow different from one's *civilian* left or right. It is not a question of one's political orientation but, rather, an acute observation of the military social milieu. Although the connotation may at first seem obscure to a reader inexperienced with the peculiar social context in which it operates, the slang phrase captures perceptively qualitative differences between military and civilian life and communicates that understanding among the troops, for whom it is essential information. Used as the title of the Fort Sam Houston underground paper, the phrase became more ambiguous. In one sense, it suggested that the paper represented a leftist political sentiment within the military. In another sense, it suggested the prospect of desertion, as if the word "left" were a verb rather than a noun.

Similar word-plays existed throughout the GI underground phenomenon. Camp Pendleton's *Attitude Check* got its title from a military slang phrase meaning to examine one's current state of mind regarding motivation and acceptable behavior within the service. A recalcitrant soldier, or one who exhibits an "attitude problem," might be encouraged to undergo such an "attitude check" or self-examination. *Gigline*, published at Fort Bliss, Texas, borrowed its name from the military term identifying the line extending down the front of a soldier's uniform. This line, formed by the edge of the uniform's belt buckle, and the uniform's fly is required to be kept straight under threat of "gigs" or demerits. As an underground title, the term "gig" suggested the more hip interpretation of an event or happening, while "line" referred to the communication function.

Shakedown, the title of an underground paper published at Fort Dix, New Jersey, was a reference to the "shakedown inspection" of enlisted men's personal belongings. "Shakedowns" are often performed without notice by commanders in search of contraband. The title suggested the possibility that the paper would reverse the process: that is, it would investigate the military command or, at least, give it a difficult time. *The Ultimate Weapon*, another Fort Dix paper, took its name from a large road sign located at the main entrance to the basic training facility. Bearing the same words, the sign also shows an infantryman in combat gear, complete with extended bayonet and threatening snarl. Adopted as the title of one of the most vehemently antiwar underground papers of the late 1960s, the epithet, while suggesting the pen is mightier than the sword, openly ridiculed an image of the American infantryman promoted virtually everywhere at Fort Dix, from road sign to post-exchange stationery. The title functioned to subvert or co-opt a symbol of military authority and esprit. The combat experience of some GI underground publishers was suggested in such titles as *Strategic Hamlet* and *The Last Incursion*, co-optations of official euphemisms.

The titles of *The Ally* and *The Bond*, two internationally distributed papers that eventually came to disagree on tactical and political matters, originated from the consensus of the Vietnam Day Committee of Berkeley, California. In 1967, this committee made the important decision to attempt the direction of antiwar propaganda at military personnel. Both titles reflect the interest of dissident civilians to build a cooperative antiwar effort between themselves and dissident service personnel, according to Clark Smith, *The Ally*'s publisher. *Aboveground* was named by publishers who hoped to communicate a sense of honesty and reliability. "We had nothing to hide," co-publisher Curtis Stocker said.

Fort Jackson's *Short Times* combined a traditional newspaper title with the term "short timer," meaning a member of the military who is about to be discharged from active duty and returned to civilian life. The title *Right On Post*, used by a California-based underground paper, performed a similar function by combining a traditional newspaper title with the slang phrase "right on," meaning "correct." The title is made more ambiguous by its reference to "post" as a military installation.

Plain Rapper, the name of a military paper published at Palo Alto, California, was a reference to the necessity of receiving in the mail underground subscriptions in plain unmarked envelopes to avoid overt or covert retaliation from military authorities. In another sense, the title connoted reliability and ease of understanding, with the term "rapper" meaning "speaker" or "communicator."

Originally a reference to the part of a ship above waterline, the term "broadside" was used as the title of an antiwar paper published at Los Angeles and distributed among navy personnel in the southern California area. Since the term can also be used to describe a denunciation, it was a likely choice for use as an underground title.

As was *Aerospaced*, the name of a paper published at Grissom Air Force Base. Without the "d," aerospace is a useful word describing both the earth's atmosphere and the space beyond. With the addition of the "d," the term "aerospaced" described the state of mind represented in the paper. Those responsible for the paper suggest in the title that they are not simply "spaced," or somewhat out of touch with conventional reality; they are specifically *aero*spaced, or somewhat traumatized by their experience in the military social environment. Thus, the title (a hybrid of military-scientific terminology and hip slang) described a particular state of mind experienced by those who published the paper and perhaps shared by readers.

Sacstrated, another Air Force underground, combined the acronym of the Strategic Air Command (SAC) with the word "castrated," the resulting title referring to the proposed effect of the paper upon the military or to the metaphorical condition of intended readers as perceived by the paper's publishers. *The Fort Polk Puke*, while not at all ambiguous, is similarly evocative.

We Got the brASS, published by dissident GIs stationed in West Germany, derived its title from "we got the ass," a somewhat esoteric military phrase meaning "we are very angry." The original phrase, of which "we got the ass" is but a variant, would be "we got a *case* of the ass," an angry or dissatisfied condition. Used as the title of a GI underground, the phrase immediately communicated the paper's orientation and added yet another twist with the placement of the lower-case letters "br" in front of the upper-case "ASS." The term "brASS," of course, referred to commissioned officers.

Slang was also incorporated into the title of an underground paper published at Chanute Air Force Base. The title, *A Four-Year Bummer*, suggested that the four-year period of active duty service in the military was similar to a bad drug-related or other unpleasant experience. *Green Machine*, a slang phrase describing the army and its predominant hue, and *Marine Blues*, a reference to both the dress uniform of Marine corpsmen as well as their possible state of mind, were used as GI underground titles.

FTA, published at Fort Knox and possibly the first GI underground produced by active duty army person-nel, made use of the military slogan, "F-T-A." This series of letters, when spoken by an army draftee in the late 1960s, meant something quite different than the paper's subtitle, *Fun, Travel, and Adventure* (derived from an army enlistment poster), might indicate. Although the publisher of *FTA* wisely chose his subtitle to avoid a possible charge of obscenity from a responsible military commander, the letters "FTA" on the masthead communicated the more common meaning among the troops: "Fuck the army."

Papers with Local Distribution

These antiwar papers, listed alphabetically, were produced and distributed by armed service personnel (often in cooperation with civilian dissidents) at military installations throughout the United States and abroad during the Vietnam War. A few were produced and distributed aboard United States war ships, including the U.S.S. Enterprise and the U.S.S. Forrestal. At least one paper, *OM*, was distributed at the Pentagon.

Many of the papers were produced by local groups affiliated with national organizations such as Movement for a Democratic Military, Pacific Counseling Service, and Vietnam Veterans Against the War. Where known, these organizational affiliations are specified in the list, along with known GI coffeehouse affiliations. Many of the papers may have had organizational and coffeehouse affiliations that remain unknown and go unlisted here.

Some listings identify both a military installation and a nearby city as a paper's base of production and distribution (as, for example, the listings for *Above-ground* and *All Ready on the Left*). Dissident GIs often found it necessary to conceal their publishing operations from military commanders and intelligence agents who attempted to suppress publication and distribution in accordance with Department of the Army memoranda and Department of Defense Directives 1325.6 (issued on September 12, 1969) and 1344.10 (issued on September 23, 1969). As a result, many of the papers developed an off-post/off-base operation in a nearby city. These off-post/off-base operations may have included affiliations with coffeehouses that, in some cases, remain unidentified here.

Because these papers were ephemeral publications, both Hayes (1975) and Haines (1976) had difficulty discovering dates of publication. The military's transient nature, as well as many successful attempts by commanders to suppress publication and distribution, often limited the papers to brief or sporadic operation. The absence of a full chronology is a weakness of the listing, and *Aboveground*'s nine-issue run (from August 1969 to May 1970) may not be typical of the GI undergrounds.

Each paper's service branch is listed according to these designations: Army (USA), Navy (USN), Air Force (USAF) and Marine Corps (USMC). Of the 212 papers listed here, 86 were produced by Army personnel, 38 by Air Force personnel, 43 by Navy personnel, and 15 by Marine Corpsmen. Coalitions of Army and Air Force personnel produced 6 papers, and coalitions of Army and Navy personnel produced 2 of them. Coalitions of Army Reservists and National Guard members produced 2 papers. A total of 20 papers are listed as "service branch unknown." A few of the listings include explanatory notes.

1. *Abandon Ship* (USN)
    Boston, Massachusetts

2. *The Abolitionist* (USN)
    Okinawa
    Pacific Counseling Service

3. *About Face* (USAF)
    Bergstrom Air Force Base

4. *About Face: The EM News* (USMC)
    Camp Pendleton and Los Angeles, California
    ("EM": enlisted men)

5. *Aboveground* (USA)
    Fort Carson
    "Home Front" Coffeehouse, Colorado Springs, Colorado

6. *ACT* (USA)
    Resisters Inside the Army
    Paris, France

7. *Aerospaced* (USAF)
    Grissom Air Force Base and Kokomo, Indiana

8. *Air Fowl* (USAF)
    Vandenberg Air Force Base

9. *All Hands Abandon Ship* (USN)
    Newport Naval Base

10. *All Ready on the Left* (USMC)
    Camp Pendleton and Oceanside-Vista, California

11. *Always Alert* (USA)
    Fort Lewis and Tacoma, Washington

12. *Anchorage Troop* (USA-USAF)
    Fort Richardson, Elmendorf Air Force Base, and Anchorage, Alaska

13. *Anti-Brass* (USA)
    Los Angeles, California

14. *Arctic Arsenal* (USA)
    Fort Greely and Delta, Alaska
    Socialist Workers and GIs United at Fort Greely

15. *As You Were* (USA)
    Fort Ord and Monterey, California

16. *Attitude Check* (USMC)
    Camp Pendleton and Oceanside-Vista, California
    Movement for a Democratic Military
    "The Green Machine" Coffeehouse, Vista, California

17. *AWOL Press* (USA)
    Fort Riley and Manhattan, Kansas

18. *Bacon* (USAF)
    March Air Force Base and Edgemont, California

19. *Barrage* (USA)
    Fort Sill and Lawton, Oklahoma

20. *Baumholder Gig Sheet* (USA)
    Paris, France

21. *Bayonet* (USA)
    The Presidio and San Francisco, California

22. *BCT Newsletter* (USA)
    Fort Ord
    ("BCT": basic combat training)

23. *Bergstrom Bennies* (USA)
    Bergstrom Air Force Base
    ("Bennies": benefits)

24. *Black Unity* (USMC)
    Camp Pendleton

25. *Black Voice* (USA)
    Fort McClellan and Anniston, Alabama

26. *Blue Screw* (USAF)
    Aurora, Colorado

27. *Bolling Other* (USAF)
    Bolling Air Force Base and Washington, DC

28. *Bragg Briefs* (USA)
    Fort Bragg, Fayetteville and Spring Lake, North Carolina
    GIs United to End the War in Indochina
    "Quaker House," "Haymarket Square," and "Mbari Cultural Center" Coffeehouses, Fayetteville, North Carolina

29. *Brass Needle* (USA)
    Fort Lee and Petersberg, Virginia

30. *Broadside* (USN)
    Los Angeles, California

31. *Broken Arrow* (USAF)
    Selfridge Air Force Base and Mount Clemens, Michigan

32. *By the Left Flank* (USMC)
Okinawa
Pacific Counseling Service

33. *The Chessman* (USMC)
Fort Beufort and Frogmore, South Carolina

34. *Chessman II* (USMC)
Paris Island Marine Base

35. *Coalition* (USAF)
Mather Air Force Base and Sacramento, California

36. *Co-Ambulation* (USAF)
Fairchild Air Force Base

37. *Come-Unity Press* (USAF)
Yokota Air Force Base, Japan
Pacific Counseling Service

38. *Common Sense* (service branch unknown)
Washington, DC

39. *Counter Attack* (USA)
Fort Carson and Colorado Springs, Colorado

40. *Counter-Military* (USMC)
Iwakuni, Japan
Pacific Counseling Service and Beheiren

41. *Counterpoint* (USA-USAF)
Fort Lewis, McChord Air Force Base, and
Seattle, Washington

42. *Cry Out* (USAF)
Clark Air Force Base and Angeles City,
Philippines
Pacific Counseling Service and National Lawyers
Guild

43. *Custer's Last Stand* (USA)
Fort Riley and Manhattan, Kansas

44. *Dare to Struggle* (USN)
San Diego, California

45. *Demand for Freedom* (USN)
Okinawa
Pacific Counseling Service and Beheiren

46. *The Destroyer* (USN)
Philadelphia Naval Yard
"Liberty Hall" Coffeehouse, Philadelphia,
Pennsylvania

47. *Different Drummer* (USA)
Fort Polk

48. *Do It Loud* (USA)
Fort Bragg and Spring Lake, North Carolina

49. *Drum* (USA)
Fort Hamilton

50. *Duck Power* (USN)
San Diego Naval Training Center and San Diego,
California

51. *Dull Brass* (USA)
Fort Sheridan and Chicago, Illinois

52. *EM-16* (USA)
Fort Knox, Fort Campbell, and Radcliffe,
Kentucky
("EM": enlisted men)

53. *Eyes Left* (USAF)
Travis Air Force Base and San Francisco,
California

54. *Fall In At Ease* (USN)
Iwakuni and Tokyo, Japan
"Hobbit" Coffeehouse

55. *Fat Albert's Death Ship Times* (USN)
Charleston Naval Base and Charleston, South
Carolina

56. *Fatigue Press* (USA)
Fort Hood
"Oleo Strut" Coffeehouse, Killeen, Texas

57. *Fed Up* (USA)
Fort Lewis
"Shelter Half" Coffeehouse, Tacoma, Washington

58. *FID* (USN)
Kodiak Island Naval Base and Kodiak, Alaska

59. *Fight Back* (USA)
Heidelberg, Germany

60. *Final Flight* (USAF)
Hamilton Air Force Base and San Francisco,
California

61. *1st Amendment* (USAF)
Yokota Air Force Base and Fussa, Japan

62. *First Casualty* (USA)
Fort Benning and Columbus, Georgia

63. *Flag-In Action* (USA)
Fort Campbell

64. *Fort Polk Puke* (USA)
Fort Polk

65. *The Forum* (USA)
Fort Sill and Lawton, Oklahoma

66. *Forward* (USA)
West Berlin, Germany

67. *Forward March* (USN)
Annapolis, Maryland

68. *A Four-Year Bummer* (USAF)
Chanute Air Force Base and Champaign, Illinois

69. *Fragging Action* (USA-USAF)
Fort Dix and McGuire Air Force Base

70. *Free Fire Zone* (USAF)
Hanscom Air Force Base

71. *Free Press* (USA-USAF)
Fort Lewis, McChord Air Force Base, and Seattle,
Washington

72. *Freedom of the Press* (USN)
Yokosuka, Japan
Pacific Counseling Service, National Lawyers
Guild
Vietnam Veterans Against the War/Winter Soldier
Organization

73. *Freedom Rings* (service branch unknown)
Tokyo, Japan
Pacific Counseling Service
Ozumi Citizens Council

74. *FTA: Fun, Travel, and Adventure* (USA)
Fort Knox and Louisville, Kentucky
"Fort Knox" Coffeehouse, Muldraugh, Kentucky

75. *FTA With Pride* (USA)
Germany

76. *GAF* (USAF)
Barksdale Air Force Base and Shreveport,
Louisiana

77. *Getting Late* (USN)
Okinawa
Pacific Counseling Service

78. *Getting Together* (USAF)
Lowry Air Force Base

79. *GI Movement in Yokosuka (GIMY)* (USN)
Yokosuka, Japan
Pacific Counseling Service
"Yokosuka David" Coffeehouse

80. *GI Organizer* (USA)
Fort Hood, Killeen and Austin, Texas

81. *GI Voice* (USA)
Fort Lewis and Tacoma, Washington

82. *Gig Line* (USA)
Fort Bliss
GIs for Peace
"GIs for Peace House," El Paso, Texas

83. *Good Times* (service branch unknown)
San Francisco, California

84. *Graffiti* (service branch unknown)
Heidelberg, Germany

85. *Grapes of Wrath* (USN)
Norfolk, Virginia

86. *The Great Lakes Torpedo* (USN)
Great Lakes Naval Training Station
Movement for a Democratic Military
"People's Place" Coffeehouse, Chicago, Illinois

87. *Green Machine* (USA)
Fort Greely and Fairbanks, Alaska

88. *Hair* (service branch unknown)
"Owl" Coffeehouse, Misawa, Japan
Pacific Counseling Service, National Lawyers
Guild, and American Servicemen's Union Beheiren

89. *Hansen Free Press* (USN)
Camp Hansen and Camp Schwab
"People's House" and "United Front"
Coffeehouses, Kin-Son, Okinawa

90. *Harass the Brass: The Airman's Voice* (USAF)
Chanute Air Force Base and Champaign, Illinois

91. *Head-On* (USMC)
Camp Lejeune and Jacksonville, North
Carolina

92. *Helping Hand* (USAF)
Mountain Home Air Force Base
"Covered Wagon" Coffeehouse, Mountain Home,
Idaho

93. *Heresy II* (USA)
Fort Leonard Wood

94. *Highway 13* (USA)
Fort Meade Military Law Project
Baltimore, Maryland, and Washington, DC

95. *HOA Binh* (service branch unknown)
Denver, Colorado

96. *Huachuca Hard Times* (USA)
Fort Huachuca and Sierra Vista, Arizona

97. *Hunley Hemorrhoid* (USN)
USS Hunley

98. *In Formation* (USA)
Fort Knox and Louisville, Kentucky

99. *In the Belly of the Monster* (service branch unknown)
Iwakuni, Japan
Pacific Counseling Service, International Counter-Military Collective and Beheiren

100. *The Intermountain Observer* (USA)
Boise, Idaho

101. *Kill for Peace* (service branch unknown)
Tokyo, Japan
Pacific Counseling Service

102. *Kitty Litter* (USN)
USS Kitty Hawk

103. *Knot* (USAF)
Minot Air Force Base and Minot, North Dakota

104. *Lackland Tailfeather* (USAF)
Lackland Air Force Base and San Antonio, Texas

105. *Last Harass* (USA)
Fort Gordon
"Home in the South" Coffeehouse, Augusta, Georgia

106. *The Last Incursion* (USA)
Fort Bragg and Fayetteville, North Carolina

107. *Left Face* (service branch unknown)
Washington, DC

108. *Left Face* (USA)
Fort McClellan
GIs United Against the War in Indochina
"GIs and WACs United" Coffeehouse, Anniston, Alabama

109. *Lewis-McChord Free Press* (USA-USAF)
Fort Lewis and McChord Air Force Base
"Shelter Half" Coffeehouse, Tacoma, Washington

110. *Liberated Barracks* (USMC)
Kailua, Hawaii

111. *Liberated Castle* (USA)
Fort Belvoir and Washington, DC

112. *Liberty Call* (USN)
San Diego, California
San Diego Concerned Officer Movement

113. *Logistic* (USA)
Fort Sheridan and Chicago, Illinois

114. *Looper* (service branch unknown)
San Francisco, California

115. *Marine Blues* (USMC)
Treasure Island Naval Station and San Francisco, California

116. *MacDill Free Press* (USAF)
MacDill Air Force Base and Tampa, Florida

117. *The Militant* (USA)
Fort Greely

118. *Military Intelligence* (USA)
Santa Monica and Venice, California

119. *Morning Report* (USA-USN)
Fort Devens and Groton, Massachusetts
"Common Sense" Bookstore, Ayer, Massachusetts

120. *Napalm* (USA)
Fort Campbell
"People's House" Coffeehouse, Clarksville, Tennessee

121. *Navy Times Are Changin'* (USN)
Great Lakes Naval Training Station
Movement for a Democratic Military
"People's House" Coffeehouse, Chicago, Illinois

122. *New England Military News* (service branch unknown)
Boston, Massachusetts

123. *New GI* (USA)
Fort Hood and Killeen, Texas

124. *New Salute* (service branch unknown)
Baltimore, Maryland

125. *The Next Step* (USA)
Heidelberg, Germany

126. *99th Bummer* (USAF)
Westover Air Force Base
"Off the Runway" Coffeehouse, Holyoke, Massachusetts

127. *Oak* (USN)
Oakland Naval Hospital and San Francisco, California

128. *Obligore* (USMC)
New York City

129. *The O.D.* (USA)
Honolulu, Hawaii

130. *Off the Brass* (USAF)
Pease Air Force Base and Portsmouth, New Hampshire

131. *Off the Bridge* (USN)
"New People's Center" Coffeehouse, Yokosuka, Japan
Pacific Counseling Service, National Lawyers Guild

132. *Offul Times* (USAF)
Offutt Air Force Base and Omaha, Nebraska

133. *Okinawa Ampo* (service branch unknown)
Tokyo, Japan
Pacific Counseling Service
Ampo Collective

134. *Okinawa Strikes* (service branch unknown)
"Freedom Family" Coffeehouse, Koza, Okinawa
Pacific Counseling Service, National Lawyers
Guild

135. *Olive Branch* (USAF)
MacDill Air Force Base and Jacksonville, Florida

136. *OM* (USN)
The Pentagon and Washington, DC

137. *Omega Press* (USN)
"Omega House" and "People's House," Koza,
Okinawa
Pacific Counseling Service, National Lawyers
Guild

138. *On the Beach* (USN)
Norfolk, Virginia

139. *Open Ranks* (USA-USN)
Fort Holabird, Bainbridge Naval Training Center,
and Baltimore, Maryland
"The DMZ" Coffeehouse, Washington, DC

140. *Open Sights* (USA)
Fort Belvoir and Washington, DC

141. *Other Half* (USN)
Glenview Naval Air Station and Glenview, Illinois

142. *Other Voice* (USAF)
Richards-Gebaur Air Force Base and Kansas City,
Missouri

143. *Our Thing* (USA)
Huntsville, Alabama

144. *Out Now!* (USA)
Long Beach, California
Movement for a Democratic Military

145. *Paper* (USMC)
Cherry Point Marine Corps Air Station and
Cherry Point, North Carolina

146. *Patriots for Peace* (USA)
Fort Benning and Columbus, Georgia

147. *The Pawn* (USA)
Fort Detrick and Frederick, Maryland

148. *Payback* (USA)
Santa Ana, California
Movement for a Democratic Military

149. *People's Press* (USA)
Fort Campbell and Clarksville, Tennessee

150. *Plain Rapper* (USA)
Palo Alto, California

151. *Potemkin* (USN)
USS Forrestal

152. *P.O.W.* (USA)
Fort Ord and Monterey, California
Pacific Counseling Service, Vietnam Veterans
Against the War, Revolutionary Union, and
American Servicemen's Union

153. *Rag* (Army Reserve and National Guard)
Chicago, Illinois

154. *Rage* (USMC)
Camp Lejeune and New River Air Station

155. *Rap!* (USA)
Fort Benning and Columbus, Georgia

156. *Rebel* (USA)
Montreal, Canada
Exiled GIs

157. *Reconnaissance* (USAF)
Forbes Air Force Base and Topeka, Kansas

158. *Redline* (Army Reserve and National Guard)
Boston, Massachusetts

159. *Right On Post* (USA)
Fort Ord, Seaside and Monterey, California
Movement for a Democratic Military

160. *Rough Draft* (USN)
Norfolk Naval Air Station and Norfolk, Virginia

161. *Sacsctrated* (USAF)
Fairchild Air Force Base

162. *Seasick* (USN)
"GI Center," Olongapo, Philippines
Pacific Counseling Service, National Lawyers
Guild

163. *Second Front* (service branch unknown)
Paris, France

164. *2nd Front International* (service branch unknown)
Stockholm, Sweden

165. *Seize the Time* (USN)
Iwakuni, Japan
Pacific Counseling Service, International
Counter-Military Collective

166. *Semper Fi* (USMC)
"Hobbit" Coffeehouse, Iwakuni, Japan
Pacific Counseling Service, Beheiren

167. *1776-Right to Revolution* (service branch
unknown)
Okinawa

168. *Shakedown* (USA)
Fort Dix
GIs United Against the War in Indochina
"Coffeehouse," Wrightstown, New Jersey

169. *Short Times* (USA)
Fort Jackson
"The UFO" Coffeehouse, Columbia, South
Carolina

170. *Skydove* (USAF)
Rickenbocker Air Force Base and Columbus, Ohio

171. *Snorton Bird* (USAF)
Norton Air Force Base

172. *SOS Newsletter* (USN)
USS Enterprise

173. *Sound Off* (USN)
Puget Sound Naval Station and Bramerton,
Washington

174. *Spaced Sentinel* (USAF)
Beale Air Force Base and Marysville, California

175. *SPD News* (USA)
Fort Dix and New York City
("SPD": Special Processing Detachment)

176. *Special Weapon* (USAF)
Kirtland Air Force Base

177. *Spread Eagle* (USA)
Fort Campbell and Clarksville, Tennessee

178. *Square Wheel* (USA)
Fort Eustis

179. *Star Spangled Bummer* (USAF)
Wright Patterson Air Force Base and Dayton,
Ohio
GIs United Against the War in Indochina

180. *Stars 'N Bars* (USN)
Iwakuni, Japan
Pacific Counseling Service, Beheiren

181. *Straight Sheet* (USAF)
Duluth Air Force Base and Duluth, Minnesota

182. *Strategic Hamlet* (USA)
Isla Vista, California

183. *Strike Back* (USA)
Fort Bragg and Fayetteville, North Carolina

184. *Stuffed Puffin* (USN)
Keflavik, Iceland

185. *Task Force B* (service branch unknown)
San Francisco, California

186. *This Is Life* (service branch unknown)
San Diego, California

187. *Top Secret* (USA)
Fort Devens and Cambridge, Massachusetts

188. *Travisty* (USAF)
Travis Air Force Base and Suisun City, California

189. *Truth Instead* (USN)
Treasure Island Naval Station and San Francisco,
California

190. *Twin Cities Protester* (USA)
Fort Snelling and Minneapolis, Minnesota

191. *The Ultimate Weapon* (USA)
Fort Dix

192. *Underground Oak* (USN)
Oakland, California

193. *Underwood* (USA)
Fort Leonard Wood

194. *Unity Now* (USA)
Fort Ord and Monterey, California
Movement for a Democratic Military

195. *Up Against the Bulkhead* (USN)
San Francisco, California

196. *Up Against the Wall* (USA)
West Berlin, Germany

197. *Up From the Bottom* (USN)
"Enlisted People's Place" and "EM Club,"
San Diego, California
Pacific Counseling Service, Movement for a
Democratic Military

198. *Up Front* (USA)
Los Angeles, California

199. *USAF News* (USAF)
Wright Patterson Air Force Base and Dayton,
Ohio

200. *Voice of the Lumpen* (USA)
Frankfurt, Germany

201. *VS & SP* (USA)
Fort Lewis

202. *We Got the brASS* (USA)
Frankfurt, Germany

203. *We Got the Brass* (USN)
Okinawa
Pacific Counseling Service, Beheiren

204. *We the People* (service branch unknown)
Iwakuni, Japan
Pacific Counseling Service

205. *Whack!* (USA)
Fort McClellan
GIs United Against the War in Indochina
"GIs and WACs United" Coffeehouse, Anniston, Alabama

206. *Where Are We?* (USA-USAF)
Fort Huachuca and Davis Monthan Air Force Base

207. *Where It's At* (USA)
West Berlin, Germany

208. *Whig* (USN)
Quezon City, Philippines
Pacific Counseling Service

209. *Woodpecker* (USA)
Fort Leonard Wood

210. *Yankee Refugee* (USA)
Vancouver, Canada
Exiled GIs

211. *Yokosuka David* (USN)
"Yokosuka David" Coffeehouse, Yokosuka, Japan
Beheiren

212. *Your Military Left* (USA)
Fort Sam Houston and San Antonio, Texas

Papers with National or International Distribution

The 15 papers listed here had national or international distribution. The list identifies the papers, their places of publication, and their organizational affiliations. Some of the publications may have had affiliations that were not discovered by Hayes (1975) and Haines (1976). Additionally, the list does not identify dates of operation. *The Ally's* lengthy publication life (1968 to 1974) was probably atypical, although Vietnam Veterans Against the War (Chicago) and Vietnam Veterans Against the War, Anti-Imperialist (New York City and Seattle) continue in 1991 to publish newspapers linking local chapters of politically active Vietnam veterans throughout the United States.

These papers were based in major cities and were often produced by coalitions of dissident civilians, active duty service personnel, and Vietnam veterans. At least three of the papers (*The Bond, GI News*, and *Winter Soldier*) functioned as organs for major organizations that provided, in varying degrees, leadership and influence in the antiwar movement. *The Bond*, established at Berkeley in 1967 by draft resister William Callison and a group of friends, was the first nationally distributed underground paper aimed exclusively at military personnel during the war. The paper promoted the organization of the American Servicemen's Union (ASU) as a collective bargaining agent, demanding the following ("We Demand," *The Bond* 24 July 1971, pp. 4-5):

1. The right to refuse to obey illegal orders—like orders to fight in the illegal, imperialist war in Southeast Asia.

2. Election of officers by vote of rank and file.

3. An end to saluting and sir-ing of officers.

4. The right of black, Latin, and other national minority servicemen and women to determine their own lives, free from the oppression of racist whites. No troops to be sent into black, Latin, or other national minority communities.

5. No troops to be used against antiwar demonstrators.

6. No troops to be used against workers on strike.

7. Rank and file control of court-martial boards.

8. The right of free political association.

9. Federal minimum wages [for service personnel].

10. The right of collective bargaining.

After raising *The Bond's* circulation to about one thousand copies a month, Callison turned over the editorship to Andrew Stapp, founder of the ASU. Stapp had been court-martialed three times at Fort Sill, Oklahoma, for offenses related to his attempts at organizing the ASU, and he eventually received a dishonorable discharge, which was subsequently overruled as illegal. Under Stapp's leadership, *The Bond* was moved to the ASU's New York City headquarters and its circulation rose to about twenty thousand.

The Bond pioneered the system of distribution that The Ally and other internationally distributed papers would modify to reach soldiers throughout the world, including units in West Germany and South Vietnam. The Bond encouraged dissident soldiers to provide the paper with unit rosters listing the names and military addresses of service personnel. The paper would then "bond" entire units, often generating conflict between lower ranking personnel and commanders who attempted to confiscate copies of the paper. Other papers, including The Ally, relied on soldiers who volunteered to distribute copies that they received through the mail in bundles camouflaged to look like "care packages" from families or church groups back home.

The GI Press Service deserves a special note for archivists and researchers. Operated by the Student Mobilization to End the War, this service functioned as a clearinghouse of articles, photographs, and political cartoons submitted by locally produced GI papers throughout the United States. The service made these materials and other features available to subscribers, including many of the 212 locally produced papers identified above. The GI Press Service acted like a "wire service," linking many of the otherwise isolated GI papers and serving their needs with packets of material that the papers received through the mail. A complete collection of the GI Press Service packets would provide a good sampling of materials characteristic of the GI underground press.

1. The Ally
    Berkeley, California

2. The Bond: The Serviceman's Newspaper
    Berkeley, California, and New York City
    GIs United Against the War in Indochina
    American Servicemen's Union

3. CAMP News
    Chicago, Illinois
    Chicago Area Military Project

4. GI News
    Chicago, Illinois
    Vietnam Veterans Against the War/Winter Soldier
        Organization
    Revolutionary Union

5. GI Press Service
    New York City
    Student Mobilization to End the War

6. GI Voice
    New York City

7. Peace and Freedom News
    New York City

8. Peace and Freedom News
    Baltimore, Maryland

9. Task Force
    Berkeley, California

10. The TET Offensive
    New York City

11. Veterans Stars and Stripes for Peace
    Chicago, Illinois

12. Vietnam GI
    Chicago, Illinois

13. War Resisters League
    New York City

14. WIN
    New York City

15. Winter Soldier
    Vietnam Veterans Against the War/Winter Soldier
        Organization
    Revolutionary Union

FAG RAG: THE MOST LOATHSOME PUBLICATION IN THE ENGLISH LANGUAGE

Charley Shively

On Friday evening, June 27, 1969, New York City police raided the Stonewall Bar on Sheridan Square; instead of going quietly into the waiting vans, the motley crowd of queers and queens attacked the police. Stonewall was closed but sporadic street rioting continued in Greenwich Village for the next few days. The event quickly became the Bastille Day of an emergent, nationwide gay and lesbian liberation movement.

In Boston, the GLF (Gay Liberation Front), through a publications collective, would soon be putting out *Lavender Vision, Fag Rag*, Good Gay Poets books, *Boston Gay Review*, Fag Rag Books, *Street Sheet*, and numerous broadsides, posters, and flyers. Boston's GLF participated in its first demonstration March 15, 1970 (against paying taxes to support the Vietnam War), organized a community center, maintained a hot line, and carried on wildly. As a formal organization Boston's GLF had ceased to exist by 1973; however, despite the obstacles of gentrification, police repression, plagues, and paradigm shifts, *Fag Rag* has continued into the nineties.

ORIGINS

Like the New Left, the Gay Liberation Fronts (GLFs) both benefited from and repudiated groups that had struggled through the dark ages of the fifties and before. During the 1920s, gay papers in Paris and Chicago were seized by the police. Catholic deputies of the Third French Republic succeeded in destroying *Inversions* (1924-25). Of the two issues of Chicago's *Friendship and Freedom*, every single copy has been

Shively is currently a member of the *Fag Rag* collective. He is the author of three books on Walt Whitman, numerous poems, and the forthcoming *Cocksucking as an Act of Revolution* (Fag Rag Books).

lost or incinerated; those working on the paper were arrested. After the 1873 Comstock law, printing presses and post offices in the United States were closed to any publication that did not denounce homosexuality. The district attorney in Boston prevented publication of an 1882 edition of Walt Whitman's *Leaves of Grass*. In 1928, Radclyffe Hall's *Well of Loneliness* was declared "obscene" and banned both in London and Boston; Hall and her lover fled England. Even such relatively uncloseted figures as John Addington Symonds, Andre Gide, and Jean Cocteau first published their defenses of homosexuality (*A Problem in Greek Ethics*, 1883; *Corydon*, 1911; *The White Paper*, 1928) anonymously and/or privately.

As late as 1958, the U.S. Post Office excluded any publication that favored homosexuality. In 1954, they busted *One Magazine* (1953-1968), a journal allied with the homosexual liberation Mattachine Society. The lower court judged *One* "obscene, lewd, lascivious and filthy"; the appeal judge called it "cheap pornography"; in 1958 the Supreme Court overturned the lower courts without comment. Even so, in 1960 postal inspectors reported several Smith College professors for receiving homosexual publications; the most famous (Whitman biographer Newton Arvin) was allowed to retire quietly; he died while the cases were still in the news.

What a contrast with the sexual liberation of the sixties. When district attorneys went after magazines and newspapers, prosecution increased circulation. Boston's *Avatar*, for instance, was busted for using the word "fuck;" and in 1964 the *Evergreen Review* ran afoul of a Long Island DA who got excited over a picture. They published my own thoughts on the DA's "Browning Evergreen 32." The poem called for closing "the (too oppressive) printing press/...Let's worship together/(without sex) and/play the electric (forgetting/the human) organ."

In his 1964 defense of the *Evergreen Review*, Edward Steichen didn't mention browning or playing with one's organ: "If human beings in the act of making love are indecent then the entire human race stands indicted. As long as the act of lovemaking is in itself not declared illegal and the extermination of the human race presented as a goal of civilization, lovers will continue to make love and babies will be born and it will be interpreted by the artist." Of course, "homosexual acts" were then illegal in every state except Illinois, which decriminalized in 1961. In the same issue in which my poem was published, there was an advertisement from *One Magazine* for "The Homosexual Viewpoint." I'm not sure why I didn't send my dollar along for a sample copy. I had few reservations about my sexuality and certainly had no plans of making babies. I was reading Allen Ginsberg, John

Wieners, Jean Genet, William Burroughs, and Simone de Beauvoir's *Must We Burn Sade*?

What I needed to pull me into gay consciousness came only with the Stonewall Rebellion. On the night of the uprising of gays against the police in New York's Sheridan Square, I wrote "Exiles' Kingdom":

1.

flower exile
filament
broken stalks
washing memories
together bracken
water lilies
disengaged
sport spurt spear
spree spent heads
wiggling for
more time

2.

Soon flowers
soon cut sleeves
open bouquets waiting
waiting awhile longer
everywhere flourishing
flooding child
finding foot
flowing mountain
    milk final finial
    flood food floor
    homecoming earth
suncaked
sunflower
shelter seed
room soon will
soon will bloom
another lagoon
other kinds of
kingdoms come
(June 27/28, 1969)

I first learned about Stonewall in *WIN*, the counterculture War Resisters League magazine; I began attending Boston's Student Homophile League, whose Wednesday night political group quickly evolved into Boston's Gay Liberation Front; the GLF group participated in the Black Panthers' Revolutionary People's Constitutional Convention and organized both a publication and a community center collective. The principles put forward at the RPC conventions in Philadelphia in September and in Washington, DC, two months later drew on gay experiences and in turn provided direction for GLFs around the country.

In November 1970, Boston's GLF published the first issue of *Lavender Vision*, with a staff that was half lesbian/half gay male. Soon after it appeared, most of the male staff members moved to San Francisco; the lesbians wanted to use the name *Lavender Vision* for an all-lesbian publication (issue number 2 came out in April 1971); the remaining male publication collective then adopted the name *Fag Rag*. Our first issue appeared in June 1971 in time for the New York Gay Pride March to commemorate the Stonewall Rebellion (see sidebar 1).

Fag Rag was one among a whole network of GLF papers that included New York's *Come Out*; Detroit's *Gay Liberator*; Toronto's *Body Politic*; Berkeley/San Francisco's *Gay Sunshine*; Washington, DC's *The Furies*; Oakland, California's *Amazon Quarterly*; and many more. All these publications offered a brisk brew of sexual liberation, anarchism, hippie love, drugs, peace, Maoism, Marxism, rock and roll, folk song, cultural separatism, feminism, effeminism, tofu/brown rice, communal living, urban junkie, rural purism, nudism, leather, high camp drag, gender fuck drag, poetry, essays, pictures, and much more.

Publication could be an act of liberation, an act of publicity for those outside the centers of power. Passive consumers of the various media came suddenly both to record and to create another reality. Even now the lesbian/gay liberation viewpoint is excluded from popular consciousness. Jill Johnston of *Lesbian Nation* wrote that the existing media provides "more an obstruction than a channel…somehow the incoming information is blocked or distorted instead of passed through intact or at all. the media is its own agency. or else it's a strict customs agency and very little cargo is permitted to pass." Even counterculture rags would at best allow an issue or a column for what they saw as a marginal viewpoint; they themselves struggled under the conservative putdown that the counterculture men were all pansies and the women all lezzies ("freaking fag revolution").

DIVISIONS AND UNITIES

Often painful conflicts arose from the individual desires of women, African-Americans, gay males, lesbians, and other groups to separate into their own collectives. Such separation was needed because of the long history of oppression, silence, and suppressed consciousness. Separation came both from hostility found in self-styled comrades and from frustration in developing a self-consciousness. Profound contradictions around race, gender, and class could not just be glossed over with well meaning but otherwise meaningless professions of a common struggle. A *Fag Rag* number 8 (Summer 1973) editorial declared, "We have to create our own existences; we have to create our own media; we have to create our own community." A first step was to find out who "we" were; what "we" wanted; who our enemies were, who our friends were; what our history was; what our future was.

Fag Rag's first great separation was to accept a division between gay men and lesbians. *Fag Rag* has never pretended to speak for more than a small group of gay men; the intellectual and political imperialists, on the other hand, want to speak for vast bodies of people, who are actually de-voiced by being conglomerated into a whole of which they are not an active, participating part. *Fag Rag* did not create the separation between men and women and *Fag Rag* has never pretended that this separation was meaningless. Where sexuality is not an issue, coed groups make sense, but the sexuality of gay men and lesbians cannot be homogenized easily.

Although a seemingly trivial issue, the different positions of men and women in body exposure cannot be covered over. For instance, at dances, some women do not feel comfortable exposing their breasts in front of other men—particularly bisexual men. And some are not happy to see men nude; the cock could represent both patriarchy and rape. Since some women don't want to expose themselves in front of any man, some demanded rules against men going topless (if not bottomless). Part of this attitude comes from a long heritage not of our making: straight men love to watch lesbians, but they freak out when they see two men making out. Women, on the other hand, have less often enjoyed watching men make out (although there is a report of one group of university wives who meet together to watch gay male porno movies). In the heterosexual society, women who expose themselves are likely to be raped; men who expose themselves are likely to be arrested for indecency.

Among lesbians some women feel uncomfortable with men around; other women seek their companionship. Likewise, among gay men, some are more companionate than others with lesbians. In addition, both lesbians and gay men relate to straight men and women in diverse ways. Homogenization tries to paper over these differences and say we are all one big group; such homogenization would wipe out differences. These differences are like dialects, which television attempts to eliminate in order to develop a single market for advertisers and manufacturers. The more separate groups there are, the better chance we have of surviving. While separate groups are needed in order to develop freedom on both sides, combinations can be made. Thus *Fag Rag* participated with a group of women who began a lesbian journal *Bad Attitude*, the first issue of which appeared with *Fag Rag* number 41 in 1984.

A group from *Fag Rag* participated in the 1971 protest at Atlantic City against the Miss America contest. Among the groups protesting were the Vietnam Veterans Against the War. Their flyer framed the position of women, men, and Vietnamese: "How to Dehumanize: a woman...enter her into a beauty contest where she is an object to be admired for her ability not to say or do anything significant; a man....enter him in the military where his individuality is crushed and where he learns to respond to the order of KILL!!!" And how to dehumanize "Vietnamese women or children...emphasize their slant eyes or their 'funny' way of life. Equate their poverty or hunger with laziness, call them GOOKS. Depersonalize their humanity to the point that they are no longer human and they become the casualties, killed by American MEN."

Feminism provided a perspective for *Fag Rag* no less than the Vietnam veterans. Allen Young, an early member of the *Fag Rag* collective, wrote that "Gay liberation without feminism...cannot really deal with the source of homosexual oppression. For that source is the system of sex roles propagated by a male supremacist society." GLF groups met in consciousness-raising and study groups that were based on the model of women's groups which themselves were based on models from the Chinese Revolution of speaking bitter tears. The links between racism, sexism, class oppression, and homophobia were studied in our groups, in our own lives, and in the society around us. One day, while we were riding in a '69 Volkswagen bug, one of the early Mattachine Society leaders from Washington, told me quite firmly that consciousness-raising groups were a waste of time. First we must become liberated, he insisted. Then we would have time for the luxuries of self-examination. I said that without changing our consciousness we would only recapitulate existing oppressions.

Style has remained an enduring division even though fashion changes every day. Men wearing "women's clothing" have petrified many faggots and not a few women; that the lines can be crossed so simply confuses philosophers who want clarity and stability in their systems. In *Fag Rag* number 3, we ran an interview with Boston's most famous drag queen, Sylvia Sydney; and several *Fag Rag*'ers—such as Clover, Maya Silverthorne, Mijo, myself, Tede Mathews, Bunny LaRue, and John Wieners—participated in cross-dressing on stage. Here is another division not of our making and perhaps more rigid in 1990 than in 1970. For instance, in businesses, the military, and universities, women can wear suits or ties but few men can survive unless they approximate the looks of straight men.

Another division (likewise not of *Fag Rag*'s making) was that between the bar gays and movement gays. Some distinction was made between "gay" and "homosexual" in the early seventies. Being gay was being liberated; being homosexual was being retrograde. *Fag Rag* from the beginning tried to avoid alienating or attacking vulnerable parts of the gay community: hustlers, drag queens, boy lovers, bath orgiasts, bar queens, leather, rest-area tea-room, and bush players were often condemned by Gay Liberation Fronts. In the first editorial (see sidebar 1), *Fag Rag* called for the creation of a new gay community: "We realize that it is very easy for any group of people to become elitist and cut off from the very people they claim to speak for and about...The fact that we are in Gay Liberation does not mean we are liberated, it means, instead that we are working towards liberation."

Those who have worked on *Fag Rag* over the years have come from diverse political directions. All have shared in some ways in the African-American liberation; from the antiwar movement; from the student revolts. And all took up a call for revolution rather than simple reform. The "front" in Gay Liberation Front came from the Algerian and Vietnamese Liberation Fronts. One of our marching slogans was "Ho Ho Homosexual, the ruling class is ineffectual; Ho Ho Ho Chi Minh, the NLF is going to win." Protesting U.S. bombing in Laos and in North Vietnam, the collective participated in the seizing of the local NBC station during the evening news. Inside the station, a statement was read (but not broadcast because they went off the air for half the program). My task in this action was to call other stations, tell them what was happening, and then hang up. As instructed, after I had finished my calls, I ate the phone numbers.

Fag Rag has, of course, never endorsed any political candidate and has never believed in begging the ruling class to grant us concessions. As close as we came to ever adopting any specific program was our "ten-point demands" (see sidebar 2), which were derived from the September 1970 "Statement of Demands from the Male Representatives of National Gay Liberation" at the Revolutionary People's Constitutional Convention in Philadelphia. Wearing a leopard skin robe (handmade by Larry Anderson), I read *Fag Rag*'s 1972 version to the Democratic Platform Committee and the demands were widely distributed in the demonstrations at the Miami conventions in 1972. Point 8 called "for the return of all United States troops to within the United States borders as the most effective way to end American imperialism." Number 10 concluded globally: "We call for the self-government and self-determination of all peoples irrespective of national, sexual, party, race, age or other artificially imposed categories....All coercion and dominance must end, equality must be

An Open Letter to Gay Brothers:

It's taken a few months to get this newspaper together. We've worked hard writing articles—informational and opinionated, taking photographs, laying out the paper. It's been especially difficult deciding what format, information, and opinion is most relevant to the Gay Community. We realize that it is very easy for any group of people to become elitist and cut off from the very people who they claim to speak for and about. We feel that the future of this paper will depend very much on your feelings and interest.

It may be naive of us to expect that people will take the time to verbalize their criticisms, but the movement for the liberation of Gay People should not belong to a small group of people with exclusive ideas. It is up to you to broaden the scope of a newspaper and the range of activities of Gay Male Liberation with your criticisms and ideas. It's not easy to accept criticism, but this is the only way we can grow, and relate to a wider range of people.

We spend lots of time in Gay Male Liberation talking about the separation we feel from the larger Gay Community. This separation seems to come in part from a whole set of political beliefs (and rhetoric we use to express those beliefs) which aren't shared by many Gay People. But there seems to be a more fundamental reason for this separation—there seems to be an unspoken sentiment among Gay People not in Gay Liberation, that coming to Gay Male Liberation means making a commitment to a certain set of political beliefs, to a certain kind of life style, most particularly a commitment to being open about Gayness all the time. This is not true—all of us live with pressure all the time, though most of us believe in theory that we should be open at all times, we often aren't—for fear of losing a job, a home, a straight friend, just for plain fear. The fact that we are in Gay Liberation does not mean we are liberated, it means instead, that we are working towards liberation.

It has been a lot of fun doing the newspaper together, sharing ideas, gaining insight into each other's experience in "coming out" and discovering the perspective of the American academic and public attitude toward Gays. We are coming closer together, overcoming fears about being Gay and attempting to create more of a communal feeling among people.

On the following page is an address and some telephone numbers which can be used to direct any comment or criticisms about the newspaper and Gay Liberation activities. Of course, this does not preclude personal contact with members of Gay Male Liberation as a means for criticism.

GAY LOVE TO ALL

NOTE

1. Reprinted from *Fag Rag* 1 (June 1971), by Mark Heumann and Kevin McGirr.

established and we must search together for new forms of cooperation."

A division between anarchists, Marxist-Leninists, Maoists, and others aroused great excitement in *Fag Rag*'s early years. The *Lavender Vision* came out just after the GML collective returned from the Revolutionary People's Constitutional Convention (November 1970) in Washington, DC. The first two issues of *Fag Rag* carried all the news of the 1971 May Day demonstrations in Washington. Various strains appeared over political differences. Thus the issue of Cuba bothered some of the returned veterans of the Venceremos Brigades. All the copies of *Out Out Damn Faggot* written by members of the 4th Brigade and highly critical of gay oppression in Cuba were "lost" by members of earlier brigades working on *Fag Rag*, but a copy of the play was recovered and published in *Fag Rag* number 3. The gay male liberation group met in the Red Book Store (named of course after Chairman Mao's pocket guide to revolution). When their Cuban posters were stickered with "This oppresses faggots," staff members of *Fag Rag* were blamed. We were also blamed when the shawls woven to raise money for the Palestine Liberation Organization disappeared. Some of the divisions from various left ideologies disappeared as the left groups disbanded or lost interest in homosexuals. In 1972, for instance, the Socialist Workers Party sent organizers into the gay community, but meeting resistance, they departed to organize the handicapped.

A division between cultural revolution and political revolution could be resolved by anarchism, which allows more room for differences. Such a position often came more from default than from consensus. In *Fag Rag* number 8 (Winter/Spring 1974), Larry Anderson summarized the dilemma *Fag Rag* faced with the passing of an active gay male liberation group. On the one hand, he asks: "Is *Fag Rag* a homosexual literary magazine which will publish anything of quality referring to writing style, regardless of content—written by homosexuals?" Or should *Fag Rag* carry on the GML struggle through the publication. "Is *Fag Rag* an anti-racist, anti-masculinist publication from some gay community of thought saying there's exploitation, needless and meaningless insults and belittling rampant in this world and it's reflected everywhere else: we

Sidebar 2: Boston GLF's 10-Point Demands
Presented to the Democratic Convention in Miami Beach, July 1972

Boston GLF urges that the following principles be incorporated in the 1972 Democratic Party Platform:

1.   We demand an end to any discrimination based on biology. Neither skin color, age nor gender should be recorded by any government agency. Biology should never be the basis for any special legal handicap or privilege.

2.   We demand an end to any discrimination based on sexual preference. Everyone should be free to pursue sexual gratification without fear of rape. Governments should neither legalize nor illegalize these forms of gratification. And no one should be restrained in movement (either immigration or emigration), in employment, in housing or in any other way for being a faggot or lesbian.

3.   The United States government should not only end discrimination based on dressing habits but should positively encourage more imaginative clothing. No member of the armed forces or other government agency should be forced to wear a "uniform" to conform to either biological gender or hierarchical position. For instance, if they prefer, women should be allowed to wear short hair and pants; males, to wear long hair and dresses.

4.   All economic discrimination against faggots and lesbians should be ended. We should not be denied either employment nor promotion because of our sexual preference or dress habits. We should have the same tax advantages as heterosexuals living in nuclear families. And like all people, we should have free access to sufficient food, housing, medical service and transportation in order to lead a full and rewarding life. We specifically support a guaranteed annual income of $5,500 for every individual, and we call for a redistribution of the national wealth. Resources and power must be taken from straight, white heterosexual men and redistributed among all the people.

5.   We call for an end to all government (or other) research on "homosexuality." Our preference is no disease; all chemical, electric or hypnotic "treatments" to "cure" us should be outlawed. Government funds now being used for "mental health" should be given to groups of lesbians, faggots and other "mental patients" so that they may organize themselves in counseling and community centers to administer to their own needs.

6.   Rearing children should be the common responsibility of the whole community. Any legal rights parents have over "their" children should be dissolved and each child should be free to choose its own destiny. Free twenty-four hour child care centers should be established where faggots and lesbians can share the responsibility of child rearing.

7.   All lesbians or faggots now imprisoned for any "sex crime" (except rape) should be released immediately from brigs, mental hospitals or prisons. They should be compensated at $2.50 an hour for each hour of their confinement and all records of their incarceration should be destroyed. Lesbians and faggots imprisoned on other charges should be protected from beatings and rape at the hands of their jailors or inmates, and no one should be denied quick release or parole for engaging in "homosexual acts" while confined.

8.   We call for an end to all aggressive armed forces. We support the Vietnamese people's Seven Point Peace Program and call for the *total* withdrawal of all United States and United States-supported air, land or naval forces from Vietnam. Moreover, we call for the return of *all* United States troops to within the United States borders as the most effective way to end American imperialism.

9.   Within the United States, we call for a disbanding of all armed forces, secret police (FBI, CIA, IRS, Narcotics squads, etc.) and uniformed police. Arms should be used only to protect the people and to prevent rape. For this purpose, we call for the formation of a people's police to be organized by those now most subject to police brutality: third world groups, women, lesbians, faggots and poor people generally.

10.   We call for the self-government and self-determination of all peoples irrespective of national, sexual, party, race, age or other artificially imposed categories. Our liberation cannot be complete as long as any person is the property or the slave of another in any way. All coercion and dominance must end, equality must be established and we must search together for new forms of cooperation.

---

don't need it here; LET'S TRY SOMETHING ELSE!?"
Fag Rag from the beginning has tried to bridge this gap. Poetry and art have provided a way of being both political and cultural emancipation, of fighting the revolution and of realizing self-expression.

PRAXIS

The difference between publishing regularly and coming out when ready expressed different lifestyles and expectations that cut across political lines. Some hoped to find emancipation from the "straight" press: murders, advertisements, puffs for the government, puffs for the middle class, all delivered on a predictable—daily, weekly, monthly, quarterly, yearly, millennial—schedule. A friend once called up and said, "Oh, I've just been talking with Susan Sontag and she says you're very interesting, but you must come out more often; you must reach a larger audience." While some wanted *Fag Rag* to become famous, others argued on the same point that we had an obligation to the movement both in Boston and elsewhere to provide regular news and comment for "all the shit coming down."

In *Fag Rag* number 1, we never promised a second issue and throughout our history no one has ever been able to bet safely that another issue would be out. Called quarterly from time to time, *Fag Rag* came out four times only in 1974. For awhile a weekly *Street Sheet* was published with regular announcements and news; it was mimeographed, given away free, and widely circulated in Boston. But despite the urging of greater regularity, *Fag Rag* never became a laxative/enema regular; we were loose from the beginning. Anyone want to bet on when the next issue will be out?

In June 1973, the Boston *Gay Community News* was founded. They relieved *Fag Rag*'s *Street Sheet* of having to come out every week and the two projects came to complement each other. I myself have participated in *GCN* from the beginning; I helped edit some articles and wrote for the paper as early as their second issue. In 1974, we rented offices together with some other gay groups (an archives, distribution agency, and campaign offices for Elaine Noble) but, while the other groups soon separated, *Fag Rag* and *GCN* have continued to share offices. The two groups did not always see eye-to-eye, however; a paroled prisoner had in fact built a wall between the two. In one squabble over religion and heterosexuals, *GCN* objected to our slogans on the wall—"God Is Dead Now Let's Kill the Church" (written by a graduate of Harvard Divinity School) and "Two, Four, Six, Eight: Kill a Straight and Masturbate"—by scribbling words like "infantile" across our part of the office. The *GCN* collective met and voted whether to demand an apology or to expel *Fag Rag* at once. The vote ended in a tie; we didn't apologize but we did cover our own and their graffiti with copies of *Fag Rag*. *GCN* responded by putting copies of their own paper on the wall.

Time and common oppression have brought *GCN* and *Fag Rag* closer together. During the June 1982 Gay Pride activities, for instance, *Fag Rag* under Tom Reeves' leadership led a march on Boston police headquarters calling for the immediate abolition of the vice squad. The next month, on July 7, our offices were torched by, we believe, a combined SWAT team of off-duty Boston firemen and policemen. Coinciden-

tally, the owner of the building was visiting China with the mayor. (We had found the mayor lingering suspiciously outside our office on the night of June 27, 1979.) Federal investigators took part of the floor to Washington for study but could only conclude there was no evidence....

The 1982 fire certainly brought us all closer together; the Glad Day Bookstore, *GCN*, and *Fag Rag* received an outflowing of goodwill and community support. With the money raised, new office space was found and new equipment was acquired. At a fundraising and information meeting at the Arlington Community Church, the charred issue of *Fag Rag* number 2 with a flaming faggot on the cover was hung over the altar.

Fag Rag has separated itself from both the rest of society and from the mainstream of the gay community in at least two ways—in a commitment to poetry and in the celebration of man-boy love. The GLF began a Good Gay Poets group who first published Aaron Shurin's "Exorcism of the Straight Man Demon." The original Good Gay Poets group included Aaron Shurin, Ron Schreiber, myself, David Eberly, Charles River, and John LaPorta. Collectively, the Good Gay Poets laid out poetry pages in *Fag Rags* number 3 and number 4. Salvatore Farinella, David Emerson Smith, and Freddie Greenfield have helped extend gay male poetry far beyond the ordinary.

From the beginning, *Fag Rag* has supported sexual freedom for people of all ages. In 1977, Anita Bryant led a campaign against the sexuality of children and was the force behind the defeat of a Dade County ordinance that would have granted human rights to homosexuals of any age. Heterosexuals and many straight-identified homosexuals suddenly turned to identify an age of consent for sexual freedom that would exclude people younger than themselves. Tom Reeves (whose "Red and Gay" was published in *Fag Rag* number 6) led the battle in Boston against a local Anita Bryant DA, whose witchhunt was stopped by the Boston Boise Committee. Out of that committee, GLAD (Gay Lesbian Advocates and Defenders) and NAMBLA (National Man Boy Love Association) were founded. Tom Reeves' vigorous leadership and forceful articles have stunned and startled the emotionally dead and have enlivened and inspired the oppressed.

LOOSE PRACTICES

Within the staff of *Fag Rag*, an anarchist commitment to having everyone participate in every part of the paper has led to many battles between the more "professional" and the more "amateur" members. This process among ourselves has been as critical to us as our public presentations, our poetry, or our struggles against a repressed and repressing society. The pro side has wanted *Fag Rag* to be better organized, to publish more regularly, to have an office, and to perform the other functions expected of a journal. "Professionalism" also involves what kind of writing gets published; the search is for "high-quality" writing, not half-digested, sloppy, lackadaisical work that would be rejected if we did not know the author. The professional also seeks "brand names" like Gore Vidal or W.H. Auden. These names inevitably sell papers because they are known and people want to know more about celebrities.

The amateur side argues that the people writing the paper are more important than any consumers or audience. They would destroy the dividing lines between author, publisher, and reader. The amateur thinks only intermittently about continuity; today I'm working on the paper, but if Alaska or Bolivia strikes my fancy tomorrow I'll be off. Freedom means not only getting away from established society but also not reduplicating that society's values within the counterculture. In writing, the amateur tends to believe not only "first thought best thought" but also that every piece submitted must be printed—word for word.

When the paper started, most of us had had little experience with publications—except as passive readers. One exception, Allen Young, who worked on several issues after number 2, brought and shared a wealth of experience from the Liberation News Service and his training at the Columbia School of Journalism. Some others had training here and there—mimeography, photography, typing—which we also shared. But for all of us on the paper, *Fag Rag* has been a virtual school of gay male journalism. We have emphatically tried to have everyone learn to share and do all tasks. Of course, in the rush of typing, layout, and printing, someone with accumulated skills might have to do more.

We have never solved the problem of unequal experience. The untrained, on the one hand, often don't want to acquire any of the accumulated wisdom about layout, writing, typing, and other skills needed to produce a newspaper. Everyone seems eager to be an "editor" (more often "the" editor)—that is, make decisions about what should be printed and how the paper should be run. But when it comes to shit work, some people are off dancing. On the other hand, the trained often hoard their skills and enjoy the leverage they gain over the unskilled.

In writing, for instance, verbal ability is a tremendous asset in getting along. Every middle-class child learns verbiage early and relatively easily; other children acquire literacy only through a struggle. Being inarticulate is a social condition in the United States. I know this firsthand since my father did not read or write and my mother only finished grammar school. But I have also learned that writing is no magic gift of the gods, given usually to the rich and well-born; it is a learned, communicable technique. (What a paradox: They tell us that the art of communication is incommunicable!)

Editing then raises problems. Some articles need rewriting, need cutting, need criticism, need help. How can that be done without the sheer exercise of power? A poem comes in from a pubescent boy, touching and beautiful, but ends disastrously with his defining his gayness by exclaiming, "at least I'm not a cunt." In a "professional" journal, a secretary (an office here called "corresponding person") just mails out a pre-printed rejection slip and that's it. But literary rejection is just as painful and horrifying as sexual rejection. And some of the same games are played in literature as in cruising places. Somebody personally explained to the youth why being a faggot did not necessarily mean hating cunts, but our cutting his poem couldn't help but increase his castration anxieties.

What we have yet to create is a "gay" or "faggot" style of writing. We might be able to finger some writing as alienating, academic, straight, impersonal, and boring—but we still lack a common style, medium, vocabulary, or even literature. There is the Queen's Vernacular but much of that is more an affectation of a saloon or salon society than a literature. Is it a first step in a new direction? Or is it only false consciousness? Perhaps the post-modern condition allows no common language to anyone? But that condition rapidly eradicates any and all vernacular (except perhaps that of the academics).

Editorial decisions have never been easy; we have always tried for the anarchist ideal of universal consensus. One trial came around the issue of whether or not we should print an interview with Gore Vidal. Those favoring publication of Vidal found defenders in the *Boston Globe* (January 19, 1974): "Any periodical that won't publish it, no matter what the reason, doesn't deserve to stay in business." In a heated meeting over the article someone got so overworked that he vomited. The interview ran with a summary statement of misgivings about some of its contents. Less easily resolved was an issue around some of the arguments derived from Michel Foucault that "homosexuals" and "homosexuality" were only recently invented. Although I wanted to print an article by a *Fag Rag*'er who had attended the master's lectures in Paris, the group rejected it and the author left. Eventually, in *Fag Rag* number 29, Mike Riegle and Giles Barbedette translated from *Le Gai Pied* number 1 (April 1979) Foucault's "The Simplest of Pleasures [Suicide]." The French celebrity's article sparkles with a wonderful irony and wit—quite alien to his many Anglophone imitators.

Typesetting underwent a revolution parallel to gay liberation; the connections between the easy access to mass production printing and the sixties movements are intimate. Without mimeograph, xerox, and photographic negatives for printing plates, the underground press would have been very different. The continuing changes in production between 1970 and 1990 have been awesome. Beginning in 1453 when moveable type was invented, type was set by hand; since 1886, newspapers have used Linotype machines. But suddenly, as microchips and other technologies have flourished, the number of people who can put out a paper has vastly multiplied. In 1970, *Fag Rag* had access to the *Old Mole* offices, which included a rented IBM Composer, a machine that had a changeable typeset ball (like the later Selectric) but that could also justify columns (right and left sides flush); to justify, the typist had to type each line twice (once ragged right edge; second time even right edge). We never justified. Everyone struggled through learning the machine; those who knew how to use it passed what they had learned on to others.

When we lost the office and the Composer, we had to fend for ourselves. By a clever improvisation, Mitzel rented an IBM executive office typewriter that used a carbon ribbon and had limited proportional spacing. We then laid out the typewritten pages and had them reduced about 10 percent in size. For *Fag Rag* number 12, we returned to an IBM Composer. David Stryker had worked many years as a typesetter at the reactionary Boston *American Herald* but, in the mid-seventies, seeing the need for typesetting in the gay community, he started a part-time business. Ken Sanchez, who worked for Stryker, was able to type out *Fag Rag* text (with some volunteer help) after hours; we paid a dollar an hour for using the machine. Stryker's business expanded and he bought a Compugraphic, a machine that uses a computer linked to a camera, which produces typeset galleys. Stryker charged basically at cost per issue; still our typesetting costs quadrupled. He saw it as a sacrifice for the movement; others saw it as an inroad of capitalism. The Compugraphic was more expensive and more complicated; only a few *Fag Rag*'ers learned to use it. In one case, when we had typeset John Wieners' *Behind the State Capitol* (1975) on a movement Compugraphic, the entire text faded and had to be reset (because the developer had not been properly changed).

After the 1982 fire, most of the relief money raised was used to buy a used Compugraphic machine, which was used until 1990, when *GCN* bought a new desktop publishing assembly and dumped the Compugraphic in the famous dustbin of history. I learned to use the Compugraphic twice but never quite mastered it. Desktop publishing almost instantly wipes away all the skills learned on the Compugraphic; and a great gap still exists between the computer-literate and those who lack access to the machines and the communication they allow. Even those skilled in one program or machine find their learning constantly obsolete with so-called upgrades and seldom find training transferrable to other machines and programs.

Page layout skills have been easier to learn and easier to share. Each page has to be assembled from galley text, photographs, headlines, page numbers, graphics, and other material. From the beginning, everyone working on the paper has taken pages for layout, sometimes in teams, sometimes alone. *Fag Rag* layouts have been in the best tradition of the underground, and each person in the collective has developed his own style of layout. The unmistakable handwritings—wild, teasing, timid, mean, giggling, quick, slow, sad, lingering, longing, panting, loving, humping, pumping, each quite distinctive—have so far always worked together.

Still, there have been some bitter divisions over layout. In *Fag Rag* number 2, some members of the collective felt the cover was too Anglo; others thought it was an exciting long-haired ideal. We finally agreed to run the cover, but we also struggled to include more non-Anglo images in the paper. Visual artists have often been uncomfortable with these discussions; they have also resented the lack of respect shown for the integrity of their work. Too often artists have felt that others have seen their work as only illustrative. For one issue, a particularly verbal person suggested that the editorial for the issue appear on the cover without any graphic. Covers have always been agreed on by the whole staff through consensus.

Printers have posed many contradictions for *Fag Rag*. Once we had decided to print in thousands of copies, we could neither do the printing ourselves nor use movement printers. Thus anti-capitalists faced off with the capitalists. A collective had to mesh with authoritarian bosses. They distrusted us (even though we paid in upfront cash) because *Fag Rag* carried no advertisements. One of the printers almost pleaded with us to take ads, do more issues, make more money. They also found it difficult to work with a whole group of people who had to make final decisions about color plates, corrections on the negatives, number of copies to be printed, and other issues. In fact, we all had to quickly learn the mechanism of presenting "camera-ready copy," "screening," "half-toning," "windows," "double-burning," "color plate," "negatives," and other mysteries of the web press. Mitzel even signed up for an adult education class on printing and we all learned to share our knowledge.

Printers exercise a great power of censorship. Supposedly they are only in business to make money, but about a dozen printers who have refused to print us have themselves gone bankrupt. A half dozen who have printed us have also gone bankrupt. Before *Fag Rag* began publishing, movement papers in Boston had used a sympathetic printer but by the time of our first issue it had gone out of business (sabotaged by the FBI, according to some reports). One printer refused to print *Fag Rag* because we carried a picture of a nude black man. Another printer submitted our copy to their most conservative daily communicant bookkeeper and asked her opinion. As luck would have it, her son had been a sexual partner of mine and we were good friends. She knew he was gay and she was grateful for support and legal help the son had received in a rest area arrest. She reported back that *Fag Rag* did not represent her way of life, but that she believed it should not be censored. We had less luck with a Brooklyn printer, which had a pressman who was a Jehovah's Witness (with a *Playboy* pinup on his desk) who threatened to shut the plant down if they printed such filth. Another printer claimed that "high school girls" had to handle the material; another said "Bibles run through those presses," without asking our opinion of bibles. In fact, one large midwestern plant told us that "Christians regularly pass through their plant" and they could not risk exposing them to *Fag Rag*.

The contradictions between a revolutionary rag and the market economy appeared even more markedly once the paper had been printed and we faced distribution. For the first issue, we debated whether to give it away free or to charge. By compromise we settled on ten cents as a fair price for those who could afford to pay. (The most recent issue costs $3.99.) Like Boston's other underground papers, we sold papers on the streets and at gay events. In June 1971 following the New York Gay Pride March, we took home two hundred dollars in dimes. We offered subscriptions for anyone who wanted to send a contribution or a request. Later we offered lifetime subscriptions for five dollars. (Currently we ask ten dollars for four issues.)

In *Fag Rag*'s first twenty years, about half our income has come from subscriptions and half from sales either on the streets or in bookstores. In 1970, few bookstores would carry *Fag Rag*. Outlets run by straights have never been very favorable. One corner store in Harvard Square took a stack of *Fag Rags*, but when we came to collect on the bill they physically threatened us. Another porno store on New York's 42nd Street took the papers, but on the four or so times we came to collect we were told that only the manager could pay us but that he was not there. Another bookstore in Atlanta (now out of business) said they couldn't sell the paper because it contained pictures of black men. Consequently, we were overjoyed as the example of the Oscar Wilde Memorial Bookstore in

New York began to spread and more and more lesbian and gay liberation bookstores have opened their doors. Gay publications helped the gay bookstores and gay bookstores helped gay publications.

CONTINUING STRUGGLES

Fag Rag may have entered the market economy and discovered a niche in that market: sex, radical, national (if not international), male, revolutionary, literary, and irregular. *Fag Rag* has never faltered in trying to find a voice for faggots and their culture. A new Berkeley, California magazine (*OUTLOOK*) by contrast promised in its prospectus "Something attractive and engaging enough that I could even hand it to a politician—or my mother—and say, 'Here, this is what gay people are thinking about these days.'" Thus the family and state become hidden censors; only god (the third part of the fascist trinity) is not mentioned. Among gay publications, respectability means money and acceptance; but most faggots bypass such sanitized writings as they look for "something a little more meaty." An issue of *Fag Rag* number 9 was placed in the Grolier Bookstore (a store devoted entirely to poetry); a priest picked it up and dropped it in shock when he opened it to Roger Stearns' drawing of a bathhouse orgy.

Fag Rag has never tried to placate our enemies nor to soft-pedal our sexuality. In 1973, I drove some cast members to the University of New Hampshire where Jonathan Ned Katz's play *Come Out!* was being presented. In return for the favor, I had been told I could sell copies of *Fag Rag*. When an official of the university intervened, I said I'd just give copies away; when he denied that, I said, "Let's just pass them out as program notes" (since the issue contained a review of the play). Police spies at the performance rushed copies of the paper to Governor Meldrin Thompson, the Manchester *Union Leader*, and Warren Rudman, then the state's attorney general. Mitzel's witty article, "How to Proselytize," caught their fancy. The governor demanded an immediate probe of *Fag Rag*, which he called "one of the most loathsome publications in the English language." (Presumably he considered all publications not in English as loathsome.) The *Union Leader* called for the immediate expulsion of all homosexuals at the university, and in an editorial publisher William Loeb suggested that god might destroy Durham, New Hampshire, as he had Sodom and Gomorrah. *Fag Rag* was labeled "unspeakably filthy," and the "most rotten, filthiest, degrading piece of literature" they'd ever seen.

The literary/movement dialectic in *Fag Rag* played itself out most pointedly in grant applications. Today, after the barbarian invasion of the eighties, few remember the days of the early seventies when the NEA (National Endowment for the Arts) began dribbling funds into African-American, women's, and gay publishing. To apply for a grant from the federal government violates fundamental anarchist principles. Lawrence Ferlinghetti of City Lights Books denounced the NEA money as contaminated and contaminating. The money, he said, could be seen as a bribe to buy out militancy and divert revolutionary energies into safer "literary" projects. The arts could be kept on a leash. Publications once dependent on the fed's trough could be brought to heel by leash tightening when the rebels began to get out of control.

Those opting for grants argued that the excluded should demand what was rightfully their own and that, while the government money was contaminated, so were all money transactions. Thus City Lights Books might not take grants but they did charge for the books and magazines that they published. In their dealings with *Fag Rag*, the bookstore acted like most other straight bookstores: suspicious of gay publications, slow to pay, and reluctant to display.

Those seeking grant support found no easy welcome in the NEA. First *Fag Rag* approached the money trough through NEA's subsidiary, CCLM (Coordinating Council of Literary Magazines), which itself was a somewhat defanged organization, less radical than COSMEP (Committee of Small Magazine Editors and Publishers), and thus funded by the NEA. In a 1974 letter to COSMEP, William Phillips, founder of the anti-Communist *Partisan Review* and then chair of CCLM, claimed that CCLM's "aim is to respect and reward quality." "Quality" was then and has remained a term to describe straight, white, middle-class literature, whose "quality" excludes the African, Asian, Native American, women's, or gay voices. CCLM nonetheless played a mediating role between the NEA and foundations which, in Phillips' words, "are afraid of the radical, experimental nature of magazines and 'dirty' things in them."

In 1972, *Fag Rag* applied to the CCLM and they threw our application away (or claimed never to have received it). In 1973, we tried again and were turned down; we then offered (threatened) to appear in person to appeal our gay rage case; consequently, *Fag Rag* received grants in the fall of '74, '75, '76, '77 and in the spring of '80. But the winds of reaction were gathering. In 1976, a new CCLM director had to fight the NEA for funding of little mags. "One of the reasons we were given for the attempt to cut off CCLM's grant," he wrote, "was that its participatory program created too much trouble and turmoil among the membership."

Fag Rag questioned some of the literary standards of the small presses no less than the grand presses. They lived by a system of mutual back-scratching: you support our grant, publication, whatever, we'll support you. In order to counter some of those politics, *Fag Rag* adopted a rule of not printing reviews or interviews since they were too often disguised advertisements or at best celebrity self-promotion. That rigorously pure stand soon gave way to our sponsoring an affiliate organization, the *Boston Gay Review*. Although the two rags were independent, they overlapped and the initial issues of *BGR* were funded entirely by *Fag Rag*. On its own the *BGR* sold slowly. I asked the manager at the East Side Bookstore (which was then selling about a hundred *Fag Rag*s per issue) why they hadn't sold a single issue of *BGR*. "The word 'gay?'" I asked. "No," he answered, "the 'Boston' kills it."

Boston Gay Review published many reviews of lesbian and gay books. The review set a high standard in reviews of poetry, which have only recently been equaled by *The James White Review* from Minnesota. And while the CCLM shut off *Fag Rag* for causing too much "trouble and turmoil," they funded *BGR*. The secret guideline for publications then included tranquility (synonymous with "quality" in their rhyme schemes), but they misread poetry who think it incompatible with agitation.

Not only did the group who put out *BGR* overlap with *Fag Rag*, but the two groups also overlapped with the Good Gay Poets. William Burroughs and John Giorno had done a benefit reading in Boston for *Fag Rag*, which had led to the publication of a volume of my own and of Sal Farinella's *San Francisco Experience*; that book had then led to John Wieners' *Behind the State Capitol* in 1975. In 1976, the Good Gay Poets received a grant directly from the NEA to publish six books of poetry. That was followed in 1978 with another NEA grant to *Fag Rag* for the publication of Arthur Evans' *Witchcraft and the Gay Counterculture*, which had appeared serially in *Fag Rag*.

One of the problems of government grants and of government surveillance has been the tracking. Even CCLM had to report in 1974: "We've been audited four times, and we are an open book to the [National] Endowment [for the Arts], the New York State Council on the Arts, the Internal Revenue Service, the General Accounting Office, the New York State Department of Social Services and the New York State Attorney General's Office." Files! Files! These not only generate information for government agencies but they also train the people to think in terms of double entry bookkeeping. Andy Warhol's clever exploitation of the government demand for monitoring his life resulted in his delightfully name-filled and profit-making diaries. But the vitiated qualities of our lives and our literatures are revealed in his telling pages; they would have us all become accountants for the office of budget and management.

Whatever the merits of grants, government funds for *Fag Rag* ceased quite abruptly with the election of Ronald Reagan. Reagan simplified the NEA so that artists could clearly identify it and the government as their out-and-out enemy. All magazines and artists should be self-supporting. To become too dependent (whether on government or foundation or spouse or patron) weakens efforts to become self-supporting. *Fag Rag* for better or worse depends on the voluntary labor of its members and on its readers. Publication for the fun of it. The *Fag Rag* number 27/28 editorial defended "self-indulgence, living our lives for ourselves, following our own desires, passions, feelings. The opposite to self-indulgence is denial, the theme of all gay oppression."

Fag Rag's relationship to prisons has in many ways defined the publication; we have not said no to grant support; we have not said no to individuals who have donated money to keep us afloat. But we have appealed beyond them to a wider audience, which too many other publications avoid. In every issue we have published writings from prisoners; and the paper is sent free to those incarcerated in prison, mental hospitals, or the armed forces. In 1972, among our demands at the Miami conventions was that "All lesbians or faggots now imprisoned for any 'sex crime' (except rape) should be released immediately from brigs, mental hospitals or prisons. They should be compensated at $2.50 an hour for each hour of confinement and all records of their incarcerations should be destroyed." The group has taken up the cases of many prisoners, such as Eddie Rastillini, who was arrested in 1970 on trumped up boy-love charges, and then killed in prison under so-called "suspicious conditions." The Massachusetts Civil Liberties Union refused even to consider his case and another more conservative gay group maintained that he was where he belonged.

The link between the sex radicals of *Fag Rag*, the movement of Chairman Mao, and the more acceptable gay movement is now epitomized in Mike Riegle who holds together the Red Book Prison Project, the *GCN* Lesbian/Gay Prisoner Project, and the *Fag Rag*. (He is also office manager for *GCN*.) Prisoners are not likely soon to take a cruise to the Caribbean, take in a play in New York, or buy a new waterfront condominium on the Pacific coast. You don't need a market researcher to tell you that they won't buy many cases

of Chilean wines or new cars. *Fag Rag* doesn't pretend to "help" prisoners, but it does provide a place where this gay voice can speak and be heard by other prisoners. Freddie Greenfield jumped from parole onto the collective and was the poetry editor for the next decade, until his death in 1989. His own book, *Were You Always a Criminal?*, was published by *Fag Rag* just before he died. At one COSMEP meeting in Philadelphia at a workshop on prisoner writings, one editor complained of the "poor quality" of writings from prisoners, and said if they just sent in something good it could be published. Half facetiously, I answered, "If you want to raise the quality of prison-writing then you should do some time."

The vision of the sixties was that the old world had died, that the divisions between good (quality, rich) and bad (poor, oppressed) could no longer hold. Some said the first shall be last and the last first; the more secular saw every threat not from the wretched of the earth but from the established powers, who controlled the press and used it to crush life, creation, and beauty. Fewer people have given up than they would like us to believe; and those who say the sixties are dead are only saying their prayers. To understand why we have struggled, you need to feel that continuing hope for a new world, which denied will only rise again. In May 1960, I went on my first march against Woolworth's segregated lunch counters; that November, I wrote the following prison/out of prison poem.

MILLENNIUM

tongue clog
drain fountain
bow broken
bed shaken
strictly still
stiff legs running

one day
love lick
lasts only
until passed

sun shadows spin
pieces disintegrate
gold leaves fallen
worm chocked apple
sudden sparrow dead
prison lock melting

BOSTON BIBLE BURNING[1]

Everything that we are
we owe to each other.
What we are
we owe in no way
to the straight society around us.
(Cheers)
I have a Harvard Ph.D., and I teach at Boston State
College: they say I'm not fit to teach gay history:
I have here the committee report calling me unqualified.
I have here my Harvard diploma.
They are worth only burning.
(Cheers for the burning papers)
In today's march, we passed by the John Hancock
Insurance and the Prudential Insurance buildings: these
companies have one hundred, two hundred, a thousand
times more space than all the gay bars and all the gay
organizations in Boston.
I have here an insurance policy and a dollar bill.
This is what they're worth: Burning.
(Cheers at the flames!)
I have here the text of the crimes against chastity,
Chapter 272, Verse 32 of the Massachusetts Criminal
Code:
"Whoever commits the abominable and detestable crime
against nature, either with mankind or with a beast,
shall be punished by imprisonment in the state prison
for not more than twenty years."
The laws of the state against us are only worth burning.
(Cheers and shouts of Burn it! burn it!)
I have here the Bible, Leviticus, Chapter 20 says: "If
a man also lie with mankind, as he lieth with a woman,
both of them have committed an abomination: they shall
surely be put to death; their blood shall be upon them."
And "A man also or woman that hath a familiar spirit,
or that is a wizard, shall surely be put to death: they
shall stone them with stones: their blood shall be upon
them."
*(Cheers and shouts of Burn it! Burn it! combine with,
No, no, Not the Bible: you can't burn the bible) after
the Bible drops into the flames and ignites, an excited
demonstrator grabs and stamps on it with his feet.)*

Nine million witches have been burnt to death under
that verse. And how many gay people we will never
know, but the word "faggot" comes from tying us to
the feet of the nine million witches as they burned to

death, which is what it means to say "burn a faggot."
So, when Anita Bryant quotes those verses, she's
talking about our MURDER!

WE CANNOT COMPROMISE; WE CANNOT SINK
INTO RESPECTABILITY. Some among us may think
you don't have to worry.

those who are Christian can blame our troubles on the
atheists and Jews

those who are rich can blame our problems on the poor

those who are white can blame the Black and Third
World peoples who are in struggle

those who are conservatives can blame the radical

those who are well-dressed can blame the sloppy
dressers

those who are educated can blame the uneducated

those who are alcoholics can blame the sober

those in their closets can blame the out-front for our
troubles

those who have sex in private can blame those in public
places

those who are monogamous can blame the promiscuous

those who are celibate can blame the sexual

those who are bisexual can say they only did it for a
lark.

We cannot remain alone and terrorized and
divided. Because we face a test: a test to see who
among us is the weakest, who among us will go first,
who among us will be destroyed first.
Some say let the weirdos go, and we will be safe.
Perhaps let the radicals go, others say, Send Susan Saxe
to jail. *(Shouts of "Free Susan Saxe!")* Some say send
the pedophiliacs to jail. Some say send the pornographers to jail.

But when the time comes, we are not going to be asked what degrees we have, how rich we are, who we know or what we have accomplished. They will only ask, "Are you queer?" And when they come for the queers, they are going to come for us all. So. WE MUST COME TOGETHER OR WE WILL SURELY BE DESTROYED.

NOTE

1. Reprinted from *Fag Rag* no. 20 (Winter 1977): 31.

— CHARLEY SHIVELY —

THE KUDZU: BIRTH AND DEATH IN UNDERGROUND MISSISSIPPI

David Doggett

Doggett is a molecular biologist engaged in basic research on aging at the Center for Gerontological Research of the Medical College of Pennsylvania in Philadelphia. He grew up in Mississippi, where he was involved in the civil rights movement in the sixties. He was the Mississippi organizer for the Southern Student Organizing Committee (SSOC) and a founder of *The Kudzu* in 1968. After leaving Mississippi in 1972 he was a freelance photographer in various places in the Southeast. He lived for two years in Nashville, where he did construction work and played bluegrass and country music (dobro and pedal steel guitar). In 1975 he went back to school to study biology at the University of Tennessee. He received a Ph.D. in molecular biology from the University of Southern California in Los Angeles and has done post-doctoral study at Harvard University, the Wistar Institute, and the University of Pennsylvania. His wife, Susan, is a Connecticut Yankee and a pediatrician, and they have two small children, Max and Charlotte.

Yes there was an underground press in Mississippi in the sixties. How could there not be writers in the land of Faulkner, Tennessee Williams, Richard Wright, and Eudora Welty? We called our paper *The Kudzu* after the notorious vine that grows over old sheds, trees, and telephone poles throughout the South. How did it come about that a bunch of Mississippi white kids, descended from rednecks, slave owners, and Bible-thumpers, published for four years in the state's capital a running diatribe of social, economic, and political revolution, a proclamation of sexual liberation, illegal drugs, and heretical mysticism? How does anyone, anywhere rise above the overpowering flow of one's native culture, the suffocating, vise-like grip of the familial and communal, birth-to-death universe view? Why and how is the swim upstream begun, and if it is abandoned, why? Such faltering steps are the progress of human ideas.

Since it is the beginnings and the ending of this phenomenon that hold the most fascination, I have chosen to go into some background history leading up to the founding of *The Kudzu*, most of it from a personal perspective. I have also included some discussion of national events, such as the disintegration of the Southern Student Organizing Committee and Students for a Democratic Society, because I believe that ultimately these events were involved in the demise of not only *The Kudzu* but the entire underground press.

From today's perspective, the fifties and early sixties were sealed in an unbelievably complete and rigid conformity, a straitjacket of convention in every area of life, which had been reinforced and tightened on our parents by the desperation of the depression, the horrors of World War II, the harsh threat of totalitarian communism, and the doomsday fear of thermonuclear destruction. Our generation knew none of this. Even The Bomb had been around since we were born; it was just part of the backdrop of life. The straitjacket didn't fit us and we slipped out of it. It was simply inevitable that such a smothering blanket of convention would be rebelled against by such a different generation as ours, even in Mississippi.

SWEET HOME MISSISSIPPI

All the horror stories about Mississippi are true, and more; yet while the reactionary face of Mississippi has appeared monolithic at times, there have always been some few, white and black, who have struggled with progressive ideas. And in spite of its notoriety, in many ways Mississippi is like other places in this country, more so now than before. Mississippi gained some ground in the Kennedy and Johnson years, and the rest of the nation has lost some ground during the Nixon-Ford-Reagan-Bush years. But before the sixties, there were things about Mississippi that were truly different. Mississippi was extreme. Segregation was state law. Most whites openly professed white supremacy, right-wing militaristic patriotism, and fundamentalist Christianity. They also had repressive, Victorian sexual attitudes and were oppressively anti-intellectual. Intellectual activity threatened the simple-minded prejudices of the lower class, and for the middle and upper classes thinking out loud was simply considered impolite. These attitudes were enforced by beatings, lynchings, shootings, and bombings.

I grew up in several small towns in North Mississippi. My father was a Methodist minister, my mother was an elementary school teacher. My first memories are of several small towns in the Mississippi Delta. The Delta is a flood plain that lies between Memphis and Vicksburg. At that time it was dominated by cotton plantations, and over half the population was black. I went to grammar school in Indianola, home of bluesman B.B. King. I went to junior high school east of the Delta in Oxford, home of William Faulkner and the University of Mississippi, Ole Miss. We moved from Oxford a few months before James Meredith entered Ole Miss and became the first black person to attend a white school in Mississippi. That accomplishment required a pitched battle by the national guard, in which a reporter was killed. I graduated from Elvis Presley's old high school in Tupelo, in northeast Mississippi.

As a small boy, growing up in small town Mississippi had been a Mark Twain-Norman Rockwell heaven, with long summers spent romping through the bayous and forests and fields. But as I entered the world of ideas in high school and college, Mississippi became a hated prison from which to escape. I loved classical music, jazz, and folk music, but on the radio was only country music and rockabilly. I read Bertrand Russell and Jean Paul Sartre; but my father was the only adult I ever met outside of a college campus who knew who they were.

In some other decade I, like so many other southerners, would have simply left the South as soon as possible and headed for one of the nation's urban, intellectual centers. But in the sixties something different happened. People from the urban, intellectual centers came to Mississippi. So I stayed for a while and struggled with Mississippi's extremism. While in college in the mid-sixties I joined up with the black civil rights struggle, the Movement.

My family went back before the Civil War in the South; some owned slaves; some were too poor for slaves. Half of my male ancestors at the time of the Civil War died defending the Confederacy. But by my grandparents' generation much of the old failed heritage had given way to strong belief in religion and education. My parents were college educated liberals. For them racism was unchristian. The religion didn't stick with me, but the fervor for good works did. So if by college I was a thoroughgoing atheist, nevertheless, I was passionately concerned with the secular struggle for moral progress, for freedom, equality, justice, and an end to economic disparity. God may have been dead, but without moral struggle history would be meaningless, just the daily rat race ending in a grave full of dirt. Racism was the product of a history that was not meaningless to me. Slavery and the fight to maintain it was a catastrophe for the South, white as well as black, and had taken lives and fortunes from my family. Racism was the vestige of this curse, the old evil still alive, just as Faulkner told of it. For Faulkner's writing to Mississippians is really not fiction but a more or less straightforward telling of our antecedents.

ANTECEDENTS, I

In 1964 I entered Millsaps College in Jackson, Mississippi's capital. Millsaps is a small Methodist affiliated liberal arts college. It has a good academic standing regionally and was a tradition in my family. All of my father's five brothers and sisters went there. One of my uncles had been editor of the school paper in the thirties and had done some verbal sparring with the reactionary Jackson daily papers. My father was on the board of trustees while I was there. During my first year, I joined a fraternity, dated a cheerleader, and hung out at jazz clubs. But it was an act I had no stomach for. My sophomore year I resigned the fraternity and moved into a dorm room with Lee Makamson, the only other overtly liberal student on campus. Lee was a political science major from a working class Jackson family. He said that, if he had been alive during the early days of the labor movement, he would have wanted to be involved in that great moment of history. So now, in his own time, he wanted to be involved in the civil rights movement. Together we made contacts with civil rights activists in Jackson.

From the beginning of my politically active years, I believed that most white people in Mississippi, like most Americans, were good people in their hearts. But they were kept isolated and ignorant by the circumstances of history and the conservative leadership of society. The only solution to the problem was massive doses of new information. Writing and publishing were the keys. Together Lee and I published a few issues of a mimeographed newsletter we called *The Free Southern Student*, which we mailed out to a handful of students around the state, white and black. It consisted mostly of civil rights news. But this really didn't catch on and we were pretty much ostracized at Millsaps, which like most schools in the South was still languishing in the apolitical, silent fifties.

That same year, I became associated with the Southern Student Organizing Committee (SSOC, pronounced "sock"). SSOC was to the Deep South what Students for a Democratic Society (SDS) was to the rest of the country. In fact SSOC and SDS became formally affiliated as "fraternal organizations," whereby members of each organization sat as token members on the other's governing council. SSOC had been founded a couple of years earlier by white southern students who were originally in the Student Nonviolent Coordinating Committee, SNCC, which was at the militant forefront of the civil rights movement. With SNCC oriented toward the black community, it became clear that there needed to be a special organization oriented toward young southern whites.

SSOC was headquartered in Nashville and also had strong groups in Atlanta and North Carolina. Like SDS, SSOC was not a political party with a set ideology, but rather a catalyst for direct action for various leftist and progressive causes and a facilitator for public education about these ideas. SSOC's main activities were publishing literature and holding conferences that brought together people from all over the South. The original focus, mostly civil rights, gradually gave way to discussions of the war in Vietnam and U.S. imperial-

ism, women's liberation, labor issues, and all the other progressive issues of the day.

My first big action in the civil rights movement was the James Meredith march from Memphis, Tennessee, to Jackson, Mississippi, in Spring 1966. Led by Stokely Carmichael of SNCC and other Movement leaders, a rag-tag group of whites and blacks marched through the Yazoo-Mississippi Delta between Memphis and Jackson. I had lived in several small towns in the Delta while growing up. The main purpose of the march was to encourage voter registration among local blacks. The cry of "black power" made its debut on this march. The climax came just above Jackson in Canton where we were teargassed by the Mississippi Highway Patrol and many people were beaten with billy clubs and gun butts. I was quick enough to escape unscathed, but I will never forget the sickening sight.

I passed that summer in Jackson working with Jan Hillegas, a northern transplant who serviced the Movement leadership and civil rights attorneys with political research and paralegal work.

TROUBLE IN SDS, PART I

At the end of the summer I went to Clear Lake, Iowa, for the national convention of SDS. While the usual topics of civil rights, the Vietnam War, and U.S. imperialism were discussed there, the most heated debate centered around an issue that had great foreboding. Membership in SDS was going ballistic at that time and it was clearly becoming the biggest and most active student organization on the American Left. Old Left, doctrinaire organizations such as the Communist Party (CP) and the Progressive Labor Party (PL) cast jaundiced eyes on SDS and saw a grand opportunity for recruitment and manipulation. Without declaring their affiliations, these people were attempting to take over SDS at the local and national levels, and were trying to enter their party lines into the SDS agenda. There was a motion to require SDS members to reveal their affiliations. The people with such affiliations claimed this would be dangerous given the anti-Communist environment in the country. SDS leaders pointed out that the FBI and the government certainly knew these affiliations, so only the SDS membership was in the dark. CP and PL cried "red-baiting." "How can that be?" responded the SDS leadership. "We are the ones being persecuted here, we are the real Communists, you guys are a bunch of failed Stalinist and Maoist hacks."

The danger was not merely that some of the conservative Old Left agenda would be foisted onto SDS at the national level, but that miring meetings in tedious parliamentary battles over the old failed dogmatisms would turn away the thousands of middle American college students who were being attracted to SDS because they wanted more participatory democracy. But CP and PL practiced dogmatic centralism. It was a case of fundamentally opposing world views. Nevertheless, SDS was an insecure "New Left" organization and was cowed by the redbaiting epithet. The move to require disclosure of outside affiliations failed to carry and the issue went unresolved. It was a mere opening skirmish in a protracted struggle that would end in disaster for everyone involved.

ANTECEDENTS, II

In the fall I was back at Millsaps College in Jackson studying sociology and cultural anthropology. That year Millsaps became the first school in the state to voluntarily integrate. In a very low key manner four black students entered Millsaps. Some minor harassment surrounded this courageous act; most memorable was an incident in which one of the black students' tires were slashed and my buddy Lee Makamson helped change the tire in front of a jeering crowd of fraternity boys. But Lee had grown disinterested in publishing, so alone I published a single issue of a newsletter called *The Mockingbird*, a play on the official Mississippi state bird. The newsletter generated little interest, and I didn't feel like carrying on completely alone.

Shortly, however, a new dynamic arose, the hippie movement. While the civil rights movement and the New Left had been my only means of escape from the straitjacket of Mississippi, increasingly those few young people in Jackson who might have joined me grew long hair and played rock music instead. Not that they felt no kinship with the Movement, but integration was moving along without their help, was actually moving faster than anyone had expected, and black separatism and the violence of ghetto riots estranged sympathetic whites. Also, the New Left leaned more and more toward a theoretical and rhetorical approach that intimidated all but the most intellectually oriented young people. Besides, the new hippie movement was far more glamorous. So, during my last two years at Millsaps, sex, drugs, and rock 'n' roll took precedence over political activism among those few young people in Jackson inclined toward rebellion. The straitjacket fifties were finally giving way to the Beatles and the Stones, the Byrds and Hendrix, grass and acid, miniskirts and the Pill, even in Mississippi.

One incident alone during this period brought the emotional impact of the civil rights struggle temporarily back to the forefront. In the spring of 1967, a sequence of loosely organized events surrounding student protest about traffic passing through the center of the predomi-

nantly black Jackson State College campus culminated in the police shooting a local black civil rights worker, Benjamin Brown. A number of facts tended to discredit the official story that Ben was part of a street crowd attacking the police. In fact he was shot in the back. At best he appeared to be a victim of typical police overreaction; at worst he had simply been recognized as someone associated with the Movement and murdered by a cop.

The following morning several of us at Millsaps made up some quick placards and organized a march to city hall. We were prepared to march with as few as five students, and were amazed to find twenty people lining up to march. Now, this may not seem like many people, but only two of us had ever been in a political demonstration before. And this was Mississippi. Everyone on the march was calling forth completely unknown consequences at the hands of school, family, friends, future employers, and the Ku Klux Klan, not to mention the police, who the night before had gunned down a man in public.

It was the first demonstration of this type in memory, maybe ever, carried out solely by Mississippi whites, and it was a little different from your usual Movement march. The president of the junior class, who was also a first string lineman on the football team, took my placard away from me and led the march, a gesture that I suppose was meant to show it was not just the usual hippie-politicos who were outraged about the killing. I guess I should have been insulted, but of course I wasn't. And the campus karate champ strolled along beside the line to protect us from any threatening bystanders we might encounter. The march went without incident. The police escorted us in a routine manner, almost politely. The public reacted with confusion and shock more than hostility.

When we arrived back at Millsaps, practically the entire student body turned out in front of the student union. Many of them were concerned that we might have been taken to represent the entire school. We replied that we never intended to give that impression, but did anyone really want to defend the killing? There were a few apologists for the police actions, but most people knew in their hearts what had really happened. There was a lot of heated debate and the scene became intense as white Mississippi confronted itself. That evening, all of our families were dragged into the turmoil when the march made NBC's evening news. The publicity also threw a kink in the school's big drive to raise funds from conservative alumni to match some promised Ford Foundation money.

That march was a powerful experience for all of us. Then something with implications for the future happened. Nothing. As organizers we blew it. We were unable to follow through with any permanent organization to capitalize on this catalyzing event. Virtually none of the new people on the march wanted to become part of the Movement, or SSOC, or the New Left. They wanted no part of our theorizing and rhetoric, our conferences and our fervent writings. The excitement settled back to the previous apolitical stupor.

TROUBLE IN SDS, PART II

That summer, while working again for Freedom Information Service, I went to an SDS workshop on power structure research at the University of Chicago and to an SDS leadership retreat in rural Michigan. The retreat was scheduled immediately before the SDS national convention in Ann Arbor and was supposed to be a strategy planning session for dealing with the Progressive Labor problem, but Abbie Hoffman showed up along with the Diggers from California, and SDS was harangued for being too stodgy and political while masses of young people were becoming hippies and Yippies. SDS was catching it from two sides, from the Old Left-style dogmatists, and from the anarchistic Yippies who wanted to revolutionize even the way political organizing was done.

Back down south, SSOC had a meeting to elect a new chair. The founding members of SSOC had by this time moved on to other activities and had left a leadership vacuum. One of the two candidates was Tom Gardner, a sincere but straight left-liberal. The other was Ed Clark, a PL hack from New Orleans. A third group led by Mike Welch of Memphis had recently moved into the Nashville office as staff members. They asked me to consider running. I was flattered but disbelieving. I had one more year of school, I said; the chair has always been a full-time position. That would be no problem, they said; it would be good for SSOC's image to have a student chair. What would my platform be, they wanted to know? I was clear on that. I would be Yippie-like; I would bring SSOC out of its straight political past into the wave of the future, the Youth Culture—sex, drugs, rock 'n' roll, and New Left politics. They weren't very happy about that, but they had to defeat Ed Clark of PL, and they had some problem with Tom Gardner that was never clear to me. However, it was all to naught, because the majority stayed true to SSOC's roots and voted in Tom Gardner. It was an odd meeting and I came away perplexed.

THE QUICKENING

That fall at Millsaps the political atmosphere finally began to heat up. We decided to start a "Free University" off campus. Bill Peltz, a cultural anthropol-

ogy instructor who had the year before come from Columbia University, joined the effort. We would have "courses" that would be self-taught discussion groups on everything from revolution to poetry. Someone stole the fraternities' freshman mailing list and we sent out a mailing about the Free University to the entire incoming freshman class. The Millsaps administration ended up with copies of the letter and freaked out, as the vernacular of the time so aptly put it.

A new president, business professor Benjamin Graves, had recently been brought in to kick off the big Ford Foundation matching grant fund drive. He summoned three of us Free University ringleaders to an intimidating meeting of the entire administration and the faculty department heads. There, he began to lecture us at great length about being irresponsible and jeopardizing the fund drive. He had no grounds for any action against us; he just wanted to browbeat us into submission. As he droned on and on, our liberal friends on the faculty shuffled their feet in embarrassment but failed to come to our defense. We could see he did not expect and did not intend to allow a response from us; I realized I had to call his bluff. When he failed to recognize my attempts to respond to his harangue, I interrupted him in mid-sentence and gave an impassioned speech, the gist of which was that fundraising to pay for an education that discouraged free inquiry was a moral travesty against the spirit of the institution and the founding principles of the nation. It was clear we would not be so easily intimidated. The meeting came to a strained conclusion.

The academic dean called up my parents and told them he thought I had mental problems and that they should take me out of school and seek psychiatric help. He even suggested a Jackson psychiatrist. My parents, bless their hearts, didn't go for it. They were having their own problems with my rebelliousness, but they knew I was not insane. We talked it over and decided to again call the administration's bluff. I would be examined by an out-of-town psychiatrist of our own choosing to settle the matter. I visited a psychiatrist in Memphis, where I went through a few standard tests and explained the situation in Jackson. He reassured my parents I was fine and he wrote a letter to the Millsaps administration giving me a clean bill of health.

Thus the Free University got off to a fiery start. Unfortunately it was overly ambitious and fizzled out before the semester was over. Nevertheless, the New Left had finally arrived in Mississippi. In addition to this new political development there was by now a very visible contingent of hippies on campus. In the spring the administration announced their intention not to renew Bill Peltz's contract. The alumni had gotten upset about his research into social change in Mississippi, and the administration was uptight about his fraternization with the most rebellious elements of the student body. In response to this and other issues, a number of us began publishing a little mimeographed publication of satire and comment called *The Unicorn*. Unlike my previous publishing attempts, this one was immensely successful. I'll never forget the experience of walking into the school cafeteria right after the first issue had been circulated and seeing a huge room full of people actively reading our writings.

The trick that made it all so different from our previous attempts at publishing, the trick it took the hippies to teach us, was to break the mold of the political tract, to make the publication more general in appeal and content. We had access to an electronic stencil maker that could copy illustrations, so we had artwork and cartoons. We also included poetry and music commentary. Writers from the censored school paper wrote for us. Everyone on campus read *The Unicorn*. We could have made money if we had sold it instead of giving it away for free. Unfortunately, we couldn't save Bill Peltz's job. He left Millsaps, but stayed in Jackson to set up Southern Media, for the purposes of documenting social change in Mississippi and training local people in documentary techniques. That spring we had an antiwar demonstration involving dozens of students. We called it a Peace Parade, decorated cars with crepe paper, and rode through downtown Jackson like a football homecoming parade.

THE BIRTH

Upon graduation in 1968 I became a full-time organizer for SSOC and was paid a subsistence salary of $15 a week. Underground papers were springing up all across the country, including the South. Atlanta's *Great Speckled Bird* had just started and many of the staff members were old SSOC friends of mine. I decided that my primary mission as an organizer would be to start an underground paper in Jackson. I felt that there were many young people ready to move in Mississippi, but that they were too cut off from what was happening around the country and around the world. It all came back to my belief that information provides the fuel for progress. I went to Atlanta and lived in the basement of the *Bird* office on 14th Street for a month while I learned how to lay out a paper for photo-offset printing. The yet unrecorded Allman Brothers played practically every night at a club down the street.

When I got back to Jackson I tried to line up a printer. Unfortunately, they were all too expensive, and they looked at me funny. I was the first hippie they had ever seen. Finally my Movement contacts put me in touch with a black printer in New Orleans who published *The Louisiana Weekly*, a regional black newspaper. The *Weekly* people were friendly, they let us print on credit, and, most important of all, they couldn't be touched by political pressure from Jackson. The four-hour drive to New Orleans was inconvenient, but it was workable.

When school started up in the fall of 1968, I gathered together about a dozen interested Millsaps students and we started *The Kudzu*. The name came out of a brainstorming session. I forget who suggested it, but once it came up it was favored virtually unanimously. Under the masthead we would run a trailer, "subterranean news from the heart of old Dixie."

At first I was the only full-time staff member; the rest were students. A mainstay of the staff was Cassell Carpenter, a woman whose family owned Dunleith, one of the premiere antebellum mansions of Natchez. My love interest at the time was Peggy Stone, a sophomore also from Natchez. She had long red hair and a rebellious spirit to match my own. We had met the previous year when she entered Millsaps. This year her parents sent her to school in Louisiana to get her away from me. But she came to town on weekends and eventually dropped out of school and moved in with me. Everett Long had transferred over to Millsaps from Mississippi College, a conservative Southern Baptist school. He had just returned from being arrested during the demonstrations at the 1968 Democratic National Convention in Chicago. He was a well-read intellectual as well as a major source of capricious humor in the early *Kudzu*. Mike Kennedy, another source of humor, was a local high school dropout who drove around in an old black Cadillac hearse. Our drug connoisseur was Mike Cassell from Canton. He had recently left New College in Sarasota, Florida, under a political cloud. He worked part-time for the Illinois Central Railroad and two years before had unloaded the tear gas that had been used on us at Canton in the Meredith March. Alan Bennett and Jeff Livesay were budding underclass intellectuals who hung around a lot. Doug and Lynn Rogers dropped out of Millsaps and got married. They had a Volkswagen bus and a Cappucine monkey. Lynn was an artist and poet and Doug was an all-round man. Several other Millsaps students, local high school students, and recent college or high school dropouts hung around and contributed intermittently.

We took out a post office box as our official address, but we had no real office at first. The first issue of *The Kudzu* was laid out on the kitchen table of Cassell Carpenter's off-campus apartment. It was eight pages, tabloid size. Our goal was to publish once or twice a month. Organizationally, the staff was small enough that a maximum of democracy could be practiced. We decided on the content of each issue more or less by consensus. There wasn't much ideological bickering simply because we tried to let everyone involved have some space to write whatever he or she wanted. We ran a fairly typical sixties smorgasbord of spacey hippie ramblings, rock music reviews, cartoons and comics, and straight political coverage of the war in Vietnam, the civil rights movement, labor struggles, and the New Left. Being in Mississippi we were naturally a little tamer than the *Berkeley Barb* or the *Rat* in New York.

There was no specialization on the staff, and no titles were ever listed with our names. People outside of the staff invariably assumed I was the editor, but in fact we never had an official editor. Some people used pen names, some of us used both our real names and pen names, and we sometimes included in the staff box the names of our cats and dogs and completely fictitious people, just to keep the police and FBI guessing. We more or less worked on all phases together throughout the publishing cycle. We would write for a few days and have a meeting or two on what was going in the issue. Unsigned articles were approved by consensus, since responsibility for them fell upon the whole paper. Signed articles were considered to be the sole opinion and responsibility of the signer. Individuals frequently took responsibility for whole pages or double pages of layout. We ran whatever state and local material we could come up with and filled remaining space with national articles from Liberation News Service. We freely ran articles, artwork, and cartoons from other underground papers, which was encouraged by the Underground Press Syndicate. Our production facility consisted of a single IBM Selectric typewriter, the kind with the little rotating ball. We started with one ball and eventually got another one that printed a sort of script italic. The machine had no margin justification or proportional spacing. It was simply an electric typewriter. We took turns typing, everyone considering it one of the more onerous chores. We pasted up the layout with household glue. Typically we finished the layout at 5 o'clock in the morning, then piled in some clap-trap car or VW bus and rushed to New Orleans to make the printer's 9 o'clock deadline. During the press run we would visit with Bob Head and Darlene Fife, the editors of the *NOLA Express*, and partake of the pleasures of hippie New Orleans.

When we got back to Jackson with the new edition, we all hand-addressed the subscriptions and then went out to the campuses and the streets to sell papers. Our initial price was fifteen cents a copy, of which the seller got to keep half. Everybody on the staff gave all the proceeds back to the paper, but there were a few people at the local high schools and at the bigger college campuses around the state who made a little pocket change in the bargain. We started with

no advertising at all, and never got very many ads. Most issues didn't make enough to pay for the press run, much less any staff salaries. If it hadn't been for the SSOC money and periodic donations from my parents, I would have starved.

THE ARRESTS BEGIN

Our first issue made a big splash at Millsaps and a few copies found their way to most college campuses around the state. With our second issue we really took off. Over a dozen arrests of *Kudzu* vendors, including virtually everyone on the staff, were made at a local high school by deputy sheriffs. Actually, the staff never made a conscious decision to sell the paper at high schools, and if the issue had been formally raised we might have decided not to make direct sales there at all. But before the issue was considered, high school students and recent graduates or dropouts started the ball rolling themselves.

At Callaway High School in a suburb where they lived just outside of Jackson, Chuck Fitzhugh, the son of a local Episcopalian rector, and Jimmy Capriotti were selling *The Kudzu*. The principal came out and started jerking the papers out of the hands of students. He then sent for a deputy sheriff who was directing traffic and had the two arrested. They were charged with obstructing traffic, a complete fabrication because they weren't even in the street. Chuck and Cap were released on bail, and the next day the whole staff went back with them to the same high school and attempted to sell papers at the close of the school day. Deputies arrived in force and all eleven of us were arrested. Chuck and Cap were singled out and beaten, although neither was seriously hurt. Bill Peltz, the former anthropology instructor, was there to document the events for Southern Media. While taking photos of the beatings, he was arrested, his camera was taken, and the film was destroyed. No charges were given for any of us, which is improper arrest procedure. When I requested that they state what the charges were, I was picked up and thrown bodily into the back of a sheriff's car. They took us to jail and thought up all the charges later. Eventually all of us were charged with vagrancy and/or blocking traffic. In typical double-think fashion, those who were beaten were charged with assault. Resisting arrest and assaulting an officer were added to my charges, presumably because of my query. My old civil rights attorney friends, with the help of a local liberal attorney, Sebastian Moore, got us out on bail right away.

On the third day following the original arrests, we all went back, accompanied by over twenty additional people, mostly Millsaps students. We sold every paper we had and no arrests were made. We had won, and the publicity was priceless. When the cases went to court the charges were dropped on all but five of us. The officers told a bunch of obvious lies that had no consistency. For one, they all denied having arrested me. The judge gave them a recess to get their stories straight. We put ten witnesses on the stand who all denied the deputies' stories. The judge—who was the state attorney general's brother—upheld the charges; in his concluding speech he claimed *The Kudzu* was a "propaganda sheet" rather than a "real newspaper" and he lamented the lack of respect for law enforcement officers. It was clear we were on trial for the content of the paper, not any illegal actions. The cases were appealed and eventually all the charges were dropped, except the two original obstructing traffic charges. The bond on these, though, was lowered to $25 each, so we forfeited bond rather than waste any further resources on the case. It was really sort of pathetic, sort of a keystone cops action.

The second round of arrests came within a month when four of us were arrested and charged with "pandering to minors." The Jackson city police came at us with crib sheets telling them how to make the arrests. The city felt our use of four-letter words and selling papers to city high school students were grounds for charges. That case eventually made it into federal court before it was dropped. An accurate account of arrests and major incidents of harassment would take a whole book. We averaged several arrests a month somewhere in the state throughout the first year of publication. Occasionally beatings were involved. There was a lot of petty harassment with traffic tickets. We had good lawyers who always got us out of jail promptly and never demanded a fee. A handful of local liberals put up their surburban homes for property bonds when the bail was set high. The charges were invariably dropped. After all, we weren't doing anything illegal. We were just trying to publish a newspaper. Equally as troubling as the arrests were the more personal incidents of harassment. A number of the students associated with the paper were financially cut off by their parents. Some high school kids were expelled from school and sent to military academies.

After initial minor confrontations over free speech the major college campuses in the state became open to us; however, a number of the smaller campuses banned us and we didn't have the resources to open them up. The police visited Cassell Carpenter's landlady and she was promptly evicted. We found other quarters and kept going. The office was nothing but the front room of a small apartment, and several of us slept in two bedrooms in back. We were afraid to sleep in the front room because of bomb threats. We lived a stressful lifestyle that was only overcome by youthful exuberance and comradery. We were charged with "vagrancy" and called lazy hippies, but we worked sixteen hours a day while welcoming a constant stream of out-of-town visitors, as well as a lot of high school runaways, sometimes followed by their parents and cops. We got threatening phone calls all day and night. Once somebody put some shots through our front window. We found the lug nuts loosened on the front wheels of the old VW bus we had bought with SSOC money. On the trips to New Orleans we had lots of breakdowns and a couple of minor wrecks. When *Rolling Stone*, the rock music magazine, did an article on the underground press, they awarded us the most courageous underground paper and said *The Kudzu* had the look of a paper actually printed on the run. The truth to tell, we did not have a slick publication, but we were alive and kicking.

We really didn't think that much about the danger of it all. In those days in Mississippi, just having long hair and doing psychedelic drugs was dangerous. The political danger didn't seem like so much on top of that. We worked hard and played hard. Every Sunday afternoon we joined an informal gathering at Riverside Park in North Jackson for free rock music and revelry. Sometimes at night we would go out with a dozen or more people to hidden clearings along the banks of the Pearl River Reservoir. There we all stripped off our clothes and went swimming and sat nude around a campfire. Once we had a late night nude party in a law office in a downtown highrise. One nude couple rode up and down the elevator opening the door at every floor just to see if there was anyone there to flash.

In the Halls of the SSS

The draft was at its height in those days. Every young male who wasn't in good standing in school was called up. Many tricks were tried to flunk the physical, but few worked. Some people moved to Canada. Liberation News Service (LNS) reported that a memo had been sent around by the Selective Service System telling local draft boards not to draft writers from underground newspapers. Underground papers were springing up inside the armed forces, and apparently the government was trying to minimize that problem. The LNS report sounded too good to be true and we didn't put much stock in it. I had applied for conscientious objector status, but I had not stated that I was an absolute pacifist, and I had not heard from the draft board. Then I was called in to take the dreaded physical. I loaded up a satchel full of *Kudzu*s and headed to the draft site on the appointed morning.

When I got there I began giving out *Kudzu*s to all the guys sitting around waiting for the procedures to start. When the officer in charge came in, he was startled to see a room full of inductees with *Kudzu*s up in front of their faces. He came over to me and told me to stop passing out the papers, and he ended with, "That's an order."

I looked him in the eye and returned, "We have freedom of the press in this country, and I am not in the army yet, and I don't take orders from anyone." The room went silent as we stared at each other. The guy clearly was accustomed to unquestioning obedience. He had no reply. He finally told me to wait there, and he left the room. He came back shortly and asked me to accompany him to see the head of the center. The top dog explained that if I continued to distribute papers they would charge me with disrupting the draft procedures, which carried the standard penalty of five years in prison and a $5,000 fine. He handed me a phone and said I could consult with my lawyers. I called one of our lawyers. He said we could fight it in court but we might lose, so I decided to go along with them. They took my satchel of papers and locked them in a locker until I was ready to leave. Then they assigned a soldier to accompany me through the entire proceedings to hold the stack of registration forms they gave me and to make sure I didn't pass out any more literature. So throughout the physical, I stand there in my underpants like everyone else, except there was this guy in uniform standing beside me holding my forms.

I was in good health, and I gave the IQ test my best shot. I didn't want them to think I was a dummy. But in the appropriate boxes I checked off that I was a bedwetter and a homosexual, and I checked off that I used several illegal drugs, none of which were addictive. They called me into the doctor's office. When I told him I quit wetting the bed as a kid, he marked through that question. Then he asked me if I loved men. I knew they could easily discover I lived with my girlfriend, so I said, "Well, I love men and women." He asked me when the last time was I had slept with a man. In the back of *The Kudzu* office I slept in a room with several men and women, so I said, "Last night." He asked me how often I did drugs. I think I said, "Often." He marked "homosexual drug addict" across the bottom of the form, and said he was sending me in to see the psychologist. I went in to see the psych. He said, "We're giving you a temporary deferment." And that was the last I ever heard from Selective Service. But none of these ploys had worked for others. Several *Kudzu* males went in for physicals within the next year, and none was drafted. Maybe there really was something to the LNS report of the memo against drafting underground press people; too bad more guys didn't take advantage of this de facto deferment.

THE BEGINNING OF THE END

In those first several months of *The Kudzu* activity rolled along at high speed. The future seemed to be opening up to us. Then, just as we were hitting our stride, politics dealt us a low blow. A call came from SSOC headquarters in Nashville. An SDS national convention was coming up in Austin, Texas, in less than a week, and Progressive Labor was campaigning to have SDS break ties with SSOC and denounce SSOC for being liberal and counter-revolutionary. There had been a lot of discussion recently within SSOC about southern consciousness, along the lines of black consciousness and women's consciousness, which had both recently become powerful organizing approaches. PL embraced a doctrine opposed to the separate organization of separate constituencies; consequently, PL opposed black separatist organizations such as the Black Panthers and even opposed national liberation movements such as Vietnam's National Liberation Front. For PL, everyone was either a worker or a capitalist; nothing else mattered.

The old reactionary southern nationalism was very much alive throughout the South. Anyone organizing in the South came up against it constantly. Few southern whites still felt slavery had been a worthwhile cause; but most southern whites had strong feelings about losing the heroic struggle of the Civil War and about the subsequent economic, political, and cultural subjugation of the region. Outside the South a southern accent generally invokes patronizing responses. Southerners are assumed to be poorly educated and ignorant, folksy and unhip. White criminals in movies and TV all too frequently have southern accents and are depraved and dumb. There was discussion in SSOC about trying to turn these pervasive feelings of inferiority and persecution into a progressive force.

Nationalism had been a potent force for revolution from the Bolsheviks to the Viet Cong. In many respects the South could be considered the first colony of Yankee imperialism. The compelling moral cause of abolition had inspired the northern states into the Civil War; but the outcome of the war was not only freedom for the slaves but also the economic subjugation of the agrarian South to the industrial North. Far from being truly free, blacks came out the poorest inhabitants of an economically devastated region.

In one of the civil rights law offices I had worked in, there hung a color-coded map of the United States, which indicated per capita income on a county-by-county basis. The thirteen states of the old Confederacy stood out clearly from the rest of the nation, and the areas of the South with the highest proportions of blacks were the poorest areas of all. It was so striking that I literally stared at the map with my mouth open the first time I saw it. At the time, I had never heard about southern consciousness. I learned an entire history lesson in an instant. The overt chains of slavery had been loosened, but the bootheel of poverty remained firmly on the black man's neck. The sincerity of the nation in this matter is open to question to this day.

This pattern of sending the troops in for a great moral cause and emerging with a colony primed for corporate exploitation and cultural domination is all too familiar in American history. In such respects southerners should feel some empathy with Third World countries, especially, in those days, Vietnam. Was there much difference between General Westmoreland's defoliation of the Vietnamese jungle with agent orange and General Sherman's burnt earth swath from Atlanta to the sea?

This powerful line of thought had tremendous appeal to many of us. A favorite SSOC button was a pair of clasped black and white hands in front of the confederate flag. That design was a spin off of an old SNCC button that had the confederate flag behind a lantern, which symbolized the light of freedom. Yet that flag and those powerful emotions of southern pride had for so long been so thoroughly submerged in the whole sordid quagmire of southern right-wing fanaticism that the prospect of raising the spectre of southern patriotism made us all a little queasy. We looked on the idea with awe; what an organizing tool! But if the beast was called up again, would it not lurch uncontrolled to the right as always before? No one knew the depth of right-wing instincts in the southern mind better than people in SSOC. We had all been in mortal combat with the monster all our lives.

Thus, although the concept had been discussed at the past couple of SSOC conferences, no one in SSOC had fully embraced southern consciousness. At one closed staff meeting, an organizer in South Carolina was criticized for participating in the burning of a confederate flag. Two of the main critics of that action were Lynn Wells, program secretary, and David Simpson, Georgia organizer. Both had taken the discussions about southern consciousness very seriously. But as I remember, no action was taken against the organizer who burned the confederate flag. There was no official SSOC policy in place regarding southern consciousness.

Mike Klonsky, SDS national secretary, had made a hasty junket to Nashville five days before the Austin SDS conference to check out SSOC. Mostly he had talked with Lynn and David. He was tentatively supporting SSOC. Considering the problems facing SDS, I couldn't believe anyone in SDS cared about this issue. I could understand that leftists outside the South might be uncomfortable about southern consciousness, so I would have understood if SDS wanted to issue a policy statement against the idea. But to try to destroy SSOC over an issue that was not official SSOC policy was an absurd overreaction. About a third of SSOC's forty staff members held a harried meeting in Austin the evening before the anti-SSOC resolution was to be introduced. Lynn and David were panicked. They convinced the rest of us that the only response we had was to thoroughly renounce southern consciousness and to put on a big show of being contrite over this grave political error. Wow, had they changed their tune. No one was happy about this response, but nobody felt like jumping up on such short notice and trying to explain the whole history and program of SSOC to a hostile SDS convention either.

When we went into the convention the next day, PL hacks from New York and Boston were everywhere putting out a line that made SSOC out to be on the verge of becoming the next Ku Klux Klan. SDSers from California and Minnesota who had never heard of SSOC before were sucking it right in. I suddenly realized we were in deep shit. Ed Clark and Fred Lacy of New Orleans PL introduced the anti-SSOC motion. PL presented southern consciousness as a major policy of SSOC. They said it was offensive to blacks and was a transparent sham revealing the true unreformed right-wing character of the white southerners in SSOC. They took a bunch of out-of-context liberal statements on various subjects from SSOC literature of years past and said that this is the way these people talk, they are not revolutionaries. Hell, that was the way everybody in the Movement had talked a few years back. But now liberalism was the kiss of death; we were all supposed to be radical revolutionaries now. Politics had become fashion; nothing was as hated as last year's ideology. PL charged that SSOC got money from liberal foundations, some of which received money from the CIA. Again, this was a problem every organization in the civil rights movement had been wrestling with in recent years. It was a twisted attack on SSOC, but it was devastatingly effective.

SDS conventions had become rigorously parliamentarian. Four speakers were allowed to speak for or against the motion and each was strictly timed for something like three minutes. Mike Klonsky had flipped his position; he got up and complained that SSOC was not sufficiently contrite about its southern consciousness error and was liberal beyond redemption. David and Lynn both gave wimpy apologetic speeches and requested that the motion be tabled until the next SDS convention. I thought we were supposed to have two more speakers, but somehow two slugs from New York Communist Party that none of us had ever seen before were given the mike. They gave horribly inane speeches to the effect that SSOC was a wonderful liberal organization with a lot of potential if given some help, and thus the CP supported SSOC. SSOC died right there. By this time everyone in SDS hated the CP. The New Left considered them a sick joke. The CP was scorned both for its slavish cowtowing to Moscow all the way back to Stalin and for its Three Stooges attempts to enter the mainstream of American politics. Nobody else in that room had given a thought to the cesspool of mainstream American politics since kindergarten. The debate was over. The motion passed. SSOC was denounced and excommunicated and, further, SDS vowed to go into the South and organize in competition with SSOC.

This was the beginning of the end—for SSOC, for *The Kudzu*, and for my involvement in the Movement and the New Left. I'm not sure when SDS's end had begun but its final act was well underway and this was just a small scene from it. There was a final meeting of SSOC in the summer of 1969. About half of the people there were from SDS, including Klonsky and Mark Rudd, fresh from the Columbia University takeover. Their dogmatism and rhetoric overpowered the fledgling southern New Left. In one memorable moment between sessions, a SSOC woman went up to Mark Rudd and took off her blouse and challenged him, "All right, Rudd, pull off your clothes and show me that you're human, too, that everything you do doesn't have to contribute to the revolution."

Rudd responded, "No, everything I do does have to contribute to the revolution, and besides, I like being repressed." Seriousness and guilt won the day. At the end of the conference SSOC dissolved itself. Within months SDS itself splintered at the infamous Chicago conference. *The Kudzu*, like the rest of the New Left, struggled on for a few more years. But the vine had been severed at the roots; it was merely a matter of time before the fruit withered.

How could this have happened? One year SSOC and SDS were raking in new members so fast they couldn't keep up with it; a year later they had both self-destructed. There are many layers to this complex tragedy. A major problem, which was obvious to all of us even at the time, was simply the superficiality and youthfulness of the participants. It was a student movement, and as long as it remained that there was action and growth. Although older people left school and left SSOC and SDS, many of them continued their activism in more permanent activities—community organizing, social work, electoral politics, journalism, civil rights and poverty law, community medicine, teaching. In fact, contrary to the popular media image of sixties activists becoming self-absorbed yuppies, most of the activists I knew in the sixties are today left-liberals involved in low-paying altruistic professions.

But in the late sixties, when the prospect suddenly loomed of transforming the New Left student organiza-

tions into a national mass movement, trouble arose in SDS and SSOC. The Old Left-style organizations that earlier had been grateful simply to purvey their wares openly in the marketplace of ideas for the first time since McCarthyism suddenly saw a historic moment approaching and began to maneuver to make a grab for the reins of control. Students, dividing their energies between school, politics, and just being young, couldn't hold off the onslaught of these professional political hacks. The students' instinctive aversion to hierarchical authoritarian organization left a wide opening for the traditional Old Left-style disciplined infiltration that occurred.

STABBED THROUGH THE BACK DOOR

Not long after SSOC's demise, it became clear that, unbeknownst to the local membership and much of the staff outside of Nashville, the Communist Party had taken over the Nashville office and many key staff positions. I knew there were people on the SSOC staff who were members of CP, but I had no idea how many until it was all over. It had seemed so harmless. As one of them put it, it was more like SSOC had organizers in CP than that CP had organizers in SSOC. Progressive Labor and the Communist Party were sworn enemies, so, once the extent of CP infiltration became clear, PL's obsession with destroying SSOC also became clear. PL had tried to take over SSOC by having Ed Clark elected chair and had failed. CP had crept in the back door and had succeeded. The whole new cohort of SSOC staffers who talked me into running for chair all turned out to be CP members. Evidently they had run me for chair so they could have an absentee chair off in Mississippi, giving them free rein at SSOC headquarters in Nashville. Tom Gardner's election was an inconvenience for them, but nevertheless the stage was set for a power struggle in SDS between PL and the CP, with SSOC as a political football. When PL saw SSOC was lost to the CP, PL decided to use its dominance in SDS to destroy SSOC. With typical clumsiness, the CP stuck those two speakers in front of the mike in Austin to defend SSOC. Due to the CP's low status in SDS, that strategy backfired and SSOC became history. The whole southern consciousness flap was a red herring thrown out by PL for gullible SDSers.

As the extent of PL's power in SDS became clear, SDSers chose one of two options. Many of the national leaders of SDS, such as Klonsky, Mark Rudd, and Bernadine Dohrn, took a "we're more revolutionary than thou" tack. They appeased PL on issues they considered of less consequence, like the SSOC question, and on other issues they sought to outflank PL with more aggressively revolutionary rhetoric and actions. This strategy eventually culminated in the Weathermen's "days of rage" in Chicago, and forced many key people into the ineffectual role of underground fugitives from the FBI. They were forced into overextending their positions beyond anything a mass movement was prepared to support. What was to have been the vanguard of a popular uprising ended up as a small isolated bunch of ineffectual extremists.

Much of SDS's local membership took another approach. In disgust they abandoned the national level of the organization to the sectarian hacks and the extremists. The national leadership splintered into several factions, none of which had any popular support. PL and the CP were left in control of only their own members. And the goose that laid the golden egg was dead. The Old Left had reached up out of the grave and engineered one last grand failure to cap half a century of impotence in the United States.

Six years after all of this, in 1975, I wrote an article about The Kudzu, SSOC, and SDS for Southern Exposure, a quarterly published by The Institute for Southern Studies of Atlanta and Chapel Hill. The entire section describing the shenanigans of PL and the CP and the deaths of SSOC and SDS was cut out by the editors. I have no idea what their motives were. Even then, after the SDS/SSOC debacle, many independent leftists and liberals looked the other way rather than stir up any controversy that might be misconstrued as anti-communism or redbaiting. To my knowledge, this full story has never been told in print.

I wrote a number of editorials in The Kudzu decrying the mindless redbaiting of right-wingers. But apparently many more people in the civil rights movement and the New Left than I cared to admit at the time were unrecognized members of doctrinaire leftist parties. They didn't state their affiliations, and good leftists and liberals were not supposed to ask. Maybe now, at the end of the Cold War, and after the economic, political, and moral bankruptcy of all the old left regimes around the world is so widely recognized and admitted, some sunlight can be shed on what happened in this country at the close of the sixties.

I am not regressing to anti-communism here. On the contrary, it appears that members of old left organizations may have to be given credit for major contributions to the birth and growth of the New Left, especially in the South. Would that they had better understood the limitations of their ideology and their machinations. The sixties were not the forties or fifties. There came a time when the Old Left should have shown its hand to the New Left, when the old ideologies should have been put forth openly to stand or fall on their own merits. They would have fallen, of course, not because of anti-Communist prejudice but because

they were out-of-date, inappropriate, and ineffectual ideologies for this country. Knowing this perhaps, the old secrecy was cravenly maintained in an unforgivable scam perpetrated on the only people in this country who had the slightest understanding and sympathy for the Old Left.

But this is still not the whole story of the death of the sixties. There was one sinister strand of this web that had not unravelled and revealed itself yet. That comes later in The Kudzu's history.

THE INK KEEPS ON FLOWING

After the traumatic ends of SSOC and SDS in 1969, and the end of The Kudzu's first year, we kept going in Mississippi. There was no more SSOC money, but that had never been an essential part of our financial base. We picked up a few paying ads and received a steady trickle of donations, most local, but some from out of state. Some staff members had outside jobs, and activity had to be scaled back somewhat. Sixteen issues appeared during The Kudzu's first year; it took us another three years to put out another 16 issues. Our writing became a little less awkward and shrill, and our layouts got a little neater and more professional looking. We continued to try for a balanced mix of culture and politics. Ironically, the real ground swell of youthful rebellion was just barely getting started in 1969. In the next few years virtually every family had at least one son or daughter who "went hippie." Radical politics was only one parental worry out of many. My own parents had more sympathy for my political activities than for the rest of the trappings of the new subculture, the wild hair and clothes, the drugs and sex.

Several Kudzu staffers had gone to one of the first pop festivals, near Miami, at the end of 1968. We had press passes to Woodstock, but passed it up because of the distance. Because of its proximity to New York, Woodstock had the biggest attendance and got all the media attention, but festivals before and after Woodstock had the same musicians and the same impact on the attendees. There were two monstrous Fourth of July festivals near Atlanta. At the second one, several hundred people tore down the fence of a swimming lake next door to the festival, stripped naked, and went for a communal skinny dip. Couples took turns assuming various positions from the Kama Sutra and going down the tall sliding board together to the applause of the nude crowd. At the climax of the festival, Jimi Hendrix played his famous version of the national anthem. But it wasn't all so beautiful; crowd facilities at all of the festivals were atrocious. We tried to come down from the clouds somewhat by pointing out the exploitive nature of the music industry as a lesson in the problems of corporate capitalism.

We put on two festivals of our own in Mississippi that we called Mississippi Youth Jubilees. We obtained use of the grounds of a former college that had been used for years as a civil rights conference site, Mt. Beulah, and brought in a bunch of local musicians. We also had political speakers and discussion groups about civil rights, the peace movement, women's liberation, and other current issues.

At the first festival, a big, fat Mississippi highway patrolman named Loyd Jones showed up taking license numbers and giving people tickets for missing tail lights and other minor infractions of the law. Jones was notorious among blacks all over the state for his alleged harassment and brutality. Many blacks called him Goon Jones. At one point he cruised onto the festival grounds in his patrol car. He refused to pay admission, but produced no search warrant. We surrounded his car and confronted him. Some people started breaking bottles in front and back of his car so he couldn't leave. A big confrontation followed between the people who broke the bottles and some pacifists. Finally the pacifists picked up the broken bottles and Jones left. We parked cars across the entrance to prevent his return. There were intense discussions about violence and pacificism all over the festival for the rest of the weekend. Jones had been a priceless catalyst.

During the next year, Nixon invaded Cambodia, National Guardsmen shot down unarmed students at Kent State University in Ohio, and in Mississippi Goon Jones and a group of fellow patrolmen marched onto the campus of Jackson State College and shot into a crowd of unarmed black students, killing two. *The Kudzu* was the only paper in Jackson that presented the students' accounts of the killings. The bullet-splattered women's dorm was my most famous photo and the *Kudzu*'s most dramatic cover (see figure 1). Among the many demonstrations following these killings was a march around the governor's mansion by Millsaps students and faculty. Three years before, when Ben Brown had been killed at almost the same spot at Jackson State, twenty Millsaps students had marched. This time it was almost two hundred. We considered that progress; still, two people had to die to get people moving. And it was still Mississippi; the patrolmen were exonerated.

NARC WARS

While arrests of *Kudzu* staffers had tapered off after the first year of publication, the increasing numbers of counterculture participants and the increasing presence of recreational drugs in Jackson gave the police both the incentive and the excuse to constantly harass *The Kudzu*, which they perceived as an instigator of the drug culture. We became more or less personally acquainted with the entire vice squad as they subjected us to constant surveillance. At one point the vice squad rented an abandoned apartment on the grounds of our office-residence. They parked in our driveway and arrested and beat staff members who also tried to park there. Many people we knew spent time in jail or prison for possession or sale of small quantities of marijuana. We were very careful ourselves and had no drug arrests of staff members during our first two years.

Nevertheless, harassment by narcotics agents resulted in my worst jail experience, but it was not in Mississippi. In May 1970, several of us covered a small pop festival and environmental rally at Denham Springs, Louisiana, near Baton Rouge. The local sheriff had deputized a bunch of his redneck cronies in this rural area, and undercover narcs disguised as hippies had been brought in from New Orleans. A hidden police compound was set up next to the festival site. Over the course of the weekend between one and two hundred people were seized, dragged into the secret compound, booked, and sent out to local jails and prisons. The pretext for the arrests was usually drugs, but most of them were bogus. Very few of those arrested were selling or even in possession of drugs. Many people were beaten as they were arrested. Inside the compound, almost everyone was beaten during the "booking procedures." Some were gassed with mace and sadistically tortured. It was a true nightmare. No announcement was made from the stage concerning this.

I started taking pictures of what I thought was a brawl between festival goers. It turned out to be one of the "arrests." I was seized, my camera was confiscated, and I was spirited into the compound. I was beaten during the strip search and not allowed to make a phone call for a day-and-a-half. Over the course of three days I was transferred to several jails. At one point I was in a Baton Rouge cell block, wearing a prison uniform, along with a *Newsweek* reporter and almost thirty other festival goers. After three days, an American Civil Liberties Union attorney finally located me and got me released on bail. After a great deal of difficulty I got my camera back but the film was gone and the camera had been maliciously damaged on the inside.

When people were finally brought up for hearings, local court-appointed lawyers tried to force innocent people to plead guilty against their wills. Charges against me were dropped. Unfortunately there was only one ACLU attorney in that rural area, and it proved too difficult to bring any charges against the law

Figure 1: Cover photo of *The Kudzu* 2, no. 6 (May 1970) showing a bullet-splattered women's dorm at Jackson State College. Photo by David Doggett.

officers responsible for this atrocity. This was one of the worst examples of the American police state gone amok I know of since the old days in the civil rights movement, when demonstrators likewise were arrested in large groups and beaten and tortured.

From today's perspective it is difficult to understand the symbolic importance of illegal drug use for both the counterculture and its persecutors. Today we look askance at the sordid abuse of addictive drugs by movie stars and rock stars, and drug use has gained an unfashionable association with inner city addicts and their petty crime, and with money crazed dealers and their violent crime. But in the sixties and early seventies, the use of illegal psychedelic drugs was an act not only of social rebellion but political rebellion, since the state forbade it. It was a line drawn in the dirt by parents and police that millions of young people stepped across in defiance of frequently severe consequences.

The drug-induced psychedelic initiation rite was like a religious awakening. But it was not really a new religion that one awoke to; rather it was chemically induced culture shock. The psychedelic experience was an instant way to step outside one's native culture and look on society from an estranged perspective. The hysterical response of the authorities served to heighten the alienating effect. While the drug tripper was trying to manipulate his or her own mind into a different perspective, the state was desperately trying to keep the minds of its youth in the old straitjacket. Thus drugs became a radicalizing political experience for millions of young people, who otherwise might never have so forcefully experienced the shocking hand of thought control in their society.

The drugs, being physical things that influenced thought, forced the thought police to step out from behind the curtain of psychological manipulation and attempt to physically control the drugs and those who used them. People who might never have made the intellectual effort to understand U.S. imperialism, or the moral effort to empathize with oppressed blacks, suddenly found themselves persecuted as outlaws because they simply wanted to alter their own mental perceptions. The drug war was a major political battleground of the sixties and seventies.

YEAR THREE

By our third year of publication we had survived 42 *Kudzu*-related arrests and were undaunted. But the financial situation was discouraging. It was clear that *The Kudzu* would not pay for itself anytime in the foreseeable future. We were taking turns holding outside jobs to support the paper. At different times, I worked full-time doing paralegal work for the

American Civil Liberties Union and other civil rights lawyers in Jackson. Except for myself, the original staff had turned over completely. Bill Rusk, on probation for draft violation in California, had become a mainstay on the staff while also working long hours as a cab driver.

We made plans to start a community center called Edge City, named after the destination of Ken Kesey's bus, Further. The hope was that the center could make money by having rock bands play on weekends and by housing some small businesses such as a craft shop and a used book and record shop. *Kudzu* staffers would try to earn a living working at the center. We sold $5 memberships, the members elected a board of directors, and the board formed a nonprofit corporation. We brought legendary bluesman Mississippi Fred McDowell down from the Delta for a fundraising concert. Jack Cohn, a local businessman, gave us several thousand dollars, which was to be paid back only if the venture was successful. We rented and renovated an old parking garage in downtown Jackson and opened for business. Edge City met with moderate success at first.

One of the people on our staff decided to go to Cuba with the Venceremos Brigade. Mike McNamara was a big red-headed guy, a former high school football guard from Vicksburg. He had been a writer and distributor of *The Kudzu* up at Ole Miss, and had moved to Jackson and joined our staff. He raised some money and went with Venceremos to Cuba to spend a summer cutting sugar cane. He cut so much sugar cane he got elected a brigade leader.

J. EDGAR'S SPOOKS

In *The Kudzu*'s third year we began to get heat from the FBI. We had always felt that the FBI had us under close surveillance. During our first year several *Kudzu* staffers and associates were questioned by FBI agents. Some people were asked to become paid informants. One of the main women on our staff came to an early staff meeting and told of being offered money to meet with FBI agents clandestinely on a regular basis to keep them informed of our activities. She would be paid $50 for each meeting. We were intrigued. We decided that she should become a double agent. She was to go along with the FBI's scheme, take the money, and try to find out as much as possible about the FBI's knowledge and operations. We weren't breaking any federal laws and had no plans to, so it was all just a game with us. Also the money wasn't bad. At the time we each lived on about $20 a month and were struggling to pay the printer's bill with each issue. Why not play a little game with them, feed them either trivial information or misleading stuff, and take some of their money to use for our own purposes?

Our staff member had one or two meetings with the FBI. They had her lie on the floor of the back seat of their car while they talked. Then she had to sign a receipt for the money. After each meeting she came back and reported at a staff meeting. After one or two meetings the FBI must have realized they had been had because they stopped setting up meetings. The main benefit we got out of the game was that we learned to recognize several agents. And from that knowledge I discovered FBI agents could be identified at demonstrations because of the brand of camera they used. Reporters and the state and local police always used Nikon cameras, the standard professional workhorse. Federal people used Beseler Topcon cameras. Topcon even advertised in photo magazines that they had a federal contract.

After those early contacts the FBI dropped into the background until our third year. Unbeknownst to us at the time, the FBI in 1970 was carrying on a national campaign called "COINTELPRO." As part of that program, informant/provocateurs all over the country were paid to both spy on activist groups and to disrupt and discredit them. In early October of 1970 we ran a statement by three Alabama attorneys which revealed that Charles R. Grimm, Jr., a Tuscaloosa Police Department undercover narcotics agent who had a close relationship with the FBI, had thrown objects at police and set fire to buildings during student disturbances at the University of Alabama the previous May. The statement noted, in fact, that Grimm had been virtually the only violent participant in some of these instances, that he had urged students to use guns and dynamite, and that he had offered to help them obtain such items. He became a member of the University Committee on Unrest and Reconciliation, where his militant approach appeared intended to divide the university community.

The article also enumerated several similar instances where apparent police and FBI agents provocateur were involved around the country. We followed the article with an editorial criticizing the FBI for vigorously pursuing the Black Panthers and white radicals alleged to be involved in violent or criminal activities, while in the South churches were bombed and burned and blacks were murdered while the FBI looked the other way and failed to successfully investigate.

Soon after that article was published, there came a knock at *The Kudzu* door. It was the first of several occasions in which FBI agents rushed into our office-residence with guns drawn, claiming they didn't need search warrants because they were "in hot pursuit of fugitives." The "fugitives" were national figures such as the SDS Weathermen or various Black Panthers. FBI agents actually looked under our beds once for Mark Rudd. We had no connection with any of these "fugitives" and the FBI well knew that, since they had us under constant surveillance. They were very hostile and spewed a lot of verbal abuse such as, "Punks like you don't have any rights." They threatened to shoot us down on the street if we had our hands in our pockets, since we might be going for a weapon. Around us they dropped the FBI's famous professional image. They were garden variety right-wing thugs to the core.

Finally, on October 26, the Jackson police marched into our house with a search warrant. Then, while holding eight of us at gun point in the front room, they ransacked the office and house, intentionally breaking several personal items and stealing address books as they worked (see figure 2). They "found" a small bag of marijuana none of us had ever seen before and off we went to spend a night in jail. They threw a few punches during the booking procedures. The local papers had a field day. However, it was one of the few times we ever got a reasonable judge, J.L. Spencer. In a surprise move he released us on our own recognizance and merely bound the case over to a grand jury for investigation. He correctly noted that there was no chance for a conviction, since the marijuana was not found on anyone's person and in fact none of us was even in the room when it was found. The charges were eventually dropped.

On the surface it was just one more case of harassment among many. But as time went by and we pieced together additional information, the incident took on a deeply sinister meaning with far-reaching implications. Word came back through the legal community that the FBI had set up the raid. The search warrant had been obtained on the grounds that an informant had witnessed the use and sale of marijuana in our house the night before the raid. At first we assumed that was a complete fabrication. But on thinking back, we realized that there had been some grass smoked in the house that night, although none was left on the premises. Further one person present at the time had not smoked any. He was a long-time acquaintance of all of us; we suddenly suspected he was almost certainly an informer-provocateur.

Don Cole was one of the first leftists I ever met. Way back in 1965, when Lee Makamson and I published our very first mimeographed newsletter, Don Cole appeared out of nowhere. He was a short nerdy guy with glasses and short hair who worked in a hardware store in the small town of Raymond, near Jackson. He claimed he was a Communist, and his first advice to Lee and me was for us to go to Vietnam and join up with the Viet Cong. We never took him seriously after that. He later claimed to be a member of the Progressive Labor Party, yet, in spite of that organization's militant Maoist image, he was never close to anyone in the Jackson activist community and he maintained his residence and job in the hardware store in Raymond. He sort of "checked in" on a regular basis but never really participated in any organizations, although he was frequently at meetings, hanging around the fringes. He showed up at demonstrations unannounced and handed out tracts containing the most embarrassing, stereotypical Communist rantings imaginable. He was always jolly and friendly to all of us, and we just sort of ignored him.

Suddenly it all made sense. In fact, Jan Hillegas of Freedom Information Service had not long before said that she suspected Don Cole of being an informer. Some photos had disappeared from her office under circumstances that convinced her Don had taken them. Don had been such a seemingly harmless fixture around town for so long that I hadn't really taken Jan seriously. But we finally became convinced that, if there was any real testimony for the search warrant that led to *The Kudzu* raid, it had to have come from Don Cole. That little snake—all those years of embarrassing us at demonstrations, and now he had gotten our house wrecked and caused us a night in jail. I was annoyed and we passed the word around, but at that point I still didn't get the really big picture.

Figure 2: The author's office after raid by Jackson police, October 26, 1970. Photo by Bill Peltz.

THE HEADLESS HORSEMAN

The Kudzu struggled on. We hosted a conference for the underground press of the Southeast at Mt. Beulah. Tom Forcade of the Underground Press Syndicate came down, and people from all over the South showed up. There was some speculation that the raid on our office had been in retaliation for our organizing this conference.

A major topic of discussion at the conference was the vacuum left at the national level by SDS and SSOC. We were all concerned that, without a strong national organization to connect with, those of us in provincial areas might sink back into isolation, and we were uncertain how long we could hold out that way. The underground press was increasingly writing about a revolution that was not happening. There were huge liberal initiatives for civil rights and peace; there were lots of hippies and Yippies pretending or naively believing that music and love and outrageous humor would cause permanent change; and there were black and white militants strutting around with guns and getting thrown in prison or forced underground. In the name of revolution, banks were being robbed and cops were being shot.

I was not a pure pacifist, and I had written in *The Kudzu* in support of violence in self-defense. We kept a loaded 12-gauge shotgun in our house. But the "vanguard" was getting way ahead of its troops. I recently read that a former SDS Weatherman confessed they had committed "the militarist error." It figures they would have a doctrinaire term for it. Too bad there's no orthodox doctrine that instills common sense. They were leading a suicidal charge that very few people were foolish enough to follow. It was all beginning to look too crazy.

There was no pre-eminent organizational vehicle with real popular support, no aggressive, but sane democratic leftist organization to fill the void left by SDS and SSOC. The New American Movement and a few other groups tried to pick up the ball where SDS had fumbled it, but somehow nothing ever took off again like SDS.

YEAR FOUR

In 1972, *The Kudzu*'s fourth and final year, the Republic of New Africa (RNA) set up house in Jackson. RNA wanted to press the United Nations for a chunk of the southeastern United States as reparations for slavery and its aftermath. Their goal was to set up a black homeland. In spite of its seeming impracticality, let's be honest, there was justice in that demand. Without much enthusiasm, we dutifully wrote about their views. But most of white Mississippi took great offense at these notions, especially the law 'n' order gang. Within months, the FBI and Jackson Police Department staged a raid on RNA's headquarters. Both sides were heavily armed. When the police fired tear gas into the building, RNA members claimed they thought it was gunshots and fired back in self-defense. A Jackson vice squad officer was shot in the head and killed. By this time we knew all of the vice squad all too intimately. As luck would have it, the officer killed, Louis Skinner, was the only member of the vice squad who treated us fairly and professionally in all of our encounters. He was a genuinely nice guy who was simply in with the wrong crowd. Now he had been at the wrong place at the wrong time. His death was totally unnecessary. The raid was purely a trumped up act of political repression. And so it goes. Everytime someone is killed, even if it is the enemy, a part of humanity dies.

After that incident, the Republic of New Africa leaders, like many other black militants, were mired in courts and prison. Activity was winding down, not only for the militant black movement and the New Left, but for the underground press and *The Kudzu* as well. Sometimes *The Kudzu* staff only consisted of Bill Rusk

and me, and we both were doing outside work. New issues came out less than once a month. We had little advertising, almost no newsstands would carry *The Kudzu*, and street sales were too poor to provide incentive to street hawkers. Jackson was simply not a large enough city to support an alternative press. We could have probably gotten more ads and sales at the major college towns around the state, but we didn't have the resources and time to do the constant traveling required for that. In the beginning we had been perceived as pioneers and martyrs and people rose up to help us. But by the fourth year, we were taken for granted as more of a business, which of course we never were. We had seen all of this by the end of the second year, which is when we started working on Edge City.

But Edge City had never really gotten off the ground. Soon after it opened, a gang of bikers started hanging out at a bar around the corner and harassing people. At one point I had to pull out a shotgun and hold off several bikers at gunpoint for almost half-an-hour while the police took their time in answering our phone call for help. The bikers weren't happy with the stand-off and immediately went over to our house, beat up Bill Rusk, and stole a bunch of stuff. They swore to see me dead. I moved out of the house and slept next to a gun for the next month. Eventually we made a strained peace with the bikers. But the whole affair did little to enhance Edge City's public image.

The biggest problem for Edge City was that the police refused to issue us a dance permit. They tried to extort us into hiring city police as security guards, but we felt that their presence would scare people away, and that having police around would simply make it easier for them to spy on people and to harass people with petty drug arrests and traffic tickets. Maybe we could have taken them to court and eventually gotten a dance permit, but, in the meantime, without dancing we couldn't keep up the rent and staff salaries. We had a band play most weekends, but most of the bands we could afford were okay as dance bands but weren't good enough to pull off an all-night concert with no dancing. Also, we didn't serve alcohol. Without dancing for the high school kids or drinks for older people, the entertainment just never took off. Edge City didn't last long.

DEATH WITH A WHIMPER

Edge City's closing was pretty much the last straw for me. We could have kept *The Kudzu* going for awhile longer with the trickle of donations we got, but when we realized that none of us would be able to quit our outside jobs to work full-time on *The Kudzu*, I decided it was time to move on to other things. In the beginning I really had thought I was starting on a lifetime career. When I finally admitted that dream was over, I was devastated. My whole identity was tied up in *The Kudzu*. I wandered for two depressing years before I got seriously involved in another career. How much revolution would occur, I had never really known. But I never envisioned that it would all just dissipate into nothing. As with the end of SDS and SSOC, again I had to ask, what had happened?

POST-MORTEM

To be sure we had changed history. Blacks were voting and electing people to office in the South. Johnson left office. The troops came home from Vietnam. Never again in our lifetime, we believed, would this country enter into war as blindly as before. Nixon was eventually to be run out of office. Women were moving out of the kitchen and into the workplace. The harsh conformity of the fifties had been broken. Everyone knew what the word "ecology" meant. Breathtaking changes had taken place in every area of culture. Thus much of what happened was not so much a dissipation as an integration of our goals into mainstream society. But there was no national structure, no comprehensive national organization or publication to carry on the original vision of the New Left and the counterculture. How could that be, when there were once so many of us with such a similar vision?

Indeed, the vision was never lost for the individuals. To this day if you talk to anyone who was active in the sixties you will discover that he or she still has that vision of racial harmony, of an economic system that nurtures those at the bottom rather than adds to their numbers, of a political system with participatory democracy rather than sham republicanism, of a culture in which work and play are fun and creative rather than desperate and destructive and there is international appreciation and cooperation in maintaining the environment. But we have been reduced to individuals when we once were a mass movement.

Several years ago I acquired my FBI file through the freedom of information act. The documents in my file were not merely about surveillance. The FBI was far more sophisticated and creative than we ever imagined them to be. We knew that they watched us. But we had no idea how much they tried to manipulate us. When *The Kudzu* started, the FBI reasoned that, since we were all students with conservative parents living in small towns throughout Mississippi, it would be a simple matter to put fear in our parents and thus enormous pressure on us. Agents visited not only our parents, but also the friends, neighbors, and employers of our parents around Mississippi. These people were questioned about us and our families in an intentionally intimidating manner. Many of my friends lost touch with their families for years after those days. People were financially cut off, transferred to other schools, forced into psychiatric treatment, and subjected to other experiences; and all of this permanently changed many people's lives. Who knows how much of the trauma we all went through in those days was intensified by this cynical meddling by the FBI?

Being young, there was a lot of amorous coupling among us in those days. The FBI sent fake letters about false infidelities in attempts to break up couples. There were FBI memos discussing who were effective leaders among us and who were ineffective, and memos about what types of rumors might turn people against the strong leaders. There was communication between the FBI, the Mississippi State Sovereignty Commission (a notorious right-wing McCarthyesque group), and state and local law enforcement organizations. There were also communications between the local FBI agents and agents further up the chain of command outside of the state.

At some point, after I had absorbed what a sophisticated campaign the FBI carried out against us in Jackson, I began to wonder what schemes they had hatched against national organizations like SDS and SSOC. SDS may have been the greatest threat to the corporate ruling class in this country in this century; not simply because the ideology of SDS, economic as well as political democracy, was so threatening, but because so many middle- and upper-class young people were flocking to SDS and the ideas SDS promulgated. At its height, there were rapidly growing SDS chapters on virtually every college campus in the country. On many campuses SDS was the biggest and most powerful student organization on campus. But although the top universities in the country had been intermittently shut down, SDS was not immediately threatening to shut down any factories or mines. Far worse, these middle- and upper-class young people were setting out to carry these ideas into the mainstream media, into electoral politics, and into all of the professions and all of the positions of influence and power that they would inevitably inherit from the older generation. J. Edgar Hoover's FBI would not stand idly by for that.

Don Cole was a member of the Progressive Labor Party. Don Cole was at the 1967 SSOC conference with Ed Clark when PL tried unsuccessfully to take over SSOC. Ed Clark and Fred Lacy of PL engineered the destruction of SSOC. The in-fighting between PL and SDS ended in the disintegration of SDS. The premiere organization of the New Left, the political manifestation of the counterculture, did not make it into the seventies.

I have talked to people from coast to coast who recall that in their city there were members of PL who were known or suspected of being informer-provocateurs. PL was universally disruptive. Possibly there were many people in PL who knew nothing about the FBI. Surely some well-intentioned people were sincerely idiotic enough to screw things up as badly as PL managed. Surely SDS's youthful ineptness contributed to its fatal inability to deal with that threat. But I would like to some day know what role the FBI had in all of this. Was PL an FBI creation from the beginning, or did the FBI merely use PL so cleverly for its own purposes? Everyone knows the FBI was in the Communist Party USA. How much of the CP's actions came from the FBI? Certainly the death of the New Left cannot be blamed solely on FBI skullduggery; there was self-inflicted damage aplenty. But how different would things have been without such disruptions? Would there have been a PL threat to SDS? Would SDS have surmounted the threat instead of splintering? Would Liberation News Service have thrived intact? Would the Black Panthers have gone further politically? Would the underground press have become a permanent part of the nation's mass media?

And what of the conclusion of *The Kudzu*'s small part in it all? Well, finally, after *The Kudzu*'s tale is told and the years have intervened, it becomes clear that Mississippi was and is not so different. It wasn't the Ku Klux Klan that stopped *The Kudzu* in the end; it was economics, the legal system, the FBI, our own youthfully superficial political polemics, the loss of an effective national connection, and changing times, the same forces that dealt killing blows in the rest of the country to the sixties' counterculture, its New Left political organizations, and its voice, the underground press.

Since I left Mississippi, I have lived in Atlanta, Washington, DC, New Orleans, Nashville, Knoxville, Los Angeles, Boston, and Philadelphia. In 1991, as I write this, a greater proportion of U.S. citizens are in prison than in any other major nation. A greater proportion of black males are in prison in the United States of America than in the Union of South Africa.

In no major nation are citizens more fearful of their own city streets than in the United States. Our cities have higher infant mortality rates than many Third World countries. In these cities today, the segregation of the white suburbs and the black inner cities is in many ways as complete as Mississippi's old segregation. We have de facto apartheid. The first slaves did not come into Mississippi; they were brought into Boston harbor. The curse of the abomination of slavery and its aftermath in America was not erased by the Civil War, and it does not fall on the South alone. The curse is alive in every major city in this country.

And there are new problems as well. The environment is more threatened than ever. The savings and loan scandal has become the biggest public theft in the nation's history, and the big banks as well have massive bad debts, both inside and outside the country. The government itself has an unthinkably huge debt. In the past decades there has been a tremendous transfer of wealth from the poor and the middle class, both inside and outside the United States, to the international upper class. Even as the old left regimes of the Cold War crumble in Eastern Europe, American capitalism can scarcely relish the victory as it wrestles with these problems and plunges into the crisis of a recession. Catastrophe continues in the Middle East because of our blind addiction to the oil of kings and dictators, and our longstanding arrogance and ignorance toward the millions of poor people in that region. And to deal with all of these problems, we have a perennially paralyzed government of peabrained right-wing Republican presidents and castrated liberal Democratic congresses.

Would history have gone in all of these directions if the counterculture, the New Left, and the underground press had continued? We will never know. We can pick over the bones and try to understand the causes of the patient's death. Many's the night some of us have lain in bed and done that. But we can scarcely imagine what the patient would have done had it lived on, what its influence would have been. It's just a small part of history now. Isn't it?

— David Doggett —

A Tradition Continues:
East Lansing's Underground Press,
1965-Present

Ken Wachsberger

Wachsberger is the author of the novel *Beercans on the Side of the Road: The Story of Henry the Hitchhiker* (Ann Arbor, MI: Azenphony Press, 1988) and co-author of the biography *The Last Selection: A Child's Journey through the Holocaust* (Amherst, MA: University of Massachusetts Press, 1991). He teaches writing at Eastern Michigan University, is managing editor of *Serials Review* and *Reference Services Review* in Ann Arbor, and is a member of the National Writers Union.

This article is an expansion of three articles that appeared in the *Lansing Star* in 1976. Appendix 2 is adapted from a talk given August 1, 1984 at the Great River Conference, Winona State University, Winona, MN.

This article is dedicated to my hometown of Lansing, Michigan. I was born in Detroit and I was raised in Cleveland. At present, I live in Ann Arbor. But I call Lansing my hometown because I became politically and philosophically aware there in 1970 after the murders at Kent State and Jackson State, the student strikes that followed, and my first political arrest. I thank then-Michigan State University President Clifton Wharton, a black member of the white power structure in this country, who ordered that student participants in a discussion on racism at the Michigan State Union (that he had been invited to) be arrested for loitering and trespassing. My brief incarceration in solitary confinement that evening was just good educational and literary fortune. My subsequent involvement in the local underground press transformed my life.

The Lansing area has a long tradition of underground and alternative newspapers, going back to December 3, 1965, when *The Paper* debuted on the campus of Michigan State University and in the East Lansing area [see "My Odyssey through the Underground Press," by Michael Kindman, in this collection]. *The Paper*'s staff were former staff members of MSU's student newspaper, *State News*, who rebelled against its refusal to deal with issues of the day. On the organizational level, they adopted the basic hierarchical structure of the *State News*, but their articles contained a new element, called "substance," and they didn't shy away from expressing opinions.

The traditional definition of "objective journalism" involves the idea that an article should contain "only the facts." Writers for underground papers, including *The Paper*, attacked this notion as a myth by pointing out that even articles that purported to be objective contained opinions simply by the terms the writers chose to use. For instance, objectively speaking, was a Black Panther described as being "militant" or "a black activist?" Were members of the Viet Cong "terrorists" or "freedom fighters?" Writers for establishment papers, such as the *State News* and the *Lansing State Journal*, carried the myth one step further by having an "editorial page." By having one page where opinions are blatantly expressed, the implication is planted that the other news articles are opinion-free.

As a breakaway paper from the *State News*, many of the local activities *The Paper* covered naturally dealt with campus issues. *The Paper* was an early champion of the previously unheard-of idea that students had rights, such as to free speech on campus, and should even have a say in their curriculum. Other campus issues *The Paper* supported then sound humorous to students of today, who often do not realize that what they accept as givens were won only through organized struggle. These issues included the right to use profanity in print, the right of women to return to their dorms whenever they wanted at night, and even the right of women to share dorms with men.

On the national and international level, *The Paper* attacked the Vietnam War and helped to define the reasons for it in terms of capitalist imperialist economics. Years later former staffer Brad Lang explained in the *Lansing Star*: "The early Sixties had seen a steady growth in the Civil Rights movement, a growing awareness of the Vietnam War, the beginnings of the youth-drug culture, and an overall growth in an understanding of the role of capitalism and imperialism. All these issues came together to virtually force the establishment of a newspaper which could express the views of the fledgling Movement in the Lansing area."

Staffers for *The Paper* represented the two political outlooks that were emerging then in the New Left. One reflected the youth-drug philosophy; the other was that of the more rigid SDS (Students for a Democratic Society). Whereas in *The Paper*'s early years these differences served as a source of intellectual and activist stimulation, by 1967, "serious cracks began to develop in the student Movement, mostly along Marxist vs. non-Marxist lines. The pressures began to make themselves felt among *The Paper* staffers, who were becoming heavily involved in psychedelics."

By the end of the 1967-68 school year, however, the SDS influence was growing. Then, SDS factional fighting caused the split that produced the Weatherman group. *The Paper* collapsed under all the splits.

The last *Paper* came out in the summer of 1969. In its time, it served, through membership in the

Underground Press Syndicate (later re-named Alternative Press Syndicate), to plug the East Lansing radical community into radical communities around the country. *The Paper* was one of the five original members of UPS. The other members were the *Los Angeles Free Press*, New York's *East Village Other*, the *Berkeley Barb*, and Detroit's *Fifth Estate*.

NEW ALTERNATIVES TO THE *STATE NEWS*

When *The Paper* folded, there was no other area newspaper to fill the void. Once again, Michigan State students had to look to the *State News* to speak for them. Once again, it didn't.

The following September, a new paper was formed, put out by "human beings in the immediate (and not so immediate) community," and called *Goob Yeak Gergibal*. In its first issue, an editorial entitled "Evolution" labeled the *State News* Michigan State University's "official administration/student newspaper," charging that it was "responsive in full measure only to the administration hand that feeds it." It described itself as "a medium that will be responsible not to the enemies of the community, but to its people. A medium which, we hope can soon be distributed free, like its quasi-competition. A medium to which you, the members of the community, can turn to for news concerning yourself more certainly, more immediately." It was a bold idea, and if *Joint Issue* and *Lansing Star* can be seen as successors, then its dream of being free was realized two years later. However, *Goob Yeak Gergibal*'s first issue was also its last.

A street paper called *Trash*, put out after the SDS split by the group that identified with the local Weatherman group, also appeared on the scene during that period, but it was very irregular and soon disappeared.

Again, students and members of the East Lansing community had no real paper to which they could relate.

By the start of the new year, 1970, a new issue was challenging the war in Vietnam for most column inches in the newspapers. Ecology had leaped overnight into our collective consciousness, and suddenly industries were being called upon to account for the waste they were dumping into our rivers and for the poisons they were spewing forth into the air. Environmentalist groups were demanding that these industries use their own profits rather than higher consumer prices to clean up this pollution since it was the industries who had caused it in the first place. Industries responded by ignoring such issues as dead streams and ecological imbalances. Instead, they blamed the populace for the worst part of the pollution and said that litterbags and anti-pollution devices in cars would solve the problem.

To deal with this new crisis, ecology teach-ins sprung up on college campuses across the country.

At Michigan State, Earth Day was set for the weekend of April 21-22 at the campus auditorium. Among the speakers were Fred Brown, billed as president of the Michigan United Conservation Clubs, but in addition, and left unstated, a daytime employee of Dow Chemical Co.; Dr. John Reynolds, of the Consumers Power Co., which at that time was preparing to build a nuclear power plant in Midland, home of Dow Chemical; Harold McClure, president of McClure Oil Co. and also head of the Independent Petroleum Association of America, a petroleum industry pressure group; John G. Winger, vice president of the Rockefellers' Chase Manhattan Bank; and Stewart Udall, who, as Secretary of the Interior under Nixon, allowed Union Oil Co. to engage in offshore drilling in Santa Barbara, California.

To protest the hypocrisy of the alleged Ecology Teach-In, Nelson Brown and Carl Stensel, working along with the New University Conference (NUC), the graduate student/faculty counterpart to SDS, wrote a 10-sided 8 1/2" x 11" pamphlet that presented NUC's official position on the teach-in and then detailed further background information on the scheduled speakers.

For the cover of their exposé, they laid out a poster showing a picture of a pig as the main speaker, an obituary for Lake Erie, and headlines like "Pollution Protest Co-opted!" "Agnew Report Criticizes Ecology," and "World Dying—Business Picks Up," along with a statement signed by the Radical Coalition for Environmental Action.

They called their paper *Swill and Squeal* and passed it out free outside the auditorium. Later, they talked about putting out a regular newspaper but nothing concrete resulted.

Two weeks later, Nixon invaded Cambodia. During the protest at Kent State University, four students were killed by Ohio National Guardsmen. Outraged by this uncalled for act of violence, campuses began shutting down across the country as students went out on strike. Although every campus had its own particular local issue, the basic demands throughout the country were: Solidarity with the students at Kent State; U.S. out of Southeast Asia now; Free Black Panther Bobby Seale; and Get ROTC off campus.

As usual, the *State News* provided only minimal coverage of national and local strike activities, so the need for a new underground became urgent. In the spontaneous style that became characteristic of political action during that whole period, a staff materialized. The name *Swill and Squeal* was retained and five issues, in tabloid form, were published out of the back room of Nelson's Park Lake Road home during the height of strike activity between May 6 and May 22.

Because of Kent State and the strike, a significant number of people were finally coming to understand the relationship between local, national, and international events and the destructive way in which the capitalist imperialist government of the United States affects these events. In addition to this, it was a period when many people were beginning to look at all aspects of their lives, due in great part to the influence of such counterculture factors as dope smoking and the sexual liberation movements. Staff members reflected the ideas of these people who were just being radicalized for the first time, and because of that the counterculture/Yippie/satirical influence was evident in *Swill and Squeal*. The paper contained news articles about local and national strike activity, research articles that spelled out background information on the various strike demands, and personal articles that expressed a deep emotional rejection of what American society was really like.

No papers appeared over the summer, but in the fall a new paper emerged. Called *Generation*, it was composed of former *Swill and Squeal* staff members and several other community folk. In volume I, number 1, a concept to which *Goob Yeak Gergibal* and *Swill and Squeal* had alluded was spelled out clearly for the first time. In a "plea for help," it stated, "We ask that readers forget the traditional way of regarding a paper as something *they* write and *I* read. This is a community paper, and to us that means that anyone who has something to say should be able to find a place to say it here. So, we are inviting everyone to help make *Generation* represent his views, by including his views in it."

No doubt if that article were written today, the third person singular pronoun would have read "his or her" instead of the sexist "his"; or else the singular antecedent "everyone" would have been made plural—perhaps "all people"—to make way for the third person plural neuter pronoun "their." Sexism in the language was only just beginning to be addressed then. Nearly two decades later, God has not yet given us a suitable third person singular neuter pronoun, although "S/He" has tried.

Two trends, according to Nelson, were beginning to emerge at that time. "A cultural understanding was beginning to develop on the paper which I think came to fruition in *Joint Issue* in terms of lifestyle questions. Issues such as women's liberation and gay liberation were starting to creep into the paper. At the same time, the paper was becoming more focused towards local politics. Some of us who had been in the East Lansing area for a while were becoming aware of our own community, the student ghetto."

The most important news event on campus at the time was the trial of the MSU 132, who had been busted on May 19, 1970, in the Student Union by President Clifton Wharton during the student strikes. This was covered extensively by *Generation*, along with events around the country, including the bombing of the Army Math Research Center in Madison, Wisconsin, and the Revolutionary People's Constitutional Convention sponsored by the Black Panther Party and held at Temple University in North Philadelphia.

And there were questions about Timothy Leary, before he turned State's evidence, whether he was part of the Movement or a fraud. "I think all of us were affected by the psychedelic movement in terms of the things Leary was doing," Nelson explained further. "Issues about food, remember the Indians. There was a sense of the mystical, a sense of how all these things tied into the death trip we were on: destroying the land, ripping off the Indians, polluting our bodies with all kinds of poisonous chemicals that Madison Avenue was trying to sell us, the whole phoniness of American culture."

Based on enthusiasm of the previous spring, their projected plan was for *Generation* to appear on the streets every two weeks supported by subscription sales. Unfortunately, enthusiasm had peaked in the strike; consequently, few subscriptions were sold. For money, they had to sell ads and hawk papers on the street for 15¢ apiece. Still, they were barely breaking even.

Meanwhile, in another part of town another underground paper, *Bogue Street Bridge*, was appearing for the first time. Volume I, number 1, the Welcome Week edition, sold for 15¢ and listed as its editorial board: Steve Crocker (who later would become an avid supporter of Lyndon LaRouche)—Social Metaphorician; Jeff McCrae—Our Man in Oregon; Pat Quayle—Staff Humanist/Marxist; and Rena Yount—Poet Liberator.

Where *Generation* favored off-campus news, the articles in *Bogue Street Bridge* were predominantly campus-based, including information on the newly formed Free U—that was the primary difference between the two papers. Like *Generation, Bogue Street Bridge* displayed a high countercultural awareness and a sensitivity to the sexual liberation movements. Like *Generation, Bogue Street Bridge* provided alternative news coverage to that of the Establishment press. And like *Generation, Bogue Street Bridge* served as a forum for communication and debate among people concerned with change.

Also, unfortunately, like *Generation, Bogue Street Bridge* understood the publishing limitations of a newspaper that had no funds. Although the East Lansing campus community was one of the largest in the country, the radical community was rather small. Had there been only one underground newspaper, it alone would have found survival to be a formidable

task. Now there were two, and, as suspected, they were both struggling.

So, with thoughts of bouncing checks and dreams of tomorrow, the two staffs, in October of 1970, held a combined meeting. Out of that meeting came the historic decision that was announced in volume I, number 3 of both papers. As an attempt to solve the money problems that were common to both papers, the two staffs had agreed that, for the next paper, they would combine personnel and resources and come out with an experimental *JOINT ISSUE*.

Voila!!

The first *Joint Issue* hit the streets on October 19, 1970. The beginning of the familial flow that would four years later produce the *Lansing Star* and then later the *Lansing Beat*, could be seen in the fact that the first *Joint Issue* was volume I, number 4 (the first *Lansing Star* was volume VI, number 1; the first *Lansing Beat* was volume 16, number 1).

The cover of the folded tabloid featured the logos of the two separate papers facing each other from opposite ends of the page. In the middle, along with a picture of a hand holding a burning joint, were the words *Joint Issue*. On the inside cover, the *Joint Issue* logo, including the Zig Zag man and the words "Qualite Superieure," appeared for the first time. Two more *Joint Issues* were printed by the middle of November and then financial hassles once again forced the East Lansing underground to stop their presses.

The change from two local papers to one brought with it its fair share of personality clashes. By the beginning of 1971, Steve Crocker from the original *Bogue Street Bridge* staff was no longer with the paper. Also missing were Carl Stensel and brothers John and Leonard Stockmann from the original *Generation*.

Overall, though, the transition was smooth, due mainly to common goals and organizational similarities. Unlike the early *Paper*, which operated under the traditional editorial board format, both *Generation* and *Bogue Street Bridge* as separate entities had attempted to work under a collective form of leadership, where all the members took equal part in the decision-making process and all the members shared all the work. Now, as a united staff, they attempted the same. The reality did not reach the ideal—as in all situations, where there is no formal leadership, informal leadership tends to emerge. Still, at this point in *Joint Issue*'s history, this was not a serious problem.

A third underground also made its debut appearance in the fall of 1970. *Red Apple News*, begun by Wendy Cahill, Ted Prato, and Don Gaudard, became the area's first Lansing-based underground. Nevertheless, finances were tight everywhere. With the same strategy as had been used four months earlier, the merger of *Joint Issue* and *Red Apple News* took place in February of 1971. It was decided at that meeting that, rather than go through another name change, the name *Joint Issue* would be kept. To clarify the transition for the community, it was agreed that the *Red Apple News* logo—a red apple housing a gun-toting, fist-waving worm—would be incorporated on the masthead for the first two combined issues.

Red Apple News brought with it a much stronger orientation to women's liberation and gay liberation than was present in *Joint Issue*. This was at least the outward reason for much of the staff dissension. Much of the friction was the result of a rivalry between certain members of *Red Apple News* and the old *Generation* that would exist as long as any of them were still on the paper.

With this second merger, *Joint Issue* was now no longer solely an East Lansing paper. Still young and innocent, with a circulation of only 3,000, they had at least begun to make inroads into the Lansing community, including the high schools and Lansing Community College. In helping to build a new countercultural community, regular features such as Seeds of Change tried to create an awareness of alternative institutions, like food co-ops and bicycle co-ops, that were in the area. At the same time, to protect this new rebellious community, descriptions and pictures of local narcs were printed at every opportunity.

The last three issues of spring provided extensive coverage of the May Day demonstrations in Washington, DC, where antiwar demonstrators shut down the city despite 12,000 arrests (see appendix 1).

And then came summer.

Joint Issue, despite ever-present financial difficulties, was still around. At a June meeting, several staff members outlined plans for summer travel. It was decided that the paper would definitely resume publication in the fall and, if the energy was there and the money could be found, those who stayed in town might put out a summer issue.

The energy was there. It came in torrents. A summer issue came out. In July of 1971, 10,000 copies of volume II, number 6 were distributed free throughout the Lansing area. A whole new era was beginning.

JOINT ISSUE BECOMES FREE

I believe every person's life is a story. History is the sum total of those stories that get recorded and preserved for the future. The events of my own story from 1970 to 1973 closely paralleled those of *Joint Issue* and for a long period events of the two were nearly synonymous. Therefore, in recalling this period in the history of the underground press in East Lansing (and by now the whole Lansing area), rather than attempting an "unbiased" analysis for the sake of an "unbiased" history, I'd like to present, simply, our story.

In January 1971, I attended my first *Joint Issue* meeting. The union between *Bogue Street Bridge* and *Generation* had been successful and they were now solidified as one newspaper; *Red Apple News* still existed in Lansing, separate from *Joint Issue*. This meeting was the first in nearly two months, since the last issue, in November, had depleted all financial resources and staff energy. The subject for discussion was: Should we attempt another issue?

Out of that meeting came two decisions. First, yes, we would attempt another issue. Second, in order to do so, the cost of one issue would have to be increased by a nickel. Volume II, number 1 appeared that week and sold for twenty cents.

Most of the participants at that meeting had experienced the first stages of our radical political consciousness during the student strike of the previous spring. Few of us had seriously studied Marx but we all knew that history was beckoning to capitalism to join feudalism and slavery as another wornout system of the past. None of us owned businesses, but we knew that the concept of "scarcity" was a myth and that competition as it was practiced in this country was no more than a divide and conquer technique that created hatred between different kinds of people. We were all young white middle-class people who were becoming aware of our own oppression and of the need for our own revolution.

An article in that first issue presented *Joint Issue*'s interpretation of "The State of the Movement." It was directed to people like us, to "young white middle class people in America who have come to realize the need for political revolution," and also to "young white middle class people who have seen the need for cultural revolution." The former were people who "have directed their efforts at altering or abolishing the various levels and forms of government that have carried out racist and militaristic policies"; the latter "have dropped, and are dropping, out of the Old Culture to begin a new, vital one based on new values, norms and morals." The article was the essence of Yippie. It called for a fusion between the two types of revolutionaries so that the revolution against the larger enemy, Capitalism, could be waged.

"Capitalism" was defined "not just as an economic system, but rather as the sum total of America's consumeristic attitude, authoritarian, pro-profit, anti-people, generally stifling social values, as an outmoded system of rules governing social and personal relations."

"Revolution" was defined as "much more than politics—it is the building of an alternate lifestyle, or better, many of them, and, perhaps most important, developing a sense of collective purpose by creating a Community."

Joint Issue saw itself as a tool in the struggle for that collective community. It would be a community newspaper, owned and operated by community people "not to 'serve' the community but to be the community."

On a lighter note, we observed the goings on around town and noted the new additions to Lansing's roadsides. As a reaction to the new countercultural term that was quickly replacing "cop" as the most derogatory description possible for a policeman, several respectable local businesses—among them Philip Dodge, Lansing Tire Co., Pollack Corp., Root Electric, Max Curtis Ford, and many others—had hired Central Advertising to devise a pro-police force campaign. Out of this campaign had come a series of billboards, each sponsored by a different business organization, that pictured a kindly policeman giving artificial resuscitation to a young boy. The caption read: "Some Call Him Pig!" *Joint Issue*'s answer featured on the cover a kindly countercultural male, bearded, with long straight hair hanging below his shoulders, giving artificial resuscitation to another young boy. The caption read: "Some Call Him Hippie!!"

Local artist extraordinaire Denny Preston made his *JI* debut with this cover, and with his version of the *Joint Issue* logo, which featured, in addition to the Zig Zag man and the words "Qualite Superieure," a marijuana stem cupped in the pocket of a flamboyant J. This logo, or revisions of it, remained the standard for the next year and three-quarters.

More than just passing reference should also be made to another article in that issue, entitled "Wharton and the U.S. Empire." Much excitement is always aroused around the subject of "firsts," and so the idea of "the first black president of a major U.S. university" got extensive coverage in the establishment media. To them, this landmark achievement symbolized just another example of how, thanks to the social greatness of this country, Horatio Alger could even be black.

This *JI* article was the second of a two-part series by Chuck Will discussing Wharton's background. The first had appeared as the cover story in the November 1970 issue and was called "Clifton Wharton—Who Pulls His Strings?" The two articles listed all of Wharton's activities previous to his becoming president of MSU and showed that he was or had been at one time or another associated with dozens of white ruling class institutions in such capacities as trustee of the Rockefeller Foundation (1970); executive associate in Agricultural Economics in Malaysia, Thailand, Vietnam, and Cambodia (ADC, 1964-66) and director or vice president of ADC (1966-70); a member of Gover-

nor Rockefeller's Presidential Mission to Latin America (1969); and a member of the Presidential Task Force on Agriculture in Vietnam (1966). Among other things. Rather than proving that America is not racist, sadly enough, Clifton Wharton was said to exemplify all that is meant by "Ya don't have to be white to be white."

The first half of 1971 was a high energy six-month period, not just for the paper but for the whole country. On the international level, the United States invaded Laos and Eldridge Cleaver placed Timothy Leary under house arrest in Algiers.

On the local and statewide level, *Red Apple News* merged with *Joint Issue*; black students at Sexton High School went on strike (not because of the *RAN/JI* merger) and 54 of them were arrested; Davey Brinn and Randy Scott appeared in court in Grand Rapids to defend themselves against separate charges stemming from protests outside a Spiro Agnew $100/plate dinner in Grand Rapids the previous summer; 25 people were arrested in Kalamazoo during a rally sponsored by the United Front; and *Joint Issue* launched its economic boycott against Min-A-Mart in East Lansing.

On the national level, May Day articles filled the last three pre-summer issues.

All these events were covered by *JI*. Unfortunately, much happened that could not be included because, in that first six-month period, only six issues were published. Again, a lack of jack was the financial fact that forced lengthy lulls between literary layouts.

In April, the staff held another meeting. Still pursued by the Poltergeist of Pecuniary Plight Past, the decision was made to raise the price of each issue another nickel. The three May Day issues each sold for 25¢.

The paper was not seen at this time as an ongoing institution. Rather, it was seen as a community organizing tool that would come out whenever money was available for a new issue. Advertisements paid for about half the costs, street and store sales for the other. In theory. In actuality, the paper printed about 3,000 copies of each issue and sold approximately half of them. A new issue would go to press when enough money had been generated through ad and paper sales to make the financial loss for the previous issue bearable. As the first half of the year had shown, this amounted to about one issue a month.

Summer was welcomed by a burnt out staff. We had survived and we were pleased by that. But too much time was being spent on hawking papers to pay the bills. There was no time left to foment a revolution when all our time was being devoted to mere survival.

In a low-energy beginning-of-summer meeting, the staff decided that, if the energy could be found, a summer issue could appear. However, with half the staff leaving for the summer, this seemed unlikely.

In any good rags to riches story, this is the time when the hidden element appears, when perseverance finally pays off, when Horatio Alger's hero gets his first break. In the story of *Joint Issue*, this was the meeting when a new idea was presented. It came from a voice in the corner, a voice that for the past six months had manifested itself in silence. Now it spoke for the first time.

"I've got an idea," he said. "If we sold enough ads, we could raise our circulation to 10,000 and give the paper away for free. If we raised our circulation to 10,000 and came out free, we would have an easier time getting ads. Then, once we got the ads, we'd be able to pay for the paper so that we could afford to come out free."

The idea created instant skepticism, and the ad campaign started the next day. Six weeks later, $300 in ads had been sold. A 16-page paper was laid out and 10,000 copies of the first free *Joint Issue* flooded the downtown shopping districts of East Lansing and Lansing on July 14, 1971. That issue, in black and white, cost $305, so the paper lost $5, mere pocket change. The staff considered that the equivalent of a profit.

The energy unleashed by this initial success propelled the staff and the paper into depths of Reality formerly believed to be beyond Fantasy level. *Joint Issue* became the most talked about news event of the summer. The incredible response in terms of community awareness and approval was so positive that ads began to come to us. By the following fall, we were able to sell ads on contract for the first time, forego street sales, and project bi-weekly dates of publication for the next three months, with a steady print run of 10,000 copies per issue. In January of 1972, we upped the ad prices 25 percent and raised the circulation to 15,000. To the best of my knowledge, *Joint Issue* was the first underground paper in the country to come out free on a regular bi-weekly basis. Underground papers in Columbus, Ohio (*Free Press*), and Madison, Wisconsin (*Free For All*), soon followed suit, directly influenced by *Joint Issue*'s success.

The revolutionary raps we had at that time centered around the possible hypocrisy of selling ads to capitalist businesses for a newspaper that advocated the overthrow of capitalism. Hard-line critics said it was liberal to accept any ads at all. We took their opinion seriously because, God forbid, the worst insult was to be called a liberal. In the end, however, we decided it was more revolutionary to provide a free community service by accepting ads than to be purists and be forced to fold. We did show some discretion, though, by purposely avoiding certain institutions that we saw as being counter-revolutionary beyond the level of acceptance, such as banks, insurance companies,

Jacobson's department stores, and barber shops. If we slipped, readers were sure to straighten us out. Thus, a barrage of mail and community complaints following our September 18, 1972, issue (volume III, number 13), in which we ran an ad for a local rental management firm, told us to never again accept a full-page ad (or any size) from them or any other of East Lansing's "rip-off apartment rental associations."

With the advent of the free paper, mere survival passed on as the crucial issue. With a new-found freedom to sit back and analyze our place in the community, the staff rose to a new level of awareness and realized that we weren't just a rag anymore. We were now coming out regularly, and we were reaching so many thousands of readers that we had a—gasp—responsibility to be credible. That meant cleaning up the rhetoric and dealing with our own hypocrisies.

In the next two years, criticism/self-criticism nearly drowned us. Tragically enough, it was our idealism that eventually doomed us.

JOINT ISSUE AND ITS SENSE OF RESPONSIBILITY

The period from 1971 to 1974 saw East Lansing's counterculture grow and expand from a campus-based protest movement to a Lansing-wide community. This was *Joint Issue*'s heyday—the time during which it was free—and, as was true with every other underground paper in East Lansing's countercultural/political history, it was a reflection of the time in which it appeared. No one knew then exactly what it meant to be countercultural—was it anyone who smoked dope? Anyone who drove a VW microbus? Anyone who ate brown rice?—but we knew it existed.

Likewise, no one knew exactly what *Joint Issue* was, least of all its somewhat amorphous staff, but there was no doubt that from its inception it was the newspaper of that community.

One fact that must be understood is that the paper that came out before July 1971 and the one that began in July 1971 were two different papers entirely, whether or not their staffs were similar. Before this first free issue, we admittedly were a naive group of freeks who, in good revolutionary faith, were trying to change the world. We meant well, but our effect was minimal. If we let slip an occasional bit of rhetoric, no harm was done because few people were reading the paper yet, and those who did were people like us who had come out of the student strikes. Their ideology, whatever it happened to be, was begun by the strike so they had a certain background that *Generation, Bogue Street Bridge, Red Apple News*, and the early *Joint Issue* just furthered along.

Coming out free with 10,000 copies changed all that. Suddenly, as a mass-produced newspaper, we became a real community force. Thousands more people were paying attention to us. To certain people, *Joint Issue* attained a position of extreme importance. For high school students, growing up in isolated communities, far from the excitement of the campus area, but nevertheless experiencing similar changes in their values, they could see this professional-looking paper that was saying the same things they were thinking and they could gain more confidence that what they were dealing with were legitimate issues and that they weren't alone. For scores of prisoners who began receiving *Joint Issue* in the mail, it became their connection to the outside world. Certain countercultural merchants were so behind the paper, they advertised just to be a part of it. And young factory workers at last had found a paper that was aware of and sensitive to the alienation that they felt from their jobs.

We were no more political heavies now than we were then, but we suddenly had an immense responsibility to be accurate. No longer could we say anything just because it sounded good. This meant, for one thing, cleaning up the rhetoric. Yes, it came as a surprise, but not everyone knew we lived in "Amerikkka." Some people were even offended by our use of the term "Pig." Still, they read *Joint Issue* because they saw it as some kind of alternative to which they could relate.

Whoever we were, we had questions—there was definitely a new consciousness in the air. We all were finding new ways to relate to our government (negatively, skeptically) and new ways to relate to each other (positively, intimately). We were searching for new ways of living together that weren't defined by oppressive sets of institutions, such as the nuclear family, the hierarchy of the university, and the military. Special issues devoted centerfolds to discussing particular countercultural values and concerns that are common today but that were still new back then, such as prisons, heroin, communal living, gays, birth control, women's self-help, and organic gardening. Volume III, number 4 (February 21-March 4, 1972) featured, in addition to an ecology special, the first community handbook.

The 18-year-old vote became a reality that year—the next step was to cut the red tape that was making it so difficult for students to register.

East Lansing City Council was in the process of trying to construct a peripheral route that would cut through East Lansing, supposedly to ease the flow of traffic from one side of campus to another. The alternatives that were raised included mass transportation and a better system of bike paths.

Marijuana laws were being challenged.

Rent control was being proposed.

And the Coalition for Human Survival was formed. The Coalition was a group of radical activists, mostly under-30 community folks who had come together earlier that year in an effort to turn this self-consciousness of community into a political force. Besides actively supporting these issues, in the summer of '71 they ran a slate of candidates for City Council.

Joint Issue saw the Coalition and all these issues as relevant to their community, and all received support, criticism, and wide coverage.

An article in the first November issue of that year, "The Youth Ghetto in East Lansing," defined this community in economic terms.

This clear visibility certainly alerted all the local authority figures to the well-founded possibility that they were being threatened (see appendix 2). *JI*'s "Police Information Guide" (PIG), a centerfold collage containing pictures and descriptions of narcs in the area, which appeared in the September '71 issue, added to their discomfort. They didn't respond, however—outside of subtle intimidation, like standing guard outside the Student Services Building on campus, where we had our office—until the paper made its first major direct attack.

This attack appeared in volume II, number 12, the last issue of 1971. The cover showed a photograph of three rows of cops dressed in riot gear, standing on the steps of the Capitol. The caption read, "What Do These Men Have To Hide?" On page 2 was an article entitled, "A Very Dangerous List." The list, carefully typed and laid out on page 3, showed the names, addresses, phone numbers, code names, and call numbers of all the state police, undercover and otherwise, in the Lansing-East Lansing area.

It was obtained by means that to this day have not been revealed, but its existence became known even before it appeared in the paper. When two staff members delivered the layout sheets to the printer, they were informed by him that his lawyer had advised him to not print the list.

With no other printer to turn to at the time, they were forced to re-layout the page. Over the list of information, they pasted a blank white sheet of paper and on that they press-typed in bold black letters, "CENSORED." In a 2" x 4" paragraph that they typed below the letters, they explained how the printer's "chicken shit liberal lawyers" had refused us freedom of the press. With a razor blade, the printer neatly—being the professional that he was—censored our explanation of the censor.

With the short-term mentality that authority figures never seem to transcend, this power play worked against them. The list got out anyhow, as *JI* stenciled hundreds of copies and gave them away to anybody who requested one. In the meantime, Detroit TV news broadcast the event, AP and UPI articles sent it all over the country, and locally this recognition turned us into a cause to unite the community. All the attention helped greatly to legitimize us further.

Another incident of harassment took place the previous month, when Associated Students of MSU (ASMSU) kicked eight student movement groups, *JI* included, out of their offices in the Student Services Building. ASMSU is the student government on campus whose officers are elected annually by a vote from approximately 10 percent of the student body. Their catch-all reason was lack of space. They did, nevertheless, allow the *State News* to retain its rent-free offices on the entire third floor of that same building.

The results of this incident were twofold. First, it brought *Joint Issue* into much closer contact with these groups, which included women's liberation, gay liberation, SDS, Vietnam Veterans Against the War, New Community, Pan African Students Organization of the Americas, and Legislative Relations. Second, it forced *JI* off campus and more deeply into the East Lansing community.

In the early years of the Movement, the major media-grabbing events were large-scale demonstrations, such as the police riots in Chicago '68, the Moratorium March in DC '69, and May Day in DC '71. Around this time, however, a change was taking place. The relevance of these media events was being called to question as community activists, aware for the first time of their own particular needs, were devoting more time and energy to local organizing. Mass demonstrations were seen as token efforts at best to create change. Whereas older folks considered themselves to be responsible citizens by voting once a year, it was being said now that, in the same way, many activists were calling themselves radical if they marched once a year. The impact on the government was about equal.

On the staff of *Joint Issue*, there were some who were opposed to these demonstrations, others who were ambivalent, and a few who were deeply involved in the national planning of them. Because of the participation of the few, *JI* gave extensive coverage to the events in Miami Beach in '72 during the Democratic and Republican presidential conventions and to the Nixon Inauguration March in DC in '73.

Nevertheless, the pattern was clear. The main focus in *JI* was becoming more and more devoted to events on the local scene. Besides regular current events articles on the co-ops in the area, *Joint Issue* was the major source of publicity for four events that took place between March and October of 1973: "The Empire's New Clothes," an educational antiwar conference sponsored by Crisis in America; Everywoman's Conference; the Male Role Workshop; and the First Annual May Daze Celebration at Valley Court Park.

JI was also in the forefront in covering such events as the trial of SDSer John Royal, the Wacousta Road pot bust, strikes at John Bean and Coral Gables, and the May 1972 blockade of East Lansing's main drag, Grand River. The blockade was one of many similar actions throughout the country that followed President Nixon's blockade of Haiphong Harbor in Vietnam.

This growth in community consciousness was not unique to East Lansing—communities around the country were experiencing the same phenomenon. The general readership of underground papers was growing rapidly as their ideas gained a broader-based acceptance. In June of 1973, members of the Underground Press Syndicate, comprised of papers from across the country, met in Boulder, Colorado, for a major convention. Here, collectively aware that their newspapers were gaining credibility even in the eyes of former skeptics, the term "underground press" gave way to "alternative press."

One month later, *Joint Issue* moved its offices for the first time into Lansing. Again, the move paralleled the general trend westward as former MSU students, no longer dependent on the university but still feeling at home in the Lansing area, began relocating closer to downtown Lansing, where rents were lower. For *JI*, the movement that began on campus had grown to encompass Lansing and several of the surrounding towns. With our press run now at 15,000, we were reaching more people than ever.

But there were problems.

The main problem was in *Joint Issue*'s structure. Or our non-structure. Or our denial of the existence of an undefined structure. It was all rather confusing because there was no constant, except for the ever-present trial and error attempt to be, in practice, a small scale of the utopian society we advocated. *JI*'s organization was a reaction to the oppressive bureaucratic closed door institutions that had guided us through childhood.

As a counterculture institution, *Joint Issue* was idealized to be "anarchistically non-structured." What this meant was that there were no hierarchical positions. People in the community were invited, urged, even begged when times were bad, to take part in all aspects of the paper process. The staff members of each issue were simply those who worked on that particular issue. No one held any titles, no one was restricted to any one job. Rather, everyone would write, everyone would type, everyone would layout, sell ads, distribute. And everyone would share in the decision-making process. This was our ideal. Unfortunately, ideals can't type.

The positive result was that activists from the different political and personal liberation groups began to contribute articles, and together they formed in *JI* a growing coalition of amalgam politics comprised of internationalist, community, and personal politics. This was a strength that encouraged further diverse input.

However, very few contributors stayed long enough to type their articles. Fewer helped to lay them out. And at *JI*'s peak, there were never more than six people selling those crucial advertisements that the paper needed to remain free. No one got paid to work on the paper so we all had to hold down other jobs as well. Further human help was essential.

To encourage new blood, *JI* individuals had to look inside ourselves for ways we might be discouraging newcomers. We knew there were personality conflicts whose vibe-puke permeated the shortest of meetings. And we copped to our collective air of elitism that no doubt was turning people off. We began announcing our meetings in the Staff Box—which we changed to Info Box to lessen the idea of us as a hardcore closed group of individuals. We made the first meeting for each issue an informal potluck dinner so interested new folks could meet *JI* regulars in a less threatening atmosphere.

Whatever changes occurred, whenever flashes of inspiration struck, we wrote articles. To explain who we were and how we operated, we wrote articles. We also would write an occasional brief history of the paper as seen not in terms of the outside events that shaped it, like the war and the strike, but rather in terms of our inner group dynamics. We publicized those dynamics because we believed we should share our weaknesses as well as our strengths with our community. Our laundry was everyone's laundry.

At this stage in the growing pangs of the counterculture, "leadership" was as yet undefined. It was, however, looked upon negatively. Leadership corresponded with all the worst aspects of the masculine image: "macho," "aggressive." Leaders were seen as "power hungry ego trippers." To deal with this charge, the regulars began to withhold opinions so as to not intimidate those who might want to become involved but were less aggressive in nature.

To some, all this concern may have been seen as force-feeding. Others, no doubt, had become disenchanted with our fluctuating politics. Whatever the reason, by the time of the move to Lansing, there were three other alternative papers in town: *Grand River Review*, put out by the folks from Goodman Free School; *Outrider*, by the Coalition for Human Survival; and *Spectacle*, by another group of local anarchists.

The move to Lansing changed little on the internal level. Burnouts were still frequent and were becoming steadily more draining. An announcement in volume IV, number 4 (Oct. 1-?) explained to the community that "Somehow, 'the system' has broken down, and we're going to lay off awhile to rebuild and reorganize."

The next issue (The "*JI* Is Back" issue) came out two months later. In an article entitled "Still Here....

Still Trying," we recognized that "structurelessness" is impossible. "It may be flexible; it may vary over time; it may evenly or unevenly distribute tasks, power and resources over the members of the group. But it will be formed regardless of the abilities, personalities, and intentions of the people involved."

We also discussed our attempt to be "leaderless." Realizing that withholding valuable guidance for fear of being seen as power hungry is ultimately as harmful as being power hungry, I wrote in that article, "I reject the idea of a 'leader' as a person who is elected to paternalistically do our thinking and acting for us. On the other hand, though, is the person who has a skill and is willing to teach others. The present type of leader is one who acts to perpetuate the notion of leadership; the other is one whose function is to make leadership obsolete." That issue schedulized on paper the entire layout procedure into a day-by-day process.

By this time, however, it was too late. Four months previous to this, two men from the community—not strangers, even, but friends of staff members—had begun working on the paper. In our eagerness to incorporate new energy, we had welcomed them heartily. Unfortunately, they had no desire to be leaderless or open. Soon after the "*JI* Is Back" issue came out, their power play took over the paper's office and equipment and they began their own paper, under the same name. They adopted what has been described as a "sort of kneejerk Marxist political line," denied access to equipment to other groups, and destroyed in less than six months the very positive reputation *JI* had earned for itself over four years.

The "*JI* Is Back" issue was the last *JI* I worked on. Soon after that, I left town, so the only veteran staffer still in town at this time was Steve Vernon. Because of intense personality conflicts, he was unable to work with the other two—hence, the takeover. Throughout that 3- to 6-month period, however, he watched the goings-on of the paper and alerted other community members to the situation. In May, there was another takeover of the paper, but this time it was the community re-ripping off its own paper. The two hightailed it westward with the *Joint Issue* typewriter and $1,000, leaving behind only the painful lesson that you don't need a uniform to be a pig.

Joint Issue was back at last in the community to which it belonged, but it had suffered in the process and it was tired. In its proud history, it had been through a lot. It had helped shape a community. Indeed, in the early years, its role was its mere existence, which served to legitimize the community. Times, however, had changed, since the day when *Generation* and *Bogue Street Bridge* first merged to put out an experimental "joint issue" in October of 1970. Personnel had changed now, too. It was time to move on.

The Return to the Womb

The *Last Joint Issue*, volume V, number 5, came out May 20, 1974. After that, the name was laid to rest forever. The first *Lansing Star—Joint Issue* with a name change—appeared June 3, 1974, as volume VI, number 1. In keeping *Joint Issue*'s legacy alive, *Lansing Star* also was free. Unfortunately, the *Star* inherited *JI*'s other legacy also: tight finances.

One of the reasons was the existence of the *State News*, Michigan State's student paper, that also was free but that came out daily and with 40,000 copies. Some competition. Credibility *JI* could deal with—few rational people have ever taken the *State News* seriously as a source of information or educated opinion. But the *State News* had the added advantage of being able to levy a one-dollar tax on every student every term. *JI* challenged the inequity of that system and questioned the legality as well in regular hard-hitting articles against the *State News,* which claimed it was stealing $120,000 every year from the students with the blessings of the MSU Board of Trustees.

One article of mine, entitled "Everyone Has Gone To The Moon: Join Us, It's On The Students," which appeared May 3, 1973, opened with this explanation: "At the beginning of every term at Michigan State University when students register, they are required to pay a $1 fee that goes to the *State News*. Michigan State is a public institution and the *State News* is a private non-profit corporation—thus, this action, quite simply, is illegal: no different than if students had to pay a $1 fee to General Motors."

This situation is no longer true today. The illegal tax is $2. If opposition forces can claim any victory at all, it is in having made the tax refundable. In order to receive that refund, students need only complete a minor bureaucratic maze before a specified deadline. History still awaits the student who will challenge in court the right of *State News* to claim that tax in the first place.

Combined with *JI*'s editorial pressure was the progressive social consciousness of Art Levin, the *State News* general manager of the time, who not surprisingly was fired midway through his one-year contract by the non-student board of directors of the alleged student newspaper. Nevertheless, before he was gone, he had succeeded in opening up a portion of the paper's reserve capital as a charity to alternative student papers. *JI* found a student to claim he was a staff member, wrote a stirring appeal for funds entitled "Up From the Basement: Or, Goodbye, Kitty Litter," satirically alluding to the wealth we were on the verge of falling into, and became the first recipient of *SN* funds.

The fund that *JI* helped to create later became known as Student Media Appropriations Board (SMAB). In 1980, SMAB funds became the property of ASMSU (Associated Students of MSU), the student government, whose Funding Board now controls handouts for not just student publications but all student groups. Because of the large number of groups applying for funds, less money is available for each group.

Unfortunately, the fund over the years became a drug on which the alternative press became dependent. *JI* had no problems finding uses for their little windfall—it amounted to about $3,000, I believe—but its survival still depended on the hustle of the ad people.

The *Lansing Star* began with remnants of *JI*'s energy but soon was relying heavily on SMAB's good graces. In addition, whereas *JI* had been born on campus and then grew to cover Greater Lansing and beyond, *Lansing Star* news coverage made a subtle return to the womb. Early issues had solid articles exposing MSU's collusion with the Shah's Iran and tracking the goings-on of Mayor Gerald Graves and the Lansing City Council. Coverage of the arts was as dynamic as our alternative press has seen.

However, in the last years of the *Star*'s existence, attention to the arts became the focus. The entertainment calendar rated with the best, but hard investigative reporting all but disappeared, as did its power as a community organizing tool. In addition, the drug of free money dulled the hunger required to conduct an ad campaign or throw a successful fundraiser. Soon, the paper's existence became nearly dependent on the ASMSU Funding Board's generosity.

In the summer of 1980, at a time when it appeared as if the *Lansing Star* had died, the *People's Voice* was born. The *Voice* was more analytical than the *Star*, being filled with well-researched thought-provoking pieces. Still, it was born as a SMAB dependent and never escaped dependency on MSU money. Then the *Star* made a comeback and East Lansing again had two alternative papers that shared a basic outlook but competed for scarce funds and resources.

In January 1983, the *Michigan Voice* was making inroads into the Lansing community with claims of being Michigan's first statewide alternative newspaper. Local coordinators—I was one of them—had joined the staff with, among other ideas, the belief that we could serve to unite the isolated local Michigan alternative papers into one dynamic network of information and activity. It was with this idea that a meeting was held on June 27 to bring together members of all three papers so we could talk about our respective papers, get to know each other as individuals, and discuss ways we could work together. Unfortunately, within a month the *Lansing Star* had ceased publication and the *People's Voice* was planning its last issue.

Meanwhile, concerns about the *Michigan Voice*'s internal organizational structure were beginning to grow among key people in the local contingent. Talking about collective goals and deals at the meeting forced us to confront our own present reality, and wince. The reason had to do with what Lansing-area activists had come to expect from the term "alternative institution."

Joint Issue, *Lansing Star*, and *People's Voice* were alternative to the *Lansing State Journal* and the *State News* not only because they were not controlled by big business but also because their non-hierarchical structures strove to give all the workers a say in the decision-making process. When the term "alternative institution" was used in Lansing, certain assumptions were included in the definition. Exact equality, à la the theory, may never be realized in reality, but progressive action is characterized by a move in that direction. After six months, key staff people from the Lansing contingent came to believe that the *Michigan Voice*, despite applying politically correct leftist analysis to issues of the day, was another hierarchical paper. Some workers in Ann Arbor and Detroit also were feeling the alienation that comes from being in the chain of command. It remained only for representatives from the three cities to make contact with each other.

On Wednesday July 27, 1983, a meeting of disillusioned *Michigan Voice* activists produced "Statement of alienation by workers on the *Michigan Voice.*" The statement began with a collectively written definition of the term "alternative newspaper": "Historically, reference to the alternative press has utilized two definitions for the word 'alternative': first, that it prints stories, news analyses, etc. 'that provide an alternative to the business-owned mass media'; and, second, that it is owned by the workers and operated, in its internal structure, in a collective non-hierarchical, non-oppressive, open manner that shows due respect for the workers."

Then, recognizing that the paper was presently owned and controlled by the Flint contingent (the roots of the *Michigan Voice* grew out of the *Flint Voice*), the statement called on the Flint people to take the first step in clarifying specifically whether decision making would remain in their hands or be opened up to the rest of the staff. At the next statewide meeting, which was held the following Saturday in Flint, the statement was presented and discussed. At the end of the discussion, ten workers, representing the contingents in Lansing, Ann Arbor, and Detroit, resigned.

Two months later, the first *Lansing Beat* appeared. The *Lansing Beat* was the product of energy not only from former local alternative press staffers but others in the community as well. Sensitive to its place in the Lansing area's underground/alternative press history going back to *The Paper*, the *Lansing Beat* began its own chapter of Lansing area alternative press history as volume 16, number 1.

In line with the Lansing area's proud tradition, the *Beat* was free. However, the staff promised to emphasize once again its own fundraising department so as to lessen its dependency on campus funds. Partly through sheer momentum generated by its twenty-year history, and partly through single-handed devotion of key individuals like Gene Hayhoe, the *Lansing Beat* managed to hang on for three years before folding at the end of 1986.

Today, no one paper directly plugs into the chain of underground newspapers that began with *The Paper* in 1965. Nevertheless, other papers that come out of that tradition do exist and enjoy their own levels of influence within their own, sometimes linking communities. Two of the best are *Peace Education Center* newsletter, put out by East Lansing's Peace Education Center, an activist organization that came straight out of the sixties and whose members often contributed directly and indirectly to the papers of that period; and *Nexus News*, a paper devoted to spiritualism and other higher levels of consciousness.

The chain's legacy can be seen further in the existence today of two dynamic food co-ops, numerous women's self-help organizations, and many other groups that received critical coverage and assistance during their formative years from the newspapers that together established that tradition.

APPENDIX 1: A PERSONAL ACCOUNT OF THE MAY 1971 DEMONSTRATIONS IN WASHINGTON, DC

by Ken Wachsberger

Life is a constant state of growing where no definitive set of boundaries ever separates one growth period from the next. Nevertheless, in retrospect, we tend to interpret our lives through a series of orderly stages. In the life of mainstream America, college is one of the key experiences, the step that launches each individual onto his or her own unique adult life path. In the life of a political revolutionary/social deviant during the Vietnam War, jail became this key experience—that and perhaps the first acid trip. It was the time when all the political theories that had been learned on the streets, and all the revolutionary courage that intellectually had been gained through personal trials, were put to the test.

Being in jail is like finals week.

For me then, May was finals week. May 1970: Nixon invades Cambodia, student strikes sweep the country, I get arrested in the Michigan State University student union, along with 131 others, and become the only one to spend the night in solitary confinement because I refuse to sign my fingerprints without first consulting my lawyer. May 1971: 20,000 antiwar activists descend on Washington, DC, for a weekend of organizing and three days of civil disobedience, 12,000 arrests are made, including 5,000 in front of the Justice Department; I'm one of the 5,000. May 1972: Nixon announces a blockade of Haiphong Harbor, uprisings again sweep the country. In Madison, Wisconsin, activity is high on both sides, I'm beat nearly senseless in a police riot and emerge from jail as—a Yippie!

Pavlovianism works. May has a different smell to me now. When I was younger, May was the first month to have no traces of snow. Summer was right around the corner. A cousin celebrated a birthday every May. Little League was a month away. Now, I see blood. I smell the dankness of sweat in an overcrowded cell, feel the suffocating heat. I probably always will.

And I laugh because Yippie is a media game and you are what you make them think you are and Stew Albert, Yippie theoretician, says to me, never realizing that the impression his words make on me will be lasting, "We can't lose because we're having too much fun."

Those years were the most intense period of my life when they were happening. The rest of my life has been and will be shaped by them. My best friends even today were veterans of the streets, and when we share war stories the mood is generally of laughter. But when I review old notes, even while I enjoy the funny memories, my mood becomes serious. The period was a constant high. It had to be because it was crazy and we were crazy and we couldn't have stopped the war if we had been any different.

The Vietnam War made accidental revolutionaries out of a significant sector of the baby boom generation. The events, the wounds of the time have not been forgotten. And though those wounds have manifested themselves in different ways—some members have become social workers, others spiritualists or health food advocates, others dropped out of society altogether—a shared cynicism of the present society is the common bond that ties this sector together eighteen years after American involvement in the war ended.

I wasn't the most revolutionary of revolutionaries—no one was—but I was totally engulfed by events of the time. Retrospective comparatives are unnecessary, although they seemed vital then—the worst enemy of the radical wasn't the conservative but the liberal. All that mattered was that you were involved. Even getting stoned and spacing out counted as activism if the alternative was holding down a respectable job.

Life was the interaction of two polarities. No, it wasn't at first. That was where liberalism came in. At a time when Jerry Rubin was saying alienation was necessary because it forced people to choose sides and Eldridge Cleaver was saying "If you aren't for us, you're against us," liberals were trying to play both sides. "Yeah, the war is wrong," they said, "but if we pulled out right away, there would be a bloodbath. I'm against ROTC personally but I believe in freedom of choice."

As disenchantment with the war grew, the polarities intensified. Liberals voted third party. The war became not the only issue but rather the focal point of a wider Movement that brought in the complete gamut of national and international, social, political, and personal issues that challenged the entire society we had come to take for granted.

In terms of my own street education, all thoughts, feelings, and actions were representative of either the death culture or the life culture. The terms, used interchangeably by me with "liberal" and "radical," were defined in keeping with the polarization of the times. The first represented the worst characteristics of the mainstream culture, those we were struggling to reject. The second possessed the best traits of the ideal anarchistic society, that which we were striving to achieve. In seeking a new lifestyle, the radical practiced Mao's creed of "criticism/self-criticism." The liberal compromised all principles to maintain ties to the mainstream death culture. Nobody belonged purely to one or the other. The journey in either direction was a personal effort fought on many fronts. When I was busted on Tuesday May 4, 1971, in Washington, DC, those definitions were just beginning to come together in my mind.

The event occurred six months after my peripheral introduction to *Joint Issue*, East Lansing, Michigan's underground paper, and immediately preceded my active involvement. "Diary of a Mad Anarchist," my written account of the week I spent in DC, was my first major effort in participatory journalism. My writing then was more colloquial at times than it is now, and included terms like "gonna" and "wanna" and "lotta" and other such deliberate misspellings that I thought were catchy then but that I cleaned up soon after I began writing articles for *Joint Issue*. It also seems, from a perspective of twenty years, to have been more rhetorical than it is now. Revolutionary phrases such as "Off the Pig" and "Smash the State" finalized many of my articles.

But in those days, these calls to action weren't rhetorical, they were new, at least to me, and to the people—friends, relatives, members of the countercultural community—who read them in early *Joint Issue* articles. More important, the terms polarized, at a time when the urgency of events didn't allow fence straddling. Street language was our way of communicating. The establishment press derided us for using meaningless rhetoric. But we knew what we were talking about. And we helped define the terms of the period.

In this published version, I've cleaned up the misspellings. I also omitted casual variations of "fuck"—"fuckin pigs," for instance—at the request of a close friend, who wanted to make sure no sensitive readers would be offended by the style and therefore miss the substance. Variations of "shit," however, were allowed to stand, a differentiation I didn't completely follow but heeded nonetheless.

Today, as a professional writer and a teacher of writing at Eastern Michigan University, I'm tempted to also change the passive verbs to active by eliminating all sentences beginning with "There was" and "There were," as I tell my students to do; but I'm getting defensive from a perspective of twenty years of writing and publishing. "Diary" was written with no intention—without even the fantasy—of being published. It was raw emotion, written with the frenzy of the time, not to define events for the Movement but just to help me figure out for myself what was going on. Today, I teach writing as a form of self-discovery; then, I was writing to discover my self.

The all lower case *shtick* was either my e.e. cummings influence or because a friend told me anarchists don't use capitals, I can't remember.

Don, by the way, is my older brother.

* * *

monday 5/24/71
12:05 P.M.

dear don,

reading the newspaper and magazine accounts of what took place in dc during the mayday activities, i really wasn't surprised at the way in which they interpreted the results. as a matter of fact, in all fairness to their sense of honesty and mine, i must admit that they were being truthful; in other words, they did do an ok job of getting the facts. but the facts aren't the issue because everyone who was there had the opportunity to see for himself or herself what happened. what is important is what this all meant in terms of the war, in terms of this fascist government (oops, i gave myself away), in terms of the life culture vs the death culture.

with this in mind, my opinion is that the straight press did a shitty job of reporting. for instance, who can deny that the government did not completely shut down on monday the third of may? after all, the workers did get to work, even though many of them were told to leave their homes at *5:00 A.M.* and this is where their interpretations end: they got to work and therefore we failed.

what they don't get into is the fact that it took 6,000 armed cops, soldiers, and mp's representing the strongest government in the world to make it all possible. and, lest i forget, there were 12,000 illegal arrests. and, of course, the tear gas.

well, let me get down to the meat of the letter. what i'm about to get into is my own long awaited-for interpretation. rather than write from memory, i'm just going to copy, as i said i would do, from my diary. so, first a brief intro to that.

my habit, after four years, is to write each night the events of that day. may day week not being exactly what one would describe as peacetime, this wasn't always possible. thus, saturday's and sunday's entries were actually written monday morning before the first battle. and the events of tuesday through friday weren't written until friday and saturday. which leaves monday, which, coincidence of all coincidences, was written monday night.

and now, without the proverbial further ado, it is my revolutionary pleasure to present to you and whoever else happens to be interested:

THE DIARY OF A MAD ANARCHIST

saturday 5/1/71

it's 5:15 A.M. now, the morning before the battle. i'm the only one up and i'm writing by the window, but, nevertheless, in the dark.

one of the essential themes here is that of unity. saturday, that was no problem. with thousands of people coming into the park and camping, there seemed to be no end in sight. traffic was already being blocked, and we weren't even trying yet. the rock concert had continuous music for those who wanted it (and, indeed, many of the campers came only for that). while we were there, there were the beach boys, jb, and linda ronstadt. also, the band was there but i didn't see them. i don't know who was there when we left.

and there were meetings. the campsites were set up by states. finding our people, we moved to the michigan section. our affinity group now has the four of us and nine others from e lansing.

organizational meetings, rap sessions, campfires, and dope—plenty of everything. all would've been perfect, but physically i felt like shit. two aspirins took care of my headache, but my hay fever was a bitch and i had a terrible sore throat. i was wondering how i'd make it through the night.

sunday 5/2/71

ATTENTION, ATTENTION: YOUR PERMIT FOR CAMPING HAS BEEN REVOKED. EVERYONE MUST LEAVE THE CAMPING AREA.

these are the folks who are running our country. and this was their plan to stop the demonstration. it's amazing how little they must think we want peace. or, it's disgusting that they think we're as dumb as they are.

that (or a paraphrase) was our alarm clock this morning at 6:30 A.M. and in no time the grounds were filled with activity. but it was in the form of meetings.

helicopters circling the area (a total joke) probably couldn't believe that instead of just splitting we were meeting. it was beautiful. yes, most of us left (50+ were arrested later on). but the various groups met at various places in georgetown u and american u.

and, in thinking about it, this futile attempt at breaking us up worked, i believe, in our favor:

1. it drove out those who came merely for the sake of the concert.
2. it *spread us out*. by doing this, the pigs couldn't guard us as a group because we were spread out throughout the city.
3. it *kept us together*. although physically we were no longer able to sleep in the same area, in spirit it brought out our strength. the meetings during the day proved that. this ludicrous move intensified the desire of those who were serious.
4. it kept the pigs busy. the city is in a total martial law state (although it hasn't been declared). there were thousands of pigs in the park as we were leaving but, by forcing us to leave there, the pigs now had to "cover" every corner. it's a joke—they look like assholes doing nothing and acting important. the beautiful thing is a lot of them know it and feel silly.
5. we were forced into the city and were thus able to learn it much better than if we had stayed in the park.

so that's my opinion of their plan, plus, of course, it was just a pig thing to do. the thirteen of us kept together the whole time and we had some good luck. but i'm going to quit writing for a while. by the next time i write, i'll know how the first battle went.

monday 5/3/71

washington dc, the capital of the land of the free, is in a virtual police state. both sides are claiming victory. as a "demonstrator," a "militant," a "radical," etc., i was overjoyed with the results.

dc pigs, mp's, cycle pigs, army men—my naivete just really had a hard time relating to all this. I know this shit happens—i've read about such stuff. but there's something about actually seeing it and being a part of it (or, better yet, a victim of it).

traffic *was* stopped. even the news conceded that the georgetown area group was effective. i didn't see much of any place other than ours, so that's all i'll comment on.

our group plan was to resist arrest. this meant that we couldn't just sit in the streets and be arrested. it was hit and run: throw a trash can into the street and run; push a car into the middle of the street, lock it, and run; break glass in the street and run; etc., and run. a lot of the pigs were pretty lenient (meaning that they just chased us) but there was some good head-beating. a lot of people were beaten and let go, and even still, estimates say there were just 5-10,000 busts. with that, the courts are going to be working round the clock for, as the radio says, probably at least a week just to get everyone out. and that's with the judges working all day and night until they fall asleep. (ed note: another scare tactic by the controlling power. by telling the radio stations, knowing that the stations will tell the world, that it will take a week to get out, they hoped to scare us into saying that our own personal comfort was more important than our reason for being there in the first place and that therefore it wasn't worth it to continue demonstrating. they just don't understand. "ed notes" aren't, by the way, part of the diary. they're just spur-of-the-moment thoughts.) the jails, of course, are full and people are being herded into rfk stadium.

the radio and tv stations are saying that the success of shutting down the city was small. i disagree so much:

1. traffic *was* held up. no, we didn't keep people from work, but we sure delayed them.
2. even though people did get to work, they hardly could keep their minds on it with all the action going on outside.
3. it showed how so many young americans are willing to put so much on the line (busted heads, jail terms, and prison records) for their ideals.
4. it cost the government an infinite amount of money: cops working overtime; judges likewise; prisons being filled, forcing guards, typists, etc. to work overtime. plus food for prisoners.

5. it showed that we could create havoc to get our point across.
6. most important, the poor blacks were behind us all the way. they know that their enemy is the same as our enemy. they cheered from windows and from their steps and many times they blocked out pigs who were chasing freeks.

we knew that the news would belittle us. people across the country are probably thinking that we failed. but dc'ers know otherwise.

a couple observations i made during the action:

1. it became more and more apparent that the pig action yesterday was a mistake. they were banking on us giving up and leaving. anything short of that would've been disastrous and such was the result. with us together, they could've raided us. with us scattered throughout dc, that's impossible.
2. differences between the life culture and the death culture become apparent in so many ways. i'm speaking now of one in particular: the death culture is an "every man for himself" thing. the life culture, on the other hand, is into unity that the pigs (the whole death culture, for that matter) just can't relate to. i already said how we organized before splitting sunday. also, i heard on the radio that the prisoners in rfk stadium got together in groups according to states. it's a mindfuck for the pigs and a source of strength for the people that points to inevitable victory.

(ed note: i've still got a couple typed pages worth of writing from monday but i'm going to let them pass so that i can begin my ego trip. what i'm ignoring is things we did after the battle, our personal emotional feelings, our hopes and fears for tuesday, which was supposed to be a continuation of what we did monday, and other such things. it actually is probably interesting and informative but i'm going to try to stick to the actual demonstrations. i'll just throw in the closing sentence from monday.)

hopefully i'll be here tomorrow night to write more—if not, i will after prison.

tuesday-saturday
5/4-8/71

"hopefully i'll be here tomorrow night to write more—if not, i will after prison." that's what i wrote in conclusion to monday's activities. and, sure enough, here i am—after prison. there's almost no sense in dividing these past few days because they were, in effect, one long day. events, as it turned out, didn't go exactly as planned, but the results—both for the

movement and for myself—far exceeded anything that our planned activities could've produced. the war hasn't yet been won, but the people gained a solid victory over the government in these past few weeks of battle.

tuesday's activities called for street tactics and confrontations with cops similar to those that took place monday. slight differences, of course, were expected based on what both sides had experienced and learned from that first day.

one thing we figured was that there would be more cops, mp's, soldiers, etc. and that they would be more violent if need be. also, they would be more prepared to counter our moves, having had experienced and survived one day. for our own part, we also had gone into the streets cold monday; for tuesday, we expected more organization.

we, of course, had one major thing going against us: with 7,000+ (that was the official count) of our people busted monday, we didn't know how many of them would be out and on the streets for a second day of the same. also, a lot of people, whether busted or not, would probably be scared away by the tear gas and the swinging billyclubs.

within our own affinity group, eleven people remained: three had returned to e lansing and t had joined us. (as ed says: good luck reader, you're about to be bombarded with initials.) going into the battle, then, were: t and p in the car (ed: to conveniently stall at intersections); k,j,m, and j; and d,c,p,d, and myself. we came with new offensive tactics, but were also ready to take the defensive.

and the defensive prevailed. apparently the fears had been effective enough to deter the masses because, when we got out, the streets were lined with cops, traffic was moving, and the good guys (those who showed up—not nearly as many as monday) were walking the sidewalks in small groups. there was no future in that—our strength is in our numbers and yet people were saying we would be busted if we got together in large groups. we were totally on the defensive, give or take a few busts and some isolated offensive instances. i was bummed out, although i knew that, even with nothing happening tuesday, the events of the two days combined were still enough to claim a victory.

my despair soon lessened as the nothing began to become a something. as the eleven of us were getting together again to eat and discuss, word was going around that at noon there was to be a march from 14th-j to the justice (that's what some people call it) dept.

to go or not to go: within our own group, there were mixed feelings because there was no permit for the march and busts were inevitable. p,c, and t decided to stay back, while the rest of us donned our armor once again.

what followed can only be described as a decisive victory of the people over the corrupt and decaying power structure (well, actually it's not the only way it can be described, but it's pretty accurate).

i walked over to the meeting place with d (we got into groups of twos so as to lessen the chances of being busted before we got there) and it was during our walk that we prepared ourselves for what we knew would happen. simply, d said, "if they try to bust us, i'm not gonna fight it" —and i replied, "farout!!" i had been ready this morning and had been disappointed that he had been so defensive. it wasn't just for the sake of saying i got busted that i decided not to resist. rather, it was for what i knew would be a fantastic learning experience. and i wasn't too worried that whatever they charged us with would hold up in court anyhow; i knew it would just amount to being detained for a while.

so, being prepared for the worst, and knowing that the worst could amount to no more than an arrest and maybe some harassment in jail and a fine, we felt only excitement and optimism.

rumors were going around that pigs were arresting freeks right off the sidewalks just because they were on the sidewalks (and, indeed, this was true in many cases); armed and uniformed men still lined the streets; and there was no permit for the march. and still the people gathered for an hour-long rally.

and the march was beautiful. my usual reaction to marches is, "big deal, what do they accomplish?" and this is usually the case. people get together for a day, march a few miles and listen to speeches, and then return home saying, "wow, was that fun." in other words, it's a social function, about as effective as a bar mitzvah. and it takes no more commitment.

yet this was different. people ran the risk of getting busted before even getting to the rally. and this was true throughout the whole illegal march. right there, then, is a certain sense of commitment. and, although it didn't stop the war, it was a victory:

1. the government said "no" but was unable to enforce its decision.
2. people lined the streets and looked out office windows. thus, even though we hadn't prevented many people from getting to work, we had prevented them from doing anything once they were there. and this was especially true during the rally at the justice dept—i'd venture to say that, with the windows filled with curious government workers (including john mitchell at one time, although i was in prison by then), virtually no work got done all afternoon.
3. maybe this is the most important thing of all—it showed the world that we do want peace and that we're willing to lay a lot on the line.

before getting into the rally and what followed, i got a kick out of the quote that is engraved on the wall of the justice dept: "justice is the great interest of man on earth. wherever her temple stands there is a foundation for social security, general happiness, and improvement and progress of our <u>race</u>." the quote itself (with the underline to help if need be) is enough to get the point across.

also, there was a point brought up at the pre-march rally that was pretty heavy. in reference to tuesday's news reports, the speaker said (paraphrasing), "what they said we failed to do today (during our rather unsuccessful street demonstrations that morning) was, in actuality, an admission of what we accomplished yesterday that they wouldn't admit then.

moving on:

i don't know how many people participated in the march, but there were at least several thousand. speakers, whoever wanted to get up there, were many: there were blacks and whites, males and females, a gay dude, some of the organizers of the activities. john froines, one of the chicago 7 and one of the most active organizers of the mayday activities, spoke and was later busted inside the crowd by six undercover pigs just before the mass busts began.

and then, sequentially speaking, came the mass busts. the rally had been high-spirited but peaceful. there had been speeches and there had been chanting—but there had been no violence. that, of course, didn't matter: the government wasn't concerned with the threat of violence. it was our mere physical presence that they feared.

and so:

over the mike, a pig broadcast: EVERYONE MUST LEAVE THE AREA IMMEDIATELY. it was nice of him to warn us but he didn't really mean it. with walls on two sides of us and cops on the other two (a couple thousand per side), there was no chance to escape. p,d, and j found that out when they tried to leave and realized that the cops wouldn't let anyone out. they rejoined k,j,d, and me, all of us having decided to be arrested peacefully.

one by one, that's what happened (with the exception of a few protesters who tried to resist). as the cops marched toward the crowd, we moved close together, joined hands, and waited. it became a ritual: a cop would walk up to a protester who would then get up and walk to the bus with him. when d got busted, i stood up to make sure i was next.

not all cops are pigs. this is a most important thing to understand because the cops themselves aren't the enemies. they do, however, represent the enemy, which is why it is essential to try to talk with them and establish whatever rapport is possible. the fact that so many cops honestly do sympathize with us shows that the good guys are winning.

anyhow, i was lucky enough to be busted by a cop, a black dude named m t gardner, #3073. he was from dc and had been on the force for two years. when i asked him what he thought of all this (meaning the mass arrests), he answered, "it's all bullshit." and he meant it, too, enough to be crying. he tried his best to get me onto the same bus as d, but when he was given the arrest form to fill out, he was also given the name of another officer, and so i had to get onto the appropriate bus.

also, in trying to help me out, he wrote down my name as "john smith." who's going to believe that a cop did all that for me? but i told him i wanted my correct name on it—i had committed myself and i wasn't concerned with faking it. we shook hands three times before i got on the bus.

remember how during the [Michigan State University] union bust [in 1970 during the student strike], i was the first one busted, the only one thrown in solitary, and almost the last one released? well, continuing, i was the last one to climb into the first bus to drive away. thus, being the closest one to the door, i was the first one out and the first one thrown in the clink out of the approximately 2,700 demonstrators arrested at that rally (unless someone was taken away before the mass arrests began—john froines is a possibility).

official arrest time, according to the arrest form, was 2:50 P.M. about twenty-five minutes later, i entered an empty cell #2 at u.s. district court cell block.

"empty," however, was a word that only i, being the first inmate, could use. by the time the guard closed the door behind the last person, we could barely see the floor.

physically, we guessed the dimensions were 40 by 21. there were two benches built into the walls of the cell extending lengthwise from the front almost to the back; in the rear on the left side were a toilet and a sink. for ten people, this would all have been sufficient; for 106 it became virtually unbearable.

and, of course, this was no accident. it just goes along with how the whole death culture thinks: "if we can make them suffer enough physically, we'll be able to break their spirit. if we succeed in doing that, we can scare them out of doing any more protesting."

they just don't understand the great difference between a radical and a liberal, one being that a radical commits himself or herself, no matter what the possible consequences, to his or her beliefs, while a liberal, although often preaching for the same things, is too intimidated by the system to be taken seriously.

i knew the conditions would be miserable and i knew that my head was strong enough to endure it—that was fortunate because things were much worse than even i expected.

throughout my stay there (arrested at 2:50 P.M. tuesday, locked up at 3:15 P.M. tuesday, taken to superior court at 5:30 A.M. thursday, arraigned at 7:00 A.M. thursday, approximately 40 hours as a political prisoner), i lived through four bologna sandwich meals (each one accompanied by a cup for water). (we managed to change wednesday's lunch, but i'll get to that.) a couple of the guards were ok dudes and occasionally we were served pineapple-grapefruit juice. but the bologna tasted horrible and the mayonnaise was rancid—we all would've been better off starving.

i spent time in three different cells, but the other two were no less crowded than the first. after being frisked and after answering a couple questions, and while waiting to be printed and mugged, i nearly passed out (very seriously) during the 2-hour+ layover as one of 52 prisoners in a 9 by 21 cell. (my mug shot number, by the way, was #247571.)

i thought at the time that being processed meant i was on my way out—i was wrong. instead, i was led to cell #13, across from #2. although being slightly smaller, it had about the same amount of people.

the crowded conditions, then, caused breathing to become a chore; with little circulation of air, each breath meant that much less fresh air; also, because of that and because each body naturally gives off a certain amount of heat, anyhow, the temperature in each cell greatly increased—someone guessed 90 degrees but that seemed pretty conservative to me.

the cells were all filthy. and with people having to sleep on the floors, this was a serious problem. of course, no one on the outside of the bars seemed to care about that—not until we had been locked up over 30 hours did they sweep the floors.

these conditions, then, plus some good hassling from some of the pigs, were what we had to put up with. it was, as i interpreted it, a psychological battle between the life culture and the death culture, with the former winning, naturally.

our long captivity brought out many differences between the two lifestyles. the death culture, to begin, is an "every man for himself/every woman for herself" culture. sandwiches given to hungry people would naturally cause a "me first" battle among them; shortages of physical space would naturally cause people to fight for whatever they could get; long stays in such overall shitty situations would naturally cause people to turn on each other.

but such was not the case. if there wasn't enough food to go around, whatever there was was shared. with cigarettes, it was a matter of taking a hit and passing it on, as was also true when drinking water out of the flask someone brought in. sharing was a reflex action; no one thought of hogging.

the life culture, then, is one of brotherhood and sisterhood. and this is in direct conflict with everything the death culture practices. throughout the long detention, there was a solid mixture of chanting, rapping, and sleeping. with only a few exceptions, there were no squabbles amongst ourselves.

as i look back at it, and, in fact, as i realized even then, it really all made sense. while the pigs were hassling us from the outside, we generally remained cool on the inside and our spirit was, for the most part, high. this is nothing surprising when thought of in terms of the two cultures. although we were held captive physically, we were able to survive because we were free mentally, relatively speaking. and, for their part, although they were free to move around, mentally they are all victims of those same middle class hangups that we, for the most part, oppose. their only weapon is physical force: hence, physical deprivations.

in comparing the liberal to the radical, i always refer to the degree of commitment. while the radical can go as far as his or her conscience allows, the liberal must always keep within the boundaries of the system. the sense of commitment shared, in whole or in part, by members of the life culture is a constant source of amazement to members of the death culture. (wow!! a flash: washington dc, capital of the *death culture*.) this in itself seems to be almost enough to explain why harassment, prison terms, etc. were unable to break our spirits.

what kind of people were busted with me? for the most part, they were college-age (probably there were as many dropouts as students). the vast majority were longhairs and only a few of them were black.

there were a handful of juveniles. bruce r was one, although he was hardly typical. at 16 years of age, he was a high school dropout with a record that consisted of two counts of auto theft, two counts of possession, and one charge of breaking and entering and grand larceny (a shitload of rifles was the haul). he lives at present with a man, three guys, and four gals, and they sell dope that they get straight from the mafia. as he put it, "i've just got too many connections for a guy 16." his full red beard made it hard to believe his age, but his driver's license convinced me. he wasn't really politically minded, but he was definitely against the war: his brother had recently died in vietnam.

there were only two men who were no longer student-aged. the first was a catholic priest from mobile, alabama. although still a priest in good standing, he had done nothing to gain the church's good favor when he opposed the pope's ruling on birth control. asking his bishop to resign didn't help any.

at the present time, he's living in a vw bus with a nun—natch, the bishop doesn't know this—and they travel the country taking part in demonstrations, etc. and living on $100/month. next year, he plans to organize a group of people to travel the country and campaign for senator mcgovern in the primaries—he asked me if i was interested but i couldn't see it.

john mathews was the other. as a reporter for the *washington evening star*, he was quite surprised to find himself all of a sudden behind bars for the first time in his life. it turned out to be a most worthwhile experience, not only because it made for an interesting article but also because it provided an opportunity for him to witness and to share a few beautiful hours with the life culture.

indeed, that's what i rapped about with him —that seems to be what i get into with everyone. we both got into each other during our talk and he took down my number (ed: where i was staying at the time) and gave me his—that turned out to be a lucky break for me.

where was i throughout the long 40 hours in an american p.o.w. camp? where was my head? how did my body react? i gave these questions a lot of heavy thought long before the bust actually took place and it was only because i was satisfied with my answers that i decided to go peacefully in the event of an arrest.

physically, the crowded cells were no comfort to anyone. the body-filled 90 degree rooms denied us all the possibilities of either breathing fresh air or finding sufficient room to relax. the vast amount of litter and dirt made free space even harder to find. drinking from the same cups, smoking the same cigarettes, etc. are things that are usually done with no second thoughts—but with so many people together, the possibility of someone being sick was high. and the possibility of an otherwise healthy person becoming ill from the shit they called food was equally high.

so who am i to physically withstand all this? my body being as sensitive as it is, i became, after many hours in the first cell, quite dizzy. but i was too emotionally involved to take much notice. with the amount of eating i do anyhow, the lack of food was no serious problem to me. the major discomforts, then, were lack of physical space and shortage of fresh air.

in the second cell, i very nearly passed out. i say that rather abruptly as if it were only because of the conditions in that cage. actually, i must have been on the verge when i went into it, and the fact that i pulled through is due only to extremely good luck—and probably the fact that i was so into the whole chain of events, the living and learning, etc. that i just didn't have time. my head, by this time, was calling my attention to an extended drum solo.

leaving the cell to be processed did much to revive me so that, by the time i was thrown back behind bars, cell #13 this time, i was feeling much stronger. by the time i left, however, dynamite was being exploded in my head and my stomach felt like the ocean at high tide.

i didn't sleep at all during the whole time as a prisoner (give or take a couple hours near the end). this quite certainly contributed to my discomfort (although i know i would've been sick anyhow) but my mind had been made up much earlier that i would sacrifice the sleep to take in whatever atmosphere prevailed—and also to see if i could influence that atmosphere.

considering that some people fainted and many got very sick, i came out of it ok. i hadn't given that much thought to my physical health anyhow—that's most likely the reason.

i *had* given thought to how my head would react. no revolutionary should be in jail—but once in jail, he should make the most of it. i've felt for the past few months that my head has come a long way. this was my first crucial test and i passed it. a lot of dudes cracked up: either they were young and scared or they just aren't yet committed to the revolution. my own spirit was never once broken, nor was it ever weakened. not only did this sustain me, but i was also able to help others through the long ordeal.

that in itself is the main reason i didn't allow myself to sleep. with the pigs trying to hassle us and to get us to turn on one another. it was essential that we keep our spirit high. with everyone chanting and rapping, this was easy—but when someone would crack up, tension found its way into the room.

this is where i first came through with anything other than a few jokes. it was by now 8:00 A.M. wednesday and we had just lived through a bologna sandwich breakfast. one dude had been complaining to me about the conditions. i turned around for a minute, and when i looked back he was hanging onto the bars yelling at an officer about our rights being denied. the officer listened calmly as he raged on. where we had just been into some heavy chanting, it all of a sudden became quiet.

so i took the floor, got everyone's attention (except the dude and whoever was sleeping) and said (although maybe not as dramatic as i'm about to write):

"people, we can't let this happen. this is just what the pigs want. they know we're in lousy conditions, that we're uncomfortable, we're tired, we're hungry. and they want nothing more than for us to crack up and turn on each other. and this is what we can't do—we have to keep our spirits high.

"to speak of rights is ludicrous. did any of you actually believe that we could come to dc with the intention of shutting down the government and then be treated as guests in the prisons of that same government? the fact that we have paper rights means nothing—those only serve to influence our cases in court. and our cases are gonna all be thrown out anyhow. so they don't have to give us anything. "we were all cool until this one dude cracked up and then it all changed. we know that the pigs will continue to hassle us so that we'll all give up and never demonstrate again. this can't be allowed to happen. we have to stick together."

—and then i suggested a food strike. actually, it was someone else's idea, but i put it together. it was beautiful. around noon, the guards came around with the bologna sandwiches and we started shouting, "no food, no food!!" the other cells spontaneously joined in and the guards walked away.

whether we were the reason or not i don't know, but they came back later with oranges and bananas. whatever the case, the strike was successful in that it gave us something to rally around.

and as for the dude—i talked to him and was able to calm him down by giving him an extended rap similar to the one i gave the group. although he was the supreme crackup case, it was satisfying to know that i was able to help others to remain calm, both from what i said and how i acted.

i'll talk about the arraignment now. when i re-read this, i may add some thoughts but i've been on this same subject for so long i'm weary.

at 5:30 A.M. thursday, we got on the bus that took us to federal court. there were about 50 of us in a 36-man bus and again i almost didn't make it. but my curiosity for what was in store sustained me.

we were taken to a room and locked up with about 80 other people, all waiting for a lawyer to take them in front of the judge. i filled out the appropriate form and then psyched myself for another long wait. shortly after, my name was called.

i went with ten other p.o.w.'s in front of judge daly. let me briefly introduce him. as our lawyer warned, "don't expect any breaks from him. he's probably the toughest of all the judges. our strategy will be to just try to stall him long enough so that he'll eventually leave and we can get an easier judge."—we had all been confidently expecting $10 collateral. what a bummer it was to hear that.

sure enough, we got what he had told us to expect. unless you could get someone to take third party custody or personal recognizance, he released us only on $250 bond. our luck to get a fascist.

but i fared well, relatively speaking. while we were in beachwood [ohio east side suburb of cleveland, where I grew up], where we had stopped on our way to dc, dad had brought up the name of a friend, h, who used to live in beachwood and now lived in dc. he had said it jokingly and i took it as seriously as he had expected me to. now i was busted in dc and h, who i didn't know at all, was who i knew best in dc. i gave the cops his name and he came down to take third party custody. and, not being satisfied with that, he said to the judge, "i have some friends from ken's hometown who are here now at a psychiatrists' convention. they're leaving tomorrow (friday). if i promise to get ken a ride with them to beachwood, will you let him off?"

well, the judge didn't quite do that (to hitler: "will you let him off if i promise to get him a plane ticket to israel?") but, in one of those rare mercy cases that are always so exciting to read about, he released me on $50 collateral.

what that means now is that, if i don't show up in court, i forfeit the fifty bucks, but they don't come out looking for me. if i do show up, and we win the case, i get it back. if i show up and we lose, i take whatever punishment they dish out. knowing that:

1. the cases will all be thrown out because there are so many, or
2. they'll be thrown out because of technicalities (like the fact that our rights were denied, we weren't given phone calls, the conditions were shitty, etc.), or
3. the cases will just be postponed indefinitely and finally dropped, or
4. we'll take it to court and win, or
5. innumerable other possibilities,

i made the decision to stick around to see what happens. my trial is set for monday. what i'm going to do, if the trial takes place at all, is watch the ones before mine. if their charges are dropped, mine will be also and my money will be returned. if they are sentenced, i won't show up and i'll just forfeit the bread.

at the arraignment, i was re-united with my people—out of our whole affinity group, i was the only one who hadn't been given a phone call, so i was the only one they hadn't been able to locate.

d walked into the courtroom around 6:00 A.M. as i was waiting to be arraigned. he had been in the courthouse all night trying to find out what was going on with p, k (they were together), and me—we were the only ones who hadn't yet been released. later, j and t came in. and, when p and k were through, we returned to the house —it was a beautiful sight to be with familiar faces and to know that everyone was safe.

of those of us who were arrested, i was the only one who had to stick around: p was given $20 or two days—and since she had already served her two days, she was let go; k was given a court date in june and released under, i believe, personal recognizance; the others had, i think, $10 collateral. having no reason to stick around, they all split that afternoon. so where am i now?

let's get back to john mathews. i noted that he took my number and gave me his. when i got to the house, i found a message for me saying that john had called and that i should call back. he had calmly wondered when i had gotten out (ed again: a little pull from the *star* had gotten him out after 20 hours)—he couldn't believe i had just gotten out.

if i had been planning on splitting that day, i would've rapped as long as possible. but seeing as i was going to be around for awhile, i asked if it might be possible if i crashed at his place —he welcomed me.

so that's where i am now. when he introduced me to a couple friends, he called me his token freek. of course, i met his wife, roberta, and their daughter, susan. and i've been treated like an honored guest.

(here's ed again: skipping the rest of thursday, and all of friday, saturday, and sunday, i take you, now, to a day in court.)

monday 5/10/71

last week i was able to witness the united states government in action. today, my government class took me to a day in court.

never for a moment did i seriously believe that i would be convicted. but i carried it to the extreme: i never even figured i'd have to appear. the government of the people, however, being truly representative of the death culture, decided otherwise. with half-ass attempts, the prosecutor tried his hand.

seventy-seven protesters, most of whom were busted tuesday, several from monday, and the rest from the week before, appeared before judge hamilton in room 17 of the superior court this morning. one by one, we were called up, each of us coming up with no lawyer and each of us getting one when we got up. i really believed the cases would be dropped, but the prosecutor tried. about six cases were dismissed outright and several were re-scheduled. after the break, this continued. i (and about five others) still hadn't been called when, at 3:45 P.M., one of our lawyers told us that the judge was accepting *nolo contendre* pleas, meaning that we didn't plead innocent or guilty. the fine, however, would be $10. most defendants were going to take that, so he went to tell the judge, a pretty liberal black dude. when he came back, he said we had a possible deal: under section 5010a of the federal youth correction act, we could get the following:

1. credit for time served
2. no fine
3. 90-day probation. to explain this: to enter a *nolo* plea, we would be considered guilty. if, after 90 days, we don't do anything wrong (get busted), the record will be expunged. if we do, the conviction will hold but there will be no further penalty. the probation would be unsupervised.

this could be used for anyone under 27. the charge was disorderly conduct.

this, of course, was even better than the first offer.

splitting up, some of us went down to room 12 to appear before judge halleck. here, the terms changed slightly:

1. we still get credit
2. there was still no fine
3. here was one difference: there would be no probation.

also, rather than a guilty plea being entered, there would be neither a "guilty" nor an "innocent." it would just kind of stay in limbo forever.

this was the best yet, but halleck was really pissed. he was just pissed at attorney general [john] mitchell, [president richard] nixon, etc. that they would make these mass arrests and then hand us over to the courts to dispose of. he said in no way could the prosecutor ever adequately try more than five cases. to do so would take, as he said, "forever and two weeks." he even got the prosecutor to admit it—this was all in an impromptu speech.

continuing, he said, "i believe in evolution, not revolution. i believe in this system and it's essential that we can prove that the law can apply equally to all." he referred to the necessity of being able to show us that we could get a "fair shake." over and over, he said he was "troubled."

it was a good speech and, mainly, it convinced us that we should try to get innocents rather than *nolos*. "remember," he warned the prosecutor, "you have to be able to prove within a reasonable doubt that each one of these people committed the alleged crime."

the prosecutor was freaked. as each defendant came up, he either dropped charges or tried to win the case. on those he tried to win, either he ended up dropping charges or the judge dismissed the case.

i got a *nol pros*, which means the prosecutor decided to not prosecute. at 6:00 P.M., i appeared and won. it was a pleasure to pick up my $50.

******

and that, brother, is my own personal account of the events that took place during the mayday week. the war isn't yet over: true. and a corrupt government is still in power: true. but we're getting it together; more people than ever are realizing that this government "of the people" doesn't represent them. and these people are turning away from the government and beginning life anew as free people. it is here, brother, with these members of the life culture, that the future of the country and of the world lies.

don, be well, be happy, and be free: your loving brother is all of these.

to the revolution
and to peace,
Ken

APPENDIX 2: GOVERNMENT HARASSMENT OF THE UNDERGROUND PRESS DURING THE VIETNAM WAR: EAST LANSING, MICHIGAN

by Ken Wachsberger

It can't happen here.

That four-word cliche of assertive apathy, born in ignorance and bred in times of economic uncertainty, has guided many a super patriot to self-righteously condemn politically threatening ideologies in other parts of the world. Ronald Reagan gained popular support in this country, for instance, by condemning Nicaragua's Sandinista government whenever the Sandinistas shut down the CIA-backed opposition newspaper, *La Prensa*.

Unfortunately, ignorance in pursuit of confidence is no substitute for knowledge in pursuit of reality; and hypocrisy is always bad policy. Government harassment of opposition points of view even in this country has been common, though not always public, throughout our own nation's short history. The campaign to destroy the underground press during the sixties is but one example.

The underground press was a network of socialist and anarchistic newspapers that arose somewhat spontaneously during the civil rights and Vietnam era.

Its growth was, for the most part, a result of the political radicalization of the white middle class youth of what was known as the counterculture. This is a general definition. One exception, for instance, was *Akwesasne Notes*, a product of the Mohawk Nation in upstate New York.

That said, the antiwar movement during the sixties never really had an underground press in the same sense as, say, the Jewish resistance in the ghettoes during the Nazi period. Certainly, the name "underground" sounded romantic, calling up images of printing presses and mimeograph machines in dingy basement offices and of daring radicals hanging up broadsheets in the middle of the night when the authorities weren't looking. But editors didn't fear for their lives. It was different.

But only to a degree—a degree too small to say "It can't happen here." There is no question that the underground press faced severe harassment from the government during the sixties, and especially during the Nixon years, in its struggle to gain legitimacy—which meant, among other things, protection under the First Amendment to the Constitution.

For instance, Mark Knops of the Madison, Wisconsin, *Kaleidoscope*, in late 1970, was the first editor to be thrown in jail for refusing to identify source material on a series of Madison bombings, and yet the issue got little or no media coverage. The next year, *Los Angeles Times* reporter William Farr was jailed for thirty days for withholding sources in a piece he wrote about the Manson Family and the establishment press proclaimed he was the first and longest jailed reporter in America. Liberation News Service, the left's alternative to AP and UPI, and *Ramparts* magazine, the left's leading national publication during the late sixties, both were victims of CIA infiltration and harassment. Columbia Records, a major advertiser in underground papers across the country, is believed to have buckled under to FBI pressure when it suddenly withdrew all its advertisements nationwide. Information sharing between government agencies was standard procedure. So was phone tapping and search and seizure of office equipment on phony drug charges.

Activists of the period were often accused of paranoia—of all things—but then, in 1981, along came a book coordinated by Geoffrey Rips, of the Freedom to Write Committee, called *The Campaign Against the Underground Press*. The book, which bases much of its information on government files obtained under the Freedom of Information Act, documents the history of the government's disunified but intense campaign of harassment, with help mostly from the CIA, the FBI, and the Army.

On college campuses and in counterculture communities around the country, papers whose members were new to the Movement—and even veterans—had no idea how many eyes were upon them. Some had entered the seventies still believing what government leaders said.

In East Lansing, Michigan, I worked on a paper called *Joint Issue*. I had become involved in the Movement when, as a junior at Michigan State University, I wandered into a meeting of striking students who were discussing racism in the Student Union just before a mass bust. I became the first of 132 students and outside agitators to be busted because I was the closest to the door. Then, I ended up in solitary confinement because I didn't sign my fingerprints, an act of daring I performed only because that's what it said to do in the bust manual that I read on the bus ride to jail and I thought everyone was going to refuse. Instantly, I achieved notoriety in the dorm where I lived, and people came to me to seek political analysis, which I didn't have. I learned the raps from the center of the storm and dropped out of school.

After I dropped out, I began to go to *Joint Issue* meetings with a friend of mine, the other bustee from the dorm, who now worked on the paper. Then, in the summer of 1971, I helped sell enough advertisements in a six-week period to triple the circulation and enable us to give the paper away for free instead of selling it for a quarter. Beginning that fall, we became the first underground paper in the country, to the best of my knowledge, to come out free on a regular bi-weekly basis. In so doing, *Joint Issue* began a tradition of free Lansing-area underground and alternative papers that is still alive and active today. Meanwhile, I became known as a political heavy because I was a good businessman.

Many of my friends and fellow paper people had also become active as a result of the student strike. Our youth was reflected in the politics of *Joint Issue*—which doesn't mean naivete was our dominant characteristic as much as it means we were free and wild and anarchistic and spontaneous and crazy. We got high full-time while we worked part-time for subsistence wages, but we still managed to get by and find time to report on what was happening or organize events to report on if nothing was happening.

We knew the police had their own secret apparatus for spying on radical activity. In Michigan, three departments of the state police were the Narcotics Unit, the Special Investigation Unit, and the Organized Crime and Wagering Unit. So we weren't surprised when we noticed the police paying close attention to us. For example, in the first free *Joint Issue* of Fall 1971, we ran a centerfold pin-up poster called Joint Issue Police Information Guide (P.I.G.). On it was featured a collage of photographs and descriptions and license plate numbers of local police and undercover officers and narcs, interspersed with caricatures of pigs. Although we don't know who informed them that we would be running it, we nevertheless, I'd say, were pleased rather than upset when they followed us into our first delivery point to grab copies for themselves and felt like we were doing our job well. What we didn't know was that this surveillance had already been going on for six months with *Joint Issue*, that it had begun nearly seven months earlier than that with *Joint Issue*'s three predecessors—*Generation*, *Bogue Street Bridge*, and *Red Apple News*—and that it was happening on a nationwide scale.

Then, a few months later, something happened that did surprise us. As a result, some of us were shocked. Others sacrificed their best political principles under the strain of fear.

In that previous week, a list had fallen into the hands of the staff. On the list were the names of every undercover police officer in the Detroit, Ann Arbor, and Lansing areas, along with his or her address, phone number, code name, and call number. To this day, it has never been revealed how the list was obtained—in the war between the Life Culture and the Death Culture, there were undercover agents on both sides. But a trusted individual on the staff convinced enough of us of the list's legitimacy that a meeting was held to decide what to do with it.

The overwhelming majority of us felt we had a revolutionary responsibility to inform the people and voted in favor of printing all the information about the individuals from the Lansing area. However, two members worried that they would get in trouble if we got caught—they were the ones we called "liberals." So, as a compromise, we ran the list but on the bottom of the page the two wrote a political analysis explaining why they voted to suppress it.

We worked all night and into the morning laying out the paper for the morning's deadline, partly because the list took so long to type and our typewriter skipped. On the cover, we put a photograph taken during an antiwar demonstration at the capitol showing the capitol steps lined with state police in full riot gear. The boldface caption asked, "What Do These Men Have to Hide?" On the inside cover, we ran an article entitled "A Very Dangerous List." That article, along with the list itself and the disclaimer, took up the entire of page three. When the sun came up, everyone went to sleep except for the two of us who were nominated to drive the layout pages to the printer.

This is what usually happened when we went to the printer: The owner, a crack craftsman who was born into the business, would come to meet us at the door if he saw us drive up. Then, together, we would walk to the nearest clean flat surface. There, one representative from the paper would go over each page

one at a time, pointing out the ones that needed special attention, which usually meant a photo had to be filtered, screened, enlarged, or reduced and then pasted down. The pages were all numbered so that they would appear numerically in the paper's final form, but they arrived at the printer's only in the order in which they hung on the clothesline during layout. The printer didn't care. He was good.

But on this day, he confronted us with immediate suspicion, as if he had been nervously expecting us. Barely had we finished our hellos when he took the box from our hands and marched to the nearby table, where he proceeded to flip pages individually as if he was a speedreader. When he got to page three, which was all the way on the bottom because it was the last one to be finished, he pressed his finger firmly onto it so that the tip turned red and his nail turned white and he said, "This can't go in."

What questions are raised by this? For one, how did he find out about the list? What he told us was that his lawyer had called him to warn him not to run it.

Why not? And how did his lawyer find out? Was there an informant on the staff? The printer said he was told only that, although he was probably protected by the First Amendment right to free speech, he had better not take chances. In other words, he was intimidated.

"But we're the ones whose asses are on the line because we wrote it," we argued.

But he didn't buy it. Further, he said we had to make a decision and have the paper back by noon or he would bump us to the back of the line and we wouldn't get the paper until the end of the week instead of the next morning. We could see he was talking out of fear, not politics, but to argue with his lawyer we knew would involve the courts and could take years. We also knew no other printer would be able to take the paper on such short notice, and there was no time to call a staff meeting and still meet the deadline.

So, we drove back to the office alone. There, we cut out a piece of white paper that was big enough to block out all the information in the list and pasted it over the page. Only the bottom line and segments of letters in the left and right extreme edges stuck out. Over the blank sheet, we press-typed in bold black letters running diagonally upward from the lower left to the upper right hand corners the word "CEN-SORED." Under it, we wrote a two-column-inch explanation telling how our printer's "chicken shit liberal lawyer" had refused to let us run the list and informing our readers that lists were available upon request.

When we got back to the printer's, he read the explanation and cut out the phrase "chicken shit liberal lawyer," thereby censoring the explanation of the censorship. However, in the next few days, news of the list circulated throughout the local and statewide media. AP and UPI picked up the story and spread it nationwide. Months later, a friend said she was in Hawaii when she read about it. And we gave away several hundred copies of the list anyhow. A victory for our side.

And in the usual pattern of zen struggles, the names of the two individuals who wrote the paragraph dissociating themselves from the decision were the only words that slipped through the shield of the white paper because they were on the bottom line. Therefore, they were the only individuals in the end who were associated with it.

This incident occurred on December 3, 1971. Unknown to us, our movements that day were well documented on three pages of *Joint Issue*'s Red Squad file.

The Red Squad was the government organization in Michigan that coordinated surveillance of at least 38,000 leftist individuals and political groups, plus countless uninvolved individuals who parked in front of houses where meetings were held or who were acquaintances of suspected subversives. It was created by the state legislature in 1950 under the name State Police Subversive Activities Investigation Unit to monitor what they called "sabotage, violence or terrorism as a means of accomplishing industrial and political reform." By the sixties, this meant mostly black and counterculture groups. In the 1970s, rock concerts became the Red Squad beat.

In 1976, the antics of the Red Squad were halted by court order in the case of *Benkert vs. Michigan*. As a result of the suit, the government was ordered to advertise the existence of the files and to notify all individuals and organizations who had files that they could receive a photocopy of it upon request. I applied for and received the files of *Joint Issue* and its immediate predecessors. Its contents were curiously sparse but nonetheless interesting.

The first two tidbits to be included blandly noted a joyous occasion. The previous March, two staffers had gotten married and so a small news article appeared the next day in the *Lansing State Journal* because she was a native of Lansing. One observant article-clipper for the police noticed that the names of the happy couple matched the names of two people mentioned in the *Joint Issue* staff box, so both the *State Journal* piece and the staff box were clipped and filed. That strikes me as an unusual first entry, but one lesson we learned from the period is that the power structure was even crazier than we were—a lesson to carry into the present.

The next entry was made six weeks later. It contained detailed information from the Ingham County Sheriff's Department about the editor of a nearby suburban weekly newspaper who, rumor had it, not only was letting the *Joint Issue* staff use the back room of one of his properties to put out the paper but who was going to become its next editor. He never did. In fact, I never heard of him until I obtained the file and saw his name.

The following month, a surveillance report stated that *Joint Issue* was one of seven radical groups on campus to sponsor a rally and picketing of the MSU placement center to protest armed forces recruiters. It identified four people in attendance at the rally.

The next three issues of the paper were included in full.

And then nothing was added until September. These months of unrecorded activity included the period when the first free *Joint Issue* appeared. Naturally, this omission of written data from the summer suggests four theories: their information-gathering network was shoddy and inefficient; not everything that was included in the files was returned to me; they kept more than one file on the paper; and all their student informants went home for the summer. I support all four.

In any case, between September 21, 1971, and the end of the year, ten more entries were made. From them, we learn that we paid our printer $367 in cash for 10,000 copies of one issue and to whom the two cars that carried the bundles were registered. Likewise, we learn the name, address, and physical characteristics of the staffer who delivered the following issue to the printer. An article about an SDS attempt to shut down the class of Wesley Fishel, former head of the MSU Vietnam project from 1956-58 that was later discovered to be a CIA front, was cut out of the campus paper because the name *Joint Issue* was included in the article. And two clips from *Joint Issue* were included because they mentioned actions we were co-sponsoring. We might imagine the police were at those two events taking notes, but no mention is made of such activity in the files. Which files do contain the information?

Following these entries were the three from December 3. Four days later, a driving record check on one of the staffers was received. Two weeks later, Detroit's *Fifth Estate* ran an article detailing their attempt to run the Detroit area information from the list. It mentioned *Joint Issue*, so a copy was clipped and filed.

No further entries of any sort were made until March 1972, when a published notice about the free high school was added. In April, notice of an upcoming rally we were co-sponsoring was filed, along with the follow-up report two days later. And in August, an article appeared in the *State Journal* entitled "Underground 'Joint Issue' Tough to Find." A copy was added to the file with no apparent effort on anyone's part. Then, for the next seven months, no entries at all were made. From the file inactivity of this past fifteen-month period, it appears as if police interest in *Joint Issue* peaked in December 1971, then quickly died.

But then, on March 23, 1973, five information-filled pages give detailed accounts of what the paper was, where it was located, and who published it, along with descriptions of key staffers, a list of our distribution contracts in the area high schools, and another list of all our advertisers. Included with this five-page entry is an article I wrote explaining how the paper is put together.

Why the sudden resurgence of interest? Where did the information come from? And then why nothing?

Fifteen months later, on June 13, 1974, the next and final entry noted that the paper had changed its name to *Lansing Star Weekly*.

Whereabouts of a Red Squad file for the *Lansing Star Weekly* or the *Lansing Star*, as it was later called, are unknown, although one is believed to exist. What is known, however, is that, in January of 1976, a pound of cocaine was found in a package that was picked up at the post office and seven members of the *Star*, none of whom had been on *Joint Issue* when the March 1973 entries were made, were thrown in jail.

According to bustee John Snyder, the *Star*'s editor at the time, the judge ruled they could not be charged with receiving mail, even if it was contraband, so the case was dropped and they were released the same day. The *Star* filed for false arrest and lost.

Snyder believes they were set up but he can only speculate as to why. "We only had five or six issues in 1975 and had just gone bi-weekly, so I don't think we had done anything to warrant that notoriety," he said.

Later that year, the Red Squad was disbanded. End of story? No, just a happy ending to one chapter.

Although the Red Squad ceased to exist in 1976, it was all along only one of many government agencies that spied on us then. Others included the FBI; the CIA; the Immigration and Naturalization Service; the Bureau of Indian Affairs; the Internal Revenue Service; and the Bureau of Alcohol, Tobacco, and Firearms. And there were others.

During the Carter and Ford years, the leash on the CIA was tightened to appease critics of the spy agency's involvement in domestic affairs during the Watergate scandal.

In addition, the Freedom of Information Act of 1966 was strengthened to allow citizens easier access to public files of government agencies.

Then the Reagan administration swept into office, hellbent on reversing those trends and shutting up all dissent for good.

Some examples:

Mother Jones, an outgrowth of the sixties and the leading national muckraking publication of the seventies and eighties, barely survived an attempt by the IRS to reclassify it as a for-profit organization, a move that would have taken away their tax-exempt status and made their operating costs prohibitive. As it was, legal fees nearly destroyed the magazine in victory.

The Civil Rights Commission was turned into an arm of the administration instead of remaining the independent investigation commission it had been since its inception during the Eisenhower years.

The call for a constitutional convention to require a balanced budget barely covered a right wing attempt to review the entire Constitution, especially the Bill of Rights.

Reagan's Supreme Court, meanwhile, turned back the exclusionary rule, a move that, according to many civil libertarians, will open the way for more police abuses, including search and seizures without warrants and planting of false evidence on anybody they want off the streets.

The Freedom of Information Act weakened under constant attack beginning with Reagan's earliest days in office; and the CIA increased its activities. Reagan's vice president during the eight years of his reign, in fact, was a former director of the CIA.

Today, we who were veterans of the counterculture can too easily recall the sixties period as a glorious period in our nation's history. Our minds expanded and so did our political consciousness. We had free drugs and free sex and brown rice and rock concerts and revolution for the hell of it.

But if we recall the period's nostalgic highpoints only, we will sterilize the sixties in the same way that "Happy Days" sterilized the fifties. When we study the past, we remember that righteous cynicism toward our government "of the people et cetera" came not from sugar and white flour or too much bad acid but from concerted efforts by our elected leaders to lie to us. When we discovered the truth and confronted them with it, they beat us with our tax dollars and smashed our presses.

Now that Ronald Reagan is out and George Bush is in, will this be a kinder, gentler nation? Only time will tell, but, lest we forget, George Bush *was* Reagan's vice president. We laughed self-righteously when former KGB head Yuri Andropov became general secretary of the Soviet Union.

And we said: "It can't happen here."

FREEDOM OF THE PRESS—
OR SUBVERSION AND SABOTAGE?

Nancy Strohl

Strohl grew up in suburban Seattle, attending Claremont College in the late sixties. She was an activist against the war in Vietnam prior to the eighteen months she spent in Yokosuka. She has continued to be politically active in a variety of progressive causes including the Jesse Jackson campaigns. She currently is executive director of Contra Costa Legal Services Foundation and lives with her husband and three children in Oakland.

In the late 1960s and early 1970s young Americans, disproportionately poor and of color, were shipped off to Southeast Asia ostensibly to fight for freedom for the Vietnamese people. They soon learned that there was precious little respect for their own freedom inside the U.S. military. Enlisted people were angry about racism, brutal conditions, lack of freedom, and the insane policies they were supposed to defend with their lives. They began to oppose the war.

Initially, these enlisted people were isolated both from the mainstream military community whose values they were beginning to question and from people outside the military who shared their opposition to the war. The nature of military duty means that people are far from home and usually have no access to support or information outside the military community. This was especially true for those stationed overseas.

Meanwhile, on this side of the ocean, antiwar activists often mistakenly attacked these same military personnel for their role in the Vietnam War. In the early seventies, however, some of us began to understand that many enlisted people were themselves victimized by the war. We also saw their opposition to fighting in Vietnam as a growing source of strength for the antiwar movement at home.

Freedom of the Press was a product of the natural coalition between the resistance movement of GIs and the antiwar movement in the United States. It was an alternative newspaper produced and distributed at the Naval Air Station in Yokosuka, Japan. Enlisted people,

Japanese activists, and American civilian organizers produced the paper.

YOKOSUKA AND THE BASE

Yokosuka Naval Air Station was the major staging area for the naval air war. After the ground war of the sixties failed to defeat the Vietnamese people, the United States switched its strategy and bombarded Vietnam from the air. Many of the planes were launched from U.S. aircraft carriers stationed or serviced at Yokosuka.

Yokosuka is one hour south of Tokyo on the coast. It is similar to other medium-sized Japanese cities with its rich history and growing prosperity. To enlistees, however, the city and the base could have been on different continents. Most enlisted people seldom left the bar strip, a six-block area that looked more like a travelling small town carnival than a Japanese street and that was known by the GIs as the Honcho. In fact, enlistees were discouraged from having any contact with "Japanese Nationals" at all. Newly stationed men were told of high prices, venereal disease, stiff drug laws, and widespread hostility to the U. S. military presence.

By the same token, most Japanese residents would not dream of visiting the Honcho. Because of widespread opposition to nuclear weapons and to the American war in Vietnam, many of the residents did not look favorably on the U.S. servicemen stationed in their city. Instead, to show their displeasure, over 20,000 Japanese protesters met the aircraft carrier U.S.S. Midway when it first arrived in Yokosuka in fall of 1973. The sailors on board were not prepared for this sort of welcome. Some sympathized with the Japanese anti-nuclear sentiment; many interpreted it on a more personal level.

For enlisted people stationed in Yokosuka, their reality was the base, the bar strip, and occasional sightseeing trips to Tokyo. Ten thousand American naval personnel were permanently stationed in Yokosuka; 4,500 were crewmembers of the U.S.S. Midway, but many other ships also came to Yokosuka after serving stints off the coasts of Vietnam or South Korea. Approximately ten percent were people of color. Less than one percent were women.

Seventy-five percent were first-termers, and most were not planning to reenlist. Most had enlisted to avoid being drafted into the Army and/or to learn a trade or finance their education. When you can't get a job and you see few prospects in your town, the military recruitment ads look very attractive.

Once in Japan, however, these enlisted people found themselves not only cut off from the Japanese people, but also alienated from one another. The civil rights movement back home was having profound effects on the Third World people in the military who were struggling daily against the institutional racism of the military. Black sailors were concentrated in the most oppressive low-skill jobs, such as those in the boiler room. Often they were supervised by white petty officers who themselves had little understanding of or tolerance for blacks. The "Brothers," which is how the black enlisted men referred to themselves, had a high degree of unity and stood up for each other. Despite some exceptions, many of the white GIs seemed to be both fascinated by and threatened by the militancy of the blacks.

For reasons whose origins were never known to the GIs, most of whom had been around fewer than two years, the bar strip was segregated into two sections, one for black GIs and one for whites. The black section was in a cul de sac off the main street and was much smaller. After six months, I was finally invited into a "black bar." By this time, *Freedom of the Press* had already made its presence known and we had been shown to demonstrate respect for black demands. The guys explained that I was a "cousin" even though I was obviously white.

YOKOSUKA IS A LONG WAY FROM SUBURBAN SEATTLE

I came to Yokosuka and New People's Center with my then-husband Richard Engle in August of 1973. I was then two years out of Clarement College; Richard was a graduate of Stanford; and we considered ourselves full-time antiwar activists. My family in the middle-class suburbs of Seattle had taught me to seek truth and stand up for justice. I also had learned that the United States was a democracy. The war shook my belief in the United States but not my belief in working for justice. Richard and I had worked with a group of antiwar enlisted people at Alameda Naval Air Station the year before and had subsequently been recruited by Pacific Counseling Service (PCS) to staff a coffeehouse and bookstore in Yokosuka. We were idealistic and had respect for the way enlisted people were putting their lives and careers on the line. We went because we felt that being in Yokosuka was the most effective way we could use our organizing skills.

Pacific Counseling Service was founded by church-connected activists in 1970 in response to the growing GI opposition to the Vietnam War. Although it sponsored projects throughout the Pacific Rim, its main focus was on the Asian bases that were the staging area for the war. Its original mission was to provide counseling to GIs who had moral objections to war and to assist them in obtaining discharges as conscientious objectors (COs). The mission expanded to include general counseling on enlisted people's rights when the National Lawyers Guild joined forces with PCS the next year. Projects were staffed by activists from both organizations. The working relationship in the field was extremely close, even though the two organizations maintained separate identities.

As the GI movement grew within the military, the counseling projects became coffeehouses, places where civilians could provide a variety of types of support to those GIs who were organizing against the war. Counseling services continued, but they were secondary. Integral to these coffeehouses were underground papers that were produced jointly by GIs and civilian antiwar activists. Papers could reach beyond the circle of activists to the growing numbers of enlisted people beginning to question the war and the military. Often they were the only alternative to the military-controlled publication, *Stars and Stripes*.

As with all of the New Left organizations I experienced in the late sixties and early seventies, PCS was collective and diverse. PCS projects were autonomously run by whatever collective was currently on the scene. In Yokosuka, the collective when we arrived included two PCS organizers and several active duty people. The politics of PCS organizers while we were there included Maoists and feminists and pacifists and trade unionists and liberals. The thread that united us was opposition to the war.

Most of the civilian organizers for PCS and NLG legal workers made a one-year commitment. The intensity of the work was hard to sustain longer than a year. Organizers often were not able to obtain visas for longer than one or two years even if they wished to stay longer. This meant that not only was each project autonomous, but its nature changed drastically as civilians and military activists ended their tours of duty and were replaced by new people with new ideas about war and peace and the military. We came as replacements for the two PCS organizers, and the active duty people were transferred soon after we arrived, so we started to build a collective from scratch.

We minimized the importance of counseling, leaving that to the two National Lawyers Guild-sponsored attorneys who worked with us. Our goal for helping to end the war was to educate and organize and provide support to the growing GI antiwar movement.

LAUNCHING *FREEDOM OF THE PRESS*

The history of the Yokosuka Project illustrates the eclectic and somewhat accidental nature of the politics of the PCS projects. The project was founded in October 1971 by an American Buddhist monk who named it Yokosuka David, a reference to David and Goliath. The project was then primarily a counseling center and producer of the *Yokosuka David*, a newspaper with a strong moral antiwar tone that had already appeared twice the previous year and that would continue to publish irregularly until August 1972. Four months later, a successor paper named *GI Movement in Yokosuka* (*GIMY*), also published by Yokosuka David, made its first of two appearances.

In April 1973, a new PCS recruit moved to Yokosuka. This new organizer renamed the coffeehouse the New People's Center and started a more political underground paper, *Off the Bridge*.

New People's Center was the only place in Yokosuka where black and white GIs, Japanese peace activists, and U.S. radicals could talk. It was, in fact, the only racially integrated establishment on the Honcho, and the only source of alternative information. PCS collective members sold books by Malcolm X, James Forman, and other civil rights leaders. We had copies of alternative papers from across the United States that people could borrow. We sponsored programs with people active in antiwar and anti-nuclear struggles in Japan and Korea and throughout Asia. Japan had a strong peace movement, galvanized in part by the experience of Hiroshima and Nagasaki. We worked with antiwar organizations there that included Beheiren, a group of primarily Japanese intellectuals formed in 1965; left student groups; local citizen groups; friends of liberation struggles; people sympathetic to Communist regimes; and even a Japanese farmland preservation group.

Although *Off the Bridge* was well read by GIs on the base, the fact that it came out only occasionally hampered its effectiveness. Richard and I believed—and we were proved correct in our assessment—that a regularly published widely distributed paper would be a more effective vehicle for making an alternative presence visible and for countering the information monopoly of the U.S. military. Soon after we arrived in Yokosuka, we began publication of *Freedom of the Press*, using the same mimeo machine that had produced *Off the Bridge*.

The only newspaper readily available on the base was *Stars and Stripes*. *Stars and Stripes*, as its name suggests, was full of jingoist patriotism but had very little content. By the early 1970s even the mainstream U.S. media generally was questioning the war in Vietnam, but this attitude was not reflected in *Stars and Stripes*. *Stars and Stripes* carried virtually no news on the civil rights movement and the general political and social upheaval in the United States.

The center only reached about a hundred people each month. Even though we were never placed off

receiving copies paid for the paper, which cost about
$40 per issue to publish. GIs could be harassed for
taking it, but so many had copies that the brass could
not officially ban it. By the second issue we were a
fixture outside the base gate and *Freedom of the Press*
was part of the reality of Yokosuka.

During this period, U.S. military brass were
reeling from impending defeat in Vietnam. The air war
conducted primarily from aircraft carriers was their
only hope for victory. They needed a patriotic and
disciplined military force on the carriers and destroyers
to accomplish their mission, so they did their best to
stifle the growing GI movement. In the first month of
publication, three enlisted people involved with *Freedom of the Press* were transferred out of the area.
When word spread that people were being sent home,
we were deluged with volunteers. Unfortunately for
them, very few were actually sent home. A number,
however, were sent to other ships operating from bases
in different parts of the world.

The navy watched us closely and changed their
tactics. Active people were subject to disciplinary
actions for the slightest infringement of other rules.
Activists were continually written up for haircut
violations and one writer was never able to crease his
sheets sufficiently to pass inspection. Still, although
Richard and I did a large portion of the writing, every
issue contained significant input from enlisted people.
The writers were from different backgrounds. Some
were black, some were white. Some dictated stories
to us, others wrote while they were at sea.

Hundreds of copies of the paper were seized by
officers. We began printing Department of Defense
Directive 1325.6 as part of our logo. This DOD
Directive guaranteed the right of active-duty service
people to possess and read "unauthorized material."
GIs threatened to write up the brass for theft of
personal property.

WHAT DID *FREEDOM* OF THE PRESS ACCOMPLISH?

In response to the first issue, several enlisted
people joined the paper staff. We wanted to create a
collective staff, but we were met with difficulties we
were unable to overcome. One difficulty was that
enlisted people were only in port half-time and their
schedules were erratic. The navy made special efforts
to transfer guys who became active with *FOP* because
they were seen as bad influences.

In addition, certain differences between the full-
time organizers and many of the enlisted people were
never adequately addressed. Richard and I were both
highly educated and, like many radicals of that period,

limits officially, GIs were discouraged from and even
harassed and questioned by superiors for coming by.
Some were told that leave requests or transfers would
be in jeopardy if they got involved with us.

The paper, however, reached a thousand people
with every issue. The twelve- to sixteen-page paper
appeared every two weeks from October 1973 to
September 1974. Donations from enlisted people

Figure 1: Cover photo of *Freedom of the Press* 2, no. 3 (February 15, 1974).

fairly self-righteous and dogmatic when it came to what we perceived as matters of principle. We also were full-time organizers and had time to write articles and produce the paper. GIs, on the other hand, were less used to writing and were newer to political activism. They tended to be more pragmatic and less dogmatic than us. As a result, meetings were fairly lively. One positive result was that our coverage of events and issues was more broadly based and balanced than it would have been without GI participation. Writers always had the final say on their own articles.

Each issue was planned by a different staff collective. By the time the paper was published, often the guys who planned it had been shipped out. The resulting paper was more eclectic than collective. An analysis at the end of the year showed that 134 pages were written by Richard and me, 180 pages were written by enlisted people, and 110 were lifted from other papers. In reviewing them fifteen years later, it is still extremely clear which articles were which. A typical issue had an article on the coup in Chile lifted from Liberation News Service, an article on trends of racism in the United States written by Richard, and an article on haircut policies on the U.S.S. Jason written by a crewmember. Occasional articles were contributed by Japanese activists from Yokosuka Citizens Group, who shared our center.

A personal disappointment was our failure to attract the American women who were in Yokosuka primarily as dependents of the men. In fact, with the exception of me, no American women were active in the project. For me, this lack of female support was difficult personally, though it was lessened when, after overcoming cultural barriers, I was accepted as a sister by several Japanese women.

Hair and liberation struggles continued as two of the most popular subjects in the paper. Navy regulations demanded that sailors have short hair. Because long hair for white and Chicano guys and Afros for blacks were signs of resistance and individuation then, this regulation branded active duty people as such even when off duty. Haircuts, therefore, became powerful symbols to the resisters and to the officers. We did not sufficiently recognize that covering these personal issues was the key to broadening our support among GIs, and we responded, only broadly as a rule, to issues of racism and harassment, lack of training the people were receiving, and poor working conditions. Looking back, I think we should have mounted even more campaigns about military conditions and responded to even more of the issues that really grabbed people. I would bet that the "political" articles Richard and I wrote were seldom read.

In retrospect, though, the paper had an effect just because it existed. Although the brass did not respond

Figure 2: Flyer distributed by crewmen aboard the U.S.S. Midway before the Midway walkoff

to us specifically—except to call us communists, which was their generic condemnation—*Freedom of the Press* was a concrete expression of protest and unity with people who were in the military but not in agreement with its politics. Sailors read the paper as an act of independence or defiance. Some people read parts of it; people trusted others who took copies. You either supported *FOP* or were part of the problem. Those GIs who knew of and trusted *FOP* often came to us for assistance when they were resisting demands made on them by the military or beginning to question the war.

Only twice, though, did actual articles become widely discussed. Both of these were joint efforts by enlisted people and organizers and came from real issues guys were facing.

The first appeared in *Freedom of the Press* 2, number 3 (February 15, 1974). "Working in a Subic Bar: 'I've Been Doing Some Hard Traveling'" was an interview with a Filipina bar woman named Gina (see sidebar 1 and figure 1). It was conducted, written, and signed by David Heiser, an enlisted man on the U.S.S. Oklahoma City. In it, Gina explains how she was

Sidebar 2: U.S. Sailors in Japan Protest "New Navy"

by Dick Engle and Nancy Strohl
from a New Asia News dispatch as reprinted
in *The Militant*, July 5, 1974

Tokyo—In one of the biggest uprisings within the U.S. military since the Vietnam cease-fire 17 months ago, more than 100 crew members of the USS Midway refused to sail when the giant aircraft carrier left its home port at Yokosuka Naval Base on June 14.

The men, about half of them Black, left the carrier within a four-hour period and quickly went underground in various parts of the Tokyo area. The spontaneous rebellion was the latest and most dramatic example of mounting discontent among enlisted men over bad living conditions and constant harassment in the new image "peacetime Navy."

"Most likely we'll go to the brig for this," one striking sailor said, "but we're together. We didn't just jump into this, we thought about it. I think our reasons are good. We're tired of the pig boat."

The walkout, talked up on board since April, was also an expression of doubts about the purpose of the U.S. Navy in Asia today. As one sailor told New Asia News, "I won't serve on it anymore. If they send me back, they'll be paying a man who won't work. In my opinion the Midway's over here for one thing: America's an aggressive nation, they always want to get ahead of other countries. It's just a Cold War."

The "new navy," inaugurated with great fanfare in 1972 to overcome the seething discontent of the Vietnam era, is meeting its most severe test at Yokosuka. The basic promise: more privileges and pay and an end to racism and petty harassment of enlisted men. Recent events suggest that the program is in a shambles.

The USN command at Yokosuka, shaken by the walkout, has tried to cover up the incident. It announced that 32 men went AWOL on June 14, and half of these had turned themselves in by June 18. However, New Asia News confirmed that 100 Midway crew members were still underground on June 20.

Several factors create an explosive situation on the Midway. The first and only carrier to be home-ported outside the United States, it is scheduled to be here through 1976. Daily demonstrations of up to 30,000 Japanese citizens preceded the ship's arrival in Yokosuka on Oct. 5, 1973. The Midway crew is well aware that most Japanese don't want the ship in Japan.

Most of the crew didn't volunteer, but were sent here from Navy schools as their first duty station. Many feel they joined the "peacetime Navy," and ask: "Why are we here if it's peacetime?"

There is deep cynicism among most first-timers about the U.S. Navy's mission. Many Midway sailors feel they are here to protect dictatorial governments from Singapore to South Korea.

Yokosuka is a lonely place for people without families or who are too low-ranking to have the military bring their families to Japan. After some of the crew volunteered last year, the Navy announced that it would not pay transportation for families of most lower enlisted men. And even with recent pay increases, these men couldn't begin to support a family in the Tokyo area.

One sailor said, "People like me have feelings, too. We don't have any families to go to, just the Honcho (bar street). All we have to do is go out there and drink, and even then the Shore Patrol harasses us."

A majority of sailors use drugs to escape the reality of life on the Midway. What is that life like? The command acts as if spit and polish can gloss over the deep discontent and low morale. There is considerable pressure on lower-ranking people.

Lack of privacy also generates pressures. While officers have private rooms, enlisted men sleep three high on bunks. Curtains which used to give some privacy were taken down as a fire hazard last fall. The Midway says new ones are not available because corners must be cut to pay for increased oil and jet fuel costs. Yet every day at sea, planes take off for nowhere and the ship steams in circles.

Blacks get more than their share of harassment. But their unity also gives them a kind of edge. Blacks were the first to talk about a walkout, and other sailors knew they had the unity to carry it off. Command racism is also a major problem for Third World people, including large numbers of Filipino sailors. "They (the commands) aren't just prejudiced against Blacks, they're prejudiced against everybody," one Black sailor commented.

The Midway's no-nonsense commander, Captain R. J. Schulte, maintains order through fear. He has the power to punish people for hundreds of infractions at Captain's Mast. A sailor is "written up" and appears before Schulte, who acts as judge, jury, and prosecutor.

There is a waiting list for the brig right now. Once sentenced at mast, there is very little recourse. An appeal is seldom granted, and even if it is, the time has already been served.

Hundreds of the Midway crew have been in the brig during the past year, and brutality is a central complaint in the current walkout. "I was pushed and hit and slammed up against the bulkheads," one sailor complained, "for no reason, for coughing, sneezing, or smiling..."

forced to drop out of college and go to work in a bar to support her family after her father lost his job.

The entire interview was only 2 1/2 mimeographed pages with virtually no editorial comment. However, it was enormously moving, and it opened the eyes of many men to a reality they hadn't known existed. The military "rewarded" crewmembers after time off the coast of Vietnam with shore time at ports in the Philippines or South Korea, where drugs of all sorts and women were readily available. Crewmembers didn't know that these women were forced into employment in bars and brothels because of the incredible poverty that was part of their daily lives. Because most young guys wanted to believe that the women were having a good time, too, they were pretty shocked by Gina's story.

The second major issue we covered revolved around events that became public on June 14, 1974. The night before, ten people—black, white, Asian, civilians, and sailors—sat in a sushi bar practically all night writing demands and mapping strategy. The next day, June 14, over one hundred crewmen of the U.S.S. Midway refused to sail (see figure 2). The men, about half of them black, left the carrier hours before it was scheduled to leave for the coast of Vietnam.

The walkout was inspired by black sailors, who felt they had tried to assert their rights through every channel, from filing grievances to meeting with race relations staff. Their demands were to end racism, harassment, and the war. The majority of enlisted people respected the guys' courage. The military leadership, however, saw potential mutiny spreading throughout the fleet and moved to crack down harshly.

The walkout and subsequent court martial trials made front page headlines all over the United States, including the *New York Times*, and led to live interviews on the "Today" show. Of course, the alternative press in the United States provided extensive coverage as well (see sidebar 2).

The incident also made headlines in Japan when one of the sailors who was on trial testified that he handled nuclear weapons on board the Midway. His testimony proved that the U.S. was violating the U.S./Japanese Security Treaty. *FOP* publicized the testimony and resulting furor in the Japanese press. Because of the trial, the ruling Liberal Democratic Party was forced to make a public promise to enforce the treaty. Nevertheless, the information was used by the opposition parties in the next parliamentary elections. When the prime minister later was forced to step down, observers of the political scene attributed his move in part to those revelations.

"On June 11, 1974, the carrier U.S.S. Midway was due to sail on a routine cruise from its home port of Yokosuka, Japan. Just prior to sailing time, a group of enlisted men from the carrier's crew assembled near the vessel and stated that they would refuse to sail at the designated time.

"On the evening of June 13, 1974, the Tokyo bureau of *Newsweek* magazine reported to the public affairs officer of the U.S. Naval Forces in Japan that the magazine had received a telephone communication from a female identified as Nancy Strohl who had stated that an undetermined number of sailors would present a petition to the commanding officer of the U.S.S. Midway on June 14, prior to departure and then they would walk out and refuse duty.

"Shortly afterward, a crewman of the carrier was apprehended on the forward mess deck distributing leaflets and stickers inciting the crewmen to participate in this seditious demonstration. Upon questioning, he revealed that the leaflets had been given to him by another crew member, and stated that he had knowledge of the walkout which was to originate in one of the engine rooms and had added that he intended to participate.

"At approximately the same time, a division officer of the carrier received an anonymous call in which plans for the demonstration on the following day were revealed in addition to threats of damage to machinery of the vessel to prevent it from sailing. Immediate steps were taken and senior petty officers were stationed at key points to prevent damage to the vessel.

"The following day, after a number of anonymous phone calls about time bombs, hidden on the vessel, the commanding officer addressed the crew on the consequences of demonstrations that were in violation of articles of the UCMJ. He also stated that he was aware that an organization identified as SOS, based at the Pacific Counseling Service Headquarters, was instrumental in fomenting the disorders. No efforts were made to forcibly restrain the crew members from abandoning ship prior to departure.

"Approximately 1 hour before departure, a group of five crewmen was observed leaving the vessel by the aft gangway and after a brief conversation with a group of unidentified persons, departed and did not return. Shortly afterwards the crewmen involved in the demonstration held a press conference at the New People's Center (NPC), the base of operations of the activists involved in the conspiracy. The NPC is located near the base and is staffed by members of the National Lawyers Guild Military Law Committee. It was manned at this time by Nancy Strohl and her husband.

"Just prior to departure, the commanding officer was advised that 51 members had missed muster at 1700 hours. Out of this number, it was ascertained that 32 had gone on unauthorized absence while about 19 were suspect of having missed ship by design.

"An ensuing investigation revealed that the principal leader of the demonstration had been observed at the NPC on the evening of June 13 and later admitted to having brought aboard a number of leaflets to be distributed for the purpose of fomenting the disturbance."

We followed the court martials in *Freedom of the Press*. While *Stars and Stripes* was reporting that the incident was being overblown, we were keeping the trial public. None of the people we were in contact with received bad conduct discharges but several did more than thirty days at hard labor.

Freedom of the Press, contrary to claims in *Stars and Stripes,* did not initiate the walkout, but we helped formulate strike demands that were broad. We also were not able to protect the guys who stood up to the Navy from brig time. We did, however, organize legal and logistical support for them. In addition, we helped publicize the walkout and demands, first aboard the ship and then, through contacts with the Tokyo press corps, in the international media. We were a small voice talking about international and racial unity. The fact that we existed showed it was possible to speak up and stand up.

We—not just *Freedom of the Press* but Pacific Counseling Services as an umbrella organization sponsoring underground newspapers on military bases throughout the Far East and the Philippines—spoke up

so loudly, and our contacts with Asian liberation struggles were so open, that on September 25, 1975, after our return, Senator Strom Thurmond suggested in Senate Internal Security Subcommittee hearings that we had committed "subversion and sabotage"[1] (see sidebar 3).

In those same hearings, star witness John Donnelly, head of the Internal Security Division of the Naval Investigative Service, testified against the politics of PCS and a group I had not heard of, until I read the transcripts of the hearings: the GI Project Alliance. He said, "There are a number of self-described revolutionary groups which are today engaged in subversive activities targeted against the military. Many of these groups are members of a loose federation of Marxist 'mass action' groups known as the GI Project Alliance or GIPA." Donnelly went on to include PCS as one group belonging to the GIPA.[2]

As proof of the conspiratorial nature of GIPA, he discussed the underground papers of each project. "[W]e know that they correspond," he asserted. "And we also know that they correspond currently by their publications. They reprint letters from each other."[3]

Donnelly and other military officers also tried to cast the project as part of the "International Communist Conspiracy," citing examples of contact between activists and Asian peace activists, both Korean and Japanese. They even contended that Beheiren was a Communist front group, an allegation they later refuted in their own appendixes.[4] The fact that we would talk to a person sympathetic to North Korea, a person active in the Japanese Communist Party (the third largest electoral party in Japan), or members of the Japanese peace movement damned us.

Later in his testimony, Donnelly gave an eloquent report of the U.S.S. Midway walkout (see sidebar 4).

The underground press was always held to different standards than the *New York Times*, whose correspondents undoubtedly had similar contacts. This showed some understanding on their part of the power of the underground press. We held positions, we sought the truth, and we were part of the movement to change this country. While the *New York Times* was reporting history, the alternative press was involved in creating history. Most of us were activists as well as writers. We did not pretend to be objective, but stood for a point of view.

The effective antiwar role played then by the people inside the military is still today not recognized by the military intelligence people. If we of PCS had been merely Marxist operatives publishing our own papers, we would not have been effective participants in a movement that was fomented primarily by racism in the military, authoritarianism, and an unjust war. We supported and assisted a resistance movement that they started.

Today, I wonder that we were not more leery of our project. We were similar to David fighting Goliath, our mimeo machine and small office positioned outside a major U.S. military base, but twenty-year-old idealists still believe they are invincible and can accomplish any goal with commitment and hard work. Certainly the antiwar energy of the times sustained our idealism. Looking back at the yellowed paper and faded mimeo ink, I still think *Freedom of the Press* was the most effective publication I was ever part of.

NOTES

1. U.S. Congress, Senate Committee on the Judiciary, "Organized Subversion in the U.S. Armed Forces, Part 1: The U.S. Navy," *Hearings before the Subcommittee to Investigate the Administration of the Internal Security Act and Other Internal Security Laws of the Committee on the Judiciary. United States Senate, September 25, 1975* (Washington, DC: Government Printing Office, 1976), 1.

2. "Organized Subversion," 5.

3. "Organized Subversion," 19.

4. "Organized Subversion," 58.

— NANCY STROHL —

THE WONG TRUTH CONSPIRACY:
A HISTORY OF MADISON ALTERNATIVE JOURNALISM

Tim Wong

The 8½ years I spent working on alternative newspapers in Madison chronicled very clearly the transition from the sixties to the eighties. In 1971, when I first worked on *Kaleidoscope*, the hippie era ("sex, dope, *Kaleidoscope*") was still in full swing. A large alternative community existed in Madison. It was clearly an alternative to the dominant community, but that alternative was not clearly defined, nor were its recognized differences destined to remain as differences. Smoking marijuana, for instance, was enough to make one "alternative," but by the end of the decade such non-political "alternative" behavior had become institutionalized. The non-political drug user was no longer implicitly attracted to the alternative political media or community.

In response to this transition, the alternative press made a similar transition. Dope columns, both glorifying drug use and evaluating goods for sale—often including those sold by staff members—were as prevalent in papers of the early seventies as they were absent by the end of the decade.

In addition, the rise of feminist and gay consciousness was challenging the heterosexual male domination of the political movement and alternative newspapers. This meant that alternative newspapers contained both more articles on feminism and the women's, gay, and lesbian movements, and fewer articles glorifying "free love" and other forms of primarily male sex. Exclusively women's and gay newspapers developed as well.

Political content changed greatly throughout the decade. The existence of the Vietnam War, the draft,

Wong is a planning analyst for the State of Wisconsin, concentrating on health care access for the uninsured, cost containment, and long-term care for the elderly and people with disabilities.

Richard Nixon, and "life drugs" (marijuana and psyche-delics) as liberators made being antiwar and anti-establishment easy, almost natural, in the early seventies. By the middle of the 1970s, the end of the draft and the war resulted in relative demilitarization; the exposure and prosecution of the main Watergate figures led to post-Watergate reforms; and the opening of the Democratic Party in 1972 and other electoral reforms led to the ventilation of the "smoke-filled rooms." All of these events led many people to make their peace with the establishment. By the end of the decade radical politics were no longer "in," even in relatively radical Madison.

THE ORIGINS OF THE "REVOLUTION"

I got my start in journalism during my college years at Carleton College in Northfield, Minnesota. The four years I was there—from 1965 to 1969—probably ushered in more changes to the college than any four years in the college's 125 years. Required chapel attendance had been abolished in 1965; men were still required to wear ties to Sunday lunch in school year 1965-66; "open houses," where members of the opposite sex could visit dorm rooms, were limited to four hours a week, and a shoe needed to be placed between the door and the jamb. By 1969 virtually nobody wore ties or went to chapel, and unlimited open houses had been instituted (dorms were integrated the following year).

These "student power" reforms coincided with a dramatic shift to the left in the predominant campus political attitudes. During my freshman year, as an early opponent to the Vietnam War, I was regularly pelted with water balloons as I walked back to my dorm. On one occasion several people came into my room and overturned my bed while I was sleeping. On another, my mattress was thrown out of my fourth-story window (fortunately I was not in bed that time). Yet three years later many of my early tormentors, whether genuinely or conveniently (due to the draft), were actively antiwar.

Carleton's student newspaper, the *Carletonian*, reflected this shift. My first story for the paper concerned the disciplining of a student for bringing a couch into his dorm room (at Carleton, there was no off-campus housing). By the time I was editor in 1969, we subscribed to Liberation News Service to give our national and international news coverage a radical slant and to College Press Service for its student power coverage.

Madison underwent a similar political conversion during the late 1960s. Mario Savio, a leader of the Free Speech Movement in Berkeley, had identified Carleton in 1965 as the midwestern campus most likely to erupt into revolt—most people at Carleton were bemused at the prospect. In reality, of course, change happened much faster in Madison. In October 1967, police violently attacked demonstrators sitting in to protest recruitment by the Dow Chemical Company, makers of napalm, at the University of Wisconsin (UW) Business School. This police attack on non-violent protesters merely served to swell the number of willing participants. Over the next three years, as many as 30,000 people took part in marches against the war, the number varying in inverse proportion to the likelihood of widespread trashing taking place.

The demonstrators felt the UW administration showed clear complicity in the Vietnam War effort by refusing to shut down the Army Math Research Center (AMRC), a campus organization that did war-related mathematical research, and the various ROTC branches. Demonstrations invariably started on the Library Mall, an open area between two libraries, with one or more incendiary speeches, followed by a march or a war-whooping run to the target building, frequently AMRC or one of the UW administrative buildings. ROTC buildings were less often the targets, primarily because they were over a mile from the Library Mall.

A black student strike in February 1969 attracted widespread white radical student support. As time went on, though, radical activity was no longer limited strictly to the campus. Many student radicals had moved several blocks southeast of campus into what was known as the Mifflin-Bassett neighborhood. When that area declared "independence" from Madison and the United States, it was renamed Miffland. In 1968 the White Front Grocery on the corner of Mifflin and Bassett closed, and a number of people organized to rent the building and establish a food cooperative, which opened on January 13, 1969. The existence of the co-op gave people the sense of controlling their own destiny; the co-op became the symbol of Miffland. The alternative community was becoming a reality.

In May 1969, Mifflin Street residents decided to have a block party to celebrate the coming of spring. While most residents were indifferent to what city reaction would be, more "responsible" types such as alderperson (and later mayor) Paul Soglin investigated getting a permit. City officials said no permit would be necessary because the 500-block of West Mifflin had very low daily traffic counts, particularly on Saturdays. Nonetheless the police department determined to keep the street open, and a three-day riot ensued, spreading to other student neighborhoods besides Miffland. Political feeling continued to become more militant. Many people began arming themselves in anticipation of the "revolution." A loose coalition of demonstrators calling themselves the Bobby Seale

Brigade, after Black Panther co-founder Bobby Seale, loaded their backpacks with rocks and trashed business storefronts during each Madison demo between 1969 and 1971 or 1972. Madison sent a large contingent of protesters to the Days of Rage protest in Chicago in the fall of 1969.

In February 1970, university teaching assistants went on strike and won a favorable settlement. Three months later, Nixon invaded Cambodia, and Madison, like most university communities, exploded, particularly as word of the Kent State and Jackson State murders spread. Numerous buildings were firebombed in various sections of town. A Kroger's supermarket, which had long drawn resentment from the student community for its perceived higher prices and lower quality than other Krogers in Madison, was burned to the ground. A week of rioting ensued, featuring barricades, pitched battles with police, and helicopters with spotlights flying overhead. The police responded with a blanket of tear gas throughout the Mifflin-Bassett neighborhood, firing tear gas canisters through windows in the Mifflin St. Co-op and most houses on the 500-block of West Mifflin and some on surrounding streets.

On August 24, 1970, the Army Math Research Center on campus was bombed by the so-called New Year's Gang, resulting in relatively little damage to AMRC but causing substantial damage to the Physics Department, housed in the same building, and killing a researcher who was working at 5 A.M. when the bomb went off.

The straight media usually portray the Army Math bombing as the beginning of the end of the antiwar movement. In reality, the Kent State and Jackson State killings—which showed people both how vulnerable and how powerless they were against an armed state—were probably more responsible for the reduced participation in antiwar protests. The leveling off and reduction in the number of U.S. troops in Vietnam and the subsequent ending of the draft succeeded in ending protest by all but the politically committed.

In Madison, though, energy flowed into creating a wide variety of alternative economic institutions. In addition to the Green Lantern Eating Co-op, which had existed for several decades, and the Mifflin St. Co-op, Whole Earth Learning Community (a food co-op) on the east side and Eagle Heights Food Co-op on the west side emerged, as did Common Market, a food "buying club," and ICC, a cooperative trucking group. There was also a book co-op, a musicians' co-op, a printing collective, an alternative publications distributor, two clothing cooperatives, a bicycle co-op, a photography co-op, and at least 21 housing co-ops.

Alternative newspapers flourished as well. Madison's first, *Connections*, published its initial issue on March 1, 1967. It was the most campus-oriented of all of Madison's undergrounds, and reflected the increasing militancy of the campus—focusing on the increasingly violent confrontations with the police during demonstrations. *Connections'* last issue appeared in May 1969. Roughly coincident with *Connections* was *The Call*, the newsletter of the UW chapter of Students for a Democratic Society (SDS), the largest radical political group in the United States during the second half of the 1960s. *The Call's* avowed purpose was to "help clarify radical thought and action on the New Left here, by providing a place for the exchange of opinions, analysis, and information." *The Call* reprinted articles by national SDS writers such as Carl Oglesby and Tom Hayden, and featured local articles on organizing, including one whose title indicates humor wasn't totally lacking: "Elephants in the Ivory Tower: The Tusk That Lies Before Us."

Other more obscure titles published in the late sixties were *Links*, the "Voice of the Wisconsin High School Underground," *Underground Underdog, Psst!, Oscar's Underground Ghetto Press, Madison Free Press*, the first community-oriented paper, *...And Beautiful*, and *Bad Moon Rising*.

Madison's second significant alternative paper, Madison *Kaleidoscope*, first appeared on June 23, 1969, less than two months after the demise of *Connections*. Some staff worked on both papers. Underground comics were a regular feature of *Kaleidoscope*. The quality of layout improved over *Connections*, and the writing reflected the increasing self-confidence of the growing counterculture. The Madison paper took its name from the Milwaukee *Kaleidoscope*, which first appeared in 1967. Milwaukee *Kaleidoscope* published a "second section" devoted exclusively to features on music, arts, and literature, which was widely distributed, including in its Madison namesake.

Shortly after the Army Math bombing in August 1970, *Kaleidoscope* received and printed a statement on the bombing by the New Year's Gang, the group that had claimed responsibility. When editor Mark Knops refused to reveal the source of the document, he was sentenced to and he served six months in jail for contempt of court. (It is certainly questionable whether Knops even knew the source—so great was our contempt for mainstream society, though, that Knops refused to cooperate on principle.)

While Knops' courageous and defiant action increased the alternative community's respect for the paper, it also hastened its demise. By late 1970, the majority of the staff was questioning the paper's hierarchical structure and some of the paper's politics that they felt exploited women. Knops' absence gave this portion of the staff the opportunity to think about (and to some extent work on) a paper without an editor and without sexism. When Knops returned from jail and tried to reimpose the *status quo ante*, a split was inevitable.

STUDENT DROPOUT GETS INVOLVED

Following my graduation from Carleton in June 1969, I moved to New York City and worked enough odd jobs to afford food and my half of the $40 rent of a dump on the Lower East Side. In September I moved to Madison to attend graduate school at the UW in Ottoman and Middle Eastern history (I had lived in Turkey and Iran for 6½ years during my childhood). I soon discovered that I was much more interested in the antiwar movement, the counterculture, and Madison in general than the stifling atmosphere at the UW History Department. I dropped out for the second semester, but discovered that employers in Madison were very conservative. I was offered two different jobs on the condition that I cut my hair—I refused, after ascertaining that women workers were not required to have short hair. My faith in the judicial system was not bolstered when my discrimination suits were dismissed.

I was seriously contemplating buying a short-haired wig when I was offered a job from a woman for whom I had worked at Columbia University the previous summer. As quickly as it took to buy my way out of my lease, I moved to New York. I got there on Sunday, May 3—the day before the Kent State murders. By Tuesday, I had persuaded my boss to let us go out on strike with full pay for a week—thank you, Stephanie, wherever you are! I also discovered I had elevated status from the Columbia students because I was a "worker." The excitement soon died down, though, and I went back to work. In September, two weeks after the Army Math bombing, I moved back to Madison to pursue my "exciting" life as a graduate student. Once again Madison proved more exciting than graduate school, and I dropped out for good at the end of the semester.

I first came into contact with Madison alternative journalism in the fall of 1970 by "hawking" Madison *Kaleidoscope*. At that time, people took bundles of 100 *Kaleidoscope*s on consignment and sold them on the street. There would be "hawkers" on every corner of State Street and on a few other university streets; good hawkers could sell 100 papers in an hour on the first day back from the printer, either by getting the "good corners" or by being obnoxious, intimidating, or persuasive. Anyone willing to invest several hours could sell a couple hundred papers every two weeks: hawkers kept a dime of the 25¢ sales price.

During the time I hawked papers, I imagined the *Kaleidoscope* staff to be very cohesive and cliquey, and

hopelessly closed to outsiders. There were probably two explanations for my feeling this way. Having come from a school of 1,300 in a town of 8,000, I was intimidated (even after a year of living in Madison and New York City) by the size of the university and the radical community. My shyness was compounded by my happening to interact with the staff at its least gregarious moment—the day staff members brought the laid out pages to the printer and returned a couple hours later with the completed bundles of papers. As I realized once I was a veteran of newspaper publishing, the core staff get less than adequate sleep the night or two before publication and feel a close affinity with their compatriots; in their burned-out condition, they might not have felt like interacting with strangers. I didn't realize this at the time, though, and thought that *Kaleidoscope* didn't need new staff. I never showed up during layout time, when I might have felt more welcome.

In the summer of 1971, I became involved in People's Office, a switchboard that provided services ranging from arranging overnight housing for visiting out-of-towners to reciting that night's campus movies to "acid rescue." That fall, as a result of a volunteer shortage, personnel from People's Office, which was housed in the same building as *Kaleidoscope*, were asked to help arrange *Kaleidoscope*'s calendar of events. I took the opportunity to work on the paper in other capacities as well.

In the four or so issues of *Kaleidoscope* I worked on, I recorded my experiences working as a corn detassler that summer along with a contingent of mostly 14- and 15-year-old boys, wrote a fantasy history of the revolution (bylined the Purple Sunlight Brigade), and compiled news shorts about government atrocities here and abroad for a feature called "In the Belly of the Monster." I was fascinated by the collection of underground papers *Kaleidoscope* had lying around and loved the stimulation.

THE *KALEIDOSCOPE* SPLIT

It was an interesting period. I happened upon *Kaleidoscope* shortly before it split into two papers. On one side was the group around editor Mark Knops, recently returned from his stint in jail for contempt. Knops was a perfectionist who felt the need to apply the editor's prerogative to have the final say over the paper's appearance. Much of the staff, having become accustomed to functioning as a collective during Knops' absence, objected to the hierarchy. While Knops' product was more graphically pleasing and coherent, the other side's was more spontaneous and their instincts definitely more democratic.

— TIM WONG —

The split, which occurred in November 1971, resulted in two bi-weekly papers, *Take Over* and the *King Street Trolley*. The two papers shared the *Kaleidoscope* office space and went to press on alternate weeks.

The faction led by Mark Knops, which became *Take Over*, was essentially unwilling to adapt to the changes brought into the movement by increased feminist consciousness. Members were predominantly male, and the ideological split brought out the worst sorts of machismo. During negotiations over the split, some of their followers showed up in motorcycle jackets and strutted around as if intent on bloodying some heads. Early *Take Over* articles glorifying prostitution probably reflected a reaction to the *Trolley* politics as much as Knops' bizarre notion that prostitution was a "revolutionary" alternative to the nuclear family. *Take Over*, during its eight years of publication, was "left-liberal" and anti-establishment in its politics but it never really embraced current leftist thinking, although it was clearly sympathetic. This gave staffers independence and the license to be more creative and irreverent, but it also isolated them politically from the radical community.

The majority faction of *Kaleidoscope*, which became the *Trolley*, felt that the hierarchy, whereby Mark Knops was editor, was antithetical to the sorts of revolutionary changes they were pursuing for society. They started the trend, followed by both *Free For All* and *No Limits*, of having no editorial staff positions on the paper. While certain people clearly fulfilled those functions, no one was credited as such. They also felt the need to reach out to people who were not white males, through the newspaper if not in person. This evolving ideology was somewhat confining, and made them easy targets for the arrogant *Take Over* antagonists. Nevertheless, the general ideology portrayed in the *Trolley* set the tone for all subsequent Madison alternative papers to this day. The *Take Over* faction dismissed them as "Stalinoid creeps." Yet the Trolleyites were neither Stalinoid nor creepy. Instead they were dedicated leftists reflecting the evolving ideology of their time.

Overall, as individuals, people on both staffs shared many common political views, including opposition to the war, support for the "revolution," and hatred of police and mainstream capitalists. Yet, the papers they produced were vastly different. The *King Street Trolley* resembled *Kaleidoscope* in its political content and its not particularly pleasing graphic appearance. This was not surprising, as the vast majority of the *Kaleidoscope* staff had migrated to the *Trolley*.

In stark contrast, *Take Over* was sensationalist. Stark headlines and *National Enquirer*-type features were the rule. A feature story about how a worker at the Madison Oscar Mayer plant had allegedly fallen into the butchery and had been ground into and mixed with the sausage product (and how Oscar Mayer officials were covering up the story) was typical. Another cover story featured an "interview" with an IRA terrorist, which I only discovered years later was completely fictitious. *Take Over* was humorous and entertaining, interested in selling newspapers, and only coincidentally interested in converting people to leftist politics. One could say that *Take Over* strived to be the Madison political establishment's underground newspaper. Relatively unconstrained with news about the alternative community, *Take Over* was perfectly suited for that role. The *Trolley* and later *Free For All* and *No Limits*, on the contrary, geared themselves to the alternative community.

After a few months, when it became clear that *Take Over* would not become a financial success and press runs dwindled from the hoped-for 10,000 to 2,000 or so, Mark Knops ceased his active participation. Knops was a sort of enigma. He had basic leftist tendencies, but he felt strongly that the "masses" were uninterested in leftist politics or ideology and that these had little or no place in an underground paper. While he was probably right that most people weren't interested in our dreams about the new society, I questioned the purpose of publishing a paper if propagandizing for the left was not a part of it. The paper soon slimmed down to a core of five people, and actually became slightly more political in content.

Having been so new to *Kaleidoscope* at the time of its demise, I was ambivalent about where to put my energy—except that I knew I was interested in working on some underground newspaper. As a result, I was the only person who actually worked on the first several issues of both *Take Over* and the *Trolley*. Because the *Trolley* had a large staff and essentially ignored me, while, on the contrary, *Take Over* had promised me several pages of copy per issue, I began working exclusively for *Take Over*. Soon, I stopped working at People's Office and even quit my typist job at University of Wisconsin.

At *Take Over*, I saw my role, in addition to the shitwork functions of circulation manager, exchange manager, main typist, and other unnamed, unglorified, but essential activities, as inserting enough leftist political news into the paper to make it palatable to the sizable leftist political community, in effect neutralizing the often sexist, usually politically irrelevant stuff in the rest of the paper. It was a tentative alliance at best. We did feel a certain kinship, as we were aware that, in these pre-Soglin days, we were under constant police surveillance, although none of us was ever personally confronted. When the *Trolley* folded in the late summer of 1972, I took it upon myself to argue for an increasing amount of leftist news. This put me in conflict with the rest of the staff, who felt such material was boring. I began to realize that I had made a mistake in ultimately siding with *Take Over*, despite the opportunity it had afforded me of filling several pages of each issue with material as I saw fit. Staff members did approve of my continuation and expansion of *Kaleidoscope*'s "Belly of the Monster," news shorts excerpted from other underground papers and, increasingly, humorous or bizarre filler stories rewritten from the straight press. I renamed the column the "World Truth Conspiracy," and changed it to the "Wong Truth Conspiracy" several issues later.

They were less taken, however, by my other contributions. As I pushed more and more strongly for additional national and international news in the paper (I wasn't yet focusing on local news), I ran into increasing resistance from Michael Fellner, the *de facto* editor who also solicited all the advertising. He didn't want to hustle more ads just to accommodate my pedestrian leftist news service stories. I began feeling resentful that my editorial (not to mention administrative) work was not being appreciated. While on vacation at the end of 1972, I realized my further participation with *Take Over* was impossible.

Take Over continued publishing on a fairly regular basis until May 1979. They maintained their humor, irreverence, and good layout until the end. *Take Over* devoted a lot of space to local politics and had a special relationship with left liberal Mayor Paul Soglin, who was in office initially from 1973 to 1979. They criticized him and his administration from the left. Yet, in 1977, when conservative challenger Nino Amato came in first in the mayoral primary (with Soglin placing second) and the pundits gave him a chance of beating Soglin in the general election, *Take Over* ran a feature story linking Amato to the mob. I don't know whether the article was true or more likely a typical *Take Over* mesh of fact and fiction, nor whether the story had a decisive impact on the outcome of the election. Amato filed suit, but Soglin won the election.

Probably the high point of *Take Over*'s existence was in about 1976 when they printed parodies of Madison's two daily newspapers. The *Capital Times* cover headline read "Nixon Suicide Attempt Fails," while the flip side *State Journal* was headlined "Nixon Recovering From Ordeal." They placed these papers inside *Cap Times* and *State Journal* vending machines, and managed to sell 10,000 copies of that well-done issue. Jim Danky summed up *Take Over* very aptly in an article he wrote for the *Harvest Quarterly* in 1977: "Needless to say, the paper has never failed to successfully call attention to itself."[1]

For instance, following the election of Paul Soglin as mayor in 1973 and his appointment of a liberal police chief, the Mifflin Street block parties became legal and institutionalized. Thousands of people descended upon Mifflin Street each May. Little known by the average partygoer was that all the profits from the party went to *Take Over*. Since *Take Over*'s demise, the Mifflin St. Co-op has taken charge of any profits made, distributing them to groups requesting donations to further their underfinanced causes.

In 1989, Michael Fellner organized a reunion for veterans of Madison's underground papers. It was billed as a celebration of the twentieth anniversary of Miffland's declaration of independence. Fellner graciously invited former *Trolley* people and others, including me, with whom *Take Over* had had difficulties. As the idea evolved, radicals from the late sixties and early seventies were invited, regardless of their involvement in alternative journalism. The event occurred around the July 4th weekend, from Friday through Tuesday the 4th, and included workshops, picnics, and parties. It concluded with a pro-choice rally and march to the Capitol. While *Kaleidoscope* and *Take Over* were adequately mentioned throughout the weekend, there was no mention of the *King Street Trolley*, *Free For All*, or *No Limits*. Those who had left Madison before 1972 and attended the get-together never learned of any other publications besides *Take Over*.

FREE FOR ALL FOUNDED

Following my split with *Take Over*, I started volunteering full-time at the Mifflin St. Co-op, which was located across the street from my house. A couple of weeks later I learned that a group of people from People's Office were seeking to start up a new alternative newspaper—one, in fact, that was alternative to *Take Over*. Interestingly, while People's Office still found out-of-towners places to "crash" and housed the Acid Rescue office, callers were no longer told what movies were being shown on campus. Differentiation between campus and commercial movie showing was no longer significant—both were considered mainstream and irrelevant to a leftist switchboard.

I was exhilarated at the prospect of working on a new paper. I was thrust into the odd position of being considered a veteran all-around journalist by the others, odd because my all-around experience stretched back less than a year and a half. At the *Carletonian*, I had been involved in all aspects of writing for a newspaper, but layout and other technical chores were done by the printer. Since coming to Madison, I had become knowledgeable about many aspects of newspaper production also, but other jobs—such as shooting a process camera—I had never done. Because I at least knew where the alternative community's process camera was and because I knew how to load it, I was a relative expert.

The first issue of *Free For All* appeared on March 1, 1973, about six weeks after the first serious organizational meetings occurred and six years to the day that Madison's first underground, *Connections*, had appeared. It was produced at night in the basement of a UW campus church basement (campus church basements have played a role in Madison leftist politics for several decades). One of the founders, a dope dealer, happened to be a very persuasive ad salesperson (he later made a fortune selling T-shirts), while the rest of us tried to pull in a few ads beyond the semi-obligatory ones from the alternative and cooperative communities. Our financial security dipped considerably after the second or third issue, when he faded from the scene.

Free For All differed from its recent predecessors in that it was circulated free and was dependent for its livelihood, after that initial two-month period, solely on advertising, plus a minimal amount from donations and subscriptions. By this time, there were enough co-ops and marginal alternative businesses in Madison to keep the paper afloat. Record companies—once the lifeblood of most underground newspapers—had by this time abandoned the political, self-avowed "revolutionary" newspapers and thrown their money instead into the less threatening and apolitical or at best quasi-political music-oriented rags such as *Rolling Stone*.

Free For All carried on the role *Kaleidoscope* and the *Trolley* had previously borne—being the newspaper for the alternative community. *Take Over*, on the other hand, with its sensationalism and its general orientation, was the "alternative" newspaper for the straight community. This explains why alternative papers with three to four times the circulation were much less well known at the time than *Take Over*.

Although I didn't recognize it at the time, the transition to *Free For All* symbolized the end of the "sixties." Staff members on Madison's earlier "underground" newspapers had been an integral part of the alternative community. While that community didn't encompass all young people, we went on the assumption that we spoke for all youth who weren't still brainwashed by their upbringing and past. Many of the people making up the *Free For All* core, however, had no ties to the alternative community. Although they had leftist politics, they decidedly were not part of the "cultural revolution"; some were even openly contemptuous of those for whom drug use was the way of life. They understood, less naively than we, that the majority of youth were not going to rally to our cause and certainly that drug use by itself was not revolutionary.

It was the end of a euphoric era, when we had assumed that only a few more excesses by the government were needed to generate a mass uprising against the state. Instead, movement was in the other direction. The Chicago police violence in 1968, the open declaration of war against the state by the Weather Underground and other revolutionary groups in 1969, the Kent State murders in May 1970, and the August 1970 Army Math bombing caused many people to wonder how committed to the struggle they really wanted to get.

By 1972 and 1973, Nixon started withdrawing U.S. troops from Vietnam, while radicals and left liberals (including Madison's Paul Soglin) found out they could get elected to public office if they really tried. Government in many places—certainly in Madison—did become more open. Radical people were appointed to city committees. In Madison, the police chief, who many in the progressive community considered to be a fascist, was replaced by a liberal one who allowed demonstrators to do virtually everything except break windows. Those who remained in the leftist community were consciously separate from mainstream society—they were convinced that "working within the system" didn't work.

Free For All put out several issues in succession. While not exceedingly well-written and falling considerably short of professional graphic standards, it had a warm feeling. Its purpose was to support and be a part of the "alternative community," which was defined as both the people who subscribed to a notion of a political lifestyle different from that they had grown up in and also the economic and political institutions—mostly cooperatives—that had sprung up to consolidate their alternative visions. At least 30 untrained but eager people worked on the first issue. It soon became apparent, though, that only a small minority of those 30 people were willing or able to commit the time needed to make a newspaper an ongoing reality.

The initial momentum of better-than-monthly publication was halted temporarily when four underground paper people from Lansing, Michigan (including Ken Wachsberger, the editor of this book), pulled up in our driveway and asked my woman friend and fellow *Free For All* staffer Marie and me if we wanted to go to Boulder, Colorado, for a conference of the Underground Press Syndicate. We rode to Colorado non-stop in the back of a "drive away"[2] pick-up truck to attend a loosely structured affair and shoot the shit with people with whose papers we exchanged.

Our return home was delayed for a series of reasons. First, we had to go to Murray, Utah, and then Denver, Colorado, to deliver the pick-up truck and then a ChemLawn truck. In both towns, we were investigated by suspicious local gendarme, and enroute to Denver the chemical fumes challenged my liver. In Denver, we had to wait for the police to release our eastbound driveaway car. That car turned out to be owned by Herb Score, the one-time phenom pitcher for the Cleveland Indians, whose career was ruined when his forehead caught a Gil McDougald line drive. Score was now working as a play-by-play announcer for the Indians in Cleveland, which was, conveniently, Ken's home town. The previous driveawayers had been stopped somewhere in Kansas and found to have a trunkful of marijuana. The car must have been held for evidence, or maybe the company couldn't find anyone who wanted to go from Denver to Cleveland. On the way back to the Midwest, I had the Michigan people drop Marie and me off in Lincoln, Nebraska. There we stayed with staffers from the Lincoln *Gazette*, including Milton Yuan, the only Asian-American I met in my years in underground journalism. He was disappointed to find out that I was not Oriental: he had hoped to find "another Chinese-American who had gone wrong." The paper later split into two, the older staff keeping the name *Gazette* and Milton and the others forming the *People's Dispatch*. The two papers shared the *Gazette*'s typesetting machine, until the *People's Dispatch* refused to give it back one time and moved to Detroit to be good Stalinists.

By the time we got back to Madison, *Free For All* had come out again. It was a graphic disaster, even by *Free For All* standards. Most of the graphics were too small and too dark; the staff hadn't rented a proportionally spaced typewriter and didn't reduce the size of the type when making negatives. The paper didn't come out again for almost three months.

We did manage to come out in September 1973, helped in large part by generous fall advertising budgets eager to greet returning students. Ads appealed directly to our perceived readership. One, from a liquor store, said, "Everybody Must Get Stoned." The graphic showed an underground comic character passed out on the street, bottle in hand, with the caption "Falling Down Drunk Stoned." A new hole-in-the-wall business that is now one of Madison's largest camping/scuba/clothing stores ran an ad exclaiming, "Good Shit!! At Great Prices," with a picture of Spiderman saying "Drop In! Or Else!"

The September issue reminded Madison that *Free For All* was back, and that we desperately needed staff. One person who answered the call, in late 1973, was Michael Kaufman. Michael was unemployed, looking for work, and had lots of energy to work on the paper, even when he finally got a job. I was paying rent with money saved from my earlier typist job, volunteering at Mifflin St. Co-op in exchange for "wages" that could be applied toward food and other co-op products, and was therefore able to live job-free. Together we did the bulk of the work for several issues.

Free For All varied from issue to issue, with few stable features. Two of them that did appear regularly were written by me: the "modestly" titled Wong Truth Conspiracy, a two-page spread of news shorts I had also written for *Take Over*, and "On the Road to Fascism," a surprisingly good (as I reread it 15 years later) summary of domestic political news, focusing, until his resignation, on Nixon, who was known in the column as Nixswine. I always considered Wong Truth Conspiracy a sort of loss leader for the alternative papers I worked on, humorous yet political writing that (I hoped) drew the reader into the more substantive, serious, and political stuff comprising the rest of the paper. Anonymous observation of people on the days the new issues came out confirmed that Wong Truth was invariably the first section people turned to. I watched to see how long they read the paper after finishing the column. Michael later also contributed a regular feature, "Revolution Abroad," a synopsis of what was going on in the Third World, particularly in countries where Marxist-Leninist regimes had taken over or where Marxist guerrilla groups were active.

In the spring of 1974, another Miffland resident and Mifflin Co-op volunteer, Rick Caprow, joined the staff, and Michael brought in some people from the housing co-op where he lived. The staff was beginning to grow, and we knew the paper was going to survive its infancy. As long as a staff is extremely small, the urge to keep that paper alive predominates, and factional disputes are kept to a minimum. Once the staff grows and stabilizes, there is time to analyze the different political viewpoints represented. Michael was talented and basically easy to work with. He also was a convinced Maoist/Communist who thought anarchism was non-revolutionary and "petit bourgeois." Phil Davis, on the other hand, the major person Michael had brought in, was of anarchist persuasion and certainly anti-Soviet and anti-China. I had libertarian instincts, but was not an overt anarchist. Rick was outspokenly anarchist, and showed me that my libertarian instincts were in line with present-day anarchist thinking.

FFA LEANS TOWARDS ANARCHISM

Rob Lerman and Nomi Schwartz, paper people from the beginning, basically were dubious about the ruling "Communist" regimes, but didn't think (Rob especially) that it was our job to attack the "left." Despite their presence and Michael's, the paper took a decidedly anarchist drift. Typical of this period was an article Rick wrote about a speech he and I had attended given by Bob Avakian, the head honcho of the Revolutionary Union (RU), a Maoist sect that had received the "China franchise" (the right to speak for China in the United States) from the Maoist regime. Because Avakian considered himself a dangerous revolutionary and therefore a ripe target for assassination, we were frisked before being allowed into the room. Chairman Bob rambled on for several hours about the need for "Communist revolution." We wrote it up under the headline, "Stalinism: RU Serious?"

The article itself was a report on Avakian's speech with frequent digressions into repudiations of the RU perspective. Along with the article was a "discussion piece" entitled "Which Way Goes the Movement?" an attack on the theory that the vanguard party should lead the "masses" to revolution, balanced with a reminder that the revolution meant destruction, not seizure, of power, and that it involved much more than just the economic question of who controlled the means of production.

Quoting from literature of another vanguard group, Detroit's Motor City Labor League, Rick expressed genuine indignation that an allegedly leftist group could talk about "lines [being] drawn so that we can precisely chart the path to revolution...[and] achieve the necessary unity of will so that the Party can impose iron discipline in order to lead the proletariat to deal the necessary death blows to decadent capitalism" (this wasn't Rick's and my idea of smashing the state). Rick added, "To get a historical perspective on the mentality I am talking about, remember that one hero of these 'vanguard parties' is none other than modern history's number two mass murderer Joseph Stalin. I am serious, they praise him and quote him in their literature. One has to struggle to keep from going blind with rage at the thought of it." To add insult to injury, one of our graphics on the pages was a profile of Stalin, designed as a mug shot, with the serial number added 5369417PIG.

The article provoked reactions. Externally, several RU adherents and/or their student affiliates, the Revolutionary Student (we always said "Stalinist") Brigade, set the papers sitting inside the doorway to our building afire. Internally, our own skepticism that China provided the guiding light for the movement, as reflected in our discussions inside the office and by our snide remarks in the paper wherever we could sneak them in (the Wong Truth Conspiracy was a natural), was distressing to Michael. He managed to convince Lucy Mathiak, his woman friend and herself a marginal contributor, and Rob and Nomi to request a meeting to discuss their futures on the paper, in light of *Free For All*'s obvious drift toward an anarchist philosophy.

At the meeting, held around November 1974, we decided that the paper should include all factions of the left, including Michael's brand of quasi-independent Maoism. In retrospect, we probably should have told the non-anarchists to fuck off and start their own paper if they needed an outlet.

The anarchists were in a position of strength in late 1974, but chose not to capitalize on it. We felt that *Free For All* would be a better paper for Michael's and Rob's contributions. In fact, the *Free For All* of 1975 was a fairly good newspaper. Following a month-long trip to the East and South around the end of the year, I helped start the Madison branch of the People's Bicentennial Commission (PBC). The idea, primarily the brainchild of Jeremy Rifkin, was to re-create scenes of the rebellion that had taken place 200 years ago, use selective quotes that made the Founders sound radical, and reenact historical events on their 200th anniversary—in general, to counteract the celebration of capitalism that the corporate mainstream was planning to commemorate the same event. I spent six months working with PBC. During that time, my involvement at *Free For All* was limited to doing the Wong Truth and inserting articles about the PBC.

When I rejoined the staff full-time in about the middle of 1975, there was a different feel to the paper. It seemed to crave more structure. We had experimented during the first half of 1975 with the idea of a paid staff by paying Rick $100 a month to coordinate all publication tasks, but he had burned out and moved to Sturgeon Bay, Wisconsin, to become a ship welder. Phil seemed to have become less of an anarchist.

At about this time *Free For All* moved from its first long-term home to an office in the University YMCA. Although the space was much bigger and the atmosphere in the Y much more leftist, the move was somehow symbolic of a change. We had been in a large room above a store on State Street, the street that bridged the eight blocks between the state capitol and the university. One neighbor was a strange character who would come next door to our office and ask, "Does anyone want to come next door and smoke a j[oint]?" Those who did—he always had good dope—were frequently subjected to a lengthy monologue on the subject of cancer.

The memories of that office are countless. The stimulating conversations we had with staffers and visitors, both from Madison and out-of-town, the arguments, the frequent all-night sessions, in short, everything that characterized the early years of *Free For All*, took place in that dingy room. One lasting annoying memory were the green flying bugs that infested our office in the summer and kamikazeed on our layout pages, the price we paid for renting a hole-in-the-wall office that had no screens on the windows.

I never felt comfortable in the new office. Michael's presence was felt very heavily. Yet that fall something happened that gave anarchism its last hurrah

Figure 1: Cover cartoon for *Free For All* 3, no. 13, September 18-October 7, 1975

on *Free For All*. A talented artist had shown up, and we had recruited him to draw some front covers for the paper. His first was a three-part graphic depicting "the Capitalist Way," "the Communist Way," and "Another Way" (see figure 1). The first two drawings were similar: in both pictures, workers at the bottom were trudging along, chained together. The air was full of pollution from numerous smokestacks. Above the trudging workers was an animal with a whip: in the "Capitalist Way," a massive pig was portrayed as the owner of Swine Works; in the "communist Way," a similar-sized rat was in charge of the People's Foundry and the People's Steel Works. Below those two drawings was "Another Way," an idyllic (definitely naive) portrayal of an apple-picking collective—the sun shining, everyone happy.

Most of our readers who contacted us loved it and supported the cover's thesis that we needed a revolutionary alternative to the twin oppressive systems of capitalism and "communism." But Michael was furious. Even though he understood (I think...I hope!) that the state-capitalist bosses were no better than the capitalist bosses from the workers' point of view, he didn't feel the left should be the ones to point that out. We thought it was exactly the left that should point it out. In reacting to reader responses, Michael redoubled his efforts to purge the anarchist ideology from the paper. Although Rick, the energetic anarchist, had moved away, several people with decidedly anarchist leanings had joined the paper. Unfortunately they played mostly minor roles and were unreliable. Many others, primarily of a leftist but nevertheless "don't rock the boat" mentality (their "boat" was the cooperative movement and the left in general), joined the staff on Michael's side.

I began to wonder whether I should spend time and effort resisting the takeover of *Free For All* by a bunch of humorless leftists. One major difference between my way of thinking and theirs was in determining when the paper should publish: my idea was that we were an "alternative" paper and therefore not a "news" paper. I felt we shouldn't publish on a specific date if we didn't have enough good material to make it worthwhile; they felt that we should publish on a regular schedule, to make our calendar of events useful and "because we promised our advertisers we'd publish." Were we a totally "alternative" newspaper or an alternative version of a regular newspaper? The development of *Isthmus* in Madison and other liberal, but definitely calendar-oriented, weeklies around the country took over that role for the "alternative" newspapers, and made "revolutionary" biweeklies that revolved around a calendar of events obsolete—most advertisers preferred a professional looking paper with no threatening politics to a graphic disaster with emphatically leftist politics.

ORIGINS OF THE SPLIT

Between January and the late summer of 1975, a new need for order and structure had descended upon the paper. We had always printed publishing schedules, but we had always been flexible as to whether we adhered to that schedule. Now, it had become an obsession to publish on the date forecast in the previous issue. More than merely irritating to someone with social plans on the night before publication (always a late night, sometimes all-night), this made volunteers think being on the paper was work, rather than fun. Naturally, when there was "work" to do, we needed to pay someone to do it. Looking back to Rick's monthly paycheck earlier in the year as precedent, staffers talked increasingly of the need to hire people to produce the paper.

The amount we could afford to pay, however, was totally inadequate for even subsistence living. Furthermore, with a paid staff, unpaid people volunteered less often—particularly for the shit jobs such as soliciting advertising. This added pressure on the paid staff assured rapid turnover. Nevertheless, the paper's reliance on whoever was paid staff made them "more equal" than the volunteer staff. Given the various political factions within the newspaper, the then-dominant faction would make sure a person of their political persuasion became the paid staff member. For these reasons, the paid staff concept at this juncture of *Free For All*'s existence really couldn't work.

In late 1975, an incident occurred that further delineated the split in thinking on the paper. An article in the December issue of *Take Over* revealed that two people involved in the movement in the early seventies had actually been police agents. One of these people, Steve Featherston, had been one of the founders of *Free For All* and had worked at People's Office before that. According to Steve, he had been recruited in Missouri by George Croal, a notorious Madison policeman who was particularly identified with spying on and harassing the left. Steve came to Madison and dutifully reported on his comrades in People's Office and *Free For All*. He stopped his work for the police some time in 1973. While he was never a major contributor to the paper, he was a frequent visitor, co-authored baseball columns with me, wrote fitness columns, and generally contributed good humor to his environment. He was genuinely working class, unlike most of the staff, and I remained a good friend of his.

In response to the *Take Over* article, Steve wrote another article, entitled "Free For All's Informer Tells His Story," for the January 1976 *Free For All*. In that article, which he signed "MPD706," Steve referred to the *Take Over* article, confessed to everything, and asked people's forgiveness for something he had done without thinking about the consequences. (The longer he hung around his informees, the more guilty he felt about his job. A few months after he quit working for the pigs, he tried unsuccessfully to hang himself.) Since Steve still hung around the paper, Michael demanded a "trial" for him, an inquisition at which this self-righteous, holier-than-thou leftist could set down the conditions for Steve's continued participation on the paper. After enduring more abuse than I would have tolerated, Steve adjourned with me and a few others to our favorite bar. This unnecessary humiliation of an obviously repentant ex-informer left a very bad taste in my mouth.

Around this time, nationwide, a movement was being organized by Marxist-Leninist types to take advantage of the hard times people were experiencing. The idea was to sponsor "Hard Times Conferences" around the country. One was held in Chicago in January 1976, and about ten people from *Free For All* attended. Simultaneously, there was a drive in Madison to establish a "Community Union" to direct political activity on the left. The anarchist community immediately dubbed it a "community onion." The CU's intent was to have a board of directors to decide what political activity was appropriate for the "community" to participate in.

The idea was not totally without merit. Politically these *were* "hard times" for the left. Several years had now passed since the left in Madison could muster more than a couple hundred people at political demonstrations. It was becoming apparent that the mass movement of the late sixties and early seventies had been the exception to the norm, rather than the beginning of a general uprising against the establishment. A central organization in town that was in contact with movements in Madison and other cities and that had a few paid full-time staff members was no doubt helpful in publicizing activities.

But more dominant was another group of people more interested in controlling the movement and establishing themselves as the vanguard of the movement, the enlightened few who could guide the wavering movement onto the correct path. To them, these hard times called for more leadership and more unity. Usually unspoken (although not always) was the fact that it would be their leadership and that they would impose the unity.

On *Free For All*, Michael viewed the Hard Times movement nationally and the Community Union locally as a godsend. A majority of the staff appeared to agree with him that the CU was a good thing. Members of *FFA*'s anarchist minority, who shared the suspicions of Madison's non-authoritarian left, argued that staff members as individuals could participate in the CU as they saw fit, but that the paper itself should not take a stand pro or con, given the differences of opinion about it among the staff. Our point of view was rejected, and *Free For All* became the major advocate and cheering section for the Community Union.

While the core staff during that time remained very small, there were 20 or 30 people who came to meetings or milled around the office during layout sessions. Structurally members didn't hold formal titles; officially, at least, we were all equal. Yet a subtle change took place during 1975: the staff had evolved into a "collective." This change involved more than semantics. While a staff was a group of individuals who gathered to produce the paper, a collective was a politically cohesive collection of individuals who met to produce the paper. The paper tried to reach agreement by consensus. Those who disagreed with the majority opinion and therefore stood in the way of consensus (as defined by the majority) were branded "consensus-blockers" and people who couldn't "work collectively."

One "collective" decision had been to keep to a regular publication schedule. To back up that schedule, they set rigid deadlines, particularly for submission of copy. Traditionally I had spent the first several days of layout hanging around the office, trying to keep volunteers busy, editing people's articles, typing them, and laying out other people's pages. About 36 hours before publication, I would go to work on my articles—the two-page Wong Truth Conspiracy and the one to four other pages I had agreed to write and lay out. My routine never caused us to miss a publication date. But this schedule was unacceptable to the "collective" under the new regime. (I would be disingenuous if I didn't admit that writing my articles late in the process irritated others I worked with over the years.)

Consistently not meeting these newly imposed deadlines cast me as an "individualist" resisting the collective will. Conveniently forgotten was the fact that I singlehandedly did more to get the paper underway during the first few days of the issue's layout than most of the people who showed up at "collective" meetings to forge the "collective will."

Although I am usually not given to conspiracy theories, in retrospect I think a conspiracy was working against me during the early part of 1976. Every staff sets copy deadlines for articles. The deadlines exist for people whose writing ability or reliability are in question and/or for people who submit their articles and let others process them further. But for those who write their articles, type them, find graphics, lay them out, and don't delay publication in so doing, a deadline seemed less necessary. It had been an unspoken agreement on *Free For All* that, unless the author asked others for feedback, articles written by members of the "core staff" were not edited by others. For instance, Michael's "Revolution Abroad" column found no fault with any two-bit dictator, as long as the dictator proclaimed himself a "Marxist-Leninist." I was a little repulsed by Michael's glorification of petty dictators, albeit proclaimed leftists, but felt he had the right to write what he believed in, especially if he awarded me that same right. Since I did all the work on my articles, solicited input from others on graphics, honored self-imposed deadlines (even if it meant staying up the last 48 hours straight), and still had time to do the camera work on the paper, I felt that the new-found insistence on deadlines for all had been specifically designed for me.

In March of 1976, a dispute during layout occurred that saw me accused of being "anti-woman" as well as an anti-collective "rugged individualist." While the story list for any given issue, although fluid, was established early on, one of the last decisions usually was on the front cover, usually due to lack of any ideas rather than a surplus. Often we solved the dilemma somewhat unsatisfactorily by printing one or more stories on the front page. For an issue in late February 1976, though, we had come up with two ideas and had agreed to do a split cover. "My" cover was a graphic accompanying an article urging people to withhold part of their utility bills to protest an illegal rate increase Madison Gas & Electric was still collecting in defiance of a court order. The organization behind the protest, People United for Responsible Energy (PURE), had asked us to help publicize the effort, and we had responded by saying we would devote part of the front page to their story. The other plan for the front cover was a graphic to introduce the centerfold, which listed the schedule of events for International Women's Day. The dispute arose when Nomi finally found a graphic she liked for the cover—because it was vertical, it could only take the whole cover or a fourth of it. Since we had promised PURE that we would publicize the bill protest on our cover, and because I thought standing up to a monopoly was as important as publicizing the upcoming celebration and series of workshops, I held out for half of the front cover.

This was the way most disputes during layout were resolved: the majority present at the time of the dispute prevailed. Because of who was in the office that night, the other side prevailed: the PURE story was relegated to page 5, and the women's day graphic took up the whole front page. I felt not giving PURE front-page publicity at a time when they were trying to build momentum for the payment withholding and for their organization was wrong. My advocacy on PURE's behalf, though, was not taken by the other staffers as advocacy on behalf of a community group who had asked us for much-needed support. Instead, my advocacy for PURE was proof positive that I was anti-woman, anti-feminist.

Another mindset gaining currency at that time—perhaps it was a new variant of white middle-class guilt about "skin privilege" that developed during the black power movement of the late 1960s—was an attitude that favored certain groups over others. For instance, women had higher status than men; gays and lesbians higher status than straights; "workers" (presumably blue-collar) higher status than non-"workers" and students; non-whites higher status than whites. The origin of these attitudes made sense—it was a rebellion against the white male (heterosexual) power structure, the system we were trying to replace with one that was more humane. Yet these attitudes, when carried to their extreme, caused friction. The quarrel cited above was one example. The paper's willingness to redo a page or two the night before we were going to press in order to accommodate the request for space of a women's or gay group (a request we denied to other groups) was another. Those of us who thought such favoritism was inappropriate were branded "anti-women," "anti-gay," or anti-whatever.

Another point of difference on the paper concerned the Wobblies. In 1974 the paper had become an Industrial Workers of the World (IWW or Wobbly) union shop. For a period, more than 20 of us carried Wobbly "red cards." As time went on, however, most staffers let their memberships lapse, but several of us stayed on. The local Wobblies were a source of fresh talent on the paper. They came as ardent proponents of anarcho-syndicalism—a point of view that rubbed the paper's Marxist-Leninists the wrong way, because of the Wobbly belief that labor unions should be revolutionary rather than business unions.

Our criticism of the Eastern European and other "Communist" regimes for their basic authoritarianism and elitism, including the fact that labor unions in "Communist" countries were docile adherents to the party line and totally subservient to the state, reignited long-expressed concerns by some that we shouldn't be criticizing the "left." We countered by saying that any government that could only stay in power through creating a police state was definitely not leftist. This tension lay mostly under the surface, but it was there nonetheless.

Although we all shared the one incentive to get the paper published, these combined tensions created a rather unpleasant atmosphere around the paper through 1975. By the beginning of 1976, we probably all realized in our subconscious at least that a split was inevitable.

The paper still consisted of about four or five people who did at least 80 percent of the work, plus a much larger group of people who came to meetings and/or hung around during layout sessions. This latter group probably considered themselves staff people even though they didn't do much. These hangers-on tended to have the politics of those who had brought them into the paper. By this time our faction had about ten adherents, the other side not quite twice as many. We thought them grim and humorless; they thought us nuisances who, through our constant questions about the paper's direction, kept the paper from realizing its true potential.

The unpleasantness led me to withdraw somewhat. On a few issues in the spring of 1976, other people on the staff wrote and laid out the Wong Truth. The first incident that led directly to the paper's eventual split occurred when I asked that the paper not use the name Wong Truth Conspiracy on those issues that I didn't work on. Rather than simply change the name, the other faction of the staff inserted a contest box saying in part, "RENAME WONG TRUTH! *Free For All* believes in change. After three years of the old one, we finally revised our masthead last January. But we've used the 'Wong Truth' name since Volume 1, Number 1, 47 action-packed issues, and *frankly, we're bored*" (my emphasis). This was inserted without my knowledge, and since the column contained my name I thought it appropriate that I see what they were running before it went to press.

I wrote a letter in response for the following issue, stating that "I was appalled to see the distortion of facts contained in the contest box in last issue's Wong Truth," and going on to delineate some of the problems I saw occurring on the paper. My letter was printed, along with seven responses (on a page entitled "Stimulus-Response") attacking me and my letter and essentially boiling the whole controversy down to a personality conflict centering on my inability to get along with the "collective" or to work "collectively." Needless to say, no one sharing my feelings about the paper was invited to write a response.

The "Stimulus-Response" page threw me for a loop and further decreased my interest in working on the paper. Ironically, at the same time that I was withdrawing voluntarily from the paper, the other side was plotting my expulsion. The "collective" (i.e., Michael, Rob, and Phil) called for a meeting to expel me. A recent Wobbly recruit, Frank Callahan, incensed at the majority's treatment of me, had vowed to increase his involvement on the paper, specifically to be confrontational and irritating to them. For his efforts over the course of just two issues, Frank was elevated to the status of "co-defendant" in the "purge trial."

The only mention in writing of this meeting was in a letter written by seven staff members who were critical of the "Stimulus-Response" page. The letter said in part, "The nature and layout of the page leads one to believe that Tim, in his rugged individualism, singlehandedly is obstructing the decisions of the otherwise unified 'collective.' This is hardly the case. In reality, over the last six months, many of us at *FFA* have been frustrated by the grim and humorless ordeal that producing *FFA* has become. We have come to question this mythical monster called the 'collective.' Is the collective the three individuals who, without

informing anyone else (not even their friends, let alone Tim) went and took Tim's name off the *FFA* [bank] account claiming that at a 'collective' meeting new officers had been elected?" It then described the upcoming meeting, and continued, "Do purges constitute collective process? How many of us will have to be removed before the paper 'functions' collectively? We urgently await the day when *FFA* will once again become the open community newspaper it once was."

THE SPLIT

The stage was set for a split, and it occurred. The expulsion meeting actually discussed four options: 1) to continue as usual; 2) to expel Frank and me; 3) to split the paper in two but continue to share the same facilities on a rotating basis; and 4) to split the assets. Although the major elements of the "collective" faction favored the expulsion option, they could not muster the two-thirds vote needed to bring that about. Since they had a paranoid distrust of our honest intentions (witness the bank account shenanigan), they rejected the office sharing option.

Being in the minority, we favored the "continue as usual" choice but this choice was unacceptable to the other side. That left only the option of splitting the assets. It passed on a 20-9 vote. The only real difference between the expulsion and assets splitting was that the latter guaranteed our side some stake in the paper. Otherwise, the effect was the same: the seven members of our group not up for expulsion would not have stayed on the paper had the two of us been expelled.

The "collective" then set a meeting to discuss how the assets would be split—they picked a day on which they knew we couldn't attend. Only one person from our side showed up, and he left before the vote. The outcome would not have been different had we been there. Considering that we were not, we were lucky to receive half the cash in the bank (our share was $750) and half of the layout supplies. They got to keep the office, the name of the paper, and, most importantly to me, the post office box. The PO box was critical, because that was where our incoming mail came, including all the other underground papers from around the country I had worked with almost exclusively from the beginning to get exchange subscriptions. They kept the two functioning typewriters and gave us one whose worth did not much exceed its value at a recycling center.

Their bitterness against us and their paranoid assumptions that we would try to destroy their paper pervaded their writings about the split. They framed the issue as a few dissidents against the otherwise unified "collective." In a guest editorial in the UW student newspaper, *The Daily Cardinal*, they wrote: "The basic division began over the role of collective action and the individual's responsibility in a collective...Some individuals have interpreted [*FFA*'s billing itself as an 'open community newspaper'] to mean 'for anyone to do whatever she/he wants'...Unfortunately, there were a few staff members who valued their individual right to dissent to the exclusion of the rights of either other individuals or the collective as a whole." Blithely ignored was the fact that over a third of the staff at the "purge trial" refused to expel these "few staff members" for their crimes against the "collective." In other words, a significant minority of the paper's staff refused to accede to the dominant faction's desire to rid itself of the nuisance minority, pious and self-righteous pronouncements about the "collective" notwithstanding.

Their editorial continued with a rewriting of history, designed to suit their political goals rather than the actual facts. They had proposed the meeting to divide the assets to occur two days hence. I and several others said we could not attend that night because of an IWW meeting. They decided to schedule the meeting for that night regardless, and their version read: "The rugged individualists once again demonstrated their contempt for the *Free For All* collective by failing to attend the meeting."

I'm not sure what Rob, Michael, Phil, and others thought we were going to do to them immediately after the split. Their *Cardinal* editorial continued: "Given these individuals' low regard for group process, however, we doubt that the last word's been spoken. [We wondered: were we to submit to their collective will even after we weren't part of the collective?] *Free For All* will likely come under heavy attack soon. It's up to readers who have enjoyed and supported what *Free For All* has been trying to do recently to demonstrate that support now....*Free For All* is still YOUR community newspaper. Accept no substitutes!"

In their next issue, late August 1976, their back page consisted of an expanded rewrite of their version of the *Free For All* split, newly entitled "How We Spent Our Summer Vacation," and what became a standard feature of the post-split *Free For All*, a whining plea for money. Their new last paragraph on the split contained this gratuitous sentence: "The rugged individualists now have the where-with-all (sic) to put out their own paper, or play the stock market if they want to, free from domination by their imagined oppressors."

Rather than feeling a need to attack their paper (physically or in writing), we felt that their humorlessness and constant whining about lack of money were their own worst enemy. We felt that unless they brought in some new staff not afflicted with the grim Hard Times/Community Union attitude, they would fall under their own dead weight.

While I was much too emotionally involved in the paper to be objective about the split, Jim Danky's article on the Madison underground press[3] seemed to affirm our point of view: "The anarchistic spirit that produced *Free For All* was only one source for its staff and readership. Other persons were interested in more controlled progress towards goals and this led to a staff division which produced [No Limits]."

Before delving into *No Limits*, a few footnotes about *Free For All* are in order. Within a year of the split, most of the people from the majority faction had stopped working on the paper. The paper underwent a steady decline in appearance, due in no small part to their essential purge of the most experienced and creative layout people. *Free For All* limped along until 1981, a slave to its calendar of events, with rarely a story worth glancing at after about 1977 or so. The begging for donations became the dominant feature of the paper along with the calendar of events, which drove the requirement to produce the paper on a regular basis. Most of the work was now done by the overworked, underpaid paid staff member. The result was a monotonous, boring paper—truly the end result of what I had predicted if *Free For All* tried to seriously pay staff in its then underfinanced position.

A typical issue appeared in April 1977, eight months after the "purge trial." It contained two quarter-page requests for money. The one on the back page, the usual location of their pleas for money, was headlined: "Did you know that we need your help!" and continued, "Hmm, you say. Two pleas for money in one issue! Things at *Free For All* must be pretty desperate. Well, they are and they aren't. *FFA* can go on the way it's been going for quite some time yet, struggling to pay for each issue and leaving a trail of burnt out staffers in its wake. But it takes a lot of money and energy to put out the paper, and right now, both are in short supply." Then they begged for $1,000 to pay two people $60 a week for two months, "by which time they will have (in theory) improved the quality of the paper, sold a bunch of new ads, and found other ways of funding *Free For All* to keep it going from there...." Judging from their continuing pleas for more money, no one bit in a significant way at their request.

A few months later, they offered to cease publication unless the community bailed them out, and held a "community meeting" to discuss their problems. The response was apparently sufficient to persuade them to limp along, which they did for another four years.

One of the more amusing (or is "pathetic" more apropos?) incidents in the history of the post-split *FFA* was when a *No Limits* staffer (a person not known to

We are a group of people who associate ourselves with the emerging movement for a free society. As part of an anti-authoritarian tradition of social revolution, we fight for an end to the tyranny of capitalism and the state over our lives, and against all forms of authority, hierarchy, and bureaucracy.

We see *No Limits* as a contribution to this movement—providing a forum for libertarian ideas and analysis of local, national, and international events from an anti-authoritarian perspective. *No Limits* will also provide news and general information which is of interest to the Madison community.

Some of us are members of the Industrial Workers of the World (IWW); others of us are members of a Madison libertarian communist group called Aurora; many of us are associated with the Social Revolutionary Anarchist Federation (SRAF).

The decision-making process at *No Limits* reflects our convictions about the structure of a free society; all decisions are made democratically and by consensus. Our view of consensus includes respect for the rights of the minority. By allowing for differences of thought and opinion within the paper, we find it possible to work together cooperatively and with a sense of unity.

No Limits will be published on a monthly basis. We will print 10,000 copies each issue, which will be distributed free at various locations in the Madison area. Unfortunately, until we become independently wealthy from your subscriptions, we will be forced to finance *No Limits* from advertisements.

If you feel any affinity for what we are doing, we encourage you to join us in working on *No Limits*!

NOTE

1. From *No Limits* 1, no. 1 (October 1976): 2.

---

them) answered a job notice *Free For All* had posted with the Job Service, the employment agency with which many unemployment compensation (UC) applicants feigned compliance in order to get their UC checks. The *Free For All* interviewer informed the applicant that the earring he was wearing in his left ear needed to be removed. Political buttons were also taboo, and a haircut was suggested. Quoting from the December 1978 *No Limits*, the story continues, "The interviewer asked the applicant if he owned a sport coat and tie. Assuming that *FFA* was somewhat left in its politics, the applicant laughed and replied, 'Good god. Of course not.' *FFA* made it quite clear that they were not joking and that the sport coat and tie were prerequisites for employment. We deal with businesses that respect a 'clean attire,' spoke the interviewer."

The final footnote on *Free For All* is what happened to Steve and Michael. Steve, the erstwhile informer, returned to St. Louis and got a job at the General Motors plant there. He was later transferred to a new GM plant in Oklahoma, and is currently a vice president of his local. In the tradition of radical unionists and contrary to customary business union practice, Steve insists on working half-time in the plant. Michael, on the other hand, the ardent "communist" who harangued Steve so about his youthful indiscretion, moved to New York and volunteered at the *Guardian*, an orthodox leftist weekly. When the staff unionized and went out on strike, Michael, I was told, crossed the picket lines and helped the "communist" managers produce scab issues until the strike was settled.

THE ORIGINS OF *NO LIMITS*

No Limits was virtually the antithesis of *Free For All*. Having received our share of the money and supplies, we saw no urgent need to produce an issue immediately. We had lost our office, our name, and our incoming mail to the other faction of the paper, which continued to produce issues under the influence of the temporary high stemming from their victory over us. Only gradually did it sink into them that getting the paper out required the same amount of energy as before, that all their loyal voters during the purge trial weren't willing to contribute energy during layout sessions, and that they needed to put out the paper without the services of several people (us) who had previously contributed essential time, energy, and talent.

A little less than three months after the purge trial, in late October 1976, *No Limits* produced its first issue. We arrived at the name *No Limits* by getting together and, quoting from the first issue, "playing the game of free association in various states of altered consciousness." Many of the 199 names were awful. Following the first list, we voted on the ones we liked best. The semi-finalists were Black Swan, Black Tornado, Black Hole, Eclipse, Constant Comment, Off My Toes, Permanent Vacation, Dispossessed, Wildcat, Subversive Times, Phlebitis Times, Total Eclipse, Under Toe, Dream World Dragon, Morning Glory, Synapse, and No Limits. Synapse and Permanent Vacation ended up being the most serious challenges to *No Limits*. Other suggestions included: Madison Mosquito, Purple Sunlight, Free For All, Long Live Death, Black Carp,

Near the end of 1975, however, *Free for All* became infected with a malaise that has threatened to relegate the Madison "movement" to the dustbin of history. Lacking an obvious focal point such as the Vietnam war or even "Free Karl [Armstrong]," the movement was floundering. The answer appeared to some to lie in increased unity among the Left—sacrificing diversity in hopes of somehow becoming more effective in organizing "the people" or "the workers." A prime focus for these frustrated intellectuals was the Community Union, an organization they hoped would "finally unify the Left." Rather than simply seeing the CU as an informal umbrella organization that could help coordinate the diverse activities of the "Left"—which might have been useful—they preferred to saddle the organization with a ready-made bureaucracy and non-debatable "principles of unity." Showing the limitations of their trust in the people, these bureaucrats ensured the CU's demise, which occurred almost immediately, despite *FFA*'s valiant attempts to portray it as something much more benign than it was.

Whether through conspiracy or not, a clique developed on *Free for All*. They maintained that *FFA* was not run efficiently and was consequently no fun to work on. Instead of quietly fading away and leaving the paper to those who still knew how to have fun and produce a good newspaper at the same time, these jerks took measures to guarantee that the paper was no fun for anybody. They insisted that all staff people conform to their methods of working at *FFA*, and laid endless guilt trips on people not "collective" enough to fall in line....Worse, they increasingly got on the cases of those who disagreed with them. Yet, consistent with their strong orientation towards leaders and refusal to believe in individualism, they tended to see most of the staff dissidents as "Tim's lackeys."

....The possibility of an open libertarian socialist community paper was denied by the advent of a bureaucracy which maintained that readers were too stupid to think for themselves. This position paraded itself as "collectivism" and "consensus" decision making. In reality it meant that the "leaders" wanted nothing they didn't like in the paper and demanded an absolute veto power. The majority faction's use of the term consensus, even on their own terms, was a joke. Their consensus could more correctly be called democratic centralism. The majority got its way and the minority was supposed to shut up to avoid problems. The junta's conception of the paper was that of a Monolith. If everything wasn't equally boring and non-controversial, the readers might get confused and the "correct line" might be lost in the richness of different ideas and perspectives. If people began to think for themselves, then what would be the point of *FFA* "leaders?"

....As for us, we refused to be sacrificed for "the cause," as though our common revolutionary project were not based upon our need for a qualitatively richer life. We will not burn ourselves out for "the revolution."...A newspaper is not an end in itself, a god to be bowed down to...."Revolution ceases to be as soon as it is necessary to be sacrificed to it" (wall painting, France, 1968). We found *FFA*'s "serve the people" mentality and its corresponding humorless guilt-tripping an altar of alienation; and we have had enough of alienation and religion.

....*Free for All* doesn't want to print anything too radical or it might scare advertisers and distributors, decreasing the budget for the paid bureaucrats. They don't want to print anything too critical of the "Left" because they are afraid of criticism from a handful of co-op Leninists. *Free for All* is to be totally "positive," pumping pages of boring uncritical monologue into the "fray" of the latest camp "struggle" of the "representatives" of "the workers."

....The majority faction's accusation that some of us are anti-feminist, anti-gay, and out to "destroy" the co-op movement is totally unfounded. It stems from their desire to smear us, thereby supposedly increasing their credibility to the aforementioned movements. As the "true" community organ of the co-op movement they have trouble understanding that there could exist more than one tendency in the wide network of alternative economic collectives and cooperatives. As guilt-ridden "leaders," any criticism of certain authoritarian tendencies within the women's movement by us is "sexist" and "anti-feminist." Where they dug up the anti-gay bit one never knows, and one wonders why they haven't accused us of being racist and anti-Martian in addition.

NOTE

1. From *No Limits* 1, no. 1 (October 1976): 8-9.

Sour Grapes, Enemy of the People, The Tyrant's Foe, Zero for Forty, Madison Hot Shot, Sugar in the Gas Tank, Black Pajamas, Rugged Individualist, Frankly We're Bored (these two were references to the *Free For All* split), Black Blood, Wicked Messenger, No Compromise, Nixon's Bloodclot, Spherical Orange, Black Orange, Swamp Gas, Bela Kun's Necktie, Methane Messenger, and Unlimited Pleasure. (Twenty-six of the names contained the word "black," reflecting

Figure 2: Bottom third of back cover cartoon for *No Limits* 1, no. 1, October 26-November 8, 1976

the fact that anarchists rallied behind the color "black," much as communists identify with the color red.)

What we discovered when we got together to produce the first issue was that, while we were all anarchists, anarchism encompassed several very different points of view. The primary distinction was between anarcho-syndicalists and other types of anarchists. Anarcho-syndicalists are anarchists who believe that the working class will rise up against the employing class and overthrow the government they dominate. Other types of anarchists oppose all types of hierarchy, including government, but do not see workers, through their control of the means of production, as the critical force in revolution. All but two of the *FFA* rejectees were in the Wobblies, and therefore sympathetic to anarcho-syndicalism. The two who weren't, Bob Brubaker and Scott McPherson, were strong advocates of their position, assuring that the paper would reflect both of these currents of anarchist thought.

The first issue had two front covers, one of *No Limits* and one of *Free For All*. The *No Limits* cover was an election cover, encouraging a "Vote for Nobody." It exhorted: "If you think nobody should run your life, vote for nobody. Nobody keeps campaign-promises. Nobody deserves to live off your taxes. Nobody can legislate your freedom. Nobody is the perfect candidate. If you *think*, vote for Nobody for President." The graphic was a picture of Gerald Ford sitting at his presidential desk, with his head whited out. The amazing feature about the cover to me was that it was graphically sophisticated—a "duotone," red on brown. *Free For All* had never had the graphic capability to produce such a cover. Scott, who had basically been scorned during the eight months or so

he had hung around *Free For All* and only had one "article" printed (a graphic of a phony UW survey of student apathy he had distributed during one student registration week), produced the cover, with the various colors in perfect registration no less. The rest of us were impressed.

The second page consisted of the list of names we had considered, several ads (including one for me, running for Dane County Registrar of Deeds on the "Abolish Private Property" ticket), and a statement of "Who We Are" (see sidebar 1). The issue was laid out in the basement of our five-bedroom cooperative house, giving us the license to say in our staff box: "Working out of a near east side basement, we are Madison's only true underground newspaper."

Page three featured a debate on voting. My article, entitled "Why You Should Vote," said that, although 95 percent of electoral candidates had essentially identical positions, some candidates, particularly in small districts such as city council or county board, are radical enough to vote for and do make a difference compared to their opposition. I contended that the mainstream media concentrate vast amounts of attention on electoral races, and that even radicals on the ballot were allowed to state their positions, an opportunity they would never have were they not candidates. I further argued that people who took not voting seriously by urging people to not vote "tend to convince those to their side who would vote most radically, leaving unaffected the traditional voters to whom the two-party system provides a choice." I made a pitch for writing in for almost all offices, suggesting that "the time spent writing-in in the booth is more annoying to the octogenarian election officials and more discouraging to voters waiting in line than simply sitting at home. Almost everyone wastes 15 minutes a day doing nothing, and voting is just another way of doing the same. The main point is: don't take voting seriously. Even more importantly, don't take *not* voting seriously."

The other point of view—entitled "Don't Vote, Revolt!"—began: "Another election, another chance to choose a leader. A chance to delegate your responsibility to one more master masquerading as the solution to the desolation and decomposition of this society." The article admonished readers to "decide if you like the flavor of not controlling the most basic aspects of your life....Choose the taste of shit or the taste of vomit; that's what capitalist elections are all about....This year less than 50 percent of the eligible voters will obediently march to the polls to give their support to class society." It continued, "As for referenda, they rarely if ever pass, and the effort spent voting could (in the instance of the marijuana referendum [to decriminalize pot, which did pass]) probably be better spent getting high illegally!" As to leftist candidates: "Naturally, there are the so-called socialist and communist candidates, the left wing of capital. These charlatans are really part of the same rotten stew as the republicans and democrats. They want to 'lead us,' they 'know what's best for us.' By reinforcing the myth of elections, these 'socialist' and 'communist' cretins are in reality the best friends of the system because they suppress the idea that people can and have run their own lives directly; without parties or bureaucrats."

This debate epitomized our positions—I at the far left of mainstream society; the writers of "Don't Vote, Revolt!" simply outside of it. I frequently felt that their position was mostly an intellectual one, one that did little to relieve the oppression felt by most people more directly affected by capitalist society. The proponents of each position were no doubt embarrassed by the other position. This dichotomy existed as long as Bob and Scott worked on the paper.

Our "back cover" was mostly a reprint of the controversial *Free For All* three-way cover, with the last panel originally entitled "Another Way" changed to read "The 'Free' for All Way" (see figure 2). The oppressor in our panel was a longish-haired person in the likeness of *FFA*'s Michael holding a whip and a *Quotations from Chairman Mao*. The factory was named "The 'Collective' Works," and had three puffs of smoke emerging from the stack labeled "repression," "guilt," and "'revolutionary' self-sacrifice." The panel also contained a "'consensus' slaughterhouse," with a door marked "Anarchists enter here." Also on the page was a box entitled "Voices of the Revolution"—graphics of Lenin, Stalin, and Mao—and a quote from Mao outlining the "discipline" of the party (i.e., the subordination of everything to the Central Committee). In addition, we ran a take-off of an inane column

by the then-editor of the *Capital Times*, Madison's afternoon daily newspaper, whose title, "Hello Wisconsin," we changed to "Hello Collective." The take-off article rambled on about people's need for a boss, and *FFA*'s willingness to be that boss. We changed *FFA*'s masthead from "the Tyrant's Foe, the People's Friend" to "the People's Foe, the Tyrant's Friend," and we changed their whining slogan "20 cents would help a lot!" to "$20 would help a lot!" The "Inside" box noted: "*FFA* Exclusive: UW Gets New Computer....[page] 3."

The centerfold was our response to the *FFA* split. In our response, we explained why we believed the formation of the Community Union and their purge of us were related (see sidebar 2). The article was entitled "Thus Spoke the 'Collective.'" It included graphics of Lenin and Stalin saying, "I'm a Libertarian Socialist"; a picture of Lenin saying (quoting *FFA*'s Phil in the *Daily Cardinal* article), "Tim's group call themselves anarchists—it's because people like him call themselves anarchists I won't call myself an anarchist anymore"; and a photo of Lenin and Stalin, with Lenin saying, "*Free For All* is still your community newspaper," and Stalin responding, "Mao, more than ever."

Reaction to the first issue was positive. We received numerous letters. A few, from doctrinaire anarchists, charged that we weren't anarchist enough, but the bulk were complimentary: "I was most pleased to find another left paper with an understanding that the revolution (and its publications) is not supposed to be boring; it's supposed to be *fun*"; "*Free For All* is clearly deteriorating (deteriorated) to unreadable crap. *No Limits* is great"; "*Free For All* seems to have lost some of its guts in the last four months. Now I know where it went—to *No Limits*. Keep up the fine work"; "I have been missing *Free For All* for many months now. It's been delivered all right, but the fun had seemed to be going out of it....We'll both keep ignoring those who think revolution only happens with clenched fists and gritted teeth"; and "Saw the new paper and I'm very impressed and I'm also looking forward to seeing *FFA* sink into a sea of mindless layout and boring articles; from the look of things, they're well under way."

The early issues (we put out two in 1976 and six in 1977) were a combination of the staff's two strains of anarchism. Bob and Scott, also known as Panda Bear and Polar Bear (we called them the Bear Brothers), produced their stuff both in *No Limits* and independently (primarily before the paper started) under the name Aurora. Polar Bear's work was graphically oriented, and given to pessimistic, macabre descriptions of society. His specialty was using other people's letterhead (e.g., Madison Mayor Paul Soglin and various UW departments and administrative offices) to have them making absurd statements. The two also did good satires of the more doctrinaire left—one poster (reprinted with different names in a later issue of *No Limits*) talked about the 57 varieties of Leninism ("all of them unfit for human consumption") and was distributed widely throughout the Midwest. Panda Bear's stuff was intellectual. As time progressed, their contributions shifted gradually from political anarchism (criticism of more authoritarian strains of the left) to situationism and nihilism, particularly the French and Italian strains. For instance, the August-September 1977 cover proclaimed: "The society that has abolished every adventure makes the only adventure the abolition of that society!" The back cover glorified the looting that took place during the 1977 blackout in New York City. Frequent features were collages of graphics and magazine and newspaper headlines that presaged the collapse of society.

The balance of the paper contained stories on the labor movement (such as Ed Sadlowski's race for president of the United Steelworkers Union), anarchist politics (articles on Spanish anarchism and anarchist political prisoners around the world), the environment (focusing on efforts in Wisconsin to defeat plans to build a fourth major nuclear power plant at several different locations and to build a copper mine in northern Wisconsin—the latter fight continues today), local election coverage (noting the candidacies of avowedly leftist candidates for political office), and, of course, the ever-popular collection of short articles, still modestly entitled the Wong Truth Conspiracy.

We occasionally gave certain people the liberty to lay out two or more pages without any editorial interference on our parts. For instance, Ben (Zippie) Masel wrote a two-page defense of his spitting on then-presidential candidate Scoop Jackson in late March 1976 coincident with his trial a year later for that heinous "crime." We allowed a member of the American Indian Movement (AIM) to lay out an eight-page spread entitled "Native Struggles Spring '77."

Because of Scott's graphic talents, the anarcho-syndicalists produced only two of the first nine covers. One was a photo of three scientists walking briskly away from a nuclear power plant with a mushroom cloud superimposed on the top and a quote from nuclear power critic David Brower: "Let's put it this way: if we're wrong, we can do something else. If they're wrong, we're dead." The centerfold consisted of a collection of short news articles on nuclear power in Wisconsin, as well as a review of McKinley Olson's *Unacceptable Risk*, a book hostile to the "peaceful atom."

The other cover was a photo of early twentieth-century electrical engineer Nikola Tesla sitting nonchalantly underneath a "Tesla coil," an oscillator that produced flame-like electrical discharges up to 125 feet long. The headline exclaimed: "How the Russians Put Us in the Deep Freeze," with the kicker, a "No Limits exclusive interview." In addition to a sidebar describing Tesla and his contributions to science, we ran an "interview" with an alleged Soviet scientist visiting the UW who claimed that Soviet use of Tesla's theory succeeded in shifting the jet stream north in the Soviet Union (and therefore south in the United States), which was responsible for the bitter-cold winter of 1976-77 in Wisconsin we were then experiencing.

The last issue of the first half of *No Limits'* existence appeared in April 1978. The cover was vintage Bear Brothers: a picture of a "comic book" cover entitled, "In the Presence of Wage Slavery." Scott had changed the captions of a militaristic comic. One terrorist thug was telling the victim, "You will get a job or you will die!!! What is your choice?" The victim says, "Here it is!" and on a piece of paper is written "Death!" Four of the background figures have their faces replaced with those of Jimmy Carter, Leonid Brezhnev, Imelda Marcos, and Idi Amin.

The issue was a nice blend of the two general schools of thought on the paper. The centerfold was a graphic argument against advertising, directed primarily against TV advertising, but basically rubbing in the fact that the Bear Brothers were not very comfortable with our reliance on advertising for the revenue needed to print the paper.

The back page was a review I did—entitled "Reader's Digest" and using *RD*'s logo—of three diverse publications: the Lyndon Larouche-led National Caucus of Labor Committees (NCLC) publication *New Solidarity*, the official North Korean newspaper *Pyongyang Times*, and a *Time* magazine "exposé" of socialism.

New Solidarity had recently determined that the villain behind everything they didn't like was now Great Britain, rather than the Rockefeller family. In just a few pages, they managed to blame Britain six different times, including for the interesting "fact" that "the Panama Canal treaty debates are little beyond a British plot to overthrow Carter and install British agent Walter Mondale in the White House." Several British agents, including Americans in high government positions, are "identified."

The second publication, the *Pyongyang Times*, devoted its space to accounts of the week's activities of the "Great Leader" Comrade KIM IL SUNG (caps in original), including receiving the Austrian ambassador and receiving a message from the dictator of Madagascar. In addition, the "Great Leader" sent telegrams to various fellow dictators around the world, including the emir of Kuwait, the shah of Iran, and Emperor Bokassa of the Central African Empire. The space devoted to something other than praise for the "Great Leader" went to attacks on South Korea, flatteringly described as "flunkeyist traitors," "the traitor for all ages," "flunkeyist splittists," "fascist hangmen," et cetera ad nauseam.

The *Time* eleven-page article on socialism divided the world into five economic systems: Marxist-Leninist, social democratic, Third World socialist, mixed economy, and capitalist. The highlight, in *No Limits'* opinion, was a "Communist" joke: "Brezhnev invites his mom to his plush villa in the Crimea. He shows her the yachts, art treasures, and his fleet of foreign cars. After a table-groaning banquet, he asks, 'Well, Mama, what do you think? Not bad for your little boy?' To which Mom replies, 'My son, it's very impressive. But what if the Communists come to power?'"

One article got us into trouble with Madison's leftist political establishment. We wrote an article entitled "Rotten Eggs in Willy-Op?" decrying the firing of Willy St. (Grocery) Co-op staffer and former IWW member Bob Steffes for political reasons. The mentality of the majority was strikingly similar to that of the gang at *Free For All* that had forced us out. The terminology was slightly different: Steffes was offensive to the "socialist feminist" rest of the staff.

We wrote: "The major point is that being a woman or a feminist is not radical per se....A woman is not inferior or superior to a man....Should a white man be miserable, ashamed, and guilt-ridden for life because he can't be a lesbian or a black militant? Obviously not, but socialist feminism is melting into liberal feminism with a double side order of guilt....Almost two years ago, the (white male) power-grabbers forced a split in the staff of *Free For All*, culminating in the founding of *No Limits*, because they could not tolerate political differences. One can choose to ignore a newspaper, but near East-siders need to shop at their co-op....Remember, it is usually those who call for political unity who make it impossible for it to exist, except under their firm tutelage."

We added parenthetically at the end of the article: "No doubt we will be accused of being 'sexist' or 'anti-feminist,' because we have refused to censor our opinions about this and other subjects—we have and are being punished financially by co-ops and other leftist businesses for our allegedly 'anti-leftist/co-op' attitudes. We deny these accusations, and reaffirm our opinion that revolutionary feminism is an essential part of any strategy for radical social change."

Of course, this attack on the co-op did piss them off; later that year when I wrote an article for the co-op newsletter, which at that time was still in the hands of the Steffes faction of the membership, the co-op staff published their own newsletter, calling our newsletter the voice of *No Limits*, a "racist, sexist, and uncon-structive local newspaper." At the time of the split, *Free For All* staffers had gone to many of *FFA's* advertisers, begging them not to advertise in *No Limits*. Many leftist businesses never advertised in *No Limits*, which was otherwise a natural market for them.

THE SECOND PHASE OF *NO LIMITS*

We didn't realize it at the time, no doubt, but that issue marked the end of an era for *No Limits*, as well as the beginning of another. That was the last issue either of the Bear Brothers worked on. Panda Bear, in an undated letter printed in our next issue, which appeared eight months later in December 1978, wrote that, because of *No Limits'* acceptance of advertising, he "no longer desire[d] to participate in the *No Limits* project." Bob stayed in town for a while longer, but Scott left town to hitchhike around the country. He was last known to be in Austin, Texas, where he personally struggled with the hopelessness of life he so frequently and eloquently expressed in *No Limits* and his other writings. Despite the political acrimony, particularly over the issue of advertising, and the frequent disdain with which we held some of each other's writings, the personal relations were completely harmonious—there was absolutely no sign of the personality conflicts the *Free For All* clique used as an excuse to purge those of us with whom they disagreed politically.

Several other changes occurred with this issue. In the spring of 1977, I had quit my "job" as a newspaper carrier for Madison's afternoon daily newspaper to take a job as a "limited term" typist with the state of Wisconsin. That job ended when state employees went on strike, and I, too, went on strike—in my case, as a benefits-less worker, essentially quitting. Several months later I landed a job as a typesetter with a fledgling publisher of academic journals. The April-May 1978 issue exhibited some of the fringe benefits of that job—typeset ads, subheads, and even a typeset Wong Truth. The sharpness of the typeset copy helped the paper shed some of its ragtag appearance.

The other major change with this issue was the emergence of a new person, Steve Spoerl, as a major contributor to the paper. He had been recruited by Panda Bear when both of them worked at one of the university libraries, and had written an article for the previous issue. Steve's bizarre interests helped him fit right in, and he wrote articles on mostly obscure subjects.

One of his stories, obscure at the time, printed in the first issue he wrote for (December 1977), was perhaps the first American mention of the Pol Pot-guided mass murder in Cambodia. The article, drawn from British sources and entitled "Cambodia Goes to

Pot," ended with a quote from Khieu Samphan, one of the country's leaders: "In five years of war, more than a million Cambodians died. The present population of the country is five million. Before the war it was seven million." When asked what happened to the other million, Samphan was annoyed: "It's incredible the way you Westerners worry about war criminals." Other articles on that two-page spread entitled "Class War in Revolt," taken mostly from other anarchist publications, were critical of Chinese repression of its critics from the left, Rumania's bloody crushing of a coal strike, and the "monolithic state-capitalist regime" in Mozambique. That latter article, entitled "Mozambique: 'Marxist' Mess," succeeded in alienating us from the Marxist People's Bookstore, another logical advertising source.

In part because I was working full-time and partly because the Bear Brothers and their graphic skills had abandoned the paper, *No Limits* did not appear again until the end of the year. A major impetus of the issue was the effort of Patrick Murfin. Murfin had, according to what he told us, been a former general secretary-treasurer (the top executive post) of the IWW and a long-time Chicago (where IWW headquarters is located) Wobbly. He was one of the more intelligent people I have ever met. He was also a heavy drinker who had been kicked out of Chicago by a few macho Chicago Wobblies, who accused him of drinking away much of the union's income during his tenure as GST. He had been "ordered" to go to New Orleans to live with a Wobbly he couldn't stand. Instead of going, however, he hitched to Madison, an "overnight" stop on his way to the Pacific Northwest. His "overnight stay" lasted four months.

Although he paid only one month's rent and didn't contribute his share toward his consumption of food and beer, he was a pleasant addition to our cooperative house. On the occasional times he found work, he typically spent his entire paycheck in various skidrow taverns following payday. But he revitalized the Madison Wobblies and was a major force behind our December 1978 issue. He organized a Wobbly lecture and film series at the State Historical Society that combined history and present-day imperatives for radical workers. He contributed two articles to *No Limits*, both incisive analyses of local politics—one about proposed bus fare increases, the other on the "ruling class blueprint for Madison." Murfin, through his incessant reading as well as conversations with townspeople, had developed an understanding of local politics far better than that of most Madisonians. We looked forward to more of Murfin's contributions in future issues, but he disappeared one day as quickly as he showed up—going down to Chicago "for a few days" over Christmas, he never reappeared in Madison.

Another newcomer to this issue was the Revolutionary Anarchist Alliance, the creation of Greg Jamrock, whom I considered to be a very neurotic individual. Greg was almost constantly accompanied by his girlfriend Mary, who, nevertheless, didn't seem to be part of the RAA effort. The RAA, which later changed its name to Count Down, subscribed to the same brand of anarchism as the Bear Brothers, but did so with considerably less graphic and semantic talent. Their departure after the February 1979 issue marked the end of any non-syndicalist anarchism on *No Limits*, and the paper developed a coherence it had never had before.

The paper's politics never really changed, though: it maintained an anti-authoritarian brand of leftism to the end, but gone (with the Bear Brothers and the cheap imitation RAA) were the anarchist polemics. What remained were articles written predominantly by Steve and me that focused on specific subjects, sprinkled with a liberal dose of "gentle asides to the reader" that revealed our political point of view. In some ways, the anarchist politics of *No Limits* of 1979 resembled the *Free For All* of 1974.

The first cover of 1979 was a photo by Diane Arbus of a white guy wearing an Indian headdress and holding an American flag—we ran it because the photo bore a striking resemblance to our then-Governor Lee Dreyfus. Page two of that issue featured a story on the strike against Checker Cab, while page 3 evaluated the various candidates for mayor three weeks before the primary. At the bottom of page 3 was a subscription ad, typical of the sub ads we had run throughout *No Limits'* existence, that featured a picture of the recently deceased Nelson Rockefeller and a caption from beyond the ad that asked, "Rocky, are you sure you renewed your subscription to *No Limits*?" Rocky answers, "I think so. I'd die before I'd let my subscription run out!" The headline on the right says, "Subscribe Now! Before You Die Too," along with the subscription rates.

The fourth page was an article by an outside contributor describing the situation in Iran between the fleeing by the Shah to take a "vacation" in the United States, and the takeover by the fundamentalist Ayatollah Khomeini. Page five featured my analysis of Carter's 1980 federal budget and my article entitled "Con-Con Is a No-No," which warned against the then-popular thrust to call a federal constitutional convention to require a balanced federal budget. None of us imagined that the Great Prevaricator Ronald Reagan, an advocate of "Con-Con," would take Jimmy Carter's relatively small $60 billion budget deficit and, through voodoo supply side economic theory, take it to four and five times that.

The next two pages were Steve's analysis of current events in China, a strong attack on the 30 years of Maoism, and a prediction that the authoritarianism would not cease even if China decided to play ball with capitalism and become one of the countries that runaway corporations in the United States moved to in order to produce their goods at slave wages to maximize profits at the expense of laid-off American workers.

The centerfold consisted of a story on Kerr-McGee and the death of Karen Silkwood and other shorter articles on nuclear power (mostly about setbacks to the nuclear industry) and how the labor establishment was doing big business' dirty work by opposing environmental goals.

The back half of the paper consisted of the Wong Truth, a story on prison revolts, and the first of a series of articles on jazz figures (in this case, Dexter Gordon) based on interviews conducted by Steve's high school friend Chuck France, who also did much of the work (but received little of the credit) on the film on Madison's antiwar movement, *The War at Home*. This was one of the few issues that did not have a baseball column and/or quiz, one of the more frequent features of *No Limits*, reflecting my obsession (and later Steve's) with baseball.

The last two inside pages were an anarchist tract entitled "Ten Theses on the Proliferation of Egocrats," an intellectual, almost incomprehensible, attack on authoritarianism, lifted from (and credited to) a brochure we had received—this was one of Greg's last contributions.

The back cover, a "genealogy" of the various authoritarian leftist splinter groups, listed 38 different "Marxist" groups and the parent groups from which they had split, presented on a time continuum. Originally printed in some sectarian leftist paper as an attack on a different strain of Leninism (Trotskyist vs. Maoist or some such), we credited it to the U.S. Association for the Study of Scientific Marxism-Leninism (Enver Hoxhaist) under the headline: "Tired of Your Present Job?"

> USASSML(EH) has recently split into three separate factions, with several careerist positions open for you, the Scientific American. All you have to do is reiterate our party line and you can become a central committee member, cadre, or rank-and-file member. We have openings for people who wish to join our central committee and make policies for our comrades around the world without regard to local conditions, and for those fluent in Albanian who could translate the latest mumblings from the great comrade leader Enver Hoxha. To show how scientific our organization is, refer to our family tree below. It took many splits to achieve our all-correct political line.

The next issue appeared in July. It featured a cover picturing traffic jams, an aerial photo showing how freeways had severed a city, an auto junkyard, and a German billboard urging everyone to wear gas masks "before we are all poisoned." It was entitled "$5.00 a Gallon and..." (on top) and "Sugar in Every Gas Tank" (on the bottom). The centerfold was a polemic on car usage and the hidden subsidies paid to the automobile and its infrastructure, along with a shorter article on the future of Amtrak. Every prediction about how catering to automotive interests would deteriorate the quality of life in cities has come true in Madison.

Several articles in the paper were written by non-staff members—an indication that the paper was beginning to be taken seriously by the leftist community—one on the Black Hills and mining, one on Nicaragua, as well as Chuck's jazz interview. Steve contributed his articles—one on the budding conflict in Yemen and another on the militarization of space. Probably the most important article in this issue, from the standpoint of an anarchist paper taking a position on current anarchist events, was about the trashing of an anarchist bookstore in Philadelphia by a group of ultra-leftist anarchists who ruined the store (by stopping up the sink and turning on the water) because they felt "a store is a store is a store." The article quoted extensively from the trashers' pamphlets and the bookstore's response and concluded that the trashers had no right to vandalize an anarchist bookstore for any reason—especially this store, which was totally staffed by volunteers. When one of the trashers came through Madison on her way to the West Coast, several of us went to a fish fry with her. Panda Bear felt favorably disposed to the vandalism, in much the same way he felt our taking advertising in *No Limits* had totally compromised everything we had to say in the paper. The rest of us were rather appalled at the self-righteousness of her attitude.

The last four issues of *No Limits* came out, amazingly enough, in regular two-month intervals. We were attracting outside articles; I was able to contribute a lot of typesetting to improve the graphic appearance. Articles in these issues dealt extensively with local issues, such as urban planning, local electoral politics, and bike trips.

But the staff responsible for producing the paper had melted to three—Steve and me, who still did the bulk of the writing, and Vicki Drenning, my "significant other," who performed much of the unheralded administrative work around the paper. When Vicki decided she was no longer interested in working on the paper, we reevaluated our purpose and decided to fold. Unlike many papers that folded, we had an adequate treasury and were in the process of producing another issue when we called it quits.

The *No Limits* of 1979 and 1980 had changed a lot from its 1976 origins. It placed a stronger emphasis on radical environmentalism; doctrinaire political preaching was less apparent. In part, I think, this resulted from our understanding that classical anarchist thinking had to be updated to deal with the present reality of the state (and we were not about to undertake this project). The state was now far more than the apparatus by which the ruling capitalist class maintained its minority stranglehold over the rest of society. Rather, the state was a major provider of social benefits to the needy elements of society. One could certainly argue about the efficiency of governmental programs and complain about the status quo nature of the two dominant political parties, but to regurgitate anarchist philosophy of the late 1800s and early 1900s in the pre-New Deal period when the state provided little other than the military for foreign excursions and wars and a police force to side with the employer against employees seemed to us a little naive.

No Limits produced 15 issues in a little over three years. The last issue was printed on January 31, 1980. *Free For All* limped along a little longer, meeting its long- and well-deserved death on December 3, 1981.

Subsequent Madison Journalism

Madison had no alternative newspaper for several years. In 1984, the other faction of *Free For All* held a reunion to which I was invited. It was fairly pleasant; the hatchets seemed to have been buried. (Michael was apparently too busy to show up from New York.) Rob tried to use the get-together as an excuse to put out one more issue, but he found no takers. Later that year he did put out an issue.

Rob kept working on the idea of putting out a paper on a regular basis. He eventually formed a staff that produced a newspaper called the *Phoenix*, which first appeared in March 1985. The paper lasted through the fall, publishing less than ten issues. Steve from *No Limits* got involved in this paper and, after Rob got

a job in New York City, almost singlehandedly put out several of the later issues. I wrote an article for the first issue on my concept of a light or heavy rail transit system for Madison and surrounding suburbs, but didn't participate beyond that. The paper was, despite Steve's valiant efforts, essentially a continuation of *Free For All*, in its gloomy politics and tone and the constant whining about the need for money. The lack of appreciation for Steve's efforts by the neo-*Free For All* clones dimmed his enthusiasm, and the paper died with the next issue.

In 1987, a two-sided, one-sheet calendar of events (along with historical remembrances of those dates) appeared under the name the *Insurgent*. After about a year, the broadside evolved into a newspaper, and it continues biweekly publication to this day, usually limited to a meager eight pages per issue. The paper suffers from a doom-and-gloom outlook with the humor prevalent in its broadside days largely gone. Also gone is one of the most useful features of its broadside days, evaluations prior to each semester of various UW professors and selected courses. Instead, with a staff dominated by white males, it reflects their all-too-familiar guilt over being white and male. While it is the most prominent leftie newspaper in town at this time, many leftists dismiss it as overly doctrinaire.

Also on the scene at the present time is a paper called the *Edge*. Published monthly since early 1990 by people formerly affiliated with the *Insurgent*, the *Edge* is less doctrinaire, and appears to be more broad-based.

Notes

1. James Danky, "Still Alive and Well: The Alternative Press in 1977. Part II," *Harvest Quarterly* no. 6 (Summer 1977): 17-22.

2. "Driveaways" were a common method of long-distance transportation in those days: car dealers or other people needed their vehicles transported from one location to another—we provided the driving; they provided the gasoline credit cards (we filled quite a few other tanks during the Boulder conference); and everyone ended up happy.

3. Danky, 17-22.

AIN'T NO PARTY LIKE THE ONE WE GOT:
THE YOUNG LORDS PARTY AND *PALANTE*

Pablo "Yorúba" Guzmán

WHO AM I?

The group of college-age Latino males who would later join with two other similar groupings to become the New York chapter of the Young Lords Organization (YLO) was called the *Sociedad de Albizu Campos* (*SAC*) when I joined in May 1969. Six or seven of us met Saturdays in Spanish Harlem—El Barrio. I was 18 at the time and had just come back from a semester of study in Mexico, part of my first year's work at the State University of New York at Old Westbury. Before leaving for Mexico, I had already been politically active for two years, organizing at my high school for citywide rallies against the Vietnam War, against outdated bureaucratic codes towards students, fighting racism, participating in mobilizations in Washington, DC, organizing among both African-American students and the radical hippies. I am a Puerto Rican and Cuban in whom the African genes are obvious; and in those pre-Young Lord days, Puerto Ricans in New York often tended to identify either with blacks or whites. From an early age, my father and maternal grandfather had instilled in me a sense of healthy skepticism towards the basic B.S. that defines this country's fundamental hypocrisy, racism, and the legacies of slavery.

For instance, my folks told me how the Japanese were rounded up during World War II, but not the Germans; how the land was stolen from the Native Americans; how Africans were brought here in chains. How separate and equal was really separate and

Guzmán is a reporter on Fox' New York television outlet, Channel 5, and a music/radio/pop culture columnist for the *Daily News*.

unequal; how the color of our skin meant we would have to work two or four times as hard as whites alongside us just to keep up. My folks spoke English at home because, they said, "We don't want you to have a Spanish accent; on top of your dark skin, that would be two strikes against you in this country."

My father often told the story of how, a naive product of El Barrio at 19, he had gone into the Navy after seeing *Anchors Aweigh* and gotten assigned to the carrier Midway shortly after the war ended; a movie was being shown on the flight deck, and he told a black friend from the South, "Let's go up front. There's some good seats there." Johnson pulled my father back and said, "Whoa, Guhz-man, that's for the white boys." "What are you talkin' about, Johnson? We just fought a war against Hitler, that stuff is dead, we're all Americans in this together—" "You been watchin' too many movies, Guhz-man." "I'm gonna sit up front."

Sure enough, my old man got his ass kicked and tossed in the back row of seats where the colored sailors were supposed to sit. Johnson helped my father up to his feet and said, "Ah *tol'* you they was only for the white boys, Guhz-man." "But I'm Puerto Rican." "They don't care what kind a nigger you is."

My parents were almost prevented from taking their room at a hotel in Atlantic City for their honeymoon because it was not for "colored." My mother started crying, but my father, now a military-trained veteran of Racism USA, began talking to her in Spanish, essentially telling her to follow his lead. The clerk bit: "Oh, pardon me," he gushed, "I didn't *know* you folks were Mexican." My folks look about as Mexican as the Huxtables. All the kids, my cousins and I, were told these stories so we could be prepared for what life unfortunately had in store. We'd be told about how my grandmother lost her thumb during an industrial accident at the garment factory where she worked in New York while the ambulance attendants argued about taking her; or how my mother was denied giving the valedictory address for her high school class, even though she had won a scholarship to the Fashion Institute of Technology (she was told she had "too much" of an accent, even though she was born and raised in East Harlem and my grandparents were bilingual).

So early in my life I learned about this country's true history. I was further influenced by reading the stories of Nat Turner, Harriet Tubman, and Frederick Douglass, by learning of W.E.B. DuBois and Marcus Garvey, by studying the life and words of Malcolm X and the southern civil rights movement, of Stokely Carmichael, H. Rap Brown, and the Black Panther Party.

This all fit in with where I was coming from culturally as well; the soul music of the era was my music, for example, in a way that the rock that I loved could never be. Not until the Lords and the expanding of my Latino consciousness could I appreciate salsa as an integral, *necessary* part of my heritage, and not "just" the dance music of my folks. My parents had been born in Spanish Harlem, and I was raised in the South Bronx, so our outlook was decidedly (North) American, as opposed to being heavily Puerto Rican. In my ghetto, (North) American meant black, baby, 'cause we certainly weren't livin' on the flip side. To be "Puerto Rican" or "Latino" before 1969 in New York, for those of us raised there and not recent immigrants from the islands, was not clearly understood. Or appreciated yet.

My entire life experience, then, pointed towards me joining the Black Panther Party. During my first semester in college, a friend and I had even worked up the nerve to go to the Panthers' Harlem branch, with the intention of inquiring about signing up. But we were totally intimidated, both by our own sense of awe and by the militant stance that often crossed over into arrogance of the members we talked to. It was something, that arrogance towards newcomers, I never forgot.

We came away with issues of the Panther paper, and my God: look at these pictures! The cartoons! The articles! References to an international struggle, Panther chapters all over the country, Panthers being attacked all over the country, Panthers in black leather picking up the gun. The rhetoric! Back at school, we slapped five over the *boldness* of these...*Niggers*, is what we said, not knowing any better. But with the kind of respect Richard Pryor used when he said (before he finally dropped the term) God, who works in mysterious ways, brought some good out of slavery, because he took the *best* out of Africa, the strongest, who survived the terrible journey, and took all the "tribes" that had been warring in Africa, the Ibos and Zulus and Masais, and in the Americas he forged one tough new tribe—*Niggas*. Now, this is a passé, even reactionary term, but back in 1968 that was the kind of audacious, charismatic, Afro-American figure we thought the Panthers were—and we wanted some of that. I had seen some other "underground" and "movement" newspapers before then, but nothing like *The Black Panther*—especially when compared to the leading black paper in the community, the *Amsterdam News*, whose coverage, to us, defined Uncle Tom.

I had gone to Mexico with this mindset, as Paul Guzman (Anglo pronunciation all the way), aspiring black militant; but after 3 1/2 months in a country where everyone was a Latino and quite conscious and proud of that heritage, I came back to the States as Pablo "Yorúba" Guzmán, ready to listen a little more to the rap fellow student Mickey Melendez had been laying down since I had gotten out to the Long Island campus in late August of '68. Inspired by Ray "Masai" Hewitt of the Black Panther Party, I took the middle name "Yorúba," from an African "tribe" whose influence was prominent in the creation of Latino culture in the Caribbean and elsewhere the slave trade functioned. For instance, the religion called santeria in Cuba and Puerto Rico (voodoo in Haiti, macumba in Brazil) has its roots in the Ife tradition of the Yorubas of Nigeria. However, my ignorance of matters was such in 1969 that for a long time I mispronounced the name, giving it a Spanish "yuh-ROO-bah" (with a light twirl of the "R") inflection; until once in late '69 or early '70, I believe, when Peter Jennings profiled us for ABC. Having spent a lot of time on assignment in the Mother Continent, it was Jennings who told me that the correct pronunciation was "yuh-roo-BAH," but that latter never really caught on among most Latinos.

Mickey Melendez had been reaching out to me, and to Felipe Luciano, another "Afro-Latino," if you will, and classmate of Mickey's at Queens Community College, and to Juan Gonzalez, a light-skinned Puerto Rican who was active at Columbia University's SDS (Students for a Democratic Society) chapter. His message to us all was that those days of identifying with either black or white North Americans, even if on a radical trip, were over; it was time to look within and without and begin organizing in our own barrios. Creating a *Puerto Rican* movement. Maybe even building into a pan-*Latino* movement.

PUERTO RICAN?

Mickey was the first guy to go into some detail with me about the *militant* history Puerto Ricans had, something to be every bit as proud of as African- (North) Americans (all this "ethnic" specification that becomes so necessary at times in this land of deliberate misinformation, this nation-hood identification in this instance, in this land where language is purposefully used to obfuscate rather than enlighten, can at times become a bit unwieldy, ¿como no?—"African- (North) American," oy...but, so long as you get the idea...and understand what kind of centuries-laden propaganda we're up against) are of their rich militant past. Mickey told us about Don Pedro Albizu Campos, president of the Nationalist Party of Puerto Rico, who fought against U.S. colonization of the island from the twenties until his death in 1965, a death very likely hastened by his exposure to x-rays while in an American prison. Mickey told us also of how Albizu Campos was Harvard-trained, and yet could not proceed as a lawyer beyond certain well-defined, racist limits; of Campos'

skills as an orator; of the blood Nationalists shed in 1937, while preparing for a peaceful march on Easter Sunday in Puerto Rico's second largest city, Ponce, when they were fired upon by U.S. imperialists. And why Oscar Collazo and other Nationalists attempted to assassinate Truman in 1950 (an erroneous news report had circulated on the island that Albizu Campos had died during one of his several incarcerations, and so it seemed logical to the *Nacionalistas* that, "Well, if they killed *our* President..."). In 1953, Lolita Lebron and her two Nationalist companions fired upon the U.S. Congress from the visitors' gallery while the Congress was debating Puerto Rico's status. Mickey explained to us that the Nationalists wanted to highlight Puerto Rico's colonial status, in particular that every important decision about the island was made, not in San Juan, but in Washington, DC, that the U.S. grip on the island's affairs was such that it had no vote in Congress, and that the highest court of appeals for a case that began on the island was in Boston not San Juan, prior to the steps that would take an ultimate appeal to the Supreme Court.

Mickey had us look into a Puerto Rican history we never knew, of a resistance first to Spanish imperialism—known as "*El Grito de Lares*": "The Shout of Lares"—led by Ramon Emeterio Betances and the other original patriots in 1868, and even of fights against the *conquistadores* by the indigenous Taino people in the 1500s, most of whom were massacred by the Spanish. We found out how Puerto Rico fell into U.S. hands, a prize won in the Spanish-American War along with Cuba, Guam, and the Philippines, even as those early nationalists of 1898 were celebrating their first month of hard-won autonomy from Spain. The U.S. Marines just dismissed what parliament Puerto Ricans had assembled. All this was contrary to what little some of us had "learned" of Puerto Rican history, that 'Ricans were practically running up to the Americans on the beach wailing "Save us!" from the nasty Spanish. What hogwash.

What our research showed us was that, by the Spirits, we *did* have a fighting history to be proud of! We *had* resisted, and fought back, against the Spanish, forging a unique Puerto Rican identity in the process that was equal parts African, Taino, and Spanish, along with some other European and Asian strains. A *Latino* identity that was new and bold to the world, as much a claimant to the mantle of the *Americas* as our large, unruly, and ever-voracious neighbor to the north. And we *continued* to fight against the *Yanquis*, from day one to the present. Our whole history was one continual line of struggle for self-determination. We found out that Puerto Ricans had been in New York since the end of the nineteenth century, had always formed political and cultural organizations, and had always fought to be treated as equals "here." We even found out that, by the 1960 census (and who knows? perhaps earlier), there were *some* Puerto Ricans in every state— including a sizable population in Hawaii, where many had been brought in the late 1800s to work the sugar cane plantations. It would not be long before we as the Young Lords Party would connect with Hawaiian activists and have an affinity group on our behalf in those islands, even as we labored to raise consciousness of the *real* story of Hawaii on our part of the mainland.

Our instrument for telling this story, as well as for passing along the Puerto Rican history we were uncovering, and the twin reasons at the root of why the Young Lords existed—liberation for Puerto Rico and equality for Puerto Ricans in a radically realigned United States—would be our newspaper, *Palante*.

PRE-YOUNG LORDS

"Palante" loosely translates into "forward," or "ahead," or even "right on!" depending on the context. Bottom line, it's a progressive, *motion* word familiar to the people. From the beginning, we took to heart the words of that noted Chinese philosopher: "Speak to the people in the language they know and love." In the early days of the Young Lords Party, we also waged a war against movement rhetoric. We *hated* rhetoric, movement jargon, and phraseology that could only be understood by "well-read" activists, and not the people we were trying to organize.

Time to back up a bit.

Excited as we all were by our research, we were also excited by current events. The year before, 1968, had been a hell of a year. The Democratic convention in Chicago, uprisings—so-called "riots"—in 150 cities following the murder of Martin Luther King, all against the backdrop of acid, acid-rock, 'Nam, the pill, Black Power, you name it—it was all happening, and happening NOW. Almost on the same Saturday, as I recall, the second or third *SAC* meeting that I attended, we got hit with two news items: two other groups of young Latins were just getting started in New York, as we were; and, in Chicago, what had been a gang had "gotten politicized" and—under the direction of the Chicago Panthers and together with a former white gang called the Young Patriots—had formed the Latino component of "the Rainbow Coalition." We read about this ex-gang in the June 7, 1969, issue of *The Black Panther*. One of our group, David Perez, whom Mickey had recruited to Old Westbury from Chicago, confirmed that these Young Lords (now the Young Lords Organization, or YLO) were indeed real, but he offered us words of caution because he knew, coming from Chicago, what we would find out later:

that the YLO had not been able to shed its gang-like ways, that they were undisciplined and not committed to radical change. Unfortunately, we didn't pay attention to his warning. Hey, it was in the *Black Panther*! And Fred Hampton and the Chicago Panthers (as everyone knew, the second-baddest Panther chapter outside of the original Oakland bunch) were behind it! Come on, Dave!

David approved of our plan to send a mini-delegation to Chicago in June 1969 to seek the green light to organize as the New York chapter of the Lords, but he continued to voice his reservations to deaf ears. At the same time, we agreed to reach out to the group we heard was trying to organize on the Lower East Side, and to the other group organizing in Spanish Harlem.

The Lower East Side group, we found out, was led by a guy named José Martinez, who seemed to be a movement pro; a Cuban from Florida who joined SDS and made contacts in Chicago when Panthers, Lords, and Patriots came to the SDS convention there in 1968. But when we got to Chicago, YLO chairman José "Cha-Cha" Jiminez told us that, contrary to what Martinez might be saying, he had not authorized Martinez to begin organizing the Lords in New York.

I was part of the group that went to Chicago in June 1969 in Mickey's Volkswagen to meet these Young Lords in the People's Church we had read about. From the start, I was excited to see that they had a newspaper, *YLO*; but all I saw were hundreds of copies of the same issue. "Does this come out weekly or monthly?" I asked, but never quite got answered. Such petty questions of detail, and anything having to do with discipline, I later found out, quickly got lost in the Viking hall environment of hale and hearty warriors surrounded by banners acknowledging their past fights against Chicago police brutality and against Mayor Richard Daley's brand of politics. We walked into this with rose-colored glasses. We *wanted* some heroes, badly. We were excited when Cha-Cha took a liking to us and said we could organize as the New York chapter. Of course, we had to fly him and another guy back out to New York to make it official. Once in that city, however, in response to our questions about what we should do and how we should begin, I remember one piece of advice he gave us: "Our people in the community are going to join us only through *observation* and *participation*. We can preach 'till we're blue in the face. But at some point, they're only going to understand after they see us throw down and after we move them to throw down themselves." This advice fit in perfectly with our already-blossoming anti-rhetoric stance.

It also was what the third grouping that would merge into the New York Young Lords was doing all along. While we in the *SAC* were meeting every Saturday like the college intellectuals most of us were, and while the José Martinez Lower East Side group was trying to get in good with the various "movement" factions that historically populated the Lower East Side, even though there was a sizable Latino population there, this third group was going out among the people of Spanish Harlem, picking a particular block, rapping with the people about the revolutionary changes going on in society at large, some of which they saw on TV or read about on the news, and then trying to connect those changes with the need to make revolutionary change in the immediate society around them. Right now. These guys pointed to the incredible garbage piling up in ghettos like East Harlem, garbage that went far beyond the bushwah that the propagandists in the society outside the ghetto tried to drill into the minds of those in and out of the ghetto, that the garbage was of "those" pigs' own making. True, barrio citizens had a certain responsibility for their/our own mess; but a greater fact of life was that garbage was only getting picked up once or twice a week—as opposed to the "high class" areas further south on Park Avenue, in the tony "Upper East Side"; or in all or nearly all-white "middle class" enclave/neighborhoods like Howard Beach, Throggs Neck, and almost all of Staten Island, where garbage pickups were more frequent. A small point, perhaps, but it sure highlighted the difference between those with access to power—those who could make politicians jump through hoops and get things done for them or those whom the politicians wanted to please with a few bones like frequent garbage pickup, more police protection, and better hospitals and schools, so they'd have something tangible to show for buying into the Great (White) American (Skin Privilege) Dream—and those who were being permanently shut out of the power game.

Garbage in the ghetto, by the way, ain't just about coffee grounds and discarded milk containers. "Garbage" is also abandoned automobiles, broken appliances like refrigerators, the squalor that surrounds burned-out buildings and rubblestone lots, which kids play in because the playgrounds have gone to seed, while rats dance and junkies shoot up. "Garbage" is refuse dumped into ghetto areas by unscrupulous, often mob-controlled private carting companies who sometimes drop hazardous medical and other industrial wastes while looking for a short end run.

So a lot of smaller issues were wrapped up in the seemingly "unglamorous" but larger issue of garbage in the ghetto. In their instinctive way, the third pre-Lord formation had hit upon the issue that would get us going, while the other two groups were still stumbling about. This third bunch was actually a photography workshop led by Hiram Maristany, a masterful photographer from El Barrio who became our first chronicler. And while all of us were certainly *young* Lords, Hiram's group was even younger, about 14-16 to our 19-23 (when we began, I was 18). Hiram's guys were also different from the other two groups in that they were *of* the barrio and destined to *remain* in the barrio, whereas guys like me had either punched a ticket to college or the service *out* of the barrio, or else weren't from the barrio at all. So from the beginning, we thrashed out a lot of class questions among ourselves, which helped us in a very real way to understand theories of class. Hiram's group had naturally proceeded from shooting pictures of their surroundings to asking questions, and Hiram encouraged them to hit the street.

Another important person in those early days was an architect named Mauricio…Gomez, I think his last name was. He was Cuban, slightly older than most of us in the *SAC*. He came to us from the Real Great Society (RGS), an anti-poverty group formed by ex-gang members with branches in El Barrio and the Lower East Side. Mickey also had been in RGS. We used their barrio offices for our Saturday meetings. At one of those meetings, Mauricio showed us a copy of "the Master Plan" for New York that a friend on the City Planning Commission had slipped him; basically it showed that the very liberal administration of Mayor John Lindsay was still tied in to the same old power elite, and was working on a plan that most New Yorkers wouldn't see manifest until a decade or two down the road, which called for "urban renewal" of ghetto areas that really amounted to "spic removal": a bulldozing of tenements and their replacement with co-op- and condo-style housing that barrio residents could not afford. We saw draft studies that pointed out how a basic transportation infrastructure of buses and trains already existed in Harlem and East Harlem, and that as apartment space dwindled in the Manhattan below 96th Street, and as costs for living in suburbia rose, perhaps efforts should be made to reclaim the untapped areas of the city—us—and make them safe for the baby boom wave to come. They weren't called yuppies then.

Within the next couple of years, as the arson fires of the South Bronx in the early seventies so vividly illustrated, speculators also got their hands on the same draft reports we were studying…which we knew would have shocked certain power brokers, who a) figured we couldn't read the tea leaves in such documents and b) were later astounded to learn we could gain access to such stuff. One of the reasons for the Young Lords' success was such class and race presumption: we were constantly underestimated, or else mistaken as some gang of semi-literate ghetto toughs. While some of us certainly *were* tough, many more of us *became* tough as a result of the Young Lords.

THE GARBAGE OFFENSIVE

For instance, one present-day media figure with a Young Lords association—though he was never a member—was Geraldo Rivera. Gerry was one of our lawyers back then; indeed, his involvement with us had as much to do with his own emerging sense of identity as any of ours. Gerry was more than ready to put not only his services but his body on the line, participating in many of the early battles with police that grew out of what were initially peaceful demonstrations by us. In fact, Gerry applied for membership a couple of times, but we kept telling him he played a more important role as one of our lawyers; we were certain that the authorities would try to find a way to discredit or disqualify Gerry from representing us if they could spear his "officer of the court" position by tarring him with some lie about the Lords. Gerry was our lawyer from about October of 1969 right up to just before he began with (local) ABC in New York; in fact, his first major assignment with ABC was getting into the Tombs, the Manhattan prison, soon after the uprising due to overcrowded conditions and the specific unclear circumstances surrounding the questionable "suicide" of one of our members, Julio Roldan, on October 15, 1970, a day after he had been picked up by cops in Spanish Harlem for "disorderly conduct." That incident had prompted an armed takeover of the People's Church following a funeral procession of 2,000 people for Julio; the resulting standoff with the city finally ended about a month later in the creation of the Board of Corrections, designed to monitor prison conditions. We were offered a choice to nominate someone for the panel; we chose Gerry, but the city said no, so closely associated was he with us already. So José "Chegui" Torres, former light-heavyweight champion, columnist, and city council ombudsman, who was the first prominent "establishment" Puerto Rican to support us, got the nod.

Mauricio was obviously experiencing some rapid changes in those early days. He was someone who could have easily bought in to privilege, a light-skinned Cuban professional from a petty-bourgeois family; but the course he had been heading on through grad school was not personally satisfying, and he came to RGS to give something back to the barrio. At first, his RGS involvement included "liberal, reform, charitable" anti-poverty work in East Harlem; but his involvement changed when to his surprise RGS led to the *SAC*, which led to the YLO. It was Mauricio who told us about Hiram's group and, if I'm not mistaken, José

Martinez' group. And it was Mauricio who became one of the important voices for unity instead of factionalism, for trying to bring the groups together and subsuming to the Chicago motion, rather than the minority view, which wanted to ego-trip on its own (obviously, you can tell where I was in the debate).

By June of 1969, the three groups had come together and had begun working as the Young Lords in New York. We had adopted the same purple berets that the Chicago Lords wore, which we later found out distinguished their "colors" from those of rival gangs. We had just thought it was to distinguish their berets from the Panthers' black ones. In the beginning, much about the YLO was based on the Panther Party, from organization ("democratic centralism") to ideology ("Marxism-Leninism-Mao Tse-tung Thought"), since we figured the Panthers were at the cutting edge of what was happening with revolution in this country, and if it was good enough for them it was OK for us. Gradually, as we gained experience of our own, we became more critical and made our own refinements. But basically, our initial revolutionary thrust was pretty much as H. Rap Brown once put it: "If Amerikka says wear a blue suit, wear a pink one; if Amerikka says be quiet, talk loud; if Amerikka says it's great, say AMERIKKA AIN'T SHIT."

We had challenged the José Martinez group's desire to begin organizing in the Lower East Side by pointing out that, with so many groups bumping into each other down there, we would have difficulty maintaining our identity, and we would wind up wasting time getting sucked up into one or another factional debate. Better, we said, and they agreed, to invest our meager resources into a well-defined community like El Barrio, the spiritual home of all New York Puerto Ricans, and a place lacking radical activity. We picked up on Hiram's group's idea of making garbage the first issue to organize around; what we in *SAC* contributed was to give it a radical edge. We would not just clean the streets; we would also point out *why* this stuff wasn't being picked up and yet *other* people's garbage *was* getting picked up when we all paid tax dollars. Sunday mornings, we picked a block and, wearing our purple berets, swept up, collected, and tried to get people to join in. We talked as we went, and at the end we summed up the experience by holding a rally. Unfortunately, our rallies were pitiful. People barely listened. And most of us were frightened to speak out loud.

Felipe Luciano, however, had no problem speaking to people. This guy had ego and personality to spare. Mickey and I desperately tried to get him to commit to us, but he had one foot in the black cultural nationalist movement in Harlem, and with the other he was testing the waters in a couple of other places.

This boy got around. A former gang member with family roots in Spanish Harlem and Brooklyn, Felipe had done time for manslaughter for killing with his fists a guy who had messed with his brother. In prison he got his GED equivalency diploma, and he was paroled to a study program at Queens College where he met Mickey. His burning intellect and exhibitionism brought him to the world of radical black theatre; he was a founding member of the Last Poets. In the black radical universe of the time, many cultural nationalists were polar opposites of the political nationalists such as the Panthers, and here Felipe and I differed; however, Felipe became tight with one of my idols, H. Rap Brown, who encouraged him to organize within his Latino community, as we were also telling him. Still, it was a long while before Felipe would commit to us on a full-time basis.

But when he did show on those early Sunday mornings when we were trying to organize through garbage collection, he energized the block. He certainly had the gift of gab. Another contribution was made by David Perez, in many ways the most inherently nationalistic Latino among us. David was born in Lares, Puerto Rico, from where Betances had launched the first fight for independence, and was brought to Chicago when he was ten. He was the most *jíbaro* of all of us, the most rooted in the peasant aspect, the rural, campesino side of the Puerto Rican experience. By comparison, the rest of us were city slickers, heavily mainland-rooted. There was a class distinction among Puerto Ricans and other Latinos, a derision by mainlanders towards island arrivals, or even by San Juan metropolitan residents towards country cousins, who were regarded as "jibaros" not with pride but as "hicks," as a putdown. Through David, we began to change how the word *jíbaro* was used, to find some pride in this part of us, even to gain some humility. David figured out that our early rallies had failed because we were still lacking that nationalist component that tied us like cement to people; when he brought out the Puerto Rican flag at the afternoon rallies that climaxed the Sunday cleanings, attendance doubled and tripled because we had hit a nerve. Still, we couldn't get people to join up afterwards. They listened, they observed, they went home. Shit continued.

Until Felipe and Juan Gonzalez hit upon an idea. Juan Gonzalez was certainly the moral and organizational engine that binded and drove us in the beginning. Once Juan decided that Mickey's message was right, that he was needed more among Latinos than white radicals, he threw himself into this thing, whatever it was going to turn out to be, full-time. With his example as an inspiration, I soon realized I wasn't going back to college. The idea he and Felipe hit upon was to take the people with us to the local sanitation facility so they could help us get more brooms and other supplies to clean up better.

For two or three weeks, people saw us get a runaround from a bureaucracy that was supposed to serve the community but could give a hang for it, and their frustration rose to a level that matched our own. We would go to one sanitation department office, and they would send us to another. That place would tell us that we weren't in their jurisdiction, or that they weren't authorized to give out brooms, or that we'd have to take it up at a higher level on the food chain...where we'd be told this was a local matter and get sent back to square one.

Finally, we took this frustration and, on Sunday, July 27, at the end of one rally, we took all the garbage—all the abandoned cars, all the refrigerators—and laid it all across Third Avenue at 110th Street, which was a major intersection. Then, with traffic blocked from all sides, we set the stuff on fire. When the police came, we took off our berets, so we could blend in. Sure enough, the cops reacted like an occupational army and began using their nightsticks on anyone hanging out on the corner. This action provoked a retaliation of bricks and bottles, which in turn prompted the cops to call for backups, who also got attacked; in minutes, the Young Lords of New York were in their first battle. Later, we signed up our first recruits.

Knowing the power of the mimeo machine from my high school and college days, I knew we had to follow up immediately so people would know that what had happened wasn't some drunken event, that it had been organized, and why; using the movement contacts of Gonzalez and Martinez, I mimeod thousands of leaflets and spent the night with a few other guys blanketing East Harlem.

This became our *modus operandi*. The police response meant we could spend no time sweeping up a block now, since they'd bust us at once; so we went right to the barricades, blocking intersections, setting fires, and, when the cops came, it was hit-and-run time, from rooftops, doorways, wherever.

The summer of '69 we called the Garbage Offensive, and it was some series of battles; our numbers grew as the cops brought in more troops to augment the two precincts that occupied El Barrio. Our battles grew from weekly to daily encounters; we called in false alarms to get cops to respond, and when they came back to their cars they'd find the cars trashed—literally, with some of the garbage we were talking about dumped in their vehicle, through broken windows and slashed tires. The police quickly became an issue, as they moved through the neighborhood seeing nothing but "hostile spics," not a disciplined small group of Young Lords. They knocked over the domino games men had been playing on the sidewalk for generations, they broke heads, they made vulgar remarks to women passing on the street. They were our best organizing tool.

And after each day's confrontation, that night would be spent leafletting. All the while, I kept calling Chicago for more than that same issue of the newspaper. We *needed* a newspaper, not just for money—to spread the word. An organizing tool. Chicago promised, but delivered I think one more new issue in the next nine months. This was unacceptable.

BUILDING AN ORGANIZATION

In our early division of labor, I was designated minister of information; actually, most of us wanted almost any job except that of chairman. Except for Diego Pabón, who came to us somehow from one of those "go-slow" type "left-wing" outfits, a la the Movimiento Pro Independencia, the "traditional," "respectable" CP (Communist Party) USA-Moscow type revisionist party of Puerto Rico. Diego became chairman by default; the rest of us really wanted Felipe, but he would not yet commit. Juan was our minister of education, and, as our best strategist, he immediately began laying down plans for what to do *after* the Garbage Offensive, even as we were still in it. Juan would take us into organizing among health workers, and, using the high tuberculosis and lead poison rates among our young people as an issue around which to organize, to raise more consciousness about why such great differences existed in this otherwise rich society. But that would come later, towards the end of 1969. David was our first minister of defense.

The last person to be added to what was the original central committee was the youngest member of the organization. Juan "Fi" Ortiz, 15, was Hiram's best photography student. Even at his young age, Juan was in many ways the most profound and even-balanced of us all. Soon after we made him chief of staff, he and his cadres became the most indispensable part of our organization, which is probably a surprise to the various police agencies infiltrating and surveilling us. Fi's staff operation, our super-personnel department, oversaw organizational development, personal problems, and other internal issues. They were our monitoring backbone.

José Martinez' Lower East Side Group, we found out, was riddled with police agents. Martinez himself soon took a hike.

Certainly not in the same category, because his contributions to our early development were enormous, but Felipe Luciano, still our best-known member, left after about ten months. The split at the time was bitter; it began with Felipe being disciplined for sexism, and ended with the realization that we were on opposite sides of an ideological gulf. The rest of us went along a more "socialist" path, while Felipe continued as a more "militant reformist," if you will. After he left, the central committee never again had a chairman. Instead, we began to decide policies democratically as a collective.

We began with a hard core of 13, plus a sole woman whom Mauricio introduced into the group, a strong Cubana named Sonia Ivanny. From the beginning we were forced to confront *machismo*, bred into the Latin culture in its own special way. As more women came into the organization, they expanded into the leadership, including what would be the core central committee of five men. Diego—too much attached to his respectable and traditional Latino background, and unable to grasp the changes taking place in the ways men and women related to each other—didn't last as chairman for more than a month; Felipe finally agreed to stay with us full-time. Women like Sonia rising to positions of leadership were part of the battle against sexism that was waged constantly in the organization. In that sense, we saw ourselves as part of the overall movement of human liberation awakening across the country, beginning, in our time, with African-Americans, and then spreading to other oppressed peoples of color; then to women, and then gays. Every step of the way, we were with it, recognizing women's and gay caucuses within the organization as legitimate forms that corresponded to various points of the organization's internal development. We made a point of building ties with women's and gay groups, just as we had with Panther chapters and I Wor Kuen, the radical Asian group in the Chinatowns of New York and San Francisco.

Interestingly, the most controversy our positions in *Palante* caused in the Latino community—as we spread in 1970 to the Bronx, Philadelphia, and Lower East Side, and in 1971 and subsequent years to Bridgeport, Connecticut, Santurce and Aguadilla, Puerto Rico, plus, through affinity groups, places like Boston and Detroit—was not over independence for Puerto Rico, opposition to the Vietnam War, or building socialism (or something *else*, at least) in America. No, the most hell we caught was in exposing the racism that affected too many Latinos and caused either some Caribbean-Latinos to deny their African heritage or some Latinos generally to despise African-Americans. We also caught hell for promoting equality between men and women, for denouncing the mocking of gays—anything on the front against sexism. Sexism and racism, those were the most sensitive buttons we pushed among those we tried to organize. And we never shrunk back from the fight.

As with anything else, though, questions and attitudes of race and class affected us within the movement even as we were supposedly about trying to fight for change in the world outside. A flash point came around late 1969 when a radical women's manifesto was published in newspapers like the *Rat*, I believe, which caused a furor among the women in the organization. The manifesto touched upon some issues that needed to be criticized in certain posturing organizations. For instance, remnants of machismo still existed in YLO at the point where a militant defiance of reactionary authority crossed over into petty toy soldiering, becoming a caricature of true militancy. In addition, a double standard was practiced by some male members, leaders in particular we were to find out, who were having affairs behind the backs of their significant others.

But when the manifesto asked sarcastically if the women in the Young Lords were Young Ladies, well, in trying to make a point they missed the mark badly. Granted, if we had had our druthers, we in New York would certainly have chosen another name; but there was a history to that gang's name, and there was something to be said about a gang that was trying to change its ways; it was not yet for us to change that name; it would have been presumptuous.

But what ticked off "the ladies" of our organization even more was that many of them had interacted with the mainly white radical women's movement and found too many of them to be essentially about bourgeois and petty-bourgeois complaints; they wanted *in* to a system the rest of us found basically corrupt. Or else their alternatives were sectarian, pitting women against men in a way that somehow still left the basic problem off the hook. The guys in the leadership barely prevailed, but we convinced the women not to go and kick ass, which they wanted to do; but their anger at being used by women who in the main were dabbling at radical change (like so many white men) but did not really want to see opportunity afforded equally to working-class women, particularly those of color, proved prophetic: I look around, for instance, at the newsrooms I have worked in (except for a period at a black-owned company), and see a great many white women, usually of petty-bourgeois background or attitude, in various positions, though it is still their male counterparts who dominate at the top; but I do not see an equal number of Latina, African-American, Caribbean, Asian, and Native American women.

The Garbage Offensive established us in El Barrio, and word of our presence zipped along *radio bembe*, the grapevine, to barrios throughout the city. Oh, we scored a victory: the fighting had made its point. Sanitation promised at a public meeting attended by Lindsay's representatives to put more garbage cans on the corners, to work with residents looking to borrow brooms and other cleaning tools, and—most importantly—to add another day of collection. Sadly, as we were about to achieve our first victory, we lost Mauricio. His rise to commitment had come full circle: what was a Cuban with skills and a commitment to social change to do if not return to Cuba, Mauricio reasoned, and help build socialism? I never saw him again.

GETTING PAST SQUARE ONE

Using a leaflet as best I could as a poor substitute for a newspaper, my energies took in all forms of media. Truth be told, I was a media freak. Still am. I wanted us to use every form of media our people were exposed to: radio, TV, live concerts, speeches, seminars, rap sessions, graffiti, posters. I was concerned with the angle Lords wore their berets, how they spoke in public, who spoke, and where. I drafted the first 13-point program (see sidebar 1) and 30 rules of discipline. I coined phrases like "poverty pimps" to define anti-poverty fat cats, and tried to blend slang into our prose whenever I could.

By September 1969, we had opened our first office, on Madison Avenue between 111th and 112th Streets, and I was determined to keep alive all of our earlier fire from our summer of fighting in the streets; everything that you have been reading until now I tried to capture in every media release that went out. The following month we opened our second office, in Newark, New Jersey.

Our second great offensive would be in late December 1969, when we occupied a church for its space so we could have breakfast and educational programs. Earlier that month on December 7, we had come to petition the church for permission to use a room there to run a breakfast program. We had been requesting permission from them for two months already with no luck. This time, they had responded by calling in the police to break our heads; thirteen arrests were made. The gauntlet was thrown. So, on December 28 we took over the church and held it for eleven days while we ran free breakfast programs, educational workshops, clothing drives, cultural events, daycare centers, and more. Three thousand people took part, and many became members. After the first day of the takeover, I looked at my performance on TV; and I didn't like it. I'd use it later as an example to our cadres of what *not* to do. I was covering up my nervousness with what had quickly become a tired image on black leather and shades (personally, I *liked* shades); much too Panther-like, and by then the Panthers were rapidly becoming a stereotype, what with their outrageous rhetoric and little actual organizing

THE YOUNG LORDS PARTY IS A REVOLUTIONARY POLITICAL PARTY FIGHTING FOR THE LIBERATION OF ALL OPPRESSED PEOPLE

1. WE WANT SELF-DETERMINATION FOR PUERTO RICANS, LIBERATION ON THE ISLAND AND INSIDE THE UNITED STATES.

For 500 years, first spain and then the united states have colonized our country. Billions of dollars in profits leave our country for the united states every year. In every way we are slaves of the gringo. We want liberation and the Power in the hands of the People, not Puerto Rican exploiters. QUE VIVA PUERTO RICO LIBRE!

2. WE WANT SELF-DETERMINATION FOR ALL LATINOS.

Our Latin Brothers and Sisters, inside and outside the united states, are oppressed by amerikkkan business. The Chicano people built the Southwest, and we support their right to control their lives and their land. The people of Santo Domingo continue to fight against gringo domination and its puppet generals. The armed liberation struggles in Latin America are part of the war of latinos against imperialism. QUE VIVA LA RAZA!

3. WE WANT LIBERATION OF ALL THIRD WORLD PEOPLE.

Just as Latins first slaved under spain and the yanquis, Black people, Indians, and Asians slaved to build the wealth of this country. For 400 years they have fought for freedom and dignity against racist Babylon. Third World people have led the fight for freedom. All the colored and oppressed peoples of the world are one nation under oppression. NO PUERTO RICAN IS FREE UNTIL ALL PEOPLE ARE FREE!

4. WE ARE REVOLUTIONARY NATIONALISTS AND OPPOSE RACISM.

The Latin, Black, Indian and Asian people inside the u.s. are colonies fighting for liberation. We know that washington, wall street, and city hall will try to make our nationalism into racism; but Puerto Ricans are of all colors and we resist racism. Millions of poor white people are rising up to demand freedom and we support them. These are the ones in the u.s. that are stepped on by the rulers and the government. We each organize our people, but our fights are the same against oppression and we will defeat it together. POWER TO ALL OPPRESSED PEOPLE!

5. WE WANT EQUALITY FOR WOMEN. DOWN WITH MACHISMO AND MALE CHAUVANISM.

Under capitalism, women have been oppressed by both society and our men. The doctrine of machismo has been used by men to take out their frustrations on wives, sisters, mothers, and children. Men must fight along with sisters in the struggle for economic and social equality and must recognize that sisters make up over half of the revolutionary army: sisters and brothers are equals fighting for our people. FORWARD SISTERS IN THE STRUGGLE!

6. WE WANT COMMUNITY CONTROL OF OUR INSTITUTIONS AND LAND.

We want control of our communities by our people and programs to guarantee that all institutions serve the needs of our people. People's control of police, health services, churches, schools, housing, transportation and welfare are needed. We want an end to attacks on our land by urban renewal, highway destruction, and university corporations. LAND BELONGS TO ALL THE PEOPLE!

7. WE WANT A TRUE EDUCATION OF OUR AFRO-INDIO CULTURE AND SPANISH LANGUAGE.

We must learn our long history of fighting against cultural, as well as economic genocide by the spaniards and now the yanquis. Revolutionary culture, culture of our people, is the only true teaching. JIBARO SI, YANQUI NO!

8. WE OPPOSE CAPITALISTS AND ALLIANCES WITH TRAITORS.

Puerto Rican rulers, or puppets of the oppressor, do not help our people. They are paid by the system to lead our people down blind alleys, just like the thousands of poverty pimps who keep our communities peaceful for business, or the street workers who keep gangs divided and blowing each other away. We want a society where the people socialistically control their labor. VENCEREMOS!

9.   WE OPPOSE THE AMERIKKKAN MILITARY.

We demand immediate withdrawal of all u.s. military forces and bases from Puerto Rico, Viet Nam, and all oppressed communities inside and outside the u.s. No Puerto Rican should serve in the u.s. army against his Brothers and Sisters, for the only true army of oppressed people is the People's Liberation Army to fight all rulers. U.S. OUT OF VIETNAM, FREE PUERTO RICO NOW!

10.   WE WANT FREEDOM FOR ALL POLITICAL PRISONERS AND PRISONERS OF WAR.

No Puerto Rican should be in jail or prison, first because we are a nation, and amerikkka has no claims on us; second, because we have not been tried by our own people (peers). We also want all freedom fighters out of jail, since they are prisoners of the war for liberation. FREE ALL POLITICAL PRISONERS AND PRISONERS OF WAR!

11.   WE ARE INTERNATIONALISTS.

Our people are brainwashed by television, radio, newspapers, schools and books to oppose people in other countries fighting for their freedom. No longer will we believe these lies, because we have learned who the real enemy is and who our real friends are. We will defend our sisters and brothers around the world who fight for justice and are against the rulers of this country. QUE VIVA CHE GUEVARA!

12.   WE BELIEVE ARMED SELF-DEFENSE AND ARMED STRUGGLE ARE THE ONLY MEANS TO LIBERATION.

We are opposed to violence—the violence of hungry children, illiterate adults, diseased old people, and violence of poverty and profit. We have asked, petitioned, gone to courts, demonstrated peacefully, and voted for politicians full of empty promises. But we still ain't free. The time has come to defend the lives of our people against repression and for revolutionary war against the businessmen, politicians, and police. When a government oppresses the people, we have the right to abolish it and create a new one. ARM OURSELVES TO DEFEND OURSELVES!

13.   WE WANT A SOCIALIST SOCIETY.

We want liberation, clothing, free food, education, health care, transportation, full employment and peace. We want a society where the needs of the people come first, and where we give solidarity and aid to the people of the world, not oppression and racism. HASTA LA VICTORIA SIEMPRE!

(in New York, anyway, where infiltration had sapped much of their strength). The Panthers, I noted, too often confronted the reporter, which became the dominant image on screen; instead, the camera should be used as an organizing tool, I thought, recalling that it is a *medium*, an avenue *to* the audience we really wanted to reach; not the reporter. For the next news conference, I adopted a more collegiate, open look, and became less confrontational with the reporters; humor, I found, went a long way.

In October 1969, we had begun publishing a mimeographed packet that we called *Palante*. Still, we looked to Chicago for leadership. They didn't produce. Their paper came out too irregularly. Finally, on May 8, 1970, a month after we opened our Bronx branch, we published *Palante* as a full-sized tabloid newspaper for the first time. We couldn't wait for Chicago anymore. Chicago threw a fit. Our printing the paper was one of the issues that led to the split with Chicago later that month. The making of the paper was in itself a liberating act for us colonized individuals. Layout, setting type, photo-ready copy, mechanicals...wow! My team was superb. Richie Perez, a young high

school teacher, had left his career to join us, and he had become deputy minister of information, my right arm. I could never have gotten that newspaper out without him...and Mecca, and Americo, and all the rest. All of us doing this work for the first time, using equipment loaned to us by supportive organizations (thank you, *Guardian*, thank you Workers World Party, thank you *Rat*, thank you Liberation News Service, thank you Joe Walker of *Muhammad Speaks*, thank all of you many others). Most of us in our teens, many of us told by the educational system to forget about it, yet here we were, following in John Peter Zenger's footsteps. To do that work, write the articles, shoot the pictures, and then see it come together as a newspaper...what a feeling.

We sold *Palante* for 25¢ an issue. It was distributed mainly by us selling it on the street; secondarily, we had about a thousand subscribers. Before long we were getting orders for subscriptions from servicemen all over the world, from prisons, from all points. We tried to get distribution on the newsstands but were told by sympathetic dealers, who *knew* we'd beat out tired *El Diario* among Latino readers, that what they sold was controlled by the Mafia, or Mafia-like outfits, along with cigarettes in vending machines and private garbage collection. While they peddled smut magazines, they blocked *Palante*.

During our peak period of 1970-71, we were selling most of the 10,000 (occasionally 20,000) copies of each issue we were printing up every other week. At one point, we hit a weekly stretch. But we could only do so much. Frankly, we were quite flexible. Who knew what our circulation was? But judging from our feedback, our circulation was great. Articles in English and Spanish dealt with local and national issues, as well as events happening in Puerto Rico. We made a point of having at least one article from every chapter—demanded it, really—so every local area would read something of interest to them while also getting a sense of how broad our struggle was. We took articles from all members, though to ensure a body of material the ministry of information crew, as well as the central committee and chapter leaders, got regular assignments. We also took articles and letters from readers outside the organization or from people in other organizations. Basically, I decided what got in after consulting with the information ministry team that produced the paper.

In October, I started hosting a weekly radio show, also called "Palante," over WBAI-FM. 'BAI is a listener-sponsored Pacifica station. We mixed talk with music, mainly salsa. We rallied around salsa, not wanting to cause the kind of political/cultural nationalist split that had affected the black movement. I saw part of my information duties to be organizing the artists, and so we reached out, successfully, to Ray Barretto, Eddie Palmieri, Tito Puente, and others.

The toughest, and yet in some ways the most exciting, issue to print came after June of 1970, when we announced our split with the Chicago group, unveiled our new symbol on the front page, and declared that we were now the YLP—Young Lords *Party*. We had debated dropping the name altogether, but figured we were the ones who had carried the organization's reputation around the planet (no lie: by this time, we were the subject of documentaries from Tokyo to Copenhagen). The previous November, I had been sent to Chicago to try and help salvage our alliance and, in particular, to try and help get a newspaper out. The problem was that, while there were a few good people in Chicago, most members of the organization there had never left the gang ways...they may not have been out committing crimes, but they knew nothing about discipline, nothing about how to organize. It was a mess. Now I remembered David's warning.

There is so much more to convey, to share...but it will have to wait. Quite simply, we tried to put all our experiences into every page of the paper and into the organization as I have tried to put some of that feeling, some of why as well as who we were, and are, in these pages.

While a few of us had been gang members, gangs went out of existence in New York by the late fifties (due either to people growing up, dying, getting locked up, or becoming strung out on heroin); most of the New York Lords had never been in a gang. The organization was always about radical politics.

And, personal liberation. Growth. Change without and change within. It was an exhilarating adventure. It had its downs—oh yeah—but overall, the period I spent as a Lord from mid-1969 to the end of 1974 was five of the best years of my life, and I know just about all the rest of us—at our peak, in New York City, we had close to 2,000 members in 1970-71—felt the same way. That period includes the nine-month stretch I would do in federal prison for resisting the draft because of Puerto Ricans' second-class citizenship status and Vietnam, while other similar offenders were getting six months' probation or community service in a V.A. hospital (I started my sentence May 30, 1973); I got tougher time precisely because of my Young Lords connection. And all the lessons I learned then have become an integral part of every aspect of my life, from what I do as a journalist to what I hope to pass on to my kids (when I have 'em).

LET A HUNDRED FLOWERS BLOSSOM,
LET A HUNDRED SCHOOLS OF THOUGHT CONTEND:
THE STORY OF *HUNDRED FLOWERS*

Ed Felien

It began for me in the summer of 1967 at the New Left Convention in Chicago. I had been hired to teach Modern European Drama at Smith College in Massachusetts in the fall, my first full-time academic appointment. On the drive there from Minneapolis, I thought I'd stop in Chicago for a few weeks and check out the state of the Left.

The New Left Convention was sponsored by a broad coalition of peace and civil rights leaders, including Julian Bond, Ivanhoe Donaldson of Student Nonviolent Coordinating Committee (SNCC), Andrew Young of Southern Christian Leadership Conference (SCLC), Richard Hatcher, and Robert Scheer. I had heard about it through my local Du Bois Club. (Remember the Du Bois Clubs? They were an alternative to Students for a Democratic Society (SDS). At this time, SDS said it didn't want any Marxists in its organization, so anyone with a developed analysis, and particularly red diaper babies of Communist Party parents, joined the Du Bois Clubs. The organization existed until Nixon personally, in classic Nixon anti-communist style, said something like, "It's typical of the Communists to try to confuse American youth with an organization that sounds like the Boys Club." After that negative endorsement by Nixon, SDS became less exclusive, welcomed radicals of any stripe, and the Du Bois club that I was staff advisor to at Hallie Q. Brown Community House disbanded.)

I went down early and met some people around Old Town. In the psychedelic spirit of love we set up

Felien still lives in South Minneapolis. He teaches occasionally at local colleges and universities. He writes sometimes for local papers, and he is still politically active.

a Free Bakery and gave away chocolate chip cookies. The convention itself was much more uptight. The blacks did not want to have anything to do with the whites. The Westside organization, with black Chicago gangster macho, wouldn't even allow the black delegations to meet with white delegations.

Martin Luther King gave the keynote address and it was typically thrilling, and only slightly enhanced by hometown clown Eddie Fassbinder's dancing up and down the aisles in time to King's cadences.

A wealthy benefactor backed the convention with enough money to provide meeting rooms in the Palmer House Hotel and free meals. Along with the local chapter of the Brotherhood of Sleeping Car Porters, I was organizing lunches and dinners. At one point the owner of the storefront we were renting on Michigan Avenue said he couldn't rent to us; he hadn't realized we were radicals and now he wanted to back out of his agreement. I told him he was going to make a lot of people unhappy, and I couldn't be responsible for what they might do to his building once they learned they weren't going to get fed. Upon reflection he graciously relented. We cooked wonderful meals, and it all worked smoothly once it got started.

Dr. Spock was at the convention. A popular idea of the time was to run King and Spock for president and vice president as an alternative to the Democratic and Republican parties. But the final consensus of the convention, one that I still agree with, was to not get caught up in a national organization at all and instead to organize locally. The big banner in the open hall read, "Don't Mourn, Organize." I left Chicago with my batteries fully charged.

On the way, a friend and I stopped off at Detroit to see the carnage wrought by the Detroit riots.

By the time I got to Northampton, I wanted action. I wanted to do something about the war, about racism, about the roar of genocide committed in my name. I knew my politics would screw up the one chance I'd have at tenure and a good gig. After all, Julie Nixon was a student at Smith at the time, and the price of job security was political compliance and a respectful silence. One of the ways I would later measure my political effectiveness (aside from not being reappointed) was that my class was visited by strange men in blue suits and white socks. These obvious Secret Service types stood out as the only men in a class of 140 women. They sat at the back and took notes.

At the time, the only political action in town was a weekly vigil sponsored by the Quakers. I went. I was able to convince myself that going was at least better than doing nothing, but I wanted to do more. I remember one time, for instance, when some local rednecks drove by and shouted at us. I shouted back, and this quiet, meek woman next to me elbowed me in the ribs and hissed, "You're supposed to be non-violent." After one of the vigils, I talked with some of the other people and asked, "Couldn't we do something a little more intense?" Jimmy Cooney said he thought we should picket the draft board.

Jimmy turned out to be probably the most important person in my life. An Irish renegade, he left the Communist Party in the thirties because they weren't radical enough, left New York City and bought a tobacco farm in Massachussetts, and began *The Phoenix*, a literary and pacifist quarterly that was the first to publish Anais Nin, Henry Miller, and others. From the first moment, we were soulmates for life.

We organized a series of meetings and had over one hundred-fifty people show up for a Monday night demonstration in front of the draft board. About fifty counter-demonstrators (many of them Vietnam Vets) from the Commercial College also showed up. We wanted the draft board to stop drafting young men for an undeclared war. At the very least we wanted the board to begin issuing deferments based on an unwillingness to fight. The board refused to meet with us. I suggested that it would be a shame to waste the momentum so, after a quick meeting, we decided we'd try to meet with the head of the draft board (who was also the chief Democratic Party political hack and town clerk) at City Hall the next day at noon. He wouldn't meet with us then, either.

That next day, a hundred of us were met by sixty counter-demonstrators. Wednesday there were sixty of us and seventy of them. Thursday there were thirty of us and seventy of them. Friday there were Jimmy, his son Gabe, a vegetarian pacifist, ten Smith young women, and me—and seventy-five angry counter-demonstrators. They started pushing us around until they had us with our backs up against the wall. The Smith women started singing "God Bless America," and I thought I was hearing angels. Then, just when I thought it all might pass, the vegetarian started singing, "Gonna Lay Down My Sword and Shield..." The Vets knew that was a Commie song and they attacked. When Gabe and I got our heads split open, I said, "O.K. you win. But we'll be back tomorrow."

Inspired by a series of meetings over the weekend, over a thousand people showed up at City Hall on Monday to march in protest against the war in Vietnam. Later, some of the Smith women went on to work for McCarthy in New Hampshire. Some formed a strong chapter of SDS. And some of the rest of us started an underground newspaper, *The Mother of Voices*, that ran for a few issues in 1968 out of Amherst, Massachussetts. The paper had gonzo antiwar politics, and it was run by a crazed collective of graduate students. I wrote a few articles, "Rabbits Underground," a parable about getting your political act together before you take it on the road; and "Summary Report from Sgt. Pepper of Colonel Cooney's Looney Army," a summary of the demonstrations. Needless to say, these were not the kind of publications that would ensure my tenure.

The Mother had a wonderful exhuberance and infectious fun. It achieved a certain notoriety when the local chief of police sent his adolescent daughter into a local leather goods shop to purchase a copy so he could bust the proprietor for obscenity and contributing to the delinquency of a minor. The lawyer defending the paper and the leather craftsman cited Constitutional guarantees of freedom of the press, but the judge said he wouldn't recognize any foreign jurisdictions. That decision better than anything demonstrated the state of the union when the U.S. Constitution was declared a foreign jurisdiction in Massachusetts.

By the spring of 1969, school was finally out for me for a while. I was leaving the tenure track, getting off the fast track, and travelling down dusty country roads. I left Northampton on a truck with a troupe of travelling actors from hometown Minneapolis. When we arrived home, we lived together in the Eater Family Commune and did some antiwar guerrilla theater. Most of them went out to San Francisco at the end of that summer. I joined some other dropped-out antiwar activists in a small rural town commune 100 miles west of Minneapolis. After six months on a rural commune, I was anxious once again for urban action, so I visited San Francisco in the spring of 1970.

There, I got caught up in a street theater group I had known from New York City. One play we performed around The Day After Demonstrations (the day after the Chicago 8 got sentenced) was a fairy tale about how it was in the interest of the ruling class in this allegorical country to keep people ignorant and fighting with each other so they wouldn't see how they were all being exploited. The demonstrators moved from downtown San Francisco to Berkeley and ended up trashing banks on Shattuck Avenue. The procedure was demonstrated for me by a Weatherman in a motorcycle helmet holding a sixteen-foot long two by four. He simply poked it through the front windows of some of the more visible banks. This was a couple days before the Bank of America was burned to the ground.

While out in San Francisco I ran across *The Dock of the Bay*, a very left-leaning agitational paper that had full-page centerfold posters of revolutionary heroes like Ho Chi Minh. I also saw *Good Times* for the first time and was impressed with its straight ahead politics and its community base. I thought that with those two ingredients and the psychedelic colors and burns of the *San Francisco Oracle* and the *Chicago Seed*, there should be enough style to sustain an underground newspaper in Minneapolis.

When I got back to Minneapolis I began asking around and found two young guys freshly dropped out of college who were game to try a sixteen-page underground tabloid. Warren was valuable to the paper's early success because he could draw, and Dickie was essential because he was the only person who had had any real production experience doing a newspaper. We agreed it should be a weekly, and I contacted another dozen or so writers. We held our first collective meeting at my old rural commune, and we decided to call the paper *Hundred Flowers*. It was to pay for itself, and sustain the working collective, by ad sales and by selling for twenty-five cents.

Our first issue came out April 17, 1970. In it were articles about strikes, upcoming demonstrations, and ongoing community struggles against developers and rapacious landlords. On the back was a picture of Mao Zedong drinking a glass of something, and under it a quote by him: "A Revolution Is Not A Dinner Party." We also quoted Mao's statement on "A Hundred Flowers," part of which predicted with tragic irony the recent events in Tiananmen Square: "In socialist society, conditions for the growth of new things are radically different from and far superior to those in the old society. Nevertheless, it still often happens that new, rising forces are held back and reasonable suggestions smothered."

Our next issue was given over to hyping the upcoming Honeywell Demonstration. One fairly conservative member of the current Minneapolis City Council who was quite the ultra-leftist back then wrote, "More and more of us are beginning to realize that we are part of a new generation, nurtured in the glutted womb of Pig Amerika's Empire and born into revolution," and he borrowed for his title the phrase "I'm going to smash down all your plate glass windows." We had music reviews of rock concerts and comics. The centerfold was a cartoon of two Viet Cong looking into the ears of a large tiger and saying, "Hey, it's not paper, it's plastic."

The cover of the third issue was a drawing celebrating May Day that was reprinted by Liberation News Service throughout the country.

The fourth issue celebrated the student strike at the university in protest of the invasion of Cambodia and the murders of four students at Kent State University. We also ran articles on the university community's resistance to the McDonald's-Burger King flash food invasion. The centerfold was a wonderful photo of a car that had been driven through the front plate glass windows of a Red Barn hamburger stand which we felt was trying to expand by buying and destroying part of an older neighborhood.

Our sixth issue upped the ante. Beyond just dropping out of society, we now wanted to secede from the Union because, we proclaimed, we could no longer be part of a tyrannical, imperialist government. A map on the cover suggested that we secede from the Union and join part of Canada to form North Country.

We rewrote the Declaration of Independence, leaving the first part, the boilerplate, and adding our own contemporary grievances (see sidebar 1). We also published the first analysis and description of the local capitalist cabal. Up to now we had been opposed to "capitalists." But it was time to get specific. Stephen Keating, president of Honeywell, the chief weapons manufacturer in Minnesota and the producer of the antipersonnel bomb, was a director of the First Bank Systems and a director of Dayton's Department Store. James Binger, chairman of the board of Honeywell, was a director of Northwest Bancorp. One Dayton brother sat on the Northwest Bancorp Board, and the other was with both the First Bank Systems and Honeywell. We named a few other names and showed how these interlocking directorships maintained economic control over Minneapolis and St. Paul.

Our next issue was devoted to women's liberation. Then we did an indepth analysis of redevelopment on the West Bank—of Minneapolis (where most of the hippies live).

Next, we did a financial issue in which we laid bare the economic realities of running a newspaper and other small businesses. *Hundred Flowers* had to gross between four and five hundred dollars a week to break even. Two hundred fifty of those dollars went to publish a 16-page tabloid with photos and two colors. Most of the rest, about two hundred a week, went to keep our urban commune in shelter, utilities, food, and so on. Our income came from two sources. We sold the paper for 25 cents. We had street vendors who got ten cents of the quarter (if they were reliable, we got the other 15 cents). After a few weeks we had three head shops that acted as drop off points. These major distributors got a nickel per paper for their trouble, so the dealers still got a dime and we got a dime. This arrangement could bring in around two hundred dollars a week, maybe a little more. We also sold ads (to be more precise, I also sold ads) that could bring in another one hundred fifty to two hundred fifty dollars a week. If it was a good week we had ice cream and could go to a movie. If it was a bad week we had brown rice and veggies into infinity.

In that issue, I wrote "A Serious Proposal for the Abolition of Money," in which I argued:

> If we truly wish to disassociate ourselves from the Federal Government then we must treat its institutions like foreigners in our land. The Federal Government has legitimacy over our lives because we give it legitimacy over our lives. It continues because we continue to support it.

Jesus stepped on the coin—"Render unto Caesar the things that are Caesar's and to God the things that are God's." We can stop the Federal Government if we understand the meaning of this simple act. If we refused to recognize the power of money, then money would cease to have power. If we developed a system of distributing goods and services that was free, then the Government would no longer have the excuse to regulate and control our lives.

The article went on to outline what specific segments of society I believed should be free—I named some of them: food, land, public and commercial buildings, universities, medical care, police and the courts....

The centerfold of that issue was a reprint of the Black Panther Manifesto that announced, "The Fascists Have Already Decided in Advance to Murder Chairman Bobby Seale in the Electric Chair." Alongside it, we ran two panels from a current issue of the comic book *Captain America*. In those panels, Captain America was saying, "Right! This is no time to quarrel amongst ourselves! Together we may hope to stand! But divided we must certainly fall! You'll notice that one of us is missing this fine morning, Thor! That one is our African Avenger...T'challa, the Black Panther." We concluded it with our own histrionics: "Bobby Seale is THE prisoner of war. He is the symbol of People's War. If White and Black America don't set Bobby free the blacks will go it alone. RACE WAR. Bobby Seale is our future on trial against America."

Two strains always coexisted in the pages and on the staff of *Hundred Flowers*: the political and the cultural. They didn't always rest easy, and eventually they were the reason we fell apart. I was one who wanted to publish stories about resistance struggles, and some of the others wanted to publish photos of themselves with LOVE written on their foreheads. We did both. The result was a bit schizophrenic but, in the early days, our differences were our twin pillars of strength.

Our eleventh issue was a religious one with a laughing Jesus on the cover and Meher Baba saying, "Don't Worry Be Happy" in the centerfold. A hippie priest declared Jesus to be a "cosmic revolutionary," and I wrote about cultural terrorists like the Marquis de Sade, Rasputin, Oscar Wilde, Jesus, and Charlie Manson in an article entitled "Revolutionary Cultural Terrorists" (see sidebar 2).

Ronald Reagan introduced issue number fourteen, our Health issue, when we reprinted on our cover a Chesterfield cigarette ad he made in the forties. Under his photo we listed our four steps to stop smoking: first, you must want to stop; second, drink lots of herbal teas; third, try chewing a sassafras root; fourth, smoke herbs like marijuana, comfrey, rosemary, thyme, and eyebright or corn silks.

As the summer wore on we became less political and a lot more cultural, part of the ebbs and flows of the times. We were best when the two merged. When a young artist was murdered in a random act of senseless violence, we wrote an obituary and served as the vehicle of grief for the community. We had a respected role in the articulation of values for the alternative culture. At least we could all agree on sex, drugs, and rock and roll. As I was laying out the paper one afternoon, I heard a local rock station DJ say, "He'd swear on a stack of *Hundred Flowers*."

We were intensely democratic in our decision making at the paper. No article could get in unless it was approved by three members of the collective. Most of the people who worked on the paper also lived in the house where it was produced. There were about twelve of us usually, but after members of the Hog Farm and another busload of migrating hippies pulled up outside one day, we had about fifty people in and out of the house for the next week. We tried to share responsibilities for housekeeping and cooking. Occasionally our domestic decisions became public policy. After a house meeting we decided to print a poster in the paper entitled "WASH YOUR DISH" so we could cut it out and put it over the sink.

By our nineteenth issue we were finding it difficult to get a printer. We had gone through about thirty printers, which included every web-fed press capable of printing a sixteen-page newspaper within 150 miles. At first, small town printers would print us, but then they'd tell us they were getting pressure from their advertisers, and they'd refuse. Once, after we had put together our Women's Liberation issue, we showed up at our printer and were met by the rightwing congressman from the district, Ancher Nelson, who personally looked over our camera-ready copy. A number of articles were critical of sexism in popular music. Another article reported on an action by some sisters who had protested sexist posters at a popular record store, The Electric Fetus. The article was entitled, "Power Failure at the Electric Cock." When the congressman saw that title, he closed the folder and looked toward heaven. The printer would not print us. As we left, we turned back and I said, "Remember what John F. Kennedy said, 'If you make peaceful revolution impossible, you make violent revolution inevitable.'" We ended up being printed by the same printer in Milwaukee, Wisconsin, who printed the *Seed*.

The police took papers away from our dealers at the state fair. We seemed to have a legitimate basis for our paranoia, our persecution mania, our delusions of grandeur. Perhaps we were being persecuted. Maybe the revolution was just around the corner. Maybe it was just what we were smoking.

In early September, we learned that Che Guevara had been killed. The Bolivian military, three years earlier and acting on orders and advice from the CIA, had assassinated him by firing a revolver bullet straight through his heart while he was in captivity, but had managed to keep it a secret until now. I cried as I typed out his final farewell letter:

> One day they asked who should be notified in case of death, and the real possibility of the fact affected us all. Later we knew it was true, that IN REVOLUTION ONE WINS OR DIES (IF IT IS A REAL ONE). Many comrades fell along the way to victory...I CARRY TO NEW BATTLE FRONTS THE FAITH THAT YOU HAVE TAUGHT ME, THE REVOLUTIONARY SPIRIT OF MY PEOPLE, THE FEELING OF FULFILLING THE MOST SACRED OF DUTIES: TO FIGHT AGAINST IMPERIALISM WHEREVER I MAY BE.

In response to this murder, the New Year's Gang of Madison blew up the Army Math Research Center on the University of Wisconsin campus. The Army Math Research Center was the training center for the CIA group that engineered the capture and assassination of Che Guevara. Members of the Gang had given sufficient warning to allow people to clear the building, but a janitor disregarded their warning and, as a result,

a researcher was killed in the explosion. Our work took on more serious implications after this.

In the same issue, Huey Newton urged everyone to choose between revolutionary suicide and reactionary suicide:

> If the penalty for the quest for freedom is death, then by death we escape to freedom. We are not alone. We have allies everywhere. We find our comrades wherever in the world we hear the oppressor's whip. People all over the world are rising up. The high tide of revolution is about to sweep the shores of America—sweeping away the evil gentry and corrupt officials.

Huey Newton was the centerfold in our next issue. On the cover was a drawing of the original seal of the United States proposed by Benjamin Franklin, John Adams, and Thomas Jefferson. It read, "Rebellion to Tyrants Is Obedience to God."

At the end of September, the death of Jimi Hendrix was the cover story for our twenty-first issue. By this time, some of our regular features were becoming standard: lead news on page three; "People Rising Up All Over," a review of international news the other papers didn't print, on pages five and six; and "Bulletin Board"—a calendar and classified ads on the back page.

Two weeks later, a couple of us were promoting a "Gathering of the Tribes," an attempt at a conference of alternative energies. We wanted to translate the newspaper into a political action, a ratification of aspirations, our agreed upon hopes. More than a hundred people showed up, at the church that was soon after permanently renamed the People's Center, for the three days of workshops and rap sessions. We had workshops on the Black Panther Party, free schools, gay liberation, women's liberation, ecology, organizing food co-ops, organic gardening, people's medical clinics, and more. We held general sessions where we talked about where we should be headed politically, and we heard reports from brothers and sisters who were facing jail and prison for anti-ROTC demonstrations and attempts to destroy draft files.

During the time we were putting together that issue, I got arrested for breach of the peace while covering a story about the demolition of single family homes to make way for two-and-a-half story walk-up apartment buildings. Some of the hippies who lived in the houses were protesting the demolition of the houses and the consequent increase in density in the neighborhood. The charges were eventually dismissed, but the police harassment was obvious: I was arrested for taking photos standing next to a television cameraman.

Finally, by the twenty-sixth issue, I snapped. I had been burning out. One or two all-nighters every week, typing copy, laying out, trying to manage circulation of 5,000 copies and sell ads, all this had taken its toll. For what seemed like the millionth time, I was the only one left at 3:00 A.M. to put the paper to bed. Was I the only one who took it seriously?

The differences between the others on the paper and me were becoming too great. I was ten years older than most of the others. I had finished my Ph.D. I had been marching against segregation and the war in Vietnam since 1963. They were bright and eager, but they had no real idea of what they were in for. We didn't share the same frame of reference or the same political commitment. They liked the music, the drugs, the lifestyle, and they enjoyed being the center of the counter-culture in Minneapolis. On the other hand, I seemed like a political fanatic.

I was typing and laying out the letters to the editor ("Readers Write On"). I had just typed a confused letter from a pacifist, a peace and love letter from a GI in 'Nam who was thankful he was in the artillery and not the infantry, and a letter from a hippie critical of the protest bombings of buildings by the Weather Underground. That was the last straw. I couldn't resist. I added a short response of my own to the first letter: "You are a chicken-shit bourgeois pacifist. Che said: 'Wherever death may surprise us let it be welcome as long as one more person comes forward to pick up the gun and intone our funeral dirge with the stacatto of machine guns.' Yours, for a just peace, thorsten dogood."

This short statement provoked a major controversy. In the next issue, a colleague and I defended our position in "Two Flowers on Violence: A Criticism of Bourgeois Pacifism." She was more eloquent than I:

> Do I dig violence? No. But tell me you don't believe in violence, and I say, "Bullshit." How much closer does Honeywell or the New Brighton Arsenal have to be before we believe in it.

I was more crude:

> We cannot any longer be pacifists: House Niggers with our heads in the sand hoping we won't get our asses shot off.

Members of the Black Panther Party were being assassinated by the Alcohol and Tax Division of the Treasury Department all over the country. Some of us were organizing a Black Panther Party chapter for Minneapolis. We had a storefront, the Kathleen Cleaver Community Information Center, and plans to start a breakfast program for children and a transportation program to help loved ones visit their friends and relatives in prison.

Our Black Panther Party issue showed the schizophrenia manifest in the paper. I supervised pages of copy about the BPP that were almost rigidly orthodox, while the cultural hippies organized pages advertising a rally of support for the Minnesota Eight who were about to be sentenced to prison for attempting to destroy draft files. They entitled their section, "Thanks for the Pie!" The centerfold was a blowup of a house fly that you were supposed to paste to a picket sign and bring to the demonstration.

The "Readers Write On" section of the paper brought the struggle out in the open. We reprinted the original pacifist letter, my response, a new response to me in which I was described as an "arrogant elitist in 'peoples' clothing," a new extended reply by me again attacking bourgeois pacifism, and a response by five members of the collective that agreed with the criticism of me as elitist and arrogant.

A few years later, the Weather Underground, in their self-criticism, said they were guilty of the Military Error. They were ultra left when they thought that quick violent acts would spark a mass uprising. Certainly, one judgment of history has to be that they were wrong.

I was wrong, too.

The way we criticize the present world is the way we build the new.

You don't fight fire with fire. You fight fire with water.

You catch more bees with honey than you do with vinegar.

All these platitudes are true. But, even though we were wrong to act angrily, violently, antagonistically, we were right to act. It was a much greater wrong to do nothing.

That was almost twenty years ago, and I'm still not repentant.

But the split in *Hundred Flowers* was irrevocable. I was purged. Some readers wrote in wanting to continue the debate, but the paper sputtered and finally folded after three more issues. The final issue came out December 11, 1970.

Those were heady days. The year 1970 was a turning point for America. Resistance to the War in Vietnam had matured into a permanent institution, a persistent and articulate counter-culture. A new consciousness was being developed about capitalism, racism, and sexism. Being a part of those struggles was exciting.

It was good work. But I have no nostalgia for the genocide, the racism, the oppression of women that made that work so immediate and necessary. There is political work enough for today and even for tomorrow. It is no less important now, even though there's new music on the radio and the tempo has changed.

THE FURIES: GODDESSES OF VENGEANCE

Ginny Z. Berson

Berson was one of the founders of *The Furies*. She co-founded Olivia Records, which she left in 1980. She was the director of women's programming at KPFA (the Pacifica Radio station) in Berkeley, and until June 1990 was the program director there. She is now working as a freelance radio producer and writer (for Chicago's *Windy City Times*, among others). Her passions include women, justice, writing, radio, and scuba diving.

Acknowledgment: I want to thank Coletta Reid for helping to jog my memory about the details, and for helping me remember the context and the times in which we lived *The Furies*. The opinions herein are mine alone.

In the winter and spring of 1972, while Richard Nixon and his minions were preparing to bug Democratic National Headquarters at the Watergate Building, 12 self-proclaimed revolutionary lesbian feminists—who were known collectively as the Furies—were putting out the first issues of what would almost instantly become *The* "legendary" *Furies*. While Washington, DC, may seem an unlikely place for the birthing of such a major contributor to the exploding underground press in this country, in retrospect, and in light of what the Furies wrote about and stood for, it all makes perfect sense.

Washington, DC, was, after all, the belly of the beast, the very seat of power of the U.S. government. As such, Washington was also the focus and locus of hundreds of protest groups and demonstrations. Government offices were regularly occupied by groups as diverse as the National Welfare Rights Organization and the Committee of Returned [Peace Corps] Volunteers. The Black Panther Party was strong and active. Gay men and (fewer) women were coming out of the closet and talking about their civil rights. As the war in Vietnam raged, hundreds of thousands of people descended regularly on the Capitol grounds to march and rally, smash windows and fight with cops, circle the Pentagon and try to levitate it, block traffic and sit in the halls of Congress. Hippies and freaks dropped acid and contemplated their visions in the reflecting pool across from the Washington Monument.

DC Women's Liberation in the early 1970s was thriving. Consciousness-raising groups enabled hundreds of women to understand a critical lesson of this second wave of feminism—the personal is political. Women took the revelations that followed and established a host of services for themselves and other women, including rape counselling and child care.

Women in the health fields began researching the pill and testified in Congress to its dangerous side effects. Others began organizing and lobbying for changes in restrictive abortion laws—*Roe v. Wade* was not decided until January 1973, so for most American women abortion was still illegal. *off our backs*, a feminist monthly, was publishing news and opinion from around the country. Women Against Racism, Women Against Imperialism, Women Against Population Control met regularly, marched together, wrote position papers, planned to change the world.

The particular confluence of forces that gave birth to *The Furies* was being duplicated all over the country. Straight women were tired of being the gofers and sperm receptacles for the white male left. Lesbians were tired of being ignored by the gay liberation movement, and were being actively told to go back in the closet or get out by the women's liberation movement. It seemed that liberation went only so far. Women's liberation was considered bourgeois by the lefties—something to take care of "after the revolution." It was not even taken seriously enough to be considered a threat. Lesbianism was considered a bedroom issue by women's liberation—but leaders like Betty Friedan were very threatened because the mainstream media were already dismissing the emerging women's movement as a bunch of "bra-burning" lesbians. If that turned out to be true, Women's Liberation would have an even harder time gaining credibility and winning converts.

The 12 original Furies came from DC, New York, and Chicago, having worked in all the movements, and having found no home in any of them. We were all white, rural and urban, working, middle, and upper middle class. Our ages ranged from 18 to 28. The primary organizer of the group was Rita Mae Brown. Rita had been a lesbian activist for years, being one of the authors of "The Woman-Identified Woman," the first authoritative definition of political lesbianism. She came to DC to organize, and she formed her first critical alliance with Charlotte Bunch, a straight (though not for long after meeting Rita) activist in the DC Women's Liberation Movement. Rita had the fire and vision, Charlotte, one of the most visible founders of DC Women's Liberation, had the credibility and contacts, and they pulled together the rest of us: Tasha Peterson and Susan Hathaway, recently arrived from Chicago where they had worked on the Chicago 7 Conspiracy trial; Nancy Myron, lesbian activist from New York; Joan Biren and Sharon Deevey, whose coming out into the DC Women's Liberation Movement had caused a major split in that organization; teenagers Helaine Harris and Lee Schwing; Coletta Reid, married mother of two who lived down the street from the first all-women's house in DC, was one of the founders of *off our backs*, and one day asked her husband to leave; Jennifer Woodul, who came out while a student at Vassar College by the organizing work of New York Radical Lesbians, including Rita Mae Brown; and me, closeted my whole life, active in the left and the women's movement.

Before the formation of the Furies, I had lived in DC's first women's house, with Tasha, Susan, and Helaine among others. We did massive quantities of grass, acid, mushrooms, and other drugs, went to meetings of Women Against (fill in the blank), and struggled endlessly about everything. I left that house after Joan and Sharon came out to me and I finally felt free to come out myself. The three of us moved in with a group of lesbians who had come from New York, one of whom was Nancy Myron. We thought that particular house would solve the problem of living among the straight "oppressor." But Joan, Sharon, and I were middle-class women with college degrees, who had no visible means of support but managed to live well. Our five housemates were working class and all had straight, 9-5 jobs. I began to develop an understanding of class in America. But the house lasted only one week. These two themes—lesbian and class consciousness—became the dominant themes of *The Furies*.

By July of 1971, the Furies had formed itself into a collective. Everyone had come out. Weekly meetings, which had begun in April as consciousness-raising sessions for the new lesbians, became more politically focused. We were going to define and build a lesbian-feminist ideology. We decided to publish a monthly newspaper—a way to reach other lesbians and would-be lesbians. In September or October of that year, we moved into three houses in (relatively) gay Southeast DC—out of hippie/male left Northwest.

By this time we had agreed to form a disciplined, revolutionary cadre. We developed an income sharing plan, by which the more privileged among us got the best jobs we could find—in direct opposition to the value being promulgated by the political and hippie middle class white male left that only "oppressors" had well-paying jobs and that we should all embrace downward mobility as a way to better relate to our working class sisters and brothers. By doing this, we were able to supplement the incomes of the less privileged, and no one had to work full-time. We each put a percentage of our wages into the common pool (the greater the privilege, the higher the percentage). One of the working class women was sent to printing school. The cars of those who had them became community property. We formed study groups that read and reported regularly on the functioning and malfunctioning of other revolutions. We stopped doing drugs.

POLITICAL LESBIANISM

We struggled among ourselves to define our politics. Out of the morass of the white male left, the hippie/freak/drug culture, the straight women's liberation movement, the male-dominated gay liberation movement, we intended to develop a truly radical lesbian-feminist ideology. We rejected the glaring weaknesses we found in each movement—the male domination, the downward mobility, the glorification of feelings over thought, the priority given to personal relationships, the lack of strategic vision and practical organization.

We chose the name "The Furies," for our collective and our newspaper, after the three Greek Goddesses—strong, powerful women, the "Angry Ones," the avengers of matricide, the protectors of women. They are part of the Orestes myth, and, according to our interpretation, their defeat marked a major victory for male supremacy; their ultimate betrayal came at the hands of Athena—"the creation of the male God, Zeus, sprung full-grown from his head, the first token woman." As I wrote in the lead article of the first issue (see appendix 1), published in January 1972:

We call our paper *The Furies* because we are also angry. We are angry because we are oppressed by male supremacy. We have been fucked over all our lives by a system which is based on the domination of men over women, which defines male as good and female as only as good as the man you are with. It is a system in which hetero-sexuality is rigidly enforced and Lesbianism rigidly suppressed. It is a system which has further divided us by class, race, and nationality.

Although we called ourselves a "newspaper," our interest in news was relatively insignificant. While that first issue did contain a full page of "What's Going On?" that reported lesbian activities from around the country, future issues devoted less and less space to that information. In fact, we were quite sure that political activity was premature until a solid ideology had been developed. And that, we thought, was our primary task. In a nutshell, again from the lead article of issue 1:

The base of our ideological thought is: Sexism is the root of all other oppressions, and Lesbian and woman oppression will not end by smashing capitalism, racism and imperialism. Lesbianism is not a matter of sexual preference, but rather one of political choice which every woman must make if she is to become woman-identified and thereby end male supremacy. Lesbians, as outcasts from every culture but their own, have the most to gain by ending race, class, and national supremacy within their own ranks. Lesbians must get out of the straight women's movement and form their own movement in order to be taken seriously, to stop straight women from oppressing us, and to force straight women to deal with their own Lesbianism. Lesbians

cannot develop a common politics with women who do not accept Lesbianism as a political issue.

These themes were developed more fully in Charlotte Bunch's first article, "Lesbians in Revolt: Male Supremacy Quakes and Quivers" (see appendix 2):

In our society which defines all people and institutions for the benefit of the rich, white male, the Lesbian is in revolt. In revolt because she defines herself in terms of women and rejects the male definitions of how she should feel, act, look, and live. To be a Lesbian is to love oneself, woman, in a culture that denigrates and despises women. The Lesbian rejects male sexual/political domination; she defies his world, his social organization, his ideology, and his definition of her as inferior. Lesbianism puts women first while the society declares the male supreme. Lesbianism threatens male supremacy at its core. When politically conscious and organized, it is central to destroying our sexist, racist, capitalist, imperialist system.

Lesbianism, we said, is a political choice, not just a matter of sexual preference. To see lesbianism as exclusively a sexual act was to strengthen the dominant view of women as only sexual beings; furthermore, the popular conception of lesbians as not being "real women" reinforced that notion: a "real woman" is one who has sex with men. Lesbianism is political, Bunch went on, "because relationships between men and women are essentially political, they involve power and dominance."

In terms of actual "sexual preference," we believed that, in an ideal world, all human beings would be bi-sexual, capable of loving, intimate relationships with people of both genders. But we did not live in an ideal world, and that natural inclination had been suppressed in most people. Still, every woman (we didn't care about the men) had the ability—and the obligation—to reclaim that part of herself, and free herself from the personal and political bonds of male domination. While lesbian singer Alix Dobkin was singing "Any woman can be a lesbian," we were saying "Every woman should be a lesbian."

But lesbianism by itself is not enough. Even billions of women coming out would still not make a revolution. At worst, lesbians could be racist, classist, oppressive to other women and lesbians. They could opt for individual solutions to political problems. They could settle for political reforms that gave them certain civil rights but did nothing to change the power structure. "Lesbians must become feminists and fight against woman oppression, just as feminists must become Lesbians if they hope to end male supremacy....The only way oppressed people end their oppression," wrote Bunch, "is by seizing power: People whose rule depends on the subordination of others do not voluntarily stop oppressing others. Our subordination is the basis of male power."

Our analysis of history concluded that sexism was the root of all oppression; the original imperialism was male over female: "the male claiming the female body and her service as his territory (or property)." Domination by men of other men, based on race, class, tribe, ensued. At the bottom of every conquered group were the women. To this day, victorious armies regard the women on the losing side as spoils of war. Even among the more "liberated" socialist and nationalist fighters, women's place is always secondary, and women's "issues" have to wait until after the "revolution." For *The Furies*, there could be no revolution until male supremacy, the primary contradiction, was resolved.

While parts of the straight women's liberation movement agreed with our analysis of sexism, *The Furies* went a step further, to a place where straight women could not go and remain straight. We defined the institution of heterosexuality as the primary underpinning of male supremacy. Charlotte Bunch wrote:

> Heterosexuality separates women from each other; it makes women define themselves through men; it forces women to compete against each other for men and the privilege which comes through men and their social standing. Heterosexual society offers women a few privileges as compensations if they give up their freedom: for example, mothers are respected and "honored," wives or lovers are socially accepted and given some economic and emotional security, a woman gets physical protection on the street when she stays with her man, etc. The privileges give heterosexual women a personal and political stake in maintaining the status quo.

The very essence of heterosexuality in the twentieth century (not to mention the previous thirty centuries) was "men first." As lesbians, therefore, we believed that to continue working with straight women in women's liberation would mean our ultimate betrayal. "Lesbians cannot grow politically or personally in a situation which denies the basis of our politics: that Lesbianism is political, that heterosexuality is crucial to maintaining male supremacy."

We hammered home those points over and over, in the first issue and in every one that followed. Sharon Deevey's first article began with her personal story of struggling with her "sensitive" husband, her first lesbian relationship, and finally her realization that "Everything around me was...heterosexual—men and women together, and men most important. Books, movies, people in the streets, my family, my friends, and especially Women's Liberation: Birth control, bad fucks, and abortions!"

Rita Mae Brown added to the discussion with "How a Female Heterosexual Serves the Interests of Male Supremacy," taking on Roxanne Dunbar, in response to Dunbar's just published article "The Movement and the Working Class." Rita was reluctant to criticize another working class woman, and acknowledged the importance of Dunbar's analysis of class in the United States and the failure of many political movements to effectively address class issues. But "Roxanne attempts to smash Lesbianism by treating it as a personal luxury rather than dealing with it as a political ideology. This sweeping us under the rug as some great apolitical, individualistic freedom is classic heterosexual blindness." Rita made the point that has been echoed by feminists ever since—class struggle, race struggle, national struggle are considered the "important" struggles because they include men. The struggle for the liberation of women in general, and lesbians in particular, is simply not taken seriously because women in this world are not taken seriously.

We tried to make *The Furies* the newspaper for the complete lesbian—with regular features on developing physical strength and self-defense tactics; short stories, including one by me on a trip to the dentist (see sidebar 1); poetry (by the likes of Judy Grahn, Pat Parker, Rita Mae, and others); discussions of the workings of capitalist economics in the United States and the world; the occasional movie review (when some political point could be made); photos (many by Joan Biren, who became JEB) and drawings of women; and history, always something about history.

We were a bit obsessed with history—we studied the Russian and Chinese revolutions and the structure of their parties, the Nazi rise to power, the Greek and Roman myths, the first wave of feminism in the United States, the beginnings of the lesbian and homophile movement in the 1940s and '50s. We looked for and found lesbians or remarkable straight women in history—women whose lives and/or loves had been kept secret from us—and we wrote about them: Queen Christina of Sweden, Emily Dickinson, Susan B. Anthony, Doña Catalina of Spain, pirates Anne Bonny and Mary Read. Part of our obsession with history was genuine curiosity about the women, especially the lesbians, who came before us. But part of it was a tribute to the serious role we believed we were taking on. We were going to create a revolution like nothing anyone had ever seen before. We had to know how other revolutionaries did it—to emulate what we could, and to avoid what we should.

Reading through *The Furies* in 1990, I was astonished to realize that we never discussed the dynamics of personal relationships (issues such as monogamy or breaking up with integrity), except to bemoan the amount of time, energy, and attention relationships were getting from other lesbians and feminists. While we seemed to have changed partners regularly, we

All the way to the dentist she thought of Jennifer. Of how it got better all the time, every night. Of how incredible it felt to love someone like that. To want them so much that her body ached at knowing that it would be hours before they would be together again. Last night had been the best, and her insides stirred and trembled at the thought of their passion—hands lips legs tongue on ears neck breasts cunt—"I am loving you." Morning coming and not wanting to get out of bed ever—to hold each other, talk, make love. Thinking with sadness now, instead of her usual anger and scorn, that all women were not Lesbians, that all women did not know, would not let themselves know, feel, love another woman—themselves. And then to Jennifer again—Jennifer of "I am loving you," never said to her like that before.

The parking lot at the clinic was half empty. The day was gray and the ground was covered with puddles. The clinic was equally gray, the magazines in the waiting room at least six months old, one of the small prices one pays for not going to a private dentist. She sat with an old *Life* open on her lap, thinking of Jennifer. Her name was called and she moved quickly to the office, eager to get it over with. The dentist was surprised to see a white woman enter, and was ashamed for her. As he poked around her mouth he poked around her life: "Are you a student?" "Why aren't you married?" "Ah, but you do have a boyfriend?" A job? A family? A life? She answered in grunts, submerging her desire to tell him to shut up, can you just fix my teeth, can't you just be a dentist instead of a man? Of course not. She knew.

The nurse filled the needle. Her mouth wide open, his finger stretching it more, he poised over her and said, "If you come to my private office, I can give you much better treatment." "I can't afford it." "It could be free." The needle went into her gum but she did not feel it. Screaming, swearing, glass smashing, heavy feet stomping his face in, knees flying to his prick, kicking kicking over and over until there was nothing left but a useless sagging mass of flesh. A knife in his guts tearing them out while he wretched on the floor in total agony and pain unimagined before. He pulled out the needle. "No thank you," she said.

He drilled and filled for the next twenty minutes, chatting all the while about his private practice, the great sacrifice he made by working at the clinic twice a week, how if any conflict arose of course his private patients came first—"A man has to make a living, doesn't he?" He only filled two—there were two more to do next week—she would have to come back. He handed her his card as she got up to leave. "Come see me some time." "Right, I will." He walked out of the office into the waiting room. "Next?"

All the way home she tried to think of Jennifer and couldn't.

NOTE

1. From *The Furies* #1 (January 1972): 4.

never allowed the comings and goings of various lovers to disrupt our political work.

Outside of the poetry and fiction, we never wrote about sex. Indeed, we made a conscious decision to specifically exclude any graphics that depicted female nudity. We were, in fact, determined to smash the popular conception of lesbianism as a purely sexual occupation; we had no intention of even acknowledging the frequently asked question, "but what do two women do in bed?"

CLASS

Class analysis and the development of class consciousness was the second dominant theme of *The Furies*. As a group, we struggled with the issues constantly, monitoring our own and each other's behavior. I cannot find a single article that did not mention class—even if class was not the point of the article. All of us were in different stages of class awareness, but we all understood that, to succeed, our revolution had to be for all women, not just the privileged.

Rita brought the clearest understanding of the workings of class to the collective, but Coletta, Tasha, and Nancy made their experiences as working class women heard as well. As a middle class woman, I was encouraged to understand my own position relative to both the working and lower classes and the upper middle and upper classes, and to not allow myself the luxury of being frozen by guilt.

Nevertheless, in retrospect it seems that class guilt was a considerable force in our group dynamics. Being accused of classism by one of the working class women in *The Furies* was tantamount to being accused of being male-identified. When in doubt about a particular issue, it was safer to shut up and follow the lead of the working class women. Needless to say, this did not make for a healthy group process.

Issue number 3 (March-April 1972) was devoted largely to class. Nancy Myron described her own "Class Beginnings" as "the trash of the community" when she was growing up. Her sister, being not only poor but endowed with large breasts, was considered a whore and an easy lay, while young women with similar physiques but higher class standing were dated and considered respectable:

> I'm not saying that the sweet magnolia blossoms of lawyers' daughters escaped objectification but that they had a less traumatic time of it. Someone has to be on the bottom to hold up the top. And in this case part of the female citizenry was projected into the shadows of alleys while the rest went steady with basketball stars.

Rita Mae Brown reviewed *The Last Picture Show* and slammed the movie as "being more dishonest than most in its packaged cinematic sensitivity":

> First the technical dishonesty: Movies shot in black and white in the 1970s are artsy fartsy. Human beings see in color....There's a class aspect to black and white movies in our times. Supposedly, the bleak screen will serve to heighten the viewer's sense of the drab, the working class, the impoverished. Those of us growing up impoverished were oppressed in living color and any deviation from that is a perversion of our lives justified in terms of "style." When our ceilings peeled they peeled from pea green to red to black to gray to blue and all together it was more hideous than anything shot in black and white.

My own contribution was "Slumming It in the Middle Class," in which I described the evolution of my class consciousness. It was important to us to describe our own processes because we desperately wanted other women to recognize themselves in us and make the changes we thought were necessary. If I had once been unaware but had learned to alter my behavior, so could others. So must others:

> For many middle class women the women's movement has meant a reprieve from working for somebody else's revolution. Having gotten in touch with their own oppression, they are unwilling to see themselves as oppressors again, especially as the oppressors of other women. It is crucial that we stop this before our movement gets torn apart by middle class women's refusal to deal with their class privilege.

Class privilege included real material issues like the amount of money one makes and the degree of economic security one has; and behavioral issues like the romanticization of poverty and downward mobility, which ran rampant in the sixties and seventies. Class background often determined who dominated meetings, as well as who had time to attend meetings.

For the middle class Furies, the sharing of material privilege with our working class sisters came much easier than changing the destructive attitudes—the ways of viewing the world, the standards of thought and action that we had learned to be the "right ways." Charlotte and Coletta wrote in "Revolution Begins at Home," in issue number 4 (May 1972):

> Class supremacy is acted out in thinking that working class women are less together, personally and politically, because they do not act and talk the way we do. Their politics may not be expressed in the same manner, their vocabulary may not be as "developed," and so they are "less articulate" and treated as less important. Or they may be hostile and emotional so one can hardly trust their political judgment; after all, we've learned to keep ourselves in check, to be reasonable, to keep things in perspective. Looking down with scorn or pity at those whose emotions are not repressed or who can't rap out abstract theories in thirty seconds flat reeks of our class arrogance and self-righteousness.

To this day, the women's movement is divided by the different needs and economic realities of the different classes. Getting past the "glass ceiling" of mid-management that so many women in the corporate world experience is not exactly a major concern to women still stuck in the pink collar ghetto. Raising the minimum wage is still not a top priority item on the agendas of most mainstream feminist groups.

We almost always mentioned race and racism in our articles, but never thought or wrote extensively about the subject. We were aware that this was a failing; indeed, the fact that our group was all white was disturbing to us. However, we did nothing about it, believing that at some future point, having successfully dealt with the class issues among us, we would be able to focus more on race. It is clear that we focused so much on class because of our internal class differences; without the leadership of the working class women in the collective, the middle-class women would have treated class issues the same way the all-white group treated race issues: important, something to be dealt with, but not urgent.

POWER

We solicited, and very occasionally printed, articles by other lesbians, particularly when they agreed with our positions. There was, however, one notable exception. In issue number 2 (February 1972), Rita wrote a perceptive article on "Leadership vs. Stardom"—a problem that was plaguing the entire women's movement, which had a tendency to trash anyone who was perceived as taking a vanguard role. Part of this tendency came from having the male, mainstream media declare our "leaders" for us. A leader was a woman like Betty Friedan or Gloria Steinem, who had "little or no political following. She has done something that the media finds noteworthy—written a book, founded a reformist organization, made a public fool of herself, etc. She serves male supremacy by being a token."

But a far more serious aspect of the problem was feminists' basic distrust of power, because of our horrendous experiences with male abuses. Many believed that power was inherently evil and corrupting. Our beliefs in egalitarianism translated into a kind of feminist lowest-common-denominator conformity. The most vivid example of this for me came while playing softball, one of my personal addictions. Every Sunday we organized softball games for women in one of DC's parks. Some of us were really good. Others weren't. I was a very good shortstop, and a number of other players insisted that I play another position—that all the good players play someplace other than at their strength in order to equal things out. I offered another solution—I and some others would come early each Sunday and spend time working with and teaching less skilled players so we could all play better. For several Sundays in a row I arrived at the park, ready to coach. Nobody else showed up. We had yet to develop an understanding of the differences between "power to" versus "power over." This was an issue *The Furies* was ready to take on.

In a very casual manner in her "Leadership" article, Rita mentioned the need to form a national feminist political party to confront the power of the State. The principal opposition to the discipline and organization required to form a party, she asserted, came from anarchists, who she accused of being middle class, cowardly, and anti-leadership. In Issue number 4, Katz (the only name she used), a white working class anarchist from Boston, responded by calling instead for a "world of man-hating-dyke-gangs," "small groups based on friendship and common politics that you are so flipply disdainful of." Katz goes on:

> Are you ready to form a party in a movement where lesbians of color are not yet fully participant? Are you willing to form a party in a movement where most of its middle class members are classist? As a leader, are you ready to risk the codification of power? Let's see you kids get all of D.C. together so fine that you can justify such a call. And then I'll show you how well you did without any damn party.

I wrote our official response, "Beyond Male Power..." We acknowledged that the mention of party in Rita's article had been fairly off-hand, without consideration given to the difficult questions that Katz raised. We also apologized for the misuses of the word "anarchy" and for its equation with emotionalism,

cowardice, and individualism. But we stuck by our call for a party:

> Individual lesbians can and do carve out little niches for themselves in which they are as "free" as possible and in as little contact with their oppressor as possible. But, by themselves, they do nothing to change the balance of power. They do nothing to change the basic system which oppresses them and forces them into that solution. Small groups, acting on their own, with no national coordination or agreed upon action do a little more. They expand the base of the niche and can improve the lot of large numbers of women. But their effectiveness is limited by their size and the degree to which they can coordinate their actions and their understandings with other groups. They still do not threaten the balance of power; they still don't bring about a major redistribution of power.

Needless to say, we never got very far with the creation of a party. In fact, some time between the fourth and fifth issues, the working collective dissolved. Many of us continued to live together, share income, work on common projects, and produce *The Furies*. By Issue number 6 (August 1972), half the people working on the paper were new. We had seen *The Furies* as an organizing tool. We were now becoming unorganized ourselves. Our demise was caused by a combination of unresolved (in some cases unacknowledged) personal/political dynamics—which is a part of the story I will not attempt to deal with in this article, and a belief that we had said what we wanted to say in the paper and it was time to move on to other work. The dream of the tight-knit cadre, the vanguard of the revolution, was gone.

Response to *The Furies* was immediate and strong. The paper hit the lesbian communities around the country like a bombshell. Much of what we were saying about political lesbianism, and male supremacy, had been said before, in the "Woman-Identified Woman" paper, *Lavender Menace* (out of New York City), and by Martha Shelley and Rita in *The Ladder*. But we were among the first to discuss heterosexuality as an institution; to devote so much thought to class analysis; and to go beyond the basic ideas of political lesbianism and male supremacy, expand them, and examine their ramifications for building a total politic. Lesbians throughout the country had experienced the same frustrations with the male left, gay liberation, and women's liberation, and we were able to articulate an explanation, a direction, a cosmology, that many others were looking for. Women waited intently for each new issue to appear, and groups were formed to read and discuss the latest words from Washington, DC. For many straight women, *The Furies* was the impetus to come out. For many lesbians, *The Furies* gave political meaning and validation.

Exact circulation figures are lost, but Coletta remembers that we printed 3,000 copies of the first issue—we mailed out 1,200 free to the *off our backs* mailing list, sold quite a few through the women's and gay bookstores that were springing up around the country, and eventually sold the rest as copies of *The Furies* became collectors' items.

We paid for the paper out of our own pockets—from the pool of money we collected each month from each woman's paycheck. We sold ads to women-owned businesses and services, but the cost for an ad was only $10, and we had very few of them. Most of our ads were, in fact, exchanges with other lesbian periodicals.

Needless to say, not all response was positive. We were accused of arrogance, elitism, communism, lesbian chauvinism, and general political incorrectness. Coletta told me a story about a trip she took to California during the summer of 1972. She was visiting a lesbian bar in San Francisco and had to get back to the East Bay, where she was spending the night. She asked a woman at the bar for a ride. When the woman found out that Coletta was a member of the Furies, she refused to give her a ride.

In all, nine issues were published over a period of 15 months, with only Lee and Helaine left at the end from the original group. We had to change printers on a regular basis; there were no lesbian print shops then, that we could find, and male printers were too afraid of lawsuits, too afraid of being picketed, or just too afraid of lesbians to stay with us for very long. In the end, the only print shop that would handle *The Furies* was a pornographic press in Long Island.

Passionate politics leave their mark, whether positive or negative, or some of both. Out of the original Furies members came some of the women who founded and ran Diana Press, which published 32 books over a ten-year period; some of the women who founded Olivia Records, the national women's record company now in its seventeenth year; some of the women who founded *Quest: A Feminist Quarterly*; some of the women who founded Women in Distribution. If we hadn't known before *The Furies*, we knew when we were done how to organize ourselves and others, and how to establish functioning, productive political projects—particularly those related to media. Some of us still hold a vision of society that is free and just. Some of us still work diligently toward turning that vision into reality.

We're all 18 years older now, and of the Furies with whom I still have contact I can say that we are not as angry, not as naive, not as self-righteous. For that reason, perhaps, I doubt that any of us would take on now what we took on then, as outlined in the lead article of the very first issue:

> We want to build a movement in this country and in the world which can effectively stop the violent, sick, oppressive acts of male supremacy. We want to build a movement which makes all people free. For the Chinese women whose feet were bound and crippled; for the Ibibos of Africa whose clitori were mutilated; for every woman who has ever been raped, physically, economically, psychologically, we take the name of the FURIES, Goddesses of Vengeance and protectors of women.

APPENDIX 1: "*THE FURIES*"[1]

by Ginny Berson

The story of the Furies is the story of strong, powerful women, the "Angry Ones," the avengers of matricide, the protectors of women. Three Greek Goddesses, they were described (by men) as having snakes for hair, bloodshot eyes, and bats' wings; like Lesbians today, they were cursed and feared. They were born when Heaven (the male symbol) was castrated by his son at the urging of Earth (the female symbol). The blood from the wound fell on Earth and fertilized her, and the Furies were born. Their names were Alecto (Never-ceasing), Tisiphone (Avenger of Blood), and Magaera (Grudger). Once extremely powerful, they represented the supremacy of women and the primacy of mother right.

Their most famous exploit (famous because in it they lost much of their power) involved Orestes in the last episodes connected with the cycle of the Trojan War. Orestes, acting on the orders of the Sun God Apollo, killed his mother Clytemnestra, because she had killed his father. Clytemnestra had killed the father because he had sacrificed their daughter Iphigenia, in order to get favorable winds so his fleet could sail to Troy. The Furies tormented Orestes: they literally drove him crazy, putting him under a spell where for days he would not eat or wash his blood-stained hands. He bit off his finger to try to appease them, but to no avail. Finally, in desperation, Orestes went before the court of Athena to plead his case.

The point at issue was whether matricide was justifiable to avenge your father's murder, or in other words, whether men or women were to dominate. Apollo defended Orestes and totally denied the importance of motherhood, claiming that women were no more than sperm receptacles for men, and that the father was the only parent worthy of the name. One might have thought that Athena, Goddess of Wisdom, would have condemned Orestes, but Athena was the creation of the male God, Zeus, sprung full-grown from his head, the first token woman. Athena decided for Orestes. Some mythologists say that Zeus, Athena, and Apollo had conspired from the beginning, ordering Orestes to kill his mother in order to put an end, once and for all, to the religious belief that motherhood was more divine than fatherhood. In any case, that was the result.

The Furies were, of course, furious, and threatened to lay waste the city of Athens. But Athena had a direct line to Zeus, King of the Gods; she told the Furies to accept the new male supremacist order or lose everything. Some of the Furies and their followers relented, the rest pursued Orestes until his death.

We call our paper *The Furies* because we are also angry. We are angry because we are oppressed by male supremacy. We have been fucked over all our lives by a system which is based on the domination of men over women, which defines male as good and female as only as good as the man you are with. It is a system in which heterosexuality is rigidly enforced and Lesbianism rigidly suppressed. It is a system which has further divided us by class, race, and nationality.

We are working to change this system which has kept us separate and powerless for so long. We are a collective of twelve lesbians living and working in Washington, D.C. We are rural and urban; from the Southwest, Midwest, South and Northeast. Our ages range from 18 to 28. We are high school drop-outs and Ph.D candidates. We are lower class, middle and upper-middle class. We are white. Some of us have been Lesbians for twelve years, others for ten months. We are committed to ending all oppressions by attacking their roots—male supremacy.

We believe *The Furies* will make important contributions to the growing movement to destroy sexism. As a collective, in addition to outside projects, we are spending much time building an ideology which is the basis for action. For too long, women in the Movement have fallen prey to the very male propaganda they seek to refute. They have rejected thought, building an ideology, and all intellectual activity as the realm of men, and tried to build a politics based only on feelings—the area traditionally left to women. The philosophy has been, "If it feels good, it's O.K. If not, forget it." But that is like saying that strength, which is a "male" characteristic, should be left to men, and women should embrace weakness. Most straight women, to say nothing of men, feel afraid or contemptuous of Lesbians. That fear and contempt is similar to the feelings middle class whites have towards Blacks

or lower class people. These feelings are the result of our socialization and are hardly worth glorifying. This is not to say that feelings are irrelevant, only that they are derived from our experience which is limited by our class, race, etc. Furthermore, feelings are too often used to excuse inaction and inability to change.

A political movement cannot advance without systematic thought and practical organization. The haphazard, nonstrategic, zig-zag tactics of the straight women's movement, the male left, and many other so-called revolutionary groups have led only to frustration and dissolution. We do not want to make those same mistakes; our ideology forms the basis for developing long-range strategies and short-term tactics, projects, and actions.

The base of our ideological thought is: Sexism is the root of all other oppressions, and Lesbian and woman oppression will not end by smashing capitalism, racism, and imperialism. Lesbianism is not a matter of sexual preference, but rather one of political choice which every woman must make if she is to become woman-identified and thereby end male supremacy. Lesbians, as outcasts from every culture but their own have the most to gain by ending class, race, and national supremacy within their own ranks. Lesbians must get out of the straight women's movement and form their own movement in order to be taken seriously, to stop straight women from oppressing us, and to force straight women to deal with their own Lesbianism. Lesbians cannot develop a common politics with women who do not accept Lesbianism as a political issue.

In *The Furies* we will be dealing with these issues and sharing our thoughts with you. We want to build a movement in this country and in the world which can effectively stop the violent, sick, oppressive acts of male supremacy. We want to build a movement which makes all people free.

For the Chinese women whose feet were bound and crippled; for the Ibibos of Africa whose clitori were mutilated; for every woman who has ever been raped, physically, economically, psychologically, we take the name of *The Furies*, Goddesses of Vengeance and protectors of women.

The Furies, January 1972

NOTE

1. This article originally appeared in *The Furies* no.1 (January 1972). It was reprinted in *Lesbianism and the Women's Movement*, ed. by Nancy Myron and Charlotte Bunch. (San Francisco: Diana Press, 1975), 15-19. It is reprinted here with permission of Diana Press.

by Charlotte Bunch

The development of Lesbian-Feminist politics as the basis for the liberation of women is our top priority; this article outlines our present ideas. In our society which defines all people and institutions for the benefit of the rich, white male, the Lesbian is in revolt. In revolt because she defines herself in terms of women and rejects the male definitions of how she should feel, act, look, and live. To be a Lesbian is to love oneself, woman, in a culture that denegrates and despises women. The Lesbian rejects male sexual/political domination; she defies his world, his social organization, his ideology, and his definition of her as inferior. Lesbianism puts women first while the society declares the male supreme. Lesbianism threatens male supremacy at its core. When politically conscious and organized, it is central to destroying our sexist, racist, capitalist, imperialist system.

LESBIANISM IS A POLITICAL CHOICE

Male society defines Lesbianism as a sexual act, which reflects men's limited view of women: they think of us only in terms of sex. They also say Lesbians are not real women, so a real woman is one who gets fucked by men. We say that a Lesbian is a woman whose sense of self and energies, including sexual energies, center around women—she is woman identified. The woman-identified-woman commits herself to other women for political, emotional, physical, and economic support. Women are important to her. She is important to herself. Our society demands that commitment from women be reserved for men.

The Lesbian, woman-identified-woman, commits herself to women not only as an alternative to oppressive male/female relationships but primarily because she loves women. Whether consciously or not, by her actions, the Lesbian has recognized that giving support and love to men over women perpetuates the system that oppresses her. If women do not make a commitment to each other, which includes sexual love we deny ourselves the love and value traditionally given to men. We accept our second class status. When women do give primary energies to other women, then it is possible to concentrate fully on building a movement for our liberation.

Woman-identified Lesbianism is, then, more than a sexual preference, it is a political choice. It is political because relationships between men and women are essentially political, they involve power and dominance. Since the Lesbian actively rejects that relationship and chooses women, she defies the established political system.

LESBIANISM, BY ITSELF, IS NOT ENOUGH

Of course, not all Lesbians are consciously woman-identified, nor are all committed to finding common solutions to the oppression they suffer as women and Lesbians. Being a Lesbian is part of challenging male supremacy, but not the end. For the Lesbian or heterosexual woman, there is no individual solution to oppression.

The Lesbian may think that she is free since she escapes the personal oppression of the individual male/female relationship. But to the society she is still a woman, or worse, a visible Lesbian. On the street, at the job, in the schools, she is treated as an inferior and is at the mercy of men's power and whims. (I've never heard of a rapist who stopped because his victim was a Lesbian). This society hates women who love women, and so, the Lesbian, who escapes male dominance in her private home receives it doubly at the hands of male society; she is harassed, outcast, and shuttled to the bottom. Lesbians must become feminists and fight against woman oppression, just as feminists must become Lesbians if they hope to end male supremacy.

U.S. society encourages individual solutions, apolitical attitudes, and reformism to keep us from political revolt and out of power. Men who rule, and male leftists who seek to rule, try to depoliticize sex and the relations between men and women in order to prevent us from acting to end our oppression and challenging their power. As the question of homosexuality has become public, reformists define it as a private question of who you sleep with in order to sidetrack our understanding of the politics of sex. For the Lesbian-Feminist, it is not private; it is a political matter of oppression, domination, and power. Reformists offer solutions which make no basic changes in the system that oppresses us, solutions which keep power in the hands of the oppressor. The only way oppressed people end their oppression is by seizing power: People whose rule depends on the subordination of others do not voluntarily stop oppressing others. Our subordination is the basis of male power.

SEXISM IS THE ROOT OF ALL OPPRESSION

The first division of labor, in pre-history, was based on sex: men hunted, women built the villages, took care of children, and farmed. Women collectively controlled the land, language, culture, and the communities. Men were able to conquer women with the weapons that they developed for hunting when it became clear that women were leading a more stable, peaceful, and desirable existence. We do not know exactly how this conquest took place, but it is clear that the original imperialism was male over female: the male claiming the female body and her service as his territory (or property).

Having secured the domination of women, men continued this pattern of suppressing people, now on the basis of tribe, race, and class. Although there have been numerous battles over class, race, and nation during the past 3,000 years, none has brought the liberation of women. While these other forms of oppression must be ended, there is no reason to believe that our liberation will come with the smashing of capitalism, racism, or imperialism today. Women will be free only when we concentrate on fighting male supremacy.

Our war against male supremacy does, however, involve attacking the latter day dominations based on class, race, and nation. As Lesbians who are outcasts from every group, it would be suicidal to perpetuate these man-made divisions among ourselves. We have no heterosexual privileges, and when we publicly assert our Lesbianism, those of us who had them lose many of our class and race privileges. Most of our privileges as women are granted to us by our relationships to men (fathers, husbands, boyfriends) whom we now reject. This does not mean that there is no racism or class chauvinism within us, but we must destroy these divisive remnants of privileged behavior among ourselves as the first step toward their destruction in the society. Race, class, and national oppressions come from men, serve ruling class white men's interests, and have no place in a woman-identified revolution.

LESBIANISM IS THE BASIC THREAT TO MALE SUPREMACY

Lesbianism is a threat to the ideological, political, personal, and economic basis of male supremacy. The Lesbian threatens the ideology of male supremacy by destroying the lie about female inferiority, weakness, passivity, and by denying women's "innate" need for men. Lesbians literally do not need men (even for procreation if the science of cloning is developed).

The Lesbians' independence and refusal to support one man undermines the personal power that men exercise over women. Our rejection of heterosexual sex challenges male domination in its most individual and common form. We offer all women something better than submission to personal oppression. We offer the beginning of the end of collective and individual male supremacy. Since men of all races and classes depend on female support and submission for practical tasks and feeling superior, our refusal to submit will force some to examine their sexist behavior, to break down their own destructive privileges over other humans, and to fight against those privileges in other

men. They will have to build new selves that do not depend on oppressing women and learn to live in social structures that do not give them power over anyone.

Heterosexuality separates women from each other; it makes women define themselves through men; it forces women to compete against each other for men and the privilege which comes through men and their social standing. Heterosexual society offers women a few privileges as compensation if they give up their freedom: for example, mothers are respected and "honored," wives or lovers are socially accepted and given some economic and emotional security, a woman gets physical protection on the street when she stays with her man, etc. The privileges give heterosexual women a personal and political stake in maintaining the status quo.

The Lesbian receives none of these heterosexual privileges or compensations since she does not accept the male demands on her. She has little vested interest in maintaining the present political system since all of its institutions—church, state, media, health, schools—work to keep her down. If she understands her oppression, she has nothing to gain by supporting white rich male America and much to gain from fighting to change it. She is less prone to accept reformist solutions to women's oppression.

Economics is a crucial part of woman oppression, but our analysis of the relationship between capitalism and sexism is not complete. We know that Marxist economic theory does not sufficiently consider the role of women or Lesbians, and we are presently working on this area.

However, as a beginning, some of the ways that Lesbians threaten the economic system are clear: In this country, women work for men in order to survive, on the job and in the home. The Lesbian rejects this division of labor at its roots; she refuses to be a man's property, to submit to the unpaid labor system of housework and childcare. She rejects the nuclear family as the basic unit of production and consumption in capitalist society.

The Lesbian is also a threat on the job because she is not the passive/part-time woman worker that capitalism counts on to do boring work and be part of a surplus labor pool. Her identity and economic support do not come through men, so her job is crucial and she cares about job conditions, wages, promotion, and status. Capitalism cannot absorb large numbers of women demanding stable employment, decent salaries, and refusing to accept their traditional job exploitation. We do not understand yet the total effect that this increased job dissatisfaction will have. It is, however, clear that as women become more intent upon taking control of their lives, they will seek more control over their jobs, thus increasing the strains on capitalism and enhancing the power of women to change the economic system.

LESBIANS MUST FORM OUR OWN MOVEMENT TO FIGHT MALE SUPREMACY

Feminist-Lesbianism, as the most basic threat to male supremacy, picks up part of the Women's Liberation analysis of sexism and gives it force and direction. Women's Liberation lacks direction now because it has failed to understand the importance of heterosexuality in maintaining male supremacy and because it has failed to face class and race as real differences in women's behavior and political needs. As long as straight women see Lesbianism as a bedroom issue, they hold back the development of politics and strategies which would put an end to male supremacy and they give men an excuse for not dealing with their sexism.

Being a Lesbian means ending identification with, allegiance to, dependence on, and support of heterosexuality. It means ending your personal stake in the male world so that you join women, individually and collectively, in the struggle to end your oppression. Lesbianism is the key to liberation and only women who cut their ties to male privilege can be trusted to remain serious in the struggle against male dominance. Those who remain tied to men, individually or in political theory, cannot always put women first. It is not that heterosexual women are evil or do not care about women. It is because the very essence, definition, and nature of heterosexuality is men first. Every woman has experienced that desolation when her sister puts her man first in the final crunch: heterosexuality demands that she do so. As long as women still benefit from heterosexuality, receive its privileges and security, they will at some point have to betray their sisters, especially Lesbian sisters who do not receive those benefits.

Women in women's liberation have understood the importance of having meetings and other events for women only. It has been clear that dealing with men divides us and saps our energies and that it is not the job of the oppressed to explain our oppression to the oppressor. Women also have seen that collectively, men will not deal with their sexism until they are forced to do so. Yet, many of these same women continue to have primary relationships with men individually and do not understand why Lesbians find this oppressive. Lesbians cannot grow politically or personally in a situation which denies the basis of our politics: that Lesbianism is political, that heterosexuality is crucial to maintaining male supremacy.

Lesbians must form our own political movement in order to grow. Changes which will have more than token effects on our lives will be led by woman-identified Lesbians who understand the nature of our oppression and are therefore in a position to end it.

The Furies, January 1972

Bunch is now chair of the Women's Studies Department at Rutgers University, New Brunswick, NJ.

NOTE

1. This article originally appeared in *The Furies* no.1 (January 1972). It was reprinted in *Lesbianism and the Women's Movement*, ed. by Nancy Myron and Charlotte Bunch. (San Francisco: Diana Press, 1975), 29-37. It is reprinted here with permission of Diana Press.

— GINNY Z. BERSON —

KARL AND GROUCHO'S MARXIST DANCE: THE *COLUMBUS* (OHIO) *FREE PRESS* AND ITS PREDECESSORS IN THE COLUMBUS UNDERGROUND

Steve Abbott

A metal canister imprinted with "No. 264 Multiple Baton Shell—For Use By Trained Police Personnel Only" stands on a bookcase in the house I now own in Old North Columbus, a neighborhood sandwiched between the ever-changing Ohio State University area and comfortably middle-class Clintonville. Loaded with short pieces of dowel, these canisters were, along with tear gas and billy clubs, standard crowd dispersal materiel for urban police departments during the civil rights and Vietnam eras. This particular relic is part of a larger story, one perhaps partially explained by the books that surround it.

The writings of Malcolm X and Martin Luther King bump up against the poetry of Allen Ginsberg and Walt Whitman. Steinbeck's *The Grapes of Wrath* offers an echo to the turn-of-the-century urban deprivation chronicled by Jacob Riis' landmark *How the Other Half Lives*. Books on mysticism and religion blend with literature that has defined much of this century; the *I Ching* and *When God Was a Woman* share a shelf with Kafka's *The Trial* and Joseph Heller's *Catch-22*. Political extremes coexist comfortably here, where Tom Wolfe's *The Electric Kool-Aid Acid Test* and Abbie Hoffman's *Revolution for the Hell of It* rub covers with Marxist and anarchist treatises. Texts on drugs and sensual massage provide a counterpoint to analyses of racism and community organizing; a book on natural foods relaxes next to transcripts of congressional proceedings of the House Internal Security Committee.

What may appear to be a library tour is, rather, evidence of a personal odyssey that represents the

Abbott, a poet, writer, and faculty member at Columbus State Community College, lives in Columbus, where he is active in human services advocacy, Amnesty International, and literary events.

myriad influences and contending philosophies that typified the alternative/underground press during its heyday in the late 1960s and early 1970s. The *Columbus Free Press* (later the *Columbus Freepress*), in both its content and its internal struggles, reflected both its community and its time, a time filled with days of agony and days of wonder as the ideals of mystical transformation and principled political struggle contended for the lives of those involved.

When the *Free Press* hit the streets of Columbus, Ohio, in October 1970, it was the most recent in a string of underground papers published in the city during the previous three years. Two issues of an underground first appeared early in 1968 as an extension of the Free University set up in the community adjoining the sprawling Ohio State campus. Put together by a mixture of counterculturalists and political activists, the first issue called itself the *Free University Cosmic Cosmic*; the second, like a new child in the family, had its own name: *Gregory*. A third issue never appeared.

Later that year, in November, a similar but decidedly more political group produced the first issue of *The People Yes*. The previous year had seen a takeover of the OSU administration building by black students demanding changes in university policies (and the subsequent indictment of 34 on charges of "kidnapping" a university vice president) and the firing of a popular professor for burning his draft card. OSU had a small but active Students for a Democratic Society (SDS) chapter, and the area abutting the campus had sprouted a large hippie community with numerous shops, many located on "Pearl Alley," a string of clothing stores, head shops, import stores, and a teahouse on nearby 13th Avenue. *The People Yes* reflected the sometimes uneasy alliance between radical politics and hippie counterculture in its first edition, which mixed license numbers of unmarked police cars and ads for roach clips with the SDS's nomination of a pig for president and an article on conscientious objector counseling at a local church.

TPY covered the 1969 Counterinaugural following Richard Nixon's election, the ever-expanding war in Indochina, national and campus developments, and the ongoing police harassment of longhairs and political activists. A regular column, "Ask Doc Pettibone," responded to questions about basic countercultural concerns such as drugs and venereal disease, and much of its local news focused on links to national political issues—antiwar demonstrations and war research on campus. Its last issue appeared in May 1969. Later that year, Howard McHale and a few former *TPY* staff members published several issues of another paper, *Renaissance*, but it, too, soon went under.

By the summer of 1970, both the cultural and political landscape had changed dramatically. Woodstock had taken rock music and its countercultural trappings—if not its fading essence—to a mass level; the dark side of the same counterculture had been exposed by the Manson clan's murder spree and the debacle at the Rolling Stones concert at Altamont Speedway, where a young black man was knifed and stomped by Hell's Angels. In November 1969, the Vietnam Moratorium Committee had brought hundreds of thousands of demonstrators to Washington for the largest national antiwar demonstration in the nation's history. The Black Panthers were under increasing attack, as reflected most notably in the murder of Chicago Panther leader Fred Hampton.

Students had been shot by National Guardsmen at Kent State and by deputy sheriffs at Jackson State in May 1970. The mind-expanding possibilities of marijuana and LSD were being compromised by adulteration and by a heavy influx of amphetamines and the notorious sopors, "prescription hypnotic" depressants (also known as Quaaludes or methaqualone) that had begun to spread quickly throughout central Ohio. In the wake of these developments, *Purple Berries* (drawn from a line in the Crosby, Stills, and Nash post-nuclear holocaust song "Wooden Ships") appeared in June of 1970.

The tone of *Purple Berries* was the tone of a youth community that had seen the naked power of the nation's military, previously directed only at nonwhites, unleashed on Blanket Hill at Kent State one month before. Indiscriminate gassings and beatings by police and the occupation of the OSU campus by National Guard troops during the student strike that coincided with the killings had pushed thousands of moderate students and community residents to question their cherished ideals of justice for all, honest government, and friendly policemen. *Purple Berries* was political, angry, and street tough, a reflection of the persona of its driving force, yippie Steve Conliff, whose expansive, insightful article-tirades represented the action-faction approach to alternative media and the most in-your-face style yet in Columbus underground writing.

Purple Berries published eight issues between June and December, during that time being an uncompromising voice promoting the antiwar/anti-imperialist movement while championing the cause of "freaks" of the socio-political counterculture community who were the constant victims of police harassment. *Purple Berries* linked the actions of the U.S. government in Vietnam and in minority communities to the day-to-day intimidation and arrest of longhairs who smoked marijuana and listened to rock music—a less polemical, less sexist, and more humorous version of White

Panther Party politics, minus the belief that rock 'n' roll was inherently revolutionary. (The paper, in fact, was printed on equipment operated by Mike Howard, a local White Panther whose Wildflower Collective became the Columbus alternative community's primary printer of leaflets and broadsides, as well as sponsor of free concerts and fundraisers for progressive community groups.) The paper's aggressiveness and total involvement with street life, however, typified the approach of the underground press: don't simply report news; *make* it and, like the corporate press, define what news is important to your community.

For example, in response to frequent police harassment and arrests of street people on petty pretexts—disorderly conduct, intoxication, possession of hallucinogens, vagrancy—in front of a popular local fast food outlet, the BBF (shortened from its sixties appellation of Burger Boy Food-o-rama), *Purple Berries* challenged the power structure in a series of articles that advocated individual rights and community control. Minor skirmishes with BBF management and Columbus police grew into a sharp clash later that summer between the police D Platoon riot squad and hundreds of street people; in the fall of 1971, the same locale and the same issue would result in a riot that rivaled those of the spring of 1970.

Unfortunately, *Purple Berries* had ceased to exist by that time. Like so many other publications, *Purple Berries* struggled with money, apathy, and the factionalism of its community. Money problems eventually pulled the paper under following its December issue, its dire financial condition noted in its printed cover and mimeographed inner pages.

By that time, though, a new voice was already rising in its place. Even as *PB* had begun publishing the previous summer, another, decidedly less radical group of people, which included me, was already planning yet another paper. A journalism student and part-time employee of the OSU Libraries, I had been approached by another library employee, Bill Quimby, early in the summer of 1970. The student riots and the 18-day shutdown of the campus that spring had changed many people's views and opened large numbers to the possibility that the radical-liberal opposition might be on to something, and he wanted to start a publication to address that group. Initially, his idea was that of a digest of radical-liberal thought, drawing from other alternative and radical publications and creating our own commentary along the way. Another OSU student, Paul Ricciardo, was also interested.

We chose the safe, hopelessly bland name *Columbus Free Press* (in some ways reflecting our own politics at the time), rented a typewriter, and set to work. Bill and Paul hustled ads, Paul recruited a few other interested folks, I wrote a piece and, being the only person with any journalism background, directed layout. With the work of Sandi Quimby, Cheryl Betz, John Hunt, Roger Doyle, and assorted artists and hangers-on, we pulled together the first issue, an 8-pager, in a garage apartment on West 8th Avenue and hit the streets on October 21, 1970, with 2,000 copies that we sold for 15 cents apiece. Articles on Vietnam Veterans Against the War, Jimi Hendrix, and a mass demonstration against Nixon at an Ohio Statehouse speech, a reprint of a Julius Lester critique of white radicals, and reflections on the indictments of 25 Kent State students for activities the prior May 3-4—supported by six paid ads and free ads for the local tenants union and drug crisis center—made up the paper's initial content.

The second issue, which we sold for 20 cents, led with a cover story on the involvement of undercover Ohio highway patrol officers in a student strike action that had precipitated a confrontation with police and led to the subsequent riots. (In a photo taken by a highway patrolman, Paul Ricciardo himself appeared standing between the two undercover agents.) Sporting a new masthead drawn by my high school friend and Cheryl Betz's roommate Jude Angelo and featuring the words "An Alternative Newspaper Serving An Alternative Culture," the paper included reports on Vietnamese opposition groups and the Revolutionary People's Constitutional Convention, an Underground Press Syndicate reprint from San Francisco's *Good Times* (on rock music as a means of social control), an Allen Ginsberg article on the destructive impact of amphetamines, and a book review of Neil Postman's *Teaching as a Subversive Activity*. Like almost every other underground of the time, it included a plea for street sellers and interested participants. The layout had improved, and the *Free Press* looked something like a newspaper.

At the time, the *Free Press* had no coherent philosophy or clear political perspective. Bill Quimby's background was old-style loyal-opposition liberal; Paul Ricciardo's and my own were vaguely left-liberal pacifist, with active participation in the antiwar movement and the previous spring's student strike and a freak lifestyle being our points in common. My own politics came out of work with the War Resisters League, my cultural interests from the blues, rock music, and poetry. Our views would always be among the more moderate of the *Free Press*' positions.

As political conditions in Columbus, and nationwide, became increasingly more repressive, those moderate views meshed uncomfortably with the demands by others on the staff for stronger response to these repressive conditions.

The fourth issue of the paper, appearing in January 1971, printed on the front page and inner pages the entire text of the Weather Underground's "New Morning, Changing Weather" communiqué; in it, they outlined the emerging types of political oppositions, many not linked to their own armed struggle except in a spirit of throwing off the control of white male domination.

The centerfold, black ink on yellow paper, was a poster of three GIs with peace symbols on their helmets walking through a rice paddy, framed by the slogan, "Smoke Pot Where You Work—They Do." The ads had the unmistakeable mark of Jude Angelo's light touch. And the general community response had been good.

The *Freep*'s situation, like its time, was full of contradictions, not the least of which was its printer. The paper was printed on the presses of *The Times*, a small weekly paper located in the rural community of Canal Winchester, southeast of Columbus. In Dick Eckleberry, its editor and publisher, the *Free Press* found a conservative who believed strongly in freedom of the press. In addition to publishing the weekly paper, he printed numerous circulars for local grocery chains; when lumber strikes in Canada threatened to reduce availability of newsprint in 1971, Eckleberry assured us that the *Free Press* would be printed even if it meant not having paper for his more lucrative commercial work. As he told us this, a framed picture of Barry Goldwater smiled at us from the wall behind his desk. Eckleberry kept his word, and he never raised any questions about the paper's content. Interesting times....

Unlike the staffs of *The People Yes* and *Purple Berries*, people working on the *Free Press* were not at that point involved closely with political groups, and the tone of the paper reflected a more detached attitude even on local issues. Still, other influences were evident. By late January, participation from representatives of OSU's Gay Liberation Front and a number of local feminists, including Mimi Morris (the pseudonymous Angela Motorman from *Purple Berries*) and OSU grad student Margaret Chisholm, was beginning to broaden the paper's perspective. New staff members Greg Frazier and Tom Moore showed up regularly to write and work on layout. Content ranged from analyses of events in Indochina to reprints of Furry Freak Brothers comix, from recipes for cooking with curry to reports of raids on local black activists.

Tradewinds, a local head shop/import store, served as the distribution point for street vendors. The store's merchandise and appearance had a definite *Free Press* feel: glass cases displayed pipes, rolling papers, handmade jewelry, and natural soaps; racks of India-print bedspreads and Mexican peasant shirts were topped with shelves holding incense, candles, massage oils, and books of Eastern philosophy and radical politics; the walls were covered with rock music silkscreens and political posters; and the bulletin board by the door was splashed with announcements of demonstrations, consciousness-raising groups, and concerts.

Tradewinds' owners had operated a shop on Pearl Alley during the days of *The People Yes*. In addition to the paper's own post office box, Tradewinds became a drop-off point for ideas, articles, and information for the *Free Press* and a gathering place for hangers-on. Owners Judy Christopher, Alice Lehman, and Libby Gregory gave the *Free Press* a highly visible presence on High Street, the main drag through the campus area. Later, when Columbus police arrested numerous staff members and its regular office seemed unsafe, the paper would be put together in Tradewinds' basement.

THE STRAINS OF CHANGE

By early 1971, internal staff conflicts that had been only subtly bothersome the previous October when the first issue hit the streets began to emerge as major psychological strains. Changes sweeping the culture of the larger Movement that the paper sought to serve added to this internal pressure.

At the time, *Free Press* content had a strong cultural/entertainment base, an undefined counterculture air buttressed by support for radical-liberal politics. Articles on growing marijuana faced reports on speeches by Angela Davis; record reviews and Sandi Quimby's wonderful (and inexpensive!) cooking recipes followed reports on demonstrations and trials. The paper was trying to maintain Bill Quimby's initial vision of being both a digest of the alternative press and a journal of its community's more immediate concerns. Its advertisers included concert promoters and "hip capitalists" of the local freak community, whose politics and attitudes were often highly suspect, but whose support helped pay our way.

In the May 17 issue, *Purple Berries* founder Steve Conliff brought his caustic, insightful style to the *Free Press* for the first time with a report on the recent Mayday actions in the nation's capital. In the same issue, an article by Margaret Chisholm and Sandi Quimby entitled "Freep Feminism: A Declaration" enumerated a series of putdowns of women by local male politicos and business owners, most evident among them being the continuing assumptions that men were the only leaders in the hip/radical community (and in the *FP*) and that women were to play traditional roles even within the so-called alternative culture. The article concluded:

> Take note, groovy-radical male chauvinist Columbus. Women of the *Columbus Free Press* hereby renounce pseudo-feminism and liberalism. No longer will we resign ourselves to piggish, put-down treatment from male movement light-weights or heavies "just for the sake of the paper." Peace and harmony, love and power, no longer take precedence over our self-respect.
>
> In the past we have endured your insults in order to preserve solidarity in the Columbus radical community. We now perceive that community built upon the subservient chattel status of half its members is a sham. We are tired of being told we do not understand "The Revolution." A revolution that excludes half the population is hardly a revolution. It is not radical.
>
> It is not even reform.

The article was accompanied by an Abbie Hoffman quote—"The only alliance I would make with the women's liberation movement is in bed"—and a passage from Mao Zedong's "Combat Liberalism." The times they were a-changin'.

And they were changing in ways none of us truly understood. How could we? All of us—female and male; gay and straight; black and white; anarchist and centralist; laid-back and revved-up; violent and pacifist; dopers and democrats; rockers and Maoists; anti-authoritarians and anti-imperialists; a confusing convergence of the disaffected, disenfranchised, disillusioned, and disestablishmentarian—were vaguely united in the belief that the country operated in direct opposition to its espoused values, and that we as individuals and collectives had to do something about it, in our own interest and in the interest of the entire globe. The dream was a command.

We were feeling our way through emotions and perceptions about the need for immediate, apocalyptic change. The essential inequities of the political and social system had led some to a principled critique of, and opposition to, the existing order; others had become simply iconoclasts opposing the structures and strictures of the predominant (white male) culture.

We were experiencing personal and political changes that we could not fully grasp even as we advocated them, changes that put us at odds with our pre-existing sense of who we were as individuals and as Americans. The future shock of history that had launched every post-World War II change—civil rights, rock 'n roll, national liberation movements, rapidly ev-

olving gender consciousness, protest actions, increased use of mind-altering drugs, growing tension between the individual and the mass society—had become a wave in the mid-1960s and, as the seventies began, had grown to a tide sweeping the world.

We believed that individually we could make a difference and collectively we could change the world. It was a rebirth of wonder.

The entire next issue of the *Free Press* was a women's issue; no male staff members worked on the 20-page paper (only the second to run 20 pages), which covered plays and music, radical motherhood, women's conferences, psychology, and struggles in the workplace, particularly offices. Its content, like other more generalized issues of the paper, combined post-hippie gentleness, anger-driven insight, and no-nonsense critique, and became the city's first public forum for a wide range of feminist concerns and an accurate reflection of the diversity of the women's movement.

Subsequent issues presented more local news and the initial appearance of Zorba the Freak, who would become one of the community's great mythic characters. Writing under the name Leon Karg, Steve Conliff created the persona of Zorba, "leader of the street people," whose utterances to "hippie fella" Karg revealed the political undertones of issues in an acerbic, wildly funny style that anyone could understand—and learn from. In his first appearance, Zorba took on the turf issue of street people vs. the BBF; the Yippies had been active all summer around the issue, and a number of demonstrations, one including flyers for a "When Will It Burn?" sweepstakes, had led to confrontations and arrests. The "community control" aspects of the conflict had even drawn support from local Marxist and anti-imperialist groups. We wanted self-determination at all levels.

By the beginning of the second year of the paper, another trend had revealed itself: individuals representing various constituencies emphasized their particular issues during brief periods of activism on the paper. When several members of OSU's Gay Activist Alliance worked on the *Free Press*, for instance, more articles on gay issues appeared.

INTERNAL DISSENSION

In volume 2, number 2, late in 1971, staff differences burst into the open with the front-page printing of an open letter from Steve Conliff under the heading "Up Against the Wall, *Free Press*" in white letters on a brick-wall background. In the previous issue, an article on the murder of revolutionary black leader George Jackson in Soledad Prison had run opposite an "Entertainment Guide"; in his letter, Conliff assailed the paper's focus on entertainment as disturbingly reflecting a "bread and circuses" approach to activism, protested the editing of references to revolutionary violence from his articles, and generally decried much of the paper's content as repetitive and liberal. His views, he said, were representative of those of many in the community "working toward a revolution in Amerika."

Although the *Free Press* had no named editor, I functioned as *de facto* editor and was largely responsible for the editing of articles. In fact, my own more liberal, culturally oriented politics had often been reflected in many articles. Coming out of a pacifist orientation which I was beginning to question seriously, I represented the less militant wing of the paper's staff. The paper's printed response acknowledged some of Conliff's criticisms and generally said it was doing the best it could, but no one knew then how true one line from the Conliff letter was: "things can't go on the way they have been going." The next few issues would make clear how rapidly "things," and the paper, were changing.

Everything was in flux. The paper was being produced in the large front room of an apartment rented by Bill and Sandi Quimby on High Street north of OSU. More people were swirling into the paper's charged, exhilarating operation and politics: photographer Evan Morris (brother of Mimi) and, occasionally, Chuck McCoy, both with experience on *The People Yes*; former marine and OSU law school professor John Quigley; gay activist Jeff Arnold; Mike Jaschik and White Panther John Miernik; Tradewinds owners Alice Lehman and Libby Gregory; and Fred Andrle, a former college media instructor who, as advisor to the Ohio Wesleyan campus radio station, had allowed the studio's on-the-air destruction after the school administration condemned the shack that housed it.

Burned out from *Free Press* work, a part-time job, and classwork for my final quarter at OSU, I temporarily withdrew from the paper early in October.

It seemed that every political and cultural activist in the country was a marked person. Official harassment, intimidation, and even outright assault by both street cops and right-wing groups were widespread, and to most of us the nation and our own community seemed to be approaching fascism. Earlier in 1971, a local white supremacist group, the Minutemen, had distributed a list of "traitors" marked for death; everyone on the list was some combination of feminist, black, liberal, or radical. Articles appearing, often buried, even in mainstream publications revealed government contingency plans for suspending elections, declaring martial law, and interning political dissidents. Antiwar demonstrators were routinely attacked by police or hardhat labor unionists. Every day brought news of a new outrage in Indochina, in the courts, or on the street, and people's public and private worlds were routinely jolted to higher levels of intensity.

Nixon had called antiwar demonstrators "bums," and within weeks soldiers on a college campus had shot protesters; Vice President Spiro Agnew incited parents against their children, and a father in Michigan killed his daughter and her "hippie" friends. In a short time, the government's COINTELPRO (Counter-Intelligence Program) operation of spying, sabotage, and disinformation against domestic political activists would be exposed. A letter to the paper claimed, "Real genocide (final-solution type) is for real here...."

The *Free Press* was not unaware that it had begun to rock the local political boat. Police harassment of street vendors and specific staff members was not uncommon. Although most of its outlets and audience were in the Ohio State area, the paper was expanding. John Miernik had begun selling ads, the advertising base was growing, and more stores around the city, even in shopping malls, were carrying the paper. We began doing outreach to local high schools and making contacts with antiwar and students' rights activists throughout the county.

Early in November, the old turf issue at the BBF exploded into a four-hour riot up and down High Street and onto the OSU campus. Hundreds of people were arrested, scores—including many uninvolved students attacked when county sheriff's deputies stormed into the Student Union building during the street battle—were beaten, and much of the area was gassed. The next issue of the *Free Press* covered both the riot and its aftermath in the courts; a separate article offered "legal self-defense" tips for use on the street or in street actions. Local labor strikes were given prominent play, and a front-page story by rock musician and music reviewer Cheryl Helm covered a different and chilling topic: a Los Angeles police informer's story of a plan by the FBI and Los Angeles police to use *agents provocateur* to justify martial law in order to thwart the rising tide of opposition to the Nixon government.

The first *Free Press* split—more accurately a purge—happened in this apocalyptic atmosphere. Several staff members as a delegation visited me and asked if I would return to the paper to lend support to an effort to oust Bill Quimby; I agreed to at least attend the meeting where a new direction for the paper would be argued. The meeting took place at the *Free Press* "office" at the Quimbys' apartment, where it quickly rose to a shouting match as various Yippies and staff feminists, most notably Cheryl Betz, with whom I was living, argued with Bill Quimby and denounced him for sexist behavior. The meeting ended with Quimby quitting and ordering everyone out of his house.

The next day, in a scene played out in many versions in the alternative press, the *Free Press* files, layout materials, mailing lists, and various equipment were spirited away in the back of a station wagon. As the winter season began, the paper found itself in the basement of John Quigley's half-double on Indiana Avenue. There, with work tables squeezed between the furnace and a wall covered with revolutionary posters (as well as our own "Smoke Pot Where You Work" exhortation), the *Free Press* began to shape a new identity.

A strong viewpoint supporting the National Liberation Front in Vietnam appeared in succeeding issues of the paper as Colin Neiburger, late of Weatherman and active in the Gay Activist Alliance, joined a staff who were in various forms connected, either by membership or frequent participation, with most of the progressive organizations in the community, regardless of their political or countercultural slant.

The left-radical community in Columbus had never been large. Although it included thousands of freaks, most were involved more in the counterculture-dropout aspect of alternatives than in the political organizing aspect. They listened to rock music, followed local bands, took drugs, worked marginal jobs, and hung out; they opposed the war because they or someone they knew might have to go, or because they didn't particularly like authority or government telling them what to do. This brand of self-determination differed significantly from the more "informed," even intellectual, approach of many "political" activists who were so serious they wouldn't dance. The social and political upheaval of the time generated a self-righteous sense of purity and certainty about how things should be even as day-to-day events and changing personal and political relationships showed how uncertain the times really were. Our collective philosophy careened between two Marxisms, Karl's and Groucho's. It was a wild dance.

THE "CRAZY HORSE APPROACH"

Strange coalitions were the order of the day. Members of the Progressive Labor Party would show up at Yippie actions against BBF; anarchists and street people would rally around Young Socialist Alliance banners at antiwar demonstrations. The Indochina Coalition, formed in the spring of 1972, was a virtual rainbow of political shadings that brought together the entire range of antiwar sentiment to organize mass actions. If any single group had organized a demonstration, ridiculous factionalism (aptly satirized later in Monty Python's movie *The Life of Brian*) might have prevented a large turnout, but when different groups worked together the impact was multiplied. Coalition groups came to support each other on issues other than the war. One radical called it "the Crazy Horse approach: it's the same warriors showing up at different points on the ridge top."

With a regular office for the paper, the staff grew. Suzie Bird provided regular artwork; Margaret Sarber, a former SDS member and now a White Panther and Indochina Coalition leader, contributed occasional articles and did layout, as did Tradewinds owner Judy Christopher. Scott Williams, a Tenants Union organizer and independent activist, covered a variety of issues. Legal worker and former *TPY* staffer Sue Urbas shot photos. Many staff wrote under both their own names and a variety of pen names to protect their identities and to create shadow personae for police to wonder about, a strategy reflective of their strong anarchist and Yippie sentiment.

Free Press staff were in the center of much of what was happening. In February of 1972, Burton Cantrell, a minister, man of peace, and director of the Wesley Foundation, the Methodist student center near the OSU campus, agreed to provide free office space to a number of community groups. The Columbus Community Food Co-op set up in the basement, and the Columbus Tenants Union and the *Free Press* moved into a shared office on the first floor. The Wesley Foundation became a center for community social and political activity where we planned, argued, celebrated, agitated, and danced.

In an effort to form its own "more perfect union," members of the Columbus Community Co-op, the Columbus Tenants Union, and the *Free Press*, along with members of the Open Door Clinic and Switchboard, the local crisis center, had formed the Community Union late in 1971. CU's goals were to provide a focal point for community alternatives—food, medical care, housing, media—and eventually to create a community center where these alternatives could be centralized and independently run. From the beginning, however, the Community Union suffered from its inability to work with large-scale democracy. The clinic and Switchboard were never very active in CU, but in the other three groups factions formed quickly.

One of the Community Union's primary issues was community control of police; as the alternative community's mouthpiece, the *Free Press* was a militant representative of the community distrust of and animosity toward police. The Columbus police were the enforcement arm of the dominant culture; its casual harassment of and violence towards blacks, gays and lesbians, freaks, and political activists were widely known in those communities and largely ignored in local media, particularly *The Columbus Dispatch*, which was owned by the powerful and conservative Wolfe family.

The *Free Press* covered CU's efforts to organize people around the need for a civilian review board to investigate police actions and exposed undercover police infiltration of community meetings. Community organizations were my "beat" in the paper; clashes between tenants and landlords or police and citizens were regular copy. The *Free Press* took straight aim at the Columbus police department, both in news articles by me and in more impassioned features by Steve Conliff. In a March 1972 issue covering a meeting demanding community control, I wrote that the police were "the best organized gang in town":

> The Police Department...runs itself. Tightly organized and ready to mobilize every civic group, news medium, and "patriotic" organization in the city against any threat to its presumptuous sovereignty posed by people it allegedly serves. The Columbus Police Department. Our very own military overseer.

In an article titled "Soporboppers: Serving the Pig," Steve Conliff drew the connection between the too-popular drug Quaalude and its impact on people's ability to resist police repression. Columbus was a popular test market for consumer products, and Conliff made an interesting case for government collusion in the "marketing" and distribution of depressants in the local freak community. Like heroin in minority communities, sopors reinforced a sense of listlessness and mindlessness, and police found users easy targets for arrest and good sources as informers. Conliff voiced the attitudes of many:

> Weed is a revolutionary drug because most people function at least as well on it as they do straight.... But I fear that catatonic sopor heads won't fare too well in the street fighting. What saves us in the streets is our mobility and our brains, and fucked-up people exhibit little of either.

All this points up how the Vietnam era was not simply political upheaval in the traditional sense of demonstrations, collectives, position papers, and cadres; it was a dizzying mix of traditional political actions and eclectic social experimentation. While many activists remained true to the models provided by radicals historically, and in turn kept themselves separate, serious, and "politically correct," the social impact of music, drugs, and a variety of alternative lifestyles, living arrangements, and relationships created a curious and sometimes perplexing blend of militant purpose, self-deprecating humor, hippie self-indulgence, cosmic flair, and the contradictions embodied in meshing them.

Bemused, we wondered aloud to what extent we were, in the words of an underground comix character, "bourgeois anarchists on an ego trip." Our *lives* were poems, political acts; how much of the re-creation we were going through was also recreation?

An "Open Letter to the Masses" in the March 15, 1972, *Free Press* noted conflicts within both the Community Union and the community at large:

> [W]hile "hippies" or "freaks" may in the early days have been predominantly middle class white kids, many of them merely out slumming prior to their eventual return to the corporate management power elite, today, through instantaneous communication and marijuana, a certain convergence of cultures has occurred. Woodstock Nation has absorbed a certain amount of input from the black experience, the Puerto Rican experience, the white greaser experience, the female experience, the military experience, the gay experience, the junkie experience, the prison experience, the daily unabating oppression of the poor experience; and the Counter-culture has increasingly come to resemble a class—a sort of cross between lumpen bourgeoisie and nouveau proletariat.
>
> But perhaps it would be more accurate to say that the Counter-culture has become a microcosm of the class system, for there exist classic Marxist class antagonisms between the penniless, vagrant, unemployed street person and the young, hip, suburban, dope-smoking liberal.
>
> Community-originating alternative institutions...have, more than anything else, fulfilled the communist slogan "Serve The People" on a practical, day-to-day basis, and have epitomized what we are supposed to be about.
>
> We are about people.
>
> But these alternative institutions are not ends unto themselves. Our food co-ops do not feed starving Latin American children—whom the US is starving; and our crashpads do not house Bengali refugees—who were driven from their homes by US-armed and -supported military; and our underground papers have not stopped the murderous bombing of Southeast Asia—by guess who. If freaks or youth or even Americans are the only people whose interests we serve, we are still imperialists, raping and pillaging the Third World for our own material comfort.

As a member of the Underground Press Syndicate, the *Freep* exchanged papers with dozens of other publications throughout the United States and Canada. We used them as sources for features, graphics, and posters, one of which encapsulated our approach to what we were doing. Reprinted from Washington, DC's *Quicksilver Times*, the poster proclaimed a determined, perhaps fatalistic, almost smug reminder: "There are two things you have to remember about making a revolution. One is that we're going to get our asses kicked. The other is that we're going to win."

As the antiwar movement grew locally and nationally, and our own community showed increasing diversity in its efforts at self-determination, the *Freep*'s staff spun through a bracing whirl of discussions, jobs, leaflets, meetings, concerts, trips, demonstrations, parties, and production work. We recognized the strength our work had generated.

When the Community Union leadership endorsed two liberal friends for local Democratic Party ward committee seats, disputes intensified. In an article titled "Unholy Alliance?" Conliff denounced the CU leadership and its exclusivity; many felt the CU was being too liberal while others, basically in agreement with the dissidents, felt the level of conflict was unraveling what was a good-faith attempt at achieving necessary goals. Most *FP* staff thought we were being co-opted. How much the community would participate in existing political structures was an issue that cut deeply—and often.

We struggled with our contradictions. One article penned by Angela Motorman noted the recent prison releases of Angela Davis and Ted Berrigan as an introduction to an article on the imprisonment of Ralph Ginzburg, publisher of *Screw* magazine, after losing a 10-year-old appeal of an obscenity conviction. "As a feminist," she wrote, "I'm no fan of skin magazines, even self-proclaimed intellectual skin magazines, and personally I don't care much for Ginzburg's style, but as a civil libertarian I can't let this one pass unnoticed....It's always easier to support the struggles of people whose politics and lifestyle you can identify with or at least admire. I still think Ralph Ginzburg is a slimy bastard, but I don't think he belongs in jail." The staff agreed to run the article with a headline chosen by the writer: "Creep Jailed."

The Indochina Coalition, many of whose members were *Free Press* staff, organized regular demonstrations against the war. The paper covered and supported efforts in state prisons to organize the Ohio Prisoners Labor Union (OPLU). In a front-page article, I wrote of the killing of an alleged drug dealer by Columbus police narcotics agents and called for a grand jury indictment of the murderers. In releases from Liberation News Service (LNS), Underground Press Syndicate (UPS), and other undergrounds, we reported on FBI informants who helped plan a break-in at the Camden, New Jersey, draft office and another agent who attempted to sell weapons to the Kent State Vietnam

Veterans Against the War. We knew that police had the paper and members of its staff under surveillance; anxiety about infiltration by informants rose and fell.

This activism and militant anti-police stance led to the arrest, in May 1972, of several staff and numerous other local activists the day after a large demonstration protesting the mining of Haiphong Harbor in North Vietnam and the resumption of saturation bombing by U.S. warplanes in Indochina. Police attacked demonstrators blocking a main street near OSU and the next day charged Margaret Sarber, John Miernik, Colin Neiburger, and former OSU student body president Jerry Friedman with inciting to riot; I was charged with riot and malicious destruction of property. Two progressive lawyers who had been at the scene prior to the street battle were also arrested, one as he was trying to obtain the release of *Free Press* staff. Still, an eight-page *Free Press*, produced in the basement of Tradewinds, hit the street on schedule, with a Suzie Bird cover drawing of Margaret and John under the heading "Staff Jailed!"

The next full issue of the paper followed the tradition of *The People Yes* and *Purple Berries* by running a list of license numbers of undercover police cars along with "Pig Pix," photos of undercover police. The license numbers had been obtained by a staff member during his lock-up in the city prison, where one range overlooked a police parking lot.

That summer, many staff joined thousands of other activists at the Republican Convention in Miami Beach. There, *Freep* women were among the most combative with right-wing locals who prowled the demonstrators' campsite in Flamingo Park, harassing gays and females. We returned to Columbus with cracked heads, bail papers, large strips of decorative patriotic bunting, and renewed energy.

The paper had an intense local focus, covering tenants' strikes, the prosecution of a local black leader, and the efforts of Ohio Penitentiary inmates to get better treatment. In the issue following our return from Miami, Steve Conliff and I described the surreal events that had taken place. The cover of that issue included a box that brought the events together: "Pigs Harass/Tenants Win/CIA Plots/Prisons Boil."

My own views had swung around. Having decided early to resist the draft, I was now convinced that the moral-witness act of turning myself in on the steps of the federal courthouse would be, in the existing political climate, an empty gesture. Nevertheless, I decided, if I was drafted I would not be pushed out of the country to Canada with other expatriates. The war was at home; I would go underground and continue to actively oppose the war from inside the United States. My draft lottery number was 116; the call-up for the year at my draft board reached 109.

The history of the underground press is incomplete without acknowledgment of the influence of drugs. Most *Free Press* staff used hallucinogens—marijuana and LSD. A few occasionally used speed, but all scorned the use of most other drugs, particularly sopors, which were prevalent on the street and regularly denounced in *Free Press* articles as counter-revolutionary because they dulled awareness rather than enhancing it. The same issue of a paper that featured gross caricatures of Nixon and Kissinger on the cover and an analysis of the politics of rape inside might have a cartoon on the back cover exhorting youth to "Build a better Amerika—Get stoned!"

We saw no contradiction; we embodied it. While more dogmatic activists shunned drugs as inherently counter-revolutionary, and while the mainstream press saw only "hippies" *or* "radicals," the *Free Press*, like its predecessors, encompassed both and included as staff members many who *were* both—not as separate viewpoints but as part of a larger liberation that included anti-imperialism, sexual freedom, and expanded consciousness, all operating to the sounds of mainstream and underground rock music and their exhortations to social and psychic change. Many a long night of layout (and countless other activities) included sessions to discuss issues and smoke a joint or two. It was a part of everyday life.

Articles on Indochina or the Black Panthers ran side by side with comix from Milwaukee's *Bugle-American*; "The Continuing Story of God" comix, from Houston's *Hooka*, might appear on the page after an analysis of racism. Hippie culture mixed with political activism, spinning a synthesis that was alternately—and even at once—impassioned, Communist, pagan, rational, flippant, mystical, hermaphroditic, anarchist, stoned, self-righteous, serious, whimsical, disciplined, and hedonistic.

We had grown up through one of the most dramatic economic expansions in history following a war in which the economic strength of every other major country in the world had been literally or virtually destroyed. We had been brought up believing in liberty and justice for all, standing up for the oppressed, and making the world a better place. We had come to take ideals seriously and "reality" less so—or maybe more so; it was difficult to tell. We saw connections between the civil rights struggle and the gay rights struggle; we saw connections between ball-and-chain slavery and wage slavery; we saw connections between our own War of Independence and the desire of other peoples for the same opportunity our young country had: to form their own govern-ment—of the *people*, by the *people*, for the *people*—and make their own mistakes.

We learned how the U.S. government had picked up the remains of the British and French colonial systems in Southeast Asia and Africa, sheltered Nazis, undermined popular governments, blacklisted and even killed its own domestic opponents, and persecuted minorities at home while propping up dictators abroad. We had come to realize that our culture was, by inertia and/or design, a machine in which we would become small cogs, automatons programmed to consume prepackaged products, prepackaged ideas, and prepackaged futures. We had seen the birth of a sexual revolution that, unlike most other social movements in the world, was out of straight men's control because women and gays had begun to challenge the male definition of sexuality.

And we had grown up with the Beats, and with music: be-bop and doo-wop, and folk music, and the gospel and spirituals of the civil rights movement, and Bob Dylan, and rock 'n' roll. We had danced to Little Richard, Janis Joplin, the Beatles, and Aretha Franklin, and gotten stoned and tripped to Pink Floyd and Jefferson Airplane. The music was the soundtrack, and sometimes the statement, of our lives: "Four dead in Ohio…Goddamn the pusher man…We can be together…Some folks inherit star-spangled eyes/Oo, they'll send you down to war…There's something happening here/What it is ain't exactly clear…Bring the boys home…And it's 1-2-3, what are we fightin' for?…War, children, is just a shot away…We got to live together…One toke over the line…I'd love to turn you on…How she walked like a woman and talked like a man…We shall overcome…."

For a while either Mimi Morris or I would call WCOL-FM, the underground radio station, and request Thunderclap Newman's "Something in the Air." As the staff labored through the night, the radio would announce a song "for the staff of the *Columbus Free Press*," and the office would fill with the song's chorus: "We got to get together sooner or later/Because the Revolution's here/And you know it's right."

And like the music itself, our lives and our beliefs were changing rapidly: how we saw ourselves as a nation in the world, as women and men, as human beings, as free individuals who were part of a larger striving for self-definition and community. For many of us, that search for self-definition included psychoactive drugs; we were both activists and psychoactivists.

A week before the 1972 election, many *Freep* staff and friends gathered for a Halloween exorcism of demons from the local headquarters of the Committee to Re-Elect the President. A massive police presence turned out to confront The Good Fairy, The Invisible Man, Aunt Jemima, several Vietnamese peasants, and a variety of wayward spirits seeking peace. Unamused police told us, "We're going to kick your asses." (Mama said there'd be days like this...) Yippie!

But always, the antiwar struggle and the resistance to repression unified us. Not planning to put out a paper at Christmas, we changed our minds and ran off a 4-page mimeographed publication, "Cow Town Times—a holiday substitute for the *Columbus Free Press*," when we received word from a serviceman that large numbers of B-52 bombers and KC-135 refueling tankers were moving through Wright-Patterson Air Force Base near Dayton as part of a massive mobilization aimed at bombing Vietnam during the holidays. Other headlines included "Juries See Police Lies—Two Acquitted," "Madness at Statehouse: New Penal Code," and "Tight Assholes Ban Gay Newsletter." On the cover, Santa Claus raised a middle finger.

(Eventually, the "Cowtown" appellation became part of the entire community's vocabulary.)

Through early 1973, the paper continued to grow, adding as regular staffers Alison "Sunny" Graff, a martial arts enthusiast and founder of Women Against Rape who often wrote as "Frieda P. Pole," and Eric Zeiters, a worker whose biker appearance, soft-spoken manner, and articulate insight brought a fresh element to the staff.

With its fiftieth issue, in March 1973, the *Free Press* changed its masthead and, at the same time, its name, to the *Columbus Freepress*. The paper began using color regularly. A new typewriter with slightly smaller type allowed us to fit in more copy; we worked harder at layout, and graphically the paper looked stronger. We ourselves felt stronger; most of the cases arising out of the previous spring's antiwar actions had resulted in dismissals or acquittals, although several Progressive Labor Party members and a few Yippies had been convicted and were spending time in jail. Roger Doyle went to Wounded Knee and sent back photos and stories on the American Indian Movement (AIM)'s showdown with federal and state police and local vigilantes; we ran a color poster commemorating Wounded Knee in the centerfold. The constitutional crisis of Watergate was exploding. Another civilian was shot by local police. The struggle continued.

SEXISM IN THEORY AND PRACTICE

Part of that struggle was with male-female relationships. Within the *Freepress*, although it was in theory collective, a number of males who wrote a great deal played powerful roles. Steve Conliff, John Quigley, and I comprised different political viewpoints (Yippie, Marxist, and stoned social democrat, respectively) that were conveyed through our many articles, which we each wrote under a variety of names. The sheer number of words carried much influence simply because the paper depended on us for articles ranging from straight news to satire to analysis of community or, in John's case, international issues. Too, certain staff concentrated on specific issues, thus becoming *de facto* "experts"—Colin Neiburger, for example, handled most writing on Vietnam. Since staff often disagreed on the specifics (though rarely the substance) of some political viewpoints, occasionally articles with conflicting analyses would appear in the same or subsequent issues.

On the other hand, the women of the *Freepress* staff—most notably Mimi Morris, Sunny Graff, Libby Gregory, Cheryl Betz, Kathy Wollard, Alice Lehman, and Judy Christopher—represented a varied cross-section of feminism. Their own articles and graphics in the paper, as well as their analyses of issues, covered a similarly wide range of viewpoints. Theirs was a continuing struggle to educate the men of the *Freepress* even as they struggled with sexism in its more general manifestations in society. Women's different sense of self, and the supportive connections they offered one another in a period of profound self-discovery, gave them a collective unity and power men did not share.

Like the use of drugs, the topic of personal relationships is often neglected in overviews of the period. For many progressives, sexuality and sexual behavior were not worthy subjects for introspection in the face of the war and racism, and discussion of complex sexual relationships and questions of identity may now seem relatively insignificant, perhaps even self-indulgent.

Today, many see the sexual revolution primarily in male terms. In some ways, the postwar sexual revolution, as typified by *Playboy*, simply reinforced the prevailing sexual double standard and served to legitimize the dominance of men in relationships. Men were allowed sexual freedom without commitment or responsibility—the requirements imposed by the economic relationship of marriage. Many "hip" and "progressive" men simply put a bell-bottomed/blue-jeaned veneer on historic male behaviors, little understanding that the real sexual revolution was happening for *women*.

For women, their liberation from psychological stereotypes and economic dependence was, in fact, the acquisition of the power to choose their relationships rather than have them imposed by tradition and necessity. It was the changing attitudes of women that defined the sexual revolution and forced changes in the attitudes of men.

The sixties and seventies were a time of experimentation—politically, economically, socially, personally. The *Freepress* staff included several monogamous couples. Too, political comrades often became lovers, and a number of staff men and women were sequentially involved in sexual relationships with other staff members or other community activists, gay and straight. The hidden dynamics of these changing relationships, combined with our underlying imperative for CHANGE NOW!, often affected the issue-to-issue atmosphere on the staff. Often, both women and men found themselves trying to separate their intellectualized principles from their immediate and deeply felt emotions.

No issue better illustrated the complexities of our attempts to remake male-female relationships than the revelation in mid-1973 that I had been secretly involved for more than a year with another woman, even as I lived with and received support from Cheryl Betz. The shock wave polarized the paper; *Freepress* women rallied around their wronged sister and isolated me; staff men, although rightly condemning my actions, recognized that sexism, male behaviors, and their own conduct were now subject to even more critical scrutiny. My own, and by extension all men's, hypocrisy was under fire. Numerous individual and group discussions followed, including one memorable four-hour meeting in which staff women ritually pilloried virtually every male staff member for various sexist behaviors. I was not purged from the staff, but my influence was irrevocably diminished.

With the loyalties of even progressive men now personally and intimately questionable, women received a powerful boost in confronting the inertia of male dominance on the *Freepress*. At the same time, they struggled with their own issues. Were women in heterosexual relationships literally sleeping with the enemy? As separatist views gained strength, could the feminism of a woman who had not explored a lesbian relationship be trusted? It was a confusing period of exploration and revelation, both of which generated ecstacy and conflict.

Women of varying politics continued to join the staff. Marianne Salcetti brought her feminism and formal journalism training to articles analyzing local labor actions and community development issues; Pat Culp provided a satirical, warped sensibility to social commentary; Sandy Sterrett, writing as "Sandra Skinner," covered ecology stories and, later, community organizing. Their personalities and contacts, and the ongoing work of other staff women in women's organizations, strengthened the paper even as it continued its struggle with identity and finances.

The dichotomy between cultural and political "change" was always apparent but never clear. Articles on Israeli crimes against Palestinians faced record reviews; reports on the sterilization of poor women and the organizing efforts of tenants bumped columns with

vegetarian recipes and advocacy of animal rights. Eric Zeiters' articles on police repression shared pages with Libby Gregory's cartoons of Polonius Potato, created after the FBI harassed local activists for "an attempt on the life of Vice-President Agnew" in the form of a potato thrown at his limousine during a fundraising visit to Columbus in 1972. The revolution was broad scale.

The paper's financial underpinning, however, was not. It had numerous advertisers but no skilled business manager. Advertising revenues were supplemented by donations from working staff members and occasionally by the then-honorable activity of dealing in marijuana and LSD. Two months after the paper's cover showed the backsides of four naked staff members over the plea "Help Save Our Asses!" a staff member worked a deal for 5,000 hits of purple microdot LSD. Many staff bought at discount, and the resulting sales allowed the paper to finish out the year more or less in the black, publishing every two weeks.

Then, in January of 1974, the *Freepress* confronted financial reality head-on by going free, dropping the 20-cent cost and expanding its press run from 2,000 to 10,000 (and ending the need to give a simple answer to "So why ain't it free?"). With a larger promised circulation, advertising increased even as the paper took a more militant stand on local and national labor conflicts and supported a strong community campaign for civilian review of police while exposing police informers. *Freepress* articles on a strike by Borden workers were the only media coverage in the city to support workers demanding compensation for a mysterious nerve ailment linked to chemicals at the Borden-owned Columbus Coated Fabrics plant.

UP AGAINST THE POLICE

The paper also exposed how Columbus police had attempted to use an informer to set up and arrest municipal judge Bill Boyland on drug charges. Boyland, a progressive lawyer for numerous community organizations as well as a number of *Freep* staff arrested for antiwar activities, had been elected in a popular campaign the previous fall, when his campaign headquarters had been kept under police surveillance; and the city's right wing, including many police, had circulated stories that the married Boyland was a secretly homosexual communist who paid campaign workers in drugs. In the same story, I reported how the lawyer who had revealed the planned frame-up had himself been arrested when police raided his office and seized marijuana and pills being held as evidence in a client's file.

The militant antigovernment, antipolice rhetoric of the *Freepress* made it a natural target for reaction and repression. Harassment by police and direct attack by right-wing groups and white supremacists continued. Death threats came by telephone and by mail. A gunshot had been fired through the window of an apartment shared by feminist activists/staff members Mimi Morris and Sunny Graff, whose basement had housed the paper in the winter of 1971; windows in the paper's office at the Wesley Foundation were broken a number of times. The homes and vehicles of staff members and other political activists had been vandalized or burglarized, and intruders killed the pet of two activists during a break-in, leaving the message "Your (sic) next" on a mirror. Both Switchboard and the Third Avenue Food Co-op were damaged by arsonists. Police "field interviews"—I.D. checks—on the street were common.

Accordingly, many staff wrote articles, particularly highly charged ones, under a variety of names which revealed a taste for irony and bad puns. John Quigley covered international stories as Vanya, legal matters as Amy Cuscuria, and tenant-landlord stories as E. Victor. Colin Neiburger wrote Indochina analyses as Colinda Tomato or Jam-Cin; Mimi Morris appeared as Liz Estrada and Angela Motorman. Stephen Sterrett covered politics and the environment under the name Stephen Skinner. Libby Gregory wrote as Norma Jean Fish, Alice Lehman as Carolina Hunt. Steve Conliff wrote as Leon Yipsky or Leon Karg, the latter surname drawn from a fatigue jacket bought in a surplus store; when Karg had another article in the same issue, "Noel Grak" authored some articles. My own pen names included [Free] Lance Ryder, Dennis Menimen, and Houston Fearless, a brand name of earthmover. The bylines of "Neil Livingston," "Patterson Blake," and "Woodrow Thurman" combined various Columbus street names. Our own names graced many articles, but each byline was a choice trying to gauge the amount of risk or ego the writer might be investing.

(Ultimately, little of this mattered. In 1976, *Freep* staff gathered for a party at the house shared by Judy Christopher and me, and together we all filled out forms requesting our FBI files under the Freedom of Information Act. When we compared files many months later, we became convinced that John Miernik, who handled much of the paper's advertising and distribution, had been an informant for both the Columbus Police Intelligence Squad and the local FBI, reporting on even our birthday celebrations and relationships with lovers. Many, though not all, of the staff's pen names appeared in the FBI's files. The Revolution had clearly provided employment for thousands of file clerks from the local to the federal level.)

Too often, though, our sense of theatre led us mistakenly to measure our impact by the amount of repression we felt from police, in effect allowing them to define our influence in the community. Criticism of this tendency would later become part of the paper's internal political struggle.

In the face of intense organizing around both local and national issues, combined with the stunning revelations of the Watergate conspiracy and the Nixon administration's extensive list of dirty tricks, the staff tried to keep its sense of humor. One issue featured, in place of page numbers, the names of radical and progressive women; thus, stories were "continued on Elizabeth Gurley Flynn" or located on "Harriet Tubman." Cartoonist Paul Volker, following other local artists Larry Hamill, Jude Angelo, and James Beoddy, began contributing humorous political comic strips and assorted artwork to the paper.

Many of us clearly were tired and overextended, but nonetheless determined to continue. Four years of intense activity; personal, political, and legal struggles; ongoing police and right-wing harassment; and the constant forming and collapsing of idealistic endeavors and personal relationships had taken a significant toll on many of us. On one hand, we felt more certain of our direction; on the other, we were dazed and confused by the whirlwind of our lives. In a gigglingly funny article on the general state of the Movement, Steve Conliff reported the activities of the "Burn-Out Liberation Front"; in the next *Freepress*, in an occasional staff column titled "Goin' Through Them Changes," we wryly denied that the BOLF consisted entirely of *Freepress* staff members past and present.

In mid-1974, after several weeks of thought and discussion with staff and other friends, I took a job working as a bailiff in the municipal courtroom of Judge Bill Boyland. The contradictions were apparent from the outset, but the opportunities to cut some slack in the system for poor and working people—again, the question of reform vs. revolution—prompted me to take the chance.

In addition to helping people get released from jail on low or recognizance bails and providing some empathetic understanding of the issues that brought them into the criminal "justice" system, I was able to work with and support a close friend whom the progressive community in the city had helped to elect. My appointment touched off a furor in the police department, whose representatives demanded my dismissal. I stayed for the next five years, and my contacts and access to information proved valuable to progressives on a number of occasions.

I was also weary of the *Freepress*. No less committed to the issues it addressed, I was exhausted (not unlike many other staff). Between the demands of the job and internal demands for a better understanding of what I myself believed independently of the group, I felt the need to leave the paper. I expanded my writing of poetry, and at a later date penned a celebratory "Poem for the Fifth Anniversary of the Columbus Tenants Union" for their annual community dinner.

GOIN' THROUGH THEM CHANGES

The *Freepress* revamped its masthead and continued making connections between local, national, and international issues. Feminists like Sunny Graff increasingly linked their anti-rape work in the community with the rape of the Third World, particularly Vietnam. And there was still power in the dictum, "The personal is political." In an article about police and media handling of several brutal assaults against women, Graff wrote:

> I am home alone and I am pissed off. I am sick and tired of being terrorized. I am tired of arming myself with mace and my whistle to take out the garbage at night. I am tired of being afraid to be alone.
>
> I'm tired of being told I have no sense of humor when men casually laugh about rape and "scoring" women. I've heard degrading comments about women from every man I've ever known. I've seen women beaten, torn, ravaged and murdered. I've seen women who press charges against their attackers degraded and humiliated by male doctors, judges, attorneys, prosecutors, police officers and reporters....
>
> I am home by myself tonight--but I am not alone. I am with all the other women who feel my anger, who are tired of being victimized....We are growing stronger every day.

In Vietnam, it was clearly only a question of time before the war would be over. Between February and May, three of the four front pages on the now-monthly *Freepress* focused on Indochina, including the printing of a communiqué from the Weather Underground following a bombing at the State Department and articles on Cambodia and, in May, the fall of Saigon. Some of us went up to Larry's Bar to celebrate, and later walked down High Street to 15th Avenue, where we encountered other folks celebrating as well.

But the next day there it was, the question the staff had debated for several years but never really confronted: without the war, and without a broader critique of society, what would hold together the anger, disaffection, and flagging energies of the disparate groups that made up the so-called underground?

The paper was facing other realities as well. Two different entertainment publications, *Focus* and *Ragazine*, had begun publishing, and their rock 'n' roll and graphics arts focuses were drawing advertisers away from the *Freepress*.

In another "Goin' Through Them Changes" column, the situation was laid out plainly but, as always, with some humor:

> We have always maintained that we are a collective and that "everybody does everything." But this is not close to the truth. In fact, a few people have done the less exciting tasks of advertising and distribution. And a relative state of order has been maintained by personality politics. Power has been held by those able to stay up all night doing layout.
>
> Last week the FREEP staff finally had the reorganizational meeting we've been dreading for years. First thing we realized is the changes we've gone through in our personal lifestyles. Two years ago we were hippies and politicos, students or part-time workers, with lotsa free time to put out a paper. Now we have all assumed straight identities and gone overground, stealthily infiltrating the work force at key points....
>
> We need distributors, advertising salespeople, and advertisers. If you've ever wanted to play underground paper, here's your chance.

The rest of the column explained the new process for handling the paper's content: articles would be submitted a week before publication, when there would be discussion and critique. Major tasks such as finances and advertising, office management, and distribution and correspondence would be handled by small staff collectives.

As 1975 began, the paper continued to be the voice of almost every revolutionary, reformist, or alternative viewpoint. An article on cultivating marijuana shared a page with a feminist critique of a proposed rape law; both faced a stern "Work Towards Socialism" piece on the opposite page. Turning the page revealed health food recipes. Other stories supported the development of community organizations—Datagang, a video collective; WFAC (Free Access Columbus), a nascent free-form radio station; the Moonshine Co-op Bar; the 16th Avenue Food Co-op, which was regularly distributing funds to other groups such as the Tenants Union, the Rape Crisis Center, and Switchboard.

Local issues—union strikes, tenant organizing, community control of police, development of alternative organizations, gay and lesbian rights—dominated *Freepress* pages, but international progressive politics remained a major element. Wedged somewhere between a political revolution and a cultural one, the paper and its content weaved wildly between seriousness and send-up.

Throughout 1975, community workers moved constantly in and out of the paper's production and writing staff. Tenant organizers Gayle Hoover and Steve Cohodas worked on several issues, and Scott Williams began writing and doing layout again; Skip Zitin contributed regular long hours. Jim Hiser played bass guitar, rhapsodized dizzily about John Lennon and Yoko Ono, helped with layout, and cranked out occasional articles. Marilyn Flower brought strong Marxist and feminist analysis. Gay activist Patrick Miller continued insightful, literate assessments of gay and lesbian issues, and Donna Smith (aka "Roxanne Role") covered rock concerts and wrote record reviews. The true responsibility for core work, however, still fell on a few.

A number of current and former staff became involved in the Prairie Fire Organizing Committee, the aboveground group supporting the Weather Underground, and local demonstrations supporting Puerto Rican independence attracted new police surveillance.

By the end of the year, however, disagreements within the paper were multiplying as the community itself saw its own struggles intensifying. Some staff, approaching issues and the paper itself from a Marxist-Leninist perspective, were increasingly impatient with the freewheeling content of the paper and its lack of coherent analysis of broader issues; debates over articles grew more pointed and prolonged.

As the *Freepress* continued into the nation's bicentennial year, some present and former staff felt the paper had lost its rebellious spirit; others countered that they sought revolution, not rebellion, and that reportage on the day-to-day economic struggles of the majority of working people was more important than radical-hippie self-indulgence.

In June of 1976, shortly before large numbers of present and former staff travelled to Philadelphia for the national demonstration coinciding with national bicentennial celebration, five staff—Mimi Morris, Kathy Wollard, Eric Zeiters, Evan Morris, and Marilyn Flower—formed a Marxist-Leninist study group and became a caucus within the paper. By then, the *Freepress* was broke and running on the energies of fewer than 10 people and the financial support of John Quigley and several members of the caucus. Ad sales had been dropping off, and what ads Eric Zeiters was able to sell were insufficient to meet expenses.

The paper's focus soon reflected a Marxist-Leninist analysis and style. By the end of summer, rock 'n' roll coverage was gone, and articles contained a more obvious internationalist approach. More and more copy was reprinted from publications such as *Workers World* and the *Guardian*. The caucus insisted on principled struggle to resolve disagreements, and many of the more free-spirited staff felt it not worth the increased effort beyond the more casual style they were accustomed to. The caucus, in fact, regularly held a voting majority, depending on how many people showed up to work on an issue, but their power and influence came as much from their determined work as from their number.

In autumn of 1976, the *Freepress* moved from its 16th Avenue location to offices above the Moonshine Co-op Bar at 11th Avenue and North 4th Street. With the move came more space, worse conditions, and numerous additional and occasional helpers. Steve and Earlene Rothman (subsequently referred to as Earlene Dennison and Earlene Rackham), Patti McFarland, Jo Hoeper, and Darrell Browning, all active in Yippie, feminist, and tenant organizations, became regular workers on the paper.

The paper lurched toward the end of the year, mainly through the efforts of the caucus and four other regular staff members—Libby Gregory, John Quigley, Steve Rothman, and Earlene Dennison. Eight to ten others occasionally put in time on articles and production, but these people had no patience with the constant staff conflict over political positions. When Marilyn Flower departed at the end of 1976, disagreements within the paper stalemated.

The four noncaucus members saw the efforts of the four remaining caucus members as an attempt to convert the *Freepress* into a militant communist party organ. The caucus sought a more concrete analysis of issues that would make the paper an organizing tool for political struggle on a mass scale, and they approached the paper's work with disciplined seriousness. Such was the appearance and tone of the paper that a reader wrote a letter beginning, "Dear *Guardian*," and saying "Why not reprint some articles from the *Columbus Freepress*?" As winter bore down on Columbus, the paper again uprooted itself to be produced from the apartment of a caucus member.

In the January 1977 issue, a full-page article written by the caucus said:

> Capitalism is the enemy....We need decent housing and food, good healthcare and childcare, jobs, education, mass transit. Things we won't get from capitalism because there's no profit in serving the people. We need a new organization of society—socialism...and only through revolution will we get socialism...In future issues the *Freepress* will develop and clarify the analysis and strategy necessary for socialist revolution. We welcome your comments and criticisms.

That statement defined the line between the caucus and the other four staff, a line with proponents of a political party on one side and a looser, less dogmatic group on the other. Thus, in early 1977, unable to reach unity on how to resolve their differences and unable to produce a February issue for lack of money, the eight agreed, after long and rancorous debate, to disband the paper after one more edition, which would be put out when money could be raised to publish it and pay off debts.

Almost immediately, however, at least two of the noncaucus staff began recruiting former staff to work on a "reconstituted" *Freepress*, apparently planning to passively sandbag the paper's "final" issue. It was not a particularly glorious moment. When the caucus found out they had been betrayed, they seized the paper's equipment and files and produced a final special edition late in April with the cover headline in bold red ink proclaiming "Celebrate Mayday!"

The 12-page paper ran a double-truck centerfold headed "The Future Belongs to Working People!" and a three-page article outlining the caucus view of the *Freepress*' problems, their efforts to change them, and the betrayal of the staff's unanimous vote to disband the paper. They correctly analyzed the paper's historic character:

The prevailing mood on the *FP* was that the important thing was to be doing something, anything in a vaguely leftist direction; to look closely at what was being done, and why, spoiled the spirit and created bad feelings.

Near the end of the critique, the statement noted:

The members of the caucus believe the "new *Freepress*" will repeat many of the errors of the "old *Freepress*" as we found it ten months ago. The new staff contains various viewpoints and perspectives that can only find unity in the eclectic style of former times. We expect a resurgence of "youth and dope" culture, of a lack of seriousness in tone and style. OSU "community" news will again become the dominant theme of the "city-wide" *FP*....But the weakness, the decisive error, will be a lack of any consideration of strategy, a return to wishful thinking and spontaneity as substitutes for organizing based on analysis.

For better or worse, it was a largely accurate prediction.

THE "RECONSTITUTED" *FREE PRESS*

When the "new" *Free Press* (separate words again) came out in mid-May of 1977, both its content and the staff/contributors box looked much like the *Free Press* of several years earlier: an assortment of, in the words of a pointed article aimed at the caucus, "socialists, communists, anarchists, feminists, eclecticists, and various kinds of et ceteras," including several long-absent former staff. For a time Conliff, Bird, Betz, Sarber, and I would contribute articles and production work. The article continued:

What the "reconstituted" *Free Press* is about is building the kind of movement that doesn't want to rule anybody, that aims to enable people to run their own lives. Everyone doesn't have to think exactly the same way, because revolution is an objective not subjective experience. There is no One Way. We look upon thinking anyone has all the "correct" answers as a mental disorder caused by reading too many books by dead men. The future belongs to the living.

The paper reflected its "et cetera" viewpoint, covering the Soweto uprising and demonstrations against the building of a gym on the site of the Kent State shootings along with rallies to legalize marijuana and efforts to preserve urban green space. When the Ku Klux Klan held rallies at the Ohio Statehouse on July 4 and Labor Day of 1977, *Free Press* staff participated in large counter-demonstrations against them; photos taken by Sue Urbas and others at the Labor Day rally, at which members of the Committee Against Racism and the Progressive Labor Party were attacked by male bystanders who turned out to be plainclothes police, later helped acquit demonstrators charged with assault for defending themselves. (Several sympathetic court bailiffs and other employees helped identify undercover police in the photos.)

In August, Steve Conliff immortalized himself by pieing Governor James Rhodes, the "butcher of Kent State," at the opening day ceremonies of the state fair. We never looked at pie judging the same way again. Charged with assault (with a deadly banana cream pie), Conliff was ultimately convicted of disorderly conduct in a jury trial and fined $100. Later, as always believing that pulling down the enemy's pants was almost as good as kicking him in them, Conliff ran as a write-in candidate against Rhodes in the Republican primary.

The paper moved into office space above Tradewinds, now two blocks north of its old location and directly across from the OSU Law School. The *Free*

Press paid no rent; Tradewinds took in-kind ads in the paper.

Over the next three years, the *Free Press* gradually changed. Still progressive but decidedly less strident in tone, it spruced up its layout and gradually moved toward more generalized "alternative" and left-progressive news. A new typesetter sharpened the paper's appearance. Coverage focused heavily on neighborhood organizing around housing, zoning, and police brutality. Antinuclear articles and coverage of other environmental issues expanded. The paper ran a regular citywide calendar of political and cultural events in a format that has since been adopted by several other local entertainment papers.

No longer on the barricades but supportive of those who were, the *Free Press* was by this time one of the few remaining "alternative" papers which had begun the seventies. It was more and more the advocate, the commentator, representative of a broad community of opposition thought. The scene had changed, but the issues hadn't. Liberation News Service (LNS) stories and strong international coverage on the Sandinista, South African, and Palestinian revolutions were highlighted by an important 1979 story by John Quigley: his *Free Press* article was the first eye-witness account by a U.S. journalist of the killing fields horror of Kampuchea after the Pol Pot regime was driven out. It was disquieting and humbling to reflect on whether I had ever voiced support for the Khmer Rouge.

Libby Gregory served as managing editor, and in 1984, with environmental activist Steve Molk, John Quigley, and yip-feminist/resident media critic Earlene Rackham as contributing editors, the paper again changed its masthead and began charging 50 cents for the 24-page monthly publication. The *Free Press* was an institution, a solid and dependable opposition voice that looked professional and more accessible to a wide audience. It began to bill itself—and does today—as "The Other Side of the News."

Some of its most unusual political education during this time was "Sexual Assault in Columbus," a regular column giving brief synopses, from police reports, of rapes reported in the previous month. Compiled by Libby Gregory, the column included reports in which women fought back or escaped, and information on whether a rapist had been charged in an attack. Sidebar articles debunked myths about rape.

It was painful, disconcerting reading. Some readers objected to the column, describing it as ghoulish and perversely pandering. Others saw it differently, believing that, by its dispassionate, relentless, page-long repetition of incidents of violence against women, it probably did more to educate its readership about the nature of rape and sexual oppression than many political analyses.

By 1987, though, core staff had dwindled to Libby Gregory, John Quigley, and Bob Roehm, who compiled the monthly calendar. All were working full-time jobs in addition to doing *FP* work. Hearing that Duane Jager, a former Tenants Union organizer, was interested in starting his own publication, they contacted him about taking over the paper.

Jager, who had more recently worked with the homeless, managed a soup kitchen, and run for Congress, set up the not-for-profit Columbus Institute for Contemporary Journalism and gradually assumed the role of publisher. In 1990, John Quigley was serving as senior editor and former Liberation News Service collective member Harvey Wasserman, now living in Columbus, was writing a regular column on environmental issues.

MOVING ON

In a somewhat different form, and in a very different time, we move on. The *Columbus Freepress* (yes, the most recent shift in the linotype), and the spirit of the people who made it happen, lives on.

In 1990 my sister, never a political activist, asked me to take her and my nieces to the Kent State 20th anniversary memorial. "I want them to understand what happened, and what it was all about," she told me. And so it is important that we explain our own history.

Part of that history was made in the streets, where like latter-day pamphleteers the members of the underground press spread the revolutionary word when even peaceful protest was often met with clubs, tear gas, and multiple-baton shells. The canister on the bookcase is, to me, a symbol of the importance of—and necessity for—dissent, and of what can happen when dissent becomes intolerable to those in power. Tiananmen Square has much in common with Kent State.

Especially today, when cynical politicians and businesses blithely manipulate national ambivalence over the legacy of Vietnam by wrapping aggression in patriotism and every imaginable product in the flag, we must not simply tolerate dissent. We must encourage it. We must question, demand answers, root out the hidden agendas, seek the other side of the story that independent media can provide. We must protect our victories and encourage further change.

The life of the underground press was a life that acknowledged the possibility of change—fundamental change in attitudes and power relationships on a global, national, local and, ultimately, personal level. Eventually, many of us realized that the heart of the struggle was not just learning to live with each other but learning to live with ourselves.

We were so much older then....

It may seem that the story of the *Free Press* and its people was solely one of conflict. To think so, however, would miss the point of how our lives themselves—political, social, spiritual—are a process, a constant testing and reshaping of our personal realities. In those lives we have marched and danced, fought and celebrated, laughed and cried, been hurt and been healed. We have worked hard to find a way for all people to live in peace, in harmony with themselves and the earth, and to have their basic needs met. We have come to understand that, as we work to create peace, whether global or personal, we have to be in it for the long haul.

We sought to live our ideals and in the process discovered our fallible humanity. We made many mistakes, but we have learned and grown, and much of what we sought has come, in some form, to fruition. And we brought all of what we were to that struggle.

Many of us still do. Take a look in the mirror. The revolution's *here*.

And you know it's right.

"RAISING THE CONSCIOUSNESS OF THE PEOPLE": THE BLACK PANTHER INTERCOMMUNAL NEWS SERVICE, 1967-1980

JoNina M. Abron

THE DEATH OF HUEY P. NEWTON

I was headed out the door to my job as managing editor of *Black Scholar* magazine in Oakland, California, when my phone rang the morning of Tuesday, August 22, 1989. The caller, a sister who had been a fellow Black Panther Party member in Oakland after first working in the party in Houston, Texas, rushed out the words.

"JoNina, have you heard? Huey's been shot. He's dead." She explained that a friend in Oakland had heard the news and called to tell her.

Shocked, I had barely hung up the phone when it rang again. On the other end was another comrade sister (in the party, women were "comrade sisters" and men "comrade brothers") calling to ask if I had heard that Huey had been killed. "I miss him already," she said.

Grief overcame me as I realized that Huey P. Newton, whose name thousands across the world once chanted in the cry "Free Huey!" and who had been an international symbol of black resistance to white oppression, was dead. Violence consumed Huey's life almost daily in the 23 years since he had co-founded the Black Panther Party, and violence finally took his life at age 47.

The following Monday afternoon, August 28, at Huey's funeral, inside and outside east Oakland's Allen Temple Baptist Church, over 2,000 people—including ex-Panthers from Baltimore, Boston, Houston, Texas, Detroit, Los Angeles, Washington, DC, Philadelphia,

Abron was the last editor of *The Black Panther Intercommunal News Service* and a member of the Black Panther Party for nine years. She is executive editor of *Black Scholar* magazine and an assistant professor of English at Western Michigan University, Kalamazoo, where she teaches journalism.

and other places—mourned Huey's death and celebrated the enduring contributions that the Panther leader and the party made to the political empowerment of black and other disenfranchised people in the United States.

I was asked to speak on the funeral program because I was an editor—the last editor—of *The Black Panther Intercommunal News Service*, the BPP's newspaper. As I stood crunched in line waiting to enter the sanctuary with Huey's family members and other speakers on the program—including ex-party leaders Bobby Seale, Elaine Brown, Ericka Huggins, David Hilliard, and Emory Douglas—I found myself looking into the faces of two Panther comrades whom I had not seen in 15 years. We embraced—sad for the occasion that had reunited us but happy to be reunited.

When I stood on the podium to speak, I nearly broke down and cried as I looked into the faces of my Panther comrades on the front pews. I thought about all the good and hard times we had gone through together "serving the people body and soul." I said that I had been privileged to serve in the Black Panther Party for nine years and that I would die a Panther. I know I said something else, but I don't remember what.

When Elaine Brown took the podium, it was the first time many ex-Panthers and party supporters had seen her since 1977, when she resigned from the party for personal reasons. Her capable leadership held the BPP together from 1974 to 1977 when Huey was in exile in Cuba after being charged with killing an Oakland prostitute. He had survived being shot by one policeman and three years of prison for killing another policeman in the same incident; other confrontations with law enforcement; and numerous trials. In her comments, Elaine said she had thought Huey was invincible and that he would live forever.

Moving to the podium and putting a black beret on his head (in the party's early days, the Panther uniform consisted of a black beret, black leather jacket, and powder blue shirt), BPP co-founder and chair Bobby Seale brought the congregation to its feet in tribute when he raised his clenched fist and shouted the Panther rallying cry, "All power to the people!" Then he recalled how he and Huey met as students at Merritt College in the early 1960s and how their mutual concerns about police brutality, poverty, and other problems in the black community led them to found the BPP in Oakland in October 1966.

Just as he had in the old days, in his familiar strident cadence, Bobby then recited from memory the entire BPP Ten Point Platform and Program. For a few minutes, it seemed as if the congregation at Allen Temple Church was at a Panther rally in 1968.

After the funeral, ex-Panthers, family members, and friends gathered for a reunion where we talked over old times and exchanged information about our lives since party days.

Later that afternoon, ex-BPP political prisoner Johnny Spain and I were among the guests on a program commemorating the legacy of the BPP on KPFA Radio in Berkeley. Johnny, who spent nearly 22 consecutive years behind bars, explained how in the late 1960s, while serving a prison sentence for murder in California, he joined the BPP because of his friendship with black prison leader George Jackson.

MURDER LINKED TO DEATH OF GEORGE JACKSON

George was legendary in the California penal system for his effective organizing of black and poor inmates. He is generally credited with starting the Black Guerrilla Family. BGF was initiated as protection for black inmates against white racist inmates and subsequently became a focus of political education for black prisoners. During Huey's three-year imprisonment for killing an Oakland policeman, he learned of George's work and appointed him to the position of BPP "field marshal," responsible for organizing and leading blacks in prison. Many BGF members became Panthers.

On August 21, 1971, George, two other prisoners, and two guards were killed in San Quentin Prison's maximum security section, the adjustment center, in what prison officials alleged was an escape attempt. Earlier in the day during a visit, the officials charged, a white attorney, Stephen Bingham, had smuggled in to George a gun, concealed in a portable tape recorder, and an Afro wig. During George's escape attempt, they maintained, he concealed the gun under the wig. This theory was questionable, given that George was thoroughly searched before and after visits from his attorneys, family, and friends.

Johnny was incarcerated at the time with George in the adjustment center. He and five other black and Hispanic adjustment center inmates—Willie Tate, Fleeta Drumgo, David Johnson, Luis Talamentez, and Hugo Pinell—were charged with assault, conspiracy, and murder in the August 21 killings. During the 18-month-long "San Quentin 6" trial, the prosecution conceded that Johnny did not kill anyone at the adjustment center, but maintained that he was trying to escape with George. He was, therefore, vicariously guilty under state law of killing the two guards. When the trial ended in August 1976, almost exactly five years after the incident, Johnny was the only one of the six convicted of murder. He was sentenced to two consecutive life prison terms. In August 1989, shortly before Huey's murder, Johnny's conviction was overturned.

What really happened at San Quentin that August day 20 years ago may never be revealed. In an affidavit signed shortly after the incident, several adjustment center prisoners declared that George risked his life to save theirs. At the time of his death, the 29-year-old prison leader was serving the eleventh year of a $70 robbery conviction and was about to go on trial with two other black inmates for the 1970 killing of a white guard at Soledad Prison. In his critically acclaimed book of 1970, *Soledad Brother: The Prison Letters of George Jackson*—in part a forceful critique of racist violence and harassment of black prisoners—George said he did not expect to leave prison alive because of his organizing of black inmates. Aware of this and determined to silence him, prison officials may have falsely led George and inmates close to him to believe that the BPP was going to break him out of prison. The party denied this rumor and charged that prison officials murdered George, a charge supported by testimony during the San Quentin 6 trial. Louis Tackwood, a black ex-police informant, testified that he was recruited to infiltrate the BPP as part of a plot by California law enforcement officials to kill George.

In any case, when George was killed, many in the BGF blamed the party, Huey in particular, and relations between the groups soured. Exactly 18 years and one day later, Huey was shot to death on a street in the same Oakland neighborhood where he and Bobby launched the party in 1966. His alleged murderer, Tyrone Robinson, is reputed to be a member of the Black Guerrilla Family.

Robinson said he shot Huey in self-defense during an argument over drugs. The truth has yet to be revealed, but there is no doubt that by 1968, three years before George Jackson was killed, then-FBI director J. Edgar Hoover had already declared war on the BPP, charging that it was "the greatest threat to the internal security of the country." [Ed. note: Robinson was found guilty of first degree murder on Wednesday October 9, 1991.]

BLACK PANTHER PARTY FOUNDED TO OPPOSE POLICE BRUTALITY

Waiting to begin the KPFA program and feeling more relaxed after the funeral celebration and more reflective from the emotions of the occasion, we laughed at the headlines as we passed around 20-year-old issues of *The Black Panther*:

"NATIONWIDE HARASSMENT OF PANTHERS BY PIG POWER STRUCTURE"
"FASCIST ACTION AGAINST THE PEOPLE OF SACRAMENTO"
"WHITE 'MOTHER COUNTRY' RADICALS"

During the program, while discussing the history of the newspaper and the party, I said that I owed Huey and Bobby a great debt for starting the BPP and allowing me to participate in one of the most important black liberation movements in United States history. As we reminisced, I recalled the party's beginnings in 1966 and my own introduction to the party six years later.

Huey and Bobby founded the Black Panther Party for Self-Defense (Self-Defense was dropped from the name in 1968 to help give the party legitimacy as a political organization) because, as they later wrote in the party's initial Ten Point Platform and Program (see sidebar 1), "We want freedom. We want power to determine the destiny of our Black Community."

The idea for the party's name came from a black self-defense group in Lowndes County, Alabama, which used a black panther as its symbol. The panther is known as an animal that only attacks in self-defense.

The two young men belonged to the community of southern blacks whose families had migrated to Oakland during World War II and afterwards in search of jobs in the naval shipyards and other industries. Huey's family came from Louisiana and Bobby's from Texas during that period. Trying to escape the rigid segregation of the South, these blacks became victims nonetheless of California-style discrimination—on the job, in housing, and in education. In addition, by the mid-1960s, the Oakland Police Department had recruited several whites, also from the South, who brought their racist attitudes with them. Police brutality in Oakland's black communities was rampant.

Huey and Bobby formed the BPP partly as a response to this rise of white police brutality—which was occurring not only in Oakland but in urban black communities across America—and partly because they believed, as did many black youth at the time, that the tactic of non-violence successfully used by the civil rights movement in the South would not be effective in the large cities of the urban North.

At the time, it was legal for a person to carry an unconcealed gun in California. Point Number 7 of the BPP platform called for "an immediate end to POLICE BRUTALITY and MURDER of black people" and advocated "organizing black self-defense groups that are dedicated to defending our black community from racist police oppression and brutality." It said further, "The Second Amendment to the Constitution of the United States gives a right to bear arms. We therefore believe that all black people should arm themselves for self-defense."

Huey, Bobby, and other Panthers conducted armed "community patrols of the police," during which they would observe police arrests and harassment of blacks and advise those arrested or harassed of their legal

Black Panther Party Platform and Program
What We Want, What We Believe *(October 1966)*

1. **We want freedom. We want power to determine the destiny of our Black Community.**
We believe that black people will not be free until we are able to determine our destiny.

2. **We want full employment for our people.**
We believe that the federal government is responsible and obligated to give every man employment or a guaranteed income. We believe that if the white American businessmen will not give full employment, then the means of production should be taken from the businessmen and placed in the community so that the people of the community can organize and employ all of its people and give a high standard of living.

3. **We want an end to the robbery by the CAPITALIST of our Black Community.**
We believe that this racist government has robbed us and now we are demanding the overdue debt of forty acres and two mules. Forty acres and two mules was promised 100 years ago as restitution for slave labor and mass murder of Black people. We will accept the payment in currency which will be distributed to our many communities. The Germans are now aiding the Jews in Israel for the genocide of the Jewish people. The Germans murdered six million Jews. The American racist has taken part in the slaughter of over fifty million black people; therefore, we feel that this is a modest demand that we make.

4. **We want decent housing, fit for shelter of human beings.**
We believe that if the white landlords will not give decent housing to our black community, then the housing and the land should be made into cooperatives so that our community, with government aid, can build and make decent housing for its people.

5. **We want education for our people that exposes the true nature of this decadent American society. We want education that teaches us our true history and our role in the present-day society.**
We believe in an educational system that will give to our people a knowledge of self. If a man does not have knowledge of himself and his position in society and the world, then he has little chance to relate to anything else.

6. **We want all black men to be exempt from military service.**
We believe the Black people should not be forced to fight in the military service to defend a racist government that does not protect us. We will not fight and kill other people of color in the world who, like black people, are being victimized by the white racist government of America. We will protect ourselves from the force and violence of the racist police and the racist military, by whatever means necessary.

7. **We want an immediate end to POLICE BRUTALITY and MURDER of black people.**
We believe we can end police brutality in our black community by organizing black self-defense groups that are dedicated to defending our black community from racist police oppression and brutality. The Second Amendment to the Constitution of the United States gives a right to bear arms. We therefore believe that all black people should arm themselves for self defense.

8. **We want freedom for all black men held in federal, state, county and city prisons and jails.**
We believe that all black people should be released from the many jails and prisons because they have not received a fair and impartial trial.

9. **We want all black people when brought to trial to be tried in a court by a jury of their peer group or people from their black communities, as defined by the Constitution of the United States.**
We believe that the courts should follow the United States Constitution so that black people will receive fair trials. The 14th Amendment of the United States Constitution gives a man a right to be tried by his peer group. A peer is a person from a similar economic, social, religious, geographical, environmental, historical and racial background. To do this the court will be forced to select a jury from the black community from which the black defendant came. We have been, and are being tried by all-white juries that have no understanding of the "average reasoning man" of the black community.

10. **We want land, bread, housing, education, clothing, justice and peace. And as our major political objective, a United Nations-supervised plebiscite to be held throughout the black colony in which only black colonial subjects will be allowed to participate, for the purpose of determining the will of black people as to their national destiny.**

When, in the course of human events, it becomes necessary for one people to dissolve the political bonds which have connected them with another, and to assume, among the powers of the earth, the separate and equal station to which the laws of nature and nature's God entitle them, a decent respect to the opinions of mankind requires that they should declare the causes which impel them to the separation.

We hold these truths to be self-evident, that all men are created equal; that they are endowed by their Creator with certain unalienable rights; that among these are life, liberty, and the pursuit of happiness. That, to secure these rights, governments are instituted among men, deriving their just powers from the consent of the governed; that, whenever any form of government becomes destructive of these ends, it is the right of the people to alter or to abolish it, and to institute a new government, laying its foundation on such principles, and organizing its powers in such form, as to them shall seem most likely to effect their safety and happiness. Prudence, indeed, will dictate that governments long established should not be changed for light and transient causes; and, accordingly, all experience hath shown, that mankind are more disposed to suffer, while evils are sufferable, than to right themselves by abolishing the forms to which they are accustomed. But when a long train of abuses and usurpations, pursuing invariably the same object, evinces a design to reduce them under absolute despotism, it is their right, it is their duty, to throw off such government, and to provide new guards for their future security.

Sidebar 1: Black Panther Party Platform and Program

rights. Huey became famous (or infamous, depending on one's perspective) for standing on street corners, armed with his gun, quoting citizens' rights from a lawbook as outraged police looked on.

WHITE POWER STRUCTURE RESPONDS

The black community had mixed reactions to gun-toting Panthers. Many, like me initially, thought they were crazy and would get themselves and innocent bystanders killed. Others believed that blacks had no recourse other than to arm ourselves against mounting police brutality.

The white power structure was less divided. To them, the sight of armed black men was terrifying. Some whites may have been reminded of slave revolts and slaves who joined the Union Army during the Civil War. The California power structure under the leadership of then-Governor Ronald Reagan struck back. Legislation aimed at disarming the BPP, known as the Mulford bill, was authored and proposed by East Bay legislator Don Mulford. The bill sought to change existing law by making it illegal for an unlicensed person to carry a loaded gun, concealed or unconcealed, in a public place.

On May 2, 1967, an armed contingent of Panthers led by Bobby Seale marched into the California legislature in Sacramento to protest the Mulford bill. Later, on the steps of the state capitol building, Bobby read the party's statement protesting the bill, "Executive Mandate No. 1," later published in *The Black Panther* (see sidebar 2). The Mulford bill was later passed.

Nearing the end of my freshman year at Baker University in Baldwin, Kansas, I saw the televised footage of armed Panthers marching into the California legislature. The BPP, which had been a local group until then, gained national attention, and Panther chapters began to appear in major cities across the country.

HOOVER BEGINS INFILTRATION PROGRAM

Unlike the Mulford bill, other attacks on the party were not so overt or legal. *War Against the Panthers: A Study of Repression in America*, Huey's 1980 doctoral dissertation at the University of California-Santa Cruz, is a detailed account of the government's harassment of the BPP—which was dominated by the FBI Counterintelligence Program (COINTELPRO). On August 25, 1967, FBI records show, the FBI launched a violent and illegal program to destroy the black liberation movement in America. In a memo, Hoover ordered 41 FBI field offices to "expose, disrupt, misdirect, discredit, or otherwise neutralize the activities of black nationalist...hate-type organizations and groupings, their leadership, spokesmen, membership and supporters."

Initial groups targeted were the Student Nonviolent Coordinating Committee (SNCC), a civil rights group that played a key role in the southern black voter registration drives of the early 1960s; Southern Christian Leadership Conference (SCLC), founded by Dr. Martin Luther King Jr.; Congress of Racial Equality (CORE); Nation of Islam; and the Revolutionary Action Movement. The BPP was added to the list in September 1968.

At Hoover's direction, FBI agents across the country planted spies and informants in the BPP and other black radical and civil rights groups in the sixties and seventies to destroy them from within. COINTELPRO was also used against white, Native American, Chicano, and Asian left groups during this period.

COINTELPRO operations against the BPP were numerous and vicious, and included:

- hundreds of false arrests. From January 1, 1968, to December 31, 1969, 739 BPP members were arrested, an average of more than one a day, with close to $5 million spent on bail;

- sending to churches whose facilities the party used for the Free Breakfast for School Children Program anonymous letters falsely accusing Panthers of teaching black children to hate whites; and

- securing respected establishment journalists to write negative articles about the BPP.

By July 1969, the BPP was the primary target of the "Black Nationalist" COINTELPRO. Ultimately, 233 of the total 295 authorized "Black Nationalist" actions had been carried out against the BPP. At least 28 Panthers were killed as a result.

The worst of the COINTELPRO activities against the party was to plant undercover informants, usually black, in party affiliates. A paid FBI informant in Chicago, William O'Neal, provided information that led to the murders by police of Illinois Panther leaders Fred Hampton and Mark Clark on December 4, 1969, in the westside Chicago apartment that was used as the local BPP headquarters. Fred, a brilliant, charismatic leader who built the Chicago BPP chapter into one of the largest and most successful in the country, was shot to death while asleep in bed, probably drugged by O'Neal. (After living under an assumed identity for 20 years, O'Neal committed suicide in January 1990.)

Details of COINTELPRO operations against the BPP were published in the April 1976 final report of the U.S. Senate committee investigating intelligence activities, known as the Church Committee for its chair, then-Senator Frank Church of Idaho. The introduction to the 989-page report concluded:

> Many of the techniques used would be intolerable in a democratic society even if all targets had been involved in violent activity, but COINTELPRO went far beyond that. The unexpressed major premise of the programs was that a law enforcement agency has the duty to do whatever is necessary to combat perceived threats to the existing social and political order.

Accusing the FBI of inciting violence between Panthers and other groups, the Church Committee declared:

> It is deplorable that officials of the United States government should engage in the activities described below...equally disturbing is the pride which those officials took in claiming credit for the bloodshed that occurred.

FIRST *BLACK PANTHER* FOCUSES ON DENZIL DOWELL KILLING

The first issue of *The Black Panther Black Community News Service*, a four-page, mimeographed sheet published April 25, 1967, focused on the killing of Denzil Dowell, a 22-year-old black man, by a white sheriff's deputy in Richmond, California. According to the official police report, Dowell was killed after he fled from the deputy, who had stopped Dowell and ordered him to show his identification. Dowell's family disputed the police account and charged that he was murdered. Residents of the area where Dowell was killed said they heard six to ten shots fired. The coroner's report said there were six to ten bullet wounds in Dowell's body, but the police said only three shots were fired. Police said Dowell jumped over a fence during their pursuit of him. Family members said a hip injury he received in a car accident some time earlier made it impossible for Dowell to jump over a fence. They also charged that the deputy who killed Dowell knew him and had previously threatened to kill him.

The family of Dowell asked the fledgling BPP to investigate the young black man's killing, which was ruled justifiable homicide. The combative editorial of the inaugural *Black Panther* set the paper's tone for the next four years. After listing "questionable facts" about the killing raised by Dowell's family, the newspaper said:

> [T]he white cop is the instrument sent into our community by the Power structure to keep Black people quiet and under control...it is time that Black People start moving in a direction that will free our communities from this form of outright brutal oppression. The BLACK PANTHER PARTY FOR SELF DEFENSE has worked out a program that is carefully designed to cope with this situation.

Former BPP "revolutionary artist" and "minister of culture" Emory Douglas coordinated layout and design of *The Black Panther* from the third issue of the paper until the last one in October 1980. In a March 1991 interview, he recalled the early days of *The Black Panther*.

"Huey compared the party's need for a publication with the armed struggle of the Vietnamese people that was going on at that time," Emory said. "He said that the Vietnamese carried mimeograph machines wherever they went to produce flyers and other literature to spread the word about their fight to free their country. The party needed to have a newspaper so we could tell our own story."

— JONINA M. ABRON —

ELDRIDGE CLEAVER BECOMES FIRST EDITOR

Eldridge Cleaver, one of the BPP's most controversial leaders, was the first editor of *The Black Panther*. In December 1966, only five months before the first issue came out, he had been paroled from prison after *Soul on Ice*, Eldridge's treatise on how being an oppressed black man in America led him to be a rapist, gained him national recognition. At Huey's invitation, he joined the party in 1967 after a BPP confrontation with police at the Berkeley office of *Ramparts* magazine, a white left publication. Eldridge was married to the former Kathleen Neal, who became BPP communications secretary and a well-known party spokesperson. Kathleen had been an activist in Nashville, Tennessee, in SNCC, and in June 1967, a short-lived merger of the BPP and SNCC began.

Huey believed that the party could become more adept at community organizing using the successful tactics SNCC had employed in the South. In "Executive Mandate No. 2" (see sidebar 3), published in the July 3, 1967, issue of *The Black Panther*, the BPP "drafted" SNCC leader Stokely Carmichael (now known as Kwame Tour) into the party with the rank of "field marshal." The alliance was formalized at a "Free Huey Rally" in Oakland on February 17, 1968, the 26th birthday of the incarcerated BPP co-founder.

"Eldridge was a flamboyant person in those days, and his writing was provocative," Emory said in characterizing *The Black Panther*'s content under its first editor. Huey, Bobby, and other party members contributed ideas and articles to the paper. The newspaper also included articles from people in the community, a practice that continued throughout the paper's existence. Members of BPP chapters throughout the country wrote articles to report news and issues in their local areas.

When Eldridge first became editor, the paper was produced at the home of his attorney, Beverly Axelrod, Emory said. Later, production moved to the apartment where Eldridge and Kathleen lived in San Francisco. Production also took place at the homes of other party members who lived in the city.

The first two issues of *The Black Panther* were done on a mimeograph machine. Afterwards, the newspaper was typed and graphics were done with instant type. Rubber cement was used to paste the galleys down. Kathleen and other BPP members typed and proofread articles.

Beginning with the third issue, Emory began to oversee the paper's format. "My job was to make the paper look appealing and to see that the art work was in line with the party's politics," he said. Under Emory's leadership, the newspaper's layout cadre used creative designs that most black newspapers had not widely used at the time. The front page of *The Black Panther* had a magazine flavor.

EMORY DOUGLAS: REVOLUTIONARY ARTIST

Emory would later outline his views as a revolutionary artist in a speech at Fisk University in Nashville, Tennessee, in October 1972. In the speech, which was printed in *The Black Panther*, the ex-BPP artist said:

> [I]f we take this structure of commercial art and add a brand new content to it, then we will begin to analyze Black people and our situation for the purpose of raising our consciousness to the oppression that we are subjected to. We would use commercial art for the purpose of educating Black people...No artist can sit in an ivory tower, discussing the problems of the day, and come up with a solution on a piece of paper. The artist has to be down on the ground; he has to hear the sounds of the people, the cries of the people, the suffering of the people, the laughter of the people—the dark side and the bright side of our lives....We must understand that when there are over 20 million people in this country, hungry, then we, as artists, have something we must deal with.

In 1968, newspaper production moved to Berkeley when the party opened an office on Shattuck Avenue. A justifax machine and later a Compugraphic machine were used for typesetting. Throughout the 13 years of its production, *The Black Panther* was typeset at party offices by BPP members or others hired by the party.

Newspaper distribution was a partywide activity. In 1967, Emory distributed *The Black Panther* in his hometown of San Francisco, where he sold papers in the then-predominantly black communities of Fillmore and Hunter's Point. Huey, Bobby, Eldridge, and other BPP members would sell papers at their speaking engagements.

"FREE HUEY" HEARD AROUND THE WORLD

The BPP gained increased national attention and membership following the October 28, 1967, shooting incident involving Huey and two white Oakland police officers, Herbert Heanes and John Frey. The officers, who recognized the license plates of the car in which Huey was a passenger as that of a BPP vehicle, ordered the car to stop. In the bloody altercation that followed, Heanes was wounded and Frey was killed. Huey, himself seriously wounded, was arrested for Frey's killing.

A picture of Huey lying wounded and handcuffed to a hospital gurney appeared on national TV and in newspapers. The BPP, charging that Heanes and Frey had tried to murder Huey, launched an international campaign to get the BPP "minister of defense" out of jail. "Free Huey," a frequent headline in *The Black Panther* at that time, became the demand of black, white, and Third World progressive and radical groups around the world. As a result, hundreds of urban black youth across America joined the party.

On September 8, 1968, Huey was convicted of manslaughter in Frey's death. Three weeks later, he was sentenced to two to fifteen years in prison and was imprisoned until his release on August 5, 1970, after his conviction was overturned.

In 1968, Sam Napier joined the BPP in San Francisco and was the party's dedicated circulation manager until his murder in New York City in April 1971. "Sam had a great desire to distribute the paper. That's what he wanted to do," Emory said. Sam traveled all over the country securing distributors for *The Black Panther*. "He would call and tell us where he was and that he had gotten another route."

In the pages of *The Black Panther*, the BPP stated its views in speeches and writings by party leaders on "the correct handling of a revolution." In an article of that name published in the May 4, 1968, issue, Huey wrote:

> The Vanguard Party must provide leadership for the people. It must teach the correct strategic methods of prolonged resistance through literature and activities....When the people learn that it is no longer advantageous for them to resist by going to the streets in large numbers and when they see the advantage in the activities of guerrilla warfare methods, they will quickly follow this example.

It was also common for the newspaper to print articles written by Cuban President Fidel Castro, Chinese leader Mao Zedong, and the late Mozambican President Samora Machel, as well as speeches and writings of party leaders.

"The paper gave black, poor, and dispossessed people a grassroots point of view on the news that they had never had before," Emory said in assessing the contribution of *The Black Panther*.

Thanks to Emory and other artists like Mark Teemer and Matilaba (Joan Lewis), *The Black Panther* published art work that most people had never seen before. The BPP's contributions to popular culture of the era included the verbal and visual depiction of police as "pigs." The pig, because it is commonly thought of as a dirty animal, was chosen by the BPP as a symbol of police brutality in the black community. Many people bought the newspaper just to see Emory's latest cartoons of pigs dressed in police uniforms, which could be found in almost every issue from 1968 to about 1970.

In its early years, the paper printed the names of BPP national and local leaders, as well as addresses of recognized chapters and branches. While this practice helped people who needed assistance to find Panthers in their local communities, it also, unfortunately, helped the FBI and police to infiltrate the party with agents provocateur, the lifeblood of Hoover's COINTELPRO.

ELDRIDGE GOES INTO EXILE

Two days after the April 4, 1968, assassination of Dr. Martin Luther King, Jr., Bobby Hutton, the first BPP member and the party's 17-year-old treasurer, was shot to death by Oakland police as he walked out of a house, hands above his head, to surrender. Eldridge and six other Panthers, including "Chief of Staff" David Hilliard, were arrested on conspiracy and murder charges in connection with Bobby's death. Fearing that he would return to prison, in late 1968, Eldridge fled with Kathleen, first going to Cuba and eventually settling in Algiers, Algeria, where he became "underground" editor of *The Black Panther* and head of the BPP's newly established international section.

By this time, the BPP-SNCC merger had begun to fall apart. In an article in the March 31, 1969, issue of *The Black Panther*, Bobby Seale and the late BPP "minister of education," Raymond "Masai" Hewitt, criticized views expressed by Stokely during a visit to Scandinavian countries. Bobby charged that Stokely had "deviated from the Party's political line." An article in the August 16, 1969, *Black Panther* reported that David Hilliard had recently met with Stokely Carmichael in Algiers, Algeria, and that it was unlikely that Stokely would continue as a party member. Writing from Algiers, in an "Open Letter to Stokely Carmichael" (*The Black Panther*, August 16, 1969), Eldridge attacked Stokely's "black power" philosophy:

> [T]here is not going to be any revolution or black liberation in the United States as long as revolutionary blacks, whites, Mexicans, Puerto Ricans, Indians, Chinese and Eskimos are unwilling to unite in some functional machinery that

can cope with this situation [capitalism, imperialism and racism].

Back in America, changes were made in the editorial staff of *The Black Panther*. After Eldridge went into exile, Raymond Lewis became managing editor of *The Black Panther* and "deputy minister of information." By January 1969, Frank Jones had replaced Lewis. In March, Elbert "Big Man" Howard and Bobby Herron became co-editors of the newspaper. By the end of March, "Big Man" replaced Frank Jones as managing editor.

During Eldridge's tenure as BPP "minister of information," which ended in February 1971, he encouraged a free speech movement in the party. Public statements by party leaders and the newspaper were filled with profanity. Although the profanity may have reflected the language of some activists of the period, it may also have offended some readers.

Newspaper sales declined, according to Emory. "We did a great disservice to the party and the people in the community," he said of the free speech movement. Huey, from prison, criticized it sharply and it was eventually stopped. While Huey did not regularly oversee the format and contents of the newspaper, even when he was not imprisoned, if he wanted particular information included, his wishes were carried out, as they were in this case.

Even after his tenure as editor ended, Eldridge remained famous for his colorful speeches and writings, often filled with expletives castigating the U.S. power structure. In one article published in the November 22, 1969, issue of *The Black Panther*, he declared:

> A dead pig is desirable, but a paralyzed pig is preferable to a mobile pig. And a determined revolutionary doesn't require an authorization from a Central Committee [BPP leadership body] before offing a pig...when the need arises a true revolutionary will off the Central Committee. In order to stop the slaughter of the people we accelerate the slaughter of the pigs.

"ONE OF THE MOST EFFECTIVE PROPAGANDA OPERATIONS"

The writings and speeches of Eldridge, Huey, Bobby Seale, and other BPP leaders that appeared in *The Black Panther* came under close government scrutiny at this time. On October 8, 1969, the Committee on Internal Security of the U.S. House of Representatives, chaired by then-Missouri Congressman Richard H. Ichord, authorized an investigation into "the origin, history, organization, character and objectives" of the

BPP as reported in *The Black Panther*. A year later, on October 6, 1970, the committee issued a report of about 150 pages detailing the newspaper's contents from June 1967 to September 1970. The report included excerpts from *Black Panther* articles, cartoons, and photos of party leaders.

For the BPP, 1970 was a critical year. In a memo of May 15, Hoover described *The Black Panther* as "one of the most effective propaganda operations of the BPP...It is the voice of the BPP and if it could be effectively hindered it would result in helping to cripple the BPP." Certainly, Hoover had cause for concern. *The Black Panther* had arguably become one of the most popular and colorful radical left publications of the era. At 25 cents per copy, *The Black Panther*'s weekly circulation had surpassed 100,000. Subscriptions and contributors came from throughout the world, including France, Sweden, Denmark, England, Japan, China, North Korea, Mozambique, Guinea-Bissau, and Cuba. Of the "alternative" publications, only *Muhammad Speaks*, newspaper of the Nation of Islam (NOI), was selling more copies.

Less than a week after Hoover's memo ordering FBI field offices to "cripple" the BPP, the San Diego FBI office proposed to spray a foul-smelling chemical called Skatol on copies of *The Black Panther*. In June, FBI headquarters concocted a plan to "ignite the fuel of conflict" between the BPP and the Nation of Islam by reducing sales of *Muhammad Speaks*. However, in July, the Chicago field office advised against pursuing this project, warning that, due to existing tensions between the two groups, "any revelation of a Bureau attempt to encourage conflict might serve to bring the BPP and NOI closer together."

In November 1970, FBI headquarters directed field offices to distribute copies of a column written by Victor Riesel, a white labor columnist, calling for a nationwide union boycott of handling *The Black Panther*, which was shipped around the country by air freight. The Church Committee could not determine the outcome of this plan.

FBI PLOT CREATES RIFT
BETWEEN HUEY AND ELDRIDGE

Earlier, in March 1970, the FBI had launched a COINTELPRO action to create a permanent rift between Huey and Eldridge. Each was isolated from the party— Eldridge in exile in Algeria and Huey in prison. Exploiting this situation, the bureau sent an anonymous letter to Eldridge saying that BPP leaders in California were trying to undermine his influence. As a result of this fake letter, Eldridge expelled three members of the BPP's international section.

Pleased with the apparent success of the first letter, the FBI followed it up with another one to David Hilliard, written to appear as if it had come from Connie Matthews, the party's representative in Scandinavia. The second letter claimed that Eldridge "has tripped out. Perhaps he has been working too hard." The letter suggested that David "take some immediate action before this becomes more serious." In May 1970, Eldridge called BPP national headquarters in Oakland and talked to David, Connie, and other BPP leaders. Suspicion was expressed that the letters had probably been sent by the FBI or CIA.

Nevertheless, the FBI continued with its campaign to cause dissension between Huey and Eldridge. About a week after Huey's release from prison on August 5, 1970, an FBI informant in Philadelphia distributed a fake "directive" to local Panthers questioning Huey's leadership ability. The fictitious COINTELPRO letters to Huey and Eldridge, alleging that each was critical of the other's leadership, continued throughout the rest of 1970 and into early 1971, and resulted in Huey's expulsion of several key members from the party, including Connie Matthews.

On February 26, 1971, during a TV interview, Eldridge criticized the expulsions and suggested that David Hilliard be removed as BPP chief of staff. As a result, Huey expelled Eldridge and the entire international section of the party. Their expulsions were reported in the March 6 edition of *The Black Panther*. The FBI program to create a permanent rift between Huey and Eldridge had succeeded.

In New York City, where animosities between the "pro-Huey" and "pro-Eldridge" groups were the greatest, several BPP members were expelled. In separate incidents there in March and April 1971, Panthers Sam Napier, *Black Panther* national circulation manager, and Harold Russell were shot to death.

In his critical essay published in the April 17, 1971, issue of *The Black Panther*, "On the Defection of Eldridge Cleaver from the Black Panther Party and the Defection of the Black Panther Party from the Black Community," Huey wrote:

> We recognize that nothing in nature stands outside of dialectics, even the Black Panther Party. But we welcome these contradictions, because they clarify our struggle. We had a contradiction with our former Minister of Information, Eldridge Cleaver. But we understand this as necessary to our growth.

While praising Eldridge for his "great contributions to the Black Panther Party with his writing and speaking," Huey accused him of joining the BPP for the wrong reasons:

Without my knowledge, he [Eldridge] took this [the *Ramparts* incident] as *the* Revolution and *the* Party...the police confrontation left him fixated with the "either-or" attitude. This was that either the community picked up the gun with the Party or else they were cowards and there was no place for them.

Criticizing the BPP for its free speech movement, which he said had isolated the party from the black community, Huey said, "The Black Panther Party defected from the community long before Eldridge defected from the Party."

PAPER EMBRACES "INTERCOMMUNAL" STRUGGLE

Two months earlier, in February, Huey had changed the name of the newspaper from *The Black Panther Black Community News Service* to *The Black Panther Intercommunal News Service*. The change was made to reflect the party's shift from a largely black nationalist perspective to one advocating an international or "intercommunal" struggle against racism and imperialism that cuts across all color lines.

Regular features of the newspaper at that time, in addition to the party's Ten Point Platform and Program, included "People's Perspective," a column on national news events affecting black and Third World people; "Black and Community News," including articles about party leaders, programs, and events; "Intercommunal News," which featured news about freedom movements in southern Africa, Central America, and the Middle East; book excerpts and reviews and movie reviews; and a list of BPP "Survival Programs," such as the Free Breakfast for School Children Program, the People's Free Medical Clinic, and the Free Food and Free Legal Aid programs. *The Black Panther* was circulated internationally. African liberation movements and many foreign embassies subscribed to it. It was also popular on college and university campuses.

ELAINE BROWN AND ERICKA HUGGINS BECOME SUCCEEDING EDITORS

Succeeding *Black Panther* editors included Elaine Brown and Ericka Huggins. The two women and Ericka's husband, John, were early party members in the Los Angeles BPP chapter founded by "deputy minister of defense" Alprentice "Bunchy" Carter, a former gang leader who had served time in prison. On January 17, 1969, Bunchy and John, the chapter's "minister of information," were shot to death during

a meeting of black students at the University of California-Los Angeles. Five members of United Slaves (US), a black nationalist organization founded by Maulana Karenga, were charged with killing the southern California BPP leaders. Two of the five remained at large. The other three, brothers George and Larry Stiner and Claude Hubert, were convicted of murder. The Church Committee on Intelligence later revealed that COINTELPRO instigated and then perpetuated rising violence between the BPP and US by sending inflammatory letters to the rival groups, claiming each was out to destroy the other. In a *Penthouse* interview published in April 1979, "Othello," an ex-agent provocateur in the Los Angeles BPP, charged that the Stiners and Hubert were police informants in US.

Following the deaths of Bunchy and John, Elaine, who had been communications secretary for the Los Angeles BPP chapter, became its deputy minister of information, the number two post in a chapter. She went to Oakland around 1970 and became editor of *The Black Panther*. Her writing and editing skills greatly improved the quality and professionalism of the newspaper. However, in late 1972, Elaine's tenure as editor ended when she ran for Oakland City Council in an historic campaign with Bobby Seale, who ran for mayor. While the two BPP leaders lost the election in April 1973, they captured 40 percent of the vote, bolstering black political power in Oakland and paving the way for the election of the city's first black mayor, Lionel Wilson, in 1977. In 1975, Elaine was defeated in a close race in her second run for city council.

Ericka, while in New Haven, Connecticut, to bury her husband, was arrested and jailed for conspiracy and murder, along with seven other Panthers, in the May 1969 death of New York BPP member Alex Rackley. Ericka and Bobby Seale, who was also charged with Rackley's murder, stood trial together in a case that was regularly covered in *The Black Panther*. They were released from nearly two years of prison on May 24, 1971, when the jury deadlocked and a mistrial was declared. Moving to Oakland in 1971, Ericka followed Elaine as editor of *The Black Panther*, a position she held until about mid-1972. In 1973, Ericka became director of the Intercommunal Youth Institute (later renamed Oakland Community School), the BPP's community-based, award-winning elementary school.

DAVID DU BOIS INSTITUTES COLLECTIVE DECISION MAKING

David G. Du Bois succeeded Ericka as editor of *The Black Panther*. During the summer of 1972, the stepson of W.E.B. Du Bois—the great African-American historian and sociologist—returned to the United States following a 13-year absence. David had spent his time abroad working as a journalist and college professor in Egypt and Ghana and traveling in Africa, Europe, the Soviet Union, and the People's Republic of China, where he was a student for a time.

"When I came to the Black Panther Party, I was no spring chicken," David wrote in a 1990 unpublished article. "I was 47 years old and had cut my revolutionary teeth on street demonstrations with other [World War II] war-weary G.I.s in the Philippines demanding our right to go home and in the east coast student and veterans' movements of the mid and late 1940's." He became frustrated with the failure of these movements to "honestly and decisively" deal with issues impacting American blacks. Thus, in 1959 David began his exile from the United States.

Back in America in 1972, David began to research the achievements of the civil rights movement of the 1960s which had taken place during his absence. At the top of his list was the BPP. Many party leaders, including David Hilliard and Eldridge Cleaver, traveled in Africa during the late 1960s and David Du Bois met some of them in Cairo, Egypt, where he lived. "Through these contacts I learned firsthand much about the Party...Most of what I learned increased an already intense admiration for these young ghetto blacks who had decided they had taken it long enough and were prepared to fight fire with fire," David wrote.

In November and December 1972, he visited the San Francisco Bay Area where he finally met Huey and toured BPP programs in Oakland and Berkeley. Later, at a dinner with other party members, Huey shared with David his "fantasy" that David would become editor-in-chief of *The Black Panther*. David was a veteran journalist, and Huey was always concerned with improving the professionalism of the newspaper. Several days later, David began his three-year association with the BPP as editor of the party's newspaper. Huey insisted that David be a party employee, not a member, "making me, he hoped, less a target for the party's enemies," David recalled.

While assured by Huey that he would have complete freedom with content and format of *The Black Panther*, David nevertheless began his work cautiously. Reflecting on his early days as editor of *BPINS*, as the paper came to be known by party members, David wrote:

> The most serious initial challenge I faced was winning the confidence and the willing cooperation of the paper's staff. None had had formal journalistic training or newspaper experience, except that they had gained getting out the party paper. Their work methods had successfully

produced the paper week after succeeding week..."So who is this aging bourgeois outsider taking over and threatening changes," they [newspaper staff] said to me with their eyes and in their manner toward me.

Being the stepson of W.E.B. Du Bois helped David's status with party members. Perhaps more important in helping him gradually win the staff's confidence, he insisted that the staff make collective decisions about the content and format of the paper. While weekly newspaper meetings were routine, David at first found it difficult to get staff members to express their opinions. With his encouragement, their reluctance abated in time, and they contributed ideas and opinions that continually improved *The Black Panther* and its status among BPP members.

In 1972 *The Black Panther* began a series of articles on sickle cell anemia, a rare blood disease that mostly afflicts people of African descent. For this reason, the party charged, medical science had made little effort to study the disease and develop a treatment for it. The party also launched a free nationwide sickle cell anemia testing program.

RECRUITED TO DETROIT BPP CHAPTER

Meanwhile, the summer of 1972 was also eventful for me. My fiancé, Joe Abron, a Detroit native and Purdue University junior, joined the local chapter of the BPP. Having recently earned my master's degree in communication from Purdue, I worked in Chicago as public information officer at Malcolm X College and later as a reporter for the *Chicago Daily Defender*. Frequently, I went to Detroit for weekends to visit Joe and to do party work. We both firmly believed that black people who wanted to make social change needed to belong to an organization in order to have the greatest impact, so I soon followed him into the BPP.

By the time I joined the party, my views about the black struggle had been shaped by the southern civil rights movement of the 1950s and early 1960s, which I observed at a distance during my childhood in Jefferson City, Missouri. I lived in the Missouri capital city with my parents and two younger sisters from 1953-1966. My father, J. Otis Erwin, a Methodist minister, taught philosophy and religion at Lincoln University, then a predominantly black school. From him and my mother, Adeline Comer Erwin, who had been a college music teacher before marrying my father, I learned that blacks with skills had a responsibility to use them to better the black race.

Watching television and reading news accounts, I was impressed by the courage of blacks and their white allies who often risked their lives to defy Jim Crow segregation laws in the South to demand the right of blacks to vote and to attend the schools of their choice. In the summer of 1964, when black and white students in SNCC and other civil rights groups launched a massive voter registration drive in Mississippi, I wanted to join them. My mother, however, told me it was much too dangerous for a 16-year-old girl like me to go to Mississippi.

At any rate, by the time I graduated from high school in May 1966, I had decided that, whatever my career would be as an adult, I would use it to help black people. I spent the next four years in college at Baker University in Baldwin, Kansas, where I majored in journalism. When Dr. Martin Luther King, Jr. was assassinated on April 4, 1968, I was near the end of my sophomore year. Dr. King's murder troubled me deeply and strengthened my resolve to get involved in the black movement.

That summer, I was one of six Baker students and a faculty member who spent eight weeks in the southern African country of Rhodesia, now Zimbabwe. Rhodesia was the first African country I had ever visited. My knowledge of Africa was so limited that I had assumed African blacks controlled their countries. In Rhodesia, I learned that the country had been under British rule since the late nineteenth century and that blacks had launched an armed struggle to win their freedom. Living on a Methodist church mission, I worked for a black newspaper that was regularly censored by the government for printing news critical of the white regime, which the U.S. government supported. Returning to Baker with increased determination to work in the black movement after graduation, I became co-editor of the campus newspaper, *The Baker Orange*, during my junior and senior years. After graduating in May 1970, I went to Purdue to graduate school.

PARTY WORK IN THE MOTOR CITY

By the time I joined the BPP in the summer of 1972, the COINTELPRO campaign against the party had taken its toll on Detroit Panthers. Many members had resigned and several were imprisoned, leaving less than a dozen members in the Motor City.

Afraid that a sheltered minister's daughter like me would not be accepted by streetwise party members, I began my apprenticeship as a would-be Panther selling *The Black Panther*. In platform shoes, I walked up and down endless drab hallways in Detroit housing projects, urging all who opened their doors to "Get your Black Panther news! Get your people's paper!" My Panther comrades and I had fun competing with Nation of Islam members for newspaper sales on Detroit street corners.

For the most part, the competition was friendly and consisted of members of the two groups trying to out talk each other for sales.

In August 1973, Joe and I were married. Four months later, in December 1973, he graduated from Purdue and we returned to Detroit to work full-time in the party. My main jobs were to work in the Free Breakfast for School Children Program; to drive for the Busing to Prisons Program, which provided transportation for relatives of prisoners to visit their loved ones at Michigan's Jackson State Prison; and to sell *The Black Panther Intercommunal News Service*. I worked hard and earned the respect of my comrades.

I became a writer for the *BPINS* in early 1974 after moving to Oakland with Joe and other members of the Detroit BPP chapter. At the time, there were 13 comrades in the newspaper cadre, as we were called, consisting of writers, led by editor David Du Bois, and layout staff (paste-up and typesetting), led by artist Emory Douglas. In a given week, writers might be assigned to cover a city council meeting, a community rally, or a speech by Bobby Seale and Elaine Brown. During my first few months there, I did a series on the party's alternative school, the Intercommunal Youth Institute.

In April 1974, shortly after my arrival in Oakland, local police raided a party facility on 29th Avenue in East Oakland where children from the Intercommunal Youth Institute often stayed. Several BPP members were arrested, and police seized party documents and files in the house. A few days later, while in a laundromat across the street from the apartment where I lived with my husband and other Panthers, I was approached by two white men who showed me badges identifying them as FBI agents.

"Hi, JoNina. We want to talk to you for a minute," one of the smiling agents said. "We know that you just came to Oakland to work with the Black Panthers. There's been trouble recently [referring to the 29th Avenue raid], and we don't think you want to be involved in that. Maybe we can help." His voice and manner were pleasant. Nevertheless, the familiar way he spoke, as if he knew all about me, terrified me.

Panthers were trained never to talk to police without an attorney present. I told the FBI agents I had nothing to say to them and tore out of the laundromat back to my apartment, where I called party headquarters to tell them what had happened. I had experienced what I believe was a COINTELPRO action.

CRISIS IN 1974

Eight months after my arrival in Oakland, in August 1974, the party underwent another crisis. In separate incidents that month, police charged Huey with beating a black tailor, Preston Callins, and shooting a black prostitute, Kathleen Smith, to death. Afraid he might return to prison, Huey disappeared. A few weeks later, he surfaced in Havana, Cuba, where he lived in exile with his wife and Panther comrade, Gwen, for the next three years. The charges against Huey and his disappearance caused considerable confusion within party ranks and severely damaged our reputation in the community. Unsure of the party's future and weary from years of courtroom trials and police harassment, party chair Bobby Seale and several other BPP Central Committee members also disappeared. With Bobby gone, Huey, from Havana, gave leadership of the party to Elaine Brown, and appointed her BPP chair.

As the party coped with the departure of its co-founders, *The Black Panther* continued its weekly publication schedule. Once again, "Free Huey" became a recurring theme in the paper. Other articles in the paper at that time reflected the expansion of the party's work and influence under Elaine's tenure as party chair. The BPP worked with such diverse groups as the United Farmworkers, the Zimbabwe African National Union, which was leading Rhodesia's armed black liberation struggle, and Oakland Concerned Citizens for Urban Renewal. She consulted frequently with David about the newspaper's coverage of the party's work with these groups.

The paper frequently reprinted articles from other left and progressive publications whose views reflected those of the BPP. Writers were given news clippings to edit. Such reprints were always attributed in an editor's note. Unlike most other left publications, however, there were no bylines on articles in *The Black Panther*.

Ideas and some copy for national and international news often came from establishment newspapers like the *New York Times, Los Angeles Times*, and *Washington Post*. However, our slant on the major news events of the day was almost always different than what appeared in the establishment papers. Under David's brilliant leadership, the quality, language, and appearance of *The Black Panther* substantially improved. The party purchased a good quality offset typesetting machine and made greater use of party members with writing skills for proofreading and copy editing.

MEMBERSHIP DROPS: *BLACK PANTHER* BECOMES BIWEEKLY

Police surveillance of the newspaper continued. According to a Los Angeles Police Department intelligence division memo of March 11, 1974, "The Black Panther has increased in journalistic quality, but decreased in circulation since the Panthers have concentrated in the Oakland area."

David's tenure as *BPINS* editor ended abruptly in early 1976 when his mother, Shirley Graham Du Bois, widow of W.E.B. Du Bois, became ill and David left Oakland to care for her. Of his work with the BPP, David later said, "It irrevocably, mercifully changed my life." Following David as editor was Michael Fultz, the talented assistant editor, a Brooklyn, New York, native who joined the party in Boston while a college student. Michael became editor of *The Black Panther* when the BPP was mounting a citywide campaign to elect Lionel Wilson as Oakland's first black mayor. Elaine told party members that Wilson's election was an essential condition for creating a favorable climate for Huey's return from Cuba to stand trial on the assault and murder charges from August 1974. The newspaper was the party's official news organ and therefore a key component in the Wilson campaign and efforts to bring Huey home. Elaine, therefore, often instructed Michael on the paper's contents. In addition to his responsibilities as editor, Michael often spoke for the party at meetings and other community events.

In April 1977, Wilson was elected mayor of Oakland, and in July, Huey returned to Oakland from Cuba. He was later acquitted of assaulting Preston Callins, but stood trial twice for the murder of Kathleen Smith. Both trials ended in mistrials and charges were dropped in 1979. As a result of Huey's three costly trials and several unrelated arrests, party resources were nearly depleted and membership further declined. By March 1978 when I became editor of the paper following Michael's resignation from the party, BPP membership, variously estimated at highs of 2,000 to 4,000 nationwide, had dropped to a couple dozen. Most members, although still dedicated to the party's principles, found it hard to stay in the organization as they got older and found themselves needing and wanting better living conditions for themselves and their families, which the party could not provide. The newspaper cadre had only six members, down from 13 in 1974. With fewer people to produce the newspaper, *The Black Panther* became a biweekly.

TRAGEDY IN JONESTOWN

The reduction in the newspaper's staff and frequency did not soften its stance on issues affecting black and poor people. One example was *The Black Panther*'s account of the November 1978 deaths of over 900 Americans, mostly black and many children, in Jonestown, a settlement in the Caribbean nation of Guyana.

The Jonestown dead were members of the San Francisco-based People's Temple, a church founded by the Reverend Jim Jones. The BPP had developed a close relationship with People's Temple, whose community programs for the poor in San Francisco and northern California were much like those of the party. I knew a few Temple members and considered them my comrades in the struggle. Charles Garry, long-time BPP attorney, was also attorney for People's Temple.

The true facts about Jonestown and People's Temple remain unknown to this day. However, the BPP, based on our ties with the church, believed that Jones and several hundred church members had exiled themselves to Guyana and established Jonestown to protest racism and poverty in the United States. To Black Panthers, Jonestown was a serious indictment of life in America. The settlement could prove to be an embarrassment to the U.S. government if allowed to continue.

California Congressman Leo Ryan, several Bay Area journalists, and attorney Garry went to Jonestown in November 1978 to investigate complaints from relatives of Jonestown settlers. Authorities said that Temple members, afraid that they would be forced to disband Jonestown, committed suicide by drinking poisoned Kool-Aid at Jones' direction. Jones was found shot to death, apparently having committed suicide. Ryan and three journalists with him were killed while boarding their plane to fly back to the United States.

The BPP questioned whether the mass deaths were really suicide. In the beginning, we had no concrete evidence to support our suspicions. However, the strident media campaign to discredit Jones and People's Temple as a "crazy cult" in the weeks following the tragedy reminded many Panthers of the FBI COINTEL-PRO campaign against the party. Some party members, including me, were convinced that the deaths at Jonestown might also be the result of COINTELPRO.

To substantiate our beliefs, *Black Panther* writers interviewed members of People's Temple and their relatives; we read dozens of news articles about the church. I went several days without sleep to gather the story on Jonestown. For me, it became a personal crusade to tell the "real" truth about how the People's Temple members died.

Six weeks in the making, an entire issue of *The Black Panther* was devoted to what we called the Jonestown "massacre." I wrote the banner headline on the front page of the paper, "C.I.A. Linked to Deaths in Jonestown." I also wrote many of the articles in the issue. One of those, quoting other news sources, charged that a top aide to Jones had once been a CIA agent.

In the editorial, which I wrote, the Black Panther Party accused the CIA of destroying Jonestown with a neutron bomb, which is colorless and odorless and doesn't leave any evidence. This was a bold charge, even for the BPP, and I knew it had to be approved prior to publication by Huey.

In all my phone conversations with him, never had I been as nervous as I was that January day in 1979 when I read the editorial on Jonestown. Despite the public damage to Huey's image from the assault and murder trials he went through after his return from Cuba, he had resumed leadership of the party, and I respected him. After I finished reading him the editorial, he said to my great relief, "Good. Print it."

Over 12 years have passed since the deaths at Jonestown. At the time, many people thought the BPP's assessment of Jonestown was crazy. One woman told me that if she accepted the party's view about CIA involvement she would have to start questioning everything the American government does. She said she was afraid to do that.

I don't know what really happened at Jonestown. I do know that *The Black Panther*'s coverage of it was but one example of the newspaper's boldness and in-depth reporting of news involving and impacting black and other disenfranchised people. Even though the programs of the Black Panther Party and its membership were all but decimated by the late seventies and *The Black Panther* was forced to go monthly in 1980, the paper was still in demand by readers who wanted a non-mainstream analysis of the news.

THE LAST *BLACK PANTHER*, THE FIRST *COMMEMORATOR*

Thus, it was with great sorrow that, after 13 years, the BPP was forced to discontinue the paper in October 1980. Much as I loved the paper, I was among those party members who persuaded Huey that we no longer had the human or financial resources to publish the "people's" paper.

Over a decade later, in November 1990, the Commemoration Committee for the Black Panther Party—composed of ex-Panthers and BPP supporters—began publication of *The Commemorator* in Oakland. The newspaper's statement of purpose reflects the original goals of the BPP and *The Black Panther*:

> The newspaper encourages grassroots organizing and networking for people empowerment and community control of the institutions effecting change...the COMMEMORATOR IS A PROGRESSIVE COMMUNITY FORUM. It offers the community at large the opportunity to help solve some of the critical problems that

affect us all....the lack of decent shelter, medical care, education and employment for all people.

The Commemorator, a monthly tabloid, averages 8 to 12 pages per issue, including photos, and is free. The paper covers local, national, and international news much in the way *The Black Panther* did, including such *BPINS* features as "Africa in Focus." "Huey's Corner," writings by the late BPP co-founder, is another regular feature. The April 1991 issue of the paper included an excerpt from Huey's doctoral dissertation, *War Against the Panthers*.

Beginning in the November 1990 issue and concluding in the March 1991 issue, *The Commemorator* reprinted an article written in May 1990 by ex-BPP chair Elaine Brown, "Responding to Radical Racism, David Horowitz Barely Remembered." Horowitz, former editor of *Ramparts* magazine, a left publication, was once a BPP ally. Elaine's article was written in response to a particularly bitter and racist article by Horowitz in the March-April 1990 issue of *Smart* magazine, in which the white ex-radical accused the BPP of being a "gang of hoodlums" and Huey of being a "thug who had terrorized the Oakland underworld in the seventies." In a stinging rebuke to Horowitz's reactionary charges Elaine wrote:

> That Horowitz chooses to dismiss the holocaustal horror of the Black experience in America in his denunciation of Huey as a "crazy nigger" serves as clear and convincing evidence of his [Horowitz's] racism.

Calling Horowitz a "racist white rabbit who tries to confuse all who enter his wonderland," Elaine then accuses him of using Huey to discredit the progressive movement:

> Depicting the support of the campaign to "Free Huey!" by Whites and non-Panthers as the development of "a cult," Horowitz clucks a reprobate tongue at the serious work of literally millions of people....There was no "cult," but a coalition by a mass of people consciously addressing yearnings and demands that came to focus on the freedom of one man, as he personified the capture of a collective freedom.

The Commemorator has been received favorably in the Bay Area, according to staff member and ex-Panther Melvin Dickson. Because the paper is free, the staff must continuously raise funds to cover production and mailing expenses.

MEMORIAL ISSUE OF *THE BLACK PANTHER*

Following on the heels of *The Commemorator*, in February 1991, in Berkeley, California, the Black Panther Newspaper Committee (BPNC), a non-profit organization of former Panthers, published a Memorial Issue of *The Black Panther Black Community News Service*. The inaugural issue of the revived *Black Panther* looks like a *Black Panther* issue of the late 1960s. Using the newspaper's original masthead from the sixties, the front page of the paper features the famous 1967 photo of Huey and Bobby dressed in the BPP uniform of black leather jackets and black berets, standing in front of party headquarters with guns, and the banner headline, "The Struggle Continues." The editorial said in part:

> We were all members of the Black Panther Party who participated in the formation, organization, and day to day operations of Black Panther Party activities...Because of our uncompromising work to build a strong Afrikan-Amerikkkan nation...many of us were forced into exile or underground, or were imprisoned by the U.S. government during its COINTELPRO war.

The editorial said that the BPNC came together out of a "compelling need" to address such critical issues in the African-American community as drugs, unemployment, inadequate housing, "miseducation, legalized police terror and murder," and institutional racism—issues addressed in the BPP Ten Point Platform and Program. The editorial concluded:

> In the past *The Black Panther Black Community News Service* was an uncompromising voice for exposing these attacks...and for advocating an implacable stand to redress them....we are proud to announce to you that uncompromising voice has returned!

The Memorial Issue is dedicated to the BPP's "Fallen Comrades," party members who were killed by police or other law enforcement agents, and political prisoners. The issue contains photos and biographies of some of the fallen comrades and articles about the cases of several political prisoners. Other articles are written by some of those prisoners, several of whom were BPP members. Also included in the Memorial Issue are the BPP Ten Point Platform and Program; a chronology of party history from 1966-1971; a description and photos of party Survival Programs; articles on current national and international news; and a financial statement.

The new *Black Panther Black Community News Service* is a quarterly publication and costs $1.00 per issue. The BPNC has offices in Illinois, New Jersey, New York, Oklahoma, and California.

TASK FOR FUTURE GENERATIONS

It has been 25 years since the founding of the Black Panther Party. The struggle of African-Americans for justice and equality, outlined in the party's Ten Point Platform and Program of October 15, 1966, continues. There is still no "land, bread, housing, education, clothing, justice and peace" for the vast majority of black people in America. For that reason, *The Commemorator* and the new *Black Panther Black Community News Service* have emerged. These publications tell the story of the Black Panther Party and its enduring contributions to the empowerment of black and disenfranchised people throughout the world. Hopefully, the two newspapers and this article will inspire former Panthers to write a complete history of the organization—a task that must be done to give future generations a thorough assessment of the Black Panther Party's important role in the history of the African-American struggle for freedom.

(Anyone wishing to contact *The Commemorator* may write the Commemoration Committee for the Black Panther Party, 4432 Telegraph Avenue, PO Box 62, Oakland, CA 94609, or call (415) 841-9063. Correspondence to *The Black Panther Black Community News Service* may be sent to the BPNC, PO Box 519, Berkeley, CA 94701-0519.)

SELECTED BIBLIOGRAPHY

Bush, Rod, ed. *The New Black Vote, Politics and Power in Four American Cities*. San Francisco: Synthesis Publications, 1984.

Carson, Clayborne. *In Struggle, SNCC and the Black Awakening of the 1960s*. Cambridge, MA: Harvard University Press, 1981.

Churchill, Ward, and Jim Vander Wall. *Agents of Repression: The FBI's Secret Wars Against the Black Panther Party and American Indian Movement*. Boston: South End Press, 1988.

Clark, Ramsey, and Roy Wilkins, chairmen. *Search and Destroy: A Report by the Commission of Inquiry into the Black Panthers and the Police*. New York: Metropolitan Applied Research Center, Inc., 1973.

Committee on Internal Security, House of Representatives. *The Black Panther Party, Its Origin and Development as Reflected in Its Official Weekly Newspaper, the Black Panther Black Community News Service*. Washington: U.S. Government Printing Office, 1970.

Donner, Frank J. *The Age of Surveillance: The Aims and Methods of America's Intelligence System*. New York: Vintage Books, 1981.

Erikson, Erik H. *In Search of Common Ground: Conversations with Erik H. Erikson and Huey P. Newton*. New York: Norton, 1973.

Foner, Philip, ed. *The Black Panthers Speak*. Philadelphia: Lippincott, 1970.

Forman, James. "The Black Panther Party." In *The Making of Black Revolutionaries*, 522-43. New York: The Macmillan Company, 1972.

Freed, Donald. *Agony in New Haven: The Trial of Bobby Seale, Ericka Huggins and the Black Panther Party*. New York: Simon and Schuster, 1973.

Huggins, Ericka, and Huey P. Newton. *Insights and Poems*. San Francisco: City Lights Books, 1975.

Jackson, George. *Blood in My Eye*. Baltimore: Black Classic Press, 1990.

____. *Soledad Brother: The Prison Writings of George Jackson*. New York: Coward-McCann, 1970.

Major, Reginald. *A Panther Is a Black Cat*. New York: William Morrow, 1971.

Marine, Gene. *The Black Panther*. New York: New American Library, 1969.

Newton, Huey P. *Revolutionary Suicide*. New York: Harcourt, Brace and Jovanovich, 1973.

____. *To Die for the People: The Writings of Huey P. Newton*. New York: Random House, 1972.

____. "War Against the Panthers: A Study of Repression in America." Ph.D. diss., University of California-Santa Cruz, 1980.

O'Reilly, Kenneth. *"Racial Matters": The FBI's Secret File on Black America, 1960-1972*. New York: The Free Press, 1989.

Seale, Bobby. *A Lonely Rage: The Autobiography of Bobby Seale*. New York: Times Books, 1978.

___. *Seize the Time: The Story of the Black Panther Party and Huey P. Newton*. New York: Random House, 1970.

Shakur, Assata. *Assata, an Autobiography*. Westport, CT: Lawrence Hill & Co., 1987.

Tannenbaum, Robert, and Philip Rosenberg. *Badge of the Assassin*. New York: Dorison House, 1979.

U.S. Senate. Select Committee to Study Governmental Operations. *Supplementary Detailed Staff Reports on Intelligence Activities and the Rights of Americans, Book III*. Washington, DC: U.S. Government Printing Office, 1976.

BOTH SIDES NOW REMEMBERED:
OR, THE ONCE AND FUTURE JOURNAL

Elihu Edelson

Edelson is an artist, calligrapher, writer, and teacher. He was listed as a critic in *Who's Who in American Art, 1976.* Alternative press watchers can find out about *BSN*'s comeback by sending return postage to Rt. 6, Box 28, Tyler, TX 75704-9712.]

Both Sides Now (*BSN*) barely made the sixties. The first issue was dated November 29, 1969. Its banner headline reflected one of the Movement's main concerns of the moment: "Paul McCartney Dead!" Two more issues managed to get squeezed in before the end of the decade.

BSN's original base, Jacksonville, Florida, was not the most fertile ground for an underground paper at the turn of the seventies. The city was ruled like a feudal fiefdom by a local machine that included the Florida Publishing Company, a monopoly that put out both the morning and evening papers. FPC, in turn, was owned by the Florida East Coast Railroad. Three nearby military bases contributed to the ultraconservative atmosphere. The St. Johns River and the intersection of Interstates 10 and 75 cut the community into pieces. Jacksonville University, a private institution, was far from a hotbed of student activism. In fact, its name appeared on a list of 500 CIA-connected institutions circulated by the Yippies.

The New Leftists could be counted on the fingers of one hand—a RYM (Revolutionary Youth Movement) Maoist and his wife, a couple of Trots (Trotskyites), and a few ACLU/Unitarian/Democrat-type liberals. A handful of blacks sporting berets and leather jackets put together a local version of the Black Panthers under the name Florida Black Front. Some good rock bands—like the Allman Brothers and Lynyrd Skynyrd—were to come out of Jax, but they had to make their names in Atlanta.

So it is not surprising that, like many other events of the time, the counterculture came belatedly to Jacksonville. The Haight-Ashbury scene had already passed its peak by the time people were getting hassled for long hair in Jax. The heads—as potheads and acidheads called themselves—had set up crash pads where people could come down gently from bad acid trips, but the cops kept harassing them. The deep Southeast had a well-established and exemplary underground paper in Atlanta's *Great Speckled Bird*, and the Jacksonville hippies wanted a publication like that as a voice for their concerns.

The Jacksonville hippies were always more an aggregation of people with related lifestyles than a coherent community. Because none of them had any journalistic experience, they went, naively, to an editor of the morning establishment paper, the *Florida Times-Union*, for advice.

This is the point in the story of *Both Sides Now* where I got sucked in. I was an art teacher in the public school system at the time, but I also wrote a weekly column of art criticism as a stringer for the evening paper, the *Jacksonville Journal*.

The counterculture had only recently entered my consciousness, as I began to pick up on the messages being communicated by rock groups like The Doors, Jefferson Airplane, and Steppenwolf. My wife, Joan, and I were introduced to a speed freak who'd done light shows for the Allman Brothers before they'd moved to Macon, and he put me up to using my press credentials to get passes for the First Atlanta Pop Festival with him as my photographer. I wrote a glowing review of the counterculture scene I saw there.

So when the hippies went to that editor, he referred them to me. I didn't know beans about the nuts and bolts of putting together a paper, but the husband of one of my art teacher colleagues was into small-scale tabloid publishing, and he taught us the basics. The first issues of *BSN* were hacked out on a number of manual typewriters, with lots of hand lettering.

Despite the lead story about Paul McCartney, *BSN*'s first issue had a variety of serious material, including an antiwar sermon by the local Unitarian minister, reviews of *Easy Rider* and *Alice's Restaurant* (by me), a drug rap interview with the vice squad honcho, and items appealing to men from the naval bases who wore long hair wigs when on shore leave. *BSN* was distributed from a combination wig and head shop.

BSN came out every two weeks for several issues into 1970 before entropy began to set in. At first it was driven by high energy and a sense of wonder as we saw our typewriter-pounding, cutting, and pasting transformed by the miracle of offset lithography into a real publication. We tackled a variety of current

issues: the Manson case, Bob Dylan's stylistic changes, high school dress codes, student rights, the draft, pollution of the St. Johns River, the emerging women's movement, the Chicago 8 trial, the first Earth Day (scorned by the same Establishment that embraced it in 1990), and the killings at Kent State and Jackson State. Street poets saw their verses in print, decorated by elaborate drawings. Local culture was viewed from the underside of society.

But after a while, the staff got into some strange trips. We held tedious discussions on how to fairly divide the proceeds among the collective staff, though the paper barely broke even. Much of our income depended on street sales by vendors who were often harassed by the police and occasionally disappeared with their bit of money. Staffers had a variety of odd jobs, but sometimes we had to "pass the hat" to pay the printing bill. In the longer run it became apparent to the dreamers that putting out a paper was mostly shitwork with very little glamour. The round-the-clock grinds every two weeks before press time were getting everyone down, and staff attrition began to set in.

In June 1970, after nine issues, the operation screeched to a halt. The situation had been essentially anarchic, not so much because we were deliberately attempting to fashion a structurally organized microcosm of an anarchistic state but because we were disorganized. A core group with various friends came together in somebody's apartment a couple of days before press time and put the assembled material into camera-ready form. Nevertheless, the group as a whole was not particularly political.

On the other hand, I—the former card-carrying ACLU member—was becoming radicalized by the information coming in from exchange underground papers, Liberation News Service dispatches, and other publications like *Ramparts*. As was true with so many other activists around the country, I was disillusioned by revelations of the U.S. political system as evidenced by the Indochina War, sabotage of peace and justice movements, frame-up trials of activists, gratuitous violence against protesters—not only at Kent State but everywhere, government alliances with organized crime, cover-ups of assassinations, and manipulation of the electoral process (Watergate).

So, as the other staff members began to drift away, I became more intense in my involvement because of my own growing awareness of a noticeable dialectic between two cultures—one oriented toward life and freedom, the other characterized by death and violence. This dialectic was analyzed in writing on the popular level by Abbie Hoffman and the underground press in general, and on the academic level by authors like Theodore Roszak, in *The Making of a Counterculture*.

The original founder of *BSN*, Larry Hanson, was a true hippie. He looked like the conventional Jesus pictures, and wore a long white robe without affectation. After getting *BSN* started he opened a head shop and was duly hassled by the police. Once he was pushed around by a cop at a Krystal diner just for the way he dressed. The staff and friends picketed the place for about a week and told the story in *BSN*.

Eventually, however, the harassment became so unbearable that Larry moved away and out of our lives. Although he was too beset by personal problems to put much energy into *BSN* toward the end anyhow, his benign presence was sorely missed by those who knew him.

Ultimately, I was the only one left of the original staff. Almost single-handedly, aided by some contributed material and reprints, I put together an anniversary issue in December 1970. A liberal Lutheran minister had given me an antique Varityper strike-on typesetter before issue number 9, and I did most of the typing after that. The small, news-size type allowed much more material to be included in the same number of pages. In much the same manner, I was able to put together two issues in 1971: number 11 in April and number 12 (a 24-page monster) for August/September.

A 1972 attempt to bring in new people and diminish my role ended in a fiasco. I believed there should be input from others besides myself, and also wished that the workload could again be shared by more people. Through a Movement "bulletin board" ad, Joan and I imported a couple from Ithaca, New York. In those days, a lot of activists were willing to work for subsistence pay. We provided room and board plus a little spending money. The man was competent at artwork and layout, and both were handy in general. At the same time, some new volunteers materialized, and it looked as though an actual staff was coming together. Two issues were put out in quick succession: number 13 for February/March and number 14 for March/April. Then a series of events led to rapid deterioration.

A cartoon the Ithaca man did for *BSN* number 14 should have given me a clue. It showed a bewhiskered man with big nose wearing a black cloak and beanie while brandishing a rolled-up *BSN*, standing next to a toady-looking little *BSN* paperboy. Joan pointed out to me that there was a decided anti-Semitic stereotype in the way the man was drawn. Despite two requests for revision, only slight improvement was made. Tired of nagging, I let the cartoon go through, for which I'm sorry. In retrospect, the drawing suggests Dickens' Fagin, who exploits little boys to do his dirty work.

The final straw came when the Ithaca couple and the new volunteers decided to use the little bit of money *BSN* had to put out a big newsprint poster instead of another issue. I was trying hard not to be the big decision maker at that time and was not involved in this idea.

Seeing that this crew was not likely to get *BSN* back on track, Joan and I angrily demanded the return of its number one asset: the old Varityper, which we'd lent to the volunteers. (I later acquired a rebuilt IBM Executive with small type that I used for most of the copy; and toward the end I added a late model Varityper.) So I had that and the *BSN* name and nothing else. The staff dissipated and the Ithaca folks went on to other pastures. I still wonder if they were screw-ups or provocateurs.

Over the remainder of the decade I put out one or two issues a year as time and finances allowed, with occasional help from friends. A rundown of the frequency of the remaining issues will give some idea of what it was like. Without any help, I was able to put out one more issue later in 1972. It was called "War Without Honor" and was largely intended for distribution at the Republican Convention in Miami, as part of the protests against Nixon's prolonging of the war. Unfortunately, issues like that come off as downers and do not help attract new readers. The count of issues for the remaining years of the decade went like this: 1973—1, 1974—3, 1975—2; 1976—2; 1977—1; 1978—0; 1979—1; 1980—1.

Part of the irregularity was due to the fact that most of the funding came out of my own pocket, with a little income from store sales, ads, and subscriptions. Street sales were a thing of the past, so *BSN* had to rely more on the mails. The economics of tabloid printing were peculiar. Most of the expense went into making the negatives and setting up the big web presses. Printing 1,000 papers cost only a little more than printing 500, and 2,000 cost just a little more than that. So I'd have 2,000 printed and give the majority away with enclosed subscription pitches.

In 1975, I got a bulk rate mailing permit, and in 1976 got a non-profit incorporation under the name Free People Inc. This last move was to end any question of anyone making money off the deal, but mostly it was made so that I could get the lowest mailing rates, which were less than 4¢ a copy back then. However, it took about two years of wrangling with the Postal Service to get the permit because Free People was not tax-exempt. All in all, one might look upon *BSN* as a somewhat expensive hobby during this period.

Publication was suspended in 1980 when Joan and I, in an attempt to de-urbanize, moved to Texas and shifted all our resources into homesteading. We're largely out of touch with Jax now but, from what I gather, new peace activists have gotten together, mainly to protest the Trident sub base just across the Georgia border—which *BSN* had warned about before it was built.

Both Sides Now put out a total of 26 issues. Minimal as that might be, some of the events, considerations, and concerns that were involved are of retrospective interest. One amusing irony was how much attention the FBI gave to such an ineffectual once or twice a year effort—I guess they had to show J. Edgar they were doing their bit to stamp out dissent.

For instance, I was informed by associates that agents had questioned them about my sex life, presumably to get some dirt to use against me, as it turned out they had done on Martin Luther King, Jr. and others also. (There was no dirt to find.) They apparently tried to have me lose my teaching job by putting the school administration up to pulling a surprise evaluation of me that no other faculty member went through. No reasons were given.

The biggest farce, however, was to have a stooge start a rival paper called *Climax!* which even subscribed to Liberation News Service. It lured away potential staffers—but no actual ones, since I was by then the only staffer—with offers of salaries. *Climax!* lasted for two issues, largely by publishing LNS reprints. Maybe the FBI realized it was a stupid waste of money and dropped it.

I didn't realize what the game was till it developed that the stooge was doing some dirty work for the FBI during the Gainesville 8 trial. The Gainesville 8 were a group of Vietnam Veterans Against the War (VVAW) leaders who were framed by the government to keep them from organizing demonstrations at the 1972 Republican convention in Miami. As reported in *BSN* number 16 (August 1973), a Jax Vietnam vet had acquired a print of the *Winter Soldier* film and was bringing Scott Camil, one of the Gainesville 8 and a prominent figure in the film, to show it at the University of Northern Florida. After a visit to the vet's home by the person who started *Climax!*, the reel disappeared. It later turned up in the hands of the FBI people who were working on the Gainesville 8 trial. Eventually it was returned and shown at the University to a very small audience—another case of the FBI going to a lot of ineffectual bother trying to hamper dissent. The FBI must have squandered millions on such trivial pursuits, and is probably still doing so.

BSN's shift from collective to autocratic management exemplifies polarities that have existed in alternative journalism from the beginning. Paul Krassner's one-man iconoclastic journal, *The Realist*, is generally acknowledged as the ancestor of the underground press. The true undergrounds that followed usually struggled with various forms of staff collectives. While these dealt broadly with movement concerns, the one-person alternatives tended to take a more personal and personalist turn. Some of my favorite personal journals have been *The Little Free Press* (anarchistic), Irv Thomas' *Black Bart Brigade* (originally for middle-aged dropouts), and *Heretic's Journal* (synthesis of radical politics and spirituality). The most substantial and enduring has been Sy Safransky's "magazine of ideas," *The Sun*, a professional-looking production that has attracted some of the best writers around. Although a staff is listed, one gets the impression that Safransky decides what the contents will be. *Little Free Press* is the only other one of these that is still around. Unknown to each other at first, the *Heretic's Journal* and *BSN* were striving for a similar synthesis—an interesting synchronicity. Other current favorites include Tris Coffin's *Washington Spectator* and Mark Satin's *New Options*.

In retrospect, *BSN*'s history is a frustrating one with respect to some good concepts that I did not have the means, support, or business sense to develop properly. At first I tried to keep up the general movement interest approach of the alternative press. In issue number 18 (June 1974) a sensational tabloid-style (*Enquirer*) treatment was given to the late Mae Brussel's analysis of the Symbionese Liberation Army—the dubious "revolutionary" group that kidnapped Patty Hearst. Brussel, a noted conspiracy investigator, believed that the SLA was fabricated by the government to discredit bona fide radical groups, which are usually nonviolent.

I still believe a nationally distributed underground-type paper is desirable, in addition to ones of local interest, just as *Time* and *Newsweek* augment the daily papers. The nearest paper to that type today is *In These Times*, with its comprehensive coverage of national and international news, as well as some fine cultural criticism.

BSN number 22 (May 1976) was a last effort to attract a local audience and support. That issue featured reprints of exposés of Jacksonville politics that had appeared in major national publications—*Rolling Stone* and *Columbia Journalism Review*.

Unfortunately, the response was virtually nil. As I indicated earlier, Jax was "from nowhere" to start with politically; by the mid-seventies, interest in the Movement was down everywhere. So *BSN* number 23 (September 1976) took up the idea of a modest national tabloid with several features on "the greatest Bicentennial scandals": the growing gap between super rich and poor, Pentagon gluttony, skyrocketing cost of nuclear power, government harassment of American Indian Movement (AIM), Watergate criminals making bucks on books, news blackout of alternative bicentennial activities, cheating at West Point, DC sex scandals... Under the front-page logo of that issue was the characterization, "An Alternative Paper and Digest." Since many of *BSN*'s features were reprints, I believed that some kind of alternative *Reader's Digest* would be a good idea. Eric Utne later proved my idea to be correct with his highly successful magazine, *Utne Reader*, whose contents include reprints from other alternative publications.

Getting back to *Rolling Stone* for a moment: though it has featured a lot of good journalism I have general contempt for the publication because of its deliberate co-optation and undermining of the underground press. *RS* developed a distinctive format that had an underground look, only slicker. It avoided taking really radical positions (though later it got into some good muckraking). This made it more attractive as an advertising vehicle for the big record labels, which subsequently placed virtually no ads in the true undergrounds—a serious setback for many shoestring operations.

My reasons for contempt are perfectly exemplified by a coffee-table-size book *RS* put out on the sixties that covered every sixties topic from Abbie Hoffman to Twiggy except the underground press. Not one word. The non-person treatment.

With *BSN* number 24 (April 1977), *BSN* was given a final editorial turn. I had been interested in esoteric spirituality, or metaphysics, long before my involvement in the Movement, but I had put that interest aside under the pressure of all the causes that had emerged in the sixties and early seventies. Around 1976-1977, I read the writings of William Irwin Thompson and Paul Hawken's account of the Findhorn community.

Thompson, a cultural historian, taught at MIT, York University, and the University of Toronto. After a visit to Findhorn, he dropped out of academe and founded the Lindisfarne Association, a sort of leading edge think tank.

Findhorn is an intentional community in northern Scotland that developed under direct spiritual guidance. Humans cooperating with nature achieved miraculous results in an organic garden grown in sandy beach soil. Cooperation, rather than competition, brought out the potentials in the varied individuals who gravitated toward this place. These people were given to understand that Findhorn was a working model of what life in the New Age could be like.

Inspired by these literary works, and aware now that the Age of Aquarius was indeed dawning, I turned *BSN* into a New Age publication.

Still, I was not prepared to give up my movement concerns. Indeed, the editorial direction of *BSN* was toward a synthesis of radical politics and New Age spirituality. *BSN* number 24 reprinted a *Berkeley Barb* essay by Louise Billotte entitled "Can the Left Find Room for Spirituality?" along with my response, which appeared in the *Barb* under the heading "The Move-ment Has a Strong Spiritual Core." This exchange was reprinted in turn by the Alternative Press Syndicate magazine *Alternative Review*.

Billotte, who said she was studying Tibetan Buddhism at the time, started out by observing that "there definitely is a conflict between politics and spirituality, one whose roots are deep and complex." She was specifically referring to the Left's longstanding suspicion of religion, which Marx had called "the opium of the people." In response to this suspicion, she stated, "What so many people on the Left seem unwilling to accept is the fact that RELIGION IS A FACT OF HUMAN CONSCIOUSNESS." If there was to be progress toward an ideal society, she added, the Left had to come to terms with the need for spiritual content. At the same time, spiritual people needed to become aware of the economic factors that were determining the kind of world we live in.

My point was to reinforce Billotte's theme and inject another viewpoint. I stated that the term "The Left" "has a tendency to narrow our definitive base" and noted a preference to "The Movement" as a name to summarize the broad spectrum of forces striving for a new society. I pointed out that many Movement groups and individuals were spiritually oriented, such as the American Friends Service Committee (AFSC), the Berrigans, and others. The counterculture itself had a definite spiritual side—sometimes lumped in with "cultural" as opposed to political—as seen in people like poet Allen Ginsberg, John Wilcock, a founder of the underground press, and Robert Anton Wilson, a fairly well-known countercultural writer, devotee of Aleister Crowley and Timothy Leary (neither of whom I care for), and student of the occult and conspiracy theories. In closing, I made a pitch for a spiritual/political synthesis to rejuvenate the Movement, which was noticeably foundering by 1977, when our exchange of articles took place.

I should mention that *BSN*'s New Age turn was strongly foreshadowed two years earlier in *BSN* number 20 (late February 1975), which carried the headline "Special Prophecy Issue 1975-2000." *BSN* had just received a review copy of *California Superquake: 1975-77*, by Paul James, who made a convincing case for the possibility that a quake of unprecedented magnitude was likely to take place within that time frame. Taking James seriously, I wrote a full-page review of his book, accompanied by a 3-page article on the national karma that might have brought on such a catastrophe, and what the rest of the century might be like if it really did come about. The term "New Age" was used several times in that feature. Of course, James' timing was way off, but there are still many indications that drastic natural cataclysms will accompany the end of the old order—possibly before the end of this century.

BSN no. 20 also saw the debut of Michael Dorian as the one and only volunteer staffer for five issues. Michael had tapped into the heady mixture of spiritual currents that were swirling around at that time, and he was a very talented pen and ink artist. For that issue, he contributed and edited a 2-2/3-page feature on Neo-Paganism that was generously sprinkled with his imaginative spot drawings. Mike had major input on *BSN* number 21, called "Earth Issue," with a cover, an editorial on planetary consciousness, and a feature on the chakras. His last major contribution was a beautiful reinterpretation of a tarot card for the cover of *BSN* number 25.

With that issue, *BSN* started billing itself as "An Alternative Journal of Aquarian/New Age Transformations." The contents were a mixture of New Age material, Movement thinking, and editorializing. Of New Age interest were an article on "The Dialectics of Astrology" by Martha Gold from *Liberation* magazine, and a long interview with Dr. Andrija Puharich on New Age children. On the Movement side were articles on "Overcoming Oppression" and "Tools for Empowerment" from the Movement for a New Society. I contributed two editorials. One, on death trips, commented on the remarkable number of notable people who died in 1977, including Elvis Presley, Bing Crosby, Groucho and Gummo Marx, Joan Crawford, Zero Mostel, Ethel Waters, Charlie Chaplin, Leopold Stokowski, Loren Eiseley, Wernher von Braun, Robert Lowell, E.F. Schumacker, and Ralph Borsodi, among others. The other editorial remarked on how we have let celebrities take the place of heroes.

Also in that issue were a short biography of Peter Maurin (co-founder with Dorothy Day of the Catholic Worker movement) and a full page of his "Easy Essays." A parable by Irv Thomas of *Black Bart Brigade* dramatized the meaning of true freedom. An experimental feature was the inclusion of an insert called *Alternative Research Newsletter*, which was produced in Canada.

The one piece I most regret having published also appeared in *BSN* number 25. It was a photocopy of a communique, purportedly from a Jonestown victim, which had been sent to a number of Movement and New Age groups and publications. At the time, I was not alert to certain indicators that would have identified this as a far-Right hoax. Fortunately, I had asked conspiracy investigator John Judge for feedback on the communique, and he sent a full-page response. In his first paragraph, he observed that the missive smacked of the U.S. Labor Party (Lyndon LaRouche) and Liberty Lobby, then proceeded to offer proof that Jonestown was a major mind control experiment conducted by fascistic elements in our government.

The last issue of *BSN* (no. 26, May 1980) featured a shift in format I had desired for some time—from tabloid to half-tabloid newsprint magazine. There is a tendency to associate the tabloid format with scandal sheets ranging from the New York *Daily News* to the *National Enquirer*, and the underground press acquired some of that stigma, due largely to uncensored language, sexual frankness, raunchy komix, and spicy classified ads. Even standard newspapers are considered to be transient publications. Magazines, on the other hand, automatically command more respect, and are often considered worth saving. *The Nation* and *The Texas Observer* are good examples of quality newsprint magazines.

BSN had been leaning more and more toward magazine-type content, and readers were encouraged to save their copies. Frequent references were made to articles in back issues.

Magazine format also had technical advantages. Pages are much easier to lay out. Reprints often came from publications with the same page size, so it was simpler to have a good photocopy made than to type the whole article over. Between reprints and original material, a new issue could be put together much more quickly and efficiently.

BSN number 26 came out at the beginning of the Iran hostage crisis and featured related concerns of the moment: Russian intervention in Afghanistan, talk of reinstituting the draft, and the possibility of war with Iran. Though the themes were essentially political, the responses (all reprints except the introductory editorial) were mostly from mainstream religious quarters: Protestant, Catholic, and Jewish. Authors included William Stringfellow, Richard Barnet, Arthur Waskow, Dave Dellinger, Jim Wallis, Charles A. Kimball, David McReynolds, and Rarihokwats.

A major theme of the issue was to recall that the Iran crisis could be traced back to 1953, when a CIA-run coup ousted the existing parliamentary government and re-established a monarchy under the late Shah. The Shah's police state gave rise to the anti-U.S. sentiment that persists to the present. When the hostages were taken, the righteous U.S. response would have been to apologize to the new revolutionary government of Iran for past injuries, and show some genuine repentance. This response might have resulted in a much faster release of the hostages, but of course nation-states never say they're sorry. My editorial introduction to the issue contributed a New Age element by observing that unholy government decisions will inevitably result in bad karma somewhere down the line.

When *BSN* started, the youth movement was saying not to trust anyone over 30, and I was over 40—44 to be exact. Max Scherr was even older when he founded the *Berkeley Barb*. Art Kunkin was 36 when he founded the *Los Angeles Free Press*. When the "kids" pooped out and left me holding the bag, why didn't I quit, too? I believe it's because some of us are truth freaks. We can't stand living in an Orwellian world of lies, distortions, doublethink, secrecy, cover-ups, and whitewashes. A need to communicate the truth becomes an obsession—an addiction, like having a monkey on your back. Some of the more notable truth freaks of our time include Noam Chomsky, George Seldes, and I.F. Stone. Even after a lapse of ten years, my monkey is still there. Though many good alternative publications exist, some bases still are not covered.

I believe that the international Green movement which started taking shape at the turn of the eighties has a potential for developing the spiritual/political synthesis that *BSN* and others had been seeking. In their 1984 book *Green Politics*, Fritjof Capra and Charlene Spretnak noted that leading founders of the German Greens—Petra Kelly and Rudolf Bahro—insisted that a spiritual element was essential to the Green movement. However, Greens who come from a Left background may not be inclined to agree. The conflict that Billotte had observed several years earlier was now reappearing in a new context. In the United States, social ecologist/anarchist Murray Bookchin has shown hostility toward any New Age elements that appear in the Green movement. Those who think like this fear that metaphysical speculation will divert attention from the economic roots of social and ecological problems. On the other hand are those like Spretnak, who believe that a change of consciousness is essential to the making of a new society.

A literary forum is much needed here to discuss such ideas. New Age magazines seldom venture into the spiritual implications of world events, and even the *Utne Reader*—whose founder, Eric Utne, was one of the founders of *New Age Journal*—has limits to its metaphysical adventurousness. In short, there's room for a New Age/Green publication in the current alternative scene—an idea toward which *BSN* was groping over ten years ago, before there was a Green movement.

The term "New Age" has been so commercialized, trivialized, misused, abused, and vilified that it has almost lost any semantic value. It has been applied to humanistic therapies, soporific music, bizarre cults, and new concepts in physics, economics, medicine, and a wide range of subjects. Most often forgotten in all the confusion is the meaning of the word "age."

An age is a specific time frame, and the New Age concept is based on astrological reckoning wherein our solar system is in a changing relationship to the constellations of the zodiac about every 2160 years. Historic times cover only three ages: Taurus, Aries, and Pisces (now in its waning years). The New Age,

as we have heard in the popular song and elsewhere, is the Age of Aquarius. While some journalists look on the New Age as a fad soon destined for the dustbin of history, the fact is that the Age of Aquarius will not really begin till the next century.

Ages do not end and start abruptly. There is a transition period like a segue as one fades out and the next makes its entrance. If we look at our times in this light, we can observe the entropy of the Old Order in political upheavals, economic instability, wars and rumors of war, plagues, famines, earthquakes, and climate changes. At the same time, we see seeds of the new order in ecological awareness, feminism, pacifism, new approaches to healing, and a fusion of old and new religious traditions. Spirituality is the unifying core behind the bewildering changes we are seeing all around us, and if we do not comprehend this we will not be able to understand these changes.

The function of *BSN*, as I saw it, was (or is) to read the "signs of the times" and interpret them in terms of the major shift from one age to another. I always liked the name "Both Sides Now" because of its many ambiguities. In this case, it conveys the idea of a bridge between the old and the new. The role of such a publication is essentially prophetic.

From the foregoing, it may be seen that the Green movement is an appropriate politic for the New Age. When the German Greens formed a party, they rested their platform on four pillars: ecology, social responsibility, grassroots democracy, and nonviolence. Capra and Spretnak discerned other implied pillars, including decentralism, feminism, and spirituality. Hence, I feel comfortable about identifying *BSN* with the Green movement, as long as it sticks to first principles.

At the same time, *BSN* should remain an independent voice, not connected to any factions or personalities in the movement. The maverick role allows one to venture into territories that are too far out for the more "respectable" journals.

At the time this is being written, I am engaged in an informal investigation of the anti-New Age movement. Over the past decade, there has been a growing body of books, articles, workshops, audio tapes, and TV broadcasts bent on discrediting the movement, which has been characterized as everything from a fascist plan for world domination to an anti-Christian heresy conjured up by Satan himself. Investigating this phenomenon takes one into a twilight zone of the paranoid style, conspiracy theories, Satanism, cults, skeptics, and spiritual counterfeits. Most of this flack comes from the fundamentalist/pentacostal axis, which has close ties to the far Right in politics, but there are also salvos from skeptical humanists. Hardly anyone is picking up on all this because so few political/spiritual minds are around.

My original idea was to put out an occasional newsletter to be called *The Tejas Light* whenever enough research material came together. This idea quickly led to the thought that, if one were to get back into publishing, why not revive *BSN* itself to cover the broader range of interests already indicated, with *TTL* serving as a department to cover the investigative material? Perhaps, by the time this essay appears in print, *BSN* could be reborn like the mythical phoenix....

[Ed. note: In fact, *BSN* did make its comeback in August 1991 with a cover story analysis of the Gulf War entitled "More Lost Than Won: A War in Retrospect." Single copies of *Both Sides Now—A Journal of Spiritual & Political Alternatives* no. 27 cost $1. Subscription rates are $9 for ten issues. For more information, send return postage to Rt. 6, Box 28, Tyler, TX 75704-9712.]

— ELIHU EDELSON —

My Odyssey Through the Underground Press

Michael Kindman

In Memoriam:

Kindman was the founder, in December 1965, of *The Paper*, East Lansing, Michigan's first underground paper and one of the first five members of Underground Press Syndicate. In early 1968 he joined the staff of *Avatar*, in Boston, unaware that the large, experimental commune that controlled the paper was a charismatic cult centered on a former-musician-turned-guru named Mel Lyman, whose psychic hold over his followers was then being strengthened and intensified by means of various confrontations and loyalty tests. Five years later, Kindman fled the commune's rural outpost in Kansas after another of many violent confrontations with irrational policy decisions over which he felt helpless and made his way to Palo Alto, California, to recover from the earlier traumas. There, he became active in the budding men's movement and on another community-based newspaper, the *Grapevine*. Later, in San Francisco, he was a home-remodeling contractor, a key activist in a gay men's pagan spiritual network, and a student. Using writing as a means of self-discovery, Kindman wrote the following story in part to try to make sense of what happened to him and why. He died, from AIDS, on November 22, 1991, two months after it was completed.

Going to College

September 1963. I'm off to East Lansing, Michigan, far from my home town on Long Island, to start college at Michigan State University, bright-eyed and enthusiastic, excited about the possibilities that await me. I'm an honors freshman in the journalism department, and one of hundreds of honors students from all over the country recruited into the freshman class. Nearly 200 of us have been awarded National Merit Scholarships underwritten by the university and usable only there; together we represent by far the largest group of Merit Scholars in any school's freshman class. At Michigan State?

Our purpose in being there, from the point of view of the university officials who created the program and the alumni who funded it, is to help upgrade the reputation and academic atmosphere of the giant school, which is still struggling to transcend its origins as an agricultural and technical school, "the pioneer land-grant college." The "land-grant act" of the 1850s offered federal land to the states for the establishment of state-sponsored schools to encourage and promote agriculture and technology. Many state universities grew from these origins. The Agricultural College of the State of Michigan, founded in 1855, happened to be the first of them. It graduated to "university" status on its hundredth birthday.

Only a few years before, MSU had begun building a national reputation by becoming a major football power in the Midwestern Big Ten, replacing the

University of Chicago in that athletic conference. Now it was striving to increase its academic reputation, particularly in the humanities and social sciences, as well as to justify its exponential growth in terms of services it could provide to the state. Competition with The University of Michigan (U-M) in Ann Arbor was in full swing, and "State" was more than a little defensive about its standing.

Attracting huge numbers of top-ranked freshmen was just one tactic in the university administration's overall strategy of challenging U-M's pre-eminence, a strategy that also included an enormously ambitious building program that had already doubled the size of the developed campus in recent years and would double it again in the next few years, as well as an aggressive lobbying campaign aimed at persuading the state to open a new medical school at State rather than expand the existing ones at U-M and Wayne State in Detroit. The tactic of attracting high-ranking high school graduates into the freshman class included, in addition to the scholarship program, grouping us together on certain floors of the gigantic new dormitories, brick monoliths along the outer edge of campus far from town, and offering us accelerated participation in the "Honors College," a special program that sounded real good in the promotional material: special library privileges, the chance to do original research work under close faculty supervision, extra recognition for our academic success, et cetera—if we kept to a certain grade-point average.

The promotional literature did not talk about the generally sterile, almost rural atmosphere of both MSU and East Lansing, a dry (no alcohol sales), conservative place that looked like a picture-postcard college town but offered little in terms of cultural opportunities or intellectual community and the stimulation these could bring. And, of course, the state capital was just a few miles away in Lansing; certainly the university fathers would not want to do anything or allow anything to occur that might raise the eyebrows of the legislature. All in all, it was sort of a company town situation, but the enthusiastic series of promotional mailings we received from Gordon Sabine, vice president for special projects, and Stanley Idzerda, director of the Honors College, did not emphasize this aspect. As a result, we showed up in droves, not only from the Midwest but from all over the country.

We honors freshmen may have suspected something was amiss, as we settled into our dormitory rooms in the farthest corners of the built-up campus, checked out the bland surroundings, and anticipated our courses, including the required freshman survey courses, American Thought and Language (ATL) and Natural Science—but if we did it was only a dim awareness at first. We were concentrating on seeking each other out for intellectual companionship and emotional support among the much larger number of more typical midwestern types surrounding us.

Most of us lacked the sophistication to really evaluate the quality of the academic programs and were simply hoping for the best. I didn't really know what to expect from college, having had very little counseling and little else in my background to prepare me for it, other than the assumption that I would do something intellectually based with my life. I didn't understand the extent to which my growing up in the New York suburbs had already colored my expectations and experience, but I had known I didn't want to stay at home for college, and had passed up opportunities to go to Berkeley and other far-flung schools. I felt quite innocent, excited about what was being offered to us at MSU, and ready to develop a loyal connection to my future alma mater.

In addition to the academic opportunities, I was also looking forward to the option those of us in journalism had to work on the *Michigan State News*, the 30,000-circulation daily paper that was the official organ of the university, published by students under the close advisorship of a professional publisher employed by the university. I got a paying job right away on the copy desk of the *State News*, final editing the articles and writing the headlines, and found it easy to keep up with my heavy course load despite the five afternoons a week I spent there.

One Saturday that fall, the university had all the freshman Merit Scholars pose for a picture for the alumni magazine, standing together to spell out "MS"—for Michigan State and for Merit Scholars; get it? The suspicion was starting to grow that we were being hoodwinked somehow. But I was making friends and gaining confidence.

THE BEGINNING OF THE BEGINNING

One Friday in November, my ATL instructor came into class late to announce he had just heard that President Kennedy had been shot and possibly killed. Class was dismissed; with it went much of our innocence and optimism. The ride was just beginning.

When first quarter ended just before Christmas, I took off for a visit to my sister's family in California. While I was there, my father had an accident at his job in New Jersey, and died a few days later of his injuries. I flew home for his funeral and the obligatory mourning period. When I returned to East Lansing to move in with my new roommate, Larry Tate, one of my honors program peers who was also a budding writer, my world had been badly shaken and I wanted deeply to be anchored in school and in my progress toward the future I was planning. I took heavy course loads through winter and spring and even summer quarters, and worked diligently on the *State News*, as copy editor and reporter and occasional editorial writer.

The journalism courses were unexciting, taught by traditionalist faculty with a heavy commitment to what we have since come to know as "the myth of objectivity," but it didn't matter much, because there was a real newspaper to play with. We got to work with wire service news about world events and to develop local angles when we could. I got to write reviews of local appearances by the folk musicians I admired. Little professional guidance was offered, but we were allowed a fair amount of room to maneuver. We had the chance to initiate coverage of issues we wanted to work on, within limits. I remember doing a series in the *State News* during the summer, when there was more freedom to experiment than during the rest of the year, on what I perceived to be the university's complicity in the pollution and degrading of the Red Cedar River that ran through campus, my first attempt at muckraking (so to speak).

By fall, I had achieved junior status and was named co-editor of the editorial page. My co-editor on the page, Sue Jacoby, was also double-timing through college (she did in fact graduate after two years, and went on to a career with the *Washington Post* and the *New York Times*). Sue had grown up locally and had worked on the *State News* since high school; she had faith in the university and, by extension, the larger government and establishment it represented. I had the viewpoint of an outsider; I was rebellious and instinctively trusted what was new and spontaneous. She was conservative; I was liberal. We got to write our differing opinions about news events as they unfolded and have thousands of people read and debate our ideas daily.

I was sure I was on a track leading eventually to the job of editor-in-chief, and then on to greater glory and success in the newspaper field. I took seriously the notions of freedom of speech and freedom of the press, and their correlate in the university context, "academic freedom," the hallowed right of instructors and students to examine any and all ideas freely and fearlessly, and to do so with the full encouragement and protection of the institution. I joined the local chapter of the American Civil Liberties Union.

IT *CAN* HAPPEN HERE

In October 1964, my friends and I all became transfixed by the drama that was unfolding in Berkeley, as students at the University of California began fighting for their right to freedom of political expression, over the opposition of their university's administration. The fight escalated for two months, and in December hundreds were arrested for sitting in at the university administration building.

The Sproul Hall sit-in had almost immediate repercussions for those of us in East Lansing who had been nurturing our growing frustrations with the situation we were in. We all felt shortchanged to one degree or another for having been tricked into doing college at Michigan State University, "Moo U," as it was sometimes known (referring to the university's origins as an agricultural college), in the conservative, teetotaling town of East Lansing, for God's sake, when we were all so brilliant and could have gone anywhere. The Honors College program that had been offered to us whiz-kid recruits had turned out to be more hype than opportunity, more the extension of Stanley Idzerda's personality and intellectual enthusiasm than a real chance to do outstanding work ahead of the ordinary academic schedule. In the sciences and technical fields MSU generally had a legitimate claim to excellence and even leadership, but those of us in the humanities and social sciences were becoming increasingly aware that MSU was something of a cultural backwater, not the center of intellectual debate we had been led to believe it was. Many of us were growing increasingly stir-crazy. Our education was working, but not in the way the university might have hoped: the more educated we became, the more frustrated we felt.

The local Socialist Club had been discussing the Berkeley situation and its parallels in East Lansing, and the time seemed right to expand the discussion beyond the club itself. A first, secret planning meeting was called for a Committee for Student Rights (CSR). I believe it was at the suggestion of Mike Price, home-grown socialist and rebel, whose parents owned one of the local department stores, that I was invited to the meeting, despite my status as a bigwig at the *State News*, and despite the need for secrecy in organizing to challenge the university's authority. Nothing like that had been done before in East Lansing. After some negotiation, I showed up at a mysterious house off-campus for the meeting. I was aware of stepping into an alternate reality of some kind. Someone played the new album by folksinger Buffy Sainte-Marie, the one with the politically inspiring songs "Universal Soldier" and "Now That the Buffalo's Gone." We talked frustrations and strategies and made plans; by the end of the evening my life had been changed forever.

CSR decided to start out by protesting the university's "in loco parentis" policies for governing students' behavior "in the place of the parents." Dormitory curfews for women and the requirement that all underclassmen live in dormitories for two years were the first targets—safe issues in terms of winning student support, and very explosive ones in the eyes of the university. I slipped a guest column into the *State News* in the name of the one member willing to go public, and we began publishing a single-sheet mimeographed newsletter for distribution in the dorms and campus buildings, along with a petition supporting our position. These publications stirred further controversy, as the university stumbled over itself trying to prevent distribution. It became clear that the "rules" governing student behavior and activities were not a clearly defined set of principles and procedures, but rather were made up arbitrarily as the need arose, by administrators whose primary interest seemed to be to stifle the debate we were inciting and to control the way students thought.

CSR sought opportunities to debate and negotiate with administrators on a wide range of university policies and, when these channels were insufficient, as was usually the case, challenged the university in our newsletters to open more channels for student participation in the governing process. When this failed, we demonstrated and sat in at various places around campus, gradually gaining support for our causes and for our right to engage in such activities. Many faculty members were happy to defend our right to express even unpopular opinions. Our protests were not just about political issues. On one occasion, we sat in at the main university library, calling attention to the low students-to-volumes ratio at MSU compared with other major universities.

That winter and spring we demonstrated and leafleted under many banners, for many causes; a political community, an indigenous piece of the counter-culture, was coming to be in East Lansing. We had a headquarters of sorts: Spiro's, a cafeteria and coffee shop across the street from campus on Grand River Avenue (everyone called the place "Kewpee's," for the "Kewpee-burgers" served there), where at any time of the day we could find some of our friends to hang out with. At last, an alternative to dorm life and bland, university-authorized activities.

Our activism jumped across the street, too, as a large number of students tried to pressure the East Lansing city government into adopting an "open housing" (anti-discrimination) ordinance. Fifty-nine were arrested in a sit-in at East Lansing city hall in May 1965.

As each of these political actions occurred, I explained and defended them in columns in the *State News*, while in news articles the university administrators and local politicians were making statements about "outside agitators" and "communist sympathizers" infiltrating the otherwise calm environment of East Lansing. I found myself leading a double life, risking everything. All my own political, intellectual, and social

assumptions were being challenged and re-examined. Whereas I formerly thought of myself as simply a liberal Democrat, now I was becoming a confirmed radical.

With a few of my political friends I participated in the Selma-to-Montgomery civil rights march inspired by Martin Luther King in Alabama. The big march on the state capitol gave me my first experience of what I have ever since felt to be the religious uplift and inspiration of masses of people calling out in unison for what they believed and needed. My more informed friends were starting to encourage the rest of us to learn about the little-known war then in progress in Vietnam. As more of us figured out what was happening there, we sought ways to organize marches and teaching efforts to let more people know about this outrage. As much as I could, I documented my changing views in the *State News*, to increasing criticism from the rest of the staff and the advisor. My grades and academic ambitions were suffering from the loss of my interest, but it was worth it for the experience. And, I was deeply enmeshed in a community of like-minded friends, an interesting, diverse, and tolerant gang; that was definitely worth it. I quickly became known among my activist friends as the "conscience" of our movement; I seemed to have an instinct for the ethics of the struggle, and for keeping our actions proportional to our demands.

During the summer, a graduate student on temporary leave from school, Paul Schiff, president of the Socialist Club and editor of *Logos*, the CSR newsletter, was refused readmission to the university in what was widely seen as retribution for his political activism. One of the accusations held against him was that he had sought to "discredit" the university by speaking out against the mayor of East Lansing, Gordon Thomas, in the campaign for the open housing ordinance; Thomas happened to be a professor of communications. Schiff decided to challenge the university in a lawsuit supported by the ACLU.

As for me, I took the summer of 1965 off from the process of school and politics and went home to Long Island to remodel my mother's house and deepen my relationship with my long-distance girlfriend, Carol Schneider. Carol and I had become friends working on our high school newspaper, at a time when we were both quite inhibited and unhappy but very successful in school affairs. We had both been offered journalism scholarships to Syracuse University in New York. A year younger than me, Carol had just finished her first year there, but she couldn't afford to return. By the end of the summer, we finally yielded our respective virginities to each other. In the fall, her college career having been stalled for the moment, Carol returned to East Lansing with me. She had come a long way from her repressive Catholic background. I wasn't sure what it meant to be living together, but I couldn't think of any reason not to.

Carol and I and my long-time roommate, Larry, rented a house off-campus. The landlady didn't protest or refuse as she signed the lease with all three of us, but then she turned right around and reported us to the university for "co-habiting." Larry and I found ourselves on "social probation," a nuisance and an insult, and a threat to our scholarships. Carol rented a room in town as a cover, mainly for her parents' benefit, but never spent a night in it. It was expensive and stupid, one more radicalizing experience. I returned to the *State News* with full responsibility for the editorial page. Carol signed up for some courses at Lansing Community College and took a job as a waitress.

CONFLICTING LOYALTIES, CONFLICTING OATHS

Returning staff members at the *State News* were greeted with a handout called "The *State News* Commandments," a list of ten behaviors that would now be required of us. This list was the invention of the new editor-in-chief, Charles C. Wells, a follow-the-rules kind of guy, and the advisor, Louis J. Berman, who in his other life was the publisher of a small-town daily in western Michigan. In addition to emphasizing such admirable newspapering qualities as excellence, truth, honesty, compassion, and accuracy, these "commandments" demanded, "You shall have no loyalty above the *State News*. If another organization claims your sympathy and you feel your membership will express that sympathy, this is permissible; but you shall exercise no leadership in any organization other than the *State News*." This was "commandment" number one. It was hard for me not to take this personally, in view of the way the previous year had gone. By October, I decided, in discussion with Carol and Larry, that it was time for me to quit the *State News*. The increasing pressure there to be either an "objective" journalist or an activist, but not both, was more than I could take. Larry had already stopped submitting the occasional reviews he had been writing.

We decided we would start our own weekly newspaper. The idea had been batted around among our circle of friends and fellow activists; it seemed clear that with my combined experience of newspapering and activism I was seen as the person most prepared to lead the way. I wrote a righteous letter of resignation and we started networking for support for *L'Étranger*, as we planned to call our paper, after Camus' existentialist hero. Someone talked sense into us and we decided on *The Paper* instead; snobbery gave way to understatement. Support was readily available, from the students

and faculty members with whom we had worked in all the campaigns of the previous year. We easily raised enough money for our first couple of issues. The biggest obstacle we seemed to be facing was our lack of a telephone; the house we were renting was brand-new and several miles off campus in a neighborhood that didn't have service yet.

The rest of the *State News* staff, with very few exceptions, scoffed at me, sure I had finally lost it. But a few weeks after my resignation, while we were still enlisting staff and support for our effort, four of the *State News*' editors and the administration beat reporter found it necessary to resign as well, in a controversy with the advisor and editor-in-chief over publication of some documents in Paul Schiff's readmission fight with the university. A number of other staff members in less responsible positions followed suit. Despite having been forced out by the party-line policies of the editor and advisor, they refused to join forces with us, and issued public statements disavowing any connection with us or any other group. They were all immediately replaced and the *State News* continued publishing without missing a beat, while both the old and the new staffs debated among themselves whether it was more important to keep publishing without missing a deadline or to stop once in a while and review what the reasons were for publishing in the first place.

Meanwhile, we were making arrangements with a small print shop in Lansing to typeset and paste up our first issue, and with a newspaper publisher in Mason, the county seat ten miles out of Lansing, who also printed the *State News*, to do our printing on their big web press. We printed 3,000 copies of our first eight-page tabloid, dated December 3, 1965. It came back from the printer on the day our telephone finally arrived. I was listed as editor and Larry was listed as arts editor. The masthead named two "inspirations": the *Michigan Daily*, the student-run paper from the University of Michigan down the road in Ann Arbor, and the *Promethean*, the off-campus paper founded at Syracuse University during the year Carol was there.

The issue included a front-page editorial, "As We Begin: A Loyalty Oath," a response to item one of the "*State News* Commandments," the complete text of which we reprinted on page two. "You shall have no loyalty above the *State News*...," the first "commandment" said. I wrote:

> I have a loyalty higher than that I once had to the *State News*....
>
> Our higher loyalty is to the practice of imaginative, creative, thoughtful journalism. We will not run a machine for processing copy which can run without people.

...We have a loyalty to the idealism on which the best journalism ever practiced has been based. We hope unabashedly to be a forum for ideas, a center for debate, a champion of the common man, a thorn in the side of the powerful. We hope to inspire thought, to attract good writing, to train newcomers in the ways of the press....

We hope never to become so sure of our position and so unaware of our real job that we will concentrate merely on putting out a paper....

And we intend to do all this in a spirit of editorial independence for which there is hardly a model on this campus. We may submit organizationally to the requirements of the university, but our editorial policies will be strictly our own....We hope most sincerely that our attempt to prove the value of independence will be a satisfying one, and that we will keep alive the interest, enthusiasm and imagination of our readers.

It is for this hope that we reserve our highest loyalty.

On page two, alongside the "*State News* Commandments," I offered an analysis of the censorship and resignation affair, "The *State News* Fiasco: A Cause Without Rebels": "[T]hey had bigger issues they might have considered....But they were afraid to shake it up...and so the establishment rushed in and proved to them they were expendable. Now, the *State News* is without a decent staff, the decent staff is without jobs, and the university is still without a good daily newspaper. They needn't have bothered to walk out."

The first issue also included articles on student government and the Committee for Student Rights, a reprint of a speech on world hunger by Georg Borgstromm, a professor of food science who was one of the first to warn of the dangers of uncontrolled population growth, film and theater and literary criticism, poetry and arty photographs, an impressionistic interview with Bob Dylan reprinted from the *Los Angeles Free Press*—and a marginal note on the back page: "Thanks...to Student Board for letting us sell this issue on campus." We had sought and received a special dispensation from student government to sell on campus under their aegis despite the lack of clear guidelines for how to obtain permission to do so; we wanted to avoid the trouble CSR had gotten into with *Logos* if we could find a way. We were off and running.

The second issue a week later included on the front page Larry's sardonic coverage of an early march on Washington against the Vietnam War; on page 2 a commentary from me on "MSU—The Closed Society,"

comparing Michigan State to segregationist Mississippi; and on page 3 a sympathetic interview with Paul Schiff, whose case for readmission to the university was heating up. Also included were more cultural coverage, a thought piece by a faculty member on "The Sick University: Is It Worth Curing?" and "Our First Letter to the Editor," a nasty piece by one of the resigned *State News* staffers, Linda Miller Rockey, briefly my successor as editorial page editor, who wrote: "The first issue of *The Paper* has clearly convinced me that a competitive newspaper in this university community is an excellent endeavor, but that you are certainly not the person to edit it...." She goes on at length to attribute complex motives of jealousy and arrogance to me in criticizing both the *State News* and the walkout, and remembers protesting an editorial I wrote for the *State News* the previous year, which proves I'm fallible, too. Et cetera, et cetera "So in view of your inaccurate chastisement of myself and my colleagues, I can only wish you all the failure in the world with *The Paper*."

Then it was time for finals and Christmas break, during which time Michigan State's highly touted football team went to the Rose Bowl for the first time in years, to compete with UCLA, which whomped them. *The Paper* returned on January 20, 1966, with Issue 3, our "first annual Rose Bowl issue"—its front page article, "The Children's Crusade," was an anonymous report ("to protect the innocent") on the partying and touristing that accompanied the football pilgrimage undertaken by hundreds of Michigan Staters. An editorial cheered Paul Schiff's "routine" readmission to school in a move clearly intended by the university to avoid the embarrassment of a court trial, and decried the lack of clear policy change that accompanied it. We had switched to a different and somewhat less expensive method of typesetting, and began developing the habit of working closely with the person hired to do our paste-up.

A news article on an inside page covered the ludicrous trial of four antiwar protestors who had been arrested for leafleting in the Student Union and whose trial in a tiny storefront courtroom in Lansing was characterized by the county prosecutor as just a routine case. The defense lawyer, Conrad Lynn, a well-known black civil libertarian imported from New York for the occasion, knew better, and called the president and one of the vice presidents of the university as witnesses, giving them their first chance to deny publicly that the university was coming down hard on antiwar protestors because it had had a role in helping create the Vietnam War. There would be more to say about that later.

By our fourth issue, we were settling into a routine. A humor piece about the competition between the *State News* and *The Paper* was on the front page;

on the inside the most interesting items were two treatments of the MSU-Vietnam connection. One, by one of our socialist friends, noted the deficiencies in the *State News'* coverage of the subject; the other was excerpts of talks given at MSU by two spokesmen from Students for a Democratic Society, then still a small and fairly reputable Ann Arbor-based "New Left" organizing project with a national perspective. Both articles made reference to the role Michigan State had played in Vietnam in the 1950s, when its political science department had sent a crew to Saigon to serve as advisors to the anti-Communist regime then being propped up by the United States, and questioned the freedom of thought and the larger political intentions of university personnel under such circumstances.

IS ANYONE IN CHARGE HERE?

The fifth issue's front page article, "Brave New MSU: University Planners Face the Future," was one of a long series of discussions we were to publish on the role of the modern university, or "multiversity" as University of California-Berkeley president Clark Kerr had called it. Long-time MSU president John Hannah was a staunch advocate of the social service model of education who had reshaped the university to help meet the needs of technological society. We felt obliged at least to question this view. The writer, Char Jolles, was a compatriot of ours from our freshman days and was the only member of the *State News* staff who had quit in the mass resignations and then joined the regular staff of *The Paper*. She became a frequent commentator on educational policy and solicited articles from faculty members, which we were attempting to include in each issue.

Inside, my editorial explored the role of the Board of Student Publications, the mysterious university committee made up of administrators, faculty, and students, and chaired by the advertising professor who served as chair of the journalism department as well. The usual job of the "pub. board" was to oversee the *State News* and the yearbook and a tame literary annual called *Red Cedar Review*. But the year before it had been the official agency hauled out to harass *Logos*, and now it was finding itself in the unaccustomed position of having to think also about *The Paper* and *Zeitgeist*, an off-campus literary magazine that had come into being about the same time we started publishing. Would these upstarts be allowed to distribute on campus, or sell advertising, or even to exist at all, with or without "authorization" from the pub. board? No one seemed to know, or to know how to find out. I wrote:

A much better system would be to have either no board at all or a board of publications which supervised the unrestricted distribution of publications, student or otherwise, around a campus increasingly difficult to reach by normal communications methods. For the moment we have merely a pub board that seems to content itself with simply making arbitrary rules which it plans neither to follow nor to follow through.

Issue 6 appears unremarkable in retrospect, further evidence that we were settling into a routine. On page 7 is a picture of one of our female volunteers staffing a card table in the Student Union, under a headline, "Is there a place in America today for the small businessman?" The caption said *The Paper* could be found each week at four locations on campus and nine stores off campus.

The next week, however, no issue was published. Instead we put out a two-page mimeographed look-alike called Vol. I No. 6-1/2, "Here We Stand: *The Paper* at the Crossroads." It turns out the student government, which had been sheltering us informally with permission to distribute on campus for "contributions" in the absence of any clear policy from the publications board to govern such circumstances, had taken offense at our decision to begin publishing advertising and "selling" copies on campus, which appeared to them to bring us within the purview of the pub. board's regulation. They had responded by hauling us before the Student Judiciary to face charges. The emergency issue invited the public to attend our "trial" that evening. "We did not set out to defy authority; we set out to survive."

Our appearance before Student Judiciary received lots of coverage in the *State News* and elsewhere. We chose to refrain from publishing for a while to see if things would clarify. They didn't, so we went back to student government for permission to conduct another "fund drive." Two weeks later we were back on the stands with Issue 7 of *THE controversial PAPER*. (The descriptive adjective, quoted from the *State News*, was pasted in, in tiny six-point type, between the words of the nearly two-inch high flag; we never again published an issue without some word play in the title.) The headline and lead read, "You Won't Believe This, But...this issue is being sold on campus by permission of Student Board. Just like in the Good Old Days." The front-page editorial went on to give the complete history again of our continuing attempts to obtain some kind of legal status from someone that would guarantee us the right to do business in a normal fashion, the attempts of which were by then being stonewalled by several different branches of the administration to which we had appealed. Student Board, the legislative branch of the student government, was choosing to step in again as a way of expressing its own disgust for the administration's delaying tactics.

What we expected to come of all this was a definition of our position by the time this issue was ready for sale....[if this didn't occur] we would have exhausted the channels and were prepared to go on selling without any authorization, in protest against a set of rules which flatly refused to recognize our existence....[W]e still need some definition of our status so we can either be legal once and for all or can be illegal and can start fighting, in total war, the obvious unconstitutionality of the whole business by which we've been held up thus far....Meanwhile, here we are, "giving away" copies of our "free" publication in a "fund drive" which is not quite a campus-wide sale of a newspaper. But almost. Someday, maybe we'll know exactly what we're doing and whether it's allowed.

The drama continued in Issue 8, *THE guilty controversial PAPER*, which appeared on the day the Board of Student Publications was scheduled to hear our latest appeal for "authorization." An editorial entitled "The Merry-Go-Round" discusses our being found guilty (without penalty) by the Student Judiciary, which also criticized the Student Board's role in half-heartedly protecting us. For our part, we pledged not to obey the latest directive from Student Board, to avoid distributing in classroom buildings, where the *State News* was routinely distributed. "Our defense derives from the unequal and unnecessarily intolerant treatment accorded any individual or group seeking to follow the university's various policies on distribution. [Soon], unless more roadblocks are thrown in our path, *The Paper* will have exhausted all possible channels in the university for authorization of a student publication. It is up to the Board of Student Publications to decide at its meeting March 10 whether or not the last remaining channel will make provision for *The Paper*. If it will not, we will be left to survive in the university on the basis simply of the mandate from students and faculty we feel we have to continue publishing."

The issue also contained a letter from Paul Krassner, editor of *The Realist*, the small left-anarchist magazine published in New York, congratulating us on our efforts and offering to come to East Lansing to do a benefit for us.

(An ironic note: I was registered for, and presumably made at least some attempt to complete, a course in "Newspaper Editorial Management" during winter quarter, the term that ended with the issue quoted above. The transcript shows I flunked the course, after first taking an "incomplete" grade, even as I was willing a functioning newspaper into existence, over the objections of the journalism school faculty, among others.)

GUILTY AND CONTROVERSIAL, AND LEGAL TOO!

As spring quarter began, we appeared as *THE guilty controversial authorized PAPER*. The pub. board had come through. It remained to be seen what benefits, if any, "authorization" would hold for us. Our editorial response, "Gratitude Will Get Us Nowhere," simply promised to keep doing the job we wanted to do all along.

On the same page, Larry had an article on Jim Thomas, a student poet we knew slightly, who had quit MSU to enlist in the Marines and go to Vietnam. He felt called there, unlike everyone else we knew, and we felt moved to publish the poetry and essays he had given us and promised to continue sending. Larry describes their only meeting, and ponders the increasing effect of the war on all of us. "I saw him only once, but I find myself speculating about him. He will be alive when this is printed. He will probably be alive when out-of-town subscribers finally get their copies. He may even be alive when the war is over. On the other hand, he may not. I am afraid for Jim Thomas. And for all of us."

Issue 10, *THE just-plain PAPER*, headlined "The Rites/Rights of Spring," was filled with reports of ongoing activism: the appeal trial and brief jail terms of the protestors arrested the previous fall for leafleting in the Student Union, and the sit-in vigil outside President Hannah's house staged in response; the trial of one of the dozens of protestors arrested the previous spring for demonstrating in East Lansing in favor of the open housing ordinance; the opening of the Free University of East Lansing; a campus conference between progressive Christians and New Leftists; the continuing good-natured rivalry between *The Paper* and *Zeitgeist*, the off-campus literary magazine; participation by East Lansing folk in the Detroit aspect of the International Days of Protest over Vietnam, considered at the time the largest peace demonstration ever; and, of all things, interviews with the candidates for Student Board elections, including several whose stated goal it was to reform the whole business.

The next issue we lightened up a bit, using the front page for a mock exposé, "Hannah Revealed to be Palindrome." (Do you know what a palindrome is? "Madam, I'm Adam," for example.) This provided brief comic relief for our readers, while we prepared ourselves for the next barrage of rebelliousness.

Ramparts, a slick progressive magazine published in San Francisco whose role resembled that of the current *Mother Jones*, had just released its April 1966 cover article on Michigan State's role in Vietnam during the 1950s, "The University on the Make, or How MSU Helped Arm Madame Nhu." We had provided support for their researcher when he was in town, leading him to information sources and giving him background information. The charge documented by *Ramparts* was that, under cover of an academic and advisory project to the puppet regime in Saigon, MSU had actually worked with the CIA to arm the Vietnamese military and help it set up the "strategic hamlet" program in which thousands of peasants were displaced from their homes into what amounted to concentration camps, thus setting the stage for the larger war that was to come.

The next week our front-page article, "*Ramparts* v. MSU v. The CIA: The University on the Run," was a compilation of excerpts from the *Ramparts* article, the media's response to it, the original university reports on the project, and earlier commentary on the project from a pamphlet by Robert Scheer, one of *Ramparts*' editors, "How the United States Got Involved in Vietnam." The effect was to support the *Ramparts* charges and refute the university's denials. We also printed a full-page ad for the *Ramparts* article, which the *State News* had refused, which was headlined, "What the hell is a university doing buying guns, anyway?"

The next issue's front page covered a press conference by MSU President Hannah, his attempt at damage control over the controversy set off by the *Ramparts* article. His defense was the "land-grant philosophy" on which his view of the university as a public servant had always been based: "When our faculty members are engaged in providing service, either within Michigan, elsewhere in our country, or overseas, we do not consider their activities as a 'diversion of the University,' but instead a recognition of a significant and defensible function of the University. International service in this day and age is a recognition by this University and a great many others that our country is a part of the larger world community. To say that a University should never undertake to serve the national policy is to deny the right of the public university to exist."

We were pleased at having helped force the university into the open on the question of exactly how it was serving the public interest. Our issue included further documentation of the charges in the *Ramparts* article, making it clear that, if university officials were not aware they were being used as a cover by the CIA, they **should** have been aware of it.

The next week we lightened up again, publishing humor articles and discussion of the university's fraternity system on the front page. We were getting ready for our next controversy; Paul Krassner's benefit appearance for *The Paper* was scheduled for May 7. The event was a success, the reception afterward was my 21st birthday party, and with our coverage of it in Issue 15 all hell broke loose.

Krassner had been his expected iconoclastic self. In attempting to cover his talk in a way we could get away with, we printed Larry's account of hosting him, alongside excerpts from his talk, including a discussion of alternative ways to say "Fuck Communism," a slogan he had popularized with a poster. We didn't actually print "the F word" at all, instead using a small picture of Krassner holding his red-white-and-blue poster, in which the word was barely readable. The caption read, "What substitutes could you have, anyway? Make love communism, sleep communism, ball communism, meaningful relationship communism...." In an unfortunate bit of timing, in the same issue we also published a lengthy, polite, thoughtful piece by Richard Ogar, one of our regular writers, on the origins and entrenched psychological underpinnings of society's prohibitions on nudity, suggesting that we might all be better off if the taboo was lifted.

EASY COME, EASY GO

The surprising upshot of this was a huge uproar and controversy, just as if we had started publishing hard-core pornography. The Board of Student Publications, which had so recently granted us "authorization" after months of waffling, summarily withdrew its seal of approval at a meeting to which we were not invited. I remember receiving a one-sentence letter announcing this news, and publishing a photocopy of that letter somewhere, but it doesn't show up in any issue of *The Paper*. I guess we must have put out a flier in our defense, as the *State News* was reporting on our "de-authorization." In Issue 16, we published yet another lengthy discussion of the irrationality and arbitrariness of the university's position, "Here We Go Again!!" We reprinted a brief excerpt from a *State News* interview with Frank Senger, chair of both the journalism department and the publications board: "Did he think that some observers might say that the board's rapid action constituted a violation of *The Paper*'s rights of due process? 'I suppose,' Senger said." The possibility didn't seem to bother him much.

The same issue included coverage of a hearing before the Higher Education Subcommittee of the Michigan House of Representatives in which MSU officials and *Ramparts* writers faced off on the subject of the MSU-Vietnam charges, and several articles on the dissolution then in progress of the university's political science department, which everyone concerned denied was related to the *Ramparts* affair; we didn't buy that explanation. After the publication of our "sensationalized and lewd material," as the *State News* called our Issue 15, the printer we had been using refused to do further business with us and published a nasty editorial about us in its own paper, the *Ingham County News*, a copy of which the publisher sent to us with an insulting cover letter. We reprinted both in Issue 17, after finding a printer elsewhere in Michigan willing to take our business, something we would have to do several more times over the next year, traveling as far afield as Chicago and Windsor, Ontario.

But Issue 17 included a couple of items more significant to us: My front-page editorial, "It's Been a Gas!" included a letter from Walter Bowart, publisher of the *East Village Other* in New York, inviting us to join him and others in forming the Underground Press Syndicate (UPS).

On the same page we published the first installment of "LandGrantMan," a Marvel Comics-style strip produced by some of our friends, in which Dr. John Palindrome, president of Midwestern Multiversity, is visited by a spirit who grants him special powers in order to fight the "vicious personifications of evil" surrounding him, in the form of student protestors, hippies, and the like. He transforms into the bungling superhero LandGrantMan, who vows, "Now to show those students whose multiversity this really is!"

With that, *The Paper* closed out its first notorious year of publication. East Lansing was never going to be the same.

I spent the summer of 1966 in an SDS organizing project in San Francisco, where some of my colleagues were students from the University of Texas. Hearing my stories of publishing *The Paper* in East Lansing, they decided they could do it, too. They returned to Austin and immediately began publishing the *Rag*, but not until one of them had guided me on my first LSD trip. The same week, I sent off my application as a conscientious objector to my draft board in New York, and *Time* magazine appeared with an article on the founding of the Underground Press Syndicate, "Underground Alliance," featuring brief interviews and photographs of the five of us who had founded the "shoestring papers of the strident left" that *Time* saw "popping up like weeds across the U.S."

Reflecting on what we had accomplished during the previous year, I was more than ever committed to carrying on the journalistic revolution we had stumbled upon. I was excited about the formation of UPS, and wrote a letter singing its praises, which I sent to the editors of every alternative paper I had come across. I found opportunities that summer to acquaint myself with the four other founding editors of UPS.

Returning to East Lansing in the fall, I definitely felt like an ambassador from a developing national counterculture, bringing news of the future back to my provincial homeland. My lady friend Carol having resumed her schooling in Albany, New York, and my accomplice Larry having chosen to rent an apartment with another friend, I needed to find a home for both myself and *The Paper*. I took over a small house near campus in whose basement was located the mimeograph on which all our movement leaflets for the previous two years had been printed; the front room became our office. We finally decided to begin doing our own paste-up; a local union activist donated a huge sheet of frosted glass that I turned into a light table big enough for three or four people to work at.

Our first issue of the year (twelve pages, circulation increased to 4,000) had a modest collage on the front page made up of our most memorable headlines and graphics of the previous year, and a piece from me that began "An Editorial (!!)...in which the editor states his preference for fun and good newspapers rather than fighting and hassling, and explains how fun and good newspapers have been pursued since he last published an issue; also including a statement of his plans for the coming year." One of our friends took one look at it and said, "Wow, Kindman's been taking acid." True enough.

But we still intended to stick thorns in the side of the MSU administration whenever we could. The opening issue for the year included our version of orientation articles on life in the multiversity, by Char ("The university is well-suited for the task of conditioning...its inhabitants psychologically for the outside world, for MSU, like American society as a whole, can be characterized by, among other things, the condition of anonymity, the pressure of conformity, and the spirit of competition") and "Culture at MSU," by Larry ("Luckily for everyone, it won't take long" to discuss).

I'm unable to remember exactly what became of the enormous controversy of the previous year concerning our distribution on campus. Reading through the issues published during that second year, I find no sign of it, although plenty of new controversy was generated and more inflammatory material than ever filled our pages. I presume the university just backed down and let us be; the times were certainly changing in many ways. We did form an organization called Friends of *The Paper* to serve as our foil when we wanted to rent rooms on campus and do that sort of thing.

Membership in the Underground Press Syndicate brought immediate benefits for us, in the form of a wealth of interesting articles available for reprinting, as all of the member papers began exchanging copies with one another, and advertising from previously unattainable sources all over the country. Later, as UPS became more established, we began receiving advance copies of books and records for review. In addition, former staff members of *The Paper* were starting to migrate to graduate schools and urban centers around the country, and they began generating original copy for us to publish on the political and social happenings occurring in their areas.

Finally, we were playing the role we had hoped for. People waited for our issues, which came out each week virtually without fail, each one looking different and more experimental than the one before. We had coverage of the antiwar movement from all over the country, of the expanding rock music scene, of the changes underway in the university. We had consumer news, arts reviews, analysis of the financial involvement of Big Business in the university, original poetry and fiction, including more poetry and commentary from Jim Thomas in Vietnam, and a new edition of Land-GrantMan each week, providing ludicrous counterpoint to our other coverage of whatever had been happening on campus. Pretty much whoever wanted to do so could comment on whatever he or she wanted to, in whatever verbal or visual form, and we would probably publish it. *The Paper* was a wide-open experimental forum, unlike anything we had seen or experienced before.

In Issue 3, I published an editorial, "The Newspaper As Art Form," each paragraph interspersed with a line from the Beatles' song "Tomorrow Never Knows" ("Turn off your mind, relax and float downstream—this is not dying," etc.). I wrote: "Being *The Paper* feels different this year. There's a spirit to it, a feeling of community and creativity and enlightened consensus about it that proves to those of us who think about these things the value of the 'underground press' as an instrument of communication....[W]e all on the staff understand now that our function is as innovative artists of journalism and that journalism is itself the art of relating importantly and currently to the concerns of people." In a way we had not anticipated but had been living for months—and for which we had lacked concepts until we started reading our fellow UPS papers and Marshall McLuhan's book, *Understanding Media: The Extensions of Man* (source of the soon-to-be-ubiquitous phrase, "the medium is the message")—we ourselves had become the news, the event worth watching. What would *The Paper* do next? What pulse would we and the community for which we spoke put our fingers on next?

One answer was going on in my small living room almost every night, after the work on the newspaper was done. More and more of us were exploring taking drugs and being stoned together. I was finding myself

skilled as a trip guide, and had plenty of work. The tripping was accompanied by the inevitable sound track of the day, the profound new music that was teaching us ever more about what we were experiencing. That season, our instructors included The Beatles' "Revolver," The Rolling Stones' "Aftermath," Bob Dylan's "Blonde on Blonde," Donovan's "Sunshine Superman," and Simon and Garfunkel's "Parsley, Sage, Rosemary and Thyme." The music contained messages far more relevant to us than anything taught in school. In Donovan's phrase, we stood "both young and old," on the brink of a new world. I remember one evening that fall when I ran out of wisdom, and one of my friends, *Paper* staff writer Gregg Hill, helped me through my first-ever confrontation with my own mortality. But most of the time, we just got off on all the fun we were having, exploring the corners of our minds and finding new meanings in everything we looked at.

ORANGE POWER DAYS

Another hint of the new pulse of the community came in a more familiar form in October, when it was learned that the American Thought and Language department, responsible for dispensing to thousands of freshmen each year the required course in literature and writing, had decided not to renew the contracts of three of its most popular young instructors, two of whom, Gary Groat and Ken Lawless, were involved in publishing the off-campus magazine *Zeitgeist*, and the third of whom, Robert Fogarty, was a talented up-and-comer in the department ranks. About the same time, we published a poem by Lawless, "The Orange Horse," which described the fantasy of an unhappy instructor, being given a magic can of spray paint and turning the entire campus orange as an expression of his frustration. As the department's decision came under increasing scrutiny over the next several weeks, in the *State News* and *The Paper* and endless discussions all over campus, the orange horse became the symbol of the dissatisfaction many students were feeling at seeing some of their favorite instructors treated so shabbily, in evident retribution for doing exactly what it seemed they should be doing.

Several articles by Char Jolles set the tone of our coverage by casting the controversy as a generational dispute within the huge and bureaucratic ATL department, in which the younger and more creative instructors were lobbying for such changes as essay rather than multiple-choice exams and whole-book readings rather than anthology selections, over the opposition of a scared and unimaginative administration. *Zeitgeist*, the magazine that Groat, especially, had inspired and of which he was the titular head, was as iconoclastic as *The Paper*, but a lot more self-consciously artsy and free-thinking, a clear challenge to entrenched authority. The popularity of the three instructors with the students did not seem to be a factor at all to the faculty committee that had made the decision to let them go.

The dissatisfaction erupted into a rally at the classroom building where the ATL department was headquartered. The rally, which was organized by one of our regular writers, Brad Lang, grew into a week-long vigil by hundreds of students, which in turn spawned an organization called United Students, of which W.C. Blanton, known as "Coon," one of the creators of LandGrantMan and more recently *The Paper*'s sports columnist, became chair. Everyone was talking "orange power," and we continued writing about the firings and the vigil and their aftermath for weeks. In one article, Brad refuted the overheard faculty comment that the vigilers were "smelly, long-haired people" by documenting just who was present one Thursday at 4 A.M. It turned out that, of 140 people sitting in at that time, over half were National Merit Scholarship winners of one sort or another, with a proportionate scattering of other academic and campus honors among the group. Protesting was no longer limited to the off-campus fringe, and it was no longer considered chic to distance oneself from the protest by demanding that there be a specific focus and reasoned strategy to any given protest action; simple frustration was a sufficient excuse for participating. The "orange power" movement was primarily a gut reaction against relentless mediocrity. The students were restless.

Meanwhile, John Hannah celebrated 25 years as president of MSU. We congratulated him with a front-page article, "Happy Anniversary," in which we excerpted dozens of his comments over the years on the subject of education and the role of the university, "so that [our] readers may know the quality of the man and the ideas we face in our president." He was an easy mark, a Michigan farmboy made good, whose only doctorate was an honorary degree in poultry science, whose politics were rock-ribbed Republican, and whose ideas for building a great university seemed to come mainly from the world of corporate development. In addition to aggressively building Michigan State up from a medium-sized and medium-grade technical and teachers college into an enormous multi-campus school with a wild and unorthodox array of professional schools and academic programs as well as business-funded training programs designed to groom personnel for particular industries, Hannah had led MSU into founding a number of overseas campuses in far-flung areas of the globe, a program with the distinct flavor of post-World War II American hegemony. Not a very inspiring leader, but one with unmistakable political ambitions and connections. An example of his thinking,

from January 1963: "The University does not belong to the students. It does not belong to the faculty. It does not belong to the administration, or even to the Trustees. MSU belongs to the people of Michigan, who established it, who have nurtured it through the long decades, and who continue to sustain it. In the final analysis, MSU belongs to the larger social organization that is the nation, and of which the State of Michigan is but a part." (A couple of years later, Hannah would finally leave Michigan State in order to accept the job of heading up the U.S. Agency for International Development in the Nixon administration.)

But stranger things than John Hannah were on our minds. On November 17, Tim Leary visited the MSU campus and spoke on the subject "LSD: Man, God and Law" to an audience of 4,000 people, most of whom knew of Leary and LSD mainly from newspaper and magazine accounts. He characterized himself as a spiritual teacher. "We seek to reaffirm the divinity of the human being, we seek to get man out of the manacles of his mind," by promoting, of course, the use of the new sacraments of psychedelic drugs, a new "visible, tangible method of finding grace," because we know now that "consciousness is a biochemical phenomenon." The front-page article in our next issue, "Turn On/Tune In/Cop Out," included our critical response to these ideas: "No religion has ever grown exclusively by the beliefs of its prophets, and the new spiritual age promised by psychedelics will be meaningless to humanity at large unless its values—and practices, which are inseparable—can be translated into many different life styles for many different groups. Many followers of the psychedelic scene seem to be realizing this, but if Leary does, he kept it hidden in what he said at MSU." We also published the first of what would be many articles on marijuana legalization, and announced an upcoming anniversary benefit dance for *The Paper* featuring—Freak Out!—the Mothers of Invention.

Our anniversary issue on December 8, "Happy Universary to Us!," included my discussion of the changes we had all been through in the preceding year, starting with that old "loyalty oath" about journalistic principles from our first issue and running through our now-active involvement in the Underground Press Syndicate and alternative culture in general. I discuss the relevance of Marshall McLuhan's ideas in making sense of this evolution and say, "What we do understand ourselves to be doing is writing living, personal subjective history—and in so doing, portraying a more accurate objective picture of the action of our time tha[n] can be given through the use of linear-oriented, formula journalism that assumes all the answers are to be had in reducing things to familiar patterns." More than 1,200 people helped us celebrate with the Mothers, as, to the best of our ability, we turned the ballroom of the Student Union into a psychedelic dance palace.

We had spent fall term publishing ten consecutive twelve-page issues. Our circulation was up to 5,000 (still small; university enrollment exceeded 38,000), and we were feeling strong. Our staff and volunteer organization numbered in the dozens. We were distributing papers in open racks in a number of campus buildings, as well as hawking them around campus; rip-offs of papers and, worse, of the coin boxes attached to the racks presented a problem, but despite that we were growing financially stronger due to the increased advertising volume.

STRANGE THINGS ARE HAPPENING

The landlady of the little house had decided to evict me, so I rented instead a much bigger house closer to the center of town, with our office and the big light table on an enclosed porch overlooking Abbott Road, one of the main streets. Behind the door, a group of us—mostly, but not all, *Paper* staffers—created a loose, chaotic communal household and tripping center. Things were getting stranger and stranger. Schoolwork was a distant memory. I had long since given up on my journalism major. Now I was in my second year as a senior, trying life as a history major and later to move on to English. But it was hard to feel any relevance in any of my courses, and it was hard for my instructors and advisors to fault me on what I was doing. I was operating in unknown territory. Sometimes I was in school, sometimes I dropped out; it didn't seem to make any difference. What *was* happening was the ongoing exploration with psychedelic drugs, informed, as ever, by the new music that kept coming out and telling us what was real. The Mamas and Papas, "If You Can Believe Your Eyes and Ears," Donovan, "Mellow Yellow," Judy Collins, "In My Life," The Beatles, "Strawberry Fields Forever." I was spending more and more of my time, money, and energy finding out just how spaced out I could get and still function in the world. I sort of functioned as the daddy of both *The Paper* and the big house, and these roles took up most of my time and energy, but I also was finding more opportunities to play and explore with my new friends. It was all a trip.

As winter quarter began, Vol. II No. 11, *THE sad-eyed PAPER of the lowlands*, featured a front-page obituary, "Jim Thomas, 1946-1966." That which Larry had feared had come to pass; Jim had been killed in battle just before Christmas. Larry wrote, "America has lost a soldier, and America can afford that. But it has also lost a poet, and no nation can afford such a loss."

The next issue criticized *State News* reporter Andy Mollison, a friend of ours and the boyfriend (later, the husband) of our staff writer Char Jolles, for jumping the gun on what might have been a reporting scoop: the East Lansing SDS was considering forming the first chapter of what national SDS anticipated would become an anti-draft union, large numbers of men willing to publicly denounce the Vietnam draft, a felony offense. Andy saw an advance copy of the plans at Char's house, in the possession of one of her roommates, an SDS officer. He ran it as a copyrighted banner story in the *State News*, even before the local SDS chapter had voted on it. We had fun embarrassing him by detailing how his "scoop" had been obtained ("Even the Best of Us Have Our Off Days"). Over the next weeks we followed the developments as the local SDS chapter did, indeed, take a public anti-draft stance, in which many *Paper* staffers of both genders (including myself) participated.

After another issue, we skipped a week due to a big snowstorm, then came back with a 20-page issue of *THE white PAPER*, headlined "Urban Renewal or, How Twenty-Four Inches of Snow Made a Better Place of East Lansing." In addition to our celebrating the unexpected winter holiday and the surprising beauty of town and campus, the article by Dale Walker, an advertising graduate student who was in the process of rethinking his values as he got to know our scene better (he lived in the attic room of the big house), commented on the failure of three "modern gods": business, government, and science. "If we are to make a better world for ourselves, we must disclaim all belief in the inevitability of progress, and we must ask of those in power that they TRY....Someone must begin to lobby for the people. Until our efforts are properly directed and humanitarian values find their place in the modern world, we will continue to be embarrassed for our failures. Pray for snow."

I don't remember for sure, but we must have changed printers again in time for that issue, because for the first time a disclaimer appeared in the corner of the front page: "NOTE: Contents of this paper do not reflect views of Printers." Inside, in the masthead, is a second note, "The opinions expressed in *THE PAPER* are solely the responsibility of *THE PAPER*."

The next issue included the first installment of "The *Paper* Forum," a chance to air our laundry in public. Trouble was brewing in paradise. Larry Tate, now listed as assistant editor but feeling increasingly alienated from the changes in our lifestyle and the content of *The Paper*, and still interested mainly in finding or writing the great American novel, had written an open letter to me. In it, he angrily tore apart one of my articles, the paean to the underground press from our anniversary issue (quoted above, in which

I credit Marshall McLuhan with formulating ideas to explain how our generation was living). Larry decried what he saw as our inexorable slide toward some anti-intellectual hippie hell. "It makes me more unhappy than I can say that *The Paper* might become just another underground newspaper."

In my response, written quickly on the way to the printer just before deadline, I was unable to counter the charge of hasty and careless writing, but I did feel the need to repeat what I had said previously about the role we were playing in exploring and defining the new culture that was coming into being around us. "I think we can easily identify an enormous impact we have had on the MSU community since we began publishing, and that impact is largely based on the loose kind of evolution I have encouraged within *The Paper*, including the movement to 'the underground.' That Larry is as blind as he seems to be to this impact simply amazes me."

The debate went on for several issues. John Sinclair, the infamous poet, community organizer, and marijuana advocate from Detroit, some of whose recent writing we had published, wrote to support my side: "I mean these guys have got to stop being so SCARED about everything that's happening—their precious intellects will still carry them through, if that's what they need....My own identity [used to be] bound up with the existence of the little magazines, but as far as I'm presently concerned the little magazine is DEAD—the papers are much more public, faster to get out, regular, get to more people, etc., etc. YES."

RUNNING ON EMPTY

Despite this testimonial to the vitality of the underground press, it was becoming clear that not all of us wanted the same thing from *The Paper* or from this phase of our lives. How would this tension resolve itself? I was slowly becoming aware that I was running down in my enthusiasm for the process. Or, at least, that something was changing, some shift in the historical moment.

In Issue 16, late in February, I started a lengthy two-part article analyzing a report by a faculty committee who had worked for a year on a proposal to rewrite all the regulations affecting student affairs in the university. This was the university's response to more than two years of student protests, and soon the faculty would vote on the proposal. I pointed out, in agonizing detail, all the report's inconsistencies and evasions, as well as the clear victories for our side, such as the proposed abolition of the ridiculous Board of Student Publications. I recommended against faculty acceptance of the proposal as offered, but acknowledged that it

would likely pass anyway, and encouraged my readers to engage in the long process of lobbying to refine the new regulations into what was needed. Clearly, this was an editorial position that implied we would be there to check up on the outcome and followthrough. Not so; the faculty report and the new regulations were barely mentioned again in *The Paper* from then until June.

Our attention was elsewhere, but it's hard to say exactly where. Certainly the continuing experiment we were living with psychedelic drugs was taking its toll. I remember waking up and/or coming down in various friends' apartments and reading *The Paper* as though for the first time; it was a hoot to read and it made me proud, but the clarity of my direction of it was waning, and it was not clear whether anything or anyone was emerging to replace me.

Winter quarter ended, and with it the ambitious communal-living-and-working arrangement I had encouraged us to explore for several months. I had found the chaotic environment too costly for comfort, both in terms of dollars and psychic energy. I don't remember whether it was my idea or the landlord's, but I gave up the big house and found another small one to rent, in the unincorporated limbo zone between Lansing and East Lansing, in the shadow of a freeway ramp, with a late-night liquor store next door. Once again, the giant light table filled half the living room. My small bedroom was painted black, the better to encourage psychedelic chalk drawings on the walls. In that room, the Beatles' "Sgt. Pepper's Lonely Hearts Club Band" and the Jefferson Airplane's "Surrealistic Pillow" would come to life. More than ever, the university seemed far away.

Our April 4 issue, the first of spring quarter, spent its front page announcing an event we were sponsoring the next week, borrowing an idea from the *Rag* of Austin for "Gentle Thursday," a one-day impromptu Summer of Love-type happening all over campus. (The actual so-called Summer of Love had yet to occur, but the mood was building.) "We are asking that on this particular Thursday everybody do exactly what they want. On Gentle Thursday bring your dog to campus or a baby or a whole bunch of red balloons." Et cetera et cetera. You get the idea.

A large ad in the same issue announced the formation of the SDS anti-draft union anticipated two months earlier. Some 42 men announced we would not go to Vietnam, would encourage others to do the same, et cetera; some 20 women signed on as supporting us. (Many years later we learned that, if it hadn't been accomplished already, signing that ad definitely opened a dossier on each of us in the secret intelligence files kept by the Michigan State Police.) Another change in that issue was in the staff listing: four of us—Larry

Tate and I, Brad Lang, and Eric Peterson, a relative newcomer to the staff who had become one of my closer friends—were now listed as the editorial board. A few weeks later we added a fifth person, Ron Diehl, who had been handling business affairs for *The Paper* for most of the year. This was a first step in the inevitable transition to new leadership, as Larry was getting ready to graduate and I was burning out.

The next issue gave our real rationale for calling for "Gentle Thursday": "It's like this: Spring had arrived. *The Paper* seemed suddenly to be a minor drag to produce each week. Radical politics had become almost totally wrapped up in the [student government election] campaigns....Serious cracks were becoming evident in the once-quasi-solid wall of the hippy community. Last term's happy college drop-outs were becoming bored with their new bohemian life. Something, in short, had to be done." Thus, Gentle Thursday.

But first, it was time for student government elections. I wrote "An Elections Handbook, or Don't Throw Out the Bath Water Just Because the Baby Is Still Dirty, or How to Survive on Brutal Wednesday." Several of our staff writers and other friends were running for positions in the student government, and the tenor of the campaigns was clearly toward incorporating some of the positions as well as the leaders of the protest organization, United Students, that had grown out of the fall sit-ins. We encouraged this trend, while continuing to promote the usefulness of direct action techniques, "for getting people involved in bringing about immediate change, both in their own lives and in their political environment."

Both "Brutal Wednesday" and "Gentle Thursday" went the way we wanted them to. Brad Lang and Jim Friel, the writer of LandGrantMan, were now on Student Board. Gentle Thursday had been a campuswide hit, supported even by the *State News*. We were no longer the out-group; suddenly our little revolution had gained some real acceptance and a measure of authority. We spent an issue celebrating the shift. A collage of Gentle Thursday photos included one of John Hannah walking across campus holding a flower someone had given him.

Our next issue covered the controversial appearance on campus of American Nazi leader George Lincoln Rockwell, and also included original coverage of the antiwar Spring Mobilization from our correspondents on both coasts. One of the articles on the New York Mobilization was from an MSU-SDS member named David Stockman, who much later would gain fame as the precocious hatchet man of Reaganomics when he headed the federal Office of Budget and Management. Still a 1967 innocent, he wrote, "It will take more than a leisurely stroll down Madison Avenue,

or even revulsion toward war atrocities to put this ghastly thing to an end. The real determinats [sic] of the war are built into the structure of the corporate system. Concomitantly, political indifference and moral insentiency are interwoven in the fabric of middle-class culture....Unless a significant process of radical humanization begins in the near future, the City will never again see giant parades, or Love-Ins or Gentle Thursdays. Neither will it see people waving balloons, nor wearing flowers in their hair, nor..." Nor what? He doesn't say.

Was there a revolution in the works? It was hard to tell, hard to know where to look. Our next issue was dedicated to reprinting pamphlets of the Diggers of San Francisco, anarchist street people who, by their way of being, challenged all the assumptions of materialism.

Then we stepped back to East Lansing and spent a long front-page article looking at the first crisis of the new student government as it flexed its muscles on—could this still be happening?—the controversial question of abolishing dormitory curfews for women. Was this the revolution we were waiting for? If so, it seemed to be spinning its wheels a bit, and I drew a parallel to the situation of *The Paper*. "I didn't feel like editing this week's issue of *The Paper*, either. There is a connection here...." I noted that, whereas we had started publishing in a desperate situation, which both stimulated and suppressed us, as simply publishing became easier and the atmosphere became more permissive, we found it more difficult in some ways to sustain interest and keep the quality of the product up. "When it looks as though we are having difficulty maintaining the spirit to exploit our uniqueness, I tend, not alone, to get bored with it. This week has been a particularly bad week in this way...."

AND NOW, SOMETHING COMPLETELY DIFFERENT...

It was by now the middle of May 1967 in my fourth year in East Lansing; many of my contemporaries were getting ready to graduate but I wasn't, because I had thrown standard college stuff overboard in order to have this revolution; and now things were sort of settling down in a funny way, or it was time to move on, or it was time to really take a stand for social change, not just pretend, or...what was it time for, anyway? I certainly wasn't sure, but something new was rumbling through my life, and I wasn't feeling like carrying *The Paper* alone. I had a new girlfriend, Candy Schoenherr, who had joined our staff a few months earlier after being brought around by Eric Peterson, and she and I were spending time with a few new friends who, in turn, were looking at their sexual identities; together we were discovering bisexuality, and it was quite a rush for all of us. I remember going to Larry Tate, who had long since acknowledged his own homosexuality, one morning after a night of discovery and saying to him, "Me, too." He responded with less than perfect enthusiasm, but I was thrilled. After so many years of mental and abstract principled activity, finally my body was beginning to speak, too.

How would we incorporate this latest craze into our newspapering, and who would see that we met the deadlines? I tried bringing these disparate elements together by devoting space in *The Paper* to activities of the various people with whom I was exploring (they were, after all, active as writers, in student government, in the various protest activities), but this did not satisfy the conflicting urges I was feeling. Despite the naming of an "editorial board," I was still feeling like the sole party responsible for meeting the deadlines, and sometimes it hurt too much. In a slightly later era, the answer to my dilemma would become obvious: explore the sexual conflicts and gender-role expectations explicitly in the newspaper. But at the time, such questions were still too new and too threatening to be examined clearly.

One week late in May, when I was particularly depressed and when the help I needed from others wasn't there, I simply didn't put an issue together at all. Instead, I put out another two-page mimeographed flier made up to look like *The Paper*, as we had done more than a year earlier when political pressure gave us no other choice. This time I raised the question, "What if there were no issue of *The Paper* this week?" It was a desperate move; I needed to know whether anyone cared. I found that they did. Andy Mollison of the *State News* paid me a visit to remind me of my responsibility to my readership. The next week a sufficient number of staff people rallied around to put out the last issue for the school year, Issue 26, 20 pages.

One of the most consistently enthusiastic staffers, Ron Diehl, wrote an article, "*The Paper* Is Dead, Long Live *The Paper*!," in which he reassured our readers that the experiment would carry on. On the subject of my mutiny the week before, he wrote, "At this point, Mike just wishes to swim back to shore and if the boat continues to float, well fine." A fair enough assessment. Somehow, it seemed I had run out of things to say, or the confidence to say them. I was burned out, that's for sure; my academic career was in ruins, and I urgently wanted the whole world to become a psychedelic wonderland so I could get some rest. But *The Paper* would continue. It was time to turn it over to a group of successors, and take a break, maybe a permanent one.

I went home to New York for a brief rest, to get ready for a summer of driving and camping around the country with Will Albert, one of my new gay friends, a would-be poet and adventurer who was just having his first coming-out experiences, and with whom I was hopelessly infatuated. While I was away, somehow, the county prosecutor decided the time had finally come to bust *The Paper* for drugs. His troops invaded my little house one night while my girlfriend Candy and nine others were partying there, and arrested everyone for possession of marijuana. Finally, the obvious had been confirmed: that we had been watched and listened to for months, and that our drug habits made us legally vulnerable. So sad for the prosecutor that I was out of the state.

Candy called me in New York to tell me about the bust. There didn't seem to be anything I needed to do. The lawyer who had been hired had sprung her after a couple of days in jail; others had done about as well. Will and I started our trip. Passing through East Lansing, we found the little *Paper* house near the freeway still functioning without me. Despite the bust, folks were putting out a summer issue of reprints from the previous year, an orientation special for the new freshmen who were starting out in summer quarter. One of the few new articles in the issue was a commentary by Ron Diehl on the bust at the *Paper* office, focusing on the admitted police surveillance that had preceded it and the violation of civil liberties that the major media took for granted, even celebrated. "[A]s each of us proceeds in this bugged, wired, voyeured life, may we have patience with those whose lives are so barren as to derive excitement from ours."

Candy headed home to spend the summer working in a factory and waiting for her trial. Will and I headed west, he with his copy of the gay-bar directory to guide him, I hoping for some clarity about something, anything to emerge from the trip. In several cities along the way, he met people and had little affairs, while I pined and waited. I felt quite unable, even ineligible, to "cruise" the bars, an activity at which Will excelled. We camped out in national parks and along roadsides. We discussed poetry and revolution. When we could, we paid brief visits to underground newspapers we knew about: the *Seed* in Chicago, *Helix* in Seattle, the *Seer* in Portland, our namesake *The Illustrated Paper* in Mendocino, California.

When we hit San Francisco, our first stop was a visit to *Vanguard*, a small, gay-oriented UPS member magazine published in the Haight-Ashbury. Will and the one-man staff, Keith St. Claire, immediately became stuck on each other, and we stayed. I had my own room in Keith's collective household, the gayest place I had been yet. I used the time to finally have some preliminary gay adventures of my own, as well as psychedelic adventures in the Haight. I remember sitting anonymously in the offices of the San Francisco

Oracle one day, tripping my brains out with the rest of the troops. That evening, I went home and tried to rest, but a voice in my brain kept reciting Candy's name to me; it seemed to be coming very powerfully from far away, but I didn't understand how or why.

One time, we picked up two hitchhikers in the Haight, "lent" them $10, and drove them to an adjoining neighborhood to see a friend for some kind of "business deal," which was supposed to get us our money back. An inordinately long time later, they reappeared at the car, shit-faced and incoherent, their eyes rolling in their heads. Loaded.

But this brief exposure to the world of hard drugs did not dissuade us from our belief in soft ones. We decided to take advantage of our proximity to Mexico, still the source of much of the available marijuana, and collected $1,000 in drug money among ourselves and from some friends in East Lansing. With that money, I went to southern California, in the company of some teenage friends of Keith's, to purchase a suitcase full of kilo bricks. All that weekend, the teenagers kept me stoned, listened to my political stories, taunted me a bit about my bisexuality, and kept the money (I'm convinced) by staging a "bust" of their contact. I felt foolish and disgraced returning to San Francisco empty-handed, but I didn't know what else to do.

After a month in San Francisco, Will and I were planning to stay on, maybe to go to school at S.F. State. During a trip back to New York with Keith to collect our goods (Will was from upstate), we stopped in Michigan for another visit.

We visited Candy at her parents' house and wound up spiriting her away and back to East Lansing, where one of the most exciting changes we discovered was the increasing number of new underground papers that had been coming in the mail. Among them were the first half dozen issues of a new paper from Boston, *Avatar*, which looked as different from the typical underground paper as the *San Francisco Oracle* did, but in an opposite way. Where the *Oracle* was lavishly decorated and colorful, setting it apart from the cut-and-paste collage style of our paper and most of the others, *Avatar* was airy and wispy, filled with pen-and-ink drawings and cloudlike, handwritten headlines. The content was unusual too: articles on the spirit of the American revolution, on personal transformation, on the morality of drugs and hippie culture, lots of personal and spiritual advice by some guy named Mel Lyman. But I'm getting ahead of my story.

MORE SCHOOL IN MY FUTURE

By the time Will and Keith and I got to New York, the bloom was off for the two of them. Will looked at me one morning and complained, "He's plastic!" That was about as bad a name as you could call anyone. Keith returned to San Francisco; his household remained a stop on all our friends' circuits for quite a while. Larry Tate even lived there for a time. Will decided to stay on in New York City, and instantly got into another affair. I had my C.O. hearing, after a year of waiting, at a draft board office in far-suburban eastern Long Island, and of course was rejected. My personal values were not a sufficient reason not to fight a war; I needed to, but couldn't, demonstrate religious reasons for refusing to be drafted. It was looking like there was more school in my future. I called Candy in East Lansing and arranged to return and live with her and try MSU again, this time joining her as a psych. major, with a radical activist professor as advisor to both of us. She found us a sublet apartment over a store on the main thoroughfare of Lansing, and we really tried hard to be a normal young couple concerned about school.

The Paper was in the hands of others, and I felt and acted like an elder statesman, as best I could. The year's publication output began on September 18, 1967, with Vol. III No. 1/2, a four-page effort (one page of which was a full-page ad for Bobbie Gentry's record, "Ode to Billy Joe"). The front page featured a picture of a billboard that had appeared at several places on campus during the summer, encouraging students and others to use a special phone number to report each other's suspicious behavior to the campus police. A letter from psychology professor Lauren Harris commented, in part:

> We can smile at it and say, "That's the police mentality for you"; but the smile would be forced. Joke about it as we might, we FEEL less free than before, and the sense of lost freedom, the atmosphere of suspicions created by such a sign, is so very destructive of ourselves and of our community....The question we should ask ourselves is, What is there about our society that produces and supports the insensitivity of the police to the people whom they are supposed to serve?

Vol. III No. 1, on October 3, had a front-page article by Ron Diehl, which continued his coverage of consumer issues begun the previous year. The subject was "SpartanTown U.S.A.," a promotional event on campus by the East Lansing Chamber of Commerce that coincided with fall registration and illegally benefited from student government funding. An inside article by Bertram Garskof, the psych. professor who was Candy's and my new advisor, described his experiences auditing a freshman ROTC class, complete with its hysterical anti-Communist propaganda. The issue had no staff listing, but a mix of familiar and new names appeared on articles.

The next issue, two weeks later, listed ten people as staff, in no particular order, but Ron Diehl's name is first, Eric Peterson's is eighth, mine is ninth. A box at the top of the front page entreatied people to "Confront the Warmakers, Washington, October 21." The lead article was a reprinted *L.A. Free Press* interview with Mort Sahl. The back page contained the return of LandGrantMan, in which John Palindrome is feeling overwhelmed by the proliferation of his duties as both a multiversity president and as LGM. Once again he is visited by the spirit who had granted him his superpowers, and who now helps him share those powers with his "most trusted stooges": the vice president for account juggling, the vice president for crowd control, the vice president for propaganda and recruiting, the chief of the occupying forces, and the head of the association of virgin females.

On page 3 was my "An Open Letter: On My Living-Learning Experiences," which I had addressed to the instructors of the four courses I was taking. Obviously, my attempt to just settle in and be a normal student was putting unfamiliar strains on me.

In the letter, I praise my professors and courses for giving me an uncharacteristically satisfying academic experience. "I find each day of classes, each week of studying, a unified experience relatively free from the isolation and fragmentation that plagues practically all formal education—and all of this seems unified with the other commitments and concerns that make up my life." I go on to discuss my pleasant living situation and my unusually satisfying work-study job as an undergraduate psychology assistant, helping counsel introductory psych. students through their first exposure to their chosen field. "I wonder how many other students would appreciate such interaction if they could find it, how many have other types of jobs or similar obstacles that prevent them from doing so—and how many are too intimidated by their schedules or by the structure of their educations even to think of the possibility." I lament the heavy course work that makes most students, and for a rare change was also making me, sacrifice other important interests and opportunities in order to meet the deadlines imposed by school. "This term, for once and at last, I really want to do all my work, but I don't see that I'm capable of it. I've already fallen so far behind that I worry even about taking the time to write this letter. But, generally, I'm not wasting time." I discuss the cutbacks I'd made in my activism, but also my continued need to remain in touch with my friends, to inform my academic learning with real experiences, with real people. "When one knows what one wants and needs, and one's commitments are designed to comprise the life one wants to lead, it is very difficult to make the adjustments sometimes required by a simple lack of time." But this is just the start of the real plaint:

I behave the way I do now because I have endured several trying years of defining myself, my interests and my world. Very little that I do seems accidental or unconscious, and it would be difficult to convince me significantly that I am making mistakes. As I have said, I like and respect your courses and recognize perhaps more strongly than ever the value of academics. But I also have strong and well-formulated ideas about how I should live, and if school happens to interfere with this I have no doubt which of the two I will favor.

I don't think there is anything wrong with this: it will take me a long time to get over the grudge I hold against Michigan State for letting me waste all the time I have spent finding my own academic direction, for forcing me to arrive with such difficulty at a tolerable compromise with the social environment here, for taking the role of adversary rather than guide through so many crucial changes I have undergone. Rather than criticizing me if I occasionally fail to perform up to par academically, I would caution you with the utmost respect to consider first the feelings of ALL your students confronting this leviathan from within the privacy of their own concerns.

I've made a temporary separate peace with the society, and I'm profiting from it. I am sure it will be temporary, however, simply because I don't trust the society to maintain for very long the conditions I'm enjoying, and because I don't trust myself to remain contented for very long. I've seen too much of both me and the society for me to expect us to remain in permanent equilibrium. Already I'm feeling the pangs that will probably lead to new involvements to save our social order from further decline; already I'm feeling concern for things my period of rest does not provide time to worry about.

CONFRONTING MACHINES, OF WAR AND OTHERWISE

Prophetic words. Four days after publication of this epistle, Candy and I and a bunch of our friends joined thousands of others in Washington, confronting the warmakers at the Pentagon, where we tasted our first tear gas but managed to avoid getting clubbed or arrested. Others did not do as well. We also dropped in on one of the first meetings of the Underground Press Syndicate and its new offshoot, the Liberation News Service, but we felt like visitors, not full-scale participants. On the way back to Michigan, my formerly dependable "Papermobile," my shiny blue 1964 Corvair, blew a gut on the highway. We spent three days in a motel in Maryland, acid-tripping with two friends while waiting for an engine rebuild. I now believe the job was sabotaged by the mechanics, but we were too stoned to know the difference. The new engine got us only as far as rural Pennsylvania, where we consigned the car to a wrecker. Friends drove down to pick us up and bring us back to East Lansing. Life was beginning to change, all right.

In the next issue, *THE American PAPER for Americans*, dated November 7, one of the new staff members, Jeffrey Snoyer, led the coverage of the Washington march with an article headlined with a mock postmark, "Washington D.C. Oct. 21, 1967—Prey for Peace." He told the story of the eye-opening and radicalizing experiences he had had on the march, intending to stay out of the fray and remain detached as a journalist, but finding himself inadvertently in the middle of a police riot and unable to keep his cool as heads were getting bashed all around him. He describes the orderly reaction of the crowd as the police repeatedly went berserk and started hitting demonstrators: "[E]ach time, there was an instantaneous uproar, then, in a few seconds, everyone would quiet down, no resisting. I was speechless whenever it happened—this was a heterogeneous, totally random group from all over the country, and such remarkable control was shown—I had never before seen a gathering of people as responsible and intelligent as these marchers were." He managed to avoid being arrested, returned to East Lansing to the disappointing, minimizing press coverage of the march, including LBJ's promise to "Keep [His] Commitment in Viet Nam," then picked up his mail and actually found a letter postmarked, "Pray for Peace."

In the same issue, a front-page note to readers offered "our sincere apologies for the slow start we have had this year. There have been several complications including disorganization and bad breaks. Beginning this issue we will strive to be weekly and to provide you with a great deal of interesting, challenging features." The staff box named an editorial board of Ron Diehl, James Ebert, and Jeffrey Snoyer, and six other "paper people," of whom I was one. The issue included a two-page reprint from *Georgia Straight, the Vancouver Free Press*, giving details of that paper's harassment and censorship at the hands of civic authorities.

Vol. III Nos. 4 and 5, *Take Me Out to THE PAPER* and *THE PAPER of Sisyphus Gathers No Moss*,

published on November 14 and November 30, respectively, contained a trio of remarkable articles by some of us long-time staffers, whose lives were in flux. The lead article of No. 4 was Larry Tate's story of having joined the draft resistance in the San Francisco Bay Area, where he had moved in order to begin graduate school at Berkeley: "BEFORE THE REVOLUTION; What to Do Till the FBI Comes, or Before the FBI; What to Do Till the Revolution Comes."

At a rally in Oakland on October 16, simultaneous with rallies all across the country on that day, Larry, who previously had of course sympathized with the antiwar movement but had stayed somewhat above its rough-and-tumble, had turned in his draft card. "I suppose I ought to feel different now, but I don't. The main problem has been what to show for identification." He recounted how the huge crowd, which had prepared itself for another police riot, had suddenly found itself in control of downtown Oakland, with the police in disarray and unsure how to respond. Nevertheless, he concludes, "What I feel most strongly most often is that the Great Tradition [of Responsible Dissent in America] has failed, period" (see sidebar 1).

GLIMPSES OF THE FUTURE

The next issue's lead article, "Sitting on a Cornflake, Waiting for the Burn to Come" (misquoting the Beatles' then-current "I Am the Walrus"), was by Dale Walker, the former advertising student who had now returned to Vermont to work as a draft counselor and was waiting for a decision on his conscientious objector application (which did come through a few months later). Reflecting on the speed of social and technological change in modern society, he wonders whether it all represents any improvement in the quality of life, but admits, "I'm frightened about other things...."

My American Hell is 1984....The military-industrial Complex makes me uneasy. But Ronald Reagan and Shirley Temple scare me out of my wits. It is the union of government with the new technology's still-crude psychology of communications which constitutes a real threat. The CIA and FBI and the electronic police are a scary supplement, but they may someday become an outdated form of control. I'm afraid that the Madison Avenue-Hollywood-Washington Complex can create a dictatorship from within the mind.

He discusses the decline in popularity of the Vietnam War and LBJ for all the wrong reasons, and the futile attempts by New Orleans Mayor Jim Garrison and others to establish the truth about the Kennedy assassination in the face of the Warren Commission's whitewash (see sidebar 2).

In 1967, the Right Wing Revolution of the 1980s was almost visible in the distance, just over the horizon. I had no way to know how relevant Dale's musings would soon become to my personal experience. For my part, I was dealing with some more current dilemmas. My contribution to the trio of life-change articles was "The Dove Has Torn Her Wing" (using the title of the Jacques Brel song popularized by Judy Collins): "This weekend has sealed it, friends. Drugs are not, repeat NOT, the Revolution." A friend of ours, a sometime *Paper* staffer and a popular musician and guitar instructor around town, Bill Kahl, had been arrested for dealing and had pleaded guilty. It looked like he was going to be in jail a long time. Not only that, but one of the people whose money I had left in southern California in my aborted drug-purchasing attempt the previous summer had decided to get even with me in the best way he could, by breaking into *The Paper*'s office (still the little house near the freeway in Lansing) over the weekend and trashing the place. The office was a wreck; the size of the issue, which was in fact the second anniversary issue, had to be reduced because of the emergency situation, and in his destructive frenzy he had broken the huge light table glass that had become almost the trademark of *The*

Paper to everyone who knew it intimately. And for what?

I wrote about my involvement in the drug-dealing experiences of both men, and exclaimed passionately, "It's hard to be just angry. WE DON'T NEED DRUGS. HEAR THAT? WE DON'T NEED THEM!" Then I explained why (see sidebar 3).

That angry and hurt declaration turned out to be my last article for *The Paper*. It was left to others to put the office back together and rebuild the spirit. Which they did; *The Paper* continued publishing for the next several years, finally achieving some recognition and assistance from the university, and eventually was supplanted by a series of successor papers. [See Ken Wachsberger's "A Tradition Continues: The History of East Lansing's Underground Press, 1965-Present" in this collection.] But I had no part in it after my anti-drug article.

I'm unable to say what became of the man who broke into our office; I'm unaware of any charges ever being filed against him. For that matter, I'm unable to say what became of the marijuana trials of the ten people, including my girlfriend Candy, who had been busted in that same little house the previous spring. I remember Candy negotiating with her lawyer for something or other, probably a reduced-sentence plea bargain that didn't require any more time served than her original couple of days, and I guess the others did something similar. Somehow it faded away. Bill Kahl

Sidebar 2: From "Sitting on a Cornflake, Waiting for the Burn to Come"[1]

by Dale Walker

They are trying to rewrite history....

America, within the next decade, may well create its own form of dictatorship. It may not appear as such because its methods may not be the traditional uses of the police and military for the suppression of dissent. It will feed upon the illusion of freedom, the reduction of fact to a question of public relations, and the manipulation of appetites (both as diversion and as substitute satisfaction). The coup from within will be effective because it will cut off debate at its source—the individual consciousness....

We as a nation are looking at the same time for a hero, for a religion and for a pleasant way out of the imposed responsibility of the Electronic Age. We have the INCLINATION to become fanatic new converts of some new cause. We would like the feeling of release, I'm sure. We have the EXCUSE: war, the race riots, the rebelling youth, the linking of dissent with "crime in the streets." And we finally have the MEANS: a new freedom from democratic restraints,

the marriage of advertising and politics, the evolution of public opinion as a creative art form....

Our foreign policy is neither right nor wrong; it is merely a question of better lighting, a different profile, more make-up, a better choice of words or more repetition. The question of truth is becoming academic. And so will the question of freedom if we don't learn quickly to resist the sell. Right now we can thank God that Johnson was no movie star and that his Texas accent finally grew to nauseate us. Maybe we can thank the War, because it proved that reality still has a bite. But Johnson wasn't that good an actor (or he would have stopped being Johnson when it stopped working). But Reagan is. And whoever Big Brother will be, he will have a lot in common with Ronnie.

NOTE

1. From *THE PAPER of Sisyphus Gathers No Moss* 3, no. 5 (30 November 1967): 1, 4-5.

Sidebar 3: From "The Dove Has Torn Her Wing

by Michael Kindman

"It's hard to be just angry. WE DON'T NEED DRUGS. HEAR THAT? WE DON'T NEED THEM!"

They don't make everyone nicer and wiser. They make nice people nicer and wiser, and send some nice people to jail. They turn some people into junkies, even when it's not junk they deal in.

WE DON'T NEED THEM! We shouldn't fight all our fights just for the drugs. We shouldn't sacrifice our friends, and then act like it's their problem when they get busted. Or burned, I guess. It's a stupid fight....

You know what? I don't like the way this article is going, and I feel like smoking some grass and sitting and thinking about it so maybe it'll come better.

WE DON'T NEED THEM!! We can't be slaves to them!

Why can't they be legal, so we wouldn't always be hiding?

Drugs are beautiful! We should have them! We should change or destroy the society that won't let us have them, but we don't need them! Not at the expense of our hopes for making it in this world, not when they split us apart from each other and get us involved in

useless fights, not when we offer our friends up on the altar of a steady supply....

Once we've learned something from the drugs, or from the drug culture, we don't need them anymore. Once we've learned how we can regulate our moods and use our talents, we don't need to be always doing something to our consciousness, in the hopes that we'll happen on something even groovier than we are already. We're it, and now we know something about how to be it. How many people know what it is to recognize a high that comes on by itself, without smoking or dropping anything?.....

Consciousness can make us a generation of sages, and can make us effective in changing the course of our history. Drugs can't, not as long as we let ourselves destroy and be destroyed in the disservice of a dead taboo.

NOTE

1. From *THE PAPER of Sisyphys Gathers No Moss* 3, no. 5 (30 November 1967): 3.

did serve some time in jail, did also try to escape to Canada at least once (I helped him get to Toronto one time, but I don't remember if that was before or after the bust discussed in my article), and did have a generally hellish time with his drug habit. He finally died of alcoholism and drug abuse in the mid-seventies. I also learned, long after the fact, of two others of our group of friends who overdosed on hard drugs during the seventies, and of course there were lots of busts for drugs. Myself, I've never had a bit of legal trouble for all my drug use over the years. Lucky, I guess.

MOVING TO THE FUTURE

Candy and I continued trying to be normal people, but to no avail. Both of us were restless and scattered, unable to concentrate very well on our school and job responsibilities; real, live people kept being more interesting to us. My friend Will came visiting from New York during December and, in a pattern that was becoming uncomfortably familiar, met a man he wanted to remain with. Candy and I also got on well with his new lover, Larry Babcock; the four of us decided to rent an apartment together when Candy's and my sublet ran out at Christmastime. We found a place in a middle-class Lansing neighborhood, a large apartment with a big attic playroom, and moved in in time for me to pay a quick visit to New York at New Year's.

When I returned in January 1968, it was time to decorate and play house. What would this phase of the experiment bring? Larry, who was an art student, and Will were busily making light fixtures and wall hangings, candles and makeshift furniture. The attic room became our tripping center and the place where the four of us could explore together sexually. Candy and I had a new crop of freshman advisees in our psych. department job. We developed the habit of bringing them to the apartment for meetings and discussions. The more daring of them became part of our tripping circle, and our tripping and our activism grew increasingly to be about pushing the limits of our sexuality and inhibitions. For this, we were receiving independent study credits in psychology.

It was winter and we were without a car. I remember long nighttime walks through Lansing to where most of our friends lived, closer to campus, to bring this person or that back to our little den for a night of space travel and discovery. During this time, Candy was going through a personal trauma, remembering and assimilating the deeply painful memory of having been forced by her family to bear an unwanted child and give it up for adoption, shortly before Eric and I had met her. She spent many hours in the attic tripping room, shouting and crying out her grief in

paroxysms I barely understood and could not penetrate with my concern.

In this context, in an LSD-induced haze one night during February, Candy and I decided that the time had come; we were done with East Lansing and had to leave. Now. But where should we go? We considered northern California, where the back-to-the-land movement was picking up momentum and we might find some commune to join. But someone (was it Will and Larry? or was it some of our young advisees?) was interested in taking that trip with us, but only after winter quarter was over. We decided to kill the few weeks until that would occur by traveling to Boston, where that interesting underground paper, *Avatar*, came from, and see who those folks were. We were gone the next morning, having made minimal apologies and arrangements. Will and Larry left, too, heading for New York. Candy and I found ourselves hitchhiking with suitcases through what turned out to be a substantial blizzard, across southern Ontario and upstate New York, finally to Boston, where we showed up at the *Avatar* office late one afternoon. It felt to us like a great, magical adventure.

In those days, people showing up unexpectedly from halfway across the country didn't raise a lot of eyebrows. But our tale of having published our own paper in Michigan did make us relatively interesting drop-ins. We quickly took in the scene around us and saw both that we could learn plenty about this urban version of our kind of newspapering and that we could offer them plenty in terms of skills and enthusiasm. But who were these people? How did it happen that their paper looked so different from all the others and affected us so differently?

DID ANYONE WRITE THESE WORDS?

I knew that, in reading issues of *Avatar* as they had arrived in East Lansing over the months, feelings had been stirred in me that no other underground papers and, Lord knew, nothing else either had stirred. Besides dealing with the usual range of underground paper subjects—the drug culture, the Vietnam War and domestic resistance to it, ongoing changes in sexual mores, organizing in the black community to fight racism, all presented in a cool, New Englandy kind of way that I liked—*Avatar* also possessed qualities that seemed absent from the other papers. There were introspective writings, private journals of people obviously struggling to improve themselves, excerpted and made into examples for all of us. There were homilies on how to live in this complex age we were experiencing. There were astrology lessons, both theory and practical applications. There was advice of the most sweeping and the most personal kind from this Mel Lyman person, who seemed to be everywhere in the paper, and lots of different kinds of reactions to his writing from others. Sometimes, reading *Avatar*, especially reading Mel Lyman, I felt that the words had always existed somewhere, that no person could have written them, or that I had written them myself and forgotten. It was eerie.

Mel's first column, "To All Who Would Know" gives a taste of his hypnotic style, and his way of stating his truths in language that allowed space for absolutely no compromise:

> To those of you who are unfamiliar with me let me introduce myself by saying that I am not a man, not a personality, not a tormented struggling individual. I am all those things but much much more. I am the truth and I speak the truth. I do not express ideas, opinions, personal views. I speak truth. My understanding is tinged by no prejudice, no unconscious motivation, no confusion. I speak clearly, simply, openly and I speak only to reveal, to teach, to guide. I have no delusions about what I am, who I am, why I am. I have no pride to contend with, no hopes, no fears. In all humility I tell you that I am the greatest man in the world and it doesn't trouble me in the least. I write here because I know that somewhere out in the jungle of the world there will be a few ears that can hear. The rest of you might just as well pass right now and write me off as an egomaniac, a madman, a self centered schmuck because I am going to attack everything you believe in, everything you cling to, I am going to shed light on your dark truths, I'm going to show you things as they REALLY ARE and not how you would like them to be....

Something about this drew me in and caused me to start reevaluating everything I believed. I could see that other people who wrote for *Avatar* were also going through their own changes and reevaluations; some of the articles attempted to convey the spirit and the feeling of these changes. Others appeared to be personal journal entries by Mel and others that illustrated a kind of sensitivity and open-heartedness I found fascinating.

Here and there in *Avatar* were short poems, mysterious and moving, otherworldly poems, unsigned and unexplained except for the line, "from the box poems."

Every issue included numerous letters to Mel and his answers. Clearly, he was having an active dialogue with his readers, whose reactions in many cases resembled mine. Above the heading of the "Letters to Mel" section in one issue, was a short poem, presumably by Mel:

> We are here to become compassionate creatures
> Father forgive them, for they know not what they do
> I am totally responsible for all the ills of mankind
> I understand, and I will do all I can to help forever
> ....
> I feel all the pain in the world in my heart AS my heart
> All this and much much more is contained in the word compassion
> We are here to become compassion
> How are YOU doing

All in all, *Avatar* made different use of the newspaper medium than anything we had seen or experienced. The results were compelling. And now Candy and I had arrived on the scene of the creation, or so we believed. It looked pretty much like a newspaper office to us, filled with the kind of people we were used to hanging around with. Where was the mystery part?

THE MAGIC SWEEPS US UP

We were invited by a young couple working at the office to spend our first night, or longer, in their apartment on "The Hill." Where? It seemed that many, but not all, of the people working on *Avatar* also lived together in a commune elsewhere in town, on a hill in the mostly black neighborhood of Roxbury, where some of them owned houses and others rented apartments, and all of them took a lot of their guidance from Mel Lyman, the person whose energy so dominated *Avatar*. If you wanted to understand what was happening with *Avatar*, we learned, you had to get to know Mel Lyman and Fort Hill. We were game. A few days later, after spending time hanging out at the office and checking out people's living spaces in the evening, we didn't feel we knew any more about what made *Avatar* and Fort Hill run, but we were intrigued by the thought of staying on and becoming part of it all. Wayne Hansen, one of the two listed co-editors of *Avatar*, was offering me a position as his assistant and encouraging us to move to Boston.

Candy and I decided to consult the *I Ching*, the Chinese oracle we were learning about from our hosts: "Work on what has been spoiled/Has supreme success./It furthers one to cross the great water./Before the starting point, three days./After the starting point, three days."

The translator's interpretive note was hard to ignore:

> What has been spoiled through man's fault can be made good again through man's work....Work toward improving conditions promises well, because it accords with the possibilities of the time. We must not recoil from work and danger—symbolized by crossing of the great water—but must take hold energetically....Decisiveness and energy must take the place of the inertia and indifference that have led to decay, in order that the ending may be followed by a new beginning.

Something magical was afoot here; we felt like the decision was being made for us. We stayed three more days, as the *I Ching* seemed to be instructing us to do, getting to know more of the people involved in both *Avatar* and Fort Hill (some people seemed loyal to both and others seemed loyal to just one or the other; very complicated) and learning the rudiments of astrology, which all of them seemed to use as their chosen language when talking about people or the unfolding of events.

We traveled by bus from Boston to New York, where I pulled some money out of the bank to buy a used station wagon and we visited Will and Larry, who were setting themselves up in a small crafts shop in Greenwich Village. Then we drove on to Michigan, where we collected our goods and our cats and, as it turned out, a young boyfriend of ours who had been one of our psychology advisees. We gave the apartment away to some friends, terminated our jobs, and, incredibly, registered for ten units of independent study in psychology and social science during spring quarter, intending to write papers about our experiences in Boston. We said our goodbyes. I put a big box in storage in the basement of a collective house occupied by several of our friends. In the box was the entire documentary record of my years in college (my *State News* clipping file, class notes, and term papers) as well as my high school yearbook and a treasured collection of several hundred 45- and 78-rpm records; I never saw it again. Then we were off to Fort Hill, Roxbury, Boston, for who knew what adventures? It was early March 1968.

A LITTLE PIECE OF HISTORY IN THE FRONT YARD

Fort Hill is named for the Roxbury High Fort that stood there during the American Revolution (the "*first* American revolution*," as the current residents called it, anticipating, as they were, an imminent second one).

A significant battle had been fought there, a victory for the colonial army, with the colonists on Fort Hill and the British across a small valley that now contained several major thoroughfares, on Mission Hill in Jamaica Plain. In commemoration of this mostly forgotten event, there was now a tall and mysterious-looking memorial, a brick water storage tower with a roof that looked like a witch's hat, built during the Civil War era and itself now an ancient and unused relic. Around this tower was a small and little-maintained city park, and around that were rows of ramshackle houses and small apartment buildings, facing the tower from several adjoining streets.

The most ramshackle of the houses were on the closest adjoining street, an unpaved public way called Fort Avenue Terrace, with the tower practically in the front yards of places known as Number One, Number Two, and so on, up to Number Six Fort Avenue Terrace. There was even a Number Four and a Half, set back slightly and looking just a bit newer than Numbers One through Four. Numbers Five and Six were two halves of a "semi-attached" house that also was a bit newer than the others. These were the houses of the Fort Hill Community. Not all of them were Community property just yet, but they would be; you could feel it. Manifest destiny. There was also a row of three-story apartment buildings, Numbers 27, 29, and 31 Fort Avenue, around the corner—actually a short walk diagonally across the park—from these houses, in which members of the community rented additional space. Candy and I had stayed in a basement apartment in one of these buildings on our visit.

We quickly made the acquaintance of Number Four, which had been the first house occupied by Mel Lyman and his friends when they had made their way to the Hill in 1966. It was rented from a disagreeable elderly woman neighbor with whom there was a continuing rivalry, and it served as a sort of community center, with a big homemade table and benches in the dining room at which twenty or so people could be served. These large gatherings in fact happened often enough, as it was to Number Four that the many visitors drawn to the Hill by *Avatar* would be shown, to have their own experience of the strange magnetism of these latter-day pioneers. The house was the home of Eben Given, the prolific, otherworldly artist whose drawings, handmade headlines, and visionary writings graced every cover and many pages of every issue of *Avatar*, bringing to them some of the windswept quality of his Cape Cod upbringing, and his Mexican-American wife Sofie, who, we learned, had been Mel's teenage bride some ten years earlier. Sofie had seven children who lived there with them: four of Mel's (one by adoption, with a different birth father) and three of Eben's. A couple other adults lived in the house as well, including Wayne Hansen, the co-editor of *Avatar* who had invited us to move to the Hill.

The other houses then owned by the group were more private, but almost as busy. Number One was the home of Jim Kweskin, long-time leader of the nationally known folk music revival act, Jim Kweskin and the Jug Band, his wife Marilyn, their two children, Marilyn's sister Alison, her husband George Peper, and their son. The basement housed a darkroom in which George produced his work as photographer for the community. The living room was a party space big enough for the whole community, fitting Jim's long-time role as entertainer and showman. But these days something was changing. Once Jim had been Mel's boss, having hired him into the Jug Band at the height of its fame, to be its banjoist and harmonica player, at a time when Mel needed a steady job in order to meet terms of probation for dealing drugs. But the tables had turned. Mel's charismatic personality and uncompromising insistence on doing things his way had given him the upper hand in the power dynamic; the Jug Band, including such talented musicians as blues guitarist Geoff Muldaur and his wife, singer Maria D'Amato Muldaur, had run aground in this shifting momentum and had recently called it quits. Now Jim was working for Mel, handling business affairs for the growing community, running errands to help produce *Avatar*, and performing music with Mel and other community members only on those rare occasions when the mood was perfect and there were no obstacles or interferences. This was all more than mysterious to me, as a newcomer to the Hill and a long-time fan of the Jug Band's records. I was a bit starstruck by the presence close at hand of a famous musician, and confused by his willingness to give up his fame and career to follow this man Mel.

Number Two was the home of David Gude, who had come into the group by working as recording engineer for Vanguard Records, the label on which the Jug Band (and many other famous folk music acts of the day) had recorded most of its work, and on which the Newport Folk Festivals, those seminal events of the folk and folk-rock scene, had been memorialized. Mel had startled the closing concert of the 1965 festival by taking the stage after the famous Bob Dylan appearance in which Dylan let loose on the world the new phenomenon of electric folk-rock music, and attempting to calm the agitated crowd by playing an unannounced harmonica solo of "Rock of Ages." David had memorialized this moment by including it in the Vanguard album of highlights from that festival. About a year later, David had been fired from Vanguard in a dispute with its owner over the proper way to mix and master the tapes of an album on which—who else?—Mel Lyman had appeared as a member of the backup band for a singer named Lisa Kindred. At Mel's urging,

David had destroyed the original tapes, leaving only the version mixed the way Mel wanted—with Mel's harmonica and Lisa's voice given equal prominence. This unorthodox version was never released by Vanguard and Lisa Kindred had moved to the West Coast for a career as a blues singer in night clubs. Leaving his job at Vanguard had left David Gude free to move to the Hill and work for Mel, bringing with him his wife, Faith Franckenstein, daughter of the famous novelist, teacher, and political activist Kay Boyle, and their two children. Faith was also foster mothering a young daughter of Mel's by Rita W., an acid casualty friend from his days as a wandering musician and spiritual seeker. Also living with David and Faith in Number Two were Faith's brother Ian, an aspiring actor, and a dreamy, rather melancholy woman named Melinda Cohn, some of whose poetry and other writings on her experiences as a mental patient had appeared in *Avatar*. Melinda was pregnant with twin girls, children of community astrologer Joey Goldfarb, whose columns explaining astrological theory and its application in the understanding of current events appeared in nearly every issue of *Avatar*. Joey lived across the way in Number 27. Faith had the idea of turning her house into a private school for all the community children. Ads had appeared in *Avatar* seeking a teacher to take on the task.

Number Three was not yet in the family, and was still occupied by others. Within months of our arrival, however, it would be purchased for the community by a couple newly moved to the Hill from Cambridge, Kay and Charlie Rose. Kay was one of the office workers for *Avatar*. For now, we would just walk past Number Three, pretending it wasn't there.

Same with Numbers Five and Six. They were still owned and occupied by a family and tenants not involved with the community. But slow and careful negotiations were under way for them to be purchased. This effort would be successful in about a year, about the time the community would finally succeed in purchasing Number Four.

And there was Number Four and a Half, the little house with the magical-looking garden in front. This was home to Mel and his current wife Jessie Benton, daughter of world-famous painter Thomas Hart Benton, an important chronicler of American country life and a muralist well known for his representational works produced for Franklin Roosevelt's WPA. Jessie had once been David Gude's wife, in fact had a son by David a mere two months older than David and Faith's son; now she was First Lady of Mel's growing family, and dark-eyed Jessie with the dark curly hair and blue-eyed Faith with the long blonde hair were the best of friends. They wrote poems for *Avatar* about their glamorous but trying lives as keepers of the spirit and the babies of the community, they oversaw the activities of all the Hill's residents and visitors with a loving kind of disdain, sort of a noblesse oblige, and they were fiercely protective of the privacy and quiet that Mel needed to do his work. Number Four and a Half was his retreat, his sanctuary from the confusion of community life, where he wrote on a typewriter no one else touched, where he kept his musical instruments and his cameras and his recording equipment in special rooms, special places where the mood would not be broken, where he occasionally guided individual members of his flock on life-transforming high-dose acid trips. Here Mel made his plans to expand his influence on the world and appear fully as the "world saviour" he had already announced himself to be, in a small, self-published book, *Autobiography of a World Saviour*, that he now advertised regularly in *Avatar*, and quoted freely from in his responses to letters sent to him by readers and seekers of all types and published in large numbers in *Avatar*. This was the home of "The Lord," as some on the Hill would have him be known.

SETTLING IN

None of this made much sense to Candy and me as we settled in from the highway, with our carload of household goods, our two cats, our young boyfriend along for the ride (who stayed only a few weeks), and our high hopes. And none of it would be made available to us just yet, either. We didn't get to live in the houses on Fort Avenue Terrace, or even in the apartments on Fort Avenue. There were other satellite houses and apartments farther away in the neighborhood, and we got to live in one of those. Rachel Brause, a slightly older, frumpy, but creative woman from New York who had somehow become a follower, but not a close friend, of Mel's, had an apartment a short couple of blocks away, with several bedrooms and a small sleeping loft. This was where we three were installed, at least until a more suitable place could be found. Rachel had endless stories about the Hill and its people, but we soon could see that she was not really an insider. With her house as our base, we set to work on *Avatar*, to the best of our ability. It was not easy to figure out what our role was.

Despite the intensity of community activity on Fort Hill, *Avatar* was headquartered in an old newspaper office in the South End, a rundown neighborhood of brownstone houses and commercial buildings close to downtown Boston, a ghetto populated mostly by blacks and hippies. Some of the people working on the paper lived in the neighborhood, which made sense to us as it resembled the way we had lived and worked in East Lansing, and some lived in Cambridge, where *Avatar*

had originally been published, operating out of the offices of a music magazine named *Broadside*, whose editor, Dave Wilson, used to be involved in *Avatar* as well but no longer was. We knew from reading the early issues in Michigan that *Avatar* had been at the center of a huge censorship controversy in Cambridge, another in the now-familiar series of attempts by local authorities to suppress the underground press on the basis of "obscenity." That attempt had failed here, as elsewhere, but in the process it had made *Avatar* a cause célèbre, giving Mel the opportunity to vent his literary spleen in wonderfully obscene tirades and Eben the chance to create a notorious centerfold with the words "fuck shit piss cunt" in giant hand lettering, all these published as challenges to the would-be censors. The notoriety of the fight had helped increase the size of the staff and the circulation, had embarrassed the city fathers of both Cambridge and Boston, as well as the governor of Massachusetts, who couldn't resist getting involved, and had caused the *Avatar* offices to be moved to Boston in order to avoid the wrathful oversight of Cambridge officials. Now the office in the South End served as a sort of meeting ground for the various communities of folks interested in *Avatar*.

This was an entirely satisfactory arrangement for us, or at least for me, as a newcomer. I felt stimulated by all the different kinds of people who came through the place, and I had fun being in an urban environment close to the center of a city I found very interesting. Wayne set me up in a small office, where I had a rather empty desk and not a lot of responsibility. *Avatar* was published every two weeks, and all I knew for sure I would be working on was layout. Candy joined the team of typists who split time on a single IBM Selectric, laboriously producing the columns of justified copy for the paper in a tiny typeface. (Ironically, there was a full-scale Linotype machine sitting in the office, sort of a museum piece that, naturally, we didn't use.) We had plenty of time to explore the geography of the area and to get to know the people we were working with. One day soon after we arrived, a guy named Abbie Hoffman showed up at the office, full of the idea he was promoting for a Youth International Party that would storm the upcoming Democratic National Convention in Chicago, that summer. Most days were quieter than that.

But troubles had by now been brewing among the several factions of the loose alliance that was *Avatar* for a long time. From the very beginning, staff members allied with Mel Lyman and Fort Hill had insisted on a very major role for Mel's writings and his perfectionist standards in the production of the paper. This role had been controversial from the start. (Mel's first column, "To All Who Would Know," excerpted above, took up a whole page in the first issue but had accidentally been printed with a line omitted, and Mel, through his lieutenants, had insisted on reprinting it, complete, in the second issue, over strong objections.) At the same time, these high expectations had established a standard of graphic excellence that had helped make the paper's reputation. It had certainly pulled *us* in. But now, nearly a year after the start of publication, the tension was intensifying. Mel's steadily increasing volume of writing—columns with such challenging names as "Contemplations," "To All Who Would Know," "Diary of a Young Artist," "Telling It Like It Is," and "Essay on the New Age," as well as a voluminous flow of letters to and from Mel and other miscellaneous writings—had both set a tone and personality for the paper that attracted many of its readers, and had caused the rest of the staff, those who were there for reasons of political organizing or to establish a more general voice for the counterculture, to feel forced into a corner of their own creation. They increasingly had the sense that Mel and his supporters were just using them and the forum of the paper to give voice to Mel's words, and that, given the chance, Mel would soon crowd them out completely.

Splitting the Baby in Two

Shortly before Candy and I arrived on the scene for our first visit, starting with issue Number 18 in February 1968, this tension had resulted in a novel compromise: *Avatar* would henceforth be published in two sections, a full metropolitan-size news section, with political and cultural content resembling that of more typical underground papers, although its visual appearance had the airy grace for which *Avatar* had become known, and a tabloid-sized inner section that contained Mel's writing and the other output from the community, including Eben Given's rambling, meditative "Journals of John the Baptist" (sometimes known as "John the Painter," "John the Wasted," or "John the Waspegg"), astrology columns by Joey Goldfarb and others, and pictures and poems of the Fort Hill children, usually with a drawing of Mel by Eben on the cover and numerous photos of Mel inside. Only the outer news section was being produced in the South End office. The Fort Hill tabloid section was being produced by Fort Hill people at Fort Hill. Candy and I had not yet entered that company in any real way.

This was part of the reason I had little work to do in my empty new office adjoining the layout room. Another reason was that I was unclear whether anyone wanted me to do any reporting or writing. Wayne's long-time co-editor, Brian Keating, was in the process of relocating back to his home town of New York to undertake publishing a separate edition of *Avatar* there,

so logically I thought there would be lots of work to do, but I couldn't find it, and nobody told me. I was given little sense of direction and, as a newcomer in town, I didn't feel I had any grounding for directing others to do anything. I remember writing one piece of commentary (I don't remember the subject) that got as far as being typeset and pasted up, until David Gude, visiting the office one day, read it in its pasted-up form and simply tore it off the page saying, "This is bullshit," or words to that effect. I didn't challenge him, didn't know how the rules worked or where the lines of authority lay, but I soon learned that this was very much the way events tended to unfold around *Avatar*. The Fort Hill behavioral model gave full authority in the moment to whoever was feeling something strongly enough to take a risk and act, no matter what action he or she took, independent of any prior system of morality. This rule was not usually put into words; only the behavior of the actors revealed what the rules were.

But both Candy and I were certainly captivated by what we saw and felt going on around us. We were both reduced emotionally to childlike conditions by the complexity of the life and subculture we had stumbled upon. We had both expressed this situation during our first visit, in letters written to Mel that were published in consecutive issues, Numbers 20 and 21, during March, about the time we arrived to stay. They give a good idea of our respective states of mind at the time. Mine, "Note from a Visitor," was laid out alone on a page with one of Mel's "Telling It Like It Is" columns:

What a waste it would have been, thinking how I came all this way and did not talk to Mel. But I sit here and I'm glad. Why am I glad? I am afraid to talk to him. I am afraid to go in and say, "Hello, I'm Mike and I came to talk to you," with big exuberant exclamation points.

But I sit here all nervous and glad to retreat unnoticed to a corner.

There is greatness in the next room...too much for me to touch without getting burned bad, burned good. I never in my life met anybody who I did not feel as if I could crush, who I was better than...didn't need to listen to.

I can't touch Mel...I just listen to low talking in the next room.

This is so good. People rap about how Mel is on an ego-trip, blowing himself up with self-importance. He is important, but it's not for him that you say it. You say it for yourself...he doesn't need it. He knows.

We all need Mel.

Candy's letter was quite different from mine, although, like mine, it also gave Mel the kind of full and easy access to the deepest aspirations of the reader-writer that he loved to work with and respond to. She wrote:

Dear Mel,

You have always touched me and reached me and probably stood watching over me during all those times when I tore my guts out and screamed and clutched because I was nothing and there was nothing but blackness and emptiness everywhere. I could take nothing though much was offered. I could only ask for love because I couldn't take it. Every moment was one quake and I was surrounded. And I surrendered. I was nothing but a scream—and so was the universe. I knew that I was the universe and I didn't want it. This was the nature of the battle.

I started writing this letter because you spoke so closely to what I had gone through and I don't seem to know how to relate my past to my present. I have rejected dying while alive and have chosen peace but I don't have it completely. Peace? If there were any forever it would have to be everywhere. The hands are always ready to grab your guts again. I know them so well. I always end up shrugging and saying "on with it" and denying a whole bunch of it but I also keep being haunted and I can't decide what to make of it. There, that's it! Is there ever an end to it? To anything? This is the always and forever question—is there an absolute? Do I need an answer? I keep living without one but I'm writing this letter and I may bake bread or move up to the hill or do lots of things before I ask the question again. So it's shelved for a while and it will haunt me intermittently, perhaps until I die, as in "What is the ultimate use."

I love you.
Candy (Cancer)

THE ONLY ABSOLUTE

Mel loved talk like this, as he had made clear in previous responses to such letters. He responded to Candy with one of his favorite aphorisms, "The only absolute is 'MORE'." In other words, don't push for meaning or clarification of the questions that bother you most deeply; just keep doing "what's right in front of you," step by step, and meaning and understanding will come in their own time. This aphorism turned out to be one of the basic tenets of Fort Hill philosophy, something we would come to have drummed into us over and over in a thousand different situations, but sometimes it was hard to see it being practiced, even by those most in a position to be doing so.

For instance, Mel was even now, in the same issue in which Candy's letter and the response to it were being published, declaring a major change in the structure of the game, for reasons that were certainly not clear. A note at the front of the tabloid section of Number 21 announced that Mel would no longer be writing his several columns for the *Avatar*, although the paper would continue printing and reprinting articles already written. He would no longer write answers to letters; these would be answered by his "friends."

On the next page, under a picture of Mel with impossibly wide-open eyes, looking haggard and world-weary, was his "Declaration of Creation":

I am going to burn down the world
I am going to tear down everything that cannot stand
    alone
I am going to turn ideals to shit
I am going to shove hope up your ass
I am going to reduce everything that stands to rubble
and then I am going to burn the rubble
and then I am going to scatter the ashes
and then maybe SOMEONE will be able to see
    SOMETHING as it really is
WATCH OUT

On the next page, his "Telling It Like It Is" declared,

The only thing I know is that people have to get together and love one another. I mean really FEEL each other. People have to look so deep inside themselves and inside of each other that they see the SAME GOD, and we can't stop looking until we KNOW we SEE it. Just knowing it's there isn't enough because it might NOT be, you've got to look until you're OVERWHELMED with how much it is there.....Please, whatever you do, don't bless ME.............CURSE me! HATE me! Do SOMETHING real!

For some reason, Mel was raising the stakes of the game he was playing with his readers. He was sounding like an angry and impatient teacher who thinks his students are defective. The next article illustrated another consequence of his mood. Mel and some of his followers had been invited—and according to advertisements had accepted the invitation—to conduct a Sunday morning service at Arlington Street

Church, one of the prominent Unitarian Universalist churches in Boston. The date had been kept, but not by Mel. Eben Given, David Gude, and another of Mel's long-time friends had shown up instead, to a mixed reception, as exemplified by two letters from members of the congregation, one harshly critical and the other warmly favorable. In a third letter, to David, the minister who had arranged the event complained of the awkward situation Mel's absence had created for him.

David's answer is especially revealing of the outlook from Fort Hill at that moment. He begins by calling the minister a "hypocrite." Mel Lyman, by contrast, is "Truth," "Life," "Love," "Consciousness," and "Christ." He then explains why the minister wasn't told about changes in Mel's itinerary and even attempts to extract some guilt from the minister:

> But neither Eben, Bob nor I could say any of this to you or your congregation because YOU DIDN'T ASK. If you had sincerely wanted to know we would have sincerely answered you. You say, "But I did ask, I asked you twice." But there was no depth to your question and so there was no depth to the response that we gave you. And it did hurt Eben and Bob and me, believe me.

A second letter from the minister good-naturedly tried to bridge the gap between the two views of what had transpired; this was clearly a doomed undertaking.

A few pages later, under a picture of himself sitting on the grass on Fort Hill, Mel gave his own version of what was happening in a letter to "Dear Readers":

> I want you to understand what I have been trying to do in *Avatar* and why it is time for me to do something else. So far I have only written what I HAD to write, I have been driven to say certain things in certain ways and I have said them, and now I am no longer driven. If I continued my writing in *Avatar* it would only be because I felt obligated to all the people who are following what I say so closely but in all honesty I must tell you that I no longer have anything to say, at least not in the present form. I have come, I have delivered my message, and now I am taking my leave. Those of you who understood me need no more words from me. Those of you who RESISTED me will find me in other people. I am the Truth, wherever, however, in whatever form it appears. As Mel Lyman writing in *Avatar* it appeared very simply and very directly.

In the "Letters to Mel" section, along with Candy's letter, a young man describes his coming to believe that Mel is indeed God, but asks whether others could be God as well. Mel's answer speaks to the "spirit that is":

> The world we see, hear, touch is one aspect of that spirit. The world we feel, sense, aspire to, is another aspect. I am totally at home in both, in me they are the same. I seek to unite them in others. I am God only in the sense that I am one with the spirit of God. The Father is in me and I know Him well. He is my leader as I am yours. I can only lead you to Him and then you are me. I am building a road into the wilderness, all other roads lead to my road, it is the LAST road, it BEGINS at the crucifixion.

The next page was devoted to yet another untitled, unsigned declaration of Mel's faith, this one faith in loneliness as "the sole motivation, the force that keeps man striving after the unattainable, the loneliness of man separated from his soul, man crying out into the void for God, man eternally seeking more of himself through every activity, filling that devouring need on whatever level the spirit is feeding, the arena of conflict, be it flesh, thoughts, aspiring to ideals...."

The issue ends with a final note from George Peper: "On Fort Hill, with Mel Lyman, our principal task is communication, to master every instrument necessary for us to become totally conscious in what Mel describes as 'the World of Sight and Sound'." He explains that henceforth work in films will supplant and "contain" all the previous expressions of Fort Hill in music, newspapering, and other media. He says that, for more than a year, Mel and others have been working and experimenting with inadequate film equipment, and solicits donations of equipment, funds, skills, and any other items that can be put to good use, in order to help them move into full-time work in their new chosen medium.

Imagine our surprise, Candy and me, invited to move from Michigan to Massachusetts to work on a newspaper we admired tremendously, in the belief that meaningful work was waiting for us, only to find ourselves walking into this turmoil of change, polarization, and redirected energies, in which it wasn't clear whether there would even be a newspaper for much longer. We didn't know what was happening, and we certainly didn't feel in control of our destinies at that point. We didn't have any way to predict what would happen next, and we weren't necessarily feeling very aligned with each other either.

TWO DIFFERENT WORLDS

I was noticing that the people on the *Avatar* staff who were based in Boston and Cambridge, rather than Fort Hill, were feeling rather threatened by the sense of impending change, in ways I didn't quite understand. I liked those people, and as I heard their versions of the story I found myself sympathizing with them and becoming confused about where my allegiance was. There was, for instance, Ed Jordan, also known as Ed Beardsley, who had been involved in the artwork and production end of *Avatar* from its beginnings, and who was the central figure in a collective household around the corner from the office, very reminiscent of my collective household in East Lansing. Ed would wonder aloud, "If Mel is God, then what about me and all of us, aren't we God, too?" This attitude didn't make him popular with the Fort Hill folks, but the question seemed like a good one to me. Besides, I enjoyed working on layout with him, with his irreverence and his zany sense of humor.

And there was Charlie Giuliano, who had known Mel for years, since the early days of psychedelic experiments at Harvard and later in Waltham, around Brandeis University. Charlie seemed sincerely interested in building *Avatar* into an alternative news source, and seemed hurt by Mel's putting him on the spot to declare his allegiance this way or that. I felt for him in his ambivalence.

Candy, however, had no such problem; she was clearly prepared to align herself with Fort Hill and its needs, whatever they would turn out to be.

Also, much more than Candy, I was enthusiastically absorbing whatever details I could about the lifestyle of the people we were getting to know. This activity filled a fair amount of my available time. I had never before thought much about the concept of "voluntary poverty," although the idea had had a certain vogue for a while among New Leftists. But here at Fort Hill, even though the phrase was seldom used and would not have been universally accepted as a description of what was happening, clearly most of these people, one way or another, had had access to lots of resources and privileges and had chosen to forego the easy life in favor of a life of principle that happened to be taking place in a poor neighborhood, in rundown houses, following a set of priorities that did not include money and what it could acquire as the primary goals. Looked like voluntary poverty to me.

Having lived for several years on relatively small amounts of money (mostly gleaned from my share of my father's rather small estate and from Social Security income that was available to me from the time he died until I turned 21) but not having had to struggle to support myself, and having been able to remain in school as long as I wanted without worrying about where the tuition would come from, I now felt somewhat flush and embarrassed by comparison to the Fort Hill folks, with their flocks of children and their patched clothing. At the same time, many of them had given up lucrative careers to live on the Hill, and they did own their houses and have some pretty nice material possessions around them. The houses had a tattered, almost magical elegance about them that fascinated me, that seemed to transcend and transform the mundane modesty of the furnishings.

And there was a certain self-righteousness to the self-imposed frugality of Fort Hill. An article in February 1968, in the local newspaper of Roxbury's black community, the *Bay State Banner*, described the attitude of this band of new white immigrants into the mostly black neighborhood:

> [L]iving without financial security is an important part of the philosophy of the Hill People. They believe that what they need they will find, and that their security comes in living for the moment at hand. "This is a way of life where you do away with everything except the moment," says Faith Gude. "The secret is to lose everything. I have to become everything that's going to happen. And then, the thing that happens is you. That's not something you can lose."

On the other hand, when I had mentioned my misgivings about my own financial status to Wayne Hansen, he had let me know there was another, seemingly less voluntary, side to the apparent poverty of Fort Hill. On that side of the issue, the lack of material goods was a real problem to be overcome; and the idea was to take advantage of whatever was available from whatever source and to make the most of it because the need was enormous. Again, this left me confused.

I did enjoy participating in the rituals of salvage and make-do that had developed under the circumstances. People from the Hill were in the habit of going to the open-air produce market that filled Haymarket Square in downtown Boston on Friday evenings. The usual practice was to go shortly before the market was to close, scout out where the surpluses were at the various stands, and make bargains for case lots or damaged goods just before they would be discarded anyway. Frequently, we would fill entire cars with huge amounts of inexpensive or free food and would be greeted as heroes upon returning to the Hill. Other types of inexpensive food, less dramatic but no less fascinating, included bulk purchases, dented cans, and day-old bread. We were clearly demonstrating the well-known and observable principle at the time that America produced huge, wasteful overabundances of everything, and that there was more than enough to go around if you knew where to look.

I learned also that the abundant supplies of building materials used to refurbish the houses on Fort Hill were also to a great extent the result of this waste and surplus. Boston's neighborhoods at the time were filled with abandoned houses, factories, and other commercial buildings, sometimes burned out in fires and not rebuilt, sometimes just abandoned for urban renewal projects that hadn't happened or for who knew what other reasons? In any case, plenty of usable construction material—frequently very attractive Victorian-style decorative mouldings, stained glass windows and mirrors, built-in cabinetry, and similar wonderful stuff—was available for the taking, and the Fort Hill men took frequently. Sometimes a slight risk would be involved if you had to break into a building to get the goods, but often doors and windows were open; all you had to do was walk in and start dismantling. I found this occupation perfectly fascinating. I had a long-time interest in architecture and construction, had in fact nearly chosen to study architecture rather than journalism in college, and had already taught myself some basic construction and remodeling skills. Hooking up with this gang of folks who had a living laboratory of half a dozen houses that they were constantly renovating, making beautiful homes for themselves, and doing it with free, salvaged construction materials—well, this was just wonderful, as far as I was concerned.

I also had a strong desire to become familiar with the culture of these people. In my mind, and in my prior experiences, the reason for choosing to live low on the economic ladder was to free up more of one's time to enjoy the pleasures of friends and of life generally. Now, here was a group of fascinating and accomplished people, many of whom were musicians, poets, visual artists, historical philosophers, all of whom had an interest in astrology, spiritual and occult matters, and personal growth. They all seemed to be in relationship with each other, and they were raising more than a dozen kids together, with more on the way. There certainly was plenty to do to fill up the time when one was not working a nine-to-five job. I did what I could to pick up on all these activities, but, curiously, discovered a certain sense of pressure, of time scarcity, that kept most of the folks on the Hill from being comfortable just hanging out and sharing all these pleasures. By contrast, I found the people in the South End contingent of *Avatar* more available for this kind of pursuit, but generally less accomplished and interesting. Another paradox.

I was not the only one struggling to make sense of these subtleties. Numbers of people around *Avatar* were considering whether or not to move to the Hill; people were examining their own lifestyle choices and were looking at the demands Mel was making on the people close to him and at the implied possibility of becoming closer to Mel if they could adapt their lives to these demands. And there was all this talk in the air of the Second American Revolution, a sense that history was moving faster and faster, that we were right on the verge of becoming active agents in one of the big historical changes, and that there wasn't time to dawdle with these little personal decisions.

Wayne wrote an article for the front page of the news section of *Avatar* Number 22, entitled "Gospel of the Good News." In laying out the page, we set an excerpt from the middle of the article in large, bold type, almost a headline itself, above a picture of Mel deep in conversation with Owen de Long, one of his close friends, a former Harvard doctoral student in international relations with connections to the Kennedy family political establishment. Owen was Fort Hill's candidate for president "in about ten years," Jessie would say.

Wayne's headlined excerpt read,

Men are coming, great men who are among us now, who will unite the extremes in to an unshakable structure, unshakable not because of its suppression of the will of the people, but because of its perfect expression of that will. And from the present bewilderment, anger and chaos a true will must arise to replace that shadow of will, that vacant greed which is now called the will of the people by the clumsy dwarves who stumble where graceful giants ought to stride.

He writes about his experience working for *Avatar* and for Mel Lyman, being besieged by offers of help and advice, but only really appreciating the contribution of those who immediately recognize the need and go right to work, without fancy talk or good ideas about how the work could be done better. He talks further about the need to sacrifice one's personal vision in preparation to do the larger work demanded by the needs of history. He makes comparisons to the time of the original American Revolution, "when a few men, who most felt the need for independence from the nation which held the great force of this nation in check, took those first steps to risk that necessary separation," and created the format for the rest of the population to follow.

[I]n our time, our revolution shall differ only in that it is a subtler thing, for the need is of a deeper nature, but its fulfillment shall be manifest outwardly at every level, in life-style, in politics, in science and in art. Men are coming, great men who are among us now....

He compares the struggle to that going on in the black community at that time, and among young whites and politicians who recognize that change is inevitable and necessary. He predicts a season of political polarization and the pre-eminence of the likes of Nixon and Reagan, even though Robert Kennedy and Eugene McCarthy could do more to unite the country if it was ready for that. "Among politicians, Robert Kennedy is the avatar," which means "the bridge between heaven and earth...pure spirit manifested in everyday reality." And this, "if you'll allow me, brings us right back home." With Mel no longer playing an active role on producing *Avatar*,

Avatar will not be less Mel Lyman. No, there will be more Mel Lyman in every issue, whether by that name or not, for there is no separation between us from where you stand. God is not dead, my friend, just now more uncreated.

He concludes optimistically with a clear statement of Fort Hill's recommended moral stance:

The greatest change humanity has ever known is upon us. Each of us must give up what we have to further that change. Evaluate your thing in that light, check it genuinely, and see what falls away and what remains. Bring what remains to us, and together we shall recreate the world.

A Season of Riots

Helping Wayne put together this front page and the rest of Issue 22, I experienced a clarity and sense of purpose that cut through a lot of the confusion I had been feeling. I felt envious of Wayne, who clearly had been living close enough to the source of all this inspiration to be able, himself, to express some of its values in terms that I found inspiring and meaningful. And change certainly was coming quickly. The "Good News" issue of *Avatar* was dated March 29-April 11. While it was still on the streets, Martin Luther King was assassinated in Memphis. I was in the *Avatar* office working on layout for the next issue when the radio announced the news. Cities across the country exploded

with rage and unleashed racial tension. In Boston, a mayor named Kevin White and an incomparably popular black entertainer named James Brown (I was struck by the coincidence of their names matching their roles in the political drama) collaborated brilliantly to keep community tempers in check by canceling a live concert Brown was to perform and televising it instead. Boston, well known as a racially polarized city, rode out the season of riots unscathed.

On the front page of the next *Avatar* we featured an essay Wayne had written—two days before King was shot—on the impending and inevitable social upheaval in America, under an oversized picture of a political demonstration on Boston Common, and alongside a headlined quote from Lyndon Johnson, of all people, who had just announced he would not run for president again: "We have talked long enough in this country about equal rights. We have talked 100 years or more. It is time to write the next chapter."

Wayne's essay discusses the tendency of society to offer diversions to the mass of the population, meaningless rivalries and preoccupations that keep people from confronting the deeper internal questions, all based in people's own desire to avoid what is real. He concludes,

They will not wake up until all they have is gone. The choice today is simple, give it all up today, or have it all taken away tomorrow, there's little difference, it feels the same either way, he who tries to hang on until tomorrow is just putting off the inevitable.

Yes, go out there and hang out in the street for an afternoon, look at the faces, if you can stand it. Then go home and look at yourself. Where do you stand in the midst of all this and what difference do you make? Precious little, I'll wager. Better get to work on yourself, my friend, become a tool of what's happening, it's willingly today or like it or not tomorrow. Nobody gets left out, there's not a way out of this one. We're all up against the same wall, and the poison gas we've been making all this time has now completely filled the air in this little room, and in a moment we shall all have to *breathe*.

This rather Calvinist message drew the connection between the steamrolling events in the world at large and the emerging philosophy of Fort Hill. Wayne seemed to be saying it was time to give up the hedonism and self-indulgence that had characterized the flowering of the hippie culture, in favor of a more purposeful and self-aware participation in the reshaping of history. I took this idea seriously, though rather innocently. It seemed to give meaning to the path Candy and I had chosen, by contrast to the aimlessness of our last days in East Lansing and of our arrival in Boston. It put the struggle for relentless self-improvement that seemed so central at Fort Hill into a context that made sense to me, joining it with the political struggle with which I had so long identified. And, it gave Candy and me a new belief to share. This would come in handy soon, as the pressure mounted on all the Fort Hill hangers-on to make a choice.

INCORPORATING AS MEL

The magazine section of issue Number 22 had featured the "United Illuminating Charter," a document created and handwritten by Eben Given and signed by him and 11 other mainstays of the Hill, declaring formally their solidarity with Mel and his purposes. This was accompanied, behind the scenes, by legal incorporation into several interlocking companies, to promote the community's media work, to hold the real estate, et cetera. (The name "United Illuminating" was borrowed from the power plant in New Haven, Connecticut, whose big red neon sign, "United Illuminating Company" lit up the highway on the route between Boston and New York.) Eben's charter reads:

Dear Friends,
I have written a charter that includes and defines everything I know. I have lived a thousand years in a day and a night, talked with you all, been still, slept, gotten up again and written—knowing through the sharpest pains of my own inadequacy and limitation—the greatest that I ever known in all my life—that what must finally be written and signed by all of us today, can only be written as my first picture of Mel could only have been drawn—when the last resources of my own separate talent had been exhausted—when I had seen so deeply, and suffered so deeply that there was finally nothing left of me to draw WITH. And the picture came.
It is not my own private pain. I suffer it as each of you has suffered it and will continue and must continue to suffer it. It is the pain of being consumed, of having every last vestige of separateness between that which we have felt and come to know more deeply than all else, which is incarnated forever, for all of us in Mel which is our heart, burned away that we may be free that HE may finally be freed. It is the pain of being born.

Today we simply incorporate ourselves as Mel Lyman. The definition rests with all that we can attest together as the larger embodiment—through us to all men—of the purpose and the practice of one pure man. Today is our birthday—March 21st, 1968.

The charter includes a horoscope for the moment of signing, high noon of the spring equinox, with the sun high in the sky in Aries and the moon in Capricorn. Not coincidentally, Mel's chart also had the sun in Aries and the moon in Capricorn.

The same issue included a lengthy transcript of a conversation between Mel, David Gude, Jim Kweskin, and Joey Goldfarb, a far-ranging conversation that occupied four pages of the magazine, under the heading "The Structure of Structure." In it, Mel elucidates for the others his way of keeping his behavior present in the moment, always feeling where the energy is attempting to move and always ready to drop whatever prior notions he may have had in order to respond to the immediacy of the emerging situation. This idea, later summarized by Ram Dass in the phrase "Be here now," was rather novel in 1968, and Mel engages in some mind-warp on the other three in order to get them to understand it. He goes on to relate this to the purpose of the Fort Hill community as he experienced it, contrasting the community to the general population, who did not yet know how to respond to Mel's way of reflecting back to them their own limitations:

[L]iving amongst men is like cosmic asthma, it's hard to breathe, and I want to BREATHE. So I have to expand the structure of man, the mind.
...There just is NOT ENOUGH LIFE on the planet EARTH for me. And I don't have any other choice, I've got to LIVE here.
...[T]he world is a dead shell on the outside and a volcano on the INSIDE. I want all that feeling OUT, I want it all AROUND me, I want it so thick I can SWIM in it, I like it THAT STRONG. Now for most people that is sheer agony, for ME it's joy. It CANNOT GET too strong. And the more structures I break down the more life there IS. That's what most people are AFRAID of, to have their structures broken down, because it HURTS. Breaking down structures is PAIN, but there is no other way to make room for more life, and I FEEL that pain, more than ANYBODY, because I am capable of so MUCH life, I KNOW that life, I FEEL it, it is ME, so I feel the limitations more than anybody does, which

is why I'm gonna DO something about it, I don't have any choice.

...[A]lready I've cleared a LITTLE space, I've broken down the structures of the people on the hill, almost to the point of being comfortable. I'll never STOP doing it, because I can't IMAGINE too much life.

Along with Wayne's two articles on the front pages of *Avatar* Numbers 22 and 23, this conversation gave still more urgency and meaning to the challenge to become part of the community, as quickly and full-heartedly as possible. We certainly didn't want to be left out of the opportunity to travel with Mel as he brought more life to Planet Earth. But I, at least, had misgivings. Mel liked to speak of his people as his creation, who in turn served as his mind and his hands, the mechanism to bring his message to the world. I didn't really know what would be involved in becoming part of his creation.

THERE'S ALWAYS ROOM FOR SACRIFICE

The magazine section of issue Number 23 illustrated again the depth of personal exploration and sacrifice that were implied by Mel's ethic and the Hill's attempt to manifest it in the world. After completing the United Illuminating charter, Eben Given had spent several days in New York helping Brian Keating fix up an office space in a Soho loft, from which to publish the New York edition of *Avatar*. While he was there, Eben had painted a mural of the tower on Fort Hill, in order to bridge the seemingly great gap between the Hill and the New York outpost. Then, after reaching a state of ecstatic creative intimacy with Brian, he had told Brian to destroy the mural by painting over it because he had realized his reasons for wanting to create it were no longer relevant or valid, and had returned to Boston. Brian had done so, leaving only a star hanging in a blank sky as a reminder of what had been. The magazine contained this story in the form of an exchange of spacey, visionary letters between the two of them, explaining to each other the mysteries of what they had just experienced, accompanied by a series of photos George Peper had taken of Eben creating the mural.

Reflecting again in yet another form the idea Mel had discussed in "The Structure of Structure," that each moment needs to be free to create itself in its own way, Eben concludes his letter by saying,

It's always seemed to me that the greatest truth of a picture is had in the painting of it—what it took to make it happen, what it *felt* like at the time. That's the part we don't see.

There are museums and they are full of pictures, but they're frozen and lifeless nearly all of them. A bad movie moves with more life than most of the famous paintings of history. But we didn't make it either. The life was there at the time and the picture is gone. The great picture is made with what we gave and so much more and most important, it must endure.

I remember that my gut reaction on reading this for the first time was to mourn for the beautiful lost picture. But the correct reaction, in terms of the lessons we were being encouraged to learn, was to forget the picture and instead to celebrate the bond that had grown between Eben and Brian, and the growth they had each experienced in the process. Candy and I were struggling, internally, to get with the demands of Hill life. In this mood, we participated in the next escalation of the struggle to make the Hill and the planet a more suitable home for Mel.

Issue Number 24 was a kind of declaration of spiritual war by Mel on the others who felt they had some claim to the paper but were not ready to move into the routine of sacrifice and blind creativity that he was advocating. Abandoning the two-section format, the larger news section wrapped around the smaller magazine, without discussion, Mel instructed those of us producing the paper to re-introduce the earlier format, a single, tabloid-sized paper. This time, though, there was a difference. This issue had an uncompromising uniformity that allowed no space for any other viewpoint. On the front page was a large, bold headline (I remember setting the press-type and thinking, "Whoa, the shit is really going to hit the fan now!"):

You know what we've been doing up here on Fort Hill? We've been building a wall around Mel's house out of *heavy, heavy stone*.

This headline was wrapped around a picture of a Fort Hill work crew celebrating after raising a heavy lintel stone over what would become the entranceway of an eight-foot-high stone wall around the front garden of Mel's house, Number Four and a Half. Such an action had become necessary because some visitor to the Hill, unaware that the red signal light meant to stay away for the moment because Mel was working, had managed to make it as far as Mel's front door at a moment when his presence wasn't welcome, and Mel had become furious. For weeks, all the available energies of the Hill's men had been devoted to learning masonry skills and building the wall, big and strong and impenetrable. The raising of the lintel was the symbolic completion of the task, and another opportunity to celebrate the unity of effort it takes to accomplish such work. Thus, four more pictures of the stages of the process appeared on the next two pages of the magazine. But that was just the beginning.

Rounding out the issue were the following features, in the sequence listed:

- a letter to Mel from a teenaged admirer, broken-hearted at the announcement of his departure. His answer compares himself to the sun, shining brightly during the day but disappearing at night, giving us the opportunity to find its light in ourselves;

- a photograph of the sun in a recent eclipse;

- a page devoted to one of Mel's "Diary of a Young Artist" passages;

- a large photograph of Alison Peper in a moment of exclamation during a recent LSD trip guided and photographed by Mel;

- a letter from Mel to David Silver, a local television programmer—who had interviewed Mel and whose work Mel admired—congratulating Silver on a recent program for its ability to convey real feelings and experience through the medium of television;

- five more full-page pictures of Alison, expressing a variety of moods at various points in her trip;

- a reprint of one of Mel's "To All Who Would Know" columns: "How much you feel is an exact measure of just how alive you are. Every time you feel pain it is just that much more of you that is trying to be born. Every time you express what you feel it is that much more of you that has just been born. We are constantly surrounded by the opportunity to give birth to more of ourselves...";

- twelve more pictures of Alison's trip, each one occupying an entire page; and

- a final picture of Mel on the back cover.

LIKE IT OR LUMP IT

What appeared in Issue Number 24 could only be interpreted as Mel and the Hill thumbing their noses at the other members of the *Avatar* alliance, challenging them to get with the Hill's program or split. I remember finding it embarrassing taking the new issue out on the streets to sell, somewhat at a loss to explain to readers why the format had changed so dramatically, so suddenly. But I guess I accepted the challenge, another early opportunity to face difficulty and let go of old ideas in Mel's name. I found it more difficult to confront the likes of Ed Beardsley and Charlie Giuliano at the *Avatar* office, quite unable to help them understand why their contributions were being undermined in this way, quite unsure of what would happen next. They were very unhappy with the turn of events.

A meeting was called to bring together the Hill community with representatives of *Avatar*'s "downtown" component, which took place around the big dining table in Eben and Sofie's house, Number Four. Candy and I attended, our first chance to share in the process of the Hill in one of its moments of yearning for a collective solution to a problem. I was struck by the intensity of the conversation and the emotions being exchanged, and by the seeming contempt in which the non-Hill people were being held. There seemed to be no room for compromise. I remember saying something about the difficulty of a person, such as myself, who didn't necessarily feel ready to commit to what was being asked, intending my comment to also apply to others in the same situation, and being cut off by Jim Kweskin, who angrily spat out, "Michael, you just want to know that you're all right," as if I were foolish and wrong for wanting that. At the same time, I could feel Candy, next to me, moving closer and closer to the Hill position and attitude, ready for anything and unquestioning of her willingness to give up whatever was necessary.

That meeting was our first encounter with Mel in the flesh. He sat around the table with the others, obviously feeling intensely whatever it was that was making this crisis necessary. At one point he insulted Jessie, telling her she was full of shit for some comment she had made. I was struck by how vulnerable he seemed, how his rather high-pitched voice sounded like that of a very young person. I had trouble integrating this with my notions of Mel the Great Man. Finally, the meeting ended, in anger and frustration, with no resolution whatsoever. I don't know how there might have been resolution, short of the "downtown" people saying they didn't really want to publish a newspaper after all and were now willing to give up their private lives and move to the Hill to do Mel's bidding. They clearly weren't ready for this. As Mel stamped out of the house, I attempted to introduce myself to him, wanting a personal encounter of some kind with him, and blatantly violating the rule he had recently been teaching about, to stay in the present and leave behind prior ideas of what might happen. He was in no mood to talk, and brushed past me to leave.

AN *AVATAR* HERE, AN *AVATAR* THERE

As a result of that meeting, the Fort Hill mainstays encouraged those of us who were equivocating to declare our allegiance to Mel; and everyone on the Hill was encouraged to rededicate ourselves to building him a more perfect media laboratory in which to develop his people and his films. From the "downtown" point of view, the meeting was further evidence that Fort Hill had declared war on them. They proceeded to pull their resources together to publish a non-Fort Hill newspaper, not exactly using the name *Avatar*, but not *not* using it either. They laid out a newspaper that looked a lot like the metropolitan-size news section of *Avatar*, but that had no flag on the front page. On page two, in reverse, was the familiar *Avatar* logo, so the page could be held up to the light to reveal its true identity.

In addition to the confrontation of wills that the fight over the name represented, there was a question of whether Fort Hill had a legal right to deny use of the name to the others, based on who had been a member of the board when, and similar details.

For his part, Mel was furious. In retaliation, he ordered his "boys" to take action. On the night the new, renegade *Avatar* was delivered to the South End office, which we from Fort Hill had all but abandoned to the other staff, after that staff had gone home for the night, several carloads of us from Fort Hill raided the office, stole all the printed copies, and took them up to Fort Hill, where we locked them in the small room at the base of the tower. (I remember having to simply put my own free-press, pro-constitution values out of my mind in order to tune in to the adventurous spirit of the raid and the camaraderie of working with the other Fort Hill men on something that was obviously important to them. Was this a sellout or a betrayal, or was this an oblique way of protecting the truth? I was confused.) The next morning, the downtown staff had its turn to be furious, and there ensued several days of negotiations and angry recriminations between the two factions. In a final deception, the downtown staff were invited to Fort Hill ostensibly to work out a deal. While representatives of the two sides were meeting, others of us from Fort Hill took the papers out of the tower and sold them for recycling. A coup!

Both sides consulted lawyers and the legal situation was worked out in favor of the downtown staffs keeping the rights to the name *Avatar*, while Fort Hill retained the right to use the word *Avatar* in other name forms. Between June 1968 and the end of the summer, the downtown staff published, on their own, about half a dozen issues of a completely reconstituted *Avatar* Vol. II, whose contents were more typical underground newspaper material—antiwar, countercultural stuff, music reviews, commentary on public events. During the same period, Brian Keating's *New York Avatar* also continued publishing, at least for a while. And, on Fort Hill, after a few months' break, there would soon appear the first of four more-or-less quarterly issues of a newly manifested magazine version of Mel's *Avatar*, under the name *American Avatar*. In other words, for a brief period, there were three different *Avatar*s all publishing simultaneously.

TIME TO GET A LIFE

With the fiction of working on the Hill's newspaper set to rest once and for all, it was time for Candy and me to figure out what else to do with our lives. She readily moved into the sisterhood of Fort Hill women, with their flocks of babies to tend and their men to take care of and make fun of. I knew then and know now little of what went on among them, other than that they were ingrown in their little society and traditional in their viewpoint. I found it strange to watch Candy, who had been as rebellious and modern a woman as I had known, relax into traditional roles and dress, but that was the Fort Hill way. The "battle of the sexes" was very much alive at Fort Hill.

The men, too, had a tight little society based on traditional roles and expectations, but I found it far from easy to merge with them. I had never had any notion whatsoever of living out a traditional man's role of any kind, didn't even have concepts like that in my mind, and certainly had no plans of playing a traditional blue-collar man's role, performing physical labor and hanging out with the boys, complaining about the women but otherwise accepting my limited lot in life. To a surprising degree, in the absence of the occasional uplift provided by association with some work of creation inspired or produced by Mel, this was all there was to the day-to-day life of the Fort Hill men. I was also surprised to find how much racism was expressed in the everyday conversation of the men, how little regard they had for the black community that surrounded us, and even for the occasional black seeker who would come visiting or looking to join the community. Sexist language was also the order of the day; the standard phrase indicating a tiny measurement was "cunt-hair," as in "Move it to the left just a cunt-hair." I had never heard or used such talk.

My first real experience with the men's society had come when I was drafted into working on the stone wall around Mel's house while we were waiting for the newspaper wars to resolve themselves somehow.

I was pleased enough to be learning a bit about cutting and setting stone. I asked one day, during a fairly demanding work session, why Mel wasn't out there with us, building this wall around his house that he had asked for. The answer, delivered in a tone of condescension, gave me one of the basic Fort Hill truths: Mel didn't work on these demeaning physical tasks because he spent his time and energy keeping us all together by doing his creative work, taking care of our spirits, as it were. Well, that made vague sense to me, but it didn't tell much about what I could expect for myself. That lesson was to come in other ways.

In the course of working on the wall, I made the acquaintance of Richie Guerin, another of Mel's closest lieutenants. Richie had come to the Hill as a dropout from architecture school, the son of a construction worker from New York, and a bit of a musician, too. He was young and brash, and talented in both design and construction supervision, a valuable asset to Mel as he imagined rebuilding the row of houses on the Hill into a multi-media production facility. The stone wall was just a necessary preliminary project. Richie was also one of the Hill's astrologers; when I learned that the graceful hand-painted charts I had seen in a number of people's private spaces had been created by him, I decided I wanted one for myself and asked for a reading. I found Richie easier to relate to, as a fellow Taurus, than Joey Goldfarb. Finally, we had our evening to discuss my chart.

TOO MANY PLANETS IN ARIES

I already knew that my sun—representing my essential self—was located in Taurus, a sign that denotes stability and consistency, determination and earthbound, practical wisdom; and that my moon—representing my personality and my way of presenting myself to others—was in Aries, a sign that suggested inspiration and creativity, individuality and unpredictability. (Remember, Mel's sun was in Aries.) This combination indicated an interesting counterpoint, a dynamic tension between my Taurus "center" and my Aries exterior. In fact, I already had developed a certain fear of what my chart would reveal because one of my first experiences of astrology, something I had in common with most visitors and newcomers to Fort Hill, was from a book called *Heaven Knows What* by Grant Lewi, one of the most successful popularizers of astrology to Americans over a period of several decades. His book enables readers to do quick, approximate personal horoscopes based on the aspects formed by the various planets in their signs, using simplified charts in the book that eliminate virtually all the calculations required for more precise horoscopes. *Heaven Knows What*

focused significantly on the 144 possible combinations of sun and moon positions, as indicators of the main dynamics of the personality. In my case, Taurus-Aries was described as a sign of great power, likely as not to walk all over other people accidentally unless held in check by a conscious discipline, which Lewi recommended if there was going to be a productive life and the possibility for relationships in which the Taurus-Aries person would not dominate. Coming out of my East Lansing phase, in which I had become a fairly charismatic personality among my circle of friends, some of whom had had difficulty with that characteristic of mine, I was taken aback by this view of my potential and made to feel I had to watch myself carefully. But I was ready to learn more about myself through the lens of astrology, and hoped Richie could guide me toward positive directions of growth.

I learned from Richie that in addition to my moon I also had my three inner planets—Mercury, representing communication skills and mental ability; Venus, representing sensitivity and appreciation of beauty and harmony, basically feminine values as those are traditionally understood; and Mars, representing assertiveness and physical energy, basically masculine values in the traditional understanding—all in Aries. Altogether, I had four of ten planets in Aries, all but overwhelming my sun in Taurus. (In most popular versions of astrology, the sun and moon are considered "planets," but the earth isn't counted because that's where we're looking out from.) Richie didn't point out to me that my four planets in Aries equaled the number of planets Mel had in that sign, or that among members of the Fort Hill community only Owen de Long also had four planets there, including his sun and moon. He didn't emphasize my inherent birthright in the realm of creativity and self-direction. I learned instead that I had lots of personal potential but a difficult path to follow, with lots of aspects indicating limitations and challenges, and that my own impulses could not be trusted much because of the way my energies were balanced one against the other. I had a nice tight square, an aspect representing difficulties and limitations, between the moon and Mars, both strong in Aries, and Saturn in Cancer, the planet representing discipline and an ordered life, located in one of the signs where it expresses most poorly. This aspect suggested a continuing struggle between creativity and spontaneity on the one hand and worldly responsibility on the other, an aspect suggestive of a personality that needs guidance from others.

Somehow Richie looked at the array of my planet placements and aspects and synthesized it into a single injunction: writing was clearly not the occupation for me; practical, physical work would serve me much better. I don't know how he found this in my chart.

Certainly it wasn't simply that my sun was located in Taurus, frequently considered a sign of builders and bankers, but also of artists and sensualists. Historically, Taurus has produced huge numbers of prominent writers, philosophers, artists, and composers—including Shakespeare, Brahms, Kant, Marx, Freud, Tchaikovsky, and Dali—as well as numerous political leaders and prominent entertainers. I think he may have been extrapolating from his own chart and his own experience, as a person with both sun and moon in Taurus and Mercury in Aries, living in the shadow of the dominant personality of Mel Lyman.

Or he may have been interpreting my chart more closely, using a method of interpreting the meanings of particular planets in a chart based on the individual degrees of the zodiac where they are located. This method, the "Sabian symbols," was a popular interpretive tool at Fort Hill. The symbols had been developed over several decades by Marc Edmund Jones, one of the most significant modern astrologers, who distilled the meanings of the 360 rough images delivered to him by a psychic medium into a cogent method of applying these images in individual chart interpretation. Jones didn't publish his version of the symbols until 1953, long after the symbols were adapted and popularized by his protégé, Dane Rudhyar, in *The Astrology of Personality*, which was published in 1936 and revised and reissued in 1963, and became one of the seminal texts in the reinterpretation of the ancient science of astrology to incorporate contemporary values and psychological understanding. Rudhyar called the resulting method "humanistic astrology," and it became the dominant trend in the field during the 1960s.

Rudhyar's book was undergoing a vogue on Fort Hill about the time I arrived and got my reading from Richie. There was one little glitch in using Rudhyar's book in interpreting charts, however. The recommended method for interpreting degree symbols, as given by both Jones and Rudhyar in their respective versions of the Sabian symbols, was to round each degree of the zodiac upward to the next whole number for purposes of interpretation. Thus, Mel's sun position of three degrees, four minutes into the sign Aries would be rounded up and interpreted as "fourth degree of Aries"—"two lovers strolling through a secluded walk," in Jones' version, a symbol of personal expression without the burden of responsibility. But on Fort Hill, it was a given that Mel was God, or at least a fully realized man, most likely an avatar for our age. And, lo and behold, there it is, in the *third* degree of Aries: "a cameo profile of a man in the outline of his country," as Jones put it, and Rudhyar's description is even more precise: "the individual self as an avatar of greater collective reality." Mel's moon position, on the other hand, made sense if rounded upward. Six degrees, 39

minutes into Capricorn became "seventh degree" Capricorn, a hierophant, or prophet, "leads a ritual of power," explained by Rudhyar as "gathering together of the power of a group to one purpose and into an individual will. 'Avatar'-ship." There was that word again. In Fort Hill logic, then, Jones and Rudhyar must be wrong; the correct way to interpret the symbols must be to round the numbers both upward and downward, as dollars and cents are rounded both upward and downward to estimate whole dollars. This forced misinterpretation of the Sabian symbols, extrapolated from a misinterpretation of Mel's sun degree as that of the avatar, became the basis for all the interpretations of charts of people on Fort Hill. Of course it was a long time later before I saw through the scam.

For the moment, I learned my chart according to an incorrect method of interpretation, and lived with a sense of my sun degree, for example, as a "symbolical battle between swords and torches," an image of the "struggle between might and enlightenment," quoting Rudhyar's version of 17 degrees of Taurus, when it really is Taurus 18, whose symbol implies continual spiritual renewal, a woman "airing a linen bag through a sunny window." In a time when I was trying to take such symbols and subtle messages deeply into myself, this misinformation encouraged me to feel afraid of my potential and to seek guidance from others rather than from my inner self. This happened to mesh well with my state of mind at the time—hesitant and confused after my long experiment with drugs and political activism, anxious for new role models and priorities to present themselves—and with the community's need for willing, compliant servants. Richie's declaration that physical work and not writing was the path for me fit this need, too, and came to me with the force of law, albeit mysterious and incomprehensible law. I assumed it meant my future would be filled with more work on the Fort Hill houses, and I prepared for that. I also started becoming accustomed to being "Michael Taurus," the name that would be used almost every time I was mentioned for the next several years. So much for the balancing influence of my Aries planets.

A PLACE OF OUR OWN

A little bit of East Lansing business remained to be taken care of, and that first spring on Fort Hill I handled it. Having given up my student deferment and lost my bid for conscientious objector status, I had to do something to guarantee that I would not be drafted into the army. I had received a notice to turn myself in for a physical. At Fort Hill I had heard several stories of people who had given themselves physical injuries or had managed to fake mental incapacity in order to be disqualified at their draft physicals.

This tactic sounded like a good deal, and the Boston Army Base sounded like a good place to use it, unlike the draft centers in Detroit and New York, where I could otherwise have chosen to turn myself in for a physical, but where it was reportedly difficult to get away with any kind of goofy tactics (Arlo Guthrie's "Alice's Restaurant" notwithstanding). On the appointed day I woke up and took a small dose of LSD to make sure I would be a little disoriented and uninhibited. I wore no underwear under my clothes, so they would either have to make me go through the physical exam line naked or with long pants on; they chose the latter option. For the written exam, I declared I had five years of college, and proceeded to answer nearly every question wrong; I scored 3 out of 100. I volunteered that I was both gay and a communist, and was unresponsive to the psychological interviewer. He made it clear I was not the kind of person they were looking for. The result was a 1-Y classification, ineligible for the draft for reasons of *physical* disability, except in times of declared national emergency, which Vietnam wasn't. I did not get the 4-F I was hoping for, but it was good enough.

Candy and I were feeling the need to create a Fort Hill house of our own, and were itching to get out of the apartment we were sharing with Rachel Brause, two blocks from the Hill, where the urgent growth of the Hill seemed far away and somehow became abstracted by talk. We wished for a place close to the main rows of Hill houses; what we found was a ground-floor apartment at 49 Beech Glen Street, facing the opposite side of the hilltop from Fort Avenue. The apartment was really just a two-minute walk up a path to the Fort Avenue Terrace houses, but it felt like another world. Our challenge was to make it feel like a Hill house. We settled on a few housemates, other newcomers to the Hill like ourselves, and painted the rooms in bright colors. I don't know what we were using for money.

I imitated Eben Given by building an oversize table for the kitchen using salvaged material. I asked David Gude if I could borrow a rasp to smooth the edge of the table, a task that would take about an hour, and was hurt by his reply that he didn't like to lend tools "off the Hill." I was also hurt by George Peper's failure to respond to my request for a print of a picture of Mel to use in our house. Every house on the Hill and all of the satellite apartments I had seen had prominently displayed on their walls large black and white photographs of Mel, usually full-frontal portraits of him staring directly into the camera or looking spiritual and exemplary; many were from a particular series shot by George and used frequently in the

*Avatar*s. I wanted a picture for our new house, too, but I had a different idea. In George's darkroom one time I saw a contact sheet with a shot of Mel standing in a circle with several of the other men, obviously planning a work project. I liked its democratic feel and asked George if he would make a print of that for our house. He simply said, "Hm, strange choice," and never made the print or mentioned it again.

One night, inspired somehow to try to put my current thoughts and feelings in writing, I stayed up late working at the big table, writing a group letter to all my friends from college and elsewhere, trying to convey the intensity of what I felt we had discovered at Fort Hill. I headlined it with a line from Paul Simon's song "America" off the new Simon and Garfunkel album, "Bookends": "Michigan seems like a dream to me now." The truth is, most everything seemed like a dream, and I could not easily tell what was real and what wasn't, but in the letter (of which I do not have a copy) I remember being explicitly insulting and abusive of some of the people to whom I was writing, whom I perceived as not having something as important or powerful going on in their lives as I now had. I wanted to impress them with the significance of what I was doing, and to inspire them to move closer to it, but I think all I did was turn them off and make them think I was crazy. Char Jolles, my journalist friend and colleague from college, wrote back a succinct post card: "Oh, come off it. Love, Char."

Soon, both Candy and I were feeling restless again and unsure how to move closer to our destinies. We settled on a plan, either individually or together, I don't remember, to ask Mel to guide us on acid trips. Like the astrological reading I had coveted and finally received, this was one of the initiation and transformation rituals of the Hill, which one sought only when one was ready for anything. The pictures of Alison Peper in the controversial "stone wall" issue of *Avatar* exemplified the wide-open emotional state that was considered the goal. I think Candy was probably ready for anything, as that notion would be understood by the Fort Hill people, and her trip with Mel bonded her closely to him in a childlike way (anticipated by her letter to him in *Avatar* a few months earlier); she came home feeling closer to Mel and to the Hill than to me. She was feeling independent and I was feeling fearful. We quarreled. Trouble.

A PURPOSE FINDS ME

My trip with Mel a week or so later made it clear I was feeling needy and unsure but probably not ready for anything, though I would have liked to be. As I was ushered into Mel's private space, he showed me his instruments, explained a bit about how he worked with them, and said something about how I would learn to work with tools and learn more about the process of creating—and eventually feel myself compelled to do real creative work—some time in the future. It was one of several cryptic and off-putting statements he made that night. But as I lifted off on his very good acid, lying on his floor looking to experience something familiar from my previous acid trips, assuming that Mel would do something amazing when he was ready, he just sat in his chair and watched me, and I felt small and unimportant. Mel apparently experienced me that way, too, and just waited until I came around enough for him to talk some sense or some wisdom into me. When he did, it was about work. He told me that when he was younger he had had to do a great deal of heavy physical work, even though he didn't have the constitution for it, and that with the kind of body I had (I'm quite small but sturdy; at that time I was also soft, but had the potential for strength) I really had no excuse to not be working and making money. This wasn't quite the elevated message I was waiting for, but it was definitely, and literally in my eyes at the time, a "dancing lesson from God," to borrow Kurt Vonnegut's wonderful phrase. I left Mel's space with a purpose, a bit let down but ready for something, if not for anything.

I stumbled home in the early morning to tell Candy this little bit of news gleaned from what I had hoped would be a major transformative experience but, to my surprise, something else was happening at the house. Our gay friends Will and Larry, from Michigan but now in New York, had shown up for an unannounced visit while I was tripping, and what a weird time it was to try to be nostalgic with them. We just couldn't pull it off. I found myself telling them (I don't know where this came from, because it had not been said to me in words by anyone) that the gay explorations I had shared with them the previous year were just not relevant to me anymore, that that wasn't my life now. Since they had come to express concern for our welfare, probably curious and a bit horrified after the letter I had sent to them and all my other friends, this was not the warmest message for them to hear, and they left rather disillusioned and worried about us. Candy wanted nothing further to do with them, and I couldn't see myself maintaining the friendship given my current beliefs and the all-encompassing nature of Fort Hill life, even though I felt a deep loss. Many years passed before we communicated again.

I was ready to get on with my new life as a worker. Another Fort Hill man and I found jobs in a furniture warehouse a short walk from the Hill, in Jamaica Plain. Was this the future? At the age of 23, I had never held such a job before. People on the Hill were fond of saying you couldn't skip any steps in your personal growth. I guessed I was making up lost time.

Candy was also making up lost time, in her way. She was becoming more and more a part of the inner social scene on the Hill, and finding me more and more irrelevant. Before long, she moved into Number One, Jim Kweskin's house. Soon she was involved with one of the men and took to offering me pointed little lessons about Hill life. I was quite unhappy. I returned to her a shirt I had given her that she had left behind when she moved out, along with a short note critical of her "social climbing"; that comment briefly became the joke of the Hill gossip circuit.

The warehouse job soon got old, and I quit to do some favors for my relatives in New York. Both my mother and an aunt needed help redecorating their houses, and helping them seemed an opportunity to make money "for the Hill" in surroundings a little more familiar and less intimidating. It also gave me a chance to visit my old girlfriend, Carol Schneider, on our home turf and update her on the latest strange developments in my life. She was between terms at Albany State and getting restless again herself. I made several long trips to New York over a period of weeks. I told Carol she had "always" been "my wife" despite our respective adventures apart. That comment came from someplace I couldn't identify, that didn't even feel like me talking. All I know is that as the words came out of my mouth I somehow felt more like a Fort Hill person for saying them.

Then I got a phone call in New York from one of the people living in my apartment on Beech Glen. She told me Mel had announced that the Aquarian Age was about to begin, on the date of a particular astrological configuration that most others didn't interpret that way. It was time to "come home," she said. I went "home" on the appointed day, and watched the sun rise over Fort Hill at the beginning of the Aquarian Age. I think it might have been September 15, 1968, when the sun in Virgo was conjunct Pluto in the early morning. (Pluto in astrology symbolizes cycles of death and rebirth, thus all deep change and unpredictable turns of events; it was one of Mel's favorite planets and concepts, and in that season lots of planets were moving through Virgo and making aspects to Pluto and each other.) Nothing seemed any different, but I was back in Boston, single and unemployed.

The Whole World Is Weeping

That summer, while I had been learning to be a blue-collar worker for the first time, and while I was getting used to living on my own, without my lady and in a rather harsh psychic environment, the nation as a whole was also going through some rather severe trauma. Robert Kennedy, by some accounts the front-runner and by any account the most exciting candidate to replace the retiring Lyndon Johnson as president, had been assassinated in June, in the moment of winning the primary election in California.

The resulting leadership vacuum had given the Democrats virtually no choice but to nominate their lackluster vice president, Hubert Humphrey, as their standard-bearer. At the same time, the Neanderthal response of the civil authorities in Chicago to the presence of thousands of antiwar and countercultural demonstrators (Abbie Hoffman's YIPpies) outside the Democratic convention there had focused the world's attention on the convention and the accompanying riots. The now-familiar phrase, "The whole world is watching," was born, and the whole world was saddened and disillusioned by what it saw. At the same time, the Republicans chose to resurrect their most morally questionable, but somehow inevitable, candidate, the eminently hatable Richard Nixon, to oppose Humphrey.

At Fort Hill, the writers and editors among the inner circle, and some of their friends, but not me, were busily at work planning the newly conceived *American Avatar*, a magazine-format reinvention of the magazine section of the earlier *Avatar* newspapers. The first issue appeared in October, in a tabloid-sized form on slightly better than newsprint paper. On the cover was a cow-eyed picture of a beautiful teenaged woman, Paula Press, who had gravitated toward the community and been wooed by Mel to be one of his many part-time "wives," but who had somehow found it in herself to resist his overtures and was attempting to be just a normal person in the community. She was living in my household on Beech Glen. Most of the issue was devoted to the community's response to the political events of the summer, mixed with a declaration of intent for this new form of the publication, under the headline "When Was There Greatness in History?":

> We, the old staff of the original AVA-TAR, are back once again. We are here under the Name, *AMERICAN AVATAR*. Before AVATAR fell into the hands of vermin we had a purpose, we are back with that purpose. Before AMERICA fell into the hands of vermin it had a purpose, we are back to fulfill that purpose. We are sick to our stomachs of counterfeit AVATARS and counterfeit AMERI-CAS, we are here to do something about them both, to DWARF them with a REAL standard, leadership.
>
> The *AMERICAN AVATAR* does not cater to any specific sociological group, do not confuse us with "hippies" or "liberals" or any

of the other current titles designating qualities of understanding and areas of congruity. We belong to no group, party, race, religion, or fervent hope. We are on the side of what is right and that, my friend, changes every moment. We will represent the right side on every side even if we are wrong....When was there greatness in history? When a man lived up to his ideals in face of the strongest opposition, there is greatness only when there is courage and courage relies on no security other than its faith in God. All great men had that courage and had that faith. It makes no friends, it transforms the world. We are here to transform the world and we begin with ourselves. We are a group of very courageous individuals. We will gladly face anyone who dares to challenge our devotion, and if they are men they will join us, and if they are boys they will follow us unwillingly.

This is clearly Mel's writing style, although the piece is unsigned. The next page features Eben's hand-drawn version of the phrase, "The whole world's watching," followed by a photo of Mel looking stern, under another unsigned piece that asserts that the "Democratic system" is outdated because the people operating under its banner no longer carry the vision represented by the idea. "Democracy" can now survive only through force, but "real men" can reawaken the spirit of democracy by the force of their conviction.

This is followed by several articles of commentary on the events of the convention and the summer by some of the community regulars and a few of their intellectual friends. My personal favorite is by Skip Ascheim, a Cambridge intellectual who had relocated to the newly acquired house, Number Three Fort Avenue Terrace, just in time to watch the convention on the television there, in the company of most of the enthralled and horrified community. His article, "All Kinds of Stuff Passing through Your Body All the Time," was written shortly after the convention in July:

> Tonight Friday there's a silence from Chicago. What's happening there, are the kids in the streets, are the spades still lying low, is anyone dead? The distance wasn't there while the convention was going on television. For four days we were in the future. The country grew even more in those four days than it did during the assassinations. It was an unbearable amount of self-revelation to take; it had to blow.
>
> No one but the muse of history could have orchestrated the week, the event grew and

shaped like an organism that knew its job. Theatre putting on life, with a script from the deepest channels of blood in the race. A very few of those delegates really knew where they were; probably not many of the demonstrators either. Certainly not the cops. Yet it was all there, the right emphasis to each gesture, everyone coming in on cue. And always in the wings, the unmentioned threat of the black uprising, a constant suspense.

...We have finally begun to use television, or rather television is beginning to understand its own use in this period of the nation, to connect us all to the same place and time, to coalesce our separate wills into energy with which to act upon the event. To focus us sharply enough to inspire the action. One of the very last gasps of the old order will be the shock of losing the myth of objectivity in television reporting. It is going fast.

He goes on to discuss the interaction between live television coverage and the unfolding of the Vietnam War and the public's reaction to it, then continues:

The old ideology will give way when there is new life to replace it; that's what's happening in television. The cameras follow where there is life, and life, in revolutionary times, favors what is being born. Sometimes, as in Chicago, there is so much birth going on that the proud life spirit rides mercilessly over what is dying.

THE MEDIA PEOPLE ARE THE MESSAGE

Skip's article offers a succinct statement of Fort Hill's view on the interplay between media and history, which was really the subject at hand on Fort Hill. Mel saw himself as creating a company of diversely talented people in a variety of media, and he saw that company as playing a key role in the phase of history that was then unfolding, in which a return to basic moral values and idealistic reinvention of the society would dominate the public awareness. As a low-life observer of all these trends from my newly acquired status as a worker and hanger-on to Mel's scene, I found what was happening here all very stimulating and heady. Some of what was published in the new magazine was familiar to me from my earlier days under the influence of Marshall Mc-Luhan's ideas, and some was so new I hardly knew how to begin thinking about it. But there could be no doubt Mel was thinking about it. He made it explicit in an article entitled "Some Enlightening News":

There is a great illusion going on in this country and that is the illusion that the government is supposed to provide leadership, supposed to set the example to the people of how to live. That was only true when government was new, when it was great, when the greatest people in the country were the statesmen. Today the great people are the musicians, the actors, the filmmakers, the COMMUNICA-TORS! The spirit that begat this country is playing a new instrument.

All things begin as inspiration, on the highest level, and must necessarily descend to the needs of the lower levels. A truly successful song is born of the heights and is only fully realized when it has reached the dullest ears of man. This is organic development....There are thousands of men today who are MUCH too great to be the president of the United States, that office can only be properly filled by much lesser men. Our new leaders will not be statesmen, we don't need a great new government to be great, we've already DONE that. We need a great new direction but not in the area of politics, we need it in the area of communications. That is where the new leaders are gathering. Let the Nixons and Humphreys and Wallaces keep house for us, we have a lot of work to do.

On Fort Hill, we undoubtedly had a lot of work to do. Mel took seriously what he was saying in this article, and he wanted to waste no time in getting ready to be there to transform the world when it was ready to be transformed, or maybe sooner. While most of us were on the street again selling the new magazine, Mel was making plans to accelerate the rate of change on the Hill, to intensify the internal struggle each of us was going through, and to undertake an ambitious building program to help manifest his vision. The word went out that fall that "the rocket ship is taking off," and one fact is clear about a rocket ship: if you're not on it when it takes off, you missed it. We found clues everywhere.

During that season, we received a large number of advance copies of the Beatles' mind-blowing new "white album," filled with four sides of songs on every conceivable subject they hadn't addressed earlier, but lacking any central vision or theme. This was, of course, a harbinger of their own impending breakup, but we didn't see it that way; these guys were the future speaking to us. Of course, like Charles Manson who later said the song "Helter Skelter" on that album gave him the inspiration to pursue the mass murders he masterminded, we heard in the background babbling in John Lennon's psychedelic patchwork song, "Revolution No. 9," a message: "Here's to Mel, king of the world." I haven't any idea what the words really were, but they probably were not an homage to Mel, any more than Mel was really "the fool on the hill" the Beatles had sung about earlier. By this time, as weird as all this was, I was feeling distant enough from my former life and concerns that I certainly didn't have any plans other than to be on Mel's rocket ship, but I wasn't too sure I knew how to be on it either.

ONE MAN'S FAMILY

One person who was only too glad to help me know what to do was Jon M., a brash, young newcomer to the community who moved into my house during that time. A Sagittarian by sun-sign, like many of Mel's favorite players, and direct and unsophisticated in a way that lets you know he couldn't possibly be lying to you because he's too simple and ingenuous, Jon quickly became a favorite among the long-timers. In their eyes, he was the person in charge of our household, even though he was new and ill-informed. On Fort Hill, emotional directness was the currency of exchange, not age or experience or information. A competitiveness developed between Jon and me that quickly dominated affairs in our little family.

Into this environment, one evening in November, came a little surprise. A taxi pulled up in front of the house and out stepped Carol Schneider, my former girlfriend from New York and Michigan, to whom I had been proselytizing about Fort Hill the previous summer. She had given me no indication then that she was ready to drop out of school and begin a new life. Now here she was, bags in hand. It seemed I wasn't single anymore, but I was disoriented.

Carol quickly adapted to life in the community and, as she had done in Michigan several years earlier, found a job and settled into the scene effortlessly. I was still having a harder time, and feeling very vulnerable. Jon instinctively knew how to take advantage of this state of mind. First, he started complaining that the living room of our apartment, which Candy and I months earlier had painted in a very traditional mode, with Victorian-style dark green walls and white trim, was too drab and boring to reflect our Fort Hill creativity. Attempting to please, Carol and I, who had decorated a bunch of rooms and houses together in the past, worked evenings with him and the other housemates painting each bit of wall and trim in the room a different pastel color, probably twenty or thirty shades in all. It certainly wasn't drab and Victorian anymore. I boasted of it to other people on the Hill, hoping to make them curious enough to come visit.

Then one day, shortly after it was done, Jon came home and started complaining about the room again, saying we had been self-indulgent and had been stealing energy that belonged to Mel and the community in order to make the room a monument to our own egos. Since the paint job had been his idea in the first place, I felt betrayed and confused. We spent the evening trying to puzzle it out, to no avail, and shortly before midnight one of us, perhaps Jon, suggested we take the problem to Mel, who we knew would still be awake. It made sense to me; if the question was whether to use all our energy directly for Mel's purposes or to somehow create a lifestyle influenced by his values, why not ask him what he wanted from us? So the whole household group, five or six of us, walked up the hill and knocked on Mel's door.

We found him and a few others sitting around his kitchen table, and they allowed us to tell them the conflicting sides of our family problem. Basically, they told us to go home and work it out among ourselves. The rest of us left, but Jon stayed behind. What they hadn't told us was that Mel was suffering from a toothache that night, and the last thing he wanted was to have to resolve interpersonal difficulties among his disciples. That became clear the next day.

That day, I went to work at my job, helping to repair electric motors at a small shop in Cambridge. As I worked, I tried to figure out what had happened the night before. I trudged home after dark, hoping to gain some clarity from the folks in the household, but when I walked in I found the living room filled not only with the entire household but with a dozen or more of the Fort Hill heavies, men and women. At first, I was pleased by the visit, although confused, but I soon realized they were not happy to see me. This was my first encounter with the "karma squad," which had recently emerged as Fort Hill's method of inner discipline for those who were having trouble getting with the program.

The phrase came from William S. Burroughs' spaced-out writings on the drug-crazed fringes of the counterculture, but the methodology was much more basic, physical and mental intimidation with no room for ambiguities or doubts. I sat down and attempted to respond to the barrage of questions and accusations, but I couldn't figure out how to be "real" in the way that was being demanded. I really had thought we were doing a good job of establishing a new household in the Fort Hill mode; these charges of ego-tripping left me again feeling confused and betrayed. Suddenly, in my confusion and paralysis, I found myself being attacked by Jon, who came flying across the room to punch me out and scream at me, while everyone else looked on. I had never before been in a physical fight with anyone and I didn't know how to react. Out of the corner of my eye, I saw Carol freaking out, too, being comforted by one of the women.

When the mood finally settled down a bit, the heavies told us what was now expected of our household: We were to find a way to purchase for the Hill a good, sturdy work truck. Maybe having a simple purpose in common would give us the means to unify ourselves, and anyway the construction projects on the Hill needed such a vehicle. This seemed a large demand, but at least they didn't ask us to leave or kill ourselves. I started looking around for possessions I could sell, unable in my guilt to imagine raising new money any other way, and feeling ashamed for wanting possessions at all. I gathered up and sold much of what remained of my book and record collections. We all resolved to work more hours. When Ian Franckenstein, one of the few people on the Hill who expressed any sympathy for our plight, offered to help me search for a truck, I felt less isolated. He and I tracked down a used Jeep pickup, and somehow we arranged a loan so we could get the truck before raising the cash. Ian became the official truck driver for the Hill, and the rest of us started making payments.

HIT THE ROAD, JACK

Within a few weeks, something was wrong again. I don't remember the details. It was probably another confrontation with Jon in the house, or something like that, but somehow I was persuaded that I just wasn't making it on the Hill, even with the new commitment to pay off the Jeep truck. Maybe it was time for me to try the "real world" again. With regret and a twinge of excitement, I found myself hitchhiking out of town late one Friday night, heading north for no particular reason. I was picked up by some teenagers in the northern suburbs of Boston, who took me to a deserted area and roughed me up, gave me a black eye and threatened to hurt me more, until one of them decided to call it off. They put me back on the highway, where I made it to Portland, Maine, the next day, then changed course and hitchhiked back into New Hampshire. A friendly couple delivered me to a college campus to find a room for the night. I found myself in a dormitory social where the privileged young people of the next generation were flirting with each other and dancing to Marvin Gaye, "I Heard It Through the Grapevine." I felt really old and disconnected, almost from another planet.

Next stop, Stowe, Vermont, where I guessed I could find work at one of the ski resorts, since it was by now January 1969. I spent the next couple weeks washing dishes, moping, eating kitchen leftovers, and hiding my heartbreak as best I could. I also exchanged letters with Carol, back on Beech Glen Street. She advised me to get out in the sun and snow and try skiing to make myself feel better, but I knew that was hopeless for me in the mood I was in.

Finally I left, and dropped in on my friend Dale Walker, who had written such wonderful articles for *The Paper* during his graduate school days at Michigan State, and had then returned to Vermont to do draft counseling as a conscientious objector. Now he was in Brattleboro, working a counseling job at the college there. He gave me access to the arts and crafts room at the college, where I couldn't quite cut loose and express myself; I did better in the evening, where I took on the job of painting the kitchen in Dale's apartment in gratitude for his hospitality. When the room was done, I hit the road again, heading for New York. I was in the mood for some urban despair, so I rented a tiny, cheap hotel room near The Bowery and found a temporary warehouse job.

A few nights later, I was walking in Greenwich Village and ran into—who else?—Jon M. and a bunch of other people from Fort Hill, selling the new issue of *American Avatar*. They were staying in Brian Keating's loft in Soho, home of the now-on-hold *New York Avatar*, and were doing such missionary work as they could on the streets of the Big Apple. My little hegira obviously had not produced much tangible change in my outlook; I wanted nothing more in the world at that moment than to join them. Reluctantly, they let me give up my hotel room and return with them to the loft. Jon especially was hard on me, testing the strength of my intention to be with them. I was not comfortable but I had a connection, and it was my ticket back to the Hill after a few days.

The new issue of *American Avatar* was Mel's way of presenting to the world his own account of how he had created a community around himself. In the mythology we heard later, the "Fort Hill Community" piece was created over a period of many days, the paper sitting in the typewriter waiting for Mel to come up with the next thought or phrase. He did so, in perfect order, never correcting or changing a word, just unfolding it in sequence. This was an example of the "conscious" writing we were told Mel engaged in.

When the piece was done, he proceeded to wrap the magazine around it, starting by offering to Eben an acid-trip photograph of Faith Gude in wide-eyed adoration to Mel, to be touched up and worked into a cover picture for the magazine's new, ever-changing format. This time it was large pages, glossy coated paper, lots of white space and wide borders, and stapled at the fold, unlike all the earlier issues. On the inside front cover was a short poem by Mel hand-lettered by Eben, evoking the feeling we were to glean from the cover picture: "and in all that time we were together/only once did I ever/see that look in her eye that gave me me/....and it's lasted me a lifetime."

Below this, was a long letter from a reader, Patti Ramsay, who writes of reading a book entitled *The Flower People* by Henry Gross, whose slightly fictionalized account of Fort Hill, under the name the "Lynch family," especially appealed to her. She had obtained from the author more information about the actual "Lyman family" and now was asking Mel to tell her more about it. "I want so bad, Mr. Lyman," she writes, "to know that there are other people who feel that there is a place for gentle love, and that there are others who not only share my belief in basic goodness, but who live it every day." Mel tells her to keep living according to her own values, regardless of the isolation this may create for her. "Continue to be an example of all you believe in and someday you'll FIND what you're searching for, don't get in a hurry, just LIVE it."

This was followed by one of Mel's poems, entitled "Contemplations," in which he explains how he applies this principle in his own creative life—"The world is a cold empty room that I seek to fill/with a life I do not own"—and by a reprint of Mel's question from the previous issue, "When was there greatness in history?" under a tranquil-looking drawing by Eben of Mel's profile, and the answer to the question: "When a man lived up to his ideals in face of the strongest opposition, there is greatness only when there is courage and courage relies on no security other than its faith in God. All great men had that courage and had that faith."

The next article, by Owen de Long, comments on the aftermath of the fiasco of the year's political campaign, which culminated in the election of Richard Nixon as president. "Perhaps all Ronald Reagan and Richard Nixon say shall come to pass for us, but it has nothing to do with my idea of leadership, nothing to do with my dream for America's future."

ANOTHER ABSOLUTE

The magazine then moves on to yet another of Mel's "Contemplations," this one on the subject of loneliness and followed by a poetic postscript under a photograph of Mel, folded into a birdlike position and quietly contemplating something off-camera: "To carry loneliness with grace is dignity./To carry loneliness with grace requires patience./A breach of dignity is an act of impatience./A breach of dignity is a lack of grace./Loneliness is an ABSOLUTE."

A section of reprints includes an old poem by Faith about "the beauties of the Atlantic" coming to visit and stealing the affections of the men of the Hill, leaving the women lonely and dependent on their own resources; and Mel's article from the previous issue

about the communication workers as the next generation of leaders. A new article by Mel on "The Democratic Process" again attributes all movement in a time of social change to the influence of the great man whose ability to contain the aspirations of the people affected makes him the leader for that time. Such a leader, Mel says, comes into being when he chooses to feel the will of the people as his own and lets himself be transformed by it.

Among these articles was a full-page photograph of one of the Fort Hill men, dark and shadowy and almost undistinguishable, standing with a rifle at night in a garden. No explanation. It was a representative photograph of a process then occurring in the Fort Hill community that was to severely test its unity. The garden was behind Mel's house, surrounded by a high fence and until recently used to cultivate marijuana. The rifle and the man standing guard were a response to a late-night ripoff, by someone from the surrounding area, of a nearly mature, eight-foot marijuana plant Mel had been nurturing for months. It was decided that Mel's most trusted lieutenants would guard the garden overnight until things calmed down.

Since we were the white and relatively affluent newcomers in a racially mixed neighborhood in a racist city in a time of rising political tensions throughout the country, this promised to be a while. In fact, the guarding of Mel's garden by his closest friends grew quickly into the guarding of the entire Hill by all of the men who could be enlisted, each serving in two-hour rotating shifts around the clock. The Hill became more and more militarized, with the front entry porch of House Number Four serving as the guard shed. We used walkie-talkies to communicate between guards in the front of the houses and others watching the rear, where the community had recently bought a set of garages with a driveway opening to the street behind, to serve as workshops and overflow storage space. (It was up this driveway that the marijuana thief had most likely come.) We had meetings to train guards, we had the usual competitions to decide who qualified to serve, and we sent delegations to attempt to build alliances with the incipient Boston Black Panther group, hoping thus to stave off racist attack on our turf. Guard duty started that fall and winter to protect one marijuana plant, but it continued for years and became part of the fabric of community life on Fort Hill. Only men stood guard; it was a privilege and responsibility of the gender, proof that we were "real men" after all.

A SIMPLE MAN

But Mel himself was gradually emerging as something both more and different from a "real man."

The "community" issue of the magazine included two articles under a joint headline, "There are a lot of illusions surrounding any truth." In these articles, both Wayne Hansen and Brian Keating present Mel as the Christ. Wayne writes as "John Wayne the Baptist" describing the out-of-this world perfection of his friend Mel: "And if you think me exquisitely eloquent in placing in your hearts these pictures of this perfectly united god and man, then your hearts would weep and your tongues melt into universes to tell of what passed when Mel Lyman spoke simply of himself." Brian simply shares an adventure with Mel and Owen in midtown Manhattan, during which Owen buys for Mel a pair of Italian leather shoes. A picture of the shoes accompanies the article, which begins, "It took the passionate Latin soul to shoe Christ."

This is all an omen of things to come, in the next issue of *American Avatar* a few months later. For now, the Mel who is offering the world his version of community building presents himself as a simple person who followed his impulses step by step to wind up where he is. The first paragraph of his article on the community is printed in the sky of a two-page panoramic photograph of the tower and houses of Fort Hill against the backdrop of the rest of Roxbury and the hills beyond:

> The largest community I am aware of is the universe but that is a very abstract kind of awareness. The community within that community that I am most familiar with is the United States, that is a much less abstract kind of awareness. The community within that community that I am most aware of is Fort Hill Community, I have to deal with that one every day. The community within that community is me, I have to deal with that one every moment. So I will start with myself and attempt to work back.

He describes his childhood and early life as a sequence of discoveries first of his essential loneliness and then of his ability to fill his loneliness by reaching out and finding companions, beginning with his mother, then his schoolmates, then his wife and family and their friends. The text is punctuated by photographs of Mel's early life and of life on Fort Hill.

After six years of marriage he sets out "into the wilderness again" because "I didn't know what I wanted but I DID know that what I had wasn't enough." Through becoming a musician, he begins "to feel close to perfect strangers."

> Thousands of people enjoyed my music, hundreds felt very close to me, and a handful

wanted to be near me all the time. They loved me and I loved their loving me. Soon we were all living together in the same house. At first it was wonderful, I played and sang and everybody sang with me. But you can't play music all the time. We had to learn to share other things. Some had to earn money, others had to cook....We all had to give things up and that was a struggle....We began to criticize each other. I found that often people were afraid to tell each other what was bothering them and would instead come to me with their problem and I encouraged them to work it out with the people involved. This brought us closer together....Now we all know each other so well that we have become as one person. We have a block of houses and we all work together on whatever needs to be done at the time. We do not need a set of rules to guarantee that everyone does his part because we trust each other and we are able to trust each other because we have come to KNOW each other.

He goes on to tell about the expansion of the community through the publication of *Avatar* and the way in which communities, either large or small, depend on people knowing each other and telling the truth to each other. "What we have evolved together is a family structure, an ideal example of the natural order inherent in the family of man," and this is a microcosm of what is going on everywhere. "We are here to create a world together, the Family is building a home," and this in turn leads to the development of systems for governing, which usually lead to restrictions of the freedom they were meant to ensure. But at Fort Hill "Our government is changed daily. Not without a struggle for conflict is a necessary step to greater understanding but it just doesn't take us very long to figure out what's wrong and then DO something about it. Things move very quickly around here, we're a fast crowd."

He continues with a rambling dissertation on how every pattern eventually is outgrown and yields to a pattern of higher order, illustrated in the article by his shifting to a very different voice to make this point and by writing of the process of writing, in order to reach across the emptiness to touch people's hearts with his words: "If I can move you deeply enough then there will be a communion between us and we will be a community, it makes things so much easier when people understand each other, then there is no need for tiresome explanations."

Sometimes people make themselves unavailable because of their own fears and doubts. Mel makes it clear that he does not put up with such limitations. This helps explain the atmosphere on Fort Hill.

> That is prison. If you cannot see beyond your own wall then you cannot see that my door is open. I will not let you shut me out, I will leap through my door and tear your wall down. You will resist me to the bitter end but I will get through because I have nowhere to go but into people. My self is YOUR self. I am inside of everybody in this community, we are as one person, that is what a community is. We all feel each other as ourself and so we all are totally responsible for each other. That is why the policy of open criticism, we are criticizing OURSELVES....It requires a great discipline to do your best. We discipline each OTHER. We drive each other NUTS!

Every community needs a leader, Mel continues, "someone who best knows the potential of that particular group of people and how to bring it into actuality. A guide. I am that leader and guide, the father at the head of this family." Further, the people of the Fort Hill community know themselves well enough to know and trust him, he says. He is all things to all men. Newcomers to the Hill usually are awed by Mel and their preconceived concepts about him.

> It always comes as a pleasant surprise to them when they discover that I am so easy to get along with. My relationships with people are solely dependent on how close they are to themselves, the closer they are the more intimate our relationship. I do not know any bounds on intimacy, if you do they are yours. All life yearns to be one.

The issue concludes with a little fictional story, by Mel, of course, of living on a life raft for months and months, just "the wife" and the writer, taking whatever comes along in the simplified environment of ocean and sky, even running out of complaints after a while and learning to accept their lot, learning to laugh uproariously about it all, not all serious like they were before. "You wouldn't believe it was really me & Margaret. It's not Margaret anymore, of course, it's Maggie the Sea Dog...or sometimes 'Lady Margaret, Queen of the Sea.' Can you imagine the things we get into together." This little nonsequitur, I suppose, is meant to illustrate the central principle of life in the Fort Hill community as Mel had just explained it, that no matter what experiences befall us, the main thing, the only thing, is to get to know ourselves better.

I remember feeling grateful for Mel's explanation of what was going on in the community, even though it didn't much match the experiences I was having. At least now I had some words and concepts against which to measure myself. I enthusiastically hit the streets with the others, selling the new issue to the people in town, who were learning not to be surprised by whatever form the published output from Fort Hill might take. I sent copies to relatives, too. If I couldn't explain to them what was happening to me, maybe Mel could.

I had one of the strangest momentary experiences of my life with this new issue shortly after returning to Fort Hill from New York. I was standing with a copy on the front steps of house Number Four, ostensibly doing an evening guard duty shift but really lost in contemplation of the community article. Suddenly I found myself upside down on the ground next to the steps, on my head. It was as though some force had picked me up, turned me over, and dropped me. I never have figured it out. Maybe I just fell asleep standing up. But it was a perfect metaphor for how my life felt in those days. I just accepted it, like the people in the life raft story.

ADVERTISEMENTS FOR OUR SELF

It's worth noting that the several pages around the centerfold of the community issue were filled with advertising, some of it national music ads similar to those found in all the underground papers but most of it ads for local businesses with whom the Hill felt allied, and some of it ads for the community itself: Joey Goldfarb's astrology, Eben Given's artwork, George Peper's photography, Mel's book *Autobiography of a World Saviour*. A letter to readers took the place of a subscription appeal: "Dear Readers, Our purpose was stated in the last issue, it is created in this one....We need to have more people know about us, we need more ways to do that, we need contributions, we need a national distribution. And you need these things too, for you need us, just as we need to do what we have to do. *Avatar* is the compassionate conscience of America. Nobody likes their conscience, but everybody has to deal with it. We're waiting for you, *American Avatar*."

There is a full-page ad for upcoming appearances, "courageously presented" in Worcester and Boston by a producer friend of the community, of "Jim Kweskin and The Lyman Family, etc." In those days, performing members of the community appeared in public as musicians only rarely. When they did, as likely as not they would not perform any music, preferring instead to dialogue with the audience until they felt confident that the audience was really present, really open-hearted and ready for whatever was to happen. The music thus became a reward for the audience for making the musicians feel welcomed and understood spiritually, far from the usual relationship between performers and audience. Not surprisingly, some of these appearances had resulted in quarreling between audience members and performers, and the reviews had grown harsh and nasty. Instead of embodying good feelings and old timey music as they used to, Jim and the other musicians had come to represent argumentativeness and unpredictability reminiscent of the misunderstandings surrounding the scheduled appearance by Mel and others at Arlington Street Church nearly a year earlier. I attended several of these appearances at clubs around Boston, playing the role of acolyte and enthusiastic fan, but confused by how they were choosing to present themselves.

An important part of living in the Fort Hill mode was proselytizing, or, what was called "learning how to talk to people." The notion was that what was happening on Fort Hill was more interesting, more important, more "real" than anything happening anywhere else. When people showed up, curious about our community or wanting more of the energy they had felt through our various outreaches, talking to them consisted of learning enough about them to then use that information to make them want to stay around and learn more. The men were invited to join the work crew, for a few hours or a lifetime. The women were introduced to the numerous children and encouraged to help with meal preparation and other chores. Little time was wasted, by anyone, although hanging out with visitors was itself considered a job and a responsibility, and if a person was clever, he or she could practically make a career of it.

FOLLOW THE LEADER

Some of the most sad and disorienting times I had during those early days on Fort Hill were when friends from East Lansing would show up and either fit in to the scene or not. I felt obliged to give them as true a Fort Hill-type experience as I could, even when I was just reciting the lines, and this feeling at times produced strange results. Larry Tate, my long-time roommate and co-founder of *The Paper*, got tired of graduate school in Berkeley after less than a year and came to Boston to check out what we were doing and to visit another friend. He visited Fort Hill a number of times over a period of months, beginning when Candy and I were living in the apartment we shared in our early days there. Predictably enough, he was not at all interested in joining the work crew, even for an hour, or in being converted to our proto-religious adoration

of Mel, or in being measured against some standard of realness.

This was really okay with me, but it was not okay with the others who observed our interactions, and eventually I was put up to challenging Larry on his "resistance." When he wouldn't budge, I accepted the inevitability of forcing him and delivered a slap across his face, which surprised and saddened both of us, and wimpily fell far short of what was expected of me. Larry left in a huff, nurturing hurt feelings and a permanent rupture in our relationship.

On the other hand, Eric Peterson, who had introduced me to Candy when he joined the *Paper* staff and then remained behind to help publish *The Paper* after we left town, graduated from Michigan State the next year and visited Fort Hill during that summer, before starting graduate school at Yale. The hierarchical authority structure, the inexorable necessity of doing "what was right in front of you," the clear truths that made it unnecessary and even undesirable to think for oneself from moment to moment—all these suited him perfectly, and he fit right in. Almost from the moment he started graduate school in New Haven, he was spending his weekends in Boston with us, and it was just a matter of time before he dropped out and moved to Fort Hill permanently.

This happened some time during the spring of 1969, roughly a year after Candy and I first arrived. Eric and I began, with some discomfort, functioning as a working unit within the larger work crew; we seemed bound to each other, which made both of us rather uncomfortable, but we remained so for years. Always obedient, he took to reminding me of the dicta of Fort Hill discipline when I would seem to be lapsing, and it made me want to scream, or kill. But on the surface we remained friends, as best we could. The work required it.

A former girlfriend of Eric's from Michigan, Linda Kendrick, also showed up during that season to see what we were up to. She quickly became involved with Randy Foote, who had moved to the Hill about the same time as Candy and I, after apprenticing with *Avatar* for quite a while, dropping out of Harvard in order to sell *Avatars* on the street and get busted during the censorship struggles. Randy and Linda set up another satellite household on Marcella Street, a few blocks downhill from the main block of houses, on the way to Jamaica Plain. Somehow, their household didn't go through the struggles our household on Beech Glen Street did, continually trying to figure out whether we were a Hill house or not. It was clear theirs was not, and it was equally clear Randy was destined to become part of the Hill inner circle.

For now, their place served as a stopover point for people curious about the Hill but not yet with it.

One of these, an unstable young man named Sandy, took a liking to Linda, and a complicated three-way relationship developed. One day, Sandy flipped out at Linda and beat her nearly to death, leaving her in a pool of blood with a badly broken jaw and numerous other injuries. Randy discovered Linda that way and rushed her to the first emergency room he could find, which happened to be at Boston Children's Hospital. There, Linda spent several months playing with the other patients, all of them young children, and gradually recovered both her health and her sanity. Her mother came to fetch her back to Michigan, but eventually she returned to Fort Hill to stay.

Another young woman from our East Lansing circle, who had been a freshman advisee of Candy's and mine in our psychology department tutoring jobs during our last days there, came to visit and never left. She was another one whom the discipline suited well, and who was ready to move into the traditional woman's role that was the only option offered her. She eventually had a child by one of Mel's musician friends, who lived at the Hill intermittently. She also played a key role in setting me up for one of my several encounters with the "karma squad," but I'll save that story until its own time.

Then there was Nancy Platt, a friend from the East Lansing countercultural circle, who arranged to spend the summer of 1968 at Fort Hill, before starting graduate school somewhere. She was simply too independent to fit in well, but her visit was pleasant enough.

And there was Dale Walker, whose curiosity brought him to Fort Hill numerous times but who was really too traditional in his own values to be taken in by the Hill's futuristic rhetoric. Eventually he stopped visiting, but we remained close enough friends that I was able to use his home in Brattleboro as a stopover when I was wandering through New England looking for myself.

All in all, so many of our friends visited and came to stay, from various phases of our past, that our East Lansing circle became an object of considerable interest and curiosity around Fort Hill. This endless supply of visitors and curiosity-seekers made it clear that we had had something fairly powerful going on in East Lansing, too, and that people there had looked up to us and learned a lot from us. Thus, it was even more mysterious that I couldn't seem to find the same thread at Fort Hill. I had these clear memories of having been a focus of community energy in the past, of having been right on about what was happening and able to move with the flow of events no matter what those events were. But at Fort Hill I couldn't seem to figure out how to be anything but a coolie, a laborer, a follower, and not a very good one at that. It was very disconcerting and disheartening, particularly in the presence of so many people who had known me before.

I remember a brief conversation with Jessie, in which she said Carol had told her about the old Michael in East Lansing, who was "full of piss and vinegar." "What happened to him?" she asked. I didn't know how to answer, but the same question was plaguing me. I used the oracle of the *I Ching* frequently for guidance and consolation, and sometimes it would help me find some direction. But with alarming frequency it would offer me the hexagram "Holding Together": "Holding Together brings good fortune....Those who are uncertain gradually join. Whoever comes too late meets with misfortune." Had I already missed my opportunity to bond with the people of the Hill? I wanted to see myself as "the superior man" mentioned throughout the *I Ching*, who understands the significance of each moment and senses the appropriate way to behave to achieve a good outcome. But I didn't seem to fit that description. I didn't want to believe that the light that I believed was shining at Fort Hill was simply too bright for me to be comfortable in its presence, even though that did seem to be what was happening. And events on the Hill were certainly moving in such a way as to test that theory.

CHRIST, YOU KNOW IT AIN'T EASY

A few months after the "community" issue of *American Avatar* was published, Mel was feeling the urge again—and this time he was in the mood to really put people through changes. A third magazine-format issue was put together, again looking different from any previous one. The "Christ" issue was on heavy, matte-finish paper, the pages wider than they were long, so that the cover could be a close-up photo of Mel surrounded by a border resembling a television screen, in working class get-up, holding a cigarette and staring into the camera. The title *American Avatar* is printed in white block letters across his chest; no ambiguity here. The next two pages are a glittering array of white stars on black background, painted by Eben, with a corner of the earth at the lower left; floating nearby is a photograph of Mel in his work clothes, sitting cross-legged on a painted-in nebula, holding a drink and grinning, with a halo around his head, and next to him is a "Message to Humanity" in white letters on black background:

Hi gang, I'm back, just like the book says. By God here I am, in all my glory, I thought I'D NEVER come. But I'm here now and getting ready to do the good work. Maybe some of ya think I aint Him. You'll see. I aint about to prove it for you, much too corny, I'm Him and there just aint no question ABOUT it. Betcha never thought it would happen like THIS did ya? Sorry to disappoint you but I've got to make the most of what's here and there sure as hell aint very much. No turnin water to wine and raisin the dead this trip, just gonna tell it like it is. You've waited a long time for this glorious moment and now that it's actually HERE I expect most of you will just brush it off and keep right on waiting, that's what those damn fool Jews did LAST time I came, in fact they're still DOING it. Oh well, what's a few thousand MORE years to people who've been suffering for MILLIONS. So while most of you turn your heads and continue sticking to your silly romantic beliefs I'll let the rest of you in on a little secret. I'm Christ, I swear to God in PERSON, and I'm about to turn this foolish world upside down....

    Love, Christ

Mel's "Message to Humanity" is followed, on the next few pages, by

- a page devoted to a painting of the "whole earth";

- another picture of Mel staring out from what looks like a small box inside a television set, telling readers that "As Christ appearing in this modern day and age I am going to take advantage of all mediums of communication," and promising his readers "another even GREATER surprise for you";

- Mel's surprise: "The Buddha is with me" for the first time "in the history of this planet....I am going to operate as the heart, the CENTER, and Buddha is going to serve as the World Mind. He will put into effect, as World Government, all that I am." Mel does not reveal his identity, but above these words is

- a large close-up picture of Owen de Long;

- another picture of Mel, in farmer garb, holding a devil's trident instead of a pitchfork, looking in Owen's direction out of the corners of his eyes;

- a silhouetted picture of the Fort Hill tower against the sky, with small figures drawn in on the ground, seeming to be a crew of workers setting up crosses for a crucifixion; and

- a tongue-in-cheek article by Les Daniels, one of the Fort Hill hangers-on, who charges, but only humorously, that "Most people who claim to be waiting for the second coming are actually perverts who are just waiting for a chance to get in on the second crucifixion," and predicting "that the twentieth-century savior is going to outfox them all by, yes, he's going to crucify *himself*," while "his loyal followers" do the same. He describes a scene of Mel's followers attaching themselves to the ground with spikes and then ascending the heavens, dragging the earth along behind them.

The issue continues with a book review written by Mel, an excerpt from Mel's *Autobiography of a World Saviour*, a couple of short poems by readers, two full-page ads (both conveniently illustrated with pictures of Mel), a sarcastic meditation by Mel on the wonders of getting lost in his television set, a lengthy semi-real autobiographical ramble, "co-written" by Wayne Hansen and Mel, about the process of getting hooked on Mel's writing and music, et cetera, that gradually turns into an angry put-down of Mel and his arrogance (just a joke, of course), and Mel's "Essay on the New Age," on the need to have discipline if one is to handle increasing amounts of freedom.

Then come a picture of Jessie with Daria, her and Mel's infant daughter; another picture of Mel alongside an exchange of letters with a reader on the nature of being God on earth; another picture of Baby Daria; and another "Essay on the New Age," on Mel's role as the bearer of a new spirit for our age.

It goes on: a picture of Mel seeming to hold the earth in his lap; an untitled essay that begins, "Patience is the test of character, you can find out just exactly how deep your understanding is by seeing how long you can wait for something you really want"; a picture of Mel looking rugged in a heavy sweater; a long poem called "Contemplations" that concludes: "God creates me, I create the world./Deep within myself I know unity, all my understanding/flows from a perfect order. In the world about me/I see fragments of this order, how can I help/but seek to unite them"; and two pictures of Mel, one of him silhouetted against the ocean at dusk, the other of him playing banjo and looking deep. End of opus.

A TEST OF FAITH

Needless to say, the "Christ" issue was not an easy one to sell on the street. I had managed to stay with all the changes up to now, but this one was really hard for me. Having grown up in a home that was both

Jewish and agnostic, and having found my own reasons as an adult to hold the church and Christianity in high disdain, it was confrontational for me to find my hero presenting himself as Christ, whatever one perceived that to be. It was even harder to find enthusiasm to purvey this version of Mel Lyman and Fort Hill to strangers, although I did dutifully work at it. Now I really felt like a weirdo from some cult. I knew that the idea of "Christ" was not the same as the historical person Jesus. One of the popular astrology books on the Hill at that time was *Meditations on the Signs of the Zodiac* by John Jocelyn, a dense and thoughtful consideration on how a person born under each of the twelve signs could consciously evolve himself to his highest potential, which in the book is called the Christ essence. This idea was okay with me, but to aggressively say to the world "I'm it, ain't no doubt about it" was sort of another thing. And, that, of course, was exactly how Mel wanted it. You're either with us, he seemed to be saying, or you're agin us.

By this time, early summer 1969, I seemed to be spending all my time trying to keep pace with the shifting and changing priorities of the Hill. My mind simply couldn't keep up with it all or make sense of it, and my heart was more and more saddened and confused, but I couldn't admit that. I tried to make sense of it somehow by keeping track of information, such as who was living in which house and why, who was in relationship with whom, which baby had been parented by which parents. (In the "serial monogamy" mode of Fort Hill, in an atmosphere in which people's spontaneous urges toward private experiences were considered suspect and risky, liable to deflect them from carrying out their responsibilities or, worse, from their devotion to the pursuit of pure spirit, lovers often got separated from each other and parents from their offspring, and couplings were constantly realigning; keeping it all straight was not easy.)

I tried to learn more about astrology and become more fluent in using it as a language of interpersonal communication, even managed gradually to acquire a set of astrology books of my own, but I was not encouraged by the others to pursue the study. I was required by peer pressure and expectations to spend more and more of my "free" time working on the building projects, and, along with most of the other men and a small number of the women, was picking up more and more skills as I did so. (The women took responsibility only for a limited range of tasks, such as removing old wallpaper or resurfacing and painting the walls.) I was trying to maintain something like a normal relationship with Carol, with whom I was still living. And both of us, and virtually everyone else who didn't have some specific defined role and responsibilities on the Hill, were going off the Hill every weekday to jobs in Boston or Cambridge to earn as much money as we could to help fund the building projects and Mel's other creative works.

The pace was quickening. There were more houses now to take care of. Number Three Fort Avenue Terrace was bought back from Kay and Charlie Rose, who had bought it the year before to make it part of the community's holdings. Now they were leaving, and Mel directed the community to buy the house from them. Faith Gude devised a scheme to connect Number Three to her house, Number Two, so the two of them together could serve as a special house and school for the growing number of children; Richie designed it and the rest of us started building. Numbers Five and Six, the duplex at the end of the row, had been bought; at first they were used as apartments for members of the community, but soon it became clear that their interiors had to be gutted and rearranged in order to fit into a grand scheme to combine them with Mel's house next door, Number Four and a Half, and have the resulting complex serve as a media center and multi-purpose living and entertainment space in which Mel could produce and display his various creations. On Fort Avenue, the set of apartment buildings—Numbers 27, 29, and 31—were being purchased and turned into full-on Hill houses, which meant still more gutting and rehabilitating, but this work had lower priority than the Fort Avenue Terrace houses; it was done in people's "spare" time.

No one, in fact, had any spare time. When we weren't off the Hill working to bring home money or selling the magazine, an endless array of tasks had to be done. Every weekend day and most evenings almost everyone worked on the construction projects, except for those women who were taking care of the houses and children, or cooking to feed the crew. We had work meetings each morning to assign tasks and plan the shopping and salvaging trips to collect materials. Visitors were enlisted into the work as quickly as possible so no time would be wasted. We were encouraged to put our personal feelings aside in order to participate more efficiently in the work. Everyone was encouraged (or badgered or driven or forced, as necessary) to learn basic skills and tricks of teamwork and group effort. We all became efficient at moving furniture and appliances. We learned to pace ourselves through heavy work, such as digging or demolition. Large tasks would be set up in lines, when possible: a truckload of lumber or bricks or sacks of cement or whatever could be unloaded and moved onto a building site in a matter of minutes by ten or twenty people in a line, passing the load from one hand to the next. We learned to watch out for each other's safety, and for the quality of each other's work. We learned to notice when too much material was being used, and to encourage frugality. We centralized collections of all materials to minimize redundancy; often one or two people would be responsible for keeping a particular collection in order and doling it out to the others.

We were all expected to maintain a set of our own tools, and to continue learning new skills. Like most aspects of life, this was used as a parable to teach a moral lesson. In this case, it was that one started with the tools that were basic and readily available to do a job, and then, as one developed more skill and took on more responsibility, one could get in a position to have more subtle and refined tools to work with. My hammer and saw might eventually become recording equipment, for example, as Mel's had. How one could learn to work with the more refined tools before one had access to them remained a mystery to me. But when it came to construction tools, access became less and less of a problem. The Hill was well equipped, and new tools were always being added. One of the garages was turned into a well-equipped woodworking shop; increasingly ambitious cabinet and furniture projects were undertaken by ever-increasing numbers of skilled workers. But lots and lots of basic grunt work also had to be done. Each of the Terrace houses needed its sewer lines dug up and rebuilt. Several of the houses needed major foundation repairs. Since the backyards of the Terrace houses were a hillside that overlooked the garages behind and below, retaining walls and fences and staircases had to be built. And every house had rooms that needed repair and remodeling, sometimes more than once as the plans changed and grew. The work never seemed to end.

HELLO, CENTRAL, GIVE ME JESUS

Increasingly, all aspects of our lives were becoming centralized. A first-floor room in Number 27 Fort Avenue became an office for the entire community. Mail delivery was coordinated from here. Finances especially became more and more centrally controlled. Everyone who worked "off the Hill" would turn in his or her paychecks to a bookkeeper who monitored all contributions and doled out money for construction purchases and other necessary expenses. Those of us still living in households outside of Hill property would handle our expenses first, then turn the balance over. Our income tax returns would get filed for us at the beginning of each year, and our refunds would simply be deposited in the Hill accounts when they arrived. A switchboard was installed in the office to connect all the houses and to receive and send all calls to the outside world. As the men rotated guard duty shifts through the 24 hours, the women took turns on the switchboard. Thus, someone always was on duty to

receive visitors or handle emergencies, and also to monitor how much time anyone spent talking to people off the Hill.

There was a fantasy going around of all the houses being interconnected with sound and even video systems, the idea being that when something particularly "real" was occurring anywhere it could be broadcast as it was happening so everyone else could share in it. This simulcasting never happened, but everything short of it did. The details of everyone's private lives were increasingly the subject for community interest, concern, and control. As Les Daniels had anticipated in his metaphor in the "Christ" issue, members of the community were nailing not only ourselves but also each other to the ground repeatedly, holding ourselves and each other to impossible standards of perfection and guarded morality, ever-vigilant for any infractions, which were perceived as opportunities to help each other live up to the standards it was assumed we all wanted to maintain.

Even our recreation became more and more directed as time went on. Mel or one of the other central figures would discover something, and suddenly it would be all the rage for everyone, or it would be a mandated necessity. We tended to read books in fads, usually biographies or memoirs of the kinds of people who embodied spirit as Mel understood it, such as *Instant Replay* by football coach Vince Lombardi, or *The Movies, Mr. Griffith and Me* by actress Lillian Gish. We all read *The Godfather* when it first appeared. Mel spent a lot of time watching old movies on TV, and the ones he especially liked became required viewing for anyone who could break free to spend time watching. Over time, we all filled our minds and our conversation with images from these classic movies and became knowledgeable about the stars and directors who made them. When Mel discovered professional football, everyone began watching the games on TV and learning the horoscopes of the players. For a while all the men played frequent touch football around the tower on the hilltop, whether we wanted to or not. (I was never one for team sports of any kind, and particularly loathed football, but I was given no choice; I have a slightly gimped finger from my required participation in one of the Hill's games, from an unfortunate encounter with a forward pass.)

Holidays and other special events were usually celebrated in large groups, often with big dinners or dance parties in Jim's house, Number One. Thanksgiving dinners would be giant potlucks where the women would pull out all the stops to make us feel well taken care of. But despite these efforts, there remained a hierarchical and manipulative aspect to it all, to which I was very sensitive, since I never did find the way to feel like an equal participant in the Hill's social circles, despite wanting that very badly. On one memorable occasion, during a summer season when a lot of random and frustrated sexual energy was floating around on the Hill, Jim and a few others put out the word that there would be an "orgy" in Number One that night, and we were all invited. Well, that would certainly be a first, and I don't think I really believed it was true, but I thought at least there would be some attempt in some form to confront and defuse the sexual frustration. At the appointed time, the more curious among us showed up at Number One and found Jim and a few of the others walking around wearing giant oversized genitals and breasts made out of balloons; apparently the whole purpose of calling the "orgy" was to tease us, and maybe themselves, for wishing to relieve our sexual energies.

Mel's role in all this was paradoxical and confusing. On the one hand, he always said, both in person and in his writings, that what he wanted most was to be surrounded by people who, like himself, could take responsibility for themselves and help create an atmosphere of creative spontaneity and inventiveness. On the other hand, he seemed to find it necessary to guide that process closely, to intervene with lessons and instructions and demands that, I felt then and am convinced now, interfered with the process. The mythology of the Hill held that Mel was in effect the source of all the riches and opportunities we enjoyed. This was understood quite literally, as though, for example, the old movies we watched on television would never have come to our attention if Mel hadn't pointed them out to us, or as though we would never have had the imagination to experiment with living in groups and alternative families if it hadn't been Mel's idea, and we certainly wouldn't have had any success in doing so if he hadn't told us what to do. I found this all contrary to the obvious truth—every one of us had arrived in the community specifically because we were actively looking for alternatives in our lives, and many of us had identified ourselves as creative, innovative people before we arrived there—and also contradictory to Mel's stated intention to have us outgrow his leadership and eventually become his equal in spiritual stature. How could we do that if we were constantly urged to follow his example and instructions rather than our own impulses?

Mel had little patience for our differing personal needs, particularly our needs to learn different lessons at our individual paces. When problems made themselves known to him, often he would use them as opportunities to issue directives or to teach particular lessons to the entire community. He might write a letter that everyone had to read. Or he might call a meeting, or direct someone else to call a meeting, to explain some need that the Hill had now, or some behavior that

would no longer be tolerated, or that would now be required. Or he might throw a tantrum in private, and then insist that whatever it was that set him off never occur again. One time Mel got angry because one of the women had become unexpectedly pregnant, when he had decided without warning that there were too many children on the Hill. He ordered an abortion for her and six months of sexual abstinence for the entire community. Incredibly, people did their best to obey. For me, this entire process of being told to take care of ourselves and then being told how to do that made it more and more difficult to know who I was, or where I ended and the community at large began. But trying to fit in gradually became all that seemed to matter.

In retrospect, it seems so superficial and futile, trying to adapt our behavior to some notion of how certain other people were living, pretending to be something we weren't in order to gain acceptance—especially when the standard of comparison kept shifting and changing. It was a hopeless, sisyphian task. Whatever behavior standard one attained, by the time one attained it the role models had moved on, sometimes for no reason other than to keep the race going, or so it seemed.

I was one of a sizable and ever-shifting population of hangers-on and hopefuls around the Hill, people who for one reason or another wanted to attach ourselves to Mel Lyman's energy and that of the glittery, resplendent people he had gathered around himself. My two lady friends, Candy and Carol, both moved easily into the inner circle and remained there (to this day, as far as I know), but I never could find the secret. One could watch certain people show up on the Hill, win the attention of the long-timers, and suddenly be part of the gang, while others, such as myself, could hang around for years struggling to be respected and appreciated, to no avail. In one particularly poignant case, a man who had been hanging around *Avatar* and Fort Hill for a couple of years simply couldn't make it, got sick and had injuries all the time, couldn't get anyone to care for him, and then his younger brother showed up and was instantly ushered into the inner sanctum, literally into Mel's presence, and figuratively into the circle of people whose energy somehow matched that of the Hill regulars. He made as many mistakes as anyone, but he was tolerated and encouraged.

Sometimes someone who had struggled for months or years to fit in would reach a limit one day and just leave. Leaving, however, sometimes involved advanced planning. For instance, a person who felt the need to have some money when leaving the Hill might go off to a job on a payday and simply never return. Or, someone who was feeling pressured to perform beyond his or her limits might decide that the only way to get out was to run away in the middle of the night. Or there might be an argument, or a fight, and the person would be allowed to leave in disgrace. Others would leave surreptitiously, and then somehow let the community know where they were, and people would go out into the world to retrieve them. It was very erratic and unpredictable, but the overall effect was to make all of us know that our presence was noticed and valued, especially if we were productive workers, even if we had to put up with intolerable demands and pressures as the price of being appreciated. The operative principle was a kind of survival of the fittest. You could almost see the pyramid of hierarchical authority around the people who got to determine what happened on the Hill, and you could equally well see it shift and change from day to day. I saw all this clearly, but could not find the way to succeed at the game.

SUPERSTARS

After returning to Fort Hill with the sales crew for the "Community" issue, I was again given the responsibility of finding a decent job off the Hill, as a source of money and, therefore, respect. After a series of short-term jobs, I answered an ad for a delivery driver for a major architecture firm in Cambridge, The Architects Collaborative (TAC), professional home during his last years of the world-famous Bauhaus architect, Walter Gropius—another great man in whose shadow I could hang out for a while, delivering blueprints to major construction sites all over the Boston area. After a few months in that capacity, I moved to a different role in the same firm, doing odd jobs in its maintenance department. This is the role I was in when "Grope" finally passed on that summer, at the age of 86; the firm hosted an afternoon celebration of his life instead of a funeral, fulfilling a clearly stated wish of the late genius.

TAC was also where I was working when, one evening that summer while I was doing a guard duty shift, I attempted to enter a conversation that was going on near the Fort Hill tower between David and Faith Gude. In my imagination, they were just sitting on the Hill appreciating the weather and the view of Boston, and I wanted to share that, too. It turned out they were negotiating the end of their long common-law marriage and felt invaded by my arrival. But instead of simply saying so, they waited until I left on my own to return to the guard shack and then continued their conversation. After a while, David joined me at the guard shack and, without ever saying what had been wrong with my behavior (I figured it out myself long afterward), told me in cold anger that I was not making it on the Hill, was clearly missing the point, and should probably move off the Hill, try the "real world" again, fall in love, fight for causes, do something real. I took this

to heart, and within a day or two had arranged housing in Cambridge, first with one of my co-workers and then in a small apartment in a working class part of town. I took one of the cats from the Beech Glen Street house with me for companionship but after a while he disappeared.

After six weeks of living and working in Cambridge, trying to reframe my life on that small and individual scale, I couldn't resist visiting Fort Hill one Sunday afternoon. Inevitably, the first person I encountered was David Gude, who asked me if I was ready to return yet and if I felt badly about how he had treated me. How and why these things happen continues to seem a mystery to me, but I said yes, I was ready to return, and of course I harbored no ill feelings toward him. (What a missed opportunity!) I immediately made arrangements to rent a studio apartment of my own facing the hilltop, in Number 23 Fort Avenue, one of several apartment buildings adjoining those owned by the community. About a third of the units in Numbers 21, 23, and 25 Fort Avenue were rented by community members. I liked the apartment a lot and enjoyed having my own vantage for observing the tower and the activities of the community houses, but I think I only lived there for a month, maybe two. The household on Beech Glen Street where Carol and several others were still living was ready to break up, and Carol and I and Eric Peterson wound up inheriting a third-floor attic apartment around the corner on Highland Avenue, probably as a way to house more of us for less rent expenditure. The apartment had previously been the home of Mark Frechette, a peripheral member of the community and an avid reader and admirer of Mel's writings in *Avatar*, whose life had taken a dramatic turn, and who no longer needed a small apartment on the back side of the Hill.

Mark, young and rugged-looking in a sensitive sort of way, with a quick temper and little use for fancy language, had found himself in a shouting match at a bus stop in Boston, intervening in a quarrel between two lovers. Miraculously (this is a true story), he had been observed in his anger by a talent scout for Italian filmmaker Michelangelo Antonioni, who had exclaimed something like "He's twenty and he hates!" and had immediately whisked Mark off for a screen test for the lead role in Antonioni's upcoming made-in-America film, *Zabriskie Point*, a fictional story of the revolutionary career of a Berkeley activist who runs off to Death Valley to escape the law and winds up confronting his destiny in the desert. Mark had indeed been given the role and had immediately pledged his devotion and the bulk of his earnings to Mel Lyman, who for his part immediately welcomed Mark into his inner circle. Mark's co-star, aspiring actress Daria Halprin, daughter of two famous creative parents from California's Marin County, landscape architect Lawrence Halprin and choreographer Anna Halprin, during the course of the filming had also become his lover, and before long they were living uneasily together in one of the Hill houses. Mark loved being one of the Hill workers, when he wasn't planning future filmmaking endeavors with Mel or going off to act in a couple of Grade-B movies; Daria had a harder time fitting in, and was really out of her element. Mel and Jessie named their baby after her, but that didn't help.

The summer afforded those of us on the work crew, the "dummies" of the Hill, two opportunities to travel out of town, feeling like emissaries from Mel's universe. For some reason, Mel and Jim Kweskin decided to try showing up one last time at the Newport Folk Festival in Rhode Island, a couple hours' drive from the Hill, with the entire performing "Lyman Family" and a gang of fans and helpers in tow. I remember that the musicians of the group were scheduled to appear at the end of one of the afternoon concerts. They started doing their make-the-audience-prove-they-really-want-it number from the stage, while Mel waited in the wings, unwilling to appear until and unless he sensed the perfect moment. The audience didn't go for this and started loudly demanding entertainment, especially some of the familiar Kweskin Jug Band songs. As the mood got worse and worse, into the breach unexpectedly came Joan Baez, no fan of Mel Lyman, suddenly assuming the role of peacemaker by singing an a capella version of "Amazing Grace" to calm the audience down and give them some of what they wanted. Jim and the others were furious and walked off stage, cursing Joan and recalling how much bitchier she could be than her more pleasant sister, Mimi Fariña, an old friend of theirs. For my part, I thought it was a delightful, subtle allusion to Mel's spontaneous "Rock of Ages" performance in a similar moment a few years earlier, when Bob Dylan had pissed off an audience that expected him to do one thing when he was in the mood to do another. In any case, we piled in our cars and headed back to Fort Hill.

Not too many weeks later, we were off again, this time several carloads of us heading for the Catskill Mountains region of New York, to represent Mel and Fort Hill at the Woodstock Festival. I haven't any idea how or why this trip got organized. I think we must have been wanting to sell copies of *American Avatar* and otherwise proselytize to the assembled masses. I remember that in preparation for the trip I bought myself a new pair of used bell-bottom jeans, white with light blue stripes, and a pale red shirt; I fancied myself looking like a sort of off-beat Uncle Sam to go with our "second American revolution" mythology. We arrived at the festival site—nowhere near Woodstock, as everyone knows, but farther into the Catskills, on

Max Yasgur's dairy farm near a town called White Lake; it happened to be just a few miles from a poultry farm where some cousins of mine had lived for many years, so it was a weird kind of homecoming for me—after the huge crowd had already gathered and established its impromptu villages and campsites, and as the now-famous rainstorm began. Our official position was that the music happening on stage was of no interest to us, and we were there to sell magazines or whatever. But with the rain coming down in buckets, Richie Guerin, who was field-marshalling the operation, decided the best thing we could do was position ourselves on the roadways and help direct traffic, because he could see mass confusion in the making. That is what we did, and it's all we did for the two or three days we were there, twenty or so of us getting muddier and muddier, directing traffic in the rain while one of the great cultural events of our generation went on all around us. Needless to say, no magazines got sold and no music was heard by any of us, except dimly in the distance.

Also during that summer, Mel started what became a long campaign of physical expansion of his community, one that went on for some years. He accepted an invitation for himself and several of his closest associates to spend the summer on Martha's Vineyard Island, off the southern coast of Massachusetts, where Jessie's father, the artist Tom Benton, and his wife had a summer home and studio. Mel needed a rest from his world saviouring, and it seemed to be time for Mel and Tom to become better acquainted. In fact, they began making a little film of Tom working in his studio and developed a friendship and mutual respect that inspired Tom to, in effect, give a portion of his summer home to Mel and the community. (I don't know the details, since I was never invited to visit the Vineyard; were there separate houses on one large property? separate quarters in one large house? adjoining properties?) The effect was to give the Hill insiders a permanent second home, to which they would retreat from time to time during appropriate seasons, inviting along those who needed a break, or with whom Mel wanted to spend more time, or, occasionally, those who needed the discipline of living in close proximity with The Lord for a while.

A Last Hurrah

While Mel and company were at the Vineyard, they began work on the next issue of *American Avatar*. This time, the magazine transmogrified into a large-format, relatively slick imitation of a journal of general culture and trendiness that was dated Summer 1969 (I believe it appeared late summer or early fall, but it might have been earlier, in time for us to take it to "Woodstock"). It was numbered "Fourth Cycle, First Issue," and was priced at $1, a high price for that era. On the cover was a photograph, by Mel, of David and Faith Gude's young daughter Clothilde and headlines announcing three of the articles inside, including an "Exclusive Interview with Antonioni's Newest Superstars." The first page of the magazine included an elaborate staff listing with no fewer than 33 members of the community listed in various positions, from editor-in-chief (Mel, of course) and executive editor (Jessie) all the way down to director of maintenance. A table of contents listed twelve articles and features, only a few of which were by Mel Lyman, and a box of publication data promised bi-monthly publication. The magazine had not yet been published bi-monthly at any time, and never would be. This was the first issue of the "fourth cycle," and the last issue ever of *American Avatar*.

The first feature was an "Editorial," untitled and unsigned but obviously Mel's work. It was yet another restatement of Mel's political philosophy of the time, and appeared facing a photograph of a statue of a Revolutionary War soldier, perhaps Paul Revere:

> Only in this country could such a wondrous revolution take place....This revolution is the test and the fruition of true democracy, of the people, by the people, for the people. There is spirit in the air again, and without a world war yet! That is encouraging. We are not uniting against an alien power, we are uniting against each OTHER! Not even north against south this time, even that won't work anymore, we are virtually eliminating geographical warfare, we are fighting man against man, we are fighting for something bombs can't buy, we are fighting for LIFE! America is getting stale, we are fighting for LIFE!

REVOLUTION OR BUST?

The next article, "No Solution to Revolution" by Wayne Hansen, tries to place Mel's message in a larger historical context. Generally speaking, Wayne describes a dialectical model of historical change in which opposing forces become more polarized through the unfolding of events until there is no choice but for a great leader to emerge spontaneously, uniting the opposites from a completely new vantage point. He attributes such a role to Hitler, whose unexpected violence in storming over Europe forced the United States and its allies to confront him, thereby ending the historical isolationism of this country.

He then discusses the early deaths by assassination of John Kennedy, Malcolm X, Martin Luther King, and Robert Kennedy, all of whom, he says, had the potential to unite and lead the country out of its despair and confusion, had the country been ready to follow their examples and the forces of the status quo not been so strong. Next he talks about the generation that developed the hydrogen bomb and, as an afterthought, went to the moon, and the generation of its sons and daughters, the young people who were now attempting to develop a new language and a new world view that could transcend the limited world of their parents.

> To a sensitive idealist it is a time of such universal agony, he must pledge his total understanding to alleviate it....The conservative pragmatist sees only the destruction of his values and his society...With these forces separating further and further every day, with men being continually thrown back upon themselves and forced into acting from the depths of what they hold most dear, the time is coming when every individual will be absolutely real, when words and concepts will be unable to mask ulterior motive, when everything will be reduced to exactly what it is, and only then will there be room on earth for entire and true creation.

I never understood what Wayne was talking about in this article. The catchy title sounded like advocacy for revolution as it was then understood, that is either violent or nonviolent thoroughgoing opposition to existing social and political structures. But the article doesn't seem to support this notion, focusing instead on cryptic generalizations about recent European and American history and offering after-the-fact rationalizations for how things had turned out, ignoring the power plays and manipulations that had produced those results. This was not my view of history.

Wayne's concluding reference to Mel's "Declaration of Creation," in which Mel promised to "burn down the world," only confused me more, unless one assumes Mel himself is the great man, the historical force who can polarize society so thoroughly that something truly new will result. I was not convinced.

Mel himself did little to clarify the issue with his latest "Essay on the New Age," which followed Wayne's article. It's a garbled statement about the place of law in governing society, and the moral authority some people have to act outside the law when they perceive a higher necessity.

> These people are on the way to becoming the new legislators of this land, the poles are

shifting....They have conceived of a wiser way to live. So far they have no legislative power, they can only resist. But they have a power far greater than the power to control action, they are invested with the future of the world.

BEING A REAL AMERICAN IS A STAGGERING TASK

Following Wayne's article is an allegorical fable about two animal kings who confront each other annually in a ceremonial war-for-a-day. Next comes the feature interview with Mark and Daria, which is actually the partial transcript of a conversation between them, several members of the community, and a visting Italian journalist who found himself unexpectedly sitting with the American stars of the latest film by one of Italy's most successful and controversial filmmakers. Over many pages of dialogue, little clarity emerges about Antonioni's film or about Mark and Daria; what does come through is that Mark and Daria (who had only been on the Hill for three days at the time of the interview, even though she reports having had powerful dream visions of it in advance) are struggling to integrate their experiences with Antonioni, Mel, and the community. Jessie and Owen seem to be doing a lot of their talking for them, fitting their comments into some prior notion of how it all fits into what is happening on the Hill. The interview ends as Mark is about to tell of a major confrontation with Antonioni during the filming; the continuation is promised in the next issue, the one that never appeared.

(My recollection from Hill gossip is that at a certain point in the months of filming, Mark, feeling compelled to bring Antonioni and Mel together, walked off the set in California and returned to Boston to rejuvenate himself with a hit of Mel. Mel, in effect, ordered him back to the filming—otherwise, all that fame and fortune would go out the window—and Mark reluctantly returned to Antonioni's influence, but never gave up trying to bring Antonioni to Fort Hill to meet a "real" filmmaker and some "real" revolutionaries. That meeting never happened. "Zabriskie Point" opened to tepid reviews; it flopped financially and critically.)

The magazine continues with several articles about current affairs and foreign policy, drawn from diverse sources. The section appears to be an attempt to present the magazine as a serious and balanced commentary on world affairs, despite its highly idiosyncratic character in other articles.

MESSAGES FROM BEYOND

The political articles are followed by several pages of letters to Mel and his responses. In the first letter, Paul Williams—former Cambridge resident, precocious editor of *Crawdaddy* magazine, and long-time friend of Mel and the community—spells out his excitement and joy at Mel's announcement that he is Christ. "I can feel no envy of your greater strength, but only great joy, knowing that you, like me, continue to choose to expand, knowing that any strength you have is my strength & my strength in turn is so much the greater because it can contribute, does contribute, to yours....Jesus, brother, you have my undivided support!" Mel responds, "[Y]our letter is the first real reply to the meat of last issue, 'The Dread Proclamation.' No one knows what it has meant or who was compelled to do it. It is a man who never knows what he will have to do next."

Mel's responses to several other letters emphasize the same point, that greatness and true creativity and spirit are only found when one pushes onself beyond one's own boundaries and capabilities.

The magazine's major feature follows. At long last, Mel and company had chosen to explain and present the "Box Poems" to the world. An introductory essay by Eben Given discusses an experience of the great psychologist Carl Jung, as described in his autobiography. Jung had found himself one day chiseling, into a large piece of stone, a poem he did not compose but that came through him automatically. The voice in the poem is of a disembodied spirit whose perceptions transcend and rise above those of mortals on earth. "It is the voice which he listened for, all ears, throughout a long and discerning life—a voice which became at times the voice, beyond words, beyond images—the voice that speaks when all the meaner voices are momentarily stilled."

He goes on to introduce the thirty Box Poems that appear in this issue:

> Written down in the early 1960s, they are as authorless as the poem at Bollingen [Jung's home at the time of his automatic writing experience]. The phenomenon of their making, which at the time attracted certain scientific minds at Duke University, is still for that factual and over-documented world to discover. To those of us who only attempt to live more closely to the message of the poems themselves, in consciousness of that place from which all whole truths, like great poems, emerge, it would be as silly as attempting to dissect the writings of Mel into vowels and consonants and saying, "Here it is—this is how he does it."

He then explains further how the Box Poems were created, drawn one word at a time from a box into

Sidebar 4: Three Box Poems[1]

No poem is this....a shadow on the page
that could have held his song
if blazing death had not seared down through all
    his bones
to bring his requiem out

I wish I could give glory to this man
but words are like the pebbles on the shore
dead
to the endless living ocean of a soul

Bear witness gates of death
that I have never ceased to knock at doors
I know will never hear

Bear witness
heaven
that my love has been as great as I could bear

and know my love
I sing of you

and always will

* * * * * * *

My face is sheeted with tears

I say
I say
that all my saints have gone

Does any other god have ears for me

or must I
unredeemed
stalk through this world wondering
why men live on and on
and gods die fast

* * * * * * *

Will you never risk me

Not ALL things live in the light
or hang in a silver sky
like a cross

A past age will tell you how beauty was hidden
in a circle of thorns

The origin of the nightbirds song
and nights kisses
and tomorrows snow
ivory bones
revolting thoughts
unsuspected love
and blazing vision
All these strange things are known only in finality

You must dare to live in darkness

NOTE

1.   From *American Avatar* "Fourth cycle, first issue" (Summer 1969): 28-41.

which hundreds of words on little slips of paper had been placed, in a moment of mysterious creativity shared by Eben himself and several of his friends. The poems had subsequently been entrusted to Mel, who, I believe, had done some editing and rearranging to make them come out as literate as they appeared, but this part of the story was not told in the magazine. The poems were presented as though complete from the moment of their creation; they speak in the same otherworldly and spiritual voice as Jung's disembodied poetic source. Many of the images seem to be Christian, that is, concerned with Jesus Christ and his life and its meaning as interpreted down through the ages.

It's easy to see from reading the examples in sidebar 4 why these mysterious poems had won the hearts of Mel and Eben. The poems speak in such a similar voice to theirs, and probably were among their teachers when they were wandering artists during the hectic and unpredictable days before they settled on Fort Hill. Laid out here on many pages of *American Avatar*, printed against photographic backgrounds of stormy and dramatic skies (photographed by Mark Frechette), they were at last being presented to the world in a cogent form. As mysterious and obfuscating as I found the rest of this issue of the magazine, I found the Box Poems a welcome and illuminating counterpoint. I had my own favorite, one that was not included in the magazine, but that Eben had painted in floor-to-ceiling glory on the living room wall in House Number Four. It was another retelling of part of the Christ story, from the mother's point of view. I think it appealed to me not because of the Christian imagery but because it reminded me of my own life story then in the making, and whose motivation neither my mother nor anyone else from my past could figure out.

My son has found truth
somewhere in a sky
that looks like one grey weeping eye to me

I bore him under a blinding star
but he comes from some land not in me

What piercing sorrow not to know
Where your one child must go.

The magazine ends with a "Contemplations" piece by Mel, in which he gives what appears to be the moral of the entire issue:

All that really matters in this life is a man's inner worth, what he still has left when all the chips are down...When a man is alone with himself and all his deeds are behind him what is there left that he can truly call his own. If there is nothing then he is nothing. If there is understanding then he has made good use of his time here.

Life is a struggle for everyone, Mel says, and no one knows how life will unfold as we take one step after another.

FIND A NICHE AND FILL IT

About the time this new magazine was published, a mysterious impulse overtook me, as suggested by Mel's essay. Mine wasn't an impulse to produce a great creative work, exactly, but it was a bold step out for me at the time. Something possessed me to give notice at my job at the architecture firm and become a freelance handyman and carpenter. I was impressed by stories of the long-time Fort Hill men occasionally hiring themselves out around town, and I felt, because of my job, I now had enough skill and personal contacts around town to successfully fill my time with freelance work. In this way, I could both bring home more money for the Hill and possibly create employment for other men from the Hill. All this easily came to pass. I put up a few signs around Cambridge announcing "The American Dream," as the little enterprise became known, and before long I was employing myself and several of the other low-status men from the Hill work crew most days of the week. I had my first-ever conversation about astrology with Joey Goldfarb, who assured me that the Mars-square-Saturn aspect in my chart was perfect for what I was doing, an aspect that would keep a person like me from ever acting boldly unless the action were perfect for the moment in which it occurred. My new venture

seemed a long way from making music or films, but it did seem to give me a purpose and a role that I could play that fit in with what was going on around me.

Haltingly at first, and then with more confidence, I found myself behaving more like a standard-issue male human, with all the accompanying mannerisms and expectations. Finally, the blue collar role seemed to fit. I found myself remembering and identifying with my father, who worked unhappily as a machinist and equipment designer all his life, never feeling he was getting ahead fast enough and always wishing he could in some way be a writer and raconteur instead, and who finally died of injuries incurred in a work accident. I seemed to be re-creating his experience, the last thing he or I ever expected me to do. Some group of us guys—as many as were needed for the day's assignment—would go off in the morning with a car full of tools and materials, and would do whatever sort of work the day demanded of us—painting, carpentry, plumbing, digging and trenching, plastering, demolition, apartment fix-up, you name it. The pleasures of the day were simple: a coffee and doughnut break from time to time, the chance to get to know a new neighborhood, sometimes a conversation with people living in the places we were working. We took pleasure from proving to ourselves that we could credibly accomplish some task we weren't sure we knew how to do. Sometimes tempers would flare, and it would suddenly seem like Fort Hill again, with clashing egos and power struggles. I tried to keep the operation upbeat and simple, but of course sometimes I made planning errors or got us into projects over our heads, and this would elicit challenges from the others. But all of us were focused on bringing home as much money as we could with as little hassle as possible.

I changed homes a few times during that fall and winter period. Carol and I, and then Eric, were living in Mark Frechette's old apartment on Highland Avenue part of the time. We made a weird, bold decision to remove several of the partitions between rooms of the apartment to make a bigger, more flexible space, without asking or telling the landlord, who lived downstairs. We used the resulting pile of scrap wood as firewood to burn in a wood stove we installed, also without his permission. (My mind reels now at the arrogance of this maneuver.) I remember all of us being under stress at the time, such that I found myself hitting and yelling at Carol a few times, another step into the world of male-patterned behavior that I hadn't experienced before. When our landlord figured out the damage we had done to his building, he evicted us, and the three of us moved back onto Fort Avenue, this time into a small rented apartment in Number 23. Carol and I had the only bedroom; Eric's space was a portion of the kitchen/living room. In these cozy quarters, I remember listening for the first dozens of times to the Beatles' "Abbey Road" album, whose enigmatic lyrics somehow came to symbolize for me the whole time period.

Then, for reasons I can't recall, our little household group broke up. Carol moved into Faith's house, Number Two, mirroring Candy's "social climbing" of a year and half earlier; Eric moved into Number 27, which was still undergoing remodeling; and I moved into Number 29, which was only now starting the remodeling process. At last, we were living in buildings owned by the community, a small step toward assimilation. I lived for a period in the top-floor apartment, which had been gutted and now had exposed framing and brick exterior walls, with my bed in the middle. I also lived in the basement apartment and a couple of other places in the building, as the several apartments were disassembled and a single kitchen and living room and numerous bedrooms were carved out of the space. Gradually, a loose family unit came together in the house, which served as an anchor for me during an upsetting time.

I had another encounter with the karma squad during the winter. I was still running a work crew five days a week and working on the Hill houses with everyone else most evenings and weekend days, trying to be a good member of the team. My crew was dependent on an old station wagon I drove, and one Sunday I felt a need to work on the car to keep it running, rather than on my appointed project of the day, which happened to be completing a portion of a decorative picket fence around the Terrace houses, obviously not an essential task. One of the men found me and insisted I work on the fence instead of the car, which I did, resentfully. Later that day, I wrote a note questioning the rigidity of the priorities and left it on the table in one of the Avenue houses, seeking support or feedback from whoever read it.

The next day, several of us went off to work in my station wagon; predictably, the car broke down during the day, and we had to call the Hill to be rescued in order to get home from where we were working. Ian came to collect us in the Jeep pickup and was inexplicably sullen as we rode home. When we arrived on the Hill, he directed us into House Number Five, which was at that time still in a stage of being remodeled for Mel's visionary use, and whose large living room was serving as a community meeting space. Practically everyone on the Hill was there waiting for us, and Richie was at the front of the room ready to pounce on me. I couldn't figure out what was happening until Richie read to the group the note I had written the day before. My former tutoring student from East Lansing had read the note and for reasons I never have figured out turned it over to Richie during the day. He

decided to make it an example of something or other, insubordination, I guess. Now that he had me on display, he wanted me to confront the person who had insisted I work on the fence, but I wasn't even willing to name who it was. To me, his behavior wasn't the problem; the problem was that the work priorities were so inflexible that we were disallowed any initiative even to choose to take care of problems for which we had assumed responsibility, such as my car. It was obvious to me that I was correct, given that the car had in fact broken down that day, but I couldn't frame this thought clearly enough to protest at the time, and I was confused and terrified being put on display that way. I simply froze and could not give Richie and the others what they wanted, any more than I could successfully defend myself. The meeting finally broke up with nothing resolved, but my status in the community was diminished again.

SUSPEND ALL THE RULES

Other incidents happened during those days on the Hill that I also just couldn't accept or rationalize. The abuse of relationships shocked me repeatedly. Couples would be thrown together or ripped apart at the whim of someone with higher standing in the community. Any withdrawal from the main group for the purpose of exploring the possibilities of a relationship was considered a violation, and if this happened to occur in combination with what was perceived as disrespect there would be hell to pay. Children were treated the same way, and were often separated from their parents or disciplined for what seemed specious reasons. I attempted a couple of times to intervene in such situations, and suddenly found all the anger and frustration focused on me. Once, in a moment when Brian Keating's former wife, Pat, was being told to leave the Hill but to leave her two young children behind because they belonged to Mel even if she didn't, I spoke up in her behalf, defending to Jim Kweskin her right to keep her family together. Jim was furious with me, and stood by while one of the other men, who saw himself as the head of our household in Number 29 and who was a great deal larger and stronger than me, punched me hard in the face, giving me a black eye that required medical attention. Pat left the Hill, with her children.

Another time, I happened to speak up in defense of Rita W., the space case who had borne one of Mel's babies (who was being raised by Faith), and who periodically would wander back to the Hill from her sojourns in the larger world. This time, she was showing up homeless and pregnant, and I felt an impulse to offer her space in Number 29. I barely knew her, but I believed she obviously was part of our family, like it or not. No one took my suggestion seriously, and Rita was told repeatedly to leave, that there was no room for her in the condition she was in. After a couple of weeks of this, Jessie finally pronounced that "we have to take care of our own," and Rita was given a space in (of course) Number 29. No one but I saw the irony in this turnabout, but now crazy Rita, and later her new baby, were part of our household.

Jon M. was the central figure in two dramas that horrified me, mainly because he was perceived as being in the right in both incidents. In one case, he reacted to what he saw as disrespectful and separating behavior on the part of one of the women, and he responded by barging in to her room and raping her, and then boasting about it. Another time, he got angry at similarly "disrespectful" and inappropriate behavior on the part of two of the children, two boys about four or five years old, and he beat them up, one of them quite seriously. In both cases, he was not criticized for what he had done; instead, he was praised for following his impulses so uncritically. I found this incredible, and impossible to condone. (I did entertain a fantasy for a time of treating another of the women, with whom I was having a running argument, the same way, but I couldn't bring myself to use force deliberately in that way.)

Equally incredible was the way in which two babies who were born to a particular couple during that period were received. They were the half-sisters of one the boys Jon had beaten, born a year or two apart from each other. Both were born with birth defects, I don't know exactly what, but they involved certain internal organs functioning irregularly and promised that the babies would need extraordinary care for a long time, perhaps permanently. The first baby was tolerated on the Hill, but when the second one was born it emerged as a necessity that both girls be given up for adoption because they were "monsters" and there was not room for them on the Hill. The babies went; the parents stayed.

I was experiencing life as more and more irrational. I was living in an authoritarian hierarchy in which the rules and priorities and power relationships were constantly shifting, and I repeatedly found my values challenged and undermined. All around me, my peers seemed to think everything was just fine, and all we had to do was keep working for Mel. In fact, that's practically all we were allowed to do, so we did. In such an environment, it goes without saying, the work was all that counted. It didn't matter if we had the right tools; it certainly didn't matter if the work was beyond our skills, or was physically risky, or exposed us to chemical fumes or other hazards. Getting it done,

somehow, and winning the attendant approval was the most important thing. We were still finding some of our building materials in abandoned houses around the area, and this opened the way to an amoral view of property ownership in which anything was okay that you could get away with.

One time, I took one of the Hill's vehicles on a lumber run, and the lumber yard personnel almost forgot to charge me for my truck load of goods. I paid, but when I told Richie about this he said I should have run for it. I couldn't quite integrate this attitude, but I did try to do so another time. Several of the other guys and I had borrowed Jim Kweskin's van to go on a "scrounging" run, looking for building materials. We came across a new building site where some large space heaters caught our eyes. The Hill had a major construction project under way at the time, rebuilding the back end of Houses Number Five and Six as part of Mel's grand scheme to create a "Magic Theater" in which to display his various works and put people through transformative changes. At this stage of the work, the crew was laboring inside a two-story plastic enclosure that was very cold and unpleasant to work in. We decided to lift the heaters and some other materials from the site. As we were loading up the truck, being as invisible as we knew how to be, police came along and busted us. Of course, the stolen goods and Jim's truck were confiscated, and we were held in jail until the Hill's lawyer could arrange bail for us. Eventually, after some skillful plea bargaining, charges were dropped against three of us, and the two who had prior records were given light sentences, probably probation. Jim and the other authorities of the Hill lectured us on our transgression, not for attempting to steal things for the Hill but for doing it clumsily and getting caught. Part of our "punishment" was digging a big hole in the driveway near the workshop buildings, in which to bury other stolen materials that were lying around, in the event the police would want to search the place. So much for morality.

By contrast, the face that the Hill presented to the world continued to be unperturbed and self-assured. Now that the magazine was no longer being published, other endeavors were receiving the attention of Mel and his close associates. The story of these endeavors was featured in an article in the *Boston Globe*, Sunday, February 1, 1970, "Fort Hill: Re-inventing Life on a Hilltop in Roxbury." Under a picture of several dozen members of the community sitting on the lawn in front of the tower on the Hill, sternly staring into the camera, the reporter, Robert L. Levey, offers the community's rationale for its treatment of both members and visitors:

The Fort Hill community has a single mind and a single heart....

[T]here is a severe authority structure on the hill. People are divided by function and they are all instruments in a plan for a new way to live that begins and ends with Mel Lyman....

[The] insistence that individuals continue to evolve and change leads to intense confrontations among those on the hill and between them and outsiders who come to visit or observe the community. There is a premium on persons being honest with each other to the point of insult. The motive is to bring people into deeper relationships of trust and common feelings.

My own presence in the community as a reporter was greeted with some suspicion and hostility. I was berated for not having the capacity to participate fully in the Fort Hill experience, for remaining rigid and aloof. I was informed that one member of the community had said of me, "He's so empty I didn't want to sit too close to him because I might fall in." Twice, when I told people it had been good meeting them I was angrily accused of lying.

This impatience with outsiders stems largely from the facts that Fort Hill residents have each gone through a series of intense changes and experiences in their own lives. They harbor massive faith in Mel Lyman and they regard most of the other three billion people in the world as infants who have not proceeded very far [a]long the path of real life.
(Reprinted courtesy of the *Boston Globe*)

The article describes the ceaseless building projects on the Hill and the "standard of perfection," as it was known, to which we were working, as well as the traditional division of labor between men and women, and the devotion by which we were giving, typically, two-thirds or more of our individual incomes to support the Hill's projects. A new project of the Hill is mentioned, as the latest creative work to take the place of the now-defunct magazine. The author seems unaware that the "new" work is really old work recently taken out of the can. The old recording done by Mel and others with Lisa Kindred, during the days when the Jug Band was intact and David Gude was the recording engineer for Vanguard Records, had resurfaced. Jim was offered a new recording contract with Reprise Records, and had asked permission to purchase from Vanguard the rights to the old recording. This was now being released by Reprise, in the only version that still

existed, the one with Mel's harmonica mixed to equal prominence with Lisa's voice, under the title "Love Comes Rolling Down," by the Lyman Family with Lisa Kindred. We on the Hill thought this was a wonderful turn of events, and we had grown quite fond of the music, which even the least of us had heard a number of times, but very few copies were sold. Much later, Lisa Kindred told another reporter she had not been consulted or even informed when the record was being prepared and released.

The *Globe* article ends with a mention of one of the more visible anomalies of Hill life at the time:

Fort Hill people are the first to point out that Mel Lyman's influence on this growing group has parallels with the case of Charles Manson and his "family," the accused mass murderers on the West Coast.

Pictures of Manson, in fact, are in evidence in some of the Fort Hill houses. Jim Kweskin was on the phone recently with an executive of the record company that will be putting out their album and the conversation got around to Manson.

"Sure, we got a lot in common," Kweskin said. "But Charles Manson talked about saving souls and he went around killing people. Mel Lyman talks about destruction and he goes around saving souls."

WE BUY ANOTHER HOUSE

The air of unreality about the record release and the *Globe* article, in the context of increasing irrationality in our daily lives, was pervading everything. The United Illuminating Realty Trust, the holding company that held title to all the buildings the community owned, had finally succeeded in acquiring title to Number Four Fort Avenue Terrace, the original home of the community, which until now had been rented from a disagreeable neighbor lady, toward whom Mel felt an irreconcilable enmity. During the negotiation process, Mel had a dream one night about fighting with Lena, the landlady. In the dream he was hitting Lena on the head; awake the next day, he interpreted this as an instruction to damage the roof of the house, so it would lose its value and she would be more ready to sell. This was done; some of the men drove nails into the roof, and then complained to Lena that the roof was leaking and needed replacing. Or she could sell to the community, cheap. To underscore the point, they removed the top of the chimney. Lena gave in and accepted the offer, one she could hardly refuse, and the house was bought, for something like $4,000 (a typical price for the neighborhood at that time). As soon as we bought the house Mel ordered it vacated and cannibalized for building parts. Before long, the instruction came to destroy the house.

The day this order came down was a special one for me, in a crazy kind of way. Feeling desperate and unable to understand why I couldn't fit in to the community, I had built up my courage and asked for a second acid trip with Mel, hoping again to glimpse some kind of truth that way. I remember the moment of asking for the trip: I let myself timidly into Mel's house and waited quietly in his living room while he finished a conversation in the kitchen with one of the men. They got talking about a mouse that had moved into the kitchen cabinets, and Mel said, "I don't mind a mouse." I was convinced the comment was aimed at me in the next room. But, whatever Mel was thinking, he agreed to arrange a trip for me. Coincidentally (or was it?) Eric had asked for an acid trip at the same time for a similar reason, and the two of us were guided through the experience one Saturday night, not by Mel but by a group of his lieutenants.

I remember sitting in the kitchen of Mel's house during the most intense part of our rush, with Faith and Jessie and some of the others, who were teasing Eric and me about the way in which we never quite seemed to get along but couldn't seem to get away from each other, either. Later in the trip, we were upstairs in the large room we had recently created in the top of Number Five, intended to be Mel's recording studio and transformational journey site. I wandered away from the group for a few minutes, to admire the city skyline through the unusual front windows, which had been reworked by Richie to resemble the cockpit of a giant airplane. David Lanier, known as David Libra, who was nominally our primary guide, came up to me and ordered me back into the group; looking deep into my eyes, he told me he finally understood why I kept myself so aloof from the community all the time. "You're afraid you might kill somebody," he said. It had never occurred to me. Then we were out on the hilltop in the middle of the night, running around the tower at top speed, flying above the ground, it seemed. All in all, a very strange night.

When the rush of the trip finally ended, very early in the morning, I went home to Number 29 to rest up for the coming Sunday work day. When I woke up, still early in the morning, I wandered over to the Terrace houses and encountered Wayne Hansen, who was doing some early morning carpentry work, and toward whom in that moment I felt a brotherly bond that I could not explain, but that feeling of mysterious brotherhood became the overriding emotion of the day for me. Wayne told me that during the night Mel had ordered the demolition of Number Four (did that have

something to do with our acid trip?), and that everyone would be working on that project as soon as the work day began. When everyone else was awake and ready to work, we went at it full throttle. I think most of the house was taken down in that one day, while the women and children played on the hilltop, and numerous strangers came wandering around. It was one of the first warm days of spring, and the hilltop park was full of baby carriages and puppy dogs, moms and dads and kids. The entire event had for me the air of an old-fashioned community celebration.

It happened that I had recently been reading one of Hermann Hesse's lesser novels, *Beneath the Wheel*, in which a socially retarded young German boy finds himself unable to fit into the vibrant life of his peers and his community and eventually dies an ambiguous death in the gutter. Is it accident or suicide? Is it inevitable or was there a choice? I felt on that Sunday as though the close-knit traditional town of the novel had suddenly come to life around me, and was I the misfit boy? I was certainly feeling disoriented, not just on that day but during all those months. A big question kept running in my mind that I couldn't discuss with anyone: Who would be the first person to die for Mel and the community? How would it happen? Would it be a work accident, or a suicide, or the result of a worse-than-usual physical fight? Would it be me? Would I find the strength of character to leave the community and expose its hypocrisies, and would I then be punished for doing so?

A LETTER HOME

A couple of months after the acid trip and house demolition adventure, I was working at a fix-up remodeling project in Brookline with Eric and Danny Oates, who had been one of Candy's and my hosts during our first visit to the Hill more than two years earlier. Two events of note happened during the few days we were on that job. Danny persuaded both Eric and me to try smoking cigarettes, something neither of us had done before. He explained that it could be almost as pleasant a high as marijuana, which we weren't getting too much of in those days and which we missed. (He was lying, of course.) Because smoking was very much the thing to do on the Hill—we were among the very few non-smokers—we gave in to Danny's urgings; for the next several years I smoked Camels, or later roll-your-own Buglers when money was especially tight, about half a pack a day. Smoking helped me feel and act like one of the folks.

The home we were working in was that of a religious but rather disorderly Jewish family. In some ways it reminded me of my family's home, not because we were religious (we were anything but) but because our home had typically been disorderly, and because the Jewishness of the home we were working in made me think of my family. For reasons that are unclear, I attempted to put the mix of my feelings in a letter to my mother. The letter paints a picture of my confused state of mind during the process I was undergoing, which can only properly be called brainwashing.

After describing my experiences in the community and the memories stimulated by my current work situation, the letter goes on to rhapsodize at some length about Mel and his mother, about whom he had written and spoken a lot, about their relationship and the lessons Mel learned from it that he was now teaching to us, and about the experience I was trying to have in his community (see sidebar 5).

THE COLONIAL ERA BEGINS IN EARNEST

It was unusual for me to attempt to put my feelings about my situation in writing. In fact, I hardly remembered how to write anything anymore. Once in a while, a directive would come from somewhere in the inner depths of the Hill, requesting or instructing that all of us write letters to tell Mel how we felt about some creative work he had produced or about our gratitude for his leadership. I would dutifully write such a letter, but doing it would be like dimly remembering something from my distant past. Less frequently, I would feel an impulse such as the one that made me write this letter to my mother, trying to put on paper some of the essence of the experience. But by far the greatest part of my energy was going into staying current with the demands of Hill life; any impulses toward a personal life or individual expression were at best an inconvenience and at worst the excuse someone else might need to humble or discipline me.

Increasingly, "dummies" like myself on the work crew were becoming just the means for Mel and his close associates to achieve more and more elaborate ends. We were no longer the "creation" that in earlier days Mel had said we were; now we were just used to produce work and money, while ever-larger projects were conceived. We were encouraged to find money wherever we could to help with the enormous expenses. During this period, the last of my inheritance from my father finally became available to me, about $2,500, the biggest single chunk of money I had had access to since shortly after his death. Unhesitatingly, I turned it over to the Hill, imagining it contributing to the studio and sleeping loft portion of the "Magic Theater" project, into which I had poured a tremendous amount of work.

Mel decided we needed a more permanent home in New York than the Soho loft that Brian Keating had kept for a couple of years. A nice two-unit brownstone was found on a quiet block of West 15th Street near Seventh Avenue, on the edge of the Chelsea district. First one unit, then the second were rented, and after a while a deal was struck to buy the building, in the name of Owen de Long and with an investment of our collective funds that equaled the total cost of all the houses on Fort Hill. We were moving into the big time, and the need for money was greater than ever. Mel started moving people between the Hill, the Vineyard, and New York—more opportunities to give people just the experiences they could use to grow in the way he thought they needed. The nicest accommodations in each location were reserved and upgraded for Mel's use.

The opportunity to recruit people in new places gave Mel the idea that some of his representatives should travel the country, seeking out souls ready for the Fort Hill experience. He dispatched Owen and a woman named Karen Poland to be the road crew. They traveled all over the country for a number of months, visiting campuses and urban centers, selling *American Avatars* and talking up the Hill and Mel. Eventually, they settled in New Orleans and established a temporary home base there in a rented apartment. Only one person joined the community from all their work, Chris Thein, known as Hercules.

Before much longer, the impulse arose to colonize California, too. I am not able to recall clearly the sequence of events, and of course no one was consulting me about any of it. But Mel's focus was definitely on collecting people and homes everywhere around the country that he felt was worth "saving," as though Mel directing energy toward a place was the only way it would be saved from certain dissolution. Definitely on his list was San Francisco, where he had settled as a very young man first leaving home, where he had met and married Sofie and become acquainted with her large and flamboyant family, where he had discovered himself as a musician. Shortly after initiating the New Orleans experiment, Owen was sent to San Francisco to rent an apartment with a view near Buena Vista Park, and a second home was obtained in the Outer Mission district, with the help of the family of one of the community's mainstays, the ex-husband of one of Sofie's sisters, who also lived on the Hill. A crew was dispatched to Los Angeles, as well, and a large house was rented in Hollywood. Before long, this house was outgrown and a second house was found, and purchased, I believe. Later, the first house was given up when a much larger house, really a mansion on a large plot of land in the Hollywood hills, was found and pur-

Today has been an especially lonely day for me, and I spent most of it wishing I had something solid and comforting in my life to hold onto, but I haven't got that right now, and it seemed like the place to start looking to build that is inside myself and my feelings. I have so much frustration and emptiness in me, years and years of it that I have held onto and almost never been willing to show anyone, that when I get lonely I hardly know how to start telling of it. I don't know what I have to hide, but somehow I've always been a secretive person, and mostly I've learned to ignore my feelings instead of opening up to them and building on the ashes of my pain, as I know I should. But these things always come home, and now I am left with only myself and the same old feelings to work with.

I guess things aren't as bad as I am making them sound. I have friends, of course, when I want them and know how to use them, and I have more work to do, really rewarding work not just drudgery, than I could ever handle, and I live in a house full of women and children who need more of everything, especially love and caring, than I am ever able to give them, and of course nothing is stopping me from growing and being more except my*self*, because that is the way our lives are arranged here—but still there is a loneliness that underlies it all that each person has to learn to overcome, and at that I am just a beginner, and my personal life is really empty.

I worked today in the home of a very religious Jewish family in Brookline, and I listened to old records on the radio all day. In some ways it put me right back 8 or 10 years to when I used to paint our house all alone just because I wanted to see it done, wanted it worse than almost anything else in my life, worse than girlfriends, worse than peace of mind or wisdom or places to go at night—or at least I was able to turn wanting these things into the spirit to do the work, and that kept me going as long as it did. That's the same way we work here, building our home and Melvin's home out of the pain of lacking all the other things we don't have yet. In some ways I am still exactly the same person I was then, only little things have changed, but I don't have an awful lot more wisdom or ease of manner or anything—except that I am surrounded by purpose and when I am empty it can carry me....

Mel had a painful and lonely childhood, but he learned things as a child that enabled him to grow into the most fantastic man alive, because he always had a clear and dependable love and strength to fall back on. A lot of what he has had to do here is to teach us first how to feel that thing coming from someone else and then how to create it and give it back to someone that needs it. Everyone needs it, everyone needs to be cared for, and it's such a simple thing as long as it doesn't get all muddled with misconceptions and as long as you accept that caring exists alongside pain and loneliness....

[T]here's something I've always missed that I'm working on getting now, and it's going to be all right. I'm finally learning to look consciously for the thing I've always thrashed about in agony trying to find, so I guess I'll live and grow after all.

I'm really pretty lucky, anyway. The people I've learned the greatest and deepest lessons from are here on Fort Hill or are connected with the Hill at our houses in New York and Martha's Vineyard. They're not far away, ever, especially if I need them. We are a great big family, and we're as close as each of us is able to make us be. I don't know what I was feeling so down about, in fact. But I'm glad I wrote this anyway, I hope it makes you feel good.

chased. It was by far the most expensive and fanciest property yet added to the increasing holdings.

Mel was moving people around between the various homes at a faster and faster pace, and was doing a lot of traveling himself, getting to know the cities, houses, and people he was now working with in his expanding creation. Also, he was pursuing new creative projects. A strong impulse had overtaken him to reassemble the documents and memories of his childhood and his early career as peripatetic musician, laborer, and spiritual explorer. He was writing to old friends, asking them to return to him letters and other writings he had sent them. He conceived the idea of revisiting the places of his formative years and reacquainting himself with people from his past.

All this activity was leading eventually toward publication of an autobiographical collection of his writings, but that took about a year to manifest. During this time, as well, the opportunity arose to bring his current company of musicians to San Francisco to record a new album to be released under Jim Kweskin's contract with Reprise. A strange musical melange was assembled: Mel and Jim and several other musicians and indispensable groupies from the Hill, along with two of the folk musicians Mel and Jim knew from the Jug Band days, bassist Reed Wasson and dobro player Mayne Smith. Together they recorded an album's worth of music in just a few days, attempting to summarize the range of the best of American popular and folk music. This, too, would take about a year to manifest commercially, but the mood of all of us now scattered around the country was excitement about the new burst of creative energy.

Back on the Hill, of course, we were noticing a severe shortage of personnel and money, as more and more of Mel's favorites were moved out to the other locations, in a time when new people were showing up only occasionally because the community was not doing a great deal of outreach. Mel himself was absent more and more. In fact, his absences also required further sacrifice and investment on our parts. Rather than continuing to spend more and more money on plane fares, he decided after a while that what he needed was a fleet of high-powered vehicles in which to drive from place to place. Over a period of a year or so, the fleet was assembled: a Lincoln Continental limousine, a Mercury cruiser, a Mustang point car, a large Travco motor home, all of these customized and outfitted for Mel's very demanding tastes and needs, all connected with CB radios, all staffed and maintained by Mel's favorite traveling companions. The process of moving him between the various locations became a major undertaking in itself, really a traveling home for a portion of the community, leaving the work responsibilities of the people traveling with him to be taken up by others in their absence.

TOPSY TURVY TIME

When Mel was on the Hill, it was often to rest up and concentrate on his own work. For this, he often preferred to work during the late night hours and sleep during the day. Much was made of the fact that Mel, who despite his strong character and presence was paradoxically increasingly frail and sickly, took hours to wake up each day, gradually descending down to the mundane planes on which the rest of us hang out and then reorienting himself here each day in order to accomplish his rarefied creative work. He was also constantly switching between aspects of his personality, which had differing needs, and dramatically different appearances. He had all his teeth—the "rocks in [his] mouth" that had given him lots of pain and trouble—pulled, and thus developed a very convincing old man persona. In fact, he had long been known as "the old man" by certain of his admirers. But he could put in his false teeth and switch back to his youthful self in minutes. All this changing and adapting, naturally, required lots of support from others, required the most detailed and exactingly maintained accommodations, required lots of privacy and insulation from other people's concerns, because anything was likely to intrude on his attention and break his concentration. And he had a way of homing in on anything that was

out of place in his environment and immediately experiencing it as a problem. I remember, for example, a time when Wayne cut and polished a new piece of glass for the top of Mel's dresser, but he left a small portion of the edge unpolished by mistake. The first time Mel entered the newly redecorated room, he put his hand precisely on that spot on the glass and cut himself; it was often that way.

One creative solution Mel came up with was to have the entire Hill move onto his schedule, so we would all be working when he was working, sleeping when he was sleeping. Beginning late in 1970, all of us who did not have daytime jobs off the Hill moved onto a day-sleeping schedule to match Mel's so the major construction work could be done at night when he was awake. My role in this endeavor was to find a way to make money on this schedule and also to be available as needed to work on the studio, or whatever the current construction project was. I don't remember phasing out the "American Dream" handyman operation but I must have, because during the period of overnight work I got a job as a cab driver with a company in Brookline, driving from late afternoon to midnight, then coming home to do construction work until morning, and sleeping days in Number 29, while the women and kids banged in and out of the house all around me.

I hope Mel got plenty of needed sleep during this time, because I sure didn't. I stayed on this schedule for over five months, as I recall, becoming more and more exhausted and frayed around the edges. Finally, one night, I fell asleep at the wheel of my cab on a side street in Jamaica Plain while heading back to Brookline to take a brief nap at a cab stand (the licensing agreements of the various cities in the area made it unacceptable for me to stop my Brookline cab within the Boston city limits); I crashed at slow speed into a parked car a few blocks from my destination. The manager of the cab company told me repairing the car would cost him everything he had made on me in five months and then some, and he fired me. Once again, I was subjected to a disciplinary talking to from Jim Kweskin and the other men on the Hill, as though I was solely responsible for having willfully cracked up the car. In the aftermath of this, I was given something I had wanted for quite a while: I was allowed to remain on the Hill full time, as a member of the in-house construction crew.

MOVING ON

During this time, one day, I got to wave goodbye to Candy and Carol and several others, who were all driving together to Hollywood to live in the new houses there. Even though I hadn't had cordial relations with either of them in quite a while, and even though both of them had long since become involved with other men of higher standing than I (in fact, Candy was pregnant with Richie's baby at the time), their departure together for a distant home left me feeling somehow uprooted and disconnected. But within a few weeks, it was my turn to be transferred. Eben and Wayne had been in New York for some months, living in the house on 15th Street and working for a range of well-off clients, doing custom carpentry for high wages. Now it was time for Eben to move on (to Hollywood? I don't recall), and Wayne needed new partners. Les Sweetnam and I drove to New York in his little car in May 1971, there to make our fortunes for Mel. I have never been back to Boston since that time.

The first period in New York was exciting and gratifying for me. At last, I felt, I had a respectable role within the community, in an environment where I was fairly certain I could perform adequately. With only a few of us in New York at the time, I also had a nice room in a nice house; it felt quite civilized. And, of course, New York was in a way my hometown. Even though I had never lived in Manhattan before I was familiar with the environment and how to function there. Wayne made Les and me feel welcome as part of his crew, and in no time we were busily working and bringing home the bucks. Quickly, though, the pressure was turned up. We weren't making money fast enough, we needed to be more scintillating conversationalists at home, Mel's rooms in the lower unit of the house needed to be fixed up, et cetera.

I had a chance to share some of my frustrations with one of our clients, an interior decorator for whom Wayne had done lots of work. She sympathized with my plight and offered to buy me a visit to a psychic friend of hers, a tarot reader with an apartment uptown. One day after work, I slipped away to keep my appointment, hoping I would hear something like "You're too good to be hanging around with that gang; here's what you should do instead." But I couldn't bring myself even to mention the community until almost the end of the reading; maybe I was testing the reader on her prescience or something, although she probably knew my story already. When I finally, shyly mentioned my dilemma and my restlessness, she just said, "You're not done with them yet," and I took that as an instruction to go home and try to adjust. When I got home that evening, of course, I was soundly criticized for having gone so far afield looking for a kind of assurance the others believed I shouldn't have been wanting in the first place. Oops.

Within a few months of our arriving, the New York handyman operation was going well enough that more people were moved down from the Hill to take advantage of the profusion of available work and the relatively high wages. Eric was among the new transferees; we were thrown into working together again. Also new in New York was Jeremy, a long-time resident of the Hill from England who seemed to me to be willing to do absolutely anything in the name of spirit and spontaneity. He was currently in the country illegally because an earlier marriage to an American woman had fallen apart. Mel decided it was time for Jeremy to marry another American, and he moved Rachel Brause, my former housemate, back to New York, her hometown, for the purpose. Rachel's parents were led to believe their daughter had finally fallen in love, and a formal wedding was held in the house, in which they participated. Rachel and Jeremy proceeded good-naturedly to live as a couple, a very odd couple; her parents even gave Jeremy a job and hired our crew to paint their apartment.

The house on 15th Street couldn't accommodate everyone, so additional space had to be found. We sublet for the summer a small loft space on West 21st Street, and several of us moved there, living and sleeping and running a shop in the tight quarters, and heading back to the other house for occasional periods of cultural R & R. In addition to working as carpenters and handymen, we also started a second business. One of Mel's long-time friends, a taciturn, reserved inventor and mathematician named John Kostick, had spent a number of years developing designs for unusually strong three-dimensional structures based on principles of multi-directional symmetry. He even held a patent on the basic design, which he called a tetraxi (four axes), and he had developed a vast line of wire sculptures based on the tetraxi and elaborations of it, which he periodically attempted to market under the name "Omniversal Design." His "stars" were everywhere in the houses on Fort Hill.

The unusual characteristic of his designs was that they were simple to make out of ordinary materials, once a person learned the principles of weaving the parts together symmetrically. Suddenly, with an entrepreneurial community of us based in a wealthy district of New York, we (John, too, was living with us in New York) were using our evenings and other "free" time learning to make his sculptures. The shop space on 21st Street was outfitted with acetylene torches for spot-welding the bronze wire we used to make the sculptures, and vats of cupric acid and plastic coating material to clean and preserve the finished products. We would take collections of sculptures out on the streets and sell them to passersby, as in the past we had sold newspapers and magazines.

We also developed furniture designs using the same principles of symmetry, gaining maximum strength from lightweight materials. I remember two specific projects: a warehouse full of storage shelves in New Jersey, that we built from very light lumber in a labor-intensive but material-shy scheme, and, quite the opposite, a heavy, carefully contoured bench made of walnut, to serve as the couch in the living room of a gentleman in Greenwich Village.

When the sublet ran out at the end of the summer, Omniversal Design seemed to be doing well enough to merit some further investment. We found a larger loft on West 18th Street, near Fifth Avenue, with large windows facing the street and a high rear space with a raised floor area that we could readily develop into a two-story living area for five or six of us. We built in a kitchen (my mother donated an extra stove out of her house on Long Island), improved the bathroom, and developed the upstairs area into several bedrooms. The front part became a shop and store for Omniversal Design, and our living room for those rare occasions when we weren't working. We filled it with samples of the furniture possibilities inherent in John's sculpture designs.

SEND OUT A LIFELINE

Meanwhile, back in the house on 15th Street, the New York community was receiving periodic infusions of news and cultural guidance from Mel and Fort Hill central. These infusions included the first of what would become a long series of music tapes prepared by Mel from a growing collection of 78 rpm records that he and Jim Kweskin were assembling in their travels around the country. The record collection was being lovingly preserved and stored in the Hollywood houses. The "Melzak" tapes were conceived as a compendium of the best popular music that had been produced in this country over the decades, carefully selected and sequenced. In choosing pieces for the tapes, Mel was looking for music that seemed to have been produced easily and spontaneously, when the spirit moved through the musicians and singers, without the labored effort of repeated takes and after-the-fact engineering. (The 78 rpm medium, in its simplicity, encouraged this possibility.) It was the same standard Mel used in evaluating his own music, and he was using the tapes to educate us in this principle, as well as to have ever more influence on what we listened to and thought about. The first tapes were of "race music," the black rhythm and blues music that Mel had listened to during his young adulthood, and which gradually evolved into rock and roll. Later tapes moved into numerous other styles, from country and western to swing to World War II-era pop and everything in between.

Tapes of the evolving music for Jim and Mel's new album also came to us from time to time, and finally the finished album itself arrived: "Richard D. Herbruck Presents Jim Kweskin's America, co-starring Mel Lyman and the Lyman Family." On the front of the jacket was a collage by one of the Hill women, composed of some of the community's favorite images of what makes America special: Marilyn Monroe, James Dean, John Kennedy, Gene Autry, Henry Miller, Billie Holiday, Vince Lombardi, Jimmie Rodgers, Lyndon Johnson, Marlon Brando as Stanley Kowalski, Henry Fonda as Tom Joad, et cetera. On the back of the jacket, Richard Herbruck, the ostensible producer of the record, describes the excitement of the recording session and the interaction of the unlikely assemblage of musicians. "All in all it was a magnificent experience, one to never be duplicated....And then we were done. The spirit of this once great country of ours had come and left its mark as minute little tracings on a plastic disc and the second American Revolution was underway." The liner notes also included a little essay from Jim, talking about the astrological sign of Cancer and its deep relationship with the musical history of this country:

My soul was born in Cancer and it was born into the great river of the American Soul, still flowing in deep strains of hope and conquest. That soul was the Freedom that the earliest American dreams of and fought for which was *the freedom to find God in themselves and follow Him*, and it was finally born on earth as the spirit of a nation which would live in men, in Cancer...the sign of the birth of God in Man.

[The American soul has been repeatedly expressed, he says, in great musicians born under the sign of Cancer]...and people who could truly hear them have felt history before it happened.

I am here once again to sing that song for you. And as this album was born in a burst of spirit and recorded simply in three days as it was sung...a new life for the world is bursting forth from the Heart of America.

The soul that is born in Cancer must always find its completion in Aries, when God and man become one. You can read the story of it in *Mirror at the End of the Road* by Mel Lyman. It is the story of life from the moment it doubts itself and receives its first intimations of immortality to the time it becomes God...as it grows from Cancer to Aries. You can hear that story in this album if you will step aside and let your soul listen. I am singing America

to you and it is Mel Lyman. He is the new soul of the world.
Jim Kweskin

You might wonder what he is talking about here. This little essay is an even more generalized, simplified, and romanticized version of American history than any that appeared in *American Avatar*. Are people expected to take this seriously? So much of the album and its liner notes is tongue in cheek, it's hard to know what Jim expected when he wrote this, if he wrote it. The truth is Mel is everywhere in this album; Jim is no more than the vehicle through whom the album became possible. Jim sings every song, but Mel's backup vocals and harmonica are frequently mixed equally with or even stronger than Jim's voice. The selection of music is surely the result of Mel's influence. The album starts on an upbeat note, with Jim singing Gene Autry's part in "Back in the Saddle," and moves through several other country music classics from various time periods, including Woody Guthrie's "Ramblin' Round Your City" and Merle Haggard's "Okie from Muskogee," the recently popular redneck anthem. The arrangements are uplifting and richly textured. The second side begins with a similarly rousing version of "Stealin'," a classic number in the jug band style, but then moves to a long, slow, somber version of the gospel song, "The Old Rugged Cross," and an equally heavy "Dark as a Dungeon," the coalminer's lament by Merle Travis. The album ends with a long, serious choral version of Stephen Foster's "Old Black Joe." Jim and Mel seem to be attempting to take the listener through a journey from simple, happy feelings into a confrontation with the real and the serious. Or something like that.

One Isn't Enough, Let's Have Two Mels

I have always found most of this album very pleasant to listen to, particularly the more upbeat songs. But I've never understood why it seems to take itself so seriously, while at the same time it's packaged in such a weird way. There are even two drawings of "monsters" adjoining the liner notes, credited to Anthony Benton Gude, the then eight-year-old son of Jessie and David. And those weird notes by Richard Herbruck, describing the epiphany of the recording session. Who is Richard Herbruck anyway, and where did he come from to become the producer of this record? The truth is, "Richard Herbruck" was just another manifestation of Mel Lyman, inexplicably using a pseudonym as a joke. Richard Herbruck was in fact the name of one of the men in the community, a rich kid from Ohio who had arrived a few years earlier.

He was known to everyone as Dick Libra, and rarely needed his legal name, which came complete with credit cards and respectability. He happened to look a bit like Mel too, similar coloring and body type. So during the days when Mel was traveling around a lot by airplane, he became Richard Herbruck in order to travel more anonymously. For some reason, it caught on, and he started being Richard more and more of the time. Soon, Richard was developing a public persona of his own.

In the period shortly before the appearance of "Jim Kweskin's America," Richard Herbruck had a brief fling with fame, as well as notoriety, through the efforts of the Hollywood branch of the family. It's a complicated and controversial story, one which I know primarily through published accounts, but it contains a number of familiar elements. In an attempt to gain media influence in the Los Angeles area, Owen de Long had applied for and been hired as program director at KPFK, the listener-supported Pacifica station in L.A. He had no radio experience, but he did have his impressive academic credentials and his self-assured manner. Joey Goldfarb was simultaneously hired as maintenance person at the station, and as part of his conscientious performance had built and provided to the station some shelves on which to store the profusion of recording tapes there. For his part, Owen generously offered to provide to the station broadcast tapes of a series called "History of Rhythm and Blues," ostensibly put together by Richard Herbruck. These were the first "Melzak" tapes that Mel had been producing and distributing to the various homes of the community. (Or maybe they were tapes in the same style produced just for this purpose, I have no way to know.)

For some reason, there was disagreement between the radio station's engineers and Owen over the sound levels at which "Richard's" tapes were put out over the air and, after a couple of disagreeable episodes, Owen simply pulled one of the tapes off the air in the middle of the program and asked listeners over the air to complain to the station about its sloppy engineering. Apparently, this was a signal to community members, who obediently called the station to make the complaint. This in turn precipitated a physical encounter between Owen and a station employee, who claimed he was injured when Owen pushed him against a wall. Owen was fired on the spot. The next day, a large crew from the community showed up at the station to reclaim their shelves and, as indicated by their behavior, to impress the KPFK staff with their seriousness. They did this by blocking all the exits, yielding only when station personnel called the police for assistance, and it was agreed the Fort Hill people would let traffic in and out of the station while they methodically removed their work. The whole episode was then exaggerated and boasted about in a column that "Richard Herbruck" wrote for the *Los Angeles Free Press*, part of a series of columns Mel as "Richard" was evidently writing in the *Free Press* and the *Berkeley Barb* at the time. These columns became controversial among the *Free Press* staff and were discontinued because "Herbruck's" defense of the KPFK episode included threats of further violence.

The facts as presented here are gleaned from two lengthy articles published in the *Free Press* by its long-time editor Art Kunkin, who made it his business in two articles, on July 30 and August 13, 1971, to investigate not only the KPFK episode but also the history and current doings of the community. He describes the commitment to excellence and perfection that he observed when visiting the community's Hollywood houses, and the pleasant interactions he had with the people there, despite their public reputation for violent and erratic behavior. He also includes "Richard Herbruck's" latest and last column for the *Free Press*, which occupies a full page of the paper, bordered by stars, with a tag line, "promises you everything, gives you nothing":

> We should be entering the new world, all the preparations have been made, it has all been written about and everybody wants it, it is so easy to imagine. A world where everybody loves each other and all motion is towards harmony and there is no more war or hate or fear and everybody is together all the time. It is very easy to imagine.
>
> Yet here we sit in a grey and tumbling world out of place and bursting with song! What happened?...Perhaps we didn't want ENOUGH. Perhaps we have settled for too LITTLE. Perhaps what we REALLY wanted had nothing to do with everything we THOUGHT we wanted. Perhaps the new world hasn't really even BEGUN yet!

Et cetera, et cetera. More of the same old diatribe against the pretentiousness and smugness of the New Age as it was emerging at the time. More complaints about the stagnancy of the government and the old institutions. A plea to stop infighting and unite against "the common enemy."

> Get together with your friends, pool your resources, make some money, buy a house, take on some responsibilities, learn to FIGHT for what you believe in, stop doping yourselves up, stop looking for a Utopia, look around you with clear eyes and make some clear decisions, THE ENEMY IS WITHIN! We have to start

a new life here, we cannot live in this dying structure, it will kill us, it has already killed itself. Our only weapon is inner strength, a small group of people with a great deal of determination can transform the world, be the NEW Christians, fight for your life, fight for love, fight for a new world, fight for room to breathe, the Heart of God is a vast darkness that only the brave can know, this is a plea for courage, WE MUST GET TOGETHER AND FIGHT THIS CREEPING DECAY!

So this was "Richard Herbruck's" message for the world of Los Angeles. Sounds a lot like all of Mel's earlier messages for the people of Boston and New York. I didn't read it until many years later—for some reason, the series of articles of which this was a part was not sent to us in New York—but it's easy to imagine such talk landing with a thud in the southern California of the early seventies. In any event, by the time "Richard Herbruck" went public as the "producer" of "Jim Kweskin's America," the entire KPFK-*Free Press* episode was in the past. The little bit of talk about it that reached us in New York focused on the spontaneity and unity of Owen and the rest of the crew as they confronted the wimpiness and low standards of KPFK. We didn't hear much about the violence or the unwillingness to reach any kind of compromise. It was a typical adventure for the community during those days. Some outreach toward the world, often through the media, would be begun with great hopes but often with unspoken ulterior motives, as Owen's "offer" of tapes was really the reason he was at KPFK in the first place, to promote Mel's work there. Then something would go slightly wrong, or the situation would be exploited beyond its tolerance, and the whole thing would come undone. After the fact, the Hill people were always right and strong, and the other people were always weak and misguided. But almost always the effect was that the high hopes would be shattered and the plans for major influence on the world would be disappointed.

Doing It All with Mirrors

By the time the news of the KPFK adventure arrived, such as it was, we in New York were busy with a new project. Mel's autobiographical collection, *Mirror at the End of the Road*, was now published, as Jim had indicated in the liner notes of "Jim Kweskin's America." The community had a distribution contract with Ballantine Books, under which they were placing it in stores but we had the right to sell it as well. We had boxes filled with books and were spending all our available time hawking copies on the streets of New York. Imagine the scene: you're walking down the street in Greenwich Village or Times Square and this young stranger approaches you, neatly dressed and looking sincere, and tries to sell you a book that is the life story of someone you've probably never heard of, who claims to be the savior for our age. It was a difficult selling assignment, but we went ahead with it, day after day when all our other work was done. I remember being on the street on the Upper East Side one day, a trendy part of town. Suddenly, around the corner came, unmistakably, Janis Joplin with two long-legged, bell-bottomed friends. I looked at her and said, "I know who you are." And, just as quickly as it takes to read these words, she fired back, "I know who you are, too," and continued walking. It was the high point of my brief book-selling career. She died a few months later.

Mel's book represented to us at the time the best opportunity yet to present what was special about him to the world. It seemed like the culmination of a long evolution, of which the *Avatars* had been a preliminary phase. The book was an assembly of his personal writings, letters and diary entries, poems, and photographs (as well as drawings by Eben of important scenes for which no photographs existed) of the years of Mel's development from a brash, frustrated young man to the spiritually accomplished person he had been just before the start of the community. Its moods cover an enormous range of emotions and diverse reactions to all kinds of situations, from silly word plays and pornographic complaints about the injustices of life, to sincere love letters and reminiscences, to contemplations about the eternal questions and little odes to his pets and his humble surroundings during difficult times.

It begins with a section called "Diary of a Young Artist" at the end of 1958, when he was first hitting the road to find himself, his marriage to Sofie on hold for the first of many times over the years. He wanders and rambles and suffers, moves his family of Sofie and a growing bunch of kids around the country trying to find some situation that works for them while he is becoming more proficient as a musician, and finds no peace. Then, in a section called "Judy" he lives through a devastating relationship over a couple of years with a young woman student at Brandeis, who eventually returns to her family in the Midwest and leaves him to "live with a broken heart," as he puts it in the dedication of the book. This experience catapults him unwillingly into a spiritual exploration, which is spelled out in the next section, "Dark Night of the Soul." As his musical career was finally taking off and he was making new homes for himself in New York and Cambridge, his longings for a higher understanding kept him restlessly seeking some meaning in life beyond the day to day adventure. Then in the last section, "Dark Night of the Spirit," it finally begins coming together for him, in the form of spiritual and personal strength to fill the emptiness all by himself if necessary, with no expectation of help from the outside or from God or anyone else. The "Contemplations" piece published in one of the *American Avatars*, the one that begins "Loneliness is the sole motivation, the force that keeps man striving after the unattainable," was written during this period. The book ends in mid-1966, with Mel's contemplation on the death by motorcycle accident—or was it suicide?—of his friend, folksinger and novelist Richard Fariña, and just before Mel and the people closest to him decided to throw in their fortunes together and move into the first house on Fort Hill. The epilogue is a playful letter to Eben, written as the book was being assembled, recalling the fun they had in their old days, of struggling unconscious with the big questions and the adventure of it all.

MORE DEMANDS, MORE OPPORTUNITIES TO GROW

About the time Mel's book and Jim's record finally made it out into the world (to resounding critical silence and sluggish sales), while we in New York were struggling to make money by any means we could—when we weren't assembling "stars" to sell or hawking books or remodeling one of our houses—a couple of events occurred to make life even more complicated for the entire bi-coastal community of us. With more and more of his people moving to the West Coast, and with his creative projects increasingly centered in the Hollywood mansion, but with the roots of the community still based in Boston and a large crew of us in New York, Mel decided that keeping in touch with all of us spread all over the place was taking too much of his time, with too long a drive between homes. The solution? Get a place in the middle of the country and move some people *there*; that way it would only take half as long to get "home" when he was on the road. Besides, he had had a fantasy for a while of a country place where his citified followers could learn to get back to basics. He and some of the others looked at a map of the country, drew lines between Boston, Los Angeles, San Francisco, and New York, and decided to find land where the lines crossed, very near the geographical center of the 48 contiguous states, in northeastern Kansas. Coincidentally, the metropolis of northeastern Kansas and the surrounding area was Kansas City, winter home of Tom Benton, Jessie's famous father. Mel dispatched David Gude to Kansas to search for land there. Tom Benton offered to help fund the project, maybe in hopes of having some of his pet hippies closer to home more of the time. Before long, David had found the perfect place, 280 acres of rolling farmland with a big old farmhouse and a broken-down but serviceable barn and other outbuildings, in the economically depressed Flint Hills area of Kansas. Now it was time to fill the place up with people and bring it to life.

At about the same time, the community was contacted by a writer from *Rolling Stone* magazine, David Felton, who wanted to do a major feature on the community. Over a period of several months, which happened to coincide with the media coverage of the KPFK incident and the purchase of the Kansas farm, he visited most of the community's homes around the country (but not New York). Somehow, he ingratiated himself to the Fort Hill people he met, sufficiently so that they shared lots of their time and information with him, expecting him to produce an article generally favorable to the Hill and its view of its role in the world. He even got to interview Mel privately at the Hollywood house.

During the period when Felton was traveling in Fort Hill circles, *Rolling Stone* published an article on another large community based in Berkeley and Oakland, which had some similarities to Fort Hill. Led by a salesman-turned-guru, Victor Baranco, the More House group offered quick, materialistic solutions to personal problems, encouraging its followers to set themselves up as paid teachers of the methods used, sort of an early version of spiritual network marketing; unlike Fort Hill it also offered its adherents lots of opportunities for sexual exploration and other hedonistic pleasures. Reading and hearing about the More Houses intrigued Mel and some of the others, and Faith Gude, who was living in the San Francisco apartment at the time, was dispatched to Oakland to meet Victor Baranco and establish friendly relations with his community, if that seemed appropriate. Faith reported back that the extensive remodeling work of the More Houses fell far short of the standards to which we were working, and that the level of interpersonal confrontation and growth was also deficient by comparison. But one of the methods used in the More Houses to keep people focused on each other and their collective responsibilities fascinated Faith, and she brought it back and taught it to people in each of the Fort Hill communities around the country. It was a structured game in which people would sit in a circle and take turns being in a "hot seat," where each one in turn would get to hear criticisms and receive praises from the others. I don't remember what this was called, or what the ostensible purpose was (and I know that in the context of our overstressed and overexamined lives, out of the context of the superficial and ego-gratifying lifestyle of the More Houses, it seemed trivial) but I do remember that, for a period of a couple months during that fall of 1971 when I was in New York, we played the game frequently, several nights a week, adding one more burden to our already very full schedules.

ON THE COVER OF THE *ROLLING STONE*

Mel got his picture on the cover of the *Rolling Stone* on the issue dated December 23, 1971. Under the headline "The Lyman Family's Holy Siege of America," for twenty pages of the magazine David Felton juxtaposed the community's glowing reports and hyperbolic claims about its greatness with interviews of people who had been burned or disappointed by Mel over the years, or who had memories of a time when Mel was just another explorer on the path, before he claimed his divinity so flamboyantly. Highlights of his article included:

- an interview with writer Kay Boyle, mother of Faith Gude and Ian Franckenstein, who was persuaded on two occasions to attempt living at Fort Hill, but found herself locked inextricably in a battle of wills with Mel and David Gude;

- a detailed story from several non-Hill veterans of the founding of *Avatar* and the faction fighting that plagued it from the beginning;

- some stories of the Hill's often violent confrontations with media people who had tried to report on the community, or with whom the community had tried to build alliances;

- the story, witnessed by Felton himself when on Fort Hill, of the persecution of a "dummie" on the work crew who was trying to decide whether or not to leave the community; and

- stories of several other people's departures under pressure from the Hill, and of the mysterious "vault" that had been rumored (correctly) to exist in the basement under one of the houses, where people due for a punishment were occasionally held in solitary confinement while they reformed themselves.

All in all, it was a detailed, well-researched, beautifully written, and less than flattering portrait of the life of the community. It was a big disappointment to the Hill, and this was only half the story. A second installment was due two weeks later. A chill went through the community; what stories would David Felton reveal next time?

The second installment again took twenty magazine pages to tell. This time, Felton was much more personal and also more explicitly critical of the community in the stories he told:

- his visit to the community's compound on Martha's Vineyard;

- his attempt to make sense of something he had witnessed on Fort Hill in Boston, the sudden decision to disassemble the addition to the houses in which Mel's "Magic Theater" was to have been housed;

- his version of Mark Frechette's brief career in films and how it intertwined with Mel's decision to colonize Hollywood;

- his story from Kay Boyle of how the community had attempted forcefully to take over her house in San Francisco, and how she had outsmarted them;

- his attempt to ferret out the truth about the community's relations with Reprise Records and Ballantine Books, and with KPFK;

- his visits with George Peper to Mel's father and his former schoolteacher, in northern California, and the fight George had picked with him about questions Felton had asked them;

- his very own visit from the "karma squad" at the *Rolling Stone* offices, where they threatened to pull out of the interview project if the reporter didn't become more real and personal; and, finally,

- his early morning visit, dinnertime at the big house in Hollywood, in which he had his long-awaited private audience with Mel, finding him both surprisingly accessible and predictably mysterious and off-putting, and in which he heard about Mel's exchange of letters with the imprisoned Charles Manson.

The overall impression given by the article is of a somewhat mad, incestuous conspiracy, a little dangerous to outsiders and inexplicable even to its own participants. Rather surreal, you could say. It even contained a full-page paid advertisement for the new record and book, headlined "Mel Lyman Is the Soul of America."

Reading the articles from within the suppressed confusion of my life in the New York community was, for me, definitely surrealistic. I wanted to feel loyalty to the community and therefore outrage at what Felton had done, but in truth I felt a lot of respect for his investigative reporting and the skillful, seamless way in which he had woven together the complex story. (*Rolling Stone* later reissued its coverage of the Mel Lyman, Victor Baranco, and Charles Manson "families" in book form, under the name *Mindfuckers* [Straight Arrow Books, San Francisco, CA, 1972, Library of Congress number 72-79032].) I was as mystified as Felton was about the demolition of the Magic Theater and the sudden shift it seemed to represent in the community's priorities, which had not been explained to us at all. And I was kept busy, to say the least, and always on the edge of burnout by the heavy demands on our time and energy. I kept my feelings to myself and continued trying to do what was expected of me.

But it was weird to feel so alone, while surrounded by my supposed friends. At one time, about 15 of us were living between the loft and the brownstone house. Many were men I had known and worked with for several years, my peers. Some were people I had learned to admire and was pleased to be with up close. Others represented continual difficulty for me. Sofie had moved to New York and in her characteristic way, part Third World bumpkin and part jaded sophisticate, had become queen of the place. I had long been fascinated by her and welcomed the chance to connect with her, but even after we found ways to talk with each other she was suspicious of me and frequently accused me of being "asleep" to the important things. Brian Keating was there with us, now completely out of his role as a writer and newspaper editor and instead directing, or you might say dictating, some of our work energies in a high-tech painting enterprise, for which he bought us airless spray equipment. On the other hand, I enjoyed the company of several of my male co-workers and several of the women who had transferred down from Boston, with whom I felt more equal. At a certain point, Les Sweetnam, the companion with whom I had moved to New York, staged a carefully planned runaway from the community, aided by one of his construction clients, a family of well-known rock and roll musicians who simply didn't understand why he was sacrificing himself as he was. The priorities were, as always, mysterious to me.

As usual, there wasn't enough of anything to go around. We had one van to use for all of us, including all the larger-scale pick-up and delivery needs of the construction and handyman business about half of us were running. Most of the time, we would travel to our jobs on subways and buses, carrying all our tools and materials with us. We would go off in the morning with just carfare and minimum food money in our pockets, often carrying a lunch of peanut butter sandwiches with us.

The financial needs of the community had grown so great there was simply no room in the budget for personal expenses or luxuries (unless they were somehow part of some scheme mandated from above), and everything we did was milked for cash at the earliest possible moment. There were even times when customers would front us advance money to buy materials for specific projects, and that money would make a mortgage payment or be sent back to Boston to be used for some overriding need of the community, such as a land payment in Kansas or a down payment on some piece of equipment Mel wanted to buy, and then we would have to arrange other work to make some new money to replace the advance so we could get back on schedule with the original job—all this without telling our customer what was happening, making excuses as necessary.

As in all the other Fort Hill homes around the country, periodically Mel and his entourage would come through and everything would be turned upside down for a time. Work schedules would instantly be revised or reduced so we could be on call to do special projects around the house; there might be screenings of Mel's latest bits of film work or a chance to listen to some of his music. The living room of the lower flat of the house had been outfitted as a small theater for this purpose. I used to call the preparations in advance of such visits "painting the roses red," in reference to the ridiculous behavior of the characters in Alice in Wonderland, but no one else seemed to get the joke, or to see the ludicrousness of these last-minute attempts to make things into something they were not. The crew traveling with Mel would use their visit to check out how things were among the locals and make adjustments as needed. Thus, the visits took on a fearsome aspect alongside their inevitable celebratory quality. On one such occasion, I inadvertently blew it one more time, and everything came crashing down again for me.

Late one night during a visit from Mel and the traveling crew, I was invited to join in a round of Mel's favorite card game, a variation of pinochle he had invented that he called—what else?—"Melvin." Group members had been playing The Game of Melvin at Fort Hill and around the country wherever he was for a number of months, and it was considered an elegantly simple way to practice the principles of cooperation and attentiveness, or something like that. We in New York had had very little chance to learn the subtleties of the game, and I felt honored to be sitting around the kitchen table in the 15th Street house with just Mel and two others. Things went along well enough for a while, although Mel did seem to be winning most of the hands somehow. Then I found myself with a hand that begged to be played as a winner; it seemed that not doing so would have been an error. So I did just that and won the hand, at which signal Mel threw down his cards and stormed out of the room, back to his private quarters downstairs. I didn't know what had happened, but suddenly I was being confronted by all the men who were present who had higher status than me; they were telling me I still hadn't learned anything from Mel and living in the community, that I was still trying to compete and win, letting my ego get in the way. I guess the message was that one was supposed to recognize that one *could* compete if one wanted to, and then back off and let someone else win instead, especially if there happened to be a World Savior present. I never have figured it out, and in an environment of almost continual competitiveness it didn't make any sense to me. In any case, I was being given a choice: I could accept demotion to the lowest position available in New York—living in the basement of the house, working all the time, no pleasures, et cetera, until I had redeemed myself, or I could leave the community immediately. As I considered the choices, I felt a physical rush up my spine, something I hadn't felt in years, and said I was ready to leave.

HIT THE ROAD AGAIN, JACK

Within an hour or so, well after midnight, I was out of there, walking to midtown Manhattan to hitchhike out of town. I decided on the spur of the moment to head for East Lansing, where I expected I still had some friends, where I hadn't been for four years, and where I believed, incorrectly, I still had a box of treasured goods in storage in someone's basement. I was, needless to say, quite disoriented and despondent.

I made it to East Lansing by the next afternoon, barely more than driving time, and started walking around town, assuming I would run into someone I knew before long. I did, indeed, find friends almost immediately, and before long I was installed as a stay-as-long-as-you-like guest in the home of two long-time friends. It was April 1972, and I thought it was the beginning of the rest of my life. I still have a letter I wrote to my mother shortly after I arrived in East Lansing, telling her the truth of why I had quickly canceled a plan to have dinner with her and my brother. Apparently I had asked for that meeting in order to press them to "invest" in Fort Hill's anticipated purchase of the house next door to the existing one in New York. In my letter I tell the story of my demotion and justify my sudden move ("This really seems like the right thing for now, even though my heart still belongs to Fort Hill and to Mel if he can ever use it again") and give the details of the investment request, which I say "would be about the kindest thing you could do for me, and for everyone in the New York community." That old fidelity dies hard.

After a few days of getting used to where I was and paying for my friends' hospitality by painting their kitchen for them, I started looking for work. I was quickly hired onto a crew that was framing a bunch of houses in Lansing, and borrowed money to buy a hammer and tape measure, the minimum tools I needed. Then came a phone call from my old friend and nemesis Eric, in New York, who had figured out where I probably was and had found me on the first attempt. He was authorized to invite me back to New York to get myself together and get ready to move to the community's farm in Kansas. Was I interested? It was another of those moments. If I had been just a little bit more established in East Lansing, or if I had achieved just a little more understanding of the psychic dilemma I had been in for years, I might have turned him down. But I did not. I immediately accepted and headed for the highway again. Back in New York, I got help from my family; my brother hired me to do some carpentry work to make traveling money, and my mother gave me an old car she no longer needed, a roadworthy Chevy sedan. I felt grateful for the chance to take "basic training" at the farm, to have an identity again. I spent a week or two getting ready, and then left for Kansas along with crazy Rita, Mel's former lady who had lived in my house on Fort Hill. Considering the unlikely twosome we made, the trip was relatively uneventful, and our reception at the farm was warm.

I remember clearly the all-American hominess of my first few days there, which made me believe, at last, the community had found a place where I could be comfortable and valued. Curiously, I have no memory of Rita after we arrived at the farm. My guess is she must have stayed only long enough to hitch a ride to one of the other "homes"; certainly she was not cut out for living in a place where one had to attend daily to the physical necessities of life.

I felt good being received into the comparatively low-pressure environment of rural Kansas, albeit Fort Hill's version of that. The few people at the farm were all familiar to me, to one degree or another, and the necessities of the moment were relatively achievable: make a home in this new place, employing simple, old-fashioned technologies as much as possible (for example, we removed an electric range from the kitchen and installed a big wood-burning cook stove; the neighbors thought we were crazy), get to know the locals, and,

in general, keep things simple. That was the point of "basic training" and it was okay with me. Wayne Hansen was there, once again acting as my guide into a new home, and we had plenty of work to do around the place. There were animals to take care of, old farm equipment to wrangle with, a big vegetable garden that the women tended, and large fields we were considering using to grow cash crops, imitating the locals. On one hand, it seemed more "real" than the concerns that had preoccupied us in Boston and New York; on the other hand, it was all kind of a sandbox situation, with no real necessities driving us to do one thing or another. Comparatively a lot of freedom.

A SIMPLER LANGUAGE

The farm had been purchased from a long-time local farmer, who owned several places in the immediate area, but who, like everyone else in the region, had come upon hard times and had put his prize place on the market. He still lived and worked in the area with his family, and, in his folksy, uneducated way and with his very limited understanding of what we were up to, gave us plenty of support and help. Through him, we met other neighbors and townspeople. We were accepted readily enough, even though our worldly ways and cross-country traveling and mysterious stories of the larger community that we were a part of must have seemed very weird and puzzling. But we were attempting to blend in as best we could, which involved learning to be interested in the things rural Kansans were interested in, trading favors when possible, and learning to speak a simpler kind of language. We learned to tend (and bully) the farm animals, to drive tractors and flat-bed trucks, to run chainsaws and baling machines, to repair barbed wire fences. We became familiar with the local landscape and some of the local history.

Much of the area had been slated to be flooded by an Army Corps of Engineers dam, and several nearby villages had been vacated and demolished, but the dam had been defective and was never filled completely, so some of the land was spared. Still, the local economy was severely damaged, both by the dislocation and by the general downturn in farm income. The county road that bisected our place came across a new bridge the Corps of Engineers had built over a small creek near our house, marking what would have been the edge of the lake if the dam had been filled. Many farms had been abandoned or had changed hands recently; some people were amassing more property and others were making do with less. It was a strange and surprising time for a flock of newcomers to arrive in the area.

I especially appreciated the chance to learn more about speaking American and acting like a down-home kind of guy. The years in Boston and New York had gone a long way toward cultivating an anti-intellectual attitude in me, but had not been very successful in replacing my former appreciation for the intellect and for precise language with something else more functional. Learning to imitate and converse with our neighbors in Kansas gave me an opportunity to do that and, surprising as it may seem, this served me well at the time and ever since. I found out that most ideas can be broken down into simple, everyday thoughts and expressed as such, and that most relationships of ideas or mechanical processes, no matter how complex, can be translated into everyday images and familiar ideas. This makes them much easier to communicate, especially if there is humor in the mix. (Later I also learned that even deep and subtle feelings can be named simply and discussed matter-of-factly, but that lesson didn't come easily or quickly for me, even at the farm.)

I appreciated working with Wayne and the others on the huge variety of maintenance and fix-up tasks we confronted, and also enjoyed a period of several months working for one of the local carpenter-builders, as his helper and sidekick. And I enjoyed the couple of women at the farm, who tended the garden and the children, and were enthusiastically learning the old skills and cultivating relations with the neighbors. But before long, the idyllic nature of this respite was put under pressure reminiscent of the burdens that all the urban communities were constantly under. Periodically we would receive a new "Melzak" tape or other communication to keep us feeling connected to the larger community we were a part of, and that was nice for us. But sometimes there would also come a directive to do something or other, that would seem to come out of the blue and just make our lives harder. Mel needs his own bedroom and bathroom at the farm; find a way to build what's needed and make space for him. Figure out some way to provide more bunk space for people to come visit. Build an outhouse and use it, instead of the indoor plumbing. Take out the telephone, learn to live more like they did in the old days. Fix one of our women up with a local bachelor farmer; maybe he'll do us more favors that way.

These kinds of directives had been hard enough to take in the city. In the country, where practicality is king, they seemed completely irrational and out of context. The result was similar to what it was in the city when people overloaded; periodically someone would up and leave, usually during or just after one of the occasional visits we received from Mel and his traveling entourage. The couple who had been the first to move out from Boston to help populate the place shortly after it was purchased took hard the first visit

from Mel and company that occurred after my arrival. Instead of welcoming the visitors and their many suggestions for how life could be improved, Neil and Judy just drew inward, resenting what they perceived as criticism. I remember George Peper complaining that Neil was lurking around like a surly farmhand instead of acting like the gracious host he was expected to be. On that visit, Sofie was being deposited at the farm to become mistress of the place, and it was a good thing, because a few days after the traveling crew left Neil and Judy were gone, too, taking Judy's young son and everything they could pack in their car. Wayne also walked away from the farm, either during that visit or the next one. Somehow the comments and suggestions from the traveling crew made him feel inadequate to the task and in some way disloyal to Mel; I felt loyal to Wayne and offered to accompany him in an expression of solidarity, but he wouldn't have me. He soon returned to the community via Hollywood.

Wayne's "replacement" as man-in-charge at the farm was a young, overconfident newcomer to the community from Boston known as Mike Aries. Mike Aries was one of those people Mel and friends loved because they wouldn't stop at anything, certainly would never let abstract thoughts or moral compunctions keep them from acting. Before long, Mike and Sofie were having an affair; I was enlisted to perform a "marriage" ceremony for them. Mike did his best to direct activities at the farm, to be the "man" around the place, but he was little more than a boy and was overly impressed by property and power. We instinctively disliked each other, and even competed for the name we shared. I lost, of course. Sofie asked me what other name I would like to use; I combined "Mike" with my middle name, Jay, and came up with "Jake," which became my name for the duration of my time at the farm.

A couple of newcomers joined the community in Kansas. A freelance journalist based in Kansas City, Dick Russell, read about us somewhere and made it his business to connect. He came visiting as frequently as he could, eventually met Mel, and was quickly encouraged to visit the other communities and generally become one of the insiders. Dick also brought along a sometime lover of his, Carol Burger, whom Sofie dubbed Carolee, who took to the place immediately, and soon moved in, with her two school-age sons. She quickly became involved with David Wilson (not the same David Wilson who worked on the earliest *Avatar*), who I considered a friend from my earliest days around the *Avatar* office, and who had recently been transferred out from the Boston work crew. When their brief affair was over, David moved into a side room in the barn, leaving Carolee free to receive flirtatious attentions from me, just in time for Christmas. We exchanged romantic gifts (I made her a hand-drawn horoscope, superimposed over a copy of a painting that resembled the local landscape in winter), and a day or two later spent the night together. It was the first time in over three years I had slept with someone, since I had broken up with Carol, and I could hardly believe it was happening.

The very next day, a car arrived on its way from Boston to Hollywood. Two of the men were moving out there and were bringing three of the little girls from Fort Hill to live with us. Sofie had to figure out the new accommodations, and announced to Carolee and me that we were moving in together. What a surprise! A couple of weeks later, we were given the job of caring for the growing number of children at the farm. To do the job, we were moved to a small house a few miles away, another one owned by the same local farmer who had sold us our farm. The arrangement was hell on a new and fragile relationship. Fortunately, it was only temporary, while David and Mike and I struggled to build a new bunkhouse on the hillside above our main farmhouse, that would serve as a children's house when no guests were present.

This disorienting arrangement was how we were living when Mel and his traveling crew came visiting again in January, with snow and ice on the ground. We all collected at the main house to have a welcoming breakfast, but Sofie was nervous that she didn't have enough maple syrup to serve with Mel's pancakes. For his part, David was nervous about seeing Mel and company at all, and volunteered to drive into town to get more syrup. He took the Toyota landcruiser that was our most reliable vehicle. But David was our least reliable driver; he didn't even have a license. He finally returned a couple of hours later, delivered by a neighbor. He had skidded on the icy road and rolled the landcruiser, landing on its roof in a ditch. All for a bottle of maple syrup in a snowstorm. David was okay but the landcruiser was quite severely damaged, and was not insured because we had been so cash-poor trying to keep up with all the other demands on our time and money. Mel's response, delivered at the breakfast table where there was in fact no shortage of syrup or anything else, was to chastise us for not placing priority on finding the money for insurance. It was another moment when I wish I had had the clarity to say the obvious: "If you hadn't placed such unreasonable demands on us, if Sofie wasn't so afraid of not pleasing you, if David wasn't so afraid of facing you, none of this would have happened, and now all you can say is that we should have insured ourselves against the loss." I didn't say a word, but my respect and appreciation for Mel's "gifts" of leadership and guidance fell still further. A few days after Mel's visit ended, while the same snow was still on the ground,

we woke up one morning to find that David had run away during the night.

It was the beginning of the end for me. Mike and I labored on to finish the new bunkhouse, working with lumber milled by a neighbor from a beech tree we had felled. We were also finishing a new bathroom for Mel's use, tucked under the eaves of the farmhouse, with a secret storage closet hidden behind the wood-paneled walls. (We had fantasies of developing a "cash crop" out of the volunteer marijuana that grew everywhere in that area, the after-effects of widespread cultivation of hemp during World War II.) Carolee and I gamely tried to act like appropriate caretakers for the flock of children in our care, but we both felt like we were in over our heads and had no time at all to explore our own relationship with each other. Sofie was being her imperious self, which by now I recognized as the personality she assumed when she felt inadequate to the role she had taken on. My best friend through this period was Dick Russell, who was splitting his time between Kansas City and the farm, and who somehow seemed able to reconcile the distance between using his mind as a working tool and otherwise operating by instinct and conviction, as Mel and company always urged us to do. I was envious of his working life as a freelance writer, and depended on him for some perspective on events at the farm.

Another visit from Mel and the road crew occurred around the time of spring equinox. The bunkhouse and Mel's new bathroom were finished just in time to be put to use. The bunkhouse was a success, and the bathroom would have been, too, if I hadn't made an error in the plumbing that prevented the drains from working properly. Uh-oh. Again, it was no excuse that I had been working under so much pressure; I should have asked all the local tradespeople what I needed to know to get it done right. As usual, the visit was the occasion to move someone new to the farm. This time it was Jeremy, the Englishman who had been with us in New York, where we staged a wedding for him in order to keep him in the country legally; now he was to have what Mel called his "American period." Jeremy and I, who had been friends for years in both Boston and New York, didn't get along at all this time. He was very committed to being an agent of positive change at the farm, and he and Mike and Sofie were gearing up to take whatever steps were necessary to make that happen.

A HISTORY LESSON

As soon as the traveling crew left, and Carolee and I reoccupied the bunkhouse with all the kids, Jeremy started questioning whether Carolee's two sons really belonged at the farm. Somehow they didn't fit in with the others; maybe they should go back to the city and live with their father. No one asked me what I thought, and I know Carolee was upset at the question being asked at all, but within a few hours, literally, the boys were gone from the farm, collected by their father's new wife, who drove up to get them as soon as she heard they were no longer welcome with us. I didn't understand this at all, and Carolee could hardly talk about it. Neither of us protested as the boys drove away; when they were gone, Carolee hid out in the bunkhouse. Then, as though nothing had happened, Jeremy made a weird request to me: could I give a little talk on American history after dinner that night to those of us who remained at the farm? It's easy now to see that this was a set-up, but at the time I just tried to do what I was asked.

Almost as soon as I began speaking, Jeremy interrupted me: why don't I say something "real," why was I just talking about all this abstract stuff? "But, Jeremy, you asked me to talk about this." That's not the point; why was I such a wimp (or whatever word was used at the time to convey that idea; "pissant," pronounced "piss-ant," was a popular one)? When was I finally going to get out of my head and start feeling? As always when confronted by this kind of attack, I didn't know what to say or do, and froze. Sofie stepped in, with a large kitchen knife in hand, and suggested that maybe it would be sufficient to elicit some reaction from me. I could hardly believe this was happening. What was she willing to do with that knife? I didn't get to find out because Jeremy came up with a new idea: what was my most precious possession? I answered that probably my copy of the *I Ching* was it. He told me to go up to the bunkhouse and get it. I did so, assuming we were going to refer to the oracle to help us out of this difficult moment, as all of us had used it many times before.

Jeremy had something else in mind. He started tearing pages out of the book. When I moved to stop him, Mike held my arms down to the table. This was not rational, of course, even in their terms. If they were trying to elicit a reaction, why stop me when I react? It made no sense. But Jeremy proceeded to destroy the book, and then he and Mike invited me down to the basement for some more discussion. Carolee ran into the living room crying, and that was the last time I saw her. In the basement, Jeremy and Mike aggressively started asking me again what it would take for me to get out of my head. They started hitting on me, and asked me what did I like and dislike? For some reason, I could only think of complaining about having to wear eyeglasses all the time, that I found them really frustrating. Jeremy suggested I just get rid of them, and I did, throwing them on the floor and breaking

them. But this was not enough to prove my conversion. They hit me some more, giving me a black eye and otherwise hurting me around the face. Then Jeremy made me look into a mirror and ordered me to "Look at what all your thinking has gotten you." My thinking? As though his fist had had nothing to do with it. He and Mike ordered me to go out to the outhouse and spend the night there, contemplating what had just happened.

I sat in the outhouse, conveniently located facing the creek near the small bridge where the county road crossed onto our property. After a short time, a voice in my head, a clear still voice speaking up for the first time in what seemed like ages, started saying, "These people want to kill me. These people want to kill me, and I'd better get out of here." As I listened to this voice, it made more and more sense to me. Here I was, at the edge of the property; all I'd have to do is slip down toward the creekbed, and it would be an easy matter to get away without being seen. But I had just broken my glasses, my wallet with ID and money were up in the bunkhouse, and I was wearing completely inappropriate clothing, including my painful, oversized cowboy boots. But it was now or never. I quietly left the outhouse and walked up the creekbed, looking back only enough to see that I wasn't being followed. I walked the several miles out to the small house owned where Carolee and I had lived briefly. I knew how to get into the basement storage room there, where there was a sleeping bag that belonged to Dick Russell and an old leather jacket that belonged to Dick Libra, the "real" Richard Herbruck. I took them both and continued walking, until I found a barn close to where the county road met the state highway, and spent the night there. I was amazed I had gotten this far without being intercepted. Was making me run away what they had in mind all along? In any case, I was gone now. The morning would be March 24, 1973, Mel Lyman's 35th birthday, and the first day of the rest of my life.

WHAT NEXT?

In the morning, I began walking south along the state highway, which would eventually take me to the interstate that ran across the state from Kansas City in the east to the Colorado border in the west. I wasn't at all sure where I was headed or what I wanted. In fact, I wasn't even sure who I wanted to be. I knew "Jake the plumber" was a thing of the past, and there was nothing on me to identify who I was or how I had gotten where I was, with my face all beat up again. I found a broken-down outbuilding on a farm alongside the road and sat down inside it to contemplate my future, if I even wanted a future. Maybe I would just sit there and die. I still wasn't sure that at any moment someone from the farm wouldn't find me and drag me home, but they did not. If I was on my own, did I want to become Michael again, or become someone new? Did I want to reconnect with people from my past, or start over? Did I want to live at all? I tried to sort it out, but couldn't.

Again, the voice inside gave me guidance: of course I wanted to be myself again; losing track of that had been the problem. But how? Somehow, I decided it would be acceptable to start out by dropping in on Dick Russell in Kansas City. I went back to the road and was immediately offered a ride by a kind gentleman, a minister from one of the nearby towns who offered me a few dollars and a small pocket bible that was his treasured possession. I had no use for a bible, but thought his gesture extraordinarily kind. I refused to tell him where I had come from or why I was in the shape I was in, other than to say some friends and I had come to a serious disagreement. Maybe he figured it out; I don't know whether he knew about our farm or not. (Months later, when I was settled in California, I returned his bible to him by mail, with an anonymous thank-you note and no return address.) A second kind driver gave me a few more dollars and took me all the way to the interstate. I was astounded, and very grateful. My feet hurt.

Before I knew it, I was in Kansas City, wandering around trying to get myself oriented, still unsure whether dropping in on Dick was a good idea. I went to a thrift shop to get some reasonable clothes and a small suitcase to travel with. When I finally saw Dick, he was gracious and reasonably understanding. We acted just like normal friends for a couple of days, sharing stories of the people we had in common, helping me figure out what to do next, going to his favorite bars and hangouts. I tried to find temporary work, and when I couldn't I sold a pint of blood to make a few dollars. Dick offered to give me a few dollars also to use on the road, but confessed he was getting worried harboring me as a runaway from the community. He asked me to leave, and gave me two mementos from the community to travel with, which I still have—a copy of Mel's book and one of the smallest of John Kostick's "tetraxi" stars. He took me out to the interstate, and I was on my own again.

It was a Friday afternoon. I easily got rides out of town and halfway across the state, but later that evening I got busted for hitchhiking on the highway near Salina, Kansas. Since I had no identification on me and my story was kind of difficult to comprehend, the arresting police found it necessary to hold me in jail for the weekend, until I could prove to an arraigning judge on Monday that I was who I said I was.

Somehow, it got worked out and I was on the road again on Monday, I think by my giving the phone number of the farm to corroborate my story and promising to send verification of my identity and payment of a fine when I got settled somewhere.

I was imagining traveling south through New Mexico, by way of Denver, and then on to California, but by the time I got to Denver a blizzard had enveloped all of Colorado and New Mexico. I spent the night in an empty semi-trailer with some other hitchhikers and a helpful truck driver, and in the morning started hitching north toward Wyoming and out of the blizzard. In Cheyenne, I met some old hoboes who encouraged me to ride a freight train out of town and told me how, but the train they put me on turned out to be a shuttle that only went back and forth between Cheyenne and a coal mine in the middle of the state. When I figured out what was happening, I shamefacedly presented myself to the engineers, and they agreed to take me back to Cheyenne. I hitchhiked out of Cheyenne, but halfway across Wyoming my highway luck ran out, and I decided to try a freight train again. This time I did it right; before long (and before my fingers froze completely), I was in Provo, Utah, north of Salt Lake City, where the train line took off around the north side of the Great Salt Lake and on westward.

It hadn't been my plan, but suddenly it made sense to hitchhike into Salt Lake City, where Sofie had two brothers and a sister, all of them relocated recently from San Francisco. I had met one of the brothers, Patrick, in Boston; now he was living an upstanding life with his Mormon convert wife and managing a hair styling salon. I knew I could find him if I tried, and even though it seemed a bit weird I couldn't think of any better way out of the cold just then.

I did find Patrick at his salon on the south side of town, and he was cordial but uneasy about putting me up in his middle-class family home. After the first night, he took me over to meet his brother James and sister Ruby, both of whom I had heard of but never met, who were living in a house much closer to downtown, where they both worked in a methadone clinic. They made me a bed on the back porch of their house, and I promised to find work as quickly as I could so I could buy my way into a place of my own. I was uncomfortable accepting these favors from the siblings of one of the people who had thrown me out of the farm, and at the same time I welcomed the sense of familiarity, and felt needy of some help if I was to get on my feet again. Within a couple of days I found a job as a laborer and ditchdigger, preparing to pour the foundations of a small apartment complex in the suburbs north of Salt Lake. My employer was a young, rather rude second-generation building contractor with family ties into the Mormon church. We had an uneasy connection, and he thought I was too strange for words, but he admired my work and quickly offered to keep me on as a carpenter if I wanted to stay. I agreed, and planned to use my first paycheck to rent a place of my own.

I wrote to Dick Russell, telling him of the amusing turn of events by which I had been kicked out of the farm by Sofie and was now hanging out with her siblings. I suggested I might want to connect with the community's house in San Francisco when I eventually got to California, and asked if he could help retrieve my wallet and ID to make my journey easier. He wrote back an angry letter, with news of more personnel changes at the farm and a strong rebuke to me:

> It seems to me you're still using people as crutches to maintain your sense of a "tie to Mel," when what you keep talking about doing is finding out if you can maintain that tie ON YOUR OWN....Goddamn it, DO what you're saying you want to—get out there in the world and bum around and make some money so you can start feeling useful, but quit expecting someone else to fill the connection you have to find YOURSELF!....If you really want to be the kind of man you told me you wanted to be, it's up to you to do it! It would seem ill-advised for you to go to the San Francisco Community until you are certain you are ready to contribute more than a physical body. You belong to the world and to yourself now, not to me or to Sofi's [sic] relatives or to San Francisco, and it is up to you to jump over that barrier and work your way back—if you want it badly enough!..I will see what I can do about your wallet. You should write soon and tell me your plans.

Dick's letter was quite a blow to me; I had thought I was behaving the way nearly anyone would when confronted with as much dislocation and separation as I was. Dick's reaction seemed based in his own fear of endorsing and supporting me in behavior the community might dislike. I saw myself humbly seeking out the help I thought I could find among the people I knew in a strange place, and was busily putting myself together as quickly as I could. When my first paycheck was imminent, I found a room in a rooming house near the University of Utah, and proudly brought that news home to James and Ruby. I then learned something very revealing about their characters that made some truths about Fort Hill clear to me as well.

It seems that on the day I brought the news home I made a blunder; I sat in on a conversation between Ruby and one of her methadone clients, thinking this was just a friendly visit and that I was welcome. Ruby said nothing to me, but asked James in an aside to announce that this was an intolerable intrusion and I would have to leave. So James took me out on a shopping errand, where I proudly told him that I had already rented a room and would be leaving in a day or two. His reply was as though I had said nothing. "Sofie called us from the farm, you know, and we knew you were coming." (Surely this was a fabrication; I didn't know myself I was coming until the weather and my hitchhiking luck made me change course.) "But Ruby says you're really getting in the way, and you'll have to leave." (But, James, I just told you I was leaving. Why didn't Ruby just ask me to give her and her client some privacy?)

The similarity to the tactics used at Fort Hill was a shock and an eye-opener to me. This was evidently the morality of the street as practiced in San Francisco's cross-cultural immigrant neighborhoods, where Sofie's family had lived for years, and where Mel Lyman too had come of age. I was not only an inept player according to these rules, I was also the kind of person—short, softspoken, educated, distinctly un-macho—who was automatically perceived as an outsider and treated with suspicion. So that's what had been happening at Fort Hill during all that painful time, I concluded. The game was stacked against me.

REBUILDING

I moved into my rooming house room and continued working my construction job. How was I going to put my life together again? My second paycheck was dedicated to new shoes and eyeglasses so I could again see what was happening around me. I asked my mother in New York to make arrangements to get a copy of my New York driver's license so I could use it to obtain a new one in Utah. It would all be a slow climb, but a possible one. But what would fill my mind, and my life? I felt unbelievably bereft.

A couple of weeks after I settled in at the rooming house, my birthday came along, and I wanted to give myself a gift of some kind. I gave myself permission to shoplift a felt-tip pen, with which to begin keeping a journal. I was busted in the attempt, and felt completely stupid about it. The first entry in the brief journal I started keeping began, "Today I turned 28. At the age of 28 I am living the life of someone who has just finished school and left home for the first time." I discuss my departure from the farm, my confusion about it, and the help I got from Sofie's family in deciding to stay on in Salt Lake, and the irony of letting myself get busted for shoplifting: "Lessons and opportunities and such things here in 'the world' tend to come in such a veiled manner, it all depends on what you make of them. It feels like I'm here for a while at least and must try like hell to be straight. [Remember when 'straight' meant 'un-hip'?] I'm so unused to this kind of thing. Thank God for the months I spent with the simple folk in Kansas...Maybe I can become such a one some time." The similarities, and the differences, between what was happening to me and the early phase of Mel's wandering life, as recorded in *Mirror at the End of the Road*, were compelling reasons to attempt to record my thoughts and feelings.

My journal entry ten days later is full of news: I got my driver's license transferred and received my third paycheck, and immediately bought an old car for $75. I have friends in the rooming house, we hang out together and harass the Mormon missionaries who come visiting us. And work for my young employer is a struggle: "[H]e irks me so much, and I piss him off so much of the time, he still treats me like a dumb shit no matter what I do. And I don't do good work for him. I'm in a fog most of the time there, he brings out the worst in me, and at least once or twice a day we just glare at each other, murder in both our eyes. It's a real bad situation." Shades of Fort Hill.   Two days later, I describe a significant dream, the first of many over the years in which I have various kinds of encounters with people from Fort Hill:

> I was with Carolee, and she came to me with the news that Faith wanted to see me up on her mountain, a ceremonious occasion. It felt like a pilgrimage or a communion meeting of some sort as we made our way to where Faith was. There were many gathered on a steep hill, and she stood in a white gown like a queen, with two similarly blond, long-haired attendants in ivory gowns. One was [a friend from high school], the other I can't remember, perhaps [someone from the community]. Carol Ann [Schneider] was there, too, behind Faith like a lady-in-waiting. I greeted Faith and teased them for being "white goddesses," but she went on talking to the others gathered there without answering me at all. After a while I asked Carolee if she knew why I'd been summoned since Faith didn't seem to intend to speak to me, and she just said it wasn't a mistake, if she was ignoring me then that must be what she intended. Then it was time to go, and we walked down the hill, separate from all the others, and got on a trolley car. The driver was my high school chemistry teacher [who in my memory resembled Carolee in appearance], who seemed to know more than she was letting on, but she was very courteous.

> While we were riding, I told Carolee that I was *trying* to be a man and do what I had to—and I was very specific about what that meant to me, like being an example, directing my loved ones toward the right way, et cetera—and I knew I was blowing it and didn't know why. Carolee listened and was both sympathetic and impassive, the way she can be, and then it was time to get off the trolley. We thanked Miss Krahm and said goodbye, and I woke up.

The next entry a few days later discusses my return to the study of astrology. I had reconstructed my own chart from memory, had found an occult bookstore from which to begin acquiring reference books and taking classes, had found the astrology section of the university library, and had begun reexamining myself in terms of the information I was finding. I describe "quite a struggle" I'd been having internally:

> Ever since the dream I had Sunday about Faith and Fort Hill, I've been feeling the Community slipping away in myself, and that is a painful change to observe, though it seems a necessary one. It is all becoming very distant, and more and more I am seeing the basic disagreements between myself and the regimen of continual sacrifice and externally imposed justice. I just can't fit in with all that, never could, it didn't fit the pattern (or lack of it) by which I have to live in order to be me. The lack of conscious understanding of who I am which I always felt in the community (and which I could never penetrate there) makes sense when I see who I am by my chart, but I feel a need and have a responsibility to live in such a way that the potential of this mysterious person becomes manifest. I cannot consciously live a lie.

Sadly, this is the last entry in my brief journal, but a couple of weeks later, I wrote a long letter to a close friend from grade school and high school, who had remained in touch with my life through all the traumas of college and the years in Boston. A letter from him had been forwarded to me by my mother; I responded with a description of my departure from the farm and a discussion of what I thought it all meant:

> Much of what I was hoping to find and attach myself to in the Community—purpose, eternal purpose, I mean, and a place in the evolution of mankind, family, security and the productivity and creativity which they can

inspire—somehow never came to me while I was there, even though I did and do believe they were there. As far as I can see, I can only blame the inadequate evolution of my soul for that fact, because I sure busted ass trying to make the grade. Others were not so charitable. They blamed my pride, egotism, stubbornness, insensitivity, stupidity, et cetera—doubtless true charges but obviously things of the moment, albeit long moments, and subject to change if we could only have come to terms with our differences. There were times when I was very close to people there and we loved each other and worked together truly, but when circumstances changed and demanded different things from us, I could not always readily adjust, and in the end I guess I just wasn't worth the effort it would have taken to bring me along.

Does that make sense to you? You have to realize that the Community has a very high and in many ways an egoless and depersonalized sense of mission and destiny for itself. In many ways the people who carry out the details of that destiny are not up to its demands, and so the means of bringing about "justice" (that is, karma) are often crude and superficially heartless or senseless, but in general the dedication to the demands of "spirit," as manifested in the creation of complete and resilient individuals, is such that what happens is somehow right despite the methods used. What I'm saying is I trust what happened to me even though it seemed a butcher-job at the time and was very difficult to go through and left a residue of bitterness, as unresolved tension and frustration always do, which I've had to live with and purge gradually and replace with a higher level of patience and understanding. I dream about people and situations in the Community very, very often, from the little kids all the way to Mel, surprising dreams, good ones, bad ones, ones in which I feel very good and useful to them, ones in which I'm a fool and a pompous ass. I miss them all, but I am far away from them. I don't know if I'll ever go back or not. I'm waiting for signals and working on my own development....

Perhaps, if I prove to have an aptitude for it and the determination which is required, astrology will become a serious study for me and will become my method of teaching which I have sought for so long. I have the feeling for teaching or communion or whatever it is

that you described so well in your letter, but as you once knew and can now see again, I have had only intermittent success in passing anything of value on to others through it. Also, someday I expect I will have to have a career, and very little appeals to me unless it serves the purpose of showing people themselves....At present, I am a carpenter again, and that and related trades are my most useful means of surviving in the material world—universally useful, in fact; I never have to want for work for very long—but I don't want to spend my whole life with a hammer or a paintbrush or a wrench in my dirty hands, so I am wishing that this delicate business of evolving a higher purpose in life would get on with itself.

MORE DANCING LESSONS FROM GOD

In my letter I discuss the probability of making my way to California to visit my sister and her family at their new home in Redwood City, near San Francisco, at a time when my mother and possibly my brother and his family would also be visiting, and then perhaps returning to New York with my mother to help her ready her house for sale so she could retire to Florida. I didn't know exactly how or when all this would happen. (In fact, it was another three years before the trip to New York occurred.) As it turned out, I stayed in Salt Lake City slightly more than another month; when my car broke down just before I was due to drive it to California, I decided instead to abandon it and take a bus to San Francisco. I left Salt Lake City on July 24, four months to the day after walking away from the farm in Kansas.

I had enlisted my mother's collaboration in keeping my plans secret from my sister, so I could surprise her by showing up unexpectedly at her door, but since I was traveling by bus and had to be collected at the terminal, it didn't happen that way. Still, it was a joyous reunion. We had been very close at times in the past, but I had only seen her and her husband and three young sons once during all my time in the community, when they had visited overnight at the farm the previous summer during a cross-country trip, and that experience was uncomfortable for everyone. They were happy to have me on their turf now and to be able to help me move on in my life. In fact, they had already arranged work for me, doing construction and decorating for the people from whom they had recently bought their house, an elderly couple who previously ran a construction business and still owned and managed a nursing home and an apartment building. There was also the possibility of purchasing used construction equipment and vehicles from the former owners, and of collaborating with my brother-in-law in putting a house on an empty lot next door that he and my sister had already bought.

I was dumbfounded. I had expected to visit briefly in Redwood City, reacquaint with my family, find out if we had anything in common, and then move on to San Francisco to reconnect with the counterculture that I had left behind years ago and assumed was still going strong there, and where I hoped to raise the question of whether I wanted to continue living as a straight man (meaning in the sense of sexual identity) or return to exploring life as a gay man. The last thing I expected was to find a congenial home in the suburbs of the San Francisco Peninsula. But there I was.

For five months I lived in an extra room in my sister's house, while I got to know the local area and while I became used to living on my own again in the regular world. In many ways I was relieved to simply move into an established household and do the things that were presented to me, which in this case meant working by day for the elderly couple and various other friends of my sister's family who offered me work, and socializing with my sister's and her husband's large circle of friends by night and on days off. I also bought an old dump truck in hopes of establishing myself in the hauling business; while that outcome did not occur, the dump truck did lead me out of my sister's circle of acquaintances and into some friendships of my own, when it blew its engine soon after I started using it for hauling.

From the elderly couple's grandson, I learned about a consumer-owned cooperative auto repair shop in nearby Palo Alto where I might be able to rebuild an engine myself with guidance from the shop personnel. I had no history at all of doing major automotive repairs—quite the opposite; my history with vehicles was filled with misadventures, poor judgments, and the pursuit of bad advice. I had never even seen an engine rebuild in progress—but this seemed like the next step at the moment. My self-image was so corrupted that I had no idea what was appropriate to do from one minute to the next, and I seemed to have a distinct inclination under the circumstances toward masculine-image adventures and involvements, toward seeing myself as capable of any feats of physical work and heroic challenges. Rebuild a truck engine? Sure, no problem!

THERE'S A PLACE IN THE SUN

Redwood City and Palo Alto are, in a sense, the twin capitals of a small suburban metropolis known as the Midpeninsula, midway down the San Francisco Peninsula from San Francisco to San Jose, both much larger metropolises in themselves and with very different characters from each other. The Midpeninsula contains a little of each—some of the urbanity and worldliness of San Francisco, some of the provincial quality of San Jose, an old agricultural capital grown into a modern industrial center—as well as a distinct personality of its own, a blend of traditional and modern styles, several small cities jammed close together, each of which runs from the wetlands of San Francisco Bay through low-lying residential and commercial neighborhoods and up into the foothills of the adjoining Santa Cruz Mountains, with their history of redwood logging and rebellious individualism. Poor and rich, intellectual and working class, Anglo, black, Mexican, and occasional Asian communities intermingle in each of the cities. Stanford University, a world-class center of scientific and cultural research, sits square in the middle of all this, the legacy of robber baron industrialist and one-time senator, Leland Stanford. An enormous endowment of land and money dominates the area with shopping centers, industrial parks, research facilities, spin-off electronics industries, and traffic problems. As host community to Stanford, Palo Alto has always been somewhat overshadowed and underfunded by its famous guest, but during the 1960s and into the 1970s the growth of the "Silicon Valley" electronics industry and the general prosperity of the area had been good to Palo Alto; a progressive city government had developed a wide range of city-funded services, and big portions of the foothills had been annexed into the city to provide for the possibility of continuing growth.

Palo Alto during those days was also home to an innovative alternative culture community, curiously scattered throughout the traditional downtown area and the surrounding neighborhoods with their more suburban character, with numerous outposts in the adjoining towns and the nearby rural hilly areas. The Briarpatch Cooperative Auto Shop was just one of the unusual expressions of that community. The *Whole Earth Catalog* was being published in the adjoining town of Menlo Park, where a retail outlet, the Whole Earth Truck Store, was also located, an early source of environmentally sensitive new technology, along with several related consulting and publishing ventures. Several consumer-operated food-buying cooperatives operated in the area, as did a string of community-based health services. The Briarpatch Network of alternative businesses linked these various enterprises together, and helped to promote a new philosophy of ecologically sound entrepreneurship.

The Stanford campus had been a significant center of antiwar organizing; its one-time student body president, David Harris, became nationally famous when he burned his draft card and later when he married folksinger Joan Baez and moved with her to a home among a group of rural communes in the Santa Cruz Mountain foothills above Palo Alto. Harris' imprisonment for draft evasion, and Baez' continuing performing and speaking in support of his cause, brought national attention to the counterculture community of which they were a part. The leftist think tank Baez helped found and to a large degree supported, the Institute for the Study of Non-Violence, was located in an old house in downtown Palo Alto. The idea of "peace conversion" was born there when the local peace movement had begun asking the question, how can we redirect the "defense"-based economy toward something more useful? A couple of research and lobbying organizations formed around this issue and a new monthly community-based newspaper, the *Grapevine*, began publishing in June 1973. The *Grapevine* spoke for all the alternative communities of the Midpeninsula, with a bias toward leftist politics, small-scale economics, and do-it-yourself socialism. It contained lots of coverage of Third World anti-colonial struggles. In format, it was a modest, even somewhat conservative tabloid.

I began learning of all these developments when I developed a friendship with Bill Duncan, the manager of the cooperative auto shop, who was deeply involved in the community. Bill was very helpful to me in getting my truck-repair project under way, though not so helpful as to help me avoid a disaster the first time I started the new engine, which burned out almost immediately and had to be rebuilt again, to my great frustration and considerable expense. (I eventually sold the truck at a loss.) He offered me remodeling work around the shop to help offset my bill, listened to my stories of the commune that went bad, and told me stories of communal life as he had experienced it. He even put out the idea of the two of us forming a cooperative home-repair business modeled after the auto shop, in which craftspeople and property owners would share responsibilities and benefits. We gave up the notion when we learned that licensing and insurance requirements were all but insurmountable.

When I expressed interest in moving out of my sister's house and closer to the Palo Alto community, Bill arranged for me to rent one of several small apartments upstairs from the Whole Earth Truck Store in downtown Menlo Park. I moved in during Christmas week of 1973. Something told me it was a good time to make other changes in my life, so on the day I moved out of my sister's house I also stopped smoking cigarettes, after about four years, and stopped eating meat, less than a year after I stopped butchering animals at the farm. Amazingly, I had no difficulty at all with these changes; I've never resumed smoking

(cigarettes, that is), remained a committed vegetarian for more than 15 years, and still shun red meat.

Moving into a place of my own forced me to examine my very negative and self-deprecating self-image. Everything in this apartment is mine, I would say to myself, and I have a right to have it. This kitchen is here just for me; all this furniture is mine and I deserve to use it. Following one of Mel Lyman's basic principles, I made sure I deserved my possessions by taking very good care of them, starting with a complete redecorating of the apartment. I collected items that reflected my innate sense of recycling and reusing, of living low on the economic ladder. I learned to shop at flea markets and thrift stores. I gave myself a few significant gifts that affirmed my right to pleasure myself at least a little, such as a waterbed to sleep on and contact lenses to replace my still-hated eyeglasses.

I was meeting lots of new people, and presented myself to all of them as a knowledgeable amateur astrologer; almost the first thing I would do was ask for people's birth information and calculate their charts, then interpret these as best I could. My offering of astrology was much deeper and more meaningful than the perfunctory "what's your sign?" that had become the standing joke of superficial pop culture, but it served almost the same purpose: if I spoke about astrology with a new friend, we wouldn't have to cast about wondering what we had in common and what we were really thinking and feeling. As I settled in and relaxed, I gradually began seeing myself in a more positive light, and even had a brief affair with a woman I met while working for a time at the nursing home owned by the elderly couple.

I was responding to notices I would see around town for freelance tradespeople, looking for possible collaborators in the remodeling cooperative Bill Duncan and I were imagining. One of the people I met in this way, Henry Jackson, proved to be a congenial collaborator in a carpentry project that was offered to me by some friends of my sister; we proceeded to become work partners and remained so for the next several years. He was a recent graduate of the rather progressive architecture program at UC-Berkeley; working with him stimulated my long-standing interest in design and unusual uses of both old and new materials. Our work days were a running conversation about architecture, construction methods, popular culture, and current events. For about a year we got to invest our creative energies in a huge remodeling and room addition project designed around a client's collection of stained glass and other antique treasures.

During the same time, we also planned major renovations on my sister's rather plain house, hiring friends to do the work when we were unavailable. When we did spend some time starting what was intended to be the major interior remodel, we discovered evidence of incompetent construction and hidden fire damage in the house, and a long period of research began in which I helped my sister and her husband bring legal charges against the former owners. Their house sat torn open for more than two years while the legal battle waited for resolution. Henry and I filled our time working for a growing network of contacts among the real estate community in Palo Alto.

IS THIS DÉJA VU, OR DO YOU JUST LOOK FAMILIAR?

My life was starting to take form. An important connection that I made during this period helped me enormously in putting the Fort Hill Community experience in perspective. During the time I was still living in my sister's house, but beginning to explore for community in Palo Alto, I answered a notice I saw in an occult bookstore for astrology classes. The instructor, William Lonsdale, immediately recognized me as having the same birthday he had (though I was two years older), and this made him curious whether our life experiences had resembled each other. I stayed late after my first class to share stories, and I was amazed to discover not only that William had grown up in circumstances fairly similar to mine and pursued a long path of exploring various aspects of the counterculture, but also that our paths had actually crossed quite directly.

He became a professional astrologer after being turned on to the subject by a person doing horoscope readings for money on a street corner in Boston. That street-corner astrologer was Joseph Dellamore, one of the more independent-minded members of the Fort Hill crew, who used to simply ignore the peer pressure to work on the building projects and go off instead to do astrology. William's first horoscope reading was actually calculated from my set of astrology books, which I had lent to Joseph when it was obvious he was going to have more use for them than I had. Joseph invited William back to Fort Hill for a visit, and William was intrigued but rather turned off by the sight of all of us working away like beavers on Mel's studio. He decided Fort Hill was not for him, but went on to live in communal groups in New York and Vermont, where he had his own share of authoritarian experiences. He was now making the study of such groups a major focus of his life, second only to astrology, in which he had become quite expert and innovative. We had plenty to talk about.

One of the most transformative moments for me in growing away from the traumas of the Fort Hill experience was the day William and I reconstructed the charts of Mel Lyman and several other key players in the community and then reinterpreted them according to his understanding of astrology, which differed considerably from the interpretations that were used among the community's members. Mel emerged not so much as an avatar and cultural leader, but more as a needy person with a very low sense of self-worth, who needed to manipulate others into supporting his self-aggrandizing fantasies. The people around him appeared similarly deficient in self-image, and seemed all to be of a personality type that would prefer to let someone else make decisions for them rather than live according to their own guidance. My chart looked not so much like that of a person unable to get himself together as it did that of a person with an undeniable independence of spirit, whose inner strength inevitably clashed with someone who could only be served by undermining that independence. What an eye-opener that was for me!

It felt like William and I had stumbled onto something terribly important that only we understood, almost conspiratorially. He told me about making the acquaintance some time earlier of Paul Williams, the former editor of *Crawdaddy* magazine and future writer of several well-received books of essays on the emerging counterculture, who had been friends with Mel for years and had lived briefly at Fort Hill (and whose sudden departure from the Hill had been the subject of the lead passage of David Felton's coverage of the community in *Rolling Stone*). Paul had had to go through a debriefing and reprogramming of himself after his experiences, not very different from what I was going through, and William had met him toward the end of that phase.

They had discussed the paradox that Fort Hill appeared to both itself and to observers to represent a new direction in collective living, a new development in culture unlike anything that had gone before, when in fact the essential energies on which the community ran were really very traditional, based deeply in patriarchal values and authoritarian power structures —not the newest of the new, but merely the latest expression of the old ways. This idea, too, seemed a revelation to me, and helped to clarify some of my ongoing confusion. It enabled me to feel better about my inability to fit in there, since I had no particular use for the values of the traditional society, and also to see more clearly why Fort Hill seemed to have so little appreciation for the various expressions of the newly emerging culture that were in fact springing up everywhere in those days. The revelation gave me new enthusiasm for exploring just how that counterculture had developed during the years while I had my back turned.

William had a theory that each oppressive charismatic community focused on and took advantage of one particular aspect of the personalities of its participants, and that aspect was the last part to heal and find its way back to normal after a person returned to regular life. In the case of Fort Hill, he hypothesized, it was the will that was undermined and thrown off course, and he guessed that my will would be the last part of myself I would be able to reclaim. This theory was difficult to hear and to understand at the time but, looking back on the many years it took me to recognize the difference between my own desires and impulses and those that came to me from outside myself, I guess his idea makes good sense.

William and his wife Diana turned me on to two expressions of the new culture that represented breakthroughs for me, one each for my body and my soul. My body loved Earth Shoes, the negative-heel shoes that were just becoming popular, and which for me represented the other end of the spectrum from the cowboy boots I had worn in Kansas and during my pilgrimage west. My body breathed a sigh of relief when it learned it didn't have to live with that kind of tension anymore. And the weekend I spent at the Living Love Center in Berkeley, the teaching space at that time of Ken Keyes (who would go on to form several other teaching centers around the country and to write *Handbook to Higher Consciousness* and *The Hundredth Monkey*, among other books), let me know that even after what I had been through I could have transformative personal experiences and achieve easy intimacy if I wanted to.

My friendship with William and our ongoing discussion about Fort Hill continued for a number of months, until he and Diana decided it was time to move back East; I did them the favor of building a customized camper on their pickup truck in which to travel and live. William paid me back by doing an extensive reading of my "progressions," the closest means to predicting the future used by humanistic astrologers. From the reading, William told me that I would only come into my own as a fully grown person some time in my middle thirties (I was then turning 29). This long-term perspective enabled me to see my difficulties up to then as simply a phase in my growth.

I made another significant friend during that time, Jonathan Rosenbloom, one of my neighbors in the apartments above the Truck Store. He and I would prepare meals together from time to time, and would discuss a variety of intellectual and countercultural topics. Through him I became familiar with *The Seth Material*, Jane Roberts' then recently published account of her developing relationship with a disembodied spirit who dictated—through Jane's voice when she was in a self-induced trance—astounding philosophical lessons about the meaning of life and the malleability of human experience, which Jane's artist husband would write down in longhand and then edit into readable manuscripts. I was fascinated, and remained devoted to Jane and Seth over the next several years as each book of the extensive and best-selling series appeared. (Jane Roberts had the same birthday as William Lonsdale and me, and this gave me a subtle but real sense of connection to her.)

Many of the key ideas in the Seth books were challenging and difficult to assimilate, but they were very stimulating. They portrayed a world with many dimensions of experience and a wide and diverse realm of interactions between living people and other kinds of spirits, all occurring in simultaneous time. The idea from Seth that I found most useful in terms of recovering from my Fort Hill experience was the notion that communications that appear to happen in dreams are in fact happening in an "alternate reality" that only touches into what we recognize as ordinary reality in momentary tangents. This idea helped me conceive of my continuing frequent dreams about the Fort Hill people in a new light; maybe I was actually working out the various incompletes and traumas from my time with them, but in ways that only penetrated my consciousness in dream form. I liked thinking that I was really communicating with Mel and the others, and not just obsessing on my memories.

I also found myself in my waking life rolling memories of Fort Hill over and over in my mind, often when I was working on repetitive tasks that required little mental attention. I would relive one experience after another, trying to make sense of all that had happened, and would compose long, often angry speeches in my mind with which to tell off this person or that, trying to give myself, internally at least, the sense that at last justice and balance had been spoken for. Gradually, over a period of years, I put the various experiences in perspective and saw that I had not been crazy or less than a whole person during all those difficulties, but that I had allowed myself to be overwhelmed by a bunch of strong personalities, most of whom had never given me the chance to express myself in my own terms, and had not recognized me when I did so spontaneously. I felt wonderful to be reclaiming myself by bits and pieces.

NEWS FROM HOME

One day during the early period in Palo Alto, while doing carpentry work for one of the *Whole Earth Catalog* operators, I got my first new information about the actual people of Fort Hill. On a break from my work, I sat down to browse through a stack of recent

Rolling Stone magazines that caught my eye. Included among the feature articles and news updates were stories about the blossoming solo career of Maria Muldaur, former singer with Jim Kweskin's Jug Band. I felt a certain connection to Maria, even though I had only seen her once at Jim's house on Fort Hill and had never met her personally. The *Rolling Stone* dated October 11, 1973, had an article on the arrest for alleged cocaine dealing of Abbie Hoffman that I wanted to read. But adjoining that article was a headline that captured my attention: "Ricky Nelson to Jimmy Dean." The article began, "Behind bars Mark Frechette is a curiously satisfied man. 'It was a good bank robbery,' he said. 'Maybe it *wasn't* a successful one, but it was *real*, ya know?'"

It seems Mark and two others from the community—Terry Bernhard, Mel's and Jim's piano-playing friend, who was the father of the two little girls given up for adoption because of their birth defects, and Chris Thein, or "Hercules," who had been recruited by Owen during his cross-country proselytizing trip and whom I had never met—had decided on the spur of the moment to rob a bank, in a personal act of revolution, or something like that. Mark and Herc had just returned from a summer working in the community's compound on Martha's Vineyard, and perhaps the pressure of the city was too much for them. Terry decided at the last minute to join them, and they had walked an easy half mile to the nearest bank, hadn't even taken a car to get away in, carrying unloaded guns. The bank they chose happened to be the one where all the community's money was deposited, but they didn't know that. A totally silly act, in other words. In the course of committing their act, they answered a question I had been considering for a long time: who would be the first to die for, or because of, Mel? Herc was shot and killed by police who responded to the alarm call. Mark and Terry were arrested.

In the article in *Rolling Stone*, the usual suspects from the Hill make several characteristically overconfident and ridiculous comments, willing to use anything at all to further their image of themselves. For example, Jessie is quoted as saying, "We're not political here. We don't have any ideas up here. But we're very aware. We're bound to the soul of the country. We *are* the soul of the country....this was the most honest thing those three boys could do." Mark is quoted as saying, "I did what I did to stay awake. This society runs amok asleep. I was running amok but I was awake."

A few months later, Mark and Terry pleaded guilty and were sentenced to prison terms of six to fifteen years. But the story had an even unhappier outcome than that. Even though they were apparently well liked in the state prison and kept their senses of humor there—an article in the *New York Times* of March 23, 1975, describes Mark directing and Terry starring in a theater production, for inmates, staff, and visiting dignitaries, of "The White House Transcripts," about the antics of Richard Nixon that led to his downfall—Mark apparently became more and more depressed in prison. The November 6, 1975, issue of *Rolling Stone* contained the final chapter of his story, "The Sorry Life and Death of Mark Frechette." Early one morning in late September, Mark, who had lost a lot of weight and strength, was found alone in the recreation room of the prison, lying dead with a 150-pound barbell across his neck that he was apparently trying to bench press. Despite the unusual circumstances, it was deemed neither suicide nor murder but merely the fitting end to an unhappy and star-crossed life.

SETTLE DOWN

I stayed in my apartment above the Truck Store for eight months, the longest time in my life of living alone, and then decided it was time to move into a collective household. I found a room at the back of a large house with a big yard and a bunch of housemates. The couple who owned the home were followers of Leonard Orr and Sondra Ray, the people who were at that time developing the new practice of Rebirthing, a New Age-style method of therapy and personal transformation based on a particular kind of "circular" controlled breathing. Shortly after I moved in, Leonard Orr came to the house to conduct their marriage ceremony, but I was not drawn into trying rebirthing (just yet; many years later I did). Another housemate was studying with Ida Rolf to become a practitioner of Rolfing, deep-tissue reconstructive massage therapy. He introduced me to some chiropractor friends, who gave me some food supplements to begin healing and strengthening my body from within. (A few years later, I went through a series of Rolfing sessions with the same friend, when he was studying a less-painful variation of Rolfing known as Aston Patterning.)

While I was living with those folks I was contacted by David Freedman, a friend from East Lansing who had worked on *The Paper* both during my time and after I left. David found me by way of my mother and invited me to visit him in Los Angeles. He had gotten caught up in radical antiwar politics of the sort I had left East Lansing partly to avoid, and had felt it necessary to go underground and live in hiding for several years. When he emerged, he met up with American followers of the Indian Sikh leader, Yogi Bhajan, and he was now wearing white robes and a turban, living in their community in L.A., with a new name, Darshan Singh, and a new wife, but he was in many ways the same gentle, goofy-humored person I knew before. We had a pleasant visit for a few days, during which time I got up before dawn and meditated with my hosts and their community-mates. I seemed to be getting a gradual introduction to all of the new spiritual and transformational disciplines that were going around in those days. Darshan indulged me in seeking out the Fort Hill houses in Hollywood to see them with my own eyes. I don't know what I expected to do; I certainly didn't have the nerve to knock on the door and say hello, but I wanted to know where they were and what they looked like.

Jonathan and I remained friends after I moved, and in January he suggested we rent a place together and start a household of our own. We found a ranch house in South Palo Alto on the day we started looking, and before long we were conducting interviews for two other housemates and choosing paint colors and furniture. During this time I got another bulletin from the real world of Fort Hill. *Time* magazine for February 3, 1975, contained an obituary for Thomas Hart Benton, who had died of heart disease at the age of 85 at his home in Kansas City. *Time* had little good to say about the lasting significance of Benton's work, but it paid him respect as an old-fashioned American individualist who had dabbled in modern art and had then resoundingly returned to traditional, even primitive forms for the bulk of his career.

Reading this account sent me into long reminiscences about his daughter Jessie and all the people around her with whom I had interacted for so long. I had never met Benton but had certainly felt his influence on Mel and all of us; his paintings and prints were everywhere in the communities. Somehow remembering all this gave me the urge to write a letter to my old partner Carol Schneider, now known as Carol Franck after partnering with Kurt Franck, mathematician-turned-photographer-turned-carpenter for the community, by whom she had been pregnant during the season when I ran away from the farm. I didn't want to reveal to her exactly where I was, but I figured out I could send my letter by way of William Lonsdale in New York and encourage her to respond by way of my mother's address if she wanted to.

In my letter I describe my current life in general terms and speak, a little defensively, of my continuing process of making sense of my experiences at Fort Hill and of rediscovering myself separate from all that. "Mainly," I write, "I realize now that we are *all* working and striving to expand ourselves in the best way we know, but my faith in the value of self-determination is (and always was) greater than that which was manifested by Fort Hill. It is clear from the way the world is moving that many, many people are acting out essentially the same intuitions about how the next phase in history and evolution is to shape itself, and the most we can do for each other is recognize our common needs and goals. Don't you agree?" I don't know if she agreed or not, as I received no response.

But my life was moving forward, with or without Carol's and Fort Hill's blessings. One of the people who moved into our new house was a young woman named Carol Settle, a student ballerina, an enthusiastic feminist, and a former follower of the teenage Guru Maharaj Ji. She and I had plenty to talk about, and were rather attracted to each other as well. After a few months of simply being friendly housemates, we decided we felt safe enough to act on our attraction and started spending more private time together. (You can bet I was struck by the coincidence of her name; it seemed practically every time I became involved with a woman, her name was Carol.)

The day we had our first definitive date together—to a nude beach on the ocean side of the peninsula—we came home to find Jonathan sitting angrily amid an enormous, outraged note he had written to us complaining about our behavior, on yards and yards of computer paper (he was a programmer) that he had taped all over the walls and ceilings of the public rooms of the house. We could hardly believe our eyes, but clearly we were dealing with a high order of jealousy. Nevertheless, we began spending our nights together. The first night, Carol asked me what my "ideal woman" looked like, and I told her I wasn't sure my ideal woman wasn't a man. She took that news bravely and we plunged forward just the same. I figured her horoscope—she had sun in Aries and moon in Taurus to match my sun in Taurus and moon in Aries, and, like me, three other planets in Aries to keep the fires going—and sent a copy of her chart to my astrologer friend William Lonsdale, who wrote back, "She's more like you than you are. Good luck."

I was still working construction, but was starting to feel restless and resentful of all the time I was spending helping affluent people improve their oversized suburban homes. One night in November I wrote a complaint to the universe about my circumstances. I had just found a copy of "Jim Kweskin's America" in a remainder bin in a record store and had heard the music for the first time in years. It left me feeling nostalgic and restive:

> It's a dark and dismal Saturday night. A night when it's impossible to remember the daylight. Has it ever been brighter than this? My imagination is at low tide, my ambition doesn't exist at all. All around me are things I "want" or "have" to do,...and what I want to do is be in New York City. Scrap the business, scrap the house and the lease and the relationship there within, and head straight for

the center of debauchery and culture. Palo Alto is so fucking boring, but I can't help but notice I'm not in the van driving to San Francisco right now. I seem pretty frozen, in fact. When I'm not playing Mr. Together, I don't really have very much going for me. Mr. Together is a builder by trade. He can do anything beautifully. The $100-a-night call girl of the building trades, he sells his time to homeowners in big chunks. "During the month of November 1975, the purpose of my life shall be to make of your barren attic a beautiful extra room with bath. I shall occupy myself with nothing else, and when the room is complete, I will leave you, and you need never think of me again." Sometimes I get tired of doing that. I want to claim myself back to myself, but I'm so out of the habit. What else do I do besides build things? I read magazines, occasionally books, and have grand theories and ineffable feelings about them. I move like a heavy mechanical object, though; all the fineness is still inside me and few if any can see it or feel it. Years ago Mel Lyman told me to go to work, to work and work and sooner or later I would find myself wanting to say and do finer, more delicate things, and I would find the way. He promised to teach me, but of course he never did. Now I am a long time away from him, and I am still looking for the fine gestures, the inexpressibly subtle and delicate word or facial expression.

Relations with Jonathan continued deteriorating, and during the fall he moved out. Carol and I wanted to move, too. In the course of looking for a new place, we interviewed with a couple named Robert and Meg Beeler, who taught in one of the experimental private schools in Palo Alto and who were involved in all sorts of interesting community affairs. They told us about the new men's group Robert and a few friends were starting, patterned after the women's "consciousness-raising" groups that characterized the seminal phase of the women's movement and inspired by a recent talk at Stanford by Warren Farrell, one of the writers exploring the new subject of men's attempts to free themselves from traditional role models. We were fascinated and immediately recognized this as an opportunity for me to do some growing.

A New Movement, a New Paper

Carol and I did not move in with our new friends, mainly because the space didn't seem adequate, but I was invited to begin meeting with the men's group, and did so promptly. On the day of the first meeting I was scheduled to attend, some particularly horrible event occurred (I don't remember whether it was another insult from Jonathan in the house or some difficulty getting paid for my work, or some combination of affronts). I told my story and related my frustration and need for support to this small group of men, most of whom I was meeting for the first time; they found my candor to be a breakthrough for their group, which they celebrated by taking me outside and hoisting me above their heads as an expression of solidarity and support. The group was off and running.

We remained together for more than two years from that point, meeting weekly and sharing every aspect of our rapidly changing lives with each other. It was a tremendously important focus for me during that time, an anchor of support, a standard of understanding against which to measure all kinds of other changes going on in my life, and a cauldron in which to explore my feelings and my willingness to allow others to see parts of myself I had always hidden. Several group members were in various stages of rethinking their sexual orientation, and over time that gave me permission to look at that subject, too, with no pressure to make a definitive decision about it.

Carol and I found a charming little two-bedroom house near downtown Palo Alto on January 1, 1976. It faced the creek that separated Palo Alto from Menlo Park, and had a low brick wall around the front yard and a small back yard with fruit trees. We were thrilled, and made the house just as homey as we could. The extra bedroom served as an office for both of us. We relished taking our place in the community as an involved young couple.

My men's group joined with other like-minded men to initiate a Palo Alto Men's Center. We rented the basement of the Institute for the Study of Non-Violence as our meeting space. Various of us from the Men's Center took turns producing a Men's Page for the *Grapevine*, partly as a device to raise interest in the activities of the center and partly to encourage people to question their own adherence to traditional roles. As other special-interest groups had done before us, we would send delegates to the monthly meetings, where editorial decisions were made by collective consensus, and to the weekend-long paste-up sessions.

My turn came up to work on the page when I wrote a description of our opening event at the Men's Center, which was heralded with a full-page article in the local daily, the *Palo Alto Times*, and was attended by 150 people. I began my article with a description of the opening night and a discussion of how the men's movement that seemed to be coming together owed a lot to both the women's movement and the history of counterculturalexplorationmanyofusshared. Playfully, I offered several different ways of describing this development, then wrote:

> These little statements are getting closer to how I'm feeling, but they still don't say it the way I would like to:
> I'm glad I'm learning to show my feelings. I'm glad I'm making so many new friends, and that it feels like home to me here. I haven't been home in so long. It's good to share again this building of something that belongs to all of us. I feel myself unfolding inside, getting ready for a rush of New and Alive. I haven't felt this way in years.
> It brings tears to my eyes to realize this; my eyes are so unused to tears, especially happy, fulfilled tears. It seems I can begin to show myself at last, and it's good not to be alone.
> Hello, brothers! Glad to see you!

It's easy for me to see Mel Lyman's influence in the writing style of this piece, but that would not have been apparent to anyone else. It's also easy to relate to the great relief I was feeling and expressing, that at last I was feeling enough courage to "go public" again after the traumas I had been through that had forced me into myself for so long. But the joyous new era did not last long.

DEAR LANDLORD

A political difference was already surfacing within the Non-Violence Institute that soon caused Joan Baez and certain others to question whether they wanted to keep the building and the institute operating in their current form. In the May issue of the *Grapevine*, just two months after I had announced the Men's Center's opening, I wrote an article entitled "'Dear Landlord': Eviction at 667 Lytton," in which I described the summary closing of the institute the previous month and the impending eviction of the Men's Center and several other community organizations. I was taking all this quite personally; in addition to participating in the Men's Center's attempts to lobby the institute board to treat us kindly as they went through their changes, I also wrote a personal letter to Baez detailing my political and social history and the numerous points at which she and her music had touched into my life, including the story of her singing Jim Kweskin and Mel Lyman off the stage at Newport and the current phase in which her political struggle seemed on the verge of putting my new movement out on the street. I hand-carried this letter to her home in the nearby town of Woodside, but received only an acknowledgment from a secretary. Baez was out of town and never answered my letter. And the effort was in vain.

In the next issue of the *Grapevine*, I wrote an article headlined "Non-Violence Institute Self-Destructs." It seems the various factions within the institute's board and its operating collective, not to mention its various tenants and related projects, were quite unable to agree on how to modernize and face the seventies, and the board decided instead to sell off the assets and reorganize under a new name in a new town, Santa Cruz, 50 miles away.

The move put a premature end to the Men's Center, but our men's group continued, and seeds of a new movement had been planted. (One of the flowers, about two years later, was the first California Men's Gathering (CMG), a weekend-long campout event at which men from around the state got together to commiserate on their experiences as men. I didn't attend that gathering or the follow-up events over the next several years, but the circle completed itself for me when I attended the Seventh CMG in 1984 and subsequent events, and became an organizer of the Ninth CMG in 1986. Many of my friends are still involved in the CMGs, which are going strong, now in their fourteenth year.)

By the time the Non-Violence Institute and the Men's Center "self-destructed," I was a confirmed member of the *Grapevine* staff, and so was Carol. We had found a purpose, and a way to participate in the community we were feeling so pleased to be part of. But trouble was brewing in the operation. Distribution was free and all labor was volunteer; printing costs were paid by advertising revenues generated mainly from local, left-oriented retail businesses and independent tradespeople. For some months the paper had contained plaintive little notices asking readers to subscribe, or to make financial donations to help the paper continue and grow. But not much was coming of these announcements. In the first several of the monthly collective meetings that Carol and I attended, we quickly perceived that lack of finances was the biggest problem for the *Grapevine*, so we offered to take over the job of selling and coordinating advertising. We persuaded the collective to pay us a commission on the ads we sold, the first time anyone had been paid for work on the paper.

The issue for July-August 1976 lists us in our new role and contains a large ad announcing our plans for a new classified column. We established higher display ad rates and began a more aggressive campaign to sell them. It became Carol's job to kick the campaign off because I spent the Bicentennial month of July in New York, finally making good on my promise from several years earlier to help my mother get her house there ready to sell.

While I was east, I visited William and Diana Lonsdale and their young daughter in Burlington, Vermont. That completely pleasurable experience proved to me that my new life in California had indeed been producing lasting results of intimacy and growth. I also got in touch with the family of my old East Lansing friend Dale Walker, in nearby Montpelier. I learned that Dale had been living in Prince Edward Island, Canada, with a new wife, but was now in a fundamentalist Bible school somewhere in New England. I gave his mother my address and a couple of months later received a long letter from him telling of his and his wife's experiences of being "born again" in Jesus, and now dedicating their life to spreading his word. I wrote a brief response, giving half-hearted approval to the changes Dale was going through and drawing parallels to the various conversions and reconversions I had lived through. I wish I had sent it to him.

My trip to New York also signaled the end of my working partnership with Henry Jackson. Our recent efforts together had produced more frustration than success, and we were starting to blame each other for having different styles. I was wanting to become more businesslike, partly because of our clients' expectations, but I also wanted to open time in my schedule to work on the *Grapevine*; Henry was wanting to do more with his architectural skills. We parted in as friendly a fashion as we could and remained friends.

I returned in August to a new solo phase of my construction career, to the new partnership with Carol selling *Grapevine* ads, and to a last-ditch attempt underway to save the Non-Violence Institute's building for community-organizing purposes, in the form of a human potential teaching organization that rented space nearby and was looking for financing to buy the building. I wrote about this for the September *Grapevine*, but nothing came of it. I also wrote an article about the city's attempt, under pressure from outraged citizens, to put limits on the burgeoning massage and adult bookstore trade in town, focusing on how the proposed ordinance then under discussion would also threaten the two legitimate therapeutic massage businesses in town, both of which were allies and advertisers of ours. (Eventually a revised ordinance was passed that made exceptions for such businesses.)

Meanwhile, Carol returned to school in order to get free of the cycle of low-paying jobs and spells of unemployment that she had been in since before I met her. She began studying psychology at Stanford that fall, funded by her parents.

Our ad-sales campaign for the *Grapevine* seemed to be paying off; the paper grew in size to twenty pages most issues. But we were frustrated by what we saw as the lack of focus and common goals among the staff, who seemed to just stumble along while the paper somehow tumbled out at a certain time each month. We wanted more, and offered a proposal to create a paid position of coordinator, who could focalize the efforts of the staff and represent the *Grapevine* publicly in the community. During October I put our thoughts in a long letter to the staff, obviously drawing heavily on my experiences with both *The Paper* and *Avatar*:

> To me, the main reason for doing a newspaper like the *Grapevine* is to carry on a dialogue on the state of things with a large number of people in the community—all those citizens whose needs and feelings are not articulated by the prevailing media. If the paper becomes distant or detached from its readers, if it fails to make itself available to them or neglects to encourage their participation, if it speaks over their heads or concentrates on matters not of interest to them, then it might as well not publish at all.
>
> On the other hand, a community-access newspaper which does perform its function well acts as an exciting and lively forum of ideas, styles, political developments, cultural and social trends. It is democracy and participation operating on the most basic level—the free expression of who we are and how we get along together. When this is happening, the newspaper staff itself becomes a community resource—a clearinghouse of ideas and technical expertise, part of a continually self-renewing process defined by the people who are using it. A good, open newspaper can be a powerful revolutionary device.

My letter lobbies for a much more aggressive stance for the *Grapevine*, challenging the monopoly of the established local media, focusing the dissatisfactions of the community into a strong alternative voice, getting over our fears and inhibitions about making and spending larger amounts of money manifesting a grander vision. I also asked for more honest dialogue among the staff members in order to fuel the other changes. None of this was very well received, and we continued stumbling forward.

For the October issue I wrote about a debate between the two candidates for Congress in the local district. Liberal Republican Pete McCloskey, who some years earlier had been the first member of his party to speak out against the Vietnam War but who had been moving to the right in recent years, was defending his seat against a famous antiwar challenger, David Harris, the former Mr. Baez and now a well-known freelance writer. "In Harris," I wrote, "as in a small number of other politicians now gaining credibility, the point of view that was the radicalism of the 1960s has become a refreshing hope for a political and ideological housecleaning in the 1970s." Would that it had been so. Despite the best efforts of most of us on the staff to help him mount a strong campaign, Harris lost to McCloskey, of course, and the only consolation prize that year was Jimmy Carter's election as president.

I took time out during election week to write another letter into the wind, aimed in the general direction of Fort Hill. I had been seeing occasional pieces of investigative reporting in the progressive media written by a Dick Russell, who I assumed was the same person I had known in Kansas. Seeing him achieve some success as a writer, and not knowing whether or not he was still with the community, I felt again the affinity for him that had been the basis of our friendship in Kansas, and I wrote to him in care of the magazine that published his latest article I ran across:

> Are you, as I am assuming, the same Dick Russell I knew out in the boonies in Kansas four years ago? Memories of Gary Griffis and grain fields and living under the work ethic gone wild and being probably the only voter for George McGovern in all of Marshall County. Everything comes full circle....The journalist in me...has been coming back to life recently. I'm very involved in a monthly community newspaper here, and have just given my heart to David Harris' attempt to get to Congress. It's a long way from here to original investigation into the machinations of history, but we all do what we have to do. I consider it a great victory in myself that I've grown back out toward the world again. I've spent all this time putting back together a personal life, a career, a point of view, and all the other things that contribute to being a whole person—like a sense of one's physical self and intrinsic value, a sense of humor, a family and friends from whom one gets support; finally, now, there seems to be enough security and enough energy left over to use some on the frivolities of political involvement, commitment to things of principle and things that draw highly evolved and articulated expressions out of oneself. I feel like a person in the world again, no longer a prisoner of my painful history, no longer bound to use all my resources just surviving....This letter is part of the process—a gradual unburdening of all those painful, frustrating, degrading memories—so that I can be here in my world...

I then give a lengthy description of the inner mental turmoil I was still going through almost daily, reliving memories of Fort Hill, sorting out the injustices done to me from the useful and pleasant memories, finding myself inadvertently reliving phases of Mel's life disguised as my own:

> I keep recreating things from the past, from my past and Mel's past, Melvin and Michael all mixed together, slowly spiraling upward through the same bugaboos and pitfalls over and over again, toward—I don't know. The instinct tells me I haven't ever been quite myself yet. I haven't found freedom yet—the real freedom, from one's own past, pride and prejudice. I believe I can, and the vision still leads me onward, but I do have to shake off all this old stuff to feel the way I want to.

I don't know for certain that I sent this letter; the copy I have is a handwritten draft, and ends abruptly. I think I did. Not that it matters; I certainly received no response. What I wrote shows that my internal process was proceeding apace, gradually freeing myself from the psychic hold Fort Hill had on me.

DEAR LANDLORD, PART II

I spent the next few weeks after the election getting to know the people who lived in a large rural commune in the Palo Alto foothills known as "The Land." A close friend of one of my carpenter buddies lived there, and through him I began hearing of the difficulties the commune was facing from the threat of eviction due to a complicated ownership dispute. The Land had been part of Palo Alto mythology for a number of years; I first heard of it when I was working on my dump truck engine at the Briarpatch garage several years earlier. Now, I decided it was time to get to know these folks and their struggles. I was invited to one of their Sunday morning public breakfasts, found myself enthralled and quite relaxed in their company, and gradually became a familiar member of the circle of regular visitors. I spent a number of evenings and whole weekend days drawing various residents out on the subject of how their community came to be, on the details of the legal entanglement they were caught in, and on what their intentions were if they could find a way to resist eviction and stay on.

I borrowed photographs and drawings from several of them and put together a lengthy front-page piece for the December *Grapevine*, in which I presented their view of the dilemma and their wishes for a happy resolution. The headline, "Digging In at the Land," was set in bold white type, superimposed over a dramatic half-page silhouette picture of Land residents confronting a bulldozer sent onto the property at dawn in an ill-fated attempt to destroy their homes. The article jumped to the centerfold and beyond of a 24-page issue, our biggest ever, where I included a brief-as-possible summary of the five separate, overlapping legal actions that were then pending, concerning the title, occupancy, and use of the property. All in all, it was the longest and most detailed single article to date in the *Grapevine*, and it was intended as the start of a series, which would go on to tell the history of how the community developed, as well as a continuing account on their current problems.

The long-time owners, Alyce and Emmett Burns, an elderly Republican couple, (she an agricultural heiress, he a disbarred lawyer), had lobbied to annex the dramatic 750-acre hilltop property into the City of Palo Alto years before as a precursor to a development plan that included a cemetery and a cattle ranch as well as housing, but had defaulted on the large assessment for utilities improvements that went with the annex-ation. They eventually agreed instead to sell to Donald Eldridge, a millionaire businessman of Democratic, progressive leanings, in a complicated deal in which title would transfer gradually as he paid off the $2 million cost in installments. He took full title to about 150 acres right away and provisional title to the rest pending completion of the payments.

Eldridge gave permission for peace activists to use the several informal buildings in the more devel-oped "frontlands" for workshops and a small residential commune, at no cost to them. This move had quickly become the entrée for a much larger group of social experimenters to move into the "backlands" and form a community there, living first in tents and tepees and later in several dozen shacks and cabins they built with recycled materials and increasingly sophisticated building skills. Hundreds of people had lived there over the years, and thousands had visited. The current population was about fifty. Eldridge had affirmed his tacit support for their presence at times over the years, particularly since he thought their being there both enhanced the chances of environmental preservation and discouraged the possibility of more serious vandal-ism, but he had otherwise kept a very low profile. The city had attempted halfheartedly over a period of time to enforce its building codes in order to outlaw the houses and evict the residents; an article by two of the residents in the *Grapevine* a year earlier had solicited community support.

The agreement for sale of the property had broken down after the city changed its zoning for the foothills, which increased the minimum parcel size for homes and thus in effect diminished the value of properties.

This action precipitated a dispute between Eldridge and the Burnses, as Eldridge withheld further payments until he could be sure of the value of what he was buying; he sued the city for relief, following the lead of other landowners similarly affected. The Burnses, in turn, refused to grant Eldridge title even to the acreage he had already paid for and ultimately fore-closed against him for title to four-fifths of the total acreage. A court gave them the right to purchase this portion of land back at a foreclosure auction, thus causing Eldridge a loss of over a million dollars. The foreclosure decision was on appeal in state courts.

The foreclosure left the community of residents without its angel, and the Burnses began attempting eviction. Their bungled attempts to serve notices of eviction and their perceived propensity toward violence when they didn't get their way precipitated the current crisis. A collective of civil rights lawyers was providing the residents with excellent legal help at minimum cost, and the eviction struggle was proceeding slowly and methodically through the courts. Meanwhile, the city was teaming up with the Burnses and the courts to crack down again on the building code violations; the residents were responding with a campaign to persuade the city to liberalize its building code to allow for such "owner-built" housing in rural areas, as several other cities and rural counties in northern California had already done, with the encouragement of the adminis-tration of Governor Jerry Brown. And, in the wings, a local regional park district was expressing interest in purchasing the entire property to add to its open-space holdings, if it could ever be obtained with a clear title and without a bunch of rowdy residents.

My article was the first time this entire complex struggle had ever been explained in one place, along with a description of the residents' visions and hopes. They were grateful for the support, and I was grateful for their friendship. I saw in my connection with them a chance to make myself part of a functioning commu-nity that offered some of the benefits and few if any of the authoritarian drawbacks of the community I had left behind at Fort Hill. It was clear I was compensat-ing, and seeking a way to balance out my earlier experiences. Here was a group of long-haired, relaxed men and strong, self-confident women easily accepting me into their ranks and welcoming my input. The Land offered a chance to be in a communal setting where free expression, spontaneity, and relaxation were the norm. I chose to overlook internal dissensions and difficulties, as I developed my alliance with them, and I especially failed to see the degree to which the relaxed exteriors of most of the men masked rather traditional values and role-model limitations. I attended Saturday night dances in the "Long Hall," the large meeting space that was the community center of the "frontlands," and there I finally learned to cut loose and let my body dance to rock and roll music, an ability that had evaded me for years. I was also interested in the fact that many of the men, and some of the women, of The Land made their livings doing carpentry and other construction work; I started seeing visions of collective enterprises.

The January *Grapevine* contained a relatively brief update on current events, telling of the latest legal entanglements between the attempts to evict the residents and the residents' response of asking the courts to hold off until the ownership dispute had moved further along. There had also been some alliance-building done with members of the Palo Alto City Council, in hopes thus of dampening the enthusiasms of the city staff to pursue the enforcement of building and health code violations.

The February *Grapevine* included my anticipated long article on the history of The Land, starting from a brief reference to its sacredness for the now-extinct local Indian tribes, through its development as a Republican political-organizing retreat from the 1920s through the 1940s, through the period of purchase and attempted development by the Burnses, their sale to Eldridge, the disagreement with the city as its intentions for the foothills gradually shifted from encouraging development to encouraging open space and conservation, the early use of the property for antiwar organizing, and the shift that gradually took place over several years to a more generalized countercultural community, complete with faction splits, influence on the larger antiwar movement at several key junctures (Daniel Ellsberg spent time there, for example, just days before he began copying and releasing to the public the Pentagon Papers), and critical roles in encouraging and hosting several of the socialist-minded enterprises that served the larger Midpeninsula community.

In recent years, all this had given way to the anarchic community that now filled the entire property, committed to as free-form a lifestyle as feasible. My concluding sentence said: "Most of the residents seem to agree that two things about The Land are special—the chance to live in close contact with a relatively unspoiled environment, and the tacit understanding that each person's life is his or her own business, which no one else can control or interfere with." Needless to say, this attitude made for a fun life, but in the current circumstances made it difficult to stay focused and together through the complex demands of the legal struggle.

I was increasingly seen as an ally of the community members most involved in this struggle, not simply a neutral observer and reporter, and was also beginning to pursue the option of employing several of the members on some larger construction projects I was

planning, including at my sister's house, where money was now coming available to continue the work we had put on hold two years earlier when we found it necessary to sue the original builders.

The March *Grapevine* again included an article on recent developments in the eviction drama. During February, the judge who was hearing the numerous preliminary motions from both sides decided to take a look for himself, to verify or deny the Burnses' claim that serving each resident with an individual proper eviction notice was impossible because of the way they lived. The judge and his assistants, and the Burnses and their lawyers, and a group of residents and observers such as myself spent several hours walking through the backlands, getting acquainted, and checking out what it was about the residents' life at The Land that made it special and worth defending and preserving. The only practical result of the tour was the opportunity it gave the Burnses' representatives to continue serving individual eviction notices.

BURNING OUT ON SUCCESS

After the March issue, the conflicts Carol and I were feeling with most of the *Grapevine* staff came due. An important Palo Alto city council election was coming up on May 10, and planning was underway to give special coverage to that election and the issues it raised. At the planning meeting at the end of March, a schedule was developed; we would give preliminary coverage as the lead of the April issue, then publish extra copies of the May issue, including a special election supplement, and distribute those copies door-to-door in selected neighborhoods in town. This was an ambitious plan for the *Grapevine*, and Carol and I saw in the relatively half-hearted acceptance of it by some of the staff a fatal problem that we no longer saw it within our power to resolve. After a year of increasing efforts on our part—selling and laying out ads, researching and writing articles, laying out pages, wrestling with staff resistance, and coordinating distribution—we were burning out. I wrote a joint letter of resignation, announcing that we would be leaving the staff after the May election issue, blaming our decision not on our work load but on:

> the prevailing short-sightedness and mistrust that is able to look at our contributions to the *Grapevine* and the personal sacrifices which have accompanied those contributions and...accuse us repeatedly of ego-tripping and trying to "take over" the paper. The increased efficiency and concern for budget-balancing that we've struggled to create has backfired two months in a row in

edit. board decisions to keep the size of the paper smaller than the available copy justified, in both cases for want of a few dollars worth of ads or the willingness to take a small risk. (A year ago, entire issues would be published with no idea of where the money was coming from to pay for them; we feel that by improving the cash flow we've created a monster, a fiscal and moral conservatism of the left that denies any of the spontaneity and faith in the process that is so essential in this kind of work).

Making good on the promise to participate in the election coverage, I wrote three major articles for the April issue. A front-page piece, "Palo Alto Chooses a Future," discussed the unusual character of this election. Five of nine seats on the council were up for grabs, and the two slate organizations that had dominated city politics for some years, a "residentialist" slate and a "commercialist" slate, had both decided to sit out the election and not run formal slates of candidates. This move opened the way for some 17 active candidates, including only one incumbent, to campaign as independents, which would have seemed to allow for more freewheeling debate on the options facing the city. But we perceived what amounted almost to a conspiracy of silence on the part of the candidates and saw it as the *Grapevine*'s role to elucidate the choices facing voters. There were important issues of foothills and baylands development or conservation, questions of mass transit versus more suburban sprawl, relations with Stanford, maintenance of city services in an impending era of budget constraints, et cetera, et cetera. With another staff member, I interviewed all the candidates and published summaries of their views on some of these issues, as well as their likely positions on a left-to-right spectrum, to help voters make sense of the choices.

My third article, "Imperial Palo Alto," discussed the city's new comprehensive plan, enforcement of which was one of the background issues in the election. Palo Alto had for years been an employment magnet for the entire Santa Clara Valley, attracting a large work force from elsewhere in the county and the surrounding area and the generous tax base and special services this funded, while the surrounding bedroom communities suffered in comparison. The comprehensive plan, prepared under the administration of a relatively development-oriented council, mainly accepted this situation without confronting its assumptions. We were challenging the candidates to break their political and moral silence on the questions this dilemma raised.

In May, as promised, we continued our analysis and gave our recommendations. An article by one of the long-time *Grapevine* staffers, one of Carol's and my conservative opponents in the ongoing planning discussions, explored the possibility that monied interests in the city, including the leadership of the Hewlett-Packard Corporation, the electronics outfit that had spun out of Stanford years earlier and begun the entire Silicon Valley revolution, were secretly supporting a slate of "commercialist" candidates in the election. I wrote an article on how the local monopoly newspaper, the *Palo Alto Times*, influenced elections in town by publishing prejudiced news coverage and refusing to publish letters critical of its policies, as well as by publishing editorial endorsements decided by two editors who didn't even live in Palo Alto and by the publisher, who did. These endorsements were considered to be worth 2,000 or 3,000 votes, which in a low-turnout election could well represent the margin of victory.

In response, we offered an endorsed slate of progressive, independent-minded candidates and encouraged our readers to review our coverage of all the candidates' policies in order to make an informed choice. Additional election coverage by a variety of staff members, including myself, discussed Palo Alto's relations with its neighboring communities, its role in planning for approach roads for a new bridge about to be built across San Francisco Bay, the deteriorating turnouts in recent city council elections and the consequences this implied for city housing policies, the city's legal involvement in the various lawsuits and zoning questions concerning the foothills, the traffic problems increasingly facing the entire Midpeninsula and Santa Clara Valley areas, child care policies and implications for the commuting work force, and solid waste disposal in the city.

Somehow I also managed to produce yet another article on The Land, this time reporting on the complex negotiations now actively underway to sell the entire property to the regional park district if the ownership and eviction disputes ever got settled. Both the Burnses and Eldridge, the two disputing owners, had signed agreements with the park district promising to give the district first dibs on the land if the other disputes could be cleared up. In the process, an internal struggle within the district's staff had precipitated the resignation of its long-time land negotiator, thus giving more political influence to its general manager, whom we found generally distasteful.

This heroic effort was indeed my, and Carol's, last for the *Grapevine*, so I did not get to write the follow-up articles over the next several months, as the dramas of The Land intensified and finally came to a dramatic conclusion. The June issue offered congratulations to the winners of the city council election: four of our five endorsed candidates won, signaling a significant turn to the left and away from a developmental majority; the fifth winning candidate, who turned out to be the swing vote for the next couple of years, was the youngest person running, a favorite son of Hewlett-Packard, which simultaneous to supporting his campaign hired him into its public relations department. But on balance, it seemed the *Grapevine* had had a salutary effect on the process. Carol and I were proud of our role in all that, and anxious for a rest.

A LETTER FROM THE LORD

Our efforts with the *Grapevine* produced an additional surprising side effect during this period. One day, a stranger knocked on our door and introduced himself to Carol as David Lerner, an acquaintance of mine from Fort Hill, who lived in Palo Alto now and had been reading my articles in the *Grapevine* for nearly a year. He finally felt ready to make contact with me, presuming I was the person he thought I was. She strongly encouraged him to come back another time so we could visit. David had never been a close friend of mine. He had moved to Fort Hill during the period of intensive work on the building projects, when I was unhappy and lonely and always working. He was at the time an eighteen-year-old from New York who had become familiar with the community through our sales efforts there. He was perceived to be a disagreeable and difficult community member, and in fact had been the first person to spend time in the infamous "vault," but the net effect of this was that he developed a strong bond with Mel and with some of the others, which continued even though he now lived on his own and was an aspiring writer. He visited regularly at the community houses in Hollywood and San Francisco.

When he and I finally saw each other in early May, it happened to be on a day when he received a new letter from Mel that contained some sad and surprising news. A close protégé of Mel's in the community, David Lanier, known as David Libra, had recently become depressed and had blown his own brains out, ostensibly because of a broken heart from a love relationship. "Libes" had been a mainstay in Mel's close-in network for years and it's easy to imagine how his suicide would have shocked the community. He had been the person whose picture standing guard with a rifle in Mel's garden had been published in the *American Avatar* community issue, and he had been the person who with Mel's encouragement had guided Eric and me on our acid trips on the fateful night before we began demolishing House Number Four, and who had told me then that I had a murderer lurking inside me. But I suspected there were other issues at work besides love-life difficulties.

I had always believed he had a bisexual component that was active before he joined the community and that had been suppressed there; he had arrived shortly before I did in early 1968, in the company of an Australian writer, now openly gay, whom he had met in California and traveled cross-country with. His brief, unhappy relationship with Alison Peper had produced a lost little girl child, who was moved to the farm for foster parenting after their relationship ended. I could imagine a sensitive person terminally overloading on the usual everyday demands of the community.

I decided to write Mel a letter about this hypothesis, relating it to my experiences with him. My letter amounted to a declaration of independence, the most honest words I had ever written to him (see sidebar 6). Despite this thoroughgoing criticism of Mel and his community, however, I concluded with praise for his original music and his music anthology tapes, and asked whether copies were available. To my great surprise, I received a response from Mel barely a week later, sent from Martha's Vineyard. It's the only letter I ever received from him, and one of the most personal communications of any kind he had shared with me. It was full of shocking news, puzzles, and confessions, including some statements that appeared to be exaggerations and untruths (see sidebar 7).

Mel's quick response, with its confusing combination of humility, confession, and arrogance, took me completely by surprise. I didn't know how to react, or whether to respond; I went to David Lerner for help, but he wasn't able to offer me much. He still saw the community in a much more favorable and unequivocal light than I did. It seemed unlikely we would remain close friends, and in fact we did not, although we did continue visiting infrequently for some months.

As was so often the case when I reflected on Fort Hill, the mix of conflicting feelings gradually gave way to one overriding emotion: deep anger, to which everything else was an afterthought. Eventually, I wrote this anger down in a draft of a return letter to Mel, which I'm quite sure I never completed or sent, though later events made me wish I had. The draft is undated, but it was evidently written late in 1977 or early in 1978, shortly before the tenth anniversary of my arrival at Fort Hill, and the fifth anniversary of my departure.

In it, I go on for a number of pages, detailing specific complaints about life in the community and how it undermined individual creativity and spontaneity, how it encouraged hierarchical power struggles, how it reflected traditional values and enforced traditional gender role models, how it abused our willingly given contributions of time, money, and energy, and created a structure in which it was impossible to claim any of those gifts back, how it was all based on an assumption of personal loyalty to Mel even when that loyalty was not present (as in my case), how the rules were enforced by violence and public humiliations, how much of this system was brought about by the creation of false expectations (such as my hope of moving to Fort Hill to work on a functioning newspaper, which was already falling apart before I arrived), and was perpetuated by the steadily increasing control of our thoughts and our access to cultural information from the world at large. I conclude with a scathing criticism of Mel's statement that he is no longer producing music, because the world is not yet ready for it. I then criticize Mel's and the community's apparent inability to achieve commercial success with any of its efforts at media or creating public influence for itself (see sidebar 8).

O Bla Di, O Bla Da, Life Goes On Now

During the months while all these intense feelings about Mel and Fort Hill were brewing in me, a number of other issues were also coming to a head. I spent the spring and summer employing a number of people from The Land, and some other friends as well, including Carol, as a crew to complete the long-awaited remodel on my sister's house, spending the money obtained in an out-of-court settlement of our suit against the former owners. When the money ran out, my sister and brother-in-law agreed to pay me some of what was due in the form of a shared title on the empty lot next to their house. My work associates and I saw this as a chance to develop a model solar house, in a financial environment in which the long cycle of real estate inflation in the area finally seemed to be slowing down but the tax benefits of solar development were increasing; it looked like our last best chance to get in on the game, after a number of disappointing overtures over the preceding years. I prepared to apply for my building contractor's license so I would be legally able to build and sell a speculation house.

My mother finally sold her house in New York and moved to Redwood City to be near my sister and me, rather than to Florida, as she had previously planned. Carol was close to finishing her work at Stanford, getting ready to graduate with a degree in psychology, which she promptly decided to apply to a career in real estate.

We watched from a distance, sadly, as the *Grapevine* proceeded to wither away. In size and format it reverted to the form it had had before we got involved, the appeals for financial and volunteer support began appearing again, but evidently to little avail. It went on like this for nearly another year, and in June 1978, an issue was published that announced there would be a publication break for the summer while the remaining

staff reviewed its plans and options. The paper never reappeared.

This was all the sadder for us because the drama of The Land's eviction struggle and the transition to a new era for the people and the property richly deserved to be covered, but we no longer felt we had outlet for this. The Burnses eventually succeeded in serving the residents with an adequate and legal set of eviction papers, and the case came to trial in county court. It was a sideshow that went on for weeks and drained everyone involved of a great deal of personal energy that all became focused, tragically, on the three-year-old daughter of two of the residents most involved in the eviction fight. They left her one day in the care of another resident, one of my close work associates who was also one of little Sierra's closest friends. He took her to the beach for the day and photographed her wistfully staring out to the ocean and the sky, then took her back to Struggle Mountain, the associated commune nearby The Land that had once been Joan Baez' and David Harris' home. While he had his back turned briefly, Sierra fell into the doughboy swimming pool; by the time she was discovered, she had suffered brain damage and nearly drowned. She was taken to the Intensive Care Unit of Stanford Hospital and remained there in a coma for several weeks while the eviction fight continued.

The Land's residents and supporters found ourselves conducting simultaneous vigils at both the hospital and the courthouse. We lost both fights. Sierra's body eventually gave out without ever regaining consciousness, and the eviction fight was lost. The Burnses proceeded to complete their sale of most of the acreage to the Midpeninsula Regional Open Space District and collaborated with city officials to conduct the eviction and nearly simultaneous demolition of all the buildings of both the "frontlands" and the "backlands," which occurred with great fanfare during October 1977. Donald Eldridge also completed his deal with the open space district, although I'm unable to remember how that transaction related to his continuing appeal in the state courts for some satisfaction on all the money he had invested.

When the demolitions occurred immediately following the eviction, they were carried out with what we perceived to be great contempt for the still relatively pristine nature of the land. A large hole was dug next to each building, and the debris unceremoniously bulldozed in and buried, causing what seemed completely unnecessary long-term damage to the environment. The springbox and gravity distribution water system that had been built many decades before and had been lovingly revived and maintained and extended by the residents was completely destroyed, leaving the land without any usable water source as it entered its new life as an open space resource for the people of the area. The entire property was fenced and kept off limits to the public for a number of months while the open space district cleared up the mess it had made and developed walking trails, marker signs, parking lots, and the like. Former residents and friends of The Land, including myself, did obtain special permission to return to the property the next Easter Sunday to have one more experience of what had become a traditional celebration on a particular hilltop, but it was a small and bittersweet victory.

I found myself that summer, while working with a friend from The Land, becoming uncontrollably infatuated with him. He was kind enough to let me talk this out with him and, I presume, to at least consider allowing some action on my infatuation, but that proved impossible. It did put me on notice that the old issue of my sexual identity was unresolved, and I raised the issue both in my men's group and with Carol, for eventual resolution. In other ways also, my relationship with Carol was becoming more tense. She was making more and more demands on my time and attention, and I was more and more unable to be available to her emotionally in the way that she wanted. A tone of psychological and occasional physical violence was creeping into the relationship that disturbed us both a great deal. I felt quite out of control with it.

During the fall, I completed my application for my contractor's license, which involved documenting years of work experience, collecting testimonials from customers and co-workers, proving my financial stability, and sending all this off with proof of a performance bond insurance policy and a passport-type picture of myself.

About the time I accomplished all this, I happened to run across a new album by Jim Kweskin, "Jim Kweskin Lives Again," a live concert album on a minor record label from the Midwest. It gave no indication of whether he was still with the community, and so, assuming that he was not, I sent off a brief fan letter to him, congratulating him on what I perceived to be his new independence and return to the music biz. I enclosed my extra copy of the passport picture taken for my license application, as a simple way of demonstrating that I too was living again. He sent back a brief note, using the return address of the record company, and mailed from Atlanta, Georgia, where he was evidently touring: "Dear Michael, Life is a ball. It's hard, but the harder it is the better I like it. If you are open to it, you shall receive it. With all sincerety [sic] Jim."

My son,

Your criticism was well taken. And how fascinating that you and brother David are in such close quarters. "He" certainly has a way of keeping kindred souls in proximity. I have become quite a "private" person in these ensuing years now upon us and therefore know little of what has been transpiring out there in the greater world. I see that you are well on your way to some manifestation of glory and fame, in contrast to my state of meditation.

I, too, have had to undergo the stress of overload, and some time back made the regrettable but unavoidable decision to withdraw from further contact and retire into the grace of my own mind to continue my efforts to root out the truth. No, there's no denying it, I'm not the man I used to be. Not that I'm giving up, mind you; only a brief respite to eventually prepare for even greater battle. I have received quite a numerous number of setbacks in my pursuits and have found, like many others in my station, that the quest is multifaceted. Consistency is a hobgoblin.

I am, basically, quite relieved that you finally saw fit to initiate contact with yours truly. How often I have questioned your fate and pondered upon your eventual outcome. Back in those days I never really knew which way the winds of fate would blow. I had my hopes, naturally, and my visions, (of which I never spoke) also. No, it was no mere whim I was following; though it may have seemed to some (yourself probably included), that my ways were strange, to say the least. And I can't now say, in all honesty, that I have learned anything or really changed radically, but I must admit that I have witnessed some unforeseen surprises and therefore can say that experience itself has been added unto me and, in a way, that may be said to be some kind of change. The people who followed me, willingly or the opposite, had, of course, to find their own way too, eventually and you might remember that, though I may have been labelled as some kind of guru or spiritual teacher, in my own secret recesses I never felt this way. Much like Charlie Manson, the interpreatation [sic] of my normal actions was in the hands of others. If I gave the unfortunate impression that I wished others to imitate my solitary acts it was involuntary. I only issued orders upon request. In my own way I was seeking, and still am, all alone. That hasn't changed, though the world has. The world (whatever that is) is fast approaching a reckoning, and my only hope is that I may be allowed to make myself ready for it. The overloading cannot continue indefinitely and examples must be set. I hope you are writing about this, for I remember your early AVATAR letters and recall you always had a way with the written word. Speaking of the early days, you remember Candy, the child you brought up to me. Well, she is still with us though I'm afraid she has grown a little withdrawn. She ought to get out on her own, like you did, but of course I will never tell her this. One must, as you say, find their own natural rhythms and instincts within the prevailing conditions and follow these impulses according to how one is individually programmed before one can really ever begin to develop their own spontaneity and creative abilities to express the holy "Self". No, it's good you got out when you did, before the continual stress and pressures built up to the inevitable overload that brought so many down. But, we bury our dead and look for a brighter day.

Jeremy, the one who held you up to the mirror to witness your squashed face, has gone off the deep end. Quite mad, as the English say. I believe he's in jail someplace for child-molesting. Now I hope you don't attribute these unfortunate events to my influence, soley (or is that "solely") but we all must shoulder our share of the blame; even you, as I'm sure you know. Sofie has gone back to her people of Mexican heritage and last I heard was drinking rather heavily. In a word, the Community is Kaput! But I'm sure you foresaw that it would turn out that way. After all, force and brutality cannot continue unimpinged forever as a normal mode of expressing life. But I do, at some future date, have plans of erecting a true space station where individuals who have only the good of humanity at heart may orbit freely. To this end I pledge myself, and only in this way do I find the courage to go on, stilted as that may sound. Not to be a teacher, not a guru, not even as a shining example but only as a free human being expressing my thanks to God and breathing the good, clean air with similar beings. If I have made mistakes, then that is a private matter and, as the *I Ching* says, there is "no blame", and if, yet, in treading my own private trail, I have, in some indistinct way or other, happened to be of some use to my fellow man, then, that is probably the most we can ever dare to hope for, for we tread alone AND together......

I almost forgot. About the music, I have given it up. Only when the compounded joy of ALL humanity is their [sic] to be born forth in song will I feel free to add my voice to the melee. My message awaits that consumation [sic].

He enclosed a fan-type picture of himself sitting naked on a lawn with his guitar covering the private parts, quite a departure for the formerly very traditional Jim Kweskin. Still no clear evidence of whether or not he was with the community.

By the time this arrived the date for my license exam had also arrived, and I spent the day in San Francisco being tested. When the exam ended early, I decided, okay, today is the day, and I went to knock on the door of the remaining Fort Hill house in San

Francisco, near Buena Vista Park in the Upper Haight-Ashbury district, with a spectacular view of downtown from the living rooms. I was greeted by three women of the house: Kay Rose, who had once owned House Number Three on Fort Hill, and who then, after divorcing her husband, had returned to the community by way of the farm, where she was a resident during the time I was there, with her young daughter in tow; Peggy McGill, a young Taurus woman with whom I had had a brief infatuation when we both were living in New York; and Nell Turner, whom I had never met before but who was the younger sister of Bess Turner, one of my close friends from the early days of working on *Avatar* in the South End. Bess was the mother of a young girl who had been born around that time, who was forcibly separated from Bess during the days of sexual behavior modification on the Hill, and was later sent to live with us at the farm while Bess was in New York being a stockbroker. Meeting Nell was a peculiar kind of déja vu for me.

All three of the women were cordial but cryptic, giving me little information about what was going on with the community but letting me know the San Francisco house was about to be given up and its personnel transferred to Hollywood. They also told me they had heard about the note and picture I had sent to Jim, and found that amusing. So the gossip network was evidently in full operation, and Jim was evidently hooked into it. When I spoke about my current life, and tried to put my relationship with Carol in a perspective that included my earlier relationships with the Carol and Candy they knew, I remember Kay just saying in an aside to Nell, paraphrasing my words, "He says he keeps having to go through the same things over and over." It must have been a reference to lessons they were experiencing, but they did not explain. One of Mel's favorite aphorisms in earlier years had been that "recapitulation is the only real learning." After a while the conversation wound down, and the women were nervous about starting dinner, so I left, thanking them for their cordiality. So that was my one and only visit to Fort Hill turf in all the years since leaving in 1973. Not too satisfying.

COME OUT, COME OUT, WHEREVER YOU ARE

That spring, I got pushed farther into exploring the question of my sexual identity. One of my men's group friends, Gordon Murray, was invited to co-facilitate a course at Stanford on the philosophy and growing body of literature of the new men's movement, through a new program at the university to encourage community participation; the course was open to both Stanford students and community members. I signed up for the course and immediately became infatuated with the other co-facilitator, a senior in the same psychology program Carol was in, who encouraged my friendship but was pretty freaked out by my amorous intentions. By the time the course ended, it was all but impossible for either of us to retain our equanimity.

I decided I had to do something about this dilemma. I wrote a letter to Don Clark, a well-known therapist and writer in the field, whose book *Loving Someone Gay* had been very helpful to me in defining the questions I was facing, and who had been Gordon's therapist while he was exploring similar issues. I asked Clark if he was available to do some work with me; he wrote back that he was not taking new clients, but recommended another local therapist, whom I had met a couple of years earlier when he "married" one of my associates in the Men's Center. I started individual therapy with him, and soon was invited to join his weekly gay men's "coming out" group, which quickly became one of the most important aspects of my ever-changing life. I did not appreciate the professional distance the therapist insisted on keeping, but the other men in the group became important new friends for me and I had affairs with a couple of them.

Carol was as supportive as she could be of this new interest in my life. For the 1978 Gay Freedom Day parade in San Francisco, I spent the weekend with my friend Gordon and some friends of his, a breakthrough for me, while Carol and her women's group from Stanford marched in the parade under a banner, "Straights for Gay Rights."

Carol graduated from Stanford. She and I signed up together for courses in real estate law and business management at the downtown Palo Alto branch of the local junior college. Soon she obtained her real estate sales license and found a job with a local office. She made new friends there and even had a brief affair with a co-worker, which was a generally unsatisfying experience, but it did affirm for her that there were other possibilities open to her.

I was exploring the gay night life scene around Palo Alto and San Jose, such as they were, and quickly concluded that to find what I was looking for I would probably have to get in the habit of commuting to the much larger and more diverse gay scene in San Francisco. I began doing this in all my available time, with a lot of encouragement but some palpable disappointment on Carol's part. It was increasingly clear our relationship was not likely to hold together, but it was equally clear that I was very happy finally letting the truth out in the air about my longings and fantasies.

Not too long into this phase I realized that I had to separate from Carol in order to have the freedom to explore freely. As ever, she was both supportive and

Dear Mel,

I'm writing in response to your letter of May 28, 1977, the one that begins, "My son, your criticism was well taken..." and goes on to explain away a lot of your current difficulties.

Let's begin by getting something straight: I'm not your son, and never have been; you're not my father, and never have been. We are *something* to each other, but it's not father and son....

I'd like to say early on that most of what you say in your letter is a shuck, and I don't believe a word of it. I don't know what purpose it serves for you to continue to fool yourself with that sort of pompous talk, if indeed you do fool yourself with it, or to continue to attempt to fool people like me with it. You're about as innocent of wrongdoing as Richard Nixon was, and about as naive.

Another thing that really bugs me is your statement that you have "pondered" my "eventual outcome"—as though I were a TV movie whose last segment you accidentally missed. My "eventual outcome" hasn't been written yet; I'm still living and changing my life, just as you are yours. What you probably meant was you have pondered the question of how I've done in the world outside your community after being *in* your community for so long. And well might you ponder. It provides telling insight into a person's character to see how they behave in the aftermath of massive trauma. You must do a lot of that sort of pondering; a great many people have passed through your community over the years, and I'm sure most have been rather intensely influenced by it.

The attitude that people's lives are curious dramas to be studied from afar—*and* **no more**—is right at the crux of what's wrong with your act, and the act of cer-

tain strong others, like your friend Charlie Manson. People like you know how to respond to the imperatives of history and spirit, at least sometimes, and you can mobilize the disorganized energies of yearning souls, but can you see the pain and confusion you cause in the people around you when you allow yourself to be blown up bigger than life?

I know you disclaim responsibility for what has happened to the people who've followed you because, after all, each of us is responsible for his or her own fate, but you must realize that is a cop-out. For one thing, if you had really "become compassion," as you admonished the readers of *Avatar* to do, you would have learned to use your personal power to urge people toward their best unfolding, rather than just watching us as though we were laboratory specimens, and using us for your own purposes. For another thing, it just isn't true that you "only issued orders upon request."

I can recall many, many incidents in which you directly ordered people to behave in ways not of their choosing, or directly forbade actions people had chosen, or demanded certain types of obeisance, or forced people into compromising positions, or interpreted people's motives in ways that violated their own intentions. And people close to you behaved in exactly the same way, often in attempts to emulate you or to do your bidding. I'm tempted to catalog some of the incidents I remember here just to get them off my chest, but if I did so my letter would threaten to become a book. Suffice it to say my head is filled with memories of weirdness and injustice perpetrated by you and yours. And while all these things were going on, you were hiding behind the same lie that your followers expected this of you, that the noblesse oblige of the

---

reluctant to see this change occur, but I began searching for an appropriate new home. I found one just before Halloween, when I interviewed with a single mother named Patricia Rain at a wonderful home in the woodsy part of Redwood City not far from my sister's home. When Patricia, almost immediately upon meeting me, lent me one of her most flamboyant dresses to wear to the upcoming obligatory drag event of my coming-out group (she and I are almost exactly the same size), I knew I had found a home and a friend. I moved in November 1 and we became instant best friends. We remained together through two years in that house and nearly two more years in another house in Los Altos and remain close friends today. I introduced her to my carpenter friend with whom I had had my infatuation the year before, and they remain a couple now ten years later.

Carol and I attempted to remain close and supportive friends, but it did not turn out to be easy. She soon became involved in a very surprising relationship with an older man, a person of some spiritual and scientific and worldly accomplishments, who was suffering from terminal cancer and blindness caused by a laboratory accident. He was still very spirited, however, and urged Carol to marry him in his last days. He proved his devotion by helping her through some amazing changes, even inducing physical growth and changes in her through processes only he seemed to understand. He remained alive through nearly a year of a marriage that was quite transformative for Carol, and when it was over she and I had little to say to each other. Her real estate career was in full swing.

Before long as I was exploring the gay scene in San Francisco, I came across the early expressions of a network of spiritually seeking and politically active

spiritually privileged required this callous behavior.

Why so many of us were ready to believe you, and others "of your station," is one of the mysteries of this age, but there is no doubt you were lying to us then and you're lying now when you say you had no choice whether to give the orders.

...I must say, it is a severe disappointment, though perfectly consistent with everything else, that you say you've given up music until "the compounded joy of ALL humanity" creates enough space for your voice to sing out again. What was wrong with being a musician, anyway, or a creative artist in any other field? What hole in your sense of self required more than that? You seem to have felt that the world owed you a living, and you've gone about insuring that you have a very nice living indeed, but why does that need to be couched inside a belief that the world at large is not even worth raising your voice in song? How do you ever expect it to become ready, and why *should* the world become more ready than it is before you sing again? Do you believe you were placed here to pass judgment on us all, rather than to participate in the process with everyone else?

I know that once you believed you were here mainly for the process of life, and you wrote eloquently about the how and why of it all. That writing drew me to you, and when I reread your words now they *still* fire my imagination and stir deep feelings in me, even though they are written with the simplistic innocence we all shared then. Who do you think you've become that using your gifts is no longer the most important thing? When you say "my message awaits" the moment when "ALL humanity" sings together, who do you think *you* are while you wait?

...Always a dream of grandeur, but the inability to let events unfold at their own pace. And always, your followers continued working at demeaning jobs and hoping for something better. It made me wonder, to say the least, how sincere you were about amassing any influence, and just how truly God was on your side.

Meanwhile, out here in the rough-and-tumble of the world, music and literature, cinema and broadcasting, politics and religion and social thought have all continued progressing and changing, no thanks to you. Do you think this is what God intends for His loyal servant, as you seem still to like to think you are?

I think you've largely missed it and wasted it, Mel, and your letter, if it represents a real belief of yours, indicates that nothing much is moving where you are. It all makes me wonder why you don't just give it up, tell everybody to take their share and go home, or do whatever they want, and get yourself back on the road or someplace where some fresh wind can blow through the old bod. Maybe take a couple of your favorite wives and kids and helpers and go back to the woods and start over. Remember how you used to threaten to do just that, every year or so? We ingrates just weren't worthy of your presence, and it was too hard to create with all these panderers around, and so forth? You never managed to make the break then; evidently you were as addicted to being followed as we were to following. I'm not sure where you are now in relation to all that, but in your letter you sure sound stuck. And, man, you sure could make music before.

---

gay men known as "radical fairies." They were coming together around the work and the philosophy of Harry Hay, a long-time political activist who in 1950 had founded the first openly gay organization of the modern era, the Mattachine Society, and Harry's long-time partner, John Burnside, among others. They wanted to offer the gay community an alternative to the assimilationist and rather materialist trend that had become dominant in the community in the decade or so since the Stonewall riots had brought "gay liberation" out of the closet. They were organizing the first of what was to become a long series of "spiritual gatherings for radical fairies," to be held in the Arizona desert in September 1979. I was invited by a friend, but I was too busy with my work to attend. But over the next months, the radical fairies became my home base in the gay scene, and I was making friends and lovers who drew me to San Francisco more and more frequently. I was also exploring actively in the gay scene generally, figuring out what I liked and didn't like. In short, I was developing a new community for

myself, this time rather better tailored to my current needs than some of my earlier efforts. One of the central principles of the radical fairies was that everyone is equal, that everyone's viewpoint is valid. All fairy groups made decisions by consensus, and all fairy events were held in circles, imitating the practice of the pagan community, which was one of the major influences on us.

I affirmed my connection with the larger gay community by traveling solo to the first National March for Gay and Lesbian Rights in Washington, DC, in October 1979, which was for me an exciting opportunity to experience the old familiar proto-religious rush of collective political action in a new context. I volunteered as a parade monitor and ushered the huge crowd from the line of march onto the Washington Monument grounds for the big rally, so I got to see the entire crowd walk past me at a distance of a few feet. I was in heaven.

After the march, I went to New York to visit my brother and other relatives and affirm my coming out to them. I also had a rare visit with some friends from high school, from whom I learned just before I was scheduled to leave that my old partner Carol Schneider-Franck was living in the Fort Hill New York house with her two children, and was keeping at least occasional contact with friends and family on Long Island. I was disappointed to learn this too late to act on it, and when I was back home in California I wrote yet another letter to her, hoping to reestablish friendly relations. This was a non-confrontational and rather wistful letter, wishing her well and telling her a little of my current life, but once again it elicited no response.

ARE YOU READY FOR THE EIGHTIES?

During this entire period of a couple of years, I continued my work relationship with a number of the people I had met at The Land, all of whom had by now long since relocated to homes in town and were paying rent each month like the rest of us and needed the cash flow. I hoped and strongly encouraged this to become a collective operation, but all the credentials and bank credits were in my name, and the truth of the relationships was that I was the employer and they were the employees. I disliked the role intensely.

Our hope of building a speculation house in Redwood City next to my sister's house fell through for several reasons; primary among them was that my sister decided to parlay a career she had developed for herself as a lecturer and color consultant into a retail decorating business, and she used the available second mortgage money from her house, which had been intended to fund our building project, to open a store in the Silicon Valley town of Cupertino. I was left with my contractor's license and a crew of employees but no major project to work on.

The fallback plan was to pursue ever-larger contracting projects through the real estate network in the Palo Alto area, and also to accept federally funded contracts to rehabilitate housing in the nearby city of Mountain View. I found myself against my will forced to compete for jobs, respect, and recognition of my own and my crew's ability to produce the work that was expected of us, despite our unorthodox appearance and behavior. Sometimes I hardly knew how to keep up the appearance, and I always resented having to make the effort to do so. I felt constantly torn between my personal impulses and the requirements of my work.

Nearly all the projects we did during this period turned out to be disasters one way or another, frequently running way over budget, frequently getting completed despite antagonistic relations with clients and employees, frequently requiring investment in tools and equipment I could scarcely afford, occasionally requiring difficult negotiations to extract payments from angry clients, and on one occasion actually tumbling unhappily into a mechanic's lien suit, which I lost. I didn't seem able to find adequate legal or accounting help, I was juggling finances with my relatives to keep my credit going, I was falling farther and farther behind in employment taxes and other overhead payments, and my stress level was going through the ceiling. And all this was going on while in the other department of my life I was actively exploring the gay counterculture and looking for a truer expression of myself free of traditional gender roles. Something had to give.

By April 1980, I finally found the courage to do an accurate accounting of how far behind I was, at the point where the owner of the largest federally funded rehab. project we had done was capriciously withholding more than $8,000 in final payments, even though the city and the federal overseers had already approved the work. I found that, even when that money came in, I would be more than $20,000 in debt. This meant that if I had sat home and lived on borrowed money for the previous two years, I would have been farther ahead than I was for all my hard work. I was devastated and completely lost the spirit to continue in the same mode, acting as employer and whip-cracker over a reluctant crew that could not perform up to my needs. I laid them all off and faced the unhappy prospect of working overtime for the next couple years to pay off the debts and get back to zero. But cutting my losses in this way seemed the only sane direction to go.

I decided that I needed to give myself a couple of gifts to assuage my broken spirits. I signed up for classes in improvisational dance and vocal expression; the dance lessons continued for several years and eventually provided me access to a gay men's contact improvisation group in San Francisco, which became another important support group for me. I began therapy sessions in a kind of regression therapy aimed at identifying and clearing up residual birth trauma, and found this very helpful in suggesting reasons I seemed to be so prone to claustrophobic and enervating karmic involvements. I checked out my intuitions about the circumstances of my birth with my mother, and she confirmed that my birth had indeed been very painful for both her and me, that a rough and unsympathetic doctor had been in charge, and that it had taken weeks to find a feeding scheme for me that did not make me ill. This all provided a new sense of the inner work I would have to do to eventually heal myself.

I also felt a need to heal on the external political level. It was the year of Jimmy Carter's downfall and Ronald Reagan's ascendancy, and I worried about the state of the economy and the rising prospects for nuclear war. I was feeling a strong urge to devote as much of myself as I could to the task of keeping the earth alive, somehow, and at the same time was feeling trapped in the task of paying off my debts and resurrecting my career. I fantasized running away, becoming an itinerant activist and handyman, but couldn't see myself voluntarily giving up the friends and family and sense of home I had developed.

To support an alternative course for the future, I aligned myself with environmentalist Barry Commoner's campaign for the presidency, under the third-party banner of the Citizens Party. I became active with the Palo Alto chapter and quickly found myself speaking for that chapter in a northern California coordinating committee, from which base—this is hardly a surprise—I also became involved in publishing an occasional tabloid newspaper for the Citizens Party, *The Citizens Voice*. We published perhaps half a dozen issues over the two-year period I remained with the party. After the rout of the 1980 election, we continued organizing various other efforts locally and statewide, hoping to create a lasting third party, but that did not come about and eventually I found other commitments more important to me than continuing the effort.

During the summer of 1980 I was offered a long-term construction job, as the foreman of a major remodel and second-story addition to a house in Palo Alto owned by a gay property developer. This was a good opportunity for steady income in a friendly environment, and relieved a bit of the pressure of constantly finding new work. On that job, I developed a friendship and then a lover relationship with a rather shy and somewhat closeted gay laborer. We dated and became increasingly close over a two-year period, living at opposite ends of the town of Los Altos and exploring in the radical fairies scene together.

We missed our second opportunity at a major fairy gathering in the fall of 1980, again because of work, but by the third opportunity, late summer of 1981, we were finally able to attend one, in the mountains of northern New Mexico. The four-day event was marked by heavy rainstorms and some other disappointments, but it was transformative for us, nevertheless. As we were getting ready to leave on the last day, I found my new name, literally in the ground at the gathering site, where the shiny, soft stone mica was in abundance. I was looking for a name that would resonate with Michael but have a character of its own. I claimed the name, and spent the next couple of years growing into it; for some years now, I have used the name Mica in nearly every part of my life.

I made a serious effort to enlist the help of my former employees in paying off the remaining debts from our business disasters, but to no avail. As part of that effort, in early 1981, I found myself obsessed

with trying to tell them more about myself, about the history that had led me into involvement with them and what it meant for me in my personal growth to be burdened by the unreasonable debts. I wrote a major chunk of autobiography for their benefit and shared it with them, along with more accounting information about how the business had failed, but it drew no financial or even much emotional support from them. I felt stung and betrayed.

Bobby Bolchalk and I remained a couple and continued working together into 1982 but in that year I decided to cut way back on my contracting career and instead to join my sister's retail business, which was going out on a financial limb to open a second location. I helped locate a building, in San Carlos, near Redwood City, and Bobby and I and other friends performed a major remodel on it. When the store opened I became its manager, receiving only minimal support from the partner with whom my sister had opened the first store. But with a great deal of creative energy and overtime, working for minimal wages, we got the store off the ground.

Bobby and I broke up on short notice when we went to our second radical fairy gathering in San Diego in late 1982 and he met someone who quickly attracted him away from me. This gave me the excuse I needed to finally move to San Francisco, since I was now commuting almost twenty miles each way on the Peninsula, and the drive from San Carlos to San Francisco was only slightly longer. One of my close radical fairy friends and I decided to start a collective household together, and we found a house in the Haight-Ashbury late in 1982. This was a homecoming, a completion of a circle for me, having decided many years earlier that I wanted to live in the Haight and then seen my life unexpectedly take a completely different direction. I am still living in that house eight years later, and it has become an institution in the radical fairy community. A great deal of community organizing work has taken place in our living rooms.

My sister split her time between the two store locations, but eventually made the San Carlos store her primary base, and she and I became closer than ever as we worked together for the next couple of years. Our mother went through a series of hospitalizations for emphysema during this period, and finally succumbed in the spring of 1983. Our business grew rapidly and looked like it was going to be successful in the long term; a third partner merged her store with us, and the three partners and I attempted to function as a "management team" for the three stores. But we were overextended financially and our personnel resources were stretched to the limit. By late 1984 there was serious dissension between me and my sister and the third partner on the one hand, and the original managing partner on the other hand. He walked out without notice one day when we were challenging his management style, leaving the rest of us to attempt to rescue the business from bankruptcy. We were unable to do so, and placed it in a Chapter 11 reorganization mode, which involved closing the San Carlos store and phasing out my job by early 1985, while also relocating and reducing the size of the other two stores we had at the time. This strategy was not enough to save the business from ultimate failure, and this failure was accompanied by the development of neurological symptoms in my sister. What at first looked like a nervous breakdown turned out to be a fatal brain tumor, which was diagnosed too late to be operable. She died in late 1985.

My response to all these developments was to reassess my own life strategy, since I was clearly at risk for the same kind of stress-induced illness that had killed my sister. I felt I had little choice but to return to freelance construction to earn my living, but I did so in as informal a fashion as I could, assuring myself that I did not have to get in over my head again as I had so many times before. I declared my intention to keep my life a little bit simpler, for a change, and did my best to live up to that intention. Doing so, however, wasn't easy or natural for me. I was already very committed to projects that were more than willing to fill all my available time.

Over the previous few years, I had become enmeshed in the San Francisco radical fairies network. I attended many gatherings of fairies in various locations up and down the West Coast, getting used to seeing myself in a wide range of roles across the spectrum of gender possibilities. Being with the fairies gave me a welcome chance to choose who to be and how to behave moment to moment, and to change at will. I decided to use my organizing abilities to make this opportunity consistently available to people who wanted it.

After playing a key role in organizing several major gatherings, I became involved in an effort within the fairies network to organize a non-profit corporation in order to collectively purchase land on which to establish a spiritual sanctuary for ourselves. We decided to seek government recognition as a religion, figuring that what we did together was the equivalent of what standard religions did. We named our sanctuary project Nomenus, making up a word that contained the sounds and implicitly the meanings of half a dozen other names we had considered. In mid-1985, I assumed the role of president of Nomenus; over the next two years I led the organization through the agonizing process of convincing the Internal Revenue Service to grant us our religious organization status (it finally did), and through the equally agonizing process of searching for

land, raising money for the down payment, buying land that was offered to us by a dying friend, and holding a "Homecoming Gathering" attended by nearly 300 people, most of whom became member-directors of the consensus organization. At the same time, I was also involved for about a year in organizing the California Men's Gatherings, helping to guide that informal consensus network of gay and straight men working together through a difficult reformulation of its purposes and way of operating. The men's contact improvisation dance group that I met and danced with weekly was an important base of support and encouragement in all these efforts.

Early in the decade, I decided to spend my activist time helping to create positive and useful alternatives rather than simply protesting and worrying about the mess that the world was in. Seeing how well my efforts with the men's movement were going, and how powerfully our efforts to offer men a wider choice of behavior models helped strengthen them to oppose the status quo of the larger society, I felt that at last I had found a meaning to all my previous experiences. Despite the financial and career difficulties I was still feeling, I felt a unity with myself that was new. And an opportunity came along to articulate this unity to some of my former tormentors.

MORE NEWS FROM THE FRONT

One of the last gifts my sister gave me before she became ill was to point out to me, on August 5, 1985, an article in the *San Francisco Chronicle* about "The Last Hippies in Boston." "I think it's about those people you used to live with," she said. That was indeed true. The article was a wire service report, datelined Boston, about the new affluence of the former hippies of Fort Hill that resulted from their construction businesses on both coasts and their substantial inheritance from Tom Benton, and about the new magazine, *U and I*, they were now beginning to publish to tell the world about what they had become and about how the visions of the old days had transformed with the community's increasing worldliness and long-term relationships with each other. The article gave the current census of the community as 72 adults and 39 children, and mentioned their homes in Boston, New York, Los Angeles, Kansas, and Martha's Vineyard. It spoke of the history of Mel Lyman's influence over them and his dominance of the community's media efforts in the early years. Most surprising, the article reported, "Group members say Lyman died in 1978, but refuse to discuss the cause of death. They deny rumors that Lyman quit the group and is now living in Europe." Two pictures accompanied the article, showing community members happily playing music after dinner one night and admiring their new magazine. All but two of the people pictured were long-familiar faces to me.

Well, well, well. What a strange and unexpected news flash. The community alive and well and reaching out to the public again. Mel reportedly dead, years ago, evidently not long after my exchange of letters with him. It was a lot to take in. I imagined Mel killing himself, or becoming depressed and dying of some mysterious disease. Who could know? In the background of the picture of the music-making that accompanied the article was someone playing harmonica, Mel's instrument, who looked for all the world like Mel himself. I had to look carefully and repeatedly to decide that it wasn't Mel after all but Richie Guerin, who had always been a near-ringer for Mel. Unless it was Mel, after all. I believed they were capable of telling the media anything, regardless of the truth.

It became very important to me to track down a copy of this magazine, but how could I do it, I wondered. I spoke to a radical fairy friend who maintains a legal practice in both San Francisco and Boston, and he gave me the name of someone who was likely to be willing to find a copy on a newsstand in Boston. That person was Charley Shively, long-time writer and editor of *Fag Rag* in Boston. [See Charley Shively's "*Fag Rag*: The Most Loathsome Publication in the English Language" in this collection.] We spoke at length by telephone; Charley was fascinated by my story and immediately went out and found me both the magazine and a copy of a poster advertising an appearance at some local clubs in Cambridge by "The U and I Band featuring Jim Kweskin."

The magazine was little more than a slicker update of the old *American Avatar* format. It was in a standard magazine-sized page, with a full-color cover and some color pages inside, front and back cover paintings clearly done by Eben Given, recognizably of himself and Candy, in a fictional country setting surrounded by friendly dragons. Much of the writing was on the theme of dragons, evidently a new archetypal symbol of life force for the community. An introductory essay inside the front cover gives the closest thing to a statement of purpose:

This publication is offered to you with no explanations, no bylines or credentials. It does not set about to sell anything, prove anything, or change anything. It is a series of open and unusual conversations about the things that concern us all. Think of it as a journey we are taking together. Pretend that we are strangers on a train, you and I traveling somewhere that we have never been before.

Let's not introduce ourselves, or ask all the usual questions like, "Who are you?" and "What do you do?" It is so much more fun to discover these things along the way. Let's begin with no preconceived ideas about each other, no judgments, no categories. Rather let us take a leap of blind faith from one reality to another, from an external world to a world of inner thoughts, feelings and experiences. This foreign land that we are traveling through is a place where one is not afraid to laugh or cry, to admit failure and defeat, to risk love and aspire to beauty. Let us ask difficult questions and give honest answers, and by no means be objective. Who knows what we will find on this uncharted voyage. Let us begin with a song, and see where it leads us.

Very little about the magazine seemed new to me, only the glimpses I could recognize of news bulletins about people I knew: Candy and Eben in tumultuous, stormy relationship, tape recording their intimate conversations to be shared with others (in the style of the electronic linking of the houses that was fantasized but never materialized when I was with them); Dick Russell writing a long paean to their newfound sport of game fishing and a corresponding interest in environmental protection; David Lerner, my Palo Alto friend, corresponding with Jessie about his developing sensitivities as a writer; stories and pictures and letters written by parents about children I've never met. Life in the community obviously goes on, anonymously except to the well connected.

After receiving and poring over the magazine, and experiencing the inevitable and by now familiar rush of nostalgia and revulsion as my memories of the community were restimulated yet another time, I wrote a thank-you letter to Charley Shively summarizing my view of the new product:

The magazine itself is no surprise at all. It's exactly in line with what they produced in years past; strikingly so, in fact. Amazing, really, that so little has changed, except their financial status. It's the same general tone, the same ideas, the same heroes and villains, the same generalized, disinterested commentary on the current scene, the same arrogance and indrawn narrowness of viewpoint, the same traditional morality presented as though it were new and different, the same adulation of Mel's thoughts and words, even some of the same articles reprinted one more time. Even, to my eye, the same Executive typewriter used to set the copy. Exactly the same, limited repertoire of graphic devices. Overall, kind of incredible, such an anachronism. Can you believe anyone still remembering Bobby Kennedy as the hero who could have made it all work out better, if only...? I really wonder what the impetus was to go public again. It clearly wasn't that they have something new to say. Some of the context suggests that the advent of Reagan, et al, has got them worried enough to look at the larger world again, but I still have a sense they'd prefer to stay in their safe little world of money-making and big-game fishing.

The magazine contained a contact card, encouraging readers to stay in touch so they could be informed of any later issues that would be published, but I couldn't quite bring myself to use it. I did alert my three grown nephews, my sister's sons who were and are all aspiring musicians living in Hollywood nearby the community's big house there, to be on the lookout for this magazine or any subsequent one that might show up in the local stores. As we talked about it, my oldest nephew, who earns his living as a carpenter, and I had a shock of recognition. It turns out that the previous year he had actually worked on one of the community's construction crews for a while. I had heard about the job he had with an outfit that did primarily fancy remodels for Hollywood stars, but I didn't make the connection at the time. We compared notes on specific people, and there was no doubt he had worked for my one-time friends; he had found them authoritarian and ungenerous, and had quit after a while. But they occasionally saw each other in the local stores, and he would watch out for a new magazine for me.

A BULLETIN FROM THE HEARTLAND

A few months later, one of his brothers did indeed come up with a copy for me of *U and I* No. 2. This issue, even thicker and slicker than the first, was dedicated to life on the Kansas farm. It stimulated deep nostalgia, even homesickness, in me, and gave lots of information about current events among the folks, again accessible to me largely because I knew more than the average reader about the context. An unsigned "Prologue" at the front of the magazine, written "six months after leaving California" and "the intense pressures of making and publishing the first magazine in Los Angeles," explained the rationale for this issue:

....This isolated spot in the center of the country was a much needed contrast. The farm was a place simply to be, and as always a place where new thoughts came to germinate in conjunction with the new spring seed.

After a few weeks of long walks through the muddy fields, planting the gardens, and getting reacquainted with the rivers, we found ourselves still there, enchanted somehow, unable to leave as we had planned. We gave ourselves up to the land, absorbed by its changing moods and rhythms, and began to write about it. In the first issue we had promised to talk about the great men of the past, about the '60s and what became of them. But because this magazine is a continuing process like our life, always changing, our earlier intentions will have to wait. Here on the farm, our heroes changed into the people who live around us, the people who make or break heroes in the first place.

A long paragraph pays homage to the land of northeastern Kansas and the rugged people who manage to survive there, and the influence both the land and the people have had on the community's members in the time they have spent there.

We came to this area almost fifteen years ago as strangers to a place that seemed formed by the wind and it captured us....Over the years we have lived through the searing summer heat, ice storms, floods, tornadoes, drought and bugs. With the help of our friends we have learned what to plant and where and when and we have a nice place here after many years of stops and starts. We've given up our horse-drawn ploughs now for an old tractor, built a few more houses, made the silo into a tower for teenagers and generally subdued the mud and weeds around the house. We raise enough grains, vegetables, meat and poultry to feed the farm and send out some for the rest of us on both coasts to have a little of this and that. And in doing this we have learned about the land and its unpredictability, its unyielding demands and the deep humility in it. It is not a place that lets you dream or forget, but concealed in its stark reality is the magic and beauty of a paradise.

The magazine is full of long narrative stories about relations with neighbors and the environment of Kansas, full of photographs and Eben Given drawings of farm life, many of scenes quite recognizable to me, some indicating the results of years of effort and increased prosperity. Articles, again recognizably by Dick Russell, speak of investigative reporting into the continuing environmental degradation of America's heartland and warn of an impending second Dust Bowl era. A long section at the back discusses relations between men and women, "He and She," with reprints of old poems and new writings on the subject, old photographs of the famous couples and lovers of Fort Hill, and new discussions of current relationships, another piece about Eben's continuing drama with Candy, and a piece about Norma Lynn Lyman, Mel and Sofie's oldest daughter, now a grown-up, and her love affair with a local man named George whom she had brought home to stay. More dragons and mythic characters. A section of letters from readers of the first magazine. An article by Owen de Long on a hypothetical "Blue Party" he is proposing to organize, another exchange of letters between David Lerner and Jessie, in which she challenges him to leave his concepts behind and get on with his life. Does anything ever change?

I couldn't seem to get beyond the nostalgia this all inspired in me and was a bit horrified to find myself thinking so kindly of those people and that place. What is there to do but respond to such strong feelings? I sat down and carefully handwrote a long letter to "Dear United Illuminating Folks," dated February 19, 1986, and sent it to the address in Kansas offered in the magazine, one among four addresses around the country where readers were encouraged to send correspondence. I went on for pages and pages, telling of my lonely journey from Fort Hill to my current life. I spoke of feeling resonance with the purposes expressed in their new magazine, how it softened for me the memories of our long-ago differences.

> What had all that suffering been for? I couldn't—and don't—believe that was the only way I was able to learn or grow. There must have been some other explanation, some karmic past-life something-or-other that tied me to you, and has kept me tied to you in a way through these years. Something about mirroring difficult aspects of ourselves to each other, I guess, or about accepting lessons for their content regardless of the packaging they come in. I know that out here in my life, somehow my confusion and aimlessness have transformed over the years into a kind of wisdom and humor, an adaptability and vitality and capability that are quite unusual and exemplary among my peers, if I do say so myself, and I'm proud of my survivorship and of my accomplishments, which are more internal than external, even though I've been working and working all these years, just like all of you have been. My life is very full, and

my life begins again empty each day. I feel like I'm ready for anything.

I discuss my sense of nostalgia at seeing new pictures and stories of some of the old friends, and wonder who is and who isn't still with them. I wonder if they wonder about me. I discuss what it has been like for me seeking and occasionally finding in the world at large the kind of security and familiarity they have created for each other in their community/family over the years. And I take a big risk by discussing one of the concerns of my current life:

> One of the really big issues for me in my life, and the area where I have come to find some of my most meaningful and public work to date, is the issue of gender, of sex "roles" and gender-related behavior, and the movement that is afoot here in the middle-class world of the 80's to open out the definitions and possibilities. If we really do have just our inner resources to rely on in life, augmented by whatever help we can elicit from the people around us, it becomes important to know what's really in there, who am I anyway?, and what do I have in me? Do I have to behave in the way my father did, or my mother, or can I create a new blend of my own?

I comment on the section of the magazine concerning gender roles, and point out the traditional interpretations of those roles on which the community's viewpoint seems to be based, something that always made me uncomfortable in the past and seemed to exclude me.

> One of the real turning points for me in the years after I left you was when I re-connected with the spirit of "feminism" and the evolutionary shift of consciousness of which it is a part. I found that men, too, could learn from exploring the ways in which our behavior and our self-images and even our thoughts are pre-programmed according to outmoded and limiting ideas of what is available to us. This is what comes up for me when I read about your ongoing Battle of the Sexes, and it sheds some light on the dilemma I was in when I was with you. People used to ask me (Randy especially comes to mind), "Don't you want to be a man?..." My answer, internally, always was, "Well, yes, but..." I did want to be strong and determined and courageous, and all that kind of thing, but I didn't want to remain locked in inarticulateness and violence and

dependency. In those terms, I wanted to be a "man," and I wanted to be something more as well, and my life with you wasn't showing me a way to do that. What about the "manly" qualities inherent in a woman, the "womanly" qualities contained in every man? When the definitions get too rigid, and get applied across the board to each person based only on their physiology, there is too much chance of the complex mix of characteristics each of us possesses getting averaged out and flattened.

I go on to question how rigid the sex roles still are in the community, and remind them that Melvin used to be in some ways a model of androgyny, a strong and yet sensitive and caring man. I point out that some hints in the magazine suggest a loosening of the gender roles; a woman plumber is mentioned, the men are obviously learning to be thoughtful and articulate. I wonder, is there room among them now for individual preferences, for "intermediate types"? I discuss how the men's movement and the gay movement have become the context of my current life, and how the range of my past experiences has become a valuable asset on which I draw constantly as I play a leadership role within those movements. I describe my work with the radical fairies, our battle to achieve recognition by the government as a religion and our struggle with ourselves to agree on buying land for a retreat center. I describe how all this is going on in the midst of the AIDS epidemic, in circumstances that suggest it could all come tumbling down in a minute, reminiscent of Germany in the thirties, or the Dust Bowl era on the Great Plains.

But in the midst of all this, one by one, we find ourselves having revelations of simple spirit and renewal, find capacities in ourselves that we didn't know were there, learn to reach out to each other and help each other through the transitions. It's quite amazing, really. There's no doubt we are living in "interesting times," as the Chinese used to say—in fact, no doubt we are living in the "last days," as the Bible still says, and, as ever, all we can expect to leave with when it's time for each of us to go, one by one or all together in a big bang, is what we have made of ourselves in our souls through the choices we've made in our lives.

After all this time and all this living, I'm pleased to say I'm still feeling a kinship with all of you and what you are doing, despite the evident differences in the external forms of our lives. And I'm wanting to receive something from you that's the same thing anyone has ever wanted from the family he, or she, has left behind: Acceptance, the knowledge that there is still a relationship across time and space. And I'm feeling, more strongly than ever before, after reading *U & I #2*, an impulse to offer what has been most difficult for me to feel in the loneliness and occasional bitterness of my memories: Forgiveness, and good wishes for your continued success.

So that was my peace offering to the community, my extension of my new self to their new selves, in 1986. Like so many attempts at communication that preceded it, it elicited no response whatsoever. But it was quite a healing for me in my own process.

By the time it was written, my life had moved forward a few more notches, and continued to do so. I became quite accustomed to the guiding role I was playing with the radical fairies, coordinating the efforts of hundreds of people up and down the West Coast and around the country, organizing gatherings and events, inevitably publishing newsletters to keep us in touch with each other. Having reluctantly returned to earning my living as a builder and contractor, after a while I found myself in a fruitful partnership with a close friend from my improvisational dance group, a contractor as skilled and jaded with it all as myself. It's a good working relationship that continues today. In my personal life, I was exploring the new forms of "safer" sexual expression that were developing in response to the spread of AIDS in the gay community, and had a number of opportunities to help friends produce videos and public events to promote this new form of expression. Increasingly, it seemed the community I had joined was finding ways to meet the basic needs of its members among ourselves.

LOOKING BACK, LOOKING FORWARD

In some ways, Fort Hill and all the traumas of the past slip farther and farther into a dim unreality of memory; in other ways it is all as real and present as ever. I seem always to be available and alert to reminders of it wherever they may show up, either from my own imagination and memories or from signals I receive from the world around me. Occasionally I see someone in a store or at a street fair selling wire sculpture stars that resemble those of John Kostick that we used to sell in New York. I always try to find out how it happens that the person selling them knows the designs, but usually it's hard to trace. Recently I met someone in Berkeley who developed some of the same designs himself many years ago by experimenting with mathematical models, the same way John did it. He told me that last year a group of people confronted him on the street in Berkeley, evidently angry and challenging his right to use the designs but not identifying themselves. Could it have been the Fort Hill crew?

In February 1988, our local listener-supported radio station, KPFA, was planning a day of commemoration of the life and work of Kay Boyle, long-time peace activist and Bay Area resident, who happens, of course, to be the mother of Faith Gude, loyal member of the Fort Hill community, and her brother Ian Franckenstein, one of my friends from back there. The advance notices said that Ian himself would be participating in the programming. I wrote a letter of introduction to Kay and a cover letter to Ian and dropped them by the station, hoping he would receive them before the programming aired and get in touch with me. When this did not happen, I ran over to the station and intercepted him as he was leaving after doing his bit on the air, reintroduced myself (he had not seen my letters), and we began a renewal of our friendship. I have been much refreshed to have a new friendship—with someone from that era. Ian lives in Marin County and is primary caretaker for his mother, who is now retired in a nursing home there. He tells me stories of his own recovery from the trauma, of various frustrating attempts to reacquaint with Faith, of people from the community who he's seen over the years.

In the time since I reacquainted with Ian, I have found myself in a new drama in my life. I learned in 1988 that I have been infected with the human immunodeficiency virus at least since 1983, based on blood work drawn then. I believe I was probably infected closer to 1980, when I was under the stress of my construction business bankruptcy and suffered a rash of other sexually transmitted diseases. I was hardly surprised to learn I was HIV-positive; knowing my history, I would have been surprised not to have somehow become caught up in the epidemic. In the last couple years, I have developed symptoms, and recently "progressed" to a diagnosis of AIDS, with Kaposi's sarcoma lesions here and there on my body, but few other major problems.

I continue to feel like a survivor and an optimist, and identify strongly with the viewpoint that AIDS need not be universally fatal. Having made it through so many setbacks and disappointments, I feel committed to making it through the epidemic as well. I'm involved in a variety of experimental treatment programs and nutritional and holistic efforts, as well as standard medical care, to keep the quality of my life intact, so far successfully. I have cut my contracting work back to half-time, and have returned to school half-time at a small progressive college, studying to become a health consultant. It seems that at last I'm going to complete a college degree, and maybe even make a career switch.

In the course of all this, I have found an old friend working in the AIDS field close by. My old collaborator on *The Paper*, Larry Tate, is now the manager of the information hotline at Project Inform, one of the most innovative and aggressive community organizations pushing for reform of the drug development process for AIDS and other diseases. After years of being aware of each other in the Bay Area and finding ourselves unable to renew our friendship, Larry and I at last have something in common in our current lives. I also recently got to reintroduce myself to Daria Halprin (now Daria Khalighi), when I took an intensive ritual and dance workshop from her mother and collaborator, choreographer Anna Halprin. "Circle the Earth" is an annual event dedicated to healing AIDS and other life-threatening illness. The key line of the performance that culminates the workshop is, "My name is (Mica) and I want to live. And I want you to live."

I don't yet feel ready to declare the "eventual outcome" of my life and circumstances, but there is no doubt that all this experience has added up to something. Getting to write about all of it has been a tremendously healing, and confrontational, experience for me. After all, as Mel Lyman used to say, "Recapitulation is the only real learning."

Stop the Presses, I Want to Get Off:

A Brief History of the

Penal Digest International

Joseph W. Grant

Prisons and Prisons, My Daughters and Sons

Penal Digest International. The *PDI*. A newspaper with two purposes: to provide prisoners with a voice that prison authorities could not silence and to establish lines of communication between prisoners and people in the free world.

Over twenty years have passed since the idea for *Penal Digest International* began to take shape. I was a prisoner in the federal penitentiary at Leavenworth, Kansas, at the time. You've heard of Leavenworth—one of the end-of-the-line prisons where feds, and even the state prisons, send their "bad boys." At that time the federal prison at Marion, Illinois, was being used as a youth joint while the feds perfected what was to become the most repressive monument to absolute security that the U.S. government could design. Back then, they used Leavenworth for the truly incorrigible. Leavenworth was where they sent the prisoners when they closed Alcatraz.

Stepping into that prison was reminiscent of the opening paragraph of *Tale of Two Cities*. It was the best and the worst place to do time. The best place to be if you wanted to serve your prison sentence and not be bothered by anyone—prisoner or guard. The worst place to be if you were hoping to make parole. The best place for quiet in the cell blocks. The worst place for informers. The best place for food. The worst place for library books. The best place if you could learn by

Grant is an artist, writer, and graphic designer living with his best friend and their daughter in the Southwest. His documentaries on El Salvador ("Prisons and Prisons: El Salvador") and author Meridel LeSueur ("Women in the Breadlines" and "The Iowa Tour") have been shown on the Time/Life and other cable networks. He believes that never before in our history has there been a greater need for the *PDI* to be publishing and providing a means for prisoners and people in the free world to communicate. He is open to suggestions.

observing and be silent until spoken to. The worst place if you had a big mouth.

I was a first-timer, a fast learner, and, in many respects, I was lucky.

So what was a first-timer—a non-violent first-timer—doing behind the walls at Leavenworth with guys who had averaged five previous incarcerations for very violent crimes? It's a long story. I've never told it before. But the memories of that period are clear. My thoughts frequently turn to the injustices that surrounded me then. I internalize them. Sometimes, when I am alone, maybe sitting on the patio late at night, I doze off. I awake suddenly, look up, and everything seems new. Fresh. The shadows on the trees are a deeper, richer, more visible green. The air is clear. The sound of the insects is sharper, crisper, vibrating. The sound waves can be felt—almost seen. In the slam, one afternoon. Very hot, the last week of July. I'm in the shade, in a slight breeze. Half asleep, I find my eyes skimming along the ground, moving fast, observing, soaring over the factories, cell houses, walls. Constantly turning back in. Lightning-like through clouds and around corners. Observing. Even the shades of gray are a miracle. Dark shadows turned into a phosphorescent green. Black prisoners, working with weights in the blinding Kansas sun, become a deep, rich blue. Blood splatters black across bleached concrete as a face is smashed and a sandfilled sock disappears. I wondered when the war would ever end. I still do.

GODLESS COUNTRY NOT THE WORST COUNTRY

Today, when conversations turn to prisons and prisoners I listen. I learned long ago that the moment the conversation turns serious, eyes (and minds) begin to glaze over in less time than it takes a Texas Ranger to kidney punch a homeless drunk. When the conversation gets around to Cuba and Castro, I remind people of writer Dorothy Day's trip to Cuba after the Cuban revolution. She had gone down to see for herself if life was as oppressive for churchgoing Catholics in Cuba as the U.S. government was reporting. In one of the columns she wrote for the *Catholic Worker* she said, "Better a Godless country that takes care of its poor than a Christian country that doesn't."

Believe me, talking to the average citizen about injustice is like walking into a white Southern Baptist church in Danville, Virginia—the last headquarters of the Confederacy—and asking for donations to the Black Panther Legal Defense Fund or the American Civil Liberties Union. Anyone present who knew what you were talking about would think you were completely mad. Those who didn't would think you were an affront to their very selective, lily white God and attempt to do to you what the Romans did to the good carpenter. Not pretty.

When I began getting phone messages in the summer of 1989 that someone interested in *Penal Digest International* was trying to contact me I was only mildly interested. Over the years I have been contacted by an occasional law student or theology student who was doing research on or volunteer work with prisoners. Invariably they had gotten a taste of prison life, and had heard about the rise and fall of the *PDI* and/or the Church of the New Song, a prisoner religion whose philosophy had been spread by the *PDI*.

These links to my *PDI* past show themselves unexpectedly. I'll notice someone staring at me. Usually I walk over and introduce myself. Not infrequently the person turns out to be a former *PDI* subscriber or a librarian. Occasionally, after I am steered away from the crowd and into a private space, the person confesses that he or she was once a prisoner. That confession is followed by a narrative of memorable moments. "Acid flashbacks," as the person says. "I remember the Sunday church service in Atlanta," or "The Terre Haute tour was a gas—whatever happened to John?" or "I was at Oklahoma Women's Penitentiary." Sometimes it's a writer, someone with a clear enough understanding of what gets into print in these United States to know that to be well informed a person has to set aside $250 a year to subscribe to *In These Times, The Progressive, The Nation, Mother Jones, Z Magazine, Utne Reader, Catholic Worker, Washington Monthly, Workers World, Dollars and Cents*, and *EXTRA* and be a member of The DataCenter,[1] publications and organizations with staff who understand the insidious Rain Barrel Theory of Politics, the theory that best describes politics in the United States—the scum rises to the top.[2] People whose names are anathema to the FBI, the Secret Service, the CIA, Nixon, Kissinger, Reagan, Bush—organizations and individuals whose existence is proof of the rain barrel theory's validity.

This most recent contact was different. Ken Wachsberger not only knew about the *PDI*, he had been part of the day-to-day insanity we had all learned to love in a sado-masochistic way. Ken had been hitching west on I-80 and was picked up by some *PDI* staff members who were on their way home. Like so many road weary wanderers, he accepted an invitation to join us for dinner and a night's rest. While waiting for dinner he wandered into the *PDI* offices—where the lights burned 24 hours a day—and went to work.

Now, 20 years later, he asked if I'd like to look back at those *PDI* years and share some thoughts. Thoughts on the *PDI*, the times, and the people. I had doubts about whether or not I was the best person to do so. For many years, friends who were witness to those three traumatic years have urged me to tell the story. I always assumed that someone else would. The *PDI* had staff members who were far better writers than I. But Ken wanted me to write the history because I was the founder. I agreed.

So what about the *PDI* years? I should include a few stories about prison experiences and observations that convinced me that the *PDI* was desperately needed; I should also include information on why I thought it would succeed and how, with the help of an unusually diverse group of people, we forced it to succeed.

The *PDI* came into existence in 1970 during politically painful times. We had caught the tail end of the Vietnam War both in and out of the can. Our detractors called us radical. We probably initiated as many lawsuits against agencies of the federal and state governments as any newspaper in history. The list of our reporters, sales agents, and prison representatives read like a Who's Who of jailhouse lawyers. Many were serving life terms with no hope for parole for committing acts that ranged from political crimes against the state to crimes for profit, revenge, you name it. In prison, they had turned to education and law as a means of self-fulfillment. They were our newspaper's strongest supporters and most committed advocates. They never gave up. They had nothing to lose. They were afraid of no one. They could be threatened, but they remained uncowed.

For over three years, with a staff that started with two and grew to 25, the *PDI* operated out of a three-story house at 505 South Lucas in Iowa City, Iowa. 505 became synonymous with *PDI*. I bought the house at 505—with the help of sympathetic realtors and a no-down-payment GI loan—so the *PDI* and the staff would have a place to live. For three years, using a variety of means, I fed, clothed, and sheltered the staff, their friends, drifters, runaways, wanted men, women, and children, and paid the bills. Well...most of the bills.

A little over four years and a couple hundred thousand dollars later, I walked away from the *PDI* with exactly what I'd walked away from the slam with. Nothing. I wasn't totally without resources, however. I owned a home in Georgeville, Minnesota, in the west central part of the state that had been home to *Hundred Flowers*, the underground newspaper edited by Eddie Felien, the Marxist scholar from the University of Minnesota who ended up on the Minneapolis city council. My home there didn't have running water or electricity, but what do you expect for $400? I also had a 1963 one-ton International pickup that looked like it had been abandoned in Watts during the riots. The pickup had been part of the junk pile out back of the $400 house. It needed tires, a battery, and six weeks worth of hard work to get it running. Along with

everything else, I considered it a gift. Hell, the *PDI* was a gift that for a long time nourished prisoners and their families. And why not? It was their newspaper. They wrote for it, produced it, paid for it pennies at a time. We never refused a prisoner a subscription. We accepted whatever they could afford. Most could afford nothing. How they got it and why they got it is part of the story I will get to.

Those years were lean, hungry years. Tough years. In many respects they were violent years. By that I mean we were witnesses to violence. Violence against men, women, and children who were prisoners. Violence against the families of prisoners. And finally, violence against the primary staff members of the *PDI* by the federal, state, and local police that culminated in murder—a murder that was committed by a man who was pushed over the "edge" by an undercover cop who sealed all of our futures by giving the man a gun and urging him to use it. Staff members were arrested for possessing drugs that were stashed by ex-prisoners who had been released from prison for the express purpose of destroying the *PDI* and the Church of the New Song. The seemingly unlimited power and resources of those three levels of government were more than a handful of unpaid, hungry men, women, and children could live with. Most took off trying to find a place to rest and restore themselves. Consequently, the *PDI* and a number of staff members were destroyed.

With the *PDI*'s voice stilled, the prisoners lost their voice. Today the conditions in prisons are more repressive. Extreme overcrowding exists mainly because of the longer prison sentences that are handed out today, so frequently for victimless crimes. Increasing numbers of prisoners are being locked up for minor drug offenses—many are denied the opportunity to earn a parole. With more of the poor, uneducated members of society ending up in prison, the need for educational and vocational programs is greater than it has ever been. Yet, cutbacks in correctional department budgets mean that fewer of these programs are available.

And the *PDI*? Today it is a mass of notes, letters, papers, and subscription lists that are safely stashed in boxes in the State Historical Society of Iowa.[3] And, of course, there are memories.

I look back, see the victories, and I'm reminded of a line Barry Hannah wrote, "Not only does absence make the heart grow fonder, it makes history your own beautiful lie."

It's not going to be easy making sure that this doesn't become my beautiful lie, but I'll try.

How brief can I be? Just the experiences inside the walls that generated the energy for the *PDI* deserve much more than I can give them here. The people, the prisoners, living and dead, deserve more. We'll just have to see where this leads us.

CUBA: POLITICAL BEGINNINGS

The foundation for the government's intense rancor against me goes back to an incident that happened in Cuba in 1952. There, I had knowledge of an exchange of some Springfield rifles from our Destroyer Squadron—old rifles that were being replaced by the new M1s—to a group of remarkable people who showed me first-hand what Fulgencia Batista, the U.S.-supported military dictator, was doing to the Cuban people. It was my first political act.

My activities in Cuba would never have surfaced if I hadn't "lost it" one night in Cedar Rapids, Iowa. That night, 12 or 13 years after Cuba, I had too much to drink at a SERTOMA Club meeting. "SERTOMA" was an acronym for "SERvice TO MAnkind." One day a former resident of Cuba visited our local branch to speak about the Cuba he had fled when Fidel Castro led the people's army into Havana. He was a *gusano*, Spanish for "worm," one of the haves who skipped to the United States with enough gold and connections to "make a new begin in the land of the free." He managed to leave with enough to steer clear of the fast money from criminal activity in Miami and had opted for banking. Another form of criminal activity. His new life began as a vice president in the bank that served eastern Iowa. Why settle in Miami and take chances being illegal when you could be a bank executive and steal with the blessing of the FDIC?

He talked about how he had fled the horrible Communists who nationalized industry, closed down the nightclubs, took over the hotels, and forced the doctors to practice the oath they took when graduating from medical school—that is, to provide medical care to people regardless of their ability to pay. His speech was gut wrenching. I could smell gun grease. The crowd was hanging on his every word. Applause interrupted him every few sentences. He was living proof to these people that Castro was a Communist who had to be eliminated—living justification for programs of assassination by U.S. agents, programs that would work better during the sixties when J. Edgar Hoover infiltrated antiwar groups through his COINTELPRO activities.

Listening to him whine his way through a litany of greed was intolerable. I turned to my bottle of Old Style and was soon retreating into my memories. My soul warmed as I left the dry, bone chilling cold of Iowa and returned to the 98 percent humidity and nighttime temperatures of 110+ that I had found in revolutionary Cuba previous to the people's victory.

When I arrived in Cuba in the early fifties, I was fresh out of high school and sincerely believed that the United States of America was the greatest country in the world. The land of opportunity. Anyone and everyone could make it. "We hold these truths to be self-evident...etc., etc."

I was in the navy to protect the world from dictators—most of whom happened to be Commies at that point in history. The generation immediately before mine had taken care of the Nazis, Il Duce's Brown Shirts, and the Japanese. Frank Sinatra was singing "I am an American, and proud of my liberty and my freedom to make derogatory remarks about Dorothy Kilgallen's chin." I was one of many young, tough Americans. I had my share of faults: no ambition, couldn't deal with routine, I bored easily, carried a book with me at all times to read as soon as the boss turned his back. On the plus side, I didn't abuse people, was generous with what little money I had, and was loyal to my friends.

KOREA IS COOKING

Korea was starting to cook and I was ready. Truman was paying big bucks to anyone who would extend his hitch for two years. The combination of patriotism and pay was all I needed. After my experiences in Cuba those additional two years would become intolerable. But the bad times were yet to come. At this point, the navy was a perfect fit.

My passion during this period in my life was the Sixth Naval District boxing team. I relished it—not just the easy life and the lack of supervision but the workouts, the sparring, and the actual fighting. At 165 pounds, I was a lanky middleweight, but I fought as a light heavyweight and occasionally as a heavyweight because the spot was empty and my coach, a redheaded chief petty officer who had once been a featherweight contender, convinced me that I was faster and better than anyone bigger than me—with the exception of my shipmate Freddie Krueger, who, using an alias, was prowling around South and North Carolina picking up pro fights and winning them.

Staying in shape was simple. Freddie would shake me awake at 4:30 A.M. and we would jog the five or six miles to the main gate of the base, make disparaging remarks to the Marine guards, and jog back to the ship in time for steak and eggs. The boxing team had no work detail assignments. As long as we worked out and won, every day was a vacation from the drudge work. Fighting wasn't work—as long as you could avoid getting kicked around in the ring. Plus, being able to take off for town every night was sweet.

Red's orders were simple: "Stay in shape and stay on the team. Get lazy and start working."

Not smoking was easy, and the second drink never tasted as good as the first so I rarely consumed enough to adversely affect my timing. I was hell in a barroom fight simply because I was usually the sober fighter. I had an extraordinary appetite for anything that moderately altered my conscious state if it enhanced the party, the love making, or the fighting. But as the man in the toga once said, "Moderation in all things." The enhancers I used in moderation; but as a middleweight in the ring with fighters who frequently outweighed me by 40 pounds, "moderation" was not a word I used or heard. It certainly wasn't part of Red's vocabulary.

If I had a reputation back then it was that I had to be pushed long and hard before I could be provoked into a fight. My best friends required less pushing. One night, Nelson King, Jim Oler, Dean Bohy, Buck, and I went over to the canteen on the base in Guantanamo, Cuba. We sat and talked and drank beer until the place closed. As we were walking back to the pier to catch the launch, Buck walked over to one of the marine barracks and ripped the thin wooden slats out of two windows. Then he leaned inside and asked if there were any marines who wanted to get their asses kicked by a sailor from the coal mines of West Virginia. We grabbed Buck and started running. By the time 30 or 40 marines came piling out of the barracks, we were about a block and a half ahead of them.

Sand burrs stopped the ones with no shoes. Three caught up with Nelson, which was like catching up with a tiger. Jim had turned around and those two were like nitro and glycerine. Buck and I stopped and watched. Nelson and Jim were two shy young men, but in a fight they were frighteningly efficient.

The next morning, with all the men lined up for muster, the captain demanded to know which men had attacked the marine barracks the night before. Fortunately, when Nelson's shirt was torn off the marines didn't get the piece with his name stencilled on it.

Back in the present, the Cuban banker droned on and on. It was easy to shut myself off from the words of this fat, soft, gusano and remain lost in memories. I could almost smell the island and feel the heavy, humid heat that made our white uniforms sag and our shoes squish with sweat.

I wondered what Bobby, Julio, and Gaby would think about this banker. I recalled the night in Cuba when I met them. Buck and I were on shore leave in Guantanamo. We had been ashore for almost 24 hours and had 24 more ahead of us thanks to his shifts in the galley and mine as a coxswain running liberty launches. It was midweek, the best time to be ashore. No military personnel were around, the shore patrol units were few and far between, and the prices were fair. Even the general pace of the people slowed down during the week, as if they were storing up energy for the make-or-break hustle of the weekend.

We had closed a couple of small clubs and were walking around trying to decide where to sleep. The heat was oppressive. The humidity steamed our glasses, softened even the landscape. You had to wade through it.

As we crossed a park I saw a hose connected to a sprinkler. The thought of cool water was irresistible. I hung my wallet on the branch of a bush, took my shoes off, aimed the sprinkler at a nearby bench, and sat down. Buck was more vocal about the cool water; his whoops and hollers attracted the attention of a young woman, who stepped out of a doorway just across a narrow street from us. She was so close Buck recognized the profile of the one-eyed Indian on her bottle of Hautuey Beer. Always the gentleman (and always thirsty), Buck stood up. As he introduced himself, water in his hat spilled down his face. She laughed so loud, I could barely hear Buck when he asked her if she had a beer he could buy. She didn't, but she offered to get some if he had the money. Buck turned to me and mimicked Hank Williams with a whining, "If you've got the money, Honey, she's got the wine—Hautuey that is!" I pointed to my wallet hanging on the branch. Buck took it, tossed it to the woman, and said, "Take what you need. Bring us as much Hautuey as you can carry." She took a twenty, tossed the wallet back to Buck, and disappeared.

She returned with a half case of beer and a small block of ice in a burlap bag. I was surprised when she handed me change.

Then she went into her house with the beer.

The house was a typical "crib" house. The door led into a long narrow room, where a second door led into another narrow, but smaller room. The backyard had just enough space for a small vegetable garden. In this part of town, and in many others, the streets were lined with hundreds of these "crib" houses. Prostitutes, many with small children, sat on the steps in a neverending hustle for enough money to live on. If she had been a hooker, twenty dollars was more than she would have made working hard on a Saturday night. But there she was with the beer—ice cold beer. When she came out of the house for the second time she had two guys with her. Each had one of my cold beers. Oh well....

I MEET A POET OF THE REVOLUTION

The woman and one of the guys joined us in the sprinkler and introduced themselves as Gabriela and Julio. They were both into the humor of the situation. The other man sat on the ground. He was not amused. Gaby and Julio were both Cuban. Although they were sister and brother they could have come from different families. Gaby was very dark skinned; Julio was blessed with a skin color George Hamilton would have killed for—the color of copper mixed with gold. He was also, like me, an amateur boxer. The other guy, Bobby Vaughn, was an Anglo, a poet from Key West.

That first night we smalltalked and drank beer. Before long, Buck and Bobby were asleep—Buck from the beer and Bobby from washing down cough medicine with wine. It was a memorable evening. I had met my first poet and turpin hydrate addict and had become friends with the first Cuban civilians I had met outside of a bar. Bobby also was the first American I met in Cuba who didn't work at the navy base.

Buck and I spent that night sleeping on pallets on the floor. After a night of listening to Bobby howling, crying, and cursing in his sleep, I arose at dawn to the sound of barking dogs. My uniform was wet and dirty and I had a headache. No one had any aspirins, but Bobby had some pain killers that worked better than anything I'd ever taken for a headache. Julio loaned Buck and me each a shirt and a pair of old pants that we wore until our uniforms could be washed and pressed.

I offered to buy breakfast but Julio was already making coffee. He said something about relaxing and enjoying the day. Buck had already had a beer and was launching into a long rambling tale about mining coal in West Virginia. His job had been to set the charges that blasted loose the coal. With each beer, the story got longer and the fuses attached to the charges got shorter. I'd heard the story many times, almost as many times as Dean Bohy's stories of Olympic wrestlers from Clarion, Iowa, stories I never tired of.

Life in Cuba had a mellow, low pressured rhythm unlike any other place I had ever been. That first day, Bobby's pain killer had me humming songs and thinking about settling down in Guantanamo. I had enough "down-home country" in me to appreciate the simple life.

We sat around for most of the day talking. Later Julio and I walked to a nearby market for beans and rice, a couple of chickens, and some vegetables. Buck almost killed himself trying to ride a bike with a bent wheel.

That night, over beans and rice, I made an offhand remark about how nice it would be to sit down to a first-class meal some day. I was speaking facetiously but it didn't come across as I intended. Bobby exploded in anger and called me an American pig. Julio told me to ignore him because he was high. Bobby started yelling poetry and cursing a U.S. political system that was killing people in Cuba and all over the world. I thought he was nuts, but I was a guest and couldn't say anything. Fortunately, I kept my mouth shut. If I had said anything, it would have been some naive comment about loyalty and being a little more respectful about the United States of America. I didn't want to offend anyone. Bobby was beyond me, but I was eager to continue the friendship with Julio and Gaby. Interesting day.

The following Wednesday I was back. Bobby was there but said nothing. For two days and two nights he listened to scratchy records by Chet Baker, Charlie Parker, Miles Davis, and Dave Brubeck. He seemed to know Chet Baker and Charlie Parker, but he wasn't in the mood to talk to me about them. During those two days, he became increasingly abusive to everyone.

Julio, Gaby, and I rode bikes out into the country and up the coast. We went swimming, brought fresh fish for supper, and made plans to go fishing the following week.

It was on the third visit that I asked Julio about the revolution that was spoken about so disparagingly by our officers. He asked me what I knew about Castro and the revolution. Not much, I told him. Castro was anti-American and Americans were good for the island's economy. He was probably a Communist. The more I said, the sillier I sounded. Julio listened calmly but Bobby turned and started yelling angrily, almost incoherently. He was spitting and sputtering, "You're a whore! Worse than Truman! Pigs!" Finally he lurched to his feet and left.

NO ROOM IN THE REVOLUTION FOR DRUGGIES

I asked Julio and Gaby if I was as ignorant of what was going on as Bobby accused me of being.

"You have to understand that Bobby is going through a very bad time in his life," Gaby explained. She looked at Julio, seemingly for permission to continue. He shrugged his shoulders and she gave me a real shock.

"Try to understand Bobby. He has been rejected by people he admires very much. Don't take what he says personally. He was with the revolutionaries for a few months. He has been with Fidel and Che."

I couldn't believe it. Vaughn was the last person in the world I would picture as a revolutionary. He was small and skinny and as physically weak as any person I had ever known. I didn't know much about what was happening in Cuba but I knew that Fidel Castro and Che Guevara were heading a small army that was involved in what officers said was a hopeless attempt to take over the island and they weren't going to get much done with an army of Bobby Vaughns. "You mean he's been fighting with the people who are trying to overthrow the government that we support?"

"Yes and no. Bobby is a poet. He's in love with the idea of the revolution. He has a strong mind for words. The problem is that he's a drug user—an addict—and nobody trusts an addict."

It seems he had been given a choice—drugs or revolution—choose one or the other; the two didn't mix.

As she continued, I learned that they were all involved with the revolution.

They didn't deny it.

"Tell me more," I asked.

And they damn sure did.

CUBA OWNED BY THE U.S.

They fed me statistics on how the Cuban people lived under Fulgencia Batista. They had no medical care, no schools, no wages, no futures to look forward to. The United States controlled 75 percent of the agriculture, all of the tourist trade, and all the gambling. Pay in the factories and on the plantations was so low people died of malnutrition.

"You see hundreds and hundreds of women lining the streets selling themselves," Julio said. "You can buy any perversion you can imagine for a dollar or less. Do you think they enjoy being whores?"

Silence.

"If you go down the street and buy a woman, do you think she likes you because you are clean and pay cash?"

Silence.

"Do you think you are special because you have money and they do not? Can you even imagine what it is like to have no money, no resources of any kind, and need a doctor for a sick baby and know that the doctor will not treat the baby unless you have cash?"

Some questions have no answers.

"Can you imagine a doctor who will let babies die because the mother has no money?"

Julio was talking softly, but his hands were trembling. Gaby got up and left the room.

Bobby returned. He had calmed down and now added bits of information that must have been poetry because I understood little of what he said. I did understand, though, that he idolized Che and called both Castro and Che fearless: "Castro the fearless warrior/Scholar" and "Che the fearless warrior/poet."

Bobby would look you in the eye and start with simple thoughts and ideas, then slowly lead you down an increasingly complex path of words and phrases and ideas. Just about the time you thought he was trying to make a fool of you he would stop. Then he'd sit there looking through you, his mouth half open. After a long pause, he would recite a poem. A sonnet. He would recite it once, twice. Play with a word. Discuss a rhyme. Go over it. Explain a sestet. Finish a sonnet with—according to Julio—a perfect sestina. Most of the time I was completely lost, but he was a hard person to dislike.

Bobby had a very serious attachment to two writers, Ezra Pound and Ernest Hemingway. I'd read all of Hemingway and nothing by Pound. Bobby shared with me his Pound books but Pound was beyond me. Gaby once asked him how he could admire Hemingway, who only wrote about fighting, fucking, and fishing. Bobby answered, "It's not what he writes about but the way he writes what he writes about." When it came to discussing literature or poetry with Bobby Vaughn, I kept my mouth shut.

(Fifteen years later, Bobby, John Eastman, and I spent many days and nights together near Marion, Iowa. John was working on film scripts and Bobby was working on getting high. By that time, Bobby had a patch covering the hole in his head where someone had beaten out one of his eyes late one night in Kansas City. He had been looking for Charlie Parker's mother.)

ANY PROSTITUTES IN YOUR FAMILY?

Julio never spoke about himself. Once when we were discussing how a poor woman survived in Cuba with only four square yards of garden to feed her family, he told me that their mother—his and Gaby's—had been a prostitute on this very street. The two of them had grown up here. He would use the word "prostitute," but he never used the word "whore." "You must be careful about the words you use," he told me seriously. "Be careful how you categorize people. A woman sells her body. Batista sells our country."

Silence.

Then, "Think about who the prostitutes are. Maybe you have a prostitute in your own family. Tell me, Joe, who in your family are selling themselves and what price are they being paid?"

I didn't like talk about having whores in my family, but I understood the point he was making.

"Which is worst, Joe, a rapist or a prostitute?"

"The rapist, of course."

"Which is worst, Joe, a pimp or a prostitute?"

"The pimp, of course."

"Don't you understand that Cuba is a woman who is being abused by your country. Cuba is being used like a prostitute. Small countries all over the world are the prostitutes and the United States is a rapist and a pimp."

Strong words.

WHY DO POETS HAVE TO CARRY GUNS?

One night Bobby announced that he was leaving and returning to Key West, or maybe New York City. He was sad that there was no place for him in Cuba—sadder still over his own drug habit. "Why does a poet have to carry a gun and be prepared to kill?" he asked.

"Because a poet of this revolution must be prepared to kill for this revolution, not just write poems about it," Julio answered.

For some reason Bobby turned to me and asked, "Who broke your nose, Joe?"

"A person who suffered far more pain doing it than I suffered having it done," I answered.

Bobby was grinning, and he didn't grin much. "A poet with a broken nose?"

Julio asked me if I would fight for the revolution. "If this was my country I would be in the mountains. But it's not my country," I answered. Then I added, "I think that I would fight for the three of you. I love you all. I even love your revolution, but I don't even know the language of your revolution—at least not yet."

Julio looked at me. "Do you know any more or any less about the Cuban people than you know about the Korean people?"

The question jolted me. I had come to know these people. I knew they were right in what they were doing—that it was the only way their lives would ever have any meaning. I was in the U.S. military, but I could never take action against them. Now Julio had made me realize that people just like Gaby and him were sitting in houses just like this one half way around the world in small towns in Korea. And I was soon to be heading over there. If we were wrong in Cuba, were we wrong in Korea also?

I didn't even have to ask.

As for Cuba's revolution, I knew at least enough of the language to understand what was happening. I learned that many other military personnel also understood. Julio worked hard at smuggling. He made regular trips into the Sierra Maestras with weapons and spare parts that came from the naval base.

The talks always went on late into the night. Bobby would be high on turpin hydrate or thorazine or heroin. He slept in the corner while I listened and learned about pain and how to kill and why they believed such actions were necessary. Bobby didn't hear many of those conversations; he'd heard them all before and may have written some of them. Occasionally he would wake with a start, grab a pencil, and start writing. Then he would look over at us like we were strangers and go back to sleep.

He awoke one night and scribbled a poem about an Anglo named Toth who would go to prison because there was a doubt and because Fidel did not have time to sort through a person's politics.

The conversations went on, broken only by the time I spent on the ship. I'd return weekly. We would ride bicycles up the coast, sometimes sleeping on the beach. We'd go fishing. Occasionally we'd buy fruit from people who were on their way to the markets. Once we were stopped by some police. While Julio talked to them, Gaby stood close to me and began acting like she was turning a trick—smiling, teasing, being irritated with the delay, asking for money to buy beer for everyone, which I gave her but which the police declined. It was a strange, yet arousing, incident. I was responding to her differently than I ever had. When the police finally left, Julio said, "More names for the list."

Gaby told me I was not a very good actor. I could have told her that.

Julio always referred to his "list" whenever he had a run-in with anyone who worked for the Batista regime. Whether he had an actual list I never knew. Years later, when the revolutionaries had successfully defeated the military dictatorship, it was said that Castro had a list of the names of people who had caused the people great suffering. It is said further that these people were arrested and executed—no questions, no trials. They were, it was said, given exactly what they had given to the Cuban people. Whether it's true or not I do not know. I do not approve of summary executions, but I can damn sure understand why it happens.

THE CASE OF THE MISSING SPRINGFIELD RIFLES

Around this time, the navy replaced the old Springfield rifles, bolt action 30-06s if I remember correctly, with the new M1s. The Springfield was becoming obsolete, we were told—a good rifle, but the M1s were superior. With the help of a chief gunner's mate, who was gay and whose passion for a beautiful man with a golden tan was greater than his fear of losing his retirement, Julio ended up with most of the old Springfield rifles from our COM DES DIV 302 destroyer group, which was made up of the USS Bronson (DD668), USS Smalley (DD565), USS Cotten (DD669), and USS Daly (DD519). "Oh yes," Julio would say, "I sure do love your old chief gunner's mate. Too bad he isn't in charge of the armory on the base."

During this particular period, Julio was always on the move. He had little to say and when I visited he was often not there. When he returned he would be relaxed, ready for bike rides, conversations, and cooking. One day, soon after returning from a trip to the Sierra Maestra Mountains, he was sitting with Gaby and me in the same park where we first had met. We were eating rice and beans and drinking Hautuey beer.

Julio asked me if I'd tell the chief gunner's mate that he wanted to see him early Sunday morning. "He knows where to meet me. Tell him it is important that he is there."

Before I could answer him, Gaby reached over and put one hand on her brother's arm and the other on mine. With a confidential tone to her voice and a smile on her face, she said, "Now I think Julio is a prostitute, just like our mother was a prostitute. I wonder if I will be next?"

Gaby laughed. Julio laughed. I laughed. I laughed out loud!

My laughter interrupted the *gusano*. People at the SERTOMA Club turned and looked at me, whispered to each other, and shook their heads.

KICKED OUT OF SERTOMA

The speaker was going on and on about "Castro and his thugs" and how they had created a grim military dictatorship on his island paradise. When he finished he asked if anyone had any questions.

I said I had a few. By then I had had a few too many Old Styles. First I asked him if he was opposed to Castro closing down the thousands of whorehouses that were run by U.S. organized crime who split the profits with Batista's military police and probably the bankers.

The room became suddenly quiet.

While he was thinking about the first question I asked him why he hadn't described how 90 percent of the Cuban people lived in abject poverty with no access to education or medical care until the Cuban people's revolution removed the U.S.-supported military dictator and the organized crime.

I asked him why he hadn't informed the SERTOMA Club of how the revolutionaries had received more help from navy personnel than from any Communist countries. And why he hadn't mentioned that U.S. corporations owned 75 percent of the farmland and paid Cuban laborers pennies a day to insure that stockholders got rich while babies died of malnutrition.

I asked him to please describe the slums, the sweat shops, and the exploitation of child labor that personified U.S. corporate involvement in Cuba.

Looking around, I could see that everyone thought I was the outrage. I'd had too much to drink and I was angry. This Cuban banker's rap had brought back too many memories, too much rage. Anger and too much beer had brought me to my feet to spill my rage. I had

a problem all right: I was unable to turn my anger into the kind of poetry my partner Tom Kuncl would spew forth when he was still sober enough to get to his feet in front of whoever was handy.

As a result of my outburst, I was kicked out of SERTOMA and labeled a crazy recalcitrant—which I was and probably am, but why scare people?

You can't be too careful. Not a good idea to mix politics, tootsie pops, and too much Old Style beer.

So the SERTOMA Club suffered an uncomfortable few minutes. They'll never know that they suffered far less listening to me than I did listening to the Cuban banker. I'm sure the banker had never been asked such questions—questions I'm sure they had all put out of their minds by breakfast.

In looking back over my life, I believe that this outburst was one more element in the government figuring out that I was speaking about my own personal involvement with assisting Cuban revolutionaries. During the period I am talking about, the navy was lecturing personnel about the revolutionaries. They were quick to use the term "Commies." We were constantly being reminded that we had to be careful about who we associated with on the island. Bobby Vaughn's presence on the island, the fact that he had spent time with the revolutionaries in the Sierra Maestra Mountains, my association with him then and later in Iowa, the possibility of the government investigating and finding out that all of the Springfield rifles from our Destroyer Squadron were never turned in when they were exchanged for M1s, all of the above may have led investigators to identify me as a subversive who may have provided Castro with weapons from our squadron's arsenals.

Little did they know.

Looking back, the one thing that I found incredibly humorous is that the chief petty officer who everyone thought was gay was straight, and the toughest old chief on the ship was gay. He had been having an affair with one of the young seamen on the ship and then had fallen hard for Julio.

BURNED DOWN AND CHARGED WITH THE CRIME

In the summer of 1966, my vehemently, pro-union weekly newspaper, the *Citizen-Times*, was deliberately burned down and I lost what little perspective I had regarding justice or even the remote possibility that "right" could prevail—at least where either the newspaper or I was concerned.

It happened in Cedar Rapids, Iowa, during a period of intense union activity involving firefighters and wholesale grocery workers. The firefighters were being fought by the city and by every fire department administrator on local and state levels. The other group was locking horns with a wealthy grocery chain owner. Our newspaper, the largest weekly in the state, was with the workers 100 percent. My partner, Tom Kuncl, had a knack for describing the anti-union groups and individuals in a way that caused them to suffer serious attacks of apoplexy—particularly in city hall. For those and other reasons we incurred the wrath of the city, the fire department hierarchy, the state fire marshall's office, and a legion of others. We had friends among the rank-and-file in the cop shop and the fire department, but everyone above the rank-and-file treated us like pariahs, troublemakers who were giving the city a bad image.

Since working on the *Citizen-Times* paid nothing, we were lumped together with the unwashed, undesirable elements and shunned by 90 percent of society. We worked hard; and frequently, after a week of hard work—thanks to the generosity of workers—we found our table loaded with cold beer and schnapps. We were less gracious drunk than sober and consequently were only welcomed in those taverns that catered to the workers.

Then the newspaper was torched and we were burned down.

While the fire was raging two firefighters smashed through a window to a second floor room where they thought I was sleeping. Not finding me they turned around and got out moments before the room exploded.

At one point, over the intercoms that connected all the vehicles, a firefighter shouted, "We're trying to find the chief. Has anyone seen him?" There was a pause. Then someone who didn't identify himself responded with a note of humor, "The chief was last seen leaving the *Citizen-Times* newspaper building by the back door shortly before the first explosion was heard."

Broke everyone up. So here was this scene. Fire trucks, hoses, flames, smoke, people risking their lives, and the rank-and-file laughing and joking about the chief. Although even from a retrospective view of some 25 years I'm confident the chief wasn't the arsonist, it was no secret that he hated the *CT*, the staff, the editorials, and particularly Tom Kuncl.

Following the fire and a lengthy investigation, I was charged with arson. The charges shocked many people, including me. We had recently spent $45,000 on a large Royal Zenith, web-fed press; we were expanding, were making money for the first time in four years, had relocated in a large building downtown, and had the financial backing of a wealthy insurance company owner. All of this carried no weight. Nor did the fact that over the objections of our backer I had dramatically cut back on our insurance policies because of the high premiums. After four years of working 16

to 20 hours a day, without pay, sleeping in the office, using petty cash for coldcuts and white bread, and pounding the pavement six days a week for nickel and dime ads and pitching the churches on Sunday, I wasn't going to spend profits on insurance policies.

Because of prejudicial actions by the prosecutor the charges were thrown out. I thought that was the end of it. However, the prosecution persisted, charges were again filed, and I was indicted for the second time. A year later, I finally appeared in court.

Over the course of that year, the harassment never ended. At times, the stress was so great that three and four days of work would just disappear from my mind. My inability to remember critically important parts of my day became a serious concern with friends. When I was "with it" I was crazy angry. When I was "out of it" I was worse—according to my staff.

One night about four months after the fire, while I was working late at our $30-a-month storefront, a couple deputies showed up with the woman who owned the local bonding company. She claimed I was preparing to leave the country; therefore, she said, she was arresting me and suspending my bond, as she had the power to do.

I told her I didn't have enough money to use the john at the bus station much less leave the country. Regardless, she said, she was pulling the bond. The deputies nodded when she repeated that I was under arrest. Further, as I knew, I'd be out the fee I had already paid her. With no money, I'd sit in the county jail until they got around to a trial. I couldn't deal with it.

As they were walking me to the car I decided I couldn't live like these people were forcing me to live. I told them they could shove their arrest warrant. I jerked loose and started walking away from them. They told me to stop. I refused. They pulled their guns and ordered me to stop and I told them exactly what I thought of them, the county attorney, the state of Iowa, and their individual parentage, and I kept walking. The sound of the hammer on the deputy's pistol being pulled back sounded like a couple of Ginger Baker rim shots. I thought they were going to kill me, and at that point in my life I didn't give a damn. I kept walking, waiting for the punch! If you have ever been shot, you know what I mean by "punch!" They waited, and waited, and finally one of them ran to their car, grabbed the microphone, and called for help. He was yelling something about an escaped prisoner and asking for backup. What a circus.

I walked across a large vacant lot to the apartment of my friends, Janie and Paul Kelso. The deputies watched where I was going.

Janie and Paul asked what all the yelling was about. I told them what was happening. The cops were going to be all over the place in a few minutes, I said.

Paul had this thing about health foods. He didn't have anything to drink with alcohol in it, so I accepted one of his special high-energy milk shakes. I knew I'd need something to help me make it through that night. I hadn't gotten half of it down before the sirens started. Seven squad cars converged on the apartment.

When the police knocked on the door I went peacefully.

The health food must have adversely affected my mind.

At the station I was informed that new charges had been filed: resisting arrest, possibly unlawful flight to avoid prosecution, escape, yaddida, yaddida, yaddida. Most of the rank-and-file cops were embarrassed. I was booked and spent the night in the can with prisoners I was beginning to know by their first names. The next morning, someone said the right words or brought enough cash and I was back on the street.

My only clear memory of leaving the jail that morning was the feeling that I was starting a new life.

The whole episode—the arrest, the second arrest—had an emotionally cleansing effect on me. There were times when the whole system had frightened me. Fear of prison; fear of having people around who you knew were trying to destroy you; not so much the fear of failure as the fear of not winning—of not being able to stand up against whomever and whatever it was you had to stand up against.

The trial began on April 18, 1966. For the first week of the trial the prosecution paraded the state fire marshall's investigators and arson experts before the jury and the news media. First to the jury and then to the news media the "overwhelming evidence" against me, which amounted to nothing more than determined speculation, was offered by a confident county attorney. After a week, the prosecutor rested his case with a round of adjectives, arm waving, and finger pointing.

Like it or not, despite the prosecutor's lack of hard evidence, I had to face the fact that it didn't look good for me. A guilty verdict would mean a 25-year sentence. With all the hell we had been raising with the city, the courts, the county attorney's office, and just about anyone who wasn't cheering for the working class, I looked for no breaks. None at all.

We asked for and received a ten-minute break to collect ourselves for the defense.

Just as we were entering the courtroom, Bob Nelson, one of my defense lawyers, was called to the phone by the bailiff. Suddenly our case became a classic Perry Mason adventure.

We had received an anonymous tip. A city detective had gotten a look into the county attorney's files and found reports that the county attorney had suppressed—scientific reports that would clear me of the arson charge. One report, he confided, was from the FBI's criminal investigation laboratory in Washington, DC, another was from an independent lab, and the third was from a chemistry department at a local college. There was no evidence in any of those reports to indicate that the fire had been set, and much to indicate that it hadn't.

Someone had set me up and it had almost worked. Whether the detective liked me or hated them I never found out. Chances are he was one of those cops who had bought into a personal honor system that couldn't be set aside. Not when the law enforcement hierarchy wanted to close down a newspaper that had been born over on the West Side in Boheme Town. The paper that published "All the News That's Pit to Frint"—one of Kuncl's favorite digs at one of New York City's "waterpumps."

He never told us his name. He just gave us the facts.

The reports had been in the hands of the county attorney within ten days after the fire and he had hidden them—suppressed them—for over a year. A classic cover-up. While I squirmed, it had been business as usual for the county attorney. I sat there with a whole new understanding of why some people kill.

With this new evidence in hand, the case for the defense was not that complex. We had brought in the top arson investigator in the country—the man who had trained the investigators the state was using in their attempt to convict me. He testified that he could not believe anyone who had attended his school could have investigated that fire and reached the conclusions they had reached. In his own opinion, he said, the fire had started probably as the result of a broken light bulb in an area far from where the state fire marshal said it had been deliberately set.

After his testimony was finished, one of the state fire marshalls was recalled and he was asked by either Bob Fassler or Bob Nelson if any outside laboratories had conducted an independent investigation into whether or not flammable agents had been used. The marshall admitted there had been at least two such investigations. He was asked where those reports were from. He said one was done at the FBI laboratories in Washington, DC, and the other was done inside the chemistry department at nearby Coe College. Upon further questioning, he admitted that the reports showed that no such agents had been found where the two fires were alleged to have been set and that those reports had been in the hands of the prosecutor within ten days after the fire had broken out.

(If you, dear reader, ever end up in court, I sure hope your day will be as sweet as mine was that day.)

With the news about the suppressed evidence in front of the jury, the state's case disappeared. The jury came back with a "Not Guilty" verdict and I was a new man. Unresolved, however, were two interesting bits of evidence: 1) a utility truck, the same as or very similar to trucks operated by the city, was seen at the rear of our building, and 2) shortly after it was seen leaving the back of the building, people living in the house next door thought they heard a muffled explosion.

Despite our own star witness' testimony about the light bulb, I believed for my own reasons that the newspaper fire had been deliberately set by someone. Why did I think so? I had studied the site for months. I had taken photos of every inch of the burned areas. I studied the textbooks on arson investigation that our own expert had authored. My conclusion was the same as his, however, that the fire had started inside the back door.

What the state investigators had failed to recognize was how the fire had spread from the first floor up to the second floor to emerge under the altar/stage area. The flames had followed the path of an "I" beam for approximately 25 feet and had burned through the floor in two places. These two burn sites "convinced" the state that the fire had been set in two places under the altar/stage. The FBI laboratory was unable to find any traces of flammable substances at or around these burn sites, however. Rather than accepting the FBI findings and continuing the investigation, as a competent investigator would have done, the fire marshall's team chose to ignore the scientific reports—actually suppressed them—and stick to their original theory. Had they acted properly they might have discovered evidence that would have led to a successful conclusion. Since they refused to do so, I can only assume that they were more interested in putting me out of business than they were in solving a crime. If they had studied the site and traced the fire to the source, they would have been looking for the utility truck and the driver.

For me to point a finger at who may have had reason to destroy the newspaper was fruitless, not because I couldn't come up with anyone but because there were so many. The only people who didn't hate us were working class people—union members.

Additional evidence we never had to use was statements that had been made by the state fire marshall's investigators at an out-of-state conference. Two of them had gotten drunk and said, "We're finally going to get rid of Kuncl, Grant, and the *Citizen-Times*."

Before the defense rested, I pointed these facts out to my attorneys and our investigators. I wanted the state witnesses recalled and questioned about the site, about their charges against me, and, more than any-

thing, about why the reports were suppressed for over a year.

They shook their heads and said, "Forget it. You're innocent. We did what we came to do. We accepted this case to prove you innocent, not to go on a crusade." I could understand their reasoning. What had to be done had to be done by me.

Some of the jury members were crying when I went over and thanked them. I thanked my lawyers, then walked out of the courtroom with a smile on my face and hatred in my heart for the local upper echelon law enforcement. The press was there and someone asked me what my plans were. I told them I was going to start a daily newspaper.

HOW TO PAY FOR A DAILY NEWSPAPER

Daily newspapers, even small dailies, cost lots of money. But, like our insurance executive investor would say, "Shoot for the stars and you might hit the moon."

Kuncl would answer, "Ya! And if a pig had wings it would fly."

As for the insurance coverage, I learned another important lesson that day: you hire an attorney as soon as you have a loss. We had held off hiring one. The thought of giving an attorney 30 percent of the money needed to replace the loss was more than we could deal with. After paying for the equipment and the building we'd be lucky if we could buy a round of beer at our 16th Avenue SW hangouts. Plus the insurance agent kept telling us that we'd get paid as soon as I was exonerated.

Needless to say, as soon as I was exonerated I called the insurance company. A few days later their attorney informed me that, since I had not filed suit within the period stipulated in the policy, they were not going to cover the loss. I learned that Daddy Warbucks, our wealthy backer, got his investment back years later. But as usual the rank-and-file got the shaft.

Back to the beginning—again. Would my worries ever end?

They ended—or appeared to end.

Living on the bottom rungs of the socio-economic ladder for the past few years and having covered the courts, the unions, fights, fires, and killings, the depths of my anger soon got to someone who saw the possibility of putting it to good use.

The right offer—rather, the wrong offer—came early in 1967.

It was no secret that I had skills as an artist: "Use your skills to print money and we will see that you make enough to do exactly what you want to do." I thought about the offer for as long as it took to drink a cup of coffee.

I went to work for a group whose desire for easy money was almost as great as my desire to get even. My knack for making the perfect copy and my knowledge about chemistry to develop a sizing agent that gave quality paper the look, feel, and flexibility of good old American currency kept me busy for a year. I desperately wanted a newspaper, but along the way my desire for the newspaper took a backseat to developing the paper and the plates. Creating money was science fiction, an addiction. I couldn't stay away from the drawing table, the plates, the chemistry. I was hooked. Strange as it may seem, I never thought of spending it, never gave any thought to the illegality of what I was doing, and never rested. I published an issue of the newspaper once a week and spent the rest of the time in a small one-room hideaway that was a combination laboratory, art studio, and printing plant. I was in another world. A world that hate had created—hate and some Chicago acquaintances.

The world was all new to me, and quite frankly it was fascinating—for a while. I became so engrossed in the work that I could do little of anything else. I was given money to run the paper and meet a modest payroll. I didn't think to pay myself. So, when I was arrested and charged with counterfeiting, I thought about it and had to face the fact that I was cursed with bad karma. No sense in making excuses or copping a plea. I called Bob Nelson and Bob Fassler again.

Later that day, I was sitting with the Bobs trying to explain what I had done. After I had answered all their questions, Fassler said to Nelson, "We won't have any trouble winning this case."

Nelson looked at Fassler like he was nutso and asked him what he had in mind for a defense.

"Why, temporary insanity. What else is there?" Fassler laughed as only he could laugh—loud, louder, loudest, and right from the heart.

I could have walked away from most of the charges but rejected adding any complications to my life that were not already there. As a result, life was considerably safer and mellower at Leavenworth—you never gain anything by dragging others to prison with you.

The trial itself was boring. I spent days answering the federal prosecutor's endless questions with a simple, "I just don't know." Every time I said "I just don't know," Nelson and Fassler would look at each other and shrug—the gesture saying, "We should have gone with the insanity plea."

The judge knew, though, and he didn't waste any time. He rewarded me with five or six ten-year sentences and tossed in an additional five for conspiracy. I

entered Leavenworth in November 1967—a Pilgrim, so to speak, a couple weeks in front of Thanksgiving.

When the two federal marshalls dropped me off at Leavenworth, one of them took me aside and gave me some advice. "You have to be mighty careful in there, Joe—there's sex-crazed men on the other side of those walls who haven't been with a woman in a long, long time. Don't let them get to you."

Don't let them get to me? I thought. If there were men in there who were so hard up they saw me as a desireable love object, I wasn't heading into a prison; I was heading into an insane asylum.

One last story about the money. Around the time I was finishing the money, a bright young high school student who had been hanging around the office getting occasional writing assignments had been given a key to the office. Being an inquisitive young man, he had discovered my hidden room and had borrowed some of the fruits of my nighttime labors. He had passed up the 10s, 20s, and 50s for the 100 dollar bills with 27 different serial numbers. He told me years later that he was working on a story of his own. After I had been cooling my heels in Leavenworth for three or four months, he and some friends got a little drunk after a football game and walked into the tavern just half a block from the old office. There, he laid a $100 bill on the bar and asked for a case of Old Style. As soon as the other patrons saw the bill, they went through the litany of jokes that my "temporary insanity" had generated.

"Check that C note!"

"Got a list of those serial numbers?"

"Let's look at that bill."

And they all did. They gathered around and studied the $100 bill that Bobby had laid down and they all agreed that it was good old American currency—the real thing—not one of Joe's bills.

When the kids were picked up for public intoxication later that night, my young friend had a couple thousand in his backpack. One of the men who had been in the tavern the night before saw the front page of the morning paper and in a letter told me about what had happened there.

I was reading the paper at about the same time he was and figured I'd hear from one of the regulars.

I wondered if it would ever go away.

BEHIND THE WALLS

The community of the walled prison is much the same as life in the big city. It's a hot, explosive environment 24 hours a day. You have to be careful what you say and do. It's a little like living in a thimble that's being held over a Bunsen burner.

The prisoners run the walled prisons. They do everything, from the cooking to much of the counting.

I'm not talking about the prisons where federal and state courts send the lawyers, doctors, preachers, financiers, and politicians—the scum who are able to buy time in the country club prisons. I'm taking about the walled prisons, where the system puts the disenfranchised—the have-nots.

To sentencing judges, the "haves," with money for the connected attorneys, are prime candidates for rehabilitation. The "have-nots," the poor with no connections or resources, end up behind the walls, where they learn how to hate. Regardless of the fact that serious, assaultive criminality, the most painful violence, crosses all economic levels, those with money end up in the country clubs with unlimited visits from loved ones who can bring in lunch. The poor fill the end-of-the-line prisons where the word "rehabilitation" has as much substance as cow shit in the springtime.

If the word "shit" continues to appear in this story about the *PDI* it's because shit is the one substance that immediately comes to mind when I think back to life inside the walls. The custody, treatment, medical, religion, and recreation departments of every prison I have ever been in, visited, or written about have been for the most part supervised by guards who have failed at life in the free world, have earned a GED, qualified with an eighth grade education, and gone to work for the government. People I have shared this observation with tell me there are exceptions to this statement. A couple have told me about good guards. They could be right. Out of the many I have known, however, I only met one.

The preachers were the worst guards. Many a prisoner, weakened physically and emotionally by the stress, has learned the hard way that you don't talk to anyone with a guard's classification. Preachers of all denominations are classified as guards. They even get guards' pay. They'll betray you faster than a guard with ulcers.

Never tell the chaplain anything you wouldn't tell a guard.

This observation, I should add, has come to be accepted by a minimum of 90 percent of the prison population worldwide—that every prison preacher, be that preacher a representative of the Baptist, Catholic, Lutheran, any and all of the Christian groups that make up world Christianity, is a guard first and a representative of all that Jesus of Nazareth held most dear second. Without exception they have obligated themselves to the state. They ALL report to the "Man." They agree to do so when they take the job. Their livelihoods, not just the food on their family tables, even their children's health insurance depends upon the state. They follow the rules or they are out.

It was hard to imagine that a group claiming to be devoted Christians could condone these conditions, condone the brutality, condone the lack of official concern.

The more I distance myself from an otherwise painful period in my life, the less painful it becomes. Consciously or unconsciously I suppress the pain and misery, the sadness, the lonesome times, the fear. On the top of the memory heap are the successes, the victories, beating the chaplains, ripping off the test answers for the college entrance exams for the prisoners who needed that college acceptance to make parole and would never have been able to pass it on their own.

I still feel a rush when I think of how we broke into the chaplain's office to find that our suspicions were true—he had been intercepting mail from free world people at the Church of the Larger Fellowship (CLF) who had been sending us our books about Unitarian Universalism (UU).

B & E BY UUS FOR CLF BOOKS

Here's the whole story. It's an important one to me because it was one of two incidents that happened behind the walls at Leavenworth that helped me gain the reputation of being a person who could be trusted. The incident stretched over a year and involved the formation of a Unitarian Universalist Fellowship in the federal prison system.

It was a community organizing experience—organizing under the most difficult, repressive conditions. Just the kind of challenge that a rag-tag group of religious malcontents needed to make their year. And what a year it was. We were surrounded by adversaries: the prisoners' "religious leader," the chaplain, who was a Baptist; the warden and the assistant wardens for custody and treatment; the ever-present guards; and a directive from the Federal Bureau of Prisons in Washington to deny the UUs everything. The highlight of the year was our publishing coup—a slick issue of an illegal underground magazine, published and distributed throughout the prison—and not a single UU group member or supporter busted.

The incident began in 1968 when a Chicano named Frank Sepulveda somehow found out I was for the most part a Unitarian Universalist. He had been trying to start a Unitarian Universalist discussion group for years with no success. He asked me if I would like to join his non-group. I was new and wary, but since Frank wasn't looking at me like I was a love object I signed on.

The group now had two members.

Our request was a simple one. We wanted to get some free thinkers together to talk about religion.

Among other topics we wanted to discuss were the conflicts between reason and creed. Frank had a way with words. Of course he had been working with words for nine years. He was serving a 15-year sentence for possession of an amount of pot that was so small it couldn't be measured—so small it couldn't even be smoked—in the bottom of a jacket pocket. Those were the days when they locked you up for not paying tax on your pot. Frank claimed that forcing a person to pay taxes on pot was unconstitutional. He had been trying to get the federal courts to stop and reread what the constitution says about self-incrimination. He had filed actions on those grounds again and again. He had a son who was nine years old whom he had only seen in the visiting room.

Frank not only had a way with words, he was patient.

Normally prisons love to see groups form. It looks good on paper. People with drinking problems had a group. Gamblers had a group. Drug, sex, and food addicts had groups. The Jaycees, Toastmasters, Catholics, Jews, and Black Muslims all had groups.

The request that we submitted and resubmitted was really quite simple. Yet the request continued to be denied.

When we pressed the chaplain for reasons we were told: 1) We didn't have a sponsor (there were no UU fellowships or churches in the area, but in such cases the chaplain automatically sponsored any group with a religious affiliation), 2) there were already too many groups in the prison, and 3) we required guard supervision because we were a security problem and they couldn't spare a guard.

Something was wrong. We called a meeting. By now we had four members. We asked Frank if we had missed something. There were many very crazy organizations in that prison. How could the religion of Thomas Jefferson and Albert Schweitzer be considered crazy or dangerous? Certainly not the religion of Walter Kellison, a poet and the minister of the People's Unitarian Church, Cedar Rapids, Iowa—the only Unitarian I personally knew until I met Frank Sepulveda.

No crazies in that crowd.

When Frank and I asked the associate warden in charge of treatment for help, he told us to go to church on Sunday if we wanted religion.

We went back to the chaplain. He was hot. In prison "No" means exactly that. "No!" When a prisoner doesn't accept the "No" he is considered either stupid or a troublemaker.

"What you two do with your lives is your business," the chaplain told us, "but as long as I'm in charge of religion around here there will be no anti-Christian groups meeting in this prison."

Unitarians are many things, but they are not anti-Christian. Since we couldn't get a room for our UU meetings we decided to meet out on the yard. We posted handwritten notices around the prison announcing the meeting.

The notices had been up about two hours when Frank and I were told to report to the captain, the man who handles discipline problems on a day-to-day basis. He told us that the notices were contraband, they had not been approved by the chaplain, we had not been authorized to enter the areas where the notices were posted—and if it happened again we would be sent to Building 63—the hole.

We resubmitted requests and sent copies to George Marshall, minister for the Church of the Larger Fellowship at UU headquarters in Boston. We also asked him for literature and books.

After about a month, we wrote to George Marshall again and asked why they hadn't sent the books. We got a fast reply. "First order was sent. Two more boxes of replacement books and literature sent today."

Another month passed. No books from UU headquarters.

By this time, six or seven months have passed. Seem strange? You have to remember that nothing happens fast in prison—except killings.

During this time other prisoners were becoming interested. But since it was becoming known that being a Unitarian Universalist wasn't going to count for points at a parole hearing, most of the prisoners who came to listen and ask questions decided it wasn't worth being hassled about.

But some stayed.

We began proselytizing. The jailhouse lawyers were informed that every time they raised a constitutional issue on behalf of themselves or a fellow prisoner they could thank a Unitarian. Since many of the best jailhouse lawyers were doing heavy time, they were unconcerned that the administration was hassling us. To some, the hassling was what attracted them.

The Black Muslims asked, "If we can meet but the Unitarians can't, just exactly what is it the Unitarians advocate? Must have 'bad' politics if you can't meet without a guard."

As a diversion our group began attending regular church services, but we refused to allow the chaplain's clerk to add our names to the attendance list. We claimed that taking attendance was only crowd insurance and that it was discriminatory. The church attendance record was part of the information given to the parole board. It took a long time to get the practice stopped. When we did, the number of prisoners attending church services declined drastically.

Meanwhile, the chaplain would scream at us when we went to his office to ask about our books. Since

George Marshall had told us he had sent the books we knew the chaplain had them. Drastic action was needed.

One day, as soon as the chaplain and his clerk left for lunch, one of our new members, who was also a lock expert, walked four of us into the chaplain's office so fast I couldn't believe my eyes. Quickly, he locked the door behind us, then picked the locks on both desks, both filing cabinets, and the closet. In the closet were the four boxes of books and literature.

Our mission was half completed.

All books of a religious nature that came into the prison had to be stamped and signed by either the chaplain or the head of education. While the books were being spread out on the floor the rubber stamp was located and the books were stamped while I signed the chaplain's name—I'd worked on duplicating his signature since we decided to take the "law" into our own hands. I signed 57 books in five minutes. The pamphlets were all stamped but I only had time to sign 15 or 20. Everything was carefully put back, desks, closet, and filing cabinets were locked, and we were out of there.

We had made it in and out in 13 minutes and 28 seconds without anyone seeing us. My first B & E had been planned perfectly, but what fascinated me most was watching a man walk up to a locked door and, with what appeared to be three little steel "toothpicks," open it in seconds, with barely a pause in our forward motion. Twelve years later, James Caan starred in a movie called *The Thief*, which used this man as a model. The man was a professional. Contrary to what the movie portrayed, though, he did not use guns in his work.

That evening we had our regularly scheduled, unofficial, non-meeting to determine a future course of action. Only four people knew about the break-in. Actually five. The chaplain knew. We decided he couldn't say anything without admitting that he had grabbed our mail. He would have been in the clear if he had simply rejected the books and returned them. Keeping them was a "no no," and that "no no" determined our course of action.

First, we sent him a letter thanking him for approving the books and literature and being so supportive. We asked him which room he wanted us to meet in.

Needless to say, he provided us with a meeting room, but only under certain conditions: We couldn't post notices that we were meeting or that the Fellowship even existed, only ten Unitarians could meet at one time, and a guard had to be present at all times to ensure that nothing threatening the security of the prison was planned.

Over a year had passed—but organizing and the risks involved had kept the juices flowing.

Once a month Emil Gudmundson, director of the Prairie Star District of the Unitarian Universalist Association, drove down from Minneapolis, 800 miles roundtrip, to lead a discussion group. Don Vaughn, minister of the First Unitarian Church of Wichita, drove over from Wichita once a month—a 400-mile round trip.

We named the group the Michael Servetus Fellowship, after the young Spanish writer who searched for, but could not find, mention of the Trinity in the Bible. Servetus not only wrote about his fruitless search, he travelled around Europe discussing it publicly. He made a serious mistake when he inadvertently wandered across the border into Switzerland, home to the infamous Calvin. Servetus, unaware that Calvin had a standing arrest warrant out for him, was arrested and brought before this godfearing, Protestant reformer. Calvin had no time for any "truths" other than his own. The kinds of truth Servetus was seeking and discussing were so abhorrent to Calvin that he promptly tied Servetus to a stake in the town square and burned him alive.

We felt a distant kinship with Servetus after being forced to interact with the chaplain for so many months. Servetus only knows, that punk chaplain would have burned our books if he'd had the cods for it.

Then, as if dealing with the chaplain wasn't enough, the Bureau of Prisons objected not only to our forming the group but to our choice of name. Don Vaughn informed the warden that the American Civil Liberties Union was taking the case. That threat removed the final barrier.

UNDERGROUND MAGAZINE FROM BEHIND THE WALLS

With the fight over, we thought we should let the entire prison population know about our fellowship. We gathered information from the books George Marshall had sent us and the chaplain had been so reluctant to part with. Then we took the information and went underground into the system that the prisoners control, the system that operates right under the noses of the guards. Books were given to typists, who passed pages on to prisoners in the print shop. There, type was set and the proofs were smuggled back into the cell blocks, where they were corrected and smuggled back into the print shop. In the print shop, pages were printed and folded. Then they were collated and covers were added. Finally, the binding crew took over.

Five weeks after we decided to go public, 1,000 28-page booklets suddenly appeared throughout the prison.

— JOSEPH W. GRANT —

"MAN'S OBLIGATIONS ARE TO MAN," the cover cautioned.

The booklets were in the cell houses, on bulletin boards, in the factories, the tunnels, everywhere. Each booklet began: "Better to believe in no God than to believe in a cruel God, a tribal God, a sectarian God...."

The book contained answers to questions that had freaked the Baptist chaplain: What is Unitarian Universalism? What do UUs think about prayer? about Jesus? God? Heaven? Questions about hell were unnecessary in Leavenworth but they were included. Like group members Artie Rachel and Frank said at the time, "What the hell, why not?"

Our Michael Servetus Fellowship was credited in the book with publishing Leavenworth's first underground publication. We swore that someone was trying to set us up. What had happened wasn't possible, we maintained. How could a 28-page booklet be typeset and printed when supervisors were around the printing presses at all times? It couldn't. How could it be collated and stapled? It couldn't. How did it get distributed? Where did the paper and cover stock come from? How was it trimmed?

No one knew. And there wasn't a snitch in the print shop underground. We had over 15 members in the fellowship and no one told the man, and neither did the men from the print shop or the men who distributed the booklets throughout the prison. It was absolutely incredible.

Frank and I were ordered to the chaplain's office. I had never seen him that color and I had never heard him scream obscenities.

"JUST WHAT THE GOD DAMNED HELL ARE YOU TWO SONS OF BITCHES TRYING TO DO?"

I'll never forget Frank's answer: "Hey, man, my boy is going to be nine in a few days. He wasn't born when I came here for less grass than a person could smoke. What am I doing? Well, today, just like yesterday, I'm trying to keep from going crazy in your circus."

I just shrugged my shoulders and said, "The Lord moves in mysterious ways, his wonders to perform."

On the way back to the cell block I said to Frank, "For a minute I thought someone had gone to Baptist confession." Frank laughed. "It's a wonder someone didn't. Hell, Jesus only had 13 members and one of them was a snitch."

For his own efforts in hiding our mail and lying about it to us, meanwhile, the chaplain was later promoted by the Federal Bureau of Prisons to head the entire chaplaincy program in Washington, DC. Interesting. Had we decided to file charges against him we would have brought the entire system down on us. Our only consolation was knowing that he knew he was spending eight hours a day exactly where he belonged: in prison.

A couple months after our meeting in the chaplain's office, Frank's conviction was overturned. Timothy Leary got credit for the Supreme Court decision, but Frank had done all the work. The Leary Decision should have been the Sepulveda Decision. Even Leary agrees to that.

The second incident that helped give me a trustworthy reputation was funny, but it could have turned out bad.

After I had been there a few months I was called into the office of the lieutenant who was in charge of custody. As soon as I entered his office I recognized him. He had called me into his office because he had remembered an incident we shared years before. Back then he had been the federal jail inspector and Tom Kuncl and I were publishing the *Citizen-Times*. His job was to inspect any jail that had been designated a place where the federal government could hold prisoners. He travelled to cities and towns all over the country, including Cedar Rapids, Iowa.

It was no secret that the Linn County jail was in poor condition. It was miserably cold in winter and stifling hot in the summer. The food was terrible. Security was so poor that prisoners were able to leave the jail for the night by crawling out and in again through heating vents.

When we learned about this I contacted one of the prisoners, who came out and brought me back in late one night. While I was inside, I interviewed a couple of prisoners, took their pictures, had my picture taken with them to prove I had been there, and then I crawled back out. I had broken into and out of jail. I thought I had a great story. But I was advised to clear it with a friend who was a member of the National Lawyers Guild. He checked the law and told me I would probably be charged with a felony crime if the story and pictures were printed. We didn't use it. It would have been a wonderful story.

Shortly after that jail "break," we learned that the federal jail inspector was arriving in town to inspect the Linn County jail. Tom Kuncl decided we had to interview him as soon as he completed his inspection. We knew the jail would be approved, but we also knew that the jail would not meet the basic requirements. Unfortunately, once he found out some newspaper reporters were trying to corner him he enlisted the aid of the deputies to avoid us.

He avoided us going in and coming out of the jail.

We staked out his hotel room.

He changed hotels.

But a room clerk tipped us off and we were waiting for him when he drove up to a motel on the edge of town.

As soon as he saw us he jumped back in his car and drove off. We were unable to find him after that. Later we learned he had driven 130 miles to Des Moines before he thought it was safe to stop and get some rest.

As soon as I recognized him sitting behind that big desk in Leavenworth's custody office, I knew I was in big trouble. If he was vindictive, he had the power to make my life a perfect hell in that prison.

I walked up to his desk and instead of waiting for him to speak—which was the rule—I said, "I hope you understand the trouble I have gone through to finally catch up to you for this interview."

Thank Servetus the man had a sense of humor. He laughed and asked me to sit down and tell him how I happened to be there.

Every administrator has a prisoner clerk. These clerks keep track of everything that transpires between prisoners and administrators. If you step into the lieutenant's office, shut the door, sit down, and start talking, it looks bad—very bad. You'll end up an outcast—regardless of what you talk about.

I told him how pleased I was that he had a sense of humor, but that if he wanted information on why I was there he would have to get it from the official record. He didn't like my answer, but he understood.

By the next day everyone knew the story. I had chased the lieutenant out of Cedar Rapids, Iowa, when he was the federal jail inspector. The population loved it.

PRISON: A MIRROR OF THE FREE WORLD

Walking those endless miles "on the yard" inside the Federal Penitentiary at Leavenworth 21, 22 years ago, I came to the conclusion that the prison population, with only a few exceptions, reflected the free world population.

Fourteen years later, in the mid-eighties, I was back in a state prison. *PDI* no longer existed. I was in the Anamosa Reformatory serving six months for manufacturing a controlled substance. That charge translated into my being held responsible for a few wild pot plants that a vindictive sheriff found growing on a farm I held the title to. The fact that I didn't live there didn't lessen my responsibility in the eyes of the court. The person who was found picking the pot took a walk by swearing he was picking it, rolling it into joints, selling them for ten cents each, and giving me the money. It was absurd and everyone knew it.

I laughed all the way to prison.

However, it turned out to be an interesting six months.

For example: I worked sorting laundry for a while. Prisoners put their socks, T-shirts, shorts, and other whites into mesh bags that were washed in huge machines. When each prisoner came back to the sorting room to pick up his clean clothes, we checked his number and put the bag in a cubicle with a corresponding number. Occasionally the guards would order us to check all the bags to make sure no prisoner had items of clothing without a number—possession of unnumbered items was illegal. We were ordered to turn the bags over to the guards. Most of the population were under age 25. Many prided themselves on how tough they were and on how much time they had done.

The first time we were ordered to check laundry bags for contraband after I had started working there, one of the prison toughs found a bag with unnumbered socks and started walking over to the guard with the bag. "Wait a minute," I said. "Let's talk about this." He came back and rejoined the circle of 10 or 15 prisoners who were inspecting the bags.

"If you give that bag to the guard someone is going to end up in trouble. We can't be causing that kind of trouble. If you find any illegal items take them out of the bag and throw them in the lost and found bin."

He thought about what I said. He had to make sure he wasn't being made to look bad. "What if I get snitched off for not turning the bag in?" The thought of getting in trouble for helping someone he didn't even know was unthinkable.

"What if you get snitched off for turning the bag in?" I answered. Now he had to think about dealing with whoever might get written up.

Damned if you do, damned if you don't.

"Look at it this way," I explained. "The guard is trying to make us do his job for him. It is not our job to arrest people. If we turn someone in for having unmarked socks, we are participating in that person's getting busted. I don't know about you, but I'm not getting paid to be a cop." Then, to make sure he didn't feel threatened by me, I added, "And I know you aren't working for the man."

Before anyone could say anything else, I asked him to give me the bag. He did. I took the items out of the bag, threw them in the lost and found bin, tied the bag shut, and went back to work.

Conversations stopped while the men thought about what had been said. Some seemed perplexed. They didn't understand their role in the peaceful order of things.

"It's interesting to watch how the prison operates," I said to the group. Then I asked them, "Who does all the work?"

"We do all the goddamned work. The prisoners do all the work and take all the crap," a number of them said all at once.

"That's why it's important that we make sure life goes as smoothly as possible for everyone. If we turn in every bag with clothes that are not numbered, 10 or 15 or more prisoners are going to get written up. A man could lose good time. Someone may get knocked off the list for a one-man cell. They may be looking for a way to stop someone from making a move to minimum security. All because the man has decided to make the prisoners snitch each other off."

"What you are saying could get you in trouble, Grant," one of the men said. "What if someone here goes to the man and snitches you off for not turning in those unmarked socks? What would you do?"

"Well, I wouldn't deny it, because the man always takes the word of a snitch over the word of the person who is being snitched on. I'd just tell them that I thought they were causing themselves more trouble than a pair of socks was worth. I didn't turn the guy in because to do so would cause me trouble—I'd be a snitch—and the guy trouble—he'd be violating rules. If I ended up in 'court' for not turning him in, I was only causing myself trouble. I'd rather be in trouble with the man for not being a snitch than in trouble with the prisoners for being a snitch. I had cut the trouble in half. They might give me a free bag of popcorn at the next movie."

The men liked my story. Lots of laughs. But I made my point.

One of the other prisoners smiled and said, "If I get caught not turning a prisoner in, I'm gonna say, 'I'm just trying to save you a bunch of paperwork, Boss!'"

Everyone laughed again, and for the rest of the afternoon we kept coming up with excuses to tell the man. Responsibility rehearsals. Memorizing your lines for the next performance. Peacekeeping practice. Helping your brothers. And that is exactly what happened. I was snitched off to the guard, he called me out, I told him exactly what I had told the prisoners, and he agreed. He tore up the report. He surprised me.

THE PRISONERS CAN VOTE...BUT!

The following week I was elected to the inmate council. Since I hadn't been a prisoner for the required amount of time, the custody officer removed my name and they had another election. The inmate population re-elected me. They took me off and filled the vacancy with an appointee.

A vote is a terrible thing to waste. "Teach your children well...," I told the warden.

It was the third inmate council I'd been denied a seat on. But I knew that a time would come when all the good, common sense rules that have developed over the past 300 years in the prisons of the world would someday come together someplace. I had hoped it would be the *PDI*, where we could refine them, get rid of the crap and the egos, and end up with a slim little volume of customary law that prisoners could use as a guide to what is right and wrong from the prisoner's perspective. Not something to make war with, but something to make peace with.

"Your vote is precious—use it," I'd tell my fellow prisoners.

This incident, as much as any, convinced me that these young prisoners could and would act responsibly if they were given reasons to do so. My talk with these guys about our obligation to look out for our brother prisoners and try to avoid creating problems had an impact. No one was ever turned in for having an unnumbered sock or T-shirt while I was still there, not because any feared me but because the decision was one they could make on their own.

One other incident took place that changed the general appearance of the population. When we sorted the shirts and pants, the clothes were jammed into the cubicles assigned to each prisoner. Each of us was assigned a block of cubicles. I decided to fold all of the clothes before I placed them in the cubicles.

When we finished the sort that day my section of cubicles stood out from the rest. It screamed "NEATNESS," and there was no way anyone could avoid seeing it. When the prisoners came for their clothes after work that day those whose numbers were in my block made a big deal out of the fact that their clothes seemed to have been pressed. They seemed pressed because we sorted when they were still warm from the dryers.

Prisoners asked, "Why go to the extra trouble?"

"Because the man wants us to look like a bunch of trashy losers," I answered.

Within a week everyone was folding the pants and shirts. The laundry room workers began taking pride in how neatly clothes were stacked in their block of cubicles.

One major population difference I could see between this prison visit and my first one 14 years earlier was the presence of an extraordinary number of prisoners who were child molesters. There had always been child molesters in the can, but in the past they were few and far between. They were considered the dregs of the population and were the recipients of every prisoner's anger or frustration. They were raped by the aggressive, beaten up by whoever took a notion, and verbally abused by everyone. Yet in the brief span of 14 years their numbers had increased so drastically that they were a significant percentage of the prison population. A group to contend with. A voting block. Old men, young men, married men, fathers, you name it—they were a group. And they were out there walking the yard like respectable prisoners.

So, does the prison population reflect the free world population before or after the proliferation of convicted child abusers? I've come to the conclusion that 14 years earlier, when I was in Leavenworth, it didn't. The prison population has been playing "catch up." Today's prison population is a more accurate reflection of society. Be that as it may.

Prisoners. A cross section of society. Living with them, constantly interacting, studying, observing, learning. It was a Philip K. Dick novel. Real. Unreal. Never have I lived in such an oppressive environment. Never have I seen "justice" meted out so swiftly. At times I felt so vulnerable it made me sick. At other times I felt invulnerable—unbeatable. For the most part, however, I was a constant witness to hopelessness, futility, and waste. At times it exhausted me. Occasionally it energized me. There were times when it inspired.

Tough Adjustments for COs

It was interesting, for instance, to watch how the conscientious objectors during the Vietnam War affected their fellow prisoners as more and more of them began showing up in the walled prisons. Suddenly the prison population had to contend with prisoners who did not lie, cheat, or steal. When a CO was asked about the conduct of another prisoner, he didn't lie to disassociate himself from what he had observed. It didn't take long for them to learn to stand on their fifth amendment rights. They simply refused to answer.

There have always been prisoners who feel an obligation to help their fellow prisoners, but the COs went public with it—taking it from the unusual to NOP—normal operating procedure. They were, with rare exception, pacifists. There were times when convict thugs—the prisoner equivalent to the guard's goon squads—who took orders from the man, would play rough with COs, but for the most part the COs earned the respect of even the toughest, most cynical cons. The fact that these gentle people were even in prison was one more example of a judicial system that had become as evil as some of the defendants who ended up before the bench, and as evil as some of the judges behind the bench.

As long as non-violent people are imprisoned for their antiwar convictions, a critically important element of civilization has been ignored or rejected by our society. We all suffer for it. Prison was a difficult adjustment for most of the COs. They were unprepared for the irrational violence that surrounded them. Unprepared for the rapes that took place during group showers with all but the participants going about their business as though nothing was happening. The insane, irrational criminality—the violence, different than any I had ever known.

I knew that rage could provoke a person to kill, but I had never, before Leavenworth, seen a killing that wasn't preceded by some show of emotion—a display of anger or rage. Not so while I was at Leavenworth. Words. Calmly spoken. And suddenly there was violence. A seemingly normal conversation ended with a person dead. And as quickly as it had happened it was over. Men walking around a body as though it wasn't there. The crowd smoothly drifting away in an ever widening circle, with no one facing in. Nothing seen. Nothing heard. It was tough on COs.

I observed their lives and the lives of others in prison. Through it all, observations provoked perplexing questions.

For example, why is it that, as soon as a person is convicted of a crime, he or she is abandoned by the law? Why do prisoners, be they convicted of pandering, prostitution, perjury, or murder, suddenly become non-humans, not worthy of an iota of attention when they are raped, assaulted, denied medical attention, starved, held in solitary confinement without trial for years, and generally treated in a manner that will guarantee that the petty offender will become tomorrow's armed robber and those carrying today's anger will walk out tomorrow harboring a potentially deadly rage?

Perhaps the most perplexing question I asked myself while on the inside looking in was this: For all the brutality (by prisoners and guards), for all the lying, cheating, and stealing (by prisoners and guards), for all the shakedowns (by prisoners and guards), how is it that so many prisoners survived the insanity and emerged to face the same situations that originally, for whatever reasons, combined to place them in jeopardy, and ultimately in prison—again, and again.

Rule by Tradition

The rule of law, which we hoped to establish in the prisons back in the seventies, does not exist in any prison in the United States. There is state law, legislated law, and the law of force, threats, and arbitrary punishment, but the "rule of law" as we think of it in the free world does not exist in prison. Prisoners, therefore, survive through guile, muscle, gangs, as informants, or by cutting deals. Nevertheless, one doesn't have to spend much time in prison to discover that an elaborate system of customs, "informal" rules, does exist. These unwritten laws, accepted simply on the strength of tradition, probably began to take shape when the Quakers released prisoners from their single, solitary cells, where isolation with only the Bible for a companion was doing then what the same treatment does to prisoners today—it drove men nuts. Once the prisoners were out of their solitary cells in Philadelphia (where prisons as we know them today were invented) and began mixing and interacting, social "agreements" began to form. A code of behavior developed.

During these hundreds of years prisoners have managed to survive the barbarity of prison with the help of these unwritten "rules." The society of prisoners, no differently than the free world society, needed a code that they could live by—could survive by.

In the dining hall at Leavenworth, for instance, if you were sitting at one of the four-person tables by yourself or with a friend and another prisoner needed a seat, he would ask if it was okay to join you. Then, he would sit quietly and not join in the conversation until he was spoken to. You could eat an entire meal with a person at your table who seemingly didn't hear a word that was said, didn't look at you, didn't seem to be there.

Whether it was a cell, a bed in a dorm, or a table in the dining hall, your personal space was something that no one entered unless he was invited. The great majority of the prisoners had a tremendous respect for another prisoner's space. You could die for not respecting it.

Usually, the longer a person had been inside, the gentler and the deadlier he became. He could respond with thoughtfulness, a totally unexpected birthday gift, or deadly force if someone broke a "law" that he lived by. "If I don't enforce my law, who will?" I was told by an old-timer a few cells down the line in B block. A new fellow had moved in and had brought a guitar with him. He was strumming the guitar. I was aware of it, but was painting and paying no attention. Suddenly a quiet voice said, "Stay out of my house with your music." And the music stopped. There were places to play your guitar. The cell block, where your music entered another person's "house," was not one of them.

Another rule: "Do your own time." This is one of the most basic rules. You hear it many ways. "If you can't do the time, don't do the crime." Defining "Do your own time" is not as simple as it first appears. One prisoner will say, "Don't let your problems spill over and affect the man in the cell next to you." Another will say, "Look out for number one, ignore what's going on around you, keep your mouth shut." Another will state, "It means that no one wants to listen to an endless litany of blaming others for the reason you're in prison. Shut up and 'do your own time'."

It's a rule that goes both ways. It benefits the administrators and the guards when prisoners "do their own time" and refuse to go to the aid of a fellow prisoner who is being treated unjustly by guard or prisoner. On the other hand, it's a very positive rule when prisoners understand that they must respect other prisoners' space, privacy, and rights.

In 1988, Professor Richard Oakes, founding dean of the Hamline University (St. Paul, Minnesota) School of Law, initiated the first systematic examination of that system when he began contacting—and being contacted by—prisoners from around the world. These prisoners are in turn carefully researching those customs in their own prisons that have literally become law (see sidebar 1).

Like Professor Richard Oakes, I believe that these unwritten rules must be collected, studied, and published, then made available to all prisoners to use in their relations with prison guards, administrators, and other prisoners. "Law and order" continues to be a major concern of people in the free world. Believe me, for much longer than anyone in the free world can imagine, it has been of paramount concern inside the walls of prisons as well.

As a union activist who had walked picket lines with the Laborers, the Packing House Workers, and the International Brotherhood of Electrical Workers (IBEW), I understood how management attempted to fragment groups of organizing workers. In the same way, the prison population were also being fragmented by the authorities. Turn the blacks against the Chicanos, the whites against the blacks, the old against the young. Keep the populations fighting amongst themselves. Keep the population from organizing. Keep the population from bringing the rule of law into the prison.

The "man" had been carefully coached by the psychologists and psychiatrists. The old stimulus/response games were being played to the hilt. Rewards and punishments. Outrageous rewards, inhuman punishments. Transfers, segregation, every tool of the trade used and learned in hundreds of years of suppressing individuality, of punishing, of breaking people's spirits were available. Many of them were common knowledge; most were not.

There was a time when a snitch was despised. Someone who could not be trusted was an outcast. However, with more and more perks being introduced to the system—good-time, parole, more liberal visits, mail, minimum and medium security prisons—the temptation for a prisoner to ingratiate himself or herself with guards became greater and greater. When a prisoner who is facing the loss of a couple of years' good time can avoid the punishment by informing on an acquaintance who is running numbers, he or she frequently does so.

My first serious mistake inside the walls was as memorable for what didn't happen as for what did. Contrary to popular thinking, and regardless of Miranda, et al., even the courts cannot help the prisoner who threatens the stability of the system. I threatened the stability of the system.

I had kicked around in a number of prison jobs until one day in 1968 the chief surgeon discovered that I had had a modest exposure to science and anatomy that had provided me with a fair degree of familiarity with medical terminology. He had been without a clerk for a couple of weeks and the paperwork on new prisoners was a mess. The job of the chief surgeon's clerk was to type medical summaries from the chief surgeon's scribbled notes that were made during the superficial physical exams that each new prisoner received. My ability to decipher his medical hieroglyphics thrust me into a job that provided me with the one possession no other prisoner in the joint had—an office of my own. My office was small, but it afforded me more privacy and freedom than I ever believed would be possible in that prison. No guards, no prisoners, no one.

Directly across the hall from my office was another small office where the psychiatrist worked. The psychiatrist was a Berkeley grad whose mannerisms were extremely effeminate. Most prisoners thought he was gay and, since most of the old-line prisoners were right-wing flagwavers who hated "draft dodgers, faggots, and longhairs," he was seen as out-of-place behind the walls. For the year or so that I worked across the hall from him I watched him gain the respect of most of the prisoners. It was not unusual for prisoners counseling with him to allow their pent-up anger and frustration at the prison and the system to explode. They would curse him, scream, jump up and down, and pound the table. One day I asked him why he put up with such abuse. "That talk means nothing. Better they get rid of the anger yelling at me than going out and killing someone."

The chief surgeon was not so sensitive. In my opinion, he was one of the coldest, most sadistic men I have ever known. He treated me like a human being simply because there was no one else available who could do the job. The job was such a cakewalk that no pay came with it. I took care of that problem within the month. I worked slowly, with a fixed pained expression on my face, until the chief surgeon asked

Section 1. Privacy and Autonomy: In the cellhouse; in the dorm; in medium and minimum security units; in the half-way house; during visitation; as both relate to personal habits and conduct, and as both relate to mail and other communications.

Section 2. Prison Rules: Rules which must be defied; rules which must be obeyed; rule enforcement and non-enforcement, and the enforcers.

Section 3. Rules of the Prison Workplace.

Section 4. Commerce and Money - Financial Affairs: Debts and debt collection; financial relationships inside the walls, and financial relationships outside the walls.

Section 5. Property Law: Ownership of property; transfer of property, and value of property.

Section 6. Contraband: Unauthorized, dope; weapons; publications, and communications.

Section 7. Sex: Sex as commodity; rules of conduct concerning: Intimate relationships, sexual commitments, and the buying and selling of people.

Section 8. Partnerships, Cliques and Gangs: Partnerships; cliques; gangs and rules within the gangs.

Section 9. Informing and Informants.

Section 10. Outside Contact Rules.

Section 11. Rules on Contact with Administration.

Section 12. Violence: Against prisoners, guards, civilians.

Section 13. Crimes and Sanctions.

Section 14. Law Enforcers and Professional Interveners: The tier boss.

Section 15. Religion and Prison Religion.

Section 16. Common Conventions of Behavior.

Prisoners, ex-prisoners, and others may send inquires to: Professor Richard T. Oakes, Customary Prison Law Project, Hamline University School of Law, St. Paul, MN 55104-1284.

Oakes is a professor of law at Hamline University, St. Paul, Minnesota. He was dean of the law school from 1972 to 1976 and has worked extensively as a criminal lawyer. Oakes has authored numerous articles on a wide range of legal topics and a text, *Oakes' Criminal Practice Guide* (New York: Wiley Law Publications, 1991). He is presently teaching criminal law and Native American law and heading a research team that is studying customary law in prisons.

---

me if $20 a month would speed me up. I said I thought it would be worth a try. He did and it was. Soon I was typing the medical histories and interviewing all new prisoners regarding their medical histories.

Since I was questioning every prisoner and the prisoner didn't know where the official questions ended, I began asking my own. I was interested in substance abuse—alcohol, drugs, and others. Had they been drinking when they committed their crime? Had they used drugs? Did other members of the family? Parents divorced? How many times? Siblings? Et cetera, et cetera, et cetera. I even initiated visits to Building 63—the hole—to get medical histories on prisoners who were never allowed to join the general prison population.

Some of the residents of Building 63 were an elite group who had committed the only unacceptable offense: they had attacked a prison guard or administrator. The ultimate crime. They got special treatment. They were endlessly transferred around the federal prison system and never saw a cell block, the mess hall, the yard, or the commissary, and rarely received mail. They lived in the hole. Prison to prison to prison. I managed to spend time with prisoners who had been in solitary for as many as 13 years. I carefully coded all of the information I gathered using a master form that enabled me to put small pencil dots on hundreds of pages of my journal. Unless you looked closely the dots were lost on the page of handwritten material. In the course of a couple of years I gathered extensive histories on over 1,000 prisoners who had served an average of five prison sentences before getting to the Big Top.

Even though I went to great lengths to keep the journals bland and free of any controversy, they were snatched when I was being transferred and I didn't realize it until I was 1,000 miles down the road. A guard later told me that much of my accumulated belongings were trashed when the guards who search prisoners' belongings before the boxes leave the prison were pissed when I showed up with five regulation-sized boxes of books and journals when the rules clearly stated that each prisoner was only allowed one. I had gotten by with breaking the rule as the chief surgeon's clerk. The transfer relegated me to the position of just another prisoner. When I dropped the boxes off, one of the old guards, an old-timer, said, "You've got more goddam shit than Bob Stroud[4] had."

The marshalls chained me and led me off. Three weeks later, my paintings and art supplies showed up, but the journals were gone. Damn near three years of research gone. Fortunately they never knew how important the material was to me.

But let's get back to my friend, the chief surgeon. Since I was able to put together a pretty good medical history, he and the director of the hospital called me in one day and told me they wanted me to document fire and emergency drills that never took place—drills that had to be held for the hospital to maintain its accreditation. They explained what they needed, showed me the forms, and sent me over to another medical clerk who had been doing them. "This is easy, fun, gives you a chance to express yourself creatively, and, if breaking the law is your idea of fun, this is the job for you," Jim explained.

So I began creating these complex drills. I'd decide on a scenario. For example: a fire breaks out in a closet, on the second floor, across the hall from where oxygen is stored. I would describe in great detail how the prisoners were evacuated, where the most serious custody cases were taken, how the ambulatory cases were moved, and on and on. For the disaster drills I even designed menus and had the cooks preparing food in the yard after a Kansas tornado had destroyed two cell blocks and the kitchen and mess hall. I would get so into these fictionalized happenings that the reports would sometimes be 8, 10, 15 typewritten pages. Designing the scenarios was fun and the surgeon, the director, and I would sometimes laugh about the complex situations the "well trained staff of the hospital was able to deal with in such a professional manner."

It was funny all right—really funny. It was part of my job. But the thought that if a real emergency ever happened the staff would not know how to evacuate that hospital began to bother me. A fire, any kind of serious emergency, could end up costing people their lives. In the midst of abject boredom a conscience reared its self-righteous head. Strange how it so frequently contributes to a person's self-destruction.

I mentioned to the director and the chief surgeon that it might be a good idea to actually hold the drills. We could really train for an emergency, I suggested. Training would not disrupt our work day, our scenarios would be documented with pictures, and the two of them would be held up as examples of how top notch hospital administrators ran a prison hospital. I was told to forget it.

Their refusal to hold actual drills, a prerequisite for a hospital to be accredited, kept digging at me until I finally decided to do something about it. A friend had documented all of the federal crimes that were being broken. All the past falsified drills were in the files. I had also researched the law. Falsifying official government documents. The signing of official forms

that contained false information. These were felony crimes. How quick I was to point a finger at officials involved in criminal activity. I sincerely believed that I had only to send the documentation to the attorney general's office to end the abuse. I was going to personally charge them with the crimes and substantiate the criminal activity by submitting the proof. It was risky. It was perfect. I was looking for action.

I didn't realize how thin the ice was.

The only difficulty would be smuggling the information out of the prison. Prisoners are allowed to send sealed mail to the attorney general. By law, prison administrators are not allowed to open mail that prisoners send to lawyers, federal officials, or members of the Senate or the House of Representatives. But they did. Fortunately, I had a friend, a fellow prisoner, whose job took him in and out of the prison a couple times a week. Frequently he would smuggle letters in and out for me. I gave him the letter with postage on it. A business envelope thick with documented evidence. He slipped it under his shirt without looking at it.

With that out of the way, I felt better.

About an hour later, a runner came to my office and told me to report to Custody. When I got there I was met by my friend and a guard. The guard took the two of us into a room, closed the door, and pulled out the letter. I had been caught and my friend nailed with me. Very serious. This was not just any letter.

The guard was the only guard I had developed any respect for. I had never seen him harass a prisoner or play any of the typical games guards play.

The letter was opened and all the copies of the last four or five fire drills and emergency drills, signed, with cover letter, were laid on the table. He folded everything up, put the material back in the envelope, and handed it to me.

The guard was being very calm about this. "I opened it because of how it was being sent. Had to be sure you guys were not planning something serious. Since this letter is addressed to the attorney general I'm not going to tell you what to do with it and I'm not going to give it to Custody. But I will tell you that if this letter gets to the attorney general's office you are going to be the most miserable prisoner in the federal system. You will do every day of your sentence. You will never see good time. You will have your cell torn apart at least once a month if you ever have a cell for a full month. You will spend hard time on the road again and again and again. You will become familiar with the hole in every maximum security joint in the system. You will not have visitors. You will get crap for food and you will have the most shit detail jobs available in this entire system. You can appeal your case to court, but you know that access to the courts takes so long you will have already lost by the time your case gets there regardless of the final legal outcome. Now if you think that kind of misery will be worth blowing the whistle on the hospital director and the chief surgeon, think again. Because nothing will change, Joe. Absolutely nothing. I'm not going to mess with any mail to the attorney general so you decide what you want to do with this letter."

With that he waved us out.

We left. Once outside my friend turned to me, and he was as white as the Johannesburg, South Africa City Hall, with a tinge of green around the edge of his jaw.

"Jesus Christ, Joe, you shudda' tol' me what you was doin'. If'n anybody else had caught me with a letter like this we'd never see daylight again! I'm too old for this kind 'a crap."

We were on the yard at the time. When we got to the rec hall I walked in and tore the entire contents of the envelope into very small pieces. Then I filled the sink with water, mashed the pieces into a mush, and flushed them down the toilet.

Lesson learned.

The more I thought about what had happened, though, the more I realized that there was no one I could have sent that information to. No one in the Federal Bureau of Prisons or its parent operation, the Justice Department, would protect the person blowing the whistle on their own system. Absolutely no one. But, I reasoned, if prisoners had their own newspaper, run by ex-prisoners who understood how vulnerable a prisoner was, that letter, that story, would have been published and I would have had the protection that comes with being able to reach the public with your story. At that point in history, 1968, there were some liberal newspapers, but their liberalism normally had a life of, if you really had a story that was dynamite, two days.

Fortunately I had smuggled a duplicate set of records out with another friend, who saw that it was sent home. Three years later, I made a copy and hand-delivered it to Norman Carlson, director of the Federal Bureau of Prisons. He was hot about some stories I had written in the *PDI* concerning conditions in the federal system. To show him I wasn't trying to make him look bad I gave him copies of the material, explained what it was about, explained what criminal acts were involved, the danger to the prisoners in the hospital, and other related pieces of information, and asked him to talk to the hospital director and the chief surgeon. I threw away a great story, but I felt it was worth it to convince him that my attacks were not personal.

After I gave him the material proving that top hospital administrators were committing a crime that carried three to five years plus fines, I sent word to a friend who worked in the hospital inside Leavenworth. I told him what I had done and asked him to keep me informed of any changes. He sent word out to me every few months for over a year. Nothing changed. The disaster and fire drills were still works of fiction, still signed by the hospital administrators and submitted as true.

No question about it. The prisoners needed a newspaper, a voice, with a second class postal permit, the same second class permit the *New York Times* and the *Washington Post* and the other daily and weekly newspapers received from the U.S. Postal Department. Only with that permit could our voice—our newspaper—get inside the walls to the prisoners. We had to have a newspaper that would allow us to spill our guts. To scream poetry and prose. To cut through the endless reams of reportorial gobble-de-gook. To write letters to the editor that you knew would get published. To sit down with cheap pens and tablets of lined paper and write exposés that you knew would be published a few weeks down the line. A newspaper to wipe our emotional asses with. Such a newspaper would be hated by all except a handful of wardens, guards, and prison administrators. Most would try to keep prisoners from subscribing. But as a newspaper with a second class permit, every establishment newspaper in the country could be coerced into asking, "If this one newspaper, a newspaper with a second class permit, can be banned, who might be next?"

A prisoner could count on no help from the courts. The free world had no way to see inside the prisons. Prisoners then and now are shut out, shut off, shut up. Everyone took the abuse. The rotten food, the sexual abuse, the psychological abuse, the beatings, the isolation in the population, and the solitary confinement were the rewards you received when you screamed for justice. The strong fought back, took their lumps, and went on. The weak folded, were crushed, ended up whipped punks or broken men and women who would never recover to regain a sense of self-worth.

The kind of suffering that is the most intolerable is the kind that holds no relief in sight. You take your lumps knowing that the longer you stand the more it's going to hurt. Giving up sometimes helps, but you always pay. And through it all you know that there is nothing you can do. If you had any resources you wouldn't be there. If you had money for an attorney good enough to take on the system, your problem would already have been taken care of.

The prisoners in the end-of-the-line prisons needed a voice. Hell, all the prisoners needed a voice.

If we were going to suffer, knowing that we would never have a day in court, we could at least suffer knowing that we had had our day in print.

Having a "day in print" is the major dream of many prisoners. That and getting out. There are many minor dreams. An unlimited supply of books to keep the sexual juices flowing. A decent meal. Some spice. A jar of hot sauce. Someone to write to. Letters. Quiet. Equity. But mostly, wanting to spill your guts about your life. Why you did or didn't do it. The arrests. The sleazy lawyers. The lying cops. The judges who neither hear nor see. The hopelessness. "If only I could tell my story!" prisoners lament. "If only someone would listen! I wish...."

But wishing isn't enough. One morning some years later, after I had been released and after *PDI* had come into existence, I was eating pancakes over by the Bronx courthouse with attorney Bill Kunstler, who was now on our advisory board. I wished for something. Bill looked up from his pancakes and said, "Tell you what, Joe, you pray in one hand and wish in the other and let me know which one fills up the fastest."

Having a day in print. Telling the prisoner's side of the story. In my cell, into my journals, I spilled my guts every day. I would rage with a pencil and my pads of lined paper. I would scream. Accuse. Threaten to file the class action suit that would end the abuse. But you file a suit and it takes 16 months getting to the judge who dismisses it quietly and sends it back and you start all over. Or else you win, which is just as bad. The judge sends the cease and desist order to the prison. The prison ignores it. You file again asking for the prison to be cited for contempt. Sixteen months later the judge sees it, reads it, and sends it back for a correction or clarification.

With a newspaper it would be different. BAM. INTO PRINT. There it would be in black and white. PRINT. People believe print. There is a magic in print. Particularly NEWSPRINT.

How often could such a newspaper be published? It would have to be a monthly. Even that might be too costly. Maybe a quarterly.

Who would buy it? Some prisoners could afford it, but for the most part the prisoners who needed it couldn't afford it.

And so, while I was still in prison, that great builder and destroyer of dreams moved in and began to take over. I said to myself, "The law schools would subscribe. Yeh! And the libraries. Yeh! And free world organizations that were concerned with the welfare of their fellow human beings. Men, women, and children who were being treated like animals. YEH! Damn right! I knew about printing costs. I knew about deadlines and layout and setting type. Boy, did I know! And I knew that in these United States I could sell three or four thousand subscriptions at, say, $6 a year. No, $9 a year. $6 for prisoners. NO! $6 for prisoners who

could afford it. $1 for prisoners who couldn't. And free to those with absolutely no resources at all.

With pencil and lined tablet I pored over the numbers. Over a million and a half people passing in and out of the city, county, state, and federal systems each year. A multi-billion dollar industry. A workforce of hundreds of thousands.

I worked on it and convinced myself that the publication would be successful. NO. Not just successful. The publication would be a steppingstone to focus the attention of the free world on the plight of the prisoner. As a result, thanks to the illuminating effect of an internationally circulated newspaper, change would come to the prison systems of the United States and the world.

If you're going to dream, dream big.

The first step was getting out. Then I had to raise money to get a publicity piece to colleges and libraries. Then, with all that money, I would have to wheel and deal for the equipment I would need to put together the camera ready copy. I would need enough left over to pay the printer. I would need a vehicle reliable enough to get us to and from the printer and big enough to haul all the newspapers back to the office for addressing and mailing.

No sweat.

"LAYING OUT MY WINTER CLOTHES"

I began seriously planning for *PDI* soon after my fellow Unitarian Universalist Frank Sepulveda was transferred. I spent more time now observing the goings on inside the prison. I paid more attention to the unwritten rules that many of the prisoners lived by. I talked with the old-timers.

What I found was, as I have said, a slice of the free world. We had it all and more. Long-smoldering feuds. A legal profession. The peacekeepers. The assassins. The poets. Capitalists, socialists, anarchists. The weak and the strong. A class of poor, a broad middle class, the wheeler-dealers hustling through their financial ups and downs. At the top, a handful of power brokers. Just as in the free world, that reliable old rain barrel theory applied inside the prison—the scum rising to the top. Many had even linked up with community organizations like the Jaycees.

One day I was sitting out in the yard watching the endless stream of prisoners walk by. One young fellow came over and sat down near me. He hadn't been there long. I remembered interviewing him when he came through the hospital. All the required questions. Have you had such and such? All the prison hospital medical stuff. Then my own questions. His was a particularly sad case. He had a serious learning disability. He had stolen a car and taken it across state lines. He had done it again and again. He was, in the eyes of the law, "incorrigible." Tell him anything and he believed you. Ask him to do anything for you and he would.

I had come across him one day a few weeks earlier. He was sitting in the middle of a driveway between two buildings. I asked him what he was doing.

"The next truck to come driving by is gonna kill me," he said.

"Why do you want to die?"

"The Bible said that if you give it'll come back to you three-fold. I've been giving away everything I get from the commissary. Nothing has ever come back to me."

"Who told you to do that?"

"The chaplain's clerk."

I explained to him that the verse didn't mean he would be rewarded here on earth. Rather, I said, "The rewards will come to you in heaven." Since he had placed so much faith in the Bible I explained that Jesus didn't want him to give to people who already had more than he did. Instead, Jesus wanted him to share with people who were suffering. I didn't have much faith in the brand of Christianity that was being peddled in that joint but with some people you have to be very gentle. He decided to go to his house instead of waiting for a truck. The chaplain's clerk was an officer in the Jaycees.

This time he looked like the problem was more than waiting for a return on donated candy bars.

"How you doin'?" I asked.

"I been makin' friends in the Jaycees. Good friends."

"Great."

"I made thirteen new friends at the meeting."

"Exactly thirteen?"

"Yeh. Exactly. Thirteen."

"Who were they?"

"I don't remember names but I counted them."

"Do you try to remember their names?"

"No. I just count. There was thirteen Jaycees that fucked me. They told me that every time I let a Jaycee fuck me he would be my friend."

He was starting to cry. He was 24. Maybe 25. Young for his age. He looked 19. The Jaycees loved him.

"I think you should tell them that you hurt real bad. Tell them that you may have to go to the doctor if anyone fucks you again. Tell them you think you have some kind of infection."

I knew how much the thought of infection would affect them. They'd all start using rubbers.

Sitting there talking. Watching him suffering. Thinking that the great majority of the Jaycees were closely associated with the church. Members of the choir. You see them with their Bibles. Their little testaments.

Like the free world. The women bleed. Without women, they manufacture substitutes and the subs bleed.

When I first arrived, I was invited to a meeting of Trailblazer Jaycees, so named because they were the first Jaycees chapter in the federal prison system. After my introduction, I was asked what I'd like to accomplish while I was in prison. I told them I'd like to convince the prison Jaycees group to drop out of the national organization because it is a sexist group that is primarily interested in the business interests and advancement of men. The president took me to the side and told me he would kill me if I ever talked like that again. The original Trailblazer charter incentive plan: do as you are told or die.

MY DILEMMA: HOBBY CRAFT OR JESUS

As my plans for the newspaper took shape I began discussing the idea with friends I could confide in. Very few of my friends encouraged the idea. Most of them had much more experience with prison populations than I did. Maybe it was my naivete that made it happen. Whatever. After some interesting escapades and scares over the next ten- or twelve-month period and a transfer to a medium security joint in Sandstone, Minnesota, I was released on parole.

Before you can "walk" you have to check out of each department in the prison. That means you have to personally go to each department head and have him sign a release form stating that you have nothing of value that belongs to that department. When I got to the chaplain's office I put on my very serious mask and asked him if I could talk to him for a moment.

He was wary, but he invited me into his office. I sat down and explained that I was leaving and that I was faced with a seemingly impossible problem. I had to make a decision that I had been struggling with for days. He was all ears. He couldn't believe he was listening to this kind of talk from the fellow who had helped shove a Unitarian Universalist Fellowship—the first inside the federal prison system—down the throat of the Federal Bureau of Prisons in Leavenworth two years earlier. I explained that I had wrestled with the problem for days. Now I had to choose. I couldn't work it out by myself and needed his help.

He came out from behind his desk and sat down beside me. The chaplain had this look of disbelief on his face. He put his hand on my shoulder and reassured me that he would help in any way he could.

"Do I have your absolute confidence?" I asked.

"My office is like the confessional, Joe. You know that," he answered.

That remark almost broke me up, but I held the serious look. My eyes were kind of watery as a result of holding back the laughter. He was in heaven. I looked him in the eye and explained, "You know I'm being released." He nodded. "You know I have to check out with all the departments." He nodded and said, "Yes, Joe. How can I help?" I explained that since yesterday I had two departments remaining to sign my release forms. My problem was that I had been going to the departments in their order of importance. With the religion and hobby craft departments the only two remaining, I couldn't decide where to go first. "Would you help me, Father?" I asked. "Should I have you sign or should I go to the hobby craft shop first?"

He froze. He took his hand away from my shoulder and stood up, walked to the chair behind his desk, turned to me, and called me a son-of-a-bitch. As I stood up to leave I added, "That's right, priest, but a son-of-a-bitch who thinks the philosophy of the good carpenter is a gas as opposed to your adulterations of Christian brotherhood and sisterhood."

He had answered my question. I headed for hobby craft.

The next day, the chaplain had the final word in the matter. Before he would sign my checkout form, he made me wait three hours.

No, I take that back: Even with the wait, it was a pleasure watching him sign his name right below the director of hobby craft's signature.

BUCK NAKED AT THE LIQUOR STORE

I stepped out of that northern Minnesota federal prison ten days in front of 1970. John Eastman was there to greet me. I had just made a terrible mistake and was in a vile mood. The associate warden had seized one of my paintings—a combination sculpture/painting that I knew was going to make me enough money to start the newspaper. I didn't find out what they had done until I picked up my parole papers and was stepping out of the prison. I had 15 or 20 paintings to load into John's station wagon. Right away, I saw that they had removed the sculpture part and given me only the painting part. I returned to the window and asked the guard on the other side about my missing art. He said I used federal property to make it. He was talking about scrap metal that had been discarded. From my papers I took out the document giving me permission to use the scrap. The guard said, "We'll let the warden decide. He'll be back in a week."

It's at times like this that the boys are separated from the men. I should have torn up my parole papers

and refused to leave. Hindsight has convinced me that if I had shoved my papers back through the slot and refused to leave I would have been given the sculpture. If I had been thinking clearly, I would have realized that they would have had to give me the sculpture—because I had already been officially paroled, the papers had been signed, and if I had refused to leave they would have had to charge me with trespassing and call the local sheriff. If they had done that, the news media would have heard about it and the story would have made the local news. Subsequently, the story would have hit the wire services and gone national: "Prisoner artist arrested for refusing to leave slam without his art."

That particular sculpture, made up of scrap metal, was a powerful piece—the best piece I had ever done. I might have turned to art full-time if I had stayed for a showdown that evening. Who knows? Who cares? Art is the grass that is always greener...Maybe it's what I'll do when I grow up.

But I was infected with "getting-out fever." I wanted out and I was one door away from freedom. I was ready to walk. John was standing there. My paintings were loaded. I turned to the guard. "Will the sculpture be safe until I call the bureau in the morning?" "Absolutely!" he answered. I believed him. Can you imagine? I believed him.

Believing a guard! Allowing your wants to override experience. I'd simply call the director of the Federal Bureau of Prisons in the morning and scream. There was no way they could take my property away—not just my property, MY ART.

Heading south toward Minneapolis I outlined my plans for a prisoners' newspaper. Money wouldn't be a problem for long. I'd sell my paintings and use the money to get started. Talk about a distorted view of reality.

I felt so good wheeling down the highway with cold beer and a little smoke that the three-hour drive to Minneapolis seemed to last just a few minutes. John has a neverending supply of stories, inspiring stuff, the good guys always lose. Approaching the Washington Avenue exit I asked John to turn off and drive west on Washington Avenue. Along the way clusters of street people were gathered around an occasional barrel nursing fires with scrap wood and rolled up copies of free weekly tabloids to keep warm. We pulled into Discount Liquors' parking lot and I ran in for a case of Linenklugle's. As I returned to the car carrying two cases, one old man asked, "Want to share a couple of those holiday beers, mister?"

"Hell, yes." I put the case down and grabbed four long-necks and motioned for John to come join us. John isn't a beer drinker but he got into the spirit of the moment. We opened the back of the wagon, set the cases inside, popped four "Linees," and we raised our beers to peace.

Christmas was only a few days away. These two men, hawking drinks in a liquor store parking lot and freezing their asses off—I knew these guys, good old guys, and they were in a worse prison than the one I had just left.

"This ain't exactly beer drinking weather," John said.

"Bullshit," the older of the two men said. "It's always beer drinking weather."

I asked them what they would be drinking if they had a choice.

"They got some Four Roses on sale that would warm us up."

I handed John my beer and came back with a couple quarts of Jack Daniels.

I handed each of them a bottle. "Merry Christmas."

The old fellow in the ratty jacket was damn near jumping up and down. I couldn't make out what he was saying until he put his teeth in. "This'll warm things up tonight."

John was stamping his feet and I was wondering what it would be like living in a prison where your heat source was a 30-gallon barrel. It must have been 10, maybe 15 degrees.

Since I had planned on changing into some of my old clothes that John had brought up from Iowa, I handed the old guy my overcoat.

"This and the bourbon will keep you warmer."

Suddenly the old guy was giving me the once over. "What ya got on your mind? You a faggot or something...?"

His partner became indignant in an almost aristocratic manner. "Shut up, fool. Ya got a new overcoat and the best bottle of booze I've ever seen you sucking on. This dude's comin' on like Santa Claus and not asking for Jack shit."

John was laughing so hard he was crying.

I handed the other guy the sport coat I had on.

"What size shoes you wear?" I asked him.

He didn't even look down. "Any size ya got."

I took my shoes off and handed them to him. He glanced at them, sized them up, put them in his coat pockets. I started unbuttoning my shirt.

The old man looked at John. "What's your friend been smoking?"

I handed him the shirt and took my pants off. "Thirty-two waist?"

"Me exactly, but what are you gonna wear?"

I took my shorts off. John handed me one of the bottles and I took a drink.

Now both of the old guys were laughing almost as hard as John. I guess it was a strange scene.

I flashed on my old Navy buddy Don Pelvit running six blocks through the snow one January night in Minneapolis, naked and barefoot. It was 33 degrees below zero.

I took my socks off. The two guys were looking at my feet like they expected my toenails to have fingernail polish on them.

A woman came out of the liquor store laughing and yelled, "You're freaking out the store manager. He just called the cops."

We all piled into the front seat. John was laughing so hard he could barely drive. I grabbed a pair of old Levis and a sweatshirt. A few minutes later we were eating burgers from White Castle and washing them down with Jack.

We dropped the old guys off some place on Lake Street and headed south on I-35.

Throughout the remainder of the trip John talked about making films. He had sent me one film to show our fellowship but custody had taken it away and returned it to custody. I asked him what it was about. "Some nuns walking around down in Mexico. Strange shit." That same film, *The Day Love Died*, was later used in a successful United Way fundraising effort.

I outlined my plans for a newspaper that would open lines of communication between prisoners and the free world.

"Who's going to buy your newspaper?"

"Libraries."

"Why?"

"Because I'll give them material that will blow their minds."

"No one cares."

"Only because the material hasn't been presented to them in an acceptable format!"

I had convinced myself! No one could reason with me. No one could change my mind. John had known me long enough to know that the stories were true. He had freaked often enough, been fired from enough jobs, stared at enough rejection slips, been married and divorced and remarried enough times that he knew how important it was to be able to tell your story.

We drove all night. It was like old times, being with a friend I could dream with.

When we reached Cedar Rapids, John asked me how I felt.

"I feel pure. Nothing to hide. No place to go but up." What I lacked in discipline I figured I could make up for with enthusiastic bullshit.

It had been a great drive. I think I'll always feel a chill across my buns whenever I think of standing naked in that parking lot by the Discount Liquors in Minneapolis. But that kind of cold I could deal with—watching the sun come up as we drove south through the rolling, snow-covered Iowa farmland, with the air so clear and sharp that it brought tears to my eyes.

This was an off period in John's life. Nothing permanent. John dropped me off at his small apartment, gave me the keys, and said he'd see me in a couple days. I went in. John's place was always as good as home and it was good being home. I needed rest and time to organize my thoughts. Another of my dearest friends was waiting to help—Marsha was one of the elements that combined to make the *Citizen-Times* an adventure. The sun on the window frost was almost blinding.

After the reunion amenities, I called the Federal Bureau of Prisons and explained about the painting and the sculpture.

Two hours later, a fellow from the bureau called me back and said that the sculpture had been destroyed. "They figured it was prison property so it was taken to the welding shop and taken apart with a cutting torch. It was junk."

I made few non-prisoner friends while I was locked up.

I'd make fewer in the next three years.

PRISON ART ATTRACTS COLLECTOR

A phone call to Eli Abodeli got me space to paint for a month in one of his downtown hideaways. Another call to the People's Church got me space for an art show.

I had left prison with enough art supplies to last me ten years. When you paint in prison an interesting thing happens. Prisoners come by and watch. They see you doing it and it looks easy. They send home for money for supplies and tell the family to send photos. "I'll have oil portraits for you in a month," they reassure the folks at home. The money arrives, they buy the oils, brushes, and a couple of "how-to" books, and everything they touch turns to mud.

They finally end up making a deal with one of the prison artists. You get the supplies and you paint them a picture they can send home.

I slapped more oil on canvas in the next 30 days than I had in my entire life. No style, no nothing. Just a hodge-podge of emotion. Pictures that I hoped would sell, if not for the art at least for the curiosity.

My show was memorable for two reasons. The first reason was that I met a person who was interested in two of my paintings, but wanted to see them hanging before making a choice. I agreed to bring them to the person's home that night.

I found the place on the east side of Cedar Rapids in a neighborhood of luxury homes. A long curved drive led to a huge entrance; just inside the entrance

was a Marvin Cone painting. Pretty heady company. On the tour of the home, I saw originals by Grant Wood, Picasso, and Matisse, and what seemed to be more early American traditional paintings by artists I didn't recognize. I was overwhelmed—not just seeing the art, but because this person was interested in my two paintings, one for $400 and a small one for $120. In my wildest prison dream of getting out and having a show I never imagined that I would ever interest anyone with this kind of an art collection.

A huge staircase led up from the front entry way. On the first landing was a prime spot for a large painting. Upon entering the house it was the first spot you saw.

"I think the large one might look good there."

I agreed with her.

"The warm colors will be complemented by the woodwork."

I had never seen that much woodwork in a home in my life. Plus it was a painting I had done in a day. "Angular Compromise." Two figures. Hard to tell if a man or a woman was compromising. John had named it. It was a steal at $400.

We went upstairs to look at it from above.

It was beautiful.

At the top of the stairs was a large area with more stairs leading off in three directions. The area was lined with bookcases and built-in seats.

"Would you care for a drink?"

"You bet!"

As the drinks were being poured I looked at the books. They were all matched sets. Some of the sets had 25 or more books in them. All appeared to be bound in leather, or at least material that looked like leather.

I didn't recognize the titles or the authors, but it didn't take me long to realize that I was not looking at the classics. *She Was Daddy's Little Girl* and *Cheerleaders Romp*. Many years would go by before we'd see a marquee with *Lawyers in Lace* on it but I'll bet the book was there if it was in print. As I gave the books a closer examination, I was aware that I was being watched. I took a book off the shelf and opened it. Clit lit. Hundreds of books. Expensive, matched sets of cheap trash. I'm not talking erotica. No Henry Miller or Anais Nin in this collection.

I couldn't believe it. The collector from hell. Grant Wood and Marvin Cone Behind the Green Door.

"You like to read books like those?" I was asked.

It was clear where this evening was headed. No sense in playing games. "Which do you prefer, the large painting or the small one?" I asked.

"I can't make up my mind. I like them both," was the response, spoken slowly while my glass was being filled with the first Calvados I'd ever tasted. I've wondered about Calvados for years. It was what Ravic always ordered in Remarque's *Arch of Triumph*. I could smell the book, see the Minneapolis Public Library. I don't think he ordered Calvados in the movie.

"I'll buy the small one because it's the better of the two paintings. I'll also buy the large one if you will spend the night."

I sat there with my Calvados. What would Ravic say? I couldn't believe this. Was it the fascination of being with a newly released prisoner? I thought about the $400. Maybe it would have been possible if she hadn't looked so much like Charles Bukowski.

"We could read to each other."

"Sorry. I'm driving a borrowed car and have to return it in half an hour."

"Could I have them until tomorrow night?"

"Sorry. I have obligations." Obligations?

I was grateful to pick up $120.

The second memorable happening was that I made $2,500 from the art show. If the sculpture that had been ripped off by the guards at Sandstone had been in the show I would have made $7,500.

Chapel Builder Busy Building Wardens

A week earlier I had moved to Iowa City and enrolled at the University of Iowa. An interesting incident happened to me when I arrived there for the first time. While in prison I had taken some correspondence courses, mostly in criminology, from the University of Iowa. The professor who I sent my lessons to, Professor Caldwell, was the author of a widely used criminology text. I had poured my heart into those lessons. Typewritten papers that would run 30 and 40 pages always returned with an "A" boldly marked across the first page, usually followed by "Remarkable" or "Good work." Years later I'd sit around with teaching assistants from that same department. The long papers only elicited groans, they told me. The papers would be passed around. Care would be taken to not spill any beer on them. The best ones were the shortest. No BS. Just the facts.

As a prisoner, I had been impressed by Dr. Caldwell. He had headed the department and authored an important text. He had praised my work. On my first trip to Iowa City to find a place to live, I stopped at his office to meet him. It was a typical office, narrow and long. Books lined the shelves from floor to high ceiling. Sitting behind a large desk that was stacked with books and papers, he looked smaller than he probably was.

He recognized my name immediately and welcomed me to Iowa City. We talked about various topics: prison, his department, what I would probably find at the University of Iowa. He failed to mention everything I learned to love and hold dear while in Iowa City: drugs of every imaginable type, fun stuff, with peyote topping the list. And love. I found love in all forms, including the permanent kind.

But at this point I revered the old professor. Finally I asked him the question I had come there to ask. Thinking that he would be the centerpiece of a lengthy article in the journal someday, I asked him, "Dr. Caldwell, you have been involved not only with the subject of criminology but with the prisons and prisoners of Iowa. What do you believe is the most important contribution you have made that has been a benefit to prisoners?"

He leaned back in his chair, shut his eyes, and was deep in thought. Finally he leaned forward and looked at me. There was a dramatic pause. Was it practiced? I'd never seen him lecture. "My most important contribution? That's easy. I'm responsible for the chapel at the Anamosa Reformatory. I'm prouder of that than anything."

It figured. He was nothing but a guard. The guard from the department head's office. It seemed like every time I turned around, some script for a grade B movie was happening before my very eyes.

I sat there looking at him. He seemed to expect a response. I didn't say anything. I just stood up and left. I couldn't believe it.

That department at the University of Iowa, I later found out, led by the likes of Caldwell, turned out more federal prison wardens than any other single institution of learning in the country. And the federal prison system, then and now, contrary to the public relations drivel that is ejaculated from Washington, is one of the most repressive systems in the world. It was bad then. It is worse now. Behind the repression, brutality, and behavior modification units are a bunch of wardens from this department.

Getting Organized

The new year found me in a small, cheap, furnished room three blocks from the University of Iowa on the southwest corner of Jefferson and Van Buren. I wasn't carrying much with me: an easel and some art supplies, a few books, and odds and ends of new used clothes. My personal needs were few.

The *PDI*, on the other hand, needed a non-profit, tax-exempt corporation, a board of directors, and money. What that added up to was a serious need for contacts and advice. I'd also need space for an office, at least one extraordinary staff member, and ultimately a home large enough for a staff that I figured would grow to 15 when we were publishing. All I had were a few ideas and the money from the sale of paintings.

That money was earmarked for emergencies. Staffing of the *PDI* was not going to be easy. I wanted ex-prisoners in key positions. I knew prisoners who had developed those necessary skills while serving long prison sentences. Unfortunately, they were still inside, with little chance of getting out.

To save money I applied for and received tuition assistance. When I learned that I could use it to help pay my rent and that I could qualify for grants to cover the rest of my rent and my living expenses, I enrolled full time.

Culturally, economically, and politically, Iowa City was the place to be. It had an excellent symphony, the best rock concerts, opera, a remarkable university drama department, the Bijou where two art movies played nightly, year around for 50 cents, and reasonable rent. You could walk anywhere in town. Politically the university campus was boiling over with antiwar activity. Opposition to the Vietnam War was drawing the kinds of crowds Vivian Stringer would draw years later with the Iowa women's basketball team. Sit-ins at Old Capitol. Gentle people making a non-violent statement while the jocks ran across their bodies. At my first sit-in, I needed every bit of restraint I could muster to keep from reaching up and smashing one of the sadists in the groin as he ran across the group. Long conversations with COs while I was a prisoner had partially prepared me for these confrontations, but I still had problems. At times, I still felt that the solution was to "take up arms against the sea of trouble."

Every night crowds would gather. Occasionally they would spill over into the streets. Banners would be unrolled, poster board would appear, and as quickly paint and brushes. An American flag appears, upside down, draped across the front of a house. The Iowa City police come pounding on the door. Jackie Blank comes out and refuses to take it down. "It's a legitimate distress signal. A nation distressed. I'm signalling for help!"

The police wanted no part of that scene. Everyday it became increasingly more difficult to break away from the discussions, the planning sessions, and the teach-ins to attend classes. That problem was soon solved when the action of the streets moved into the classrooms. With increasing frequency students were challenging instructors about the significance of what they were teaching. "If universities are teaching people to think, why are we in Vietnam? Why are there people without food, housing, jobs...?"

Some students who objected to the interruptions would counter with, "We're trying to get an education! Why don't you take your rhetoric some place else?"

To them, activists responded, "What the hell do you think I'm here for? I'm paying tuition just like you are—but I want more for my money!"

Endless questions, accusations, and confrontations.

One day a group of students challenged an instructor about a comment he had made in an offhand manner. After some give and take the instructor finally got angry and told the students, "If you don't like what I'm teaching or how I teach it, you can get out."

One of them jumped up and said, "Wrong! Either you begin to deal seriously and responsibly with these issues or you can get out."

Thinking he was involved with just three loud-mouthed radicals, the instructor called the university police. When they arrived, the three students were addressing the entire lecture hall about the use of police to back up instructors who "were out of touch with reality." As the police advanced on the three, 95 percent of the rest—over 300 students in all—got up and began to leave the hall. The three disappeared in the crowd. When calm returned, only 20 or so students remained. The great majority agreed that changes were needed.

I had been away from school for a long time. What I saw now was more than students demanding an end to a war they believed was unjust and illegal. They were demanding the right to participate in the decision-making process. They wanted some say in what they were being taught. The most vocal students were being singled out as troublemakers, and no doubt they were. But the trouble they were causing had been a long time coming.

In many ways the university's attempt to stifle dissent reminded me of my recent life in prison. Prisons have always been intractable as far as rules are concerned. You do as the state tells you, or else. In prison, you refuse an order and you land in solitary confinement. You don't get kicked out—you get kicked farther in. When prison personnel find themselves in a situation where they are wrong and a prisoner is right, they simply change the rules. No discussion permitted.

Traditionally, neither prisoners nor students had any say in how their institutions were run. But now, as I became acclimated to my new environment, I saw that educational institutions were changing. The *PDI* would act as a catalyst to open prisons to greater public scrutiny, I vowed. As a result, change in the prisons would be possible also. Making prisons more democratic would not be easy. Once people realized that only a small percentage of the prisoners were a serious danger to society, change would come.

Punishment for radical activity was a reality on the campus. Some of the more conservative students, especially from the fraternities and the athletic department, would catch antiwar activists alone and attack them. During sit-in demonstrations, the leaders invariably ended up getting kicked around, stepped on, and punched when they were being carried or dragged away. Vietnam veterans who were opposed to the war were often attacked. A young bearded veteran with a flag sewn on his sleeve upside down was set upon one night by a group of ROTC students who ripped his dog-tags off and whipped them across his face again and again. He was cut rather badly, but he refused to press charges against them or tell anyone their names even though he knew the students who had attacked him. He had seen and participated in all the violence he could endure in Vietnam, he told me. "There is nothing anyone can do that will cause me to fight—ever again."

Sobering. Your anger would rage. Understanding would be almost impossible. But finally, painfully, you realized that he and others like him were right. The resolution of disputes through the use of force and violence accomplished nothing positive and led only to more violence.

And just as it was tough for the most active protesters, it was also tough for many of the instructors. I was awed by the sophisticated methods young students used to pin instructors down on issues pertaining to the war. There were groups that seemed to be devoting all of their time to the war. They were constantly producing and distributing fliers and making amazing demands on instructors.

In my previous life as a full-time student many years before, I had always viewed professors as intelligent, dedicated, educated people. Frequently, we students didn't like their regimen or their methods, but we never thought to challenge them, to treat them like equals. Now I was watching professors being dragged out of their ivory towers and knocked off their pedestals.

For example, at the beginning of one semester, a professor who had been head of the department the previous year was putting everyone to sleep. Finally a young man stood up and started making his way to the aisle. "Pardon me. Excuse me. Pardon, etc. etc," he was saying in a conversational voice as he squeezed by the students seated in the cramped lecture hall seats. The professor stopped speaking and was watching him work his way past students.

"May I ask where you are going?" he said to the young man.

The student stopped, looked at the professor, and said, "Yes." And stood there.

"Well?" the professor asked.

"No, I'm not well," he answered. "I signed up for this course thinking I'd get my mind fucked. I'm

certainly not going to listen to this drivel for the rest of the term." And out he went.

I had never heard the word used in reference to mind stimulation and gratification, but I understood.

A number of other students must have understood as well. About 20 percent got up and left.

Interesting.

DUSTY ROADS BETWEEN PRISONS

During the summer of 1970, I made a month-long swing through Nebraska, Colorado, Texas, Oklahoma, and Kansas. Unfortunately, because I didn't have a van, I had to travel by bus. I had picked up an assistantship from the University of Iowa Communications Department to produce a series of half-hour radio shows. I was tape recording editorials written and read by editors of prison newspapers. The tape recorder weighed 45 pounds.

With no money for cabs or rent-a-cars, I walked miles from the bus station to the walls at Huntsville, Texas, got in, recorded a couple of editorials, talked, planned, listened, and left to walk more miles up and down those hot Texas roads swearing that a time would come when there would be money for a taxi, a van, or a rented car.

Back on the bus. Over to Dallas and a visit with Judge Sarah T. Hughes, the federal judge who made the news when she administered the oath of office to Lyndon Johnson after Jack Kennedy was assassinated. Jackie, stunned and bloodied, looked on. Judge Hughes would provide us with a feature article for the front page of the first issue: "LAW AND SOCIETY: Where Do We Go from Here?" It was a thoughtful article by a person who was looked upon by the public as a venerable member of the judiciary and by those who had been tried in her court as either a blessing or a curse. Most important, every warden in the country knew Judge Sarah T. Hughes. If any wardens decided to ban the *PDI* or to seize issues from prisoner subscribers, as I anticipated could easily happen in Texas, I wanted the National Lawyers Guild to wave that front-page story at some federal judge when we demanded that the first amendment rights of prisoners were as sacred as those of a judge.

On my trip through Texas, I rested a few days with Paul and Janie Kelso in Dallas, caught my breath, cursed the 45 pounds of tape recording equipment, took in a Janis Joplin concert, and continued crisscrossing the country visiting prisons.

My last stop before returning to Iowa City was Leavenworth, Kansas. The walk from the bus station to the "Big Top" was a long one. I always seemed to be arriving around noon. The sun was as unmerciful as it had been when I walked the yard behind the walls. Now I had no more luck getting in than I had once had getting out. I waited a long time. When I was given the final no, I left. Out on the front walk I stopped and looked back. Through the windows, five stories high, I could see my old tier. I heard a "Yo, Joe" and it sounded like my friend, the Green Lizard, a most remarkable, gentle, thoughtful artist who had lived a few cells down from me. From a nearby speaker came the admonishing, "Move it, Grant."

A woman with two young boys was leaving and asked where I was going. I split the cost of a tank of gas and they dropped me at the bus station in Kansas City.

By the time I arrived back in Iowa City an extraordinary amount of mail had accumulated, mostly from prison editors who had interviewed me and prisoners who had read about me in their newspapers. All of their letters encouraged us to publish—to get that first issue out.

The response from prison editors was more than I had hoped for. Some who sent me editorial contributions were Mary Vangi, editor, *The Clarion*, California Women's Institution, Fontera, California; Henry Moore and raulrsalinas, *The New Era*, U.S.P., Leavenworth, Kansas; Jerry Nemnich, *The Interpreter*, Colorado State Pen, Canon City, Colorado; Erik Norgaard, Danish Prison System, Denmark; Arnett Sprouse, *Georgia State Prison News*, Reidsville, Georgia; Verna Wyer and Mark Suchy, Sandstone Coffeehouse Organizing Committee, Minnesota Federal Prison, Sandstone, Minnesota; Cathy Kornblith, *Connections*, San Francisco, California; Harley Sorenson, *Prison Mirror*, Minnesota State Pen, Stillwater, Minnesota (Harley went on to become a top-notch journalist working for major dailies. Years later he would meet up with Becky, the *PDI*'s first full-time employee, who was on her way to support the Indians at Wounded Knee. Harley was covering the story for the *Minneapolis Star*); James Farnham, *The Presidio*, Iowa State Pen, Fort Madison, Iowa; Lee Harg (aka Wesley N. Graham, who would make it out in time to share the editor's job with Rex Fletcher, who, as you'll read, we were able to get out), *The Signet*, U.S.P. Leavenworth, Kansas; James R. Caffey, editor, and Jim Bishop, *The Jefftown Journal*, Missouri State Pen, Jefferson City, Missouri; James Williams, *The Voice*, Southhampton Prison Farm, Virginia.

Poetry came from Celeste Clark, Jerry Nemnich, Linda (a resident of Hillcrest School for Girls), Johannes von Gregg, Bones Kennedy, Gary Ayers, Freda Pointer, S.L. Poulter, E.M. Matzko, and a fellow named Benavidez.

Other contributions came from Oregon, Rhode Island, Israel, Michigan, Maryland, Illinois, Ohio, and Indiana. Not all were from prisoners. Walter E. Kellison, the Unitarian Universalist minister at Peoples Church in Cedar Rapids, sent us an inspirational Easter sermon to share with the many readers we hoped to have in prisons.

One of our big surprises was an article from United States Senator Hubert H. Humphrey, who wrote, "Let's listen to ex-cons for a change." (An interesting note to share about Hubert Humphrey: I met him briefly once in 1970. I told him about my plans for the *PDI* and he shared some of his thoughts with me. I never saw him again until 1976, when we passed each other at Washington National Airport. I knew he had been ill so I walked over and said, "It's good to see that you are feeling well, Senator." "Thanks, Joe," he answered, "I wish I had some time to talk. I'd like to hear more of your ideas about changing the prisons." And he was gone. I couldn't believe that he really knew who I was. I later learned that he never forgot a face or a name.)

For the next few weeks, I spent more time than usual in my room, recuperating from my exhausting trip. The window by my work table gave me the opportunity to observe a young woman who lived next door. When the weather was mild she would sit out on the back porch of her second floor apartment and study. Observing led to sketching and soon I had the oils out and was running down one of my favorite escape routes—painting.

When it was finished I looked at the painting for a few weeks, then finally walked over and introduced myself. We became close friends despite our more obvious differences—Sharlane was attractive, intelligent, and quiet, and she paid her bills. Just what I needed: a role model to fall in love with. In the following months our relationship grew into a commitment to each other that continues to this day.

Also during this period, I was leaving for a 7:00 class one morning when I saw a wild rabbit get hit by a car. I brought the rabbit into my room, sterilized the cuts, and closed them. The rabbit was a quick learner. Within two weeks it was depositing its pellets on newspaper in the corner of the bathroom.

One morning I woke up to find that the book I had laid on the floor the night before was covered with pellets. The book was *The Arms of Krupp*, about the German military industrialist Alfred Krupp. This was certainly a special rabbit, I thought. I named it Israel.

Israel did one other thing that I will never forget: he discovered a small stash of hashish behind a chest of drawers next to my front door. I had moved the drawers in myself, so I knew a previous resident hadn't left it. I hadn't left it. But if I were caught with any drugs I would get a minimum of five years with no chance to defend myself in court. Within ten minutes,

I wrapped the package securely, walked to the post office, and mailed it to my parole officer in Des Moines. I then wrote a brief note, stuffed it in an envelope, and tacked the envelope to the front door. On the envelope I wrote: "ATTENTION INVESTIGATORS WITH SEARCH WARRANT. PLEASE READ BEFORE ENTERING." The note explained that the stash had been found and had been mailed to a federal law enforcement agency in Des Moines. They came that day, saw the note, didn't search the place, but did contact my parole officer.

COMMUNITY SUPPORT GROWS FOR *PDI*

Given the political environment at the university during this period, I had thought that most of my support for the *PDI* would come from there. I was wrong. The departments where I thought I'd find interest and support turned a deaf ear: Criminology and Sociology had many interests, but communicating with prisoners was not one of them. The most interest came from folks in the Psychology Department, the Writer's Workshop, and the Poetry Workshop. Vance Bourjaily, from the Writer's Workshop, was genuinely interested, both in opening lines of communications and in the space I'd be devoting to poetry and art in the publication. Not only did he put me in touch with ex-prisoners in the workshop, he also agreed to take a seat on my board of directors.

Despite the lack of further interest on campus, my own increasing commitment to antiwar activism and the increasing commitment of so many others was leading me effortlessly to resource people throughout the city, including a group of business people who appeared willing to front some money for a newspaper. Or, as I had come to refer to it, a monthly journal.

In my daily contacts with them, I'd describe the desperate need for a newspaper that would open lines of communications with prisoners and people in the free world. It was the right time to talk about prisons. Liberals were everywhere. Normal, law-abiding people were spending nights in the can for demonstrating, smoking some pot, acting up in magistrate's court. Young innocents were going to the can and a straight, free world society didn't like what they were hearing about prisons, or the city and county jails.

It was, to be perfectly honest, the ideal place to be, and the perfect environment for the *PDI*.

Through it all I indicated, but didn't specifically say, that such a newspaper would make money. At the thought of a return, chipping in $500 to a $5,000 nut looked okay. It all depended on how much money you had and whether you had a social conscience.

Within a few months, I was living a couple blocks south of Burlington on Van Buren, the one block in Iowa City that was as close to a slum as any street in Iowa City could get. (Now it's all apartment buildings—no character at all.) On both sides of me were welfare families and a corps of kids ranging in age from five to sixteen. Most of the families were in trouble with the police. Some of the teens had spent time in Iowa's juvenile prison.

In the winter of 1970-71, Joe Johnston, a young attorney, agreed to help me form a non-profit, tax-exempt corporation. I decided to call it PHASE IV. In a feature article that appeared Saturday January 2, 1971, in the Des Moines *Register*, Larry Eckholt explained:

> The purpose of the Penal Digest International is reflected in the meaning of...the corporation's name—Phase IV.
>
> "First, a man commits a crime and is arrested; that's phase one," said Grant. "Phase two is incarceration, at which time, hopefully, you decide you don't want to continue phase two.
>
> "Phase three is education. And the fourth phase is assuming an obligation to your fellow offenders—helping to find solutions to the problems."

The four phases: violation, incarceration, education, and obligation. In that first article Eckholt wrote, "Libraries are enthused, Grant said, because 'there's nothing else like [the *PDI*] in the country.'" I would get a real surprise when we did our first promotional mailing to libraries, universities, and wardens.

Around this time, two new friends who had a small public relations firm—Jerry Mansheim and Loren Bivens—met with me and listened to my ideas. We spent the evening talking. A couple days later, I met again with Loren to see the plan he and Jerry had laid out for presenting those ideas to a carefully chosen group of business people, educators, elected officials, and possible investors. Their roughed-out presentation would use slides and possibly film. He asked me for a theme, I gave him one—the plight of the prisoner with no way to communicate grievances—and we went to work.

They became my advertising agency, public relations agency, idea board, and source of unlimited help. All the good ideas in the world are worthless if you lack organization and the necessary experience to present them to the people who can help turn them into working projects.

Loren and Jerry designed an attractive packet containing news articles, carefully written press releases, professional photographs by Jerry, information about the non-profit corporation that was forming, and a description of the *PDI* and its goals. When I presented my plans for an international journal that would open lines of communications with prisoners, the news media moved right in for a story.

The importance of the press releases cannot be overstated. They are the difference between a reporter getting all the carefully thought out statements—the "phrases" and "buzzwords" that stick in his or her mind and sell your idea—and the reporter missing important points altogether. Reporters use releases as backup. Often a complete article is no more than an edited version of a press release that you yourself write.

Not that writers are lazy or incompetent—on the contrary, they are always incredibly busy and writing against deadlines. They'll spend enough time with you to be sure they are not being led down some "primrose path." Once they're satisfied they have a good story they will get the information they feel is important to the story. Later, when they are writing the story, the press release provides them with answers to all the unasked questions. The more information you provide, the better your chances are the story will touch on the subjects you believe are most important.

While the formal presentation was being planned I was busy contacting the local and regional representatives of companies that manufactured typesetting equipment. When approaching a manufacturer about possibly purchasing very expensive equipment, you have to achieve one of two missions to get that equipment on a trial basis: convince them that you are absolutely trustworthy and will not cheat them—or convince them that you are absolutely trustworthy and will not cheat them.

When the packets were ready, I personally delivered them to all the representatives I had contacted.

Jerry also designed our stationery. Pure art. It screamed "stability."

Knowing we were going to need top flight legal advice, I contacted nationally respected lawyers, authors, and activists to make up our advisory board. Some I called, some I wrote. All accepted. Our advisors were front line activists: William "Bill" Kunstler, Stan Bass, Julian Tepper, Diane Schulder, Jessica Mitford, and Kitsi Burkhart. Like the commercials would claim years later, "It doesn't get any better than that."

Meanwhile, news articles, feature pieces, poetry, fiction, and other items of interest continued to come in from prisoners.

Some of these prisoners were standouts. One, Rex Fletcher, had been in prison for 19 years. He was editor of the newspaper at the Oklahoma State Pen. His column was humorous and filled with insights. Often,

Oklahoma dailies reprinted his columns. By the end of the year I had decided I wanted him for an editor. He informed me that his chance of making parole was zero.

Another person I wanted was Charles DuRain, a cartoonist who had become a fixture in the Kentucky State Pen. The parole board had been laughing at him for over twenty years.

This wasn't going to be easy.

Hawkeye Foods owned a large building at 405 South Gilbert, a few blocks from the university (in Iowa City, everything is a few blocks from the university). There, I set up the *PDI*'s first office. The space was split down the middle. We were on the left. On the right was the Crisis Center that Howard Weinberg had started. A few years down the line, Howard would head the Iowa Civil Liberties Union.

Howard was sitting around the office one day and saw a poem by Jerry Nemnich, editor of the Colorado State Penitentiary *Interpreter*, that was scheduled to go into the first issue. He read it and wanted a copy:

> "Worth"
>
> avocado seeds turn
> black
> for the chisel.
> &
> someday
> I'll carve a rose
> a black rose
> the mythical kind
> you always hear about
> but never see.
> I'm no carver of ironwood or teak.
> I'd be of no use at the monument works
> &
> I'd be hopeless & even frightened
> at the thought of shaping jade,
> but
> an avocado seed....

Before long, I was getting calls about Jerry. Local poets and bookstore owners wanted to hear him read. He would have loved it, but the warden at Colorado State Penitentiary had other ideas.

Soon, wardens throughout the state heard about my plans and began inviting me to visit their prisons. My initial relationship with the wardens was fairly good—not until the *PDI*'s second year did some of them begin to actively oppose our existence.

Laurel Rans was the warden of the Women's Penitentiary at Rockwell City. The first time I heard from her was in a letter asking if we could help a young woman, an ex-prisoner, relocate in Iowa City.

I drove to Rockwell City to meet her and talk to her about the *PDI* and about using our headquarters as a halfway house for prisoners—men, women, and children—who were returning to the community.

Laurel was the ideal warden. Open and direct, she was a no-nonsense administrator. The prisoners respected her and I believed her to be trustworthy and a person whose counsel would be valuable. I was right. Again and again she proved that she was as willing to trust a group of ex-prisoners to help other prisoners as she was to trust the established state agencies.

During that first visit sometime in mid-1970, I told her also of my plans to participate in a workshop on corrections at the university and asked if some of the women from the prison could participate with me. I'd asked that same question to the wardens at the men's reformatory in Anamosa and the penitentiary in Ft. Madison but they couldn't, or wouldn't, cut through all the red tape to give me any men.

Laurel, however, thought the idea was excellent. When I asked her if I would have a problem keeping them for a weekend she said, "Just stay out of trouble. I'm releasing them to your custody."

Pretty heavy. I'm living under the supervision of a federal parole officer with the admonition to not associate with other ex-prisoners and suddenly I'm given custody of four women from the women's penitentiary for a long weekend. I checked my parole papers and found no mention of having prisoners in my care so I figured "Why not?"

As it turned out we spent our days on campus participating in panel discussions, our evenings listening to good music and making the rounds of the clubs, and our nights in the home of the woman who had been arrested for hanging the flag upside down to signal that the ship of state was in a state of distress.

In the end, we had a terrific, and productive, weekend, the first of many that would follow. Panel participants impressed the audience, we partied afterward in a secure section of town, the fireplace roared, and the food was exceptional. But most important, a warden had decided to take a chance with a group of society's losers. A circle of friends formed that weekend that continued long into the future. And the trust that Warden Rans placed in those women and in me did as much to help get the *PDI* going as did the investment in time and money by our board of directors, advisors, and friends.

The news coverage from that weekend was a great help, too. I wish we could have held a press conference and told them the whole story. How we had sat on the panels, spilled our guts, emotionally naked, and escaped to some dance and laughing, talking, quietly, gently, lovingly. Reaching into each other. Answering questions normally left unasked. Nothing to hide. At home for the first time in a long time. Relaxed. Responsibility's rewards.

Had the truth been known, Laurel Rans would have had more trouble from the correctional department than any warden as considerate and trusting as she deserved.

Following that weekend, John Clark, a computer consultant at Westinghouse Learning Corporation, introduced me to the right man at the right time and Westinghouse Learning Corporation gave us the desks and chairs we needed. It was remodeling time. They even loaned us a truck.

Permanent transportation, however, was becoming a problem. With our non-profit status secured and our federal tax exemption status working its way through the IRS, I started looking around for a van. Once again we benefited from favorable media coverage. I found what I was looking for, a large Chevy van, and the dealer was enthusiastic about leasing it to the corporation. Unfortunately all of our money was earmarked. The van had to wait.

One day shortly after the Eckholt article came out, I received a call from a William McDonald. Bill had read about my plans and wanted to sit down with me to see how he could help. The next day he drove to Iowa City and we spent a few hours talking about prisons, prisoners, rehabilitation, jobs, and my plans for the *PDI*. Bill was a typical Iowa farmer, plain-spoken and sincere. He had helped a number of people who had had problems with the criminal justice system and was especially interested in helping children. He was, without question, a good man.

Around that time, I had just received a folder of poetry and short stories from some of the youngsters doing time at the Hillcrest School for Girls in Salem, Oregon. Bill was looking at the poetry and came across a poem I had decided to use in the first issue of the *PDI*. It was a poem by a young girl named Ellen:

> PEOPLE, so busy bein' black, that they never
> be people;
> PEOPLE, gettin' their kicks, kickin' others
> while down;
> PEOPLE, getting their kicks, kickin' man in
> thorn crown.
> PEOPLE, wonderin' what to do with, rather
> than for, kids;
> PEOPLE, coverin' superficial topics deeply
> and deep topics superficially
> PEOPLE, coverin' superficial topics deeply
> and deep topics artificially
> PEOPLE, drawin' immoral morals from lives
> best left unled;
> PEOPLE, drawin' immoral morals from books
> best left unread.

PEOPLE, sayin' "how is he?" meanin' "can
I get his bread yet?"
PEOPLE, sayin' "how is he?" meanin' "is he
dead yet?"
PEOPLE, lovin' people whose love is all a lie;
PEOPLE, lovin' people whose love will never
die.

The entire folder of material, but especially that poem, struck a responsive chord with Bill. He knew that he would not be able to initiate any kind of a rehabilitation program on his own, but he wanted to help. His concern was genuine enough that I asked him if he would like to take a seat on the board of directors.

By that time, my board consisted of the following individuals: attorney Joe Johnston; Vance Bourjaily; John Clark; Sharm Scheuerman, a former University of Iowa basketball coach who was now a realtor; Richard E. (Dick) Myers, Jr. a onetime Republican legislative candidate and the owner of Hawkeye Truck Stop on I-80; Miles (Mace) Braverman, vice president of Hawkeye Wholesale Foods; Myra Mezvinsky, wife of our district congressman; Dr. Magorah Maruyama of the Social Science Research Institute, University of Hawaii; and prison poet/editor Jerry Nemnich. Bill's response was positive and enthusiastic.

While he was there I received a call from the manager of the Davenport office of a major manufacturer of typesetting equipment. The manager offered to loan me all the equipment we needed to get the publication ready to go to press. The problem was we had to pick up the equipment ourselves.

When I hung up the phone, Bill said, "You need some wheels...."

Two hours later the van was ours. Bill had given us money for the first and last lease payments, and enough extra for the next two payments.

I drove to Davenport, picked up the equipment—with enough supplies for the first three issues thrown in for good luck—and that evening I was setting type. By the next morning, I knew I had to have someone working with me who could type.

Since I was in the business of opening lines of communication between the free world and prisoners I figured I might as well employ as many ex-prisoners as could fill jobs. I called a parole officer I knew. She was working with a huge case load. I asked her if she knew of any typists looking for work.

The next day, Becky Evans walked into the office. When I asked her where she lived, she said she lived two houses up from me. We were neighbors. She was a little on the shy side, quiet, not much to say, but she could type like a whiz and was on probation. Perfect. The only problem was, I needed a full-time employee and this kid was only 15 years old.

"Call my probation officer," she said.

I did and the next thing I knew I was a foster parent and Becky was the *PDI*'s first paid employee. I never asked her what particular problems she'd had with the law; I think they had something to do with her having a yen for travel and not placing school very high on her list of priorities. But when I told her my ideas about the *PDI* she loved them. She bought the whole concept and worked two hours for every hour I paid her. A believer.

No, she was family. She never left; and she could do it all.

Over the next few months, Becky and I took care of everything. Between school and the *PDI*, neither Becky nor I had time for recreation.

Loren and Jerry helped design a mailer to send to prospective subscribers. The first issue was shaping up. The presses we were using could print a 24-page tabloid. We had material for three 24-page signatures—a total of 72 pages for that first issue. The front page was reduced and used on the first page of the flier. Seven pages in total were on card stock. The last three pages were postage paid return mailers: "Check the box and we'll send you the first issue free. If you like it subscribe, if you don't write cancel on the invoice and return it." The potential subscriber had nothing to lose. The mailer was beautiful. I was convinced that it would convince and we'd be in business.

In March of 1971, with a little fanfare and a small addressing party, we sent out 7,000 mailers. Cost us an arm and a leg. An important step.

THE FIRST ISSUE

After mailing out the flyer I sat back and waited for the postage paid return mail cards to flood in. In a few weeks we would have a return of at least 50 percent. Why not? It was free—gratis. If you don't like it, just write cancel on the invoice and forget it. No obligation to inspect a 72-page tabloid—written, designed, edited, and marketed by prisoners and ex-prisoners. Curiosity alone would have people returning the postage paid card. We couldn't miss.

When a direct mail campaign brings in a 3 percent return it is considered successful. I believed that the *PDI*'s uniqueness alone would bring us a return of 50 percent or more. Not all of them would subscribe, but I knew that most intelligent respondents would at least consider $6 a fair investment. Prisoners could subscribe for $1, although we were encouraging them to spend $6 if they could afford to do so.

The response during the first five weeks was less than exciting. Three weeks after the mailing, two cards came in. A few days later we received three more. Another week passed and two more came in. Seven in five weeks, out of 7,000.

Hello, I thought. Is anyone out there?

With the response to the mailing in my hand, I understood clearly that the only people I could count on to support the *PDI* were the people who were unable to do so—the prisoners.

The lack of response from the libraries I could understand. In their eyes, our content was so specialized that no one besides prisoners and correctional employees would be interested. I had failed to convince them that 20 to 25 percent of the general population was interested in the problems facing prisoners and their families.

My greatest disappointment was the lack of response from the colleges, particularly those with criminology departments. I had fine-tuned my list so that the mailer was sent directly to the department heads as well as to those professors who were well known because of books they had written.

What also mystified me was that no one called or wrote to ask questions about what I was doing. The *PDI* was the only newspaper dealing directly with incredibly serious problems—problems that concerned the public as well as prisoners. Our initial presentation to prospective subscribers had been professionally done. Yet it generated no response.

Equally distressing was my not being able to discuss the problem with anyone. Becky and I were the only people who knew. If I mentioned what was happening to anyone else, I would never be able to undo the damage. For those few weeks while I waited for postage paid cards to arrive, I had imagined a flood of so many cards that I would have to borrow money to pay the postage. During that time I would occasionally find myself sitting in the office late at night. Becky would be typing articles. I'd reach to the rear of the bottom drawer and take out the seven return mailers that we had received. Becky would glance over, see what I was looking at, and shake her head.

"I simply cannot believe that there are not more people who are curious enough to drop a postage paid card in the mail to get a free copy of a publication of any kind," I would say for the fiftieth, sixtieth, or hundredth time.

Becky would shrug her shoulders and respond, over and over, "No one gives a damn about prisoners, or about you or about me."

One night, just as she was saying that to me for the umpteenth time, an Iowa City police car slowly drove by the office. Becky smiled and added, "At least not anyone willing to spend $6 on a year's subscription."

She was absolutely right. It took over a month for the facts to sink in—for me to understand and admit to myself that my dream of a widely circulated and subscribed to monthly journal that would provide a power base to bring change to one of the most repressive prison systems in the world was not happening. There would be no wages for staff and travel and lobbying. There would be no research department, nothing for correspondents behind the walls. If the *PDI* was going to happen it would have to be done on sheer determination, bluff, and a willingness to work without pay. The question was, how much determination could a person generate when the bank account had only enough money to cover a couple months' expenses.

We were in trouble.

"Let's get a pizza."

Over pizza Becky and I discussed options.

"If the *PDI* is going to press, it will happen because we make it happen, Becky."

"If we print the issue, who will we send it to? Surely you'll print more than seven copies."

"Somehow we have to generate some excitement."

Becky had been to all the board meetings. She had heard the details of my dream. More than anyone, besides me, she was a believer. Becky I could confide in. I explained what I was going to do and asked her if she wanted to help. Since it was a week night and she wasn't allowed to party she said, "Let's go do it."

We returned to the office—our sanctuary—and started filling out postage paid return mailers. By morning we had filled out about 3,000.

We were tired- but we felt satisfied. Every person, every department, every college and university that I had believed would request the first issue was going to get that first issue. So were the television networks, the top newspapers and magazines, some carefully selected wardens of federal and state prisons, chiefs of police, congressional representatives, a few authors, and some prisoners.

Believe me I had my lists.

We locked up, had breakfast, and walked over to Van Buren for a quick rest. Becky still lived two doors up the street. A couple hours later we walked to the office, filled some brown bags with the postage paid cards, and then went to the board meeting.

Everyone was eager to hear about the mailing. Becky and I walked in like we'd just hit the lottery. All smiles. Shaking with what everyone thought was excitement—instead of exhaustion. Not being one to waste words, I just emptied the bags on the table and announced that we had a 43 percent return. These were business people and they were stunned by the return. It was a higher return than any direct mail solicitation they had ever heard of.

After a general discussion about what was next I said that I felt safe in projecting a paid subscription base of around 20,000 by the end of the first year.

Then I explained that I needed $1,500 to pay for the return mailers and $2,500 to print and mail the first edition of the *PDI*. The vote was unanimous. Combined loans from Dick Myers, Mace Braverman, Sharm Scheuerman, and John Clark totalled the $4,000. Becky and I walked back to the office and went to work.

We had the money now for the first issue. We even had enough money to pay Becky. But we were only three months into the lease on the van and I knew I'd be unable to generate the $225 needed to keep it. Not with the office rent, utilities, and printing costs—plus two separate places of residence.

The problem of housing was solved with the help of Sharm Scheuerman and his partner Steve Richardson. Using my GI loan, that I picked up from my time in the navy, I bought a large three-story house at 505 South Lucas Street. The combined rent that we were already paying on separate places almost covered the monthly payment. I still had money stashed from the sale of my paintings. We were going to have financial problems, but we were going to get out at least two issues.

505 became synonymous with *PDI*.

With more room, a large house, a yard, and a great kitchen, more people began spending time at the *PDI*. Included, in particular, were some of the kids from welfare families I had been helping out.

OATMEAL AND LOVE

The number of people who were living and working at 505 previous to our printing the first issue fluctuated between five and eight. That number, plus the constant flow of visitors, forced us to locate sources for large quantities of food. I think we were one of the first groups to check out the commercial food wholesalers around closing time each day. Staff members would show up to pick over the fruits and vegetables that were too ripe to be sold to the stores the next day.

Hawkeye Wholesale Foods provided us with tremendous additional quantities of food, thanks largely to David Braverman, patriarch of the Braverman clan, the founder of Hawkeye Foods, and a genuine friend. David's generosity was legend throughout the area. During the holidays he would load up our van with turkeys and hams. Our staff, the welfare families, and the homeless, helpless drifters always knew where the groceries were. Maybe the old man liked us so much because he knew two things: that we could have all been working 8 to 5 making good livings for ourselves but chose instead to devote our lives to the only

prisoner-owned and operated halfway house in the country, and that we shared everything we had no matter how much or how little. David recognized that we didn't share a religion, but we damn sure shared a philosophy.

As a result we set a dinner table that was second to none and always had food to share with a dozen or so other poor families. We were the largest welfare family in Iowa City. We housed runaways, escapees, wanteds, people who were walking to the beat of a different emotional drummer, and children from preschool on up.

Although we applied for and used food stamps regularly, many of them went to families who came to us for emergency help. Families also came to us when they felt they were not being treated fairly by Human Services. When that happened I was the one who usually accompanied them back to the office to lodge a complaint. I would listen to the long list of regulations concerning food stamp eligibility, then argue my response. I'd listen and argue, listen and demand, listen and threaten, but I would never leave. Finally I'd walk over and start pounding on Director Cleo Marsolais' door.

"Come," Cleo would call.

The aide would open the door. Cleo would be sitting at her desk, buried behind stacks of paperwork; all you could see was the top of her head.

I'd start right off, "Cleo, these people are desperate. I've never lied to you and I'm not lying now..."

Cleo would just raise a hand and wave for us to go away, yelling, "Just give Grant the goddam food stamps."

If we could have cloned a Human Services army of Cleo Marsolaises we would be living in a more equitable world today.

We became expert on living well with an incredibly small amount of money thanks to the *PDI*'s first vegetarians, Warren and Cathy Dearden. Warren and Cathy came to us in 1971 after Warren won a scholarship to the Writer's Workshop at the University of Iowa. Grove Press had just published *A Free Country*, a book by Warren that was not only entertaining, it resounded with the ring of personal experience. They hadn't been in Iowa City more than a few hours before hearing about the activities at 505 from a woman at the workshop. That afternoon, they wandered in and introduced themselves (see sidebar 2).

Warren had taken an early pot bust and done some federal time. He was quiet, had a great sense of humor, and seemed to know what he was doing. For a person so small and slight, he moved around with deliberation and authority. That first night, we didn't even have floor space so they ended up on the living room floor at the home of Elinor Cottrell, who was one of the most interesting and remarkable women I met in Iowa City and whose friendship is one of the highlights in my life.

Early the next morning, when Elinor came downstairs, Warren had just awakened and was standing in the middle of the living room, naked, facing away from her. Just as she was about to say good morning he bent over, and it appeared that he was mooning her. Had she spoken, she recalled to me later, she would have been talking to Warren's butt. She turned and walked back upstairs, then came down a few minutes later when he was dressed.

Some time later, she asked me if I thought he had done that deliberately. I wasn't sure. He and Cathy hadn't been long off a desert commune in New Mexico where food and water had to be carefully conserved. Elinor was living in what appeared to be rather affluent surroundings. He might have decided to let her take a good look at the skinny ass of a man who wasn't impressed with the surroundings, or he may have been bending over to see what Elinor looked like coming down the stairs upside down. Maybe he was picking up his socks. I never asked him.

The next day they were back at 505. Cathy checked the kitchen, the stove, and the refrigerator, and walked through the house. After about a half hour she indicated that she wanted to talk.

"We'll prepare two meals a day, breakfast and dinner, make out the grocery lists, and see that someone does the shopping or do it ourselves," she offered. "We all clean up for ourselves and Warren and I will live in the attic."

There was no question in my mind that Cathy was exactly what 505 needed. I was right. Soon Cathy and Warren were cooking two meals a day at 505. Cathy was also working part-time at a pseudo-Mexican restaurant, the Taco Vendor, across from Keith Dempster's Mill Restaurant, and playing out a whole host of roles at the house: to Warren she was a wife and lover, to the women in the house she was a sister, to the kids she was a mother, to the men she was damned attractive, quick with a smile, always a pleasure to be around, and absolute boss in the kitchen and dining room.

At Taco Vendor, she scrubbed pots and pans during the lunch rush. Her boss was a man who seemed to have trouble with women who thought for themselves and expected answers to questions.

Women like Cathy. Cathy would do her job, but when he started laying "trips" on her she would just look at him and smile. Finally he decided that she had to wear a bra when she washed the dishes—in effect, "Wear one or lose your job." I recall her getting that slight, lopsided grin on her face, slowly shaking her head from side to side, raising one eyebrow quizzically, and saying, "He is really screwed up." We assumed at 505 that her boss was having hormonal problems—among other things.

Meanwhile, the meals at 505 became legendary. The evening meal soon developed into the most important meal socially. Often, 20 or more people would sit together around our long dining room table. There, over casserole and salad, we caught up on incidents of interest that had been happening around Iowa City and the state and federal prison systems via news reports from our correspondents in prisons around the world. Conversations touched on deaths, births, and suicides. One of the main thoroughfares from the east coast to the west was I-80; it was a rare evening meal that didn't find a traveler or two sharing dinner with us and bringing us news from the road.

Breakfast was always my most important meal. I had been raised on substantial breakfasts. My mother was a tyrant when it came to breakfast. As soon as you were old enough to work, play, or go to school, you left the breakfast table with the nourishment to carry your share of the load for the day. Fortunately for me, Cathy had graduated from that same nutritional school. Breakfast consisted of cooked cereal made up of a variety of grains, raisins, and nuts with gallons of raw whole milk from Moss' Dairy. It always appeared that Cathy had made more than the regulars and visitors could eat. Yet invariably the last person to eat would be cleaning out the second of the two huge cast iron kettles that were seasoned to perfection.

Breakfast was spread out over a three-hour period, beginning about 6 A.M., as people wandered in from the six upstairs bedrooms and the two basement bedrooms. It wasn't unusual in the morning to find people sleeping on the porch or in the backyard, or neighborhood kids walking in for breakfast on their way to the elementary school a few blocks away. With Cathy's touch, the house at 505 became a home. Of course she had a pretty responsive crew gathering for those meals. Many had spent long years lining up for food in prison mess halls; they knew what it was like living on a diet of "cake and wine" in solitary confinement.

The kids who came for breakfast not only were welcomed, but they became close enough to us that we started filling in for parents. Often teachers contacted us if there was a problem. We'd stop in and discuss grades, behavior, all of the issues that parents normally discussed.

One observation I made was that when the kids spent time at 505 their behavior and also their grades seemed to improve. I could easily understand why: they had people around them who were genuinely concerned about their welfare. They were getting good breakfasts and attention in a friendly, laidback environment. Being by Warren Dearden

There's no way to talk about the *Penal Digest International* without talking about Joe Grant. For Joe wasn't simply the paper's founder and publisher, or simply the fundraiser and organizer who made the paper possible. Joe was literally the *sine qua non* of *PDI*—the only person on the planet, probably, who could have gotten such an unlikely enterprise off the ground, and the exemplar of the wholeheartedly altruistic dedication that characterized its staff. In a profound way, *PDI* was Joe Grant—a newspaper that reflected his radical analysis of American society and its justice system, dedicated to improving the lot of its most abused, most oppressed bottom rung.

"Oh, you've got to meet Joe Grant!" the receptionist in the Writer's Workshop office told me the day after my wife and I arrived in Iowa City when she learned that I was an ex-convict. Joe was also an ex-con, she told me, a dynamic, fascinating character, who'd started an underground newspaper for prisoners. "You'll really like Joe," she said, and offered to put me in touch with him. I think it was that very night when we met. I remember that he telephoned late one steamy August afternoon, introduced himself, and invited us for dinner at his friend Elinor's house: I know it was impromptu because I remember Elinor remarking that she'd given us her kids' dinners. After dinner, we sat on the porch and smoked, watched a lightning storm explode the torrid day, and laughed our asses off.

Joe and I were non-violent, amateur criminals who'd both struck out at the outset of our criminal careers, me before I could get my thirty kilos of marijuana into the United States, Joe before the currency he had created got into the hands of its wrongful owners. We'd have probably been cohorts if we'd done our time in the same joint. But Joe came into my life at just the time I was reading Ferdinand Lundberg's *The Rich and the Super Rich*, grasping for the first time the full implications of an oligarchical society, grasping that the law and the government were *always* tools of the ruling class, always used to oppress the commonfolk. Joe was a patented hero for my money in the struggle for the rights of the most oppressed, incarcerated victims of that system, playing for all he was worth a game that could end only in defeat, playing it for the sake of the difference it might someday make.

I pegged Joe for a con man the minute I met him: handsome, amiable, and amusing, with a head full of ambitious, improbable schemes and an absolutely mesmerizing voice, a syrupy radio baritone that dripped sincerity, that could charm the birds out of the trees. Yet I liked him enormously, somehow sensing that he was at heart the altruist he pretended to be and that his concern for prisoners was genuine. Joe was a working class, intellectual anarchist, like me, a freethinking, iconoclastic, idealistic revolutionary, full of goodwill and good humor, charity and fun. He was kind and tolerant of practically anybody he met, yet ready to ridicule any institution, especially those he believed in. I laughed at all of Joe's jokes and he laughed at all of mine, and on that very sound basis our friendship was founded. If my memory serves me right, it was that first night that Joe invited Cathy and me

to move into the attic of his new *PDI* headquarters at 505 South Lucas Street.

My part of the bargain was to insulate and drywall the ceiling and so convert the bare attic into a living space. I'd never applied insulation or hung drywall before, but I was handyman enough to do a decent job—though hanging drywall on a sloping ceiling, professional drywall hangers have since told me, is one of the trickiest jobs they have to do. I boxed in the eaves at chest height, building chests of drawers so they were flush with the walls, storage compartments and shelves into the wall, and a desk where I could write under the front windows. The result was a big, bare space, 12' x 30' maybe, with sunny yellow ceiling and walls, no furniture but the desk and chair at one end, a mattress on the floor at the other end, and a rocking chair beyond it near the back windows. A very Zen garret.

One entered by a narrow, dangerously steep, head-bumping, railingless stairway from the second floor of the house. The electricity came up the stairs via a heavy-duty extension cord, from an outlet on the second floor, to power an electric heater at my feet in the daytime, or by our bed at night; our light was kerosene lamps. But Cathy and I were hippies in 1971 who'd spent the past summer in a dirt-poor, beans and tortillas commune a mile and a half high in the Jemez Mountains of New Mexico, sleeping under a roof that didn't even keep the rain off. A warm, dry place was heaven to us. We actually called it our "log cabin home in the sky," after an Incredible String Band song Cathy liked me to sing to her. I wrote a couple hundred pages of *Children of All Ages* at that desk, including "The Little Boy Who Never Got Anything for Christmas Except Underwear" and "Little Lost Creek." Two or three times a day, a crew of *PDI* staffers would assemble there to smoke a joint. Shortly after dawn on March 11, 1972, my daughter Nimblewill was born in *PDI*'s attic.

Joe probably counted on my getting caught up in *PDI* and joining the production staff, although we agreed specifically before I moved in that I would be busy writing fiction for the workshop and working on my novel. If he did, he was disappointed. But Joe got something from Cathy and me that he wanted in the Lucas Street residence: an example that made the house a home. We'd been living in communes for a couple of years between us so we were practiced at the communal spirit and were able to draw together an extended family out of a bunch of strangers. That was, to a large extent, what transpired among a core group—Joe, Merrily Megletsch, Dick Tanner, Becky Evans, and Bob Copeland—who worked selflessly in that basement like slaves for *PDI* all through that winter of 1971-72. And Cathy and I (not to mention Nimble) were the instigators of it.

Buying and preparing the food was a big part of our contribution. We spent our food stamps and my tiny fellowship stipend on beans and tortillas, rice and vegetables, spinach lasagna, and other bulk foods and grains.

Cathy baked fresh bread every other day. Other people would rebel against the vegetarian fare occasionally and cook a meat dish for us all, but Cathy and I did probably 90 percent of the food preparation between us, and she did two-thirds of that, as well as probably two-thirds of the housecleaning.

All of this only reinforced the mother role her swollen stomach cast her in. A sweet, pretty mother-to-be in her 23-year old prime, she was the spiritual center of the commune. Happy as she was to be in love and pregnant, she drew that *PDI* core into a tight, cozy family.

Joe was blessed in the people he attracted to *PDI*; although there were a few who couldn't fit, the best were absolute bricks. Bob Copeland was a relentlessly genial Lake Forest graduate who'd somehow convinced his draft board to let him do his alternative service working for *PDI*. Dick Tanner was a Leavenworth graduate, a mercurial madman/genius from Oklahoma who'd been in jail the last ten years.

Dick Tanner rode his temper like a tiger, high on brotherhood and selflessness. Merrily was an artist and a junior high school English teacher whose marriage had recently gone on the rocks, a woman looking for a place to live, an important job to do, and someone to love, who found 505, *PDI*, and Joe Grant. These talented people worked long hours for nothing under the worst conditions, in a windowless basement—much harder and longer, I daresay, than they've ever worked at paying jobs. Thanks largely to their unpaid labor, Joe was able to publish *PDI* nearly every month for the two years or so of its life.

Joe, as I've said, was the *sine qua non* of *PDI*: the provider of the means for housing and feeding the staff, of the paper, printing, and postage necessary to produce and deliver a newspaper without a line of advertising in it. Joe himself had not a pot to piss in, so he did it all on credit: on his own credit, as far as that would take him (not far); on the credit of his benefactors, mostly some Iowa City businessmen whom Joe had persuaded to join the *PDI* board of directors. Entirely on credit he leased the typewriters, composing machines, and photocopiers, plus the van he drove around in; with a no-down-payment VA loan he'd purchased the Lucas Street headquarters. He of course charged the rolls of insulation and the drywall I hung in the attic. He bought his gasoline and tires on a credit card, naturally, and maybe the heating oil as well. "Charge it," he said airily, for as long as he could get away with it. What else do you say when you can't pay?

Subscription revenues at *PDI* were seldom more than $10 to $20 per day, money diverted by whomever got to the post office first, so very few of these bills were being paid. Overdue bills mounted around him the winter long; the clamor of unsatisfied creditors steadily swelled. Joe charmed them, cajoled them, made rosy, empty promises, and fended them off as well as he could. But the concerned inquiries of his board members began to swell also, and sometime around February or March 1972 the board assembled to question Joe about his finances and to take *PDI* away from him.

I knew nothing of *PDI*'s finances: Joe kept them to himself, if he kept them at all. I never used credit: at 30 years of age, I'd paid cash for everything I ever bought. But for some reason—call it Joe's instinct for survival—he asked me to come along to the board meeting with him, and hence gave me an opportunity to repay him some of the debt I owed him.

It was clear from the moment we walked in that tossing Joe out on his ear was the basic conspiracy: a disaffected ex-*PDI* staffer, Wesley Nobel Graham, was there, ready and eager to succeed him. I don't recall the details of its unfolding over the next couple of hours, and I don't remember why they had to do it just this way, but eventually the basic shape of their plot became clear. They wanted Joe to produce a financial statement that would detail accounts payable; with that in hand, they were going to assume responsibility for *PDI*'s debts and replace Joe as publisher. Up against the wall, Joe agreed to produce a financial statement after a two-hour lunch break.

I don't recall the total debt, but I remember that it wasn't enough: the board had a fairly accurate idea of its size and was prepared to swallow it. By dinner time, Joe was going to be out on his ass, and with him gone the *PDI* family would disintegrate. Dick and Merrily and Bob were devoted to the cause, but they weren't going to work for nothing if their room and board weren't provided. Without them, *PDI* was doomed.

Maybe it was that realization that fired off my brainstorm: inflating *PDI* into a spiky, unappetizing blowfish in the very jaws of its predator. By accounting for the labor costs that had gone into *PDI*, I realized, we could effectively triple the debt. And because labor liabilities take precedence over other liabilities, Merrily, Dick, Bob, and Joe himself would each be entitled to between $5,000 and $10,000 in payoffs before any of the other bills could be paid.

You would've loved to see their faces after lunch when they got a look at that financial statement. Everybody knew that none of the labor that went into *PDI* had ever been paid. Nobody had ever suggested before that it would or should be: Joe had never made any promises; no one who worked for the paper ever hoped to get paid. No one had ever thought of it till I did. But it was a legitimate debt just because Joe had put it down there, and each of the board members knew it as soon as he saw it. Watching them pass it around, seeing them change color as they read it, Joe and I had all we could do to keep from laughing. We heard nothing about assuming *PDI*'s debts the rest of that afternoon, nothing more about replacing Joe as publisher. Firmly in command of his sinking ship, but with enough energy to bail water frantically for another eight months, he sailed bravely on toward oblivion, cranking out issues until it finally submerged.

Dearden is an author who is raising fruit on Haiku, Maui, and keeping a fatherly eye on daughter Nimblewill and son Lightnin'.

---

with the kids, I learned this important lesson: the best way to rehabilitate screw-up A was to give screw-up A the job of helping screw-up B. I had the kids looking out for the grown-ups and the grown-ups looking out for the kids. I impressed upon the kids how important it was that they set a good example for the men and women who arrived at 505 fresh out of prison—and incidentally, I also carefully impressed upon these same men and women how important it was that they set a good example for the kids. The result was that the cons looked out for the kids and the kids looked out for the cons.

During this time, I was frequently driving between Iowa City and Chicago because we had contacts there for bulk food—mostly 25- and 50-pound bags of rice, beans, and flour and cases of canned peanut butter. On one of my trips, we struck it rich and were given much more than we would be able to use before the next shipment was ready. I asked around and ended up dropping some beans and rice off with the Black Panthers for their breakfast program. I observed their program in operation and found that where we were feeding three or four kids they were feeding hundreds, and the results were the same. The kids were healthier, their behavior in the classroom was more laidback, and consequently they were learning more and they were learning faster.

I was impressed.

And I was depressed—because I knew that we could not mount that kind of an offensive against hunger in Iowa City. To begin with, as far as 99 percent of the population was concerned, there was no hunger in Iowa City.

I was determined to get a breakfast program going in Iowa City but couldn't figure out how to do so while keeping the *PDI* going and making sure enough money was raised each month to make the house payment, keep the folks who had no resources in shoes and clothing, and care for the kids who came by for breakfast.

One night I was making notes in my journal about some incidents that had happened to me and a few other Korean War veterans while studying at Boston University. The money we got from the GI Bill barely covered tuition. We had to earn what we needed for food, but on top of our academic loads we had little time to work. As a result we each made due with coffee for breakfast, a peanut butter and jelly sandwich and a half-pint carton of milk for lunch, and whatever we could hustle at jobs for dinner.

One morning, my friend Eddie Doyle and I were having our coffee at the school cafeteria when a couple of young women from my college sat down next to us. On each woman's tray was a cup of coffee and a gigantic cinnamon roll with raisins. As we talked, one of them decided she couldn't eat her cinnamon roll.

"Will you eat that roll, Joe?" she asked. "I hate to see it go to waste."

Eddie and I looked at each other and smiled. Then, like John Belushi with his samurai sword, we split it—and it was gone.

"We should pay you for it," I offered.

"Why bother? Daddy has already paid for it."

With that we headed for class. But the fact that "Daddy has already paid for it" kept echoing through my hunger-crazed brain. If Daddy had paid for it, why didn't I ask her to go through and get a tray full of food? Why didn't I ask four or five of those diet conscious young women to do the same for all of us who simply had no money for meals.

During lunch I brought the subject up and they thought it was a great idea.

"No reason to let that money go to waste" was the unanimous decision. From that point on, breakfast was eggs, ham, bacon, potatoes, toast, fruit juice, coffee, and cinnamon rolls.

School became a joyous experience. As a result of enabling those fine young women to become nurturing caretakers to a pack of insane veterans, and helped along by my own weird sense of humor, I was elected president of the Humanities Workshop at the College of General Education. CGE was referred to as the Tire Factory. With me, and with most of my friends, CGE was an affair filled with as much hate as love. I had been given a choice of either accepting CGE or taking a walk. My poor high school grades gave me no rebuttal.

As if the academic load wasn't enough to drive me nuts, the VA messed up some paperwork. Everyday I would race home to the abandoned closet I rented at 529 Beacon and ask my landlady if my checks had arrived. Each day for four months Mrs. Lusier would shake her head "no" and look at me with the ever-present question in her eye, "Is this guy for real?" Rent was accumulating at the rate of $7 a week (for a small room with a broken window; a piece of 1/4" plywood separated my small room from my neighbor Jim) and only breakfast and lunch kept me sane.

I vowed daily that when my checks came I would go out for a steak dinner and follow that up with a bottle of wine. When my checks finally came, two days before Christmas, I paid my tuition and rent, then called all my friends for a party at a corner tavern. I was there having a beer when they arrived, ready to party. Before they could yell for the bartender to send over a round a beer, I stood up and told them that I was here to spend every damn cent I had left after paying my tuition and back rent. I laid down two dollars.

"Have you had your steak?" Eddie asked.

"No money for food," I answered.

"You don't think that $2 is gonna fund a party, do ya, Joe?"

"Look at it this way," I said. "There's five of us. Two pitchers of beer will cost $1.50. That leaves each of us with a dime to make a phone call. If I can come up with the idea that is keeping us in food for the next four years, it seems to me that collectively we can come up with enough money for a few beers and, if not steak, at least pizza."

But that's another story and the Boston scene was what reminded me that there were full-time students at Iowa whose parents paid for meals that were not being eaten. That being the case, why not give the meals to kids who needed the nutrition, the friendship, and a little adventure?

I contacted a few friends at Iowa and we met to figure out how we could make it work. To begin with someone pointed out that the laws of the University of Iowa made it illegal to transfer a meal.

"It would upset the computerized figures that have been worked out over many, many years," Al Frost said. "If people who didn't eat their breakfasts suddenly showed up and gave them to hungry kids, the balance would be upset and the system would go a little haywire."

"That means we can only allow people who always eat breakfast to participate in the program!" I offered.

Correct.

Everyone at the meeting always ate breakfast. All agreed to give them up anytime a kid showed up for breakfast. Together they were confident they could get as many other students as we needed so that a college student would be available for every kid we brought to the school.

I had put out the word that I would pick up, feed, and deliver to school any kids who wanted to challenge the system. Specifically I asked for kids who were hungry, who wanted nutritional breakfasts so their grades would improve, or who wanted excitement.

Little did we know how much excitement we would get.

We started out one Monday morning with about twenty kids, about half boys and half girls. We all met at the Burge Hall cafeteria, and there each student was teamed with a child. After introductions and an explanation of the game plan, the teams headed for the cafeteria.

Now you have to understand that these kids lived in a small, midwestern college town. The university was the town's number one employer. It was where all the action was: the best concerts, the best movies, the best of everything. Yet these kids were strangers to the school. Certainly they had never been in one of the cafeterias. Some of them would sneak around stealing whatever wasn't nailed down or checking coin return slots on phones and pop machines (they'd come away with a couple of dollars for an hour's work). With rare exception they were not welcomed on campus.

And now we told them that they could have anything they wanted and as much as they wanted—just like the students who were there for the full ride.

The first ones through the line were taking a sweet roll and a couple of cartons of chocolate milk apiece. I sat down with Lester Holderness and asked him why he didn't fill up with food like he did at 505.

"I dunno."

The idea of having that much food, or that kind of a variety of food, was beyond their understanding.

"Have some fun," I said. "Try a little of everything. Let's see who can sample a little bit of everything being served."

Suddenly it became a game. They headed back to the food line. Lester jumped in with a friend who was just starting and soon everyone was trying everything.

After breakfast, I loaded them into the *PDI* van and got them to school on time. About mid-afternoon, some of the teachers called to find out what we were doing. I told them. They liked the idea and asked if they could recommend additional kids. I said, "There's always room for one more."

We had already decided to feed the kids every Monday, Wednesday, and Friday: Monday to get their week off to a good start, Wednesday for a mid-week boost, and Friday to give them a good start for the weekend. On Wednesday, the news media was there to greet the kids. I think it was Al Frost who told the press that every care had been taken to insure that the computerized balance wouldn't be affected. He and the other students, he said, were only giving away the breakfasts they had been eating regularly since coming to the University of Iowa. The kids talked about their new friends at the university and admitted that they enjoyed trying the different kinds of food.

When the news media asked me if the kids were participating because they were not being fed at home, I told them it wasn't so much a matter of getting them food as it was helping them increase their commitment to education. I couldn't say that they were not eating nutritiously at home because I knew their mothers were doing the best they knew how. "This breakfast program is our way of making them feel that they are part of the system, and not outsiders," I said. "I want them to feel that the university is as much theirs as it is the students who are enrolled."

The press liked my answer and gave us good publicity. No parents were made to look bad, and the kids were excited about the publicity. Normally the only time they paid attention to newspapers was when a relative had been busted.

The second week went by without incident, but during the third week we were tipped off that university security was going to be at Burge cafeteria to stop the students from giving the kids their breakfasts.

To avoid security, we went across campus to another cafeteria. By the time they arrived, the kids had eaten and were on their way to school.

Still, we knew the university wanted to stop the program so we arranged to meet with a high-level university administrator. At that meeting, the students explained again that they had designed the program carefully, that only those students who had always eaten breakfast were involved, that they had the computerized lists to substantiate this assertion, and that they were going to be at Burge the following morning with the kids.

They were, and so were all four network TV affiliates plus photographers and reporters from all the newspapers. When the students arrived, hand in hand with the kids, the police just stepped aside. The next morning, the university informed all the participating students that their final grades would be withheld and they would not graduate unless they stopped giving their breakfasts away.

The students called a meeting. About half were seniors. Some of their parents had been notified by the school. The thought of a year's tuition being wasted and their children's degrees being held up caused them concern. Even some of the kids heard about the meeting and showed up.

I remember one of the kids saying, "I don't want any more of their goddamned food." It was probably Lester. There was no question about how the kids felt. They were turning their hurt into anger. The teams had developed a tremendous affection for each other, more than we had ever anticipated, but it was the kids who would end up being harmed if the program stopped—not because they would be losing those three breakfasts every week, but because they were once again ending up on the outside. The university was rejecting them. We talked about the rules and how rules for the most part should be obeyed. But this time the students decided that the university was being too inflexible. After weighing the worst that could happen—no grades and a year down the drain—the students asked the kids to stick with them for the rest of the semester.

When the university students announced that they were not backing down the kids cheered them. It was an incredibly courageous act, but as Al Frost said to one of the university administrators, "Look into the future. Do you want these kids to feel that they are a part of the educational system of this state, or do you want them to feel like rejects—feel like outsiders?"

As usual the answer was, "I understand how you feel but we have rules that must be followed."

It was an amazing semester. No more hassles from the university. Occasionally a television camera would show up, or a reporter from somewhere who wanted to do a human interest story, but for the most part the kids simply became part of the normal Monday, Wednesday, and Friday morning breakfast routine.

During that semester we began to take kids with us when we travelled around the country filling speaking engagements. They went for the ride and the sights. I recall one trip to Miami with Lester, Jeanie, Patrick, and Brenda Holderness, Chris and Diane Stockman, and Becky. A friend of a friend had learned that we were in town. He called a friend, Jim Montgomery, and suddenly these kids were looking out the top floor window of the best beachfront hotel on Miami Beach. The phone lines to room service were hot. I didn't sleep for three days and nights; one night, two of the kids were missing until dawn and then had the nerve to walk into the hotel as though nothing had happened.

Drive a pseudo father nuts.

When the semester ended, the university told the students they could have their grades if they agreed not to continue the program in the fall. The students met, discussed the offer, and rejected it. Talk about hard-assed, never-give-an-inch students.

In the end, the university relented. The students got their grades. Those who were seniors got their diplomas. Their looks of satisfaction at having successfully confronted the university were unforgettable.

Although it was a major victory I had the feeling one or more of the administrators had secretly supported the program but had been entangled in the rules and regulations that had been in place for decades. Although they now were backing down, they didn't want students to view this breakfast program—this Oatmeal and Love—as a student victory. They also didn't want the television cameras and the newspaper reporters making heroes out of students who had sacrificed grades and graduation to feed some hungry young kids. So when they learned that we might hold a press conference, I was asked to try and discourage any news that would make the university look as though they had been "beaten." For the sake of those university administrators who were trying to help—and I later learned that Phil Hubbard had been the force that tilted the decision in favor of the students—the press conference was called off. I didn't have to mention anything to anyone because the students did it all on their own—for which I was grateful.

The university was relieved when the term ended and the students left. They were doubly relieved that no one called a press conference to boast about the victory. After the confrontations that took place on campus after the Kent State murders the year before, the administration feared the *PDI* would attempt to use the breakfast program to our own advantage. In fact, we used the van to pick up and deliver students to breakfast and then to school, but early on I had stepped aside and let the students deal with the media. We were always there, but students like Al Cloud, who would move on from Iowa to work for Liberation News Service, provided leadership that was so calm and laidback we never had to step in throughout the crisis.

FIRST *PDI* GENERATES FIRST SUBSCRIBERS

Meanwhile, the staff continued to expand. For six months, beginning in the middle of 1970, I worked hard with correctional officials and the legislators from Oklahoma to get Rex Fletcher paroled from prison. He had been in longer than was necessary. He didn't deny that prison was a just reward for armed robbery or that his escape warranted an extension on his sentence. However, 33 years in the can was a bit much for a man in his 50s. He was writing and loving it. He had a job waiting for him in Iowa City and enough politicians urging a positive response to our petition that the parole board had to give serious thought to releasing him. The state of Iowa had already agreed to accept him as a parole transfer.

Finally I was notified that Rex would be released on March 24, 1971. He came straight to Iowa City and the *PDI*.

A few weeks later, Wes Graham arrived from Leavenworth.

A couple months after our two ex-prisoner editors were in place, we added our first "non-offender" to the staff—a junior high school English teacher, artist, and close friend of friends named Merrily Megletsch. In a series of interesting events that all of us were grateful for because we desperately needed someone with an English degree, she left teaching, her marriage broke up, and she joined us at 505. She was pure sunshine.

By now our first issue was almost ready to print—morale was high, we were attracting more and more prison writers and artists.

One of the slickest check passing artists I'd heard of wrote a wonderful article, "CHECKMATE: The Trade Secrets of a Professional Check Passer." Some of the ex-cons on the staff didn't like it—they thought we were giving away trade secrets.

I had some photographs by John Ricardo, a prisoner from the Florida State Penitentiary who had taught himself photography while doing time. One dramatic photo we turned into a poster that we used as the centerspread in the first 24-page section. It showed the electric chair at Raiford, Florida, with the caption "You think speed kills...."

Our entire staff participated in an all-day seminar on prisons and corrections at Scattergood, a Quaker school east of Iowa City. Artist Phyllis Lehrman photographed the day's activities for a feature in the second issue. Media coverage of the activities gave us more press.

LAW SECTION ATTRACTS JAILHOUSE LAWYERS

With the addition of a law section, the best writers in the system—the jailhouse lawyers—began to get involved. The law section in the first issue made public an important ruling: The Arkansas prison system was in such terrible shape that a federal district court judge, J. Smith Henley, had declared it unconstitutional to sentence people to prison there. Of course the state was given time to make changes, but the decision was an important one that would help us later.

The law section also included another decision that concerned a black man who had been arrested for armed robbery in Cedar Rapids. The man had never before committed a crime. His record was absolutely clean. Further, even though armed robbery by a black man normally meant that he would go to prison for a minimum of ten years, in front of District Court Judge Ansel Chapman the accused admitted that he had committed the robbery. An exhaustive pre-sentence investigation report followed. In the end, because the circumstances surrounding the case were so unusual, and despite the severe criticism he knew he would come under from the news media, Judge Chapman gave the man a suspended sentence and placed him on probation. The judge made the right decision. The man never committed another crime. It took a judge with incredible courage to do what Chapman did. Iowa wasn't easy on him, but he weathered that storm.

To insure that there was no opposition to the *PDI* when we sent it to carefully selected prisoners, we added a third story to the front page: "Why should any inmate or ex-offender be interested in a college education?" by board member Dr. Magoroh Maruyama.

Jackie Blank, an Iowa City friend, approached me one day and handed me a note. "I think this describes what you are doing better than anything I've read," she said. On the slip of paper was written, "Our life's mission is to be impatient—to push social progress a little faster than it is prepared to go." We placed it on the front page of the newspaper above the title and went to press in June 1971.

It had taken us a year and a half to get out this 72-page tabloid that no one seemed to be interested in. Regardless, we were a non-profit corporation, we had tax exempt status, and I was confident that we were going to rock some boats.

Just before going to press the American Correctional Association called me and ordered a copy of the first issue for everyone who was signed up to attend that year's convention in Miami Beach—well over a thousand extra copies. Maybe some people *were* interested.

Our staff had grown too. Board member Myra "Mickey" Mezvinsky was taking more time from the demands of her busy family life to sort through folders of poetry; board member Bill McDonald was helping us turn our headquarters at 505 South Lucas into a halfway house for recently paroled men, women, and children. To the best of our knowledge it was the first of its kind. Paul D. Burian, an incredibly resourceful jack-of-all-trades from Westinghouse Learning Corporation and a good friend of John Clark, joined the board of directors.

Within a couple of weeks subscriptions began coming in from law professors, senators and representatives, prisoners, and libraries. Meeting the expenses of printing on a regular basis suddenly became feasible.

On a trip to New York City I met with directors of the Famous Artists School, whose home study courses seemed to be in great demand but were too expensive for prisoners to afford. The directors agreed to donate to the *PDI* $300,000 worth of art and writing scholarships for us to award to prisoners. In retrospect, I believe that, when they agreed to donate the scholarship money, they already knew they were going to declare bankruptcy but they made the offer anyhow to get good publicity for themselves. As it turned out, the school declared bankruptcy in less than six months and the prisoners got zip.

A young woman showed up one day with a story that she wanted us to publish. She and her husband had been so jacked around by the correctional system in Iowa that she wanted to share their experience. Although her story was typical, we felt that her ability as a writer would inspire others. "The Guilty and the Fumbling" shared the front page with a story that came up the day before we were going to press with our July 1971 issue.

PDI STOPS EXTRADITION OF ARKANSAS ESCAPEE

That second story involved a prisoner who had been picked up in Cedar Rapids after escaping from Tucker Prison Farm in Arkansas. I read in the Cedar Rapids *Gazette* that he had waived extradition. He obviously had not read the first issue of the *PDI*, I thought.

I rushed to Cedar Rapids and drove directly to the Linn County jail. No one was inclined to do me any favors so I asked to visit the escapee from Arkansas to do a story on prisons down there. They agreed but they wouldn't let me bring my tape recorder into the jail. They wouldn't even let me have my notebook. Nothing. Zip. I left all my material in my van, but as I started in I said, "Hell, let me take them a copy of our newspaper. I'll just leave it inside."

The guard said "Okay."

Roy Daniel Childers was called out. He had no idea who I was or why I was there. I didn't waste any time.

"Why did you waive extradition and agree to go back to Tucker?" I asked him.

"What else could I do? I have no money. No lawyer. Nothing."

"Do you want to go back?" I asked.

"Are you nuts? It's crazy down there. I'm going to end up doing heavy time for running."

I introduced myself and showed him a copy of the first issue of the *PDI*. I explained why I thought he should not go back to Tucker Farm. Then I told him that I had an attorney who was willing to take his case and money to pay the attorney. I didn't have either. What I did have was a decision from Federal District Court Judge J. Smith Henley stating unequivocally that serving a prison sentence at Tucker or Cummins Farm in Arkansas constituted cruel and unusual punishment.

I told him I would have an attorney working on this first thing Monday morning.

"No good," Roy told me. "I'm being picked up at 6 A.M. by Arkansas deputies and taken back to Tucker."

There was no time for lawyers; I had to go directly to a judge. With a black marker I turned the front page of the *PDI* into a legal brief:

9:20 A.M. 7/31/71. I, Roy Daniel Childers, wish to state publicly that I retract my waiver of extradition to Arkansas on the following grounds: 1) that I was not represented by counsel during my hearing in Judge Maxwell's court on or about July 29th, and that, whether or not I have a right to counsel, I was ignorant of the court decisions that have ruled that imprisonment in Tucker or Cummins prison constitutes cruel and unusual punishment; 2) that I was forced to be a trustee at Tucker which is a violation of J. Smith Henley's U. S. Dist. Ct. decision of Feb 18, 1970; 3) that returning me to either Tucker or Cummins prison will constitute sentencing me to death either at the hands of inmates, or the hands of trustees, or the hands of guards. Let it be known that I wish to appear before Judge Maxwell, or any Dist. Ct. Judge in Linn County on Monday morning, or before, with my attorney Joseph Johnston, of Iowa City, Ia., and 4) I, Roy Daniel Childers, refuse to return to Arkansas and will fight extradition.

It was signed by Roy and witnessed by me. I told him I would do my best to get to a judge.

I called Judge William R. Eads from the pay phone at the jail. He was home and agreed to see me. He issued the following order:

> In the matter of the
> Extradition of
> Roy Daniel Childers
> The sheriff of Linn County, Iowa is hereby ordered to not release Roy Daniel Childers to the State of Arkansas, or any legal representative or law enforcement officer thereof, until the matter of the waiver of extradition is set for hearing. The court shall issue further orders to the Linn County Sheriff subsequent to the time and date of hearing concerning the extradition of Roy Daniel Childers.
> Signed, William R. Eads, Judge, 8th Judicial District of Iowa
> 1:28 P.M. July 31, 1971

The next morning the deputies from Arkansas were turned away from the jail.

Later that day, Roy's wife called me and we discussed options. I decided to appeal to the judge at the hearing and request that Roy be released on bond. I was advised by lawyers that there were no provisions to allow bond for escaped prisoners. "Face it, Joe, he's already proven to the world that he runs. No one will put up the money. The risk is too great."

I answered, "Let's get him released on his own recognizance." And we did, with help from Joe Johnston. Johnston was the young attorney who had helped me form PHASE IV, our non-profit, tax-exempt corporation, when I was first laying plans to begin the *PDI*. Now he came to our aid again. He was incredible. Not only did he stop extradition, he asked that Roy be released on bond. This was unheard of unless the bond was so high that the courts were absolutely assured that he wouldn't run again. But Johnston was eloquent. Not only was Roy released, he was released on his own recognizance—just his and our collective promises that he would stay for whatever was coming up.

The news media picked up the case at once. It was a compelling story: an escaped prisoner, a wife, twin daughters who were 7 or 8. Great kids. With signs in their hands that said, "FREE MY DADDY," they captivated the press photographers.

By the time the second issue went to press, we were sending out subscriptions as fast as we could process them. Everytime I would check the fast increasing numbers, I'd catch Becky glancing over at me with a sly grin on her face. Many a time over lunch or dinner or on the road, we would recall the time we stayed up all night filling out return mailers so it appeared that more than seven people wanted to see the *PDI*. In this bio of the *PDI* I'm sharing this secret for the first time.

Once, many years later, I asked Becky if she had ever mentioned it to anyone. She was bouncing her beautiful little baby girl on her knee. She flashed that quiet smile at me and said, "I ain't no snitch."

Success Was Killing Us

With subscriptions skyrocketing, we should have been coasting but we weren't. The more we received, the more we struggled because on most we were losing money. The vast majority were from prisoners, who were allowed to subscribe for a dollar down and the rest when they could afford it. Exactly what we had hoped for was now happening with one exception—we couldn't make it on one dollar per subscription. Or, in the case of prisons where there were no jobs, and consequently no pay, 25 cents for a year's subscription. Each issue we mailed to those subscribers cost us at a minimum the price of postage. In addition, many prisoners who had no money got the paper for free. Fortunately, a large number of supporters began sending in an extra dollar apiece with their own subscriptions to help us out.

We learned that the average number of prisoners to read an issue of the *PDI* was 12. Groups were subscribing. The first person would write the names of all the participants on the front page. As each section was finished it was passed on. By the time the last prisoner was looking at an issue, the next issue would be arriving.

In the second issue, which came out in July 1971, letters to the editor increased in number. The first was from a young conscientious objector from Florida. Robert Copeland was more qualified to be running a newspaper than any of us at the *PDI*. I contacted Bob's draft board and they agreed that he could serve alternative service working with the *PDI*. No other person was to have a greater influence on the development of the *PDI* into a respected, international journal (see sidebar 3).

We also had letters from Congressmen John Culver and Fred Schwengle; law professor Herman Schwartz (whom we would next see at Attica Prison during the riots, when so many prisoners were murdered); Celeste West of the San Francisco Public Library; Dr. Karl Menninger; Reverend Walter Kellison (whose daughter was one of the university students who helped make the breakfast program a success); and many prisoners.

We were also beginning to hear from political prisoners. Political prisoners were, for the most part, extremely radical. They condemned the prison administrations, advocated the use of force to gain equity, and used such forceful language that, in order to avoid the label of "dangerous troublemaker," I had to edit out of their letters any comments about "prisoners rising up" or "prisoners organizing to take control of their lives." Two or three subscribers in the New York prison at Attica were killed when the National Guard stormed the prison. Sam Melville wrote letters to us that we could not print.

Correspondents joined us from prisons in South Carolina (Gary Addis), San Quentin (John Severenson Watson and Donald Chenault), Wisconsin (S.L. Poulter and Bruce Brandi), Minnesota (Jim Bosley), Virginia (James Williams), Florida (Thomas Winberry), Illinois (Harold Sampson and Dean Hill), Missouri (Earl Guy), and Iowa (Barry McDaniel). Other outstanding writers were taking their places as regulars, including Tom Puchalski (New Jersey State Pen) and Gordy Peterson (Minnesota State Pen).

The Mad Writer from Cell 1616 in San Luis Obispo, James Ralph Williamson, was back again in issue two and would continue with the *PDI* until its demise. I will never forgive the California correctional officials who refused to allow me to visit this remarkable writer and full-time character.

Cartoon panels by an old friend from Leavenworth were back in issue two also. "The Concrete Bungle," by Drummond, never failed to entertain.

Stanley Eldridge, from behind the walls of Indiana State Penitentiary, was emerging as an important American poet. His poem "A Tear for Darryl" had University of Iowa Poetry Workshop students hanging around the office reading from the ever-growing pile of poems arriving from prisons around the world.

One complete 24-page section devoted to the Florida prison system was enlightening. Written by reporters from the *St. Petersburg Times*, it allowed the voices of prisoners to be heard when few newspapers were listening to prisoners. The series (actually a tabloid section) was probably a circulation builder for them but it was a sincere attempt to bring change to the prisons of Florida. We picked it up because it was the kind of coverage that appealed to the people in the free world.

The law section of the July 1971 issue provided prisoners with information about the *Palmagiano vs. Travisono*, et al. (317 F.Supp. 776 1970) case. Thomas Ross, assistant editor of *The Challenge*, Adult Correctional Institution, Rhode Island, provided insights and analysis of the case that was pending in the United States District Court for the District of Rhode Island.

In that case, U.S. District Court Judge Pettine, in a 43-page opinion, ordered that prison officials "shall not open or otherwise inspect the contents of any incoming or outgoing letters" between a long list of specified individuals, embracing federal and state officials, court officers, and Rhode Island attorneys. The temporary order also stated that mail inspected for contraband could not be read and that letters to approved correspondents from prisoners could not be opened and inspected. The order was to stand until a three-judge panel could meet in October for a trial.

Also in the Law Section, Richard G. Singer provided a lengthy article entitled "Censorship of Prisoners' Mail and the Constitution." The article included 31 footnotes of cases supporting Singer's views that censorship of mail is dehumanizing, demeaning, unconstitutional, and unnecessary. He closed his article with a thought we all hoped was true: "Prison reform is in the air. Let us hope the humanizing breath will invigorate us all."

As I page through back issues of the *PDI*, reading the articles, remembering the authors, I am struck by the number of contributors I met in the living room of the house where the flag flew upside down signaling a nation in distress. In this house I was able to hold meetings when more people were involved than I could fit into my one small room. Here my friends from the women's prison rested in a manner to which they were most assuredly not accustomed. Frequently I found myself being introduced to people who became significant contributors to the *PDI*.

One such individual was a young assistant law professor from the University of Iowa. Phillip J. Mause was able to listen to a legal problem and, without moving from his chair, provide endless citations, analyses, and sound opinions.

In our July issue, Mause reviewed two books: *Criminal Law: Cases, Comment, Questions* and *Criminal Process: Cases, Comment, Questions*, by Lloyd L. Weinreb, professor of law, Harvard University. Mause's comments eloquently enabled jailhouse lawyers to better grasp and use the legal tools that Weinreb discussed. Again, the use of footnotes provided prisoners with the roadmaps so frequently denied them in prison—citations and explanations of cases and how they related to points of law. In the end, however, Mause took the books and the law schools to task, pointing out, "Our historic failure to ask and answer...basic questions in the law schools has contributed significantly to the current breakdown of our criminal justice system."

Around the time our July issue appeared, the "David Susskind Show" featured a group of ex-prisoners who were working with the Fortune Society, a New York City-based prisoner-support organization that took its name from a play, "Fortune in Men's Eyes," a graphic description of life inside a maximum security prison. Mel Rivers, Danny Keane, Prentice

Sidebar 3: Drafted into Service at the *PDI*

by Bob Copeland

I was drafted into service at *PDI*, but if Uncle Sam's left hand had known that his right hand had put me there, I would have been moved quickly to a VA hospital and handed a bedpan to clean. I know I contributed far more to the greater good at *PDI*.

As a college junior at Lake Forest (Illinois) Collge in 1970, I was disgusted by the lies from Washington, the carnage in Southeast Asia, the violence and poverty and racism in American towns and cities. My world view and plans for my future were radicalized by the ferment of the times. They peaked with the U.S. invasion of Cambodia, the killings at Kent State and Jackson State, and the ensuing turmoil on campuses across the nation. I vowed then to forsake careerism upon graduation and to find an honest organization through which I could work for peace and social change.

One month before leaving college I mailed my Florida draft board my claim for conscientious objector status. Shortly after my induction physical that summer, I was amazed to learn that Selective Service had approved my petition on first reading. I was classified as a C.O. and required to perform two years of alternative service.

One afternoon that summer, my father brought home from the newspaper office where he worked a copy of a prison newspaper from McAlester, Oklahoma. I read with interest a back-page ad for the *Penal Digest International*, a slick monthly published in the country's first ex-convict-owned and operated halfway house in Iowa City, Iowa. I thought it seemed the perfect opportunity to apply my journalism experience and revolutionary impulses while working for social and personal changes.

I wrote *PDI* and Joe Grant responded by welcoming me to join them. Again I was amazed when my draft board agreed to send me to Iowa City for my service stint. Selective Service would have been more amazed had they foreseen all that my work at *PDI* would entail.

From the moment the door at 505 South Lucas Street opened to me, I felt both at home and swept up in a tide of heroic effort, high hopes, and boundless collective energy, pushing, pushing for change, with the dark unknown always lurking around the corner, at the edges and under the surface.

The living was communal, vibrant, and in constant flux. A core group of people worked nearly around the clock to get out the *PDI* and maintain its links with prisoners around the world. Other workers came and went. Cross-country travelers stopped by for a night or several months. We were a rainbow of personalities: ex-prisoners fresh from the joint, college professors, teenage runaways, artists, aging alcoholic vagabonds, writers, fugitives, do-gooders, lawyers, con-men, and musicians.

Money always was too tight to mention, but we lived well. We took care of each other, ate together, shared dreams and fears, clothes and beds, hopes and shortcomings. We were a family constantly redefining ourselves, our circumstances, and our destination. Personal growth in such a setting was guaranteed.

Then there was the mail. The letters, letters, letters kept our kaleidoscopic free-world lives rooted in the shadows of a separate reality—the prisons of the world. The mail came in torrents, outpourings of hope and rage and suffering and great creativity. Prisoners sensed that our family was open to them, that our founders saw with their eyes, that our voice was intended to be theirs.

We received eloquent poetry, astute legal analyses from jailhouse lawyers, cartoons and drawings, news reports, humor columns, helpful critiques of our own efforts, and harrowing accounts of brutality and injustice behind the walls. The latter were far too numerous, and they kept coming, insinuating their painful details into our psyches, galvanizing our allegiance to our constituents, strengthening our determination to make their plight known, to effect some change in their conditions.

We corresponded with thousands and we were changed deeply by the exchanges. Talk of prison reforms gave way to essays on abolition. We became *Prisoners' Digest International*. Our editorials took on a sharper edge. Issues of *PDI* continued to be banned at certain institutions and we were denied personal access to a growing number of prisons. Friction with local authorities increased. One night we awoke to waving flashlights and cops walking through our house looking for a fugitive their teletype said might stop by our house. Outside other officers waited, guns drawn.

We saw the American prison as a microcosm of the whole society. In the dynamics of the relationship between keeper and kept were crystallized potent truths about power and poverty, right and wrong, privilege and prejudice, fear and forgiveness in our culture. Ultimately the fundamental questions were spiritual, which led us into alliance with a group of federal prisoners who had forged their own religion, a vision of truth and unity called the Church of the New Song. Once judicially recognized as protected under the Constitution, New Song spread quickly through federal and state prison systems. We assisted the process and became ministers ourselves, finally gaining personal access to the people we had been serving from outside the walls.

I stayed at *PDI* beyond my required tour of duty because the work and the people had become part of me. We truly believed in the power of non-violent conflict resolution to create a new approach to criminal justice. We devoted all our energies to living our convictions and we changed many lives.

When I left *PDI*, it was to serve as New Song resident minister for the men in the Iowa State Penitentiary. Ultimately, I burned out. What I read of prisons today is dishearteningly familiar, even more frightening than the horrors we faced 20 years ago. I hope those who are working for change there today have access to back copies of the *PDI*. I know there is enough truth and inspiration in those pages to be of help for generations.

Copeland was an editor of *PDI* from October 1971 until the final issue was published in April 1973. As a Church of the New Song Sealed Revelation Minister he worked for two years inside the walls of the Iowa State Penitentiary as minister to the Prison Purlieu, Fort Madison, Iowa. For the past 15 years he has been part of a farming collective in southern Minnesota where he composes music and lives with his family in a recently completed earth home.

Williams, Chuck Berganski, George Freeman, and Stan Telega discussed the horrors of prison and the incredible difficulties faced by ex-prisoners when they were released. The show was originally seen in the New York area, but it was subsequently seen in many parts of the country. Repeated calls to local television stations finally got Iowa a showing of the program. David Rothenberg was the steady, hard-working force behind the success of the Fortune Society. Years later, he would run for a New York city council seat and be narrowly defeated. David's was one of the few political campaigns I personally contributed to. He is a remarkable person who has done an extraordinary amount of good for prisoners and ex-prisoners.

THE KIDS AND THE CONS

Shortly before the second issue went to press, Rex Fletcher, who had been paroled from prison in Oklahoma in March to become a *PDI* co-editor, was busted on a trip to Oklahoma. He had left Iowa with a woman friend and the pickup in which they were driving was involved in an accident. Rex had violated his parole by being there. Nothing serious, a rule was broken but no crimes were committed—except for the crime of Rex not being where he was told to be. So be it. The real crime was that Rex was back in the slam.

Rex was only with us for a few short months. During those months he had a difficult time adjusting to life outside of prison. Rex was older than most of us, in his early fifties. He had been locked up a long time, 33 years to be exact. As a young man, according to what I heard, he had been involved in armed robberies. I never questioned people about past crimes, but I knew that he had never killed anyone, nor had he ever harmed any women or children.

Before he arrived I told my little pal Patrick (age 5 or 6) and his older brother Lester (10 or 11) that Rex was coming to Iowa City and he needed a couple of friends more than even he realized. He's got a temper, maybe drinks more than he should when drinking anything at all could get him sent back to prison, and he tended to believe, like a lot of people then both young and old, that we should go forward and win the war in Vietnam. He thought pot smokers should be disciplined and he respected the flag.

Lester and Patrick sat there looking at me waiting for more information.

Lester said, "Dammit, next thing you'll tell us he drinks Coke."

Lester was something else. All the kids who hung around 505 were a little unusual. At the time, Coca Cola products were being boycotted and no one we knew was drinking Coke, particularly the kids. If they saw anyone with a Coke they would start their rap. I was always telling Lester to watch his language. That kid could embarrass the crew waiting for work at the Laborers Union hall. After he learned about the boycott he went to one of the supermarkets in town and asked to see the manager. When the manager came out to the front of the store, Lester asked him why he had all that Coke on the shelf when there was a boycott. The manager told him to run along. Lester raised his voice about twice its normal decibel level and asked him again. Now some customers had stopped and were listening. The manager told him he wasn't interested in any boycott. Lester was appalled. He started to leave, but about halfway to the door he turned around and said, "You oughta be ashamed of yourself!" He stood there for a moment thinking of what else he could say and obviously could think of nothing, so he simply yelled, "GODDAMMIT!" And he left. One of the cashiers told me about it.

Years later whenever I bumped into Lester I would ask him if he wanted something to drink. "Maybe a Coke, Lester?" I'd ask. He'd look at me and say, "I don't drink Coke."

Lester was a good kid. All his little brother Patrick wanted in life was to be with him.

"Damn kids," Lester would say.

Rex Fletcher needed help to stay out of trouble. Plus he was a good guy—generous, loved to go swimming, liked to work out. He was a tough guy, took care of himself, but he was a good friend and actually a gentle person.

The kids were looking forward to his arrival. When he arrived it was late at night. We hadn't moved into 505 yet. Joe Johnston, the lawyer who had agreed to take Roy Childers' case, had recently bought a house that he didn't plan to occupy for three or four months so he was letting us stay there. In those days one typesetting unit punched the tape. Then the tape was fed into the unit that set the type. Work went on all the time. Some of our typesetting equipment was in the den along with a massive pile of punched paper tape that went with it. Other equipment was scattered around town. With more people arriving to work on the *PDI* we needed more space. Joe's house was a comfortable temporary residence. "I'm living high as an Oklahoma hog," Rex would say.

We showed Rex around the office, and took him for a walk around town. We all loved Iowa City and he sensed it. I told Rex that he could start work as soon as he felt ready. I explained that he had two jobs: helping me with a couple of young kids who needed a friend and relaxing and getting used to life in Iowa City.

Rex received what was to him a strange welcome in Iowa City. In the afternoon he would take a walk and stop in some of the working class taverns in Iowa City. There he'd meet some of the good old boys and everything would be fine until they realized who he was. Once they knew they were talking to a dude who had spent 33 years behind bars, they were gone. They wanted no part of that potential scene. So the older, working class conservatives who Rex could relate to didn't want anything to do with him. The hippies, the freaks, the peaceniks, and the antiwar activists, on the other hand, were in love with Rex. He had spent more time in a cell than they had on earth. He was articulate, a handsome old guy, in great physical shape, and clean. The young women admired him. Some even tried to take advantage of him. They understood why he was a conservative and they were forgiving. Rex, however, thought the hippies, Yippies, etc. etc. were a bunch of Commie sympathizers and borderline traitors. He was uncomfortable with them, but after we moved into 505 he couldn't avoid them.

Every afternoon Rex would go to the Iowa City Recreation Center for a swim. Patrick never missed that trip even though he couldn't swim. He would flail and fight and churn his way around the shallow end for a few yards like he had 25 pounds of rocks jammed in his bathing suit. Then he would call to Rex. Rex would swim over to Patrick, Patrick would grab hold around Rex's neck, and Rex would start to swim laps, back and forth, never tiring, for 30 minutes or more. Patrick loved it and so did Rex.

Rex never had a family. Suddenly there were kids who depended on him. Co-workers, who were more family than employees, were around day and night. The large meal gatherings were more festive than crowded, and people worried if you were gone longer than expected.

Walking home late one night, I saw Lester hanging around outside a tavern on the edge of downtown.

"What are you doing up this late, Lester?" I asked.

"Waitin' for Rex?"

"Does he know you're out here?"

"I dunno."

I went in. Rex was sitting by himself at the bar. I walked over and ordered a beer. Small talk. He was lonesome. Finally I said, "I'm worried about Lester. It's a school night and I just saw him up the street."

Rex looked worried. "Lester? Downtown at this time of night? Drink up. Let's find out if something's wrong."

And out we went. Lester was checking the coin return slots on a bank of pay phones.

"Hey, Partner!" Rex called. "What gives?"

"I dunno," Lester responded with a shrug. And we all walked home together. That happened more than once.

But the most serious problem was that the people Rex admired and wanted to be with rejected him while the people he rejected or wasn't fond of being around loved him. The hippies and the antiwar activists were kind, considerate, generous, friendly. These "outlaws" would gather at 505 for dinner and Rex was the senior member of the group. He was gracious and had wonderful stories. But Rex wanted to be telling the stories to his peers, to the "good old boys" at the taverns where the older workers hung out, and they didn't want to listen.

Somewhere along the line things got distorted. Rex had been too long in prison. He may have been a robber but he was a patriotic American. The flag was an important symbol of his love of country. It was a symbol that many of the people who were in and out of 505 had little time for. Life was out of balance for Rex: "Koyaanisqatsi," as the Hopi say and as Phillip Glass described so eloquently in his music for the film of the same name. When Rex arrived in Iowa City he was already in an emotional spin from his sudden change in lifestyles. He had read nothing to prepare himself for what he was walking into. His magazine of choice had been *Playboy*. If we had known we might have been able to find him a few issues of *off our backs*, *The Progressive*, and a few other publications of the Left.

Then we were notified that Rex would have to return to Oklahoma because of a paperwork mixup. We had lobbied everyone from the federal office holders right down to the warden for Rex and we were successful, but the paperwork had been pushed through too fast. Rex was convinced they were going to revoke the parole approval and never release him. He discussed taking off. His voice was edged with panic. Rex couldn't sit down and relax. He paced the office, the dining room, the streets. He was like a leopard who was cornered and was looking for a way to avoid the net.

Making a run for it meant he would have to leave the country. "I don't think I can go back," he told me. He had spent too much time in the can already. The thought of going back was more than Rex could deal with.

I sat with Rex and listened to him as he mulled over the choices of the Oklahoma State Penitentiary or a boat to Jamaica, where the extradition situation was fair. I had close friends down there and had occasionally thought of making the move myself, though I never did. There's too much of the North Country in my soul.

Rex asked, "If I run, what will it do to the *PDI*, Joe?"

"It would be a great feature. We'd defend you and get you a pardon."

Rex laughed and said, "A pardon? How would you do that?"

"I figure if we could get you released we can do anything." Rex liked hearing that.

"The *PDI* will be dead in Oklahoma," he said.

"'Is,' not 'will be,'" I answered.

I called the governor, the warden, and parole board members; everyone reassured me that it was a technicality that would be worked out.

Rex was skeptical, and he knew I had been lied to before.

But running was so serious that I made Rex an offer. I promised him that if the state of Oklahoma revoked the approved parole I would come to the prison and not leave the front gate until they gave Rex back to us. He was family and he believed. Rex headed back.

When we next heard from Oklahoma, the news was good. Rex had returned calmly. He just walked into the front office of the state penitentiary and sat down to wait. He was soon back in his cell at night and in the prison newspaper office during the day. Support for Rex poured in from all over the state and the country. He was back in the slam because of red-tape "screw-ups." It was as simple as that. After a few weeks he was back on the street and on his way to Iowa City.

The reunion was special for all of us, but mostly for the kids. Unfortunately, the same problem persisted: Rex was lost in the middle ground of two opposing political forces, unable to accept the New Radical Left, whose membership wanted him as a friend, and not accepted by the conservative right, whose friendship he wanted. After a few weeks, Rex started to miss Oklahoma and his friends down there who shared his politics and accepted his past transgressions.

He finally reached a point where he had to go home for a few days.

One day, a woman drove up from Oklahoma to see Rex. She was an antique dealer and absolutely striking—short, solid, an Oklahoma Indian who drove her pickup and camper around the country buying collectibles. She and Rex had been corresponding for years and when she arrived we could see that much more than simple friendship was involved here. When they left for Oklahoma I realized Rex might be on a path that would take him away from the *PDI*. I wished them the best, assured Rex that this was his home, and told them to be cool. He said they would be back in a week or so, and I think that was their plan. Then they were gone.

If he had applied for permission the state of Iowa would have let him make the trip, but the process would have taken a few weeks, and Rex was feeling desperate. He had to "go home or go nuts," as he put it.

On the way, they had a minor accident. While checking the car, the police found some guns. The fact that they were civil war relics cleared Rex of a serious possession of firearms charge, but not of the charge of violation of parole. He had some blind spots, we all do, but I know Rex went back asking himself, "What's the sense of trying?" There were times during those *PDI* years when I asked myself the same question.

NATIONAL LAWYERS GUILD: "GIVE PRISONERS *PDI*"

Bad news was arriving from around the country. Some prisoners had been denied the first issue of the *PDI* despite our efforts to not be seen as "troublemakers." Others were contacting us to say that their wardens were not allowing them to draw money out of their accounts to subscribe to the *PDI*. Some prisons quickly passed a new rule: you couldn't draw just one dollar out of your account.

Our lawyers went to work at once. National Lawyers Guild attorneys in the cities closest to the offending prisons were contacted. They were in the offices of the wardens the next morning. We had discussed how we wanted them to deal with the wardens. First, they were to find out exactly which articles in the *PDI* the wardens objected to. Second, they were to have copies of the *PDI* with them so they could read the objectionable articles.

Invariably the wardens were concerned about some innocuous statement or article they had taken out of context or something they had been told that turned out to be untrue. Talking about their concerns and looking at a copy of the *PDI* sometimes was enough to make them change their minds. If they had arbitrarily decided to keep the newspaper out because it was published by an ex-prisoner, they quickly were told what was going to happen if they persisted. No warden relished the idea of the news media following the likes of William Kunstler and Stan Bass and our other heavy hitters into his office bright and early some Monday morning. Looking back, I believe I might have been able to print everything, even pieces by Sam Melville and other political prisoners, if I had made enough use of this threat.

Some prisons were set so far back from civilization's road that names like Kunstler and Bass didn't mean anything to them. The administrators of the Florida State Pen at Raiford epitomized this group. Gene Jones was removed from his job as editor of the *Raiford* (Florida) *Record* because he was determined to write an article for the *PDI*. Lawyers were notified and they in turn notified Gene that he would have whatever counsel he needed—counsel to defend him and counsel to ensure that retaliation by prison administrators against *PDI* contributors was stopped immediately wherever it happened.

The warden at Statesville Prison in Illinois looked me in the eye and told me the *PDI* was too radical to be allowed inside the walls. When I asked him which articles he was talking about he told me, "I forget!" I asked him if any of his prisoners were allowed to subscribe to the *New York Times*.

"That's different," he answered. "The *New York Times* is a newspaper."

Over the next few months, I came to enjoy conversations like this. "That's right. The *New York Times* is a newspaper. But it's a newspaper that has a special privilege: a second class postal permit that only subscribed-to newspapers can get from the federal government," I answered.

I had with me the page from the *Times* that stated "Second Class Postage Paid at, etc. etc." Then I opened the *PDI* and showed him where it said, "Second Class Postage Paid at, etc. etc."

"The fact of the matter is that the only difference between the *Penal Digest International* and the *New York Times* is this: they are a daily and we are a monthly. If you can keep us out because you don't like the idea that a newspaper is concerned about how prisoners are treated, then you can keep the *Times* out because you don't like their editorial policy."

Looking around his office was like looking at a history of oppressive penology in the United States: leg irons and remnants of all that seemed dear to the old boys who ran their prisons with absolute authority. They even thought they could kick newspapers around. This warden still thought that wardens could play God.

There are still wardens like that. And guards. And prisoners, too.

Our lawyers moved quickly and effectively.

With the Roy Childers case taking up more of our time, the question came up about how much energy and time we should devote to free-world issues. To me the answer was automatic; we had an obligation to help prisoners, ex-prisoners, and any members of their families. Decision-making support was always available from Merrily, Richard Tanner, and community friends. Our staff was still growing. The first people released to my custody as halfway house residents were two women from the Iowa Women's Reformatory who had participated as *PDI* representatives in discussion groups and as panelists at recent conferences that addressed prisoner issues. They were right at home at 505. Soon we had others.

A Halfway House Like Home

This halfway house business had happened quite by accident. I had been critical of the halfway house programs that the states were slowly developing. Coming out of prison and readjusting to life in the free world was difficult at best. If the period of adjustment was going to be effective, prisoners had to live in an environment that would be as close to real life as possible. It was to the advantage of both prisoners and society then that halfway houses had men, women, and children living in them. If a person had problems living with children and persons of the opposite sex, then the time to work them out was while they were in a minimum custody environment.

Our home at 505 was perfect. The most serious problem we faced was not being able to apply for financial assistance from state or federal agencies that had funds available. The house was in a quiet, residential neighborhood. An application for financial assistance would have meant publicity, which would have brought an end to everything we were doing. People thought of us as just another group of people, no different from the many large houses around town that contained mixes of students.

When ex-prisoners arrived they had to check in with the local state parole office. As more and more arrived we attracted the attention of the police. One day the chief of police came by with a couple of detectives. I welcomed them into the house and we sat in the living room talking about the *PDI*, the staff, and the number of ex-prisoners who were living with us. He asked me what kinds of rules we had for the people living with us. I said that we had the same rules in effect in our house that he had in his: Respect people's privacy and property, clean up after yourself, and don't break the law.

They had come to 505 to inquire about a young runaway. They had all the information they needed except for a picture of the girl, which was a good thing since she just happened to be serving them coffee.

Hers was a sad case of parental abuse. We were able to verify that she was telling us the truth by contacting a social service caseworker in her hometown. Anyone who came to 505 could count on help and a meal, but everyone had to be honest with us. We were determined that the respect we were building in the neighborhood not be jeopardized. It's worth noting that this young girl worked at the house for a few months, started back to school, got her high school degree, went on to the University of Iowa, got her college degree, and is still in Iowa City working as a counselor helping young kids.

My most vivid memory about the police chief's visit that day is when he asked if he could look around the house.

"By all means," I answered. "Anything you will let me do in your home you can do in mine."

His look told me that he didn't understand. He was working on it, but it wasn't coming together, so I explained. "What I'm saying, Chief, is you can look around our house any time you want, as long as I can look around your house anytime I want. That's fair, isn't it?"

I gave him credit for seeing my intended humor. He chuckled, thanked us for the coffee, and left. He never came back.

The folks at 505 were not impressed by uniforms. Here again, the subject of customary law would come up. A number of men at 505 had done long prison terms in the toughest prisons in the country. They had spent long periods in solitary confinement, they had been beaten, they had been in life and death situations. Some, while serving sentences for non-violent crimes, had been forced to kill while defending themselves from aggressive prisoners. It was not possible to frighten them. They were always prepared to defend themselves. And that, I always pointed out to our residents, is not a laidback way to live your life. Again and again I stepped forward to defuse potentially dangerous situations when I was out with people from 505.

One night I was walking around Iowa City with a friend who hadn't been on the street for more than a month. We were walking and talking and found ourselves in front of a very active nightclub, Gabe'n Walker's. There, we sat down on some park benches that were built into the landscaped area. We had been sitting there for 30 minutes or so when two police officers came by and started talking to the people who were hanging around. They were part of the new public relations program. Humanizing the police force. Just friendly folks trying to help.

We sat there silently, watching the two officers, and I could see that Freddie was becoming increasingly tense. They were speaking to everyone, one at a time, and we were part of the scene so it was just a matter of time. Finally one officer said to Freddie, "Hi. Sure is a nice night." Freddie looked at him but did not answer. The officer said again, "Sure is a nice night." Freddie was not making conversation.

The officer looked at me. He knew who I was.

"How ya' doing?"

"Fine," I answered.

"Have I done something to alienate your friend?"

"What makes you think I'm Grant's friend," Freddie asked before I could answer. And then, before the officer could answer, Freddie added, "And what makes you think I have an obligation to answer any of your questions?"

At that point I sincerely believed the officer would excuse himself and leave. He didn't. His partner overheard the conversation and stepped over. He looked at Freddie and said, "I'd like to see your identification."

Freddie looked up at him and said, "I don't carry identification and there is no law that says I have to carry identification. And if you didn't already know it I'll quote you the law that says that you have no right to arbitrarily ask me for identification. I was sitting here enjoying myself when you"—Freddie nodded to the other officer—"and you interjected yourselves into my space, and quite frankly I don't like it. I don't know either of you, have no desire to make your acquaintance, and would appreciate very much if both of you would catch a rabbit"—which means, "Get your ass outta here!"

One of the officers looked at the other and asked, "Catch a rabbit?"

Freddie looked at me. I couldn't hold back the laughter.

Nationally, *PDI* lines of communication were being quickly established in prisons throughout the United States and Canada. By the time the third issue was ready to print, we had prisoners subscribing, or attempting to subscribe, from every state and federal prison in the country. Letters of support, for Roy and his family, were arriving from people and organizations both in and out of prison. But we were discovering an unexpected problem: Roy had a temper. On two occasions he had struck his wife during arguments. He had been drinking on both occasions. We didn't set down any rules about what people did on their own time. We only asked that they didn't break any laws. We didn't expect more of our staff and residents than we did of the general public. We met with Roy and explained what a serious setback it would be to his case if his family left him, which is what would happen if he didn't learn to control his temper. He reassured everyone that he would control his temper.

GEORGE JACKSON MURDERED IN SAN QUENTIN

Prison activists were stunned by the news of George Jackson's death on August 21, 1971, during what the California Department of Corrections head, Raymond Procunier, described as an attempted escape. Procunier blamed the increasing prison violence on the access prisoners had to underground newspapers.

Again and again, wardens of U.S. prisons laid the blame for their problems on "outside agitators" and any newspapers that were fighting for recognition of prisoners as human beings who deserved basic human rights. Meanwhile, they did everything in their extraordinary power to avoid talking about overcrowding, absence of rehabilitation and education programs, unhealthy prison diets, and prison employees who lacked the interpersonal skills necessary to work in ethnically and racially mixed environments. When Hispanic, black, and Indian prisoners from inner city slums and ghettos were supervised by small town, predominantly poor, conservative white guards, prisoners and guards both suffered from emotionally and physically disabling degrees of stress. Prisons often were isolated and difficult for families to visit; prison industries still manufactured license plates, shoes, and furniture—which taught prisoners job skills that were nonexistent in the free world.

Tragedies like the killing of George Jackson brought the issue of prison violence to the public in splashy headlines and lengthy interviews with wardens and directors. Rarely available to the public were articles by writers who were familiar with the prison systems—writers who had investigated prison conditions, listened to prisoners AND the administrators, and written stories that dealt not only with the violence that took place but with the root causes of that violence.

What Procunier never mentioned when he attacked underground newspapers was that these same newspapers and others like them had been warning him of impending violence and rebellion that would be built not upon what prisoners were reading but upon what wardens and administrators were not reading. These incidents would be triggered by what was being done to ensure that "rehabilitative" prison systems were not only punitive, but were excessively punitive.

In colonial times, sanctions against people who violated customary or legislated law were purely punitive. The most effective way to deal with crime was "Red Hannah"—the whipping post. It was public, it was swift, and it was over. Offenders of public norms rarely committed acts that took them back to Red Hannah. The Quakers built the first penitentiaries in Philadelphia because they thought the existing form of punishment was barbaric and they believed that to punish with acts more violent than the crime was wrong, unChristian, and lacked the element that would cure the criminal and satisfy the ever present Christ: forgiveness. "Penitentiaries"—where offenders could be "penitent"—were thought to be more humane methods of punishment. The Quakers believed that a person who had committed a crime—sinned, so to speak—would repent that "sin" if kept in a cell where he or she would be exposed to the Bible and religious teachings and kept reasonably active. This was the beginning of rehabilitation.

Unfortunately, the punishment models persisted within the penitentiary until well into the 1900s. Prisoners were locked up and forgotten about. There were no such things as parole, time off for good behavior, education departments, vocational training, or anything that helped a prisoner prepare for his or her return to the free world. Prisoners were being released from penitentiaries in worse shape than when they went in.

Theoretically, the forties and fifties saw a change in the way legislators and the public perceived the "criminal." At the insistence of religious organizations and humane groups, some legislators began to challenge the policies of lock-step and silence. The "rehabilitative" approach was to reward a prisoner for abiding by prison rules, for studying, for working conscientiously—for becoming a better person. When rehabilitation programs were started, prisons saw an emergence of education departments where prisoners could get high school diplomas or college degrees and vocational training programs that actually trained prisoners for useful vocations outside prison. Prisoners were able to be released on parole long before the original sentence was served. Church services, libraries, and recreational facilities were brought into the prisons. Other changes included parole programs, revisions in the sentencing codes, and the awarding of good time, whereby prisoners who did not violate prison rules could have two days taken off the end of their sentences for every 30 days of good behavior.

All these steps toward a more humane, rehabilitative model were accompanied by publicity and a favorable acceptance from prisoners and the public. Unfortunately, the programs were never fully funded, never entered into with the kind of conviction necessary to bring about meaningful change in the system. While the public believed that prisoners were being treated humanely and were being given the opportunity to rehabilitate themselves, most programs in fact were cosmetic.

Violence in the prisons was caused by the refusal of correctional administrators to deal with legitimate prisoner complaints. Prisoners learned about demonstrations not from the radical, alternative, or underground newspapers but from the TV evening news, where they saw the country's youth demonstrating against racism and the war in Vietnam. Demonstrations that began peacefully were quelled with high-powered water hoses, dogs, and clubs. The greater the violence, the greater the numbers of demonstrators. It was a "war" the government could not win because it was a public war. At the same time, many of these demonstrators and war resisters were ending up in prison. As the prisoners spoke with these political activists and learned of their success in ending first segregation and then the Vietnam War, they became convinced that the same course of action was open to them.

Little did they know. The wars that erupt inside the prisons are private wars. Outsiders only see and hear what the government allows.

Many prisoners, like students of psychology, sociology, criminology, or penology, learn that the number of poor and non-white prisoners is disproportionately greater than their numbers in the general population. Murderers from Park Avenue homes are treated differently than murderers from poor families with no resources. When one criminal walks and another faces a lengthy prison sentence simply because one can afford the best lawyers and the other cannot, justice is not served. The persons who do the time realize that they are as much prisoners of an economic system as they are of a judicial system.

During the Attica uprising, which happened the month after George Jackson was murdered, one of the prisoners yelled to us, "When both have done the crime but only one does the time, that one becomes a political prisoner." He was right. A day later he was dead.

Although the *PDI* never pinned specific blame on capitalism and the U.S. judicial system for the plight of all prisoners in this country, there is no doubt that many prisoners are indeed victims and have committed crimes because of what society has done to them personally. For many years I have used, as my political mentor, Eugene V. Debs. Debs was a man workers could talk to and understand. On the subject of prisons he stated clearly, upon his release from a federal penitentiary where he had served a lengthy sentence for speaking out against the United States entering World War I, "As long as there is a soul in prison, I am not free." The reason so few people understand the truth about prison conditions is because the public is not allowed inside the prison walls. In-depth, investigative feature stories that expose conditions and make demands do not find favorable reception in mainstream daily newspapers.

As for the death of George Jackson during the "escape attempt," anyone who had ever been in San Quentin as a prisoner or a visitor knows that what Procunier described was not possible. The idea of Jackson hiding a gun in his Afro hairstyle was preposterous. The "shootout" was a brutal assassination. It was one more act of violence in what seemed to be a neverending conflict between guards and prisoners.

Playboy Kicks in Cash, Boosts Subscription

With circulation growing, publications began calling 505 for interviews. One call came from a *Playboy* magazine editor, who invited me to submit a request for a foundation grant. The application was successful and we were given $2,500. Equally important was *Playboy*'s mention of the *PDI* in one of their issues. We only rated a paragraph, but with a circulation in the millions the response from the free world and from prisoners was remarkable.

I visited the foundation's office at *Playboy*'s headquarters in Chicago two or three times and became acquainted with some of the writers and photographers. Three people I remember quite well were Jill Parsons, secretary to the foundation director; Craig Vetter, author and feature writer; and Don Myrus. Jill and her husband Roy became supportive, resourceful friends. Craig introduced me to people in the photography department who helped us out with film, paper, and a variety of supplies that, though dated, were perfectly usable.

Don Myrus was editorial director of Playboy Press. One day I mentioned the sorry state of prison libraries. Not only did they lack books, I pointed out, but almost every book they had was dated or damaged. I was glancing at some of the books Playboy Press had published. In those days the list was small—12 to be exact: some science fiction, a few horror, and the *Bedside Playboy Advisors and Readers*. Not exactly literary classics, but entertaining. I asked him if Playboy would donate a set of the books to any prison libraries that requested a set. Don asked how many prisons might ask for sets. I honestly did not know and told him so. I did mention, though, that such an offer might get more responses than he or I would ever imagine. He liked my idea and said he would get back to me.

On July 27, he wrote me a letter stating that Playboy Press would send three sets of the 12 books to any prison library that sent the request on library or prison stationery. The offer terminated 60 days after publication of the ad, which appeared in our July issue. (During the first year, it wasn't unusual for issues to be published late, as was obviously the case here.)

During that 60-day period letters arrived from prison libraries not just in the United States but from around the world. The prison grapevine had picked up the news. Dollar subscriptions were flooding 505 and book requests were flooding Playboy's Chicago headquarters.

Up to that point in our brief history—the July issue was only our second issue—we had not had a chance to statistically measure our actual impact on anyone or anything. The ad gave us our first opportunity. In the end, it cost Playboy somewhere between 80 and 100 thousand dollars. It also cost Don Myrus his job. Don thought it was rather humorous. I was bummed.

As a result of accepting grant money from the Playboy Foundation I took considerable heat from colleagues—particularly women. Maybe I deserved it. Although I wasn't a reader of *Playboy*, I recognized that it was not possible to disassociate yourself from the people or organization you accepted money from. They wanted to help and we needed help. But in a way, accepting a person's money is like saying "You are okay!" All of the people I met there were okay. They were gracious, helpful, professional, damned interesting, and fun to be around.

A couple years later, while passing through Chicago around Christmas, Sharlane and I were invited to a party that the photo editor was having at his loft. When we arrived, we found a fellow in a large lot across from the loft waving us into a parking spot. The parking fee for the night was only $2, a real bargain in Chicago. Two hundred cars at least were lined up neatly. Later I found out that no arrangements had been made for parking. Some street dude had seen a vacant lot and cars piling up on the street, had broken the lock on a chain that kept cars out of the lot, and had gone into business for himself. When I asked him later how he happened to get into the parking lot business, he laughed. "Man, this street was a mess until I snapped that lock and helped you folks out. Hope you don't think $2 is high." I assured him that $2 was more than fair.

Playboy helped us and, in a strange way, harmed us. The rapid increase in circulation was dramatic, certainly relative to underground newspaper standards; however, 90 percent of the increase was to prisoners who were taking me up on my offer of "Pay $1 now and the rest when you can afford it." With no financial backing it was clear that our seemingly successful newspaper would be running out of money much sooner than I ever suspected.

ATTICA

Perhaps the most interesting feature in issue number 3, which appeared in September, was about a Minnesota prisoner. Dick Mitchell arrived at Minnesota State Penitentiary in 1959 and immediately set a record for the number of consecutive days spent by a Minnesota prisoner in solitary confinement—900 days. For months he was told that he would be moved back to the general population if he would simply make the request. He refused. "I didn't do anything to get placed in solitary and I refuse to do anything to get out." Actually, any prisoner who whistled in a Minnesota State prison hallway went to the hole. Mitchell whistled.

No prisoner, until Dick Mitchell was sent to the hole, was ever gassed for refusing to eat. Mitchell was gassed so many times that whenever guards were going to punish another prisoner with gas they would move him to Mitchell's cell first.

Mitchell was an amazing man. After his release, he finished school and became a counselor. When his cell mate, Frank Eli, later wrote his book, *The Riot*, he based the character of Indian Joe on Mitchell. How many Frank Elis and Dick Mitchells are still around?

Shortly after issue 3 went to press I was called to New York City for a series of interviews with radio and television stations. I drove there with Merrily Megletsch and Warren Levicoff, our photographer, in Elinor Cottrel's old Volvo station wagon.

Our primary purpose was to speak out on behalf of the Attica prisoners. Conditions there were intolerable. Prisoners worked in shops where temperatures were over 115 degrees, the food was poor, they were allowed one shower a week—the list of complaints was long, and the prisoners were justified in requesting changes.

On the morning of September 9, 1971, I was on the air at a radio station in Harlem. We hadn't been on the air for long when a group of men who were members of the Black Panther Party entered the station and announced that a revolt was in progress inside the prison at Attica and that the prisoners had taken over.

We immediately took a break to get the details. What we learned was that the takeover had in fact happened and that 49 guards and civilian employees had been taken hostage.

Merrily, Warren, and I were facing a dilemma. We were in New York City and we had to get to Attica—in upstate New York, 350 miles away—as quickly as possible. We had no money but we had a credit card for gas. One of the Panthers offered to loan me enough for one airline ticket to Attica and I took it. I thought it would be best if Warren was on the scene to take pictures so he got the ticket.

At 10 A.M., Merrily and I started driving. We opted for the interstates that crossed Pennsylvania. We stopped in Elmira to refill the thermos with coffee and arrived in Attica at 5:00 P.M.

On the way we had followed the radio news bulletins. Most of the news was coming from stations in Buffalo. Mutual Broadcasting, from New York City, had no reporters on the scene, so as soon as we arrived I ran to a pay phone, called Mutual, and made a deal to cover Attica for them, via telephone and tape, while we were there. Over the next three days, Merrily and I took turns on the phone.

Warren had caught a ride to the airport and was on a flight immediately. When he landed in Buffalo the first people he ran into were Herman Schwartz, the law professor from Buffalo, and lawyer Bill Kunstler, who was a member of both our national advisory board and our legal defense team. Warren didn't have to look for photo opportunities; they came to him. He was at the main gate of the prison when we arrived.

With the Mutual contact I thought we could afford a place with a roof rather than Elinor's station wagon. Across the street from the prison were homes. On the front porch of one was an older couple sitting and watching the action at the prison. I walked over and introduced myself. Not wanting to ruffle any local feathers, I mentioned my need for a room, a table for a typewriter, and a telephone to make collect calls. "Who are you working for?" the man asked me. "Mutual. The radio network for all America," I answered. "Come right in," was his reply. "We have a room overlooking the prison."

We shook hands on it. A few minutes later, while we were unloading the wagon, Fred Ferretti, from the *New York Times*, walked up and asked if there was any extra room. The *Times* didn't have a better feature writer than Ferretti. We welcomed him.

The prison had been taken at a few minutes before nine that morning. During the takeover a guard had been critically injured. He died from his injuries—the first casualty.

By nightfall we had made contact with people at the prison. A negotiating team was forming. The prisoners wanted Bill Kunstler and *New York Times* columnist Tom Wicker. Herman Schwartz became part of the team also, as did Clarence Jones, editor of the *Amsterdam News*; Arthur Eve, a New York assembly-man; David Rothenberg, Ken Jackson, and Mel Rivers, from the Fortune Society; Juan Ortiz and "G.I." Paris, from the Young Lords; Lewis Steel, from the National Lawyers Guild; Julian Tepper, another of our board members from the National Law Office; and Tom Soto, from the Prisoners' Solidarity League. Three others on the team were state senators John Dunne and Thomas McGowan and U.S. Congressman Herman Baddillo and there were others whose names I have forgotten. This remarkable group was at the prison day and night for the four days between the time the prisoners took the hostages and the time the National Guard and the state police launched their attack to retake the prison.

About 100 state police had taken back part of the prison and rescued some of the hostages late that first day.

By the next morning, family members of prisoners began showing up at the prison. They knew that the lives of everyone in the prison were at risk. Only a short space separated these parents, wives, and children from the parents, wives, and children of the hostages. Late the second day, an older woman, the mother of one of the prisoners, came down to the area in front of the main entrance and asked if there was any news

about her son. A state trooper turned and said, "Get outta here, Nigger."

The woman was stunned. Merrily ran over to her and walked her back to the group that had gathered waiting for news of prisoners. As they walked back, people in the group who were waiting for news of the hostages were yelling, "Go home, whore!" "Go back to New York City, bitch!" Those taunts accurately reflected the feelings of most of the state police, the National Guard, and the townspeople who had gathered. It was an incredibly ugly scene.

Each day the tension became greater. Each day corrections superintendent Vincent Mancusi and Walter Dunbar, a deputy director who reported directly to Russell Oswald, New York State director of corrections, answered fewer questions. Each day the number of guardsmen and state troopers arriving at the prison became greater.

It was clear that the guardsmen and troopers were becoming impatient. Cooler heads were encouraging the negotiators to keep everyone talking, hoping that the discussion would continue and that more newsmen would be allowed into the prison.

From the beginning, objective reasoning would have concluded that this riot, the prison takeover, and the taking of hostages were all the end result of many attempts by the prisoners to get Oswald and the state of New York to initiate changes at Attica.

Requests had been submitted again and again. Requests had become demands. Finally, the takeover.

ONLY CHANCE TO AVOID A MASSACRE

What were the prisoners' demands? On the list of demands by prisoners holding hostages at Attica were the formation of a grievance committee, a doctor to examine and treat prisoners, daily showers, religious freedom, fresh fruit daily, an end to pork every day, more recreation time and recreational equipment, education programs, vocational training, an end to the censorship of newspapers, magazines, and letters, and an end to slave labor.

There were also two demands—amnesty for all prisoners and transportation to a non-imperialistic country—that the prisoners knew would never be met. Amnesty may have been possible if trust could have been established between both sides, but that was not going to happen. The prisoners had the hostages, but the state had the upper hand. And Nelson Rockefeller's state had no intention of allowing these prisoners to force the state into making basic humane changes.

Helicopters had arrived with tanks of tear gas aboard. Warren was everywhere with his cameras. His pictures were pure art, his energy unlimited.

— JOSEPH W. GRANT —

Early in the evening on September 12, as it was beginning to get dark, the media were gathered around a flatbed truck. For three days I had been listening to the guards, the state troopers, the national guardsmen, and New York Department of Corrections administrators. I had spoken with Warren and he agreed with me. The guard and the police were preparing to storm the prison. Many people were going to die. The most perplexing puzzle was this: how could an army enter a tear gas-filled yard, with or without gas masks, and be able to differentiate between prisoner and hostage when the shooting started? They couldn't—and that meant that both hostages and prisoners would die during the raid and sole blame would be laid on the prisoners. The inhumane treatment that had precipitated the takeover would be lost to history.

With these thoughts I stepped up on the platform and asked the media to listen for a moment. I explained what I sincerely believed was about to happen: a takeover that would result in the deaths of hostages and prisoners. A slaughter. I told them there was only one way to stop the killing that would surely take place the next day: representatives of the nation's news media must demand the right to be exchanged for the guards who were being held hostage. I explained that—regardless of the rhetoric by the radical prisoners, regardless of the threats to kill the hostages—the solution was for the media to spend the next few days in the prison, on the yard, as hostages. The prisoners wanted to talk. They wanted us to see what it was like, to feel what it was like, to listen to the horror stories about life inside the walls of Attica.

Someone said, "The state wouldn't allow it."

"Nonsense!" I replied. "If we do it to free the guards, the families, the town, every cop in the country will say, 'Let them in.' We can demand the right to free the hostages on the front page of every paper in the country."

"Who will join me?" I asked.

There was one, then two, then a couple more. Four others were all I could convince. The others in the media turned away. They wanted no part of that story. They refused to believe what was about to happen right in front of them. And I'm sure many were simply afraid. John Linstead from the *Chicago Daily News* believed what I was saying. So did Fred Ferretti and a couple more, but not anywhere near the number necessary. From Mancusi I got a curt "Out of the question!" and a look that convinced me I was right.

The next morning, September 13, at 9:45, helicopters dumped the gas cannisters, snipers opened fire, and the police moved in. Thirty minutes or so later, ten guards and 28 prisoners were dead. Two prisoners and one guard died before the police moved in.

When the bodies of the hostages were carried out of the prison, Oswald indicated to a group of reporters that all had died at the hands of prisoners who had cut their throats, emasculated them, and stuffed their genitals in their mouths. Warren Levicoff was one of the few people covering the riots who refused to believe that the prisoners had killed the hostages. He followed the bodies to the coroner's office and he would not leave until the autopsies were completed. Sure enough, he was right. The coroner personally told him that all of the hostages had been killed by "friendly" gunfire. Their genitals were all intact.

Two months later, an article by Linstead appeared in the November 1971 *Chicago Journalism Review*. In it, Linstead noted that the exchange of newsmen for hostages might have avoided the massacre. More important, he pointed out that the establishment press had, again and again, accepted information from the state, without question, and printed it as a fact.

Almost immediately after the massacre, Bill Kunstler had been condemned by wardens, correctional officials, columnists, and an endless lineup of elected officials. Some wanted him disbarred. Again and again he would raise his voice and cry, "Remember Attica!" He would condemn Rockefeller, Oswald, and everyone who had a hand in the the shootout. Very few people would ever be aware of how long Kunstler agonized over those deaths. He and a few others understood that as long as people were talking there was hope for a settlement, as long as solutions were being discussed. As long as there was even a remote hope that a resolution was possible, the talking had to continue.

He and others who tried so desperately to avoid the bloodbath felt that they had failed all the people who suffered because of the inhumane conditions the state of New York forced upon the prisoners in Attica.

Charles Dickens once visited the Cherry Hill prison in Philadelphia and remarked that those who had devised the system didn't understand it and did not have the right to inflict such suffering on other human beings.

A society can be judged by the way its members treat its prisoners.

TWENTY-YEAR AFTERMATH TO ATTICA

Investigations into why and how the massacre took place began immediately and continue up to the present. I feel I must share the following information with you since it probably will not be carried by the mainstream media.[5]

To begin, even though Oswald had promised there would be no retaliation against prisoners, and even though he was assured that the huge amount of CS tear gas that would be dropped would totally incapacitate everyone in the yard, he sent in 150 heavily armed state troopers with orders to use whatever force they felt necessary.

Further, even though he had been ordered by the state to exclude all Attica prison guards from the assault force because of their proven record of brutality against prisoners who disobeyed orders, he allowed them to participate. The troopers and guards were joined by sheriff's deputies, park police, and unknown others.

To ensure that there were no impartial witnesses, Oswald refused to allow any members of the Observers Committee to monitor the retaking of the prison. He even denied access to those individuals Governor Rockefeller had selected to be inside the prison when the assault took place.

The state-mandated obligation to account for every round of ammunition that is expended during any law enforcement action was ignored. No attempt was made to publicly inventory weapons going into the prison before the assault.

During the assault itself, which lasted six minutes, only 450 shots were fired, according to the official report. If we only counted the 150 state troopers, 450 shots in six minutes translates to each trooper firing one shot every other minute. Outside, we heard a continuous barrage of gunfire.

Not until seven hours after the assault ended were the first wounded prisoners treated. Some prisoners bled to death waiting for medical help.

The Second Circuit Court, more than a month after the massacre, ordered that injunctive relief be granted against further brutality by guards. Proof was provided the court that

- prisoners—including those who were wounded—were stripped naked and forced to run and crawl through a gauntlet of guards, across floors covered with broken glass, while guards beat them with clubs and guns;

- both Warden Mancusi and Deputy Assistant Warden Pfeil were identified as being in the yard and cell blocks observing the beatings, yet neither exercised his supervisory authority to stop them;

- Deputy Assistant Warden Pfeil supervised the beating of prisoners in the segregation unit. He personally threatened prisoners with death and prevented doctors and lawyers with court-ordered access from entering the prison;

- all evidence was quickly destroyed by the state. Neither ammunition nor weapons were accounted for; bodies of dead prisoners were moved before

being photographed; shell casings and spent bullets were not saved. The entire scene was bulldozed over. Videotapes and photographs of the assault and its aftermath disappeared, were altered, or were destroyed.

At that hearing the barbarous conduct testified to by witnesses was taken as true by Judge Curtin and ruled as being wholly beyond any amount of force needed to maintain order. According to Curtin, "It far exceeded what our society will tolerate on the part of officers of the law in custody of defenseless prisoners."

Now, in the fall of 1991, almost twenty years to the day later, the federal civil rights action brought against Oswald, Mancusi, and Pfeil by the prisoners will be heard in federal court. The prisoners, the outside doctors, the National Guardsmen, and the observers will finally detail what the state of New York has attempted to cover up.

TOM MURTON LEADS RALLY FOR ESCAPEE

Our drive back to Iowa after the Attica massacre was slow and arduous. Physically and emotionally we were completely exhausted. We had first returned to New York City to discuss what had happened with other prisoners' rights advocates and to take care of some TV obligations we had made. On one of the network panel shows, I found myself sitting next to attorney Roy Cohn. I asked him if his years as a hatchetman for right-wing Wisconsin senator Joe McCarthy during the Communist witchhunt years of the early fifties had made it difficult to spend time alone. So that the microphones wouldn't pick up his voice, he leaned close to me and asked, "What's real, Grant? What's really real?" After Attica I had no answers.

On our way back home, we stopped for meetings in Columbus, Ohio, and in Chicago. Finally we were back in Iowa City and surrounded by our *PDI* family at 505.

We were pleased to learn that the Roy Childers case was moving forward. A report from the Hawkeye chapter of the Iowa Civil Liberties Union had "taken a stand behind [the] escaped convict who [was] fighting extradition back to the Arkansas prison he had broken out of last July."

In the meantime, Joe Johnston was devoting most of his time to Roy's case. By the time we got back, he had made arrangements for a meeting with Governor Robert Ray. Since Iowa and Arkansas had extradition agreements, the only way we could keep Roy in Iowa indefinitely was with Governor Ray's help. Ray was a conservative Republican, but we were holding rallies around the state, the national press was showing up, and we had a cause célèbre on our hands.

Tom Murton came to Iowa for a series of rallies. Murton, the first Ph.D. penologist ever, and the former warden at Tucker Prison Farm (on his way to being appointed Arkansas Director of Corrections), had shaken up the state of Arkansas and the nation when he took over and did away with the rifle-carrying inmate trustees (who could win parole by shooting an escapee) and the Tucker telephone (where guards would connect electrical leads to a prisoner's genitals and crank up the electricity—just for fun), ended the selling of young men to the wheeler-dealers who used them as prostitutes, and discovered the field of buried prisoners who were thought to have escaped but in reality had been murdered by guards and trustees.

It was a scandal that was heard around the world. As Tom's reward for cleaning up the prison system, ending the graft, and making one of the most barbaric prison systems in the world a more humane place to serve a prison sentence, Arkansas Governor Winthrop Rockefeller betrayed and fired him. Rockefeller buckled under to those who condoned the most brutal criminality and profited by it. Think of this: Murton ended the sale of young, 14- and 15-year-old juveniles to end-of-the-line hardtimers for sexual purposes. These kids were used like whores. It was done openly with the approval of the prison administrators who received a share of the profits. Rockefeller kept the good old boys, and not only got rid of Murton, he helped blackball him.

Tom wrote a book about his experiences as superintendent of the Arkansas Prison System from February 1967 to March 1968. *Accomplices to the Crime* is not easy reading. Years later, Robert Redford would star in a movie that was Murton's story. To avoid having to pay Murton for the movie rights, Hollywood changed the name of the prison, called the main character "Brubaker," and made a ton of money. Really soured me on Redford. Terrible rip-off of a man who placed his life in jeopardy to singlehandedly clean up one of the most corrupt prison systems in the country.

He tried to teach for a while but his heart wasn't in it. Later, he moved to a small farm in Oklahoma. I spoke to him not long ago about some dates I couldn't remember clearly, an incident here and there where our paths had crossed, and I needed help remembering the name of a mutual friend. We spoke for a while. I asked him if I could drive down and videotape a series of interviews with him. He wasn't interested. "I can't do it."

I know burnout when I hear it. Tom had been in the thick of it for many, many years. He had been marked for death by proven killers and prisoners who were as bad as the worst his adversaries could recruit, assassins who had killed other prisoners and, to save work, cut up the bodies so they could be stuffed into smaller holes.

He had had enough.

But he was major force in helping us with Roy's case. With Murton describing the Arkansas prison system, and with Roy, his wife, and the twins standing by for interviews and photos, we generated tremendous favorable publicity. By the time I returned from Attica, we had petitions with over 5,000 signatures from all over the United States supporting Roy. We felt confident Governor Ray would bend to the will of the people and refuse to sign the extradition papers.

Roy, however, was still acting up and making life difficult for Jeanne, his wife. We met with him and asked him to understand that successfully fighting the extradition was not only keeping him out of prison, it was also forcing Arkansas to rush forward with the changes they had to make in their entire prison system to bring it within the constitutional guidelines that Federal Judge Henley had set forth.

Roy was having an impact on correction in the United States whether he liked it or not. Sitting here today remembering Roy, Jeanne, and the twins, I'm amazed at the inconsistencies of so many of the causes we championed. Roy was a former trustee and unquestionably a bully, a wife beater, and not an easy person to deal with. It helped that I was a pacifist because again and again I wanted to grab him and kick his ass. We were trying to use his case, his plight, to make a point about all prisons, not just the prisons of Arkansas. A damn good attorney was not only spending a great deal of time on his case and getting no fee, the attorney was spending his own money on the case.

SUBSCRIPTION DRIVES INSIDE THE WALLS

As usual during this period, lack of money was a persistent problem. Subscriptions were still coming in from prisoners—at a dollar each. In meetings to discuss the problem, we would resolve to work harder so that prisoners who didn't have six dollars could get a subscription for a dollar.

While we were laying out the October issue—issue number five—Becky and I were invited to visit the Federal Penitentiary at Lewisburg, Pennsylvania, by John Wagner, a prisoner who had been the chaplain's clerk at Leavenworth and was now an active Jaycee in Lewisburg. He had lobbied the prison chapter of Jaycees to have a subscription drive for the *PDI* and wanted me to tour the prison, speak to a gathering of the prisoners, and meet with the chapter members.

A few years after inciting the boycott of French wines through my article in issue 5 of the *PDI*, I would organize another action that would result in all South African wines being removed from all Iowa liquor stores. Our state legislator at the time had married into a South African family and afterwards was responsible for the lobbying effort that caused the state of Iowa to purchase the South African wine. Unfortunately, his South African connection was never investigated, so I planned what I thought was an interesting tactic to get him into court and at the same time make a "joyful" noise about Iowa doing business with a racist country. After all the South African wine was pulled off the shelf I contacted the commissioner in charge of that department and told him I was willing to buy all the wine. After buying it, I was going to destroy it in a public spectacle that would be part of our educating the public about South Africa.

Actually, I was going to arrive with a truck and a team of "workers" to load the wine, but instead of paying for it and loading it we were going to video tape the team destroying the wine, which was state property, and then leave. Our video record would be the best evidence against what was clearly a criminal act. The tape also would insure that the destruction of the South African wine would be seen on TV news shows across the country with an explanation of why it took place. We would plead not guilty in order to get into court for a trial. During the trial the legislator would be forced to testify about the lobbying effort and the strings that were pulled to get the state to buy the wine. Once that was done, I would pay for the wine—make restitution, so-to-speak.

On the day of the action I was called by the commissioner, who informed me that the wine had been moved to a location that he would not reveal until I paid him in advance. Someone who was part of my team of seven had informed them of our plans. One in seven. Bad odds. But the wine was off the shelves and the state cancelled all future orders. So it goes.

This visit became the first of a series of subscription drives that would pay the monthly printing bills. That night, we were the featured guests at a banquet. Jimmy Hoffa presented Becky and me with bricks from the prison wall to commemorate the work we were doing to tear down the walls that restricted prisoners from viewing the free world and prevented members of the free world from better understanding what was happening inside.

I had met Jimmy Hoffa once years before and believed him to be a remarkable man who, contrary to what most people were led to believe, never mishandled a penny of Teamster union money. Hoffa ended up in prison because certain members of the federal attorney general's office had an extraordinary dislike for him. They disliked him because he was a strong union organizer who had stood toe-to-toe with the goon squads hired by the giant corporations to crush the unions.

Hoffa liked the *PDI*, but most of all he liked the idea that a group of people had gathered together to work for no pay on a cause they collectively cherished. He knew about working for a cause. That evening during dinner he slipped me a note and told me to call the people on the list.

"What do you want me to tell them?" I asked.

"Tell them you are a non-profit, tax-exempt corporation, and that I asked you to call them."

Later, I would do just that. Every call I made resulted in a contribution from a Teamster local.

Our visit to Lewisburg was the first of many trips that Becky and I took around the country. She loved to drive and could drive for long periods of time. The energy of youth.

As a result of John Wagner's efforts, we received $2,000 in new subscriptions. Less than 10 percent of the prisoners had opted for the dollar subscription price. Most had spent six dollars; some had spent nine. That plus a tour of the prison plus a banquet: I couldn't believe that a prisoner had pulled it off. Later I learned that John had been a super wimp for the better part of his prison life. He had been abused and used. He was weak. But something happened to him when he contacted us after seeing the first issue of the *PDI*. He believed it gave him a broader perspective on prison life and his social status as a prisoner. Reading about the political activism of other prisoners, and gaining a better perspective of his own position in the pecking order, he decided to make a change. As an inmate editor on the *PDI* staff he had found himself. He had taken up a cause, and the cause, so to speak, had set him free. Being able to involve himself in something outside of himself—and outside of the prison itself—had freed him from the limitations of the prison, he told me. His activism increased his stature in the eyes of a respected and responsible element of the prison's population. He was never going to be a fighter in the physical sense, but he became a fighter for prisoner rights, and in that role he became fearless. He wasn't afraid of anyone.

A few months later, during a prisoner strike in Lewisburg, he emerged as a spokesperson for the prisoners. He would pay dearly for stepping into that leadership role.

With issue number 5 we once again alienated some of the prisoners who felt it was wrong to "blow the whistle" on anyone for any reason. I spoke of what we were going to do when Becky and I were at Lewisburg. Many prisoners were upset.

Here's what happened: The use of heroin had been growing more serious with each passing year. I had seen on many occasions the hell addicts went through when they were locked up with no access to drugs. On a trip to the East Coast I met two ex-cons I had known at Leavenworth who were involved in some illegal activities that put them in contact with the drug trade. One of them was a courier who, by a variety of circuitous routes, was involved with smuggling. Both had recently been "burned" and asked me what I would do if I had a list of the main heroin processing plants in two of the major port cities.

I had to think about that for a while. When I questioned them and learned that the plants were condoned by the French government, I thought of a way we could bring more information about drug trafficking to the public. Most people know that the great majority of drug sellers who end up in prison are the users who sell to support their habits. These are the people who are the least dangerous and the least important. They are also the most vulnerable, and they receive the most publicity. But people never hear about the protection the processors and large suppliers get from governments. I decided I wanted the list, provided they would vouch for the authenticity of the list. They did, and they gave me the addresses and phone numbers.

In the lead story of issue 5, we called for a boycott of French wines until the labs were closed down. When I broke the news of the soon-to-be-published story at one of the federal maximum security prisons, some felt that I had violated the code of silence, one of those customary laws of prison behavior that are so damned interesting. Most, however, liked that I was breaking with that tradition. I liked the idea of closing the processing plants and doing so with considerable publicity.

There was much picketing of liquor stores that carried French wines. In Iowa City the picket lines were made up of *PDI* staff, college activists, and union members, and the ensuing publicity was effective. The plants were soon vacant and the *PDI*'s circulation increased. No one with any knowledge of the drug trade, me included, thought that the closing of the plants would mean anything positive in the end. It didn't. They moved. At the most our "publicity drive" created a minor inconvenience. That we had any effect was gratifying (see sidebar 4).

WOMEN PRISONERS PROTEST

The lead story in issue number six was a letter about the demonstrations that had been taking place inside the Oklahoma State Prison for Women at McAlester. For two years, incident after incident had created an anger among the prisoners that finally led to a riot. A letter from a black prisoner reflected the desperation that the prisoners felt. Fights between blacks and whites, she wrote, were resolved with the blacks being locked in solitary confinement in the cells that Oklahoma uses to teach prisoners conformity.

The letter addressed issues that went back to 1969 when a woman died because the prison doctor refused to give her medical care. "She is faking," the doctor had maintained. The woman had spent three days in the "hospital" room—a room with six beds and a toilet. Although she was unable to eat, no attempts were made to provide her with nourishment intravenously or to take her to the local hospital. Shortly after her death a sister prisoner went before the parole board. Instead of appealing to the board for parole, however, she chose to inform the board of the senseless death. She was labeled a "troublemaker" and denied parole.

While Rex Fletcher was still a prisoner he attempted to alert the public to what was happening in the women's prison, but to no avail. In the free world, letters from prisoners generate no media interest unless they contain specific information that concerns some sexual aberration. The media generally follow up such an instance by calling the warden for an explanation—which they invariably get. But they never get the truth, because the media have neither the inclination nor the internal channels.

After learning of this death we drove to McAlester to meet with the warden and personally ask questions. We were called "troublemakers and instigators." He added, "You people cannot come down here and tell me how to run my institution!"

Early in 1971, a woman with a history of two previous heart attacks had another attack in the hall just outside the dining room. The doctor who answered the call said there was nothing he could do for her. He returned to the dining room to finish his lunch. Then he called an ambulance. In November 1971, a woman with epilepsy suffered an attack at 10 A.M. in the same area. She was left on the floor until 5:30 P.M. when the doctor returned from Springtown.

Copies of the letter and copies of the *PDI* were sent to all the state legislators, the governor, and the elected federal officials. Our Lawyers Guild contacts and the Oklahoma Civil Liberties Union were also informed. As a result of our efforts, the medical facilities were upgraded somewhat and treatment of prisoners showed some improvement. Hardly enough, but something.

The staff of the *PDI* was being called to emergency situations involving prisoners in every part of the country. The stress on us all was great. What kept people going was the knowledge that fellow human beings were living in situations that made our lives look like dream jobs. We were free, Cathy was providing us with two of the best meals we could ask for each day, and we had our evenings together, along with a constant stream of visitors from around the country and the world.

And we had a purpose. Fulfilling that purpose kept us on our toes 24 hours a day.

PDI ENDS INNOCENT INDIAN BOY'S SIX YEARS IN PRISON

I was asked by a prisoners group to speak at the Iowa reformatory in Anamosa. When requests like that arrived I tried to turn the session into more than me speaking. I'd ask to bring musicians and singers because prisoners seldom heard live entertainment.

On this occasion I spoke, the band played, and everyone had a good time. As we were leaving a young Indian approached me.

"Do you have a minute?"

I said I did and he told me he was 19 years old. "They are going to transfer me to Fort Madison tomorrow because I will not cooperate with them."

"What's the problem," I asked him.

"To begin with I have been locked up since I was 13 and I have never committed a crime, been charged with a crime, or been tried for a crime."

As soon as you have any indication that there is a serious problem you get the person's name and number as fast as you can. Invariably the guards will see you with a "troublemaker" and they will come over and tell the prisoner to "move it on out."

With his name and number I asked him what had happened.

He said he had been sent to Eldora, the Iowa youth prison, when he was 13 because he ran away from home. He couldn't handle life at Eldora so he ran away from there. They caught him and brought him back. He ran away again and they caught him again. And again. After three years of this, when he turned 16, they sent him to Anamosa. He was no more cooperative there than he had been at Eldora. Now the state of Iowa was going to teach him the ultimate lesson. They were going to send him to Fort Madison to do some time with the men. He'd damn sure regret not cooperating at Anamosa.

I asked him my stock question. "Is everything you have told me the truth?" He said it was. "If anything you've told me isn't exactly the way you said it was, please tell me now."

"Everything I have told you is the truth."

He knew what was in store for him at the Fort and it wasn't going to be pretty. He didn't have a friend to turn to for help. He was trying to save his emotional life when he walked up to me that day.

I told him he would hear from me before the day was over. Or, if I didn't get back to him today I would be at the prison personally first thing in the morning.

Anamosa is only 45 minutes from Iowa City. Back at 505 I called around to verify that he had no criminal record or outstanding charges. His record was clean. The kid had never committed a crime and had been locked up for six years. I called the director of corrections and explained to him the young man's situation. I assured the director that I was certain he had been unaware of the problem. However, I said, "Now you *are* aware of the problem. If you don't place that young man in a minimum security situation NOW, we will drive to your office with a TV crew first thing tomorrow morning."

"Does the prisoner have a lawyer yet?" he asked.

"I'm making arrangements now. What civil actions will be taken I do not know."

The young man walked out of the prison less than an hour later, spent a few days on the farm, and was discharged.

I called the director back that night and thanked him for acting immediately.

"That young man was lucky he met you today," he said.

"No," I answered, "You and I are lucky I met him today, because if anything had happened to that boy it would have been bad for everyone in the state of Iowa—particularly you."

He agreed. We spoke for a while and before the conversation ended he mentioned that he had already set the wheels moving to determine if any other people were doing time in Iowa who had not committed a crime.

In the Law Section we ran the complete decision in the case of a Virginia prisoner, Robert J. Landman, who had filed a civil action against the director of the Virginia Department of Corrections, M.L. Royster, et al.—the "et al." in this case being the superintendent of the state penitentiary and the superintendent of the state farm.

This case was important because it forced the state to stop using certain forms of punishment, including bread and water diets, chains, leg irons, and others. The case contained a number of important court orders, but perhaps the most important was that the state list the rules and regulations concerning standards of expected prisoner behavior and minimum and maximum punishments that could be accorded those who violated these rules and regulations. In addition, the court ordered that the rules had to be posted and made available to all prisoners.

That step was an important tool in ending the arbitrary and capricious use of rules and non-rules by guards against prisoners. Now, if it wasn't in the book, it didn't exist.

With the assistance of Steve Fox, a psychology professor from the University of Iowa, we formed the National Prison Center (NPC). According to our original statement of purpose for the NPC's formation, which was published in the November/December 1971 issue of the *PDI*: "The Center's activities would be conducted in a 'closed-loop' manner, with constant cooperation and reciprocation between prisoners, ex-convicts and professionals and paraprofessionals on the NPC staff. Central emphasis [would be] on the removal of barriers between those working for prison change on the inside and their brethren outside the walls." Someone asked, "What about the sistern?"

Response was favorable.

GRATEFULLY, HE DIDN'T ORDER 1,000 SUBSCRIPTIONS

Early one morning, Merrily found me sitting quietly in the office. I had been up all night trying to figure out how I was going to pay for the January issue. When she saw me she said, "Is it that bad?" I nodded and she handed me the morning mail.

As usual the envelopes were filled with cashier's checks and one-dollar bills. One envelope contained a typed letter with the check. I added the check to the pile and read the letter. The writer, a lifer at the Wisconsin State Penitentiary in Waupon, was more articulate than most prisoners in his praise for the *PDI*. When I got to the final paragraph I looked up at Merrily, caught her eye, and pointed to the check on the top of the stack.

"What is it?" she asked.

"I think I know, but I'm afraid to look."

Merrily reached over and picked it up. The look on her face told me I was right. "How about an early morning walk to the bank?"

"Exactly what I was thinking." I handed her the letter.

These are the final two paragraphs:

If we expect meaningful reform within the prisons of this country, and help for our wives and families, we can't just sit back, as most of

our brethren outside the walls seem to be doing these days, and "Let the other guy do it." If ever self-help is God's help had any meaning, it does in the instant case. We gotta put our money where our mouths are.

Your publication must not fail. It is with pleasure and with hope that I have instructed Mr. William Konkel of the Marine National Exchange Bank to place a certified check made out to the Penal Digest International along with this letter in the sum of $1000, as my contribution toward your fine efforts. I only wish at this time that it could be more.

Good wishes and good luck,
August K. Bergenthal

Merrily, Sam, and I walked to the bank, dropped the deposit in the night depository, circled back by Hamburg Inn #1, and returned to 505.

Sam had been a resident of 505 for the past few months, since he was dropped off there by a fellow who had lost an appeal. "Would you take care of him until I get back?" the fellow asked. We couldn't say no and Sam became Iowa City's best-known dog. Actually Sam was more hobo than dog. Every day after breakfast with Margie Staack and Shar, he would make the rounds of the construction sites looking for handouts. He'd begin on the north side of downtown, where he'd visit the sites during morning coffee breaks. Then he would hang around the downtown sites for lunch. Afternoon breaks would find him in the area of Blackhawk mini park. Drive by the park after 3:30 and Sam might jump through your car window for a ride back to 505. Whenever I saw him sniffing around downtown I expected him to pick up a cigar butt, get up on his hind legs, and ask for a light.

Sam's fearlessness could send the biggest, most aggressive dogs running for their lives. Ranging ahead of us to check for strays, he'd suddenly make a quick turn and race past us to check the rear. If a dog was within 100 feet Sam would charge. Dogs always turned and ran.

Groucho Marx once said, "Outside of a dog a book is man's best friend. Inside of a dog it's too dark to read," or something to that effect.

When we got back to 505 I called the warden at Waupon and arranged for an immediate visit with August K. Bergenthal.

Augie was a tall, thin man in his sixties. I never ask prisoners what they're serving time for; however, early in our conversation Augie told me he'd been found guilty of murder one. I believed him when he insisted he was innocent, not because he had given us a thousand dollars but because as I came to know him

I became convinced that he was not capable of taking a life. A few years later, after many years in prison, it was learned that evidence had been suppressed and witnesses had perjured themselves in his case. He was released.

We spent our time together that day talking about the business end of the *PDI*. He was bright and alert, an astute businessman and a natural teacher; I had no business experience and was becoming discouraged. People were responding to the *PDI*, but they all had no money. Still, when I spoke to him, I expressed enthusiasm and recapped our fairly successful track record.

After our talk he shook his head and offered a sad appraisal of our chances for survival. "You have wonderful ideas, Joe, and the *PDI* is probably the most important single tool to help prisoners that has ever come along, but you'll never make it without foundation help or government help. You'll never get government help because government is the cause of the problem and you'd have to get in bed with them to get their money. If the foundations haven't rejected you yet, they will. They rarely give money to radicals. You can't ask for money for your halfway house because as soon as you do the public will know who the people at 505 are and they'll chase you out of town. You're wise to reject advertising because no one would advertise with you anyway. If you don't already understand how serious your problem is, I'm going to regret having given you a thousand dollars."

I was completely amazed. Through my forced enthusiasm, he had seen the weak foundation upon which the *PDI* had been built.

"What should I do?" I asked him.

"Do you want the truth?" I nodded.

"Unless you can find a business manager and someone who knows the magazine business and someone with the financial ability to fund a subscription drive, you won't make it."

"How come my board of directors hasn't seen what you've seen?"

"Because they haven't been looking."

One thing I liked about Augie—he gave us money first and advice second. I was quick to admit we needed both.

"I know," he said.

We talked for the full three hours we were allowed. When we parted, he invited me back and said he would be thinking of ways he could help us.

Back in Iowa City the *PDI* staff was busy with issue number seven. With the $2,000 from the Lewisburg subscription drive, and now the donation from Augie, we were solvent again, possibly for as long as two months. A benefit concert was being planned. As

I recall, Country Joe and the Fish and five or six other groups wanted to help.

Having money to pay bills was a great feeling. I hated to part with the money, of course, but I loved the act of paying bills. I detested the collectors, but I would walk in with a smile, a handshake, and a good word for everyone. They didn't care as long as the money was there. The most critically important public relations plan you have to develop if you are barely solvent is with the companies who can shut you down. In our case it was the printer, the utilities, and the bank where we made our house payment. Their collectors were people who had heard every story, knew all the scams, and had sat through the tears, screams, and curses.

For them, I worked hard to choreograph a production number. I made it a point to always pay our utility bills a few days late. Whenever possible I'd pay them in person. It cost a little extra but I got to know the staff. After a few months it became a standing joke. I'd be late, but they knew I would show up and they'd get their money. I'd write out a check that was a few dollars less than the bill and make up the difference in cash and change. I'd even show up if I didn't have money. Showing up to talk to a creditor before the creditor showed up to talk to me was a MUST. At times, I was able to keep the utilities turned on even when we had gone far past the point when they normally pulled the plugs.

The front page of number seven was a powerful photograph by George Armitage that showed the silhouette of a prisoner in his cell, his hands on the bars. That photo would be used by publications all over the world. It was one of five or six that I thought were award winners. This issue also included more of Warren Levicoff's photos from Attica.

The cartoons included many more by Chas DuRain, editor of the newspaper inside the Kentucky penitentiary. DuRain and Drummond, from Leavenworth, had become favorites with prisoners. Both were talented artists who had that unique ability to spot unusual incidents and render them as editorial cartoons. By using humor they were able to comment on many of the ugly, painful situations inside the walls and get by with it.

In this issue John Severenson Watson took the journalism department at Southern Illinois University (SIU), in Carbondale, to task for the awards they handed out as part of the 1971 Penal Press Contest, which SIU sponsored. He started off by pointing out that Joe Milani, editor of the *Joliet-Statesville TIME* "had been screaming for years about the inequities of the Urbandale [sic] thing." Topping Watson's list of complaints was that *The Presidio*, from Iowa State Penitentiary, came in third in the magazine category but was awarded the Charles Clayton Award, which is the highest prison journalism award SIU gives. Watson wrote that the "Sweepstakes Divisions" included printed newspapers and magazines and mimeographed publications, which pitted weeklies against monthlies. "The time element alone concerning deadlines makes it two different worlds."

Watson complained further that the judges must wear blindfolds to choose *The Weekly Scene* and *The Vacavalley Star* over *The Advocate*. He also took exception to the fact that Donald Chenault, cartoonist for the *San Quentin NEWS*, only received an honorable mention. Since Chenault was reprinted in more prison publications than any prison cartoonist and restricted his themes to prison, Watson wrote, he deserved better.

Finally, Watson pointed out that only 51 institutions in 27 states submitted material to SIU for judging, an indication that many other editors shared his views.

A couple of long-timers at *PDI* believed Watson was right on all counts. The outstanding journalists within the walls were starting to question "the Urbandale thing" and the *PDI* had plans for a prison press awards program. Unfortunately, the lack of financial resources made it impossible to develop. Still, Watson was correct in his appraisal of the Penal Press Awards program from SIU's journalism department; not only were improvements needed, but there should have been more input from committed prison journalists behind the walls who were award winners.

A news article noted that Judge Leo Oxberger, from the Ninth Judicial District of Iowa, handed down a decision that took the most important step yet to end censorship in the prisons of Iowa. It started in the Polk County jail when an attorney for an inmate brought the prisoner his personal books, including many by Chairman Mao. Quoting those cases that made prisoners slaves of the state (*Price vs. Johnson*, 1948; *Ruffin vs. Commonwealth*, 1871; *Fortune Society vs. McGinnis*, 1970; *Younger vs. Gilmore*, 1971; and *Sostre vs. Otis*, 1971), Judge Oxberger cut through the crap and told the Polk County sheriff to give the man his books.

Our staff was growing. Augie had agreed to become our corporate consultant even while he was still in prison. Authors Kitsi Burkhart, Jessica Mitford, and Diane Schulder joined our national advisory board. Al Cloud, Jill Donaldson, and Becky Hensley joined the staff. Connie Klotz joined us as editorial assistant. Merrily Megletsch took on the position of assistant to the director. Richard Tanner, in charge of circulation, was training Shirley Randall and Jody Hinds to take over while he was on the road. Soon we would add Dick Hayward of the *J-S* (Joliet-Stateville) *TIME* and Donald Chenault of the San Quentin *NEWS*, two award-winning artists.

And the *PDI* was getting better. The layout was more attractive, the editing was better, and Bob Copeland carefully scrutinized every detail. With each issue, we had more to be proud of. Every month the numbers of subscribers increased.

NIMBLEWILL IS BORN AT 505

Meanwhile, the long-awaited event finally took place and life at 505 would never be the same. Cathy gave birth to a 6 1/2 pound, 17-inch baby girl.

For weeks Warren and Cathy had been pouring over books on home childbirth. They felt confident they could handle a normal birth. If an emergency arose they were five minutes away from one of the top medical centers in the country. The rest of us continued our normal level of activity. During the day of March 10, 1972, Bob and Brother Richard were at Lake Forest College for a speaking engagement. Richard had been calling in regularly to check on Cathy; when late that afternoon he was told that Cathy was in labor, he ran to the auditorium where Bob was speaking and announced that they had to leave. They thanked the folks for their hospitality and promised to return another time, jumped in a borrowed wreck of a car, and were in Iowa City four hours later. No one complained. They knew Bob Copeland at Lake Forest.

When Bob and Richard arrived at 505, Warren, Merrily, and local artist/photographer Connie Hanson were on the third floor attending to Cathy. Throughout the night they sang, held hands, toked, timed contractions, and got themselves into the spirit of the occasion.

Early the next morning, March 11, at 6:40 A.M., with Bob, Richard, and Merrily as official greeters, Warren as catcher, and Connie as official photographer, Nimblewill was born. One of Connie's extraordinary photos, of Cathy holding her little Nimblewill, back lighted against the west window, was used in issue seven, which, because we were running late as usual, was the January issue. Brother Richard described the occasion and the birth:

> Suddenly there was a body bathed in juices and already abuses from the journey just begun from there to infinity as the cord reached from the child back into yesterday and was cut away leaving only the present and the delicate administerings of Father Warren working with seven hands across the body of his and her woman-child taking mucus from the mouth and nose that grows like a button there on the face which has already opened its eyes to the world to greet we five with the flash of blue from the waters somewhere and the child was looking for somewhere to hide

away from today while Mother Cathy's sobs subsided into a soft blues-song of begging for her child to lay upon her breast to feel and see and smell and hear the senses of nature played lively upon the instrument of good faith and good vibes and... good morning, Sister Nimblewill.

One paragraph from a page of paragraphs with picture—Cathy and Nimblewill, our 505 people, a beautiful little child—a birth. What incredible good fortune for us all.

The next day Becky and I returned home from Washington, DC, to that new, special feeling. The birth of Nimblewill was a magic moment that lingered long after she, Cathy, and Warren moved to Maui.

Another article that was to take on a growing significance informed prisoners all over the world that the Church of the New Song (CNS) had held its first church service on March 6 inside the federal prison in Atlanta, Georgia. Six hundred prisoners attended. Prisoner church ministers who spoke at this first gathering were co-founder Jerry Dorrough (fellow co-founder Harry Theriault had been transferred to an undisclosed federal prison and was in solitary confinement) and Herbert E. Juelich. Church members referred to themselves as Eclatarians, from the French "eclater," meaning "to break forth with brightness." Eclatarians were to live naturally, avoid loneliness, and strive for inner peace. Part of this "living naturally" was interpreted by the group that had gathered as never having to shave or to subject themselves to haircuts.

In the middle of the meeting a black prisoner stood up and asked why there were no black members on the CNS Central Committee. Dorrough pointed out that blacks had been invited to sit on the committee. Another black prisoner stood and said, "As long as we got conflicts with one another, we're doing what the administration wants."

At the end of the brief article prisoners were invited to send requests for information to the church's prison address.

This was the first time prisoners had been asked to respond to another group of prisoners. With the exception of married couples who were locked up, such correspondence was against the rules of every prison in the country without special permission. After the invitation appeared in issue number seven, every state and federal prisoner in the United States and Canada knew about CNS. The response would send a shock wave throughout the federal and state prison systems.

ON THE ROAD WITH THE *PDI*

In the February 1972 issue John Wagner emerged as a man who was much more than a huckster who could promote a successful subscription drive within the walls of the federal prison at Lewisburg. John had come a long way from his days in Leavenworth where he was involved with the choir, the chaplain, and the Trailblazer Jaycees. He had probably heard the words "prisoners rights" previous to picking up his first copy of the *PDI*, but he had never given it a second thought. That he had obligations to other prisoners had never crossed his mind. His was a life of "doing his time" with as little pain and discomfort as possible.

When he became involved with the *PDI* he did so to help promote what he thought was a good idea. What he didn't understand then was that many duties and obligations came with the job. He learned that truth in the best way possible, by getting in the thick of the Lewisburg prison strike when it started in the spring.

With the peaceful strike in progress the population was split down the middle. You were either with the strikers or against them. Many prisoners headed for their cells and stayed there. John spoke out for the strikers. In the February issue, we published his first of two articles in a series called "Anatomy of a Prison Strike." Two months later, on April 14, he was awarded with "the road trip," the famous punitive transfer gig that the Federal Bureau of Prisons gives to any prisoner whose refusal to cooperate is deemed serious.

First *PDI* Associate Editor Wagner was forced to don travel coveralls. Then he was placed in leg irons, chained from his ankles to his waist to his wrists, handcuffed, and seated on the bus heading west. His worldly belongings were thrown into a box. His mail would never catch up to him during his solitary life on the road. Every night he stayed in solitary confinement in a different county jail or federal prison. It wasn't enough that you were a prisoner. The bureau wanted more. They wanted to make examples of people who wouldn't lie, cheat, and steal for the man. They wanted these carefully selected prisoners to spend hours chained to the seat of a bus that was either freezing cold or sweltering hot. No letters, no showers, no toothbrush, no decent meals. Just hour after hour of pounding down the highway toward another solitary cell, eating cold burgers and greasy fries twice a day, and arriving at each night's scheduled destination too late to even get a county jail meal.

Many have made the trip and many more will.

During that road trip, John spent time in solitary confinement in Terre Haute, Indiana; Leavenworth, Kansas; El Reno, Oklahoma; La Tuna, Texas; Tucson, Arizona; Terminal Island, California; and Lompoc,

California, as well as in some county jails along the way. Five weeks after he began, he arrived at the federal penitentiary on McNiel Island in the state of Washington.

There are ways to communicate in the jails and prisons—even from a solitary cell. Along the way he spoke to prisoners and shared information about the *PDI*, the folks at 505, and the strike. In return, prisoners went out of their way to bring John a cup of coffee, something to smoke, and news from the prison grapevine. In Terre Haute, he met Nat Warden, a frequent contributor to *PDI*, Pun Plamondon of the Rainbow People, John Maybery, Jay Vidovich, Johnny Sullivan, Tamie Sargis, Billy Silvers, and Rocky Bijeol. Billy "Duchess" Thompson paid him a visit in Leavenworth, as did Arthur Rachel, the *PDI* associate editor and former tier boss in the Cook County jail. John would be gone the next morning but the prisoners would contact us by mail, by phone, through family visitors, and even through guards who had not bought into the system. According to the prisoners, John told them to "Contact the *PDI* and tell 'em I'm working on a series." He didn't have pen and paper so he was writing the series in his head. His third and final article for *PDI*—his first called "On the Road: Time on the Transfer Circuit"—would appear in our June 1972 issue.

Richard Tanner and I contacted the Bureau of Prisons in Washington, DC, and were given permission to visit with John when the bus got to Leavenworth. We were there when the bus arrived, but the warden overruled the bureau and would not let us visit with John.

Instead, we sat in the van in front of the prison and wondered at the warden's enormous stupidity. Every prisoner knew why we were there. They knew we had permission from the bureau to enter and visit. Half the cells from A and B block were faced out to where we sat, so hundreds of prisoners saw us being turned away. John's status inside and ours outside the prison were both enhanced. Such arbitrary acts by prison administrators gave prisoners a hook to hang their anger on. With the *PDI*, however, the message was, "Don't react with violence—sell subscriptions, share your copy of the *PDI*, help your Brothers and Sisters."

When John arrived at McNiel Island our attorneys greeted the United States marshalls and the warden with legal briefs. However, before we could stop the harassment they had John back on the bus for a return trip to Lewisburg, Pennsylvania.

John's response was, "Let's go." He wasn't going to give them the satisfaction of thinking he was having anything but fun out there on the road. The first five weeks hadn't softened him up. He was a model prisoner, a *PDI* associate editor we were proud to have on the staff. At every stop he talked about the right of a prisoner to subscribe to the prisoners' newspaper. After every stop prisoners would send us the news about John's "visit" and their conversations with him from his solitary cell at the other end of the tier.

Our lawyers met that bus a few more times with legal briefs and just about the time they were going to drop him back in Lewisburg the bureau decided it would be to their best interests if they let John settle down a few miles from home to finish his sentence. The long journey ended in Sandstone, Minnesota, 75 miles from his home. It was a good place to finish a sentence if you didn't mind noise, bland food, giant, bloodthirsty mosquitoes in the summer, and unimaginable cold in the winter.

I FIND A RELIGION AND CHALLENGE CONTEMPORARY-PRISON-NORMAL

A few weeks after the article about the Church of the New Song (CNS) meeting in Atlanta appeared in the January issue, Richard Tanner and I were invited to join the church, become ministers, and address prisoner members in Atlanta.

I can't speak for Richard, but religion didn't, and doesn't, hold much interest for me. While at Leavenworth I had become a member of the Unitarian Universalist (UU) Fellowship because they are an organization more concerned with improving the human condition on earth than sweating out life to get a seat in heaven. I found them and their brand of religion acceptable, more acceptable than they ultimately found me. A few years later I would become the first UU to be formally excommunicated by the Unitarian Universalist church in Iowa City after I let the Air Force know what I thought of an F-86 jet fighter that was being turned into a shrine at the Iowa City airport.

Still, I welcomed the invitation because, while CNS was looked upon by prison administrators as a religious "con job," I saw it as the safest means of getting us inside the prisons under the U.S. constitution's guarantee of religious freedom so we "clergy" could discuss the rule of law with prisoners.

When we arrived at the federal prison the administrators refused to allow Richard inside. Prison administrators frequently did this to us. They would approve a request to speak at or visit a prison and then change their minds at the gate and leave us standing in the parking lot, where we were not allowed to stand for very long. I was allowed into the auditorium, but I was searched first and all my notebooks were taken away.

Before the prisoners were allowed into the hall a row of guards lined up and formed a complete semi-circle around the stage. When the doors opened to this Free Exercise Seminar, as the organizers referred to the gathering, over 1,200 prisoners, more than had ever attended a church service in a federal prison, poured into the hall to share with me three of the most memorable hours I have ever spent in prison. Many others were turned away because there weren't enough seats.

With the help of friends from Atlanta's underground newspaper, the *Great Speckled Bird*, I had arranged for some musicians to appear with us that day. The musicians were sensational. They rocked that auditorium like it had never been rocked. Then it was my turn.

Earlier at the gate, Richard had written and given me a note to the prisoners when he learned he was being barred from entering the prison. Somehow when I was searched, his note had been missed. I read Richard's message to the prisoners. Then I asked them to let Richard know how much they appreciated his coming all the way from Iowa City only to be refused admittance.

The roar so exceeded my expectation that I was stunned. The guards in front of the stage damn near turned and ran. They were nervously glancing at the prisoners, then at each other, then at me, and all the while trying to speak to each other, trying to be heard over the deafening roar of the prisoners. The solid stone and steel surfaces caused the sound to ricochet back and forth across the hall. Whistles and screams bouncing off the floor, the ceiling, and the walls magnified the sound.

After eight or ten minutes, when the prisoners were back in their seats and quiet, I spoke about the obligation we as prisoners and ex-prisoners had to bring the rule of law into the prisons. With my outline gone I simply shared with them what we had been writing about in the *PDI* and planning back at 505, ideas about how to negotiate conflict in this violent environment that prisoners had been forced to believe was contemporary-prison-normal.

I talked about the concerns prisoners were writing us about and told them how legislators were sitting down with us to discuss the beatings and killings and violence that could be controlled only by prisoners. I shared the discussions that went on late into the night at 505 and mile after mile on the road as we drove from prison to prison to prison.

I could hardly believe what was happening. There were no divisions in the crowd, no cliques. This spontaneous "coming together" of 1,200 hearts and minds and shared concerns seemed to generate its own revolutionary energy. You could actually see the ground and walls move.

Outside, Richard heard the roar slowly building and the ground beginning to shake. He watched as tower guards called security to find out what was happening and picked up their rifles in preparation for what sounded like trouble.

"I thought it was time to circle the wagons," a guard told me a few hours later.

The cordon of guards lining the front of the stage locked their arms and tightened up into a human wall, but as the band picked up the rhythm of the crowd with a closing song the prisoners simply walked through the line of guards. No one was pushed or hurt, they just walked through.

The stage was suddenly packed with prisoners. As a result of the front gate shakedown my pockets had been emptied. Suddenly I had eight or ten letters, some of them dangerously thick, and many small, folded notes stuffed in my pockets, socks, and belt. The guards couldn't possibly see what was happening, but then it didn't matter. I had been searched coming in and would probably be searched going out. If I was caught with signed letters there would certainly be trouble for the prisoners who had written them and trouble for me. By the time the guards cleared the stage I was standing there with my pockets loaded, holding five oil paintings that prisoners had also given me along with a half dozen books and a large walnut plaque that proclaimed me head of the church in the free world.

The guards surrounded me before I could get rid of the letters and they led me out a side door. Once we were outside the auditorium I was able to feel what had been happening. The roar from the crowd had not diminished. I leaned close to one of the guards so he could hear me. "These paintings have been cleared by the AW (Associate Warden). Security has cleared the books, but you guys will have to take them through the gate for me. I came in with nothing and that's the way I'm leaving."

It was a gamble. They nodded and I divided all the paintings, the books, and the plaque between them while we stood in the hall waiting for the band and their prison guard escorts. As soon as they joined us, we were walked to the front gate and then through to the outside. There, the guards handed me the books, the paintings, the engraved plaque, and, whether they knew it or not, a tremendous sense of relief that I was walking without a search. I was so sick with the anxiety and fear of the anticipated search that I almost threw up.

Richard was pacing up and down the sidewalk at the base of the long flight of stairs. When the door swung open and he saw us he ran up the stairs and helped me with the paintings.

"I thought there was trouble, Bro. It sounded like a riot was starting."

Richard chuckled at the thought. "We do not need a riot!" He didn't seem surprised at all the paintings

I was carrying but then again Richard rarely showed surprise.

Late that night we sat with friends from the *Great Speckled Bird* and talked about what had happened. The musicians had never had that kind of an experience. They speculated that it was going to be happening right across the country.

"Let's call Reidsville and see if we can do this down there," one of them offered.

"And then on to 1600 Pennsylvania Avenue," I said. "The White House will be easier than Reidsville."

Certainly we had the means and we had the message, but Reidsville, where the Georgia State Prison was located, would later refuse to let the *PDI* inside.

We talked about elections inside the prisons, not just of representatives on an inmate council but of tier bosses, real representatives, elected on ability and merit, to head negotiating teams that resolved conflicts in their immediate living area.

We would develop teams of "ministers" who were serious about opening up the prisons and bringing the rule of law to the prisoners. We'd need access to educational programs for prisoners who wanted to help. Conflict resolution must become as important as showers. If the prisoners could keep the prison clean, keep it organized, and keep everyone fed, they should be able to work out a way to keep the environment peaceful. With teams from the free world coming into the prisons on a regular basis, there was a good chance that we could counter the ongoing efforts by administrators and guards to fragment the population along racial lines.

We were positive that the means had been handed us to bring the issues and the solutions directly to the prisoners. On the drive back to 505 we stopped in Chattanooga, Nashville, Evansville, St. Louis, Jefferson City, and Leavenworth. We couldn't get into any of the jails and prisons but we always parked the van where the prisoners could see that the *PDI* was there trying to get back in.

When we got back to 505, we learned that the Federal Bureau of Prisons had issued an order that I was never to be allowed back into a federal prison as a speaker. A year later I would be allowed into Leavenworth to watch prisoners get GED certificates, but I had four guards with me at all times. If 25 prisoners had shown up to the church service in Atlanta and we had given them all gift prayerbooks and hummed a few bars of "Onward Christian Soldiers" we would have been welcomed back into every joint in the country.

Our experience in Atlanta was reported in the March issue. The entire trip had seemed too good to be true. Prisoner response to the idea of having their own religion was greater than we had even dreamed it would be. Other prisoners would learn of it through the *PDI*. The power of the newspaper was apparent. We had to use that power carefully. As it turned out we wouldn't be careful enough.

Peter Breggin, M.D., wrote the front-page article, "Psychiatry in the Prisons." As a faculty member of Washington School of Psychiatry, he had campaigned vigorously and extensively against psychosurgery. His book, *After the Good War*, reflected his political concerns and his ability to tell a great story.

Another article, by Dr. Richard Korn, a professor from the Berkeley School of Criminology, was built around Korn's testimony before the Senate Judiciary Committee. Dr. Korn was an energetic man with a keen sense of humor and an eloquent voice that was frequently raised on behalf of prisoners and other underdogs. In Cleveland one afternoon he gave me a copy of a poem he had written about his father. The poem had been enlarged and silk-screened on heavy, poster-sized, paper. Later, framed and matted, it was too much of a temptation to someone and was ripped off.

THE TOTAL PARTICIPATION PUBLICATION

The April/May issue had 56 pages and two supplements. In the January issue, we had informed our prison readers that Tom Murton was planning to publish a monthly journal, *The Freeworld Times*, under the sponsorship of The Murton Foundation for Criminal Justice. To inform prisoners that the new publication was available, our first supplement was a 12-page insert edition of Tom's first issue. At the time Tom was a criminology professor at the University of Minnesota. For some reason the prisoners never accepted *The Freeworld Times*.

This was a painful time for Tom. He had challenged some of the most dangerous, most corrupt politicians and had won the battle while losing the war. He had stood up to assassins with pens, assassins with knives and guns, and the elected assassins with the power to legislate. I remember Tom saying that his newspaper would "pierce the facade of reform and shed some light on the efficacy of prison reform efforts." He never had a chance. In Arkansas he proved that he was a reformer who could not be bought. For thanks, he was thrown out on his ear and blackballed.

I had not missed a single move the establishment made in their treatment of Tom Murton. When people in the Federal Bureau of Prisons, in the courts, in Des Moines around the capitol, and in many a foundation office told me that I would get financial assistance from funding agencies if I would be less outspoken, I knew they were wrong. They may have believed what they were telling me, but I knew that if a legitimate reformer and now university teacher like Tom couldn't get help, there was nothing anyone could do to get help. We'd proceed as originally intended. We'd be the free world voice for the imprisoned for as long as we could. We were not going to modify our message or refuse to print the letters and articles from our prison editors for any reason.

CREATION: The Arts in Prison, a slim little magazine of poetry, art, and fiction by prisoners, also premiered in this issue. In order to add *CREATION* to this press run without busting our budget, I had to come up with some way to cut the costs without offending our subscribers. Here's what I did:

CREATION started out as a 12-page tabloid with a quarterfold. The gutter of the quarterfold was glued on each page and the other sides were untrimmed, giving us a 24-page magazine that couldn't be opened. But trimming would have cost us more money—and we didn't have it. So, I drew a dotted line across the top of the cover, down the right edge, and across the bottom to the bottom left corner. Printed along this dotted line were the instructions: "Cut along dotted line and become the final participant in a total participation publication."

As soon as some of our graphic designer friends at Playboy saw *CREATION* they called us to say it was the first really original idea they had seen in many years. I told them there wasn't much originality in having your readers slice the pages ("Instead of each other," as someone at my elbow offered). It was just an interesting way to get them to participate in the creation of *CREATION*.

The next time I saw Don Myrus; he was holding an uncut copy of *CREATION*. "It's a great idea, Joe. I wish I had thought of it."

"Yeh," I said, "but you also thought it was a great idea to offer a set of Playboy books to prison libraries and look where that got you."

One other article in the April/May issue contained the results of a special survey on county jail conditions. Extensive information had been gathered by prisoners who had spent time in the jails. This issue contained much information that was picked up by free world dailies from cities whose county jails made the survey.

THE *PDI* GOES TO COLLEGE

The next issue, June, marked our first anniversary. It was an exciting anniversary for us all, despite our financial strains.

The two months leading up to the June issue had been one of the busiest periods in the life of the *PDI*. We were involved with all the day-to-day work and we were helping with the development of the Church of the New Song. A few weeks earlier I had been in Clinton, Iowa, for some reason, being shown around the town by a fellow some of the folks at 505 called White Man, not because he was a racist but because he was so absolutely Mr. Average, straight, American male that he just didn't appear to fit in with the 505 crowd.

Clinton is a working class river town with a rich political history of supporting labor and regularly electing Socialist mayors. On the drive through town that day we passed a beautiful old campus that had been John Neumann College for many years and then, for a while, a Catholic girls school, Our Lady of Angels Academy. Now, it was closed and for sale by the Redemptorist Order. I asked my friend to stop so I could explore my sudden inspiration for a home, a printing plant, a college, and government funding.

The college sat on a hill overlooking the Mississippi River. The main building was a huge, old mansion with rooms for about 300 students and faculty. It had two cafeterias, a large chapel, an auditorium, and an endless number of furnished rooms. A caretaker told me that it was heated with water and that one of the boilers needed some work done on it.

The college was on nine of the most expensive residential acres in the town. Most of the land was lawn, but there were also tennis courts and a small stream. Scattered around the grounds were typical Catholic college statuary of Jesus and a few of the saints. The entire place was pure art. I spent the rest of the day, that night, and the next day studying every inch of the buildings, the boilers, electrical systems, the kitchens. It crossed my mind that some developer was going to buy this place, tear the building down, tear up the trees, and build ticky tacky. At the end of the second day, I drove back to Iowa City and picked up Sharlane. We returned to Clinton to look at the place together.

Finally I called Bishop Lowery who was head of the Redemptorist Order and made plans to see him the next day to discuss purchasing the college.

We found the Redemptorist Order with no trouble and were welcomed into the bishop's study. There, I told him about the *PDI*, our phenomenal growth, our lack of money, and my belief that with the college I could attract top teachers and a student body who would live together, work together, teach together, and learn together in this ideal environment. In doing so, I added, we could attract the attention of private and government money to run the college. The *PDI* was already tax exempt.

The bishop was genuinely excited about the idea. He even asked if he could join the faculty to help get the college started. He had a graduate degree in sociology and all the theology a bishop of the Redemptorist Order needed. I told him that Richard Korn, from the University of California at Berkeley, had already accepted my invitation to join the faculty as well.

Bishop Lowery and I discussed price and down payment. We agreed on $63,000 for the entire property. He took $1,000 as a down payment. I had three months to arrange financing for the remaining $62,000. Meanwhile, half of our staff moved to Clinton right away and half stayed at 505. Artists from Ohio State University donated paintings and sculpture that turned the hall inside the front entrance into an art gallery. New Song began to feel like a home.

In the June issue we devoted more space to the Church of the New Song than to any other single topic or organization. My purchase of the college in Clinton dominated the front page and two pages inside, while individual articles from prisoners spoke to the effect the *PDI* was having spreading the CNS story to prisons across the country and in other countries. I had corresponded with co-founder Harry Theriault and asked him to try to simplify the religion rather than make it increasingly complex—page after page after page of doctrine and new names to describe women, men, titles, and positions of church officials flowed from his solitary cell. I wondered if it might not save us time if individuals could become members simply by assuming an obligation to respect and cherish all living things.

In the brief time the church had existed prison administrators were already committed to breaking it. To do so they attacked anyone who stepped into a leadership role. Each issue from this point on would be dominated by CNS, its court cases, meetings, and prison ministers.

At the time we could not see the adverse effect this would have on our financial situation. Even the number of dollar subscriptions began to fall off drastically. This issue had only 44 pages. Bob Copeland reduced the size of the type. Still, the *PDI* was the only place to find the kind of information prisoners had come to depend on.

JAILHOUSE LAWYERS: THAT SPECIAL GROUP OF PRISONERS

One of the most interesting articles in the anniversary issue involved the establishment of Buddhist services within the Texas prison system. Frederick Cruz, *PDI* associate editor and a competent jailhouse lawyer, had been ordained as a lay minister by the Buddhist church while he was an inmate there. After being released from prison he accompanied the Reverend Calvin Chan Vassallo and two nuns on an official visit, during which Buddhist services were held in

Goree Unit and at the Walls Unit (the Texas State Prison is referred to as the Walls). At the completion of each service a number of prisoners signed a request that the services continue on a regular basis and that they be allowed to learn more about Buddhism, and even become members.

Prison officials responded angrily to the appearance of their four visitors, especially the ex-Texas state penitentiary prisoner with the Buddhist minister ID card. Barring Cruz from future services directly violated a U.S. Supreme Court decision that had concluded the case of *Cruz vs. Beto*, which Cruz himself had initiated and won while in prison. Nevertheless, according to Cruz, Assistant Director of Treatment W. Dee Kutach and Warden Bobby Morgan vowed that they were prepared to spend the rest of their lives in prison before they would allow Frederick Cruz to enter any unit of the Texas Department of Corrections in his present capacity.

It was interesting to me that our man Cruz elicited such a violent response from prison administrators. The possibility of Buddhist services attracting much interest in the Texas prison system was certainly remote. But, as with CNS, Buddhism provided prisoners a means to stability in their lives that administrators could not control.

Anyone can enter a prison to preach the traditional Christian message of "forgive sin, give yourself to God, be born again, and dig down deep to help us spread the word"; but arrive with the literal message of Jesus—sharing, rejecting violence, being your brothers' and sisters' keeper, living the message through actions that help the poor, finding a closet to pray in—and you are out on your ass.

The actions by Frederick Cruz further convinced me that the freedom of religion clause in the Constitution—and a battalion of ACLU and jailhouse lawyers—was going to provide us with the means to get our message into the prisons. A message stressing unity would attract the leaders and ultimately the rank-and-file. The Christians I most respected—Phil and Dan Berrigan, Liz McAlister, Dave Dellinger, and the thousands of activists from Catholic Worker houses across the country, the Unitarian Universalists, Mennonites, Church of the Brethren, the Quakers—all understood that equity and the peaceful resolution of conflict were the foundation of Jesus of Nazareth's teachings. Suddenly we had a Buddhist challenging a prison system as the Muslims had challenged the system in the sixties. The Muslims exemplified the kind of discipline that enabled their members to prevail over the most brutal treatment. The body and the mind had to be clean and well exercised to measure up to the expectations of their God. Individuals understood that to be looked upon favorably by God demanded full-time commitment, a communal approach to belongings, and a recognition that the condition of the least able member reflected the whole.

The Church of the New Song stressed peace, freedom, and justice and was attracting thousands every month. Whether or not its spiritual leaders would provide inspiration and stability was yet to be seen. Whether or not CNS would attract members disciplined enough to stand up to prison administrators and hold with their religion was also a test that was coming.

Carlos Porras, Jr., chairman of La Causa de La Raza, El Reno (Prison), Oklahoma, provided us with an excellent article, filled with information about the disproportionate number of Chicano soldiers who had been killed in Vietnam. He wrote, "For a people who comprise six percent of the population, we represent 18 percent of Viet Nam's casualties. An equally astonishing statistic is that roughly 22 percent of La Raza is behind bars in prisons throughout America. After arrest we do an average of 23 months more than the Anglo...one out of every five Chicanos is incarcerated...in La Tuna, where the Chicanos comprise roughly 80 percent of the population all of the policy makers are Anglo."

After writing a letter documenting and formally requesting an investigation into a savage beating of a Chicano prisoner by Anglo guards, Carlos was transferred, along with the inmate who was beaten, the witness to the beating, and the chairman and vice chairman of the Americans of Latin Extraction (ALE), a self-help organization within the prison. It was a typical response by prison officials from all the states who were faced with demands by intelligent articulate prisoners. Transfer them. Keep them moving. Hide them in the dreaded county jails where uneducated guards earn their jobs through political favoritism and hold their jobs by following orders.

A lengthy report detailed the formation and development of the National Prisoners Coalition (NPC). After the initial meeting in Washington, DC, it was agreed that Richard Tanner would complete a white paper on the concept of the coalition and the history of past efforts to organize; Hy Cohen would draft the constitution and by-laws; Dan Karger would prepare a position paper on prison industry and labor; and Becky Hensley would correlate all information coming into 505 from members of the committee. Mary Jean Erickson was to prepare a white paper on social services as they affect prisoners, ex-prisoners, and would-be prisoners, while David Miller, *PDI*'s man in Washington, was checking federal and state legislation that could affect the NPC. Ron Daigneault was being sent to Providence, Rhode Island, to check out the Prisoners Reform Association.

John van Geldern provided us with an extraordinary article about prison lawyers, that special group of prisoners who took up the study of law from the confines of a cell. Attorney Fay Stender, a friend and ally of John, provided him with encouragement and sisterly legal advice when he needed it. John was himself one of the most highly respected prison lawyers in the country, particularly in California. He had locked horns with the best and the brightest lawyers the state and federal governments had throughout a career that had spanned the days when a jailhouse lawyer would be thrown in the hole for helping a fellow prisoner. John recalled the skills of his friend Willie Hill, a black prisoner with a fifth grade education, whose remarkable memory enabled him to cite from over 5,000 cases.

John wrote, "[Mr. Hill's] phenomenal legal recall has helped to unravel the ineffective representation afforded to prisoners by numerous graduate lawyers. Many an indigent California prisoner owes his freedom to Willie Charles Hill, Jailhouse Lawyer extraordinaire."

To give readers some idea of how effective John was as an attorney, a partial list of his accomplishments in 1970 included the writing of some 176 briefs relating to eight prisoner class action cases and 96 individual cases. His work resulted in the change or repeal of a number of unjust, unlawful prison rules and relief for 47 of the 96 individuals. The relief ranged from outright release to modified sentences. He ended the article by pointing out that he was proud to be a member of such distinguished company as Willie Hill, Chuck Warnocks, Tony Citrinos, Rodney Nunes, and Frenchy Martins.

FEDS SUPPORT SOPHISTICATED BRAINWASHING

In the July issue we printed our second *CREATION: The Arts in Prison*.

Jose Teseta, a former Leavenworth prisoner, wrote:

> Go
> to the ghetto.
> A garden where
> talons
> grow and
> harden
> and the whetstone
> of
> hate
> is much used.

A number of poems by "Wilkerson & Williamson" appeared also in this issue. James Ralph Williamson was one of *PDI*'s most prolific writers. We never met, but his and Wilkerson's letters arrived regularly at 505 and we always had space for the comments of these remarkable writers who shared a "View from Cell 1616" at San Luis Obispo.

Alex Kulikoff's art should have earned him the top awards from Southern Illinois University. The two drawings he sent us for this issue were reprinted in newspapers around the world.

The next month, we dedicated a full page to the memory of those who had died at the Attica Massacre the year before. The prisoners had been responsible for two deaths. The guards had gone in shooting and left 41 dead. It was noted that a memorial had been placed outside the gates of Attica but that no prisoner's name was on the memorial.

Also in that issue, we published an article by *PDI* Associate Editor L. A. Ramer, a prisoner in Marion who had gathered information to document the Federal Bureau of Prisons' commitment to brainwashing and the modification of prisoners' behavior. When he submitted the material to the *PDI* he sent it also to the United Nations Economic and Social Council in New York. Responses to the article came from readers around the world.

The federal prison in Marion, Illinois, housed those who were considered to be the most dangerous prisoners: political prisoners, prisoners who had developed organizing skills while in prison, and prisoners who had assaulted prison guards and/or administrators. Beginning in 1962, the Marion facility had been a youth prison. During this time the experts had developed a prison where prisoners could be moved from one part of the prison to another without the need for guard escorts. Every move could be monitored with television cameras. Some of the cameras were stationary. Others were mounted on tracks that could follow individuals or groups as they were being moved. This constant monitoring plus cells with barred doors backed up with solid steel doors and a highly trained guard corp with a SWAT team mentality made this prison the most secure, escape-proof prison in the United States.

On the first day that adult prisoners were transferred into the institution in 1968, two men were being escorted to their cells by cameras mounted on tracks. One of the men flipped a tightly rolled up piece of a matchbook cover onto the track and jammed the camera. Suddenly two high-risk prisoners were missing. Actually they had walked a few steps and then, out of sight of the jammed camera and not in range yet of the next, they had simply stopped. They could not be seen or heard. As far as the control room was concerned

they were gone. While the whistles blasted and the horns hooted and the guards scrambled, the prisoners stood calmly waiting for the emergency teams to arrive in their SWAT outfits. When the teams arrived, neither prisoner would admit responsibility for jamming the cameras. Instead, they maintained that they knew nothing. The videotapes of the prisoners were studied and neither could be seen throwing the wad of paper; neither had made a move that could have been construed as throwing or flipping anything. When blame cannot be pinpointed the bureau's behavior modification policy is to punish everyone who was in a position to do whatever was done. Thus, the prisoners had the distinction of being not only the first to get cells, but the first to get solitary cells.

A few years before these first adults were transferred to the Marion prison, Associate Editor Ramer learned, James V. Bennett, director of the Bureau of Prisons, had sponsored a three-day seminar for all senior staff and administrators in the federal prison system. The main speaker was Dr. Edgar H. Schein, associate professor of psychology, Massachusetts Institute of Technology's School of Industrial Management. His theme was, "Man Against Man: Brainwashing." Intentionally or not, Dr. Schein gave the bureau a powerful weapon. The message he delivered from his treatise was, as quoted in the *PDI*: "In order to produce marked behavior and/or attitudes it is necessary to weaken, undermine or remove the supports to the old patterns of behavior and the old attitudes...it is often necessary to break emotional ties...this can be done by...preventing communication with those [the prisoner] cares about, or by proving to him that those he respects are not worthy of it and...should be mistrusted."

Then the seminar participants were given a list of tactics that he considered to be the most effective in modifying behavior in the prison setting. These tactics, which were later adopted by the bureau, are listed in sidebar 5 so free world people can judge how the "rehabilitation" models were being run by the feds.

At the conclusion of the seminar Federal Bureau of Prisons Director Bennett gave his staff the go-ahead to experiment with methods of behavior modification. In his own words, as quoted by Ramer in his article, "The Bureau's Brainwashing Tactics": "[W]e are a large organization with [many] thousands [of employees] in 31 different types of institutions and we have a tremendous opportunity here to carry on some experimenting to which the various panelists have alluded. We can manipulate our environment and culture. We can perhaps undertake some of the techniques that Dr. Schein discussed. What I am trying to say is that we are a group that can do a lot of experimenting and research and we can change our methods,

Sidebar 5: Dr. Edgar Schein's List of Behavior-Modifying Tactics

1. Physical removal of prisoners to areas sufficiently isolated to effectively break or seriously weaken close emotional ties.

2. Segregation of all natural leaders.

3. Use of cooperative prisoners as leaders.

4. Prohibition of group activities not in line with brainwashing objectives.

5. Spying on the prisoners and reporting back private material.

6. Tricking men into written statements which are then shown to others.

7. Exploitation of opportunists and informers.

8. Convincing the prisoners that they can trust no one.

9. Treating those who are willing to collaborate in far more lenient ways that those who are not.

10. Punishing those who show uncooperative attitudes.

11. Systematic withholding of mail.

12. Preventing contact with anyone unsympathetic to the method of treatment and regimen of the captive populace.

13. Building a group conviction among the prisoners that they have been abandoned by and totally isolated from their social order.

14. Disorganization of all group standards among prisoners.

15. Undermining of all emotional supports.

16. Preventing prisoners from writing home or to friends in the community regarding the conditions of their confinement.

17. Making available and permitting access to only those publications and books that contain materials which are neutral to or supportive of the desired attitudes.

18. Placing individuals into new and ambiguous situations for which the standards are kept deliberately unclear and then putting pressure on them to conform to what is desired in order to win favor and a reprieve from the pressure.

19. Placing individuals whose will power has been weakened or eroded into a living situation with several others who are more advanced in their thought-reform and whose job it is to further the undermining of the individual's emotional supports which has begun by isolating him from family and friends.

20. Using techniques of character invalidation (e.g., humiliation, revilements, shouting to induce feelings of guilt, fear, and suggestibility) coupled with sleeplessness, an exacting prison regimen, and periodic interrogational interviews.

21. Meeting all insincere attempts to comply with cellmates pressures with renewed hostility.

22. Repeatedly pointing out to the prisoner, by cellmates, that he has not in the past lived up to his own standards and values, and that he still is not in the present.

23. Rewarding of submission and subservience to the attitudes encompassing the brainwashing objective with a lifting of pressure and acceptance as a human being.

24. Providing social and emotional supports which reinforce the new attitudes.

---

our environments, and perhaps come up with something more specific. What I am hoping is that [you] will believe that we here in Washington are anxious to have you undertake some of these things. Do things on your own—undertake a little experiment with what you can do with the Muslims—undertake a little experiment with what you can do with some of the sociopathic individuals.

"If there is one thing that you can get out of this visit to Washington, let it be that you are thoughtful people with lots of opportunity to experiment. There

is a lot of research to do—do it as individuals, do it as groups, and let us know the results."

In 1968 and 1969, Dr. Martin Groder, the psychiatrist at Marion, introduced the U.S. Bureau of Prisons' behavior-modification program there by semantically camouflaging the language and goals so that the public and our elected officials would think they were reading about transactional analysis, encounter groups, marathon sensitivity sessions, and psychodrama instead of what it was—brainwashing.

The August 1972 issue of the *PDI* contained more documentation of inhuman treatment of prisoners than any single document I have ever been able to find. Ramer's article and others, such as "The Manifesto of Dehumanization: Neo Nazi," "The United Black Front vs Brutality in Atlanta," and "Myth and Reality in Walla Walla," documented a lifetime of suffering and make this issue one of the most important we ever published.

Perhaps our best example of how the behavior modification programs of the federal government were used is the case of Eddie Sanchez, a friend of mine, who was typical of many prisoners in the end-of-the-line prisons. He had been arrested first as a young teen, spent his formative years in a juvenile institution, and graduated to the reformatories and then to the penitentiaries. His case was a classic example of what poverty, lack of education, and racism do to a child. Eddie was one of many prisoners placed in the S.T.A.R.T. program, a program based on the theory that behavior desired by the prison administrators can be strengthened by rewards and inappropriate behavior can be ended with punishment.

According to what Eddie told me personally, when he refused to participate in the program, he was denied showers, recreation, exercise, mail, books, and magazines. He still refused. His clothes and bedding were taken from him. He still refused. Finally he was spread-eagled face down on the metal of his bed with handcuffs on each wrist and ankle. For seven days and nights he remained in this position. He was not allowed to use the toilet or to wash. No fecal matter or urine was cleaned up during the seven days and nights. He was finally released. That night he managed to break the lightbulb behind the heavy mesh screen in his cell. With a sliver of glass from the broken bulb he methodically sliced through his achilles tendon. He was transferred to the Federal Medical Center at Springfield the next day.

Meanwhile, on August 22, Merrily stuffed 35 pounds of belongings into a backpack and hitchhiked to LaTuna Federal Prison in Anthony, New Mexico, on the Texas-New Mexico border, where she had been given permission to visit Harry Theriault. Merrily had recently returned from a visit to the federal prison at Sandstone, Minnesota, where she had visited with John Wagner.

In the August issue, which was not printed until close to the end of October, we published a collage of stories about the wardens and the prisoners and how a remarkably mellow *PDI* staffer was able to slip into and out of a prison that had systematically barred the *PDI* since we began publishing. Merrily was unaware of it, but her travels around the country by herself just scared the hell out of all of us. When she returned, a collective sigh of relief was breathed. This diminutive young teacher with the shock of tightly curled hair had become as important to *PDI* as our second class permit.

NEIGHBORS PLAY HARDBALL WITH THE *PDI*

I had thought that buying a college was going to get us some press. I wasn't prepared for the kind of press we were going to get. It didn't take long before we discovered that the folks living in the neighborhood were not pleased to learn that a group of people associated with prisoners had purchased a college. Our neighbors were getting ready to play hardball.

In September, the community laid siege to the college. An organized effort was underway to gather hundreds of signatures demanding that we be driven out. Petition leaders were charging that wives, mothers, and little girls were no longer safe while the killers, drug addicts, perverts, and rapists were living across the street.

The petition circulators convinced many people, but they didn't convince everyone. We had immediately opened a drug counselling service staffed by people who knew how to help substance abusers. I was quick to point out that, if anything, we had gathered many of the people Clinton considered to be problems and were housing them under one roof and keeping them busy. Not that they needed my direction. The great majority of the people who joined us at the college were innovative, intelligent, family-oriented mothers and fathers who just didn't have the resources to survive being out of work for two or three months. These were the forerunners of the tens of thousands who would end up on the streets during the Reagan administration.

As a way to protest the treatment our people were getting from many of the people of Clinton I went on a fast. After three weeks without food I felt great. I was thinking clearer and feeling better than I had in a long time. Unfortunately, the few bucks we saved on food that I didn't eat during that period did little to boost our ailing budget and in September I missed the first deadline on partial payment for the college.

At the time, I didn't panic because I was certain that in our negotiations I had discussed the possibility that this might happen and believed the bishop had indicated that he was flexible with the dates set forth in the contract. Unfortunately, at the time we discussed "flexibility" the bishop wasn't being bombarded with letters, phone calls, and petitions from a very Catholic Clinton flock.

As soon as it became clear that Bishop Lowery was going to start eviction proceedings I raced across town to retain attorney Donald Seneff. When Bishop Lowery beat me to him by minutes, I resolved to defend myself. I spent the next couple of days researching the Redemptorist Order's beginnings. I learned that the order's founder, St. Alphonsus, had established his "new institute" in Italy in 1732. In his day, he had gathered the beggars, drifters, and thieves around him. If St. Alphonsus had been living in Clinton in 1972 he probably would have done one of two things. He would have joined us or he would have convinced us to join him. The good St. Alphonsus would certainly have quoted scripture to the city of Clinton and to the members of the Redemptorist Order about what the college should be used for.

We divided up the defense. Anne Garza, a staff member from the Iowa City community who had moved into the center with us, was defending herself; John Price, a *PDI* staff member who also lived at the center, was defending himself and five others; I was defending *PDI*, CNS, and approximately twenty other individuals.

Although the odds seemed to be heavily against us we had a good case. Verbal agreements between the bishop and I did not follow the letter of the written contract; however, I believed that the bishop under oath would have to admit that we had agreed on flexible payment deadlines; in our talks we concluded that the most important item on the college agenda was to get the college started. Being in court would also give me a chance to set forth our goals under oath and answer the many questions I had not yet been able to address. I knew that the city would feel much better about the *PDI* purchasing the college when I finished testifying.

A short way into the trial, with the bishop on the stand, I asked him about our conversation concerning the deadlines. He said that the only agreements he had made with me were the written agreements in the contract.

That finished us. I believed he wasn't conveying the whole truth, but I had nothing in writing; it was just my word against his. For a while I wasn't sure how to proceed. One part of me wanted to go after him, to really dig into him about the Commandments. I wanted to have him re-sworn to make sure he understood. I wanted to tell him he was going to fry for his lie. But there was no reason to grandstand. I'm convinced to this day that everyone in the courtroom knew what he had done. I think I asked him if there was anything about our conversations that he wanted to share with the court. He said there wasn't. I said I had no more questions. The bishop left the stand, sat down next to his attorney, folded his arms, and put his head down so his forehead was resting on his forearms. He didn't look up for the rest of the trial.

Annie and John presented their cases and then I called myself as a witness.

Normally, when you are in front of a judge who you know is on the "other side" you wait for him or her to make a mistake that will give you grounds to appeal the decision. With this judge it happened as soon as I got on the stand. I had already been talking for a while, so when I began questioning myself my throat became very dry. I asked the judge to call a brief recess so I could get a drink of water.

The judge replied, "Why don't you have one of your cohorts bring you a drink, Mr. Grant."

Ruth Harty, a Clinton resident who was living with us at the center, was on her feet instantly. "Where do you get off labelling us 'cohorts?' We are sisters and brothers!"

I was prepared to move for a mistrial and walk out of the courtroom. Doing that would have given us another couple of weeks—if nothing else we might have gotten the ten acres of grass cut again.

But then the judge did the unexpected. He apologized to Ruth and to everyone in the crowded courtroom. Since there wasn't a jury we had to live with his apology.

I continued questioning and answering myself. I have never been involved in such an emotional courtroom experience. I'm certain everyone in the courtroom believed that the sadness in my voice and the tears in my eyes were based on the conflict between the bishop and me about the college. Not so. I was watching four years of work slowly come apart. I didn't have any less money in my pocket than I had two years earlier. We never really had any money, but we had always had enough to keep the bills partially paid. Now we were close to the end of the rope.

I had a difficult time answering my own questions because I was talking dreams. The college was to have been staffed by faculty and their families, the students were to have been ex-offenders, and all participants and their families would live at the college. Everything was to have been shared—the teaching, the cooking, the cleaning, the maintenance. We would have room for daycare, art, counselling, the *PDI*, the National Prison Center, a publishing operation. We only needed time and cooperation. And money.

Part of my appeal was to the community to allow us to save the Redemptorist Center, which had been rezoned for single-family dwelling and was sure to be destroyed if someone didn't take it for the school it was meant to be.

The bishop's face was still buried in his folded hands. He couldn't watch. I realized that his hands were tied. Making him suffer would accomplish nothing. The city wanted us out, the police were standing by with a SWAT team to evict us, and the only thing that would have saved us was cold hard cash.

On the stand that afternoon, I learned that I could no longer generate hatred, not for the bigots, the liars, or the racists. I saw what these people were doing—through their campaign of hate mail, petitions, obscene phone calls, trespassing charges, breaking and entry charges, court orders, legal notices, constant threats, and, through it all, lies by people from whom you do not expect lies—to keep a small group of ex-prisoners from buying a vacant college in their neighborhood. That the Redemptorist fathers could turn their backs on the teachings of their founder was disappointing. I would think for many years about the kind of pressure Bishop Lowery had to have been under to deny us the college.

The Karma was bad in Clinton, and if we had had a hundred of our best it wouldn't have made any difference. We had certainly shown greater restraint than our neighbors. We could leave the courtroom, the college, and the city of Clinton knowing that we had harmed no one and had helped many.

I asked all of our people if there was anything they wanted to add and we rested our case. John Price, Ruth Harty, and others had been eloquent. The judge commended us for our presentation and mentioned that our grasp of the law and our knowledge of court procedure had surprised and pleased him.

Then he retired to his chambers to reach a decision. Less than three minutes later he emerged with a five-page typewritten decision. He had ruled against us. He gave us until sundown to get out of town.

The headline in the *Clinton Herald* said, "Grant and followers given until sundown to leave." Talk about the bench shooting from the hip.

That night we sat together at the art gallery and discussed our options. In the end, we narrowed our options down to two. Everyone had a vote: should we barricade the entrances and fight eviction as non-violently as we could, and in so doing create a media event that would have the networks there in helicopters; or should we just leave? We smoked some Iowa pot that someone had brought, then contemplated quietly as we thought about what the next few days would be like if we stayed. Three of us had witnessed Attica a year earlier. We knew how mean the police could get. We were not frightened. There would never be serious rough stuff, but heads would get busted if we stayed, families would be separated, paroles would be violated.

It was during a period of extended silence that we suddenly heard what sounded like many people running toward us down one of the long corridors in the college. The noise became louder. It sounded like 15 or 20 police in riot gear thundering down the hallway. I said, "It looks like we should have nailed the doors shut earlier."

Suddenly the entire building was shaking and the floor of the art gallery was moving us ever so slightly up and over and down and back to where we were. "The Lord moves in mysterious ways, Her wonders to perform." I think Ruth or Ma Jones had the presence of mind and the wit to offer that gem.

Actually we had just experienced my first earthquake. It was a rather frightening experience. Someone said, "I wonder if it means that God wants us to stay or to leave." Nikki and Lisa Levicoff, two youngsters who were wise beyond their years, looked at each other and broke up laughing.

Soon everyone was laughing. A short time later we gathered for our last dinner at "New Song." There was some wine, a little smoke, and, eventually, consensus. We were tired, in no mood for another siege, more confrontations, and lengthy court actions. We decided to stay one day past the deadline, just to let them know that we were not impressed with ultimatums. Our Clinton brothers and sisters proposed that we camp on the edge of town for a few days to get organized and to relax.

"There's a place a couple miles north of Clinton on the banks of the Mississippi River called Bulger's Hollow," said Stan Mortenson. "Legend has it that the place is haunted."

Sounded like a perfect place for a vacation.

A NIGHT IN BULGER'S HOLLOW

Some 45 men, women, and children gathered in Bulger's Hollow late that first day. Spirits were high as we pitched tents, arranged logs, and positioned the tripods so that the huge cast iron cooking pots filled with rice and vegetables hung directly over the fires. Small smudge fires circled the hollow to discourage mosquitos as young children played and older kids lined the bank with fishing tackle. Warren Levicoff was taking pictures, Joan "Ma" Jones was organizing dinner, and someone was planning a family concert for the evening. All our problems, including our uncertain financial future, were set aside. We were free of Clinton, the courts, and creditors for at least a few days. As I watched everyone settling in I was struck by our group's resemblance to the Sunday family and church outings I had attended as a young child.

My hope, as I told reporter Harley Sorenson, who had been sent down to Clinton from the Minneapolis *Star Tribune* to write a series of feature pieces about our attempt to buy the college, was to find a place with homes for everyone, enough space so we could raise our own food, and a central location to publish the *PDI* and maybe do job printing to help raise additional revenue.

That evening storm clouds began to gather. Warren wondered if we should maybe take the tents down and prepare to crowd into the cars. Many of the kids were already sleeping in the tents so we decided to pack away and tie down everything else right away. We could quickly take the tents down later when the storm broke.

Then we gathered around a central fire to await the storm. The clouds were boiling and the lightning was getting closer. Suddenly the lights of Clinton disappeared as a wall of water rushed up from the south. It reached us so fast we had no time to wake the children and take the tents down. But just as suddenly, it separated and passed us by. We stood there watching rain pour down on all sides of us like it was happening on a movie screen. The storm lasted for an hour. We speculated that Clinton must have suffered from the incredible downpour.

I went over to the fire for another plate of rice and veggies. While standing by the cast iron pot I glanced down river and saw a line of nine cars slowly driving up the road from Clinton. I pointed to the caravan and told people to get ready for trouble. We knew they were not coming out to invite us back. Half of the adults walked over and stood blocking the small road. The rest stayed back with the children.

As the caravan pulled up to the front of the camp, the passengers in the first car rolled down their windows. We walked over and asked them if there was something they needed.

"We came out to see if you needed any help," the driver said. "We had such a terrible flood in Clinton that some cars were washed into the river. We thought your camp would be completely torn up."

They started getting out of their cars to help, but as they looked over the camp they couldn't believe what they were seeing. The tents were up, fires were blazing, pots still hung over two of the fires, and people were walking around like nothing had happened.

Someone from the first car walked back and told the others that we were okay. We invited them to share our food. The last car on the line left and returned a few minutes later with some beer. We introduced ourselves, fed our guests, enjoyed the beer, and swapped stories.

It was a perfect evening.

The next morning when Harley checked in with his editors at the *Star Tribune* he learned that a Larry Johnson was trying to get hold of me. I called Larry and was offered a couple of houses, some property for more houses, all the land we needed for gardens, and a large two-story office building up in west central Minnesota, all of which represented a good section of Georgeville, a small town that had gone broke during the Great Depression. He wanted $400.

Late the next day, Sharlane and I left for Iowa City on our way to Minnesota with Judy and Warren Levicoff, their daughters Nikki and Lisa, Ma Jones, Bill Smith, and Jerry Samuels.

THEY'RE COMING TO TAKE US AWAY, HA HA

505 had always been home to a musician or two. Becky Hensley was an accomplished singer, guitarist, and composer. Bob Copeland, when he finally found time to concentrate on music, played guitar, sang, and composed like he wrote—extremely well. Over the brief time we were in business we hosted many musicians who had been booked into Iowa City. Biff Rose was a 505 favorite. However, the person who stayed for the longest period of time was Jerry Samuels. Jerry had an international following as a result of his recording, "They're Coming to Take Me Away, Ha Ha," which he recorded under the name Napoleon XIV. Jerry called us when he learned that he had been booked into the Carousel Lounge, on the "Coralville Strip," the business community's garbage can of fast food establishments crowded in between motels and gas stations and restaurants just outside of Iowa City. We invited him to stay with us during his three-week appearance in Coralville.

Jerry was an incredibly active man who appeared to be moving at all times. The day he arrived, he announced that we were going to eat "Chinese" for dinner that night. He had already driven off and returned with wine for dinner, so we figured he had also been grocery shopping and was planning to take over the kitchen and prepare his specialties.

Later that day, Jerry called down the basement stairs and announced that dinner was ready. On the dining room table, completely covering it, were carry-out containers from one of the local Chinese restaurants. Jerry was busy opening them. On the table were all of Cathy's wooden serving spoons, most of which would not fit into the containers. While we were gathered around eating I noticed a shocked look on Becky's face. I asked her if she was okay. She didn't say anything; she just handed me the bill for the food. That dinner had cost Jerry almost $200, which was more than we spent on food in a week. When we explained that to Jerry, he explained to us that he spent 80 percent of his time in recording studios and control rooms or on stages, none of which came with kitchens. When he was hungry he reached for the phone.

After dinner Jerry asked if anyone was interested in dessert and promptly pulled out a small bag of what he called Lamb's Breath. "This is the best Jamaican pot I have ever tasted," he said and began rolling joints.

In those days it was not unusual to see marijuana around 505. Hard drugs were never tolerated, but pot was lumped together in the same category as beer.

After enjoying Jerry's "dessert," someone asked Jerry if he had ever tried Iowa pot. Jerry laughed and pointed out that he had been seeing tons of Iowa pot, or ditch-weed, on his drive in from Chicago. Of course this wasn't the same brand of marijuana that had been grown in Iowa during World War II and harvested for the fibers that made great rope. This was the amazing end result of many years of genetic manipulation by local botany professors. Jerry tried it and couldn't believe its potency. He touched it, smelled it, tasted it, and smoked a little more. Then he just sat there with his feelings and thoughts until finally he got up, walked to the piano, and wrote "I Owe a Lot to Iowa Pot" in about 20 minutes.

Over the next three days, while he was waiting to begin his Friday night gig, Jerry spent all his time at 505. By the time Friday arrived he had learned much about prison. He opened his first set at the Carousel with a medley of sixties protest songs interspersed with his own compositions. At the end of the evening the Carousel manager told him he was not to sing any protest songs or political songs.

"Get your act together, Mr. Samuels," he was warned, "or tomorrow night will be your last night at the Carousel."

Jerry didn't threaten well. He returned to 505, told us what had happened, and informed us of what he was going to do. The next night Jerry opened to a packed house. In every seat was someone directly or indirectly involved with the *PDI*. A couple of musician friends had driven over from Chicago to sit in with Jerry, including Warren Levicoff's 18-year-old brother Steve, who had collaborated with Jerry in the past and who, twenty years later, would write his college dissertation on the history of the Church of the New Song for a doctorate in theology and law (see sidebar 6). The most difficult task for each of us in the audience was sitting there for six hours nursing one beer. Never had the Carousel had such a crowd or made less money. A memorable evening—Jerry's last in that club.

Jerry was to stay with us for a couple of months in Iowa City, join us in Clinton, and continue on with us to Minnesota. During his stay he also composed "Children, Oh Children," "Prisons and Prisons (My Daughters and Sons)," and "Sing a New Song." Before he left, he gave me the songs to copywrite and told me to use any revenue for social action projects and give away copies of the sheet music, which I do to this day.

FOLLOWING THE HIPPIES INTO GEORGEVILLE

During our meeting with the staff in Iowa City we learned that only ten copies of our August issue had been allowed inside Leavenworth. Issues for our approximately 140 other subscribers had been destroyed. Late that night we left for Minnesota to look at the property in Georgeville.

Georgeville is located in Sterns County, about 90 miles northwest of Minneapolis. In *Zen and the Art of Motorcycle Maintenance*, Robert Pirsig describes the area's most distinctive feature as being its lack of anything distinctive. Sterns County was unique for a number of reasons as far as I could tell. It was home to some of the largest granite quarry operations in the Midwest. According to a University of Minnesota doctoral study, it also was home to more mentally retarded residents per capita than any county in the United States, due to its concentration of German emigrants who had come to work in the quarries and then had intermarried for a number of generations. Finally, Sterns County had one of the largest turnouts for George Wallace when he ran for president in the seventies. I never researched these "unique" characteristics, but I saw enough quarries and met so many impoverished, emotionally disturbed, conservative racists of all ages that I never questioned the hearsay evidence.

The property in Georgeville had been owned by Larry Johnson, a Minneapolis investor and real estate speculator who had taken a critical look at his life in the late sixties. What he saw was a very successful middle-aged man who was getting more than his fair share of the profits while others were getting zip. Upon closer examination, he saw that his substantial taxes were supporting a U.S. military that was on a rampage of death and spending in Vietnam. Having two draft age sons helped him with his non-violent coming-of-age and inspired him to get rid of all his income-generating property. One month he notified his tenants that beginning with the next rent payment they were buying the property at a bargain price. When the checks rolled in the following month he realized that he was still in a high income ballpark so he signed the property over to the tenants, threw away his razor, cleaned the polyester out of his closet, and started concentrating on greens from the garden instead of greens from the bank.

Larry had originally rented the Georgeville property for $100 a month to a communal group that included Eddie Felien, editor of *Hundred Flowers* [see Ed Felien's "Let a Hundred Flowers Blossom, Let a Hundred Schools of Thought Contend: The Story of *Hundred Flowers*" in this collection], who recently had become the first avowed Marxist to be elected to the

Minneapolis City Council. Larry ended up spending considerable time with the group; subsequently his life became washed in the purifying waters of their democratic socialist politics. His son had taken the same political bath and had changed his name from Alan Johnson to Foster Goodwill. A few months later Larry would change his name to Ernest Mann. He had cut his income so drastically that he did not have to pay taxes. As a means of sharing his conversion and economic philosophy he began publishing a small underground newspaper called *The Little Free Press* with a you-pay-the-postage subscription fee. He continues to do so today (Route 1, Cushing, MN 56443-9712; 218-575-2007) in a small one-room house trailer just down the road from where Bonnie Raitt's brother had a recording studio.

The original Georgeville Commune had been settled by a small group of antiwar activists from the Twin Cities who were approaching burnout from the intensity of their activity there; three needed a quiet "nest" where their soon-to-arrive babies could be born. The two primary "movers" were Keith Ruona and Suzy Shroyer. Suzy's three sisters were also part of the group. Stephen Mickey was a master potter and pottery teacher whose oil-fired kiln produced income-generating pottery that attracted visitors from the surrounding areas.

After a couple of years, with the babies born and energies replenished, the core group moved on. As Eddie described it, they had experienced the "rural thing," but had no intentions of spending their lives there. Without the productive energies of a few far-sighted, hardworking people, the garden became overrun with weeds; the lethargy of cheap wine and pot soon had the remaining "trippies" ("hippies" who spent most of their time looking for a place to get a handout) crossing the tracks to Highway 55 in search of easier digs.

The commune wasn't Georgeville's first major closing. According to old-timers, the bank had gone broke during the Great Depression and the post office had closed soon after when the majority of residents left to seek work elsewhere. Georgeville was an end-of-the-line, economically deprived town now, made up of people with no resources and no place to go. I had read about rural poverty but had not witnessed it or lived this close to it. Later, when I came to know the remaining 25 or so residents, I was surprised to find ex-offenders making up the majority of the population. To residents in the outlying area, however, the commune had been a bad memory. They would welcome us heartily at first, but when they found out who we were many added extra security bolts to their doors.

Directly behind the large two-story building was the pottery. Across the alley was a Phillips 66 gas station that was owned and operated by an elderly man who lived next door to the station with his wife. The wife had considered members of the Georgeville Commune to be so sinful that when she walked from the house to the station she would cover her eyes with her hand. When I asked Pete Wendt, a local farmer, why she shielded her eyes, he told me that the women in the commune would work in the garden wearing miniskirts with no underpants on. When they weeded they would bend from the waist with their rear ends facing the gas station. Pete said that the gas station owner and his wife didn't like it, but lots of folks would stop, buy gas, and stand around taking in the sights while a soft drink got warm in their hands.

The only other business in the town was a small frame tavern that catered to a few locals.

After carefully checking the various structures and the property, I believed that we would never find a better opportunity to fulfill our needs. The two houses and the large building where the bank had been needed insulation, electrical wiring, plumbing, and a heating source, but the building was open and solid and large enough to support a printing plant and shops. Where the bank had been located a large bank vault remained. The front door to what was once the general store led to an area that could easily seat 300 people.

Thanks to farm sales and a weekly auction in Belgrade I had the houses habitable within a month for less than $200. By Christmas, we had furnished the former bank area with a stove, an antique pocket pool table, and a pinball machine someone had given us. I bought the last two available wood-burning Ashley stoves in Minneapolis for $86 each. We became the tax-exempt Georgeville Community Project.

Jerry Samuels spent most of his time writing music. He also performed briefly at the Sunwood Inn in Morris, Minnesota. With the money he earned, he bought chicken feed, people feed, and a 1942 Model B John Deere tractor that Pete Wendt said would run forever. We had hoped Jerry would spend the rest of the winter with us, but he met Petronella "Pete" Ludwina Vesters, a North Country woman with a flawless complexion and a keen mind, and together they headed for Los Angeles, where Jerry enjoyed some relaxing moments with his friend from New York, studio engineer/musician Jeff Cooper, and Jeff's Roto-Rooter Goodtime Street Band. Jerry tried to sell some of his recent compositions but was told the new material was too political. This was a disappointment to us because we held the copyrights to three of the best songs. Jerry and Pete sang their way across the country—Jerry doing the singing and Pete providing him with inspiration. Eventually they settled in Philadelphia.

Sidebar 6: Reflections on *Penal Digest International*

by Steve Levicoff

The prison reform movement that was active from 1960 to the early 1980s saw more success than at any other period in the nation's history. Civil liberties advocates enjoyed success in the judicial system and generated a public awareness that has not been matched since. *Penal Digest International* played a strong role in that public awareness.

The *PDI* was a publication written by a group of ex-convicts and social activists and circulated not only within federal and state prison systems but also to the outside community. More than anything else, the *PDI* was a vehicle for communication, ensuring that those who were inside the prison walls did not lose touch with the reality that they were not alone, that men and women in other penitentiaries and correctional facilities were going through the same oppression that they were, and that people in the outside world were willing to put themselves on the line to do something about it.

As a voice of the prisoner, the *PDI* had qualities that were both an advantage and a detriment. It was brazenly honest about conditions inside the prison walls, unabashedly angry about the fact that those conditions could exist, and forthright in its demands for immediate change. The *PDI* often challenged people by offending their sensibilities, shocking them into the reality of knowing that prison was not a pretty picture.

At the same time, there is another reality: anger tends to overcompensate for conditions as they exist, and expressing too much anger often has a reverse effect in terms of the goals that are sought.

The Church of the New Song provides a striking example. Founded in 1969 by prisoners, for prisoners, CONS (an accidental acronym with an appropriate touch of tongue in cheek) was originally formed as a tool to gain prisoner rights through the freedom of religion clause in the First Amendment to the Constitution. Its proponents raised a plethora of concerns about freedom of expression and effectively addressed the religious rights of prisoners for the first time since the Black Muslims had done so in the 1960s. The constitutional issues addressed by CONS were legitimate, regardless of what one thought of the tenets of their faith system.

PDI, as the most visible voice in the nationwide community of prisoners, provided a voice of communication that spread the CONS message. Yet along with that message came expressions of anger at the tradition-al religions that CONS members felt oppressed them. As CONS' "minister of political correspondence" Norman Gorham wrote in *PDI*, CONS was "a faith, not of Christ, a dude who may have existed in 33 A.D., or his invisible, pound-of-air Father, but of people—convict people...a bastard group of hard-core cons who were sought for various crimes that never took place by the forces of Caesar." CONS, another member wrote, was a church that "does away with the bullshit, the mysticism, life hereafter." And therein laid the problem.

There was never a doubt that members of CONS had the right to hold or not to hold whatever religious tenets they chose. But in their often self-righteous anger, they ended up offending many people who would otherwise have defended their rights.

So it was with other issues addressed in *PDI* by those who were being burned in the prison system. Hands were reaching in to help ensure the rights of those behind bars, but when those hands were bitten they retreated. By the time the anger began to subside, society as a whole had changed.

During the late 1970s and into the 1980s, society's desire to effect positive change was replaced by what Tom Wolfe would call "The Me Decade." Liberal social causes that had been emphasized in earlier years were replaced by a conservative politic that remains with us today. In the 1990s, a war that would have generated peace protests and resistance resulted in resurging pride and a plethora of yellow ribbons.

Penal Digest International served a purpose in its time that may not be duplicated for another decade or more. The late Lenny Bruce once reflected, "One generation saves up to buy their children galoshes. When the storm finally comes, the kids are outside barefoot, digging the rain." When that new generation comes that has a higher priority in terms of human rights for those who are behind bars, let's hope that a new *PDI* exists to act as a voice in the wilderness.

Levicoff is director of the Institute on Religion and Law in Ambler, Pennsylvania, and specializes in legal issues impacting religious rights. He holds a Ph.D. in religion and law from The Union Institute, and his books include *Building Bridges: The Prolife Movement and the Peace Movement* and *Christian Counseling and the Law*.

Also during this period, Warren, Judy, Nikki, and Lisa Levicoff returned to Chicago. Shar and I remained along with five others.

In Iowa City, meanwhile, the staff decided on a slight name change. While all agreed that the word "penal" did refer to punishment, its closeness to "penis" caused discomfort among some. Brother Richard had been using the replacement word "prisoners'" for months. Finally, everyone agreed that "penal" had to go, and Bob Copeland made the change.

PRISONERS WITH FAMILIES ARRIVE

In the September/October 1972 *PDI*, our first issue under the new name *Prisoners' Digest International* and our first since being given "until sundown to leave" Clinton, we carried my article about our move and the Georgeville Community Project. In that article, I outlined my plans for an expanded *PDI* operation that would work within a community and be the watchdog for the rights of all prisoners—economic, political, and criminal. My primary goal was to make ourselves self-sufficient by cutting our expenses and finding a means to generate income. By this time, we hadn't published an issue during the month that was printed on the front page for a long time. The September/October issue was mailed shortly before Christmas.

One way we cut back on our expenses was by travelling less. Our lone exception was National Prison Center board member Dr. Stephen S. Fox, a professor of neuropsychology from the University of Iowa, Because his specialty was sensory deprivation, he was with increasing frequency being called as an expert witness in cases where prisoners were filing legal actions against state and federal authorities. His travel expenses were covered by the fees he was being paid to testify.

Also in this issue, we reprinted a lengthy article that Rev. Anthony Mullaney, one of the Milwaukee 17, wrote for the *National Catholic Reporter*. "Chaplains...play an important role in the machinery of control presided over by the [authorities]," wrote Mullaney. Then he methodically pointed out how they were used by wardens to keep other religious leaders out of the prisons in order to deprive political prisoners and prisoners in general of the right to be served by religious activists who were sympathetic to their plight. In Mullaney's important article, a respected minister and antiwar activist was saying what Frank Sepulveda and I had said four years earlier when we broke into the chaplain's office inside Leavenworth.

Another article covered the protest over inadequate food inside the federal prison in Marion, Illinois in October. The protest was ultimately put down with mace, beatings, and solitary confinement inside solid, windowless cells that had the psychological effect upon some prisoners of being welded inside a steel box without a blow torch. When an attorney from the People's Law Office in Carbondale arrived on October 17 to visit prisoner Eddie Adams, he was shocked to see two guards dragging Eddie down a hall. The constitutional right of an attorney and client to meet privately was violated in the Marion prison that day when attorneys and clients were separated by a thick glass in the visiting room and permitted to communicate only by means of monitered phones. By the attorney's

next visit the following day, Eddie had been beaten so badly he could only get around in a wheelchair.

We carried the full decision by Federal District Court Judge Edward Weinfeld regarding the injunction to lift the ban on the newsletter published by The Fortune Society. Stanley Bass, legal counsel for the NAACP Legal Defense Fund, and Stephan Shestakofsky represented prisoners Roger Campen and Nathan Wright and the Fortune Society. This decision was important because it prevented individual wardens from arbitrarily seizing and censoring publications that had been approved by the state department of corrections.

A letter to Senator Quentin Burdick from Federal Bureau of Prisons Director Norman Carlson, dated October 13, 1972, stated that all solitary confinement prisoners in the Leavenworth prison have commissary privileges and hot and cold water in their cells. In this issue, we also published a note by *PDI* Associate Editor Joseph Harry Brown to Carlson in which he wrote, "Really, Norm, you've got to be kidding."

With this issue Walter Plunkett took over circulation, John Price moved to prisoner affairs, Jean Schneller became editor of *CREATION*, and editorial assistants included Becky Hensley, Ruth Harty, John Honeywell, John Adams, and Anne Garza. Our National Prison Center board of directors included Richard Tanner, Penny Baron, Robert D. Bartels, Jane and Steve Fox, Joseph C. Johnston, Donald Mazziotti, Thomas Renwick, Mark E. Schantz, William Simbro, and me.

Members of the *PDI* Prisoner Advisory Board (PAB) represented state prisoners in California, Colorado, Florida, Georgia, Indiana, Iowa, Kentucky, Minnesota, Missouri, New York, Ohio, Oklahoma, Oregon, Pennsylvania, and Texas. Federal prisoners came from Allenwood, Atlanta, El Reno, La Tuna, Leavenworth, Lorton, Lompoc, Marion, McNiel Island, Sandstone, Terminal Island, and Terre Haute. S.J. Delaney was a PAB member from Leicestershire, England. Our national associate editor was John Wagner, in Sandstone. These prisoners were constantly harrassed by guards and prison administrators. Signed articles by PAB members reporting assaults on prisoners by guards got some of them weeks in solitary confinement. Many were confined simply because of their association with the *PDI*.

PDI mail came to Georgeville and to Iowa City. An artist I remembered from Leavenworth wrote and asked if he could come to Georgeville to do nothing but paint when he was released: "I have saved enough money to support myself for two years while I concentrate on my painting." I had hoped that *CREATION* would get the attention of serious artists. It seemed to be happening.

One day, Twin Cities attorney Richard Oakes visited the Georgeville Project. While he was there, we discussed a proposal that would allow prisoners with children to be sent to Georgeville instead of prison so the families could stay together. A few weeks later our first prisoner/probationer arrived with a one-year-old child. By spring, we would have seven probationers living with us. Our most serious problem was that we were given no financial assistance from the state, even though we were saving the state around $10,000 a year for each person we kept out of prison. During our first year we would save the government over $100,000.

Meanwhile, in the general Sterns County community, an elderly retired woman came to us to ask if we would look at the linoleum a Belgrade merchant had installed in her kitchen. He had sold it to her at $7 a square yard and installed it without preparing the old floor. A few days after the installation, the old nails were already coming through the linoleum. We took the merchant to small claims court, where he was ordered by the judge to replace the linoleum after cleaning and refinishing the floor. It wasn't much, but it showed the community that we were willing to help anyone who needed help.

A DIFFICULT EXISTENCE

The November 1972 issue was published in early 1973. This was the smallest issue since the *PDI* was founded: one section of twelve pages, two of which were *CREATION: The Arts in Prison*. The front page and much of the issue was devoted to articles by Hans W. Mattick, co-director of the Center for Studies in Criminal Justice, University of Chicago Law School ("The Prosaic Sources of Prison Violence") and Daniel Glaser, Ph.D. from the University of Southern California ("Casual Processes in the Development and Control of Prison Riots").

All income that came in to the *PDI* was being used by the staff in Iowa City. I was supporting the Georgeville Community Project and the growing number of participants—which by now included approximately 15 adults and children—by accepting speaking engagements and participating in seminars. In the *PDI* I wrote, "For the past three months it has been what some would term a difficult existence. I have been on the move constantly. Sleeping on the ground, in the van, in the back seats of cars, on floors in mansions and shacks. It has been cold, wet, hot, bug infested, dirty, windy and sometimes downright miserable. And through it all, right there and not complaining, has been Sharlane. An independent human being, a woman, a partner and a mother-to-be, who values truth above all else."

I was looking for printing equipment, tools, supplies, seeds for spring planting, anything that could be used to improve the houses and the property. I built a greenhouse across the front of the old post office where Shar and I were living. On sunny days so much heat was generated that we didn't burn wood in the house.

Our financial problems were not looking any better when a young parolee who had helped us in the past called me in Georgeville. Eight or ten months earlier Tommy Terrill had stopped by 505 on his way to spending the $500 he had saved on work release. Before he left, he graciously loaned us the $500 to help pay printing bills. Now Tommy needed it back. He was married. He and his wife had just had a baby boy. Medical bills were mounting. "If you have it," he added.

We didn't, but as luck would have it the University of Wisconsin called and asked me to chair a panel discussion during a two-day seminar on corrections. I accepted and we were able to pay Tommy and fix up a frightning looking one-ton pickup that would carry us all over the country when I finally returned the *PDI* van.

In the January and February 1973 issues of *PDI* we began reducing the size of the type to get more news into the twelve-pages of each issue. In the February issue the Iowa City group pointed out to readers that we only had money for one more issue. They also explained that the Georgeville Project and the Iowa City group were totally separate entities and that some of the Iowa City group believed more energy had to be directed to the Church of the New Song.

Four pages were devoted to defining the new language of the new religion and explaining how a group could organize a purlieu (local "church" headquarters) where the redactor (preacher) or sealed revelation minister (member of the CNS clergy) could meet with the mavorites (men) and sporades (women), who could learn how to accept their candid functions (responsibilities) and ponder the exigenic missives (letters) from the Bishop of Tellus (Shiloh Harry Theriault), who was located in the fountainhead seminary (ministerial school of Eclarianity) and was busy explaining the inverse crucible (basic eclatarian belief) to CNS members.

Although I believed too much energy was being devoted to complicating the language of the Church of the New Song, I did open a church in Georgeville. We were located in Crow River Township so I called it the Crow River Church of the New Song. All of my community service there was performed as a CNS minister because I believed that the fastest way to "gather a flock" (so to speak) was to become a community resource and let them see the tangible results of my work. If I couldn't inspire them to donate enough food and/or money to allow the ministry to survive, it simply meant that I hadn't become an indispensible resource to the community.

GEORGEVILLE PROJECT FINDS OUTSIDE FUNDING

Soon after the legal hassles began in Clinton, I was contacted by Dr. Alan Green, director of the Irwin Sweeney Miller Foundation, a non-profit organization funded by Cummins Diesel Engines in Columbus, Indiana. His interest, he said, was in finding out what I was planning for the community and how I planned to tie it into the *PDI*. He asked me to contact him when I found a home. When we settled in Georgeville in early fall, Sharlane and I wrote a description of our plans, mailed it off, and forgot about it. Then one day in the early weeks of 1973, we were notified that he was flying in to discuss financial support for the project.

We met Dr. Green at Minneapolis International Airport. There, over coffee, we discussed the proposal and he offered the foundation's help. Dr. Green told us they would give us enough money so Shar and I could pay ourselves a modest salary with a little left over for the project if we abided by certain conditions, namely that Shar and I had to attend a week-long transactional analysis seminar in Lynchberg, Virginia, and that we had to account for all the money, none of which could be used for the Church of the New Song. When I asked him about the second condition, I was told bluntly, "Because it's bullshit!" Unfortunately the foundation had seen the February issue. Although I saw more potential in CNS than he did, I could see he was a bright man, and so I had no problem with his conditions. I accepted on the spot. When I asked him why the foundation was supporting us, he said, "This money is an investment in Sharlane and you. It will help you do the things you are doing." On our drive back to Georgeville, Shar and I discussed Dr. Green's proposal. We tried to be positive about the *PDI* and the project, but we were not generating much excitement with the folks at 505, who felt I should be living in Iowa City and concentrating all my energy there.

A few days after the support from the foundation began I was contacted by someone at the Good Thunder, Minnesota weekly newspaper. The long-time owner was selling the entire printing plant so he could retire but the owners-to-be wanted no part of the old equipment. I drove immediately to Good Thunder, a few miles south of Mankato, and was met by the newspaper's owner, the mayor, and members of the town council, who asked me to consider moving to Good Thunder. "We have a vacant building for any

business you might want to start," I was told. "Plus, there are many vacant homes."

They said they were willing to help us with promotion and fundraising while providing cheap rent. They also had a library and proximity to Mankato State University. What they didn't mention was the potential for community development funds that might be available from the federal government. Good Thunder was a beautiful, traditional small town in southern Minnesota, similar to the one nearby which I had grown up. But now Good Thunder was a depressed area.

I drove alone to Mankato to think about their incredible offer. Then I called Sharlane. Together we decided we didn't want to be responsible for what might happen if we relocated all our people to Good Thunder. In the end, without talking to the staff in Iowa City, I decided to turn down the offer.

Instead, with money Shar and I were not paying ourselves, I made the fellow an offer for everything in the plant, which included a 17' x 22' Harris offset press and two huge Linotype machines. The townspeople obviously were disappointed to be losing the only printing equipment in town. Nevertheless, he accepted my offer. I returned with a borrowed truck and hoist and removed three printing presses, 100 drawers of type, two Linotype machines, and all the odds and ends of "stuff" that accumulates in a printing plant that has been serving a community since the turn of the century.

One month later we were completely set up to print in Georgeville. I found out that it was much easier going from hot type to cold than from cold to hot. My plans were to have both—letter press and offset.

It was now almost spring. The fifteen of us were living in four homes, along with a regular stream of temporary residents who were sent to us through corrections' agencies in Minnesota. We were set up to raise our own food on our own land. A coop full of chickens provided us with eggs. The five windows needed for the bank, each seven feet by three feet, were donated to us by a Minneapolis window company.

GOODBYE, 505; GOODBYE, *PDI*

One day I was shocked to find out that payments at 505 were many months in arrears. I had purchased the house with my GI loan from the Korean War. The payments were only $225 a month, but by the time I became aware of how many payments had been missed I had already bought the Good Thunder printing plant. It was too late now to stop foreclosure and I didn't have any money anyhow. Still, I called Iowa City and told them we would be down within a week.

A few days later I received a letter from Merrily telling me she had earlier been given the job by the Iowa City staff of investigating our books because some of the staff were convinced I had embezzled money from the *PDI*. Our books were not in the best order, of course, but after several weeks Merrily was able to find no improprieties. The staff were amazed to find out that there never was any money. Her letter informed me that "the investigation has cleared you of any wrongdoing."

By the time we got to Iowa City, 505 was gone and the staff had moved to a large house on Linn Street, where they were paying considerably more rent than they had at 505.

Our meeting there was interesting for a couple of reasons. First, many new unfamiliar people were present. Richard Tanner had called Georgeville to warn me that some of the new staff members were dangerous and that I should consider staying away from Iowa City. For that warning, I later learned, he was rewarded with a vicious ass-kicking by a couple of the new members. At the time I wasn't worried.

At the meeting, which was attended by the entire staff, I outlined how the *PDI* could be saved and shared what I had put together in Georgeville. There was some concern about my being so far away from a city, but I pointed out that the mail was delivered to Georgeville just as regularly as it was to Iowa City.

I asked staff members if any were interested in moving to Minnesota. A new staffer named Jack Kime saved everyone the trouble of answering by telling me, "If you move any part of the *PDI* to Minnesota I will personally guarantee that you will not live to see that baby born," and he pointed to Sharlane who was sitting next to me and unquestionably pregnant.

We were all sitting on the floor in a large circle. I looked around the room to see if there was consensus. Jane Fox, a board member at our National Prison Center as well as a CNS Jurisconsult and Sporade, said nothing because of her commitment to CNS; no one else did either. Richard had warned me about several CNS members, including Kime, who had recently joined the *PDI* staff after being released from Fort Madison. I could see now that he had been correct in his warning—*PDI* decisions were now being made by the Church of the New Song.

One lesson I had learned in the can was this: when someone said he was going to kill you if you did something, you had two choices; you could kill him first and then do what you were going to do, or you could say screw it, chalk one up for the killers, and walk away.

"Looks like you folks have yourselves a newspaper; when you close down let me know." I took Shar's

hand and helped her up. We walked out of the house and that ended our contacts with them.

When we got in the van, Shar said, "Good riddance."

I agreed.

We had one more stop to make before we returned to Georgeville. The three-year lease on our van allowed us to drive 10,000 miles a year. In two years, I had put 100,000 miles on its odometer and had only made three or four payments on it. For some unknown reason the company had never billed me. I wondered why, but I had an idea. With that idea, I devised a plan. There had been an electrical fire in the wires under the dash a couple months earlier. The body was in good shape and the engine burned less than a quart of oil a month, but the wiring was a problem.

When we got to the company, I said to the sales manager, "I want you folks to rewire the van and give it back to me, and then I'll start making payments on it."

He looked at me like I was nuts and told me my proposal was the stupidest thing he had ever heard.

I raised my voice. When I did he got a panicked look on his face, motioned with his hands to "please keep this quiet," and looked around nervously to see if any other potential customers were listening. Then he ran over to his boss' office and shut the door.

As I watched him, I thought about the fact that I had never received a payment due bill or a warning about possible repossession. His need to keep this discussion from his boss indicated to me that he and possibly others were leasing vehicles and pocketing the payments. It was an old scam. I was only guessing, but I thought they were dirty.

When he sat back down, he looked at me and said "How are we going to get this worked out, Joe? You owe us over $4,000."

I took a chance. I spoke as seriously as I could under the circumstances and said, "I think that everyone, including you, is going to be much better off if you take the van, fix it up, put it on the lot, and forget about the lease and the money you say I owe you."

He sat there looking at me.

I added, "When I think of the endless hassles we'll be going through over this—lawyers, court dates, all of that legal stuff—I want to keep it as simple as possible."

He said, "Let's just forget about it."

I stood up and reached out to shake his hand. "Is there anything I should be having you sign, or can I trust you to take care of all the paper work?"

"Trust me," he said. And I did. I never heard from them again. Part of the floor boards on the passenger side of our pickup were missing, but it was all ours—free and clear. For the first time in four years

I had no debts. When those new staff members decided they wanted the *PDI* bad enough to kill for it, they got a hell of a lot more than circulation—they walked into the opportunity to meet some businesspeople who had to see cash before the presses rolled. From the attitudes of everyone at the meeting it appeared that they had developed connections for financial support, possibly from the Teamsters. Regardless of what the future held for the *PDI* it was depressing to see people taking over who took the shortcuts they were taking.

As we left Iowa City, Shar and I looked back over the past three years. In some respects the *PDI* had been more demanding than my jailers. One had exacted about as much of my time as the other. Exactly how much money I had raised over the past three years was hard to figure out—we never had a worthwhile accounting system. All I do know is that we never wasted any money—but at the same time I was never able to tap into the kind of money it takes to do what we were doing. The demise of the *PDI*, though, was directly proportional to the very temporary rise of the Church of the New Song. We became overwhelmed by the response of a vocal minority, and I was as turned on by the response as anyone. I saw the church as a chance to get into the prisons. I sincerely believed, for a while, that the "Truth, Peace, and Freedom" lingo being bandied around was believed by the bandiers. Without a doubt some did. But others didn't.

In the process of leaving Iowa City, death threats or no death threats, I picked up a printout of the subscription list.

A month later, Richard Tanner sent me a small bundle of the April 1973 issue of the *PDI*. That issue consisted of one eight-page section. All copy was set in seven-point type.

The lead story indicated that the federal government's parent behavior modification project (S.T.A.R.T.) would soon be closed. The story, which was datelined "SPRINGFIELD, MO. PRISON, Federal Prison Colonies," began

> The Federal Bureau of Prisons, headed by the neo-nazi Commandant, Norman A. Carlson, was dealt a grievous blow in Federal court in a hearing investigating prisoner complaints of gross atrocities...In a week of testimony given by such professional witnesses as Dr. Stephen S. Fox, Ph.D., world renowned professor of neuropsychology at the University of Iowa; Dr. Richard Korn, Ph.D., professor of criminology, University of California; and Dr. Roger Ulrich, Ph.D., the most respected name in the science of behavior modification, the entire system contrived by the federal prisoncrats to violently modify the behavior of federal prisoners was found to be an insidious conspiracy by federal officers acting under the color of federal office to commit and cause to be committed, crimes against humanity and the constitutional welfare of American citizens.

> Numerous prisoners testified to beatings and gassings; the illegal use of potent, untested drugs that rendered victims almost dead and wishing they were; the chaining of prisoners to iron cots for long periods of time, where they were forced to lay in their own shit and piss, eating only what they could lick from their faces where the federal guards threw what little food was offered. Long, long lists of blatant atrocities and excuses by the federal prisoncrats of why these crimes against humanity were justified in the United States of America in modern times.

But just as the parent program was being closed down, the article reported, federal behavior modification forces were regrouping at the new Butner, North Carolina federal prison. On the state level, at the Marquette (Michigan) Intensive Program Center, a "two-million dollar behavior modification unit has been built" to hold as many as 85 "highly disruptive men." Further, in Clinton, New York, the prison's Special Housing Unit 14 had been designed to hold "militants, radicals and natural leaders."

Prison authorities were continually improving their methods of isolating these specially skilled prisoners, who included those able to articulate how the criminal justice system is set up to oppress the poor, those whom other prisoners could trust to represent them in conflicts with prison authorities, and jailhouse lawyers. Those methods of isolation included solitary confinement within one prison and lengthy transfers by bus from one prison to another.

The tone in *PDI* articles had over the past year become much more dramatic and angry. Our critics described the language and writing styles as inflammatory. What most people did not understand was that many of the prisoners who were being subjected to the tortures of the behavior modification programs were our friends. Many friends were dying. The anger and frustration felt by the staff increased with each issue. Add that pain to our lack of financial support that was causing the *PDI* to face closing down and the tone became not only understandable but justified.

This might have been a more painful and difficult time for me if it hadn't been for the demands of the Georgeville Community Project. Vegetable gardens were planted and demanded daily care. More people were joining the project.

CHAS DuRAIN

One of the most talented cartoonists in the prison press network was Charles DuRain. Chas, as Charles called himself, had been in prison for over 20 years. He was a small fellow, slight of build, in his late forties, who was self-educated as a cartoonist. Ever since his first cartoons arrived at the *PDI* early in 1972, I had been trying to convince the Kentucky Parole Board to give him a parole date.

In my initial correspondence with Chas, when I first told him I was going to get him his walking papers, he had responded, "Hey, I appreciate all you are doing, but you're wasting your time." His letters continued like that for a long time.

Not until the fall of 1973, was I able to get them to seriously consider releasing him. What they said was that they would agree to releasing him to Minnesota if no one objected. I got Minnesota to agree. All plans were in place. Then suddenly all plans were cancelled. In a letter from Chas dated September 24, 1973, he told me he hadn't lost hope. "Six months ago I wouldn't have given a plug nickle for my chances, now I'm sure....I have absolute faith in you."

It was then that I called Senator Hubert Humphrey and asked for help. First he called the two Kentucky senators and asked them to help "Get the wrinkles ironed out of this parole plan." Then he wrote to the Kentucky Parole Board.

His request prompted immediate action. A letter from Chas dated October 12, 1973, was the first handwritten letter I had ever received from him:

> I was transferred suddenly. No typewriters here. Joe, you wouldn't believe this place. Absolutely no locks anywhere! No fences, no guards—nothing like a prison; or at least, nothing like any prison I ever heard of...it's now 10:30 P.M.—that's the latest I've been up for 20 years. If I wanted to I could walk straight across the pastures from here to I-65. There's nothing between me and the highway but a three strand barbed-wire fence. But, of course, I won't leave.

While he was waiting he was presented with the top Penal Press Award by Southern Illinois University. A few weeks later, when Chas arrived in Minnesota, Senator Humphrey was on hand to personally hand him the award.

Another award, this one for special public service, was given by Senator Humphrey to another important *PDI* contributor. To thank Augie Bergenthal for the help he had given us—he loaned me $15,000 a few months after he had given us the $1,000—we created the award ourselves. Senator Humphrey presented the award to Augie's daughter in Washington, DC. Augie would remain in prison for another couple of years. Finally, the weight of support for his case from the *PDI* and the Georgeville Community Project paid off and he was exonerated and released.

The primary challenge of our Georgeville Project, meanwhile, was to cut expenses. Had the *PDI* staff moved to Georgeville, in theory we would have been able to raise all our food. The garden was growing more vegetables and fruit than we could use. I had purchased an old used freezer. What we couldn't can we froze. Our chickens were providing us with a surplus of fresh eggs and meat. When the Georgeville caravan headed for Minneapolis we would bring along four or five large baskets of eggs. When you ate at the Riverside Cafe you paid what you could afford. We ate there and paid for our meals with fresh eggs.

CHARITY BEGINS AT HOME

Christmas 1973 came and went. I look back on that period with many regrets. The project was taking so much of my time that we never really took time to Christmas shop or prepare for the holiday celebration. Sharlane was only a few weeks away from giving birth and it would have been a perfect time to drop everything, shop for gifts, and settle down for an old-fashioned Christmas.

We had decided on a home birth. Sharlane was healthy and strong. She had read everything on the subject and I had read enough to feel confident that together we could handle the birth. Still, I kept the one local doctor's phone number handy and was grateful that he had promised to be standing by in case we needed help. An intern in obstetrics from the St. Cloud hospital called. He had delivered over six hundred babies, he told us, but he had never seen a home birth. He asked if he could observe. We welcomed his expertise.

Just before Chas arrived in Georgeville I had bought two more small homes and moved them onto the property. Chas was living and working in one of them. We were sending his fine editorial cartoons out to weekly newspapers and syndication services.

On January 14, in the afternoon, Sharlane told me that the baby would probably be born within the next few hours. We were still heating with wood, but we now had electricity and a phone. I brought the oxygen tank from my welding unit to our upstairs room in the post office to provide Sharlane with additional oxygen in case she needed it during the birth.

By 6:30 P.M., Sharlane was in labor. The intern hadn't arrived, so I called the doctor. There was no answer. Upstairs I was alone with Sharlane and Kitty the cat. Downstairs was Sam the dog. Chas was working across the street; the rest of the folks were stuffing wood into stoves.

The sun by this time had already gone down for the day and it was thirty degrees below zero, but in our room we were warm and cozy. Shar was laying back, supported by a pile of pillows.

Three hours later, three inches of the baby's crown were already there in front of me. Then suddenly progress stopped. Sharlane was working and I was waiting. Occasionally I would turn the valve on the oxygen tank and wave the hose in Sharlane's direction.

"Just a little extra oxygen," I would say.

"Don't distract me," she would answer.

After about thirty minutes of looking at the top of the baby's head I became concerned. We had made such good progress. Now we seemed to be at a standstill.

Just then we heard someone drive up. A moment later the intern and a nurse were climbing up the ladder to join us. I explained what had happened and where we were. The intern looked over my shoulder and said, "Wow! The baby is being born with the caul intact."

He explained that what we had thought was the baby's head was really the caul, or what we knew as the waterbag. He had never seen a baby born with the caul intact.

"Do you want me to help?" he asked me.

"Not if it isn't necessary," I answered.

But I welcomed his explanation of how to break the caul using the hemostat. As soon as the caul broke the birthing continued. The intern asked about the oxygen tank. I waved some oxygen Sharlane's way.

"Stop it," Sharlane ordered. I did.

Outside the wind was howling. It had been snowing for hours and the wind had turned the snowfall into a blizzard.

"For a while we didn't think we'd make it," the nurse said. "Drifts are building up and some are all the way across the highway." In addition, she said, the plows hadn't gotten to all the main roads yet; Georgeville was not high on local government's list of priorities.

Sharlane was pushing hard and I was ready. All of a sudden, in a move that happened quickly and smoothly, our baby, our little girl, our Charity, was in my hands.

"This is the first time I have ever seen a baby born pink," the intern said to the nurse, "Look at her. She's pink instead of blue, and she hasn't started breathing yet."

He was kneeling beside me. "Give her a little slap on her butt and she'll start to breathe."

"Not a chance," I answered. I reached for one of her incredibly tiny feet. "This child is going to start

her new life with a little tickle." She gave a little start, took a deep breath, and I couldn't do anything except kneel there holding and looking at that amazing little creature. Sharlane reached down and I handed Charity to her. She held her while I tied off the umbilical cord and cut it. Sharlane lay back in the pile of pillows with Charity cuddled up on her breast.

I started taking pictures. The intern and the nurse were right down next to Sharlane looking at Charity.

"She appears to be a perfectly healthy little girl," the intern said. Then he added, "It's very rare that a baby is born with a caul. I've never seen one and I've delivered hundreds and hundreds of babies. Many cultures consider a child that is born with a caul to be a special child—a child that has been blessed."

Sounds good to me, I thought.

I think there was a bottle of wine, but I'm not certain. We sat around and talked newborn-infant talk. After an hour, Sharlane finally let me hold Charity again while she got up, walked over to the phone, and called her folks in Chicago Heights.

Charity seemed right at home all wrapped up in a warm cotton blanket. I wanted to tell her about her wonderful mom so we ignored everyone and I told her a story.

Later that evening after the intern and nurse were gone, we took a few more pictures. Then I took the oxygen tank downstairs and carried it across the street. When I returned to the room, Shar and I settled down to look the baby over carefully and to give her a gentle bath with a soft cloth and olive oil. Soon Charity was nursing and sleeping and nursing and sleeping; the *PDI* and the Georgeville Community Project took a backseat to our new addition.

PRISONER'S DEATH SPARKS PROTESTS AT LEAVENWORTH

The last part of 1973 and all of 1974 was to be a period filled with tremendous satisfactions and difficult problems. People with felony convictions arrived from the courts with their families, spent the necessary time with us, then moved on to training programs and jobs.

As spring approached, visitors drifted in off Highway 55. It wasn't hard to determine which visitors were workers and which weren't. Usually they would arrive on foot, introduce themselves, and get a drink of water. Workers would look around, see a task that needed doing—like gardening or weeding or repairing vehicles—and pitch right in. Those who weren't working within the hour would stay for one meal and move on.

The *PDI*, meanwhile, was being published regularly from Iowa City. Issues were small, usually eight or twelve pages. A one-page *CREATION: The Arts in Prison* was still being edited by Jeanne Schneller, who would work on the *PDI* until her nursing career eventually took her away to the poor, volatile Far East and Third World countries.

Merrily was heading up special projects. In that position, she had gained permission for the *PDI* to reprint *The Jailhouse Lawyer's Manual*, by Brian Glick and the Prison Law Collective in San Francisco. Although that book was written for California prisoners, with minor modifications it provided prisoners in any state with the information they needed to "fight mistreatment or bad conditions" in federal court without an attorney.

John Price, a prisoner at the Atlanta federal prison when I spoke to the first mass meeting of the Church of the New Song, was in charge of prisoner affairs.

For all practical purposes, the *PDI* was now a Church of the New Song publication. It was clear, though, that Bob Copeland was firmly in the editor's chair and doing a great job without interference.

With each passing month I felt we were closer to resuming responsibility for the *PDI*. Our Harris press and the two Linotype machines were restored and ready to operate. Although our money from the foundation had been approved and we were now receiving around a thousand dollars a month, we were housing, feeding, and caring for a population that numbered from eight to 20 people. Their needs became a forced priority over personal salaries. Still, I felt what others described as "insane optimism." I still believed that at least one level of government would one day realize not only that our project was saving them money by keeping people out of prison but also that our programs were contributing to the betterment of society by keeping people out of trouble. Sooner or later, I was positive, the government would reward our successful programs with at least a partial subsidy.

The September 1973 *PDI* had an aerial photo of the Oklahoma State Pen being burned to the ground. The riot began at 2:30 p.m on Friday, July 27 when a prisoner grabbed a microphone and announced over the P.A. system, "This is a revolution!" The story was written by George Knox, our associate editor in the federal prison at El Reno, Oklahoma, where some of the riot participants were quickly sent. Again and again he and other *PDI* associate editors had provided informative articles on existing or impending problems at McAlester prisons. These articles were always sent to the wardens. The wardens never listened. In this particular instance, not listening was going to cost the taxpayers of Oklahoma about 30 million dollars.

Another article reported grim news from Leavenworth. Here's what the article said:

In the early morning of July 29, prisoner Della-Rocca was brought to Leavenworth on his way to Danbury, Connecticut, from the medical center prison in Springfield, Missouri. When he arrived at Leavenworth, he was so weak he had to be moved from the marshall's car to a prison cell in a wheelchair.

DellaRocca had been labeled a malingerer while he was at Springfield. At Leavenworth, when he complained of pain to my old boss, he was stripped naked and placed in a hospital isolation cell on the concrete floor with no bedding. A bowl of food was placed in his cell. When a prisoner nurse was caught helping him eat, a guard ordered him to "Get out of there! This bastard can feed himself if he wants to eat." Three on-duty physician's assistants ignored Della-Rocca's pleas for medical help. A medical technical assistant named Anderson was one of the few who tried to help.

At 9 a.m. my boss stated, "It is my opinion that there isn't a damn thing wrong with that man. Let him stay where he is and I will have him transferred back to Danbury in a few days. Personally I don't think there's a damn thing wrong with that fellow, either mentally or physically."

The next day, a serious argument took place between prison nurses and a physician's assistant over the need to bathe DellaRocca. The prisoners prevailed. While they were giving DellaRocca a bath he stated that he was being murdered and didn't know what he could do or who he could turn to for help. Then he became incoherent and lost consciousness. He was returned to the concrete floor of the cell. By afternoon he was comatose and appeared to be paralyzed except for slight movement in his left arm.

Early on July 31, when he appeared to be dying, DellaRocca was quickly moved from the concrete floor of the strip cell to a cell with a bed. A few minutes later he was dead. Without consulting DellaRocca's family, the doctor performed an autopsy. All of DellaRocca's medical records were gathered together and given to the doctor to ensure that nothing was in them that would reflect unfavorably on the prison hospital or the staff.

No one is certain exactly how the protest started—although it is known that the "sanitization" of DellaRocca's records was an immediate provocation—and I'm not positive how a guard died during the protest, but suddenly, two days after DellaRocca died, in the dining hall, trays, cups, anything prisoners could throw were in the air. Windows shattered and guards were hit. William Hurst, who was in the prison laundry with Armando Miramon, ordered four guards to sit down. "You are hostages," he told them. "Be quiet, don't cause any problems, and you will not be hurt."

Then Hurst called Warden Daggett and asked him if he was ready to listen to the grievances. At first Daggett was belligerent, but when he learned that four guards were in the laundry he agreed.

The list of 13 demands that were submitted to the warden were the exact same reasonable demands the prisoners had been trying to get Daggett to look at for many months. They included

- an end to racist policies now in effect;

- freedom of religion for all prisoners;

- an end to arbitrary lockup of all prisoners and the right to due process at all disciplinary hearings, counsel, and the right to cross-examine and confront witnesses;

- more minority group guards;

- reorganization of the mechanical (medical) staff within the walls, including psychiatric staff. Three prisoners had died through medical neglect during the previous nine months;

- an end to discrimination by the parole board. Only one percent of prisoners were being paroled from the Leavenworth Federal Prison Camp; none were being paroled from behind the walls;

- the right to confidential correspondence with attorneys, the courts, and the press;

- an end to the ban on political books;

- an end to exploitation of prison factory workers;

- returning to all prisoners the interest on their savings;

- an investigation of Federal District Court Judge Stanley, who constantly denied petitions for redress under law;

- better food and an end to cutbacks on food allotments; and

- abolition of the hole.

Hurst, who wrote the *PDI* article with Miramon and Associate Editor John Alkes, agreed to release the hostages as soon as Daggett met with a committee of prisoners in the presence of members of the press.

Daggett consented to that arrangement. Committee members—three Chicanos, three blacks, and three whites—were chosen by their fellow prisoners. They included Jesse Lopez, Juan Fernandez, George Santiago, Dennis Kniss, Alvin Jasper, Frank Harris, Robert Butcher, Odell Bennett, and Jack Abbott.

At the end of the meeting, Daggett promised that no reprisals would be taken against committee members if the hostages were released unharmed. Although the hostages were brought in unharmed, news media were forbidden to take pictures of them because two of the guards had been so frightened they lost control of their bowels.

As soon as the press left the room, the nine committee members were taken to Building 63, Leavenworth's "hole," stripped, and locked in solitary cells, along with Bill Hurst, Armando Miramon, and 50 other prisoners.

As soon as the rest of the prison was secured, the goon squad went to work on the prisoners in solitary. Many of them were clubbed into unconsciousness. Although committee member and negotiator Jesse Lopez was not one of the prisoners who had initiated the riot, he was charged with being its leader.

When Associate Warden A.W. Putnam was called to testify before the House Internal Security Committee that was investigating subversion in the prisons, he said, "Certain literature calls for unconventional warfare because it is, in effect, an attack on the integrity of the prison system." Putnam named the literature he considered the most dangerous: the *Prisoners' Digest International; Midnight Special*, from the National Lawyers Guild in San Francisco; and *Outlaw*, from the Prisoners Union in San Francisco.

It is impossible for free world people to comprehend the courage it takes for a prisoner to write an article critical of a prison administrator, to describe the senseless death of a prisoner, to lay out details of a prison revolt, and then sign the article and request that it be bylined. Reading the reports from John Alkes and the others, I remembered an incident that had happened years before, in the same prison hospital where DellaRocca died, when I was clerking for the chief surgeon. I had read one of his reports but had been unable to understand it so I walked down the hall to the medical examination room where he was working on a prisoner. Another prisoner was lying against the wall on a gurney, a collapsible stretcher on wheels.

I told my boss I didn't understand what he meant.

"Come here and I'll show you," he said. He walked over to the prisoner on the gurney and grabbed his left leg. He raised the leg suddenly.

The prisoner's face turned white. The pain must have been excruciating. He clutched at the sides of the gurney and what started out as a scream ended up a sharp expulsion of breath and a sickening groan.

My boss took his pen and added a notation to the physical exam form as he said, "This describes how far the leg can be raised before the pain is so great the prisoner cannot stand it."

"Why didn't you just tell me?" I said.

"It took less time showing you than explaining it."

THE FBI VISITS GEORGEVILLE

Toward the end of 1973 the FBI made its first appearance in the area. Agents stopped at nearby farms and introduced themselves. After the people had been duly impressed they were asked questions about the project and about me. Two who were questioned were Pete Wendt and his old friend who farmed nearby. Pete was an old German farmer with roots deep in the grange movement. He was a pro-union activist who had openly fought the packing house barons. He was as quick to loan you his farm equipment as he was to shake your hand.

His friend had once chased some government people off his land with his 30-06 and spent a little time in the lock-up for it. Both Pete and his friend were hardcore Debs Socialists.

The two men listened to the government's concern about law and order in the prisons, answered what questions they could, and just nodded their agreement to anything the agents said. As soon as the "G-men" (Pete's term to describe all law enforcement officials who were not in uniform) left, the two men drove over and filled me in.

"They seem to think you're not a good-old law and order man, Joe," said Pete.

His friend, who had a streak of frontier stubbornness and independence that was a yard wide, said, "I didn't give that slicker the time of day."

The next time I was in Belgrade I made it a point to have a cup of coffee with Henry Roos, who was the town marshall. Henry was the ideal lawman. He believed that he could solve problems in his town better than the county sheriff and the courts over in St. Cloud and he was right.

One of the fellows in our project was a young Chicano from Chicago named Humberto de la Rosa. Humberto had spent a few years in an Illinois youth prison. When he was arrested the cops didn't like his name so they changed it to Bill Smith. Illinois had shipped him to Iowa City to work in a shoe repair. He couldn't read, write, or count his money but he knew he was being ripped off so he walked over to the university and told them he thought some education would help him. The officials sent him to me. He had been living under one of the bridges in downtown Iowa City. He moved into 505 with us, we got his name straightened out, and he became part of the family. When we moved to Georgeville, he was one who moved with us.

One night Humberto was insulted and pushed around by a few "toughs" in Belgrade. He walked the four miles to Georgeville, put some sand in an old sock, grabbed a knife, and walked back to Belgrade. Henry had heard him threaten to come back so he was watching for him. Before Humberto got to the three fellows, Henry stopped him, sat down and talked to him, and ended up giving him a ride back to Georgeville. Henry liked to head off trouble before it started.

Henry wasn't one to betray a confidence and he didn't talk business much, but I felt he would tell me if something was seriously wrong. As we sat and talked now, he was his usually amiable self so I figured things were okay as far as our end of the township was concerned. I wasn't worried about raids. The project was clean and Henry knew it. Once, when I discovered a person from the project selling barbiturates, I tossed his belongings into a bag and escorted him to the bus station in Belgrade. On the way into town he kept running his mouth off about how he wasn't afraid of me because he knew I was a pacifist. I took it for almost four miles, but just short of the bus station I slammed on the brakes, kicked him through the passenger door, and was waiting for him when he hit the ground. Then I kicked his ass about every third step he took for the final block to the bus station. Henry was across the street. When I started back to the van he asked, "What was that all about?"

"If it was something I couldn't handle, you know I'd call ya, Henry."

That fall Pete Wendt and Henry launched a secret write-in campaign to get me elected Crow River Township constable. The constable is the low man on the law enforcement ladder. People called him before they called Henry. Henry used him to do the chores he was too busy for. I lost the election by one vote and raised hell with Pete for not telling me what he was doing so I could have voted for myself. My vote would have given my opponent and me three votes each. Elections for constable in Crow River Township were not high priorities for the voters.

It was the closest I ever came to being elected to public office.

ENTER JERRY TETERUD AND BUD WILLARD

In the November 1973 *PDI*, which was published late in January 1974, there is an announcement of the death of Jackson "Curly" Fee, one of 140 prisoners who took part in a peaceful work stoppage at the

Marion federal prison. Eddie Sanchez reported to us that a group of guards entered Curly's cell, beat him severely, and dragged him to the "boxcars" (strip cells). A few days later, Curly wasn't talking or eating. Then, on October 27, he was found dead in his cell. The death was labeled a suicide by hanging. Ignored by prison administrators, guards, and news media was the fact that he was in a strip cell with nothing to hang himself with.

On the masthead of the November issue, a new name appeared as a board member of the National Prison Center. Jerry Teterud had been active with the *PDI* and the Church of the New Song while he was in the Iowa State Penitentiary. As soon as he was paroled he joined Steve Fox, Merrily, Bob Copeland, Richard Tanner, Ma Jones, Betty Ebert, William Corrado, and Becky Hensley on the *PDI* and moved in with Steve and Jane Fox over on River Street.

Bud Willard, another CNS member, also moved in with Steve and Jane around this time after being paroled from Leavenworth.

At the meeting where Teterud was elected to the board, much of the discussion centered around whether the *PDI* should continue publishing. "As our readers are aware, the Digest has never paid for itself and our dismal financial situation has been a consistent topic of discussion on these pages," wrote one staff member.

At this same meeting, the collective agreed on a list of priorities for the coming year that included "Support and development of projects aimed at the abolition of all institutions, relationships and conditions which imprison people; consciousness raising communications to the people on the level of mass behavior; educational and supportive projects relative to returning the solution of 'crime' problems to the communities where they occur; developing a legal resources center to handle problems of incarcerated persons; providing for the immediate needs of prisoners; seeking spiritual solutions to universal problems."

Of the core *PDI* staff people, Bob Copeland announced that he was moving to Fort Madison to be the Church of the New Song minister at the Iowa State Penitentiary. Jim Crawford and Ma Jones wanted to continue publishing the *PDI*. Merrily was willing to work on whatever publication the collective decided to publish. Randall Knoper was willing to stay and work with the others. Had I known at the time that only Merrily, Jim, Ma, and Randall had chosen to continue publishing, I would have invited them to join us in Georgeville. Unfortunately, the collective didn't send us any copies of the November issue.

Years later, when the *PDI* was history, I picked up copies of the last few issues from the Historical Society of Iowa, with whom I had made arrangements to microfilm each issue. I discovered that the *PDI* staff,

the National Prison Center board, and the local Church of the New Song (the latter group was made up of members of the first two groups) were concerned that I had never resigned any of my "positions" with the organizations. Perhaps their hard feelings were the result of their inability to keep enough money and energy flowing into the organizations. Membership in the Church of the New Song was declining, even as the *PDI* devoted increasing space to endless litanies and exhortations by the CNS leadership. Fewer prisoners and free world people were renewing their subscriptions. When the November issue was refused by the warden at Leavenworth and returned to Iowa City, no lawyers filed suits in Kansas on behalf of prison subscribers.

THE LAST *PDI*

At the Georgeville Community Project work continued. I was accepting a few speaking engagements. A group of musicians joined us from California. Their harp player wanted to grow up and play with Willie and the Bumble Bees. Great goal, but he had a ways to go.

We thought less about what was happening in Iowa City as our lives became more oriented to solving our own immediate problems. Still, I can recall discussing with Sharlane what my obligations were to the *PDI*. We could see that they were going to suspend publication soon. I felt that I had to pick up the equipment and give it another try. My original intention was to just reprint the most important articles from progressive publications, from other prison publications, and from our associate editors who were located in every prison in the country. With a staff of three and a concentrated drive to re-establish ties with my original supporters, national board members, and sources of financial help, I felt I could successfully rebuild the *PDI*.

Sharlane, on the other hand, questioned the advisability of continuing to develop either the Georgeville Community Project or the *PDI*. We both felt much satisfaction in what we were doing, but we were living in a depressed area, with average or below average schools.

"Is this where we should be raising Charity?" Shar asked.

I knew the answer.

In March of 1974, a package of *PDI*s arrived. The *PDI*'s fourth excerpt from *The Jailhouse Lawyer's Manual* ended with a simple "(To Be Continued.)." It never was. That issue, dated December 1973, was to be the last. In Iowa City there was no money, nor was there enough energy to raise any.

Merrily and Randall, under a headline that read "News From Us—Statements by Two Collective Members," wrote eloquently about what they felt the *PDI* staff, past and present, had accomplished and learned. Merrily ended her article with a simple drawing of a hand with a finger pointing into the future. It was perfect. She headed for California and art school. Jim Crawford headed for the Northwest and ended up working the fishing boats in Alaska. Ma Jones returned to Clinton. I don't know where Randall went.

There was nothing to decide now. I believed I was the only person who could salvage the *PDI*. Even though I wasn't in Iowa City at the end, the *PDI* was as much a part of me as Charity was. I was tired and burned out. Yet I didn't think I could refuse to try to do it all again.

I planned to visit Iowa City during the first week of April to pick up the pieces of the paper. Only a few hours before I was ready to leave Georgeville, Richard Tanner called me to explain why I shouldn't bother to come down. "All of the equipment, files, furniture, everything, has been taken to the Quad Cities [Davenport, Bettendorf, Moline, and Rock Island] by Kime and sold," he said.

Again there was nothing to decide. The decision had been made for us. It was over.

Richard's only mistake was calling from a place where his conversation with me was overheard. He ended up taking a serious beating from Kime and two of his friends. I saw Richard about a month later and he was still in rough shape.

So much animosity.

NEVER A GREATER NEED

Over the next few months we would all learn how inevitable the closing of the *PDI* was. Had our own burnout and financial failure not brought us down when it did, the government was standing by with an elaborate plan that they were already developing. It's an ending to the story that I must share with you.

On November 6, 1975, drug arrests were made of Michael Remmers and Fletcher Henderson "Sonny" Lott. Both men were Church of the New Song activists. Lott was, in addition, a political activist and musician and had been a fundraiser for the *PDI*. Remmers was living with Kay Mesner at the time. Six days after the arrest, on November 12, he was released on bond and returned home.

Exactly one week later, on November 19, odds and ends of drugs—heroin, cocaine, MSD, LSD, marijuana, and a variety of barbiturates—were planted in the home of Jane and Steve Fox. When the house was raided the next day, Jane and Steve, Betty Ebert,

Mickey Matyka, Bill Corrado, Bud Willard, and Jerry Teterud were arrested on charges of possession. Willard and Teterud were also charged with possession of burglary tools and stolen property that were found at the Fox home along with the drugs.

By this time, the paper had long since folded but people were still living and talking together and letters were still arriving from prisoners and others around the country.

As for the garbage bags full of marijuana that a cooperating Johnson County deputy sheriff held up for the news cameras, they turned out to contain only—garbage. And no one got excited over the small quantities of actual pot that were found. But because heroin, cocaine, MSD, LSD, and barbiturates were found, the defendants started calling lawyers. The Iowa City *Press-Citizen* reported, on November 20, that "Attorneys outnumbered defendants" at the arraignments.

Only the defendants understood just how serious the arrests were since they knew the drugs had been planted. The perplexing question was, "Who was working with the feds and/or the state?"

A few weeks after he was released on bond, Remmers, depressed and unable to find work, bought a pistol. When Mesner found out about the pistol, she asked him to get rid of it. Remmers gave the pistol to Bud Willard, who took it to Sheriff Gary Hughes. Hughes tested the gun, kept on file bullets fired from the gun, and told Willard, a convicted felon, to return the gun to Remmers, a convicted felon.

During this period, Mesner and Remmers were arguing frequently. It was a touchy situation and many of Mesner's friends were concerned because Remmers' temper was well known in state and federal prisons. While serving a sentence in the Iowa State Penitentiary, he was attacked by two prisoners who had been hired to kill him. Although they stabbed him 19 times, Remmers outlasted them; when the fight was over, both of the men were dead.

On the night of January 9, 1976, Mesner told Remmers to move out. On that same day, Willard finally returned the gun to Remmers. The next day, Remmers became despondent and angry and murdered Mesner with that same pistol.

As convicted felons, it was against the law for either Willard or Remmers to have a gun in his possession. It also was general knowledge that Remmers was not in complete control of himself.

Ultimately, the drug arrests were resolved with fines. Sonny Lott ended up going to prison for a few months because he was in the wrong place at the wrong time.

Later in the year, Bud Willard sent a letter to the editor of the Iowa City *Press-Citizen*. At the time, he was a prisoner again, this time in Illinois. In his letter, which was published on November 9, 1976, he claimed he had been working undercover for the government. "I came up with the double agent plan. I simply convinced the authorities that I would be the best informant they ever had, and give them all the information they needed, if I could be released on my own recognizance....It worked."

Later we would learn that Teterud also was working for the government. In fact, according to my information, they both had been released to come to Iowa City as informants for the government.

Willard went on to tell how Sgt. Bob Carpenter of the Johnson County Sheriff's Department had personally told him, "We've been trying to get all these people for a long time...*we were lucky to get them through your arrest.*" [Author's emphasis]

At one point nearly a year before, it looked like the government was going to seize all Church of the New Song funds. When the *PDI* collective members found out that Steve Fox and John Price had nearly ten thousand dollars of money Steve had received in testimony fees stashed in a special CNS bank account in Wisconsin, Steve and John headed for the bank late one night, got the money, and invested it in a 300-acre farm in northeast Iowa. The purchase was justified as a way to protect the money from being seized and to provide a retirement plan for the prisoners who had donated so much free time and energy to the *PDI*, NPC, and CNS. Because the price of land was low at the time, it was a great investment that has continually paid for itself. Unfortunately, today Steve Fox is the sole owner and the ex-prisoners have been completely excluded.

As much as I disliked Jack Kime, his own action during this period at least convinced many people that he wasn't working with the law. If he had been, he would have delivered the *PDI* to me in Minnesota. The government had a long-range plan that was working to destroy independent voices around the country. In the case of the *PDI*, their plans were wasted. We were gone before they had their people in place to affect us. However, if I had moved in and taken the paper back before everything was moved to the Quad Cities, I'm sure we would have been arrested along with the others.

Over the years from the time I started the *PDI*, I had been warned by a number of people that the *PDI* was high on the government's hit list. The warnings intensified when we used the *PDI* to inform the prison world about the Church of the New Song. The last serious warning that I received before the bust, in fall 1975, was from Bob Beecroft, a news correspondent for Mutual Radio Network in Washington, DC. He told me that my days were numbered unless I made an occupational change. He then told me who to call for a job that appeared to have been designed for me. I called and was hired to be national program director for Offender Aid and Restoration in Charlottesville, Virginia.

Preparing to close down the Georgeville Community Project we made 110 gallons of homemade sauerkraut, Charlie and Anne Kukuk turned the hogs into sausage, and we held an auction that had cars parked along the roads for a mile in four directions. We gave the retired folks free lunch. Everything went for a song. We kept the property and still have it, so if there are people out there who are thinking "pottery works" or who want a home with a garden that will support a Catholic Worker house, drop me a line.

As for the *PDI*, I occasionally ask myself if it can be done again. There has never been a time in the history of prisons when there was a greater need for a *PDI*, a greater need for questions to be asked concerning our total disregard for proven methods of humane punishment.

I have a fantasy: through a series of carefully placed classified ads I notify the associate editors, board members, advisors, and, yes, the subscribers—wherever they may be. The response is overwhelming. The directors of the foundations that helped in the past are on the phone: "Glad you're back. How much do you need to get going?" Country Joe McDonald calls: "Sure we'll do another fundraiser." The next call doesn't surprise me; it's Richie Havens: "Let's set up another benefit, shoot some more video, and let prisoners know that they will soon have a voice to the free world!"

With my own dream desktop operation in my home office I could cut production costs tremendously...and payroll costs wouldn't be that much...and...

NOTES

1. For current prices, contact the following numbers: *In These Times*, 1912 Debs Avenue, Mt. Morris, IL 61054, (312) 772-0100; *The Progressive*, Box 421, Mt. Morris, IL 61054-0421, (608) 257-4626; *The Nation*, Box 10791, Des Moines, IA 50347-0791, (212) 242-8400; *Mother Jones*, Box 58249, Boulder, CO 80322-8249, (415) 558-8881; *Z Magazine*, 150 West Canton Street, Boston, MA 02118, (617) 236-5878; *Utne Reader*, Box 1974, Marion, OH 43306-2074, (612) 338-5040; *Catholic Worker*, 36 East 1st Street, New York, NY 10003, (212) 777-9617; *Washington Monthly*, 1611 Connecticut Avenue NW, Washington, DC 20077-3865, (800) 926-6980; *Dollars and Cents*, 1 Summer Street, Sommerville, MA 02143, (617) 628-8411; *Workers World*, 46 West 21st Street, New York, NY 10010, (212) 255-0352; *EXTRA*, 175 5th Avenue, Suite 2245, New York,

NY 10010, (212) 633-6700; and The DataCenter, 464 19th Street, Oakland, CA 94612, (415) 835-4692.

2.   One of these days you will read that I have finally gotten enough prize money together to invite artists to submit works for the "Rain Barrel Art Classic." Artists can portray the scum in oils, watercolors, clay, whatever. And with five-dollar contributions from the folks who were ripped off by the Keatings, et al., we will have big money to hand out for prizes and purchases. We'll save enough to put all the submitted works together in a book so the scum will be given a permanent place in history. The artists will do a better job of exacting equity for the servant class (With the cost of the savings and loan debacle costing every man, woman, and child around $4,000 we have all been turned into servants working, without recourse, to bailing out the wealthy) than the justice department will ever do.

3.   Odds and ends of information continue to be sent to the *PDI* archives and CNS archives, Historical Society of Iowa, 402 Iowa Avenue, Iowa City, Iowa 52240. Any documents, letters, or information about the *PDI* and/or CNS that you have access to should be sent to them. Include a letter stating that the material is to be added to the *PDI* or

CNS collections. Legal documents concerning actions over issues of SPEECH and RELIGION are particularly important.

4.   Robert Stroud was the prisoner who did extensive research on canaries while at Leavenworth. A movie, typically Hollywood as far as the facts were concerned, was made of Stroud's years in prison. Burt Lancaster starred. Stroud's hobby had started at Alcatraz. Old-timers at Leavenworth described him as "...strange...very bright ...crazy...reclusive...dangerous...non-dangerous...good guy...weird..." The only thing everyone agreed on was, "His birds created a smell that permeated the cell block." He also collected more "stuff" than regulations allowed.

5.   Information about what happened after the assault comes from several sources, including New York State Appellate Division documents; Court of Claims documents; the McKay Commission; Second Circuit Court documents; *Police Misconduct and Civil Rights Law Report* 3., no. 9 (May/June 1991): 98-104; the Attica Justice Committee; conversations with observers; and letters from prisoners and attorneys.

Campen, Roger 564
Campos, Pedro Albizu 295
Camus, Albert 373
Cantrell, Burton 331
Capital Times 274, 287
Capra, Fritjof 367
Capriotti, Jimmy 219
Caprow, Rick 276-77, 279
Captain America 309
Carleton College 270
Carletonian 270, 274
Carlson, Norman A. 503, 564, 568
Carmichael, Stokely 215, 294, 349, 351
Carnegie Foundation 75
Carpenter, Bob 576
Carpenter, Carol 64
Carpenter, Cassell 218, 220
Carpenter, Craig 150
Carpenter, Edward 144
Carpenter, Liz 113
Carson, Barbara 21-22, 25
Carter, Alprentice "Bunchy" 353
Carter, Bob 24
Carter, Jimmy 60, 62, 120, 258, 288, 290, 460, 471
Casimere 92
Cass Corridor 13, 17
Cass Technical High School 37
Cassady, Neal 135
Cassell, Mike 218
Castro, Fidel 19, 83, 350, 480, 482, 484-86
Catalina, Doña 316
Catch-22 325
Catholic Worker 480
Catholic Worker House (see Catholic Worker
        Movement)
Catholic Worker Movement (Catholic Worker
        House) 12, 366, 553, 576
Cavanagh, Jerome 13
CCLM (see Coordinating Council of Literary Magazines)
Cell 16 125
Center for Constitutional Rights 71
Center for Investigative Reporting 71
Center for Studies in Criminal Justice 565
Central Advertising 238
Central Intelligence Agency (CIA) xxiii, 5, 39, 58, 65-
        66, 70-71, 86-87, 116, 128, 141, 157, 161, 222,
        254-55, 258, 308, 310, 352, 357, 361, 377,
        387, 480
Challenge, The 528
Chanute Air Force Base 190
Chaplin, Charlie 310, 366
Chapman, Ansel 525
Chapman, Frances 69, 108
Chapman, Kent 145
Charles Clayton Award 547
Charlotte Observer 70
Chase Manhattan Bank 235
Chat n' Shoot Pool Hall 25
Chavez, Cesar 24
Chavis, Ben 87
Checker Cab 290
Cheerleaders Romp 508
Chessman, The 192
Chessman II 192

Chenault, Donald 528, 547
Cherry Hill 539
Chesterfield 309
Chicago 7 128, 249
Chicago 8 trial 362
Chicago Area Military Project 188
Chicago Daily Defender 81, 354
Chicago Daily News 539
Chicago Journalism Review 68, 539
Chicago Seed (*Seed*) 57, 66, 149, 307, 309, 384
Chicago Sun-Times 98
Chicago-area High School Independent Press
        Service (CHIPS) 74
Childers, Jeanne 541
Childers, Roy Daniel 526-27, 530, 533-34, 540-41
Children of All Ages 520
Chinese Communist Party 26
Chinmayananda 156-57
Chinook 68
CHIPS (see Chicago-area High School Independent
        Press)
Chisholm, Margaret 328
Chisholm, Shirley 115
Chomsky, Noam 367
Christian Science Monitor 56, 84
Christina, Queen 316
Christopher, Judy 328, 331, 335, 337
Christopher Street 49
Chrysler Corporation 24, 34, 39
Chrysler Jefferson Assembly Plant 23-24
Church Committee 348, 352-53
Church, Frank 348
Church of the Larger Fellowship (CLF) 492-93
Church of the New Song (CNS) 480-81, 529, 548-49,
        552-54, 558, 561, 563, 565-68, 571, 574-76
CIA (see Central Intelligence Agency)
CIA Diary 70
Cincinnati Independent Eye xxii
CIO (see Congress of Industrial Organizations)
CISPES (see Committee in Solidarity with the People of
        El Salvador)
"Circle the Earth" 478
Cisler, Lucinda 114
Citadel Underground Press 66
Citizen's Commission to Investigate the FBI 67
Citizen-Times 487-88, 490, 495, 508
Citizens Voice, The 472
Citrinos, Tony 554
City Hall Auditorium (Detroit, Michigan) 26
City in History 158
City Lights Books 209
City Sun 81
Civil Rights Commission 258
Clarion, The 512
Clark, Celeste 512
Clark, Don 468
Clark, Ed 217, 222-23, 231
Clark, John 515-16, 518, 526
Clark, Mark 310, 348
Clark Park 25
Clarke, Shirley 52
Cleage, Albert 11
Cleaver, Eldridge 238, 245, 349-54
Cleaver, Kathleen 351

Notes

Notes

Notes

Notes

Notes

Notes

Notes

Notes